D1224267

# MATHEMATICS AND *MATHEMATICA* FOR ECONOMISTS

# Mathematics and *Mathematica* for Economists

Cliff J. Huang and Philip S. Crooke

BLACKWELL
Publishers

Copyright © Cliff J. Huang and Philip S. Crooke, 1997

The right of Cliff J. Huang and Philip S. Crooke to be identified as author of this work has been asserted in accordance with the Copyright, Designs and Patents Act 1988.

First published 1997

First published in USA 1997
2 4 6 8 10 9 7 5 3 1

Blackwell Publishers Inc.
350 Main Street
Malden, Massachusetts 02148
USA

Blackwell Publishers Ltd
108 Cowley Road
Oxford OX4 1JF
UK

All rights reserved. Except for the quotation of short passages for the purposes of criticism and review, no part of this publication may be reproduced, stored in a retrieval system, or transmitted, in any form or by any means, electronic, mechanical, photocopying, recording or otherwise, without the prior permission of the publisher.

Except in the United States of America, this book is sold subject to the condition that it shall not, by way of trade or otherwise, be lent, resold, hired out, or otherwise circulated without the publisher's prior consent in any form of binding or cover other than that in which it is published and without a similar condition including this condition being imposed on the subsequent purchaser.

***Library of Congress Cataloging in Publication Data***

Huang, Cliff J., 1938–
Mathematics and Mathematica for economists / Cliff J. Huang and Philip S. Crooke.
p. cm.
Includes bibliographical references and index.
ISBN 1-57718-034-8 (alk. paper)
1. Mathematica (Computer file) 2. Economics, Mathematical—Computer programs. 3. Economics, Mathematical. I. Crooke, Philip.
HB143.5.H8 1997
330′.0285′5369—dc21 96-37456
CIP

*British Library Cataloguing in Publication Data*

A CIP catalogue record for this book is available from the British Library.

Typeset in 10 on 11½pt Times
by Graphicraft Typesetters Limited Hong Kong
Printed in Great Britain by Hartnolls Ltd., Bodmin, Cornwall

This book is printed on acid-free paper

To our families . . .

Elizabeth, Tricia, Cynthia, Mark
and
Barbara, Alex, Neelie

# Contents

# Preface

This book grew out of the authors' experience in teaching mathematics over several years at Vanderbilt University. It was written in response to the university's effort to integrate the computer into teaching. For many first-year graduate students and advanced undergraduates in economics, obtaining mathematical proficiency is a grueling task. Computer software, such as *Mathematica* or Maple, with their sophisticated graphics and ability to perform symbolic computations, promises to make this learning process more efficient and bearable for both the student and the instructor. With software that allows visualization and experimentation, students can construct their own graphs, changing parameter values and functional forms, until underlying concepts are understood. In this mode of instruction, the limiting factor is the student's imagination and willingness to experiment. Moreover, a course in mathematics for economists typically involves a significant amount of tedious computations that often obscure the underlying mathematical and economic principles. The computer software can relieve the student of this tedium and allow him or her to concentrate on the conceptual steps necessary to understand the underlying principles.

The accelerating pace of software development has placed in the hands of researchers and teachers, capabilities that were hardly imagined only a few years ago. In fact, the difficulty today is not a lack of software, but rather selecting the best software for the task at hand from among many with similar capabilities. Though no single program is dominant in the software market, *Mathematica* was chosen over other programming languages (FORTRAN, BASIC, Pascal, C, etc.) that are used by economists, because of its high-level structure that allows the user to perform sophisticated operations – numerical, symbolic, and graphical – through many built-in functions. Also, the *Mathematica* interface (*Mathematica* notebooks) is suited for interactive tutorials.

The material covered in this book constitutes the core of a one-semester course in mathematics for economists at the first-year graduate or advanced undergraduate level. Special effort has been made to select mathematical topics that are useful to economists. Although its coverage of the mathematics is suitable for students in many fields, the applications are naturally biased toward economics. The only prerequisite for the mathematics present in this text is a basic understanding of one-variable differential and integral calculus, material that is usually found in an introductory calculus course. Chapter 1 begins with an introduction to *Mathematica*. Chapter 2 reviews one-variable differential calculus. Chapters 3–9 deal with topics from advanced calculus and linear algebra. Chapters 10–12 present the mathematics of optimization, including material on constrained and unconstrained optimization. Chapters 13–15 serve as introductions to ordinary differential equations and difference equations.

Many of the repetitive computations that are performed in the text are done by *Mathematica* functions that the authors have prepared. These functions have been grouped into a package called **MathEcon**. This package is a useful adjunct to this book and students should be encouraged to use them. The package is not meant to be a state-of-the-art computational tool, but rather a means to explore problems typically found in a course on mathematics for economists.

We are indebted to many friends, colleagues, and students who have helped bring this project to fruition. We are especially grateful to Malcolm Getz, who suggested, encouraged, and supported the project of integrating *Mathematica* into teaching mathematics for economists. We also want to express our appreciation to John W. Gray of the University of Illinois at Urbana-Champaign, Martha L. Abell and James P. Braselton of Georgia Southern University, Michael Arnold of the University of Delaware, Chihwa Kao of Syracuse University, John C. Eckalbar of California State University, William Barker of Bowdoin College, Hui-Shyong Chang of the University of Tennessee, Phil Haun of the Air Force Academy, Sheng-Cheng Hu of the Purdue University, Mark Huang, and Chyong-Chiou Lin of the University of Pittsburgh, for their comments and suggestions. Steven Tschantz of Vanderbilt University was a valuable resource on the *Mathematica* language. The support of ***Mathematica* across the Curriculum** by the Pew Charitable Trust was an integral part of this project. Finally, our gratitude goes to our wives for their patience and understanding throughout the entire project.

## □ **About** MathEcon □

The **MathEcon** package is a collection of *Mathematica* programs that can be used with the text. As with any *Mathematica* package, it must be read by the kernel so that functions that are defined in the package are available. Information about how this can be done can be found in Chapter 1. The **MathEcon** package contains definitions for many functions. For example, the function **rank** computes the dimension of the subspace spanned by the vectors in its argument. After the package has been loaded, on-line help about the functions is available by using the information function (**?**).

## □ Special Acknowledgment □

This book was conceived in 1990 when the authors and Andrew W. Horowitz responded to Vanderbilt University's initiative to integrate the computer into classroom teaching. In 1993 a decision was made to expand the project from a collection of *Mathematica* notebooks to a self-contained, full-fledged text book. This decision resulted in a much higher opportunity cost than any of us anticipated. Professor Horowitz withdrew from the project after an initial draft. However, we have benefited tremendously from his ideas and contributions. We wish to express our special gratitude to Professor Horowitz for his effort in the early development of this project.

C.J.H.
P.S.C.

# 1

# Introduction to *Mathematica*

*Mathematica* is a computer algebra system that performs numeric, symbolic, and graphical computations. As characterized by the developers, Wolfram Research, Inc. *Mathematica* is "a system for doing mathematics by computer." *Mathematica* is different from other programming languages that are used by economists (FORTRAN, BASIC, Pascal, C, etc.). It is an interpreted language, i.e., each input statement produces immediate output. Although *Mathematica* can be used as a programming language, its high level structure is more appropriate for performing sophisticated operations through the use of built-in functions. For example, *Mathematica* can find limits, derivatives, integrals, and determinants, as well as plot the graphs of functions and perform symbolic computations. The number of built-in functions in *Mathematica* is enormous. Our goals in this introductory chapter are modest. Namely, we introduce a small subset of *Mathematica* commands necessary to explore the mathematics discussed in this book.

*Mathematica* is composed of two parts: the *Mathematica* front end and the *Mathematica* kernel. The *front end* accepts input, displays output, and generally organizes information in a *Mathematica* session. The *kernel* is the part of the program that does the actual calculations. The front end and kernel communicate through a communications protocol called **MathLink**. It is possible to run the front end and kernel on different computers, although most people run them on the same machine. There are three basic types of front ends: Microsoft Windows, Macintosh, and UNIX. These front ends use *Mathematica* notebooks as the interface between the user and the kernel. *Mathematica* notebooks are analogous to electronic worksheets that allow the integration of *Mathematica* input statements, kernel output, and text. Except for minor differences, *Mathematica* notebooks for each front end appear quite similar. We will not discuss *Mathematica* notebooks in this text, but it will be necessary to familarize yourself with the notebook features on your machine before you try to use *Mathematica*.

## □ 1.1 Doing Arithmetic with *Mathematica* □

At its most primitive level, *Mathematica* can be viewed as a calculator. It can perform the five basic operations of arithmetic: addition (+), subtraction (–), multiplication (*, or a blank space), division (/), and exponentiation (^). Later we will discuss how to perform these arithmetic computations. Unlike a basic calculator, however, *Mathematica* does rational arithmetic and keeps a history of the operations that are performed by the kernel.

### 1.1.1 The **In** and **Out** tags

*Mathematica* keeps track of each input expression sent to the kernel and each output statement that it produces in a session. This bookkeeping of statements is displayed in the front end by the use of **In** and **Out** tags. To add 5 to 3, we type 5+3, then press the <enter> key on the Macintosh front end, or the <shift> and <enter> keys on the Microsoft Windows front end.

*In[1]:=*
```
5+3
```

*Out[1]=*
```
8
```

Notice that in addition to the input to the kernel, 5+3, and the output, 8, from the kernel, the front end has attached the tags, **In[1]:=** and **Out[1]=**. This is the sequencing scheme to keep track of inputs and outputs to and from the kernel.

To multiply 13 by 203.8, we type 13*203.8 or 13 203.8 (a space in an expression is interpreted as multiplication) and press the <enter> key.

*In[2]:=*
```
13*203.8
```

*Out[2]=*
```
2649.4
```

Since this was the second input to the kernel (in this session), it has been tagged as **In[2]:=** and its output as **Out[2]=**. The *Mathematica* kernel keeps track of all input and output statements in a *Mathematica* session (a session is defined as the interval between launching and quitting a *Mathematica* kernel).

It is possible to refer to an input statement as **In[k]** or an output statement as **Out[k]** where **k** is an integer that refers to the *k*th statement in the *Mathematica* session. **In** and **Out** are, in fact, *Mathematica* functions that can be used in input expressions. For example, we can ask *Mathematica* to execute the second input statement again.

*In[3]:=*
```
In[2]
```

*Out[3]=*
```
2649.4
```

Note that the second input instructed *Mathematica* to multiply 13 by 203.8. Next, we add the previous two outputs.

*In[4]:=*
```
Out[1] + Out[2]
```

*Out[4]=*
```
2657.4
```

This result is the same as 8 + 2649.4. You can refer to the $k$th previous output and input statements as **Out[-k]** and **In[-k]**, respectively. A short form of **Out[-1]** is **%**, and **Out[-2]** is **%%**. Also, **%k** is a short form for **Out[k]**. For example, here is a sequence of *Mathematica* statements:

*In[5]:=*
```
3-4
```

*Out[5]=*
−1

Multiply 5 to the last result, i.e., 5*(−1).

*In[6]:=*
```
5*%
```

*Out[6]=*
−5

Multiply 6 to the last result, i.e., 6*(−5).

*In[7]:=*
```
6*%
```

*Out[7]=*
−30

Give the third previous result, i.e., −1.

*In[8]:=*
```
In[-3]
```

*Out[8]=*
−1

Generally speaking, blank spaces are ignored by *Mathematica* unless they can be interpreted as multiplication. For example, **2+3** is treated the same as **2 + 3**.

It is important to remember that the sequence of statements inputed to and outputed from the kernel in a *Mathematica* session, is not necessarily the literal sequence of input and output statements that appear in the *Mathematica* notebook. *Mathematica* commands do not have to be executed in a top to bottom fashion in a *Mathematica* notebook.

### 1.1.2 Numbers, symbols, and assignment

*Mathematica* does arithmetic differently than ordinary calculators. It does its calculations using rational arithmetic. This allows certain types of calculations to be performed with infinite precision. For example, the computation of an expression such as (4+1)/3 on a calculator would produce the decimal approximation 1.666666666 and not the exact answer 5/3. *Mathematica* treats 5/3 as a symbol in the rational number system and does not approximate it by its decimal expansion. Another example of *Mathematica*'s representation of numbers as symbols is computing the area of a circle of radius 3.

*In[9]:=*
```
Pi*3^2
```

*Out[9]=*
9Pi

Here **Pi** is the symbol for irrational number $\pi$. There are other special symbols in *Mathematica*. Here is a table of some of the important ones.

| | |
|---|---|
| **Pi** | $\pi \approx 3.14159$ |
| **E** | $e \approx 2.71828$ |
| **I** | $i = \sqrt{-1}$ |
| **Infinity** | $\infty$ |
| **-Infinity** | $-\infty$ |

Notice that the *Mathematica* built-in constants always begin with a capital letter (or $). *Mathematica* is case sensitive, e.g., **Pi** is different from **pi**, and **E** is different from **e**. Since all the built-in constants and functions in *Mathematica* begin with a capital letter, it is a good practice to start with a lowercase letter for user-defined constants or functions.

To assign *Mathematica* expressions to user-defined symbols, we use the **Set** operator (=), or the **SetDelayed** operator (:=). These two operators differ in the way the assignment is made. We will discuss the differences between the two operations once we learn how to use the **Set** function.

Let us assign the symbol $u$ to $-3$ and the symbol $v$ to $(1-9)\pi$.

*In[10]:=*
```
u = -3
```

*Out[10]=*
-3

*In[11]:=*
```
v = (1-9)*Pi
```

*Out[11]=*
-8Pi

Parentheses in *Mathematica* input and output expressions are used as algebraic deliminators. We can now use $u$ and $v$ in other *Mathematica* expressions. For example, let us calculate $3u-5v$ and assign its value to the symbol $w$.

*In[12]:=*
```
w = 3*u - 5*v
```

*Out[12]=*
-9 + 40Pi

One can always ask *Mathematica* what expression has been assigned to a symbol by entering the symbol. Let us inquire about the assignment to $v$.

*In[13]:=*

```
v
```

*Out[13]=*

−8Pi

To remove any assignments to a symbol, we use the **Clear** function.

*In[14]:=*

```
Clear[v]
```

Now we ask what expression is presently assigned to the symbol *v*.

*In[15]:=*

```
v
```

*Out[15]=*

v

When *Mathematica* returns the name of the symbol, it indicates that any assignment to this symbol cannot be evaluated, or in this case, no expression has been assigned to *v*. An alternative method to clear a symbol assignment is to use the **Unset** operator (**=.**). For example, to remove any assignments to the symbol *v*, we could use the following expression:

*In[16]:=*

```
v =.
```

In any of the above assignment of symbols, we could have used the **SetDelayed** operation (**:=**) instead of the **Set** operation (**=**).

We now demonstrate the differences between the **Set** and **SetDelayed** functions. When we enter a *Mathematica* statement of the form *symb* = *expr*, *Mathematica* evaluates the right-side expression (*expr*) and assigns the symbol *symb* the value of *expr*. In the statement *symb* **:=** *expr*, the evaluation of the right-side *expr* is delayed until the symbol *symb* is used in another *Mathematica* statement. Here is an example that shows the difference. Let *b* denote a constant which we initially assign the value –3.

*In[17]:=*

```
b = -3
```

*Out[17]=*

–3

Let us assign the expression 1+*b* to two new symbols: *immediate* and *delayed.* Since both symbols are user-defined variables, lowercase letters are used. The statement

*In[18]:=*

```
immediate = 1 + b
```

*Out[18]=*
```
-2
```

uses the **Set** operator and as expected, 1+b was immediately evaluated and assigned to the symbol *immediate*. However, the statement

*In[19]:=*
```
delayed:= 1 + b
```

uses the **SetDelayed** operator and produces no output. The right-side expression of the **SetDelayed** statement, 1+*b*, is not evaluated until the symbol *delayed* is actually used. Now we inquire about what is stored in the symbol *delayed*.

*In[20]:=*
```
delayed
```

*Out[20]=*
```
-2
```

This is expected since the calculation 1+(–3) was performed in this last input statement. Suppose we change the value of *b*, say, to 5.

*In[21]:=*
```
b = 5
```

*Out[21]=*
```
5
```

What is assigned to the symbols **immediate** and **delayed**?

*In[22]:=*
```
immediate
```

*Out[22]=*
```
-2
```

*In[23]:=*
```
delayed
```

*Out[23]=*
```
6
```

Notice the differences: immediate was assigned a value of –2; on the other hand, delayed, 1+*b*, was recalculated in the last statement with $b = 5$ and now has the value of 6.

## □ 1.2 Functions □

*Mathematica* has an impressive list of built-in mathematical functions. It also allows users to define their own functions.

### 1.2.1 Built-in *Mathematica* functions

*Mathematica* built-in functions have names that are similar to the standard mathematical notations. All built-in functions in *Mathematica* start with a capital letter and the arguments are enclosed in brackets. For example, the sine function, sin $x$, is represented as **Sin[x]** in *Mathematica*. Here is a table of commonly used functions.

| | |
|---|---|
| **Abs[x]** | absolute value, $\|x\|$ |
| **Sqrt[x]** | square root, $\sqrt{x}$ |
| **Exp[x]** | exponential, $e^x$ |
| **Log[x]** | natural logarithm, ln $x$ |
| **Log[a,x]** | logarithm to base a, $\log_a x$ |
| **Sin[x],Cos[x],Tan[x], . . .** | trigonometric functions with arguments in radians |
| **ArcSin[x], ArcCos[x], . . .** | inverse trigonometric functions |
| **Factorial[n] (n!)** | factorial function |
| **Random[ ]** | uniform pseudorandom number between 0 and 1 |
| **N[x]** | numerical value of $x$ |
| **N[x,n]** | value of $x$ with $n$-digit precision |
| **Re[z]** | real part of the complex number $z$ |
| **Im[z]** | imaginary part of the complex number $z$ |
| **Conjugate[z]** | conjugate complex number of $z$ |

*Mathematica* has a built-in help feature that allows us to obtain information about any function. To obtain information about a function, we enter the expression **?** *functionname*. For example, if we want to find information about the function **Log**, we would input the following expression.

*In[24]:=*
```
?Log
```

**Log[z] gives the natural logarithm of z (logarithm to base E). Log[b, z] gives the logarithm to base b.**

As we can see, *Mathematica* describes two forms for the logarithm function, **Log[z]** for the natural logarithm, log $z$, and the **Log[b,z]** for logarithm to base $b$, $\log_b z$.

Functions may have other functions as their arguments. For example, to enter the expression sinh(log(sin $\pi/4$)), we would use the following *Mathematica* statement.

*In[25]:=*
```
Sinh[Log[Sin[Pi/4]]]
```

*Out[25]=*
```
   -1
---------
2Sqrt[2]
```

*Mathematica* often is aware of certain fundamental properties of a mathematical function. For example, it knows that the exponential function and the natural logarithm function are inverses.

*In[26]:=*
```
Clear[x];
Exp[Log[x]]
```

*Out[27]=*
```
x
```

*Mathematica* possesses a built-in function that will compute the decimal representation of an expression. The numerical function **N** will compute the numerical value of an expression.

*In[28]:=*
```
?N
```

**N[expr] gives the numerical value of expr. N[expr, n] does computations to n-digit precision.**

For example, we can find a numerical approximation to $\pi$.

*In[29]:=*
```
N[Pi]
```

*Out[29]=*
```
3.14159
```

Alternatively, **N** with two arguments computes the numerical value of the first argument to the precision specified by the second argument.

*In[30]:=*
```
N[Pi,25]
```

*Out[30]=*
```
3.141592653589793238462643
```

*Mathematica* functions may accept complex numbers as arguments and the values of these functions may be complex numbers (even with arguments that are real numbers).

*In[31]:=*
```
Sqrt[-2]
```

*Out[31]=*
```
I Sqrt[2]
```

*In[32]:=*
```
Sqrt[-4*I]
```

*Out[32]=*

$$-2(-1)^{3/4}$$

To input a complex number we use the symbol **I**, which denotes the imaginary number $\sqrt{-1}$. Suppose that the symbol $a$ is assigned the expression 4+3i and the symbol $b$ the expression 2−i. *Mathematica* can then perform various arithmetic operations on these complex numbers.

*In[33]:=*
```
a = 4+3*I
```

*Out[33]=*
```
4 + 3I
```

*In[34]:=*
```
b = 2-I
```

*Out[34]=*
```
2 - I
```

*In[35]:=*
```
a + b
```

*Out[35]=*
```
6 + 2I
```

*In[36]:=*
```
a/b
```

*Out[36]=*
```
1 + 2I
```

We can also find a numerical approximation to a complex expression.

*In[37]:=*
```
N[Exp[a]]
```

*Out[37]=*
```
-54.0518 + 7.70489I
```

The functions, **Re**, **Im**, and **Conjugate** compute the real part, imaginary part, and conjugate of a complex number, respectively.

*In[38]:=*
```
Re[a]
```

*Out[38]=*
```
4
```

*In[39]:=*
```
Im[b]
```

*Out[39]=*
```
-1
```

*In[40]:=*
```
Conjugate[a]
```

*Out[40]=*
```
4 - 3I
```

An alternate way to apply a function to an expression is to use the operator (//). The statement, *expr // fct*, is interpreted as *fct*[*expr*]. For example, the following statement is identical to **Sin[Pi/4]**:

*In[41]:=*

```
Pi/4 // Sin
```

*Out[41]=*

$$\frac{1}{\text{Sqrt[2]}}$$

The following is the same as **N[Pi]**:

*In[42]:=*

```
Pi // N
```

*Out[42]=*

3.14159

### 1.2.2 User-defined functions

In addition to built-in functions, *Mathematica* allows users to define their own functions. To define a function, we must specify the symbol that will represent the name of the function (in *Mathematica* lingo, the **Head** of the function) as well as the rules that prescribe its action on its arguments. The format of defining a function of one variable is:

*symb0*[*symb1*_] := definition in terms of *symb1*.

*symb0* represents the **Head** of the function, i.e., the name of the function. *symb1* is the independent variable, or argument, of the function. The expression *symb1*_ (with an underscore at the end) denotes a pattern. *symb1* may be a number, a symbol, or another function. For example, to define the function $f(x) = x^2-3x+4$, we would use the following statements:

*In[43]:=*

```
Clear[f,x];
f[x_]:= x^2 - 3*x + 4
```

We could use the **Set** operator (=) or the **SetDelayed** operator (:=) in the defining statement. As a general rule, it is better to use **SetDelayed**. The symbol **x_** is a pattern. This means that the argument of the function can be anything, not just *x*. For example, consider the following:

*In[45]:=*

```
f[4]
```

*Out[45]=*

8

*In[46]:=*

```
f[x^2]
```

*Out[46]=*

$4 - 3x^2 + x^4$

*In[47]:=*
```
f[z]
```

*Out[47]=*

$4 - 3z + z^2$

Suppose we did not use the underscore (_) in the definition.

*In[48]:=*
```
Clear[g];
g[x]:=  x^2  -  3*x  +  4
```

When we ask *Mathematica* to evaluate this function when its argument is 4, we find the following:

*In[50]:=*
```
g[4]
```

*Out[50]=*
```
g[4]
```

*Mathematica* returns the input as output since it does not know how to evaluate **g[4]**. The only thing that has been defined with regards to **g** is the symbol **g[x]**.

Functions of more than one variable are defined in a similar manner. For example, to define a Cobb-Douglas production function with labor ($L$) and capital ($K$) as inputs,

$$f(L,K) = 10L^{0.6}K^{0.3},$$

we would use the following *Mathematica* definition:

*In[51]:=*
```
Clear[f,L,K];
f[L_,K_]:=  10*L^0.6*K^0.3;
```

The function is then evaluated at different values of $L$ and $K$.

*In[53]:=*
```
f[5,8]
```

*Out[53]=*

49.0127

*In[54]:=*
```
f[6,3]
```

*Out[54]=*

40.7406

When we define a function in *Mathematica*, it is sometimes necessary to include some conditions on the domain for the function. For example, suppose we define the function

$$f(x) = \begin{cases} x^2, & x < 0 \\ 2x, & x > 0 \end{cases}$$

To define this function in *Mathematica*, we use the **Condition** function (/;). Here is the description of this function.

*In[55]:=*
```
?Condition
```

**patt /; test is a pattern which matches only if the evaluation of test yields True. lhs :> rhs /; test represents a rule which applies only if the evaluation of test yields True. lhs := rhs /; test is a definition to be used only if test yields True.**

As we can see from the description, the format for using this operator in a definition is *patt* /; *test*. *patt* is a pattern and the expression test must be in the form of a logical expression such as **x > 0** or **x == 0**. These logical expressions are evaluated by *Mathematica* as **True** or **False**, or unevaluated if the expression cannot be determined to be either **True** or **False**. For example, consider the following logical expressions:

*In[56]:=*
```
-3 < 4
```

*Out[56]=*
True

*In[57]:=*
```
3 == 5
```

*Out[57]=*
False

*In[58]:=*
```
Clear[y];
y < 3
```

*Out[59]=*
y < 3

In the last example, *Mathematica* could not evaluate this expression as either **True** or **False** and it thus returned the input statement unevaluated. We use the condition operator to define $f(x)$ given above.

*In[60]:=*
```
Clear[f,x];
f[x_ /; x < 0]:= x^2
f[x_ /; x > 0]:= 2*x
```

We now inquire about the values of $f(x)$ for different values of $x$.

*In[63]:=*
```
f[-1]
```

*Out[63]=*
```
1
```

*In[64]:=*
```
f[2]
```

*Out[64]=*
```
4
```

*In[65]:=*
```
f[0]
```

*Out[65]=*
```
f[0]
```

One can always inquire about the definition of a symbol. Suppose we ask *Mathematica* what definitions it has attached to the **Head** *f*. This is accomplished by using **?**.

*In[66]:=*
```
?f
```

**Global`f**

**f[x_ /; x < 0] := x^2**

**f[x_ /; x > 0] := 2*x**

**Global`f** refers to the context of the symbol *f* and is something that we generally can ignore.

### 1.2.3 Algebraic manipulations

*Mathematica* has several built-in functions to manipulate expressions. These functions will perform the algebraic tasks of expanding products, factoring, finding common denominators, and doing partial fraction expansions. The most important manipulation functions are **Expand**, **Factor**, **Together**, **Apart**, and **Simplify**. Below a description of these functions is given along with an example.

- **Expand**

*In[67]:=*
```
? Expand
```

**Expand[expr] expands out products and positive integer powers in expr. Expand[expr, patt] avoids expanding elements of expr which do not contain terms matching the pattern patt.**

*In[68]:=*
```
Clear[x]
Expand[(x-2)*(x+1)^2]
```

*Out[69]=*

$-2 - 3x + x^3$

- **Factor**

*In[70]:=*

```
?Factor
```

**Factor[poly] factors a polynomial over the integers. Factor[poly, Modulus->p] factors a polynomial modulo a prime p.**

*In[71]:=*

```
Clear[x]
Factor[x^3  -  3*x  -  2]
```

*Out[72]=*

$(-2 + x)(1 + x)^2$

- **Together**

*In[73]:=*

```
?Together
```

**Together[expr] puts terms in a sum over a common denominator, and cancels factors in the result.**

*In[74]:=*

```
Clear[x]
Together[1/(x+1)^2  -  2/(x-2)  +  9/x]
```

*Out[75]=*

$$\frac{-18 - 31x - 3x^2 + 7x^3}{(-2 + x)\,x\,(1 + x)^2}$$

- **Apart**

*In[76]:=*

```
?Apart
```

**Apart[expr] rewrites a rational expression as a sum of terms with minimal denominators. Apart[expr, var] treats all variables other than var as constants.**

*In[77]:=*

```
Clear[x]
Apart[(-18-31*x-3*x^2+7*x^3)/((-2+x)*x*(1+x)^2)]
```

*Out[78]=*

$$\frac{-2}{-2 + x} + \frac{9}{x} + (1 + x)^{-2}$$

- **Simplify**

*In[79]:=*

```
?Simplify
```

**Simplify[expr] performs a sequence of transformations on expr, and returns the simplest form it finds.**

*In[80]:=*

```
Clear[x]
Simplify[Sin[x]^2 + Cos[x]^2 - 1/x + 1/(x+1)]
```

*Out[81]=*

$$1 - \frac{1}{x} + \frac{1}{1+x}$$

## 1.2.4 Lists and tables

A list in *Mathematica* is a collection of objects enclosed by braces { }. The collection can be quite general. It may contain numbers, functions, symbols, graphics, or other lists. Here is an example of a list in *Mathematica.*

*In[82]:=*

```
Clear[apple,x,y,w,z];
a = {-5, apple, 3^(-4), {x,y,{w,z}}}
```

*Out[83]=*

$$\{-5, \text{apple}, \frac{1}{81}, \{x,y,\{w,z\}\}\}$$

The *n*th element of a list is referenced by using double brackets, **[[ ]]**. This is a shorthand notation for a built-in function called **Part**. If **a** is a list, then its first element is **a[[1]]**, its second element is **a[[2]]**, etc. If some elements of a list are themselves lists, then the elements of the sublists can be referenced by using more than one argument in the double brackets [[ ]]. The following examples illustrate this referencing:

*In[84]:=*

```
a[[1]]
```

*Out[84]=*
-5

*In[85]:=*

```
a[[4,2]]
```

*Out[85]=*
y

*In[86]:=*

```
a[[4,3,1]]
```

*Out[86]=*
w

Some basic entities of mathematics are often represented as lists in *Mathematica.* For example, vectors and matrices are represented as lists in *Mathematica.* Furthermore, *Mathematica* allows the basic arithmetic operators to be applied to lists. Here is the addition operator with two lists.

*In[87]:=*

```
a = {2,9,5};
b = {-3,1,-6};
a + b
```

*Out[89]=*

{-1, 10, -1}

We can even apply some functions to lists.

*In[90]:=*

```
Sqrt[a]
```

*Out[90]=*

{Sqrt[2], 3, Sqrt[5]}

Some built-in functions in *Mathematica* produce lists as their output. One of these functions is called **Table**.

*In[91]:=*

```
?Table
```

**Table[expr, {imax}] generates a list of imax copies of expr. Table[expr, {i, imax}] generates a list of the values of expr when i runs from 1 to imax. Table[expr, {i, imin, imax}] starts with i = imin. Table[expr, {i, imin, imax, di}] uses steps di. Table[expr, {i, imin, imax}, {j, jmin, jmax}, ...] gives a nested list. The list associated with i is outermost.**

As we can see, the **Table** function has several different forms. Let us consider the form: **Table**[*expr*,{*i*,*imin*,*imax*,*di*}]. It generates a list of the values of *expr* when *i* runs from *imin* to *imax* incremented by *di*. Here is an example of a list generated by the **Table** function.

*In[92]:=*

```
Table[i^2,{i,2,10,1.5}]
```

*Out[92]=*

{4, 12.25, 25., 42.25, 64., 90.25}

## □ 1.3 Algebra and Calculus □

*Mathematica* is capable of performing many algebraic and calculus problems symbolically. It can compute sums and products of sequences, find roots of a polynomial or solve equations, and differentiate and integrate functions.

### 1.3.1 Sums and products

*Mathematica* can be used to compute the sum and product of a sequence. To compute the sum

$$\sum_{i=n}^{m} x_i$$

we use the *Mathematica* **Sum** function. Let us inquire about its format.

*In[93]:=*

```
?Sum
```

**Sum[f, {i, imax}] evaluates the sum of f with i running from 1 to imax. Sum[f, {i, imin, imax}] starts with i = imin. Sum[f, {i, imin, imax, di}] uses steps di. Sum[f, {i, imin, imax}, {j, jmin, jmax}, ...] evaluates a multiple sum.**

For example, to compute 1+2+3+ . . . +100, we use the following *Mathematica* expression.

*In[94]:=*

```
Sum[i,{i,1,100}]
```

*Out[94]=*

5050

The sum

$$1+\frac{2}{3}+\left(\frac{2}{3}\right)^2+\left(\frac{2}{3}\right)^3+\ldots+\left(\frac{2}{3}\right)^{10}$$

is evaluated using the following expression.

*In[95]:=*

```
Sum[(2/3)^i,{i,0,10}]
```

*Out[95]=*

$$\frac{175099}{59049}$$

Symbolic sums are also allowed.

*In[96]:=*

```
Clear[f];
Sum[f[i],{i,1,3}]
```

*Out[97]=*

f[1] + f[2] + f[3]

For a multiple sum,

$$\sum_{i=n}^{m}\sum_{j=p}^{q}x_{ij}$$

we again use the **Sum** function with a different form for its arguments, namely, two iterators.

*In[98]:=*

```
Clear[x];
Sum[x[i,j],{i,1,3},{j,1,i}]
```

*Out[99]=*

x[1, 1] + x[2, 1] + x[2, 2] + x[3, 1] + x[3, 2] + x[3, 3]

*Mathematica* cannot symbolically sum many infinite series, say,

$$s = \sum_{i=0}^{\infty} \left(\frac{2}{3}\right)^i$$

*In[100]:=*

```
s = Sum[(2/(3*i))^(i),{i,1,Infinity}]
```

*Out[100]=*

$$\text{Sum}[(\frac{2}{3})^i (\frac{1}{i})^i, \{i, 1, \text{Infinity}\}]$$

However, it can often provide an approximation to a sum.

*In[101]:=*

```
N[s]
```

*Out[101]=*

0.789567

To compute products such as

$$\prod_{i=n}^{m} x_i \quad \text{or} \quad \prod_{i=n}^{m}\prod_{j=p}^{q} x_{ij}$$

we use the **Product** function. Here is a description of this function.

*In[102]:=*

```
?Product
```

**Product[f, {i, imax}] evaluates the product of f with i running from 1 to imax. Product[f, {i, imin, imax}] starts with i = imin. Product[f, {i, imin, imax, di}] uses steps di. Product[f, {i, imin, imax}, {j, jmin, jmax}, ...] evaluates a multiple product.**

Here are two examples.

*In[103]:=*

```
Clear[x,y];
Product[(i+x)^i,{i,1,5}]
```

*Out[104]=*

$(1 + x) (2 + x)^2 (3 + x)^3 (4 + x)^4 (5 + x)^5$

*In[105]:=*

```
Product[(i+x)(j+y),{i,1,3},{j,1,2}]
```

*Out[105]=*

$(1 + x)^2 (2 + x)^2 (3 + x)^2 (1 + y)^3 (2 + y)^3$

## 1.3.2 Solving equations

The **Solve** function in *Mathematica* attempts to find exact solutions of an equation or a system of equations.

*In[106]:=*

```
?Solve
```

**Solve[eqns, vars] attempts to solve an equation or set of equations for the variables vars. Any variable in eqns but not vars is regarded as a parameter. Solve[eqns] treats all variables encountered as vars above. Solve[eqns, vars, elims] attempts to solve the equations for vars, eliminating the variables elims.**

As we can see, in the format of this function, the first argument contains the equations to be solved and the second argument contains the variable(s) for which we want solutions. The following *Mathematica* statements solve the cubic polynomial equation $x^3 + 2x^2 - x - 2 = 0$. Notice that in *Mathematica* the equal sign is represented by the logical operator ==.

*In[107]:=*

```
Clear[x];
solution = Solve[x^3+2*x^2-x-2==0,x]
```

*Out[108]=*

$\{\{x \to -2\}, \{x \to -1\}, \{x \to 1\}\}$

The output, **solution**, of the **Solve** function is a list of replacement rules in the form $x \to a$. It states that the equation, $x^3 + 2x^2 - x - 2 = 0$, is satisfied if $x$ is replaced by either $-2$ ($x \to -2$), $-1$ ($x \to -1$), or 1 ($x \to 1$). If we like the solutions to be expressed as a list, $\{-2, -1, 1\}$, instead of a list of rules, we can use the **ReplaceAll** operator (/.) (no space between the / and .). Here is a description of this built-in function.

*In[109]:=*

```
?ReplaceAll
```

**expr /. rules applies a rule or list of rules in an attempt to transform each subpart of an expression expr.**

One can view the **ReplaceAll** function as the function that does a replacement or substitution. For example, the following statement replaces $y$ by 9 in the expression $y^2 + 5$.

*In[110]:=*

```
Clear[y];
y^2 + 5 /. y->9
```

*Out[111]=*
    86

Similarly, the following statement sequentially replaces $y$ by 9, –2, and 4 in the expression. The result is a list of numbers.

*In[112]:=*
```
y^2 + 5 /. {{y->9},{y->-2},{y->4}}
```

*Out[112]=*
    {86, 9, 21}

The following statements replace the list of three rules obtained from solving the cubic polynomial equation by the list of solutions, {a,b,c} = {–2, –1, 1}.

*In[113]:=*
```
Clear[x];
solution = Solve[x^3+2*x^2-x-2==0,x]
```

*Out[114]=*
    {{x → –2}, {x → –1}, {x → 1}}

*In[115]:=*
```
{a,b,c} = x /. solution
```

*Out[115]=*
    {–2, –1, 1}

For many equations, *Mathematica* cannot find exact solutions. In fact, there are no general mathematical methods for finding explicit solutions of a polynomial equation of degree five or more. For example, *Mathematica* is not able to find the roots of the polynomial $x^5 + x^3 + 1 = 0$.

*In[116]:=*
```
Clear[x];
Solve[x^5+x^3+1==0,x]
```

*Out[117]=*
    {ToRules[Roots[$x^3$+ $x^5$ == –1, x]]}

This output indicates that **Solve** could not find the solutions to the equation. However, there is a companion function to **Solve**, called **NSolve**, that attempts to find numerical solutions. Here is a description of this function.

*In[118]:=*
```
?NSolve
```

**NSolve[eqns, vars] attempts to solve numerically an equation or set of equations for the variables vars. Any variable in eqns but not vars is regarded as a parameter. NSolve[eqns] treats all variables encountered as vars above. NSolve[eqns, vars, prec] attempts to solve numerically the equations for vars using prec digits precision.**

Using **NSolve** to find approximations to the roots of the above polynomial, we find that it is has one real root and four complex roots.

*In[119]:=*

```
Clear[x];
NSolve[x^5+x^3+1==0,x]
```

*Out[120]=*

```
{{x → -0.83762}, {x → -0.217853 - 1.16695 I},
  {x → -0.217853 + 1.16695 I}, {x → 0.636663 - 0.664702 I},
  {x → 0.636663 + 0.664702 I}}
```

Finding solutions of transcendental equations, it is often necesary to employ a numerical scheme such as Newton's Method. *Mathematica* implements other such numerical methods in the function **FindRoot**.

*In[121]:=*

```
?FindRoot
```

**FindRoot[lhs == rhs, {x, x0}] searches for a numerical solution to the equation lhs == rhs, starting with x == x0.**

The first argument of **FindRoot** contains the equation to be solved. The second argument is a list that includes the variable for which we want to solve and some initial guess to the solution. For example, let us find an approximation for the solution of the equation $x = \log(x) + 2x^2$.

*In[122]:=*

```
Clear[x];
FindRoot[x==Log[x]+2*x^2,{x,1}]
```

*Out[123]=*

```
{x → 0.723576}
```

We note that there may be other solutions. To find them, we choose different initial guesses.

A system of equations can also be solved with the functions **Solve**, **NSolve**, and **FindRoot**. For example, the system of equations

$$x + y = 1$$
$$xy = -2$$

has two solutions, (–1,2) and (2,–1).

*In[124]:=*

```
Clear[x,y];
Solve[{x+y==1,x*y==-2},{x,y}]
```

*Out[125]=*

```
{{x → -1, y → 2}, {x → 2, y → -1}}
```

### 1.3.3 Calculus

Three basic calculus operations are evaluating limits, derivatives, and integrals. *Mathematica* has the functions, **Limit**, **D**, and **Integrate**, to perform these operations.

The **Limit** function attempts to evaluate the limit of an expression as one of the symbols in the expression approaches a particular value.

*In[126]:=*

```
?Limit
```

**Limit[expr, x→x0] finds the limiting value of expr when x approaches x0.**

Here is an example of finding the limit of a rational expression.

*In[127]:=*

```
Clear[x];
Limit[(x^3-3*x^2+3*x-1)/(x-1),x->1]
```

*Out[128]=*

```
0
```

Derivatives in *Mathematica* are computed using the **D** function.

*In[129]:=*

```
?D
```

**D[f, x] gives the partial derivative of f with respect to x. D[f, {x, n}] gives the nth partial derivative with respect to x. D[f, x1, x2, ...] gives a mixed derivative.**

In its most basic form, the first argument of **D** is the function to be differentiated and the second argument is the variable of differentiation. For example, to differentiate the function $x\cos(2x)$ with respect to $x$, we would use the following expression.

*In[130]:=*

```
Clear[x];
D[x*Cos[2*x],x]
```

*Out[131]=*

```
Cos[2x] - 2xSin[2x]
```

An alternative method of differentiating functions of a single variable is to use the prime notation (′) for the derivative.

*In[132]:=*

```
Clear[f,x];
f[x_]:= x*Cos[2*x];
f'[x]
```

*Out[134]=*

```
Cos[2x] - 2xSin[2x]
```

Higher order derivatives can be computed by nesting the **D** function, using multiple primes, or specifying a list in the second argument of **D**. The list should be of the form $\{x, n\}$ where n is a positive integer that denotes the order of the derivative. For example, to compute the third derivative of the above function, we could use any of the following expressions.

*In[135]:=*
```
Clear[x];
D[D[D[x*Cos[2*x],x],x],x]
```

*Out[136]=*

−12Cos[2x] + 8xSin[2x]

*In[137]:=*
```
f'''[x]
```

*Out[137]=*

−12Cos[2x] + 8xSin[2x]

*In[138]:=*
```
D[x*Cos[2*x],{x,3}]
```

*Out[138]=*

−12Cos[2x] + 8xSin[2x]

If an expression involves more than one variable, then the **D** function computes partial derivatives. Higher order partial derivatives are found by adding arguments to the **D** function. For example, to compute the partial derivative

$$\frac{\partial^3}{\partial x \partial y^2}(x^3y^2 + x^4)$$

we would use the following *Mathematica* statement.

*In[139]:=*
```
Clear[x,y];
D[x^3*y^2+x^4,y,y,x]
```

*Out[140]=*

$6x^2$

The total differential of a function can be computed with the **Dt** function. Here is *Mathematica*'s description of this function.

*In[141]:=*
```
?Dt
```

**Dt[f, x] gives the total derivative of f with respect to x. Dt[f] gives the total differential of f. Dt[f, {x, n}] gives the nth total derivative with respect to x. Dt[f, x1, x2, ...] gives a mixed total derivative.**

Let us compute the total differential of $xy^2+z^3$.

*In[142]:=*
```
Clear[x,y,z];
Dt[x*y^2+z^3]
```

*Out[143]=*

$y^2Dt[x] + 2xyDt[y] + 3z^2Dt[z]$

In this output, **Dt[x]** plays the role of d$x$, **Dt[y]** the role of d$y$, and **Dt[z]** the role of d$z$.

*Mathematica* is a very powerful integrator. The **Integrate** function can be used to evaluate both definite and indefinite integrals. Here is the description of this function.

*In[144]:=*
```
?Integrate
```

**Integrate[f,x] gives the indefinite integral of f with respect to x.
Integrate[f,{x,xmin,xmax}] gives the definite integral.
Integrate[f,{x,xmin,xmax},{y,ymin,ymax}] gives a multiple integral.**

As an example, we compute the definite integral

$$\int_0^{\pi} x\cos(x)\mathrm{d}x$$

*In[145]:=*
```
Clear[x];
Integrate[x*Cos[x],{x,0,Pi}]
```

*Out[146]=*

–2

Let us find an antiderivative (indefinite integral) of $x^2 \sin x$.

*In[147]:=*
```
Clear[x];
Integrate[x^2*Sin[x],x]
```

*Out[148]=*

$2Cos[x] - x^2Cos[x] + 2xSin[x]$

Notice that *Mathematica* does not include an arbitrary constant of integration. Our last example is the following iterated integral

$$\int_{-1}^{2}\left[\int_{x}^{x^2} xy^2\mathrm{d}y\right]\mathrm{d}x$$

*In[149]:=*
```
Clear[x,y];
Integrate[Integrate[x*y^2,{y,x,x^2}],{x,-1,2}]
```

*Out[150]=*

$$\frac{337}{40}$$

# □ 1.4 Graphics in *Mathematica* □

One of the outstanding features of *Mathematica* is its graphing capabilities. It can graph functions of one or two variables or even functions specified parametrically.

## 1.4.1 **Plot**

To graph a function of a single variable, $y = f(x)$ on an interval $[a,b]$, we use the **Plot** function. Here is *Mathematica*'s description of this function.

*In[151]:=*

```
?Plot
```

**Plot[f, {x, xmin, xmax}] generates a plot of f as a function of x from xmin to xmax. Plot[{f1, f2, ...}, {x, xmin, xmax}] plots several functions fi.**

In its most basic form, the first argument of **Plot** is the function to be plotted and the second argument is a list that specifies the interval over which the function is to be plotted. The following expression graphs the function $f(x) = x^3+2x^2-3x-5$ over the interval $-3 \leq x \leq 2$.

*In[152]:=*

```
Plot[x^3+2*x^2-3*x-5,{x,-3,2}];
```

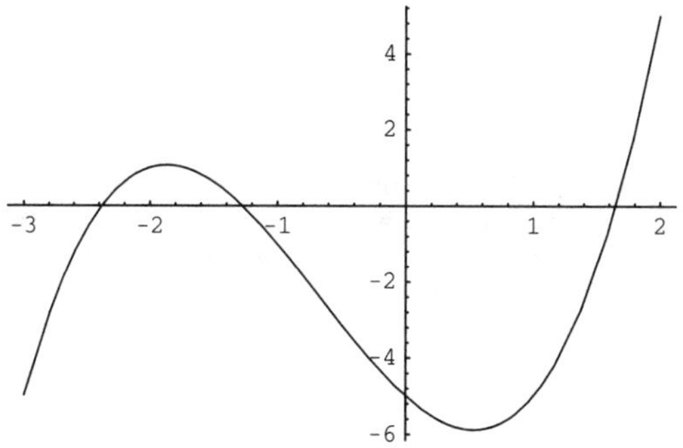


The **Plot** function may have more than two arguments. These additional arguments are called *options* and are used to enhance the graph. There are several plotting options available in *Mathematica.* We can inquire about them by using the *Mathematica* function **Options**.

*In[153]:=*

```
Options[Plot]
```

*Out[153]=*

{AspectRatio → $\frac{1}{\text{GoldenRatio}}$, Axes → Automatic,
AxesLabel → None, AxesOrigin → Automatic,
AxesStyle → Automatic, Background → Automatic,
ColorOutput → Automatic, Compiled → True,

```
DefaultColor → Automatic, Epilog → { }, Frame → False,
FrameLabel → None, FrameStyle → Automatic,
FrameTicks → Automatic, GridLines → None, MaxBend → 10.,
PlotDivision → 20., PlotLabel → None, PlotPoints → 25,
PlotRange → Automatic, PlotRegion → Automatic,
PlotStyle → Automatic, Prolog → { }, RotateLabel → True,
Ticks → Automatic, DefaultFont :> $DefaultFont,
DisplayFunction :> $DisplayFunction}
```

Notice that the options are in the form of rules and these rules represent the default settings. Many of these are self-explanatory. The default settings of these options suffice for plotting most functions. Some of the more useful options are **AxesLabel** (labels the horizontal and vertical axes), **AspectRatio** (determines the scaling of the axes with respect to one another), **PlotRange** (specifies the range of the vertical and/or horizontal axes), **PlotStyle** (specifies the line style used to draw the graphs), and **PlotLabel** (puts a title on the graph). Here are the descriptions of some of these options.

*In[154]:=*

```
?AxesLabel
```

**AxesLabel is an option for graphics functions. With AxesLabel → None, no labels are drawn on the axes in the plot. AxesLabel → label specifies a label for the y axis of a two-dimensional plot, and the z axis of a three-dimensional plot. AxesLabel → {xlabel, ylabel, ... } specifies labels for different axes.**

*In[155]:=*

```
?AspectRatio
```

**AspectRatio is an option for Show and related functions. With AspectRatio → Automatic, the ratio of height to width of the plot is determined from the actual coordinate values in the plot. AspectRatio → r makes the ratio equal to r.**

*In[156]:=*

```
?PlotStyle
```

**PlotStyle is an option for Plot, ParametricPlot and ListPlot. PlotStyle → style specifies that all lines or points are to be generated with the specified graphics directive, or list of graphics directives. PlotStyle → {{style1}, {style2}, ... } specifies that successive lines generated should use graphics directives style1, style2, ... .**

As an example, let us plot the function $y = \sin(2x)\cos(2\pi x)$ over the interval $-1 \le x \le 2$ using several options.

*In[157]:=*

```
Plot[Sin[2*x]*Cos[2*Pi*x],{x,-1,2},
     AxesLabel->{"x","f(x)"},PlotRange->{-1,2},
     AspectRatio->Automatic,
     PlotStyle->Dashing[{0.015}]];
```

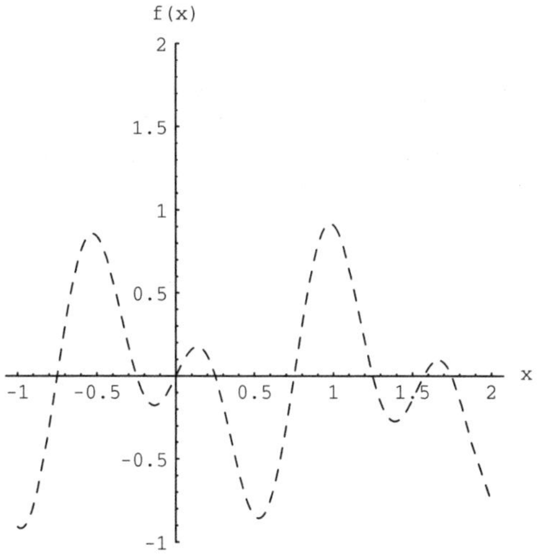


In the above input statement, we have indented the second, third, and fourth lines of the **Plot** expression for clarity. When a single *Mathematica* expression extends over more than one line, we will indent the beginning of each line beyond the first line to indicate this situation.

It is possible to plot two or more functions on the same set of axes. The functions to be plotted must be grouped as a list {*f1*,*f2*, . . }. Each function can have a different **PlotStyle**. This is accomplished by entering the plot option in the form of **PlotStyle→**{*plotsty1*, *plotsty2*, ..}. The following example plots two functions, $x^2\cos x$ and sin $x$, over the interval $-\pi \le x \le \pi$ with the first graph using the default style and the second graph using a dashed style. The default style is denoted as the empty list { }.

*In[158]:=*
```
Plot[{x^2*Cos[x],Sin[x]},{x,-Pi,Pi},
        PlotStyle->{{},Dashing[{0.005,0.02}]}];
```

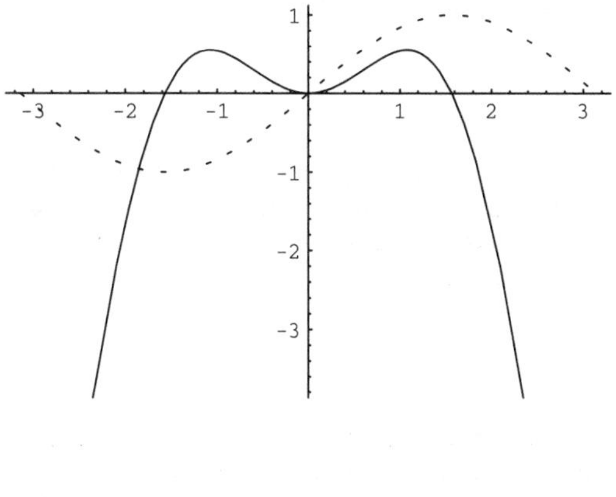


## 1.4.2 Plot3D

Functions of two variables are plotted using the **Plot3D** function. The function **Plot3D** is very similar to **Plot** in its format.

*In[159]:=*

```
?Plot3D
```

**Plot3D[f, {x, xmin, xmax}, {y, ymin, ymax}] generates a three-dimensional plot of f as a function of x and y. Plot3D[{f, s}, {x, xmin, xmax}, {y, ymin, ymax}] generates a three-dimensional plot in which the height of the surface is specified by f, and the shading is specified by s.**

Some options are different because the graph will be a surface in a three-dimensional space. Here are the default settings for these options.

*In[160]:=*

```
Options[Plot3D]
```

*Out[160]=*

```
{AmbientLight → GrayLevel[0], AspectRatio → Automatic,
  Axes → True, AxesEdge → Automatic, AxesLabel → None,
  AxesStyle → Automatic, Background → Automatic, Boxed → True,
  BoxRatios → {1, 1, 0.4}, BoxStyle → Automatic,
  ClipFill → Automatic, ColorFunction → Automatic,
  ColorOutput → Automatic, Compiled → True,
  DefaultColor → Automatic, Epilog → { }, FaceGrids → None,
  HiddenSurface → True, Lighting → True,
  LightSources →
   {{{1., 0., 1.}, RGBColor[1, 0, 0]},
    {{1., 1., 1.}, RGBColor[0, 1, 0]},
    {{0., 1., 1.}, RGBColor[0, 0, 1]}}, Mesh → True,
  MeshStyle → Automatic, PlotLabel → None, PlotPoints → 15,
  PlotRange → Automatic, PlotRegion → Automatic,
  Plot3Matrix → Automatic, Prolog → { }, Shading → True,
  SphericalRegion → False, Ticks → Automatic,
  ViewCenter → Automatic, ViewPoint → {1.3, -2.4, 2.},
  ViewVertical → {0., 0., 1.}, DefaultFont :> $DefaultFont,
  DisplayFunction :> $DisplayFunction}
```

Some of these options require some explanation. For example, let us check the meaning of the options **BoxRatios** and **ViewPoint**.

*In[161]:=*

```
?BoxRatios
```

**BoxRatios is an option for Graphics3D and SurfaceGraphics. BoxRatios → {rx, ry, rz} gives the ratios of side lengths for the bounding box of the three-dimensional picture. BoxRatios → Automatic determines the ratios using the range of actual coordinate values in the plot.**

*In[162]:=*

```
?ViewPoint
```

**ViewPoint is an option for Graphics3D and SurfaceGraphics which gives the point in space from which the objects plotted are to be viewed. ViewPoint → {x, y, z} gives the position of the view point relative to the center of the three-dimensional box that contains the object being plotted.**

To illustrate this function, let us plot the graph of the function

$$f(x,y) = (x^2+2y^2)\,e^{-(x^2+y^2)}$$

over the rectangle $-3 \le x \le 1$ and $-2 \le y \le 2$.

*In[163]:=*
```
Plot3D[(x^2+2*y^2)*Exp[-(x^2+y^2)],{x,-3,1},{y,-2,2},
                     AxesLabel->{"x","y","z"},
                    ViewPoint->{-2.270,  0.910,  2.580}];
```

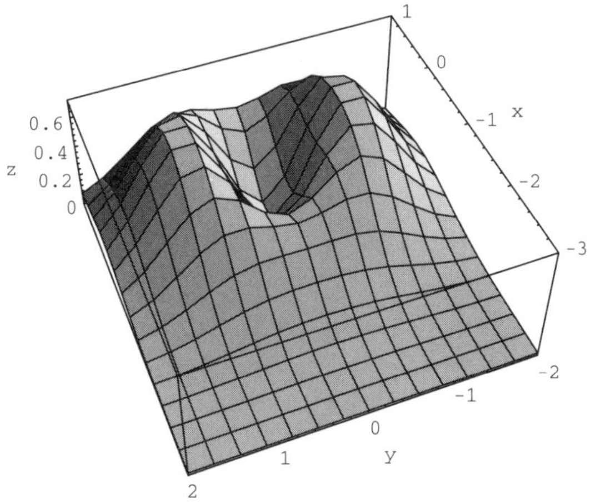


## 1.4.3 **ParametricPlot** and **ParametricPlot3D**

Parametrically defined functions such as $x = f(t)$, $y = g(t)$, $a \le t \le b$, in two-dimensions, and $x = f(t)$, $y = g(t)$, $z = h(t)$, $a \le t \le b$, in three-dimensions can be graphed using **ParametricPlot** and **ParametricPlot3D**, respectively. *Mathematica* provides the following information on these functions.

*In[164]:=*
```
?ParametricPlot
```

**ParametricPlot[{fx, fy}, {t, tmin, tmax}] produces a parametric plot with x and y coordinates fx and fy generated as a function of t. ParametricPlot[{{fx, fy}, {gx, gy}, ...}, {t, tmin, tmax}] plots several parametric curves.**

*In[165]:=*
```
?ParametricPlot3D
```

**ParametricPlot3D[{fx, fy, fz}, {t, tmin, tmax}] produces a three-dimensional space curve parameterized by a variable t which runs from tmin to tmax. ParametricPlot3D[{fx, fy, fz}, {t, tmin, tmax}, {u, umin, umax}] produces a three-dimensional surface parametrized by t and u. ParametricPlot3D[{fx, fy, fz,**

**s}, ...] shades the plot according to the color specification s. ParametricPlot3D[{{fx, fy, fz}, {gx, gy, gz}, ...}, ...] plots several objects together.**

Options for these functions are similar to **Plot** and **Plot3D**. Here are three examples.

*In[166]:=*

```
ParametricPlot[{Sin[3*t]*Cos[t],Sin[t]*Sin[3*t]},
                    {t,-Pi,Pi},AspectRatio->1];
```

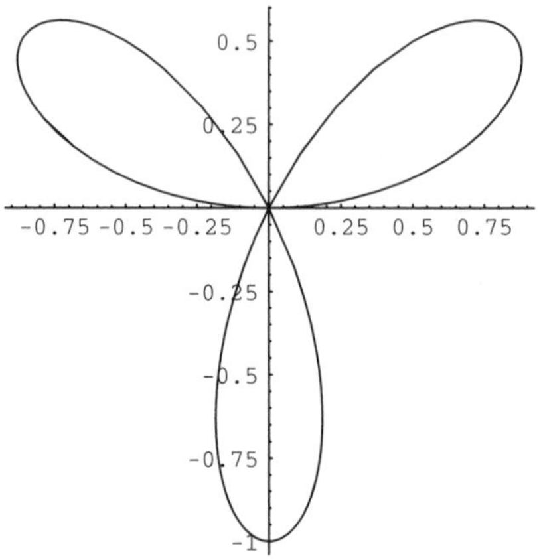


*In[167]:=*

```
ParametricPlot3D[{t*Sin[3*t],t*Cos[3*t],t},{t,0,15},
            PlotPoints->200,ViewPoint->{2.737,-3.416,0.906},
        Boxed->False,AxesLabel->{"x","y","z"}];
```

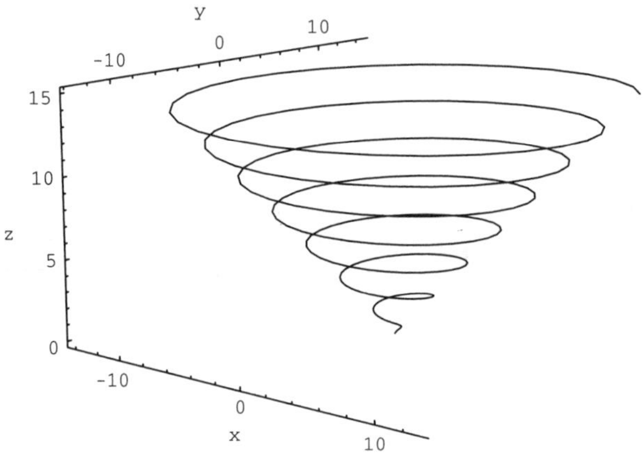


*In[168]:=*

```
ParametricPlot3D[{t*Cos[u],t*Sin[u],t},{t,0,10},
     {u,-2Pi,2Pi},ViewPoint->{1.368,-4.101,1.712}];
```

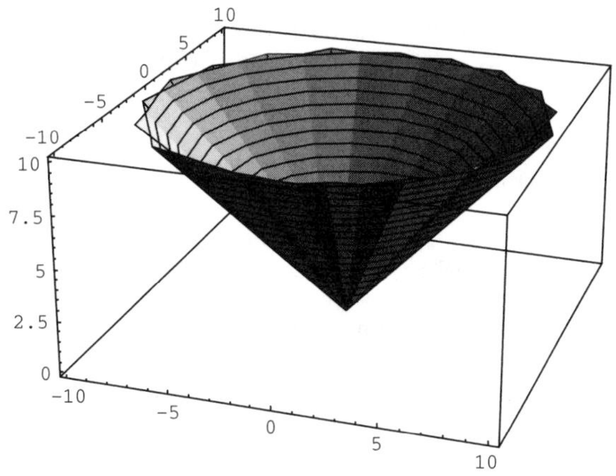


## 1.4.4 ContourPlot

The **ContourPlot** function produces a contour map of a surface defined by an equation $z = f(x,y)$ for various values of $z$. The following is the *Mathematica* information on **ContourPlot**.

*In[169]:=*

```
?ContourPlot
```

**ContourPlot[f, {x, xmin, xmax}, {y, ymin, ymax}] generates a contour plot of f as a function of x and y.**

This function has several options.

*In[170]:=*

```
Options[ContourPlot]
```

*Out[170]=*

```
{AspectRatio → 1, Axes → False, AxesLabel → None,
  AxesOrigin → Automatic, AxesStyle → Automatic,
  Background → Automatic, ColorFunction → Automatic,
  ColorOutput → Automatic, Compiled → True,
  ContourLines → True, Contours → 10, ContourShading → True,
  ContourSmoothing → True, ContourStyle → Automatic,
  DefaultColor → Automatic, Epilog → { }, Frame → True,
  FrameLabel → None, FrameStyle → Automatic,
  FrameTicks → Automatic, PlotLabel → None, PlotPoints → 15,
  PlotRange → Automatic, PlotRegion → Automatic, Prolog → { },
  RotateLabel → True, Ticks → Automatic,
  DefaultFont :> $DefaultFont,
  DisplayFunction :> $DisplayFunction}
```

Let us check the meaning of **Contours** and **ContourShading**.

*In[171]:=*

```
?Contours
```

**Contours is an option for ContourGraphics specifying the contours to use. Contours → n chooses n equally spaced contours between the minimum and maximum z values. Contours → {z1, z2, ... } specifies the explicit z values to use for contours.**

*In[172]:=*

```
?ContourShading
```

**ContourShading is an option for contour plots. With ContourShading → False, regions between contour lines are left blank. With ContourShading → True, regions are colored based on the setting for the option ColorFunction.**

As an example, let us plot the contour of $f(x,y) = \sqrt{x^2+2y^2}$ . The contour plots are by default shaded in such a way that regions with higher $z$ values are shaded more lightly than those lower $z$ values.

*In[173]:=*

```
Clear[f,x,y];
f[x_,y_]:=  Sqrt[x^2  +  2*y^2];
               ContourPlot[f[x,y],{x,-2,2},{y,-1,1},
               PlotPoints->25];
```

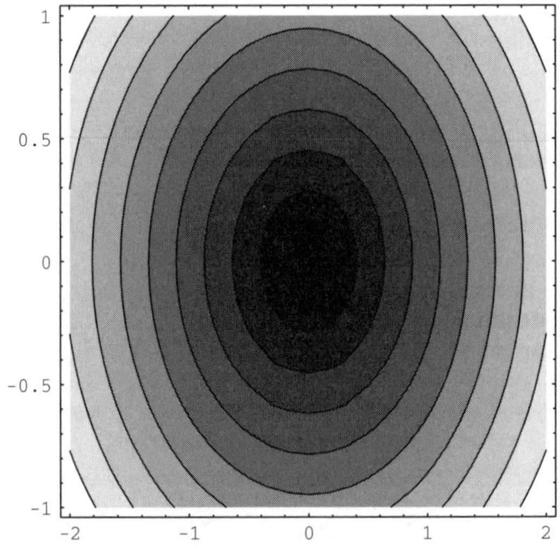


## 1.4.5 Graphics primitives and the **Show** function

Graphics in *Mathematica* are composed of graphics primitives. In two dimensions, the graphics are constructed using some basic graphics objects: points, lines, polygons, circles, and text. These graphics primitives are constructed using the *Mathematica* functions **Point**, **Line**, **Polygon**, **Circle**, and **Text**. Below are descriptions of these primitives.

*In[176]:=*

```
?Point
```

**Point[coords] is a graphics primitive that represents a point.**

*In[177]:=*
```
?Line
```

**Line[{pt1, pt2, ...}] is a graphics primitive which represents a line joining a sequence of points.**

*In[178]:=*
```
?Polygon
```

**Polygon[{pt1, pt2, ...}] is a graphics primitive that represents a filled polygon.**

*In[179]:=*
```
?Circle
```

**Circle[{x, y}, r] is a two-dimensional graphics primitive that represents a circle of radius r centered at the point {x, y}. Circle[{x, y}, {rx, ry}] yields an ellipse with semi-axes rx and ry. Circle[{x, y}, r, {theta1, theta2}] represents a circular arc.**

*In[180]:=*
```
?Text
```

**Text[expr, coords] is a graphics primitive that represents text corresponding to the printed form of expr, centered at the point specified by coords.**

Graphics directives such as **Thickness**, **RGBColor**, **PointSize**, **Dashing**, etc., control the ways these basic objects are constructed. Let us check two of these directives.

*In[181]:=*
```
?Thickness
```

**Thickness[r] is a graphics directive which specifies that lines which follow are to be drawn with a thickness r. The thickness r is given as a fraction of the total width of the graph.**

*In[182]:=*
```
?RGBColor
```

**RGBColor[red, green, blue] is a graphics directive which specifies that graphical objects which follow are to be displayed, if possible, in the color given.**

The graphics primitives and their directives are assembled by another *Mathematica* function. In two-dimensions, this function is **Graphics** and in three-dimensions it is **Graphics3D.** As an example, we construct a two-dimensional graphic that contains a point at (1/4,1/2), a thick line between the points (0,0) and (1,1), a circle of radius 1/4 centered at (–1/2,1/2), and the text "Dog" centered at the point (3/4,1/2).

*In[183]:=*
```
picture = Graphics[{Point[{1/4,1/2}],Thickness[0.01],
                     Line  [{{0,0},  {1,1}}],
                   Circle[{-1/2,1/2},1/4],
                   Text["Dog",{3/4,1/2}]}];
```

**Graphics** constructs the graphics named **picture**, but it does not display it. To display the graphics, *Mathematica* uses the **Show** function.

*In[184]:=*
```
Show[picture];
```

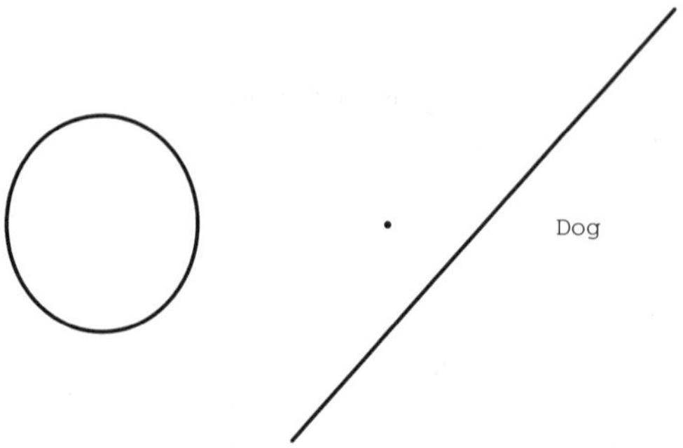


Notice that the directive **Thickness[0.01]** is in effect for both the line and the circle. The **Show** function has several options. We will display the above graphic using two of these options.

*In[185]:=*
```
Show[picture,Axes->True,AspectRatio->Automatic];
```

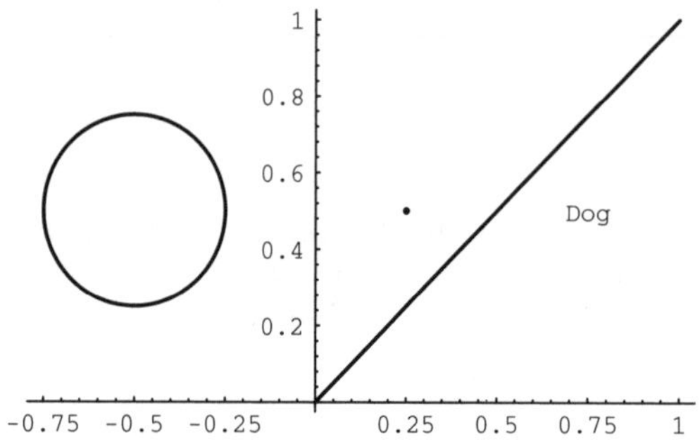


Options can also be placed in the **Graphics** and **Graphics3D** function. For example, here are the options for Graphics.

*In[186]:=*
```
Options[Graphics]
```

*Out[186]=*

$\{\text{AspectRatio} \to \frac{1}{\text{GoldenRatio}}$, Axes → False, AxesLabel → None,
AxesOrigin → Automatic, AxesStyle → Automatic,
Background → Automatic, ColorOutput → Automatic,
DefaultColor → Automatic, Epilog → { }, Frame → False,
FrameLabel → None, FrameStyle → Automatic,
FrameTicks → Automatic, GridLines → None, PlotLabel → None,
PlotRange → Automatic, PlotRegion → Automatic, Prolog → { },
RotateLabel → True, Ticks → Automatic,

```
DefaultFont :> $DefaultFont,
DisplayFunction :> $DisplayFunction}
```

## □ 1.5 Modules and Packages □

Often, we would like to group a number of *Mathematica* statements together to perform a specific task. One easy way to do this is to use the **Module** function. Here is *Mathematica*'s description of this function.

*In[187]:=*

```
?Module
```

**Module[{x, y, ...}, expr] specifies that occurrences of the symbols x, y, ... in expr should be treated as local. Module[{x = x0, ...}, expr] defines initial values for x, ....**

The first argument of **Module** is a list of symbols that are used internally in the the module. The second argument contains the instructions that *Mathematica* is to follow in the module. We can thus define a function that requires several steps. For example, the following function generates a circle that is centered at $(a,b)$ with radius $R$ and places a label at the point. We will call this function **labeledcircle**. The first argument **pt** is a list that represents the point $(a,b)$, the second argument **rad** is the radius $R$, and the third argument **label** is a label.

*In[188]:=*

```
Clear[labelcircle,pt];
labelcircle[pt_,rad_,label_]:=
      Module[{round,txt},round=Circle[pt,rad];
                              txt=Text[label,pt];
             Graphics[{round,txt}]]
```

Thus, the following statement creates a graphics object, named **picture**, which is a circle centered at {−1,1} with radius 2 and a label, "My Circle." To display the output of this function, we use the **Show** function with a couple of options.

*In[190]:=*

```
picture = labelcircle[{-1,-1},2,"My Circle"];
Show[picture,AspectRatio->Automatic,Axes->True];
```

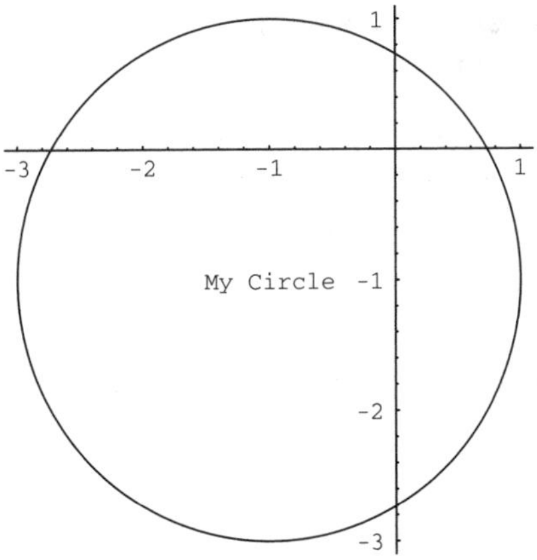

A module is a convenient way to organize a group of *Mathematica* statements. Many of the special functions that we use in this book have function definitions that are defined as modules. We have collected these function definitions into a package called **MathEcon**. This package is defined in a *Mathematica* notebook (file) called **MathEcon.m**. The package can be loaded into the kernel by using the **Needs** function. However, before the **MathEcon** package can be loaded, a path must be established to inform *Mathematica* of the location of the package. Suppose the notebook **MathEcon.m** is stored in a folder named **MathFunctions** on the hard-disk drive called **mydisk**. The following statement establishes a path to the package.

```
AppendTo[$Path,"mydisk:MathFunctions"];
```

Once the path is established, we can load the **MathEcon.m** package into the *Mathematica* kernel using the **Needs** function.

```
Needs["MathEcon`"]
```

The functions that are defined in **MathEcon.m**, are now available to use. We ask *Mathematica* to give us a description of the package.

*In[192]:=*

```
?MathEcon
```

**MathEcon is a package of functions that is used with the book:**

**Mathematics and Mathematica for Economists**
**by Cliff Huang and Philip Crooke.**

**It contains the following functions:**

**fibprime directed directed3d**
**vector2d vector3d addition2d**
**subtraction2d projection2d projection3d**
**rotation2d rank rowop**
**colop submatrix minor**
**cofactor aug colrep**
**signQ signQL borderB**
**gradf hessian conhess**
**arc2d tangentline fjohn**
**separableode linearode tangentfield**
**wronskian wis trajectory**

As an example, we have created a function called **fibprime** that will find all of the Fibonaci numbers that are prime and less than or equal to a given integer. The Fibonaci numbers $z_k$ are those integers that satisfy the the difference equation

$$z_k = z_{k-1} + z_{k-2},\ k = 0,1,2,\ldots$$

with $z_0 = z_1 = 1$. Let us look up the format of this function.

*In[193]:=*

```
?fibprime
```

**fibprime[n] calculates the prime Fibonaci numbers that are less than or equal to an integer n. For example,**

**fibprime[37].**

For example, the first 6 Fibonaci numbers are {1, 1, 2, 3, 5, 8}. Having loaded the file **MathEcon.m**, we can use this function to find the prime Fibonaci numbers less than or equal to a given integer. Let us find the prime Fibonaci numbers that are less than or equal to 100.

*In[194]:=*
```
fibprime[100]
```

*Out[194]=*
```
{2, 3, 5, 13, 89}
```

To distinguish between the functions defined in the **MathEcon** package and the built-in functions of *Mathematica*, all the **MathEcon** functions start with a lower case letter. Once these functions have been loaded, they are available in the **Function Browser** of the **Help** menu.

*Mathematica* comes with many other specialized packages that the user can read into the kernel. For example, the normal and other continuous probability distributions are contained in the **Statistics`ContinuousDistribution`** package. Let us first load the package into the kernel.

*In[195]:=*
```
Needs["Statistics`ContinuousDistributions`"]
```

We evaluate the probability density function, **PDF**, of the variable $x$ having the normal distribution with zero mean and unit standard deviation, **NormalDistribution[0,1]**.

*In[196]:=*
```
normal=PDF[NormalDistribution[0,1],x]
```

*Out[196]=*

$$\frac{1}{E^{x^2/2}\,\mathrm{Sqrt}[2Pi]}$$

The probability density function is plotted for $-3 \leq x \leq 3$.

*In[197]:=*
```
Plot[normal,{x,-3,3},AxesLabel->{"x","f(x)"}];
```

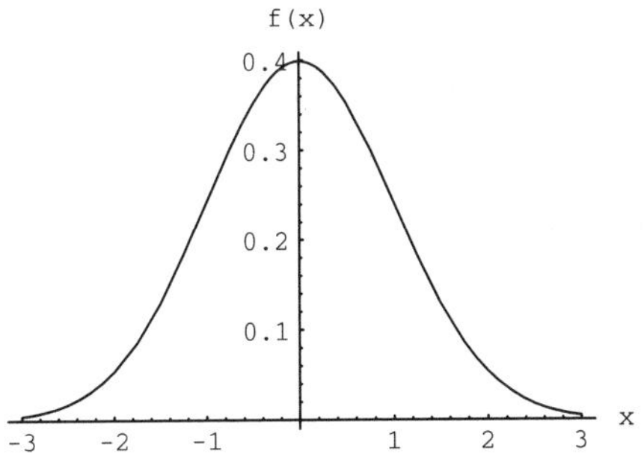

# 2

# A Review of Calculus

This chapter contains a brief review of topics in the calculus of functions of a single variable. Although the basic principles of differential and integral calculus are familiar to most students in economics, we will show how *Mathematica* can be used both to enhance our understanding of these basic concepts, and to facilitate computation.

Since the fundamental characteristics of calculus are based on the notion of limiting processes, this chapter begins with a review of limits and derivatives of functions of a single variable. We introduce the built-in *Mathematica* functions for computing limits, derivatives, and integrals. With the aid of the **Plot** function, we examine the properties of monotonicity and concavity and their implications on local extrema.

The second limiting process in calculus involves the Riemann integral. This integral is evaluated by a process called integration. The Fundamental Theorem of Calculus relates the concepts of differentiation and integration. Differentiation of a function $f(x)$ produces the function $f'(x)$. The function $f(x)$ is called the antiderivative of $f'(x)$. Antidifferentiation or integration is essentially a process that reverses differentiation. We review indefinite and definite integrals, and demonstrate the use of the *Mathematica* function, **Integrate**, for computing the antiderivative.

## □ 2.1 Limits and Continuity of Functions □

### 2.1.1 Limits

Suppose $f(x)$ is a function which is defined over an interval which may or may not contain the point C. We are interested in the values of $f(x)$ as $x$ approaches $c$.

> **DEFINITION 2.1** *A function f(x) has a* ***limit*** *A at the point c if for any* $\varepsilon > 0$ *there exists a* $\delta > 0$ *such that*
>
> $|f(x) - A| < \varepsilon$ *if* $0 < |x - c| < \delta$.

The symbolic form of the definition is

$$\lim_{x \to c} f(x) = A$$

Note that $0 < |x - c|$ means that $x \neq c$. Furthermore, $|f(x) - A| < \varepsilon$ implies that $A - \varepsilon < f(x) < A + \varepsilon$, and $0 < |x - c| < \delta$ implies that $c - \delta < x < c + \delta$. The variable $x$ may approach $c$ from either the left side or the right side. We use notation $x \to c^-$ to indicate that $x$ approaches $c$ from the left, and $x \to c^+$ from the right. One can prove that $f(x)$ has a limit $A$ at $c$ if and only if

$$\lim_{x\to c^-} f(x) = \lim_{x\to c^+} f(x) = A.$$

These are called *one-sided limits.* A function may have one-sided limits at a point even if the limit itself does not exist. However, if both one-side limits exist and are equal, then the limit itself must exist and have the same value as the one-sided limits.

**Example 2.1** Does the limit of the function

$$f(x) = \frac{x^2 + 4x - 5}{x^2 - 1}$$

exist at the point $x = 1$? We use the **Table** function to evaluate $f(x)$ near the point $x = 1$, and to give evidence that as $x \to 1^-$, $f(x)$ approaches 3, and as $x \to 1^+$, $f(x)$ approaches 3. We note that one can give a formal proof that

$$\lim_{x\to 1} f(x) = \lim_{x\to 1^-} f(x) = \lim_{x\to 1^+} f(x) = 3.$$

*In[1]:=*

```
Clear[f,x];
f[x_]:= (x^2+4*x-5)/(x^2-1);
leftside = Table[{x,f[x]},{x,0.999,0.9999,0.0001}]
```

*Out[3]=*

```
{{0.999, 3.001}, {0.9991, 3.0009}, {0.9992, 3.0008}, {0.9993, 3.0007},
  {0.9994, 3.0006}, {0.9995, 3.0005}, {0.9996, 3.0004}, {0.9997, 3.0003},
  {0.9998, 3.0002}, {0.9999, 3.0001}}
```

The table for $x$ and $f(x)$ are more readable if we rearrange them in columns with headings given by using the **TableForm** function and its option **TableHeadings** for placing headings on the table.

*In[4]:=*

```
TableForm[leftside,TableHeadings->{{},{"x","f(x)"}}]
```

*Out[4]//TableForm=*

| x | f(x) |
|---|---|
| 0.999 | 3.001 |
| 0.9991 | 3.0009 |
| 0.9992 | 3.0008 |
| 0.9993 | 3.0007 |
| 0.9994 | 3.0006 |
| 0.9995 | 3.0005 |
| 0.9996 | 3.0004 |
| 0.9997 | 3.0003 |
| 0.9998 | 3.0002 |
| 0.9999 | 3.0001 |

Note that the option, **TableHeadings→{{},{"x", "f(x)"}}**, gives an empty label, { }, for the rows, and **{"x", "f(x)"}** for the column. The output shows that as $x$ approaches 1 from the left side, $f(x)$ approaches 3. Below we tabulate $x$ and $f(x)$ as $x$ approaches 1 from the right side.

*In[5]:=*

```
rightside = Table[{x,f[x]},{x,1.001,1.0001,-0.0001}];
TableForm[rightside,TableHeadings->{{},{"x","f(x)"}}]
```

*Out[6]//TableForm=*

| x | f(x) |
|---|---|
| 1.001 | 2.999 |
| 1.0009 | 2.9991 |
| 1.0008 | 2.9992 |
| 1.0007 | 2.9993 |
| 1.0006 | 2.9994 |
| 1.0005 | 2.9995 |
| 1.0004 | 2.9996 |
| 1.0003 | 2.9997 |
| 1.0002 | 2.9998 |

We graph the function $f(x)$ around $x = 1$. Since the function is not defined at $x = 1$, we vary $x$ from 0 to 0.999 for the left-sided limit, and vary $x$ from 1.001 to 2 for the right-sided limit. The option **DisplayFunction→Identity** in **Plot** suspends the display of the graph. The option **DisplayFunction→$DisplayFunction** redisplays the graph. We observe that the curve does approach to 3 from both sides of $x = 1$.

*In[7]:=*

```
leftgraph=Plot[(x^2+4*x-5)/(x^2-1),{x,0,0.999},
          PlotStyle->{Thickness[0.008]},
          DisplayFunction->Identity];
rightgraph=Plot[(x^2+4*x-5)/(x^2-1),{x,1.001,2},
          PlotStyle->{Thickness[0.008]},
          DisplayFunction->Identity];
Show[leftgraph,rightgraph,AxesLabel->{"x","f(x)"},
          DisplayFunction->$DisplayFunction];
```

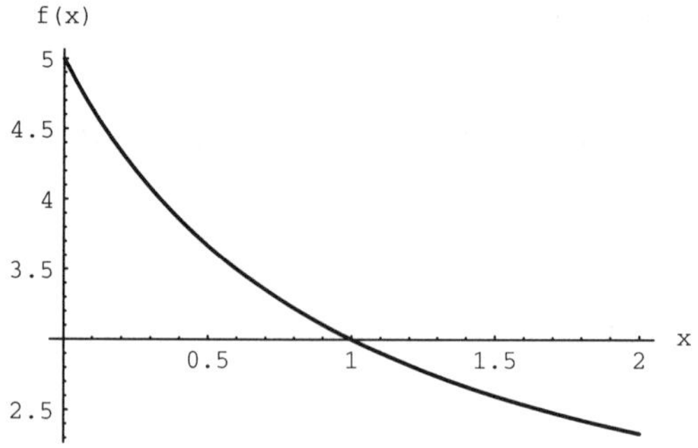


**Example 2.2** The function

$$f(x) = \begin{cases} 1/x, & \text{if } x < 1 \\ x^2 + 1, & \text{if } x > 1 \end{cases}$$

has no limit at $x = 1$. From its graph it is clear that the left-sided limit at $x = 1$ is not equal to the right-sided limit:

$$\lim_{x \to 1^-} f(x) = 1 \neq \lim_{x \to 1^+} f(x) = 2.$$

*In[10]:=*

```
leftgraph=Plot[1/x,{x,0.1,0.999},
               PlotStyle->{Thickness[0.008]},
               DisplayFunction->Identity];
rightgraph=Plot[x^2+1,{x,1.001,2},
               PlotStyle->{Thickness[0.008]},
               DisplayFunction->Identity];
Show[leftgraph,rightgraph,AxesLabel->{"x","f(x)"},
               DisplayFunction->$DisplayFunction];
```

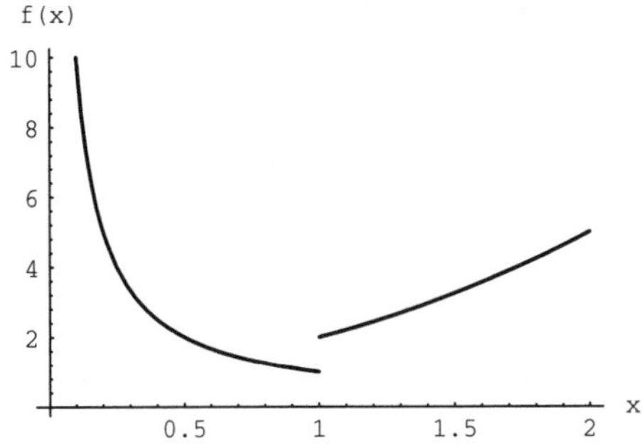


Two special cases of the limit of a function $y = f(x)$ are significant. Consider the function $f(x) = 1/x$. As $x$ becomes large, $f(x)$ tends to zero. A function is said to approach the limit $A$ as $x$ approaches $+\infty$ if for every $\varepsilon > 0$, there is a positive number $N$ such that

$$|f(x) - A| < \varepsilon, \quad \text{for all} \quad x > N.$$

If the limit exists, then we write

$$\lim_{x \to \infty} f(x) = A.$$

A corresponding concept holds as $x$ approaches $-\infty$ and we write

$$\lim_{x \to -\infty} f(x) = A.$$

In either situation, the horizontal line $y = A$ is called a *horizontal asymptote* of the function.

Consider another function $f(x) = 1/(x–2)$. The function becomes large as $x$ tends to 2 from the right side. We write this fact as

$$\lim_{x \to 2^+} f(x) = \infty.$$

In general, the expression

$$\lim_{x \to c^+} f(x) = \infty$$

means that for any positive number $M$, there is an $\delta > 0$ such that

$$f(x) > M, \quad \text{if} \quad c < x < c + \delta.$$

The function $f(x) = 1/(x-2)$ exceeds $M$ if $2 < x < 2 + 1/M$. In this case, $\delta = 1/M$ and $c = 2$. Hence

$$\lim_{x \to 2^+} f(x) = \infty.$$

In a similar manner, the following situations:

$$\lim_{x \to c^+} f(x) = -\infty, \quad \text{or} \quad \lim_{x \to c^-} f(x) = \infty, \quad \text{or} \quad \lim_{x \to c^-} f(x) = -\infty$$

have similar interpretation. The line $x = c$ is called a *vertical asymptote*.

A function $f(x)$ is said to approach $+\infty$ as $x \to +\infty$,

$$\lim_{x \to +\infty} f(x) = +\infty$$

if for any positive number $M$, there is a positive number $N$ such that $f(x) > M$ when $x > N$. Similar definitions can be given to

$$\lim_{x \to -\infty} f(x) = +\infty, \ \lim_{x \to +\infty} f(x) = -\infty, \ \lim_{x \to -\infty} f(x) = -\infty.$$

We now state some basic theorems about limits without proof.

**THEOREM 2.1** *Suppose the limits*

$$\lim_{x \to c} f(x) = A \quad \text{and} \quad \lim_{x \to c} g(x) = B$$

*exist with* $|A|,|B| < \infty$. *c may be infinite. Then,*

*(1) The limit of the sum is the sum of the limits; that is,*

$$\lim_{x \to c} (f(x) + g(x)) = \lim_{x \to c} f(x) + \lim_{x \to c} g(x) = A + B$$

(2) *The limit of the product is the product of the limits; that is,*

$$\lim_{x \to c} (f(x)\, g(x)) = \left(\lim_{x \to c} f(x)\right)\left(\lim_{x \to c} g(x)\right) = AB$$

In particular, if $f(x) \equiv k$, a constant function, then

$$\lim_{x \to c} k g(x) = k\left(\lim_{x \to c} g(x)\right) = kB$$

(3) The limit of the ratio is the ratio of the limits; that is,

$$\lim_{x \to c} \frac{f(x)}{g(x)} = \frac{\lim_{x \to c} f(x)}{\lim_{x \to c} g(x)} = \frac{A}{B}$$

provided that $B \neq 0$.

*Mathematica* contains a built-in function, **Limit**, for taking limits. Here is the *Mathematica* description of this function.

*In[13]:=*
```
?Limit
```

**Limit[expr, x→x0] finds the limiting value of expr when x approaches x0.**

In the following example, we use the **Limit** function to find the limit at a specific point.

**Example 2.3** Use the function **Limit** to show that the limit of $f(x) = (2x+5)/(x+2)$ as $x \to 0$ is 5/2.

*In[14]:=*
```
Clear[f,x];
f[x_]:= (2*x + 5)/(x + 2);
Limit[f[x],x->0]
```

*Out[16]=*

$$\frac{5}{2}$$

Now let us examine the limit of this function at $x = -2$. By inspecting the denominator of $f(x)$, it is clear that the values of function change dramatically as $x \to -2$. Plotting $f(x)$, we find that $x = -2$ is a vertical asymptote and neither right- or left-sided limits exist. Thus the limit of $f(x)$ does not exist at $x = -2$.

*In[17]:=*
```
Plot[f[x],{x,-3,-1},AxesLabel->{"x","f(x)"}];
```

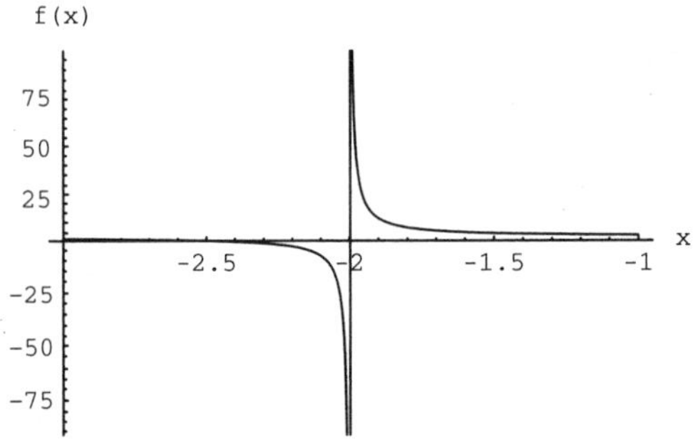


In cases such as this, *Mathematica* has the ability to take one-sided limits. To do so, simply add an option to the **Limit** function. The option is called **Direction**.

*In[18]:=*
```
?Direction
```

**Direction is an option for Limit. With Direction → 1, the limit is taken from below. With Direction → -1, the limit is taken from above. Direction → Automatic uses Direction → -1 except for limits at Infinity, where it is equivalent to Direction → 1.**

We now compute the one-sided limits of our function at $x = -2$.

*In[19]:=*
```
Limit[f[x],x->-2, Direction->1]
```

*Out[19]=*
```
-Infinity
```

*In[20]:=*
```
Limit[f[x],x->-2, Direction->-1]
```

*Out[20]=*
```
Infinity
```

Notice that *Mathematica* correctly distinguished between the left-sided limit $-\infty$, and the right-sided limit $+\infty$.

**Example 2.4** (The Compound Interest Formula) If the annual effective rate of interest is $i$, then the compound interest rate $r$ is defined as

$$1 + i = \lim_{x \to \infty} \left(1 + \frac{r}{n}\right)^n = \mathrm{e}^r.$$

Using *Mathematica*, compute this limit.

*In[21]:=*
```
Clear[r,n];
Limit[(1+r/n)^n,n->Infinity]
```

*Out[22]=*
```
E^r
```

Thus, a compound interest rate of $r = 0.1$ (or 10%) is equivalent to the annual effective rate of $i = \mathrm{e}^{0.1} - 1 \approx 0.1052$ (or 10.52%).

**Example 2.5** (The Box-Cox Transformation) The Box-Cox transformation of a variable $x$ is defined as

$$f(x) = \frac{x^b - 1}{b}$$

where $b$ is a parameter. Each value of $b$ defines a new transformation. Although it is not obvious, it can be shown that

$$\lim_{b \to 0} f(x) = \log x.$$

Let us check this using *Mathematica*.

*In[23]:=*
```
Clear[f,x,b];
f[x_]:= (x^b-1)/b;
Limit[f[x],b->0]
```

*Out[25]=*
```
Log[x]
```

Thus the Box-Cox transformation includes a variety of functional forms as special cases. We plot the function $f(x)$ and observe its variation with respect to various values of $b$. The solid line corresponds to $b = 2$, the large dashed line to $b = 1$, the medium dashed line as $b \to 0$, and the small dashed line to $b = -1$.

*In[26]:=*
```
Plot[{(x^2-1)/2,(x-1),Log[x],-(1/x-1)},{x,0.1,2.5},
                PlotStyle->{{},Dashing[{0.03}],Dashing[{0.02}],
               Dashing[{0.01}]},AxesLabel->{"x","f(x)"}];
```

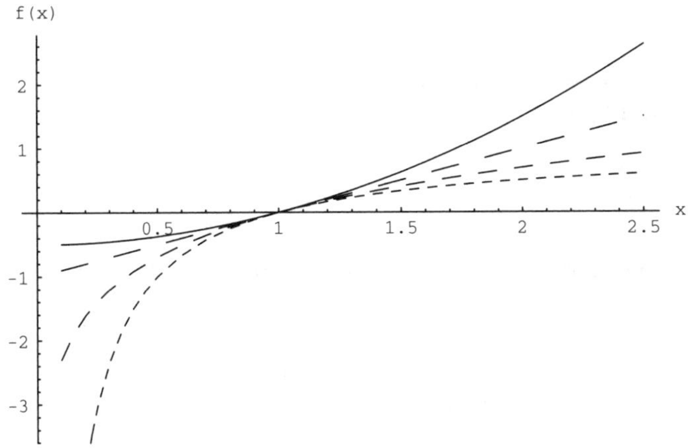


**Example 2.6** One important application of the Box-Cox transformation in economics is in production theory. Consider the production of $Q$ units of output using $K$ units of capital input and $L$ units of labor input. Suppose the following relation holds for the Box-Cox transformation in $Q$, $K$, and $L$.

$f(Q) = af(K) + (1-a)f(L)$, or

$$\frac{Q^b-1}{b} = a\left(\frac{K^b-1}{b}\right) + (1-a)\left(\frac{L^b-1}{b}\right)$$

where $0 < a < 1$. Expressing the above relation in term of the production function, i.e., $Q$ as a function of $K$ and $L$, we find that

$$Q = [aK^b + (1-a)L^b]^{1/b} \equiv g(b).$$

This is a function of the parameter $b$ and is called the *constant elasticity of substitution (CES)* production function in $K$ and $L$. It is evident when $b = 1$ that

$$g(1) = Q = aK + (1-a)L$$

is an arithmetic mean of $K$ and $L$, and is a *linear* production function. When $b = 2$,

$$g(2) = Q = \sqrt{aK^2 + (1-a)L^2}$$

is a root mean square. Furthermore,

$$g(-1) = Q = \frac{1}{a/\mathrm{K} + (1-a)/L}$$

is a harmonic mean. As shown in the following *Mathematica* calculation, we find the limit of $g(b)$ as $b \to 0$ is

$$\lim_{b \to 0} g(b) = Q = K^a L^{1-a}.$$

*In[27]:=*

```
Clear[g,b,a,K,L];
g[b_]:=(a*K^b+(1-a)*L^b)^(1/b);
Limit[g[b],b->0]
```

*Out[29]=*

$$E^{a\mathrm{Log}[K] + \mathrm{Log}[L] - a\mathrm{Log}[L]}$$

This expression can be simplified to the expression $K^a L^{1-a}$. This function is called the *Cobb-Douglas production function.*

**Example 2.7** (Standard Normal Density) A standard normal density function of a random variable $x$ in statistics has the following form:

$$f(x) = \frac{1}{\sqrt{2\pi}} e^{-x^2/2}, -\infty < x < \infty.$$

We calculate the horizontal asymptotes as $x \to \pm\infty$.

*In[30]:=*

```
Clear[f,x];
f[x_]:= Exp[-x^2/2]/Sqrt[2*Pi];
Limit[f[x],x->-Infinity]
```

*Out[32]=*

0

*In[33]:=*

```
Limit[f[x],x->Infinity]
```

*Out[33]=*

0

Plotting this function, we confirm these calculations.

*In[34]:=*

```
Plot[f[x],{x,-4,4},AxesLabel->{"x","f(x)"}];
```

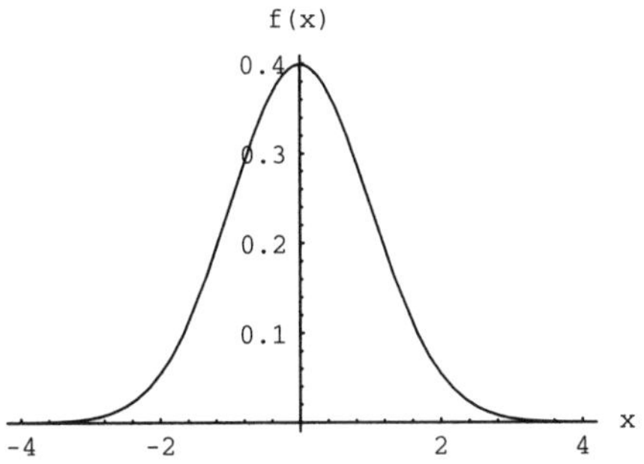


## EXERCISES

1. Consider the following function

$$f(x) = \frac{(1+x)^2 - 1}{x}, \quad \text{for} \quad x \neq 0.$$

   (a) Use the **Table** function of *Mathematica* to show that

   $\lim_{x \to 0^+} f(x) = 2$

   (b) Plot the function to confirm this limit.

2. Find the limits of the following functions, if they exist.

   (a) $\dfrac{1-x}{1+x}$ as $x \to \infty$

   (b) $\dfrac{e^x - 1}{x}$ as $x \to 0$

3. Show the following limits.

   (a) $\lim_{x \to 0^+} \sqrt{x} = 0$

   (b) $\lim_{x \to 0^+} x \log(x) = 0$

   (c) $\lim_{x \to 0} \dfrac{\sin x}{x} = 1$

   (d) $\lim_{x \to 0} \dfrac{1 - \cos x}{x} = 0$

4. Graph the following functions and verify the horizontal asymptotes.

   (a) $\lim_{x \to \infty} \left(1 - \dfrac{1}{x}\right) = 1$

   (b) $\lim_{x \to -\infty} \left(1 - \dfrac{1}{x}\right) = 1$

   (c) $\lim_{x \to \infty} \dfrac{3}{x^2} = 0$

   (d) $\lim_{x \to -\infty} \dfrac{3}{x^2} = 0$

5. By plotting, show that

(a) $\lim_{x \to 0^-} \frac{1}{x} = -\infty$

(b) $\lim_{x \to 0^+} \frac{1}{x} = \infty$

6. Consider the functions,

$$f(x) = \frac{x^2 - 1}{x - 1} \quad \text{and} \quad g(x) = x^2 - 4x$$

Show that

(a) $\lim_{x \to 1} (f(x) \pm g(x)) = \lim_{x \to 1} f(x) \pm \lim_{x \to 1} g(x)$

(b) $\lim_{x \to 1} \frac{f(x)}{g(x)} = \frac{\lim_{x \to 1} f(x)}{\lim_{x \to 1} g(x)}$

(c) $\lim_{x \to 1} [f(x)]^3 = \left[\lim_{x \to 1} f(x)\right]^3$

7. A manufacturer of plastic bags finds that due to volume discounting, the cost of producing $x$ tons of the product is given (in thousands of dollars) by the function:

$$C(x) = \left(\sqrt{x - 8} + [[x + 1]]\right), \; x > 8.$$

What is the cost as $x \to 8^+$? Here [[.]] denotes the greatest integer function. In *Mathematica*, this function is **Floor**.

## 2.1.2 Continuity

A continuous function is a function whose graph does not have any breaks. This is a good intuitive definition, but it is often difficult to apply for complicated functions. Hence, we use a definition that involves the limit.

> **Definition 2.2** *A function is said to be continuous at a point in its domain* x = c *if and only if*
>
> $$\lim_{x \to c} f(x) = f(c)$$

If $f(x)$ is continuous at all points $x$ on an interval $I$, it is said to be *continuous on I*. From the definition of the limit, continuity implies that for each $\varepsilon > 0$, there corresponds a $\delta > 0$ such that

$$|f(x) - f(c)| < \varepsilon \quad \text{if} \quad |x - c| < \delta.$$

**Example 2.8** $f(x) = x^2 + 3x - 2$ is continuous at $x = 1$ since

$$\lim_{x \to 1} f(x) = 2 = f(1).$$

**Example 2.9** Let us define $f(x) = (1 - \cos x)/x$ if $x \neq 0$. This definition excludes the point $x = 0$. Suppose we make the additional definition $f(0) = 0$. Is the function then continuous at $x = 0$? We use *Mathematica* function **Limit** to compute the limit of the function at $x = 0$.

*In[35]:=*
```
Clear[x];
Limit[(1-Cos[x])/x,x->0]
```

*Out[36]=*
```
0
```

Since the limit of $f(x)$ at $x = 0$ is $f(0)$, the function is continuous at this point. We plot the function below to confirm this. Note that the **Condition** function (**/;**) and the logical function **Unequal** (**!=**) are used to define $f(x)$. As shown in the plot, $f(x)$ has no break at $x = 0$ and hence it is continuous there. It is also continuous at every other point of the real line and hence, it is continuous on $(-\infty, \infty)$.

*In[37]:=*
```
Clear[f,x];
f[x_ /;  x!=0]:=  (1-Cos[x])/x;
f[x_ /;  x==0]:=  0 ;
Plot[f[x],{x,-2,2.1},AxesLabel->{"x","f(x)"}];
```

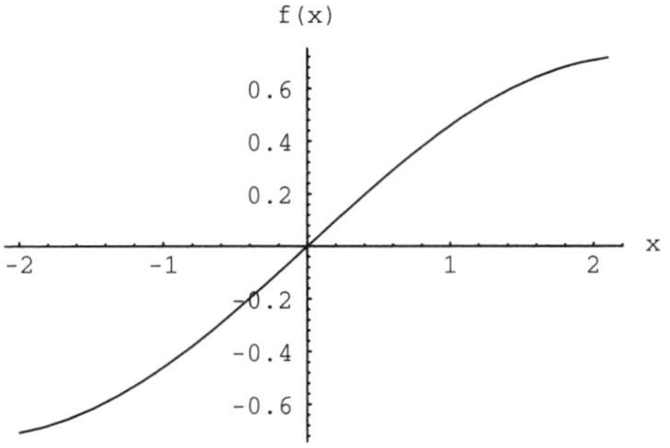


**Example 2.10** The following function is not defined at both $x = -1$ and $x = -1.5$.

$$f(x) = 1+\cfrac{1}{1+\cfrac{1}{1+\cfrac{1}{1+x}}}$$

How should one define $f(-1)$ and $f(-1.5)$ so that $f(x)$ is continuous at these points? The following *Mathematica* computation shows that

$$\lim_{x\to-1} f(x) = 2; \quad \lim_{x\to-1.5^+} f(x) = \infty; \quad \lim_{x\to-1.5^-} f(x) = -\infty.$$

*In[41]:=*
```
Clear[x];
f[x_]:=  1+(1/(1+(1/(1+(1/(1+x))))));
Limit[f[x],x->-1]
```

*Out[43]=*
```
2
```

*In[44]:=*

```
Limit[f[x],x->-1.5,Direction->-1]
```

*Out[44]=*

Infinity

*In[45]:=*

```
Limit[f[x],x->-1.5,Direction->1]
```

*Out[45]=*

–Infinity

Thus, $f(x)$ is continuous at $x = -1$ if $f(-1) = 2$. However, since the limit of $f(x)$ at $x = -1.5$ does not exist, the function cannot be made to be continuous at $x = -1.5$. We plot the function to illustrate the case.

*In[46]:=*

```
Clear[f,x];
f[x_ /; x!=-1]:= 1+(1/(1+(1/(1+(1/(1+x))))));
f[x_ /; x==-1]:= 2;
Plot[f[x],{x,-2,0},AxesLabel->{"f(x)","x"}];
```

Power::infy : Infinite expression $\frac{1}{0}$ encountered.

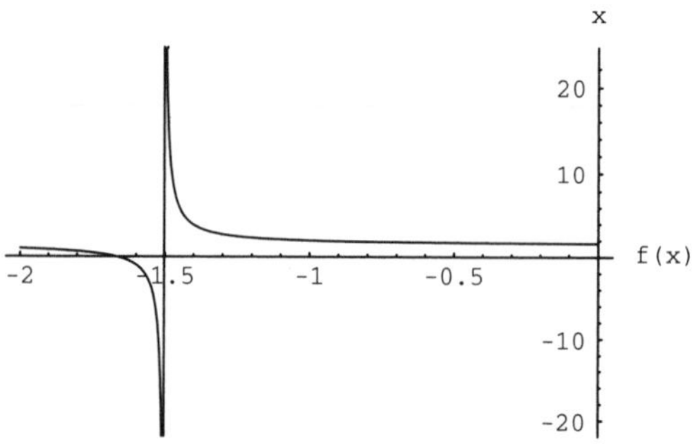


## EXERCISES

1. Use *Mathematica* to graph each of the following functions and then answer the questions about the continuity.
   (a) $f(x) = 2x - 1$ if $x \le 1$ and $f(x) = 3 - 2x$ if $x > 1$. Is $f(x)$ continuous at $x = 1$?
   (b) $f(x) = x^2/4 - 1$ if $0 < x < 2$, and $f(x) = 1 - 4/x^2$ if $2 < x$. Does the limit exist at $x = 2$? How should $f(2)$ be defined so that $f(x)$ is continuous at $x = 2$?
   (c) $f(x) = (x^2 - 1)/(x^3 - 1)$. Is $f(x)$ continuous over the interval $-2 \le x \le 2$?

2. The following functions are defined only if $x \ne 0$. How should $f(0)$ be defined so that $f(x)$ is continuous at $x = 0$?
   (a) $f(x) = \dfrac{\cos x}{x}$
   (b) $f(x) = \dfrac{(x-2)^3 + 8}{x}$
   (c) $f(x) = e^{-1/x^2}$

## □ 2.2 Differentiation of Functions □

### 2.2.1 Derivatives

**DEFINITION 2.3** *The function* $f(x)$ *is said to be* ***differentiable*** *at the point c if and only if the following limit,* $f'(c)$, *exists,*

$$f'(c) = \lim_{x \to 0} \frac{f(x) - f(c)}{x - c}$$

The number $f'(c)$ is called the *derivative* of $f(x)$ at $x = c$. If $f(x)$ has a derivative at each point of an open interval $I$, then the function $f'(x)$ is called the derivative of $f(x)$ on $I$.

Differentiability is a stronger condition than *continuity*. Namely, a function can be continuous at a point and not be differentiable there. Letting $h = x - c$, the derivative at point $x$ can be stated as

$$f'(x) = \lim_{h \to 0} \frac{f(x+h) - f(x)}{h}.$$

The derivative is sometimes written as

$$f'(x) = \frac{df}{dx}(x).$$

**Example 2.11** Show that the function $f(x) = a + x^2$ where $a$ is a constant, is differentiable at each point of its domain. We use the definition of the derivative to show that this function is differentiable for every $x$.

*In[50]:=*

```
Clear[f,x,a,h];
f[x_]:= a + x^2;
Limit[(f[x+h]-f[x])/h,h->0]
```

*Out[52]=*

```
2x
```

**Example 2.12** (Elasticity) The elasticity of a function $y = f(x)$ measures the percentage change in $y$ divided by the percentage change in $x$. That is,

$$\frac{\dfrac{f(x+h) - f(x)}{f(x)}}{\dfrac{h}{x}} = \frac{f(x+h) - f(x)}{h} \frac{x}{f(x)}.$$

If the derivative of the function exists, then the *elasticity* at the point $x$ is

$$\lim_{h \to 0} \left[ \frac{f(x+h) - f(x)}{h} \frac{x}{f(x)} \right] = f'(x) \frac{x}{f(x)}.$$

We evaluate the elasticity of the function $f(x) = xe^x$.

*In[53]:=*
```
Clear[f,x,h];
f[x_]:=  x*Exp[x];
Limit[((f[x+h]-f[x])/h)(x/f[x]),h->0]
```

*Out[55]=*
```
1 + x
```

Derivatives of $f(x)$ in *Mathematica* can be computed using the function **D**. Here is a description of this function.

*In[56]:=*
```
?D
```

**D[f, x] gives the partial derivative of f with respect to x. D[f, {x, n}] gives the nth partial derivative with respect to x. D[f, x1, x2, ...] gives a mixed derivative.**

**Example 2.13** Find the derivative of the function $f(x) = (x^2 + 3)/x$, and evaluate the derivative at $x = 2$.

*In[57]:=*
```
Clear[f,x];
f[x_]:=  (x^2+3)/x;
D[f[x],x]
```

*Out[59]=*

$$2 - \frac{3 + x^2}{x^2}$$

Since the derivative is itself a function of $x$, we could evaluate the derivative at a point by using the **ReplaceAll** (`/.`) function.

*In[60]:=*
```
D[f[x],x]  /.  x->2
```

*Out[60]=*

$$\frac{1}{4}$$

Alternatively we could use the prime notation for the derivative to compute directly the derivative at $x = 2$.

*In[61]:=*
```
f'[2]
```

*Out[61]=*

$$\frac{1}{4}$$

The *Mathematica* command **D[f[x],2]** is not equivalent to **D[f[x],x] /.x→2**. It would result in an error since the derivative of $f(x)$ with respect to a constant 2 has no meaning as shown below.

*In[62]:=*

```
Clear[f,x];
D[f[x],2]
```

General::ivar : 2 is not a valid variable.

*Out[63]=*

D[f[x], 2]

**Example 2.14** The total cost function of producing $Q$ units of output is found to be:

$$TC(Q) = Q^3 - 10Q^2 + 50Q + 20.$$

The marginal cost ($MC$) is defined as the derivative of $TC(Q)$, and the average cost ($AC$) is equal to $TC(Q)/Q$. The relationship between the average cost(solid line) and the marginal cost(dashed line) is plotted below. The $MC$ curve intersects the minimum point of the $AC$ curve.

*In[64]:=*

```
Clear[TC,MC,AC,Q];
TC[Q_]:= Q^3 - 10*Q^2 + 50*Q + 20;
MC[Q_]:= TC'[Q];
AC[Q_]:= TC[Q]/Q;
Plot[{AC[Q],MC[Q]},{Q,0.1,10},
        AxesLabel->{"Q","AC(Q),MC(Q)"},
         PlotStyle->{{},Dashing[{0.01}]}];
```

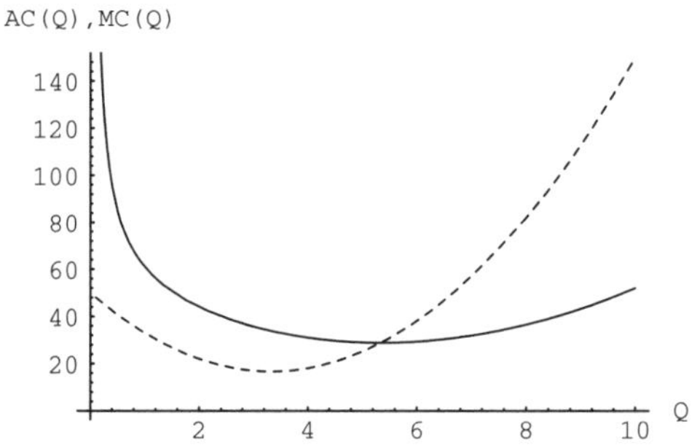


The derivative of a function $f(x)$ at a point $x = c$ is related to the slope of the tangent line $T(x)$ to the graph at the point, $(c,f(c))$. The slope of the tangent line is called the *gradient* of $f$ at $c$. The equation for the tangent line passing through $(c,f(c))$ is

$$T(x) = f(c) + f'(c)(x - c).$$

Hence, the gradient of the tangent is equal to $f'(c)$, which is the derivative of $f(x)$ at the point $x = c$.

**Example 2.15** Graph the exponential function $f(x) = e^x$ and the tangent line at $c = 2$. The tangent gradient at $c$ is equal to $f'(2) = e^2 \approx 7.389$.

*In[69]:=*

```
Clear[f,x,c,T]; c = 2;
f[x_]:= Exp[x];
T[x_]:= f[c] + f'[c]*(x-c);
Plot[{f[x],T[x]},{x,1,3},
        AxesLabel->{"x","f(x)"},
           PlotStyle->{{},Thickness[0.008]}];
```

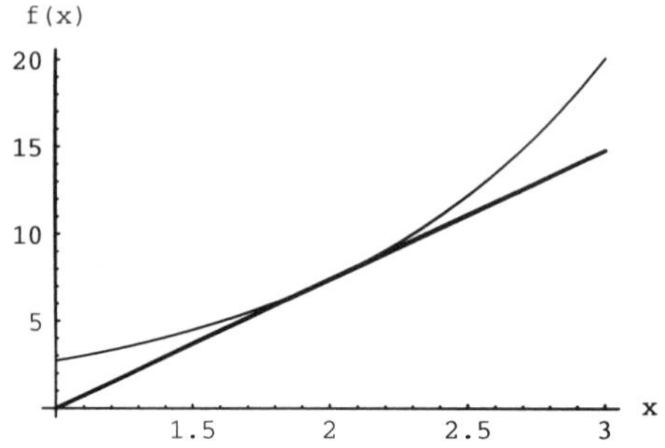


**Example 2.16** Graph the total cost, $T(Q)$, and the tangent line at $c = 6$ units of output. The tangent gradient is the marginal cost at $c$, $MC(c)$.

*In[73]:=*

```
c = 6;
Plot[{TC[Q],TC[c]+MC[c]*(Q-c)},{Q,0.1,10},
      AxesLabel->{"Q","TC(Q)"},
         PlotStyle->{{},Thickness[0.008]}];
```

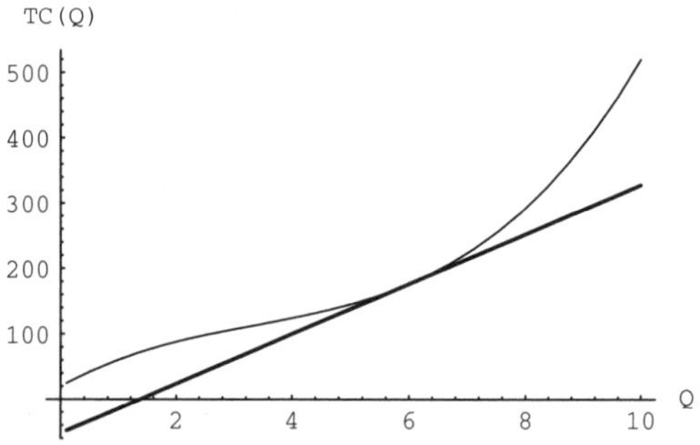


The derivative $f'(x)$ measures the rate of change of $f(x)$. A positive derivative on an interval $I$, i.e., $f'(x) > 0$, $x \in I$, indicates that the values of $f(x)$ increase as $x$ increases through the points on $I$. This can be observed through the relationship between the derivative and the slope of the tangent line. Similarly, if the derivative is negative on an interval $I$, then the values of the function decrease as $x$ increases through the interval.

In the case when $f'(c) = 0$ for some point $c$ in $I$, the rate of the change of the function is momentarily stationary and the tangent line is horizontal. The point $x = c$ is called a *stationary* or *critical point* of the function. These stationary points might be points where the function is changing from increasing to decreasing or vice-versa or neither. For example $f(x) = x^3$ increases on any interval that contains $x = 0$, yet $x = 0$ is a stationary point.

**Example 2.17** The function $f(x) = x^3 - 3x^2 + 5$ has the derivative $f'(x) = 3x^2 - 6x = 3x(x-2)$ and the sign of the derivative is as follows

$$f'(x) = \begin{cases} \text{positive}, & x < 0 \text{ or } x > 2 \\ \text{zero}, & x = 0 \text{ or } x = 2 \\ \text{negative}, & 0 < x < 2 \end{cases}$$

As shown in the following plot, $f(x)$ (solid line) is increasing on the interval $x < 0$ or $x > 2$ when $f'(x)$ (dash line) is positive; $f(x)$ is decreasing on the interval $0 < x < 2$ when $f'(x)$ is negative; and $f(x)$ has stationary points at $x = 0$ or $x = 2$.

*In[75]:=*

```
Clear[f,x];
f[x_]:= x^3-3*x^2+5;
Plot[{f[x],f'[x]},{x,-1,3},AxesLabel->{"x","f(x)"},
          PlotStyle->{{},Dashing[{0.01}]}];
```

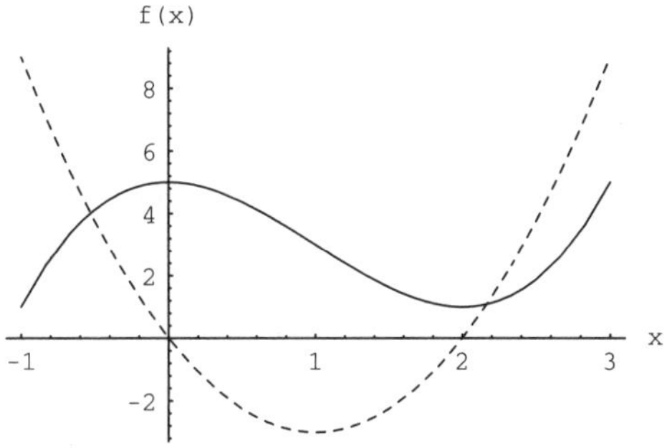


## EXERCISES

1. Using the **Limit** function, find the derivatives of the following functions.
   (a) $(x^2 + 1)^2$
   (b) $\left(\dfrac{x}{1 + e^{2x}}\right)^n$
   (c) $\dfrac{2x + 1}{x - 1}$
   (d) $xe^x$
2. Using the derivative function **D**, confirm the results obtained in Exercise 1.
3. The **logistic distribution function** of a random variable $x$ in statistics is defined as

$$f(x) = \frac{1}{1 + e^{-x}}$$

The derivative $f'(x)$ is called the **logistic density function**. Find the density function.

4. Total cost is defined as $TC(Q) = Q\ AC(Q)$. Use *Mathematica* to calculate the marginal cost, $MC(Q) = TC'(Q)$, and show that

$$AC'(Q) = (MC(Q) - AC(Q))/Q.$$

In other words, if $MC(Q) < AC(Q)$, then $AC(Q)$ is decreasing ($AC'(Q) < 0$); and if $MC(Q) > AC(Q)$, then $AC(Q)$ is increasing ($AC'(Q) > 0$).

5. If the average cost function is

$$AC(Q) = Q^3 - 3Q + 5,$$

plot the functions $AC(Q)$ and $AC'(Q)$ and show that $AC(Q)$ is increasing (decreasing) when $AC'(Q)$ is positive (negative). Find the stationary points.

6. If $\eta$ is the elasticity of total cost, $TC(Q)$, find the elasticity of the average cost, $AC(Q) = TC(Q)/Q$.

7. Find the tangent line for the following functions at the indicated points.

(a) $f(x) = \dfrac{x}{1 + x^2}$ at $c = 1.5$

(b) $f(x) = xe^x$ at $c = 1$

## 2.2.2 General rules of differentiation

Computing derivatives using limits can be quite tedious. The following properties of differentiation can be used to facilitate these computations. *Mathematica* automatically applies these rules when taking derivatives of a function.

*1. Addition rule* The derivative of the sum (difference) of two differentiable functions is the sum (difference) of the derivatives of the two functions. That is, if $f(x) = g(x) \pm h(x)$, then $f'(x) = g'(x) \pm h'(x)$.

**Example 2.18** Both the total revenue $TR(Q)$ and total cost $TC(Q)$ are functions of quantity, $Q$. The total profit $TP(Q)$ is then the difference $TP(Q) = TR(Q) - TC(Q)$. The marginal profit, $TP'(Q) = TR'(Q) - TC'(Q)$, is the difference between the marginal revenue and the marginal cost.

*In[78]:=*

```
Clear[TR,TC,TP,Q];
TP[Q_]:= TR[Q] - TC[Q];
D[TP[Q],Q]
```

*Out[80]=*

```
-TC'[Q] + TR'[Q]
```

*2. Product rule* The derivative of the product of two differentiable functions is equal to the derivative of the first function times the second function plus the derivative of the second function times the first function. That is, if $f(x) = g(x)h(x)$, then $f'(x) = g'(x)h(x) + g(x)h'(x)$.

**Example 2.19** The total revenue $TR(Q) = QP(Q)$ is the product of the quantity $Q$ and the inverse demand function $P(Q)$. The marginal revenue is then equal to $TR'(Q) = P(Q) + QP'(Q)$.

*In[81]:=*
```
Clear[TR,Q,P];
TR[Q_]:= Q*P[Q];
D[TR[Q],Q]
```

*Out[83]=*
```
P[Q] + Q_P'[Q]
```

If we define the elasticity of demand as

$$\eta = -\frac{dQ}{dP}\frac{P}{Q}$$

one can show that the marginal revenue is equal to

$$TR'(Q) = P\left(1 - \frac{1}{\eta}\right).$$

From this we deduce the following important results:

(1) If the demand is elastic, i.e., $\eta > 1$, a small increase in price results in increase in total revenue since the marginal revenue is postive, $TR'(Q) > 0$.

(2) If the demand is unitary elastic, i.e., $\eta = 1$, a small increase in price will not change the total revenue since the marginal revenue is 0.

(3) If the demand is inelastic, i.e., $\eta < 1$, a small increase in price results in decrease in total revenue since the marginal revenue is negative, $TR'(Q) < 0$.

*3. Quotient rule* If $g(x)$ and $h(x)$ are differentiable functions, then the function $f(x) = g(x)/h(x)$ is differentiable at the points $x$ where $h(x) \neq 0$, and the derivative is

$$f'(x) = \frac{h(x)g'(x) - g(x)h'(x)}{[h(x)]^2}.$$

**Example 2.20** The average cost $AC(Q)$ is defined as the ratio of total cost $TC(Q)$ to quantity $Q$ when $Q > 0$, i.e., $AC(Q) = TC(Q)/Q$. The derivative of the average cost can be obtained from *Mathematica* calculation.

*In[84]:=*
```
Clear[AC,Q];
AC[Q_]:= TC[Q]/Q;
D[AC[Q],Q] // Simplify
```

*Out[86]=*

$$\frac{-TC[Q] + Q\,TC'[Q]}{Q^2}$$

This result can be further simplified by noting that

$$AC'(Q) = \frac{TC'(Q)\,Q - TC(Q)}{Q^2} = \frac{1}{Q}\left[TC'(Q) - \frac{TC(Q)}{Q}\right]$$
$$= \frac{1}{Q}[TC'(Q) - AC(Q)].$$

The last expression shows that

$$AC'(Q) = \begin{cases} \text{positive}, TC'(Q) > AC(Q) \\ \text{zero}, TC'(Q) = AC(Q) \\ \text{negative}, TC'(Q) < AC(Q). \end{cases}$$

That is, the average cost is increasing (decreasing) when the marginal cost $MC(Q) = TC'(Q)$ is greater (less) than the average cost $AC(Q)$. $MC(Q)$ intersects $AC(Q)$ when $MC(Q) = AC(Q)$. Example 2.14 in section 2.2.1 shows this result.

4. *Chain rule* If $z = g(y)$ and $y$ itself is a function of $x$, $y = h(x)$, then $z = g(h(x)) = f(x)$ is called the *composite function* of $g$ and $h$. The derivative of $f$ with respect to $x$ can be computed if both $g(x)$ and $h(x)$ are differentiable functions. The rules for differentiating composite functions are called *chain rules*. For the above composite function, the chain rule states

$$\frac{dz}{dx} = f'(x) = g'(h(x))\,h'(x).$$

Alternatively, we can express the derivative as

$$\frac{dz}{dx} = \frac{dz}{dy}\frac{dy}{dx} = g'(y)\,h'(x).$$

**Example 2.21** Let $TR = g(Q)$ be the total revenue function where the output $Q$ is a function of labor input $L$ specified in a production function $Q = h(L)$. Then the total revenue is a function of $L$, i.e., $TR = g(h(L)) = f(L)$. The marginal revenue product of labor is the derivative of $TR = g(h(L))$ with respect of $L$, i.e.,

*In[87]:=*
```
Clear[TR,g,h,L];
TR[L_]:= g[h[L]];
D[TR[L],L]
```

*Out[89]=*
```
g'[h[L]] h'[L]
```

Thus the marginal revenue product of labor is equal to the marginal revenue, $g'(Q) = g'(h(L))$, times the marginal physical product of labor, $h'(L)$.

5. *Inverse function rule* If a differentiable function $f(x)$ has an inverse $f^{-1}(y)$ i.e., $f^{-1}(f(x)) = x$ and $f(f^{-1}(y)) = y$, then the inverse function is differentiable provided that $f'(x)$ does not vanish. In particular,

$$(f^{-1})'(y) = \frac{1}{f'(f^{-1}(y))}.$$

If we use the Liebnitz notation for the derivative, i.e., $dy/dx = f'(x)$ and $dx/dy = (f^{-1})'(y)$, then this formula can be written in the compact form:

$$\frac{dx}{dy} = \frac{1}{\frac{dy}{dx}}$$

**Example 2.22** The demand function $Q = f(P)$ expresses the quantity $Q$ as a function of price $P$. The inverse demand function expresses price as a function of the quantity, $P = f^{-1}(Q) = g(Q)$. The demand elasticity $\eta$ can be expressed in terms of the derivative of the demand function,

$$\eta = -\frac{dQ}{dP}\frac{P}{Q} = -f'(P)\frac{P}{f(P)}$$

or in terms of the derivative of the inverse demand function,

$$\eta = -\frac{1}{dQ/dP}\frac{P}{Q} = -\frac{1}{g'(Q)}\frac{g(Q)}{Q}.$$

*6. Implicit differentiation* To find the derivative of a function $y = f(x)$ defined implicitly by an equation in $x$ and $y$ such as

$$x^2y + y^2x = 2,$$

we take the derivative $dy/dx$ by treating $y$ as an unknown but nonetheless differentiable function of $x$. Differentiating both sides of the equation, we obtain

$$\frac{d}{dx}(x^2y) + \frac{d}{dx}(y^2x) = \frac{d}{dx}(2) = 0.$$

Using the product and chain rules, we have

$$\left[x^2\frac{dy}{dx} + y(2x)\right] + \left[x(2y)\frac{dy}{dx} + y^2\right] = 0.$$

Solving for $dy/dx$,

$$\frac{dy}{dx} = \frac{-y^2 - 2xy}{x^2 + 2xy}.$$

This is called *implicit differentiation*. By denoting $y(x)$ as the function of $x$ implicitly, the above implicit differentiation is easily accomplished using *Mathematica*.

*In[90]:=*

```
Clear[y,x];
equation = (x^2)*y[x] + (y[x]^2)*x == 2;
Solve[D[equation,x],y'[x]]
```

*Out[92]=*

$$\{\{y'[x] \to -(\frac{2xy[x] + y[x]^2}{x^2 + 2xy[x]})\}\}$$

To help us visualize our result, we can produce a graph of the equation $x^2y + y^2x = 2$ using the **ImplicitPlot** function that is in the **ImplicitPlot package**.

*In[93]:=*

```
Needs["Graphics`ImplicitPlot`"];
```

*In[94]:=*

```
ImplicitPlot[y*x^2+x*y^2==2,{x,-5,5},{y,-5,5},
  AxesOrigin->{0,0},PlotPoints->100];
```

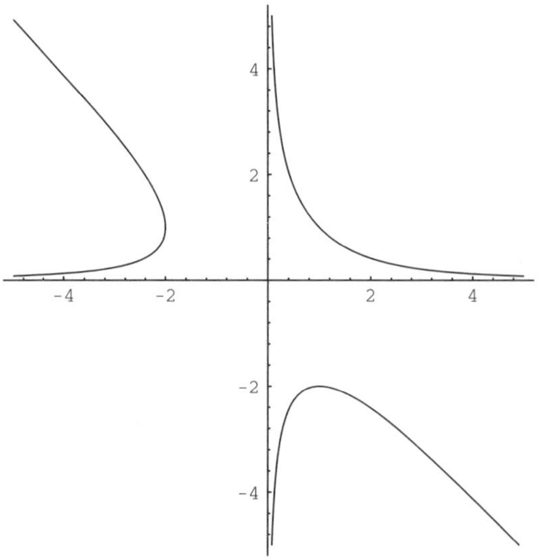


Notice how the slope of the tangent line to the curves becomes infinite as $x \to 0^+$, $y \neq 0$, and at the point (–2,1). This agrees with our formula for $y'(x)$.

**Example 2.23** Consider a utility function of two goods, $x$ and $y$.

$$u = f(x, y) = \log x + \log y.$$

An indifference curve (an iso-utility curve) is a functional relation between $x$ and $y$ at a constant level of utility, say $u = k$, where $k$ is a constant. Taking the derivative of $f(x, y) = \log x + \log y = k$ implicitly, we have

$$\frac{1}{x} + \frac{1}{y}\frac{dy}{dx} = 0.$$

Now the slope of the indifference curve, $dy/dx$, is

$$\frac{dy}{dx} = -\frac{y}{x}.$$

The negative of the derivative, $-dy/dx = y/x$, is called the *marginal rate of substitution* of good $x$ for good $y$.

*In[95]:=*

```
Clear[y,x,k];
equation = Log[x] + Log[y[x]] == k;
Solve[D[equation,x],y'[x]]
```

*Out[97]=*

$$\{\{y'[x] \to -(\frac{y[x]}{x})\}\}$$

## EXERCISES

1. Find derivatives of the following functions at $x = c$.
   (a) $f(x) = \log\left(\frac{1}{1+x^2}\right)$ at $c = 1$
   (b) $f(x) = (e^x + e^{-x})^2$ at $c = 0$
   (c) $f(x) = \frac{1}{1+e^{1+2x}}$ at $c = 0$
   (d) $f(x) = x^x(1 + \log x)$ at $c = 1$
   (e) $f(x) = \frac{(x-1)(x+2)}{(x+1)(x-2)}$ at $c = 0$
2. Find the derivative $dx/dy$ of the inverse function.
   (a) $y = 2x$
   (b) $y = \frac{1}{1+e^{-x}}$
   (c) $y = \log x$
3. It is known that
   (a) $e^{(a+b)x} = e^{ax}e^{bx}$
   (b) $\log(ax) = \log(a) + \log(x)$
   (c) $\cos(a+b)x = \cos(ax)\cos(bx) - \sin(ax)\sin(bx)$
   (d) $\sin(a+b)x = \sin(ax)\cos(bx) + \cos(ax)\sin(bx)$
   Take the derivatives of the both sides and show that the results are equal.
4. Using implicit differentiation, find $dy/dx$.
   (a) $x^3 + y^3 = 3xy$
   (b) $e^x + e^y = 100$
   (c) $\log(x^2 + y^2) = 2$
5. Consider a production function $Q = f(L,K)$ with labor $L$ and capital $K$ inputs. At a given constant output $Q$, the marginal rate of technical substitution (MRTS) is the negative of the derivative $dK/dL$. Find the MRTS at $Q = 10$ units for the following two production functions.
   (a) CES (constant elasticity of substitution production function)

   $$Q = A[aL^b + (1-a)K^b]^{1/b}$$

   (b) GPF (generalized production function)

   $$Qe^{rQ} = AL^aK^b$$

### 2.2.3 Higher-order derivatives

The derivative of a function is itself a function. Therefore, it seems reasonable to be able to take the derivative of a derivative. Namely,

$$\lim_{x\to c}\frac{f'(x)-f'(c)}{x-c}.$$

If this limit exists, we call it the second derivative of $f$ at $x = c$ and denote it by $f''(c)$ or, in Liebnitz notation,

$$\frac{d^2f}{dx^2}(c).$$

Taking the derivative of the second derivative gives the third derivative, which is denoted by $f'''(c)$ or

$$\frac{d^3f}{dx^3}(c).$$

We can continue this process as long as the derivatives are differentiable at $x = c$. We call $f''(c)$, $f'''(c)$, etc., *higher derivatives* of $f(x)$ at $x = c$.

The *Mathematica* commands for higher-order derivatives are **D[f[x],{x,2}]** or **f''[x]** for the second derivative, **D[f[x],{x,3}]** or **f'''[x]** for the third derivative, etc.

**Example 2.24** Compute the first three derivatives of the function $f(x) = 2x^3 + 3$.

*In[98]:=*
```
Clear[f,x];
f[x_]:= 2*x^3+3;
f'[x]
```

*Out[100]=*
$6x^2$

*In[101]:=*
```
f''[x]
```

*Out[101]=*
12x

*In[102]:=*
```
D[f[x],{x,3}]
```

*Out[102]=*
12

**Example 2.25** Given that $f(x) = e^x$, show that $f'(x) = e^x$, $f''(x) = e^x$, and so forth.

*In[103]:=*
```
Clear[f,x];
f[x_]:= Exp[x];
D[f[x],{x,1}]
```

*Out[105]=*

$E^x$

*In[106]:=*

```
D[f[x],{x,2}]
```

*Out[106]=*

$E^x$

*In[107]:=*

```
D[f[x],{x,3}]
```

*Out[107]=*

$E^x$

The first derivative of a function $f(x)$ at a point measures the slope of the tangent line at that point, or the rate of change of the function at that point. It can be used to determine if a function is increasing or decreasing on an interval. The second derivative, $f''(x)$, measures that rate of change of the first derivative, $f'(x)$. Furthermore, it has implications about the shape of the graph of $f$. We say that the graph of $f$ is *convex* on an interval $I$ when $f'(x)$ is increasing on $I$, i.e., $f''(x) > 0$ for $x \in I$, and *concave* when $f'(x)$ is decreasing on $I$, i.e., $f''(x) < 0$ for $x \in I$.

If a function changes from being convex to being concave, or vice versa, at some point $c$, then the sign of the second derivative change from positive to negative, or vice versa. If $f''(x)$ exists in a neighborhood of $x = c$, then $f''(c) = 0$. The point $c$ is called an *inflection point* of $f$.

**Example 2.26** The function $f(x) = x^4 - 6x^2 - 8x + 10$ is plotted (thick line) along with $f'(x)$ (solid line) and $f''(x)$ (dashed line).

*In[108]:=*

```
Clear[f,x];
f[x_]:= x^4 - 6*x^2 - 8*x + 10;
Plot[{f[x],f'[x],f''[x]},{x,-2,3},
      PlotStyle->{Thickness[0.008],{},Dashing[{0.02}]},
      AxesLabel->{"x","f(x), f'(x), f''(x)"},
      AspectRatio->0.8];
```

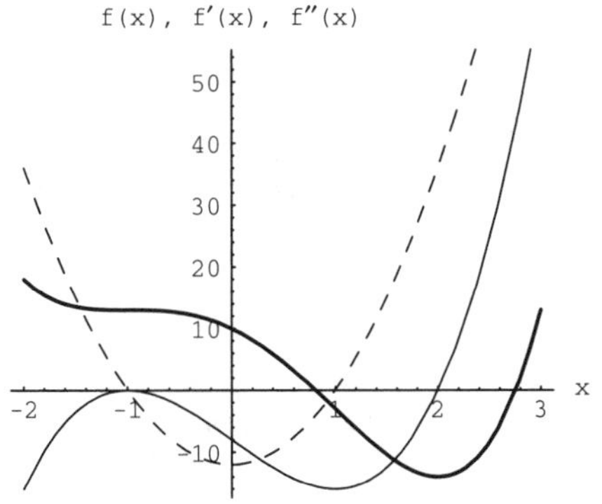

The graphs show the following properties:

(1) $f'(x) < 0$ and $f''(x) > 0$ for $x < -1$.
$f(x)$ is decreasing and convex.

(2) $f'(x) = 0$ and $f''(x) = 0$ at $x = -1$.
$x = -1$ is both a critical and inflection point.

(3) $f'(x) < 0$ and $f''(x) < 0$ for $-1 < x < 1$.
$f(x)$ is decreasing and concave.

(4) $f''(x) = 0$ at $x = 1$.
$x = 1$ is an inflection point.

(5) $f'(x) < 0$ and $f''(x) > 0$ for $1 < x < 2$.
$f(x)$ is decreasing and convex.

(6) $f'(x) = 0$ for $x = 2$.
$x = 2$ is a critical point.

(7) $f'(x) > 0$ and $f''(x) > 0$ for $x > 2$.
$f(x)$ is increasing and convex.

## EXERCISES

1. Find $f''(x)$ and $f'''(x)$ for the following functions at $x = c$.
   (a) $f(x) = \log\left(\dfrac{1}{1+x^2}\right)$ at $c = 1$
   (b) $f(x) = (e^x + e^{-x})^2$ at $c = 0$
   (c) $f(x) = \dfrac{1}{1+e^{1+2x}}$ at $c = 0$
   (d) $f(x) = x^x\,(1+\log x)$ at $c = 1$
   (e) $f(x) = \dfrac{(x-1)(x+2)}{(x+1)(x-2)}$ at $c = 0$

2. Plot the following functions and examine the sign of second derivatives to determine intervals where the function is convex or concave. Find the inflection points.
   (a) $f(x) = x^2(x - 2)$
   (b) $f(x) = xe^x$
   (c) $f(x) = \dfrac{1}{1+e^{1+2x}}$

### 2.2.4 Relative maxima and minima

One of the most important applications of differentiation in economics is locating *relative maxima* and *minima* of a function.

**Definition 2.4** *Let $f(x)$ be a function, and let $c$ be a point in its domain. If $f(c) \geq f(x)$ for all $x$ in an open interval containing $c$, then $f(c)$ is called a **relative maximum** of $f$ and $c$ is called a **relative maximum point**. A **relative minimum** and a **relative minimum point** are defined in a similar fashion. A **relative extremum** is either a relative maximum or a relative minimum.*

**Example 2.27** Consider the graph of the function

$$f(x) = \begin{cases} 1 + |x-1|, & 0 \le x < 2 \\ (3-x)^3 + \dfrac{3}{4}x - \dfrac{1}{2}, & 2 \le x \le 4 \end{cases}$$

on the interval [0,4].

*In[111]:=*

```
Clear[f,x];
f[x_ /; 0<=x<2]:=1+Abs[x-1];
f[x_ /; 2<=x<=4]:=(3-x)^3 + 3/4*x - 1/2;
Plot[f[x],{x,0,4},AxesLabel->{"x","f(x)"}];
```

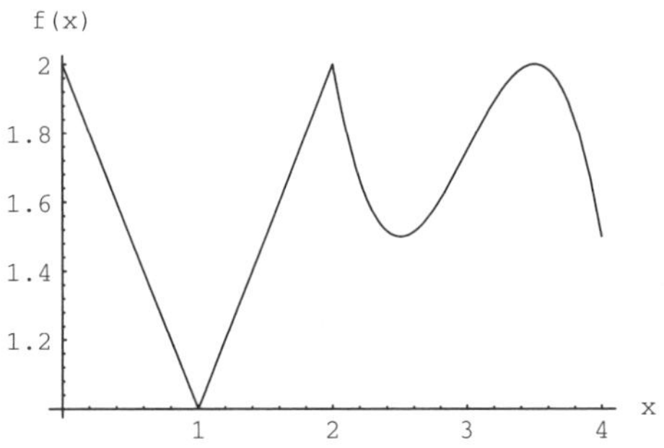


We note that this function is not differentiable at $x = 1$ and $x = 2$. The graph shows that the function has relative maxima at $x = 2$ and $x = 3.5$ and relative minima at $x = 1$ and $x = 2.5$. We have not included the endpoints of the interval [0,4], however. Technically, an endpoint cannot be a relative extremum since the open interval on which the function is defined does not include the endpoint.

This example demonstrates that a relative extreme point needs not be at a point where the function is differentiable. However, the following theorem gives a necessary condition for a differentiable function to have a relative extremum.

**THEOREM 2.2** *(Necessary Condition) Suppose $f(x)$ is differentiable in a neighborhood of the the point c. If f has a relative extremum at c, then $f'(c) = 0$.*

Since the above condition is related to the first-order derivative, it is often referred to as a *first-order condition.* The theorem provides a convenient way of locating relative extrema. If $f(x)$ is differentiable, the relative extreme points are the stationary or critical points of the function.

**Example 2.28** The function

$$f(x) = 2x^3 - 3x^2 - 12x + 5$$

is differentiable on the interval $-2 < x < 3$. To find the critical points, we solve the equation $f'(x) = 0$.

*In[115]:=*

```
Clear[f,x]
f[x_]:= 2*x^3 - 3*x^2 - 12*x + 5;
Solve[f'[x]==0,x]
```

*Out[117]=*
```
{{x → -1}, {x → 2}}
```

As shown in the following plot, we observe that the critical point $x = -1$ is a relative maximum point, and $x = 2$ is a relative minimum point.

*In[118]:=*
```
Plot[f[x],{x,-2,3},AxesLabel->{"x","f(x)"}];
```

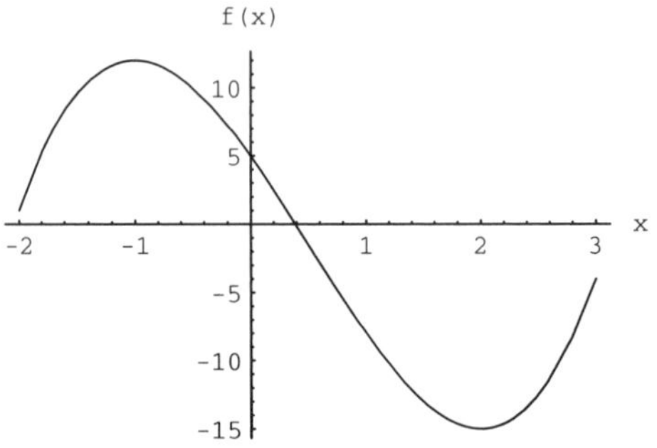


Of course, the mere fact that $f'(c) = 0$ does not guarantee that $f(x)$ has a relative extremum at $c$. For example, consider the function $f(x) = x^3$. Then $f'(x) = 3x^2$, and hence, $f'(0) = 0$. But $f$ does not have a relative extremum at $x = 0$. The following plot confirms this assertion.

*In[119]:=*
```
Plot[x^3,{x,-1,1},AxesLabel->{"x","f(x)"}];
```

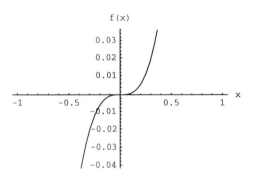

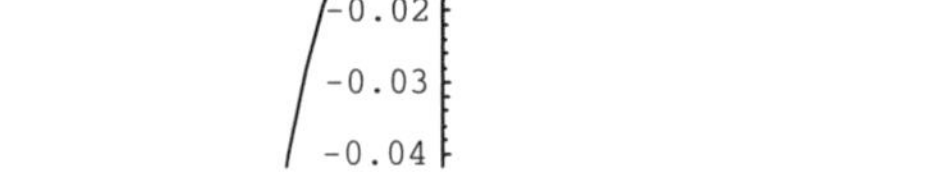


If a function is differentiable at $c$, $f'(c) = 0$ is a necessary condition that $f(x)$ has a relative extremum at $x = c$, but it is not a sufficient condition.

**THEOREM 2.3** *(Sufficient Condition) Suppose $f(x)$ is twice differentiable on an open interval containing a critical point $c$. Then $f(x)$ has a relative maximum at $c$ if $f''(c) < 0$, and $f$ has a relative minimum* at *$c$ if $f''(c) > 0$.*

The sufficient condition is sometimes called the *second-order condition*. This theorem is easily shown by observing that the second derivative is related to the concavity of the function. For a relative maximum, the function $f(x)$ must be concave on an open interval containing the critical point $c$ and convex for a relative minimum. Concave ($f''(x) < 0$) indicates a relative maximum and convex ($f''(x) > 0$) indicates a relative minimum.

**Example 2.29** Find the relative extrema of the function

$f(x) = x^4 - 4x^3 + 4x^2$

on the open interval $(-\infty,+\infty)$.

*In[120]:=*
```
Clear[f,x];
f[x_]:= x^4 - 4*x^3 + 4*x^2;
Solve[f'[x]==0,x]
```

*Out[122]=*
$\{\{x \to 0\}, \{x \to 1\}, \{x \to 2\}\}$

The critical points are at $x = 0$, 1, and 2. We check the second-order condition by evaluating the second derivative at the critical points.

*In[123]:=*
```
f''[0]
```

*Out[123]=*
8

*In[124]:=*
```
f''[1]
```

*Out[124]=*
−4

*In[125]:=*
```
f''[2]
```

*Out[125]=*
8

Since $f''(0) = f''(2) = 8 > 0$, $x = 0$ and $x = 2$ are points where $f$ has a relative minimum; and since $f''(1) = -4 < 0$, $x = 1$ is a relative maximum point. The following plot shows that $f(x)$ is convex in the neighborhood of $(0,f(0))$ and $(2,f(2))$ and concave in the neighborhood of $(1,f(1))$.

*In[126]:=*
```
Plot[f[x],{x,-2,3},AxesLabel->{"x","f(x)"}];
```

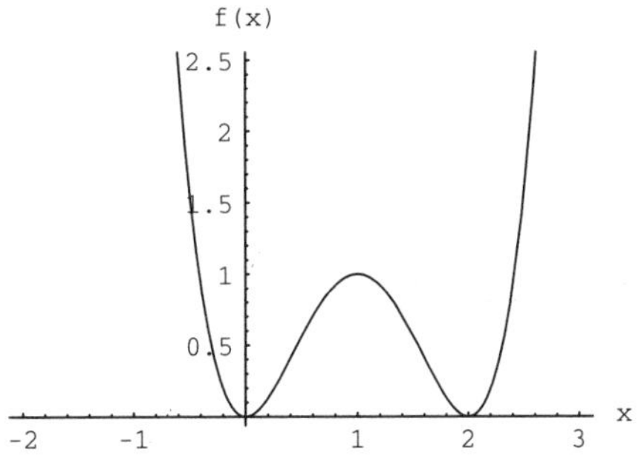

**Example 2.30** The function

$$f(x) = 3x^4 - 16x^3 + 30x^2 - 24x + 12$$

has two critical points at $x = 1$ and 2. The point $x = 2$ corresponds to a relative minimum since $f'(2) = 0$ and $f''(2) = 12 > 0$. The point $x = 1$ is an inflection point since $f''(1) = 0$ and $f''(x)$ changes signs at $x = 1$.

*In[127]:=*
```
Clear[f,x];
f[x_]:= 3*x^4 - 16*x^3 + 30*x^2 - 24*x + 12;
Solve[f'[x]==0,x]
```

*Out[129]=*
{{x → 1}, {x → 1}, {x → 2}}

*In[130]:=*
```
f''[2]
```

*Out[130]=*
12

*In[131]:=*
```
f''[1]
```

*Out[131]=*
0

*In[132]:=*
```
Plot[f[x],{x,0,3},AxesLabel->{"x","f(x)"}];
```

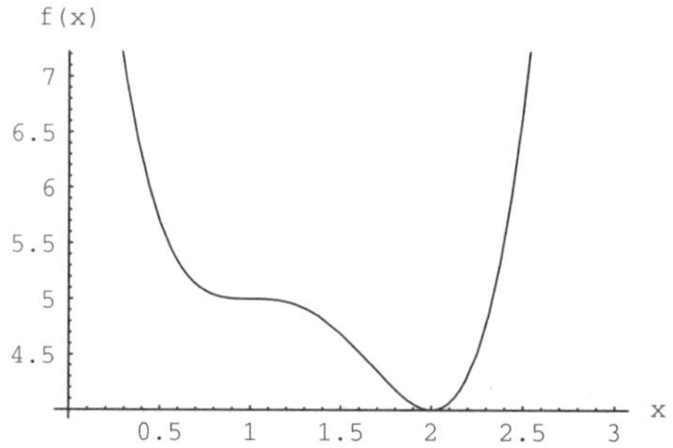


## EXERCISES

1. Find the relative extrema (if any) of the following functions. Graph the functions to confirm it.
   (a) $f(x) = x^3 - 6x^2 + 12x + 10$.
   (b) $f(x) = x^4 - 4x^3$
   (c) $f(x) = (x^2 - 75)/(x - 10)$ for $0 < x < 10$.

2. Find the relative extrema of the function

$$f(x) = \frac{x}{(x^2 + a^2)^{3/2}}$$

3. Consider a linear demand function, $Q = a + bP$, and a total cost function, $C = Q^2 + kQ + f$, where $a$, $b$, $k$, and $f$ are fixed constants. Find the profit, $(PQ - C)$, maximizing price ($P$) and quantity ($Q$).

4. The Red Apple Orchard Corporation estimated if 24 apple trees are planted per acre, then each mature tree will yield 500 apples per year. For each additional tree planted per acre, the number of apples produced per tree is decreased by 11 per year. How many trees should be planted per acre to obtain the most apples per acre?

5. A psychologist measures the learning performance of workers by a numerical score on a standardize test. He determines that this score as a function of time spent in traning is given by

$$S(t) = 15t^2 - t^3, \ t \geq 0.$$

What is the optimal training time?

## □ 2.3 Integration □

### 2.3.1 Indefinite integral

Differentiation of a differentiable function $F(x)$ produces the function $F'(x)$. $F(x)$ is called an *antiderivative* of $F'(x)$. Antidifferentiation (integration) is essentially a process that reverses differentiation. Many applications of calculus in economics requires the determination of an antiderivative. For example, let $F(x)$ be the total cost of producing $x$ quantity of a good. If the marginal cost $F'(x)$ is known to be $F'(x) = 3 + x$, then the total cost function, $F(x)$ can be found using integration.

**DEFINITION 2.5** *A function $F(x)$ is an* ***antiderivative*** *of a function $f(x)$* if $F'(x) = f(x)$.

**Example 2.31** The total cost functions

$$F(x) = 3x + x^2$$
$$F(x) = 3x + x^2 + 5$$
$$F(x) = 3x + x^2 - 10$$

are all antiderivatives of the marginal cost function, $f(x) = 3 + 2x$, since each function $F(x)$ has the derivative $F'(x) = 3 + 2x$.

From the above example, it is clear that if $F(x)$ is an antiderivative of $f(x)$, then $F(x) + c$ is also an antiderivative, where $c$ is an arbitrary constant. If $F(x)$ is an antiderivative, i.e., $F'(x) = f(x)$, then

$$\frac{\mathrm{d}}{\mathrm{d}x}(F(x) + c) = f(x) + 0 = f(x).$$

The set of all antiderivatives of $f(x)$ is called the *indefinite integral* of $f$ with respect to $x$ and is denoted as

$$\int f(x)\,\mathrm{d}x = F(x) + c.$$

The symbol $x$ in the indefinite integral, is called the *variable of integral*, and $f(x)$ is called the *integrand.*

**Example 2.32** Find the antiderivatives of the function, $f(x) = 1/x$. It can be shown that the antiderivative of $f(x) = 1/x$ is $F(x) = \ln|x| + \mathrm{c}$. If $x > 0$, then $F(x) = \ln x + c$ and hence, $F'(x) = 1/x$; if $x < 0$, then $F(x) = \ln(-x) + \mathrm{c}$ and hence, $F'(x) = 1/x$. In the indefinite integral notation, we have

$$\int \frac{1}{x}\,\mathrm{d}x = \ln|x| + c.$$

Indefinite integrals satisfy the same linearity properties as derivatives.
(1) The integral of sums is the sum of integrals:

$$\int (f(x) + g(x))\,\mathrm{d}x = \int f(x)\,\mathrm{d}x + \int g(x)\,\mathrm{d}x.$$

(2) A constant can be moved across integral:

$$\int k f(x)\,\mathrm{d}x = k \int f(x)\,\mathrm{d}x.$$

**Example 2.33** Suppose the price elasticity of demand is constant, say

$$\frac{\mathrm{d}Q}{\mathrm{d}P}\frac{P}{Q} = -k$$

where $Q$ and $P$ are quantity and price, respectively, and $k$ is a constant. What is the demand function? We rearrange the above equation as

$$\frac{\mathrm{d}Q}{Q} = -k\frac{\mathrm{d}P}{P}.$$

Taking the indefinite integral of both sides, we have

$$\int \frac{\mathrm{d}Q}{Q} = -k\int \frac{\mathrm{d}P}{P}$$

which in turn yields

$$\ln|Q| + c_1 = -k\ln|P| + c_2$$

where $c_1$ and $c_2$ are arbitrary constants. Assuming $P$ and $Q$ are positive, we have the demand function

$Q = cP^{-k}$

where $c$ is a new arbitrary constant. The function is a general form of a constant price elasticity of demand function.

*Mathematica* provides the built-in function, **Integrate**, for computing the indefinite integral.

*In[133]:=*
```
?Integrate
```

**Integrate[f,x] gives the indefinite integral of f with respect to x. Integrate[f,{x,xmin,xmax}] gives the definite integral. Integrate[f,{x,xmin,xmax},{y,ymin,ymax}] gives a multiple integral.**

**Example 2.34** Find an antiderivative of $f(x) = xe^x$.

*In[134]:=*
```
Clear[f,x];
f[x_]:=  x*Exp[x];
F[x]=Integrate[f[x],x]
```

*Out[136]=*
```
E^x(-1 + x)
```

We can check the answer by differentiating it and seeing if $F'(x) = f(x)$.

*In[137]:=*
```
D[F[x],x]  //  Simplify
```

*Out[137]=*
```
E^x x
```

Note that the *Mathematica* **Integrate** function does not automatically add an arbitrary constant to the antiderivative. As we shall see in later chapters on differential equations, this arbitrary constant plays an important role. Hence it is a good practice to include it. This can be accomplished by appending it to the **Integrate** function.

**Example 2.35** Find the indefinite integral of $f(x) = \ln x$.

*In[138]:=*
```
Clear[x,c];
Integrate[Log[x],x]  +  c
```

*Out[139]=*
```
c - x + x Log[x]
```

**Example 2.36** The net investment $x(t)$ is the rate of change in capital stock $y(t)$ over time $t$, i.e., $x(t) = dy/dt$. The capital stock is then the antiderivative of the investment flow,

$$y(t) = \int x(t)\,dt.$$

Suppose the investment flow at time $t$ is given by the function

$$x(t) = a\,t^b$$

where $a$ and $b$ are constant. The capital stock is calculated by integrating $x(t)$.

*In[140]:=*

```
Clear[x,t,a,b,c];
x[t_]:=  a*t^b;
Integrate[x[t],t]  +  c
```

*Out[142]=*

$$c + \frac{a t^{1+b}}{1+b}$$

## EXERCISES

1. Evaluate the indefinite integrals using the **Integrate** function.
   (a) $\int\left(x^2 - \sqrt{x}\right)dx$
   (b) $\int x \ln x \, dx$
   (c) $\int x^2 e^{-3x} dx$
   (d) $\int x \sin(2x^2)\,dx$
   (e) $\int \frac{e^x}{1 + e^x} dx$
   (f) $\int \frac{e^x + e^{-x}}{e^x - e^{-x}} dx$

2. The marginal revenue function $f'(Q)$ is the derivative of the total revenue function $f(Q)$. Find the total revenue functions for the following marginal revenue functions:
   (a) $f'(Q) = 25 - Q$
   (b) $f'(Q) = \frac{10}{Q}$
   (c) $f'(Q) = 2e^{-Q/2}$

### 2.3.2 The definite integral

Integral calculus was introduced originally to measure the area under a curve. Suppose a function $f(x)$ is a non-negative function and is defined over an interval $[a,b]$. A *uniform partition* of the interval $[a,b]$ is a set points $\{x_0, x_1, \ldots, x_n\}$ such that

$$a = x_0,\ x_1 = x_0 + \Delta x,\ x_2 = x_0 + 2\Delta x,\ \ldots,\ x_n = x_0 + n\Delta x = b$$

where $\Delta x = (b-a)/n$ is the length of each subinterval. The sum

$$\sum_{i=1}^{n} f(x_i)\Delta x$$

is an approximation for the area under the curve and is called a *Riemann sum*. The actual *area under the curve* is defined as

$$I = \lim_{n\to\infty} \sum_{i=1}^{n} f(x_i)\Delta x$$

provided this limit exists. This limit is a simple version of the *Riemann integral*. The integral is denoted as

$$I = \int_a^b f(x)\,\mathrm{d}x$$

and is called the *definite integral* of $f(x)$ over $[a,b]$. The *lower* and *upper limits* of integration are $a$ and $b$, respectively. If the definite integral of $f(x)$ over $[a,b]$ exists, then we say that $f(x)$ is *integrable* on $[a,b]$.

**Example 2.37** The Standard Normal Distribution Density Function of a random variable $x$ is defined as

$$f(x) = \frac{1}{\sqrt{2\pi}} \mathrm{e}^{-x^2/2}, \ -\infty < x < \infty$$

and its graph was displayed in example 2.7 of section 2.1.1. The probability that $x$ is between $a$ and $b$ is defined as the area under the curve between $a$ and $b$,

$$P(a \le x \le b) = \int_a^b f(x)\,\mathrm{d}x.$$

To find an approximation to the probability $P(1 \le x \le 2)$, we partition the interval [1,2] into $n = 100$ subintervals of equal length $\Delta x = 1/100$. The partition points are

$$x_0 = 1.00,\ x_1 = 1.01,\ x_2 = 1.02,\ \ldots,\ x_{100} = 2.00.$$

The Riemann sum is then

$$S_{100} = \sum_{i=1}^{100} f(x_i)\,\Delta x.$$

We use *Mathematica* function, **Sum**, to calculate the sum.

*In[143]:=*

```
Clear[f,x,a,b,n,dx,i];
f[x_]:= Exp[-x^2/2]/Sqrt[2*Pi];
a=1;  b=2;  n=100;  dx=(b-a)/n;
S  =  Sum[f[a+i*dx]*dx,{i,1,n}]  //  N
```

*Out[146]=*

```
0.134966
```

The probability that $1 \le x \le 2$ is approximately equal to 0.134966. The accuracy of the approximation can be improved by choosing larger values of $n$.

From a computational point of view, the above method of calculating the definite integral as a limiting process is formidable. However, we could use the *Mathematica* function, **Integrate**, to calculate the definite integral by specifying the lower and upper limits. Here is *Mathematica*'s description of this function.

*In[147]:=*
```
?Integrate
```

**Integrate[f,x] gives the indefinite integral of f with respect to x. Integrate[f,{x,xmin,xmax}] gives the definite integral. Integrate[f,{x,xmin,xmax},{y,ymin,ymax}] gives a multiple integral.**

The second form is used to calcuate a definite integral.

**Example 2.38** Evaluate the definite integral

$$\int_0^{\pi} x\cos(2x - \frac{\pi}{2})\,dx.$$

*In[148]:=*
```
Clear[f,x];
f[x_]:= x*Cos[2*x-Pi/2]
Integrate[f[x],{x,0,Pi}]
```

*Out[150]=*
```
-Pi
---
 2
```

**Example 2.39** (The Present Value) The present value of \$100 to be received two years from now is $\$100e^{-2(0.07)}$ if the discount rate (interest rate) is 7% per year. The present value of an income stream lasting for $t$ years with income $f(x)$ in year $x$ and a discount rate $100r$ percent per year is equal to

$$\int_0^t f(x)e^{-rx}\,dx.$$

If a retirement income stream is \$40,000 a year for the next 10 years, the present value is \$314,775 if the discount rate is 5% per year.

*In[151]:=*
```
Clear[f,x,t];
f[x_]:= 40000; t=10;
Integrate[f[x]*Exp[-0.05x],{x,0,t}]
```

*Out[153]=*
```
314775.
```

The following theorem gives a method for evaluating the definite integral of a function if an antiderivative of the function can be found.

**THEOREM 2.4** *(Fundamental Theorem of Calculus) If $f(x)$ is continuous on $[a,b]$ and if $F(x)$ is any antiderivative of $f(x)$, then*

$$\int_a^b f(x)\,dx = F(b) - F(a)$$

The theorem tells us that in order to calculate the definite integral of $f(x)$ over $[a,b]$, we first find an antiderivative of $f(x)$. The definite integral can then be evaluated in the following manner.

$$\int_a^b f(x)dx = F(x)\,|_a^b = F(b) - F(a).$$

**Example 2.40** Evaluate the definite integral

$$\int_{-2}^{3}(x^2-2)dx = \left(\frac{x^3}{3} - 2x\right)\Big|_{-2}^{3} = \left(\frac{27}{3} - 6\right) - \left(\frac{-8}{3} + 4\right) = \frac{5}{3}.$$

The definite integral also satisfies the same linearity properties as the antiderivative. Suppose $f(x)$ and $g(x)$ are integrable over $[a,b]$, and $k$ is a constant. Then

(1) $\int_a^b (f(x) \pm g(x))\,dx = \int_a^b f(x)\,dx \pm \int_a^b f(x)\,dx$

(2) $\int_a^b k\,f(x)\,dx = k\int_a^b f(x)\,dx$

Moreover,

(3) $\int_a^a f(x)\,dx = 0$

(4) $\int_a^b f(x)\,dx = \int_a^c f(x)\,dx + \int_c^b f(x)\,dx$ for each $c$ in $[a,b]$

(5) $\int_a^b f(x)\,dx = -\int_b^a f(x)\,dx$

(6) if $f(x) \geq 0$ on $[a,b]$, then $\int_a^b f(x)\,dx \geq 0$

**Example 2.41** Consumer's surplus and producer's surplus play an important role in welfare economics. Suppose $p = f(x) = 350 + x - 2x^2$ is the demand equation where $x$ is quantity and $p$ is price. A consumer is willing to pay $p = f(1) = 349$ dollars for the first unit, $x = 1$, of a good. In order to buy 2 units, he is willing to pay $p = f(2)$ = \$343 for the second unit and \$349 for the first unit, and so on. Thus the total dollars he is willing to pay for $x^*$ units if he has to buy one unit at a time is the sum

$$\sum_{x=1}^{x^*} f(x).$$

If quantity $x$ is a continuous variable, then it is the definite integral,

$$\int_0^{x^*} f(x)dx.$$

However, if he buys $x^*$ units, he actually pays only $x^*f(x^*)$. The difference

$$\int_0^{x^*} f(x)\,dx - x^* f(x^*)$$

is called the *consumer surplus*. Similarly, suppose $p = g(x) = 50 + x + x^2$ is the supply equation. A producer is willing to supply the first unit if he receives $p = g(1) = \$52$, and is willing to supply two units if he receives $p = g(2) = \$56$ for the second unit, and so on. The producer is willing to supply $x^*$ units, one at a time, if he receives

$$\int_0^{x^*} g(x)\,dx.$$

Since the producer is actully receiving $x^*g(x^*)$ for supplying $x^*$ units, the difference

$$x^*g(x^*) - \int_0^{x^*} g(x)\,dx$$

is called the *producer surplus*. At market equilibrium, quantity demand and supply are equal. The equilibrium quantity $x^*$ is the solution of $f(x) = g(x)$. The *total surplus*, the sum of both consumer surplus and producer surplus, is the integral

$$\int_0^{x^*} f(x)\,dx - \int_0^{x^*} g(x)\,dx = \int_0^{x^*} (f(x) - g(x))\,dx.$$

To evaluate the total surplus for $f(x) = 350 + x - 2x^2$ and $g(x) = 50 + x + x^2$, we first find the equilibrium quantity $x^*$ by solving $f(x) = g(x)$ for $x$. There are two solutions, $x^* = -10$, and 10.

*In[154]:=*

```
Clear[f,g,x]
f[x_]:= 350 + x - 2*x^2;
g[x_]:= 50 + x + x^2;
Solve[f[x]==g[x],x]
```

*Out[157]=*

{{x → −10}, {x → 10}}

Since quantity is supposed to be nonnegative, we identify $x^* = 10$ to be the equilibrium quantity. We plot the demand $f(x)$ and supply $g(x)$ equations below and observe that $x^* = 10$ is the intersection of $f(x)$ and $g(x)$. In the picture below, the demand function's graph is the solid curve and the supply function's graph is the dashed curve.

*In[158]:=*

```
Plot[{f[x],g[x]},{x,0,12},AxesLabel->{"x","p"},
        PlotStyle->{{},Dashing[{0.02}]}];
```

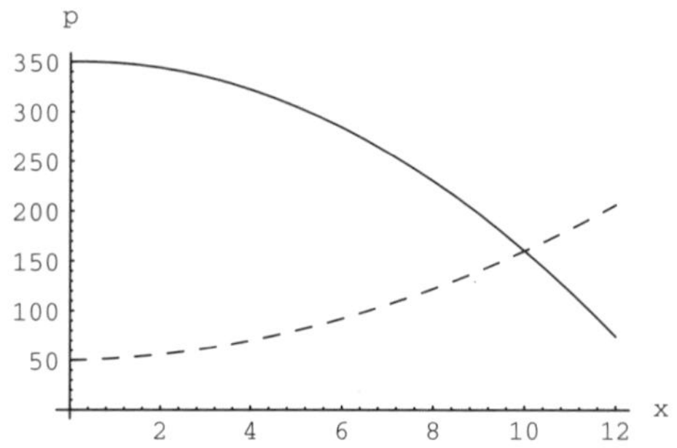

The total surplus, which is equal to 2000, is the area between $f(x)$ and $g(x)$ for $x$ between 0 and $x^* = 10$.

*In[159]:=*
```
Integrate[f[x]-g[x],{x,0,10}]
```

*Out[159]=*
```
2000
```

In the above discussion, the lower and upper limits of the definite integral are assumed to be constant. The limits can be generalized to allow them to be functions of some independent variable $t$. The definite integral

$$\int_{a(t)}^{b(t)} (f(x)\,\mathrm{d}x = F(b(t)) - F(a(t))$$

is then a function of $t$. By the chain rule of differentiation, we have

$$\frac{\mathrm{d}}{\mathrm{d}t}\left[\int_{a(t)}^{b(t)} f(x)\,\mathrm{d}x\right] = f(b(t))\,b'(t) - f(a(t))\,a'(t).$$

**Example 2.42** In example 2.37, the probability that $0 \le x \le t$ is defined as

$$P(0 \le x \le t) = \int_0^t f(x)\,\mathrm{d}x$$

where

$$f(x) = \frac{1}{\sqrt{2\pi}}\mathrm{e}^{-x^2/2}.$$

The derivative of the probability is simply the standard normal density function evaluated at $t$,

$$\frac{\mathrm{d}}{\mathrm{d}t}\left[P(0 \le x \le t)\right] = \frac{1}{\sqrt{2\pi}}\mathrm{e}^{-t^2/2} = f(t).$$

The following *Mathematica* calculation confirms the result.

*In[160]:=*
```
Clear[f,x,t];
f[x_]:= 1/Sqrt[2*Pi]*Exp[-x^2/2];
D[Integrate[f[x],{x,0,t}],t]
```

*Out[162]=*

$$\frac{1}{\mathrm{E}^{t^2/2}\,\mathrm{Sqrt}[2\mathrm{Pi}]}$$

Now consider the definite integral

$$\int_0^1 \frac{1}{\sqrt{x}}\mathrm{d}x.$$

Notice that the integrand is not defined at $x = 0$. This type of integral is called a *improper integral*. We can sometimes evaluate an improper integral as the limit. In this case, we compute

$$\int_0^1 \frac{1}{\sqrt{x}}\mathrm{d}x = \lim_{a \to 0^+} \int_a^1 \frac{1}{\sqrt{x}}\mathrm{d}x$$
$$= \lim_{a \to 0^+} 2\sqrt{x}\,\Big|_a^1 = \lim_{a \to 0^+} \left[2 - 2\sqrt{a}\right] = 2.$$

Confirming this calcuation with *Mathematica* we obtain the same result.

*In[163]:=*
```
Clear[f,x];
f[x_]:= 1/Sqrt[x];
Integrate[f[x],{x,0,1}]
```

*Out[165]=*
```
2
```

**Definition 2.6** *An integral*

$$\int_a^b f(x)\,\mathrm{d}x$$

*is called an* ***improper integral*** *if*

(1) *$f(x) \to \pm\infty$ at one or more points in the interval of integration*, $[a,b]$, *or*

(2) *either a and/or b are infinite.*

A point in $[a,b]$ where the integrand becomes unbounded is called a *singularity* of $f$. To evaluate an improper integral, we transform the problem into one of taking the limit of a proper integral. We say that the improper integral *converges* if the appropriate limit exists. Otherwise, we say that it *diverges*. The various types of improper integrals and the corresponding limits that must be examined for convergence are presented below.

$$\int_a^{+\infty} f(x)\,\mathrm{d}x = \lim_{M \to +\infty} \int_a^M f(x)\,\mathrm{d}x$$
$$\int_{-\infty}^a f(x)\,\mathrm{d}x = \lim_{M \to -\infty} \int_M^b f(x)\,\mathrm{d}x.$$

If $c$ is a singularity of $f$ in $[a,b]$, then we examine the limit

$$\int_a^b f(x)\,\mathrm{d}x = \lim_{x \to c^-} \int_a^c f(x)\,\mathrm{d}x + \lim_{x \to c^+} \int_c^b f(x)\,\mathrm{d}x.$$

If the improper integral converges, then we define the improper integral to be the value of the limit.

**Example 2.43** The definite integral

$$\int_1^\infty \frac{1}{x^2}\mathrm{d}x$$

is an improper integral since $b = \infty$. The improper integral is equal to 1 since

$$\lim_{b\to\infty} \int_1^b \frac{1}{x^2} dx = \lim_{b\to\infty} \frac{-1}{x} \Big|_1^b = \lim_{b\to\infty} \left[ \frac{-1}{b} + 1 \right] = 1.$$

*In[166]:=*
```
Clear[f,x]
f[x_]:= 1/x^2;
Integrate[f[x],{x,1,Infinity}]
```

*Out[168]=*
```
1
```

**Example 2.44** Let $x$ be the insurance claim on an automobile accident. The distribution of $x$ above $x_0$ = \$250 deductable is assumed to be,

$$f(x) = \frac{a x_0^a}{x^{1+a}}, x > x_0, a > 0$$

where $a$ is a positive constant. Suppose $a = 2.5$, the distribution of $x$ is plotted below.

*In[169]:=*
```
Clear[f,x,a,x0];
a = 2.5; x0 = 250;
f[x_]:= a*x0^a/x^(1+a);
Plot[f[x],{x,x0,1000},
        AxesLabel->{"x","f(x)"},AxesOrigin->{250,0}];
```

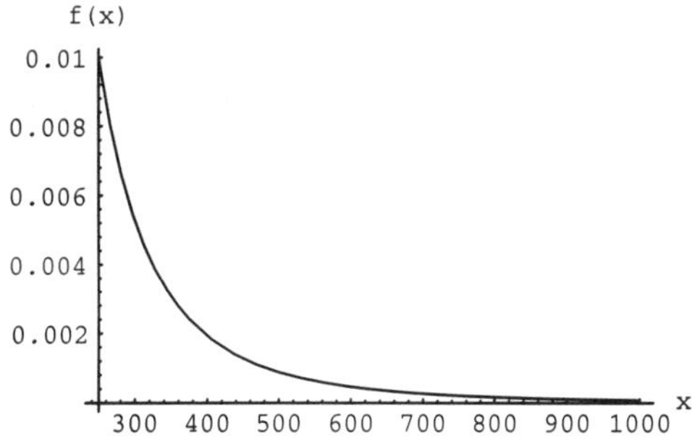


The average claim or the mean of $x$ is defined as the definite integral

$$\mu = \int_{x_0}^{\infty} x f(x) dx.$$

The mean is equal to \$416.67.

*In[173]:=*
```
mu = Integrate[x*f[x],{x,x0,Infinity}]
```

*Out[173]=*
```
416.667
```

The variation of the claims, measured by the variance, is defined as the definite integral

$$\sigma^2 = \int_{x_0}^{\infty} (x - \mu)^2 f(x)\,dx.$$

Computing this integral, we find that $\sigma^2 = 138889$.

*In[174]:=*
```
sigma2 = Integrate[(x-mu)^2*f[x],{x,x0,Infinity}]
```

*Out[174]=*
```
138889.
```

## EXERCISES

1. Evaluate the following definite integrals
   (a) $\int_0^1 (x+1)^2\,dx$
   (b) $\int_{-4}^{4} |x|\,dx$

2. Find $F'(0)$, $F''(0)$, and $F'''(0)$ for the function

$$F(t) = \int_0^t (2 + x^3)^{-2}\,dx$$

3. Find the relative extreme points of the function $F(t)$

$$F(t) = \int_0^t x(x-1)\,e^{-x^2}\,dx.$$

4. Find the mean and variance of $x$ with the following density functions $f(x)$:
   (a) Chi-square density:

$$f(x) = \frac{1}{\sqrt{2\pi}} x^{-1/2} e^{-x/2} \quad \text{for} \quad x > 0$$

   (b) Standard Normal density

$$f(x) = \frac{1}{\sqrt{2\pi}} e^{-x^2/2} \quad \text{for} \quad -\infty < x < \infty$$

# 3

# Vectors

Students of economics often encounter systems of equations. Among the most familiar is a two-equation linear system used to describe supply and demand. As we move beyond such introductory examples, however, it becomes necessary to acquire mathematical tools capable of describing more general and complicated systems. As a first step in this direction, we will learn how to view systems of linear equations at a higher level of abstraction. For example, the equilibrium price–quantity pair of a two-equation supply and demand model can be thought of as a point, say ($10, 8 apples), or a *vector* in price–quantity space. More generally, we will see that vectors provide a convenient notation for manipulating large systems of linear equations.

This chapter begins with the definition of a vector, which is simply a collection or a list of objects. When the lists are composed of numbers, vectors have a simple geometric interpretation as arrows in $n$-space. When a vector is a collection of two or three numbers, it can be viewed using the functions, **vector2d** and **vector3d**, contained in the **MathEcon** package. The algebra of vector operations – addition, subtraction, scalar multiplication, and the dot product – are studied in this chapter with the aid of several **MathEcon** functions to help visualize these operations.

## □ 3.1 Vectors □

### 3.1.1 Some terminology

We begin with a definition of vectors.

**DEFINITION 3.1** *A vector is an ordered collection of objects.*

The vector below is composed of 3 numbers.

$$\mathbf{v} = \begin{bmatrix} 2 \\ -4 \\ 1 \end{bmatrix}$$

By "ordered," we mean that "2" is the first element, "−4" is the second element, and "1" is the third element in the collection of numbers that makes up the vector. The objects that make up a vector are called *components* or *elements* of the vector. We will use boldface letters to denote vectors, in order to distinguish them from other types of symbols. The number of elements in a vector is called the *dimension* of the vector. The particular vector **v** has three elements and is a 3-dimensional vector. When the elements are arranged in a column, it is called a *column vector*. A vector may be written as a column, as above, or as a row. When the elements are arranged in a row, the ordered collection is called a *row vector*. For example,

$$\mathbf{w} = [2 \quad -4 \quad 1]$$

We note that **v** and **w** have the same elements. The only difference between the two vectors is how the elements are arranged (in **v** as a column and in **w** as a row). **w** is called the transpose of **v** and is denoted as $\mathbf{v}^T$. Similarly, **v** is the transpose of **w** and is the same as $\mathbf{w}^T$. That is, $\mathbf{w} = \mathbf{v}^T$ and $\mathbf{v} = \mathbf{w}^T$, and hence, $(\mathbf{v}^T)^T = \mathbf{v}$. Note that we use square brackets to enclose the elements of a vector. Some authors use parentheses and commas to separate the elements of the vector, $\mathbf{x} = (x_1,x_2, \ldots ,x_n)$, or even braces, $\mathbf{x} = \{x_1,x_2, \ldots ,x_n\}$, to represent vectors. We will use square brackets and spaces between elements.

**Example 3.1** If the row vector **a** is the ordered collection of the ages of four individuals, say, 45,6,23,60,

$$\mathbf{a} = [45 \quad 6 \quad 23 \quad 60]$$

then the transpose of the vector, $\mathbf{a}^T$, is the column vector,

$$\mathbf{a}^T = \begin{bmatrix} 45 \\ 6 \\ 23 \\ 60 \end{bmatrix}$$

The arrangement of a vector as row or column is indicated by specifying how many rows and columns are in the vector. We adopt the terminology $m \times n$ to indicate that the vector has $m$ rows and $n$ columns. Using this terminology, the row vector $\mathbf{v}^T$ above would be a $1 \times 3$ vector, and the column vector **v** is a $3 \times 1$ vector. Similarly, the above age vector **a** is $1 \times 4$, and $\mathbf{a}^T$ is $4 \times 1$.

**Example 3.2** Let the quantity of $n$ goods purchased be denoted as the sequence, $x_1,x_2, \ldots ,x_n$, and the price paid for each good as $p_1,p_2, \ldots ,p_n$. The quantities and the prices of the bundle of goods can then be represented by a quantity vector, **x**, and a price vector, **p**:

$$\mathbf{x} = [x_1 \quad x_2 \quad \ldots \quad x_n] \quad \text{and} \quad \mathbf{p} = [p_1 \quad p_2 \quad \ldots \quad p_n].$$

The *zero* vector is a vector whose elements are all zero. For example, the $1 \times 3$ zero vector is

$$\mathbf{0} = [0 \quad 0 \quad 0].$$

## EXERCISES

1. Last week Tricia, Cynthia and Mark earned $20, $15, and $10, respectively.
   (a) Write an earning vector to represent the earnings of the three.
   (b) How many other earning vectors with different ordering can be constructed?
2. The dimension of a vector **x** is $1 \times 5$.
   (a) How many rows and columns does **x** have? Is **x** a row or column vector?
   (b) What is the dimension of $((\mathbf{x}^T)^T)^T$? Is it a column or row vector?

### 3.1.2 *Mathematica* representation of vectors

*Mathematica*'s representation of a vector is somewhat different from the mathematical one that we discussed in the last section. As defined above, a vector is an ordered collection of objects. The elements are enclosed in a pair of square brackets. In *Mathematica*, however, a vector is represented as a list, and lists are always enclosed in curly braces. Square brackets in *Mathematica* are used for specifying arguments of functions.

To represent the vector [2 –4 1 5] in *Mathematica*, we use the expression **{2,–4, 1,5}** with curly braces and commas between elements.

*In[1]:=*
```
w = {2,-4,1,5}
```

*Out[1]=*
```
{2, -4, 1, 5}
```

*Mathematica* does not distinguish between row and column vectors. Both of these types of vectors are stored as lists.

*Mathematica* is capable of building a general vector, $\mathbf{a} = [a_1, a_2 \ldots, a_n]$ using the **Array** function. Here is the description of this function.

*In[2]:=*
```
?Array
```

**Array[f, n] generates a list of length n, with elements f[i]. Array[f, {n1, n2, ...}] generates an n1 X n2 X ... array of nested lists, with elements f[i1, i2, ...]. Array[f, dims, origin] generates a list using the specified index origin (default 1). Array[f, dims, origin, h] uses head h, rather than List, for each level of the array.**

Here is an example for $n = 3$.

*In[3]:=*
```
Clear[a];
Array[a,3]
```

*Out[4]=*
```
{a[1], a[2], a[3]}
```

The *i*-th element or component of a vector can be extracted by the **Part** function which has the shorthand notation [[ ]]. Here is its description.

*In[5]:=*
```
?Part
```

**expr[[i]] or Part[expr, i] gives the ith part of expr. expr[[-i]] counts from the end. expr[[0]] gives the head of expr. expr[[i, j, ...]] or Part[expr, i, j, ...] is equivalent to expr[[i]] [[j]] .... expr[[ {i1, i2, ...}] ]gives a list of the parts i1, i2, ... of expr.**

**Part**[**v**,2], and **v**[[2]] both extract the second element of a vector **v**.

*In[6]:=*
```
v = {2,-4,1,5};
Part[v,2]
```

*Out[7]=*
−4

*In[8]:=*
```
v[[2]]
```

*Out[8]=*
−4

Contrary to the **Part** function, the **Range** function is used to generate elements of a vector.

*In[9]:=*
```
?Range
```

**Range[imax] generates the list {1, 2, ..., imax}. Range[imin, imax] generates the list {imin, ..., imax}. Range[imin, imax, di] uses step di.**

For example, **Range**[1,15] gives a list of integers from 1 to 15, and **Range**[1,15,4] creates a list from 1 to 15 with increments of 4.

*In[10]:=*
```
Range[1,15]
```

*Out[10]=*
{1, 2, 3, 4, 5, 6, 7, 8, 9, 10, 11, 12, 13, 14, 15}

*In[11]:=*
```
Range[1,15,4]
```

*Out[11]=*
{1, 5, 9, 13}

The **Range** function can be used in conjunction with the **Part** function to extract elements of a vector. Let **v** = [5 0 −3 12 −6 7]. **v**[[**Range[1,3]**]] gives a list of the first three elements of **v**, and **v**[[**Range [2,6,2]**]] creates a list starting from the second element to the sixth with increment 2.

*In[12]:=*
```
v = {5,0,-3,12,-6,7};
v[[Range[1,3]]]
```

*Out[13]=*
```
{5, 0, -3}
```

*In[14]:=*
```
v[[Range[2,6,2]]]
```

*Out[14]=*
```
{0, 12, 7}
```

## EXERCISES

1. Given a quantity vector **q** = [28 16 18], and the corresponding price vector **p** = [$p_1$ $p_2$ $p_3$]. Use *Mathematica* commands to:
   (a) write both **q** and **p** vectors;
   (b) determine the dimensions of both vectors; and
   (c) extract the second element of **q** and the third element of **p**.
2. Create a vector of 10 elements and extract:
   (a) the fourth element;
   (b) the seventh element; and
   (c) from the fifth to the eighth elements.

### 3.1.3 Geometric interpretation of a vector

Geometrically, a $1 \times n$ vector can be viewed as a *directed line segment* in *n*-space. It has a *length* (the length of the line segment) and an *orientation* (from starting point of line segment to its terminal point). For example, **v** = [1 2] is identified with the directed line segment that starts at the origin of the plane and ends at the point (1,2). The orientation of the directed line segment can be view as a *direction*, as we see below. In figure 3.1, we have drawn this vector.

We know from elementary geometry that the length of the line segment that forms the vector **v** = [1 2], is the distance from the origin (0,0) to (1,2); that is, the square root of 5. We denote the length of **v** by ||**v**|| and call it the *length* or *magnitude* or *modulus* of the vector. In this case, we have

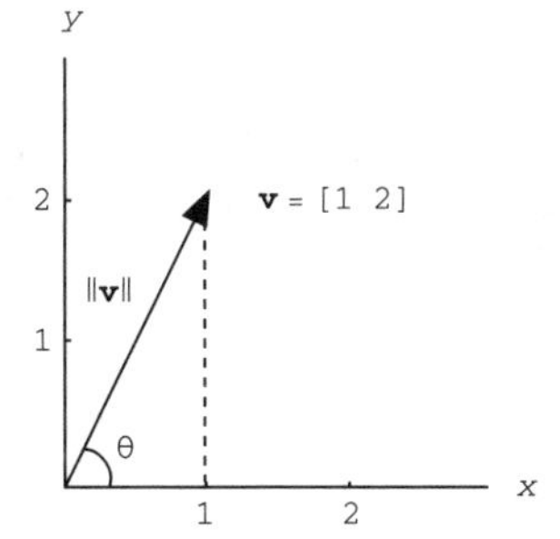


**Figure 3.1** Illustration of a vector

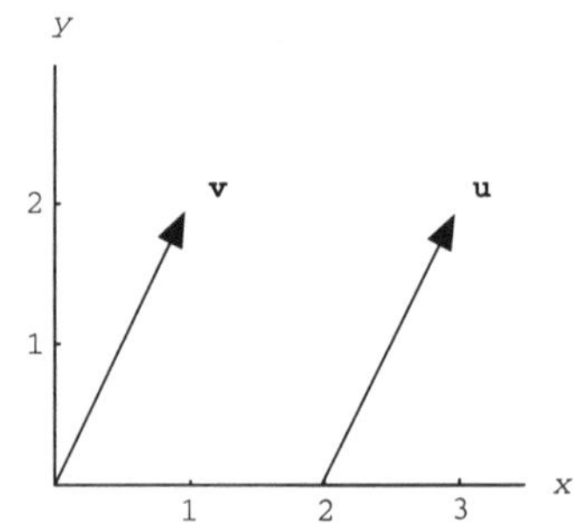


**Figure 3.2** Identical vectors with different origins

$$\|\mathbf{v}\| = \sqrt{1^2 + 2^2} = \sqrt{5}.$$

What is the direction of a vector? The direction of a vector is defined as the angle θ between the $x$-axis and the vector. From trigonometry, the cosine of angle θ is the ratio of the adjacent side to the hypotenuse of the triangle formed by the vector. Hence,

$$\cos(\theta) = \frac{1}{\|\mathbf{v}\|} = \frac{1}{\sqrt{5}}.$$

The angle θ is given by the equation:

$$\theta = \cos^{-1}\left(\frac{1}{\sqrt{5}}\right) \approx 1.10715 \text{ radians or } 63.43 \text{ degrees.}$$

From a geometric viewpoint, **v** is a directed line segment with length √5 and with the direction approximately 63.43 degrees with respect to the $x$-axis. Once the direction and the length are set, the vector is defined. Even if we move the starting point of the directed line segment from (0,0) to (2,0) as shown in figure 3.2, **u** has the same direction and length as **v**. Thus, geometrically speaking, **u** with the starting point at (2,0) is equal to **v** with the starting point at (0,0). In other words, two parallel line segments running in the same direction and with same length are equal.

If we restrict ourselves to the same starting point, say at (0,0), then two vectors, $\mathbf{v} = [a\ b]$ and $\mathbf{u} = [2\ 4]$ are equal if and only if $a = 2$, and $b = 4$. This is obvious since there is one and only one directed line segment with equal length and direction, starting from the same point.

Any vector whose length is 1 is called a *unit vector*. For example, vectors [0 0 1 0] and [√3 0 √3 0 √3 0] are unit vectors. While $\mathbf{I}_1 = [1\ 0]$ and $\mathbf{I}_2 = [0\ 1]$ are both unit vectors, they have different directions. The angle with the $x$-axis of the first one is 0 degress and the second is 90 degress.

Three-dimensional vectors have a similar geometric interpretation. A 1 × 3 vector is a directed line segment in three-dimensional space. Figure 3.3 shows $\mathbf{v} = [2\ 3\ 2]$ as the directed line segment from the origin to the point (2,3,2).

More generally, although we are unable to provide graphical representation, an $n$-dimensional vector, $\mathbf{x} = [x_1\ x_2\ \ldots\ x_n]$, can be deemed as a directed line segment from the origin to the point $(x_1\ x_2\ \ldots\ x_n)$. It has a length that is given by the number

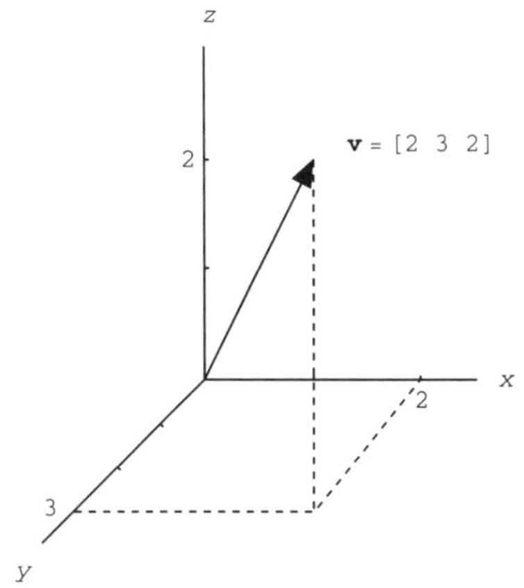


**Figure 3.3** A three-dimensional vector

$$\|\mathbf{x}\| = \sqrt{\sum_{i=1}^{n} x_i^2}$$

and a direction which is specified by certain angles that the line segment makes with the coordinate axes. We will discuss later how the direction is specified in this case.

## EXERCISES

1. Given **u** = [2 5] and **v** = [5 3],
   (a) plot **u** and **v** in the *xy*-plane;
   (b) calculate the length of each vector; and
   (c) give the direction of each vector.
2. Two vectors are *equal* if and only if they have the same direction and length. Suppose vector $\mathbf{x} = [x_1\ x_2\ x_3]$ and $\mathbf{y} = [y_1\ y_2\ y_3]$ are plotted on the same diagram and with same starting point at (0,0,0). State the condition under which the vectors are equal.
3. Suppose the elements of vector **v** are multiples of a constant $k$, i.e., $\mathbf{v} = [kx_1\ kx_2\ \ldots\ kx_n]$. What shall be the value of $k$ be, such that **v** has unit length?
4. Find two vectors having the same direction as **x** = [2 5 3].

### 3.1.4 Displaying vectors with *Mathematica*

To further convey the geometric interpretation of two-dimensional vectors, a function **vector2d** in the package **MathEcon** creates a graphic object that represents a two-dimensional vector. Here is the description of this function.

*In[15]:=*
```
?vector2d
```

**vector2d[pt,"label",opt] generates a 2D Graphics object for a vector from the origin to the point specified in the first argument. It allows the**

**vector to have a label (a string) and a dashed line style is used when the third argument is present. For example,**

**vector[{3,4},"a",dash].**

Note that **vector2d** function assumes that the starting point of the vector is at the origin. The second argument of **vector2d** is a string and hence, it is enclosed by quotes ("). To display the graphic object created by **vector2d**, one must use the **Show** function.

**Example 3.3** Display the vector **v** = [2 1] using **vector2d**.

*In[16]:=*

```
vector = vector2d[{2,1},"v"];
Show[vector,Axes->True];
```

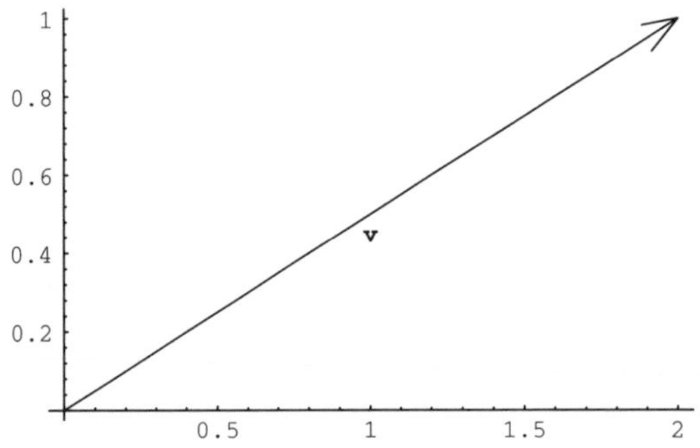


Alternatively, we could define the vector **v** first and use the vector's name as the argument of the function. For example,

*In[18]:=*

```
v = {2,1};
Show[vector2d[v,"v"]];
```

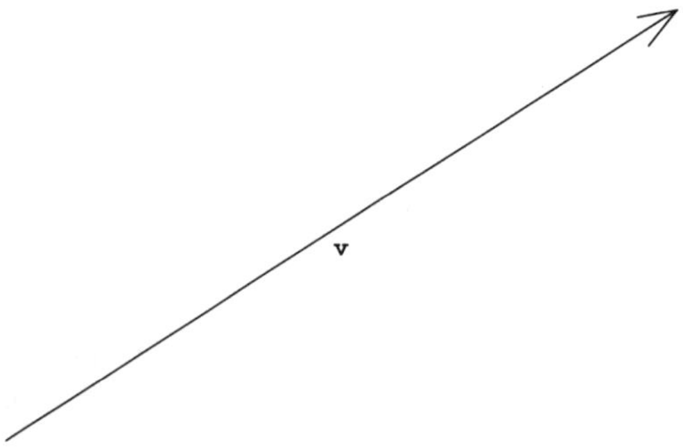


Note that we did not use the option **Axes→True** to draw the coordinate axes in the **Show** function and hence, the axes were not drawn.

**Example 3.4** Display the vectors, **v** = [–2 1] and **u** = [1 3] using **vector2d**.

*In[20]:=*
```
v = {-2,1}; u = {1,3};
vectv = vector2d[v,"v"];
vectu = vector2d[u,"u",dash];
Show[vectv,vectu,Axes->True,AxesLabel->{"x","y"}];
```

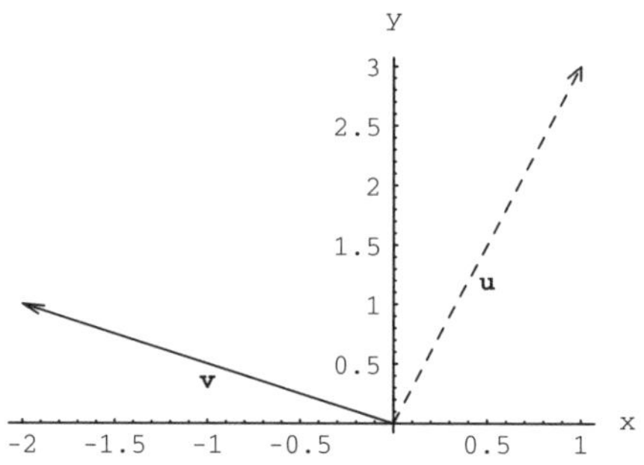


Note that we have used dashing option for **u**.

For 3-dimensionsal vectors, there is another **MathEcon** function to generate a graphic; it is called **vector3d**. It has the same format as **vector2d**.

*In[24]:=*
```
?vector3d
```

**vector3d[pt,"label",opt] generates a 3D Graphics object for a vector from the origin to the point specified in the first argument. It allows the vector to have a label (string) and a dashed line style is used when the third argument is present. For example,**

**vector3d[{1,-9,0},"a",dash].**

**Example 3.5** Display the vectors **v** = [1 2 1], **u** = [−2 1 1] in 3-space using **vector3d**.

*In[25]:=*
```
v = {1,2,1}; u = {-2,1,1};
vectv = vector3d[v,"v"];
vectu = vector3d[u,"u",dash];
Show[vectv,vectu,Axes->True,
      AxesLabel->{"x","y","z"}];
```

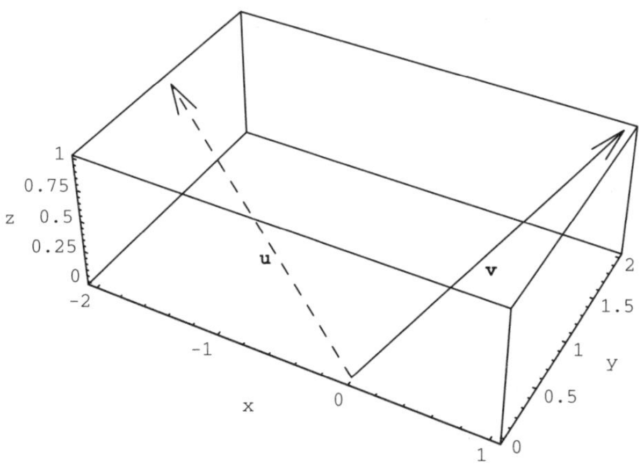

## EXERCISES

1. Plot the vectors $\mathbf{v}_1$ = [1.8 2.3], $\mathbf{v}_2$ = [1.8 −2.3], $\mathbf{v}_3$ = [−1.8 2.3], and $\mathbf{v}_4$ = [−1.8 −2.3] using **vector2d**.

2. Plot the three unit vectors, $\mathbf{I}_1$ = [1 0 0], $\mathbf{I}_2$ = [0 1 0], and $\mathbf{I}_3$ = [0 0 1] using **vector3d**.

## □ 3.2 Vector Operations □

### 3.2.1 Addition

Consider the vectors $\mathbf{a} = [a_1\ a_2\ a_3]$ and $\mathbf{b} = [b_1\ b_2\ b_3]$. The *sum* of two vectors **a** and **b** is defined as the vector

$$\mathbf{a} + \mathbf{b} = [a_1+b_1 \quad a_2+b_2 \quad a_3+b_3].$$

Notice that the sum of the two vectors is calculated by adding the corresponding components. For example, if $\mathbf{v}_1$ = [1 2] and $\mathbf{v}_2$ = [2 1], then

$$\mathbf{v}_1 + \mathbf{v}_2 = [1+2 \quad 2+1] = [3 \quad 3].$$

Note that only row (column) vectors that have the same number of components can be added. Thus, neither $\mathbf{a}^T + \mathbf{b}$ nor $\mathbf{a} + \mathbf{b}^T$ are conformable for addition, but $\mathbf{a} + \mathbf{b}$ and $\mathbf{a}^T + \mathbf{b}^T$ are. The vector $\mathbf{a} + \mathbf{b} = [a_1+b_1\ a_2+b_2\ a_3+b_3]$ is a row vector, but

$$\mathbf{a}^T + \mathbf{b}^T = \begin{bmatrix} a_1 \\ a_2 \\ a_3 \end{bmatrix} + \begin{bmatrix} b_1 \\ b_2 \\ b_3 \end{bmatrix} = \begin{bmatrix} a_1 + b_1 \\ a_2 + b_2 \\ a_3 + b_3 \end{bmatrix}$$

is a column vector.

Vector addition obeys the commutative and associative laws:

(1) Commutative law: $\mathbf{a} + \mathbf{b} = \mathbf{b} + \mathbf{a}$.

(2) Associative law: $(\mathbf{a} + \mathbf{b}) + \mathbf{c} = \mathbf{a} + (\mathbf{b} + \mathbf{c})$.

*Mathematica* performs the addition of vectors automatically. That is, vector addition is the same as the addition of lists in *Mathematica*.

**Example 3.6** Compute the sum of the vectors $\mathbf{a} = [a_1\ a_2\ a_3]$ and $\mathbf{b} = [b_1\ b_2\ b_3]$, using *Mathematica*.

*In[29]:=*

```
a = {a1, a2, a3}; b = {b1, b2, b3};
a + b
```

*Out[30]=*

```
{a1 + b1, a2 + b2, a3 + b3}
```

**Example 3.7** Using the **Array** function, add two four-dimensional vectors **x** and **y**.

*In[31]:=*
```
Clear[x,y];
Array[x,4]  +  Array[y,4]
```

*Out[32]=*
```
{x[1] + y[1], x[2] + y[2], x[3] + y[3], x[4] + y[4]}
```

To create a graphical representation of the addition of two vectors, we use the **MathEcon** function **addition2d**.

*In[33]:=*
```
?addition2d
```

**addition2d[pt1,"label1",pt2,"label2"] generates a 2D Graphics object that illustrates the addition of two vectors from the origin that terminate at the points pt1 and pt2, respectively. Each vector has a label (string) and the vector that is the sum is labeled. For example,**

**addition2d[{-1,2},"a",{0,-1},"b"].**

**Example 3.8** Show graphically the sum of **u** = [1 2] and **v** = [2 1].

*In[34]:=*
```
s = addition2d[{1,2},"u",{2, 1},"v"];
Show[s,Axes->True];
```

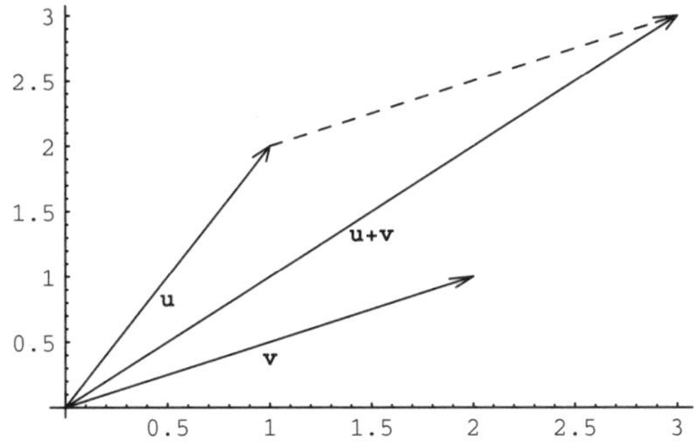


As illustrated above, the sum of **u** and **v** can be found by attaching **v** to the tip of **u** (denoted by the dashed vector), and then drawing the vector from the origin to the new tip of translated **v**. The parallel attachment is necessary in order to maintain the same direction of the vector. The order of the vector addition is not important and the same vector, **u** + **v**, can be found by attaching **u** to **v**.

**Example 3.9** Show graphically the sum of **u** = [–1 1/2] and **v** = [2 3/2].

*In[36]:=*
```
s = addition2d[{-1,1/2},"u",{2,3/2},"v"];
Show[s,Axes->True];
```

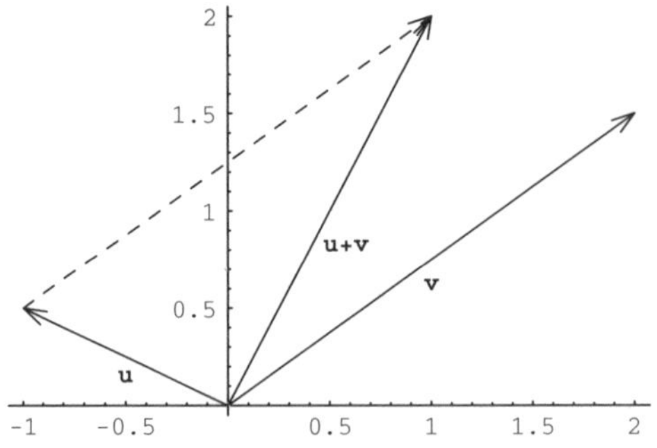


## EXERCISES

1. Given vectors $\mathbf{a} = [1\ 3\ 5]$, $\mathbf{b} = [2\ 4\ 6]$, and $\mathbf{c} = [1\ 2\ 3]$,
   (a) find $\mathbf{a} + \mathbf{b} + \mathbf{c}$;
   (b) find $(\mathbf{a} + \mathbf{b} + \mathbf{c})^T$; and
   (c) illustrate that $(\mathbf{a} + \mathbf{b} + \mathbf{c})^T = \mathbf{a}^T + \mathbf{b}^T + \mathbf{c}^T$.
2. Given vectors $\mathbf{x} = [1\ 2]$, $\mathbf{y} = [-2\ 3]$,
   (a) graph the addition $\mathbf{z} = \mathbf{x} + \mathbf{y}$; and
   (b) graph the addition $\mathbf{w} = \mathbf{x} + \mathbf{z}$;
3. Find the vector $\mathbf{x}$ such that $[1\ 3] + \mathbf{x} = [2\ 4]$. Graph the vector addition to confirm the result.
4. Show the length of $\mathbf{a} + \mathbf{b}$ is less than or equal to the length of $\mathbf{a}$ plus the length of $\mathbf{b}$, i.e., $\|\mathbf{a}+\mathbf{b}\| \leq \|\mathbf{a}\| + \|\mathbf{b}\|$.

### 3.2.2 Scalar multiplication

Let $\mathbf{v}$ be a vector and $k$ a scalar (number). *Scalar multiplication* of $\mathbf{v}$ by $k$ is the vector obtained by multiplying each component of $\mathbf{v}$ by $k$. It is sometimes called the *scalar multiple* of $\mathbf{v}$ and $k$, and is denoted by $k\mathbf{v}$.

**Example 3.10** Given $\mathbf{v} = [1\ 2]$ and k = 2, the scalar multiple of $\mathbf{v}$ and $k$ is the vector

$2\mathbf{v} = [2\quad 4]$.

The scalar $k$ could be negative. If $k = -1.5$, then

$-1.5\mathbf{v} = [-1.5\quad -3]$.

*Mathematica* does scalar multiplication automatically. We could write scalar multiplication in *Mathematica* either as **k a** with a space in between or **k*a** with "*" representing multiplication. However if we leave out space or *, and type "*k***a**", *Mathematica* will interpret **ka** as a new variable or a new vector.

**Example 3.11** Compute the scalar multiple of the vector $\mathbf{a} = [a_1\ a_2\ a_3]$ with a scalar $k$.

*In[38]:=*
```
Clear[a1,a2,a3,k];
a  =  {a1,  a2,  a3};
k*a
```

*Out[40]=*

```
{a1k, a2k, a3k}
```

Geometrically, the multiplication of a vector **v** by the scalar $k$ produces a vector $k\mathbf{v}$ that lies along the same line that contains **v**. Its length is $k$ times the length of **v**. If $k$ is negative, then the direction of $k\mathbf{v}$ is the opposite of **v**.

**Example 3.12** Given **v** = [1 2], display the vector −0.5*v.

*In[41]:=*

```
k = -0.5; v = {1,2};
vect1=vector2d[v,"v"];
vect2=vector2d[k*v,"-0.5v",dash];
Show[vect1,vect2,Axes->True];
```

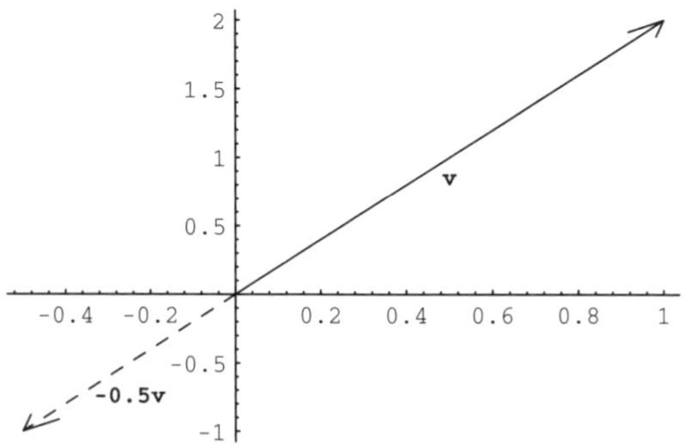


**Example 3.13** Consider the *production plan* (vector) **p** = [Q L K], where $Q$ is units of output, $L$ and $K$ are units of labor and capital inputs. A production plan is *feasible* if $Q$ units of output can be produced by using $L$ and $K$ units of labor and capital. For example, suppose the production technology is such that, $Q = L(L+K)$. The vectors, $\mathbf{p}_1$ = [2 1 1], $\mathbf{p}_2$ = [6 2 1], and $\mathbf{p}_3$ = [5 2 2] are feasible even though $\mathbf{p}_3$ is not *efficient* since it could produce $Q = 8$ units. The vectors, [3 1 1], [6 1 2], and [5 1 2], are not feasible. The collection of all feasible production plans, **S**, is called *production possibility set*. The production possibility set **S** is said to exhibit a *constant returns to scale* if a positive multiple of **p**, $a\mathbf{p}$, is also feasible, i.e., $a\mathbf{p} \in \mathbf{S}$. Since $0.5\mathbf{p}_2$ = [3 1 0.5] is not feasible, $Q = L(L+K)$ is not a constant returns to scale production technology. Suppose the capital $K$ is fixed at some level, say $K^0$. The vector $\mathbf{p} = [Q\ L\ K^0]$ is called a *short-run production plan*, and the corresponding set **S** is called a *short-run production possibility set*.

## EXERCISES

1. Given $\mathbf{v}_1$ = [4 3 8], $\mathbf{v}_2$ = [3 2 5], and $k_1 = 2$, $k_2 = 3$, and $k_3 = -1$, compute:
   (a) $k_1\mathbf{v}_1$ and $k_2\mathbf{v}_2$.
   (b) $k_1\mathbf{v}_1 + k_2\mathbf{v}_2$.
   (c) $k_1\mathbf{v}_1 + k_3\mathbf{v}_2$.

2. Plot the following vectors:
   (a) $k_1\mathbf{u}_1$ and $k_2\mathbf{u}_2$.
   (b) $k_1\mathbf{u}_1 + k_2\mathbf{u}_2$.
   (c) $k_1\mathbf{u}_1 + k_3\mathbf{u}_2$.
   where $\mathbf{u}_1 = [-3\ 1]$, $\mathbf{u}_2 = [2\ 3]$, and $k_1 = 2$, $k_2 = 3$, and $k_3 = -1$.
3. Suppose the length of vector $\mathbf{x}$ is 5.
   (a) Find the length of $\mathbf{y} = 3\mathbf{x}$.
   (b) Find the length of $-\mathbf{x}$.
4. Let $\mathbf{a} = [1\ 2]$ and $\mathbf{b}$ be a vector in the opposite direction of $\mathbf{a}$ with length $\|\mathbf{b}\| = 2$. Find the vector $\mathbf{b}$.

### 3.2.3 Subtraction

The *subtraction* or *difference* of two vectors is a vector whose components are the difference of the correspondent elements in the two vectors.

**Example 3.14** Given $\mathbf{v}_1 = [1\ 2]$, $\mathbf{v}_2 = [2\ 1]$, $\mathbf{a} = [a_1\ a_2\ a_3]$, and $\mathbf{b} = [b_1\ b_2\ b_3]$, we have

$$\mathbf{v}_1 - \mathbf{v}_2 = [1{-}2 \quad 2{-}1] = [-1 \quad 1],$$
$$\mathbf{a} - \mathbf{b} = [a_1{-}b_1 \quad a_2{-}b_2 \quad a_3{-}b_3].$$

**Example 3.15** Subtraction of two vectors in *Mathematica* follows the same rule as the subtraction of two lists.

*In[45]:=*
```
u = {1,2}; v = {2,1};
u - v
```

*Out[46]=*
```
{-1, 1}
```

*In[47]:=*
```
Clear[a1,a2,a3,b1,b2,b3];
a = {a1, a2, a3}; b = {b1, b2, b3};
a - b
```

*Out[49]=*
```
{a1 - b1, a2 - b2, a3 - b3}
```

We can view the difference of two vectors as the addition of the negative of one of the vectors to the other vector. That is,

$$\mathbf{u} - \mathbf{v} = \mathbf{u} + (-1)\mathbf{v}.$$

To show this, we use a **MathEcon** function **subtraction2d**. It has the same format as **addition2d**.

*In[50]:=*
```
?subtraction2d
```

**subtraction2d[pt1,"label1",pt2,"label2"] generates a 2D Graphics object that illustrates the difference of two vectors from the origin that**

**terminate at the points pt1 and pt2, respectively. Each vector has a label (a string) and the vector that is the difference is labeled. For example,**

**subtraction2d[{-1,2},"a",{0,-1},"b"].**

**Example 3.16** Using **subtraction2d**, display

$\mathbf{u} - \mathbf{v} = [1 \quad 2] - [2 \quad 1] = [-1 \quad 1]$

geometrically.

*In[51]:=*

```
u = {1, 2}; v = {2,1};
vect = subtraction2d[u,"u",v,"v"];
Show[vect,Axes->True];
```

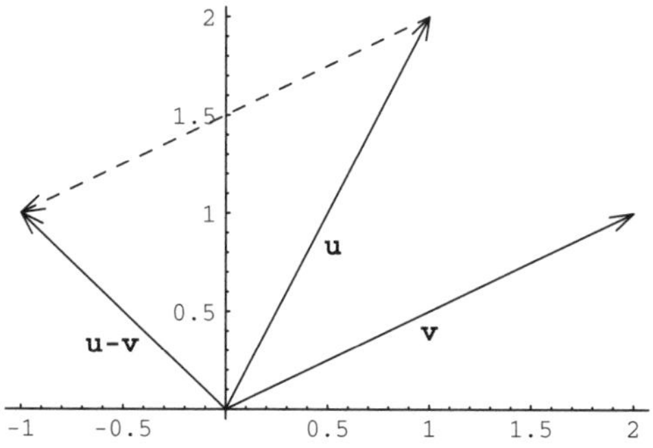


In the above graph the dashed vector represents $-\mathbf{v}$, which has been translated to the tip of $\mathbf{u}$.

## EXERCISES

1. Given vectors $\mathbf{a} = [1\ 3\ 5]$, $\mathbf{b} = [2\ 4\ 6]$, and $\mathbf{c} = [1\ 2\ 3]$,
   (a) find $\mathbf{a} - \mathbf{b} - \mathbf{c}$;
   (b) find $(\mathbf{a} - \mathbf{b} - \mathbf{c})^T$; and
   (c) show that $(\mathbf{a} - \mathbf{b} - \mathbf{c})^T = \mathbf{a}^T - \mathbf{b}^T - \mathbf{c}^T$.
2. Given vectors $\mathbf{x} = [1\ 2]$, $\mathbf{y} = [-2\ 3]$,
   (a) plot $\mathbf{v} = \mathbf{x} - \mathbf{y}$;
   (b) plot $\mathbf{z} = 1.5\mathbf{x} - 0.5\mathbf{y}$;
   (c) plot $\mathbf{w} = 1.5\mathbf{x} - \mathbf{z}$.
3. Show the length of $\mathbf{a} - \mathbf{b}$ is less than or equal to the length of $\mathbf{a}$ plus the length of $\mathbf{b}$, i.e., $\|\mathbf{a}-\mathbf{b}\| \le \|\mathbf{a}\| + \|\mathbf{b}\|$.

### 3.2.4 Dot product

The *dot product* or *inner product* of two vectors $\mathbf{a}$ and $\mathbf{b}$ is a scalar and is defined as the sum of the products of the corresponding components of $\mathbf{a}$ and $\mathbf{b}$. For example, if $\mathbf{a} = [a_1\ a_2\ a_3]$ and $\mathbf{b} = [b_1\ b_2\ b_3]$, then the dot product, denoted as $\mathbf{a} \cdot \mathbf{b}$, is the sum: $a_1b_1 + a_2b_2 + a_3b_3$. The order of vectors in a dot product is not important, i.e., $\mathbf{a} \cdot \mathbf{b} = \mathbf{b} \cdot \mathbf{a}$.

**Example 3.17** Let $\mathbf{q} = [q_1\ q_2\ \ldots\ q_n]$ denote the quantity vector of $n$ goods that a consumer purchased during the last week, and $\mathbf{p} = [p_1\ p_2\ \ldots\ p_n]$ the correspondent price vector. The total expenditure for the week is then the dot product

$$\mathbf{p} \cdot \mathbf{q} = p_1q_1 + p_2q_2 + \ldots + p_nq_n = \sum_{i=1}^{n} p_iq_i.$$

In *Mathematica*, the function **Dot** computes the dot product of two or more vectors. Here is a description of this function.

*In[54]:=*
```
?Dot
```

**a.b.c or Dot[a, b, c] gives products of vectors, matrices and tensors.**

**Example 3.18** Find the dot product $\mathbf{v} = [4\ 2\ -1]$ and $\mathbf{u} = [1\ -1\ 3]$.

*In[55]:=*
```
v = {4,2,-1}; u = {1,-1,3};
v.u
```

*Out[56]=*
−1

We could also use the function **Dot**.

*In[57]:=*
```
Dot[v,u]
```

*Out[57]=*
−1

**Example 3.19** Using the **Array** function, the dot product of a price vector and a quantity vector of three goods is computed below.

*In[58]:=*
```
Clear[p,q]
Array[p,3].Array[q,3]
```

*Out[59]=*
p[1]q[1] + p[2]q[2] + p[3]q[3]

The dot product of a vector and itself is equal to the square of the length of the vector. If $\mathbf{v} = [4\ 2\ 1]$, then $\mathbf{v} \cdot \mathbf{v} = 21$. If we denote the length by $\|\mathbf{v}\|$, then

$$\|\mathbf{v}\| = \sqrt{\mathbf{v} \cdot \mathbf{v}} = \sqrt{21}.$$

The length of a vector is sometimes called the *norm* of the vector.

**Example 3.20** Find the norm of $\mathbf{v} = [-3\ 5\ 1]$.

*In[60]:=*
```
v  =  {-3,5,1};
norm  =  Sqrt[v.v]
```

*Out[61]=*
```
Sqrt[35]
```

The vector $\mathbf{v} = [1\ 2]$ has length $\|\mathbf{v}\| = \sqrt{5}$. Dividing each element of **v** by the length $\sqrt{5}$ gives the new vector $\mathbf{y} = [1/\sqrt{5}\ 2/\sqrt{5}]$, which has unit length $\|\mathbf{y}\| = 1$ but the same direction as **v**. Any nonzero vector **v** can be transformed into a unit vector by dividing each component by $\|\mathbf{v}\|$.

$$\mathbf{y} = \frac{\mathbf{v}}{\|\mathbf{v}\|}$$

The vector **y** has the same direction as **v**. The process of creating a unit vector that has the same direction as the original given vector is called *normalization*.

For any two nonzero vectors such as the ones displayed in figure 3.4, one can show that

$$\mathbf{u} \cdot \mathbf{v} = \|\mathbf{u}\|\,\|\mathbf{v}\| \cos\theta$$

where $\theta$ is the smaller angle between the vectors **u** and **v**. The dot product is equal to the product of the lengths of the vectors and the cosine of the angle between them. The above equation can be used to calculate the angle between two vectors. In particular, we have the following formula for the angle between two vectors **u** and **v**,

$$\theta = \cos^{-1}\left(\frac{\mathbf{u} \cdot \mathbf{v}}{\|\mathbf{u}\|\,\|\mathbf{v}\|}\right).$$

**Example 3.21** Plot the vectors, $\mathbf{u} = [3\ 1]$ and $\mathbf{v} = [1\ 1]$, and use the *Mathematica* function **ArcCos** to calculate the angle between them.

*In[62]:=*
```
u  =  {3,1};  v  =  {1,1};
theta  =  ArcCos[u.v/Sqrt[(u.u)*(v.v)]]  //  N
```

*Out[63]=*
```
0.463648
```

Thus $\theta = 0.463648$ radians or $180\ \theta/\pi = 26.5651$ degrees.

*In[64]:=*
```
vectu  =  vector2d[u,"u"];
vectv  =  vector2d[v,"v"];
Show[vectu,vectv,Axes->True];
```

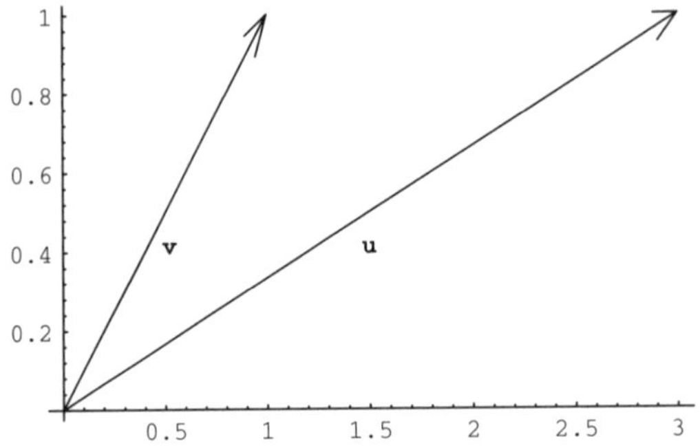


## EXERCISES

1. Given **a** = [1 2 3], **b** = [2 3 4], **c** = [3 4 5], and **d** = [4 5 6].
   (a) Find **a** · **b** and **c** · **d**.
   (b) Is **a** · **b** = **b** · **a**, and **c** · **d** = **d** · **c**?
   (c) Show that (**a** + **b**) · **c** = **a** · **c** + **b** · **c**
   (d) Show (**a** + **b**) · (**c** + **d**) = **a** · **c** + **b** · **c** + **a** · **d** + **b** · **d**.
2. Use *Mathematica* to check (a)–(d) in exercise 1.
3. Find the norms of **a**, **b**, **c**, and **d** in exercise 1.
4. Normalize the vectors **a**, **b**, **c**, and **d** so that each has a unit length.

## □ 3.3 Projection Vectors □

### 3.3.1 Geometric view

The dot product has its own geometric interpretation. It is related to the projection of one vector upon the other vector.

The *projection vector* of **u** onto **v**, the vector **p** in figure 3.4, is the vector obtained by projecting **u** onto the line that contains **v**. The length of **p** is a function of the angle between **u** and **v** and the length of **u**. Let θ be the angle between **u** and **v**. If the angle θ is acute, then

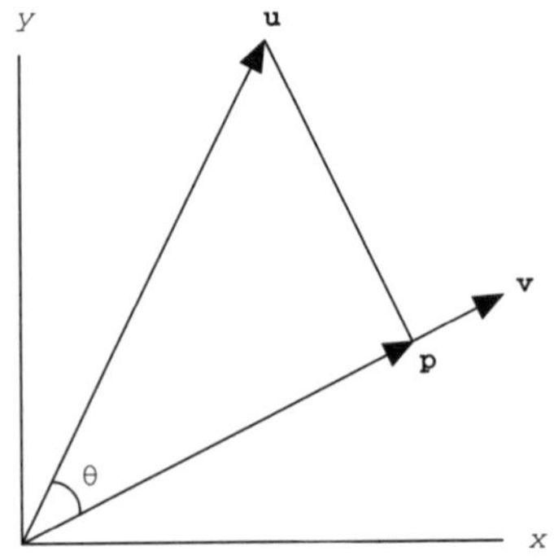


**Figure 3.4** Projection of **u** onto **v**

$$\cos\theta = \frac{\|\mathbf{p}\|}{\|\mathbf{u}\|}.$$

The length of **p** is

$$\|\mathbf{p}\| = \|\mathbf{u}\|\cos\theta.$$

Since **p** lies on and points in the same direction as **v** when θ is acute, **p** must be a scale multiple of **v**, i.e., $\mathbf{p} = k\mathbf{v}$ with $k = \|\mathbf{p}\|/\|\mathbf{v}\|$. Thus

$$\mathbf{p} = k\mathbf{v} = \frac{\|\mathbf{p}\|}{\|\mathbf{v}\|}\mathbf{v}.$$

If the angle θ is obtuse, then the projection vector points in the opposite direction of **v**. Thus

$$\mathbf{p} = -k\mathbf{v} = -\frac{\|\mathbf{p}\|}{\|\mathbf{v}\|}\mathbf{v}$$

and its length is

$$\|\mathbf{p}\| = -\|\mathbf{u}\|\cos\theta.$$

In either case, $\|\mathbf{u}\|\cos\theta$ is called the *scalar component* of **u** in the direction of **v**. Subtituting $\|\mathbf{u}\|\cos\theta$ (or $-\|\mathbf{u}\|\cos\theta$ in obtuse angle case) for $\|\mathbf{p}\|$, the projection vector **p** becomes

$$\mathbf{p} = \frac{\|\mathbf{u}\|\cos\theta}{\|\mathbf{v}\|}\mathbf{v} = \frac{\|\mathbf{u}\|\|\mathbf{v}\|\cos\theta}{\|\mathbf{v}\|^2}\mathbf{v} = \frac{\mathbf{u}\cdot\mathbf{v}}{\mathbf{v}\cdot\mathbf{v}}\mathbf{v}.$$

**Example 3.22** Find the projection vector **p** of **u** = [1 2] onto **v** = [2 1]. Since $\mathbf{u}\cdot\mathbf{v} = 4$ and $\mathbf{v}\cdot\mathbf{v} = 5$, **p** is equal to 4/5 [2 1] = [8/5 4/5].

**Example 3.23** Use *Mathematica* to find the projection vector **p** of **u** = [2 2 –2] onto **v** = [3 1 0] and calculate the angle in radians between the vectors.

*In[67]:=*
```
u = {2,2,-2}; v = {3,1,0};
p = (u.v)/(v.v)*v
```

*Out[68]=*

$$\{\frac{12}{5}, \frac{4}{5}, 0\}$$

*In[69]:=*
```
ArcCos[(u.v)/(Sqrt[v.v]*Sqrt[u.u])] //N
```

*Out[69]=*

0.75204

To graph the projection of a two-dimensional vector onto another two-dimensional vector, we have the **MathEcon** function **projection2d**.

*In[70]:=*
```
?projection2d
```

**projection2d[pt1,“label1”,pt2] generates a 2D Graphics object that illustrates the projection of a vector that starts at the origin and ends at pt1 onto another vector that starts at the origin and ends at pt2. The first vector can have a label (a string). For example,**

**projection2d[{-2,1},“a”,{1,4}].**

**Example 3.24** Show the projection vector **p** of **u** = [2 2] onto **v** = [3 1].

*In[71]:=*
```
u = {2,2}; v = {3,1};
p = projection2d[u,"u",v];
Show[p,Axes->True];
```

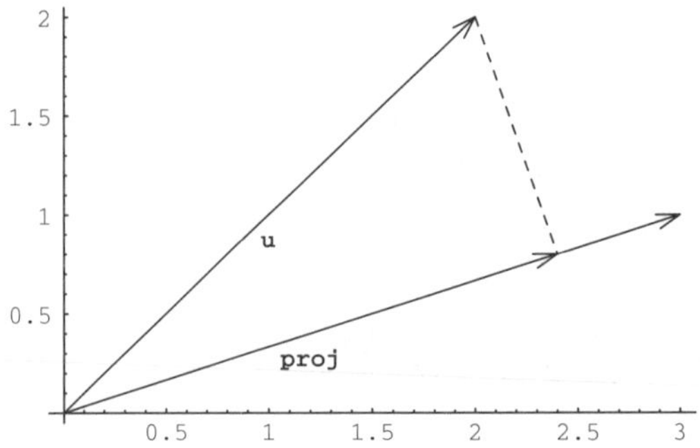


**Example 3.25** Show the projection vector **p** of **u** = [2 1] onto **v** = [–1 –1].

*In[74]:=*
```
u = {2,1}; v = {-1,-1};
p = projection2d[u,"u",v];
Show[p,Axes->True,AspectRatio->1];
```

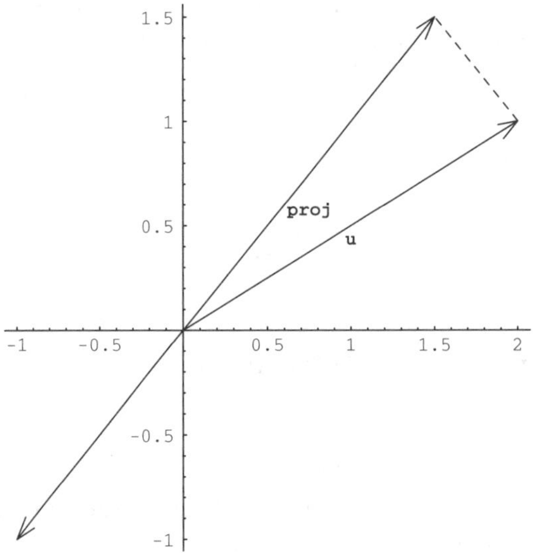

Note that in this example the projection vector of **u** onto **v** is a vector that points in the opposite direction to **v**.

We also have a three-dimensional version of **projection2d** which we call **projection3d**.

*In[77]:=*

```
?projection3d
```

**projection3d[pt1,"label1",pt2] generates a 3D Graphics object that illustrates the projection of a vector that starts at the origin and ends at pt1 onto another vector that starts at the origin and ends at pt2. The first vector can have a label (a string). For example,**

**projection3d[{1,0,2},"a",{3,1,2}].**

**Example 3.26** Display the projection vector **p** of **u** = [1 1 1] onto **v** = [−1 2 2].

*In[78]:=*

```
p=projection3d[{1,1,1},"u",{-1,2,2}];
Show[p,Axes->True,AxesLabel->{"x","y","z"}];
```

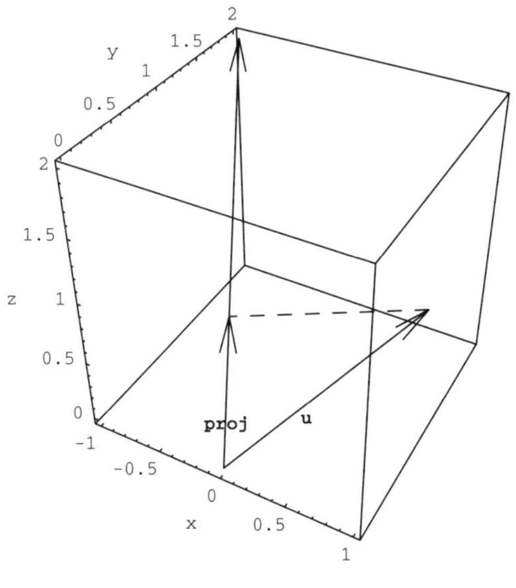


The projection vector **p** depends on the angle between the two vectors **u** and **v**. Therefore, another way of thinking of the projection of a vector **u** onto a vector **v** is to envision the rotation of **u** through the angle between **u** and **v** onto the line that contains **v**. As **u** changes, i.e., as the angle between **u** and **v** changes, the projection will change. If the angle is less than $\pi/2$ (90 degress), then the rotation is counterclockwise; if it is greater than $\pi/2$ (90 degress), then the rotation is clockwise.

**Example 3.27** The following graph shows the projection vectors on **v** = [3 1] and their lengths as we rotate counterclockwise from $\mathbf{u}_1$ = [2.4 1.5] to $\mathbf{u}_2$ = [1.5 2.4].

*In[80]:=*

```
u1 = {2.4,1.5}; u2 = {1.5,2.4}; v = {3,1};
p1=projection2d[u1,"u1",v];
p2=projection2d[u2,"u2",v];
Show[p1,p2,Axes->True,AspectRatio->Automatic];
```

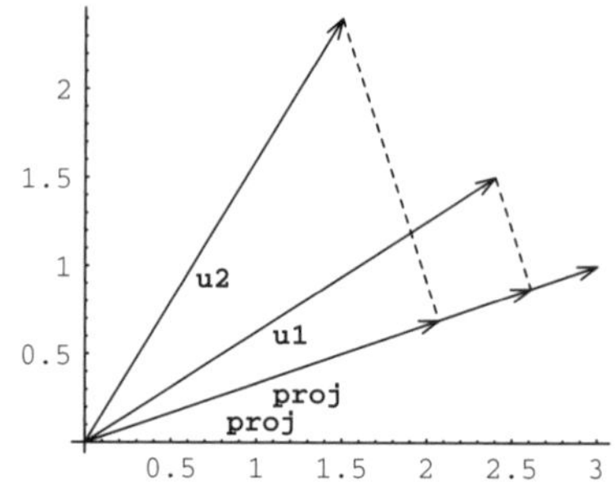


**Example 3.28** Let $\mathbf{v} = [2\ 1]$. How does the projection vector change when we rotate $\mathbf{u}_1 = [1\ 1]$ to $\mathbf{u}_2 = [-1\ 1]$?

*In[84]:=*

```
u1 = {1,1}; u2 = {-1,1}; v = {2,1};
p1 = projection2d[u1,"u1",v];
p2 = projection2d[u2,"u2",v];
Show[p1,p2,Axes->True,AspectRatio->Automatic,
                Ticks->None,PlotRange->{-1,2}];
```

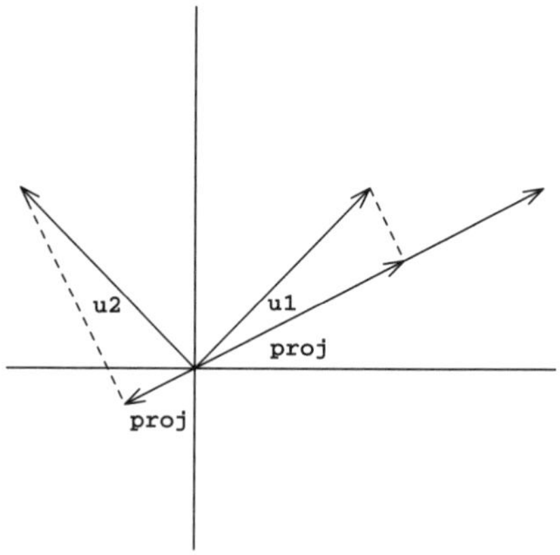


## EXERCISES

1. Given $\mathbf{v}_1 = [2\ 1\ 3]$ and $\mathbf{v}_2 = [3\ 1\ 2]$,
   (a) find the projection vector $\mathbf{p}$ of $\mathbf{v}_1$ onto $\mathbf{v}_2$;
   (b) find the angle $\theta$ in radians between $\mathbf{v}_1$ and $\mathbf{p}$;
   (c) find the norms of $\mathbf{v}_2$ and $\mathbf{p}$; and
   (d) find the vector $\mathbf{x} = \mathbf{v}_1 - \mathbf{p}$.

2. Let **a** = [1 1 2] and **b** = [3 2 −3] represent the vectors associated with the sides *XY* and *XZ* of the following triangle *XYZ*.
   (a) Find the vector associated with *XM* where *M* is the midpoint on *YZ*.
   (b) Find the vector associated with *NZ* where the length of *XN* is equal to one-third of the length of *XY*.

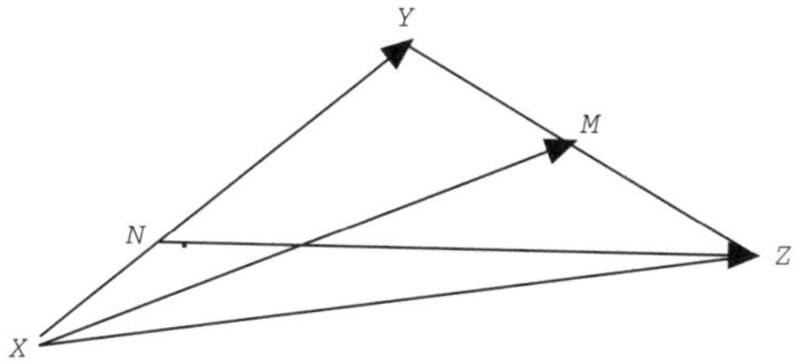


3. Graph $\mathbf{v}_1$ = [2 3] and $\mathbf{v}_2$ = [1 0] and find the angle θ between them.

### 3.3.2 Orthogonal vectors

Two vectors are said to be *orthogonal* when they are perpendicular to each other (i.e., the angle between the vectors is π/2 or 90 degrees). Since $\mathbf{u} \cdot \mathbf{v} = \|\mathbf{u}\| \|\mathbf{v}\| \cos\theta$ and the cosine of π/2 is zero, the dot product of two orthogonal vectors is equal to zero. Furthermore, the projection vector of two orthogonal vectors, $\mathbf{p} = (\mathbf{u} \cdot \mathbf{v})/(\mathbf{v} \cdot \mathbf{v})\,\mathbf{v}$, is the zero vector since $\mathbf{u} \cdot \mathbf{v} = 0$.

**Example 3.29** The vectors **v** = [1 2 3] and **u** = [−1 −1 1] are orthogonal since the dot product, $\mathbf{v} \cdot \mathbf{u} = (1)(-1) + (2)(-1) + (3)(1) = 0$.

**Example 3.30** Use *Mathematica* to show that **v** = [1 2 3] and **u** = [−1 −1 1] are orthogonal vectors by computing the dot product **v** · **u**, the angle θ between **u** and **v**, and the projection vector **p**.

*In[88]:=*
```
v = {1,2,3}; u = {-1,-1,1};
v.u
```

*Out[89]=*
```
0
```

*In[90]:=*
```
theta = ArcCos[v.u/Sqrt[(v.v)*(u.u)]]
```

*Out[90]=*
$$\frac{\text{Pi}}{2}$$

*In[91]:=*
```
p = (v.u)/(v.v)*u
```

*Out[91]=*
```
{0, 0, 0}
```

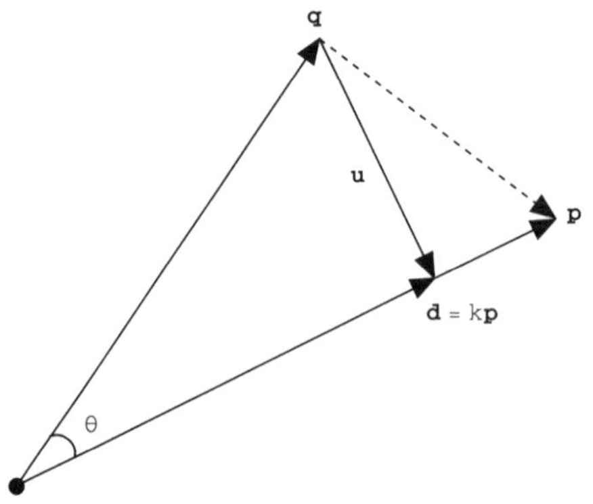


**Figure 3.5** Projection of **q** onto **p**

**Example 3.31** Let $\mathbf{d} = [d_1\ d_2 \ldots d_n]$ and $\mathbf{s} = [s_1\ s_2 \ldots s_n]$ be the demand and supply vectors of $n$ goods in $n$ markets, respectively. If the $n$ markets are in equilibrium, then there exists a price vector $\mathbf{p} = [p_1\ p_2 \ldots p_n]$ such that the aggregate demand value, $\mathbf{p} \cdot \mathbf{d}$, is equal to the aggregrate supply value $\mathbf{p} \cdot \mathbf{s}$. That is,

$$\mathbf{p} \cdot (\mathbf{d}-\mathbf{s}) = p_1(d_1-s_1) + p_2(d_2-s_2) + \ldots + p_n(d_n-s_n) = 0.$$

Hence, the price vector **p** and the excess demand vector (**d**–**s**) are orthogonal. Since prices $p_i \geq 0$ are nonnegative, if the $j$th market has excess demand $(d_j-s_j) > 0$, then there is at least one market has excess supply $(d_k-s_k) < 0$. This phenomena is called the *Walras's law* and **p** is the *Walrasian equilibrium price* vector if there is no market with excess demand.

**Example 3.32** One important application of the vector projection in economics is prediction and estimation. Consider a simple demand equation, $d_t = kp_t$, where the quantity demanded $d_t$ at the time period $t$ is proportional to price $p_t$ with the constant scalar, or *coefficient* $k$. We are interested in estimating the scalar $k$ so that the quantity demand could be predicted once the price is known. However, the observed quantity purchased $q_t$ may differ from the $d_t$ due to the randomness of observations. The difference, denoted as $u_t$, is called the *residual*,

$$q_t = d_t + u_t = kp_t + u_t.$$

Suppose we have $n$ periods of data on $q_t$ and $p_t$. Let $\mathbf{q} = [q_1\ q_2 \ldots q_n]$ and $\mathbf{p} = [p_1\ p_2 \ldots p_n]$ be the quantity and the price vectors observed in $n$ periods, respectively. We have then,

$$\mathbf{q} = \mathbf{d} + \mathbf{u} = k\mathbf{p} + \mathbf{u}$$

where $\mathbf{d} = [d_1\ d_2 \ldots d_n] = \mathrm{k}\mathbf{p}$ is the demand vector and $\mathbf{u} = [u_1\ u_2 \ldots u_n]$ is the residual vector. The estimation of the demand coefficient $k$ is done by finding the value $k$ such that the length of the residual vector, or the norm of **u** is minimized. As shown in figure 3.5, the demand vector $\mathbf{d} = k\mathbf{p}$ with the shortest length of **u** corresponds to the projection vector **q** on **p**. Other values of $k$, such as the one with the dashed line, would result in longer length than the residual vector **u**. Thus the projection vector **d** and the coefficient $k$ are equal to

$$\mathbf{d} = \frac{\mathbf{q}\cdot\mathbf{p}}{\mathbf{p}\cdot\mathbf{p}}\mathbf{p} \quad \text{and} \quad k = \frac{\mathbf{q}\cdot\mathbf{p}}{\mathbf{p}\cdot\mathbf{p}}.$$

Furthermore, when the vectors **q** and **p** are orthogonal, the length of the projection vector is zero, or k = 0, and the angle between the quantity vector and the projection vector is $\pi/2$. In this case, prices do not predict demand, or demand is not a function of **p**, $\mathbf{d} = 0\mathbf{p} = \mathbf{0}$. Thus, the cosine of the angle $\theta$ between **q** and **p** serves as a measure of goodness of prediction,

$$\cos\theta = \frac{\mathbf{q}\cdot\mathbf{p}}{\|\mathbf{q}\|\|\mathbf{p}\|} = \frac{\mathbf{q}\cdot\mathbf{p}}{\sqrt{(\mathbf{q}\cdot\mathbf{q})(\mathbf{p}\cdot\mathbf{p})}}.$$

Since $|\cos\theta| \le 1$, its value serves as an index of the goodness of predicting demand **d** based on the price **p**. A perfect prediction will have $\cos\theta = \pm 1$. A positive (negative) value of $\cos\theta$ implies a positive (negative) relation between price and quantity.

**Example 3.33** Weekly family food expenditure varies with family income. The following vectors **y** and **x** represent the 10 families' food expenditure and income, respectively.

$\mathbf{y} = [36 \quad 45 \quad 58 \quad 50 \quad 55 \quad 72 \quad 60 \quad 64 \quad 88 \quad 95]$,
$\mathbf{x} = [120 \quad 132 \quad 236 \quad 158 \quad 195 \quad 310 \quad 284 \quad 246 \quad 355 \quad 402]$

By calculating the coefficient $k$ from the following equation, we shall be able to predict the food expenditure, $k\mathbf{x}$, based on income **x**,

$$\mathbf{y} = k\mathbf{x} + \mathbf{u}.$$

The following *Mathematica* calculation shows that $k = 0.247416$. We predict a family with weekly income \$200 will spend \$49.48 ($k$*200) on food.

*In[92]:=*
```
y = {36, 45, 58, 50, 55, 72, 60, 64, 88, 95};
x = {120,132,236,158,195,310,284,246,355,402};
k = (x.y)/(x.x) //N
```

*Out[94]=*
```
0.247416
```

The index of the goodness of prediction, $\cos\theta = 0.99384$, is close to one. Thus, income is a good predictor of food expenditure.

*In[95]:=*
```
index = x.y/Sqrt[(x.x)(y.y)] //N
```

*Out[95]=*
```
0.99384
```

## EXERCISES

1. Given vectors $\mathbf{a} = [1\ 1\ 1]$, $\mathbf{b} = [2\ 0\ -1]$, and $\mathbf{c} = k\mathbf{b}$ where k is a scalar,
   (a) find the vector $\mathbf{c}$ such that the length of the vector $\mathbf{a}-\mathbf{c}$ is minimized; and
   (b) find a vector $\mathbf{v}$ with unit length which is orthogonal to the vector $\mathbf{c}$.
2. Given $\mathbf{v} = [2\ 1\ 3]$ and $\mathbf{u} = [3\ 1\ 2]$, find a vector $\mathbf{w}$ which is orthogonal to both $\mathbf{v}$ and $\mathbf{u}$.
3. If the vectors **a** and **b** are orthogonal, and **b** and **c** are orthogonal, then are **a** and **c** orthogonal?
4. Let $\mathbf{a} = [1\ 2]$ and **b** be a vector orthogonal to **a** and having $\|\mathbf{b}\| = 4$. Find the vector **b**.
5. Job performance rating (**r**) is believed to be predictable from the employee's grade-point average (**g**) in school. Based on the following data, find the projection vector, $k\mathbf{g}$, and the index of the goodness of prediction.

   $\mathbf{r} = [5\quad 4\quad 7\quad 8\quad 4\quad 6\quad 6\quad 8]$
   $\mathbf{g} = [2.5\quad 1.8\quad 3.6\quad 3.5\quad 1.5\quad 2.2\quad 3.2\quad 2.6]$

## □ 3.4 Vector Spaces □

### 3.4.1 Definition

A *vector space*, denoted by the symbol **V**, is a collection of vectors $\{\mathbf{v}_1, \mathbf{v}_2, \ldots\}$ such that

(1) the sum of any two vectors is also a vector in **V**; and

(2) the scalar multiplication of any vector is a vector in **V**.

**Example 3.34** Let $x$ and $y$ be real numbers. The collection of all three-dimensional vectors of the form $[x\ y\ 0]$ forms a vector space **V**. To prove this, suppose $\mathbf{v} = [a_1\ a_2\ 0]$ and $\mathbf{u} = [b_1\ b_2\ 0]$ are arbitrary vectors in **V**. It is obvious that $\mathbf{v} + \mathbf{u} = [a_1{+}b_1\ a_2{+}b_2\ 0]$ is of the form $[x\ y\ 0]$ and hence is in **V**. Any scalar multiple $k\mathbf{v}$ is also of the form $[x\ y\ 0]$ and is also in **V**.

**Example 3.35** The collection of all three-dimensional vectors of the form $[x\ y\ 1]$ where the third element is equal to 1 is not a vector space. For example, both $\mathbf{v} = [5\ 4\ 1]$ and $\mathbf{u} = [-3\ 2\ 1]$ are in the collection, but $\mathbf{v} + \mathbf{u} = [2\ 6\ 2]$ and $-3\mathbf{v} = [-15\ -12\ -3]$ are not.

**Example 3.36** The collection of all vectors that are scalar multiples of a vector **w** forms a vector space **V**. Suppose $\mathbf{u}_i = c_i\mathbf{w}$ and $c_i$'s are scalars. The collection $\mathbf{V} = \{\mathbf{u}_1, \mathbf{u}_2, \mathbf{u}_3, \ldots\}$ is then a vector space. It is obvious that $k_i\mathbf{u}_i$ and $k_i\mathbf{u}_i + k_j\mathbf{u}_j$ are in **V** since $k_i\mathbf{u}_i = k_ic_i\mathbf{w} = a\mathbf{w}$ with $a = k_ic_i$, and $k_i\mathbf{u}_i + k_j\mathbf{u}_j = (k_ic_i{+}k_jc_j)\mathbf{w} = b\mathbf{w}$ with $b = k_ic_i{+}k_jc_j$ are both scalar multiplications of **w**. Furthermore, since the $\mathbf{u}_i$'s in **V** are scalar multiples of **w**, the vector space **V** is the line extended on both directions of **w**. Let $\mathbf{w} = [1\ 2]$ and $\mathbf{u}_i = k_i\mathbf{w}$ for any real number $k_i$. The following *Mathematica* plot shows the geometric view of the vector space $\mathbf{V} = \{\mathbf{u}_1, \mathbf{u}_2, \mathbf{u}_3, \ldots\}$ which is the line extended on both directions of **w**. For example, $\mathbf{u}_1 = -0.7\mathbf{w}$, and $\mathbf{u}_2 = 4\mathbf{w} + \mathbf{u}_1$ are both on the extended line.

*In[96]:=*

```
w  =  {1,2};
u1  =  -0.7*w;
u2  =  4*w  +  u1;
vectw  =  vector2d[w,"w"];
vectu1  =  vector2d[u1,"u1"];
vectu2  =  vector2d[u2,"u2",dash];
Show[vectw,vectu1,vectu2,Axes->True];
```

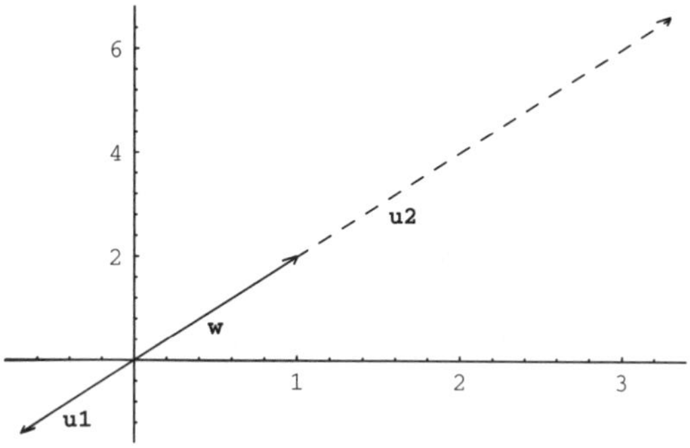


Since addition and scalar multiplication are used to form a linear combination of vectors, the above definition implies the following theorem.

**THEOREM 3.1** *If* $\mathbf{v}_1, \mathbf{v}_2, \ldots, \mathbf{v}_p$ *are vectors in a vector space* **V** *and* $k_1, k_2, \ldots, k_p$ *are scalars, then the linear combination of these vectors,*

$$\mathbf{u} = k_1\mathbf{v}_1 + k_2\mathbf{v}_2 + \ldots + k_p\mathbf{v}_p$$

*is also a vector in the vector space* **V**.

**Example 3.37** Let $\mathbf{v}_1 = [1\ 2]$ and $\mathbf{v}_2 = [-2\ 1]$. The collection $\mathbf{V} = \{\mathbf{u}_1, \mathbf{u}_2, \mathbf{u}_3, \ldots\}$, where $\mathbf{u}_i = k_{1i}\mathbf{v}_1 + k_{2i}\mathbf{v}_2$, forms a vector space. The vector space **V** is in fact a plane. Scalar multiplication of any vector in the plane, say $3\mathbf{u}_1 = 3k_{11}\mathbf{v}_1 + 3k_{21}\mathbf{v}_2$, is also in the plane, and so is a linear combination of any two vectors, say $3\mathbf{u}_1 - 2\mathbf{u}_2 = (3k_{11}-2k_{12})\mathbf{v}_1 + (3k_{21}-2k_{22})\mathbf{v}_2$. Two such vectors, $\mathbf{u}_1 = \mathbf{v}_1 + \mathbf{v}_2$ and $\mathbf{u}_2 = \mathbf{v}_1 - \mathbf{v}_2$ are plotted below.

*In[103]:=*

```
v1={1,2};  v2={-2,1};  u1=v1+v2;  u2=v1-v2;
vectv1=vector2d[v1,"v1"];
vectv2=vector2d[v2,"v2"];
vectu1=vector2d[u1,"u1",dash];
vectu2=vector2d[u2,"u2",dash];
Show[vectv1,vectv2,vectu1,vectu2,Axes->True];
```

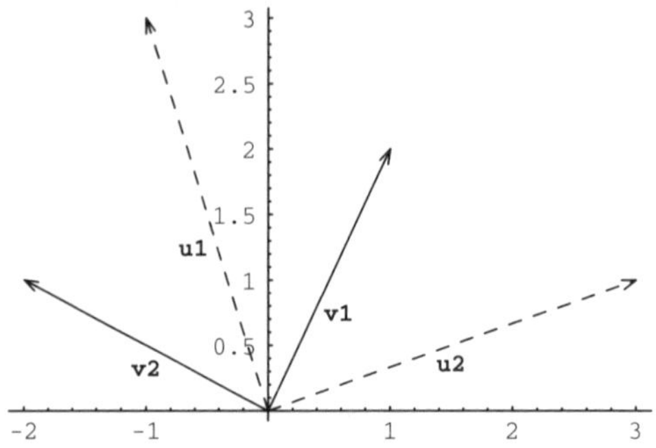


## EXERCISES

1. For the real numbers $x_i$, determine which of the following collections of four-dimensional vectors form a vector space:
   (a) $\mathbf{v} = [x_1\ x_2\ x_3\ x_4]$, where $x_1 + x_2 + x_3 + x_4 = 0$.
   (b) $\mathbf{v} = [x_1\ x_2\ x_3\ x_4]$, where $x_1 + x_2 + x_3 + x_4 = 1$.
   (c) $\mathbf{v} = [x_1\ x_2\ x_3\ x_4]$, where $x_1 = x_4$.
   (d) $\mathbf{v} = [x_1\ x_2\ x_3\ x_4]$, where $x_1 = x_2 x_3$.
2. Does the collection of all $n$-dimensional zero vectors form a vector space?
3. Does the collection of all $n$-dimensional unit vectors form a vector space?

### 3.4.2 Linear dependence

**DEFINITION 3.2** *The vectors $\mathbf{v}_1, \mathbf{v}_2, \ldots, \mathbf{v}_p$ are said to be **linearly dependent** if there are scalars $k_1, k_2, \ldots, k_p$, not all zero, such that*

$$k_1\mathbf{v}_1 + k_2\mathbf{v}_2 + \ldots + k_p\mathbf{v}_p = \mathbf{0}.$$

*On the other hand, the vectors $\mathbf{v}_1, \mathbf{v}_2, \ldots, \mathbf{v}_p$ are said to be **linearly independent** if all $k_i$'s must be zero for the linear combination to be the zero vector. Hence a collection of vectors is either linearly dependent or independent.*

**Example 3.38** Let $\mathbf{v}_1 = [1\ 2\ 3]$, $\mathbf{v}_2 = [2\ 4\ 6]$, and $\mathbf{v}_3 = [1\ 1\ 1]$. Show that $\mathbf{v}_1$ and $\mathbf{v}_2$ are linearly dependent, and $\mathbf{v}_1$ and $\mathbf{v}_3$ are linearly independent. It can be shown that

$$k_1\mathbf{v}_1 + k_2\mathbf{v}_2 = [k_1{+}2k_2 \quad 2k_1{+}4k_2 \quad 3k_1{+}6k_2] = [0 \quad 0 \quad 0]$$

for some nonzero $k_1$ and $k_2$; for example, $k_1 = -2$, and $k_2 = 1$. Hence, the vectors $\mathbf{v}_1$ and $\mathbf{v}_2$ must be linearly dependent. In fact, a linear combination of $\mathbf{v}_1$ and $\mathbf{v}_2$ is a zero vector as long as $k_1 = -2k_2$. On the other hand, $\mathbf{v}_1$ and $\mathbf{v}_3$ are linearly independent since $k_1\mathbf{v}_1 + k_2\mathbf{v}_2 = 0$ requires

$$k_1 + k_2 = 0$$
$$2k_1 + k_2 = 0$$
$$3k_1 + k_2 = 0$$

These three equations imply $k_1 = k_2 = 0$. Also, note that the three vectors $\mathbf{v}_1$, $\mathbf{v}_2$, and $\mathbf{v}_3$ are linearly dependent since a subset of them is linearly dependent.

**Example 3.39** The vectors, $\mathbf{a} = [1\ 2]$, $\mathbf{b} = [2\ 1]$, and $\mathbf{c} = [2.2\ 2.3]$, are linearly dependent since, for example, $0.8\mathbf{a} + 0.7\mathbf{b} - \mathbf{c} = \mathbf{0}$. The vector $\mathbf{c}$ can be written as a linear combination of vectors $\mathbf{a}$ and $\mathbf{b}$, i.e., $\mathbf{c} = 0.8\mathbf{a} + 0.7\mathbf{b}$. We graph all three vectors using **vector2d**.

*In[109]:=*

```
a={1,2};  b={2,1};  c={2.2,2.3};
vecta  =  vector2d[a,""];
vectb  =  vector2d[b,""];
vectc  =  vector2d[c,""];
s  =  addition2d[0.8*a,"0.8*a",0.7*b,"0.7*b"];
Show[vecta,vectb,vectc,s,Axes->True,
                        PlotRange->{{0,2.5},{0,2.5}}];
```

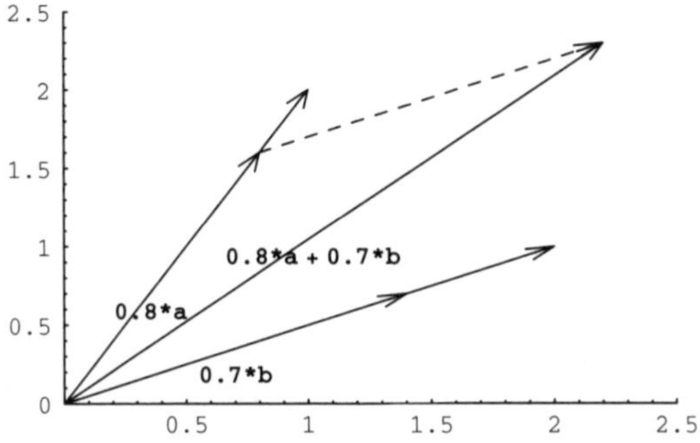


More generally, to determine whether a set of $n$-dimensional vectors, $\mathbf{v}_1,\mathbf{v}_2, \ldots ,\mathbf{v}_p$, are linearly dependent entails solving for $k_1,k_2, \ldots ,k_p$ in the following $n$ simultaneous linear equations,

$$k_1\mathbf{v}_1 + k_2\mathbf{v}_2 + \ldots + k_p\mathbf{v}_p = \mathbf{0}$$

where $\mathbf{0}$ is the zero vector. Any set of vectors, $\mathbf{v}_1,\mathbf{v}_2, \ldots ,\mathbf{v}_p$ that contains the zero vector cannot be linearly independent. We use **Solve** to solve for $k_i$'s in the following example.

**Example 3.40** $\mathbf{v}_1 = [1\ 2\ 3\ 4]$, $\mathbf{v}_2 = [-1\ 1\ 1\ -1]$, and $\mathbf{v}_3 = [0\ 3\ 4\ -3]$ are linearly independent, since $k_1\mathbf{v}_1 + k_2\mathbf{v}_2 + k_3\mathbf{v}_p = \mathbf{0}$ only if $k_1 = k_2 = k_3 = 0$ as shown below.

*In[115]:=*

```
v1={1,2,3,4};  v2={-1,1,1,-1};  v3={0,3,4,-3};
Solve[k1*v1+k2*v2+k3*v3  =={0,0,0,0},{k1,k2,k3}]
```

*Out[116]=*

{{k3 → 0, k1 → 0, k2 → 0}}

## EXERCISES

1. Given $\mathbf{v}_1 = [3\ \ 1/2\ \ -1]$, $\mathbf{v}_2 = [3/2\ \ 1\ \ 0]$, and $\mathbf{v}_3 = [1\ \ 0\ \ 0]$,
   (a) show that $\mathbf{v}_1$, $\mathbf{v}_2$, and $\mathbf{v}_3$ are linearly independent; and
   (b) find the scalars $k_1$, $k_2$, and $k_3$ such that

   $$k_1\mathbf{v}_1 + k_2\mathbf{v}_2 + k_3\mathbf{v}_3 = [13/2\quad -3/2\quad -2].$$

2. If $\mathbf{v}_1$,$\mathbf{v}_2$, and $\mathbf{v}_3$ are linearly independent vectors, then are the vectors $\mathbf{x} = \mathbf{v}_1 + \mathbf{v}_2 + \mathbf{v}_3$ and $\mathbf{y} = \mathbf{v}_3 + \mathbf{v}_1$ linearly independent?
3. Determine a value $x$ that makes the following vectors linearly dependent,

   $$[1\quad 2\quad x],\ [0\quad 1\quad x{-}1],\ [3\quad 4\quad 3].$$

4. Show that $\mathbf{c} = [7\ 4]$ is a linear combination of vectors $\mathbf{a} = [5\ 4]$ and $\mathbf{b} = [10\ 4]$.

### 3.4.3 Basis and rank of a vector space

Consider two linearly independent 2-dimensional vectors,

$$\mathbf{v}_1 = [-1\quad 1],\ \mathbf{v}_2 = [1\quad 1].$$

It is easy to show that $\mathbf{v}_3 = [-1\ 3]$ is a linear combination of $\mathbf{v}_1$ and $\mathbf{v}_2$. That is, there are nonzero scalars, $k_1 = 2$ and $k_2 = 1$ such that

$$\mathbf{v}_3 = k_1\mathbf{v}_1 + k_2\mathbf{v}_2 = 2\mathbf{v}_1 + \mathbf{v}_2.$$

In other words, the two linearly independent vectors, $\mathbf{v}_1$ and $\mathbf{v}_2$, “generate” or “span” the vector $\mathbf{v}_3$. This can be seen in the following graphic.

*In[117]:=*

```
v1  =  {-1,1};  v2  =  {1,1};
v3  =  addition2d[2*v1,"2*v1",v2,"v2"];
Show[v3,Axes->True,AspectRatio->1];
```

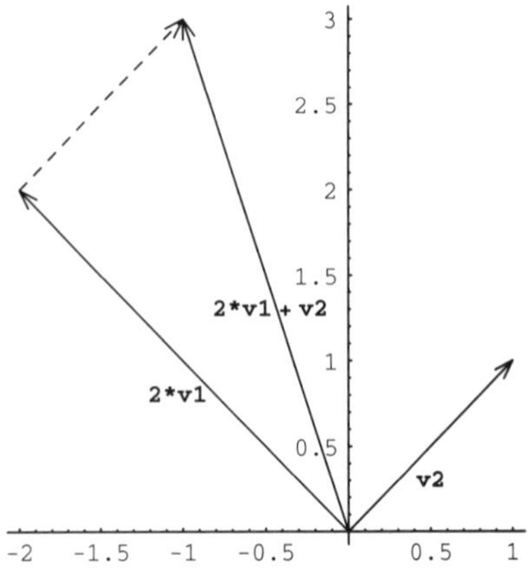

In fact, any two-dimensional vector can be expressed as a linear combination of $\mathbf{v}_1$ and $\mathbf{v}_2$. For example, for any $a$ and $b$

$$\mathbf{v} = [a \quad b] = k_1{*}\mathbf{v}_1 + k_2{*}\mathbf{v}_2,$$

we can determine values for $k_1 = (-a+b)/2$ and $k_2 = (a+b)/2$. By the definition of a vector space $\mathbf{V}$, the collection of all two-dimensional vectors generated by $\mathbf{v}_1$ and $\mathbf{v}_2$ (including $\mathbf{v}_1$ and $\mathbf{v}_2$ themselves) constitutes a vector space. The vectors $\mathbf{v}_1$ and $\mathbf{v}_2$ generate each vector in this vector space and is called a *basis* of the vector space. The *dimension*, or the *rank*, of the vector space $\mathbf{V}$ is the maximum number of linearly independent vectors that are able to generate all vectors in $\mathbf{V}$. A vector space $\mathbf{V}$ of rank $n$, or an $n$-dimensional vector space, is denoted as $\mathbf{V}^n$.

**Example 3.41** Let $\mathbf{v}_1 = [1\ 2\ 3\ 4]$ and $\mathbf{v}_2 = [-1\ 1\ 1\ -1]$. The collection of all vectors $\mathbf{u}$ such that

$$\mathbf{u} = k_1\mathbf{v}_1 + k_2\mathbf{v}_2$$

constitutes a two-dimensional vector space $\mathbf{V}^2$. Note that $\mathbf{v}_1$ and $\mathbf{v}_2$ are linearly independent. The rank of $\mathbf{V}^2$ is 2. One of the vectors in this vector space is $\mathbf{u} = [5\ 4\ 7\ 14]$ since if $k_1 = 3$ and $k_2 = -2$, then

$$\mathbf{u} = 3\mathbf{v}_1 - 2\mathbf{v}_2.$$

The unit vectors

$$\mathbf{I}_1 = [1 \quad 0 \quad 0],\ \mathbf{I}_2 = [0 \quad 1 \quad 0],\ \mathbf{I}_3 = [0 \quad 0 \quad 1]$$

are linearly independent. Any vector in $\mathbf{V}^3$ can be written as a linear combination of $\mathbf{I}_1$, $\mathbf{I}_2$, and $\mathbf{I}_3$. Hence $\mathbf{I}_1$, $\mathbf{I}_2$, and $\mathbf{I}_3$ form a basis for $\mathbf{V}^3$. We call this basis the *natural basis*. All 3-dimensional vectors can be expressed as a linear combination of this basis. If $\mathbf{v} = [x_1\ x_2\ x_3]$, then

$$\mathbf{v} = x_1\mathbf{I}_1 + x_2\mathbf{I}_2 + x_3\mathbf{I}_3.$$

The function **rank** in the **MathEcon** package computes the rank of a collection of vectors. Here is its description.

*In[120]:=*

```
?rank
```

**rank[lst] calculates the dimension of the space spanned by the vectors contained in its argument (list). For example,**

**rank[{{1,-1,9},{1,-2,-3}}].**

**Example 3.42** Find the number of independent vectors or the rank of the vector space generated from the following collection.

$\mathbf{v}_1 = [1 \quad 2 \quad 3 \quad 4]$, $\mathbf{v}_2 = [-1 \quad 1 \quad 1 \quad -1]$,
$\mathbf{v}_3 = [5 \quad 4 \quad 7 \quad 14]$, $\mathbf{v}_4 = [5 \quad 7 \quad 11 \quad 17]$.

*In[121]:=*

```
v1 = {1,2,3,4}; v2 = {-1,1,1,-1};
v3 = {5,4,7,14}; v4 = {5,7,11,17};
rank[{v1,v2,v3,v4}]
```

*Out[123]=*

```
2
```

## EXERCISES

1. Find a basis of the vector space spanned by

$$\mathbf{v}_1 = [1 \quad 0 \quad 2 \quad -1],\ \mathbf{v}_2 = [2 \quad 0 \quad 1 \quad 4],\ \mathbf{v}_3 = [-1 \quad 0 \quad 7 \quad -17].$$

2. Find a basis of the vector space spanned by

$$\mathbf{v}_1 = [2 \quad 3],\ \mathbf{v}_2 = [4 \quad 1],\ \mathbf{v}_3 = [3 \quad 2].$$

   Show geometrically that $\mathbf{v}_3$ is a linear combination of $\mathbf{v}_1$ and $\mathbf{v}_2$.

3. Find a basis and the rank of the vector space spanned by

$$\begin{aligned}
\mathbf{v}_1 &= [1 \quad -3 \quad 3 \quad 4] \\
\mathbf{v}_2 &= [0 \quad 2 \quad 1 \quad -3] \\
\mathbf{v}_3 &= [1 \quad 1 \quad 4 \quad 1] \\
\mathbf{v}_4 &= [3 \quad -5 \quad 8 \quad 9].
\end{aligned}$$

# 4

# Matrices

In the last chapter we learned the basic properties and some applications of vectors and vector spaces. In this chapter we study the properties and applications of collections of vectors called *matrices*. For example, an equation, such as $2x_1 - x_2 + 5x_3 = 5$, can be written as the dot product of two vectors, $\mathbf{a} \cdot \mathbf{x} = 5$, with $\mathbf{a} = [2\ -1\ 5]$ being a coefficient vector and $\mathbf{x} = [x_1\ x_2\ x_3]$ being a variable vector. A system of $m$ linear equations can thus be viewed as a collection of $m$ dot products composed of $m$ coefficient vectors and a variable vector. This generalization leads us to the definition of a matrix. The algebraic operations of matrices are similar to operations of vectors. In this chapter we discuss the algebra of matrices. This discussion paves the way for the study of the methods of solving a system of linear equations in the next chapter.

## □ 4.1 Matrices □

### 4.1.1 Definition

A *matrix* is an ordered collection of row (or column) vectors. An $n \times m$ matrix has $n$ rows and $m$ columns. For example, The matrix $\mathbf{A}$ below is a $2 \times 3$ matrix – it has 2 rows and 3 columns. It can be viewed as an ordered collection of two, three-dimensional row vectors, $\mathbf{v}_1^T$, and $\mathbf{v}_2^T$. Alternatively, $\mathbf{A}$ can be viewed as an ordered collection of three, two-dimensional column vectors: $\mathbf{u}_1$, $\mathbf{u}_2$, and $\mathbf{u}_3$.

$$\mathbf{A} = \begin{bmatrix} a_{11} & a_{12} & a_{13} \\ a_{21} & a_{22} & a_{23} \end{bmatrix} = \begin{bmatrix} \mathbf{v}_1^T \\ \mathbf{v}_2^T \end{bmatrix}$$
$$= [\mathbf{u}_1 \quad \mathbf{u}_2 \quad \mathbf{u}_3]$$

In the matrix $\mathbf{A}$ we have used the notation

$$\mathbf{v}_1^T = [a_{11} \quad a_{12} \quad a_{13}]$$
$$\mathbf{v}_2^T = [a_{21} \quad a_{22} \quad a_{23}]$$

and

$$\mathbf{u}_1 = \begin{bmatrix} a_{11} \\ a_{21} \end{bmatrix};\ \mathbf{u}_2 = \begin{bmatrix} a_{12} \\ a_{22} \end{bmatrix};\ \mathbf{u}_3 = \begin{bmatrix} a_{13} \\ a_{23} \end{bmatrix}$$

If the elements of a matrix $\mathbf{A}$ are $a_{ij}$, then we write $\mathbf{A} = [a_{ij}]$. The first subscript $i$ indicates the row and the second subscript $j$ indicates the column in which the element $a_{ij}$ resides. Lastly, we note that a vector is a special type of matrix. A row vector $\mathbf{v}^T = [a_{11}\ a_{12}\ \ldots\ a_{1n}]$ is a $1 \times n$ matrix and the column vector

$$\mathbf{v} = \begin{bmatrix} a_{11} \\ a_{12} \\ \cdot \\ \cdot \\ a_{1n} \end{bmatrix}$$

is an $n \times 1$ matrix.

When the rows and columns of a matrix $\mathbf{A}$ are interchanged, the new matrix is called the *transpose* of $\mathbf{A}$, and is denoted by $\mathbf{A}^T$. Thus,

$$\mathbf{A}^T = \begin{bmatrix} a_{11} & a_{21} \\ a_{12} & a_{22} \\ a_{13} & a_{23} \end{bmatrix} = \begin{bmatrix} \mathbf{v}_1 & \mathbf{v}_2 \end{bmatrix}$$

Hence, if $\mathbf{A}$ is an $n \times m$ matrix, $\mathbf{A}^T$ is an $m \times n$ matrix. Notice that the transpose is the same operation that was introduced in the previous chapter for vectors.

**Example 4.1** John bought 3 gallons of milk, 5 loaves of bread, and 6 apples last week. Nancy bought 6 gallons of milk, 4 loaves of bread, and 3 apples. This data can then be arranged as a matrix. The rows of the matrix $\mathbf{A}$ below indicate John's and Nancy's purchases, respectively. The columns correspond to the 3 goods that they bought.

$$\mathbf{A} = \begin{bmatrix} 3 & 5 & 6 \\ 6 & 4 & 3 \end{bmatrix}$$

**Example 4.2** There are two ways of making a chair. One is more labor intensive and the other is more machine intensive. The labor intensive method requires 6 hours of labor, 1 hour of machine time, and 2 units of material. The machine intensive method needs only 3 hours of labor, 2 hours of machine time, and the same 2 units of material. The methods for making a chair can then be represented by the $3 \times 2$ matrix

$$\mathbf{A} = \begin{bmatrix} 6 & 3 \\ 1 & 2 \\ 2 & 2 \end{bmatrix} = \begin{bmatrix} a_{ij} \end{bmatrix}$$

The elements $a_{ij}$ are called *input coefficients.*

A *zero* or *null matrix* is a special matrix whose elements are all zero. For example, the $2 \times 3$ zero matrix is

$$\mathbf{Z} = \begin{bmatrix} 0 & 0 & 0 \\ 0 & 0 & 0 \end{bmatrix}$$

A *square* matrix is a matrix that has the same number of rows and columns. The elements of a square matrix $a_{ii}$ are called the *main diagonal elements*. Among different types of matrices, the class of square matrices plays a key role in later chapters. Four special matrices are important and are defined here.

The *identity matrix* is a square matrix whose elements are zero except the main diagonal elements which are 1. The $3 \times 3$ identity matrix is

$$\mathbf{I} = \begin{bmatrix} 1 & 0 & 0 \\ 0 & 1 & 0 \\ 0 & 0 & 1 \end{bmatrix}$$

A *diagonal matrix* is a square matrix whose elements are all zero except the main diagonal elements. The general $3 \times 3$ diagonal matrix has the form

$$\mathbf{D} = \begin{bmatrix} \mathrm{a} & 0 & 0 \\ 0 & \mathrm{b} & 0 \\ 0 & 0 & \mathrm{c} \end{bmatrix}$$

A square matrix $\mathbf{A} = [a_{ij}]$ is said to be *upper (lower) triangular* if $a_{ij} = 0$ for all $i > j$ $(i < j)$. That is, all elements below (above) the main diagonal are zero. Triangular matrices with $a_{ii} = 0$ for all $i$ are called *strictly triangular*. The following matrices **A**, **B**, and **C** are an upper, lower, and strictly upper triangular, respectively.

$$\mathbf{A} = \begin{bmatrix} a_{11} & a_{12} & a_{13} \\ 0 & a_{22} & a_{23} \\ 0 & 0 & a_{33} \end{bmatrix}; \ \mathbf{B} = \begin{bmatrix} b_{11} & 0 & 0 \\ b_{21} & b_{22} & 0 \\ b_{31} & b_{32} & b_{33} \end{bmatrix}; \ \mathbf{C} = \begin{bmatrix} 0 & c_{12} & c_{13} \\ 0 & 0 & c_{23} \\ 0 & 0 & 0 \end{bmatrix}$$

## EXERCISES

1. Suppose

$$\mathbf{A} = \begin{bmatrix} 1 & 2 & 3 \\ 4 & 5 & 6 \\ 7 & 8 & 9 \end{bmatrix} = [a_{ij}].$$

   (a) What are the elements $a_{23}$, $a_{32}$?
   (b) Find the transpose matrix $\mathbf{A}^T$. Is the element in the 2nd row and 3rd column of $\mathbf{A}^T$ equal to $a_{23}$?

2. A *symmetric* matrix is a square matrix such that $\mathbf{A}^T = \mathbf{A}$.
   (a) Give an example of a $3 \times 3$ symmetric matrix.
   (b) Is it true that a symmetric matrix requires $a_{ij} = a_{ji}$?

3. The *dimension* of the matrix **A** with $m$ rows and $n$ columns is defined as symbol $m \times n$.
   (a) What is the dimension of $((\mathbf{A}^T)^T)^T$?
   (b) Show that $(\mathbf{A}^T)^T = \mathbf{A}$.

### 4.1.2 Creating matrices with *Mathematica*

Just as with vectors, matrices in *Mathematica* are represented by lists. The vector $[a\ b\ c]$ is represented in *Mathematica* by **{a,b,c}**. In *Mathematica* a matrix is represented as a list of lists where the sublists are the rows of the matrix. The number of sublists corresponds to the number of rows in the matrix and the number of elements in each sublist corresponds to the number of columns of the matrix. For example, the matrix

$$\mathbf{A} = \begin{bmatrix} a & b & c \\ d & e & f \end{bmatrix}$$

is represented in *Mathematica* as the list **{{a,b,c},{d,e,f}}**. Here is a specific example.

**Example 4.3** Define the symbol **A** to be the $2 \times 3$ matrix

$$\mathbf{A} = \begin{bmatrix} 3 & 2 & 3 \\ 1 & -2 & 0 \end{bmatrix}$$

*In[1]:=*

```
A = {{3,2,3},{1,-2,0}}
```

*Out[1]=*

```
{{3, 2, 3}, {1, -2, 0}}
```

The *Mathematica* function **MatrixForm** displays the list as a rectangular array. We can display **A** as a rectangular array with **MatrixForm**.

*In[2]:=*

```
MatrixForm[A]
```

*Out[2]//MatrixForm=*

```
3  2   3
1  -2  0
```

Note that the output from the **MatrixForm** function is for display purposes only. The output is not enclosed with braces, and hence cannot be used for other calculations.

There are several *Mathematica* functions that are useful in constructing matrices. Some of these functions were introduced in the last chapter.

**Example 4.4** The **Array** function can be used to construct both symbolic vectors and matrices. Below we construct an $m \times n$ matrix with the elements **a[i,j]**.

*In[3]:=*

```
Clear[a]
Array[a,{2,3}] //MatrixForm
```

*Out[4]//MatrixForm=*

```
a[1, 1]  a[1, 2]  a[1, 3]
a[2, 1]  a[2, 2]  a[2, 3]
```

One can think of **a[i,j]** as representing the element $a_{ij}$.

**Example 4.5** The individual row vector or element $a_{ij}$ of a matrix **A** can be extracted by the *Mathematica* **Part** function which has the shorthand notation [[ ]]. Let us apply this function to the following matrix **A**.

*In[5]:=*
```
A = {{4,5,-1,3},{0,-4,8,7},{1,2,9,10}};
```

The first row is

*In[6]:=*
```
A[[1]]
```

*Out[6]=*
```
{4, 5, -1, 3}
```

The second element of the first row is

*In[7]:=*
```
A[[1,2]]
```

*Out[7]=*
```
5
```

The third element of the second row is

*In[8]:=*
```
A[[2,3]]
```

*Out[8]=*
```
8
```

**Example 4.6** The function **Table** can be used to construct matrices. Here we construct a 3 × 2 matrix $\mathbf{A} = [a_{ij}]$ where $a_{ij} = i+j$.

*In[9]:=*
```
A = Table[i+j,{i,3},{j,2}]
```

*Out[9]=*
```
{{2, 3}, {3, 4}, {4, 5}}
```

Let us display this matrix as a rectangular array.

*In[10]:=*
```
A // MatrixForm
```

*Out[10]//MatrixForm=*
```
2  3
3  4
4  5
```

**Example 4.7** The function **Transpose** interchanges the rows and columns of a matrix.

*In[11]:=*
```
A={{1,2},{3,4}};
A // MatrixForm
```

*Out[12]//MatrixForm=*

```
1   2
3   4
```

*In[13]:=*

```
Transpose[A]  //  MatrixForm
```

*Out[13]//MatrixForm=*

```
1   3
2   4
```

**Example 4.8** The *Mathematica* function **IdentityMatrix** creates an identity matrix. The $3 \times 3$ identity matrix is constructed below.

*In[14]:=*

```
IdentityMatrix[3]  //  MatrixForm
```

*Out[14]//MatrixForm=*

```
1   0   0
0   1   0
0   0   1
```

**Example 4.9** The function **DiagonalMatrix** creates a diagonal matrix.

*In[15]:=*

```
Clear[a,b,c]
DiagonalMatrix[{a,b,c}]  //  MatrixForm
```

*Out[16]//MatrixForm=*

```
a   0   0
0   b   0
0   0   c
```

## EXERCISES

1. Using *Mathematica* to construct the matrix

$$\mathbf{A} = \begin{bmatrix} 3 & a & -2 \\ b & 5 & 0 \\ 1 & x & z \end{bmatrix}$$

Find its tranpose. Is **A** a symmetric matrix?

2. A symmetric matrix of the following form is called an *autocorrelation matrix*,

$$\mathbf{A} = \begin{bmatrix} 1 & a & a^2 & a^3 \\ a & 1 & a & a^2 \\ a^2 & a & 1 & a \\ a^3 & a^2 & a & 1 \end{bmatrix}$$

Use the **Table** function to construct it.

3. Use *Mathematica* to extract the elements containing $a^2$ of the autocorrelation matrix.

4. Use *Mathematica* to construct a general $4 \times 4$ upper triangular matrix **A**. Transpose the matrix **A** to obtain a lower triangular matrix.

## □ 4.2 Matrix Operations □

### 4.2.1 Matrix addition and subtraction

Consider the matrices

$$\mathbf{A} = \left[a_{ij}\right] = \begin{bmatrix} a_{11} & a_{12} & a_{13} \\ a_{21} & a_{22} & a_{23} \end{bmatrix}; \ \mathbf{B} = \left[b_{ij}\right] = \begin{bmatrix} b_{11} & b_{12} & b_{13} \\ b_{21} & b_{22} & b_{23} \end{bmatrix}$$

The *sum (difference)* of **A** and **B** is defined as the sum (difference) of the corresponding elements in the matrices. That is, we define the sum and difference of two matrices as

$$\mathbf{A} \pm \mathbf{B} = \left[a_{ij} \pm b_{ij}\right] = \begin{bmatrix} a_{11} \pm b_{11} & a_{12} \pm b_{12} & a_{13} \pm b_{13} \\ a_{21} \pm b_{21} & a_{22} \pm b_{22} & a_{23} \pm b_{23} \end{bmatrix}$$

Note that the sum and difference of two matrices only makes sense when the matrices are of the same dimension.

**Example 4.10** Calculate $\mathbf{A} + \mathbf{B}$ and $\mathbf{A} - \mathbf{B}$ where

$$\mathbf{A} = \begin{bmatrix} 1 & 2 & 3 \\ 3 & 4 & 5 \end{bmatrix}; \ \mathbf{B} = \begin{bmatrix} 2 & -1 & 4 \\ 1 & -3 & 3 \end{bmatrix}$$

*In[17]:=*

```
A = {{1,2,3},{3,4,5}}; B = {{2,-1,4},{1,-3,3}};
A + B // MatrixForm
```

*Out[18]//MatrixForm=*

```
3  1  7
4  1  8
```

*In[19]:=*

```
A - B // MatrixForm
```

*Out[19]//MatrixForm=*

```
-1  3  -1
2   7  2
```

In matrix algebra the sum or difference of a matrix with a scalar has no meaning. However, in *Mathematica*, the sum of a matrix and a scalar is allowed. Specifically in *Mathematica*, the addition or subtraction of a scalar to a matrix produces a new matrix where each element is added to (or subtracted from) by the scalar. Thus,

$\mathbf{A} + 3 = [a_{ij} + 3]$; $\mathbf{B} - 4 = [b_{ij} - 4]$.

**Example 4.11** Add a constant k to each element of $\mathbf{A} = \begin{bmatrix} 1 & -1 & 3 \\ -9 & 2 & 1 \end{bmatrix}$.

*In[20]:=*
```
Clear[k];
A = {{1,-1,3},{-9,2,1}};
A + k // MatrixForm
```

*Out[22]//MatrixForm=*
```
1 + k    -1 + k   3 + k
-9 + k   2 + k    1 + k
```

Matrix addition obey the commutative and associative laws:

(1) Commutative law: $\mathbf{A} + \mathbf{B} = \mathbf{B} + \mathbf{A}$

(2) Associative law: $(\mathbf{A} + \mathbf{B}) + \mathbf{C} = \mathbf{A} + (\mathbf{B} + \mathbf{C})$

The trace of a square matrix is the sum of the diagonal elements of the matrix. For example, if

$$\mathbf{A} = \begin{bmatrix} 3 & -2 & 1 \\ 0 & 4 & 2 \\ 1 & 2 & 1 \end{bmatrix}$$

then the trace of **A**, denoted as tr(**A**), is 3+4+1 = 8. In general, an $n \times n$ matrix $\mathbf{A} = [a_{ij}]$ has the trace

$$\text{tr}(\mathbf{A}) = \sum_{i=1}^{n} a_{ii}$$

It is easy to use the *Mathematica* functions **Sum** and **Part** applied to a matrix to calculate the trace. For example

*In[23]:=*
```
A = {{3,-2,1},{0,4,2},{1,2,1}};
tr = Sum[A[[i,i]],{i,3}]
```

*Out[24]=*
```
8
```

If both **A** and **B** are square matrices, then it is obvious that

$$\text{tr}(\mathbf{A} \pm \mathbf{B}) = \text{tr}(\mathbf{A}) \pm \text{tr}(\mathbf{B})$$

## EXERCISES

1. Does the commutative law of addition apply to subtraction, i.e., $\mathbf{A} - \mathbf{B} = \mathbf{B} - \mathbf{A}$?
2. Can $\mathbf{A} + \mathbf{A}^T$ be calculated for any matrix **A**?
3. Show that $(\mathbf{A} + \mathbf{B} + \mathbf{C})^T = \mathbf{A}^T + \mathbf{B}^T + \mathbf{C}^T = (\mathbf{C} + \mathbf{B} + \mathbf{A})^T$.

4. Does $(\mathbf{A} - \mathbf{B})^T = \mathbf{A}^T - \mathbf{B}^T$? If not, give a counterexample.

5. Prove that $\mathbf{A} - \mathbf{B} = \mathbf{0}$ if and only if $\mathbf{A} = \mathbf{B}$.

6. Given $\mathbf{A} = [\mathbf{a}_1\ \mathbf{a}_2\ \mathbf{a}_3]$ and $\mathbf{B} = [\mathbf{b}_1\ \mathbf{b}_2\ \mathbf{b}_3]$ where $\mathbf{a}_i$ and $\mathbf{b}_i$ are $n$-dimensional column vectors. Compute $\mathbf{A} + \mathbf{B}$ and $\mathbf{A} - \mathbf{B}$. What are the dimensions of these matrices?

## 4.2.2 Matrix multiplication

Since a matrix is an ordered collection of vectors, the rule governing the product of two matrices is similar to the dot product in vector operation. Recall that the dot product of two vectors is a scalar. This product is a special case of matrix multiplication, namely, the multiplication of a $1 \times n$ matrix (row vector) with a $n \times 1$ matrix (column vector). By the same token if the matrix $\mathbf{A}$ is $2 \times 3$ and $\mathbf{B}$ is $3 \times 2$, i.e.,

$$\mathbf{A} = \left[a_{ij}\right] = \begin{bmatrix} a_{11} & a_{12} & a_{13} \\ a_{21} & a_{22} & a_{23} \end{bmatrix};$$

$$\mathbf{B} = \left[b_{ij}\right] = \begin{bmatrix} b_{11} & b_{12} \\ b_{21} & b_{22} \\ b_{31} & b_{32} \end{bmatrix}$$

then the pre-multiplication of $\mathbf{B}$ by $\mathbf{A}$ (or, equivalently the post-multiplication of $\mathbf{A}$ by $\mathbf{B}$) is a $2 \times 2$ matrix $\mathbf{C}$ and is defined as

$$\begin{aligned} \mathbf{C} &= \mathbf{A}\mathbf{B} \\ &= \left[c_{ij}\right] = \begin{bmatrix} a_{11}b_{11}+a_{12}b_{21}+a_{13}b_{31} & a_{11}b_{12}+a_{12}b_{22}+a_{13}b_{32} \\ a_{21}b_{11}+a_{22}b_{21}+a_{23}b_{31} & a_{21}b_{12}+a_{22}b_{22}+a_{23}b_{32} \end{bmatrix} \end{aligned}$$

The element in the $i$-th row and $j$-th column of $\mathbf{C}$ is calculated by multiplying each element in the $i$-th row of $\mathbf{A}$ by each corresponding element in the $j$-th column of $\mathbf{B}$ and summing the resulting terms. That is, the dot product of the $i$-th row vector of the first matrix $\mathbf{A}$ and the $j$-th column vector of the second matrix $\mathbf{B}$.

**Example 4.12** Suppose

$$\mathbf{A} = \begin{bmatrix} 1 & 2 \\ -3 & 4 \end{bmatrix};\ \mathbf{B} = \begin{bmatrix} 1 & 2 & 3 \\ 1 & -3 & 4 \end{bmatrix}$$

The pre-multiplication of $\mathbf{B}$ by $\mathbf{A}$ is equal to

$$\begin{aligned} \mathbf{A}\mathbf{B} &= \begin{bmatrix} 1 & 2 \\ -3 & 4 \end{bmatrix}\begin{bmatrix} 1 & 2 & 3 \\ 1 & -3 & 4 \end{bmatrix} \\ &= \begin{bmatrix} 1(1)+2(1) & 1(2)+2(-3) & 1(3)+2(4) \\ -3(1)+4(1) & -3(2)+4(-3) & -3(3)+4(4) \end{bmatrix} \\ &= \begin{bmatrix} 3 & -4 & 11 \\ 1 & -18 & 7 \end{bmatrix} \end{aligned}$$

In *Mathematica*, matrix multiplication is performed by the **Dot** function.

*In[25]:=*

```
?Dot
```

**a.b.c or Dot[a,b,c] gives products of vectors, matrices and tensors.**

We see that it has a short-hand form using a period. To multiply the matrices **A** and **B**, *Mathematica* requires a period between matrices, i.e., **A . B**.

*In[26]:=*

```
A = {{1,2},{-3,4}}; B = {{1,2,3},{1,-3,4}};
A.B // MatrixForm
```

*Out[27]//MatrixForm=*

```
3   -4    11
1   -18   7
```

**Example 4.13** Suppose the quantity matrix $\mathbf{Q} = [q_{ik}]$ represents the $i$-th consumer's purchase of $k$-th commodity. The price of each commodity varies from week to week. The price matrix $\mathbf{P} = [p_{kj}]$ represents the unit price of the $k$-th commodity in week $j$. There are $n$ consumers, $r$ commodities, and $m$ weeks. The total cost to the $i$-th consumer in $j$-th week is then the element of the $i$-th row and $j$-th column of the matrix **C**,

$$\mathbf{C} = [c_{ij}] = \mathbf{QP}$$

where

$$c_{ij} = \sum_{k=1}^{r} q_{ik} p_{kj}; \; i=1,2, \ldots ,n, \quad \text{and} \quad j=1,2, \ldots ,m$$

The following diagrams illustrate the multiplications of elements which results in $c_{ij}$.

$$\begin{bmatrix} q_{11} & q_{12} & \cdot & \cdot & \cdot & q_{1r} \\ \cdot & \cdot & \cdot & \cdot & \cdot & \cdot \\ \cdot & \cdot & \cdot & \cdot & \cdot & \cdot \\ \boxed{q_{i1}} & \boxed{q_{i2}} & \cdot & \cdot & \cdot & \boxed{q_{ir}} \\ \cdot & \cdot & \cdot & \cdot & \cdot & \cdot \\ \cdot & \cdot & \cdot & \cdot & \cdot & \cdot \\ q_{n1} & q_{n2} & \cdot & \cdot & \cdot & q_{nr} \end{bmatrix} \begin{bmatrix} p_{11} & \cdot & \boxed{p_{1j}} & \cdot & p_{1m} \\ p_{21} & \cdot & \boxed{p_{2j}} & \cdot & p_{2m} \\ \cdot & \cdot & \cdot & \cdot & \cdot \\ \cdot & \cdot & \cdot & \cdot & \cdot \\ \cdot & \cdot & \cdot & \cdot & \cdot \\ p_{r1} & \cdot & \boxed{p_{rj}} & \cdot & p_{rm} \end{bmatrix} = \begin{bmatrix} c_{11} & \cdot & c_{1j} & \cdot & c_{1m} \\ \cdot & \cdot & \cdot & \cdot & \cdot \\ \cdot & \cdot & \boxed{c_{ij}} & \cdot & \cdot \\ \cdot & \cdot & \cdot & \cdot & \cdot \\ \cdot & \cdot & \cdot & \cdot & \cdot \\ c_{n1} & \cdot & c_{rj} & \cdot & c_{nm} \end{bmatrix}$$

**Example 4.14** Suppose the quantity matrix $\mathbf{Q} = [q_{ik}]$ is $4 \times 3$ and the price matrix $\mathbf{P} = [p_{kj}]$ is $3 \times 2$. The element $c_{32}$

$$c_{32} = q_{31}p_{12} + q_{32}p_{22} + q_{33}p_{32}$$

of the total cost matrix, **cost** = **QP**, can be computed using *Mathematica*.

*In[28]:=*

```
Clear[q,p]; Q = Array[q,{4,3}]; P = Array[p,{3,2}];
cost = Q.P;
cost[[3,2]]
```

*Out[30]=*

```
p[1, 2]q[3, 1] + p[2, 2]q[3, 2] + p[3, 2]q[3, 3]
```

**Example 4.15** A simple model of demand ($D$), supply ($S$) and market equilibrium ($D = S$) are the equations:

Demand: $D = -P + 5;$
Supply: $S = 0.5P + 2;$
Equilibrium: $D = S$

where $P$ is the price. These three equations can be rearranged as

$$\begin{aligned} D + P &= 5 \\ -0.5P + S &= 2 \\ D - S &= 0. \end{aligned}$$

The equation can be written as the matrix equation

$$\begin{bmatrix} 1 & 0 & 1 \\ 0 & 1 & -0.5 \\ 1 & -1 & 0 \end{bmatrix} \begin{bmatrix} D \\ S \\ P \end{bmatrix} = \begin{bmatrix} 5 \\ 2 \\ 0 \end{bmatrix}$$

If we call the above $3 \times 3$ matrix $\mathbf{A}$, the $3 \times 1$ vector (of elements $D$, $S$, and $P$) $\mathbf{x}$, and the $3 \times 1$ vector of constants $\mathbf{b}$, then we can write the equation system as

$$\mathbf{A}\mathbf{x} = \mathbf{b}.$$

We make the following observations about matrix multiplication:

(1) Two matrices, $\mathbf{A}$ and $\mathbf{B}$, are said to be *comformable* for multiplication if and only if the numbers of columns in $\mathbf{A}$ is equal to the numbers of rows in $\mathbf{B}$. Thus if $\mathbf{A}$ is $m \times n$ and $\mathbf{B}$ is $n \times q$, then it is meaningful to multiply $\mathbf{AB}$, which is a $m \times q$ matrix. However, the product $\mathbf{BA}$ is not defined unless $q = m$.

(2) Matrix multiplication is not in general commutative, i.e.,

$$\mathbf{AB} \neq \mathbf{BA}.$$

For example,

*In[31]:=*

```
A = {{1,2,3},{4,5,6}}; B={{-2,5},{2,1},{-3,2}};
A.B // MatrixForm
```

*Out[32]//MatrixForm=*

```
-7    13
-16   37
```

*In[33]:=*

```
B.A // MatrixForm
```

*Out[33]//MatrixForm=*

```
18  21  24
6   9   12
5   4   3
```

Matrix multiplication may not be commutative even when both matrices are square.

(3) Matrix multiplication is associative; this is,

$$(\mathbf{A}\mathbf{B})\mathbf{C} = \mathbf{A}(\mathbf{B}\mathbf{C})$$

(4) Matrix multiplication satisfies the following distributive properties.

$$\mathbf{A}(\mathbf{B} + \mathbf{C}) = \mathbf{A}\mathbf{B} + \mathbf{A}\mathbf{C}$$
$$(\mathbf{A} + \mathbf{B})\mathbf{C} = \mathbf{A}\mathbf{C} + \mathbf{B}\mathbf{C}.$$

(5) The transpose of the product of matrices satisfies the identities:

$$(\mathbf{A}\mathbf{B})^T = \mathbf{B}^T\mathbf{A}^T$$
$$(\mathbf{A}\mathbf{B}\mathbf{C})^T = \mathbf{C}^T\mathbf{B}^T\mathbf{A}^T.$$

For example,

*In[34]:=*

```
A = {{1,2,3},{4,5,6}}; B = {{-2,5},{2,1},{-3,2}};
Transpose[A.B] == Transpose[B].Transpose[A]
```

*Out[35]=*

```
True
```

The *scalar multiple* of a matrix **A** with a scalar k is defined to be the matrix formed by multiplying each element of **A** by k. Thus,

$$\mathrm{k}\mathbf{A} = \begin{bmatrix} \mathrm{k}a_{11} & \mathrm{k}a_{12} & \mathrm{k}a_{13} \\ \mathrm{k}a_{21} & \mathrm{k}a_{22} & \mathrm{k}a_{23} \end{bmatrix}$$

Scalar multiplication is commutative,

$$\mathrm{k}\mathbf{A} = \mathbf{A}\mathrm{k}$$

Scalar multiplication in *Mathematica* is performed with either "*" or a space in between the scalar and the matrix.

**Example 4.16** Show the scalar multiplication of 2**A** where $\mathrm{A} = \begin{bmatrix} 1 & 2 & 3 \\ 1 & -3 & 4 \end{bmatrix}$.

*In[36]:=*

```
A = {{1,2,3},{1,-3,4}};
2*A // MatrixForm
```

*Out[37]//MatrixForm=*

```
2   4   6
2  -6   8
```

Suppose

$$\mathbf{P} = \begin{bmatrix} p_{11} & p_{12} & p_{13} \\ p_{21} & p_{22} & p_{23} \end{bmatrix}; \ \mathbf{Q} = \begin{bmatrix} q_{11} & q_{12} & q_{13} \\ q_{21} & q_{22} & q_{23} \end{bmatrix}$$

are the price and quantity matrices of three commodities purchased in two weeks, respectively. Thus, $p_{ij}$ and $q_{ij}$ are, respectively, the price and quantity of the $j$-th commodity purchased in the $i$-th week. Occasionally, we might be interested in the cost of each individual commondity in each week. The matrix **C**,

$$\mathbf{C} = \begin{bmatrix} c_{11} & c_{12} & c_{13} \\ c_{21} & c_{22} & c_{23} \end{bmatrix} = \begin{bmatrix} p_{11}q_{11} & p_{12}q_{12} & p_{13}q_{13} \\ p_{21}q_{21} & p_{22}q_{22} & p_{23}q_{23} \end{bmatrix}$$

gives us this information. The element $c_{ij}$ of **C** is obtained by the multiplication of $p_{ij}$ of **P** and $q_{ij}$ of **Q**. This is an *element by element multiplication* of two matrices. When using *Mathematica*, the element by element multiplication of two matrices is denoted as **P Q**, without a dot. The product, **P*Q**, with *, is also used to represent the element by element multiplication. We adopt the notation **P*Q** for an element by element multiplication to distinguish it from matrix multiplication **P . Q**.

**Example 4.17** The following is the element by element multiplication of the matrices **P** and **Q**.

*In[38]:=*

```
Clear[p,q];
P  =  Array[p,{2,3}];  Q  =  Array[q,{2,3}];
P*Q  //  MatrixForm
```

*Out[40]//MatrixForm=*

```
p[1, 1] q[1, 1]   p[1, 2] q[1, 2]   p[1, 3] q[1, 3]
p[2, 1] q[2, 1]   p[2, 2] q[2, 2]   p[2, 3] q[2, 3]
```

In more advanced calculations, we may also encounter the *outer* or *Kronecker product* of two matrices. This product is calculated by multiplying each element of one matrix by the other matrix. For example, let **A** be an $m \times n$ matrix and **B** a $p \times q$ matrix. The outer product of **A** and **B**, denoted as **A⊗B**, is defined as

$$\mathbf{A}\otimes\mathbf{B} = \begin{bmatrix} a_{11}\mathbf{B} & a_{12}\mathbf{B} & \ldots & a_{1n}\mathbf{B} \\ a_{21}\mathbf{B} & a_{22}\mathbf{B} & \ldots & a_{2n}\mathbf{B} \\ \cdots & \cdots & \cdots & \cdots \\ a_{m1}\mathbf{B} & a_{m2}\mathbf{B} & \ldots & a_{mn}\mathbf{B} \end{bmatrix}$$

Each element of **A** multiplies the matrix **B**. The outer product is a $mp \times nq$ matrix.

**Example 4.18** Find the outer product of the matrices

$$\mathbf{A} = \begin{bmatrix} 1 & 2 \\ 3 & 0 \end{bmatrix} \quad \text{and} \quad \mathbf{B} = \begin{bmatrix} 2 & -1 \\ -2 & 3 \end{bmatrix}$$

The outer product is a $4 \times 4$ matrix.

$$\begin{bmatrix} 1 & 2 \\ 3 & 0 \end{bmatrix} \otimes \begin{bmatrix} 2 & -1 \\ -2 & 3 \end{bmatrix} = \begin{bmatrix} 1\begin{bmatrix} 2 & -1 \\ -2 & 3 \end{bmatrix} & 2\begin{bmatrix} 2 & -1 \\ -2 & 3 \end{bmatrix} \\ 3\begin{bmatrix} 2 & -1 \\ -2 & 3 \end{bmatrix} & 0\begin{bmatrix} 2 & -1 \\ -2 & 3 \end{bmatrix} \end{bmatrix} = \begin{bmatrix} 2 & -1 & 4 & -2 \\ -2 & 3 & -4 & 6 \\ 6 & -3 & 0 & 0 \\ -6 & 9 & 0 & 0 \end{bmatrix}$$

The outer product can be calculated by using the *Mathematica* function **Outer** in conjunction with the function **Times**. Here is the description of the **Outer** function.

*In[41]:=*

```
?Outer
```

**Outer[f, list1, list2, ...] gives the generalized outer product of the listi.**

To compute the outer product of two matrices we use the following format:

**Outer[Times,***matrix1*,*matrix2*]

where *matrix1* and *matrix2* are two matrices in the product. For example,

*In[42]:=*

```
A = {{1,2},{3,0}};  B = {{2,-1},{-2,3}};
Outer[Times, A, B] // MatrixForm
```

*Out[43]//MatrixForm=*

```
2    -1   4    -2
-2   3    -4   6

6    -3   0    0
-6   9    0    0
```

**Example 4.19** If **A** is a $2 \times 3$ matrix with elements $a_{ij}$, then what is the outer product of **A** and a $2 \times 2$ identity matrix, i.e., **A**⊗**I**? Will **A**⊗**I** be equal to **I**⊗**A**? The answer is no, as shown below.

*In[44]:=*

```
Clear[a,b,c,d,e,f];
A = {{a,b,c},{d,e,f}};
Outer[Times,A,IdentityMatrix[2]] // MatrixForm
```

*Out[46]//MatrixForm=*

```
a 0   b 0   c 0
0 a   0 b   0 c

d 0   e 0   f 0
0 d   0 e   0 f
```

*In[47]:=*

```
Outer[Times,IdentityMatrix[2],A] // MatrixForm
```

*Out[47]//MatrixForm=*

```
a b c   0 0 0
d e f   0 0 0
```

```
0 0 0   a b c
0 0 0   d e f
```

## EXERCISES

1. Given

$$\mathbf{A} = \begin{bmatrix} 5 & 6 & -4 \\ -1 & 1 & 2 \end{bmatrix};\ \mathbf{B} = \begin{bmatrix} 2 & 1 \\ 1 & -3 \\ 0 & 4 \end{bmatrix};\ \text{k} = 3.$$

   find **AB**, k**A**, and k**B**. Is **BA** = **AB**?

2. Show $(\mathbf{AB})^T = \mathbf{B}^T\mathbf{A}^T$.

3. If **I** is an $n \times n$ identity matrix and **A** is a $n \times n$ square matrix, what dimensions are **IA** and **AI**?

4. If **D** is an $n \times n$ diagonal matrix with $d_i$ as the $i$-th diagonal element and **A** is an $n \times n$ square matrix, find the product **DA**. Is **DA** = **AD**?

5. Suppose

$$\mathbf{A} = \begin{bmatrix} a & b \\ c & d \end{bmatrix}$$

   use *Mathematica* to construct the matrix

$$\mathbf{B} = \begin{bmatrix} a^3 & b^3 \\ c^3 & d^3 \end{bmatrix}$$

6. A skew-symmetric matrix **B** is defined as $\mathbf{B}^T = -\mathbf{B}$. Give an example of a $4 \times 4$ skew-symmetric matrix.

7. Let **A** and **B** be $n \times n$ matrices and let $k$ be any scalar. Show that
   (a) $\text{tr}(k\mathbf{A}) = k\text{tr}(\mathbf{A})$
   (b) $\text{tr}(\mathbf{AB}) = \text{tr}(\mathbf{BA})$

### 4.2.3 Matrix inversion

Consider an $n \times n$ matrix **A**. If there exists a matrix **B** such that **AB** = **BA** = **I** where **I** is an $n \times n$ identity matrix, then **B** is called the *inverse matrix* of **A**, and is denoted by $\mathbf{A}^{-1}$. For example,

$$\mathbf{A} = \begin{bmatrix} 4 & 6 \\ 1 & 2 \end{bmatrix};\ \mathbf{A}^{-1} = \begin{bmatrix} 1 & -3 \\ -1/2 & 2 \end{bmatrix}$$

since $\mathbf{A}^{-1}\mathbf{A} = \mathbf{A}\mathbf{A}^{-1} = \mathbf{I}$ as shown by the following calculation.

*In[48]:=*

```
A = {{4,6},{1,2}}; B = {{1,-3},{-1/2,2}};
A.B // MatrixForm
```

*Out[49]//MatrixForm=*

```
1  0
0  1
```

*In[50]:=*

```
B.A // MatrixForm
```

*Out[50]//MatrixForm=*

```
1  0
0  1
```

**Example 4.20** One of the most important applications of the inverse matrix is solving a system of equations such as the one in Example 4.15 in section 4.2.2.

$$\begin{bmatrix} 1 & 0 & 1 \\ 0 & 1 & -1/2 \\ 1 & -1 & 0 \end{bmatrix} \begin{bmatrix} \mathrm{D} \\ \mathrm{S} \\ \mathrm{P} \end{bmatrix} = \begin{bmatrix} 5 \\ 2 \\ 0 \end{bmatrix}; \quad \text{or} \quad \mathbf{Ax} = \mathbf{b}$$

The matrix **A** has the inverse,

$$\mathbf{A}^{-1} = \begin{bmatrix} \frac{1}{3} & \frac{2}{3} & \frac{2}{3} \\ \frac{1}{3} & \frac{2}{3} & -\frac{1}{3} \\ \frac{2}{3} & -\frac{2}{3} & -\frac{2}{3} \end{bmatrix}$$

since $\mathbf{A}^{-1}\mathbf{A} = \mathbf{A}\,\mathbf{A}^{-1} = \mathbf{I}$. If we pre-multiply the equation, $\mathbf{A}\,\mathbf{x} = \mathbf{b}$, by $\mathbf{A}^{-1}$ we obtain the solution for $D$, $S$, and $P$.

$$\mathbf{A}^{-1}\mathbf{A}\,\mathbf{x} = \mathbf{A}^{-1}\mathbf{b}, \quad \text{or} \quad \mathbf{x} = \mathbf{A}^{-1}\mathbf{b}$$

That is

$$\mathbf{x} = \begin{bmatrix} D \\ S \\ P \end{bmatrix} = \mathbf{A}^{-1}\mathbf{b} = \begin{bmatrix} \frac{1}{3} & \frac{2}{3} & \frac{2}{3} \\ \frac{1}{3} & \frac{2}{3} & -\frac{1}{3} \\ \frac{2}{3} & -\frac{2}{3} & -\frac{2}{3} \end{bmatrix} \begin{bmatrix} 5 \\ 2 \\ 0 \end{bmatrix} = \begin{bmatrix} 3 \\ 3 \\ 2 \end{bmatrix}$$

The solutions for the system indicate that equality of demand and supply occurs at $D = S = 3$ and price $\mathrm{P} = 2$.

Many techniques exist for matrix inversion. We shall discuss them later in the chapter. The *Mathematica* function for finding the inverse matrix is **Inverse**.

*In[51]:=*

```
?Inverse
```

**Inverse[m] gives the inverse of a square matrix m.**

**Example 4.21** Find the equilibrium quantity and price described in the previous example.

*In[52]:=*

```
A = {{1,0,1},{0,1,-0.5},{1,-1,0}};
b = {5,2,0};
x = Inverse[A].b
```

*Out[54]=*

```
{3., 3., 2.}
```

**Example 4.22** Consider a simple (Keynesian) national income model with two equations – an equilibrium condition for income, and a consumption function:

$$Y = C + I_0 + G_0$$
$$C = a + bY$$

where $Y$ is national income, $C$ is consumption. The symbol $a$ is a constant, and $b$ is the marginal propensity to consume. $I_0$ and $G_0$ are investment expenditure and government spending that are exogenously determined. Shifting the $Y$ and $C$ to the left sides of equations, we rewrite the system as:

$$Y - C = I_0 + G_0$$
$$-bY + C = a.$$

In matrix form the system is

$$\begin{bmatrix} 1 & -1 \\ -b & 1 \end{bmatrix} \begin{bmatrix} Y \\ C \end{bmatrix} = \begin{bmatrix} I_0 + G_0 \\ a \end{bmatrix}; \quad \text{or} \quad \mathbf{Ax} = \mathbf{k}$$

The coefficient matrix **A** has inverse $\mathbf{A}^{-1}$ if $b \neq 1$,

$$\mathbf{A}^{-1} = \begin{bmatrix} \frac{1}{1-b} & \frac{1}{1-b} \\ \frac{b}{1-b} & \frac{1}{1-b} \end{bmatrix}$$

Premultiplying the equations by $\mathbf{A}^{-1}$, we obtain the solutions for equilibrium $Y$ and $C$,

$$\begin{bmatrix} Y \\ C \end{bmatrix} = \begin{bmatrix} \frac{1}{1-b} & \frac{1}{1-b} \\ \frac{b}{1-b} & \frac{1}{1-b} \end{bmatrix} \begin{bmatrix} I_0 + G_0 \\ a \end{bmatrix} = \begin{bmatrix} \frac{a + I_0 + G_0}{1 - b} \\ \frac{a + b(I_0 + G_0)}{1 - b} \end{bmatrix}$$

The solutions are confirmed in the following *Mathematica* calculation.

*In[55]:=*

```
Clear[Io,Go,a,b];
A = {{1,-1},{-b,1}}; k = {Io + Go, a};
Inverse[A].k // Simplify
```

*Out[57]=*

$$\{\frac{\text{a + Go + Io}}{1 - \text{b}}, \frac{\text{a + bGo + bIo}}{1 - \text{b}}\}$$

As government expenditure $G_0$ increases, so does the equilibrium national income $Y$ and the consumption $C$. The partial derivatives of the equilibrium $Y$ and $C$ with respect to $G_0$ are the government-expenditure multipliers, which are positive if $0 < b < 1$,

$$\frac{\partial Y}{\partial G_0} = \frac{1}{1 - b} > 0; \quad \frac{\partial C}{\partial G_0} = \frac{b}{1 - b} > 0.$$

We now list several important properties about the inverse of a matrix:

(1) For a matrix **A** to have an inverse it must be square, i.e., it must have the same number of rows as columns. However, squareness is a necessary, but not sufficient, condition for a matrix to have an inverse. Since a matrix is an ordered collection of vectors, the conditions for the existence of the inverse depend upon the nature of the collection. More precisely, they depend upon the linear independence of the vectors. If the vectors in the collection are linearly independent, then the inverse exists. Otherwise, it does not. For example,

$$\mathbf{A} = \begin{bmatrix} 1 & 2 \\ 2 & 4 \end{bmatrix}$$

does not have an inverse since the two rows of the matrix are linearly dependent. A matrix is *singular* if it does not have an inverse. Otherwise, the matrix is said to be *nonsingular*. We shall discuss this condition in greater detail shortly. Attempting to find the inverse of a singular matrix using *Mathematica* will result in an error message.

*In[58]:=*

```
A = {{1,2},{2,4}};
Inverse[A]
```

LinearSolve : : nosol :
Linear equation encountered which has no solution.

*Out[59]=*

```
Inverse[{{1, 2}, {2, 4}}]
```

(2) If the matrix **A** has an inverse, then the inverse is unique. If **B** and **C** are both inverse matrices of **A**, so that

$$\mathbf{BA} = \mathbf{CA} = \mathbf{I}$$

then $\mathbf{B} = \mathbf{C} = \mathbf{A}^{-1}$.

(3) $(\mathbf{A}^{-1})^{-1} = \mathbf{A}$. The inverse of the inverse matrix is equal to the original matrix. For example,

*In[60]:=*

```
A = {{1,2},{-1,1}};
Inverse[Inverse[A]] == A
```

*Out[61]=*

True

(4) The inverse of the product of two nonsingular matrices is equal to the product of the inverse matrices in reverse order. In other words,

$$(\mathbf{AB})^{-1} = \mathbf{B}^{-1}\mathbf{A}^{-1}.$$

*In[62]:=*

```
A = {{1,2},{3,4}}; B = {{2,3},{1,4}};
Inverse[A.B] == Inverse[B].Inverse[A]
```

*Out[63]=*

True

(5) $(\mathbf{A}^T)^{-1} = (\mathbf{A}^{-1})^T$. The inverse of the transpose is equal to the transpose of the inverse.

*In[64]:=*

```
A={{1,2,3},{3,4,5},{5,4,1}};
Inverse[Transpose[A]] == Transpose[Inverse[A]]
```

*Out[65]=*

True

## EXERCISES

1. Use *Mathematica* to answer the following questions with respect to the matrices

$$\mathbf{A} = \begin{bmatrix} 2 & 3 & 1 \\ 4 & 1 & 2 \\ 5 & 3 & 4 \end{bmatrix}; \mathbf{B} = \begin{bmatrix} 2 & 7 & 0 \\ 5 & 8 & 1 \\ 6 & 7 & 0 \end{bmatrix}$$

   (a) Find $\mathbf{A}^{-1}$ and confirm that $\mathbf{A}^{-1}\mathbf{A} = \mathbf{I}$. Is $\mathbf{A}\,\mathbf{A}^{-1} = \mathbf{I}$?
   (b) Show $(\mathbf{A}^{-1})^{-1} = \mathbf{A}$. What is $((\mathbf{A}^{-1})^{-1})^{-1}$?
   (c) Show $(\mathbf{A}^T)^{-1} = (\mathbf{A}^{-1})^T$. What is $((\mathbf{A}^{-1})^T)^{-1}$?
   (d) Show $(\mathbf{AB})^{-1} = \mathbf{B}^{-1}\mathbf{A}^{-1}$. Compute $((\mathbf{AB})^{-1})^{-1}$.
   (e) Is $(\mathbf{A} + \mathbf{B})^{-1} = \mathbf{A}^{-1} + \mathbf{B}^{-1}$?

2. Let $\mathbf{D}$ be an $n \times n$ diagonal matrix with $d_i \neq 0$ as the $i$-th diagonal element. What is the inverse of $\mathbf{D}$?

3. A matrix $\mathbf{M}$ is called *idempotent* if $\mathbf{M} = \mathbf{MM} = \mathbf{M}^2$. If $\mathbf{X}$ is an $n \times k$ matrix, and I is the $n \times n$ identity matrix, then show that

$$\mathbf{M} = \mathbf{I} - \mathbf{X}(\mathbf{X}^T\mathbf{X})^{-1}\mathbf{X}^T$$

   is idempotent.

4. Find the inverse matrix of

$$\mathbf{A} = \begin{bmatrix} a & b \\ c & d \end{bmatrix}$$

   when it exists. When does it exist?

5. Suppose we expand the national income model in example 4.22 by treating the investment $I$ as a dependent variable to be determined within the model. The level of investment is assumed to be a function of both income $Y$ and an interest rate $R_0$ which is determined exogenously. In addition, consumption is assumed to be affected by $R_0$ also. With these modifications the system becomes:

$$Y = C + I + G_0$$
$$C = a + bY - dR_0$$
$$I = gY - hR_0.$$

Find the government-expenditure multipliers, $\partial Y/\partial G_0$, $\partial C/\partial G_0$, $\partial I/\partial G_0$.

## □ 4.3 Rank, Elementary Operations and the Inverse Matrix □

### 4.3.1 Rank of a matrix

The number of linearly independent row (column) vectors in a matrix **A** is called the *rank* of **A**, and is denoted as $\rho(\mathbf{A})$. In other words, the rank is the dimension of the vector space spanned by the row or column vectors that make up **A**. The following matrix **A** is constructed of three row vectors, $\mathbf{v}_1$, $\mathbf{v}_2$ and $\mathbf{v}_3$.

$$\mathbf{A} = \begin{bmatrix} 0 & 1 & 1 & 0 \\ 1 & -1 & 1 & 1 \\ 2 & -4 & 0 & 2 \end{bmatrix} = \begin{bmatrix} \mathbf{v}_1 \\ \mathbf{v}_2 \\ \mathbf{v}_3 \end{bmatrix}$$

Since

$$-2\mathbf{v}_1 + 2\mathbf{v}_2 - \mathbf{v}_3 = 0$$

the three vectors are linearly dependent. However,

$$k_1\mathbf{v}_1 + k_2\mathbf{v}_2 = 0$$

if and only if $k_1 = k_2 = 0$. Thus $\mathbf{v}_1$ and $\mathbf{v}_2$ are linearly independent, and they form a basis of a two-dimensional vector space. The rank of **A** is therefore 2, i.e., $\rho(\mathbf{A}) = 2$. One method of finding the rank of an $n \times m$ matrix **A** is to find the maximum number of linearly independent vectors that can be found among the $n$ row vectors that make up the matrix, $\mathbf{v}_1, \mathbf{v}_2, \ldots,$ and $\mathbf{v}_n$ as shown in Chapter 3. Alternatively, the **MathEcon** function **rank** can be used to find the rank of a matrix.

*In[66]:=*
```
?rank
```

**rank[lst] calculates the dimension of the space spanned by the vectors contained in its argument (list). For example,**

**rank[{{1,-1,9},{1,-2,-3}}].**

**Example 4.23** Find the rank of the following matrix,

$$\mathbf{A} = \begin{bmatrix} 1 & 2 & 3 \\ 2 & 1 & 4 \\ 1 & -1 & 1 \\ 4 & 2 & 8 \end{bmatrix} = \begin{bmatrix} v_1 \\ v_2 \\ v_3 \\ v_4 \end{bmatrix}$$

*In[67]:=*

```
A = {{1,2,3},{2,1,4},{1,-1,1},{4,2,8}};
rank[A]
```

*Out[68]=*

```
2
```

The rank of a matrix can also be determined using elementary operations which will be discussed in the next section.

## EXERCISES

1. Use *Mathematica* to determine the rank of the matrix

$$\mathbf{A} = \begin{bmatrix} 2 & 1 & -3 \\ -4 & -2 & 6 \\ -16 & -8 & 24 \end{bmatrix}$$

2. Determine the rank of the matrix

$$\mathbf{A} = \begin{bmatrix} 1 & 1 & 1 \\ y+z & z+x & x+y \\ x & y & z \end{bmatrix}$$

### 4.3.2 Elementary operations

The number of linearly independent vectors and hence the rank of a matrix are invariant with respect to certain operations, called *elementary operations*. An elementary row operation on a matrix is one of the the following operations:

(1) interchanging two rows;

(2) multiplying a row by a nonzero scalar;

(3) adding a scalar multiplication of one row to another.

Consider the following matrices:

$$\mathbf{A} = \begin{bmatrix} \mathbf{v}_1 \\ \mathbf{v}_2 \\ \mathbf{v}_3 \end{bmatrix}; \ \mathbf{B} = \begin{bmatrix} \mathbf{v}_2 \\ \mathbf{v}_1 \\ \mathbf{v}_3 \end{bmatrix}$$

Since **A** and **B** are comprised of the same collection of vectors, $\rho(\mathbf{A}) = \rho(\mathbf{B})$. If **u** is a vector in the vector space spanned by the vectors in **A**, i.e.,

$$\mathbf{u} = k_1\mathbf{v}_1 + k_2\mathbf{v}_2 + k_3\mathbf{v}_3$$

then **u** must also be generated by the vectors that make up **B**. That is,

$$\mathbf{u} = k_2\mathbf{v}_2 + k_1\mathbf{v}_1 + k_3\mathbf{v}_3.$$

This illustrates that the rank is unaltered by interchanging row vectors of a matrix.

Consider another matrix

$$\mathbf{C} = \begin{bmatrix} \mathbf{v}_1 \\ \mathbf{v}_2 \\ \mathbf{v}_3^* \end{bmatrix} = \begin{bmatrix} \mathbf{v}_2 \\ \mathbf{v}_1 \\ h\mathbf{v}_3 \end{bmatrix}$$

where $h$ is a nonzero scalar. The matrix **C** is obtained by a scalar multiple of the third row vector of **A**. The vectors in **C** span the same set of vectors as the vectors in **A** since

$$\mathbf{u} = k_1\mathbf{v}_1 + k_2\mathbf{v}_2 + \frac{k_3}{h}(h\mathbf{v}_3) = k_1\mathbf{v}_1 + k_2\mathbf{v}_2 + k_3^*\mathrm{v}_3^*.$$

Again, this illustrates that the elementary operation of multiplying a row by a nonzero scalar does not change the rank of the matrix.

Lastly, consider the matrix

$$\mathbf{D} = \begin{bmatrix} \mathbf{v}_1 \\ \mathbf{v}_2 \\ \mathbf{v}_3^{**} \end{bmatrix} = \begin{bmatrix} \mathbf{v}_1 \\ \mathbf{v}_2 \\ \mathbf{v}_3 + h\mathbf{v}_2 \end{bmatrix}$$

The vectors of **D** span the same vector space as the vector of **A** since

$$\begin{aligned} \mathbf{u} &= k_1\mathbf{v}_1 + (k_2 - k_3h)\mathbf{v}_2 + k_3(\mathbf{v}_3 + h\mathbf{v}_2) \\ &= k_1\mathbf{v}_1 + k_2^*\mathbf{v}_2 + k_3\mathbf{v}_3^{**}. \end{aligned}$$

Hence, the rank of **A** is invariant with respect to the elementary operation of adding a scalar multiplication of one row to another.

We shall give an example of the three elementary row operations. Consider a matrix

$$\mathbf{A} = \begin{bmatrix} 0 & 1 & 1 & 0 \\ 1 & -1 & 1 & 1 \\ 2 & -4 & 0 & 2 \end{bmatrix}$$

By interchanging the first and the third rows of **A**, we have a new matrix

$$\mathbf{A}_1 = \begin{bmatrix} 2 & -4 & 0 & 2 \\ 1 & -1 & 1 & 1 \\ 0 & 1 & 1 & 0 \end{bmatrix}$$

Multiplying the first row of $\mathrm{A}_1$ by (1/2) results in the new matrix

$$\mathbf{A}_2 = \begin{bmatrix} 1 & -2 & 0 & 1 \\ 1 & -1 & 1 & 1 \\ 0 & 1 & 1 & 0 \end{bmatrix}$$

Subtracting the first row from the second row, gives us a new matrix

$$\mathbf{A}_3 = \begin{bmatrix} 1 & -2 & 0 & 1 \\ 0 & 1 & 1 & 0 \\ 0 & 1 & 1 & 0 \end{bmatrix}$$

Subtracting the second row from the third row results in the matrix

$$\mathbf{A}_4 = \begin{bmatrix} 1 & -2 & 0 & 1 \\ 0 & 1 & 1 & 0 \\ 0 & 0 & 0 & 0 \end{bmatrix}$$

Lastly, adding two times the second row to the first produces the matrix

$$\mathbf{A}_5 = \begin{bmatrix} 1 & 0 & 2 & 1 \\ 0 & 1 & 1 & 0 \\ 0 & 0 & 0 & 0 \end{bmatrix}$$

It is obvious that the rank of $\mathbf{A}_5$ is 2, since the third row is a zero vector. Clearly, the rank of a matrix is unaltered by a succession of elementary row operations. The rank of the original matrix $\mathbf{A}$ is also 2. Thus, $\rho(\mathbf{A}) = \rho(\mathbf{A}_5) = 2$.

Matrices obtained by these elementary operations can also be constructed through matrix multiplication. An *elementary matrix* is a matrix that is obtained from an identity matrix by exactly one elementary row operation. Let $\mathbf{I}$ be the $3 \times 3$ identity matrix

$$\mathbf{I} = \begin{bmatrix} 1 & 0 & 0 \\ 0 & 1 & 0 \\ 0 & 0 & 1 \end{bmatrix}$$

Interchanging the first and the third rows of $\mathbf{I}$ results in an elementary matrix,

$$\mathbf{E}_1 = \begin{bmatrix} 0 & 0 & 1 \\ 0 & 1 & 0 \\ 1 & 0 & 0 \end{bmatrix}$$

Since $\mathbf{A}_1$ is obtained from the same elementary operation as in $\mathbf{E}_1$, $\mathbf{A}_1$ is in fact the result of the *pre-multiplication* of $\mathbf{A}$ by $\mathbf{E}_1$,

$$\mathbf{A}_1 = \mathbf{E}_1\mathbf{A}.$$

Similarly, $A_2$ is obtained by multiplying 1/2 to the first row of $\mathbf{A}_1$. The elementary matrix $\mathbf{E}_2$ is then obtained by the same operations applied to the identity matrix,

$$\mathbf{E}_2 = \begin{bmatrix} 1/2 & 0 & 0 \\ 0 & 1 & 0 \\ 0 & 0 & 1 \end{bmatrix}$$

Thus, the pre-multiplication of $\mathbf{E}_2$ to $\mathbf{A}_1$ results in

$$\mathbf{A}_2 = \mathbf{E}_2\mathbf{A}_1.$$

The elementary matrix for the third operation applied to $\mathbf{A}_2$ is

$$\mathbf{E}_3 = \begin{bmatrix} 0 & 0 & 0 \\ -1 & 1 & 0 \\ 0 & 0 & 1 \end{bmatrix}$$

and

$$\mathbf{A}_3 = \mathbf{E}_3\mathbf{A}_2.$$

In general, a sequence of $t$ elementary row operations can be performed upon an $m \times n$ matrix $\mathbf{A}$,

$$\mathbf{E}_t\mathbf{E}_{t-1} \ldots \mathbf{E}_2\mathbf{E}_1\mathbf{A} = \mathbf{PA} = \mathbf{B}$$

where $\mathbf{P}$ is the product of the elementary matrices and $\mathbf{E}_i$ is an elementary matrix.

Two matrices $\mathbf{A}$ and $\mathbf{B}$ are said to be *row equivalent* if $\mathbf{B}$ can be obtained by performing a finite number of elementary row operations on $\mathbf{A}$. Since the rank of $\mathbf{A}$ is unaltered by the succession of elementary operations, the rank of $\mathbf{A}$ is equal to the rank of $\mathbf{B}$, $\rho(\mathbf{A}) = \rho(\mathbf{B})$. The matrix $\mathbf{B}$ obtained in this manner has a special form. A matrix $\mathbf{B}$ is called an *echelon matrix* if

(1) $\rho(\mathbf{B}) = \mathrm{k}$, then only the first k rows of $\mathbf{B}$ are nonzero vectors;

(2) the first nonzero element of each nonzero row vector is 1 and its position is always to the right of the first nonzero element of the preceding row.

**Example 4.24** The following matrices **A** and **B** are echelon matrices, but **C**, **D**, and **E** are not.

$$\mathbf{A} = \begin{bmatrix} 0 & 1 & 2 & 3 & 4 \\ 0 & 0 & 1 & -1 & 0 \\ 0 & 0 & 0 & 1 & 3 \\ 0 & 0 & 0 & 0 & 0 \\ 0 & 0 & 0 & 0 & 0 \end{bmatrix}; \mathbf{B} = \begin{bmatrix} 1 & 2 & -1 & -4 \\ 0 & 1 & 2 & 3 \\ 0 & 0 & 0 & 1 \\ 0 & 0 & 0 & 0 \end{bmatrix}$$

$$\mathbf{C} = \begin{bmatrix} 1 & 2 & 1 & 4 \\ 0 & 0 & 1 & 2 \\ 0 & 0 & 1 & -1 \\ 0 & 0 & 0 & 1 \end{bmatrix}; \mathbf{D} = \begin{bmatrix} 0 & 1 & 2 & 3 \\ 0 & 0 & 2 & 1 \\ 0 & 0 & 0 & 0 \end{bmatrix}; \mathbf{E} = \begin{bmatrix} 0 & 1 & 2 & 3 \\ 0 & 0 & 0 & 0 \\ 0 & 0 & 2 & 1 \end{bmatrix}$$

The first nonzero element on the third row of **C** is not to the right of the first nonzero element of the second row. Moreover, the first nonzero element on the second row of **D** is not 1. The nonzero rows of the **E** matrix is not in the first two rows of **E**.

Elementary row operations can be performed by using the **MathEcon** function **rowop**.

*In[69]:=*
```
?rowop
```

**rowop[rowlist] generates the elementary row operation matrix that are dictated by its argument which is a list of elementary row operations that are to be performed. For example,**

**rowop[{row[3],row[2],row[1]}].**

Note that the argument of **rowop** is a list of elementary row operations using the function **row[i]** that denotes the *i*th row. In using the function **rowop** to construct a sequence of elementary row matrices, one must clear the definition of the function **row**.

**Example 4.25** Consider the 3 × 3 identity matrix **I**. Interchanging the first and the third rows of **I** yields the elementary matrix $\mathbf{E}_1$.

$$\mathbf{I} = \begin{bmatrix} 1 & 0 & 0 \\ 0 & 1 & 0 \\ 0 & 0 & 1 \end{bmatrix}; \ \mathbf{E}_1 = \begin{bmatrix} 0 & 0 & 1 \\ 0 & 1 & 0 \\ 1 & 0 & 0 \end{bmatrix}$$

We use the function **rowop** to create $\mathbf{E}_1$.

*In[70]:=*
```
Clear[row];
E1  =  rowop[{row[3],row[2],row[1]}];
E1  //  MatrixForm
```

*Out[72]//MatrixForm=*
```
0  0  1
0  1  0
1  0  0
```

The elementary matrix $\mathbf{E}_2$ is created by multiplying 1/2 to the first row of **I**. The elementary matrix $\mathbf{E}_3$ is created by adding the negative of the first row to the second row of **I**.

*In[73]:=*
```
E2  =  rowop[{row[1]/2,row[2],row[3]}];
E2  //  MatrixForm
```

*Out[74]//MatrixForm=*

$$\begin{matrix} \frac{1}{2} & 0 & 0 \\ 0 & 1 & 0 \\ 0 & 0 & 1 \end{matrix}$$

*In[75]:=*
```
E3  =  rowop[{row[1],-row[1]+row[2],row[3]}];
E3  //  MatrixForm
```

*Out[76]//MatrixForm=*

```
1   0  0
-1  1  0
0   0  1
```

**Example 4.26** Consider the $3 \times 4$ matrix.

$$\mathbf{A} = \begin{bmatrix} 0 & 1 & 1 & 0 \\ 1 & -1 & 1 & 1 \\ 2 & -4 & 0 & 2 \end{bmatrix}$$

In the following sequence of elementary operations, we obtain an echelon matrix $\mathbf{B} = \mathbf{E}_5\mathbf{E}_4\mathbf{E}_3\mathbf{E}_2\mathbf{E}_1\mathbf{A}$. Interpret each of the elementary matrices $\mathbf{E}_i$.

*In[77]:=*

```
Clear[row];
A  =  {{0,1,1,0},{1,-1,1,1},{2,-4,0,2}};
E1  =  rowop[{row[3],row[2],row[1]}];
A1  =  E1.A;  A1  //  MatrixForm
```

*Out[80]//MatrixForm=*

```
2  -4  0  2
1  -1  1  1
0   1  1  0
```

*In[81]:=*

```
E2  =  rowop[{row[1]/2,row[2],row[3]}];
A2  =  E2.A1;  A2  //  MatrixForm
```

*Out[82]//MatrixForm=*

```
1  -2  0  1
1  -1  1  1
0   1  1  0
```

*In[83]:=*

```
E3  =  rowop[{row[1],row[2]-row[1],row[3]}];
A3  =  E3.A2;  A3  //  MatrixForm
```

*Out[84]//MatrixForm=*

```
1  -2  0  1
0   1  1  0
0   1  1  0
```

*In[85]:=*

```
E4  =  rowop[{row[1],row[2],row[3]-row[2]}];
A4  =  E4.A3;  A4  //  MatrixForm
```

*Out[86]//MatrixForm=*

```
1  -2  0  1
0   1  1  0
0   0  0  0
```

*In[87]:=*

```
E5  =  rowop[{row[1]+2*row[2],row[2],row[3]}];
B  =  E5.A4;  B  //  MatrixForm
```

*Out[88]//MatrixForm=*

```
1  0  2  1
0  1  1  0
0  0  0  0
```

Since there are two nonzero rows in **B**, $\rho(\mathbf{B}) = \rho(\mathbf{A}) = 2$. The product of the elementary matrices in the above operations is equal to the matrix **P**,

$$\mathbf{P} = \mathbf{E}_5\mathbf{E}_4\mathbf{E}_3\mathbf{E}_2\mathbf{E}_1 = \begin{bmatrix} 0 & 2 & -1/2 \\ 0 & 1 & -1/2 \\ 1 & -1 & 1/2 \end{bmatrix}$$

*In[89]:=*

```
P = E5.E4.E3.E2.E1
```

*Out[89]=*

$$\{\{0, 2, -(\frac{1}{2})\}, \{0, 1, -(\frac{1}{2})\}, \{1, -1, -(\frac{1}{2})\}$$

We check the result that **PA** equals the echelon matrix **B**.

*In[90]:=*

```
P.A // MatrixForm
```

*Out[90]//MatrixForm=*

```
1  0  2  1
0  1  1  0
0  0  0  0
```

If you are not interested in the intermediate steps of the elementary operations and are only concerned with obtaining an echelon matrix **B**, the function **RowReduce** produces the echelon matrix directly.

*In[91]:=*

```
?RowReduce
```

**RowReduce[m] gives the row-reduced form of the matrix m.**

**Example 4.27** Find an echelon matrix of the following $3 \times 4$ matrix

$$\mathbf{A} = \begin{bmatrix} 0 & 1 & 1 & 0 \\ 1 & -1 & 1 & 1 \\ 2 & -4 & 0 & 2 \end{bmatrix}$$

*In[92]:=*

```
A = {{0,1,1,0},{1,-1,1,1},{2,-4,0,2}};
RowReduce[A] // MatrixForm
```

*Out[93]//MatrixForm=*

```
1  0  2  1
0  1  1  0
0  0  0  0
```

Analogously, an *elementary column operation* on an $m \times n$ matrix **A** refers to either interchanging two columns, multiplying a column by a nonzero scalar, or adding a multiple of one column to another column. An *$n \times n$ elementary column matrix* is obtained from the $n \times n$ identity matrix by applying an elementary column operation. For example, to replace the fourth column of **A** in example 4.27 by subtracting the first column from the fourth column will require the $4 \times 4$ elementary matrix

$$\mathbf{H}_1 = \begin{bmatrix} 1 & 0 & 0 & -1 \\ 0 & 1 & 0 & 0 \\ 0 & 0 & 1 & 0 \\ 0 & 0 & 0 & 1 \end{bmatrix}$$

and the *post-multiplication* of $\mathbf{H}_1$ to **A** results in

$$\mathbf{A}\mathbf{H}_1 = \begin{bmatrix} 0 & 1 & 1 & 0 \\ 1 & -1 & 1 & 0 \\ 2 & -4 & 0 & 0 \end{bmatrix}$$

A series of elementary column operations upon a $m \times n$ matrix **A** is represented by a series of post-multiplications by the $n \times n$ elementary matrices, $\mathbf{H}_1, \mathbf{H}_2, \ldots, \mathbf{H}_s$,

$$\mathbf{A}\mathbf{H}_1\mathbf{H}_2 \ldots \mathbf{H}_s = \mathbf{A}\mathbf{Q} = \mathbf{R}$$

where **Q** is the product of the elementary column matrices. The matrices **A** and **R** have the same rank. A matrix **R** is called a *column echelon matrix* if

(1) only the first $k$ columns of **R** are nonzero vectors; and

(2) the first nonzero element in each nonzero column vector is 1 and its position is always below the first nonzero element of the preceding column.

The elementary column operations can be performed by using the **MathEcon** function **colop**. It has the same format as **rowop** except that it uses a function **col**[i] to denote the *i*th column.

*In[94]:=*

```
?colop
```

**colop[collist] generates the elementary column operation matrix that are dictated by its argument which is a list of elementary column operations that are to be performed. For example,**

**colop[{col[2],col[3],col[1]}].**

As in the case of **rowop**, one must clear the definition of the function **col** the first time you use it to construct a sequence of the elementary column matrices.

**Example 4.28** Find an elementary column matrix that replaces the third column by subtracting 2 times the first column from the third.

*In[95]:=*

```
Clear[col];
H1 = colop[{col[1],col[2],col[3]-2*col[1]}];
H1 // MatrixForm
```

*Out[97]//MatrixForm=*

```
1  0  -2
0  1  0
0  0  1
```

**Example 4.29** The following operations find a column echelon matrix for the matrix,

$$\mathbf{A} = \begin{bmatrix} 0 & 1 & 1 & 0 \\ 1 & -1 & 1 & 1 \\ 2 & -4 & 0 & 2 \end{bmatrix}$$

*In[98]:=*

```
Clear[col];
A  =  {{0,1,1,0},{1,-1,1,1},{2,-4,0,2}};
H1  =  colop[{col[3],col[1],col[2],col[4]-col[1]}];
F1  =  A.H1;  F1  //  MatrixForm
```

*Out[101]//MatrixForm=*

```
1  0  1   0
1  1  -1  0
0  2  -4  0
```

*In[102]:=*

```
H2  =  colop[{col[1],col[2],col[3]-col[1],col[4]}];
F2  =  F1.H2;  F2  //  MatrixForm
```

*Out[103]//MatrixForm=*

```
1  0  0   0
1  1  -2  0
0  2  -4  0
```

*In[104]:=*

```
H3  =  colop[{col[1],col[2],col[3]+2*col[2],col[4]}];
F3  =  F2.H3;  F3  //  MatrixForm
```

*Out[105]//MatrixForm=*

```
1  0  0  0
1  1  0  0
0  2  0  0
```

*In[106]:=*

```
H4  =  colop[{col[1]-col[2],col[2],col[3],col[4]}];
R  =  F3.H4;  R  //  MatrixForm
```

*Out[107]//MatrixForm=*

```
1   0  0  0
0   1  0  0
-2  2  0  0
```

By taking the transpose of

$$\mathbf{A}\,\mathbf{H}_1\mathbf{H}_2 \ldots \mathbf{H}_s = \mathbf{A}\,\mathbf{Q} = \mathbf{R},$$

we obtain

$$\mathbf{H}_s^T \ldots \mathbf{H}_2^T \mathbf{H}_1^T \mathbf{A}^T = \mathbf{Q}^T\mathbf{A}^T = \mathbf{R}^T$$

Hence, the elementary column operations on **A** are equivalent to row operations on $\mathbf{A}^T$. Furthermore, since $\mathbf{R}^T = \mathbf{Q}^T\mathbf{A}^T$, $\mathbf{R}^T$ and hence the column echelon matrix **R** can be obtained by the same *Mathematica* **RowReduce** function applied to $\mathbf{A}^T$.

**Example 4.30** Find a column echelon matrix **R** for the matrix **A** given in Example 4.29. We calculate $\mathbf{R}^T$ first by applying **RowReduce** to $\mathbf{A}^T$. The transpose of $\mathbf{R}^T$ is the same column echelon matrix **R**.

*In[108]:=*

```
A  =  {{0,1,1,0},{1,-1,1,1},{2,-4,0,2}};
RT  =  RowReduce[Transpose[A]];
R  =  Transpose[RT]  //  MatrixForm
```

*Out[110]//MatrixForm=*

```
1    0   0   0
0    1   0   0
-2   2   0   0
```

This shows that $\rho(\mathbf{A}) = \rho(\mathbf{R}) = 2$.

A sequence of both row and column operations can be applied to a matrix A at the same time. Thus,

$$\mathbf{E}_t\mathbf{E}_{t-1} \ldots \mathbf{E}_2\mathbf{E}_1\mathbf{A}\mathbf{H}_1\mathbf{H}_2 \ldots \mathbf{H}_s = \mathbf{PAQ} = \mathbf{T}.$$

The matrices **A** and **T** are still equivalent in some senses, and $\rho(\mathbf{A}) = \rho(\mathbf{T})$. We now have shown the following important theorem.

**THEOREM 4.1** *An $m \times n$ matrix* **A** *of rank* k *can be reduced by a sequence of elementary row and column operations to a matrix* **T** *where the first* k *diagonal elements of* **T** *are* 1 *and every other element in* **T** *is zero. The matrix* **T** *is called the **canonical form** of* **A**. *Furthermore, the number of nonzero rows in* **T** *is the rank of* **A**.

**Example 4.31** Given the matrix **A**, the following elementary row operations reduce **A** to a row echelon matrix **B**

$$\mathbf{A} = \begin{bmatrix} 1 & 0 & 1 \\ 3 & 1 & 2 \\ 6 & 2 & 4 \\ 3 & 0 & 3 \end{bmatrix} \rightarrow \mathbf{A}_1 = \begin{bmatrix} 1 & 0 & 1 \\ 3 & 1 & 2 \\ 0 & 0 & 0 \\ 3 & 0 & 3 \end{bmatrix} \rightarrow \mathbf{A}_2 = \begin{bmatrix} 1 & 0 & 1 \\ 3 & 1 & 2 \\ 0 & 0 & 0 \\ 0 & 0 & 0 \end{bmatrix} \rightarrow \mathbf{B} = \begin{bmatrix} 1 & 0 & 1 \\ 0 & 1 & -1 \\ 0 & 0 & 0 \\ 0 & 0 & 0 \end{bmatrix}$$

The following elementary column operations further reduce **B** to the canonical matrix **T**.

$$\mathbf{B} = \begin{bmatrix} 1 & 0 & 1 \\ 0 & 1 & -1 \\ 0 & 0 & 0 \\ 0 & 0 & 0 \end{bmatrix} \rightarrow \mathbf{B}_1 = \begin{bmatrix} 1 & 0 & 0 \\ 0 & 1 & -1 \\ 0 & 0 & 0 \\ 0 & 0 & 0 \end{bmatrix} \rightarrow \mathbf{T} = \begin{bmatrix} 1 & 0 & 0 \\ 0 & 1 & 0 \\ 0 & 0 & 0 \\ 0 & 0 & 0 \end{bmatrix}$$

The following elementary matrices correspond to the above operations

*In[111]:=*
```
Clear[row,col];
E1=rowop[{row[1],row[2],row[3]-2*row[2],row[4]}];
E2=rowop[{row[1],row[2],row[3],row[4]-3*row[1]}];
E3=rowop[{row[1],row[2]-3*row[1],row[3],row[4]}];
H1=colop[{col[1],col[2],col[3]-col[1]}];
H2=colop[{col[1],col[2],col[3]+col[2]}];
```

We check the calculation by showing $\mathbf{E}_3\mathbf{E}_2\mathbf{E}_1\mathbf{A}\,\mathbf{H}_1\mathbf{H}_2 = \mathbf{T}$.

*In[117]:=*
```
A  =  {{1,0,1},{3,1,2},{6,2,4},{3,0,3}};
T  =  E3.E2.E1.A.H1.H2  //  MatrixForm
```

*Out[118]//MatrixForm=*
```
1  0  0
0  1  0
0  0  0
0  0  0
```

Notice that this indicates that the rank of **A** is 2.

## EXERCISES

1. Let $\mathbf{A} = [a_1\ a_2\ a_3\ a_4]$ be a $3 \times 4$ matrix with column vectors $a_i$. Let $\mathbf{B} = [a_1{-}a_2\ a_2{-}a_3\ a_3{-}a_4\ a_4{-}a_1]$. Find the elementary matrix **E** that should be applied to **A** to obtain **B**.
2. Let

$$\mathbf{A} = \begin{bmatrix} 4 & 6 & -2 \\ 2 & 3 & -4 \end{bmatrix}$$

Find the elementary matrices that reduce **A** to the canonical matrix **T**. What is the rank of the matrix?

3. Derive the echelon matrix of

$$\mathbf{A} = \begin{bmatrix} 1 & 1 & 1 \\ y+z & z+x & x+y \\ x & y & z \end{bmatrix}$$

and determine its rank.

### 4.3.3 Gauss elimination method and inverse matrix

Suppose an $n \times n$ matrix **A** is nonsingular, i.e., $\rho(\mathbf{A}) = n$. The canonical matrix of **A**, which we denote as **T**, then has rank $n$. Hence, **T** must be an identity matrix. This leads us to a method for constructing the inverse of a nonsingular matrix.

**THEOREM 4.2** *Every nonsingular $n \times n$ matrix* **A** *has as its canonical form, the $n \times n$ identity matrix. Furthermore, this canonical form is achieved through multiplication by elementary row or column matrices:*

$$\mathbf{E}_t\mathbf{E}_{t-1} \ldots \mathbf{E}_2\mathbf{E}_1 = \mathbf{PA} = \mathbf{I} \quad \text{or} \quad \mathbf{AH}_1\mathbf{H}_2 \ldots \mathbf{H}_s = \mathbf{AQ} = \mathbf{I}.$$

The above theorem implies **P** and **Q** are the inverses of **A**. Since we have shown that an inverse is unique, we have that $\mathbf{P} = \mathbf{Q} = \mathbf{A}^{-1}$. To find the inverse matrix of **A**, we then apply a sequence of elementary operations. Each step of the operation attempts to reduce the diagonal elements of **A** to 1 and all others elements to 0. This is called the *Gauss Elimination Method* of finding the inverse.

**Example 4.32** Use the Gauss Elimination Method to find the inverse of the matrix

$$\mathbf{A} = \begin{bmatrix} 4 & 2 \\ 1 & 1 \end{bmatrix}$$

We shall use row operations only.

$$\mathbf{A} = \begin{bmatrix} 4 & 2 \\ 1 & 1 \end{bmatrix} \to \mathbf{A}_1 = \begin{bmatrix} 1 & 1/2 \\ 1 & 1 \end{bmatrix} \to \mathbf{A}_2 = \begin{bmatrix} 1 & 1/2 \\ 0 & 1/2 \end{bmatrix} \to \mathbf{A}_3 = \begin{bmatrix} 1 & 0 \\ 0 & 1/2 \end{bmatrix} \to \mathbf{T} = \begin{bmatrix} 1 & 0 \\ 0 & 1 \end{bmatrix}$$

The first operation involves the division of the first row of **A** by 4.

*In[119]:=*

```
Clear[row]; A = {{4,2},{1,1}};
E1 = rowop[{row[1]/4,row[2]}];
A1 = E1.A; A1 // MatrixForm
```

*Out[121]//MatrixForm=*

$$\begin{matrix} 1 & \frac{1}{2} \\ 1 & 1 \end{matrix}$$

In the second operation, we subtract the first row of $\mathbf{A}_1$ from the second row.

*In[122]:=*

```
E2 = rowop[{row[1],row[2]-row[1]}];
A2 = E2.A1; A2 // MatrixForm
```

*Out[123]//MatrixForm=*

$$\begin{matrix} 1 & \frac{1}{2} \\ 0 & \frac{1}{2} \end{matrix}$$

Subtract the second row from the first row of $\mathbf{A}_2$ to obtain $\mathbf{A}_3$ in the third step of the operation.

*In[124]:=*

```
E3 = rowop[{row[1]-row[2],row[2]}];
A3 = E3.A2; A3 // MatrixForm
```

*Out[125]//MatrixForm=*

$$\begin{matrix} 1 & 0 \\ 0 & \frac{1}{2} \end{matrix}$$

Lastly, multiply the second row of $\mathbf{A}_3$ by 2. This results in an identity matrix **T**.

*In[126]:=*

```
E4 = rowop[{row[1],2*row[2]}];
T = E4.A3; T //MatrixForm
```

*Out[127]//MatrixForm=*

$$\begin{matrix} 1 & 0 \\ 0 & 1 \end{matrix}$$

Since **T** is an identity matrix, the product of the elementary matrices, $\mathbf{P} = \mathbf{E}_3\mathbf{E}_2\mathbf{E}_1$, must be the inverse matrix of **A**.

*In[128]:=*

```
P = E4.E3.E2.E1; P // MatrixForm
```

*Out[128]//MatrixForm=*

$$\begin{matrix} \frac{1}{2} & -1 \\ -(\frac{1}{2}) & 2 \end{matrix}$$

We confirm the result by using the *Mathematica* function **Inverse**.

*In[129]:=*

```
Inverse[A] // MatrixForm
```

*Out[129]//MatrixForm=*

$$\begin{matrix} \frac{1}{2} & -1 \\ -(\frac{1}{2}) & 2 \end{matrix}$$

The above inverse is obtained through elementary row operations. As an exercise, try to obtain the same inverse through column operations.

## EXERCISES

1. Use the Gauss elimination method to find the inverse of **A** and **B**. Use the *Mathematica* function **Inverse** to check your results.

$$\mathbf{A} = \begin{bmatrix} 1 & x & 0 \\ x & 1 & x \\ 0 & x & 1 \end{bmatrix}; \ \mathbf{B} = \begin{bmatrix} 1 & x & 0 & 0 \\ x & 1 & x & 0 \\ 0 & x & 1 & x \\ 0 & 0 & x & 1 \end{bmatrix}$$

2. Express the following system of equations in matrix form, $\mathbf{Ax} = \mathbf{b}$, and solve for $\mathbf{x}$ by using the inverse, $\mathbf{x} = \mathbf{A}^{-1}\mathbf{b}$.

$$\begin{aligned} 4x_1 + 3x_2 + 5x_3 &= 27 \\ x_1 + 6x_2 + 2x_3 &= 19 \\ 3x_1 + x_2 + 3x_3 &= 15 \end{aligned}$$

## □ 4.4 Determinants □

### 4.4.1 The determinant

In this section, we introduce the *determinant* of a square matrix. If $\mathbf{A}$ is an $n \times n$ matrix, then the determinant of $\mathbf{A}$ is denoted by $|\mathbf{A}|$. The determinant of a general $2 \times 2$ matrix

$$\mathbf{A} = \begin{bmatrix} a_{11} & a_{12} \\ a_{21} & a_{22} \end{bmatrix}$$

is defined as

$$\begin{aligned} |\mathbf{A}| &= a_{11}a_{22} - a_{12}a_{21} \\ &= \Sigma(-1)^t a_{1i}a_{2j} \end{aligned}$$

where the sum is taken over the two possible permutations of the set (1,2). These permutations are ($i$=1,$j$=2) and ($i$=2,$j$=1). The sign of each product of elements is determined by the number of inversions in the permutation, which we denote by $t$. For example if

$$\mathbf{A} = \begin{bmatrix} 1 & 2 \\ 3 & 4 \end{bmatrix}$$

then the determinant of $\mathbf{A}$ is

$$|\mathbf{A}| = \begin{vmatrix} 1 & 2 \\ 3 & 4 \end{vmatrix} = 1(4) - 2(3) = -2$$

If $i$=2 and $j$=1, the permutation (2,1) is said to have an inversion of the natural order and $t$=1. The product term, $a_{12}a_{21}$, in the determinant $|\mathbf{A}|$ is then attached a negative sign in the definition. If $i$=1 and $j$=2, then the permutation (1,2) has zero inversion and $t$=0, and the product term $a_{11}a_{22}$ has a positive sign attached.

Consider a permutation of (3,1,4,2) taken from the set (1,2,3,4). The permutation is not in the natural order since (3,1), (3,2), and (4,2) are all in reverse order. The total number of inversions in this permutation is 3. However, for the permutation (3,4,1,2), there are 4 inversions. These are (3,1), (3,2), (4,1), and (4,2). A permutation is an *even permutation* if it has an even number of inversions, and an *odd permutation* if it has an odd number of inversions.

**DEFINITION 4.1** *The determinant of an $n \times n$ square matrix* **A** *is*

$$|\mathbf{A}| = \begin{vmatrix} a_{11} & a_{12} & \dots & a_{1n} \\ a_{21} & a_{22} & \dots & a_{2n} \\ \dots & \dots & \dots & \dots \\ a_{n1} & a_{n2} & \dots & a_{nn} \end{vmatrix} = \sum^{n!} (-1)^t a_{1i}\, a_{2j} \dots a_{nk}$$

*where the sum is extended over the $n!$ possible permutations of the column indices $(i,j, \dots ,k)$, and where $t$ is the number of inversions of the column indices from the natural order $(1,2, \dots ,n)$.*

The determinant of the $3 \times 3$ matrix **A** is

$$|\mathbf{A}| = \begin{vmatrix} a_{11} & a_{12} & a_{13} \\ a_{21} & a_{22} & a_{23} \\ a_{31} & a_{32} & a_{33} \end{vmatrix}$$
$$= + a_{11}a_{22}a_{33} + a_{12}a_{23}a_{31} + a_{13}a_{21}a_{32} - a_{11}a_{23}a_{32} - a_{12}a_{21}a_{33} - a_{13}a_{22}a_{31}$$

Obviously, it is not an easy task to find the determinant of a large matrix. However, the *Mathematica* function **Det** calculates the determinant for us.

*In[130]:=*
```
?Det
```

**Det[m] gives the determinant of the square matrix m.**

**Example 4.33** Build a $3 \times 3$ matrix **A** with the *Mathematica* function **Array** and then find its determinant. Compare and check the solution with the definition given above for its consistency in sign and the permutations of column indices.

*In[131]:=*
```
Clear[a]
A = Array[a,{3,3}]; MatrixForm[A]
```

*Out[132]//MatrixForm=*
```
a[1, 1]  a[1, 2]  a[1, 3]
a[2, 1]  a[2, 2]  a[2, 3]
a[3, 1]  a[3, 2]  a[3, 3]
```

*In[133]:=*
```
Det[A]
```

*Out[133]=*
```
-(a[1, 3]a[2, 2]a[3, 1]) + a[1, 2]a[2, 3]a[3, 1]
  + a[1, 3]a[2, 1]a[3, 2] - a[1, 1]a[2, 3]a[3, 2]
  - a[1, 2]a[2, 1]a[3, 3] + a[1, 1]a[2, 2]a[3, 3]
```

**Example 4.34** Find the determinant of the matrix

$$\begin{bmatrix} 1 & x & y+z \\ 1 & y & z+x \\ 1 & z & x+y \end{bmatrix}$$

*In[134]:=*
```
Clear[x,y,z];
A = {{1,x,y+z},{1,y,z+x},{1,z,x+y}};
Det[A]
```

*Out[136]=*
```
0
```

**Example 4.35** Find the determinant of the $5 \times 5$ matrix

$$\mathbf{A} = \begin{bmatrix} 1 & 1 & -1 & 0 & 4 \\ 2 & 1 & 3 & -1 & 2 \\ 0 & -4 & 5 & -2 & 4 \\ 1 & 0 & 3 & 0 & -1 \\ 4 & 2 & -2 & -5 & 3 \end{bmatrix}$$

*In[137]:=*
```
Det[{{1,1,-1,0,4},{2,1,3,-1,2},{0,-4,5,-2,4},
        {1,0,3,0,-1},{4,2,-2,-5,3}}]
```

*Out[137]=*
```
-260
```

**Example 4.36** Show that the determinant of the matrix

$$\mathbf{B} = \begin{bmatrix} x^2-y^2 & x+y & x \\ x-y & 1 & 1 \\ x-y & 1 & y \end{bmatrix}$$

is zero.

*In[138]:=*
```
Clear[x,y];
B={{x^2-y^2,x+y,x},{x-y,1,1},{x-y,1,y}};
Det[B]
```

*Out[140]=*
```
0
```

The determinants of the following special matrices illustrated in examples 4.37 through 4.39 are direct consequences of the definition,

$$|\mathbf{A}| = \sum^{n!} (-1)^t a_{1i}\, a_{2j} \ldots a_{nk}.$$

The proofs are simple and left as exercises.

**Example 4.37** The determinant of a zero matrix is 0 and the determinant of an identity matrix is 1. Define **A** as a $5 \times 5$ identity matrix and then calculate its determinant.

*In[141]:=*

```
A = IdentityMatrix[5];
Det[A]
```

*Out[142]=*

1

**Example 4.38** The determinant of a diagonal matrix is equal to the product of the diagonal elements. For example,

$$|\mathbf{D}| = \begin{vmatrix} a & 0 & 0 \\ 0 & b & 0 \\ 0 & 0 & c \end{vmatrix} = abc$$

**Example 4.39** The determinant of a triangular matrix is equal to the product of the diagonal elements. If it is a strictly triangular matrix, then the determinant is zero. For example,

$$|\mathbf{A}| = \begin{vmatrix} a_{11} & a_{12} & a_{13} \\ 0 & a_{22} & a_{23} \\ 0 & 0 & a_{33} \end{vmatrix} = a_{11}a_{22}a_{33}; \ |\mathbf{B}| = \begin{vmatrix} b_{11} & 0 & 0 \\ b_{21} & b_{22} & 0 \\ b_{31} & b_{32} & b_{33} \end{vmatrix} = b_{11}b_{22}b_{33};$$

$$|\mathbf{C}| = \begin{vmatrix} 0 & c_{12} & c_{13} \\ 0 & 0 & c_{23} \\ 0 & 0 & 0 \end{vmatrix} = 0.$$

We now present some properties of determinants. These properties apply to determinants of square matrices of any dimension, although we only illustrate them for some specific matrices.

(1) The determinant of **A** is equal to the determinant of its transpose, $\mathbf{A}^T$. Thus, $|\mathbf{A}| = |\mathbf{A}^T|$. We show this property for the following $3 \times 3$ matrix

$$\mathbf{A} = \begin{bmatrix} 1 & 2 & 3 \\ 3 & 2 & 4 \\ 5 & 4 & 3 \end{bmatrix}$$

*In[143]:=*

```
A = {{1,2,3},{3,2,4},{5,4,3}};
Det[A] == Det[Transpose[A]]
```

*Out[144]=*

True

(2) If all elements of any row(column) are zero, then $|\mathbf{A}| = 0$. For example,

$$|\mathbf{A}| = \begin{vmatrix} 0 & 0 & 0 \\ a & b & c \\ x & y & z \end{vmatrix} = 0$$

*In[145]:=*
```
Clear[a,b,c,x,y,z];
Det[{{0,0,0},{a,b,c},{x,y,z}}]
```

*Out[146]=*
```
0
```

(3) Interchanging any two rows(columns) changes the sign of the determinant. For example, consider the 3 × 3 matrix

$$\mathbf{A} = \begin{bmatrix} 1 & 2 & 3 \\ 3 & 2 & 4 \\ 5 & 4 & 3 \end{bmatrix}$$

Let **B** be the matrix obtained from **A** by interchanging the first and the third rows. Then

$$|\mathbf{B}| = \begin{vmatrix} 5 & 4 & 3 \\ 3 & 2 & 4 \\ 1 & 2 & 3 \end{vmatrix} = -18 = -|\mathbf{A}|$$

*In[147]:=*
```
A  =  {{1,2,3},{3,2,4},{5,4,3}};
B  =  {{5,4,3},{3,2,4},{1,2,3}};
Det[B]  ==  -Det[A]
```

*Out[149]=*
```
True
```

(4) Multiplying a row by a scalar $k$ results in the determinant being multiplied by $k$. Multiplying the second row of **A** by $k$ results in k times $|\mathbf{A}|$.

$$\begin{vmatrix} 1 & 2 & 3 \\ 3k & 2k & 4k \\ 5 & 4 & 3 \end{vmatrix} = k \begin{vmatrix} 1 & 2 & 3 \\ 3 & 2 & 4 \\ 5 & 4 & 3 \end{vmatrix} = 18k$$

*In[150]:=*
```
Clear[k];
A  =  {{1,2,3},{3,2,4},{5,4,3}};
B  =  {{1,2,3},{k*3,k*2,k*4},{5,4,3}};
k*Det[A]==Det[B]
```

*Out[153]=*
```
True
```

(5) If the elements of two rows(columns) of a matrix **A** are proportional, then $|\mathbf{A}| = 0$. For example, consider the following 3 × 3 matrix

$$\mathbf{A} = \begin{bmatrix} a & b & c \\ 2a & 2b & 2c \\ x & y & z \end{bmatrix}$$

The first and second rows of **A** are proportional and

$$|\mathbf{A}| = \begin{vmatrix} a & b & c \\ 2a & 2b & 2c \\ x & y & z \end{vmatrix} = 0$$

*In[154]:=*
```
Clear[a,b,c,x,y,z];
Det[{{a,b,c},{2*a,2*b,2*c},{x,y,z}}]
```

*Out[155]=*
```
0
```

(6) If the $i$-th row(column) of a matrix **A** consists of elements, $[a_{i1}+b_1\ a_{i2}+b_2 \ldots a_{in}+b_n]$, then the determinant of **A** is equal to the sum of the determinants of two matrices, one of which has $[a_{i1}\ a_{i2} \ldots a_{in}]$ as its $i$-th row(column), and the other has $[b_1\ b_2 \ldots b_n]$, as its $i$-th row(column). The remaining rows(columns) in both matrices are the same as **A**. For example, the following determinant of **A** is equal to the sum of the determinants of $\mathbf{A}_1$ and $\mathbf{A}_2$.

$$|\mathbf{A}| = \begin{vmatrix} 1 & 2 & 3 \\ 3+x & 2+y & 4+z \\ 5 & 4 & 3 \end{vmatrix} = \begin{vmatrix} 1 & 2 & 3 \\ 3 & 2 & 4 \\ 5 & 4 & 3 \end{vmatrix} + \begin{vmatrix} 1 & 2 & 3 \\ x & y & z \\ 5 & 4 & 3 \end{vmatrix} = |\mathbf{A}_1| + |\mathbf{A}_2|$$

*In[156]:=*
```
Clear[x,y,z,A,A1,A2];
A  =  {{1,2,3},{3+x,2+y,4+z},{5,4,3}};
A1  =  {{1,2,3},{3,2,4},{5,4,3}};
A2  =  {{1,2,3},{x,y,z},{5,4,3}};
```

*In[160]:=*
```
Det[A]
```

*Out[160]=*
```
18 + 6x - 12y + 6z
```

*In[161]:=*
```
Det[A1]  +  Det[A2]
```

*Out[161]=*
```
18 + 6x - 12y + 6z
```

(7) Adding the elements of one row(column) to another row(column) will not change the determinant. This property follows from properties (5) and (6) above. For example, consider adding the first row to the second row in the following determinant:

$$\begin{vmatrix} 1 & 2 & 3 \\ 3 & 2 & 4 \\ 5 & 4 & 3 \end{vmatrix} = \begin{vmatrix} 1 & 2 & 3 \\ 3+1 & 2+2 & 4+3 \\ 5 & 4 & 3 \end{vmatrix}$$

Having *Mathematica* calculate each determinant, we find that they have the same value.

*In[162]:=*

```
Det[{{1,2,3},{3,2,4},{5,4,3}}]
```

*Out[162]=*

```
18
```

*In[163]:=*

```
Det[{{1,2,3},{3+1,2+2,4+3},{5,4,3}}]
```

*Out[163]=*

```
18
```

(8) The determinant of the product of two square matrices is equal to the product of the determinants. Thus, $|\mathbf{A}\,\mathbf{B}| = |\mathbf{A}||\mathbf{B}|$. For example,

$$|\mathbf{A}\,\mathbf{B}| = \left|\begin{bmatrix} a & b \\ c & d \end{bmatrix}\begin{bmatrix} 1 & 2 \\ 3 & 4 \end{bmatrix}\right| = |\mathbf{A}||\mathbf{B}| = \begin{vmatrix} a & b \\ c & d \end{vmatrix}\begin{vmatrix} 1 & 2 \\ 3 & 4 \end{vmatrix} = 2(bc - ab)$$

*In[164]:=*

```
Clear[a,b,c,d];
A={{a,b},{c,d}};  B={{1,2},{3,4}};
Det[A.B]  ==  Det[A]*Det[B]  //  Simplify
```

*Out[166]=*

```
True
```

The following two theorems are direct consequences of these properties.

**THEOREM 4.3** *Suppose* $\mathbf{E}_1$, $\mathbf{E}_2$, *and* $\mathbf{E}_3$ *are the elementary matrices applied to an identity matrix* $\mathbf{I}$. $\mathbf{E}_1\mathbf{I}$ *interchanges two rows of* $\mathbf{I}$, $\mathbf{E}_2\mathbf{I}$ *multiplies a row of* $\mathbf{I}$ *by* $k$, *and* $\mathbf{E}_3\mathbf{I}$ *adds one row of* $\mathbf{I}$ *to another row. The determinants of these elementary matrices are then* $|\mathbf{E}_1| = -1$, $|\mathbf{E}_2| = k$, *and* $|\mathbf{E}_3| = 1$.

The theorem is derived directly from properties (3), (4), and (7) above. The theorem is also applicable to elementary column operations. Thus, in general, the determinants of elementary matrices are nonzero.

**THEOREM 4.4** *An* $n \times n$ *square matrix* $\mathbf{A}$ *is non-singular if and only if the determinant of* $\mathbf{A}$ *is nonzero,* $|\mathbf{A}| \neq 0$.

To prove this theorem, recall that a square matrix $\mathbf{A}$ can be reduced by a sequence of elementary operations to a canonical matrix $\mathbf{T}$, and the ranks of $\mathbf{A}$ and $\mathbf{T}$ are equal. That is,

$$\mathbf{E}_t\mathbf{E}_{t-1} \ldots \mathbf{E}_2\mathbf{E}_1\mathbf{A}\,\mathbf{H}_1\mathbf{H}_2 \ldots \mathbf{H}_s = \mathbf{T}.$$

If $\mathbf{A}$ is nonsingular, then $n = \rho(\mathbf{A}) = \rho(\mathbf{T})$. Furthermore, $\mathbf{T}$ is the identity matrix $\mathbf{I}$. We have from property (8) the following equation:

$$|\mathbf{E}_t||\mathbf{E}_{t-1}| \ldots |\mathbf{E}_2||\mathbf{E}_1||\mathbf{A}||\mathbf{H}_1||\mathbf{H}_2| \ldots |\mathbf{H}_s| = |\mathbf{T}| = 1.$$

Since $|\mathbf{E}_i| \neq 0$ and $|\mathbf{H}_i| \neq 0$, we must have $|\mathbf{A}| \neq 0$. On the other hand, since $|\mathbf{E}_i| \neq 0$ and $|\mathbf{H}_i| \neq 0$, and if $|\mathbf{A}| \neq 0$, then $|\mathbf{T}| \neq 0$. **T** must be the identity matrix with $\rho(\mathbf{T}) = n$. Thus $\rho(\mathbf{A}) = n$, and **A** is nonsingular.

## EXERCISES

1. Prove that if **A** is nonsingular, then $|\mathbf{A}^{-1}| = 1/|\mathbf{A}|$.
2. Let **A** be an $n \times n$ matrix and $k$ be any scalar. Show that $|k\mathbf{A}| = k^n|\mathbf{A}|$.
3. Using both the definition of determinants and *Mathematica* function **Det**, calculate

$$|\mathbf{A}| = \begin{vmatrix} 1 & x & x^2 & x^3 \\ x & 1 & x & x^2 \\ x^2 & x & 1 & x^2 \\ x^3 & x^2 & x & 1 \end{vmatrix}$$

4. Let **A** be a $5 \times 5$ matrix with $|\mathbf{A}| = 4$.
   (a) Find the determinant of $3\mathbf{A} + 2\mathbf{A}$.
   (b) Find the determinants of $\mathbf{A}^3 = \mathbf{A}\mathbf{A}\mathbf{A}$, and $\mathbf{A}^k$ where $k$ is a positive constant.
   (c) Find the determinant of $-\mathbf{A}$.
5. Use the properties of determinants to show that

$$\begin{vmatrix} 1 & x & y+z \\ 1 & y & z+x \\ 1 & z & x+y \end{vmatrix} = 0$$

$$\begin{vmatrix} yz & x^2 & x^2 \\ y^2 & xz & y^2 \\ z^2 & z^2 & xy \end{vmatrix} = \begin{vmatrix} yz & xy & xz \\ xy & xz & yz \\ xz & yz & xy \end{vmatrix} = 0, \quad \text{if} \quad xyz \neq 0$$

### 4.4.2 Submatrices, minors, and cofactors

A submatrix $\mathbf{A}_{ij}$ of the elements $a_{ij}$ of an $n \times m$ matrix **A** is an $(n-1) \times (m-1)$ matrix obtained by deleting the $i$th row and the $j$th column of **A**. For example,

$$\mathbf{A} = \begin{bmatrix} a_{11} & a_{12} & a_{13} & a_{14} \\ a_{21} & a_{22} & a_{23} & a_{24} \\ a_{31} & a_{32} & a_{33} & a_{34} \end{bmatrix}$$

The submatrix $\mathbf{A}_{21}$ is

$$\mathbf{A}_{21} = \begin{bmatrix} a_{12} & a_{13} & a_{14} \\ a_{32} & a_{33} & a_{34} \end{bmatrix}.$$

The **MathEcon** function **submatrix[A,i,j]** can be used to calculate the submatrix $\mathbf{A}_{ij}$.

*In[167]:=*

```
?submatrix
```

**submatrix[mat,irow,jcol] calculates the submatrix of a given matrix mat by removing row irow and column jcol. For example,**

**submatrix[{{1,9},{6,-5}},1,2].**

**Example 4.40** The submatrices $\mathbf{A}_{12}$, and $\mathbf{A}_{23}$ of respective elements $a_{12}$ and $a_{23}$ of the matrix $\mathbf{A}$ are

$$\mathbf{A} = \begin{bmatrix} 1 & 2 & 3 \\ 3 & 4 & 5 \\ 5 & 6 & 7 \end{bmatrix}; \mathbf{A}_{12} = \begin{bmatrix} 3 & 5 \\ 5 & 7 \end{bmatrix}; \mathbf{A}_{23} = \begin{bmatrix} 1 & 2 \\ 5 & 6 \end{bmatrix}.$$

*In[168]:=*

```
A  =  {{1,2,3},{3,4,5},{5,6,7}};
A12  =  submatrix[A,1,2];  A12  //  MatrixForm
```

*Out[169]//MatrixForm=*

```
3  5
5  7
```

*In[170]:=*

```
A23  =  submatrix[A,2,3];  A23  //  MatrixForm
```

*Out[170]//MatrixForm=*

```
1  2
5  6
```

A *minor* $m_{ij}$ of elements $a_{ij}$ of a square matrix $\mathbf{A}$ is the determinant of the submatrix $\mathbf{A}_{ij}$. Thus,

$$m_{ij} = |\mathbf{A}_{ij}|.$$

A signed minor is called a *cofactor*. The cofactor, denoted as $c_{ij}$, is defined as

$$c_{ij} = (-1)^{i+j} m_{ij} = (-1)^{i+j} |\mathbf{A}_{ij}|.$$

Thus, in the above example,

$$m_{12} = \begin{vmatrix} 3 & 5 \\ 5 & 7 \end{vmatrix} = -4; \; c_{12} = (-1)^{1+2} m_{12} = -(-4) = 4.$$

Both minors and cofactors of a matrix $\mathbf{A}$ can be evaluated by the **MathEcon** functions, **minor** and **cofactor**.

*In[171]:=*

```
?minor
```

**minor[mat,irow,jcol] calculates the (irow,jcol) minor of a given matrix mat. For example,**

**minor[{{1,9},{6,-5}},1,2].**

*In[172]:=*
```
?cofactor
```

**cofactor[mat,irow,jcol] calculates the (irow,jcol) cofactor of a given matrix mat. For example,**

**cofactor[{{1,9},{6,-5}},1,2].**

**Example 4.41** Use **minor** and **cofactor** to compute the minors and the cofactors of the elements $a_{12}$ and $a_{23}$ for the matrix **A** in example 4.40.

*In[173]:=*
```
A = {{1,2,3},{3,4,5},{5,6,7}};
minor[A,1,2]
```

*Out[174]=*
−4

*In[175]:=*
```
cofactor[A,1,2]
```

*Out[175]=*
4

*In[176]:=*
```
minor[A,2,3]
```

*Out[176]=*
−4

*In[177]:=*
```
cofactor[A,2,3]
```

*Out[177]=*
4

**Theorem 4.5** *(Laplace expansion) The determinant* $|\mathbf{A}|$ *is equal to the sum of the products of the elements of a row (or column) of* **A** *and its own cofactors. That is,*

$$\begin{aligned}|\mathbf{A}| &= a_{i1}c_{i1} + a_{i2}c_{i2} + \ldots + a_{in}c_{in},\ i = 1,2,\ldots,n\\ &= a_{1j}c_{1j} + a_{2j}c_{2j} + \ldots + a_{nj}c_{nj},\ j = 1,2,\ldots,n\end{aligned}$$

The first equation is obtained by a row expansion, and the second by a column expansion.

**Example 4.42** Show that the Laplace expansion of the determinant of **A** below is equal to the products of the elements on the second ($i$=2) row and its cofactors. Use the *MathEcon* function **cofactor** and the built-in function **Det** to confirm this result.

$$|\mathbf{A}| = \begin{vmatrix} 4 & 1 & 2 & 5 \\ 5 & 3 & 1 & 3 \\ 8 & 6 & 0 & 4 \\ 3 & 2 & 1 & 2 \end{vmatrix} = 5c_{21} + 3c_{22} + 1c_{23} + 3c_{24}$$

$$= 5(-1)^3\begin{vmatrix} 1 & 2 & 5 \\ 6 & 0 & 4 \\ 2 & 1 & 2 \end{vmatrix} + 3(-1)^4\begin{vmatrix} 4 & 2 & 5 \\ 8 & 0 & 4 \\ 3 & 1 & 2 \end{vmatrix}$$

$$+ 1(-1)^5\begin{vmatrix} 4 & 1 & 5 \\ 8 & 6 & 4 \\ 3 & 2 & 2 \end{vmatrix} + 3(-1)^6\begin{vmatrix} 4 & 1 & 2 \\ 8 & 6 & 0 \\ 3 & 2 & 1 \end{vmatrix} = -8$$

*In[178]:=*

```
A = {{4,1,2,5},{5,3,1,3},{8,6,0,4},{3,2,1,2}};
laplace = 5*cofactor[A,2,1] + 3*cofactor[A,2,2] +
          1*cofactor[A,2,3] + 3*cofactor[A,2,4]
```

*Out[179]=*

```
-8
```

*In[180]:=*

```
Det[A]
```

*Out[180]=*

```
-8
```

It can also be shown that the cofactors satisfy the following properties.

**THEOREM 4.6** *The sum of the products of the elements of a row (or column) by the elements of the cofactors from another row (or column) is zero. That is,*

$$a_{i1}c_{k1} + a_{i2}c_{k2} + \ldots + a_{in}c_{kn} = 0, \quad \text{for} \quad i \neq k.$$
$$a_{1j}c_{1k} + a_{2j}c_{2k} + \ldots + a_{nj}c_{nk} = 0, \quad \text{for} \quad j \neq k.$$

The above two theorems may then be summarized as

$$\sum_{j=1}^{n} a_{ij}c_{kj} = \delta_{ik}|\mathbf{A}|, \; i = 1,2, \ldots, n; \; k = 1,2, \ldots, n.$$

$$\sum_{i=1}^{n} a_{ij}c_{ik} = \delta_{jk}|\mathbf{A}|, \; i = 1,2, \ldots, n; \; k = 1,2, \ldots, n.$$

where $\delta_{ik}$ and $\delta_{jk}$ are *Kronecker deltas*, defined by $\delta_{mn} = 1$ if $m = n$, and $\delta_{mn} = 0$ if $m \neq n$.

**Example 4.43** Show that the expansion of the determinant of **A** in exercise 4.42 by the products of the elements on the first ($i$ = 1) row and the cofactors from the second ($k$=2) row is equal to zero.

$$|\mathbf{A}| = \begin{vmatrix} 4 & 1 & 2 & 5 \\ 5 & 3 & 1 & 3 \\ 8 & 6 & 0 & 4 \\ 3 & 2 & 1 & 2 \end{vmatrix} = 4c_{21} + 1c_{22} + 2c_{23} + 5c_{24}$$

$$= 4(-1)^3 \begin{vmatrix} 1 & 2 & 5 \\ 6 & 0 & 4 \\ 2 & 1 & 2 \end{vmatrix} + 1(-1)^4 \begin{vmatrix} 4 & 2 & 5 \\ 8 & 0 & 4 \\ 3 & 1 & 2 \end{vmatrix}$$

$$+ 2(-1)^5 \begin{vmatrix} 4 & 1 & 5 \\ 8 & 6 & 4 \\ 3 & 2 & 2 \end{vmatrix} + 5(-1)^6 \begin{vmatrix} 4 & 1 & 2 \\ 8 & 6 & 0 \\ 3 & 2 & 1 \end{vmatrix} = 0$$

We confirm this calculation with the **cofactor** function.

*In[181]:=*

```
4*cofactor[A,2,1]  +  1*cofactor[A,2,2]  +
2*cofactor[A,2,3]  +  5*cofactor[A,2,4]
```

*Out[181]=*

```
0
```

## EXERCISES

1. Use the **cofactor** function to evaluate the determinants:

$$\begin{vmatrix} 2 & 4 & 6 & 4 \\ 0 & 4 & 6 & 9 \\ 2 & 1 & 4 & 0 \\ 1 & 2 & 3 & 2 \end{vmatrix}; \begin{vmatrix} x^2-y^2 & x+y & x \\ x-y & 1 & 1 \\ x-y & 1 & y \end{vmatrix}$$

2. If $\mathbf{A} = [a_{ij}]$ is an $n \times n$ matrix, show that the determinant of **B** is

$$|\mathbf{B}| = \begin{vmatrix} 0 & b_1 & b_2 & \dots & b_n \\ d_1 & a_{11} & a_{12} & \dots & a_{1n} \\ \cdot & \cdot & \cdot & \dots & \cdot \\ d_n & a_{n1} & a_{n2} & \dots & a_{nn} \end{vmatrix} = \sum_{i=1}^{n} \sum_{j=1}^{n} b_j d_i c_{ij}$$

where $c_{ij}$ are cofactors of **A**. The matrix **B** is called the *bordered matrix*. Use *Mathematica* to check the result for $n = 3$.

3. If **A** should be an $n \times n$ matrix and $k$ is any scalar, then show that $|k\mathbf{A}| = k^n|\mathbf{A}|$.

4. A *skew-symmetric* matrix **B** is one with the proporty $\mathbf{B}^T = -\mathbf{B}$.
   (a) Give an example of a $4 \times 4$ skew-symmetric matrix.
   (b) If **B** is a $9 \times 9$ skew-symmetric matrix, find $|\mathbf{B}|$.

### 4.4.3 The cofactor, adjoint, and inverse matrices

The *cofactor matrix* of an $n \times n$ matrix **A** has the cofactors of **A** as its elements. Thus, the cofactor matrix of **A** is

$$\mathbf{C} = \begin{bmatrix} c_{11} & c_{12} & \cdots & c_{1n} \\ c_{21} & c_{22} & \cdots & c_{2n} \\ \cdots & \cdots & \cdots & \cdots \\ c_{n1} & c_{n2} & \cdots & c_{nn} \end{bmatrix}$$

where $c_{ij}$ is the cofactor of the element $a_{ij}$ of **A**.

**Example 4.44** Consider the matrix

$$\mathbf{A} = \begin{bmatrix} 1 & 2 & 3 \\ 2 & 5 & 4 \\ 4 & 3 & 1 \end{bmatrix}$$

The cofactor matrix of **A** is

$$\mathbf{C} = \begin{bmatrix} -7 & 14 & -14 \\ 7 & -11 & 5 \\ -7 & 2 & 1 \end{bmatrix}$$

We confirm this with *Mathematica*. Since the notation **C** is a reserved symbol in *Mathematica* we use **CF** for **C** in the following *Mathematica* calculation.

*In[182]:=*

```
A = {{1,2,3},{2,5,4},{4,3,1}};
c11=cofactor[A,1,1];
c12=cofactor[A,1,2];
c13=cofactor[A,1,3];
c21=cofactor[A,2,1];
c22=cofactor[A,2,2];
c23=cofactor[A,2,3];
c31=cofactor[A,3,1];
c32=cofactor[A,3,2];
c33=cofactor[A,3,3];
CF = {{c11,c12,c13},{c21,c22,c23},{c31,c32,c33}};
CF // MatrixForm
```

*Out[193]//MatrixForm=*

```
-7   14   -14
7    -11  5
-7   2    1
```

An easier way to generate this cofactor matrix is to use the **Table** function.

*In[194]:=*

```
CF = Table[cofactor[A,i,j],{i,1,3},{j,1,3}];
CF // MatrixForm
```

*Out[195]//MatrixForm=*

```
-7   14   -14
7    -11  5
-7   2    1
```

> **DEFINITION 4.2** *The adjoint of an $n \times n$ matrix* **A**, *denoted as* adj **A**, *is defined as the transpose of the cofactor matrix* **C** of **A**:
>
> $$\text{adj}\,\mathbf{A} = \mathbf{C}^T$$

**Example 4.45** Find the adjoint of matrix **A** in the previous example.

*In[196]:=*

```
adj = Transpose[CF]; adj // MatrixForm
```

*Out[196]//MatrixForm=*

$$\begin{matrix} -7 & 7 & -7 \\ 14 & -11 & 2 \\ -14 & 5 & 1 \end{matrix}$$

> **THEOREM 4.7** *The inverse matrix* $\mathbf{A}^{-1}$ *of a nonsingular matrix* **A** *is equal to*
>
> $$\mathbf{A}^{-1} = \frac{1}{|\mathbf{A}|}\text{adj}\,\mathbf{A}$$

The proof is simple and is left as an exercise.

**Example 4.46** Find the inverse of the above matrix **A** by the cofactor method. Check the result obtained directly from the *Mathematica* function **Inverse**.

*In[197]:=*

```
B = adj/Det[A]; B // MatrixForm
```

*Out[197]//MatrixForm=*

$$\begin{matrix} \frac{1}{3} & -(\frac{1}{3}) & \frac{1}{3} \\ -(\frac{2}{3}) & \frac{11}{21} & -(\frac{2}{21}) \\ \frac{2}{3} & -(\frac{5}{21}) & -(\frac{1}{21}) \end{matrix}$$

*In[198]:=*

```
Inverse[A] // MatrixForm
```

*Out[198]//MatrixForm=*

$$\begin{matrix} \frac{1}{3} & -(\frac{1}{3}) & \frac{1}{3} \\ -(\frac{2}{3}) & \frac{11}{21} & -(\frac{2}{21}) \\ \frac{2}{3} & -(\frac{5}{21}) & -(\frac{1}{21}) \end{matrix}$$

When the dimension of a matrix is large, it is often advantageous to invert the matrix by partitioning. Partitioning involves grouping certain parts of the matrix together. Suppose that (for convenience) we partition **A** as follows:

$$\mathbf{A} = \begin{bmatrix} 4 & 1 & 2 & . & 5 & 0 \\ 5 & 3 & 1 & . & 3 & 2 \\ 8 & 6 & 0 & . & 4 & 1 \\ & & \cdots & \cdots & & \\ 3 & 2 & 1 & . & 2 & 0 \\ 1 & 4 & 3 & . & 5 & 1 \end{bmatrix} = \begin{bmatrix} \mathbf{A}_{11} & \mathbf{A}_{12} \\ \mathbf{A}_{21} & \mathbf{A}_{22} \end{bmatrix}$$

The dotted lines indicate that **A** has been partitioned into four parts, which may be regarded as submatrices, $A_{11}$, $A_{12}$, $A_{21}$, and $A_{22}$. If the partitioning is done so that $A_{22}$ is nonsingular, as it is in this case, then the inverse is given by

$$\mathbf{A}^{-1} = \begin{bmatrix} \mathbf{B}^{-1} & -\mathbf{B}^{-1}\mathbf{A}_{12}\mathbf{A}_{22}^{-1} \\ -\mathbf{A}_{22}^{-1}\mathbf{A}_{21}\mathbf{B}^{-1} & \mathbf{A}_{22}^{-1} + \mathbf{A}_{22}^{-1}\mathbf{A}_{21}\mathbf{B}^{-1}\mathbf{A}_{12}\mathbf{A}_{22}^{-1} \end{bmatrix}$$

where

$$\mathbf{B} = \mathbf{A}_{11} - (\mathbf{A}_{12}\mathbf{A}_{22}^{-1}\mathbf{A}_{21})$$

We leave the proof of $\mathbf{A}^{-1}\mathbf{A} = \mathbf{I}$ as an exercise.

**Example 4.47** Use partitioning to denote the system of equations

$$\begin{aligned} 4x_1 + x_2 + 2x_3 + 5x_4 \phantom{+ 2x_5} &= -1 \\ 5x_1 + 3x_2 + x_3 + 3x_4 + 2x_5 &= 2 \\ 8x_1 + 6x_2 \phantom{+ x_3} + 4x_4 + x_5 &= 0 \\ 3x_1 + 2x_2 + x_3 + 2x_4 \phantom{+ 2x_5} &= 4 \\ x_1 + 4x_2 + 3x_3 + 5x_4 + x_5 &= 1 \end{aligned} \quad \text{or} \quad \mathbf{Ax} = \mathbf{k}$$

The partitions are:

$$\mathbf{Ax} = \begin{bmatrix} 4 & 1 & 2 & . & 5 & 0 \\ 5 & 3 & 1 & . & 3 & 2 \\ 8 & 6 & 0 & . & 4 & 1 \\ & & \cdots & \cdots & & \\ 3 & 2 & 1 & . & 2 & 0 \\ 1 & 4 & 3 & . & 5 & 1 \end{bmatrix} \begin{bmatrix} x_1 \\ x_2 \\ x_3 \\ \cdots \\ x_4 \\ x_5 \end{bmatrix} = \begin{bmatrix} -1 \\ 2 \\ 0 \\ \cdots \\ 4 \\ 1 \end{bmatrix} \quad \text{or} \quad \begin{bmatrix} \mathbf{A}_{11} & \mathbf{A}_{12} \\ \mathbf{A}_{21} & \mathbf{A}_{22} \end{bmatrix} \begin{bmatrix} \mathbf{x}_1 \\ \mathbf{x}_2 \end{bmatrix} = \begin{bmatrix} \mathbf{k}_1 \\ \mathbf{k}_2 \end{bmatrix}$$

where

$$\mathbf{x}_1 = \begin{bmatrix} x_1 \\ x_2 \\ x_3 \end{bmatrix}; \ \mathbf{x}_2 = \begin{bmatrix} x_4 \\ x_5 \end{bmatrix}; \ \mathbf{k}_1 = \begin{bmatrix} -1 \\ 2 \\ 0 \end{bmatrix}; \ \mathbf{k}_2 = \begin{bmatrix} 4 \\ 1 \end{bmatrix}$$

Premultiplying the equations by $\mathbf{A}^{-1}$, we have the solution partitioned as

$$\begin{bmatrix} \mathbf{x}_1 \\ \mathbf{x}_2 \end{bmatrix} = \mathbf{A}^{-1}\mathbf{k} = \begin{bmatrix} \mathbf{B}^{-1} & -\mathbf{B}^{-1}\mathbf{A}_{12}\mathbf{A}_{22}^{-1} \\ -\mathbf{A}_{22}^{-1}\mathbf{A}_{21}\mathbf{B}^{-1} & \mathbf{A}_{22}^{-1} + \mathbf{A}_{22}^{-1}\mathbf{A}_{21}\mathbf{B}^{-1}\mathbf{A}_{12}\mathbf{A}_{22}^{-1} \end{bmatrix} \begin{bmatrix} \mathbf{k}_1 \\ \mathbf{k}_2 \end{bmatrix}$$

In particular, we have

$$\mathbf{x}_1 = \begin{bmatrix} x_1 \\ x_2 \\ x_3 \end{bmatrix} = \mathbf{B}^{-1}\mathbf{k}_1 - \mathbf{B}^{-1}\mathbf{A}_{12}\mathbf{A}_{22}^{-1}\mathbf{k}_2 = \mathbf{B}^{-1}(\mathbf{k}_1 - \mathbf{A}_{12}\mathbf{A}_{22}^{-1}\mathbf{k}_2).$$

The solution $\mathbf{x}_1$ is calculated below, but we leave the calculation of the solution $\mathbf{x}_2$ for the reader to work out.

*In[199]:=*

```
A11  =  {{4,1,2},{5,3,1},{8,6,0}};
A12  =  {{5,0},{3,2},{4,1}};
A21  =  {{3,2,1},{1,4,3}};
A22  =  {{2,0},{5,1}};
k1  =  {-1,2,0};
k2  =  {4,1};
B  =  A11-(A12.Inverse[A22].A21);
x1  =  Inverse[B].(k1-A12.Inverse[A22].k2)
```

*Out[206]=*

$$\{\frac{297}{188}, \frac{61}{94}, \frac{23}{4}\}$$

Inversion by partitioning has important theoretical implications. Also, if the matrix can be partitioned so that $\mathbf{A}_{12}$ and $\mathbf{A}_{21}$ are zero matrices, then

$$\mathbf{A}^{-1} = \begin{bmatrix} \mathbf{A}_{11} & 0 \\ 0 & \mathbf{A}_{22} \end{bmatrix}^{-1} = \begin{bmatrix} \mathbf{A}_{11}^{-1} & 0 \\ 0 & \mathbf{A}_{22}^{-1} \end{bmatrix}$$

## EXERCISES

1. Consider the matrix

$$\mathbf{A} = \begin{bmatrix} 1 & 0 & -1 \\ -3 & -1 & 6 \\ 2 & 1 & -5 \end{bmatrix}$$

   (a) Find the adjoint matrix, adj $\mathbf{A}$.
   (b) Find the inverse matrix from the adjoint matrix.
   (c) Find the inverse by partitioning $\mathbf{A}$ so that $\mathbf{A}_{22} = -5$.

2. Prove that

$$\mathbf{A}^{-1} = \frac{1}{|\mathbf{A}|}\operatorname{adj}\mathbf{A}$$

3. Show that $\mathbf{A}^{-1}\mathbf{A} = \mathbf{I}$ where $\mathbf{A}$ is partitioned as

$$\mathbf{A} = \begin{bmatrix} \mathbf{A}_{11} & \mathbf{A}_{12} \\ \mathbf{A}_{21} & \mathbf{A}_{22} \end{bmatrix}$$

and

$$\mathbf{A}^{-1} = \begin{bmatrix} \mathbf{B}^{-1} & -\mathbf{B}^{-1}\mathbf{A}_{12}\mathbf{A}_{22}^{-1} \\ -\mathbf{A}_{22}^{-1}\mathbf{A}_{21}\mathbf{B}^{-1} & \mathbf{A}_{22}^{-1} + \mathbf{A}_{22}^{-1}\mathbf{A}_{21}\mathbf{B}^{-1}\mathbf{A}_{12}\mathbf{A}_{22}^{-1} \end{bmatrix}$$

where

$$\mathbf{B} = \mathbf{A}_{11} - (\mathbf{A}_{12}\,\mathbf{A}_{22}^{-1}\,\mathbf{A}_{21})$$

## □ 4.5 Applications of Matrix Algebra to Economics □

### 4.5.1 Leontief input–output models

In a modern economy, many goods serve as both intermediate and final products. For example, electricity is used as an input in the production of many goods but is also demanded by consumers as a "final" product. Likewise, motor vehicles may be both an intermediate as well as final good. *Leontief input–output models* provide a means of tracking the interactions of goods that are both inputs and outputs in production processes. The models are represented as a system of linear equations, which in turn can be expressed and manipulated conveniently using matrix notation.

We begin by defining an *input coefficient matrix*

$$\mathbf{A} = \begin{bmatrix} a_{11} & a_{12} & \cdots & a_{1n} \\ a_{21} & a_{22} & \cdots & a_{2n} \\ \cdots & \cdots & \cdots & \cdots \\ a_{n1} & a_{n2} & \cdots & a_{nn} \end{bmatrix}$$

The elements, $a_{ij}$, indicate the value, say in dollar units, of the good $i$, required to produce a dollar's worth of the good $j$. The sum of the elements in $j$-th column represents the "cost" of producing a dollar's worth of good $j$, and is assumed to be less than one,

$$a_{ij} > 0 \quad \text{and} \quad \sum_{i=1}^{n} a_{ij} < 1$$

for all $j = 1,2, \ldots ,n$. Since each good is potentially an input in the production of the other goods, including its own, $\mathbf{A}$ is a square matrix. Let $x_i$ be the total quantity of good $i$ produced and let $a_{ij}x_j$ be the portion demanded by the production of the other good $j$. In addition, assume that there is a final consumer demand of quantity $d_i$ for the consumption of good $i$. For the market to be at equilibrium, the total supply $x_i$ must be equal to the total demand for good $i$ both as an input of production and as a final demand for consumption,

$$x_i = a_{i1}x_1 + a_{i2}x_2 + \ldots + a_{in}x_n + d_i$$

for $i = 1,2, \ldots ,n$. Expressed in matrix form, we have

$$\begin{bmatrix} x_1 \\ x_2 \\ \vdots \\ x_n \end{bmatrix} = \begin{bmatrix} a_{11} & a_{12} & \ldots & a_{1n} \\ a_{21} & a_{22} & \ldots & a_{2n} \\ \ldots & \ldots & \ldots & \ldots \\ a_{n1} & a_{n2} & \ldots & a_{nn} \end{bmatrix} \begin{bmatrix} x_1 \\ x_2 \\ \vdots \\ x_n \end{bmatrix} \begin{bmatrix} d_1 \\ d_2 \\ \vdots \\ d_n \end{bmatrix}; \quad \text{or} \quad \mathbf{x} = \mathbf{A}\mathbf{x} + \mathbf{d}$$

Rewriting the above equations, we have $(\mathbf{I} - \mathbf{A})\mathbf{x} = \mathbf{d}$. The matrix $\mathbf{I} - \mathbf{A}$ is called the *technology matrix*. If $\mathbf{I} - \mathbf{A}$ is nonsingular, then we have the solution for the total output $\mathbf{x}$ needed to satisfy the final demand $\mathbf{d}$,

$$\mathbf{x} = (\mathbf{I} - \mathbf{A})^{-1}\mathbf{d}.$$

For example, consider the input coefficient matrix and the final demand

$$\mathbf{A} = \begin{bmatrix} 0.2 & 0.6 & 0.3 \\ 0.2 & 0.1 & 0.6 \\ 0.4 & 0.1 & 0.0 \end{bmatrix}; \ \mathbf{d} = \begin{bmatrix} 250 \\ 140 \\ 100 \end{bmatrix}$$

The economy needs to produce $x_1 = \$1228.57$ of good 1, $x_2 = \$881.63$ of good 2, and $x_3 = \$679.59$ of good 3, in order to meet the final demands, $d_1 = \$250$, $d_2 = \$140$, and $d_3 = \$100$, of the three goods:

$$\mathbf{x} = \begin{bmatrix} x_1 \\ x_2 \\ x_3 \end{bmatrix} = (\mathbf{I} - \mathbf{A})^{-1}\mathbf{d} = \begin{bmatrix} 1228.57 \\ 881.63 \\ 679.59 \end{bmatrix}$$

We use *Mathematica* to confirm this calculation.

```
In[207]:=
    A  =  {{.2,.6,.3},{.2,.1,.6},{.4,.1,0}};
    d  =  {250,140,100};
    x  =  Inverse[(IdentityMatrix[3]  -  A)].d

Out[209]=
    {1228.57, 881.633, 679.592}
```

For the Leontief input–output models to make economic sense, we need to assume that:

(1) the technology matrix $\mathbf{I} - \mathbf{A}$ is nonsingular; and

(2) the elements of the solution $\mathbf{x} = (\mathbf{I} - \mathbf{A})^{-1}\mathbf{d}$ are nonnegative.

We will discuss the nonsingularity of $\mathbf{I} - \mathbf{A}$ in Chapter 6 when we study the eigenvalues of a matrix. However, we present here a heuristic explanation of the nonnegativity of the solution.

Consider the *matrix power sequence,*

$$\mathbf{A}, \mathbf{A}^2, \mathbf{A}^3, \ldots, \mathbf{A}^m, \ldots$$

where $\mathbf{A}^2 = \mathbf{A}\mathbf{A}$, $\mathbf{A}^3 = \mathbf{A}^2\mathbf{A}$, and so on. For example,

$$\mathbf{A}^2 = \begin{bmatrix} a_{11} & a_{12} & \cdots & a_{1n} \\ a_{21} & a_{22} & \cdots & a_{2n} \\ \cdots & \cdots & \cdots & \cdots \\ a_{n1} & a_{n2} & \cdots & a_{nn} \end{bmatrix} \begin{bmatrix} a_{11} & a_{12} & \cdots & a_{1n} \\ a_{21} & a_{22} & \cdots & a_{2n} \\ \cdots & \cdots & \cdots & \cdots \\ a_{n1} & a_{n2} & \cdots & a_{nn} \end{bmatrix}$$

$$= \begin{bmatrix} \sum_{k=1}^{n} a_{1k}a_{k1} & \sum_{k=1}^{n} a_{1k}a_{k2} & \cdots\cdots & \sum_{k=1}^{n} a_{1k}a_{kn} \\ \sum_{k=1}^{n} a_{2k}a_{k1} & \sum_{k=1}^{n} a_{2k}a_{k2} & \cdots\cdots & \sum_{k=1}^{n} a_{2k}a_{kn} \\ \cdots & \cdots & \cdots & \cdots \\ \sum_{k=1}^{n} a_{nk}a_{k1} & \sum_{k=1}^{n} a_{nk}a_{k2} & \cdots\cdots & \sum_{k=1}^{n} a_{nk}a_{kn} \end{bmatrix}$$

If the elements of $\mathbf{A}$ are nonnegative, $a_{ij} \geq 0$, then the elements of $\mathbf{A}^2$ are also nonnegative,

$$a_{ij}^{(2)} = \sum_{k=1}^{n} a_{ik}a_{kj} \geq 0$$

Furthermore, if the column sums of $\mathbf{A}$ is less than one, for example,

$$0 \leq \sum_{i=1}^{n} a_{ij} \leq \mathrm{t} < 1, \; j = 1,2, \ldots, n$$

then the column sum of $\mathbf{A}^2$ is less than or equal to $t^2$ since

$$\sum_{i=1}^{n} a_{ij}^{(2)} = \sum_{i=1}^{n} \sum_{k=1}^{n} a_{ik}a_{kj} = \sum_{k=1}^{n} \left( \sum_{i=1}^{n} a_{ik} \right) a_{kj} \leq t \sum_{k=1}^{n} a_{kj} \leq t^2$$

for $j = 1,2, \ldots, n$. Every element of $\mathbf{A}^2$ is nonnegative and every column sum is less than or equal to $t^2$. Hence, every element of $\mathbf{A}^2$ is

$$0 \leq a_{ij}^{(2)} \leq t^2$$

Continuing the process, we can show that for $\mathbf{A}^m$,

$$a_{ij}^{(m)} = \sum_{k=1}^{n} a_{ik}^{(m-1)} a_{kj}^{(m-1)} \geq 0 \quad \text{and} \quad \sum_{i=1}^{n} a_{ij}^{(m)} \leq t^m$$

Hence, in general, we have

$$0 \leq a_{ij}^{(m)} \leq t^m$$

If $0 \le t < 1$, then

$$\lim_{m\to\infty} a_{ij}^{(m)} \le \lim_{m\to\infty} t^m = 0$$

Thus, every element of $\mathbf{A}^m$ approaches zero,

$$\lim_{m\to\infty} \mathbf{A}^{(m)} = \lim_{m\to\infty} [a_{ij}^{(m)}] = 0$$

The *Mathematica* function, **MatrixPower**, calculates the matrix power sequence, $\mathbf{A}^m$.

*In[210]:=*

```
?MatrixPower
```

**MatrixPower[mat,n] gives the nth matrix power of mat.**

For example, $\mathbf{A}^{30} \approx \mathbf{0}$, where $\mathbf{A}$ is the Leontief coefficient matrix defined earlier.

*In[211]:=*

```
A = {{.2,.6,.3},{.2,.1,.6},{.4,.1,0}};
MatrixPower[A,30]
```

*Out[212]=*

```
{{0.00131141, 0.00128, 0.00140822}, {0.000987593, 0.000963939, 0.0010605},
 {0.000755779, 0.000737678, 0.000811576}}
```

Let us consider the following *matrix power series*,

$$\mathbf{B}_m = \mathbf{I} + \mathbf{A} + \mathbf{A}^2 + \mathbf{A}^3 + \ldots + \mathbf{A}^m$$

It is easy to show that

$$\begin{aligned}(\mathbf{I} - \mathbf{A})\mathbf{B}_m &= (\mathbf{I} - \mathbf{A})(\mathbf{I} + \mathbf{A} + \mathbf{A}^2 + \mathbf{A}^3 + \ldots + \mathbf{A}^m) \\ &= (\mathbf{I} + \mathbf{A} + \mathbf{A}^2 + \mathbf{A}^3 + \ldots + \mathbf{A}^m) \\ &\quad - (\mathbf{A} + \mathbf{A}^2 + \mathbf{A}^3 + \ldots + \mathbf{A}^m + \mathbf{A}^{m+1}) \\ &= \mathrm{I} - \mathbf{A}^{m+1}\end{aligned}$$

Since $\mathbf{A}^{m+1} \to \mathbf{0}$ as $m \to \infty$, $\mathbf{B}_m$ approaches the inverse of $\mathbf{I} - \mathbf{A}$, and

$$(\mathbf{I} - \mathbf{A})^{-1} \approx \mathbf{B}_m = \mathbf{I} + \mathbf{A} + \mathbf{A}^2 + \mathbf{A}^3 + \ldots + \mathbf{A}^m$$

The solution to the Leotief input-output model is approximately

$$\begin{aligned}\mathbf{x} &= (\mathbf{I} - \mathbf{A})^{-1}\mathbf{d} \\ &= \mathbf{d} + \mathbf{A}\mathbf{d} + \mathbf{A}^2\mathbf{d} + \mathbf{A}^3\mathbf{d} + \ldots + \mathbf{A}^m\mathbf{d}\end{aligned}$$

The total output $\mathbf{x}$ required to meet the final demands is the sum of

(1) $\mathbf{d}$, the final demand itself;

(2) $\mathbf{A}\mathbf{d}$, the input demand needed to produce $\mathbf{d}$; and

(3) $\mathbf{A}^2\mathbf{d}$, the input demand needed to produce $\mathbf{A}\mathbf{d}$; etc.

Since all elements of $\mathbf{A}^n$ and $\mathbf{d}$ are nonnegative, the intermediate demands $\mathbf{A}^n\mathbf{d}$ are nonnegative. The total output $\mathbf{x}$ is therefore nonnegative. Below, we tabulate $n$ and $\mathbf{A}^n$ $\mathbf{d}$ for various $n$ from 0 to 3. The intermediate demands are arranged in a table form with headings.

*In[213]:=*

```
d = {250,140,100};
demand=Table[{n,MatrixPower[A,n].d}, {n,0,3,1}];
TableForm[demand,
          TableHeadings->{{},{"n","Int. Demand"}}]
```

*Out[215]//TableForm=*

```
n   Int. Demand
    250
    140
0   100

    164.
    124.
1   114.

    141.4
    113.6
2   78.

    119.84
    86.44
3   67.92
```

## 4.5.2 Regression equation and estimation

Economists frequently estimate how one variable is related to, or affected by, other variables. For example, we might seek to identify how family food expenditure is related to family income and family size. To estimate such a relationship, economists employ *regression* techniques. Suppose $y_i$ is the $i$-th family's weekly food expenditure, and $w_i$ and $s_i$ are the corresponding weekly family income and family size, respectively. The relationship between the dependent variable, food expenditure, and the independent variables, income and family size, are written as a regression,

$$y_i = b_0 + b_1 w_i + b_2 s_i + u_i$$

where $u_i$, called the *residual*, represents a "composite" factor other than income and family size that affects the expenditure. The constants, $b_i$, indicate the impacts of the independent variables on the dependent variable.

Regression analysis is used to determine the constants $b_i$ based on a set of sample observations. Suppose that for $n$ families, weekly expenditures, income, and family size are observed. The regression equation for the sample family can be written in a matrix form,

$$\begin{bmatrix} y_1 \\ y_2 \\ \vdots \\ y_n \end{bmatrix} = \begin{bmatrix} 1 & w_1 & s_1 \\ 1 & w_2 & s_2 \\ & \vdots & \\ 1 & w_n & s_n \end{bmatrix} \begin{bmatrix} b_0 \\ b_1 \\ b_2 \end{bmatrix} + \begin{bmatrix} u_1 \\ u_2 \\ \vdots \\ u_n \end{bmatrix}$$

or written more compactly, $\mathbf{y} = \mathbf{X}\mathbf{b} + \mathbf{u}$.

The *method of least square* is frequently used to estimate the vector **b**. Given the observations on the vector of dependent variable **y** and the independent variable matrix **X**, the least squares technique finds the coefficient vector **b** that minimizes the squares of the length of the residual vector **u**, $\mathbf{u}^T\mathbf{u}$, The minimization, which will be discussed in Chapter 11, results in the least square estimation

$$\mathbf{b} = (\mathbf{X}^T\mathbf{X})^{-1}\mathbf{X}^T\mathbf{y}.$$

The following data represent observations of five families' weekly food expenditure, income, and family size.

$$\mathbf{y} = \begin{bmatrix} 16.12 \\ 22.97 \\ 24.83 \\ 26.79 \\ 29.18 \end{bmatrix};\ \mathbf{X} = \begin{bmatrix} 1 & 30.92 & 1 \\ 1 & 66.38 & 2 \\ 1 & 85.60 & 2 \\ 1 & 103.94 & 3 \\ 1 & 123.35 & 3 \end{bmatrix}$$

The least squares estimates of the regression coefficients are calculated from matrix operations.

*In[216]:=*

```
y  =  {16.12,  22.97,  24.83,  26.79,  29.18};
X  =  {{1,  30.92,  1},{1,  66.38,  2},{1,  85.60,  2},
       {1,  103.94,  3},{1,  123.35,  3}};
b  =  Inverse[(Transpose[X].X)].Transpose[X].y
```

*Out[218]=*

```
{12.4874, 0.12577, 0.533036}
```

The least squares estimates based on the sample data result in the regression equation

$$y_i = 12.49 + 0.126w_i + 0.533s_i.$$

For every dollar increase in weekly family income, the weekly food expenditure is estimated to increase 12.6 cents. And for every additional member in the family, the weekly expenditure increases 53.3 cents. The regression equation can be used to make a prediction for the family food expenditures. Suppose a family of four has weekly income of \$100. The estimated weekly food expenditure is then

$$\begin{aligned} y_i &= 12.49 + 0.126(100) + 0.533(4) \\ &= \begin{bmatrix} 1 & 100 & 4 \end{bmatrix} \begin{bmatrix} 12.490 \\ 0.126 \\ 0.533 \end{bmatrix} = \$27.20 \end{aligned}$$

## EXERCISES

1. Consider an economy consisting of three industries where the input coefficent matrix is

$$\mathbf{A} = \begin{bmatrix} 0.2 & 0.2 & 0.3 \\ 0.5 & 0.5 & 0 \\ 0 & 0 & 0.2 \end{bmatrix}$$

and the demand vector is $\mathbf{d} = [9\ 12\ 16]^T$ which is given in millions of dollars. Find the output levels required of each industry to meet these demands.

# 5

# Systems of Linear Equations

Economic variables often have linear relationships. The Leontief input–output model describes linear relationships among demands and productions of various goods in an economy. Geometrically, a linear equation defines a hyperplane in an Euclidean space. Solutions of a system of linear equations are viewed as intersections of these hyperplanes. However, we can also view a linear equation such as $2x_1 + x_2 - 3x_3 = 5$ as the dot product $\mathbf{ax} = 5$ between a coefficient vector $\mathbf{a} = [2\ 1\ -3]$ and a variable vector $\mathbf{x} = [x_1\ x_2\ x_3]^T$. A system of $n$ linear equations is then a collection of the $n$ dot products. In this chapter, we use vectors and matrices to represent systems of linear equations, and then use the theory that was developed in Chapter 4 to find solutions of these systems.

## □ 5.1 Systems of Linear Equations □

### 5.1.1 Definition and solutions

A *system of linear equations* consists of a set of linear equations of the form:

$$
\begin{aligned}
a_{11}x_1 + \ldots + a_{1n}x_n &= k_1 \\
a_{21}x_1 + \ldots + a_{2n}x_n &= k_2 \\
\ldots\ldots\ldots\ldots\ldots\ldots & \\
a_{m1}x_1 + \ldots + a_{mn}x_n &= k_m
\end{aligned}
$$

The constants, $a_{ij}$ and $k_i$, are assumed to be independent of the variables, $x_1, x_2, \ldots, x_n$. As we learned in Chapter 4, this system can be represented as a matrix equation

$$\mathbf{Ax} = \mathbf{k}$$

where $\mathbf{A}$ is a m × n matrix, $\mathbf{x}$ is an $n \times 1$ column vector, and $\mathbf{k}$ is the $m \times 1$ column vector. In particular, they are defined as

$$
\mathbf{A} = \begin{bmatrix} a_{11} & a_{12} & \ldots & a_{1n} \\ a_{21} & a_{22} & \ldots & a_{2n} \\ \ldots & \ldots & \ldots & \ldots \\ a_{m1} & a_{m2} & \ldots & a_{mn} \end{bmatrix}; \quad \mathbf{x} = \begin{bmatrix} x_1 \\ x_2 \\ \cdot \\ \cdot \\ x_n \end{bmatrix}; \quad \mathbf{k} = \begin{bmatrix} k_1 \\ k_2 \\ \cdot \\ \cdot \\ k_m \end{bmatrix}
$$

**A** is called the *coefficient matrix* of the linear system.

**Example 5.1** The linear system

$$\begin{aligned} 3x_2 - 4x_3 \quad &= -20 \\ x_1 - x_2 + x_3 \quad &= 15 \\ x_2 - x_3 - x_4 &= 10 \end{aligned}$$

can be written as $\mathbf{Ax} = \mathbf{k}$ where

$$\mathbf{A} = \begin{bmatrix} 0 & 3 & -4 & 0 \\ 1 & -1 & 1 & 0 \\ 0 & 1 & -1 & -1 \end{bmatrix}; \ \mathbf{x} = \begin{bmatrix} x_1 \\ x_2 \\ x_3 \\ x_4 \end{bmatrix}; \ \mathbf{k} = \begin{bmatrix} -20 \\ 15 \\ 10 \end{bmatrix}$$

**Example 5.2** A simple macroeconomic model consists of three linear equations:

(1) Consumption equation: $C = a_0 + a_1Y + a_2T$

(2) Investment equation: $I = b_0 + b_1Y + b_2K$

(3) Income identity: $Y = C + I$

Consumption ($C$) is a linear function of income ($Y$) and government tax ($T$); investment ($I$) is determined by income and accumulative capital stock ($K$). Income identity is an accounting equality. Both $T$ and $K$ are assumed to be constant. We express the model in the following matrix form,

$$\begin{bmatrix} 1 & 0 & -a_1 \\ 0 & 1 & -b_1 \\ -1 & -1 & 1 \end{bmatrix} \begin{bmatrix} C \\ I \\ Y \end{bmatrix} = \begin{bmatrix} a_0 + a_2T \\ b_0 + b_2K \\ 0 \end{bmatrix}$$

A *solution* of a system of linear equations is a vector **x** that satisfies the equation $\mathbf{Ax} = \mathbf{k}$. There are two ways of conceptualizing solutions of linear systems:

(1) A linear equation can represent either a line ($n$=2), a plane ($n$=3), or a hyperplane ($n$>3) in an Euclidean space. A system of linear equations can then be viewed as a collection of these lines, planes, or hyperplanes. When viewed in this manner, the solution, if it exists, will be the intersection of these entities. The absence of a solution will indicate the absence of a common intersection.

(2) The system of equations is a linear combination of vectors,

$$x_1 \begin{bmatrix} a_{11} \\ a_{21} \\ \cdot \\ \cdot \\ a_{m1} \end{bmatrix} + x_2 \begin{bmatrix} a_{12} \\ a_{22} \\ \cdot \\ \cdot \\ a_{m2} \end{bmatrix} + \ldots + x_n \begin{bmatrix} a_{1n} \\ a_{2n} \\ \cdot \\ \cdot \\ a_{mn} \end{bmatrix} = \begin{bmatrix} k_1 \\ k_2 \\ \cdot \\ \cdot \\ k_m \end{bmatrix}$$

or, more compactly,

$$x_1\mathbf{a}_1 + x_2\mathbf{a}_2 + \ldots + x_n\mathbf{a}_n = \mathbf{k}$$

where $\mathbf{a}_i$ is the $i$-th column vector of the coefficient matrix $\mathbf{A}$. From this prospective, the solution $\mathbf{x} = [x_1\ x_2\ \ldots\ x_n]^T$ is a vector of scalars chosen so that the linear combination of the column vectors of $\mathbf{A}$ equals the constant vector $\mathbf{k}$.

**Example 5.3** Consider the following system of equations:

$$x_1 + x_2 = 1$$
$$3x_1 + 6x_2 = 4$$

Rewriting them as vectors, we have

$$\mathbf{x}_1\begin{bmatrix}1\\3\end{bmatrix} + \mathbf{x}_2\begin{bmatrix}1\\6\end{bmatrix} = \begin{bmatrix}1\\4\end{bmatrix} \quad \text{or} \quad x_1\mathbf{a}_1 + x_2\mathbf{a}_2 = \mathbf{k}$$

We use the *Mathematica* function **Plot** to graph both equations. The first equation, $x_2 = 1 - x_1$, is represented by a solid line, and the second, $x_2 = 4/6 - 3/6x_1$ is represented by a dashed line.

*In[1]:=*

```
Clear[x1,x2];
Plot[{1-x1,4/6-(3/6)*x1},{x1,-1,2},
       AxesLabel->{"x1","x2"},
        PlotStyle->{{},Dashing[{0.01}]},
       AspectRatio->Automatic];
```

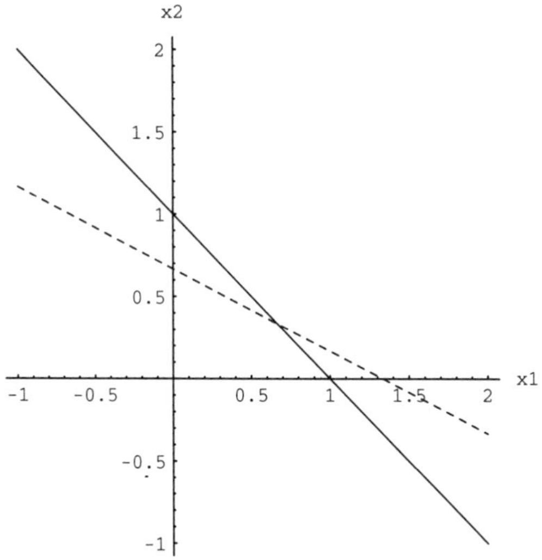


The point of intersection of the two lines at $(x_1,x_2) = (2/3,1/3)$ satisfies both equations simultaneously, and is therefore the solution of the system. Substituting $x_1 = 2/3$, and $x_2 = 1/3$ into $x_1\mathbf{a}_1 + x_2\mathbf{a}_2 = \mathbf{k} = [1\ 4]^T$ $\mathbf{k}$ is expressed as a linear combination of $\mathbf{a}_1$ and $\mathbf{a}_2$:

$$\frac{2}{3}\begin{bmatrix}1\\3\end{bmatrix} + \frac{1}{3}\begin{bmatrix}1\\6\end{bmatrix} = \begin{bmatrix}1\\4\end{bmatrix}$$

**Example 5.4** Consider the system of equations:

$$2x_1 + 3x_2 = 1$$
$$4x_1 + 6x_2 = 4$$

By plotting the two equations, $x_2 = 1/3 - 2/3\,x_1$ and $x_2 = 4/6 - 4/6\,x_1$, we observe that these two lines are parallel. The system thus has no intersection, and consequently, no solution to the system exists.

*In[3]:=*
```
Clear[x1,x2];
Plot[{1/3-(2/3)*x1,4/6-(4/6)*x1},{x1,-1,2},
        AxesLabel->{"x1","x2"},
         PlotStyle->{{},Dashing[{0.01}]}];
```

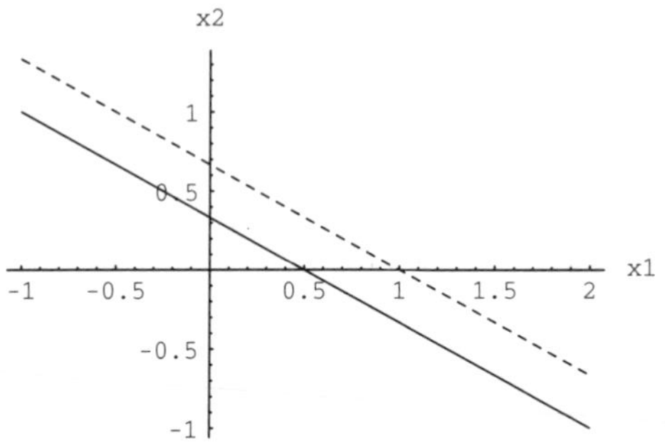


Additionally, the nonexistence of a solution implies that no scalars ($x_1$ and $x_2$) exist such that the linear combination

$$x_1\begin{bmatrix}2\\4\end{bmatrix} + x_2\begin{bmatrix}3\\6\end{bmatrix} = \begin{bmatrix}1\\4\end{bmatrix}$$

holds.

**Example 5.5** Consider a system of three equations in two unknowns:

$$x_1 + x_2 = 1$$
$$4x_1 + x_2 = 2$$
$$x_1 + 4x_2 = 2$$

Again, we plot the three equations and observe that the three lines do not intersect at the same point.

*In[5]:=*
```
Clear[x1,x2];
Plot[{1-x1,2-4*x1,2/4-(1/4)*x1},{x1,0,1},
        AxesLabel->{"x1","x2"},
           PlotStyle->{{},Dashing[{0.01}],Dashing[{0.02}]}];
```

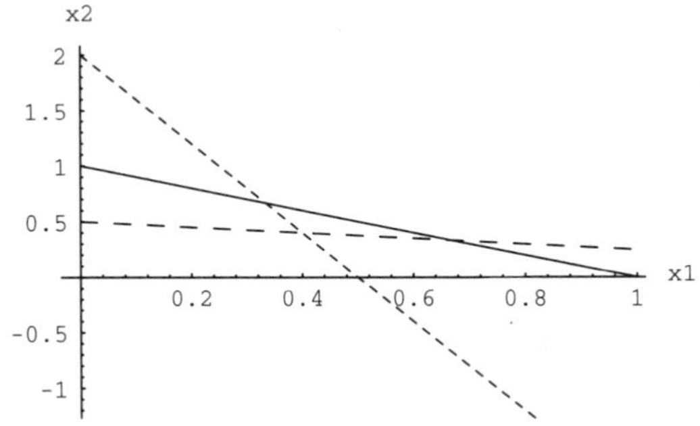


In other words, it is not possible to find scalars $x_1$ and $x_2$ that can simultaneously satisfy the equation

$$x_1\begin{bmatrix}1\\4\\1\end{bmatrix} + x_2\begin{bmatrix}1\\1\\4\end{bmatrix} = \begin{bmatrix}1\\2\\2\end{bmatrix} \quad \text{or} \quad x_1\mathbf{a}_1 + x_2\mathbf{a}_2 = \mathbf{k}.$$

**Example 5.6** Consider the system

$$\begin{aligned} 2x_1 + 3x_2 + x_3 &= 3 \\ x_1 - 6x_2 + x_3 &= 6 \end{aligned}$$

Each equation in the system is a plane in three-dimensional space. We plot the two equations, $x_3 = 3 - 2x_1 - 3x_2$, and $x_3 = 6 - x_1 + 6x_2$, using the *Mathematica* **Plot3D** function. We use the **Plot3D** option, **Mesh→False**, to omit the drawing of a mesh on the graphic surface so that the intersection of the planes can be seen more clearly.

*In[7]:=*

```
Clear[eq1,eq2,x1,x2];
eq1  =  Plot3D[3-2*x1-3*x2,{x1,-2,2},{x2,-2,2},
                    Mesh->False,DisplayFunction->Identity];
eq2  =  Plot3D[6-x1+6*x2,{x1,-2,2},{x2,-2,2},
                    Mesh->False,DisplayFunction->Identity];
Show[eq1,eq2,AxesLabel->{"x1","x2","x3"},
                    ViewPoint->{2.592,-1.914,1.033},
                    DisplayFunction->$DisplayFunction];
```

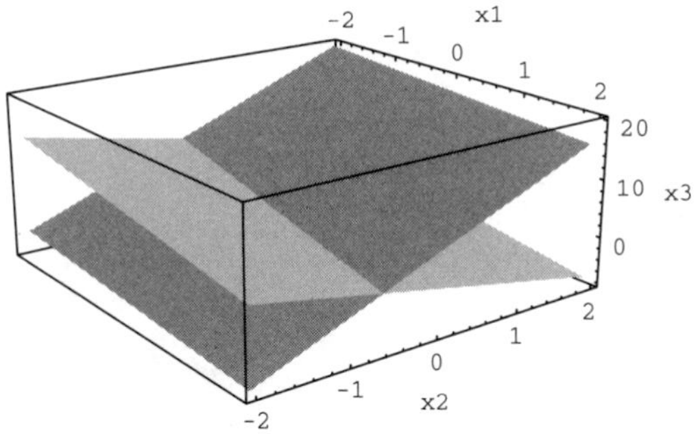

As illustrated, the intersection of these planes is a line. Since any point on the line created by the intersecting planes satisfies both equations, an infinite number of solutions exist. For example, $(x_1, x_2, x_3) = (0, -1/3, 4)$ and $(-3, 0, 9)$ are both solutions. In fact, the linear combination

$$x_1\begin{bmatrix}2\\1\end{bmatrix} + x_2\begin{bmatrix}3\\-6\end{bmatrix} + x_3\begin{bmatrix}1\\1\end{bmatrix} = \begin{bmatrix}3\\6\end{bmatrix}$$

can be satisfied by any value for $x_1$ as long as

$$\begin{aligned} x_2 &= -1/3 - 1/9x_1 \\ x_3 &= \ \ 4 \ \ - 5/3x_1. \end{aligned}$$

## EXERCISES

1. Write the following linear system of equations in matrix form: $\mathbf{Ax} = \mathbf{k}$.
   (a) $$\begin{aligned} x_1 - 3x_2 + 2x_3 - 4 &= 0 \\ x_1 + x_2 - x_3 - 2 &= 0 \\ 2x_1 \qquad + 4x_3 \qquad &= 0 \end{aligned}$$
   (b) $$\begin{aligned} x_1 + x_2 + x_3 &= 0 \\ x_1 - x_2 - x_3 &= 0 \end{aligned}$$
   (c) $x_1 - 2x_2 + 3x_3 - 4x_4 = 0$
   (d) $$\begin{aligned} a_{11}x_1 + a_{12}x_2 + a_{13}x_3 &= x_1 \\ a_{21}x_1 + a_{22}x_2 + a_{23}x_3 &= x_2 \\ a_{31}x_1 + a_{32}x_2 + a_{33}x_3 &= x_3 \end{aligned}$$

2. If the macroeconomic model in example 5.2 is expanded to include a tax equation,

   $$T = d_0 + d_1Y,$$

   then express the model in a matrix form, $\mathbf{Ax} = \mathbf{k}$.

3. Plot the following equations and determine whether the systems have solutions.
   (a) $$\begin{aligned} 3x_1 - x_2 &= 7 \\ -x_1 + 2x_2 &= -4 \end{aligned}$$
   (b) $$\begin{aligned} 5x_1 - 4x_2 &= 1 \\ x_1 + x_2 &= 2 \\ 4x_1 - 5x_2 &= 1 \end{aligned}$$
   (c) $$\begin{aligned} x_1 - x_2 + x_3 &= 2 \\ x_1 + x_2 - x_3 &= 2 \end{aligned}$$

4. Show that the system of equations

   $$\begin{aligned} x - z &= 1 \\ x + y - z &= 2 \\ y &= 1 \end{aligned}$$

   has an infinite number of solutions.

5. Show that the system of equations

$$x\begin{bmatrix}1\\0\\1\end{bmatrix} + y\begin{bmatrix}2\\1\\3\end{bmatrix} + z\begin{bmatrix}-1\\3\\2\end{bmatrix} = \begin{bmatrix}0\\0\\0\end{bmatrix}$$

has the solution $(x,y,z) = (7t,-3t,t)$ for any scalar $t$.

6. Consider a system of equation

$$x_1\mathbf{a}_1 + x_2\mathbf{a}_2 + x_3\mathbf{a}_3 = \mathbf{0}$$

where $\mathbf{a}_i$ is the $i$-th column of a coefficient matrix $\mathbf{A}$. If both $\mathbf{c}_1$ and $\mathbf{c}_2$ are solutions, i.e., $\mathbf{Ac}_1 = \mathbf{0}$ and $\mathbf{Ac}_2 = \mathbf{0}$, then prove that any linear combination of the two solutions is itself a solution. For example, $\mathbf{c}_3 = 3\mathbf{c}_1 - 2\mathbf{c}_2$ is a solution.

## 5.1.2 Existence of solutions

We have demonstrated that a system of linear equations may have a unique solution, multiple solutions (infinitely many), or no solution. A system of linear equations that has at least one solution is called *consistent*. A system that does not have a solution is called *inconsistent*. Though the graphical examples provided an intuitive interpretation for these various scenarios, we cannot rely upon graphs to check or to obtain solutions of general systems of linear equations. Instead, examining the coefficient matrix $\mathbf{A}$ and constant vector $\mathbf{k}$ can answer most questions regarding the existence and uniqueness of solutions to linear systems of equations.

Consider a system of equations, $\mathbf{Ax} = \mathbf{k}$. An *augmented matrix* $\mathbf{M}$ is an $m \times (n+1)$ matrix obtained by appending the constant vector $\mathbf{k}$ to the coefficient matrix $\mathbf{A}$, as the $(n+1)th$ column. That is,

$$\mathbf{M} = [\mathbf{Ak}] = \begin{bmatrix} a_{11} & a_{12} & \dots & a_{1n} & k_1 \\ a_{21} & a_{22} & \dots & a_{2n} & k_2 \\ \dots & \dots & \dots & \dots & \dots \\ a_{m1} & a_{m2} & \dots & a_{mn} & k_m \end{bmatrix}$$

The augmented matrix can be created by using the **MathEcon** function **aug**.

*In[11]:=*

```
?aug
```

**aug[mat,vect] forms the augmented matrix of the matrix mat and the vector vect. For example,**

**aug[{{1,2},{0,1}},{-3,2}].**

**Example 5.7** Create the augmented matrix **M** for the following system of linear equations:

$$x_1 + 3x_2 + 4x_3 = 14$$
$$x_1 + 7x_2 + 9x_3 = 3$$

*In[12]:=*

```
A = {{1,3,4},{1,7,9}}; k = {14,3};
M = aug[A,k] // MatrixForm
```

*Out[13]//MatrixForm=*

```
1  3  4  14
1  7  9  3
```

A system of $m$ linear equations in $n$ unknowns can be written as a linear combination of vectors:

$$x_1\mathbf{a}_1 + x_2\mathbf{a}_2 + \ldots + x_n\boldsymbol{a}_n = \mathbf{k}$$

where $\mathbf{a}_i$ is the $i$-th column vector of $\mathbf{A}$. Hence the equation system possesses a solution if and only if the vector $\mathbf{k}$ is a linear combination of the $n$ vectors, $\mathbf{a}_1, \mathbf{a}_2, \ldots,$ $\mathbf{a}_n$. In other words, the vector $\mathbf{k}$ must belong to the vector space spanned by the vectors $\boldsymbol{a}_i$'s. Furthermore, if the rank of $\mathbf{A} = [\mathbf{a}_1, \mathbf{a}_2, \ldots, \mathbf{a}_n]$ is equal to $r$, and if $\mathbf{k}$ is a linear combination of $\mathbf{a}_i$'s, then the rank of the augmented matrix $\mathbf{M}$ must be exactly $r$. Conversely, if the rank of $\mathbf{M}$ is equal to the rank of $\mathbf{A}$, then the vector $\mathbf{k}$ is a linear combination of $\mathbf{a}_i$'s. In this case the system of equations is solvable. Therefore, we have proven the following theorem.

**THEOREM 5.1** *A solution exists for a system of m linear equations in n unknowns* $\mathbf{Ax} = \mathbf{k}$ *if and only if the rank of the coefficient matrix* $\mathbf{A}$ *is equal to that of the augmented matrix* $\mathbf{M} = [\mathbf{A}\ \mathbf{k}]$.

**Example 5.8** Does the linear system of equations

$$x_1 + 3x_2 + 4x_3 = 14$$
$$x_1 + 7x_2 + 9x_3 = 3$$

have a solution? We use the **MathEcon** function **rank** to compute the ranks of **A** and the augmented matrix of the system.

*In[14]:=*

```
A = {{1,3,4},{1,7,9}}; k = {14,3};
M = aug[A,k];
rank[A] == rank[M]
```

*Out[16]=*

True

Since the rank of $\mathbf{A}$ is equal to the rank of $\mathbf{M} = [\mathbf{A}\ \mathbf{k}]$, the system of equations is consistent and solutions exist.

**Example 5.9** Show that system of linear equations

$$2x_1 + 3x_2 = 1$$
$$4x_1 + 6x_2 = 4$$

is inconsistent. We simply have to check the ranks of the coefficient and augmented matrices.

*In[17]:=*

```
A = {{2,3},{4,6}}; k = {1,4};
M = aug[A,k];
rank[A] == rank[M]
```

*Out[19]=*

False

## EXERCISES

1. Use the rank test to determine whether the following systems have solutions:

   (a) $$\begin{aligned} 2x_1 + 3x_2 + 4x_3 &= 2 \\ x_1 + x_2 - 2x_3 + 6x_4 &= 8 \\ -x_1 + 3x_2 + 4x_3 + 5x_4 &= 12 \end{aligned}$$

   (b) $$\begin{aligned} 4x_1 + x_2 - x_3 &= 4 \\ x_1 + 3x_2 &= 1 \\ x_2 + x_3 &= 0 \end{aligned}$$

   (c) $x_1 + x_2 - x_3 - x_4 = 3$

   (d) $$\begin{aligned} x_1 + x_2 + x_3 &= 0 \\ 2x_1 + 2x_2 + 2x_3 &= 0 \\ 3x_1 + 3x_2 + 3x_3 &= 0 \end{aligned}$$

2. Prove that the system $\mathbf{Ax} = \mathbf{k}$ always has solutions if $\mathbf{k}$ is a zero vector.

# □ 5.2 Nonhomogeneous Linear Systems of Equations □

## 5.2.1 Case of $n$ equations in $n$ unknowns

A system of linear equations $\mathbf{Ax} = \mathbf{k}$ is said to be nonhomogenous if $\mathbf{k} \neq \mathbf{0}$. If $\mathbf{A}$ is an $n \times n$ square matrix, then the augmented matrix of the system, $\mathbf{M} = [\mathbf{A}\ \mathbf{k}]$, is an $n \times (n+1)$ matrix. Suppose $\rho(\mathbf{A}) = \rho(\mathbf{M}) = n$. By theorem 5.1, a solution exists for the system. In fact, the solution is unique and is equal to $\mathbf{x} = \mathbf{A}^{-1}\mathbf{k}$ since $\mathbf{A}^{-1}$ is unique.

**Example 5.10** Solve the following system of three equations,

$$\begin{aligned} x_1 + 3x_2 + 4x_3 &= 14 \\ x_1 + 7x_2 + 9x_3 &= 3 \\ 6x_1 + 5x_2 + 4x_3 &= 2 \end{aligned}$$

We first observe that $\rho(\mathbf{A}) = \rho(\mathbf{M}) = 3$.

*In[20]:=*

```
A = {{1,3,4},{1,7,9},{6,5,4}}; k = {14,3,2};
M = aug[A,k];
rank[A] == rank[M]
```

*Out[22]=*

True

Hence a unique solution $(x_1,x_2,x_3) = (72/5,-42,157/5)$ exists.

*In[23]:=*
```
x = Inverse[A].k
```

*Out[23]=*

$$\{\frac{72}{5}, -42, \frac{157}{5}\}$$

Let us check this solution to make sure that it satisfies the system.

*In[24]:=*
```
A.x == k
```

*Out[24]=*
True

An alternative method to find solutions of linear systems is called *Cramer's rule.* To understand Cramer's rule, we first recall from Chapter 4 that the inverse of **A** can be expressed in terms of the cofactor matrix:

$$\mathbf{A}^{-1} = \frac{1}{|\mathbf{A}|}\begin{bmatrix} c_{11} & c_{21} & \cdots & c_{n1} \\ c_{12} & c_{22} & \cdots & c_{n2} \\ \cdots & \cdots & \cdots & \cdots \\ c_{1n} & c_{2n} & \cdots & c_{nn} \end{bmatrix}$$

Each element of the solution vector $\mathbf{x} = \mathbf{A}^{-1}\,\mathbf{k}$ can be expressed as a linear combination of cofactors and the constant vector **k**, i.e.,

$$x_i = \frac{1}{|\mathbf{A}|}(k_1c_{1i} + k_2c_{2i} + \ldots + k_nc_{ni})$$

which, by using the Laplace expansion given in Chapter 4, can be expressed as:

$$x_i = \frac{|\mathbf{A}_i|}{|\mathbf{A}|}$$

where $|\mathbf{A}_i|$ is the determinant of the matrix derived from **A** by replacing the $i$-th column of **A** with the vector **k**. Hence, we have the following formulas for the components of the unique solution:

$$x_1 = \frac{\begin{vmatrix} k_1 & a_{12} & \cdots & a_{1n} \\ k_2 & a_{22} & \cdots & a_{2n} \\ \cdots & \cdots & \cdots & \cdots \\ k_n & a_{n2} & \cdots & a_{nn} \end{vmatrix}}{\begin{vmatrix} a_{11} & a_{12} & \cdots & a_{1n} \\ a_{21} & a_{22} & \cdots & a_{2n} \\ \cdots & \cdots & \cdots & \cdots \\ a_{n1} & a_{n2} & \cdots & a_{nn} \end{vmatrix}}, \quad x_2 = \frac{\begin{vmatrix} a_{11} & k_1 & \cdots & a_{1n} \\ a_{21} & k_2 & \cdots & a_{2n} \\ \cdots & \cdots & \cdots & \cdots \\ a_{n1} & k_n & \cdots & a_{nn} \end{vmatrix}}{\begin{vmatrix} a_{11} & a_{12} & \cdots & a_{1n} \\ a_{21} & a_{22} & \cdots & a_{2n} \\ \cdots & \cdots & \cdots & \cdots \\ a_{n1} & a_{n2} & \cdots & a_{nn} \end{vmatrix}}, \ldots, x_n = \frac{\begin{vmatrix} a_{11} & a_{12} & \cdots & k_1 \\ a_{21} & a_{22} & \cdots & k_2 \\ \cdots & \cdots & \cdots & \cdots \\ a_{n1} & a_{n2} & \cdots & k_n \end{vmatrix}}{\begin{vmatrix} a_{11} & a_{12} & \cdots & a_{1n} \\ a_{21} & a_{22} & \cdots & a_{2n} \\ \cdots & \cdots & \cdots & \cdots \\ a_{n1} & a_{n2} & \cdots & a_{nn} \end{vmatrix}}$$

Though this rule may seem complicated, in practice it provides an easily implementable procedure for computing the solution of a system of linear equations. Since only the variables of interest are computed, it is particularly efficient when some variables of a system have important economic significance and others do not. To replace a column of a matrix, we use the **MathEcon** function **colrep** which replaces a column of a matrix by another column vector. Here is the form for this function.

*In[25]:=*

```
?colrep
```

**colrep[mat,vect,icol] replaces the icol column of a given matrix mat by the vector vect. For example,**

**colrep[{{1,2},{0,1}},{-3,2},2].**

**Example 5.11** Find value of $x_2$ of example 5.10, using Cramer's rule. We create a new matrix, $\mathbf{A}_2$, by replacing the second column of **A** with **k**.

*In[26]:=*

```
A = {{1,3,4},{1,7,9},{6,5,4}}; k = {14,3,2};
A2 = colrep[A,k,2]; MatrixForm[A2]
```

*Out[27]//MatrixForm=*

```
1  14  4
1  3   9
6  2   4
```

According to Cramer's rule, $x_2 = |\mathbf{A}_2|/|\mathbf{A}|$. We compute this ratio of determinants using the *Mathematica* function **Det**.

*In[28]:=*

```
x2 = Det[A2]/Det[A]
```

*Out[28]=*

```
-42
```

The result is identical to that obtained by using matrix inversion directly in Example 5.10.

*Mathematica* has a function that may be used to obtain solutions of systems of linear equations. This function is called **LinearSolve**. Here is *Mathematica*'s description of this function.

*In[29]:=*

```
?LinearSolve
```

**LinearSolve[m, b] gives the vector x which solves the matrix equation m.x==b.**

**Example 5.12** Use **LinearSolve** to find the solution of the following system of equations:

$$\begin{aligned} x_1 + 2x_2 - 3x_3 + 4x_4 &= 19 \\ x_1 \quad\quad + 4x_3 - x_4 &= 6 \\ -x_1 + 4x_2 - x_3 - x_4 &= -6 \\ 10x_2 \quad\quad - 2x_4 &= 0 \end{aligned}$$

We first observe that $r(\mathbf{A}) = r(\mathbf{M}) = 4$.

*In[30]:=*
```
A = {{1,2,-3,4},{1,0,4,-1},{-1,4,-1,-1},{0,10,0,-2}};
k = {19,6,-6,0}; M = aug[A, k];
rank[A] == rank[M]
```

*Out[32]=*
True

*In[33]:=*
```
rank [A]
```

*Out[33]=*
4

Since **A** is nonsingular, a unique solution $(x_1,x_2,x_3,x_4) = (3,1,2,5)$ is obtained using **LinearSolve**.

*In[34]:=*
```
x = LinearSolve[A,k]
```

*Out[34]=*
{3, 1, 2, 5}

It is possible for a nonhomogeneous system to have infinitely many solutions. Consider the following two linear equations,

$$\begin{aligned} x_1 + x_2 &= 2 \\ 2x_1 + 2x_2 &= 4 \end{aligned}$$

The coefficient matrix

$$\mathbf{A} = \begin{bmatrix} 1 & 1 \\ 2 & 2 \end{bmatrix}$$

is singular since $|\mathbf{A}| = 0$. The second equation in the system is a multiple of the first equation. However, solutions to the system exist since the rank of **A** and the corresponding augmented matrix are equal.

*In[35]:=*
```
A = {{1,1},{2,2}}; k={2,4};
rank[A] == rank[aug[A,k]]
```

*Out[36]=*
True

There are an infinite number of solutions vectors $(x_1, x_2)$ in this case. For example, (–2,4), (0,2), (1,1), (2,0), etc., are solutions. Although the *Mathematica* function **LinearSolve** is still capable of finding a solution in this case, it does not list all possible solutions. As shown below, it gives a single solution (2,0).

*In[37]:=*
```
x = LinearSolve[A,k]
```

*Out[37]=*
```
{2, 0}
```

In general, when a system of $n$ equations in $n$ unknowns has a singular coefficient matrix, certain equations in the system are linear combinations of other equations of the system. The next section discusses a method of finding solutions in a more general situation of $m$ equations in $n$ unknowns.

## EXERCISES

1. Consider the following system of three equations:

$$2x_1 - x_2 = 2$$
$$3x_2 + 2x_3 = 16$$
$$5x_1 + 3x_3 = 21$$

(a) Use Cramer's rule to find a solution. Check the solution by using the column-replace function **colrep**.
(b) Use the *Mathematica* function, **LinearSolve**, to find a solution.

2. Use **LinearSolve** to find a solution for the consumption ($C$), investment ($I$), and income ($Y$) in the following macroeconomic model.

$$C = a_0 + a_1 Y$$
$$I = b_0 + b_1 Y$$
$$Y = C + I$$

3. Verify that the system of equations $\mathbf{Ax} = \mathbf{k}$ has a unique solution which can be written as

$$\frac{x_1}{d_{11}} = \frac{x_2}{d_{12}} = \ldots = \frac{x_n}{d_{1n}} = -\frac{1}{d_{1,n+1}}$$

where $d_{ij}$ are the cofactors of the elements $z_{ij}$ of the following determinant.

$$\begin{vmatrix} z_{11} & z_{12} & \ldots z_{1n} & z_{1,n+1} \\ a_{11} & a_{12} & \ldots\ a_{1n} & k_1 \\ a_{21} & a_{22} & \ldots\ a_{2n} & k_2 \\ \cdots & \cdots & \cdots & \cdots \\ a_{n1} & a_{n2} & \ldots\ a_{nn} & k_n \end{vmatrix}$$

### 5.2.2 Case of $m$ equations in $n$ unknowns

Assume that the $m \times n$ coefficient matrix **A** and the $m \times (n+1)$ augmented matrix **M** have the same rank $r$. Since there are $r$ linearly independent rows in **A** and in **M**, there are exactly $r$ linearly independent equations in the system of $m$ equations, $\mathbf{Ax} = \mathbf{k}$. A solution to the linear system exists, and the following procedure will yield the set of solutions.

We begin by rewriting the $m$ equations as functions:

$$\begin{aligned}
f_1(\mathbf{x}) &= a_{11}x_1 + a_{12}x_2 + \ldots + a_{1n}x_n - k_1 = 0\\
&\vdots\\
f_r(\mathbf{x}) &= a_{r,1}x_1 + a_{r,2}x_2 + \ldots + a_{r,n}x_n - k_r = 0\\
f_{r+1}(\mathbf{x}) &= a_{r+1,1}x_1 + a_{r+1,2}x_2 + \ldots + a_{r+1,n}x_n - k_{r+1} = 0\\
&\vdots\\
f_m(\mathbf{x}) &= a_{m1}x_1 + a_{m2}x_2 + \ldots + a_{mn}x_n - k_m = 0.
\end{aligned}$$

Suppose the $m$ equations are arranged so that the first $r$ equations are linearly independent. The last $(m-r)$ equations must then be linear combinations of the first $r$ equations. That is,

$$f_j(\mathbf{x}) = c_{1j}f_1(\mathbf{x}) + c_{2j}f_2(\mathbf{x}) + \ldots + c_{rj}f_r(\mathbf{x}),\ j = r+1, \ldots, m.$$

Suppose $\mathbf{x}_0 = (x_{10}, x_{20}, \ldots, x_{n0})$ is a solution of the first $r$ equations, $f_i(\mathbf{x}_0) = 0$, for $i = 1,2, \ldots, r$. Then $\mathbf{x}_0$ is also a solution of the last $(m-r)$ equations, i.e., $f_j(\mathbf{x}_0) = 0$, for $j = r+1, \ldots, m$. To show this, we observe that

$$\begin{aligned}
f_j(\mathbf{x}_0) &= c_{1j}f_1(\mathbf{x}_0) + c_{2j}f_2(\mathbf{x}_0) + \ldots + c_{rj}f_r(\mathbf{x}_0)\\
&= c_{1j}(0) + c_{2j}(0) + \ldots + c_{rj}(0) = 0,\ j = r+1, \ldots, m.
\end{aligned}$$

From the viewpoint of solving the system of $m$ linear equations, the last $(m-r)$ equations are redundant and can be discarded. The coefficient matrix of the remaining $r$ equations is

$$\begin{bmatrix}
a_{11} & a_{12} & \cdots & a_{1r} & a_{1,r+1} & \cdots & a_{1n}\\
a_{21} & a_{22} & \cdots & a_{2r} & a_{2,r+1} & \cdots & a_{2n}\\
\cdots & \cdots & \cdots & \cdots & \cdots & \cdots & \cdots\\
a_{r1} & a_{r2} & \cdots & a_{rr} & a_{r,r+1} & \cdots & a_{rn}
\end{bmatrix}$$

Since this matrix has rank $r$, there are $r$ linearly independent columns. Assuming the first $r$ columns are linearly independent (if not, it can always be so arranged), rewrite the $r$ equations by moving the variables $x_{r+1}, \ldots, x_n$, and $k_1, \ldots, k_r$ to the right-hand side. The system of $r$ equations is reduced to

$$\begin{aligned}
a_{11}x_1 + \ldots + a_{1r}x_r &= k_1 - a_{1,r+1}x_{r+1} - \ldots - a_{1n}x_n\\
&\vdots\\
a_{r1}x_1 + \ldots + a_{rr}x_r &= k_r - a_{r,r+1}x_{r+1} - \ldots - a_{rn}x_n.
\end{aligned}$$

Written in matrix notation, the above system is

$$\mathbf{A}_r\mathbf{x}_r = \mathbf{k}_r - \mathbf{A}_{n-r}\mathbf{x}_{n-r}$$

where

$$\mathbf{A}_r = \begin{bmatrix} a_{11} & a_{12} & \cdots & a_{1r} \\ a_{21} & a_{22} & \cdots & a_{2r} \\ \cdots & \cdots & \cdots & \cdots \\ a_{r1} & a_{r2} & \cdots & a_{rr} \end{bmatrix}; \ \mathbf{A}_{n-r} = \begin{bmatrix} a_{1,r+1} & a_{1,r+2} & \cdots & a_{1n} \\ a_{2,r+1} & a_{2,r+2} & \cdots & a_{2n} \\ \cdots & \cdots & \cdots & \cdots \\ a_{r,r+1} & a_{r,r+2} & \cdots & a_{rn} \end{bmatrix}$$

$$\mathbf{x}_r = \begin{bmatrix} x_1 \\ x_2 \\ \cdot \\ \cdot \\ x_r \end{bmatrix}; \ \mathbf{x}_{n-r} = \begin{bmatrix} x_{r+1} \\ x_{r+2} \\ \cdot \\ \cdot \\ x_n \end{bmatrix}; \ \mathbf{k}_r = \begin{bmatrix} k_1 \\ k_2 \\ \cdot \\ \cdot \\ k_r \end{bmatrix}$$

Since $\mathbf{A}_r$ is a square matrix composed of linearly independent row and column vectors, $|\mathbf{A}_r| \neq 0$ and $\mathbf{A}_r^{-1}$ exists. We can therefore solve the system by finding the inverse of $\mathbf{A}_r$ so that

$$\mathbf{x}_r = \mathbf{A}_r^{-1}(\mathbf{k}_r - \mathbf{A}_{n-r}\mathbf{x}_{n-r}).$$

The elements of the vector $\mathbf{x}_{n-r}$ may be assigned arbitrary values. If the elements are assigned a value of $\mathbf{x}_{n-r}^0$, then the corresponding equation is $\mathbf{x}_r^0 = \mathbf{A}_r^{-1}(\mathbf{k}_r - \mathbf{A}_{n-r}\mathbf{x}_{n-r}^0)$. The *general solution* of the system of $m$ equations, $\mathbf{Ax} = \mathbf{k}$, is then

$$\mathbf{x} = \begin{bmatrix} \mathbf{x}_r \\ \mathbf{x}_{n-r} \end{bmatrix} = \begin{bmatrix} \mathbf{A}_r^{-1}(\mathbf{k}_r - \mathbf{A}_{n-r}\mathbf{x}_{n-r}) \\ \mathbf{x}_{n-r} \end{bmatrix}$$

where $\mathbf{x}_{n-r}$ is arbitrary.

The above procedure suggests that if a system of $m$ linear equations in $n$ variables is consistent and has $r$ linearly independent equations, then it is only necessary to find solutions for the $r$ linearly independent equations. Solutions are obtained by solving for $r$ variables in terms of the $n{-}r$ variables whose values can be arbitrarily assigned. The solutions so obtained are also solutions of the other $n{-}r$ equations.

**Example 5.13** Consider the following system:

$$\begin{aligned} x_1 + x_2 + x_3 + x_4 + x_5 &= 3 \\ 2x_1 + 2x_2 + 2x_3 + 2x_4 + 2x_5 &= 6 \\ x_1 + x_2 + x_3 + 3x_4 + 2x_5 &= 8 \end{aligned}$$

Expressed in matrix notation, we have

$$\begin{bmatrix} 1 & 1 & 1 & 1 & 1 \\ 2 & 2 & 2 & 2 & 2 \\ 1 & 1 & 1 & 3 & 2 \end{bmatrix} \begin{bmatrix} x_1 \\ x_2 \\ x_3 \\ x_4 \\ x_5 \end{bmatrix} = \begin{bmatrix} 3 \\ 6 \\ 8 \end{bmatrix}; \quad \text{or} \quad \mathbf{Ax} = \mathbf{k}.$$

We first check if the system is consistent by checking the ranks of $\mathbf{A}$ and the augmented matrix $\mathbf{M}$.

*In[38]:=*

```
A = {{1,1,1,1,1},{2,2,2,2,2},{1,1,1,3,2}}; k = {3,6,8};
rank[A] == rank[aug[A,k]]
```

*Out[39]=*

True

*In[40]:=*

```
rank[A]
```

*Out[40]=*

2

Since $\rho(\mathbf{A}) = \rho(\mathbf{M}) = 2$, solutions exist for the system and only two of the equations are independent. We rearrange the equations and variables necessary to express the system as $\mathbf{A}_r\mathbf{x}_r = \mathbf{k}_r - \mathbf{A}_{n-r}\mathbf{x}_{n-r}$. Interchanging the order of the second and third equations (the second and the third rows of **A**), and the second and fourth variables (the second and the fourth columns of **A**), we have

$$\begin{aligned} x_1 + x_4 + x_3 + x_2 + x_5 &= 3 \\ x_1 + 3x_4 + x_3 + x_2 + 2x_5 &= 8 \\ 2x_1 + 2x_4 + 2x_3 + 2x_2 + 2x_5 &= 6 \end{aligned}$$

We disregard the third equation since it is a multiple of the first equation. Moving $x_3$, $x_2$ and $x_5$ to the right-hand sides of the equations, we have

$$\begin{aligned} x_1 + x_4 &= 3 - x_2 - x_3 - x_5 \\ x_1 + 3x_4 &= 8 - x_2 - x_3 - 2x_5 \end{aligned}$$

Expressed in matrix notation, we have

$$\begin{bmatrix} 1 & 1 \\ 1 & 3 \end{bmatrix} \begin{bmatrix} x_1 \\ x_4 \end{bmatrix} = \begin{bmatrix} 3 \\ 8 \end{bmatrix} - \begin{bmatrix} 1 & 1 & 1 \\ 1 & 1 & 2 \end{bmatrix} \begin{bmatrix} x_2 \\ x_3 \\ x_5 \end{bmatrix}$$

or,

$$\mathbf{A}_r\mathbf{x}_r = \mathbf{k}_r - \mathbf{A}_{n-r}\mathbf{x}_{n-r}$$

Since $\mathbf{A}_r$ is nonsingular, the solution $\mathbf{x}_r = \mathbf{A}_r^{-1}(\mathbf{k}_r - \mathbf{A}_{n-r}\mathbf{x}_{n-r})$ is obtained.

*In[41]:=*

```
Clear[x2,x3,x5];
Ar = {{1,1},{1,3}}; Anr = {{1,1,1},{1,1,2}};
kr = {3,8}; xnr = {x2,x3,x5};
xr = Inverse[Ar].(kr- Anr.xnr);
Simplify[xr] // MatrixForm
```

*Out[44]//MatrixForm=*

$$\begin{pmatrix} \frac{1}{2} - x2 - x3 - \frac{x5}{2} \\ \frac{5 - x5}{2} \end{pmatrix}$$

That is

$$\mathbf{x}_r = \begin{bmatrix} x_1 \\ x_4 \end{bmatrix} = \begin{bmatrix} \frac{1}{2} - x_2 - x_3 - \frac{1}{2}x_5 \\ \frac{5}{2} - \frac{1}{2}x_5 \end{bmatrix}$$

The general solution **x** depends on the arbitrary values for $x_2$, $x_3$ and $x_5$,

$$\mathbf{x} = \begin{bmatrix} x_1 \\ x_2 \\ x_3 \\ x_4 \\ x_5 \end{bmatrix} = \begin{bmatrix} \frac{1}{2} - x_2 - x_3 - \frac{1}{2}x_5 \\ x_2 \\ x_3 \\ \frac{5}{2} - \frac{1}{2}x_5 \\ x_5 \end{bmatrix}$$

When we set $x_2 = 1$, $x_3 = 0$, and $x_5 = 0$, we obtain a particular solution

$$\mathbf{x} = \begin{bmatrix} -1/2 \\ 1 \\ 0 \\ 5/2 \\ 0 \end{bmatrix}$$

When we set $x_2 = -1$, $x_3 = 1$, and $x_5 = 4$, we have another particular solution

$$\mathbf{x} = \begin{bmatrix} -3/2 \\ -1 \\ 1 \\ 1/2 \\ 4 \end{bmatrix}$$

By varying the values of $x_2$, $x_3$, and $x_5$, an infinite number of particular solutions can be obtained.

A second means of solving systems of linear equations is using the *Mathematica* function **Solve**.

*In[45]:=*

```
?Solve
```

**Solve[eqns, vars] attempts to solve an equation or set of equations for the variables vars. Any variable in eqns but not vars is regarded as a parameter. Solve[eqns] treats all variables encountered as vars above. Solve[eqns, vars, elims] attempts to solve the equations for vars, eliminating the variables elims.**

The first argument of **Solve** is a list of equations, $\mathbf{Ax} = \mathbf{k}$, to be solved and the second argument is a list of the variables, **x**. Although we currently use this function to solve systems of linear equations, it can also be used to solve nonlinear systems as well. The example below demonstrates the use of this function on the same system of linear equations given in example 5.13.

**Example 5.14** From the linear equations in example 5.13, we first define the system as a list of equations and then solve for $\mathbf{x}_r = [x_1\ x_4]^T$ by treating $\mathbf{x}_{n-r} = [x_2\ x_3\ x_5]^T$ as parameters.

*In[46]:=*
```
Clear[x1,x2,x3,x4,x5];
eqn1  =  x1  +  x2  +  x3  +  x4  +  x5  ==  3;
eqn2  =  2*x1  +  2*x2  +  2*x3  +  2*x4  +  2*x5  ==  6;
eqn3  =  x1  +  x2  +  x3  +  3*x4  +  2*x5  ==  8;
Solve[{eqn1,eqn2,eqn3},{x1,x4}]
```

*Out[50]=*

$$\{\{x1 \to 3 - x2 - x3 + \frac{-5 + x5}{2} - x5,\ x4 \to \frac{5 - x5}{2}\}\}$$

**Solve** gives the same results obtained in example 5.13,

$$\mathbf{x}_r = \begin{bmatrix} x_1 \\ x_4 \end{bmatrix} = \begin{bmatrix} \frac{1}{2} - x_2 - x_3 - \frac{1}{2}x_5 \\ \frac{5}{2} - \frac{1}{2}x_5 \end{bmatrix}$$

The list of equations in the first argument of the **Solve** function can be more conveniently expressed in matrix notation, $\mathbf{Ax} = \mathbf{k}$. For example,

*In[51]:=*
```
Clear  [x1,x2,x3,x4,x5];
A  =  {{1,1,1,1,1},{2,2,2,2,2},{1,1,1,3,2}};
k  =  {3,6,8};  x  =  {x1,x2,x3,x4,x5};
Solve[A.x  ==  k,{x1,x4}]
```

*Out[54]=*

$$\{\{x1 \to 3 - x2 - x3 + \frac{-5 + x5}{2} - x5,\ x4 \to \frac{5 - x5}{2}\}\}$$

**Example 5.15** Consider the following demand and supply equations for an automobile, and the market clearing equation of equating demand and supply.

$$D_1 = a_{11}P_1 + a_{12}P_2 + a_{13}Y + a_{14}Z + a_{10}$$
$$S_1 = a_{21}P_1 + a_{22}W + a_{23}P_3 + a_{20}$$
$$D_1 = S_1.$$

The coefficients $a_{ij}$ are constant, and

$D_1$ = quantity demanded for automobile,
$S_1$ = quantity suppled for automobile,
$P_1$ = automobile price,
$P_2$ = gasoline price,

$P_3$ = steel price,
$Y$ = income,
$Z$ = interest rate,
$W$ = wage rate.

Suppose we are solving the equations for $D_1$, $S_1$, and $P_1$. Expressed in a matrix form, the system is

$$\begin{bmatrix} 1 & 0 & -a_{11} \\ 0 & 1 & -a_{21} \\ 1 & -1 & 0 \end{bmatrix} \begin{bmatrix} D_1 \\ S_1 \\ P_1 \end{bmatrix} + \begin{bmatrix} -a_{12} & -a_{13} & -a_{14} & 0 & 0 \\ 0 & 0 & 0 & -a_{22} & -a_{23} \\ 0 & 0 & 0 & 0 & 0 \end{bmatrix} \begin{bmatrix} P_2 \\ Y \\ Z \\ W \\ P_3 \end{bmatrix} = \begin{bmatrix} a_{10} \\ a_{20} \\ 0 \end{bmatrix}$$

or

$$\mathbf{A}_r \mathbf{x}_r + \mathbf{A}_{n-r} \mathbf{x}_{n-r} = \mathbf{k}_r .$$

The solution for $D_1$, $S_1$, and $P_1$ of automobiles is then

$$\mathbf{x}_r = \mathbf{A}_r^{-1}(\mathbf{k}_r - \mathbf{A}_{n-r}\mathbf{x}_{n-r})$$

which we calculate using *Mathematica*.

*In[55]:=*
```
Clear[Y,Z,W,P2,P3];
Clear[a10,a11,a12,a13,a14,a20,a21,a22,a23];
Ar  =  {{1,0,-a11},{0,1,-a21},{1,-1,0}};
Anr  =  {{-a12,-a13,-a14,0,0},{0,0,0,-a22,-a23},
        {0,0,0,0,0}};
kr  =  {a10,a20,0};
xnr  =  {P2,Y,Z,W,P3};
xr  =  Inverse[Ar].(kr-Anr.xnr)
```

*Out[61]=*

$$\{\frac{\text{a11(a20 + a23P3 + a22W)}}{\text{a11} - \text{a21}} - \frac{\text{a21(a10 + a12P2 + a13Y + a14Z)}}{\text{a11} - \text{a21}},$$
$$\frac{\text{a11(a20 + a23P3 + a22W)}}{\text{a11} - \text{a21}} - \frac{\text{a21(a10 + a12P2 + a13Y + a14Z)}}{\text{a11} - \text{a21}},$$
$$\frac{\text{a20 + a23P3 + a22W}}{\text{a11} - \text{a21}} - \frac{\text{a10 + a12P2 + a13Y + a14Z}}{\text{a11} - \text{a21}}\}$$

With minor rearragement, the solutions become

$$D_1 = S_1 = \frac{1}{a_{11} - a_{21}} [(a_{11}a_{20} - a_{21}a_{10}) - a_{12}a_{21}P_2 - a_{13}a_{21}Y - a_{14}a_{21}Z + a_{11}a_{23}P_3 + a_{11}a_{22}W]$$

$$P_1 = \frac{1}{a_{11} - a_{21}} [(a_{20} - a_{10}) - a_{12}P_2 - a_{13}Y - a_{14}a_{21}Z + a_{23}P_3 + a_{22}W].$$

Alternatively, we may use the **Solve** function,

*In[62]:=*

```
eqns = {D1==a11*P1+a12*P2+a13*Y+a14*Z+a10,
         S1==a21*P1+a22*W+a23*P3+a20,
        D1==S1};
Solve[eqns,{D1,S1,P1}]
```

*Out[63]=*

$$\{\{D1 \to a20 + a23P3 + a22W - \frac{a21(-a10 + a20 - a12P2 + a23P3 + a22W - a13Y - a14Z)}{-a11 + a21},$$
$$S1 \to a20 + a23P3 + a22W - \frac{a21(-a10 + a20 - a12P2 + a23P3 + a22W - a13Y - a14Z)}{-a11 + a21},$$
$$P1 \to -(\frac{-a10 + a20 - a12P2 + a23P3 + a22W - a13Y - a14Z}{-a11 + a21})\}\}$$

## EXERCISES

1. Given the following system of equations, determine in each case whether or not the system is consistent. If so, find the general solution.

   (a)
   $$\begin{aligned} x + 2y - 3z &= -4 \\ 4x - y + 2z &= 8 \end{aligned}$$

   (b)
   $$\begin{aligned} x + 2y - 3z &= -4 \\ 4x - y + 2z &= 8 \\ 5x - 8y + 13z &= 25 \end{aligned}$$

2. Use the **Solve** function to solve the macroeconomic model given in example 5.2 in section 5.1.1 for the consumption $C$, investment $I$, and income $Y$.

3. Rearrange the equations given in example 5.13 so that $\mathbf{x} = [x_2\ x_5]$ and $\mathbf{A}_r$ is the coefficients of $x_2$ and $x_5$ in the first and third equations. Is this solution consistent with the solution given in example 5.13?

4. What happens if one uses the **LinearSolve** function on the systems in exercise 5.13?

# □ 5.3 Homogeneous Systems of Equations □

## 5.3.1 Solutions to homogeneous systems

A homogeneous system of linear equations is a set of equations of the form:

$$\begin{aligned} a_{11}x_1 + \ldots + a_{1n}x_n &= 0 \\ a_{21}x_1 + \ldots + a_{2n}x_n &= 0 \\ &\ldots\ldots\ldots\ldots\ldots \\ a_{m1}x_1 + \ldots + a_{mn}x_n &= 0. \end{aligned}$$

In matrix notation, it is written as $\mathbf{Ax} = \mathbf{0}$, where $\mathbf{0}$ is the $n \times 1$ zero vector.

Homogeneous systems always have the *trivial solution*, $\mathbf{x} = \mathbf{0}$, as a solution. Hence, a homogeneous system is always consistent. We also know that if $\mathbf{A}$ is square and nonsingular, that is, $m = n$ and $\rho(\mathbf{A}) = n$, then the system has a unique solution which must be the trivial solution, $\mathbf{x} = \mathbf{A}^{-1}\mathbf{0} = \mathbf{0}$. However, if $m \neq n$ or $\rho(\mathbf{A}) < n$, then it is possible to have a nontrivial solution.

For homogeneous systems with $m \neq n$, and $\rho(\mathbf{A}) = r$, there are $r$ linearly independent equations. Suppose that the first $r$ equations are linearly independent and that the variables of these $r$ equations are rearranged so that the first $r$ columns of $\mathbf{A}$ are linearly independent. Thus,

$$\begin{matrix} a_{11}x_1 + \ldots + a_{1r}x_r = -a_{1,r+1}x_{r+1} - \ldots - a_{1n}x_n \\ \vdots \qquad\qquad \vdots \qquad\qquad \vdots \qquad\qquad \vdots \\ a_{r1}x_1 + \ldots + a_{rr}x_r = -a_{r,r+1}x_{r+1} - \ldots - a_{rn}x_n. \end{matrix}$$

Expressed in matrix notation,

$$\mathbf{A}_r\mathbf{x}_r = -\mathbf{A}_{n-r}\mathbf{x}_{n-r}$$

where $\mathbf{A}_r$ is a nonsingular $r \times r$ matrix. The solution can then be written as

$$\mathbf{x}_r = -\mathbf{A}_r^{-1}\mathbf{A}_{n-r}\mathbf{x}_{n-r}.$$

The elements of the vector $\mathbf{x}_{n-r}$ may again be assigned arbitrary values, say $\mathbf{x}_{n-r}^0$. We then obtain a solution $\mathbf{x}_r^0 = -\mathbf{A}_r^{-1}\mathbf{A}_{n-r}\mathbf{x}_{n-r}^0$. The general solution to the system of $m$ equations is then

$$\mathbf{x} = \begin{bmatrix} \mathbf{x}_r \\ \mathbf{x}_{n-r} \end{bmatrix} = \begin{bmatrix} -\mathbf{A}_r^{-1}\mathbf{A}_{n-r}\mathbf{x}_{n-r} \\ \mathbf{x}_{n-r} \end{bmatrix}$$

**Example 5.16** Find a non-trivial solution of the homogeneous system of equations:

$$\begin{aligned} x_1 + x_2 + x_3 + x_4 &= 0 \\ x_1 + x_2 + 3x_3 + 4x_4 &= 0 \\ 2x_1 + 2x_2 + 4x_3 + 5x_4 &= 0 \end{aligned}$$

The coefficient matrix $\mathbf{A}$ is

$$\mathbf{A} = \begin{bmatrix} 1 & 1 & 1 & 1 \\ 1 & 1 & 3 & 4 \\ 2 & 2 & 4 & 5 \end{bmatrix}$$

and $\rho(\mathbf{A}) = 2$.

*In[64]:=*

```
A = {{1,1,1,1},{1,1,3,4},{2,2,4,5}};
rank[A]
```

*Out[65]=*

```
2
```

Since the third equation (third row of **A**) is a linear combination of the first and second equation, it can be discarded. Rearranging variables and moving $x_2$ and $x_4$ to the right side of equations, we have

$$x_1 + x_3 = -x_2 - x_4$$
$$x_1 + 3x_3 = -x_2 - 4x_4.$$

Thus

$$\begin{bmatrix} 1 & 1 \\ 1 & 3 \end{bmatrix}\begin{bmatrix} x_1 \\ x_3 \end{bmatrix} = -\begin{bmatrix} 1 & 1 \\ 1 & 4 \end{bmatrix}\begin{bmatrix} x_2 \\ x_4 \end{bmatrix}; \quad \text{or} \quad \mathbf{A}_r\mathbf{x}_r = -\mathbf{A}_{n-r}\mathbf{x}_{n-r}$$

We have the solution $\mathbf{x}_r = -\mathbf{A}_r^{-1}\mathbf{A}_{n-r}\mathbf{x}_{n-r}$.

*In[66]:=*

```
Clear[x2,x4]
Ar = {{1,1},{1,3}}; Anr = {{1,1},{1,4}}; xnr = {x2,x4};
xr = - Inverse[Ar].Anr.xnr // Simplify;
xr // MatrixForm
```

*Out[68]//MatrixForm=*

$$\begin{matrix} -x2 + \frac{x4}{2} \\ \frac{-3\,x4}{2} \end{matrix}$$

In other words, $x_1 = -x_2 + x_4/2$ and $x_3 = -3x_4/2$. The general solution **x** depends on the arbitrary values of $x_2$, and $x_4$:

$$\mathbf{x} = \begin{bmatrix} -x_2 + \frac{1}{2}x_4 \\ x_2 \\ -\frac{3}{2}x_4. \\ x_4 \end{bmatrix}$$

For example, if we set $x_2 = 1$ and $x_4 = 0$, then we obtain a particular solution

$$\mathbf{x}_1 = \begin{bmatrix} -1 \\ 1 \\ 0 \\ 0 \end{bmatrix}$$

If $x_2 = 0$ and $x_4 = 1$, then we have another particular solution

$$\mathbf{x}_2 = \begin{bmatrix} \frac{1}{2} \\ 0 \\ -\frac{3}{2} \\ 1 \end{bmatrix}$$

There are an infinite number of solutions.

We can solve this system with the **Solve** function to obtain the same result.

*In[69]:=*

```
Clear[x1,x2,x3,x4];
A = {{1,1,1,1},{1,1,3,4},{2,2,4,5}}; x = {x1,x2,x3,x4};
Solve[A.x == 0,{x1,x3}]
```

*Out[71]=*

$$\{\{x1 \to -x2 + \frac{x4}{2},\ x3 \to \frac{-3\,x4}{2}\}\}$$

## EXERCISES

1. What is the augmented matrix **M** for a homogeneous system? Is $\rho(\mathbf{A}) = \rho(\mathbf{M})$ in a homogeneous system?

2. Find the general solutions of the following homogeneous systems:
   (a) $x_1 + 2x_2 + 3x_3 = 0$
   $x_1 = 0$
   (b) $2x_1 - x_2 = 0$
   $10x_1 - 5x_2 = 0$
   $-2x_1 + x_2 = 0$
   (c) $2x_1 + x_2 - 3x_3 + x_4 = 0$
   $-x_2 + x_4 = 0$

3. Rearrange the equations given in example 5.16 so that $\mathbf{x}_r = [x_2\ x_4]$ and $\mathbf{A}_r$ is the coefficients of $x_2$ and $x_4$ in the second and fourth equations. Is this solution consistent with the solution given in Example 5.16?

4. A set of three price equations is
   $a_{11}P_1 + a_{12}P_2 + a_{13}P_3 = 0$
   $a_{21}P_1 + a_{22}P_2 + a_{23}P_3 = 0$
   $a_{31}P_1 + a_{32}P_2 + a_{33}P_3 = 0$

Use **Solve** to find the general solution of the prices $(P_1,P_2,P_3)$.

### 5.3.2 Fundamental sets of solutions

In the previous discussion we saw that a homogeneous system of linear equations may have an infinite number of solutions. In fact, any linear combination of the solutions is also a solution of the homogeneous system. If $\mathbf{x}_1$ is a solution vector of the equation, then any scalar multiple of the $\mathbf{x}_1$, $c\mathbf{x}_1$, is also a solution vector since

$$\mathbf{A}(c\mathbf{x}_1) = c\mathbf{A}\mathbf{x}_1 = \mathbf{0}.$$

If both $\mathbf{x}_1$ and $\mathbf{x}_2$ are solution vectors, then any linear combination of them, $c_1\mathbf{x}_1 + c_2\mathbf{x}_2$, is also a solution vector since

$$\mathbf{A}(c_1\mathbf{x}_1 + c_2\mathbf{x}_2) = c_1\mathbf{A}\mathbf{x}_1 + c_2\mathbf{A}\mathbf{x}_2 = \mathbf{0}$$

**Example 5.17** Consider the following homogeneous system,

$$\begin{aligned} x_1 + 6x_2 - 5x_3 + 2x_4 &= 0 \\ 3x_1 + 20x_2 - 15x_3 + 10x_4 &= 0 \\ 2x_1 + 10x_2 - 10x_3 \qquad &= 0 \end{aligned}$$

The coefficient matrix **A** has rank 2.

*In[72]:=*

```
A = {{1,6,-5,2},{3,20,-15,10},{2,10,-10,0}};
rank[A]
```

*Out[73]=*

```
2
```

Since the first two rows and first two columns of **A** are linearly independent, we choose $\mathbf{x}_r = [x_1\ x_2]$ to be solved in terms of $\mathbf{x}_{n-r} = [x_3\ x_4]$, using the **Solve** function.

*In[74]:=*

```
A = {{1,6,-5,2},{3,20,-15,10},{2,10,-10,0}};
x = {x1,x2,x3,x4};
Solve[A.x=={0,0,0},{x1,x2}]
```

*Out[76]=*

```
{{x1 → 5x3 + 10x4, x2 → -2x4}}
```

The general solution is

$$\mathbf{x} = \begin{bmatrix} 5x_3 + 10x_4 \\ -2x_4 \\ x_3 \\ x_4 \end{bmatrix}$$

Choosing $x_3 = 1$ and $x_4 = 0$, we have obtained a particular solution $\mathbf{x}_1$; choosing $x_3 = 0$ and $x_4 = 1$, we have another particular solution vector $\mathbf{x}_2$; that is,

$$\mathbf{x}_1 = \begin{bmatrix} 5 \\ 0 \\ 1 \\ 0 \end{bmatrix}; \ \mathbf{x}_2 = \begin{bmatrix} 10 \\ -2 \\ 0 \\ 1 \end{bmatrix}$$

Thus, for $c_1 = 2$ and $c_2 = -1$, the following vectors are also solutions:

$$c_1\mathbf{x}_1 = \begin{bmatrix} 10 \\ 0 \\ 2 \\ 0 \end{bmatrix}; \ c_2\mathbf{x}_2 = \begin{bmatrix} -10 \\ 2 \\ 0 \\ -1 \end{bmatrix}; \ c_1\mathbf{x}_1 + c_2\mathbf{x}_2 = \begin{bmatrix} 0 \\ 2 \\ 2 \\ -1 \end{bmatrix}$$

Let **X** be the collection of all solutions of $\mathbf{A}\mathbf{x} = \mathbf{0}$.

**X** is a vector space. In this context we refer to this vector space as the *solution space* of $\mathbf{Ax} = \mathbf{0}$. The dimension of the vector space is precisely the maximum number of linearly independent solution vectors in **X**. A basis for the solution space of a homogeneous system of equations is called a *fundamental set of solutions.*

The solution of the homogeneous system can be written as

$$\mathbf{x}_i = \begin{bmatrix} \mathbf{x}_r \\ \mathbf{x}_{n-r} \end{bmatrix}; \; i = 1,2,\ldots$$

where

$$\mathbf{x}_r = -\mathbf{A}_r^{-1} - \mathbf{A}_{n-r}\,\mathbf{x}_{n-r}.$$

The solution $\mathbf{x}_i$ depends upon the arbitrary assignment of the values for $\mathbf{x}_{n-r}$. The dimension of these vectors is $(n-r) \times 1$. We may set the vectors $\mathbf{x}_{n-r}$ to be any one of the following $(n-r) \times 1$ unit vectors,

$$\mathbf{x}_{n-r} = \begin{bmatrix} 1 \\ 0 \\ 0 \\ \cdot \\ \cdot \\ 0 \end{bmatrix}; \begin{bmatrix} 0 \\ 1 \\ 0 \\ \cdot \\ \cdot \\ 0 \end{bmatrix}; \ldots \begin{bmatrix} 0 \\ 0 \\ 0 \\ \cdot \\ \cdot \\ 1 \end{bmatrix}$$

It is obvious that these $n-r$ unit vectors are linearly independent. The corresponding solution vectors associated with these unit vectors must also be linearly independent and form a basis for the solution space. We therefore have the following theorem.

**THEOREM 5.2** *If the coefficient matrix* **A** *in a homogeneous system of linear equations* $\mathbf{Ax} = \mathbf{0}$ *is of rank r, then the dimension of the solution space is n–r.*

**Example 5.18** In the previous example, the general solution was found as

$$\mathbf{x} = \begin{bmatrix} 5x_3 + 10x_4 \\ -2x_4 \\ x_3 \\ x_4 \end{bmatrix}$$

By setting $\mathbf{x}_{n-r}$ to be either one of the following two vectors,

$$\mathbf{x}_{n-r} = \begin{bmatrix} x_3 \\ x_4 \end{bmatrix} = \begin{bmatrix} 1 \\ 0 \end{bmatrix} \text{ or } \begin{bmatrix} 0 \\ 1 \end{bmatrix},$$

we define a fundamental set of solutions:

$$\mathbf{x}_1 = \begin{bmatrix} 5 \\ 0 \\ 1 \\ 0 \end{bmatrix}; \; \mathbf{x}_2 = \begin{bmatrix} 10 \\ -2 \\ 0 \\ 1 \end{bmatrix}$$

Of course, any $n-r$ linearly independent solutions can be chosen as a basis of the solution space.

The implications of the rank of the coefficient matrix of $m$ homogeneous equations in $n$ unknowns on the dimension of the solution space are listed below.

(1) If $\rho(\mathbf{A}) = n$, then $\mathbf{x} = 0$ is the unique solution.

(2) If $\rho(\mathbf{A}) = r < n$, then the dimension of the solution space is $n-r$. That is, there are $n-r$ linearly independent solution vectors.

(3) If $m < n$, then $\rho(\mathbf{A}) = r \leq m < n$. The dimension of the solution space is again $n-r$. That is, if the number of equations is less than the number of unknowns, a nontrivial solution always exists.

(4) If $m = n$, then a nontrivial solution exists if and only if $\mathbf{A}$ is singular, i.e., $\rho(\mathbf{A}) = r < n$.

For any $m \times n$ matrix $\mathbf{A}$, the *null space* of $\mathbf{A}$ (also sometimes called the *kernel* of $\mathbf{A}$) is defined as the set of vectors $\mathbf{x}$ such that $\mathbf{Ax} = \mathbf{0}$ and is denoted as $N(\mathbf{A})$,

$$N(\mathbf{A}) = \{\mathbf{x} \mid \mathbf{Ax} = \mathbf{0}\}.$$

Notice that $\mathbf{x} = \mathbf{0}$ is always in the null space of $\mathbf{A}$. It can be shown that $N(\mathbf{A})$ is a vector space. Furthermore, the null space of $\mathbf{A}$ is identical to the solution space of $\mathbf{Ax} = \mathbf{0}$. Since the null space is a vector space, we can seek a basis for it. The dimension of the null space or the solution space is equal to $n-\rho(\mathbf{A})$. If $n = \rho(\mathbf{A})$, then the zero vector is the only solution vector and in this case the dimension of the null space is $\mathbf{0}$. The *Mathematica* function **NullSpace**, can be used to find a basis for the null space of $\mathbf{A}$.

*In[77]:=*
```
?NullSpace
```

**NullSpace[m] gives a list of vectors that forms a basis for the null space of the matrix m.**

**Example 5.19** Consider the homogeneous system

$$\begin{aligned} x_1 + x_2 + x_3 + x_4 &= 0 \\ x_1 + 2x_2 - x_3 - x_4 &= 0 \\ 2x_1 + 3x_2 \qquad &= 0. \end{aligned}$$

We first compute the rank of the coefficient matrix.

*In[78]:=*
```
A = {{1,1,1,1},{1,2,-1,-1},{2,3,0,0}};
rank[A]
```

*Out[79]=*
```
2
```

Hence the dimension of the solution space is 2. The **NullSpace** function returns a basis for the solution space.

*In[80]:=*

```
NullSpace[A]
```

*Out[80]=*

```
{{-3, 2, 0, 1}, {-3, 2, 1, 0}}
```

Thus, a basis of the solution space consists of two linearly independent solution vectors,

$$\begin{bmatrix} x_1 \\ x_2 \\ x_3 \\ x_4 \end{bmatrix} = \begin{bmatrix} -3 \\ 2 \\ 0 \\ 1 \end{bmatrix}; \begin{bmatrix} x_1 \\ x_2 \\ x_3 \\ x_4 \end{bmatrix} = \begin{bmatrix} -3 \\ 2 \\ 1 \\ 0 \end{bmatrix}$$

Alternatively, the solutions can be obtained using the **Solve** function. Since the first two rows and the first two columns of **A** are linearly independent, we select $\mathbf{x}_r = [x_1\ x_2]$ to be solved as a function of $\mathbf{x}_{n-r} = [x_3\ x_4]^T$.

*In[81]:=*

```
Clear[x1,x2,x3,x4];
A = {{1,1,1,1},{1,2,-1,-1},{2,3,0,0}};
x = {x1,x2,x3,x4};
Solve[A.x == 0,{x1,x2}]
```

*Out[84]=*

```
{{x1 → 3(-x3 - x4), x2 → -2(-x3 - x4)}}
```

Thus,

$$\mathbf{x}_r = \begin{bmatrix} x_1 \\ x_2 \end{bmatrix} = \begin{bmatrix} -3(x_3 + x_4) \\ 2(x_3 + x_4) \end{bmatrix}$$

Setting $x_3 = 0$ and $x_4 = 1$, we obtain a solution. Setting $x_3 = 1$ and $x_4 = 0$, we obtain a second linearly independent solution.

**Example 5.20** Consider the homogeneous system of equations:

$$\begin{aligned} -x_1 + x_2 + x_3 &= 0 \\ x_1 - x_2 + x_3 &= 0 \\ x_1 + x_2 - x_3 &= 0. \end{aligned}$$

We first compute the rank of the coefficient matrix.

*In[85]:=*

```
A = {{-1,1,1},{1,-1,1},{1,1,-1}};
rank[A]
```

*Out[86]=*

```
3
```

Since $\rho(\mathbf{A}) = 3$, the only solution is a zero vector. Therefore, the null space contains only the zero vector and a basis for the null space of **A** is the empty set.

*In[87]:=*
```
NullSpace[A]
```

*Out[87]=*
```
{ }
```

## EXERCISES

1. Find a basis of the solution space for each of the following systems of equations. Use the **NullSpace** function to check your answers.
   (a)
   $$\begin{aligned} 3x_1 + 2x_2 + 5x_3 &= 0 \\ x_1 - x_2 + x_3 &= 0 \\ 5x_1 + 7x_3 &= 0 \\ 9x_1 + x_2 + 13x_3 &= 0 \\ 2x_1 - x_2 + 8x_3 &= 0 \end{aligned}$$
   (b)
   $$\begin{aligned} x_1 + 2x_2 + x_3 - 2x_4 + x_5 &= 0 \\ x_2 - x_3 + x_4 &= 0 \\ 2x_1 + 3x_2 + x_3 - 5x_4 + 2x_5 &= 0 \end{aligned}$$

2. Suppose the homogeneous system of equations $\mathbf{Ax} = \mathbf{0}$ has a nontrivial solution. Does a solution exist for the nonhomogeneous system $\mathbf{Ax} = \mathbf{k}$? If so, is the solution unique?

# □ 5.4 Economic Applications □

## 5.4.1 Linear programming problems

Imagine a firm that produces two goods, each of which requires three factors of production: labor$(L)$, capital$(K)$, and energy$(E)$. Suppose it takes one unit of $L$, two units of $K$, and 15 units of $E$ to produce one unit of good 1. Similarly, it requires 2 units of $L$, one unit of $K$, and 3 units of $E$ to produce one unit of good 2. Furthermore, suppose the firm has a fixed endowment on inputs for production: 20 units of $L$, 15 units of $K$, and 100 units of $E$. Given the fixed endowment, any production of these two goods must satisfy the following inequality constraints,

$$\begin{aligned} x_1 + 2x_2 &\le 20 \quad \text{(labor input constraint)} \\ 2x_1 + x_2 &\le 15 \quad \text{(capital input constraint)} \\ 15x_1 + 3x_2 &\le 100 \quad \text{(energy input constraint)} \end{aligned}$$

where $x_1 \ge 0$ and $x_2 \ge 0$ are quantities of good 1 and good 2, respectively. The objective of the firm is to maximize the revenue (R) of its two outputs of the goods that are priced at \$3 for good 1 and \$2 for good 2. That is, we want to find the maximum value of

$$R = 3x_1 + 2x_2$$

subject to the above inequality constraints.

As we will discuss in another chapter, the problem of maximizing a linear objective function (the revenue) subject to a set of linear constraints (the endowments restric-

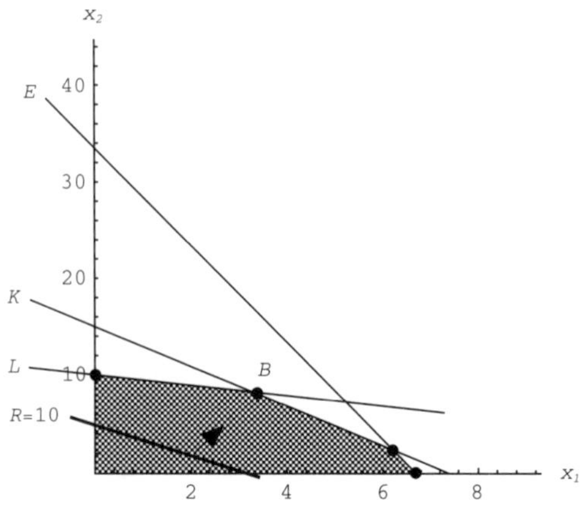


**Figure 5.1** Linear programming

restriction) is called a *linear programming problem*. In this section we shall illustrate the solution of the linear programming problem using the technique of finding feasible solutions of a nonhomogeneous linear system of equations. Before we proceed, however, take a geometric view of the problem. As shown in figure 5.1, the feasible output combination of $x_1$ and $x_2$ are restricted within the shaded area bordered by the three input endowments that must be satisfied simultaneously. The heavy line, $10 = 3x_1 + 2x_2$, represent an iso-revenue line at $R = \$10$. As the line shifts outward in a parallel fashion, higher revenue $R$ is obtained. Clearly, the higest attainable iso-revenue line will pass through the point $B$. Point $B$ is the solution of the linear programming problem. We will show that the maximum revenue is reached when $x_1 = 10/3$ and $x_2 = 25/3$.

We first observe that the linear constraints on input utilizations can be rewritten by introducing a new set of variables, called *slack variables*. For example, if $x_1 = 5$ and $x_2 = 6$, then a total of $17 = 5 + 2(6)$ units of labor is used. That leaves 3 units of labor input unused, or "slack." We define $s_1$ be the slack variable for labor input, the inequality in labor endowment can now be rewritten as the equality

$$x_1 + 2x_2 + s_1 = 20.$$

Obviously, the slack variable $s_1$ is nonnegative, $s_1 \geq 0$. Similarly, we define $s_2$ and $s_3$ be the slack variables for capital and energy inputs as

$$\begin{aligned} 2x_1 + \phantom{3}x_2 + s_2 &= 15 \\ 15x_1 + 3x_2 + s_3 &= 100. \end{aligned}$$

These three equality constraints form a system of three nonhomogeneous linear equations in five unknowns: $x_1$, $x_2$, $s_1$, $s_2$, and $s_3$. The equations can be expressed in a matrix form as

$$\begin{bmatrix} 1 & 2 & 1 & 0 & 0 \\ 2 & 1 & 0 & 1 & 0 \\ 15 & 3 & 0 & 0 & 1 \end{bmatrix} \begin{bmatrix} x_1 \\ x_2 \\ s_1 \\ s_2 \\ s_3 \end{bmatrix} = \begin{bmatrix} 20 \\ 15 \\ 100 \end{bmatrix}$$

That is

$\mathbf{Ax} = \mathbf{k}$

where the vector $\mathbf{x}$ includes the slack variables. The linear progamming problem becomes

maximize $R = 3x_1 + 2x_2$
subject to $\mathbf{Ax} = \mathbf{k}$

Below we show that the rank of $\mathbf{A}$ and the augmented matrix $\mathbf{M}$ is three, and hence, solutions to $\mathbf{Ax} = \mathbf{k}$ exists. The constraint system, $\mathbf{Ax} = \mathbf{k}$, can now be solved for a particular solution, say, $x_r = [x_1\ x_2\ s_1]^T$ by treating $x_{n-r} = [s_2\ s_3]^T$ as parameters with $s_2 = s_3 = 0$.

*In[88]:=*
```
A={{1,2,1,0,0},{2,1,0,1,0},{15,3,0,0,1}};
k={20,15,100};
rank[A]
rank[aug[A,k]]
```

*Out[90]=*
3

*Out[91]=*
3

*In[92]:=*
```
x={x1,x2,s1,s2,s3};
Solve[A.x  ==  k,  {x1,x2,s1}]  /.{s2->0,s3->0}
```

*Out[93]=*

$$\{\{s1 \to \frac{25}{3},\ x1 \to \frac{55}{9},\ x2 \to \frac{25}{9}\}\}$$

Since $x_1 = 55/9$, $x_2 = 25/9$, and $s_1 = 25/3$, are all nonnegative, and are within the input restriction,

$$\begin{aligned} 55/9 + 2(25/9) &= 35/3 < 20 \\ 2(55/9) + (25/9) &= 15 \\ 15(55/9) + 3(25/9) &= 100. \end{aligned}$$

The particular solution, $\mathbf{x} = [55/9\ 25/9\ 25/3\ 0\ 0]^T$, is feasible. This particular production results in a total revenue, R = 3(55/9) + 2(25/9) = 215/9 ≈ \$23.88. Other particular solutions are also feasible. For example, setting $\mathbf{x}_r = [x_1\ x_2\ s_3]^T$ and $\mathbf{x}_{n-r} = [s_1\ s_2]^T = [0\ 0]^T$, we obtain the particular solution, $\mathbf{x} = [10/3\ 25/3\ 0\ 0\ 25]^T$, which yields R = 3(10/3) + 2(25/3) = 80/3 ≈ \$26.66. This particular production plan, $x_1 = 10/3$, $x_2 = 25/3$, has higher revenue than the previous plan with $x_1 = 55/9$, $x_2 = 25/9$.

*In[94]:=*
```
Solve[A.x  ==  k,  {x1,x2,s3}]  /.{s1->0,s2->0}
```

*Out[94]=*

$$\{\{s3 \to 25,\ x1 \to \frac{10}{3},\ x2 \to \frac{25}{3}\}\}$$

In search for maximum revenue, other solutions need to be explored. For example,

$$\begin{array}{llll}
\mathbf{x}_r = [x_1 \quad x_2 \quad s_2]^T & \text{and} & \mathbf{x}_{n-r} = [s_1 \quad s_3]^T = [0 \quad 0]^T, \\
\mathbf{x}_r = [x_1 \quad s_1 \quad s_2]^T & \text{and} & \mathbf{x}_{n-r} = [x_2 \quad s_3]^T = [0 \quad 0]^T, \\
\mathbf{x}_r = [x_2 \quad s_1 \quad s_2]^T & \text{and} & \mathbf{x}_{n-r} = [x_1 \quad s_3]^T = [0 \quad 0]^T, \\
\mathbf{x}_r = [x_2 \quad s_2 \quad s_3]^T & \text{and} & \mathbf{x}_{n-r} = [x_1 \quad s_1]^T = [0 \quad 0]^T, \text{ etc.,}
\end{array}$$

are all possible particular solutions. However, not all of the particular solutions are feasible. For instance, $\mathbf{x}_r = [x_1\ x_2\ s_2]^T$ and $\mathbf{x}_{n-r} = [s_1\ s_3]^T = [0\ 0]^T$ is not feasible since the slack variable $s_2 = -25/9$ is negative.

*In[95]:=*

```
Solve[A.x == k, {x1,x2,s2}] /.{s1->0,s3->0}
```

*Out[95]=*

$$\{\{s2 \to -(\frac{25}{9}),\ x1 \to \frac{140}{27},\ x2 \to \frac{200}{27}\}\}$$

A solution by solution search of all feasible solutions yields the maximum revenue of $R = 3(10/3) + 2(25/3) = 80/3 \approx \$26.66$ with the output combination $x_1 = 10/3$, $x_2 = 25/3$. This is the point $B$ in figure 5.1.

## 5.4.2 Leontief input–output closed model

In this section we look at the "closed" variant of the Leontief input–output model presented in section 4.5.1 of Chapter 4. Departing from the previous model, the "closed" model contains no final demand or consumption by consumers. The consumers, or households, are treated just as any other sector or industry in an economy that produces output (labor). The households demand other sectors' output as input for producing "labor," and other sectors need labor service as an input of production. Viewing households as a production sector, say sector 0, expands the input coefficient matrix $\mathbf{A}$ to an $(n+1) \times (n+1)$ square matrix,

$$\mathbf{A} = \begin{bmatrix} a_{00} & a_{01} & a_{02} & \dots & a_{0n} \\ a_{10} & a_{11} & a_{12} & \dots & a_{1n} \\ a_{20} & a_{21} & a_{22} & \dots & a_{2n} \\ \dots & \dots & \dots & \dots & \dots \\ a_{n0} & a_{n1} & a_{n2} & \dots & a_{nn} \end{bmatrix}$$

The element $a_{ij}$ indicates the dollar value of good $i$ required to produce a dollar's worth of good $j$. The sum of the elements in the $j$-th column represents the "cost" of producing a dollar's worth of good $j$. Since there is no outside sector, all outputs, including labor, are used up somewhere in the input–output production process. Any column sum of $\mathbf{A}$ must be equal to 1, that is,

$$a_{0j} + a_{1j} + a_{2j} + \dots + a_{nj} = 1, \quad \text{for} \quad j = 0,1,2, \dots ,n.$$

Let $x_i$ be the total quantity of good $i$ produced and $a_{ij}x_j$ be the portion used as input in producing good $j$. At market equilbrium, the total output $x_i$ must be equal to the total demand for good $i$,

$$x_i = a_{i0}x_0 + a_{i1}x_1 + a_{i2}x_2 + \ldots + a_{in}x_n$$

for $i = 0,1,2, \ldots ,n$. Expressed in matrix form, the system is thus

$$\begin{bmatrix} x_0 \\ x_1 \\ x_2 \\ \cdot \\ \cdot \\ x_n \end{bmatrix} = \begin{bmatrix} a_{00} & a_{01} & a_{02} & \ldots & a_{0n} \\ a_{10} & a_{11} & a_{12} & \ldots & a_{1n} \\ a_{20} & a_{21} & a_{22} & \ldots & a_{2n} \\ \ldots & \ldots & \ldots & \ldots & \ldots \\ a_{n0} & a_{n1} & a_{n2} & \ldots & a_{nn} \end{bmatrix} \begin{bmatrix} x_0 \\ x_1 \\ x_2 \\ \cdot \\ \cdot \\ x_n \end{bmatrix}$$

or,

$$\mathbf{x} = \mathbf{A}\mathbf{x}, \quad \text{or} \quad (\mathbf{I} - \mathbf{A})\mathbf{x} = \mathbf{0}.$$

The Leontief "closed" model is in fact a homogeneous system of linear equations.

The Leontief closed model can also be viewed as a set of market price equations. The solutions of the system are the general equilibrium prices in an economy. The element $a_{ij}$ of $\mathbf{A}$ represents the value of the $i$-th input used in producing a dollar's worth of good $j$. Suppose $P_i$ is a unit price of good $i$. The product, $a_{ij}P_j$, is the dollar value of good $i$ used in the production of one unit of good $j$. The total dollar value of good $i$ used in the production of one unit of each good is the sum $a_{i0}P_0 + a_{i1}P_1 + a_{i2}P_2 + \ldots + a_{in}P_n$. This sum must be equal to a unit value, or the price $P_i$, for the market to be at equilbrium. The general equilibrium conditions for all markets is then

$$a_{i0}P_0 + a_{i1}P_1 + a_{i2}P_2 + \ldots + a_{in}P_n = P_i$$

for all $i = 0,1,2, \ldots ,n$. Expressing the $n$+1 conditions in matrix notation, we have

$$\begin{bmatrix} P_0 \\ P_1 \\ P_2 \\ \cdot \\ \cdot \\ P_n \end{bmatrix} = \begin{bmatrix} a_{00} & a_{01} & a_{02} & \ldots & a_{0n} \\ a_{10} & a_{11} & a_{12} & \ldots & a_{1n} \\ a_{20} & a_{21} & a_{22} & \ldots & a_{2n} \\ \ldots & \ldots & \ldots & \ldots & \ldots \\ a_{n0} & a_{n1} & a_{n2} & \ldots & a_{nn} \end{bmatrix} \begin{bmatrix} P_0 \\ P_1 \\ P_2 \\ \cdot \\ \cdot \\ P_n \end{bmatrix}$$

Or

$$(\mathbf{I} - \mathbf{A})\mathbf{P} = \mathbf{0}$$

The general equilibrium prices in an economy are the solutions of the homogeneous system of linear equations.

As an illustration, suppose an economy consists of three sectors, household, agriculture, and manufacture, which are designated as sectors 0, 1, and 2, respectively. Suppose the input coefficient matrix $\mathbf{A}$ is

$$\mathbf{A} = \begin{bmatrix} a_{00} & a_{01} & a_{02} \\ a_{10} & a_{11} & a_{12} \\ a_{20} & a_{21} & a_{22} \end{bmatrix} = \begin{bmatrix} 0.2 & 0.5 & 0.6 \\ 0.5 & 0.3 & 0.1 \\ 0.3 & 0.2 & 0.3 \end{bmatrix}$$

The household sector, for example, uses up $a_{10} = 0.5$ dollars of agricultural goods to produce a dollar's worth (wage rate) of one hour of labor service. The manufacturing sector uses $a_{02} = 0.6$ dollars of labor service as input in producing a dollar's worth of manufacturing good. The general equilibrium prices of labor service, agricultural good, and manufacturing goods are then the solutions of the homogeneous system

$$(\mathbf{I} - \mathbf{A})\mathbf{P} = \begin{bmatrix} 0.8 & -0.5 & -0.6 \\ -0.5 & 0.7 & -0.1 \\ -0.3 & -0.2 & 0.7 \end{bmatrix} \begin{bmatrix} p_0 \\ p_1 \\ p_2 \end{bmatrix} = \begin{bmatrix} 0 \\ 0 \\ 0 \end{bmatrix}$$

The null space of $\mathbf{I} - \mathbf{A}$ provide a basis of the solution space for $\mathbf{P}$.

*In[96]:=*

```
A  =  {{0.2,0.5,0.6},{0.5,0.3,0.1},{0.3,0.2,0.3}};
P  =  NullSpace[IdentityMatrix[3]-A]
```

*Out[97]=*

```
{{0.691925, 0.559429, 0.456376}}
```

How do we interpret the solution? Obviously it is difficult to interpret the negative prices in the price vector,

$$\mathbf{P} = \begin{bmatrix} p_0 \\ p_1 \\ p_2 \end{bmatrix} = \begin{bmatrix} -0.691925 \\ -0.559429 \\ -0.456376 \end{bmatrix}$$

However, the above basis of the price vector is not unique. Any scalar multiplication of the above solution is a solution. In general equilibrium models, we are concerned with *relative*, rather than *absolute* prices. It is the agricultural good (food price) relative to the household good (wage rate) that is important in an economy. It is possible to set the price $p_0$ to be equal to one, i.e., to choose the wage rate as the numeraire and obtain the relative prices of the other two goods in terms of the price of labor service. The general equilibrium prices with $p_0 = 1$ is then

$$\mathbf{P} = \begin{bmatrix} p_0 \\ p_1 \\ p_2 \end{bmatrix} = \begin{bmatrix} \dfrac{-0.691925}{-0.691925} \\ \dfrac{-0.559429}{-0.691925} \\ \dfrac{-0.456376}{-0.691925} \end{bmatrix} = \begin{bmatrix} 1 \\ 0.808511 \\ 0.659574 \end{bmatrix}$$

# 6

# Eigenvalues and Eigenvectors

In the previous three chapters, we have discussed some of the fundamental aspects of vectors, matrices, and systems of linear equations. A linear system of equations, $\mathbf{A}\mathbf{x} = \mathbf{k}$, can be thought of as a transformation of a vector $\mathbf{x}$ into a vector $\mathbf{k}$ by the matrix $\mathbf{A}$. When $\mathbf{A}$ is a square matrix we study a special set of vectors $\mathbf{x}$ that are mapped into scalar multiples of themselves; that is, $\mathbf{k} = \lambda\mathbf{x}$ where $\lambda$ is some constant. The constant is called an eigenvalue of $\mathbf{A}$ and $\mathbf{x}$ is called an eigenvector. Eigenvalues and eigenvectors are important concepts in economics for solving optimization problems, difference equations, and differential equations. These topics will be discussed in later chapters.

We first discuss linear transformations or mappings from one vector space to another vector space. These mappings are called linear transformations if they satisfy certain identities. Since any linear transformation on a vector space can be represented by a matrix, these properties will be given in terms of matrices.

## □ 6.1 Linear Transformations □

### 6.1.1 Definition

A real-valued function of a single variable $y = f(x)$ can be thought of as a rule for transforming a point $x$ in the domain of $f$ to a point $y$ in the range of $f$. The domain and range of $f$ are subsets of the real line. A generalization of $y = f(x)$ is a function (sometimes called a transformation) $T$ that assigns an $n$-dimensional vector $\mathbf{x} = [x_1\ x_2\ \ldots\ x_n]^T$ to an $m$-dimensional vector $\mathbf{y} = [y_1\ y_2\ \ldots\ y_m]^T$. We use the shorthand notation $\mathbf{y} = T(\mathbf{x})$. For example,

$$T(\mathbf{x}) = \begin{bmatrix} \sum_{i=1}^{n} x_i \\ \sum_{i=1}^{n} x_i^2 \\ \cdot \\ \cdot \\ \sum_{i=1}^{n} x_i^m \end{bmatrix} = \mathbf{y}$$

The set of all vectors **x** on which the transformation is defined is called the *domain* of $T$ and the set of all vectors **y** which come from the vectors in the domain is called the *range* of $T$. If $D$ denotes the domain of $T$, then the range of $T$ is the set $\{\mathbf{y}: T(\mathbf{x}) = \mathbf{y}, x \in D\}$.

The system of linear equations introduced in Chapter 5, $\mathbf{Ax} = \mathbf{y}$ is an example of a transformation, $T(\mathbf{x}) = \mathbf{y}$. If **A** is an $m \times n$ matrix, **x** is an $n \times 1$ vector, and **y** is an $m \times 1$ vector, then the transformation essentially associates each $n$-dimensional vector point **x** in the domain to a single $m$-dimensional vector point **y** in the range such that the components of **y** are given by

$$y_i = a_{i1}x_1 + a_{i2}x_2 + \ldots + a_{in}x_n, \quad \text{for} \quad i = 1,2, \ldots ,m$$

This transformation is an example of a linear transformation. A linear transformation satisfies two important properties:

(1) If $T(\mathbf{x}) = \mathbf{y}$ and $T(\mathbf{x}^0) = \mathbf{y}^0$, then $T(\mathbf{x}+\mathbf{x}^0) = \mathbf{y}+\mathbf{y}^0$.

(2) If $T(\mathbf{x}) = \mathbf{y}$, then $T(k\mathbf{x}) = k\mathbf{y}$, for any scalar $k$.

**Example 6.1** Consider the mapping of $T$ from 3-space into 1-space such that $y = T(\mathbf{x}) = x_1+x_2-2x_3$ where $\mathbf{x} = [x_1\ x_2\ x_3]^T$. This mapping is a linear transformation since

(1) $$\begin{aligned} T(\mathbf{x}+\mathbf{x}^0) &= (x_1+x_1^0) + (x_2+x_2^0) - 2(x_3+x_3^0) = (x_1+x_2-2x_3) + (x_1^0+x_2^0 -2x_3^0) \\ &= T(\mathbf{x}) + T(\mathbf{x}^0) = y+y^0 \end{aligned}$$

(2) $$\begin{aligned} T(k\mathbf{x}) &= (kx_1+kx_2-2kx_3) = k(x_1+x_2-2x_3) \\ &= kT(\mathbf{x}) = ky \end{aligned}$$

**Example 6.2** The transformation $y = T(\mathbf{x}) = x_1x_2 + x_2$ is not a linear transformation since

(1) $$\begin{aligned} T(\mathbf{x}+\mathbf{x}^0) &= (x_1+x_1^0)(x_2+x_2^0) + (x_2+x_2^0) \\ &= (x_1x_2+x_2) + (x_1^0x_2^0+x_2^0) + (x_1^0x_2+x_1x_2^0) \\ &= T(\mathbf{x}) + T(\mathbf{x}^0) + (x_1^0x_2+x_1x_2^0) \neq y+y^0 \end{aligned}$$

(2) $T(k\mathbf{x}) = (kx_1kx_2+kx_2) \neq kT(\mathbf{x})$

**Example 6.3** Suppose **A** is a $2 \times 2$ square matrix, and **x** is a vector in a 2-space such that

$$\mathbf{A} = \begin{bmatrix} 2 & 1 \\ 1 & 2 \end{bmatrix}; \ \mathbf{x} = \begin{bmatrix} 2 \\ 1 \end{bmatrix}$$

The linear transformation $T(\mathbf{x}) = \mathbf{Ax} = \mathbf{y}$ maps the vector $\mathbf{x} = [2\ 1]^T$ into the vector $\mathbf{y} = [5\ 4]^T$ as shown in figure 6.1.

**Example 6.4** The following four vectors $\mathbf{x}_i$ ($i = 1,2,3,4$) form a square in a two-dimensional space. As shown in figure 6.2 the linear transformation $\mathbf{Ax}_i = \mathbf{y}_i$ stretches and shifts the square formed by the **x**'s to the right and transforms it into a parallelogram.

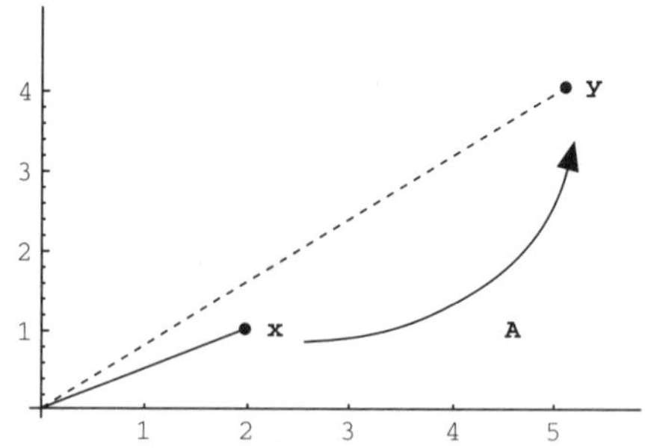


**Figure 6.1** Linear transformation from **x** to **y**

$$\mathbf{A} = \begin{bmatrix} 1 & 2 \\ 0 & 1 \end{bmatrix};\ \mathbf{x}_1 = \begin{bmatrix} 1 \\ 1 \end{bmatrix};\ \mathbf{x}_2 = \begin{bmatrix} 2 \\ 1 \end{bmatrix};\ \mathbf{x}_3 = \begin{bmatrix} 2 \\ 2 \end{bmatrix};\ \mathbf{x}_4 = \begin{bmatrix} 1 \\ 2 \end{bmatrix}$$

$$\mathbf{y}_1 = \begin{bmatrix} 3 \\ 1 \end{bmatrix};\ \mathbf{y}_2 = \begin{bmatrix} 4 \\ 1 \end{bmatrix};\ \mathbf{y}_3 = \begin{bmatrix} 6 \\ 2 \end{bmatrix};\ \mathbf{y}_4 = \begin{bmatrix} 5 \\ 2 \end{bmatrix}$$

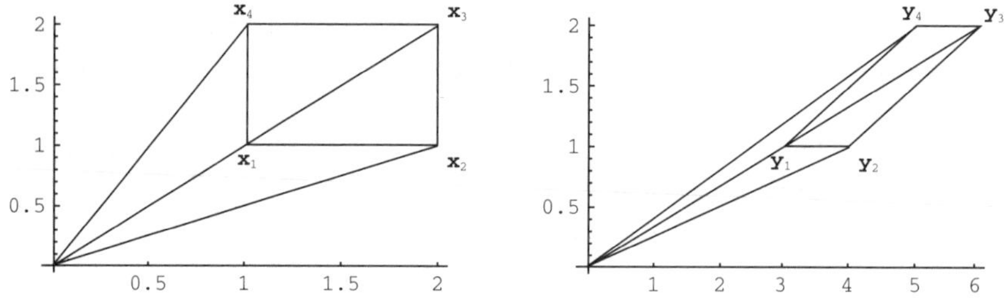


**Figure 6.2** Linear transformation from a square to a parallelogram

**Example 6.5** Let $\mathbf{x} = [x_1\ x_2\ \ldots\ x_n]^T$. The transformation $T(\mathbf{x}) = \mathbf{Ax}$ where $\mathbf{A} = [1/n\ 1/n\ \ldots\ 1/n]$ maps **x** to the mean of **x**, i.e.,

$$\mathbf{Ax} = \frac{1}{n}\sum_{i=1}^{n} x_i \equiv \bar{x}$$

and is linear. Let **B** be the $n \times n$ matrix

$$\mathbf{B} = \frac{1}{n}\begin{bmatrix} 1 & 1 & \ldots & 1 \\ 1 & 1 & \ldots & 1 \\ \ldots & \ldots & \ldots & \ldots \\ 1 & 1 & \ldots & 1 \end{bmatrix}$$

and $\mathbf{D} = \mathbf{I} - \mathbf{B}$. The linear transformation

$$\mathbf{Dx} = \begin{bmatrix} x_1 - \bar{x} \\ x_2 - \bar{x} \\ \cdot \\ \cdot \\ x_n - \bar{x} \end{bmatrix}$$

maps a vector onto the deviations from the mean.

## EXERCISES

1. Determine which of the following transformations $T(\mathbf{x}) = \mathbf{y}$ are linear transformations:
   (a) $\mathbf{x} = [x_1 \quad x_2]^T$ and $\mathbf{y} = [1+x_1 \quad x_2]^T$.
   (b) $\mathbf{x} = [x_1 \quad x_2]^T$ and $\mathbf{y} = [0 \quad 0]^T$.
   (c) $\mathbf{x} = [x_1 \quad x_2]^T$ and $\mathbf{y} = [x_1 \quad x_2^2]^T$
   (d) $\mathbf{x} = [x_1 \quad x_2]^T$ and $\mathbf{y} = [x_1^2 \quad x_2^2]^T$

2. Let the vector $\mathbf{x} = [x_1\ x_2]^T$. Find the matrix $\mathbf{A}$ such that $\mathbf{A}\mathbf{x} = \mathbf{y}$ in the following linear transformation.
   (a) $\mathbf{y} = [x_2 \quad x_1]^T$.
   (b) $\mathbf{y} = [0 \quad x_2]^T$.
   (c) $\mathbf{y} = [x_1+x_2 \quad x_2-x_1]^T$.
   (d) $\mathbf{y} = [x_1 \quad x_2 \quad x_1+x_2 \quad x_1-x_2]^T$.

### 6.1.2 Orthogonal transformations

If a matrix $\mathbf{A}$ satisfies the equation $\mathbf{A}^T\mathbf{A} = \mathbf{A}\mathbf{A}^T = \mathbf{I}$, then $\mathbf{A}^{-1} = \mathbf{A}^T$. Such a matrix is called an *orthogonal matrix*. For example,

$$\mathbf{A} = \begin{bmatrix} \frac{1}{\sqrt{2}} & -\frac{1}{\sqrt{2}} \\ \frac{1}{\sqrt{2}} & \frac{1}{\sqrt{2}} \end{bmatrix}$$

is an orthogonal matrix since $\mathbf{A}^T\mathbf{A} = \mathbf{I}$. Its inverse is

$$\mathbf{A}^{-1} = \mathbf{A}^T = \begin{bmatrix} \frac{1}{\sqrt{2}} & \frac{1}{\sqrt{2}} \\ -\frac{1}{\sqrt{2}} & \frac{1}{\sqrt{2}} \end{bmatrix}$$

It is obvious that if $\mathbf{A}$ is an orthogonal matrix, then $\mathbf{A}^{-1}$ is also an orthogonal matrix since

$$(\mathbf{A}^{-1})^T(\mathbf{A}^{-1}) = (\mathbf{A}^T)^T(\mathbf{A}^T) = \mathbf{A}\mathbf{A}^T = \mathbf{I}.$$

The linear transformation $T(\mathbf{x}) = \mathbf{A}\mathbf{x}$ where $\mathbf{A}$ is an orthogonal matrix is called an *orthogonal transformation.*

**Example 6.6** Consider the orthogonal matrix

$$\mathbf{A} = \begin{bmatrix} \frac{1}{\sqrt{2}} & -\frac{1}{\sqrt{2}} \\ \frac{1}{\sqrt{2}} & \frac{1}{\sqrt{2}} \end{bmatrix}$$

We can check that it is orthogonal by computing its inverse and comparing it with the transpose of $\mathbf{A}$.

*In[1]:=*

```
A = {{1/Sqrt[2],-1/Sqrt[2]},{1/Sqrt[2],1/Sqrt[2]}};
Inverse[A] == Transpose[A]
```

*Out[2]=*

```
True
```

The matrix **A** transforms the vector $\mathbf{x} = [2\ 1]^T$ into the vector $\mathbf{y} = [1/\sqrt{2}\ 3/\sqrt{2}]^T$ and is shown in the following plot using the **MathEcon** function **vector2d** introduced in Chapter 3.

$$\mathbf{Ax} = \begin{bmatrix} \frac{1}{\sqrt{2}} & -\frac{1}{\sqrt{2}} \\ \frac{1}{\sqrt{2}} & \frac{1}{\sqrt{2}} \end{bmatrix} \begin{bmatrix} 2 \\ 1 \end{bmatrix} = \begin{bmatrix} \frac{1}{\sqrt{2}} \\ \frac{3}{\sqrt{2}} \end{bmatrix} = \mathbf{y}$$

*In[3]:=*

```
x = {2,1}; y = A.x;
vecx = vector2d[x,"x"];
vecy = vector2d[y,"y"];
Show[vecx,vecy,Axes->True,AspectRatio->1];
```

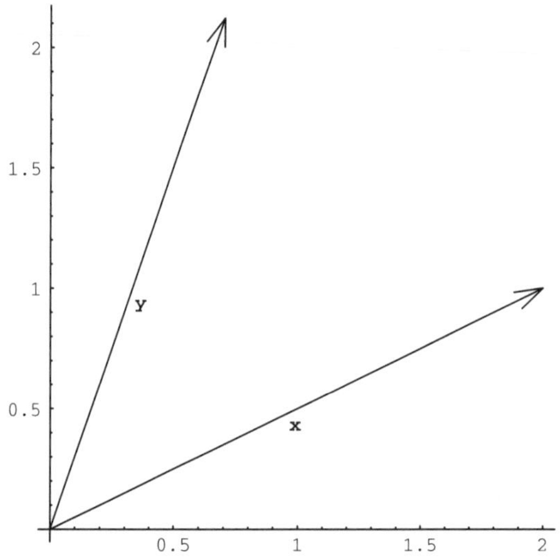


Several important properties of an orthogonal transformation $T(\mathbf{x}) = \mathbf{Ax} = \mathbf{y}$ exist. One property states that the lengths of the vectors **x** and **y** are equal. To see that this property holds true, we pre-multiply both sides of $\mathbf{Ax} = \mathbf{y}$ by its own transpose.

$$\mathbf{y}^T\mathbf{y} = (\mathbf{Ax})^T(\mathbf{Ax}) = \mathbf{x}^T\mathbf{A}^T\mathbf{Ax} = \mathbf{x}^T\mathbf{x}$$

This confirms that $\mathbf{y}^T\mathbf{y} = \mathbf{x}^T\mathbf{x}$, i.e., $\|\mathbf{y}\|^2 = \|\mathbf{x}\|^2$, or $\|\mathbf{y}\| = \|\mathbf{x}\|$. Geometrically, the orthogonal transformation rotates **x** without changing its length. In Example 6.6, the length of **x** is $\sqrt{5}$, which is equal to the length of **y**.

Furthermore, since $\mathbf{B} = \mathbf{A}^{-1}$ is an orthogonal matrix, the linear transformation from $\mathbf{y}$ to $\mathbf{x}$, $\mathbf{B}\mathbf{y} = \mathbf{A}^{-1}\mathbf{y} = \mathbf{x}$, also defines an orthogonal transformation. That is, if $T(\mathbf{x}) = \mathbf{y}$ is an orthogonal transformation, then so is $T^{-1}(\mathbf{y}) = \mathbf{x}$.

Finally, suppose $\theta$ is the angle between two vectors $\mathbf{x}_i$ and $\mathbf{x}_j$. From Chapter 3, the angle $\theta$ is equal to

$$\theta = \cos^{-1}\left(\frac{\mathbf{x}_i \cdot \mathbf{x}_j}{\|\mathbf{x}_i\| \, \|\mathbf{x}_j\|}\right)$$

where $\|\mathbf{x}_i\|$ and $\|\mathbf{x}_j\|$ are the lengths of vectors $\mathbf{x}_i$ and $\mathbf{x}_j$, respectively. Consider an orthogonal transformation of the vectors,

$$\mathbf{A}\mathbf{x}_i = \mathbf{y}_i \quad \text{and} \quad \mathbf{A}\mathbf{x}_j = \mathbf{y}_j$$

The angle $\phi$ between $\mathbf{y}_i$ and $\mathbf{y}_j$ must be equal to the angle $\theta$ between $\mathbf{x}_i$ and $\mathbf{x}_j$ since

$$\phi = \cos^{-1}\left(\frac{\mathbf{y}_i \cdot \mathbf{y}_j}{\|\mathbf{y}_i\| \, \|\mathbf{y}_j\|}\right) = \cos^{-1}\left(\frac{\mathbf{A}\mathbf{x}_i \cdot \mathbf{A}\mathbf{x}_j}{\|\mathbf{A}\mathbf{x}_i\| \, \|\mathbf{A}\mathbf{x}_j\|}\right)$$
$$= \cos^{-1}\left(\frac{\|\mathbf{A}\mathbf{x}_i\| \, \|\mathbf{A}\mathbf{x}_j\| \cos\theta}{\|\mathbf{A}\mathbf{x}_i\| \, \|\mathbf{A}\mathbf{x}_j\|}\right) = \cos^{-1}(\cos\theta) = \theta.$$

Thus, an orthogonal transformation preserves angles. The following two examples illustrate this property more clearly.

**Example 6.7** An orthogonal transformation, $\mathbf{A}\mathbf{x}_i = \mathbf{y}_i$, that is applied to the following four vectors, $\mathbf{x}_i$ ($i = 1,2,3,4$), will rotate a square formed by the tips of four vectors $\mathbf{x}_i$ into a square formed by the tips of corresponding four vectors $\mathbf{y}_i$ without altering the size (i.e., $\|\mathbf{x}_i\| = \|\mathbf{y}_i\|$) and the shape of the square (i.e., the angle between the vectors $\mathbf{x}_i$ and $\mathbf{x}_j$ is equal to the angle between the correspondent vectors $\mathbf{y}_i$ and $\mathbf{y}_j$). Notice in figure 6.3 that the rotation of vectors under orthogonal transformations is different from the rotation under non-orthogonal transformations as illustrated in figure 6.2.

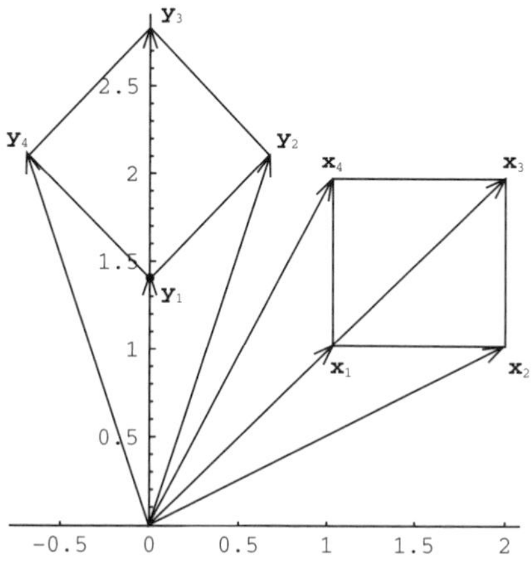


**Figure 6.3** Orthogonal transformation

**Example 6.8** The matrix

$$\mathbf{A} = \begin{bmatrix} \cos\theta & \sin\theta \\ -\sin\theta & \cos\theta \end{bmatrix}$$

is an orthogonal matrix for any θ. We can easily show that **A** is othogonal by computing its inverse and transpose.

*In[7]:=*

```
Clear[theta];
A = {{Cos[theta],Sin[theta]},{-Sin[theta],Cos[theta]}};
Inverse[A] == Transpose[A] // Simplify
```

*Out[9]=*

```
True
```

Imagine a set of vectors **x** whose vector tips form an ellipse. For $\theta = \pi/3$ (60 degrees), the orthogonal transformation rotates the ellipse (shown by the thicker line in figure 6.4) clockwise. The vectors $\mathbf{x}_1$ and $\mathbf{x}_2$ are rotated to $\mathbf{y}_1$ and $\mathbf{y}_2$, respectively. Again, the size and the shape of the ellipse remains unchanged.

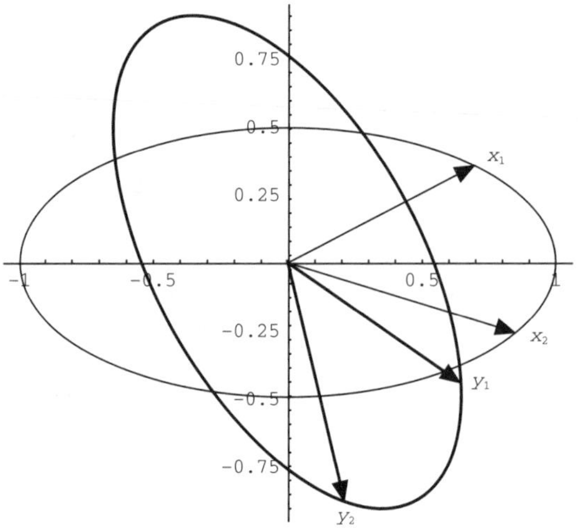


**Figure 6.4** Orthogonal transformation of an ellipse

## EXERCISES

1. Consider the linear transformation

$$\begin{bmatrix} y_1 \\ y_2 \\ y_3 \end{bmatrix} = \begin{bmatrix} \frac{2}{3} & \frac{1}{3} & -\frac{2}{3} \\ \frac{1}{3} & \frac{2}{3} & \frac{2}{3} \\ \frac{2}{3} & -\frac{2}{3} & \frac{1}{3} \end{bmatrix} \begin{bmatrix} x_1 \\ x_2 \\ x_3 \end{bmatrix}$$

(a) Show that the transformation is orthogonal.
(b) If $\mathbf{x} = [1\ 2\ 3]^T$, then find the vector $\mathbf{y}$ and show that the length of $\mathbf{x}$ is equal to the length of $\mathbf{y}$.
(c) Show that the angle between $\mathbf{x}_1 = [1\ 2\ 3]^T$ and $\mathbf{x}_2 = [-1\ 2\ 1]^T$ is equal to the angle between $\mathbf{y}_1 = \mathbf{A}\mathbf{x}_1$ and $\mathbf{y}_2 = \mathbf{A}\mathbf{x}_2$.

2. Show that the following transformations satisfy the equation $\mathbf{A}\mathbf{x} = \lambda\mathbf{x}$, where $\lambda$ is a scalar:

(a) $\mathbf{A} = \begin{bmatrix} 2 & 1 & -1 \\ 0 & 1 & 1 \\ 2 & 0 & -2 \end{bmatrix}$; $x_1 = \begin{bmatrix} 2 \\ 1 \\ 1 \end{bmatrix}$; $x_2 = \begin{bmatrix} 1 \\ -1 \\ 2 \end{bmatrix}$ $x_3 = \begin{bmatrix} 1 \\ -1 \\ 1 \end{bmatrix}$

(b) $\mathbf{A} = \begin{bmatrix} 1 & 1 \\ 2 & -1 \end{bmatrix}$; $\mathbf{x}_1 = \begin{bmatrix} 1-\sqrt{2} \\ 1 \end{bmatrix}$; $\mathbf{x}_2 = \begin{bmatrix} 1+\sqrt{2} \\ 1 \end{bmatrix}$

3. Suppose $\mathbf{A}\mathbf{x} = \lambda\mathbf{x}$, where $\lambda$ is a scalar. Find a scalar $\alpha$ in the transformation, $\mathbf{B}\mathbf{x} = \alpha\mathbf{x}$ where $\mathbf{B} = (\mathbf{A} - k\mathbf{I})$.

## □ 6.2 The Eigensystem of a Matrix □

### 6.2.1 Eigenvalues and eigenvectors

The *eigenvalues (characteristic roots)* and *eigenvectors (characteristic vectors)* of an $n \times n$ matrix $\mathbf{A}$ are scalars $\lambda$ and the $n \times 1$ nonzero vectors $\mathbf{x}$ that satisfy the equation

$$\mathbf{A}\mathbf{x} = \lambda\mathbf{x}.$$

For any square matrix $\mathbf{A}$, the above equation is equivalent to the system of $n$ homogeneous linear equations:

$$\mathbf{A}\mathbf{x} - \lambda\mathbf{x} = (\mathbf{A} - \lambda\mathbf{I})\mathbf{x} = \mathbf{0}.$$

These $n$ equations can be written as

$$\begin{aligned} (a_{11} - \lambda)x_1 + a_{12}x_2 + \ldots + a_{1n}x_n &= 0 \\ a_{21}x_1 + (a_{22} - \lambda)x_2 + \ldots + a_{2n}x_n &= 0 \\ \ldots\ldots\ldots\ldots\ldots\ldots\ldots\ldots\ldots\ldots\ldots \\ a_{n1}x_1 + a_{n2}x_2 + \ldots + (a_{nn} - \lambda)x_n &= 0 \end{aligned}$$

where $x_i$'s are the components of the vector $\mathbf{x}$. The set of $n$ equations has the trivial solution, $x_i = 0$. Thus, the zero vector, $\mathbf{x} = \mathbf{0}$, is always a solution. However, we are interested in only the nontrivial solutions. From Chapter 5, a necessary and sufficient condition for having a nontrivial solution is that $\lambda$ be so chosen that $|\mathbf{A} - \lambda\mathbf{I}| = 0$.

**DEFINITION 6.1** *Let $\mathbf{A}$ be an $n \times n$ square matrix, and $\lambda$ a scalar. The determinant $f(\lambda) = |\mathbf{A} - \lambda\mathbf{I}|$ is called the* ***characteristic polynomial*** *of $\mathbf{A}$. The equation $f(\lambda) = |\mathbf{A} - \lambda\mathbf{I}| = 0$ is called the* ***characteristic equation*** *of $\mathbf{A}$. The roots of the characteristic polynomial are called the* ***eigenvalues (characteristic roots,*** *or* ***eigenroots)*** *of the matrix $\mathbf{A}$. The nonzero vectors $\mathbf{x}$ which are the solutions $(\mathbf{A} - \lambda\mathbf{I})\mathbf{x} = \mathbf{0}$ are called* ***eigenvectors (characteristic vectors)*** *of the matrix $\mathbf{A}$.*

**Example 6.9** Find the characteristic equation and eigenvalues of the matrix

$$\mathbf{A} = \begin{bmatrix} 4 & -1 \\ 2 & 1 \end{bmatrix}$$

Since the characteristic polynomial is of second degree,

$$f(\lambda) = |\mathbf{A} - \lambda\mathbf{I}| = \begin{bmatrix} 4-\lambda & -1 \\ 2 & 1-\lambda \end{bmatrix} = \lambda^2 - 5\lambda + 6 = 0$$

it has two roots: $\lambda_1 = 3$, and $\lambda_2 = 2$. In the following *Mathematica* calculations, we use $k$ to denote an eigenvalue, $\mathbf{B} = \mathbf{A} - \lambda\mathbf{I}$, and $f$ as the characteristic polynomial.

*In[10]:=*

```
Clear[k,f];
A = {{4,-1},{2,1}};
B[k_]:= A - k*IdentityMatrix[2]; B[k] // MatrixForm
```

*Out[12]//MatrixForm=*

```
4 - k   -1
2       1 - k
```

*In[13]:=*

```
f[k_]:= Det[B[k]];
f[k]
```

*Out[14]=*

$6 - 5k + k^2$

*In[15]:=*

```
Solve[f[k]==0,k]
```

*Out[15]=*

```
{{k → 2}, {k → 3}}
```

If $\lambda_i$ is a eigenvalue so that $|\mathbf{A} - \lambda_i\mathbf{I}| = 0$, then the matrix $\mathbf{A} - \lambda_i\mathbf{I}$ associated with $\lambda_i$ is singular. The eigenvector $\mathbf{x}_i$ is a solution of the system of homogeneous linear equations,

$$(\mathbf{A} - \lambda_i\mathbf{I})\mathbf{x}_i = \mathbf{0}$$

**Example 6.10** Find the eigenvectors associated with the two eigenvalues, $\lambda_1 = 3$, and $\lambda_2 = 2$, in the previous example. For $\lambda_1 = 3$, the two homogeneous linear equations, $(\mathbf{A} - \lambda_1\mathbf{I})\mathbf{x}_1 = \mathbf{0}$, are

$$\begin{aligned} x_{11} - x_{12} &= 0 \\ 2x_{11} - 2x_{12} &= 0 \end{aligned}$$

where $x_{11}$ and $x_{12}$ are the components of $\mathbf{x}_1$. Hence, $x_{11} = x_{12}$. The eigenvector corresponding to $\lambda_1 = 3$ is

$$\mathbf{x}_1 = \begin{bmatrix} a \\ a \end{bmatrix}$$

where $a$ is an arbitrary nonzero constant. Suppose we let $a = 1$. The eigenvector associated with $\lambda_1 = 3$ is

$$\mathbf{x}_1 = \begin{bmatrix} 1 \\ 1 \end{bmatrix}$$

Since the value $a$ is arbitrary, the eigenvector is not unique. The eigenvector associated with $\lambda_2 = 2$ can be found to be

$$\mathbf{x}_2 = \begin{bmatrix} a \\ 2a \end{bmatrix}$$

for any arbitrary nonzero constant $a$. For $a = 1$, the second eigenvector becomes

$$\mathbf{x}_2 = \begin{bmatrix} 1 \\ 2 \end{bmatrix}$$

**Example 6.11** Demonstrate graphically the transformation, $\mathbf{A}\mathbf{x}_i = \lambda_i \mathbf{x}_i$, in example 6.10. The transformations extend the lengths of $\mathbf{x}_i$ without changing its directions. In the diagram below, the eigenvectors, $\mathbf{x}_1$ and $\mathbf{x}_2$, are shown with solid lines, and $\mathbf{y}_i = \lambda_i \mathbf{x}_i$ are shown with dashed lines.

*In[16]:=*

```
A = {{4,-1},{2,1}}; x1 = {1,1}; x2 = {1,2};
y1 = A.x1; y2 = A.x2;
vecx1 = vector2d[x1,"x1"];
vecx2 = vector2d[x2,"x2"];
vecy1 = vector2d[y1,"",dash];
vecy2 = vector2d[y2,"",dash];
Show[vecx1,vecx2,vecy1,vecy2,Axes->True];
```

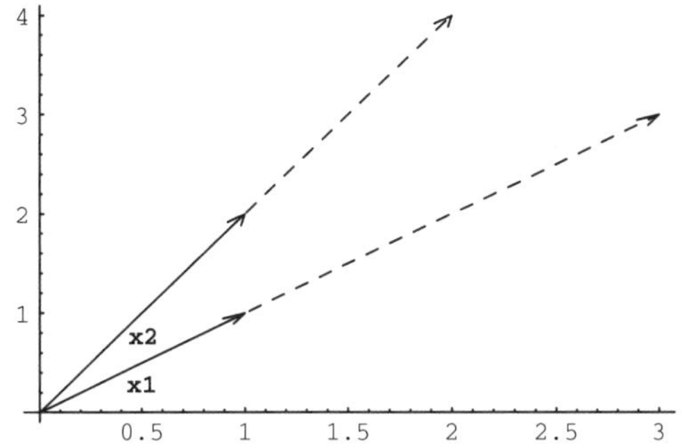


Since the eigenvectors are not unique, *normalized vectors* are frequently used to represent them. A normalized vector is a vector of unit length. The length of the vector $\mathbf{x}_1 = [a\ a]^T$ is equal to $a\sqrt{2}$. It is possible to normalize the vector $\mathbf{x}_1$ so that it has unit length. Dividing each component of the vector by its length, will result in a vector with unit length. Thus the normalized eigenvectors for $\mathbf{x}_1 = [a\ a]^T$ and $\mathbf{x}_2 = [a\ 2a]^T$ are

$$\begin{bmatrix} \dfrac{a}{\sqrt{2}a} \\ \dfrac{a}{\sqrt{2}a} \end{bmatrix} = \begin{bmatrix} \dfrac{1}{\sqrt{2}} \\ \dfrac{1}{\sqrt{2}} \end{bmatrix}; \begin{bmatrix} \dfrac{a}{\sqrt{5}a} \\ \dfrac{2a}{\sqrt{5}a} \end{bmatrix} = \begin{bmatrix} \dfrac{1}{\sqrt{5}} \\ \dfrac{2}{\sqrt{5}} \end{bmatrix}$$

**Example 6.12** Normalize the above eigenvectors $\mathbf{x}_1$ and $\mathbf{x}_2$ and display them. The two normalized vectors with unit length are labeled as $\mathbf{v}_1$, and $\mathbf{v}_2$ in the following graphic generated by *Mathematica.*

*In[23]:=*

```
A  =  {{4,-1},{2,1}};  x1  =  {1,1};  x2  =  {1,2};
v1  =  x1/Sqrt[x1.x1];  v2  =  x2/Sqrt[x2.x2];
y1  =  A.v1;  y2  =  A.v2;
vecv1  =  vector2d[v1,"v1"];
vecv2  =  vector2d[v2,"v2"];
vecy1  =  vector2d[y1,"",dash];
vecy2  =  vector2d[y2,"",dash];
Show[vecv1,vecv2,vecy1,vecy2,Axes->True];
```

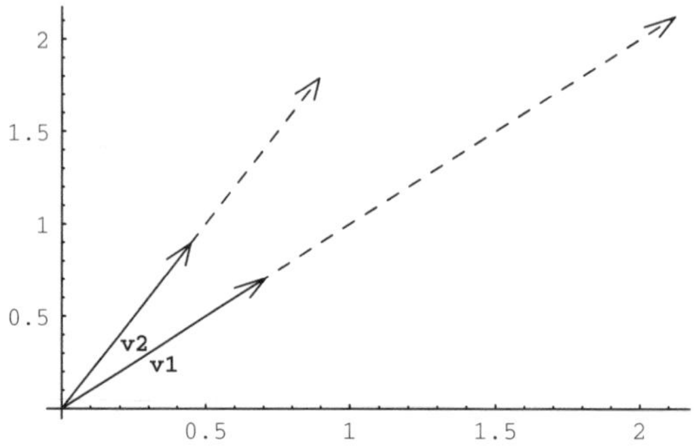


## EXERCISES

1. Consider the matrix

$$\mathbf{A} = \begin{bmatrix} 1 & 0 & 2 \\ 6 & -1 & 3 \\ 0 & 0 & 2 \end{bmatrix}$$

Find
(a) its characteristic equation; and
(b) its eigenvalues and associated normalized eigenvectors.

2. Find the eigenvalues and eigenvectors of

$$\mathbf{A} = \begin{bmatrix} 3 & 2 \\ 2 & 6 \end{bmatrix}$$

and using **vector2d**, plot its eigenvectors.

### 6.2.2 Finding eigenvalues and eigenvectors with *Mathematica*

Several functions are available in *Mathematica* to find the eigenvalues and eigenvectors of a square matrix **A**. For example, we have the *Mathematica* function **Eigenvalues** that computes the eigenvalues of a square matrix.

*In[31]:=*

```
?Eigenvalues
```

**Eigenvalues[m] gives a list of the eigenvalues of the square matrix m.**

*In[32]:=*

```
?Eigenvectors
```

**Eigenvectors[m] gives a list of the eigenvectors of the square matrix m.**

*In[33]:=*

```
?Eigensystem
```

**Eigensystem[m] gives a list {values, vectors} of the eigenvalues and eigenvectors of the square matrix m.**

**Example 6.13** Use *Mathematica* to find the eigenvalues and eigenvectors of the matrix

$$\mathbf{A} = \begin{bmatrix} -1 & -2 & -2 \\ 1 & 2 & 1 \\ -1 & -1 & 0 \end{bmatrix}$$

*In[34]:=*

```
A = {{-1,-2,-2},{1,2,1},{-1,-1,0}};
Eigensystem[A]
```

*Out[35]=*

```
{{-1, 1, 1}, {{2, -1, 1}, {-1, 0, 1}, {-1, 1, 0}}}
```

The eigenvalues and the corresponding eigenvectors are

$$\lambda_1 = -1;\ \lambda_2 = 1;\ \lambda_3 = 1$$

$$\mathbf{x}_1 = \begin{bmatrix} 2 \\ -1 \\ 1 \end{bmatrix};\ \mathbf{x}_2 = \begin{bmatrix} -1 \\ 0 \\ 1 \end{bmatrix};\ \mathbf{x}_3 = \begin{bmatrix} -1 \\ 1 \\ 0 \end{bmatrix}$$

We make the following observations:

(1) **Eigensystem** computes the eigenvalues and vectors at the same time. The output from **Eigensystem** is a list of two sublists. The first sublist contains the eigenvalues of **A** and the second sublist contains lists which are the eigenvectors of **A**. In the following calculations the symbol **roots** is a list of the eigenvalues and **vectors** to the eigenvectors.

*In[36]:=*

```
A = {{-1,-2,-2},{1,2,1},{-1,-1,0}};
{roots,vectors} = Eigensystem[A]
```

*Out[37]=*

```
{{-1, 1, 1}, {{2, -1, 1}, {-1, 0, 1}, {-1, 1, 0}}}
```

We can verify the result by picking the first root and the first vector and see if $\mathbf{A}\mathbf{x}_1 = \lambda_1\mathbf{x}_1$ is true.

*In[38]:=*
```
A.vectors[[1]]  ==  roots[[1]]*vectors[[1]]
```

*Out[38]=*
```
True
```

(2) For $n > 4$, the roots of the characteristic polynomial cannot, in general, be found. Even for a simple $2 \times 2$ matrix, the explicit form may be quite complicated,

*In[39]:=*
```
A  =  {{c,b},{-b,2c}};
Eigensystem[A]
```

*Out[40]=*

$$\{\{\frac{3c - \text{Sqrt}[-4b^2 + c^2]}{2}, \frac{3c + \text{Sqrt}[-4b^2 + c^2]}{2}\}, \{\{\frac{c + \text{Sqrt}[-4b^2 + c^2]}{2b}, 1\}, \{\frac{c - \text{Sqrt}[-4b^2 + c^2]}{2b}, 1\}\}\}$$

(3) Eigenvectors computed by *Mathematica* are not normalized. To normalize the vectors, divide each vector by its length.

*In[41]:=*
```
vectors[[1]]/Sqrt[vectors[[1]].vectors[[1]]]
```

*Out[41]=*

$$\{\text{Sqrt}[\frac{2}{3}], -(\frac{1}{\text{Sqrt}[6]}), \frac{1}{\text{Sqrt}[6]}\}$$

(4) Not all eigenvalues are real numbers. Consider the matrix

$$\mathbf{A} = \begin{bmatrix} 1 & 2 \\ -1 & -1 \end{bmatrix}$$

The characteristic equation, $f(\lambda) = \lambda^2 + 1 = 0$, has two complex roots which imply that the eigenvalues are $\lambda_1 = -i$, and $\lambda_2 = i$. However, *Mathematica* is still capable of finding the eigenvalues and eigenvectors in this case.

*In[42]:=*
```
A  =  {{1,2},{-1,-1}};
{roots,vectors}  =  Eigensystem[A]
```

*Out[43]=*
```
{{-I, I}, {{-1 + I, 1}, {-1 - I, 1}}}
```

## EXERCISES

1. Calculate the numerical eigenvalues and the normalized eigenvectors of the following matrices:

(a) $\mathbf{A} = \begin{bmatrix} 1 & 0 & 2 \\ 6 & -1 & 3 \\ 0 & 0 & 2 \end{bmatrix}$

(b) $\mathbf{A} = \begin{bmatrix} 1 & -1 & -1 \\ 2 & -2 & -2 \\ -1 & 1 & 1 \end{bmatrix}$

(c) $\mathbf{A} = \begin{bmatrix} 1 & -1 & -1 \\ -1 & -1 & -2 \\ -1 & -2 & 1 \end{bmatrix}$

2. Prove that eigenvalues of a real symmetric orthogonal matrix **A** are ±1. Using *Mathematica*, illustrate this fact with the matrix

$$\mathbf{A} = \begin{bmatrix} \frac{1}{\sqrt{2}} & \frac{1}{\sqrt{2}} & 0 \\ \frac{1}{\sqrt{2}} & -\frac{1}{\sqrt{2}} & 0 \\ 0 & 0 & 1 \end{bmatrix}$$

3. Prove that

$$\mathbf{A} = \begin{bmatrix} \cos(x) & \sin(x) \\ \sin(x) & -\cos(x) \end{bmatrix}$$

is an real symmetric orthogonal matrix. Using *Mathematica*, calculate the eigenvalues and the normalized eigenvectors.

4. Consider the $n \times n$ matrix

$$\mathbf{A} = \begin{bmatrix} 5 & -1 & -1 \\ -1 & 3 & 1 \\ -1 & 1 & 3 \end{bmatrix}$$

with an eigenvalue $\lambda$. Prove the following statements and use *Mathematica* to illustrate them for this specific **A**.
(a) $\lambda^n$ is an eigenvalue for $\mathbf{A}^n$, for any positive or negative rational number $n$.
(b) If **A** is nonsingular, then $1/\lambda$ is an eigenvalue of $\mathbf{A}^{-1}$.

### 6.2.3 An economic example

In this example we introduce a special type of matrix, called a *stochastic matrix.* Stochastic matrices and vectors are often used in the study of random phenomena where the exact outcome of events is unknown, but the probability of the outcome can be determined. In this example, we use a stochastic matrix to study the buying habits of gasoline customers of a fictitious oil company. First, we introduce the concepts of a stochastic vector and a stochastic matrix.

**DEFINITION 6.2** *A vector* $\mathbf{v} = [v_i]$ *is called a* ***stochastic vector*** *if* $0 \le v_i \le 1$ *and* $v_1 + v_2 + \ldots + v_n = 1$. *An* $n \times n$ *matrix* $\mathbf{A} = [a_{ij}]$ *is called a* ***stochastic matrix*** *if* $0 \le a_{ij} \le 1$, *and* $a_{1j} + a_{2j} + \ldots + a_{nj} = 1$, $j = 1,2, \ldots ,n$.

The elements of a stochastic vector or the columns of a stochastic matrix are usually associated with the probabilities of the outcome of a given event. For this reason, a stochastic matrix is often called the *matrix of transition probabilities*.

Let us consider the following situation which involves a stochastic matrix. The C-H Oil Company distributes three different grades of gasoline – Regular, Extra, and Super. The marketing department of C-H Oil Company has done a study of the purchasing habits of their customers. This study predicts the probabilities that customers will purchase a certain grade of gasoline based on the grade they chose in their last purchase. Here are the results of the study:

(1) Sixty percent of the customers who previously purchased the Regular grade will again purchase Regular. Twenty percent of the customers will switch to the Extra grade and 20 percent will buy Super.

(2) Seventy percent of the customers who previously purchased the Extra grade will again purchase Extra. Twenty percent of the customers will switch to the Regular grade and 10 percent will buy Super.

(3) Fifty percent of the customers who previously purchased the Super grade will again purchase Super. Twenty percent of the customers will switch to the Regular grade and 30 percent will buy Extra.

We can construct a stochastic matrix of transition probabilities. Namely,

$$\mathbf{A} = \begin{bmatrix} 0.6 & 0.2 & 0.2 \\ 0.2 & 0.7 & 0.3 \\ 0.2 & 0.1 & 0.5 \end{bmatrix}$$

The component $a_{ij}$ is the probability that a customer who bought the $j$-th grade will switch to the $i$-th grade. Thus $a_{23} = 0.3$ indicated a 30 percent chance of switching from Super grade ($j$=3) to Extra grade ($i$=2). This transition probability matrix may be regarded as describing the relative frequency distribution of change in grade loyalty. Let the vector, $\mathbf{x}_0 = [R_0\ E_0\ S_0]^T = [900\ 400\ 200]^T$, be the numbers of customers who purchase the Regular, Extra, and Super grades, respectively, initially ($t$=0). It is predictable that out of the 900 customers who purchase Regular initially, 540 of them, $a_{11}R_0 = 0.6(900)$, will still purchase Regular grade again at next purchase ($t$ = 1), 180 of them, $a_{21}R_0 = 0.2(900)$ will switch to Extra grade, and another 180 to Super grade. The relative frequency distribution of these 1500 customers' brand preference at the next purchase ($t$ = 1) will be

$$\mathbf{x}_1 = \mathbf{A} \cdot \mathbf{x}_0 = \begin{bmatrix} 0.6 & 0.2 & 0.2 \\ 0.2 & 0.7 & 0.3 \\ 0.2 & 0.1 & 0.5 \end{bmatrix} \begin{bmatrix} 900 \\ 400 \\ 200 \end{bmatrix} = \begin{bmatrix} 660 \\ 520 \\ 320 \end{bmatrix}$$

*In[44]:=*

```
A={{0.6,0.2,0.2},{0.2,0.7,0.3},{0.2,0.1,0.5}};
x0={900,400,200};
x1=A.x0
```

*Out[46]=*

```
{660., 520., 320.}
```

By repeated application, the relative frequency distribution the customers brand preference at various purchase ($t$=$n$) can be computed. For example, after two rounds of purchases ($t$=2), the distribution among the three grades is

$$\mathbf{x}_2 = \mathbf{A} \cdot \mathbf{x}_1 = \begin{bmatrix} 0.6 & 0.2 & 0.2 \\ 0.2 & 0.7 & 0.3 \\ 0.2 & 0.1 & 0.5 \end{bmatrix} \begin{bmatrix} 660 \\ 520 \\ 320 \end{bmatrix} = \begin{bmatrix} 564 \\ 592 \\ 344 \end{bmatrix}$$

*In[47]:=*

```
x2=A.x1
```

*Out[47]=*

```
{564., 592., 344.}
```

By iteration, this can be written as

$$\mathbf{x}_2 = \mathbf{A} \cdot \mathbf{x}_1 = \mathbf{A} \cdot (\mathbf{A} \cdot \mathbf{x}_0) = \mathbf{A}^2 \cdot \mathbf{x}_0$$

The process can be continued and the relative frequency distribution of the customers' brand preference at $t = k$ will then be

$$\mathbf{x}_k = \mathbf{A} \cdot \mathbf{x}_{k-1} = \mathbf{A}^k \cdot \mathbf{x}_0$$

An interesting fact about stochastic matrices is that products and powers of stochastic matrices are again stochastic. Hence, in this example, $\mathbf{A}^2$,$\mathbf{A}^3$, . . . will again be stochastic matrices. For example, the components of $\mathbf{A}^2$ and $\mathbf{A}^3$ are nonnegative and the columns sum to one.

*In[48]:=*

```
A2=A.A  //MatrixForm
```

*Out[48]//MatrixForm=*

```
0.44   0.28   0.28
0.32   0.56   0.4
0.24   0.16   0.32
```

*In[49]:=*

```
A3  =  A.A.A  //MatrixForm
```

*Out[49]//MatrixForm=*

```
0.376   0.312   0.312
0.384   0.496   0.432
0.24    0.192   0.256
```

We could use the *Mathematica* function **MatrixPower** to compute the integer powers of **A**. For example, to calculate $\mathbf{A}^4$ we use

*In[50]:=*

```
MatrixPower[A,4]  //MatrixForm
```

*Out[50]//MatrixForm=*

```
0.3504   0.3248   0.3248
0.416    0.4672   0.4416
0.2336   0.208    0.2336
```

Another interesting aspect of the stochastic matrix is the question of stability. Given $\mathbf{A}$ and $\mathbf{x}_0$, we would like to determine if the relative frequency distribution becomes stable after a finite number of iterations. This is called *finite stability*. That is, if $\mathbf{x}_{t+1} = \mathbf{A}\mathbf{x}_t$, does there exist a positive integer $N$ such that $\mathbf{x}_{N+1} = \mathbf{x}_N$ or $\mathbf{x}_N = \mathbf{A}\mathbf{x}_N$. After $N$ periods, the relative frequency distribution becomes constant. We now turn our attention to the finite stability condition that is closely related to the eigenvalues of the stochastic matrix $\mathbf{A}$. Here is an important characteristic of stochastic matrices.

**THEOREM 6.1** *Every stochastic matrix has $\lambda = 1$ as an eigenvalue.*

The theorem is easy to prove. Suppose $\mathbf{A} = [a_{ij}]$ is a stochastic matrix. If $\lambda = 1$ is an eigenvalue, then $|\mathbf{A} - \lambda\mathbf{I}| = |\mathbf{A} - \mathbf{I}| = 0$. That is,

$$|\mathbf{A} - \mathbf{I}| = \begin{vmatrix} a_{11}-1 & a_{21} & \cdots & a_{1n} \\ a_{21} & a_{22}-1 & \cdots & a_{2n} \\ \cdots & \cdots & \cdots & \cdots \\ a_{n1} & a_{n2} & \cdots & a_{nn}-1 \end{vmatrix}$$

Adding columns 2 to $n$ to the first column, we have

$$|\mathbf{A} - \mathbf{I}| = \begin{vmatrix} \sum_{j=1}^{n} a_{1j}-1 & \sum_{j=1}^{n} a_{2j}-1 & \cdots & \sum_{j=1}^{n} a_{nj}-1 \\ a_{21} & a_{22} & \cdots & a_{2n} \\ \cdots & \cdots & \cdots & \cdots \\ a_{n1} & a_{n2} & \cdots & a_{nn} \end{vmatrix}$$

Since the sum of elements in each column of a stochastic matrix $\mathbf{A}$ is 1, the first row of $|\mathbf{A} - \mathbf{I}|$ is zero and hence $|\mathbf{A} - \mathbf{I}| = 0$, which proves that $\lambda = 1$ is an eigenvalue.

Now we prove another theorem that will provide a necessary condition for finite stability.

**THEOREM 6.2** *Consider $\mathbf{x}_{N+1} = \mathbf{A}\mathbf{x}_N$. A necessary condition for finite stability, $\mathbf{x}_N = \mathbf{A}\mathbf{x}_N$, is that $\mathbf{A}$ is singular.*

Again this is easy to prove. Suppose that there exists a positive integer $N$ such that $\mathbf{x}_N = \mathbf{A}\mathbf{x}_N$. Since $\mathbf{x}_N = \mathbf{A}^N\mathbf{x}_0$, we have that $\mathbf{A}^{N+1}\mathbf{x}_0 = \mathbf{A}^N\mathbf{x}_0$. That is,

$$(\mathbf{A}^{N+1} - \mathbf{A}^N)\mathbf{x}_0 = \mathbf{A}^N(\mathbf{A} - \mathbf{I})\mathbf{x}_0 = 0.$$

Define $\mathbf{z}_0 = (\mathbf{A} - \mathbf{I})\mathbf{x}_0$. Since $\mathbf{x}_0$ is arbitrary, so is $\mathbf{z}_0$. Thus $\mathbf{A}^N\mathbf{z}_0 = 0$ implies that $\mathbf{A}^N$ is a singular matrix, and $|\mathbf{A}^N| = |\mathbf{A}| \cdot |\mathbf{A}| \ldots . |\mathbf{A}| = 0$. This is equivalent to $\mathbf{A}$ being singular.

In the gasoline example, let us check to see if finite stability exists.

*In[51]:=*

```
Det[A]
```

*Out[51]=*

```
0.16
```

Since, **A** is nonsingular, stability cannot be achieved in a finite number of purchases.

The economic applications of the stochastic matrix are enormous. For example, the distribution of wealth at any time period $t$ can be described by a vector $\mathbf{x}_t = [L_t\ M_t\ H_t]^T$, where the component gives the proportion of the population whose wealth falls into the categories of "low," "medium," and "high" classes, respectively. Suppose the stochastic matrix of transition from one category to another can be estimated. It is possible then to predict the distribution of wealth in the future. Other applications such as population migration, age distribution, business cycle, etc., have all been studied in using stochastic matrices.

## □ 6.3 Diagonalization of a Square Matrix □

### 6.3.1 Similar matrices

It is obvious that the eigenvalues of a diagonal matrix

$$\mathbf{D} = \begin{bmatrix} \lambda_1 & 0 & 0 & \dots & 0 \\ 0 & \lambda_2 & 0 & \dots & 0 \\ \dots & \dots & \dots & \dots & \dots \\ 0 & 0 & 0 & \dots & \lambda_n \end{bmatrix}$$

are precisely the elements on the diagonal. We will show that under some circumstances a square matrix **A** can be transformed into a diagonal matrix **D** using a nonsingular matrix, say **P**, with the transformation

$$\mathbf{P}^{-1}\mathbf{A}\mathbf{P} = \mathbf{D}.$$

This transformation is called a *similarity transformation.* We will then show that **A** and **D** have the same eigenvalues.

> **DEFINITION 6.3** *Two matrices* **A** *and* **B** *are said to be* ***similar*** *if there exists a nonsingular matrix* **P** *such that*
>
> $$\mathbf{P}^{-1}\mathbf{A}\mathbf{P} = \mathbf{B}.$$

Three important properties of similar matrices can be deduced from this definition. If **A** and **B** are similar matrices, then

(1) the determinants of **A** and **B** are equal;

(2) the two matrices have the same rank;

(3) **A** and **B** have the same characteristic polynomial and hence they have the same set of eigenvalues.

**Example 6.14** The following matrices

$$\mathbf{A} = \begin{bmatrix} 1 & 4 \\ 0 & -1 \end{bmatrix};\ \mathbf{B} = \begin{bmatrix} -1 & 4 \\ 0 & 1 \end{bmatrix}$$

are similar. The matrix in the similarity transformation is

$$\mathbf{P} = \begin{bmatrix} 2 & -3 \\ -1 & 2 \end{bmatrix}$$

First, we show that $\mathbf{P}^{-1}\mathbf{A}\mathbf{P} = \mathbf{B}$. Next we show that their determinants are equal, $|\mathbf{A}| = |\mathbf{B}| = -1$, as well as their ranks, $\rho(\mathbf{A}) = \rho(\mathbf{B}) = 2$.

*In[52]:=*
```
A = {{1,4},{0,-1}}; B = {{-1,4},{0,1}};
P = {{2,-3},{-1,2}};
Inverse[P].A.P == B
```

*Out[54]=*
True

*In[55]:=*
```
Det[A]==Det[B]
```

*Out[55]=*
True

*In[56]:=*
```
rank[A]==rank[B]
```

*Out[56]=*
True

Furthermore, the characteristic polynomials are identical.

*In[57]:=*
```
Det[A - k*IdentityMatrix[2]] == 0
```

*Out[57]=*
$-1 + k^2 == 0$

*In[58]:=*
```
Det[B - k*IdentityMatrix[2]] == 0
```

*Out[58]=*
$-1 + k^2 == 0$

A word of caution is in order. If **A** and **B** are similar matrices, then they have the same rank, the same characteristic polynomial, and the same eigenvalues, but not necessarily the same eigenvectors. As shown in the following calculation, the eigenvalues for **A** and **B** of the above example are –1 and 1, but the eigenvectors for **A** are $[-2\ 1]^T$ and $[1\ 0]^T$, while those for **B** they are $[1\ 0]^T$ and $[2\ 1]^T$.

*In[59]:=*
```
A = {{1,4},{0,-1}};
Eigensystem[A]
```

*Out[60]=*
{{–1, 1}, {{–2, 1}, {1, 0}}}

*In[61]:=*

```
B  =  {{-1,4},{0,1}};
Eigensystem[B]
```

*Out[62]=*

```
{{-1, 1}, {{1, 0}, {2, 1}}}
```

If a square matrix **A** is similar to a diagonal matrix **D**,

$$\mathbf{P}^{-1}\mathbf{A}\mathbf{P} = \mathbf{D}$$

then we say that **A** is *diagonalizable*. A diagonalizable matrix has eigenvalues equal to the diagonal elements of **D**. Not every square matrix is diagonalizable. The following theorem gives a condition under which a matrix is diagonalizable.

**THEOREM 6.3** *An $n \times n$ matrix* **A** *is diagonalizable if and only if it has n linearly independent eigenvectors.*

We will not prove the theorem, but will rather state an important implication of the theorem for finding the matrix **P**. Suppose $\mathbf{x}_1,\mathbf{x}_2, \ldots ,\mathbf{x}_n$ are the linearly independent eigenvectors with the corresponding eigenvalues $\lambda_1,\lambda_2, \ldots ,\lambda_n$. The $n$ equations, $\mathbf{A}\mathbf{x}_i = \lambda_i\mathbf{x}_i$, $i = 1,2, \ldots ,n$, can be expressed in matrix form:

$$\mathbf{A}[\mathbf{x}_1 \quad \mathbf{x}_2 \quad \ldots \quad \mathbf{x}_n] = [\mathbf{x}_1 \quad \mathbf{x}_2 \quad \ldots \quad \mathbf{x}_n]\begin{bmatrix} \lambda_1 & 0 & 0 & \ldots & 0 \\ 0 & \lambda_2 & 0 & \ldots & 0 \\ & \ldots & \ldots & \ldots & \\ 0 & 0 & 0 & \ldots & \lambda_n \end{bmatrix}$$

Define the $n \times n$ matrix

$$\mathbf{P} = [\mathbf{x}_1 \quad \mathbf{x}_2 \quad \ldots \quad \mathbf{x}_n]$$

The matrix **P** is called the *modal matrix* of **A**, which is a collection of the $n$ linearly independent eigenvectors and hence is nonsingular. Now let **D** be the diagonal matrix with the eigenvalues of **A** along the diagonal. Then the above $n$ equations can be written as

$$\mathbf{A}\mathbf{P} = \mathbf{P}\mathbf{D}$$

Pre-multiplying both sides by $\mathbf{P}^{-1}$, we find

$$\mathbf{P}^{-1}\mathbf{A}\mathbf{P} = \mathbf{D}.$$

Thus the matrix **A** is similar to a diagonal matrix **D** with the eigenvalues of **A** as the diagonal elements of **D**.

**Example 6.15** The $3 \times 3$ matrix

$$\mathbf{A} = \begin{bmatrix} -1 & -2 & -2 \\ 1 & 2 & 1 \\ -1 & -1 & 0 \end{bmatrix}$$

has the eigenvalues and the corresponding eigenvectors:

$$\lambda_1 = -1;\ \lambda_2 = 1;\ \lambda_3 = 1$$
$$\mathbf{x}_1 = \begin{bmatrix} 2 \\ -1 \\ 1 \end{bmatrix};\ \mathbf{x}_2 = \begin{bmatrix} -1 \\ 0 \\ 1 \end{bmatrix};\ \mathbf{x}_3 = \begin{bmatrix} -1 \\ 1 \\ 0 \end{bmatrix}$$

A modal matrix is

$$\mathbf{P} = \begin{bmatrix} 2 & -1 & -1 \\ -1 & 0 & 1 \\ 1 & 1 & 0 \end{bmatrix}$$

The following *Mathematica* calculations diagonalize the **A** matrix. Since the eigenvectors are arranged in rows in *Mathematica*, we need to take the transpose to obtain the modal matrix **P**. Lastly we show that

$$\mathbf{P}^{-1}\mathbf{A}\mathbf{P} = \begin{bmatrix} -1 & 0 & 0 \\ 0 & 1 & 0 \\ 0 & 0 & 1 \end{bmatrix} = \begin{bmatrix} \lambda_1 & 0 & 0 \\ 0 & \lambda_2 & 0 \\ 0 & 0 & \lambda_3 \end{bmatrix}$$

*In[63]:=*
```
A = {{-1,-2,-2},{1,2,1},{-1,-1,0}};
{roots,vectors} = Eigensystem[A]
```

*Out[64]=*
```
{{-1, 1, 1}, {{2, -1, 1}, {-1, 0, 1}, {-1, 1, 0}}}
```

*In[65]:=*
```
P = Transpose[vectors]; P // MatrixForm
```

*Out[65]//MatrixForm=*
```
2   -1  -1
-1  0   1
1   1   0
```

*In[66]:=*
```
Inverse[P].A.P // MatrixForm
```

*Out[66]//MatrixForm=*
```
-1  0  0
0   1  0
0   0  1
```

**Example 6.16** The following $3 \times 3$ matrix

$$\mathbf{A} = \begin{bmatrix} 2 & -1 & 1 \\ 3 & 3 & -2 \\ 4 & 1 & 0 \end{bmatrix}$$

has the eigenvalues $\lambda_1 = 1$, $\lambda_2 = 1$, $\lambda_3 = 3$, and eigenvectors $\mathbf{x}_1 = [0\ 1\ 1]^T$, $\mathbf{x}_3 = [2\ 1\ 3]^T$, namely, only two eigenvectors. We confirm this with *Mathematica*.

*In[67]:=*

```
A  =  {{2,-1,1},{3,3,-2},{4,1,0}};
{roots,vectors}  =  Eigensystem[A]
```

*Out[68]=*

```
{{1, 1, 3}, {{0, 1, 1}, {0, 0, 0}, {2, 1, 3}}}
```

Hence, we cannot construct a modal matrix $\mathbf{P} = [\mathbf{x}_1\ \mathbf{x}_2\ \mathbf{x}_3]$. This is an example of a matrix that cannot be diagonalized.

## EXERCISES

1. Are the following matrices similar?

   (a) $\mathbf{A} = \begin{bmatrix} 1 & 2 \\ 2 & 1 \end{bmatrix}$; $\mathbf{B} = \begin{bmatrix} -21 & -32 \\ 15 & 23 \end{bmatrix}$

   (b) $\mathbf{A} = \begin{bmatrix} 3 & 2 & 1 \\ 0 & 1 & 2 \\ 6 & 4 & 6 \end{bmatrix}$; $\mathbf{B} = \begin{bmatrix} -3 & -1 & -3 \\ 6 & 5 & 8 \\ -3 & -2 & -5 \end{bmatrix}$

2. Prove that the determinants of **A** and **B** are equal if they are similar.

3. Prove that $\mathbf{A}^T$ and $\mathbf{B}^T$ are similar if **A** and **B** are similar.

4. If there is one, find a modal matrix **P** that diagonalizes the matrix **A**. Show the eigenvalues of **A** are the diagonal elements of **D**.

   (a) $\mathbf{A} = \begin{bmatrix} 2 & 1 & -1 \\ 0 & 1 & 1 \\ 2 & 0 & -2 \end{bmatrix}$

   (b) $\mathbf{A} = \begin{bmatrix} 1 & 0 & 2 \\ 7 & -1 & 5 \\ 1 & 0 & 4 \end{bmatrix}$

   (c) $\mathbf{A} = \begin{bmatrix} 0 & 1 \\ 0 & 0 \end{bmatrix}$

   (d) $\mathbf{A} = \begin{bmatrix} 0 & 1 & 1 \\ 1 & 0 & 1 \\ 1 & 1 & 0 \end{bmatrix}$

   (e) $\mathbf{A} = \begin{bmatrix} 1 & 1 & 1 \\ 0 & 1 & 1 \\ 0 & 0 & 1 \end{bmatrix}$

### 6.3.2 Diagonalization of a real-symmetric matrix

An $n \times n$ matrix **A** is a *real-symmetric* matrix if its elements are real numbers, and $\mathbf{A}^T = \mathbf{A}$. Note that the matrix $\mathbf{A} = [a_{ij}]$ is symmetric if and only if $a_{ij} = a_{ji}$, $i,j = 1,2, \ldots ,n$. Two properties of a real-symmetric matrix are particularly relevant.

(1) The eigenvalues of a real-symmetric matrix are real.

(2) There exists $n$ eigenvectors of unit length and they are orthogonal to each other. This implies that a real-symmetric matrix is diagonalizable. Furthermore, the

modal matrix $\mathbf{P}$ is orthogonal, $\mathbf{P}^T\mathbf{P} = \mathbf{I}$, or $\mathbf{P}^T = \mathbf{P}^{-1}$. Hence, the diagonalizing transformation is

$$\mathbf{P}^T\mathbf{A}\,\mathbf{P} = \mathbf{D}.$$

**Example 6.17** Consider the real-symmetric matrix

$$\mathbf{A} = \begin{bmatrix} 3 & 1 \\ 1 & 3 \end{bmatrix}$$

The eigenvalues are $\lambda_1 = 2$, and $\lambda_2 = 4$. The corresponding two eigenvectors are the linearly independent vectors

$$\begin{bmatrix} -1 \\ 1 \end{bmatrix}; \begin{bmatrix} 1 \\ 1 \end{bmatrix}$$

Dividing each element of the eigenvectors by the length of the vector, $\sqrt{2}$, we obtain the normalized modal matrix

$$\mathbf{P} = [\mathbf{x}_1 \quad \mathbf{x}_2] = \begin{bmatrix} \frac{-1}{\sqrt{2}} & \frac{1}{\sqrt{2}} \\ \frac{1}{\sqrt{2}} & \frac{1}{\sqrt{2}} \end{bmatrix}$$

It is easy to show that $\mathbf{P}^T\mathbf{A}\,\mathbf{P} = \mathbf{D}$.

*In[69]:=*

```
A  =  {{3,1},{1,3}};
P  =  {{-1/Sqrt[2],1/Sqrt[2]},{1/Sqrt[2],1/Sqrt[2]}};
Transpose[P].A.P  //  MatrixForm
```

*Out[71]//MatrixForm=*

```
2  0
0  4
```

**Example 6.18** Consider the matrix $\mathbf{A}$ below. The eigenvalues $\lambda_i$, the modal matrix $\mathbf{P}$, and the diagonalization $\mathbf{P}^T\mathbf{A}\,\mathbf{P} = \mathbf{D}$ are presented in decimal form.

$$\mathbf{A} = \begin{bmatrix} 2 & 1 & 2 & 1 \\ 1 & 1 & 4 & 2 \\ 2 & 4 & 1 & 1 \\ 1 & 2 & 1 & 2 \end{bmatrix}; \; \lambda_1 = -3.326; \; \lambda_2 = 1.236; \; \lambda_3 = 0.837; \; \lambda_4 = 7.162$$

$$\mathbf{P} = \begin{bmatrix} -0.162 & -0.688 & 0.573 & 0.413 \\ -0.688 & 0.162 & -0.413 & 0.573 \\ 0.688 & -0.162 & -0.413 & 0.573 \\ 0.162 & 0.688 & 0.573 & 0.413 \end{bmatrix}$$

$$\mathbf{P}^T\mathbf{A}\,\mathbf{P} = \mathbf{D} = \begin{bmatrix} -3.236 & 0.000 & 0.000 & 0.000 \\ 0.000 & 1.236 & 0.000 & 0.000 \\ 0.000 & 0.000 & 0.837 & 0.000 \\ 0.000 & 0.000 & 0.000 & 7.162 \end{bmatrix}$$

These calculations are obtained using *Mathematica*. To save space, we have used the decimal representation of numbers. *Mathematica* function **Chop** replaces numbers less than $10^{-10}$ by 0.

*In[72]:=*

```
A = {{2,1,2,1},{1,1,4,2},{2,4,1,1},{1,2,1,2}};
{values,v} = Eigensystem[N[A]];
P = Transpose[Table[v[[i]]/Sqrt[v[[i]].v[[i]]],{i,4}]];
Chop[P] //MatrixForm
```

*Out[75]//MatrixForm=*

| | | | |
|---|---|---|---|
| 0.413453 | 0.16246 | −0.688191 | 0.573635 |
| 0.573635 | 0.688191 | 0.16246 | −0.413453 |
| 0.573635 | −0.688191 | −0.16246 | −0.413453 |
| 0.413453 | −0.16246 | 0.688191 | 0.573635 |

*In[76]:=*

```
Chop[Transpose[P].A.P] // MatrixForm
```

*Out[76]//MatrixForm=*

| | | | |
|---|---|---|---|
| 7.16228 | 0 | 0 | 0 |
| 0 | −3.23607 | 0 | 0 |
| 0 | 0 | 1.23607 | 0 |
| 0 | 0 | 0 | 0.837722 |

**Example 6.19** Home mortgage interest rates vary from one bank to another, yet they are highly correlated. Suppose the correlation matrix of mortgage rates charged by four banks is

$$\mathbf{A} = \begin{bmatrix} 1 & a_{12} & a_{13} & a_{14} \\ a_{21} & 1 & a_{23} & a_{24} \\ a_{31} & a_{32} & 1 & a_{34} \\ a_{41} & a_{42} & a_{43} & 1 \end{bmatrix} = \begin{bmatrix} 1.0 & 0.7 & 0.9 & 0.8 \\ 0.7 & 1.0 & 0.6 & 0.9 \\ 0.9 & 0.6 & 1.0 & 0.7 \\ 0.8 & 0.9 & 0.7 & 1.0 \end{bmatrix}$$

where the element, $a_{ij} = a_{ji}$, is the correlation coefficient between the $i$-th and $j$-th banks' rates. The vector $\mathbf{r} = [r_1\ r_2\ r_3\ r_4]^T$ represents interest rates charged by four banks. It is of interest to economists to obtain a market or composite rate, say $y$. The market rate is a weighted average of the four mortgage rates, $y = \mathbf{w}^T\mathbf{r}$, with the weights being the vector $\mathbf{w}$. In the statistical analysis of principal components, the weight vector $\mathbf{w}$ is the eigenvector of the largest eigenvalue of $\mathbf{A}$. In the following *Mathematica* calculation, we show that $\mathbf{w} = [0.515\ 0.484\ 0.484\ 0.515]^T$, which is the first eigenvector associated with the eigenvalues $\lambda_1 = 3.30312$. Thus the market or the weighted average rate is equal to

$$y = 0.515r_1 + 0.484r_2 + 0.484r_3 + 0.515r_4$$

*In[77]:=*

```
A = {{1.0, 0.7, 0.9, 0.8},{0.7, 1.0, 0.6, 0.9},
    {0.9, 0.6, 1.0, 0.7},{0.8, 0.9, 0.7, 1.0}};
Eigensystem[A]
```

```
Out[78]=
    {{3.30312, 0.523607, 0.096878, 0.0763932},
     {{0.515359, 0.484154, 0.484154, 0.515359}
      {0.371748, -0.601501, 0.601501, -0.371748},
      {-0.484154, 0.515359, 0.515359, -0.484154},
      {-0.601501, -0.371748, 0.371748, 0.601501}}}
```

## EXERCISES

1. Diagonalize the following matrices:

(a) $$\mathbf{A} = \begin{bmatrix} 2 & 0 & 1 \\ 0 & 1 & 0 \\ 1 & 0 & 1 \end{bmatrix}$$

(b) $$\mathbf{A} = \begin{bmatrix} 2 & 1 & 1 \\ 1 & 3 & -2 \\ 1 & -2 & 3 \end{bmatrix}$$

(c) $$\mathbf{A} = \begin{bmatrix} \cos(x) & \sin(x) \\ \sin(x) & -\cos(x) \end{bmatrix}$$

2. Suppose **A** is a $3 \times 3$ real-symetric matrix with eigenvalues $\lambda_i$ and vectors $\mathbf{x}_i$. Let the matrix $\mathbf{B} = k\mathbf{I} - \mathbf{A}$, where $k$ is a constant scalar. Does **B** have same eigenvectors as **A**? If so, are the eigenvalues of **A** also eigenvalues of **B**? Using *Mathematica*, demonstrate your conclusion with $k = 4$ and

$$\mathbf{A} = \begin{bmatrix} 2 & 1 & 1 \\ 1 & 1 & 0 \\ 1 & 0 & 1 \end{bmatrix}$$

### 6.3.3 Orthogonal transformation and change of basis

Consider a vector $\mathbf{x} = [x_1\ x_2]^T$. Obviously the vector can be expressed as a linear combination of two linearly independent unit vectors, $\mathbf{I}_1 = [1\ 0]^T$, and $\mathbf{I}_2 = [0\ 1]^T$. That is,

$$\mathbf{x} = \begin{bmatrix} x_1 \\ x_2 \end{bmatrix} = x_1\begin{bmatrix} 1 \\ 0 \end{bmatrix} + x_2\begin{bmatrix} 0 \\ 1 \end{bmatrix} = x_1\mathbf{I}_1 + x_2\mathbf{I}_2$$
$$= \mathbf{Ix}$$

where **I** is the $2 \times 2$ identity matrix. The two unit vectors, $\mathbf{I}_1$ and $\mathbf{I}_2$, are a basis for a two-dimensional vector space, say $\mathbf{V}^2$, and we shall call them the **I**-*basis* for $\mathbf{V}^2$. The elements, $x_1$ and $x_2$, are the coordinates of the vector **x** with respect to this basis.

Now consider two orthogonal vectors of unit length

$$\mathbf{p}_1 = \begin{bmatrix} -\frac{1}{\sqrt{2}} \\ \frac{1}{\sqrt{2}} \end{bmatrix}; \ \mathbf{p}_2 = \begin{bmatrix} \frac{1}{\sqrt{2}} \\ \frac{1}{\sqrt{2}} \end{bmatrix}$$

Since these two vectors $\mathbf{p}_1$ and $\mathbf{p}_2$ are linearly independent, the vectors can also serve as a basis on the same $\mathbf{V}^2$. The vector **x** can then be expressed as a linear combination of $\mathbf{p}_1$ and $\mathbf{p}_2$,

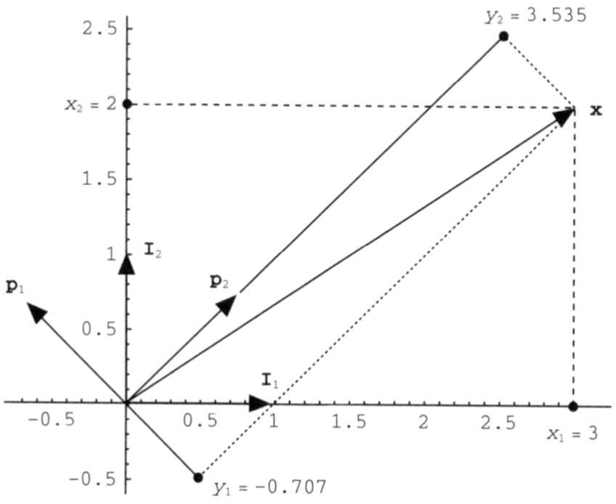


**Figure 6.5** Change of basis

$$\mathbf{x} = y_1\mathbf{p}_1 + y_2\mathbf{p}_2 = \mathbf{P}\mathbf{y}.$$

Let $\mathbf{P}$ denote the $2 \times 2$ matrix $[\mathbf{p}_1\ \mathbf{p}_2]$. The coordinates of $\mathbf{y}$, $y_1$ and $y_2$, are then the coordinates of $\mathbf{x}$ with respect to the $\mathbf{P}$-basis. To obtain the vector $\mathbf{y}$, we pre-multiply both sides by $\mathbf{P}^{-1}$, which is equal to the transpose $\mathbf{P}^T$ since $\mathbf{P}$ is an orthogonal matrix,

$$\mathbf{y} = \mathbf{P}^T\mathbf{x}$$

From an algebraic point of view, the above equation is a change of basis formula. That is, the matrix $\mathbf{P}^T$ gives a way of converting the coordinates of $\mathbf{x}$ with respect to the $\mathbf{I}$-basis to the coordinates of $\mathbf{x}$ with respect to the $\mathbf{P}$-basis.

**Example 6.20** The vector $\mathbf{x} = [3\ 2]^T$ has the coordinates $x_1 = 3$ and $x_2 = 2$ with respect to the $\mathbf{I}$-basis. It has coordinates with respect to the $\mathbf{P}$-basis

$$\mathbf{y} = \begin{bmatrix} y_1 \\ y_2 \end{bmatrix} = \mathbf{P}^T\mathbf{x} = \begin{bmatrix} \frac{-1}{\sqrt{2}} & \frac{1}{\sqrt{2}} \\ \frac{1}{\sqrt{2}} & \frac{1}{\sqrt{2}} \end{bmatrix} \begin{bmatrix} 3 \\ 2 \end{bmatrix} = \begin{bmatrix} \frac{-1}{\sqrt{2}} \\ \frac{5}{\sqrt{2}} \end{bmatrix}$$

The coordinate $y_1$ of $\mathbf{y}$ is $-1/\sqrt{2} \approx -0.707$, and the coordinate $y_2$ of $\mathbf{y}$ is $5/\sqrt{2} \approx 3.535$. That is, $\mathbf{y} = y_1\mathbf{p}_1 + y_2\mathbf{p}_2$. In figure 6.5 we show how the vector $\mathbf{x}$ is represented in the $\mathbf{I}$-basis with coordinates $(x_1,x_2)$ and in the basis $[\mathbf{p}_1\ \mathbf{p}_2]$, which we will call the $\mathbf{P}$-basis, with coordinates $(y_1,y_2)$.

We now extend this idea to $n$-space. A new basis $\{\mathbf{p}_1\ \mathbf{p}_2 \ldots \mathbf{p}_n\}$ for an $n$-dimensional vector $\mathbf{x}$ does not have to be composed of orthogonal vectors. It is necessary and sufficient that the vectors $\{\mathbf{p}_1\ \mathbf{p}_2 \ldots \mathbf{p}_n\}$ are linearly independent and span the vector space $\mathbf{V}^n$. Consider the vector space $\mathbf{V}^n$. The $\mathbf{I}$-basis of $\mathbf{V}^n$ consists of the $n$ unit vectors $\mathbf{I}_i$ from which we can construct the $n \times n$ identity matrix $\mathbf{I} = [\mathbf{I}_1\ \mathbf{I}_2 \ldots \mathbf{I}_n]$. With the $\mathbf{P}$-basis in mind, we then we construct the matrix $\mathbf{P}$ such that

$$\mathbf{P} = [\mathbf{p}_1 \quad \mathbf{p}_2 \quad \ldots \quad \mathbf{p}_n]$$

where the $n$ basis vectors $\mathbf{p}_i$ are linearly independent and span $\mathbf{V}^n$. One can show that if $\mathbf{x}$ is a vector represented in the **I**-basis, i.e., $\mathbf{x} = \mathbf{I}\mathbf{x}$, then this same vector can be represented in the **P**-basis, i.e.,

$$\mathbf{x} = \mathbf{P}\mathbf{y}.$$

The new coordinates of $\mathbf{y} = [y_1\ y_2 \ldots y_n]^T$ for the vector $\mathbf{x}$ with respect to the **P**-basis is then equal to

$$\mathbf{y} = \mathbf{P}^{-1}\mathbf{x}.$$

To geometrically show the change of coordinates of a vector $\mathbf{x}$ with a new basis, we have the **MathEcon** function **changebasis** which draws the analogue of figure 6.5. Here is the description of this function.

*In[79]:=*

```
?changebasis
```

**changebasis[vect1,bas,"label1","basislabel"] creates a graphic that illustrates how the vector vect1 given in the usual basis {{1,0},{0,1}} appears in the basis bas. The given vector and the basis vectors can have labels (strings). For example,**

**changebasis[{-1,3},{{-1,1},{0,1}},"a","b"].**

The first argument is the vector that will be expressed in the new basis, and the second argument is the new basis. The third and fourth arguments are optional and they represent the symbols for the vector in the first argument and the symbol for the vectors in the basis. If they are omitted, they are assumed to be **x** and **P**. The function **changebasis** produces a graphic that must be displayed with the **Show** function.

**Example 6.21** The new coordinates of $\mathbf{x} = [3\ 4]^T$ with respect to the **P**-basis

$$\mathbf{P} = [\mathbf{p}_1 \quad \mathbf{p}_2] = \begin{bmatrix} 2 & 1 \\ 1 & 2 \end{bmatrix}$$

are:

$$\mathbf{y} = \mathbf{P}^{-1}\mathbf{x} = \begin{bmatrix} \frac{2}{3} & \frac{-1}{3} \\ \frac{-1}{3} & \frac{2}{3} \end{bmatrix} \begin{bmatrix} 3 \\ 4 \end{bmatrix} = \begin{bmatrix} \frac{2}{3} \\ \frac{5}{3} \end{bmatrix}$$

*In[80]:=*

```
x = {3,4}; P = {{2,1},{1,2}};
basis = changebasis[x,P,"x","p"];
Show[basis,Axes->Automatic,AspectRatio->Automatic];
```

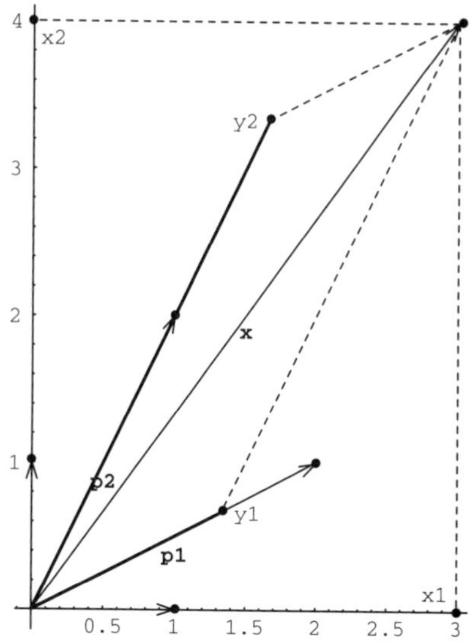


As we can see from the graphic above, the vector $\mathbf{x} = [3\ 4]^T$ in $\mathbf{V}^2$ can be represented as a linear combination of vectors in two ways:

$$\begin{aligned}\mathbf{x} &= x_1\mathbf{I}_1 + x_2\mathbf{I}_2 = \mathbf{I}\mathbf{x}\\ &= y_1\mathbf{p}_1 + y_2\mathbf{p}_2 = \mathbf{P}\mathbf{y}\end{aligned}$$

Suppose we have the linear transformation $\mathbf{z} = \mathbf{A}\mathbf{x}$. The vector $\mathbf{x}$ is mapped onto $\mathbf{z}$ by the matrix $\mathbf{A}$. Suppose both the vectors $\mathbf{x}$ and $\mathbf{y}$ are expressed in terms of the $\mathbf{I}$-basis. The transformation can be written more precisely as

$$(\mathbf{I}\mathbf{z}) = \mathbf{A}(\mathbf{I}\mathbf{x}).$$

Suppose $\mathbf{A}$ can be diagonalized and the modal matrix of $\mathbf{A}$ is the matrix $\mathbf{P}$. That is, $\mathbf{D} = \mathbf{P}^{-1}\mathbf{A}\mathbf{P}$ is a diagonal matrix with the eigenvalues of $\mathbf{A}$ along its diagonal. Let $\mathbf{P}$ be the change of basis matrix. Since $\mathbf{P}$ is composed of eigenvectors of $\mathbf{A}$, the new $\mathbf{P}$-basis will also consist of the eigenvectors of $\mathbf{A}$. Let $\mathbf{x} = \mathbf{P}\mathbf{u}$ and $\mathbf{z} = \mathbf{P}\mathbf{v}$. $\mathbf{u}$ and $\mathbf{v}$ are the representations of $\mathbf{x}$ and $\mathbf{z}$, respectively, in the new basis. The linear transformation then becomes

$$(\mathbf{P}\mathbf{v}) = \mathbf{A}(\mathbf{P}\mathbf{u}).$$

We may view the two linear transformations as

$$(\mathbf{I}\mathbf{z}) = \mathbf{A}(\mathbf{I}\mathbf{x}) \quad \text{and} \quad (\mathbf{P}\mathbf{v}) = \mathbf{A}(\mathbf{P}\mathbf{u})$$

which represent the same transformation, but with respect to two different bases. The former is with respect to the $\mathbf{I}$-basis and the latter with respect to the $\mathbf{P}$-basis. Furthermore,

$$\mathbf{v} = (\mathbf{P}^{-1}\mathbf{A}\mathbf{P})\mathbf{u} = \mathbf{D}\mathbf{u}$$

since $\mathbf{P}^{-1}\mathbf{A}\mathbf{P} = \mathbf{D}$. We may also view the two linear transformations,

$$(\mathbf{I}\mathbf{z}) = \mathbf{A}(\mathbf{I}\mathbf{x}) \quad \text{and} \quad (\mathbf{I}\mathbf{v}) = \mathbf{D}(\mathbf{I}\mathbf{u})$$

as representative of two different transformations, one with the matrix **A** and the other with the matrix **D**, but both with respect to the same **I**-basis.

In summary, the linear transformations $\mathbf{z} = \mathbf{A}\mathbf{x}$ can be viewed in two ways:

(1) $\mathbf{z} = \mathbf{A}\mathbf{x}$ and $\mathbf{P}\mathbf{v} = \mathbf{A}(\mathbf{P}\mathbf{u})$ are identical transformations with different bases. The former is with the **I**-basis and the latter with the **P**-basis.

(2) $\mathbf{z} = \mathbf{A}\mathbf{x}$ and $\mathbf{v} = \mathbf{D}\mathbf{u}$ are different transformations but with the same basis (**I**-basis). The transformations are similar since the matrices **A** and **D** are similar.

## EXERCISES

1. Show the coordinates of the vectors **x** and **z** with respect to the **P**-basis of the following linear transformation, $\mathbf{z} = \mathbf{A}\mathbf{x}$.

   (a) $\mathbf{A} = \begin{bmatrix} 4 & 2 \\ 2 & 7 \end{bmatrix}$; $\mathbf{x} = \begin{bmatrix} 2 \\ 1 \end{bmatrix}$

   (b) $\mathbf{A} = \begin{bmatrix} -2 & 1 \\ 1 & 3 \end{bmatrix}$; $\mathbf{x} = \begin{bmatrix} -1 \\ 1 \end{bmatrix}$

   (c) $\mathbf{A} = \begin{bmatrix} 2 & 0 \\ 0 & 1 \end{bmatrix}$; $\mathbf{x} = \begin{bmatrix} 1 \\ 1 \end{bmatrix}$

2. Determine the coordinates of the vectors **x** and **z** with respect to the **P**-basis of the following linear transformation, $\mathbf{z} = \mathbf{A}\mathbf{x}$.

   (a) $\mathbf{A} = \begin{bmatrix} 2 & -2 & 3 \\ -2 & 1 & 1 \\ 3 & 1 & 3 \end{bmatrix}$; $\mathbf{x} = \begin{bmatrix} 1 \\ 1 \\ 2 \end{bmatrix}$

   (b) $\mathbf{A} = \begin{bmatrix} 3 & 4 & 0 \\ 4 & 1 & 1 \\ 0 & 1 & 3 \end{bmatrix}$; $\mathbf{x} = \begin{bmatrix} 1 \\ -1 \\ 3 \end{bmatrix}$

# 7

# Real Quadratic Forms

In the previous chapter, we studied the linear transformation $T(\mathbf{x}) = \mathbf{A}\mathbf{x}$ where $\mathbf{A}$ is an $n \times n$ matrix and $\mathbf{x}$ is a $n \times 1$ vector. In this chapter we will examine a nonlinear transformation that also employs a matrix. Of special significance in economic analysis is the nonlinear transformation known as a *quadratic form*, $Q(\mathbf{x}) = \mathbf{x}^T\mathbf{A}\mathbf{x}$, where $\mathbf{A}$ is a real, symmetric matrix. We will learn how the eigenvalues of $\mathbf{A}$ reveal the properties of this transformation. In particular, we will investigate conditions under which $Q(\mathbf{x})$ is always positive (or nonnegative) or always negative (or nonpositive), for any nonzero vector $\mathbf{x}$. Determination of the signs of quadratic forms is a fundamental problem of optimization in economic theory. Utility maximization in demand analysis or cost minimization in theory of firm, for example, both require the knowledge of the signs of quadratic forms.

## □ 7.1 Definitions □

### 7.1.1 Linear, bilinear, and quadratic forms

A scalar-valued function of $n$ variables

$$L(\mathbf{x}) = L(x_1,x_2, \ldots ,x_n) = a_1x_1 + a_2x_2 + \ldots + a_nx_n$$

where $a_i$, $i = 1,2, \ldots ,n$, are constants is called a *linear form*. This function can be written in vector notation as

$$L(\mathbf{x}) = \mathbf{a}\mathbf{x}$$

where $\mathbf{x} = [x_1\ x_2 \ldots x_n]^T$ and $\mathbf{a} = [a_1\ a_2 \ldots a_n]$. It is easy to show that $L$ satisfies the following properties:

(1) $L(\mathbf{x}+\mathbf{y}) = L(\mathbf{x}) + L(\mathbf{y})$,

(2) $L(k\mathbf{x}) = kL(\mathbf{x})$ for any scalar $k$.

Hence, $L$ is a linear transformation.

Now let $\mathbf{A} = [a_{ij}]$ be an $m \times n$ matrix, $\mathbf{x} = [x_1\ x_2 \ldots x_m]^T$, and $\mathbf{y} = [y_1\ y_2 \ldots y_n]^T$ vectors. A *bilinear form* in **x** and **y**, denoted as $B(\mathbf{x},\mathbf{y})$, is a function having the following form:

$$\begin{aligned} B(\mathbf{x},\mathbf{y}) = &\ a_{11}x_1y_1 + a_{12}x_1y_2 + \ldots + a_{1n}x_1y_n \\ &+ a_{21}x_2y_1 + a_{22}x_2y_2 + \ldots + a_{2n}x_2y_n \\ &+ \ldots\ldots\ldots\ldots\ldots\ldots\ldots\ldots \\ &+ a_{m1}x_my_1 + a_{m2}x_my_2 + \ldots + a_{mn}x_my_n \\ = &\ [x_1\quad x_2\quad \ldots\quad x_m]\begin{bmatrix} a_{11} & a_{12} & \ldots & a_{1n} \\ a_{21} & a_{22} & \ldots & a_{2n} \\ \ldots & \ldots & \ldots & \ldots \\ a_{m1} & a_{m2} & \ldots & a_{mn} \end{bmatrix}\begin{bmatrix} y_1 \\ y_2 \\ \cdot \\ \cdot \\ y_n \end{bmatrix} \\ = &\ \mathbf{x}^T\mathbf{A}\,\mathbf{y} \end{aligned}$$

**Example 7.1** The function

$$\begin{aligned} \mathbf{B}(\mathbf{x},\mathbf{y}) = &\ 3x_1y_1 + 2x_1y_2 - x_1y_3 \\ &+ 5x_2y_1 - 3x_2y_2 + x_2y_3 \\ = &\ [x_1\quad x_2]\begin{bmatrix} 3 & 2 & -1 \\ 5 & -3 & 1 \end{bmatrix}\begin{bmatrix} y_1 \\ y_2 \\ y_3 \end{bmatrix} \end{aligned}$$

is a bilinear form in the variables $\mathbf{x} = [x_1\ x_2]^T$ and $\mathbf{y} = [y_1\ y_2\ y_3]^T$.

A special case of bilinear form occurs when the matrix **A** is square, $m = n$, and the two vectors are equal, $\mathbf{x} = \mathbf{y}$. In such a case the bilinear form is called a *quadratic form*. The quadratic form, denoted as $Q(\mathbf{x})$, is then the function

$$\begin{aligned} Q(\mathbf{x}) = &\ a_{11}x_1x_1 + a_{12}x_1x_2 + \ldots + a_{1n}x_1x_n \\ &+ a_{21}x_2x_1 + a_{22}x_2x_2 + \ldots + a_{2n}x_2x_n \\ &+ \ldots\ldots\ldots\ldots\ldots\ldots\ldots\ldots \\ &+ a_{n1}x_nx_1 + a_{n2}x_nx_2 + \ldots + a_{nn}x_nx_n \\ = &\ [x_1\quad x_2\quad \ldots\quad x_n]\begin{bmatrix} a_{11} & a_{12} & \ldots & a_{1n} \\ a_{21} & a_{22} & \ldots & a_{2n} \\ \ldots & \ldots & \ldots & \ldots \\ a_{n1} & a_{n2} & \ldots & a_{nn} \end{bmatrix}\begin{bmatrix} x_1 \\ x_2 \\ \cdot \\ \cdot \\ x_n \end{bmatrix} \\ = &\ \mathbf{x}^T\mathbf{A}\,\mathbf{x} \end{aligned}$$

**Example 7.2** The function

$$\begin{aligned} Q(\mathbf{x}) &= x_1^2 + 4x_1x_2 + 5x_2^2 \\ &= \mathbf{x}^T\mathbf{A}\,\mathbf{x} = [x_1\quad x_2]\begin{bmatrix} 1 & 4 \\ 0 & 5 \end{bmatrix}\begin{bmatrix} x_1 \\ x_2 \end{bmatrix} \end{aligned}$$

is a quadratic form in $x = [x_1\ x_2]^T$. Note that the above matrix **A** in the expression $Q(\mathbf{x}) = \mathbf{x}^T\mathbf{A}\mathbf{x}$ is not unique. Other matrices and expressions are possible. For example, by writing $4x_1x_2$ as $3x_1x_2 + 1x_1x_2$, we have

$$\begin{aligned} Q(\mathbf{x}) &= x_1^2 + 4x_1x_2 + 5x_2^2 \\ &= x_1^2 + 3x_1x_2 + 1x_2x_1 + 5x_2^2 \\ &= \mathbf{x}^T\mathbf{A}\mathbf{x} = [x_1 \quad x_2]\begin{bmatrix} 1 & 3 \\ 1 & 5 \end{bmatrix}\begin{bmatrix} x_1 \\ x_2 \end{bmatrix} \end{aligned}$$

It is often convenient, however, to specify a symmetric matrix **A** as the matrix for the quadratic form. In this case we write $4x_1x_2$ into $2x_1x_2 + 2x_1x_2$, and hence,

$$\begin{aligned} Q(\mathbf{x}) &= x_1^2 + 4x_1x_2 + 5x_2^2 \\ &= x_1^2 + 2x_1x_2 + 2x_2x_1 + 5x_2^2 \\ &= \mathbf{x}^T\mathbf{A}\mathbf{x} = [x_1 \quad x_2]\begin{bmatrix} 1 & 2 \\ 2 & 5 \end{bmatrix}\begin{bmatrix} x_1 \\ x_2 \end{bmatrix} \end{aligned}$$

**Example 7.3** Express the quadratic form

$$Q(\mathbf{x}) = 2x_1^2 + x_2^2 + x_3^2 + 2x_1x_2 + 2x_1x_3$$

in the form $Q(\mathbf{x}) = \mathbf{x}^T\mathbf{A}\mathbf{x}$ with a symmetric matrix **A**. The representation of the quadratic form is

$$Q(\mathbf{x}) = \mathbf{x}^T\mathbf{A}\mathbf{x} = [x_1 \quad x_2 \quad x_3]\begin{bmatrix} 2 & 1 & 1 \\ 1 & 1 & 0 \\ 1 & 0 & 1 \end{bmatrix}\begin{bmatrix} x_1 \\ x_2 \\ x_3 \end{bmatrix}$$

## EXERCISES

1. Express the following linear, quadratic, and bilinear forms in terms of matrices:
   (a) $L(\mathbf{x}) = 3x_1 - 2x_2 + 4x_3$
   (b) $B(\mathbf{x},\mathbf{y}) = x_1y_1 - x_1y_2 + 3x_1y_3 + 4x_3y_1 - 2x_3y_3$
   (c) $B(\mathbf{x},\mathbf{y}) = (x_1 + x_2 + x_3)(y_1 + y_2 + y_3)$
   (d) $Q(\mathbf{x}) = x_1^2 - 2x_1x_2 + x_2^2$
   (e) $Q(\mathbf{x}) = -x_1^2 + 2x_3^2 + x_1x_2 - 4x_2x_3$
   (f) $Q(\mathbf{x}) = 2(x_1x_2 + x_1x_3 + x_2x_3)$
2. Express the following quadractic forms as $(\Delta\mathbf{x})^T\mathbf{A}\,(\Delta\mathbf{x})$:
   (a) $Q(\Delta\mathbf{x}) = (x-3)^2 + 2(y+2)^2 - 3(z-1)^2 + 3(x-3)(y+2) + 2(x-3)(z-1) + 5(y+2)(z-1)$
   where $\Delta\mathbf{x} = [\Delta x \;\Delta y \;\Delta z]^T = [(x-3) \;\; (y+2) \;\; (z-1)]^T$
   (b) $Q(\Delta\mathbf{x}) = x^2 + y^2 - 3(z+2)^2 + xy - x(z+2) + y(z+2)$
   where $\Delta\mathbf{x} = [\Delta x \;\Delta y \;\Delta z]^T = [x \; y \; (z+2)]^T$
3. If $x_1, x_2, \ldots, x_n$ are observations of $n$ prices, then the variance of these $n$ prices is defined as

$$S^2 = \frac{1}{n}\sum_{i=1}^{n}(x_i - m)^2$$

   where $m = (x_1 + x_2 + \ldots + x_n)/n$ is the mean price. Is $S^2$ a quadratic form? If so, what is the symmetric matrix **A**?

### 7.1.2 Geometric view of quadratic forms

The graph of a quadratic form is a surface. It is obvious that the quadratic form $Q(\mathbf{x}) = \mathbf{x}^T \mathbf{A}\mathbf{x}$ is equal to zero when $\mathbf{A}$ is the zero matrix. In this case, the quadratic surface is "flat," i.e., $Q(\mathbf{x}) \equiv 0$. We plot the graph of this special quadratic form in the following example.

**Example 7.4** Plot $Q(\mathbf{x}) = \mathbf{x}^T \mathbf{A}\mathbf{x}$ when $\mathbf{A} = \mathbf{0}$.

*In[1]:=*

```
Clear[x1,x2];
A = {{0,0},{0,0}}; x = {x1,x2};
Q = x.A.x;
plane = Plot3D[Q,{x1,-1,1},{x2,-1,1},
               AxesLabel->{"x1","x2","Q"}];
```

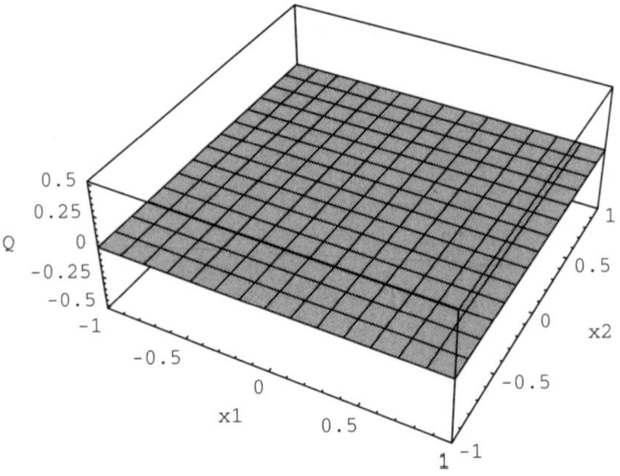


**Example 7.5** Plot the quadratic form

$$Q(\mathbf{x}) = 2x_1^2 + 2x_1x_2 + x_2^2 = \mathbf{x}^T \mathbf{A}\mathbf{x}$$

where $\mathbf{x} = [x_1\ x_2]^T$, and

$$\mathbf{A} = \begin{bmatrix} 2 & 1 \\ 1 & 1 \end{bmatrix}$$

Here is the graph of this quadratic form.

*In[5]:=*

```
Clear[x1,x2];
A = {{2,1},{1,1}}; x = {x1,x2};
Q = x.A.x;
pdef = Plot3D[Q,{x1,-1,1},{x2,-1,1},
              AxesLabel->{"x1","x2","Q"},
              ViewPoint->{1.300, -2.400, 1.330}];
```

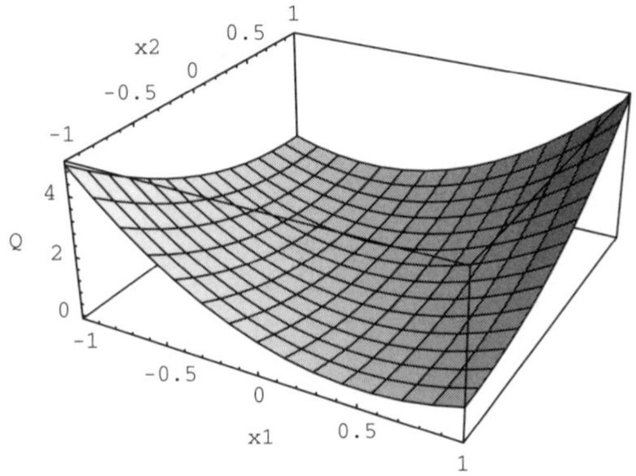


The quadratic surface bends upward. It is obvious that $Q(\mathbf{x}) = 0$ when $\mathbf{x} = \mathbf{0}$. As $\mathbf{x}$ moves away from the origin in any direction, the value $Q(\mathbf{x})$ increases. In fact, $Q(\mathbf{x})$ is always positive, except at $\mathbf{x} = \mathbf{0}$, i.e., $x_1 = x_2 = 0$. This can be shown algebraically,

$$\begin{aligned} Q(\mathbf{x}) &= 2x_1^2 + 2x_1x_2 + x_2^2 \\ &= x_1^2 + (x_1 + x_2)^2 \geq 0. \end{aligned}$$

Since $Q(\mathbf{x})$ is always positive for any $\mathbf{x} \neq \mathbf{0}$, the quadratic form $Q(\mathbf{x})$ is called a *positive definite* quadratic form.

To illustrate the positivity of $Q(\mathbf{x}) = 2x_1^2 + 2x_1x_2 + x_2^2$, we superimpose the flat surface $Q(\mathbf{x}) \equiv 0$ with this quadratic surface. As shown, the entire quadratic surface $Q(\mathbf{x}) = 2x_1^2 + 2x_1x_2 + x_2^2$ lies above the flat surface. Thus, $\boldsymbol{Q}(\mathbf{x}) > 0$, for any value of $\mathbf{x} \neq \mathbf{0}$.

*In[9]:=*

```
Show[pdef,plane];
```

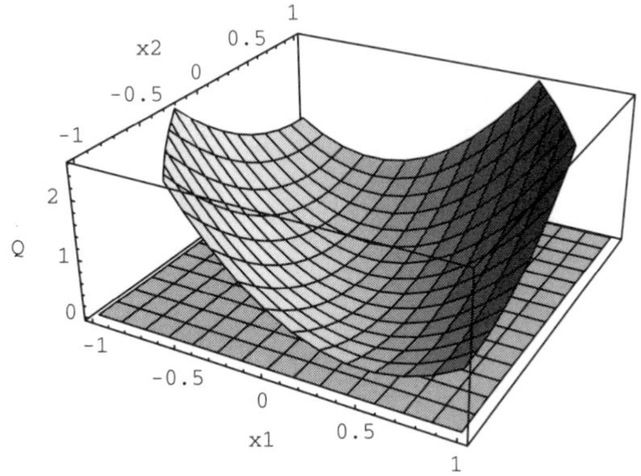


**Example 7.6** Consider the quadratic form,

$$\begin{aligned} Q(\mathbf{x}) &= x_1^2 - 2x_1x_2 + x_2^2 \\ &= [x_1 \quad x_2]\begin{bmatrix} 1 & -1 \\ -1 & 1 \end{bmatrix}\begin{bmatrix} x_1 \\ x_2 \end{bmatrix} = \mathbf{x}^T\mathbf{A}\mathbf{x}. \end{aligned}$$

Since the quadratic form can be rewritten as

$$Q(\mathbf{x}) = \mathbf{x}^T \mathbf{A}\,\mathbf{x} = (x_1 - x_2)^2 \geq 0,$$

the values of the quadratic form are nonnegative. It is zero along the line $x_1 = x_2$ as shown in the following plot.

*In[10]:=*

```
Clear[x1,x2];
A = {{1,-1},{-1,1}}; x = {x1,x2};
Q = x.A.x;
Plot3D[Q,{x1,-1,1},{x2,-1,1},
        AxesLabel->{"x1","x2","Q"},
       ViewPoint->{1.300, -2.400, 1.330}];
```

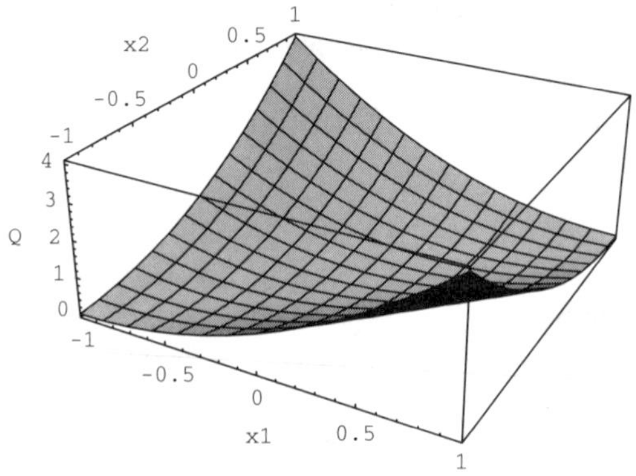


This quadratic form is called a *positive semidefinite* quadratic form.

**Example 7.7** Let

$$\begin{aligned} Q(\mathbf{x}) &= -2x_1^2 + 2x_1x_2 - x_2^2 \\ &= [x_1 \quad x_2]\begin{bmatrix} -2 & 1 \\ 1 & -1 \end{bmatrix}\begin{bmatrix} x_1 \\ x_2 \end{bmatrix} = \mathbf{x}^T \mathbf{A}\,\mathbf{x}. \end{aligned}$$

The quadratic form can be written as

$$Q(\mathbf{x}) = \mathbf{x}^T \mathbf{A}\,\mathbf{x} = -x_1^2 - (x_2 - x_1)^2 \leq 0.$$

Thus $Q(\mathbf{x})$ is always negative for any values of $x_1$ and $x_2$, unless both are zero. This quadratic form is called a *negative definite* quadratic form. The graph of $Q(\mathbf{x}) = -2x_1^2 + 2x_1x_2 - x_2^2$ is plotted below.

*In[14]:=*

```
Clear[x1,x2];
A = {{-2,1},{1,-1}}; x = {x1,x2};
Q = x.A.x;
negdef=Plot3D[Q,{x1,-1,1},{x2,-1,1},
                        AxesLabel->{"x1","x2","Q"},
                         ViewPoint->{-0.090,-5.731,0.885}];
```

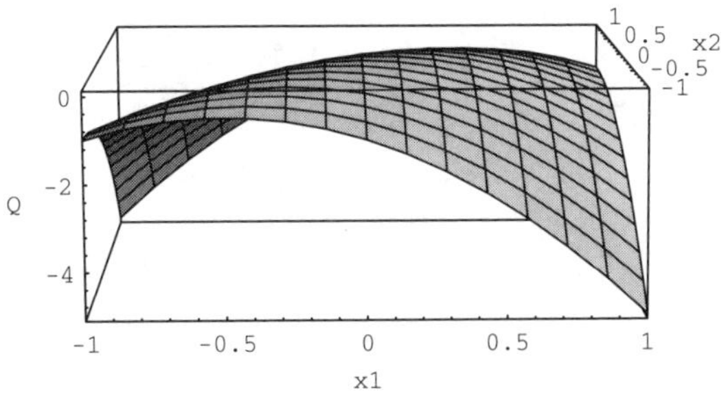


Combining it with the quadratic form $Q(\mathbf{x}) \equiv 0$, we see that $Q(\mathbf{x}) = -2x_1^2 + 2x_1x_2 - x_2^2$ lies below the graph of $Q(\mathbf{x}) \equiv 0$.

*In[18]:=*

```
Show[negdef,plane];
```

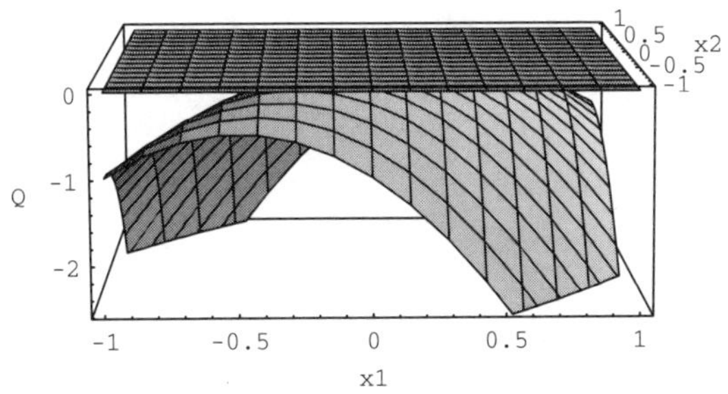


**Example 7.8** Suppose

$$\begin{aligned} Q(\mathbf{x}) &= -x_1^2 + 2x_1x_2 - x_2^2 \\ &= [x_1 \quad x_2]\begin{bmatrix} -1 & 1 \\ 1 & -1 \end{bmatrix}\begin{bmatrix} x_1 \\ x_2 \end{bmatrix} = \mathbf{x}^T\mathbf{A}\,\mathbf{x} \end{aligned}$$

which can be rewritten as

$$Q(\mathbf{x}) = \mathbf{x}^T\mathbf{A}\,\mathbf{x} = -(x_2 - x_1)^2 \le 0.$$

The quadratic form is nonpositive. Along the line $x_2 = x_1$, $Q(\mathbf{x}) = 0$. Thus, $Q(\mathbf{x}) = \mathbf{x}^T\mathbf{A}\,\mathbf{x}$ is called a *negative semidefinite* quadratic form. Here is the graph of this quadratic form.

*In[19]:=*

```
Clear[x1,x2];
A = {{-1,1},{1,-1}}; x = {x1,x2};
Q = x.A.x;
Plot3D[Q,{x1,-1,1},{x2,-1,1},
            AxesLabel->{"x1","x2","Q"},
             ViewPoint->{-0.090,-5.731,0.885}];
```

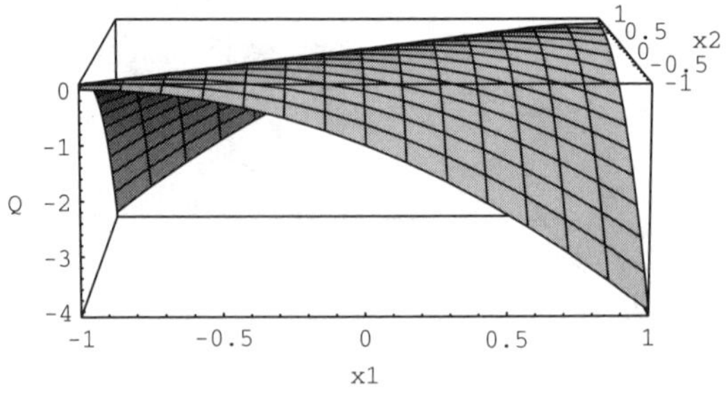


**Example 7.9** Consider the quadratic form

$$Q(\mathbf{x}) = x_1^2 + 4x_1x_2 + x_2^2 = \mathbf{x}^T\mathbf{A}\mathbf{x}$$

where

$$\mathbf{A} = \begin{bmatrix} 1 & 2 \\ 2 & 1 \end{bmatrix}$$

It can also be written as

$$Q(\mathbf{x}) = \mathbf{x}^T\mathbf{A}\mathbf{x} = (x_1 + x_2)^2 + 2x_1x_2.$$

The sign of $Q(\mathbf{x})$ depends upon whether $x_1$ and $x_2$ have the same sign. When both $x_1$ and $x_2$ are positive or both negative, $Q(\mathbf{x})$ is positive. However, if one is positive and the other is negative, then $Q(\mathbf{x})$ may be positive or negative, depending upon the magnitudes of $(x_1 + x_2)^2$ and $2x_1x_2$. In this case, $Q(\mathbf{x}) = \mathbf{x}^T\mathbf{A}\mathbf{x}$ is called an *indefinite* quadratic form. The following graph shows that $Q(\mathbf{x})$ takes both positive and negative values.

*In[23]:=*
```
Clear[x1,x2];
A = {{1,2},{2,1}}; x={x1,x2};
Q = x.A.x;
indef = Plot3D[Q,{x1,-1,1},{x2,-1,1},
                 AxesLabel->{"x1","x2","Q"},
                 ViewPoint->{-0.090,-5.731,0.885}];
```

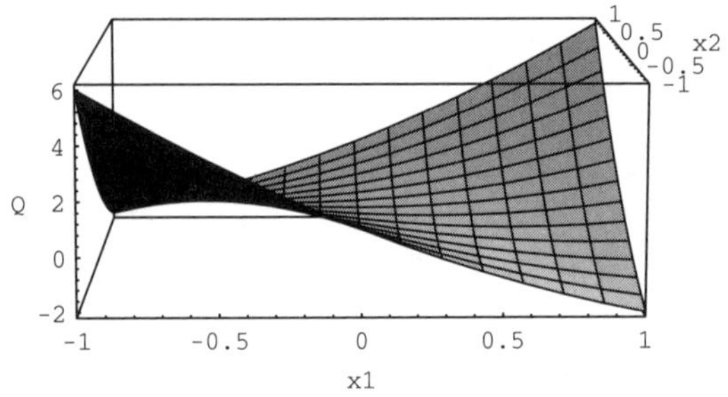

## EXERCISES

1. Use *Mathematica* to plot the quadratic form and determine the sign of $Q(x,y)$.
   (a) $Q(x,y) = x^2 + y^2 + 2xy$
   (b) $Q(x,y) = 2xy$
   (c) $Q(x,y) = x^2 + 2xy$

2. Show that $Q(x,y) > 0$ for all $(x,y)$ except at $(1,2)$ where

$$\mathbf{Q}(x,y) = (x-1)^2 + (y-2)^2 + (x-1)(y-2)$$

# □ 7.2 Signs of Quadratic Forms □

## 7.2.1 Definitions

The sign of a quadratic form, $Q(\mathbf{x}) = \mathbf{x}^T\mathbf{A}\mathbf{x}$, depends upon the matrix $\mathbf{A}$. Using this observation, we make the following definitions.

**DEFINITION 7.1** *Let* $Q(\mathbf{x}) = \mathbf{x}^T\mathbf{A}\mathbf{x}$, *where* $\mathbf{A}$ *is a real, symmetric matrix.*

(1) $Q(\mathbf{x})$ *is said to be a* ***positive (negative) definite quadratic form*** *if* $Q(\mathbf{x}) > 0$ $(< 0)$ *for all* $\mathbf{x} \neq 0$. *In this case* $\mathbf{A}$ *is called a* ***positive (negative) definite matrix***.

(2) $Q(\mathbf{x})$ *is said to be a* ***positive (negative) semidefinite quadratic form*** *if* $Q(\mathbf{x}) \geq 0$ $(\leq 0)$ *for all* $\mathbf{x}$. *In this case,* $\mathbf{A}$ *is called a* ***positive (negative) semidefinite matrix***.

(3) $Q(\mathbf{x})$ *is said to be an* ***indefinite quadratic form*** *if it is positive for some* $\mathbf{x}$ *and negative for others.*

Obviously, if $Q(\mathbf{x})$ is positive (negative) definite, it is always positive (negative) semidefinite. The converse is not true.

**Example 7.10** The quadratic form

$$\begin{aligned} Q(\mathbf{x}) &= x_1^2 - 2x_1x_2 + x_2^2 + 2x_1x_3 - 2x_2x_3 + x_3^2 \\ &= (x_1 - x_2 + x_3)^2 \end{aligned}$$

is positive semidefinite quadratic form since $Q(\mathbf{x}) \geq 0$ for all $\mathbf{x}$, and $Q(\mathbf{x}) = 0$ for $x_1 - x_2 + x_3 = 0$. Hence,

$$\mathbf{A} = \begin{bmatrix} 1 & -1 & 1 \\ -1 & 1 & -1 \\ 1 & -1 & 1 \end{bmatrix}$$

is a positive semidefinite matrix.

**Example 7.11** The quadratic form

$$Q(\mathbf{x}) = 3x_1^2 - 2x_2^2$$

is indefinite since, for example, $Q(\mathbf{x}) = 1 > 0$ for $x_1 = x_2 = 1$, and $Q(\mathbf{x}) = -5 < 0$ for $x_1 = 1$ and $x_2 = 2$.

## EXERCISES

1. In exercise 3 at the end of Section 7.1.1, what is the sign of the variance $S^2$?
2. Let $Q(\mathbf{x}) = Q_1(\mathbf{x}) + Q_2(\mathbf{x})$ be the sum of two quadratic forms, $Q_1(\mathbf{x}) = \mathbf{x}^T\mathbf{A}\mathbf{x}$ and $Q_2(\mathbf{x}) = \mathbf{x}^T\mathbf{B}\mathbf{x}$. Determine the sign of $Q(\mathbf{x})$ of the following:
   (a) $Q_1(\mathbf{x})$ and $Q_2(\mathbf{x})$ are positive definite.
   (b) $Q_1(\mathbf{x})$ is positive definite and $Q_2(\mathbf{x})$ is positive semidefinite.
   (c) $Q_1(\mathbf{x})$ is positive definite and $Q_2(\mathbf{x})$ is negative definite.

### 7.2.2 Eigenvalues and the sign of $Q(\mathbf{x}) = \mathbf{x}^T\mathbf{A}\mathbf{x}$

Consider a quadratic form

$$Q(\mathbf{x}) = \mathbf{x}^T\mathbf{A}\mathbf{x}$$

where $\mathbf{A}$ is an $n \times n$ real, symmetric matrix. Since $\mathbf{A}$ is symmetric, it can be diagonalized. Hence, there exists an orthogonal modal matrix $\mathbf{P}$ such that

$$\mathbf{P}^T\mathbf{A}\mathbf{P} = \mathbf{D} = \begin{bmatrix} \lambda_1 & 0 & 0 & \ldots & 0 \\ 0 & \lambda_2 & 0 & \ldots & 0 \\ \ldots & \ldots & \ldots & \ldots & \ldots \\ 0 & 0 & 0 & \ldots & \lambda_n \end{bmatrix}$$

The elements $\lambda_i$'s of the diagonal matrix $\mathbf{D}$ are the (real) eigenvalues of $\mathbf{A}$. The matrix $\mathbf{P}$ is orthogonal, $\mathbf{P}^T = \mathbf{P}^{-1}$, and the column vectors of $\mathbf{P}$ are the normalized eigenvectors of $\mathbf{A}$.

Suppose we define an orthogonal transformation with the matrix $\mathbf{P}^T$ and apply it to the $\mathbf{x}$ vector. That is, set

$$\mathbf{y} = \mathbf{P}^T\mathbf{x}, \quad \text{or} \quad \mathbf{x} = \mathbf{P}\mathbf{y}$$

where $\mathbf{y} = [y_1\ y_2\ \ldots\ y_n]^T$. Replacing $\mathbf{x}$ in the quadratic form, we have

$$\begin{aligned} Q(\mathbf{x}) &= \mathbf{x}^T\mathbf{A}\mathbf{x} = \mathbf{y}^T(\mathbf{P}^T\mathbf{A}\mathbf{P})\mathbf{y} \\ &= \mathbf{y}^T\mathbf{D}\mathbf{y} \\ &= \lambda_1 y_1^2 + \lambda_2 y_2^2 + \ldots + \lambda_n y_n^2. \end{aligned}$$

Thus, any quadratic form $Q(\mathbf{x}) = \mathbf{x}^T\mathbf{A}\mathbf{x}$ where $\mathbf{A}$ is diagonalizable can be reduced to a simple quadratic form that contains only quadratic terms, $y_i^2$, and no cross product terms. Since $\mathbf{y} \neq \mathbf{0}$ when $\mathbf{x} \neq \mathbf{0}$, the sign of the quadratic form $Q(\mathbf{x}) = \mathbf{x}^T\mathbf{A}\mathbf{x}$ can be determined from the signs of the eigenvalues $\lambda_i$ of $\mathbf{A}$. We have proven the following theorem.

**THEOREM 7.1** *Let $Q(\mathbf{x}) = \mathbf{x}^T\mathbf{A}\mathbf{x}$ be a real, symmetric quadratic form with $\lambda_1, \lambda_2, \ldots, \lambda_n$ as the (real) eigenvalues of* **A**. *Then,*

(1) *$Q(\mathbf{x})$ is positive (negative) definite if and only if $\lambda_i$'s are all positive (negative), $\lambda_i > 0$ ($\lambda_i < 0$).*

(2) *$Q(\mathbf{x})$ is positive (negative) semidefinite if and only if $\lambda_i$'s are all nonnegative (nonpositive), $\lambda_i \geq 0$ ($\lambda_i \leq 0$).*

(3) *$Q(\mathbf{x})$ is indefinite if and only if some eigenvalues of* **A** *are positive and others are negative.*

**Example 7.12** Determine the sign of

$$Q(\mathbf{x}) = x_1^2 + 5x_2^2 + 6x_3^2 + 4x_1x_2 - 2x_1x_3.$$

The matrix for this quadratic form is

$$\mathbf{A} = \begin{bmatrix} 1 & 2 & -1 \\ 2 & 5 & 0 \\ -1 & 0 & 6 \end{bmatrix}$$

We use the *Mathematica* function **Eigenvalues** to calculate the numerical eigenvalues of **A**.

*In[27]:=*
```
A = {{1,2,-1},{2,5,0},{-1,0,6}};
Eigenvalues[N[A]]
```

*Out[28]=*
```
{6.39543, 5.57653, 0.0280392}
```

Since all of the eigenvalues are positive, the quadratic form is positive definite.

**Example 7.13** Determine the sign of the quadratic form

$$Q(\mathbf{x}) = \mathbf{x}^T\mathbf{A}\mathbf{x} = 2x_1^2 + x_2^2 + x_3^2 + 2x_1x_2 + 2x_1x_3.$$

Also, express $Q(\mathbf{x})$ in the form $\mathbf{y}^T\mathbf{D}\mathbf{y} = \lambda_1 y_1^2 + \lambda_2 y_2^2 + \lambda_3 y_3^2$ and find the orthogonal transformation $\mathbf{x} = \mathbf{P}\mathbf{y}$ or $\mathbf{y} = \mathbf{P}^T\mathbf{x}$.

*In[29]:=*
```
A = {{2,1,1},{1,1,0},{1,0,1}};
Eigenvalues[A]
```

*Out[30]=*
```
{0, 1, 3}
```

Since the eigenvalues are 0, 1, 3, the quadratic form

$$Q(\mathbf{x}) = \mathbf{x}^T\mathbf{A}\mathbf{x} = \mathbf{y}^T\mathbf{D}\mathbf{y} = 0y_1^2 + y_2^2 + 3y_3^2$$

is positive semidefinite. We proceed to calculate the eigenvectors of **A**.

*In[31]:=*
```
vecs = Eigenvectors[A]
```

*Out[31]=*
```
{{-1, 1, 1}, {0, -1, 1}, {2, 1, 1}}
```

Recall that the eigenvectors in *Mathematica* are not normalized and are arranged in rows. We need to normalize and to transpose them to obtain the orthogonal modal matrix **P**.

*In[32]:=*
```
Clear[x1,x2,x3];
P = Table[vecs[[i]]/Sqrt[vecs[[i]].vecs[[i]]],{i,3}];
P = Transpose[P];
x = {x1,x2,x3};
y = Transpose[P].x; y // MatrixForm
```

*Out[36]//MatrixForm=*

$$\begin{array}{l} -(\frac{\text{x1}}{\text{Sqrt[3]}}) + \frac{\text{x2}}{\text{Sqrt[3]}} + \frac{\text{x3}}{\text{Sqrt[3]}} \\ -(\frac{\text{x2}}{\text{Sqrt[2]}}) + \frac{\text{x3}}{\text{Sqrt[2]}} \\ \text{Sqrt}[\frac{2}{3}]\text{x1} + \frac{\text{x2}}{\text{Sqrt[6]}} + \frac{\text{x3}}{\text{Sqrt[6]}} \end{array}$$

The orthogonal transformation $\mathbf{y} = \mathbf{P}^T\mathbf{x}$ is

$$\begin{aligned} y_1 &= -\frac{1}{\sqrt{3}}x_1 + \frac{1}{\sqrt{3}}x_2 + \frac{1}{\sqrt{3}}x_3 \\ y_2 &= -\frac{1}{\sqrt{2}}x_2 + \frac{1}{\sqrt{2}}x_3 \\ y_3 &= \sqrt{(2/3)}\,x_1 + \frac{1}{\sqrt{6}}x_2 + \frac{1}{\sqrt{6}}x_3 \end{aligned}$$

**Example 7.14** Determine the sign of $Q(\mathbf{x}) = \mathbf{x}^T\mathbf{A}\mathbf{x}$ where

$$\mathbf{A} = \begin{bmatrix} 0 & 1 & 2 & 3 \\ 1 & 0 & 1 & 2 \\ 2 & 1 & 0 & 1 \\ 3 & 2 & 1 & 0 \end{bmatrix}$$

We first calculate the numerical eigenvalues of **A**.

*In[37]:=*
```
A = {{0,1,2,3},{1,0,1,2},{2,1,0,1},{3,2,1,0}};
Eigenvalues[N[A]]
```

*Out[38]=*
```
{5.16228, -3.41421, -1.16228, -0.585786}
```

One eigenvalue is positive and the others are negative. Thus the quadratic form is indefinite.

## EXERCISES

1. Use the eigenvalues of **A** to determine the signs of the following quadratic forms. Express them in the form $Q(\mathbf{x}) = \mathbf{y}^T\mathbf{D}\mathbf{y}$ and find the orthogonal transformation, $\mathbf{y} = \mathbf{P}^T\mathbf{x}$:
   (a) $Q(\mathbf{x}) = 2x_1^2 + 4x_1x_2 + 6x_2^2$.
   (b) $Q(\mathbf{x}) = 2(x_1^2 + x_2^2 + x_3^2) - 2(x_1x_2 + x_1x_3 + x_2x_3)$.
   (c) $Q(\mathbf{x}) = ax_1^2 + bx_1x_2 + cx_2^2$, where $a$, $b$ and $c$ are constant.
   (d) $Q(\mathbf{x}) = [x_1 \quad x_2 \quad x_3 \quad x_4]\begin{bmatrix} 0 & 2 & 1 & 3 \\ 2 & 3 & 1 & 2 \\ 1 & 1 & 2 & 0 \\ 3 & 2 & 0 & 1 \end{bmatrix}\begin{bmatrix} x_1 \\ x_2 \\ x_3 \\ x_4 \end{bmatrix}$
2. Suppose $Q_1(\mathbf{x}) = \mathbf{x}^T\mathbf{A}\mathbf{x}$ is positive definite. Is $Q_2(\mathbf{x}) = \mathbf{x}^T\mathbf{A}^{-1}\mathbf{x}$ positive definite? If so, does this observation apply to the cases of negative definite and semidefinite?
3. If the matrix **A** is positive definite, is $\mathbf{A}^n$ also positive definite? If so, does this extension apply to negative definite?

### 7.2.3 Determinants and the sign of $Q(\mathbf{x}) = \mathbf{x}^T\mathbf{A}\mathbf{x}$

The diagonalization of a real, symmetric matrix **A** by the orthogonal modal matrix **P**,

$$\mathbf{P}^T\mathbf{A}\mathbf{P} = \mathbf{D}$$

means that the determinant of **A** must be equal to the determinant of **D** since the matrices are similar. This can be inferred from the identities:

$$|\mathbf{P}^T\mathbf{A}\mathbf{P}| = |\mathbf{P}^T|\,|\mathbf{A}|\,|\mathbf{P}| = |\mathbf{P}^T\mathbf{P}|\,|\mathbf{A}| = |\mathbf{I}|\,|\mathbf{A}| = |\mathbf{A}| = |\mathbf{D}|.$$

Furthermore, the determinant of the diagonal matrix **D** is equal to the product of the eigenvalues,

$$|\mathbf{A}| = |\mathbf{D}| = \lambda_1\,\lambda_2\ldots\lambda_n$$

This proves that a necessary condition for a quadratic form

$$Q(\mathbf{x}) = \mathbf{x}^T\mathbf{A}\mathbf{x}$$

$$= [x_1 \quad x_2 \quad \ldots \quad x_{n-1} \quad x_n]\begin{bmatrix} a_{11} & a_{12} & \ldots & a_{1,n-1} & a_{1n} \\ a_{21} & a_{22} & \ldots & a_{2,n-1} & a_{2n} \\ \cdots & \cdots & \cdots & \cdots & \cdots \\ a_{n1} & a_{n2} & \ldots & a_{n,n-1} & a_{nn} \end{bmatrix}\begin{bmatrix} x_1 \\ x_2 \\ \cdot \\ x_{n-1} \\ x_n \end{bmatrix}$$

to be positive definite is that the determinant of **A** must be positive.

Suppose one of the variables is zero, say $x_n = 0$. In the quadratic form, we have

$$Q(\mathbf{x}) = \mathbf{x}^T\mathbf{A}\mathbf{x}$$

$$= [x_1 \quad x_2 \quad \dots \quad x_{n-1} \quad 0]\begin{bmatrix} a_{11} & a_{12} & \dots & a_{1,n-1} & a_{1n} \\ a_{21} & a_{22} & \dots & a_{2,n-1} & a_{2n} \\ \dots & \dots & \dots & \dots & \dots \\ a_{n1} & a_{n2} & \dots & a_{n,n-1} & a_{nn} \end{bmatrix}\begin{bmatrix} x_1 \\ x_2 \\ \cdot \\ x_{n-1} \\ 0 \end{bmatrix}$$

Notice that this can be rewritten as

$$Q(\mathbf{x}_{n-1}) = \mathbf{x}_{n-1}^T\mathbf{A}_{n-1}\mathbf{x}_{n-1}$$

$$= [x_1 \quad x_2 \quad \dots \quad x_{n-1}]\begin{bmatrix} a_{11} & a_{12} & \dots & a_{1,n-1} & a_{1n} \\ a_{21} & a_{22} & \dots & a_{2,n-1} & a_{2n} \\ \dots & \dots & \dots & \dots & \dots \\ a_{n1} & a_{n2} & \dots & a_{n,n-1} & a_{nn} \end{bmatrix}\begin{bmatrix} x_1 \\ x_2 \\ \cdot \\ \cdot \\ x_{n-1} \end{bmatrix}$$

where $\mathbf{x}_{n-1} = [x_1\, x_2 \dots x_{n-1}]^T$ is a vector with only $n-1$ elements. That is, $\mathbf{x}_{n-1}$ is obtained by dropping $x_n$ from the $\mathbf{x}$ vector, and $\mathbf{A}_{n-1}$ is the principal submatrix of $\mathbf{A}$ obtained by deleting the $n$-th row and the $n$-th column of $\mathbf{A}$. If $Q(\mathbf{x}) = \mathbf{x}^T\mathbf{A}\mathbf{x}$ is positive definite, then this implies that the reduced quadratic form $Q(\mathbf{x}_{n-1}) = \mathbf{x}_{n-1}^T\, \mathbf{A}_{n-1}\, \mathbf{x}_{n-1}$ must also be positive definite, and hence its determinant must be positive, $|\mathbf{A}_{n-1}| > 0$. In other words, the principal minor of the element $a_{nn}$ of $\mathbf{A}$ must be positive.

By setting both $x_n = x_{n-1} = 0$, we further reduce the quadratic form to

$$Q(\mathbf{x}_{n-2}) = \mathbf{x}_{n-2}^T\mathbf{A}_{n-2}\mathbf{x}_{n-2}$$

where $\mathbf{A}_{n-2}$ is an $(n-2)\times(n-2)$ matrix obtained by deleting the last two rows and the last two columns of $\mathbf{A}$. Its determinant must also be positive, $|\mathbf{A}_{n-2}| > 0$.

The determinants $|\mathbf{A}_1|$, $|\mathbf{A}_2|$, ... , $|\mathbf{A}_{n-1}|$ and $|\mathbf{A}_n|$ are called the *leading principal minors* of $\mathbf{A}$. $|\mathbf{A}_i|$ stands for the determinant of the upper left-hand corner, $i \times i$ submatrix of $\mathbf{A}$. In particular, $|\mathbf{A}_n| = |\mathbf{A}|$. We now present the following theorem:

**THEOREM 7.2** *The quadratic form $Q(\mathbf{x}) = \mathbf{x}^T\mathbf{A}\mathbf{x}$ is positive definite if and only if all of its leading principal minors are positive:*

$$|\mathbf{A}_1| = a_{11} > 0;\ |\mathbf{A}_2| = \begin{vmatrix} a_{11} & a_{12} \\ a_{21} & a_{22} \end{vmatrix} > 0;\ |\mathbf{A}_3| = \begin{vmatrix} a_{11} & a_{12} & a_{13} \\ a_{21} & a_{22} & a_{23} \\ a_{31} & a_{32} & a_{33} \end{vmatrix} > 0;\quad \dots ;$$

$$|\mathbf{A}| = \begin{vmatrix} a_{11} & a_{12} & \dots & a_{1n} \\ a_{21} & a_{22} & \dots & a_{2n} \\ \dots & \dots & \dots & \dots \\ a_{n1} & a_{n2} & \dots & a_{nn} \end{vmatrix} > 0.$$

**Example 7.15** Determine the sign of

$$Q(\mathbf{x}) = 2x_1^2 + 2x_2^2 + 2x_3^2 + 2x_1x_2 + 2x_1x_3 + 2x_2x_3.$$

The matrix $\mathbf{A}$ and the leading principal submatrices are

$$\mathbf{A} = \begin{bmatrix} 2 & 1 & 1 \\ 1 & 2 & 1 \\ 1 & 1 & 2 \end{bmatrix}; \ \mathbf{A}_2 = \begin{bmatrix} 2 & 1 \\ 1 & 2 \end{bmatrix}; \ \mathbf{A}_1 = [2]$$

To obtain the submatrix $\mathbf{A}_2$, we use the **MathEcon** function **submatrix** which deletes the $i$-th row and $j$-th column of a matrix.

*In[39]:=*

```
?submatrix
```

**submatrix[mat,irow,jcol] calculates the submatrix of a given matrix mat by removing row irow and column jcol. For example,**

**submatrix[{{1,9},{6,-5}},1,2].**

The determinants can then be calculated.

*In[40]:=*

```
A = {{2,1,1},{1,2,1},{1,1,2}};
Det[A]
```

*Out[41]=*

4

*In[42]:=*

```
A2 = submatrix[A,3,3];
Det[A2]
```

*Out[43]=*

3

*In[44]:=*

```
A1 = submatrix[A2,2,2];
Det[A1]
```

*Out[45]=*

2

Since all determinants are positive, the quadratic form must be positive definite. We can confirm this by computing the eigenvalues of **A**.

*In[46]:=*

```
Eigenvalues[N[A]]
```

*Out[46]=*

{4., 1., 1.}

Although the conditions for $Q(\mathbf{x}) = \mathbf{x}^T\mathbf{A}\mathbf{x}$ to be positive definite are stated in terms of the leading principal minors of **A**, these conditions technically apply to all other principal minors as well. For example, consider a $3 \times 3$ symmetric matrix **A**. By sequentially setting some $x$'s to be zero, we have

$$|\mathbf{A}_3| = \begin{vmatrix} a_{11} & a_{12} & a_{13} \\ a_{21} & a_{22} & a_{23} \\ a_{31} & a_{32} & a_{33} \end{vmatrix} > 0 \quad \text{if} \quad x_1 \neq 0,\ x_2 \neq 0,\ x_3 \neq 0$$

$$|\mathbf{A}_2| = \begin{vmatrix} a_{11} & a_{12} \\ a_{21} & a_{22} \end{vmatrix} > 0 \quad \text{if} \quad x_1 \neq 0,\ x_2 \neq 0,\ x_3 = 0$$

$$|\mathbf{A}_1| = |a_{11}| > 0 \quad \text{if} \quad x_1 \neq 0,\ x_2 = 0,\ x_3 = 0.$$

We can derive a criterion for $Q(\mathbf{x}) = \mathbf{x}^T\mathbf{A}\mathbf{x}$ to be positive definite by setting some $x$'s to be zero in different sequences. For example,

$$|\mathbf{A}_3| = \begin{vmatrix} a_{11} & a_{12} & a_{13} \\ a_{21} & a_{22} & a_{23} \\ a_{31} & a_{32} & a_{33} \end{vmatrix} > 0 \quad \text{if} \quad x_1 \neq 0,\ x_2 \neq 0,\ x_3 \neq 0$$

$$\begin{vmatrix} a_{11} & a_{13} \\ a_{31} & a_{32} \end{vmatrix} > 0 \quad \text{if} \quad x_1 \neq 0,\ x_2 = 0,\ x_3 \neq 0$$

$$\begin{vmatrix} a_{22} & a_{23} \\ a_{32} & a_{33} \end{vmatrix} > 0 \quad \text{if} \quad x_1 = 0,\ x_2 \neq 0,\ x_3 \neq 0$$

$$|a_{22}| > 0 \quad \text{if} \quad x_1 = 0,\ x_2 \neq 0,\ x_3 = 0$$

$$|a_{33}| > 0 \quad \text{if} \quad x_1 = 0,\ x_2 = 0,\ x_3 \neq 0.$$

This shows that the necessary and sufficient conditions for $Q(\mathbf{x}) = \mathbf{x}^T\mathbf{A}\mathbf{x}$ to be positive definite is that all principal minors (not just the leading ones) must be positive.

Let $|\mathbf{P}k|$ denote any principal minor of $\mathbf{A}$ of order $k$. For example, a $3 \times 3$ symmetric matrix A has 3 principal minors of order 1,

$$|\mathbf{P}_1|\text{: } |a_{11}|,\ |a_{22}|,\ |a_{33}|;$$

$|a_{11}|$ is the leading principal minor. The matrix $\mathbf{A}$ also has 3 principal minors of order 2,

$$|\mathbf{P}_2|\text{: } \begin{vmatrix} a_{11} & a_{12} \\ a_{21} & a_{22} \end{vmatrix},\ \begin{vmatrix} a_{11} & a_{13} \\ a_{31} & a_{33} \end{vmatrix},\ \begin{vmatrix} a_{22} & a_{23} \\ a_{32} & a_{33} \end{vmatrix}$$

The first is the leading principal minor of order 2. $\mathbf{A}$ has one principal minor of order 3, which is the determinant $|\mathbf{A}|$.

$$|\mathbf{P}_3|\text{: } |\mathbf{A}| = \begin{vmatrix} a_{11} & a_{12} & a_{13} \\ a_{21} & a_{22} & a_{23} \\ a_{31} & a_{32} & a_{33} \end{vmatrix}$$

All seven principal minors must be positive for $Q(\mathbf{x}) = \mathbf{x}^T\mathbf{A}\mathbf{x} > 0$. For a $5 \times 5$ matrix $\mathbf{A}$, there are 31 principal minors. Determining all of them can be computationally burdensome. However, it can be proven that if all leading principal minors are positive, then all other principal minors will be positive, and therefore there is no need to examine the sign of other principal minors if the leading ones satisfy the condition for positive definiteness. This fact reduces the computations considerably. Theorem 7.2 is stated only in terms of the leading principal minors. As will be discussed later, however, this equivalence in sign does not hold in the case of semidefinite quadratic forms. This is the reason why we distinguish between leading principal minors and principal minors here.

**Example 7.16** The 4 × 4 symmetric matrix

$$\mathbf{A} = \begin{bmatrix} 2 & -1 & 1 & 1 \\ -1 & 3 & -1 & 2 \\ 1 & -1 & 4 & 1 \\ 1 & 2 & 1 & 5 \end{bmatrix}$$

has 15 principal minors, and they are all positive. Hence **A** is a positive definite matrix.

$|\mathbf{P}_1|$: $|2| = 2$; $|3| = 3$; $|4| = 4$; $|5| = 5$

$$|\mathbf{P}_2|: \begin{vmatrix} 2 & -1 \\ -1 & 3 \end{vmatrix} = 5; \begin{vmatrix} 2 & 1 \\ 1 & 4 \end{vmatrix} = 7; \begin{vmatrix} 2 & 1 \\ 1 & 5 \end{vmatrix} = 9; \begin{vmatrix} 3 & -1 \\ -1 & 4 \end{vmatrix} = 11; \begin{vmatrix} 3 & 2 \\ 2 & 5 \end{vmatrix} = 11; \begin{vmatrix} 4 & 1 \\ 1 & 5 \end{vmatrix} = 19$$

$$|\mathbf{P}_3|: \begin{vmatrix} 2 & -1 & 1 \\ -1 & 3 & -1 \\ 1 & -1 & 4 \end{vmatrix} = 17; \begin{vmatrix} 2 & -1 & 1 \\ -1 & 3 & 2 \\ 1 & 2 & 5 \end{vmatrix} = 10; \begin{vmatrix} 2 & 1 & 1 \\ 1 & 4 & 1 \\ 1 & 1 & 5 \end{vmatrix} = 31; \begin{vmatrix} 3 & -1 & 2 \\ -1 & 4 & 1 \\ 2 & 1 & 5 \end{vmatrix} = 32$$

$$|\mathbf{P}_4|: |\mathbf{A}| = \begin{vmatrix} 2 & -1 & 1 & 1 \\ -1 & 3 & -1 & 2 \\ 1 & -1 & 4 & 1 \\ 1 & 2 & 1 & 5 \end{vmatrix} = 29$$

The **MathEcon** package contains a function **signQ** that calculates all principal minors of a matrix **A**. Here is a description of this function.

*In[47]:=*
```
?signQ
```

**signQ[mat] creates a list of the principal minors of the matrix mat. For example,**

**signQ[{{2,3,1},{4,3,1},{0,9,-3}}].**

The above 15 principal minors of **A** are calculated by **signQ** in the following *Mathematica* statements.

*In[48]:=*
```
A = {{2,-1,1,1},{-1,3,-1,2},{1,-1,4,1},{1,2,1,5}};
P = signQ[A]; TableForm[P]
```

*Out[49]//TableForm=*

| | | | | | |
|---|---|---|---|---|---|
| 2 | 3 | 4 | 5 | | |
| 5 | 7 | 9 | 11 | 11 | 19 |
| 17 | 10 | 31 | 32 | | |
| 29 | | | | | |

The first row of the output is the four principal minors of order 1, $|\mathbf{P}_1|$. The second row is of order 2, $|\mathbf{P}_2|$, and so on. The leading principal minors are given first in each row. Note that we use the *Mathematica* function **TableForm**, instead of **MatrixForm**, to tabulate the principal minors since **P** does not have the same number of columns in each row. The principal minors of order $k$ can be extracted by using the **Part** function. For example, here are the second order ones.

*In[50]:=*

```
P[ [2] ]
```

*Out[50]=*

```
{5, 7, 9, 11, 11, 19}
```

Alternatively, we can use the **MathEcon** function **signQL** to calculate only the leading principal minors of a matrix **A**.

*In[51]:=*

```
?signQL
```

**signQL[mat] creates a list of the leading principal minors of the matrix mat. For example,**

**signQL[{{2,3,1},{4,3,1},{0,9,-3}}].**

We use this function on **A**.

*In[52]:=*

```
LP = signQL[A]
```

*Out[52]=*

```
{2, 5, 17, 29}
```

We now examine the condition for $Q(\mathbf{x}) = \mathbf{x}^T\mathbf{A}\mathbf{x}$ to be negative definite. The condition for negative definiteness can be derived from the fact that if $Q(\mathbf{x})$ is negative definite, then $-Q(\mathbf{x})$ must be positive definite. Since

$$-Q(\mathbf{x}) = \mathbf{x}^T(-\mathbf{A})\mathbf{x},$$

the determinant of $(-\mathbf{A})$ and all the leading principal minors of $(-\mathbf{A})$ must be positive. However, since **A** is an $n \times n$ matrix, and from the properties of a determinant introduced in Chapter 4, we have

$$|-\mathbf{A}| = (-1)^n|\mathbf{A}|$$
$$|-A_{n-1}| = (-1)^{n-1}|\mathbf{A}_{n-1}|$$
$$\cdots\cdots\cdots\cdots$$
$$|-\mathbf{A}_2| = (-1)^2|\mathbf{A}_2|$$
$$|-\mathbf{A}_1| = -|\mathbf{A}_1|$$

We have developed a criterion for a quadratic form to be negative definite.

**THEOREM 7.3** *The quadratic form $Q(\mathbf{x}) = \mathbf{x}^T\mathbf{A}\mathbf{x}$ is negative definite if and only if the sign of the leading principal minor of order k is $(-1)^k$; that is,*

$(-1)^k|\mathbf{A}_k| > 0.$

*In other words, the successive leading principal minors $|\mathbf{A}_k|$ ($k = 1, 2, \ldots, n$) must alternate in sign with the first one being negative.*

$$|\mathbf{A}_1| = a_{11} < 0;\ |\mathbf{A}_2| = \begin{vmatrix} a_{11} & a_{12} \\ a_{21} & a_{22} \end{vmatrix} > 0;\ |\mathbf{A}_3| = \begin{vmatrix} a_{11} & a_{12} & a_{13} \\ a_{21} & a_{22} & a_{23} \\ a_{31} & a_{32} & a_{33} \end{vmatrix} < 0;\ \ldots\ldots;$$

$$(-1)^n|\mathbf{A}| = \begin{vmatrix} a_{11} & a_{12} & \ldots & a_{1n} \\ a_{21} & a_{22} & \ldots & a_{2n} \\ \ldots & \ldots & \ldots & \ldots \\ a_{n1} & a_{n2} & \ldots & a_{nn} \end{vmatrix} > 0$$

Satisfying the conditions, $(-1)^k|\mathbf{A}_k| > 0$ for $k = 1,2, \ldots ,n$, in terms of the leading principal minors automatically guarantees that all other principal minors satisfy the same conditions. That is, $(-1)^k|\mathbf{P}_k| > 0$. There is no need to examine the sign of $|\mathbf{P}_k|$ if $|\mathbf{A}_k|$ meets the conditions for negative definite.

**Example 7.17** Show that the quadratic form

$$Q(\mathbf{x}) = -2x_1^2 - x_2^2 - 2x_3^2 - 3x_4^2 + 2x_1x_2 - 2x_1x_3 + 2x_1x_4 + 2x_2x_3 - 2x_2x_4 + 2x_3x_4$$

is negative definite. The function **signQ** shows the alternating signs of the principal minors. $Q(\mathbf{x})$ is thus negative definite. In particular, we have

$|\mathbf{A}_1| = -2;\ |\mathbf{A}_2| = 1;\ |\mathbf{A}_3| = -1;\ |\mathbf{A}| = 2.$

*In[53]:=*
```
A = {{-2,1,-1,1},{1,-1,1,-1},{-1,1,-2,1},{1,-1,1,-3}};
P = signQ[A]; TableForm[P]
```

*Out[54]//TableForm=*
```
-2   -1   -2   -3
1    3    5    1    2    5
-1   -2   -7   -2
2
```

The leading principal minors are given first in each row. They can also be calculated directly by using **signQL**.

*In[55]:=*
```
LP = signQL[A]
```

*Out[55]=*
```
{-2, 1, -1, 2}
```

The condition for $Q(\mathbf{x}) = \mathbf{x}^T\mathbf{A}\mathbf{x}$ to be positive or negative semidefinite involves the examination of all principal minors of **A**, not just the leading principal minors. The following theorem states the conditions for a semidefinite quadratic form:

**THEOREM 7.4** *The quadratic form $Q(\mathbf{x}) = \mathbf{x}^T\mathbf{A}\mathbf{x}$ is positive semidefinite if and only if all principal minors of order* k *are nonnegative, i.e.,* $|\mathbf{P}_k| \geq 0$ $(k = 1,2, \ldots ,n)$. *The quadratic form $Q(\mathbf{x})$ is negative semidefinite if and only if* $(-1)^k|\mathbf{P}_k| \geq 0$ $(k = 1,2, \ldots ,n)$, i.e., *the principal minors of successive order alternate in sign.*

**Example 7.18** The quadratic form

$$Q(\mathbf{x}) = 2x_1^2 + x_2^2 + x_3^2 + 2x_1x_2 + 2x_1x_3 + 2x_2x_3$$

is positive semidefinite. We show that all the principal minors are nonnegative in the following calculation.

*In[56]:=*

```
A = {{2,1,1},{1,1,1},{1,1,1}};
signQ[A] // TableForm
```

*Out[57]//TableForm=*

```
2  1  1
1  1  0
0
```

The 3 principal minors $|\mathbf{P}_1|$ of order 1 are 2, 1, and 1; the 3 principal minors $|\mathbf{P}_2|$ of order 2 are 1, 1, and 0; and the principal minor of order 3, $|\mathbf{P}_3| = |\mathbf{A}|$, is 0. All principal minors are nonnegative.

**Example 7.19** The quadratic form $Q(\mathbf{x}) = \mathbf{x}^T\mathbf{A}\mathbf{x}$ with

$$\mathbf{A} = \begin{bmatrix} -1 & 2 & 0 \\ 2 & -5 & -1 \\ 0 & -1 & -1 \end{bmatrix}$$

has the eigenvalues, $\lambda = 0, -1$, and $-6$. Hence $Q(\mathbf{x})$ is known to be negative semidefinite. The 3 principal minors $|\mathbf{P}_1|$ of order 1 are negative, $-1$, $-5$, and $-1$. The 3 principal minors $|\mathbf{P}_2|$ of order 2 are positive, 1, 1, and 4. Finally, the principal minor of order 3, $|\mathbf{P}_3| = |\mathbf{A}|$, is 0. This is shown in the following calculation.

*In[58]:=*

```
A = {{-1,2,0},{2,-5,-1},{0,-1,-1}};
signQ[A] // TableForm
```

*Out[59]//TableForm=*

```
-1  -5  -1
1   1   4
0
```

It is important to emphasize that the necessary and sufficient conditions for a (positive or negative) semidefinite quadratic form should be examined using all principal minors and not just the leading principal minors. A matrix **A** with nonnegative (nonpositive) leading principal minors does not imply positive (negative) semidefinite. For example, $Q(\mathbf{x}) = (x_1+x_2)^2 - (x_3)^2$ is clearly indefinite, but the associated matrix

$$\mathbf{A} = \begin{bmatrix} 1 & 1 & 0 \\ 1 & 1 & 0 \\ 0 & 0 & -1 \end{bmatrix}$$

has the nonnegative leading principal minors, $|\mathbf{A}_1| = 1$, $|\mathbf{A}_2| = 0$, and $|\mathbf{A}_3| = 0$. By checking the principal minors, however, we find: $|\mathbf{P}_1| = 1$, 1, and $-1$; $|\mathbf{P}_2| = 0$, $-1$, and $-1$; and $|\mathbf{P}_3| = 0$.

*In[60]:=*

```
A = {{1,1,0},{1,1,0},{0,0,-1}};
signQ[A] // TableForm
```

*Out[61]//TableForm=*

```
1   1   -1
0  -1   -1
0
```

## EXERCISES

1. Use the principal minors to determine the sign of $Q(\mathbf{x})$ in exercise 1 at the end of section 7.2.2.

2. Examine the sign of $Q(\mathbf{x}) = \mathbf{x}^T\mathbf{A}\mathbf{x}$.

   (a) $\mathbf{A} = \begin{bmatrix} 2 & -1 & 1 & 1 \\ -1 & 3 & -1 & -1 \\ 1 & -1 & 4 & 1 \\ 1 & -1 & 1 & 5 \end{bmatrix}$

   (b) $\mathbf{A} = \begin{bmatrix} 0 & -1 & 1 & 1 \\ -1 & 0 & -1 & -1 \\ 1 & -1 & 0 & 1 \\ 1 & -1 & 1 & 0 \end{bmatrix}$

# □ 7.3 Constrained Quadratic Forms □

## 7.3.1 Geometric view

In determining the sign of $Q(\mathbf{x}) = \mathbf{x}^T\mathbf{A}\mathbf{x}$, the components of $\mathbf{x} = [x_1\ x_2\ \ldots\ x_n]^T$ are allowed to vary and to take any value as long as they are not all zero simultaneously, i.e., **x** is not the zero vector. We now consider the sign of $Q(\mathbf{x})$ in which the variables are subject to constraints.

Consider the indefinite quadratic form $Q(\mathbf{x}) = x_1^2 + 4x_1x_2 + x_2^2$ given previously. The graph of this quadratic form shows that some of the surface is positive, and some negative. Suppose we restrict the variation of the variables $x_1$ and $x_2$ to be positive only, i.e., $x_1 > 0$ and $x_2 > 0$. In this region of 2-space we have $Q(\mathbf{x}) > 0$. We plot the graph of $Q(\mathbf{x})$ on the region: $0 \leq x_1 \leq 1$ and $0 \leq x_2 \leq 1$.

*In[62]:=*

```
Clear[x1,x2];
A  =  { {1,1},{1,-1} };  x  ={x1,x2};
Q  =  x.A.x;
indef=Plot3D[Q,{x1,0,1},{x2,0,1},
                    AxesLabel->{"x1","    x2","Q"},
                     ViewPoint->{-0.090,-5.731,0.885}];
```

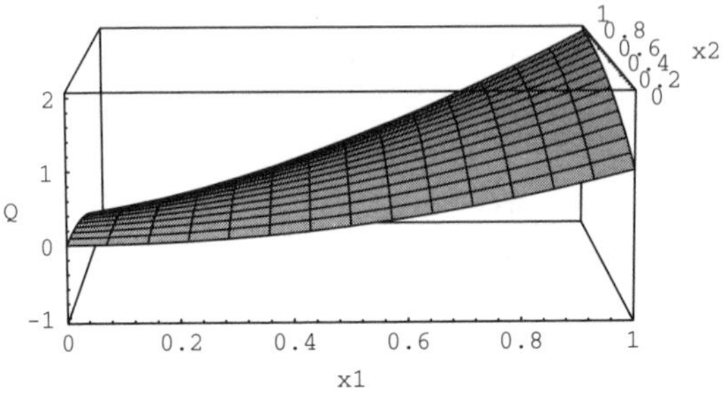


The $Q(\mathbf{x})$ subject to the positive constraints, $x_1 > 0$ and $x_2 > 0$, is thus positive definite.

Again the determination of the sign of quadratic forms, subject to constraints in variables, is a fundamental question in constrained optimization. Utility maximization in demand analysis, or cost minimization, both require the examination of signs of quadratic forms subject to a budget constraint or an output constraint. We are often interested in linear constraints.

**Example 7.20** The quadratic form

$$Q(\mathbf{x}) = x_1^2 + 2x_1x_2 - x_2^2 = 2x_1^2 - (x_2 - x_1)^2$$

is indefinite as illustrated in the following *Mathematica* plot.

*In[66]:=*

```
Clear[x1,x2];
A  =  {{1,1},{1,-1} };  x  ={x1,x2};
Q  =  x.A.x;
indef=Plot3D[Q,{x1,-1,1},{x2,-1,1},
                    AxesLabel->{"x1","    x2","Q"},
                     ViewPoint->{-0.090,-5.731,0.885} ];
```

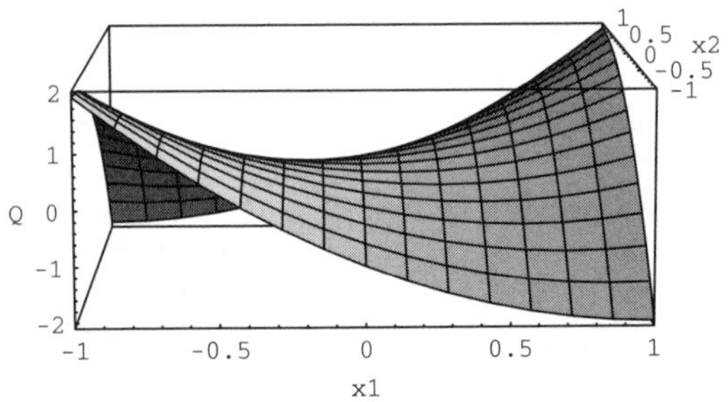

Since $Q(\mathbf{x}) = 2x_1^2 - (x_2 - x_1)^2$, it is obvious that if the linear constraint, $x_2 - x_1 = 0$ is imposed, then the quadratic form is positive i.e., $Q(\mathbf{x}) = 2x_1^2 > 0$. Hence $Q(\mathbf{x})$ is positive definite on the line $x_2 - x_1 = 0$. Geometrically, we examine the quadratic form along the line $x_1 = x_2$. To show this graphically, we first construct a cutting plane that contains the line, $x_1 = x_2$, using the **ParametricPlot3D** function.

*In[70]:=*

```
Clear[x1,z,const];
const  =  ParametricPlot3D[{x1,x1,z},{x1,-1,1},{z,-2,2},
              AspectRatio->0.5,
              AxesLabel->{"x1","x2","Q"}];
```

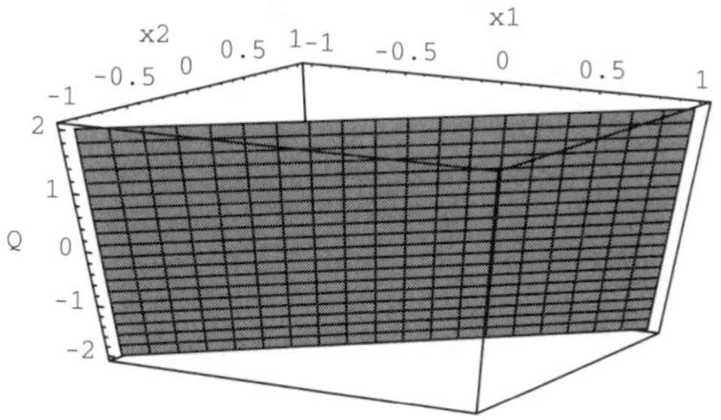


The cutting plane is then superimposed on the graph of $Q(\mathbf{x})$ to trace out the graph of the quadratic form restricted to the constraint. The quadratic form on this constraint, $Q(\mathbf{x}) = 2x_1^2$ is obviously above zero, and hence the quadratic form is positive definite.

*In[72]:=*

```
Show[indef,const];
```

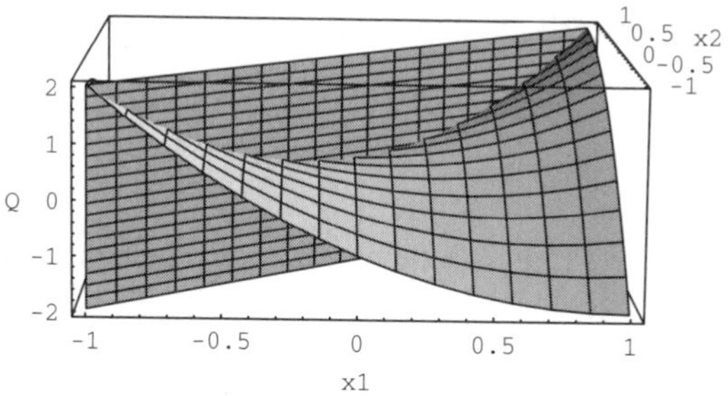


## EXERCISES

1. Given $Q(\mathbf{x}) = 2x_1x_2$ subject to the constraint, $ax_1 + bx_2 = 0$:
   (a) Prove that $Q(\mathbf{x})$ is positive definite if $a$ and $b$ are opposite in sign.
   (b) Prove that $Q(\mathbf{x})$ is negative definite if $a$ and $b$ have the same sign.
2. Use **Plot3D** to show the following statements.
   (a) $Q(\mathbf{x}) = 2x_1x_2$ is indefinite.
   (b) $Q(\mathbf{x}) = 2x_1x_2$ subject to $2x_1 - x_2 = 0$ is positive definite,
   (c) $Q(\mathbf{x}) = 2x_1x_2$ subject to $2x_1 - x_2 = 0$ is negative definite.

## 7.3.2 Sign of quadratic forms with constraints

Consider a quadratic form in two scalar variables

$$Q(\mathbf{x}) = \mathbf{x}^T\mathbf{A}\mathbf{x} = a_{11}x_1^2 + a_{22}x_2^2 + 2a_{12}x_1x_2$$

We wish to determine the condition for $Q(\mathbf{x})$ to be positive definite subject to a linear constraint of the form:

$$\mathbf{b}\cdot\mathbf{x} = b_1x_1 + b_2x_2 = 0, \quad \text{or} \quad x_2 = -(b_1/b_2)x_1.$$

Here $\mathbf{b} = [b_1\ b_2]^T$.

The direct substitution of the constraint in the quadratic form gives

$$\begin{aligned} Q(\mathbf{x}) &= a_{11}x_1^2 + a_{22}\frac{b_1^2}{b_2^2}x_1^2 - 2a_{12}\frac{b_1}{b_2}x_2^2 \\ &= (a_{11}b_2^2 + a_{22}b_1^2 - 2a_{12}b_1b_2)\frac{x_1^2}{b_2^2} \\ &= -\frac{x_1^2}{b_2^2}\begin{vmatrix} 0 & b_1 & b_2 \\ b_1 & a_{11} & a_{12} \\ b_2 & a_{21} & a_{22} \end{vmatrix} \end{aligned}$$

where $a_{12} = a_{21}$. It is obvious now that $Q(\mathbf{x})$ is positive (negative) definite if the determinant, denoted as $|\mathbf{B}_2|$, is negative (positive)

$$|\mathbf{B}_2| = \begin{vmatrix} 0 & b_1 & b_2 \\ b_1 & a_{11} & a_{12} \\ b_2 & a_{21} & a_{22} \end{vmatrix}$$

The matrix $\mathbf{B}_2$ is composed of elements of $\mathbf{A}$ with a border added to the first row and column. The determinant of $\mathbf{B}_2$ is thus called a *bordered determinant*.

**Example 7.21** Determine the sign of the quadratic form

$$Q(\mathbf{x}) = -x_1^2 + 4x_1x_2 + 3x_2^2$$

subject to the constraint, $x_1 + 2x_2 = 0$. Since the bordered determinant is positive, $Q(\mathbf{x})$ is negative definite on the constraint.

$$|\mathbf{B}_2| = \begin{vmatrix} 0 & 1 & 2 \\ 1 & -1 & 2 \\ 2 & 2 & 3 \end{vmatrix} = 9 > 0$$

Here is a picture of this situation.

*In[73]:=*

```
Clear[x1,x2];
A = {{-1,2},{2,3}}; x = {x1,x2};
Q=x.A.x;
quad = Plot3D[Q,{x1,-2,2},{x2,-1,1},
            AxesLabel->{"x1","x2","Q"},
            ViewPoint->{4.000,-0.250,0.890},
            DisplayFunction->Identity];
```

```
const  =  ParametricPlot3D[{-2*x2,x2,z},{x2,-1,1},
                  {z,-2,6},DisplayFunction->Identity];
Show[quad,const,DisplayFunction->$DisplayFunction];
```

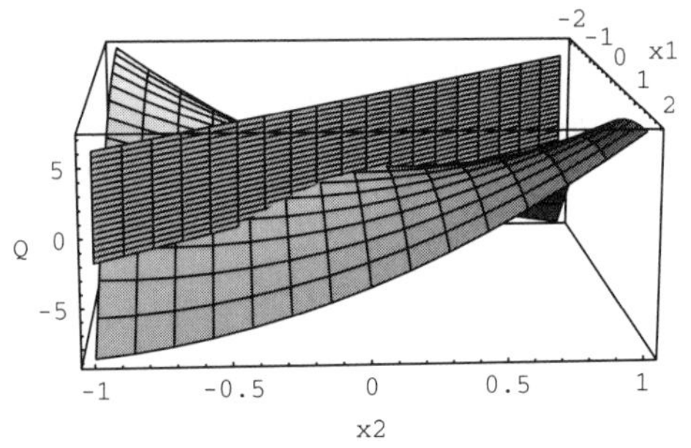


In general, consider a quadratic from in $n$-variables

$$Q(\mathbf{x}) = \mathbf{x}^T \mathbf{A}\,\mathbf{x}$$

$$= [x_1 \quad x_2 \quad \ldots \quad x_{n-1} \quad x_n] \begin{bmatrix} a_{11} & a_{12} & \ldots & a_{1,n-1} & a_{1n} \\ a_{21} & a_{22} & \ldots & a_{2,n-1} & a_{2n} \\ \ldots & \ldots & \ldots & \ldots & \ldots \\ a_{n1} & a_{n2} & \ldots & a_{n,n-1} & a_{nn} \end{bmatrix} \begin{bmatrix} x_1 \\ x_2 \\ \vdots \\ x_{n-1} \\ x_n \end{bmatrix}$$

subject to a linear constraint

$$\mathbf{b} \cdot \mathbf{x} = b_1 x_1 + b_2 x_2 + \ldots + b_n x_n = 0.$$

Here $\mathbf{b} = [b_1 \; b_2 \; \ldots \; b_n]^T$.

The condition for $Q(\mathbf{x})$ to be positive definite subject to the constraint is that the following leading bordered determinants are negative:

$$|\mathbf{B}_2| = \begin{vmatrix} 0 & b_1 & b_2 \\ b_1 & a_{11} & a_{12} \\ b_2 & a_{21} & a_{22} \end{vmatrix} < 0; \; |\mathbf{B}_3| = \begin{vmatrix} 0_1 & b_1 & b_2 & b_3 \\ b_1 & a_{11} & a_{12} & a_{13} \\ b_2 & a_{21} & a_{22} & a_{23} \\ b_3 & a_{31} & a_{32} & a_{33} \end{vmatrix} < 0 \ldots ;$$

$$|\mathbf{B}_n| = \begin{vmatrix} 0 & b_1 & b_2 & \ldots & b_n \\ b_1 & a_{11} & a_{12} & \ldots & a_{1n} \\ \ldots & \ldots & \ldots & \ldots & \ldots \\ b_n & a_{n1} & a_{n2} & \ldots & a_{nn} \end{vmatrix} < 0$$

Note that $Q(\mathbf{x})$ must be positive for any $\mathbf{x}$ as long as $\mathbf{x} \neq \mathbf{0}$. For example, we could set $x_3 = x_4 = \ldots = x_n = 0$. Then the reduced quadratic form

$$Q(\mathbf{x}) = [x_1 \quad x_2] \begin{bmatrix} a_{11} & a_{12} \\ a_{21} & a_{22} \end{bmatrix} \begin{bmatrix} x_1 \\ x_2 \end{bmatrix}$$

subject to

$$\mathbf{b} \cdot \mathbf{x} = b_1 x_1 + b_2 x_2 = 0$$

must still be positive. Thus, the condition becomes $|\mathbf{B}_2| < 0$. However, it is not legitimate to expect $Q(\mathbf{x})$ to be positive by setting all $x$'s to be zero except $x_1$, i.e., $x_2 = x_3 = \ldots = x_n = 0$. Doing so would automatically imply that $x_1 = 0$. This follows from the constraint that $\mathbf{b} \cdot \mathbf{x} = b_1x_1 = 0$. That is, setting $x_2 = x_3 = \ldots = x_n = 0$, implies $x_1 = 0$. We expect the quadratic form $Q(\mathbf{x}) = 0$ when $\mathbf{x} = \mathbf{0}$. Consequently, the smallest meaningful dimension of the leading bordered determinant is $3 \times 3$. The subscript $k$ in $|\mathbf{B}_k|$ indicates the number of nonzero $x$'s in the elimination.

The condition for negative definiteness (subject to the same constraint) is that the leading bordered determinants be alternatively positive and negative with the first one being positive.

$$|\mathbf{B}_2| > 0,\ |\mathbf{B}_3| < 0,\ \ldots,\ (-1)^n|\mathbf{B}_n| > 0$$

**Example 7.22** Determine the sign of

$$Q(\mathbf{x}) = 5x_1^2 + x_2^2 + x_3^2 + 4x_1x_2 - 4x_1x_3 - 2x_2x_3$$

subject to

$$\mathbf{b} \cdot \mathbf{x} = 2x_1 + 2x_2 - x_3 = 0.$$

We first set up the bordered matrix $\mathbf{B}$ and then calculate the determinants:

$$|\mathbf{B}_2| = \begin{vmatrix} 0 & 2 & 2 \\ 2 & 5 & 2 \\ 2 & 2 & 1 \end{vmatrix} = -8 < 0; \quad |\mathbf{B}_3| = \begin{vmatrix} 0 & 2 & 2 & -1 \\ 2 & 5 & 2 & -2 \\ 2 & 2 & 1 & -1 \\ -1 & -2 & -1 & 1 \end{vmatrix} = -1 < 0$$

Since $|\mathbf{B}_2| = -8 < 0$ and $|\mathbf{B}_3| = -1 < 0$, $Q(\mathbf{x})$ is positive definite subject to the constraint. We could use the **MathEcon** function **borderB** to form the bordered matrix. Here is the description of this function.

*In[79]:=*
```
?borderB
```

**borderB[mat,vect] generates the border matrix of the matrix mat and the vector vect. For example,**

**borderB[{{2,3,1},{4,3,1},{0,9,-3}},{-1,0,4}].**

The first argument in **borderB** is the matrix **A** and the second argument contains the constraint coefficients vector **b**.

*In[80]:=*
```
A = {{5,2,-2},{2,1,-1},{-2,-1,1}}; b = {2,2,-1};
B = borderB[A,b]; B //MatrixForm
```

*Out[81]//MatrixForm=*
```
0   2   2   -1
2   5   2   -2
2   2   1   -1
-1  -2  -1  1
```

Once the bordered matrix **B** is obtained, we then use the function **signQL** to calculate the leading principal minors of the bordered matrix and to check for the signs.

*In[82]:=*

```
signQL[B]
```

*Out[82]=*

```
{0, -4, -8, -1}
```

As discussed above, the first two leading principal minors

$$|\mathbf{B}_0| = |0| = 0, \quad \text{and} \quad |\mathbf{B}_1| = \begin{vmatrix} 0 & 2 \\ 2 & 5 \end{vmatrix} = -4$$

can be ignored. Since both $|\mathbf{B}_2| = -8$ and $|\mathbf{B}_3| = -1$ are negative, $Q(\mathbf{x})$ is negative definite subject to $\mathbf{b} \cdot \mathbf{x} = 0$.

**Example 7.23** Show that $Q(\mathbf{x}) = \mathbf{x}^T \mathbf{A}\,\mathbf{x}$ subject to $\mathbf{b} \cdot \mathbf{x} = 0$ is negative definite where

$$\mathbf{A} = \begin{bmatrix} 1 & -1 & 1 & 4 \\ -1 & -4 & -3 & 2 \\ 1 & -3 & -5 & 1 \\ 4 & 2 & 1 & -4 \end{bmatrix}; \ \mathbf{b} = [1 \quad 1 \quad 1 \quad 1\,]^T$$

We use *Mathematica* to do the necessary calculations.

*In[83]:=*

```
A  =  {{1,-1,1,4},{-1,-4,-3,2},{1,-3,-5,1},{4,2,1,-4}};
b  =  {1,1,1,1};
B  =  borderB[A,b];
signQL[B]
```

*Out[86]=*

```
{0, -1, 1, -2, 13}
```

Ignoring the first two values ($|\mathbf{B}_0| = 0$ and $|\mathbf{B}_1| = -1$), the leading principal minors of the bordered matrix **B** are $|\mathbf{B}_2| = 1 > 0$, $|\mathbf{B}_3| = -2 < 0$, and $|\mathbf{B}_3| = 13 > 0$. Thus the quadratic form $Q(\mathbf{x})$ is negative definite subject to $\mathbf{b} \cdot \mathbf{x} = 0$.

We now examine the general problem of determining the sign of a quadratic form with multiple linear constraints. Consider

$$Q(\mathbf{x}) = \mathbf{x}^T \mathbf{A}\,\mathbf{x}$$

subject to $m$ linear constraints

$$\begin{aligned} b_{11}x_1 + b_{12}x_2 + \ldots + b_{1n}x_n &= 0 \\ b_{21}x_1 + b_{22}x_2 + \ldots + b_{2n}x_n &= 0 \\ \cdots\cdots\cdots\cdots\cdots\cdots\cdots & \\ b_{m1}x_1 + b_{m2}x_2 + \ldots + b_{mn}x_n &= 0 \end{aligned}$$

We assume that these $m$ linear constraints are linearly independent. Define the $m \times n$ matrix $\mathbf{b}$ to be the coefficient matrix for the constraints

$$\mathbf{b} = \begin{bmatrix} b_{11} & b_{12} & \dots & b_{1n} \\ b_{21} & b_{22} & \dots & b_{2n} \\ \dots & \dots & \dots & \dots \\ b_{m1} & b_{m2} & \dots & b_{mn} \end{bmatrix}$$

The linear independence of the constraints implies that the matrix $\mathbf{b}$ is of rank $m$. We are interested in the sign of the quadratic form,

$$Q(\mathbf{x}) = \mathbf{x}^T \mathbf{A} \mathbf{x}$$

subject to

$$\mathbf{b}\mathbf{x} = \mathbf{0}$$

for $\mathbf{x} \neq \mathbf{0}$.

Similar to the single constraint case, the sign of $Q(\mathbf{x})$ must be consistent for any $\mathbf{x}$ value as long as $\mathbf{x} \neq \mathbf{0}$. For a positive definite case, this implies that even with $x_{k+1} = x_{k+2} = \dots = x_n = 0$, the reduced quadratic forms must be positive also. That is

$$Q(\mathbf{x}_k) = \mathbf{x}_k^T \mathbf{A}_k \mathbf{x}_k > 0, \quad \text{subject to} \quad \mathbf{b}_k \mathbf{x}_k = \mathbf{0}$$

where $\mathbf{x}_k = [x_1\ x_2 \dots x_k]^T$, $\mathbf{A}_k$ is a submatrix obtained by deleting the last $(n-k)$ rows and the last $(n-k)$ columns of $\mathbf{A}$, and $\mathbf{b}_k$ is the submatrix with the last $n-k$ columns of $\mathbf{b}$ dropped. Of course, $k$ must be at least $m+1$. Otherwise, if $k = m$, for example, the reduced constraints, $\mathbf{b}_m \mathbf{x} = \mathbf{0}$, will force $\mathbf{x}_m = \mathbf{0}$ since $\mathbf{b}_m$ is nonsingular.

We define the reduced leading bordered matrix $\mathbf{B}_k$ as

$$\mathbf{B}_k = \begin{bmatrix} 0 & \dots & 0 & b_{1k} & \dots & b_{mk} \\ \dots & \dots & \dots & \dots & \dots & \dots \\ \dots & \dots & \dots & \dots & \dots & \dots \\ 0 & \dots & 0 & b_{m1} & \dots & b_{mk} \\ b_{11} & \dots & b_{m1} & a_{11} & \dots & a_{1k} \\ \dots & \dots & \dots & \dots & \dots & \dots \\ \dots & \dots & \dots & \dots & \dots & \dots \\ b_{1k} & \dots & b_{mk} & a_{k1} & \dots & a_{kk} \end{bmatrix}; \; k = m+1,\ m+2, \dots, n$$

The following theorem gives a sufficient condition for asserting the sign of $Q(\mathbf{x}) = \mathbf{x}^T \mathbf{A} \mathbf{x}$, subject to $m$ linear constraints, $\mathbf{b}\mathbf{x} = \mathbf{0}$.

**THEOREM 7.5** *A sufficient condition for $Q(\mathbf{x}) = \mathbf{x}^T \mathbf{A} \mathbf{x}$ to be positive definite subject to m linear constraints $\mathbf{b}\mathbf{x} = \mathbf{0}$ is that*

$$(-1)^k |\mathbf{B}_k| > 0, \; k = m+1,\ m+2, \dots, n$$

*The corresponding sufficient condition for $Q(\mathbf{x}) = \mathbf{x}^T \mathbf{A} \mathbf{x}$ to be negative definite with the same constraints is that*

$$(-1)^k |\mathbf{B}_k| > 0, \; k = m+1,\ m+2, \dots, n$$

**Example 7.24** The quadratic form $Q(\mathbf{x})$ with $n = 5$ variables is positive definite

$$Q(\mathbf{x}) = \mathbf{x}^T\mathbf{A}\,\mathbf{x}$$

$$= [x_1 \quad x_2 \quad x_3 \quad x_4 \quad x_5]\begin{bmatrix} 2 & 1 & -1 & 1 & -1 \\ 1 & 3 & -1 & 1 & -1 \\ -1 & -1 & 2 & -1 & 1 \\ 1 & 1 & -1 & 1 & -1 \\ -1 & -1 & 1 & -1 & 1 \end{bmatrix}\begin{bmatrix} x_1 \\ x_2 \\ x_3 \\ x_4 \\ x_5 \end{bmatrix}$$

subject to the constraints

$$\mathbf{b}\,\mathbf{x} = [x_1 \quad x_2 \quad x_3 \quad x_4 \quad x_5]\begin{bmatrix} 2 & 1 & 1 & -1 & 3 \\ 1 & 1 & 1 & 1 & 1 \end{bmatrix}\begin{bmatrix} x_1 \\ x_2 \\ x_3 \\ x_4 \\ x_5 \end{bmatrix}$$

To show this we need to construct the bordered matrix $\mathbf{B}_5$.

$$\mathbf{B}_5 = \begin{bmatrix} 0 & 0 & 2 & 1 & 1 & -1 & 3 \\ 0 & 0 & 1 & 1 & 1 & 1 & 1 \\ 2 & 1 & 2 & 1 & -1 & 1 & -1 \\ 1 & 1 & 1 & 3 & -1 & 1 & -1 \\ 1 & 1 & -1 & -1 & 2 & -1 & 1 \\ -1 & 1 & 1 & 1 & -1 & 1 & -1 \\ 3 & 1 & -1 & -1 & 1 & -1 & 1 \end{bmatrix}$$

This can be accomplished using **borderB**.

*In[87]:=*

```
A  =  {{2,1,-1,1,-1},{1,3,-1,1,-1},{-1,-1,2,-1,1},
{1,1,-1,1,-1},{-1,-1,1,-1,1}};
b  =  {{2,1,1,-1,3},{1,1,1,1,1}};
B  =  borderB[A,b];  B  //  MatrixForm
```

*Out[89]//MatrixForm=*

| | | | | | | |
|---|---|---|---|---|---|---|
| 0 | 0 | 2 | 1 | 1 | −1 | 3 |
| 0 | 0 | 1 | 1 | 1 | 1 | 1 |
| 2 | 1 | 2 | 1 | −1 | 1 | −1 |
| 1 | 1 | 1 | 3 | −1 | 1 | −1 |
| 1 | 1 | −1 | −1 | 2 | −1 | 1 |
| −1 | 1 | 1 | 1 | −1 | 1 | −1 |
| 3 | 1 | −1 | −1 | 1 | −1 | 1 |

We then evaluate the determinants of the submatrices $\mathbf{B}_k$, for $k = m+1, m+2, \ldots, n$. The evaluation can be done using the function **signQL**. The output of the function **signQL** is the $m+n$ leading principal minors of the bordered matrix $\mathbf{B}_n$. Since we are interested in the signs of $|\mathbf{B}_k|$ for $k = m+1, \ldots, n$, only the last $(n-m)$ leading principal minors are of significance. The first $2m$ leading principal minors of the output should be ignored. Following this procedure we see that $|\mathbf{B}_3| = 7 > 0$, $|\mathbf{B}_4| = 118 > 0$, and $|\mathbf{B}_5| = 152 > 0$. The quadratic form is thus positive definite.

*In[90]:=*

```
signQL[B]
```

*Out[90]=*

```
{0, 0, 0, 1, 7, 118, 152}
```

It is important to note that the conditions stated in the theorem are sufficient but not necessary. It is possible for the bordered determinant $|\mathbf{B}_n|$ to be zero and the quadratic form $Q(\mathbf{x})$ with constraints still to be positive definite as shown in the following example.

**Example 7.25** $Q(\mathbf{x}) = x_2^2 + 2x_3^2 + 2x_1x_2 + 2x_1x_3 + 2x_2x_3$ subject to the constraint $x_2 + x_3 = 0$. Direct substitution of the constraint to $Q(\mathbf{x})$ shows that $Q(\mathbf{x}) = x_3^2 > 0$, which is positive definite. However, the bordered determinant $|\mathbf{B}_3| = 0$.

*In[91]:=*

```
A = {{0,1,1},{1,1,1},{1,1,2}}; b = {{0,1,1}};
B = borderB[A,b];
signQL[B]
```

*Out[93]=*

```
{0, 0, 0, 0}
```

## EXERCISES

1. Find the sign of $Q(\mathbf{x}) = \mathbf{x}^T\mathbf{A}\mathbf{x}$ subject to $\mathbf{b}\mathbf{x} = \mathbf{0}$.

   (a) $\mathbf{A} = \begin{bmatrix} 1 & 2 \\ 2 & -4 \end{bmatrix}$; $\mathbf{b} = [1 \quad -2]$

   (b) $\mathbf{A} = \begin{bmatrix} 1 & 2 & 3 & 4 \\ 2 & 2 & -1 & 0 \\ 3 & -1 & 3 & 1 \\ 4 & 0 & 1 & 4 \end{bmatrix}$; $\mathbf{b} = [1 \quad -2 \quad 1 \quad 3]$

   (c) $\mathbf{A} = \begin{bmatrix} 1 & 2 & 3 & 4 \\ 2 & 2 & -1 & 0 \\ 3 & -1 & 3 & 1 \\ 4 & 0 & 1 & 4 \end{bmatrix}$; $\mathbf{b} = \begin{bmatrix} 1 & -2 & 1 & 3 \\ 0 & 2 & 1 & -1 \end{bmatrix}$

# 8

# Multivariable Differential Calculus

We reviewed the calculus of functions of one variable in Chapter 2. Most economic relations, however, are usually modeled with functions of several variables. For example, the demand for a product typically depends upon income, the price of related goods, and advertising, among other factors. In this chapter we discuss the calculus of functions of several variables, in preparation for the development of other mathematical concepts presented in subsequent chapters.

We shall begin with a discussion of limits and continuity of functions of several variables. In applications, we are often interested in isolating the effects of a particular variable upon a function, while holding all other variables constant. This process of isolation is called *partial differentiation*, and the rate of change of the values of a function with respect to the isolated variable is called the *partial derivative*. Partial derivatives are sometimes grouped together in a vector, called the *gradient vector*, or a matrix, called the *Hessian matrix*. These quantities are used to determine extrema of functions of several variables.

Lastly, we shall introuduce an important class of functions known as *homogeneous functions* which play an important role in economic modeling. Many economic functions are assumed to be homogeneous. A constant returns to scale production function is linearly homogeneous. A consumer demand function is homogeneous of degree zero in income and prices.

## □ 8.1 Limits and Continuity □

### 8.1.1 Limits

Consider a function $f(x,y)$ which is defined over a set $S$ and let $(x_0,y_0)$ be a point which may or may not be in $S$. We are interested in the values of $f(x,y)$ as $(x,y)$ approaches to $(x_0,y_0)$.

**DEFINITION 8.1** *A function $f(x,y)$ is said to have a limit A at the point $(x_0,y_0)$ if for any $\varepsilon > 0$ there exists a $\delta > 0$ such that*

$$|f(x,y) - A| < \varepsilon \quad \textit{whenever} \quad 0 < \sqrt{(x-x_0)^2 + (y-y_0)^2} < \delta$$

*The symbolic form of the statement is*

$$\lim_{(x,y)\to(x_0,y_0)} f(x,y) = A$$

As shown in figure 8.1, $\sqrt{(x-x_0)^2+(y-y_0)^2} < \delta$ means that $(x,y)$ is in a "disk" or $\delta$-neighborhood of $(x_0,y_0)$. The above definition of the limit closely parallels the definition of the limit of a single variable function given in Chapter 2, yet there is a fundamental difference. In the single-variable case, a function has a limit $A$ as $x \to x_0$ if it has one-sided limits (right or left) and these limits equal $A$. However, in the case of two variables, $(x,y)$ can approach $(x_0,y_0)$ from any direction within the $\delta$-neighborhood as shown in figure 8.1.

If $f(x,y)$ approaches different values as $(x,y)$ approaches $(x_0,y_0)$ in different directions, then the limit does not exist. This situation is demonstrated in the following example.

**Example 8.1** Consider the function

$$f(x,y) = \frac{(x^2-y^2)}{(x^2+y^2)}$$

This function is defined everywhere except at the origin. We want to see if this function has a limit at the origin. The following *Mathematica* plot of $f(x,y)$ shows the behavior of $f(x,y)$ around (0,0).

*In[1]:=*

```
Clear[f,x,y];
f[x_,y_]:= (x^2-y^2)/(x^2+y^2);
Plot3D[f[x,y],{x,-1,1},{y,-1,1},PlotPoints->35,
                    ViewPoint->{0.960, -2.900, 0.580},
                    AxesLabel->{"x","y","f(x,y)"}];
```

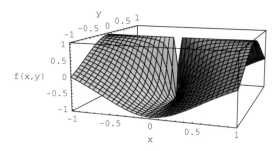

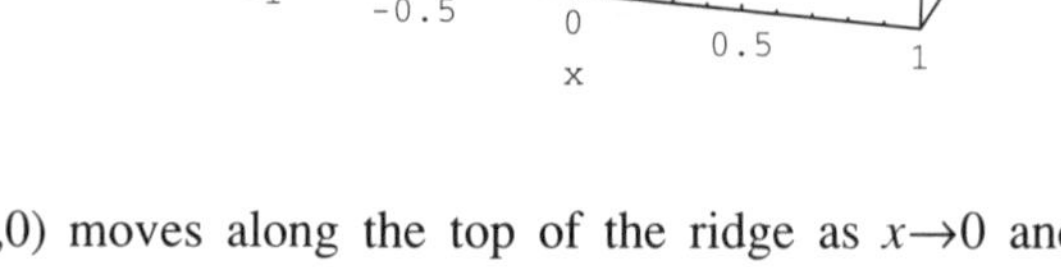


The function $f(x,0)$ moves along the top of the ridge as $x \to 0$ and $\lim_{x\to 0} f(x,0) = 1$. Now let $(x,y)$ approach (0,0) parallel to the $y$-axis, i.e., let $y$ approach 0 along the line $x = 0$. Then $f(0,y) = -y^2/y^2 = -1$ for all $y \neq 0$ and $\lim_{y\to 0} f(0,y) = -1$. Finally, let $(x,y)$ approach (0,0) along the arbitrary line $y = mx$. Then

$$\lim_{x\to 0} f(x,mx) = \frac{(x^2-y^2)}{(x^2+y^2)} = \frac{(x^2-m^2x^2)}{(x^2+m^2x^2)} = \frac{(1-m^2)}{(1+m^2)}$$

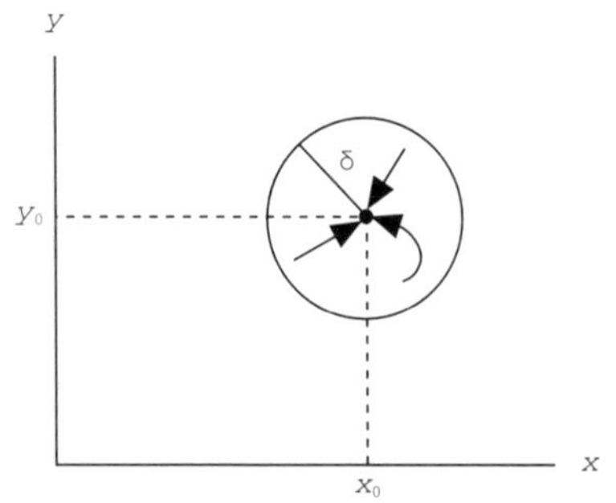


**Figure 8.1** δ-neighborhood

As we can see, when $(x,y)$ moves along the line $y = mx$, the limit depends upon the slope of the line. Since the limit changes with the direction of approach, the limit of the function $f(x,y)$ at the point of origin $(x,y) = (0,0)$ does not exist. The following *Mathematica* calculation confirms this observation.

*In[4]:=*

```
Clear[f,x,y];
f[x_,y_]:= (x^2-y^2)/(x^2+y^2);
Limit[f[x,y] /.{y->m*x}, x->0]
```

*Out[6]=*

$$\frac{1-m^2}{1+m^2}$$

Hence, this function does not have a limit at (0,0).

**Example 8.2** The following function is defined everywhere except at (0,0),

$$f(x,y) = \frac{(2x^3 - y^3)}{(x^2 + y^2)}.$$

From the previous example, we might expect that this function does not have a limit at (0,0). However, it can be shown that

$$\lim_{(x,y)\to(0,0)} \frac{(2x^3 - y^3)}{(x^2 + y^2)} = 0.$$

To prove the existence of the limit, consider the following inequalities,

$$|2x^3 - y^3| \leq 2|x|x^2 + |y|y^2 \leq 2[\,|x|x^2 + |y|y^2\,]$$

Furthermore, since

$$|x| \leq \sqrt{(x^2 + y^2)} \quad \text{and} \quad |y| \leq \sqrt{(x^2 + y^2)}$$

we have

$$\left|2x^3 - y^3\right| \leq 2\left[|x|x^2 + |y|y^2\right] \leq 2\sqrt{(x^2 + y^2)}\,(x^2 + y^2)$$

Thus,

$$\left|\frac{2x^3 - y^3}{x^2 + y^2}\right| \leq 2\sqrt{x^2 + y^2} \quad \text{whenever} \quad 0 < x^2 + y^2.$$

Suppose we are given ε and we choose δ such that

$$0 < \sqrt{x^2 + y^2} < \delta = \frac{\varepsilon}{2}$$

Then have

$$\left|\frac{2x^3 - y^3}{x^2 + y^2} - 0\right| \leq 2\sqrt{x^2 + y^2} < \varepsilon \quad \text{whenever} \quad 0 < \sqrt{x^2 + y^2} < \delta$$

This last step completes the proof that

$$\lim_{(x,y)\to(0,0)} f(x,y) = 0$$

The following *Mathematica* plot confirms the existence of the limit at (0,0).

*In[7]:=*

```
Clear[f,x,y];
f[x_,y_]:=  (2*x^3-y^3)/(x^2+y^2);
Plot3D[f[x,y],{x,-1,1},{y,-1,1},
                    AxesLabel->{"x","y","f(x,y)"}];
```

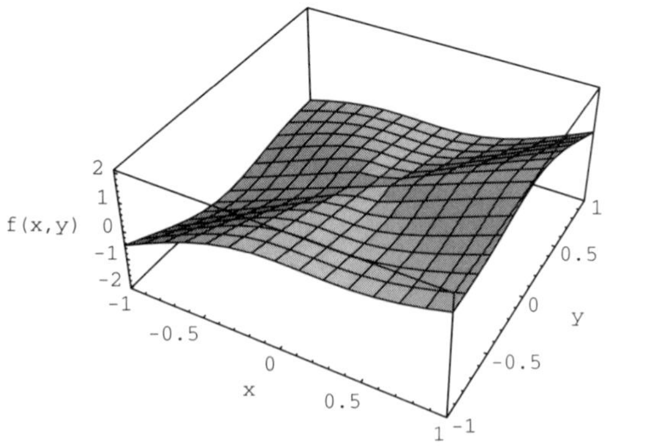


The definition of the limit of a function at a point can be generalized to functions of several variables. If a function of $n$ variables $f(\mathbf{x}) = f(x_1,x_2, \ldots ,x_n)$ is defined at each point in a δ-neighborhood about the point $\mathbf{c} = (c_1,c_2, \ldots ,c_n)$, except possibly at $\mathbf{c}$ itself, then $f(\mathbf{x})$ has limit $A$ as $\mathbf{x}$ approaches $\mathbf{c}$ if for every $\varepsilon > 0$, there exists a $\delta > 0$ such that

$$|f(\mathbf{x}) - \mathbf{A}| < \varepsilon \quad \text{whenever} \quad 0 < \|\mathbf{x}-\mathbf{c}\| < \delta$$

where $\|\mathbf{x}-\mathbf{c}\|$ is the the distance between the two points $\mathbf{x}$ and $\mathbf{c}$.

The algebra of limits for functions of several variables is analogous to that of limits for functions of a single variable. We state below, without proof, some algebraic properties of limits of functions of two variables. These properties are also true for functions of more than two variables.

**THEOREM 8.1** *Let f and g be functions of two variables such that*

$$\lim_{(x,y)\to(x_0,y_0)} f(x,y) = A \quad \textit{and} \quad \lim_{(x,y)\to(x_0,y_0)} g(x,y) = B.$$

*(1) Limit of a sum and difference:*

$$\lim_{(x,y)\to(x_0,y_0)} [f(x,y) \pm g(x,y)] = \lim_{(x,y)\to(x_0,y_0)} f(x,y) \pm \lim_{(x,y)\to(x_0,y_0)} g(x,y) = A \pm B$$

*(2) Limit of a product:*

$$\lim_{(x,y)\to(x_0,y_0)} [f(x,y)\, g(x,y)] = \left[\lim_{(x,y)\to(x_0,y_0)} f(x,y)\right]\left[\lim_{(x,y)\to(x_0,y_0)} g(x,y)\right] = AB$$

*In particular, if $f(x,y) = k$ is constant, then*

$$\lim_{(x,y)\to(x_0,y_0)} [kg(x,y)] = k\left[\lim_{(x,y)\to(x_0,y_0)} g(x,y)\right] = kB$$

*(3) Limit of a quotient: if $B \neq 0$, then*

$$\lim_{(x,y)\to(x_0,y_0)} \frac{f(x,y)}{g(x,y)} = \frac{\lim_{(x,y)\to(x_0,y_0)} f(x,y)}{\lim_{(x,y)\to(x_0,y_0)} g(x,y)} = \frac{A}{B}$$

**Example 8.3** Evaluate the limit

$$\lim_{(x,y)\to(1,2)} (x^2 + 2xy + 3y^2)$$

Using the properties of the limit, we have:

$$\lim_{(x,y)\to(1,2)} (x^2 + 2xy + 3y^2)$$

$$= \lim_{(x,y)\to(1,2)} x^2 + \lim_{(x,y)\to(1,2)} 2xy + \lim_{(x,y)\to(1,2)} 3y^2$$

$$= \left[\lim_{(x,y)\to(1,2)} x\right]^2 + 2\left[\lim_{(x,y)\to(1,2)} x\right]\left[\lim_{(x,y)\to(1,2)} y\right] + 3\left[\lim_{(x,y)\to(1,2)} y\right]^2$$

$$= (1)^2 + 2(1)(2) + 3(2)^2 = 1 + 4 + 12 = 17$$

**Example 8.4** Does the limit

$$\lim_{(x,y)\to(1,2)} \frac{2xy}{x^2 + y}$$

exist? The following calculation shows that it does exist.

$$\lim_{(x,y)\to(1,2)} \frac{2xy}{x^2+y} = \frac{\lim_{(x,y)\to(1,2)} 2xy}{\lim_{(x,y)\to(1,2)} (x^2+y)} = \frac{2\left(\lim_{(x,y)\to(1,2)} x\right)\left(\lim_{(x,y)\to(1,2)} y\right)}{\left(\lim_{(x,y)\to(1,2)} x^2\right)+\left(\lim_{(x,y)\to(1,2)} y\right)} = \frac{2(1)(2)}{1+2} = \frac{4}{3}$$

**Example 8.5** Suppose $D_A(P_A,P_B)$ denotes the demand function for a product $A$ and depends on its own price $P_A$ and the other product price $P_B$. If

$$D_A(P_A,P_B) = 105 - 4P_A^3 + 2\sqrt{P_B}$$

does the demand function have a limit at $(P_A,P_B) = (2,100)$? It is clear that $(2,100)$ is in the domain of the demand function $D_A(P_A,P_B)$ and as $P_A \to 2$, $P_B \to 100$, $D_A(P_A,P_B) \to 93$. We draw the graph of $D_A(P_A,P_B)$ in a neighborhood of $(2,100)$

*In[10]:=*

```
Clear[DA,PA,PB];
DA[PA_,PB_]:= 105 - 4*PA^3 + 2*Sqrt[PB];
Plot3D[DA[PA,PB],{PA,1,3},{PB,95,105},
        AxesLabel->{"PA","PB","DA"}];
```

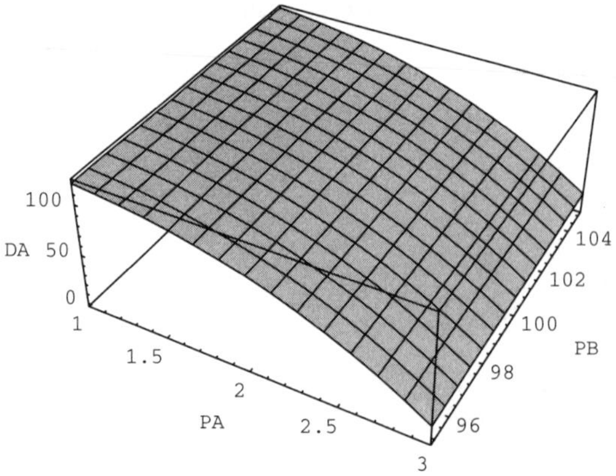


*In[13]:=*

```
DA[2,100]
```

*Out[13]=*

```
93
```

## EXERCISES

1. Find the limits of the following functions at the specific points (if they exist):
   (a) $\lim_{(x,y)\to(1,3)} (x^2 + xy - y^2)$
   (b) $\lim_{(x,y)\to(0,0)} e^{x^2-y^2}$

(c) $\lim_{(x,y)\to(0,0)} \frac{(\sin x)(\cos y)}{x}$

(d) $\lim_{(x,y)\to(3,2)} \frac{x^2 - y^2}{x - y}$

2. Calculate the limits of the following functions at the origin: (1) along the $x$-axis; (2) along the $y$-axis; (3) along $y = 2x$; (4) along $y = x^2$.

(a) $\lim_{(x,y)\to(0,0)} \frac{xy^2}{x^2 + y^4}$

(b) $\lim_{(x,y)\to(0,0)} \frac{x^2 + xy}{x^2 + y^2}$

(c) $\lim_{(x,y)\to(0,0)} \frac{x - y}{x^2 + y^2}$

3. Plot the following functions and show that their limits do not exist.

(a) $\lim_{(x,y)\to(0,0)} \frac{xy}{x^2 + y^2}$

(b) $\lim_{(x,y)\to(0,0)} \frac{2x^2 + y^2}{x^2 + y^2}$

## 8.1.2 Continuity

**DEFINITION 8.2** *Let $f(x,y)$ be a function defined on a open set S and suppose $(x_0,y_0)$ is a point in S. The function $f(x,y)$ is said to be* ***continuous at the point*** *$(x_0,y_0)$ if*

$$\lim_{(x,y)\to(x_0,y_0)} f(x,y) = f(x_0,y_0)$$

*Otherwise, the function is said to be* ***discontinuous*** *at $(x_0,y_0)$.*

A function that is continuous at every point in $S$ is said to be *continuous on the set S*.

**Example 8.6** The function

$$f(x,y) = \begin{cases} \dfrac{2}{x - y^2}, & x - y^2 \neq 0 \\ 0, & x - y^2 = 0 \end{cases}$$

is discontinuous at each point on the parabola $x = y^2$. The values of $f(x,y)$ approach infinity as the points $(x,y)$ approach points on the parabola. We observe this behavior in the following *Mathematica* plot of the function.

*In[14]:=*
```
Clear[f,x,y];
f[x_,y_ /; x-y^2 != 0]:= 2/(x-y^2);
f[x_,y_ /; x-y^2 == 0]:= 0;
Plot3D[f[x,y],{x,-2,2},{y,-2,2},PlotPoints->35,
        ViewPoint->{-4.000, -2.900, 2.330},
        AxesLabel->{"x","y","f(x,y)"}];
```

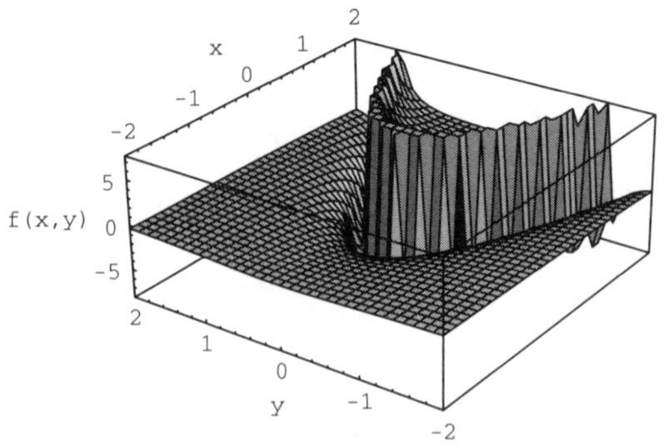


**THEOREM 8.2** *Suppose $f(x,y)$ and $g(x,y)$ are both continuous at $(x_0,y_0)$. If $k$ is a real number, then the following functions are continuous at $(x_0,y_0)$:*

*(1) sum and difference: $f(x,y) \pm g(x,y)$*

*(2) scalar multiple: $kf(x,y)$*

*(3) product: $f(x,y)\, g(x,y)$*

*(4) quotient: $f(x,y)/g(x,y)$* if $g(x_0,y_0) \neq 0$.

*Furthermore, if the function $h(x)$ is continuous at $f(x_0,y_0)$, then the composite function $h(f(x,y))$ is continuous at $(x_0,y_0)$.*

**Example 8.7** The function

$$f(x,y) = \frac{xy^2}{x^2 + y^2}$$

is continuous at all points $(x,y)$ except (0,0). This follows from the following computation

$$\lim_{(x,y)\to(x_0,y_0)} f(x,y) = \frac{\lim_{(x,y)\to(x_0,y_0)} (xy^2)}{\lim_{(x,y)\to(x_0,y_0)} (x^2+y^2)} = \frac{x_0 y_0^2}{x_0^2+y_0^2} = f(x_0,y_0)$$

where $(x_0,y_0) \neq (0,0)$. The function can be defined at (0,0) so that it is a continuous function on $\mathbf{R}^2$. Since $y^2/(x^2+y^2) \leq 1$, $(x,y) \neq (0,0)$, we have

$$\left|\frac{xy^2}{x^2 + y^2}\right| \leq \frac{|x|y^2}{x^2 + y^2} \leq |x| \leq \sqrt{x^2} \leq \sqrt{x^2 + y^2}.$$

This indicates that $\lim_{(x,y)\to(0,0)} f(x,y) = 0$.

Given $\varepsilon > 0$, we choose $\delta = \varepsilon$. If $0 < (x^2 + y^2)^{1/2} < \delta$, then

$$\left|\frac{xy^2}{x^2 + y^2}\right| \leq \sqrt{x^2 + y^2} < \delta = \varepsilon$$

and hence,

$$\lim_{(x,y)\to(0,0)} f(x,y) = \frac{xy^2}{x^2 + y^2} = 0$$

If we define $f(0,0) = 0$, then $f(x,y)$ is a continuous function everywhere. The following *Mathematica* plot demonstrates the continuity of this function.

*In[18]:=*
```
Clear[f,x,y];
f[x_,y_ /; x^2+y^2 !=0]:= x*y^2/(x^2+y^2);
f[x_,y_ /; x^2+y^2 ==0]:= 0;
Plot3D[f[x,y],{x,-2,2},{y,-2,2},PlotPoints->35,
        ViewPoint->{-3.840, -1.300, 1.410},
        AxesLabel->{"x","y","f(x,y)"}];
```

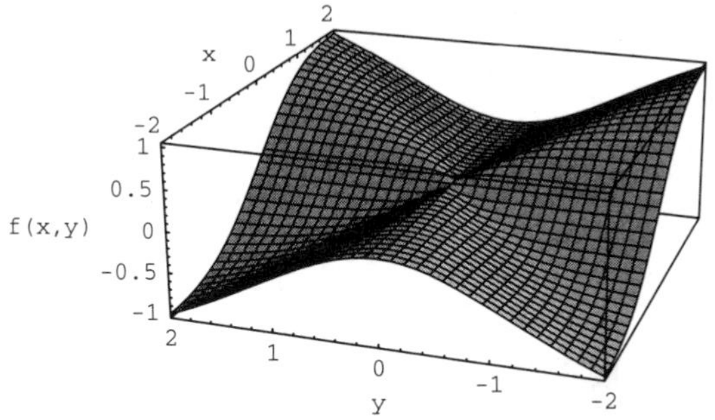


Continuity of functions of more than two variables is similar to that of functions of two variables. Here is an example of a function of three variables.

**Example 8.8** The function

$$f(x,y,z) = x^2 - y^2z^2$$

is continuous everywhere since

$$\lim_{(x,y,z)\to(x_0,y_0,z_0)} f(x,y,z) = x_0^2 - y_0^2z_0^2 = f(x_0,y_0,z_0)$$

## EXERCISES

1. Find the limits and discuss the continuity of the following functions at the indicated points:
   (a) $\lim_{(x,y)\to(1,2)} (x^2 + 3xy)$
   (b) $\lim_{(x,y)\to(1,3)} \dfrac{x+y}{x-y}$
   (c) $\lim_{(x,y)\to(0,0)} e^{xy}$
   (d) $\lim_{(x,y,z)\to(1,2,3)} \sqrt{x+y+z}$
2. Plot and discuss the continuity of the following functions on the indicated sets:
   (a) $f(x,y) = \dfrac{\sin xy}{xy}, \quad -1 < x,y < 1$
   (b) $f(x,y) = \sin x + \cos y, \quad -2 < x,y < 2$
   (c) $f(x,y) = \dfrac{x}{x^2 + y^2}, \quad -2 < x,y < 2$

# □ 8.2 Partial Differentiation □

## 8.2.1 Partial derivatives

We begin with the definition of the partial derivative of a function of two variables.

**DEFINITION 8.3** *The partial derivatives of $f(x,y)$ with respect to x and with respect to y are the functions $f_x$ and $f_y$, respectively, and are defined as*

$$f_x(x,y) = \lim_{\Delta x \to 0} \frac{f(x+\Delta x,y) - f(x,y)}{\Delta x}$$

$$f_y(x,y) = \lim_{\Delta y \to 0} \frac{f(x,y+\Delta y) - f(x,y)}{\Delta y}$$

*provided these limits exist.*

**Example 8.9** We use the definition and the *Mathematica* function **Limit** to calculate the partial derivative of $f(x,y) = x^2 - 3y$ with respect to $x$. In the following calculation, **dx** stands for $\Delta x$.

*In[22]:=*
```
Clear[f,x,y,dx];
f[x_,y_]:= x^2  -  3*y;
Limit[(f[x+dx,y]-f[x,y])/dx,dx->0]
```

*Out[24]=*
```
2x
```

**Example 8.10** Show that $f(x,y) = xe^{xy} + x^2y$ has the partial derivatives:

$$f_x(x,y) = (1+xy)e^{xy} + 2xy$$
$$f_y(x,y) = (1+e^{xy})x^2$$

Again we use the definition.

*In[25]:=*
```
Clear[f,x,y,dy];
f[x_,y_]:= x*Exp[x*y]  +  x^2*y;
Limit[(f[x+dx,y]-f[x,y])/dx,dx->0]
Limit[(f[x,y+dy]-f[x,y])/dy,dy->0]
```

*Out[27]=*

$E^{xy} + 2xy + E^{xy}xy$

*Out[28]=*

$(1 + E^{xy})x^2$

It is not necessary to use limits to compute partial derivatives. The definition indicates that $f_x$ is a measure of how $f$ changes with respect to $x$ if $y$ is held constant.

Similarly, $f_y$ is a measure of how $f$ changes with respect to $y$ if $x$ is held constant. Hence, to compute the partial derivative of $f$ with respect to $x$, we differentiate $f(x,y)$ with respect to $x$, treating $y$ as a constant. Similarly, to compute $f_y$ we differentiate $f(x,y)$ with respect to $y$ with $x$ treated as a constant. To verify this, we find the partials in Example 8.10.

*In[29]:=*

```
D[f[x,y],x]
```

*Out[29]=*

```
E^(xy) + 2xy + E^(xy)xy
```

*In[30]:=*

```
D[f[x,y],y]
```

*Out[30]=*

```
x^2 + E^(xy)x^2
```

We will show in section 8.2.2 that the **Mathematica** function D can be used to compute partial derivatives.

Since the process of finding a partial derivative of a function of two variables is essentially the same as the differentiation of a single variable function, the usual rules (sum, difference, product, quotient, and chain) of finding derivatives are applicable.

Another notation for the partial derivatives is frequently used. It is similar to representing $f'(x)$ as $df/dx$. If $z = f(x,y)$, then

$$f_x(x,y) = \frac{\partial f}{\partial x} = \frac{\partial z}{\partial x}$$

$$f_y(x,y) = \frac{\partial f}{\partial y} = \frac{\partial z}{\partial y}$$

The symbols $\partial/\partial x$ and $\partial/\partial y$ denote operators for finding the partial derivative of a function with respect to $x$ and to $y$, respectively. When a partial derivative is evaluated at a point $(x_0,y_0)$, we denote it as

$$\left.\frac{\partial f}{\partial x}\right|_{(x_0,y_0)} = \left.\frac{\partial z}{\partial x}\right|_{(x_0,y_0)} = f_x(x_0,y_0)$$

$$\left.\frac{\partial f}{\partial y}\right|_{(x_0,y_0)} = \left.\frac{\partial z}{\partial y}\right|_{(x_0,y_0)} = f_y(x_0,y_0)$$

In Example 8.10, the partial derivatives evaluated at (1,2) are equal to:

$$\left.\frac{\partial f}{\partial x}\right|_{(1,2)} = \left.\frac{\partial z}{\partial x}\right|_{(1,2)} = f_x(1,2) = 3e^2 + 4$$

$$\left.\frac{\partial f}{\partial y}\right|_{(1,2)} = \left.\frac{\partial z}{\partial y}\right|_{(1,2)} = f_y(1,2) = 1 + e^2$$

Consider a function of $n$ variables, $f(\mathbf{x}) = f(x_1,x_2, \ldots ,x_n)$. The partial derivative of $f$ with respect to $x_i$ is defined as

$$f_{x_i} = \lim_{\Delta x_i \to 0} \frac{f(x_1, \ldots, x_i+\Delta x_i, x_{i+1}, \ldots, x_n) - f(x_i, \ldots, x_i, x_{i+1}, \ldots, x_n)}{\Delta x_i}$$

providing the limits exist.

**Example 8.11** Consider a function $w = f(x,y,z) = x^2y + y^3z + z^4x$. The partial derivatives with respect to $x$, $y$, and $z$ are:

$$\frac{\partial f}{\partial x} = \frac{\partial w}{\partial x} = f_x = 2xy + z^4$$

$$\frac{\partial f}{\partial y} = \frac{\partial w}{\partial y} = f_y = x^2 + 3y^2z$$

$$\frac{\partial f}{\partial z} = \frac{\partial w}{\partial z} = f_z = y^3 + 4z^3x$$

*In[31]:=*

```
Clear[f,x,y,z,fx,fy,fz,dx,dy,dz];
f[x_,y_,z_]:= x^2*y + y^3*z + z^4*x;
fx[x_,y_,z_] = Limit[(f[x+dx,y,z]-f[x,y,z])/dx,dx->0]
fy[x_,y_,z_] = Limit[(f[x,y+dy,z]-f[x,y,z])/dy,dy->0]
fz[x_,y_,z_] = Limit[(f[x,y,z+dz]-f[x,y,z])/dz,dz->0]
```

*Out[33]=*

$2xy + z^4$

*Out[34]=*

$x^2 + 3y^2z$

*Out[35]=*

$y^3 + 4xz^3$

It is obvious from examining the above example that the partial derivatives are themselves functions of $x$, $y$, and $z$. It is thus possible to take partial derivatives of the partial derivatives, $f_x$, $f_y$, and $f_z$. The *second-order partial derivatives* of $f_x$ with respect to $x$, $y$ and $z$ are:

$$\frac{\partial}{\partial x}\left(\frac{\partial f}{\partial x}\right) = \frac{\partial^2 f}{\partial x^2} = f_{xx} = 2y$$

$$\frac{\partial}{\partial y}\left(\frac{\partial f}{\partial x}\right) = \frac{\partial^2 f}{\partial y \partial x} = f_{xy} = 2x$$

$$\frac{\partial}{\partial z}\left(\frac{\partial f}{\partial x}\right) = \frac{\partial^2 f}{\partial z \partial x} = f_{xz} = 4z^3$$

We can verify this with *Mathematica*.

*In[36]:=*

```
Limit[(fx[x+dx,y,z]-fx[x,y,z])/dx,dx->0]
Limit[(fx[x,y+dy,z]-fx[x,y,z])/dy,dy->0]
Limit[(fx[x,y,z+dz]-fx[x,y,z])/dz,dz->0]
```

*Out[36]=*

2y

*Out[37]=*

2x

*Out[38]=*

$4z^3$

Note that symbol $f_{xy}$ is interpreted as the partial derivative of the function $f(x,y,z)$ with respect to $x$ first, and then $y$ second. This derivative is called a *mixed(cross) partial derivative*. Here the mixed partial derivative is

$$\frac{\partial}{\partial x}\left(\frac{\partial f}{\partial y}\right) = \frac{\partial^2 f}{\partial x \partial y} = f_{yx} = 2x$$

is the same as the partial derivative $f_{xy}$. A proposition, known as *Young's theorem*, states $f_{xy} = f_{yx}$, as long as $f$, and the first-order and second-order partial derivatives are continuous. The proposition holds for functions of three or more variables. For example, if $f(x,y,z)$, its first-order, and second-order partial derivatives are contintuous, then

$$f_{xz} = f_{zx}, \quad \text{and} \quad f_{yz} = f_{zy}.$$

In principle, partial derivatives of any order can be taken. Young's theorem also holds true for any higher-order partial derivatives, provided all of the partial derivatives are continuous.

A function $f(x)$ is said to be *differentiable* at a point $x_0$ if there exists a constant $A$ such that

$$\Delta f = f(x_0+\Delta x) - f(x_0) = A\Delta x + \mathrm{K}(\Delta x)\Delta x,$$

where $\mathrm{K}(\Delta x)$ is a function of $\Delta x$ and

$$\lim_{\Delta x \to 0} \mathrm{K}(\Delta x) = 0.$$

In other words,

$$\lim_{\Delta x \to 0} \frac{\Delta f}{\Delta x} = A + \lim_{\Delta x \to 0} \mathrm{K}(\Delta x) = A.$$

Thus, if $f(x)$ is differentiable at $x_0$, then it has a derivative at $x_0$ and $f'(x_0) = A$. The differentiability of a function $f(x,y)$ of two variables requires a stronger condition than merely having partial derivatives. A function $f(x,y)$ is said to be *differentiable* at a point $(x_0,y_0)$ if there exist constants $A$ and $B$ such that

$$\Delta f = f(x_0+\Delta x, y_0+\Delta y) - f(x_0,y_0)$$
$$= A\Delta x + B\Delta y + K_x(\Delta x,\Delta y)\Delta x + K_y(\Delta x,\Delta y)\Delta y$$

where $K_x(\Delta x,\Delta y)$ and $K_y(\Delta x,\Delta y)$ are functions of $\Delta x$ and $\Delta y$ such that

$$\lim_{(\Delta x,\Delta y)\to(0,0)} K_x(\Delta x,\Delta y) = 0, \quad \lim_{(\Delta x,\Delta y)\to(0,0)} K_y(\Delta x,\Delta y) = 0$$

The expression $A\Delta x + B\Delta y$, denoted as d$f$, is called the (*total*) *differential* of $f$ at $(x_0,y_0)$, and we write

$$df = A\Delta x + B\Delta y$$

If $f$ is differentiable at $(x_0,y_0)$, then the first partials of $f$ at $(x_0,y_0)$ exist, and $f_x(x_0,y_0) = A$ and $f_y(x_0,y_0) = B$.

We shall discuss the differential further in section 8.4. We would like to point out here, however, that there exist functions which are not differentiable at a point even though their partials may exist. If $f$ is differentiable at each point of a set $S$, then the function is said to be *differentiable on S*. If the partial derivatives exist, then

$$df = f_x dx + f_y dy$$

where $dx = \Delta x$ and $dy = \Delta y$ denote the increments, or differentials, of the independent variables.

## EXERCISES

1. Use the function **Limit** to compute the partial derivatives, $f_x$, $f_y$, and $f_z$, for the following functions:
   (a) $f(x,y) = x^2y + y^2x$
   (b) $f(x,y,z) = \log(x^2 + y^2 + z^2)$
   (c) $f(x,y,z) = \sqrt{x^2 + y^2 + z^2}$
2. Use **Limit** to find the second-order and mixed partial derivatives of the functions in exercise 1. Check Young's theorem for these functions.

### 8.2.2 Computing partial derivatives with *Mathematica*

To compute partial derivatives with *Mathematica* we use the **D** function.

*In[39]:=*

```
?D
```

**D[f, x] gives the partial derivative of f with respect to x. D[f, {x, n}] gives the nth partial derivative with respect to x. D[f, x1, x2, ...] gives a mixed derivative.**

As we can see, there are various formats of the function. We illustrate formats in the following examples.

**Example 8.12** Find the first, second and mixed partial derivatives of the function $f(x,y) = x^2y + e^{-xy}$.

*In[40]:=*
```
Clear[f,x,y];
f[x_,y_]:= x^2*y + Exp[-x*y];
D[f[x,y],x]
```

*Out[42]=*

$$-(\frac{y}{E^{xy}}) + 2x\,y$$

*In[43]:=*
```
D[f[x,y],{x,2}]
```

*Out[43]=*

$$2y + \frac{y^2}{E^{xy}}$$

*In[44]:=*
```
D[f[x,y],x,y]
```

*Out[44]=*

$$-E^{-(xy)} + 2x + \frac{xy}{E^{xy}}$$

**Example 8.13** A general form of the Cobb-Douglas production function is

$$Q = f(x_1,x_2, \ldots ,x_n) = \prod_{i=1}^{n} cx_i^{a_i}$$

where $Q$ is output, the $x_i$'s are inputs, and $c$ and the $a_i$'s are constants. The *marginal product* of an input is defined as the change in output associated with the change in the quantity of the input while holding all other inputs constant. Thus, the marginal product of $x_i$ is simply the partial derivative of $Q$ with respect to $x_i$. Now consider a special case with $n = 2$ and rewrite the Cobb-Douglas form as

$$Q = f(L,K) = cL^aK^b$$

The marginal product of labor (L) and capital (K) are, respectively,

$$f_L = a\,cL^{a-1}K^b$$
$$f_K = bcL^aK^{b-1}$$

These partial derivative are computed by *Mathematica* as follows.

*In[45]:=*
```
Clear[f,L,K,a,b,c,fL,fK];
f[L_,K_]:= c*(L^a)*(K^b);
fL  =  D[f[L,K],L]
fK  =  D[f[L,K],K]
```

*Out[47]=*

$$acK^bL^{-1+a}$$

*Out[48]=*

$bcK^{-1+b}L^{a}$

The mixed partial derivative, $f_{LK}$, which measures the change in the marginal product of labor when there is an incremental change in capital, is equal to $f_{KL}$ by Young's theorem.

*In[49]:=*

```
fLK  =  D[f[L,K],L,K]
fKL  =  D[f[L,K],K,L]
```

*Out[49]=*

$abcK^{-1+b}L^{-1+a}$

*Out[50]=*

$abcK^{-1+b}L^{-1+a}$

**Example 8.14** A production function $Q = f(L,K)$ of the form

$$\log f(L,K) = a_0 + a_1 \log L + a_2 \log K + a_3(\log L)^2 + a_4(\log K)^2 + a_5(\log L)(\log K)$$

is called a *translog* or *transcendental logarithmic* production function. Suppose $a_0 = 1.5$, $a_1 = 0.9$, $a_2 = 0.2$, $a_3 = -0.03$, $a_4 = -0.01$, and $a_5 = 0.02$. Evaluate the marginal product $f_L$ of labor, and the marginal product $f_K$ of capital at the input level $(L,K) = (20,30)$ units. In the following *Mathematica* statements, we note that $f(L,K) = e^{\log f(L,K)}$.

*In[51]:=*

```
Clear[f,L,K,fL,fK,a0,a1,a2,a3,a4,a5];
a0=1.5;a1=0.9;a2=0.2;a3=-0.03;a4=-0.01;a5=0.02;
f[L_,K_]:=  Exp[a0+a1*Log[L]+a2*Log[K]+a3*(Log[L])^2+
                a4*(Log[K])^2+a5*Log[L]*Log[K]];
fL  =  D[f[L,K],L]/.{L->20,K->30}  //  N
```

*Out[54]=*

4.31299

*In[55]:=*

```
fK  =  D[f[L,K],K]/.{L->20,K->30}  //  N
```

*Out[55]=*

0.69994

## EXERCISES

1. Use *Mathematica* to find the first-order, second-order and mixed second partial derivatives of the following functions. Evaluate the partial derivatives at the indicated points.

(a) $f(x,y) = e^x \log(1+y)$, $(x_0,y_0) = (1,2)$.
(b) $f(x,y) = x\sin y + y\sin x$, $(x_0,y_0) = (\pi,-\pi/2)$.
(c) $f(x,y,z) = xy^2 + yx^2 + zx^2$, $(x_0,y_0,z_0) = (1,-2,1)$

2. A CES (constant elasticity of substitution) utility function has the form,

$$f(x,y,z) = [a_1x^b + a_2y^b + (1-a_1-a_2)z^b]^{1/b}$$

Find the marginal utilities: $f_x$, $f_y$, and $f_z$.

### 8.2.3 Geometric interpretation of partial derivatives

A function of $n$-variables can be thought of as a surface in an $(n+1)$-dimensional space. The partial derivative with respect to the $i$-th variable measures the slope of the surface as the value of the $i$-th variable changes, while holding the values of all other variables constant. More insight into partial derivatives can be gained by examining the surface of the function

$$z = f(x,y) = 0.5(x-1)y - (x-1)^2 - y^2$$

*In[56]:=*

```
Clear[z,f,x,y];
f[x_,y_]:=  0.5*(x-1)*y  -(x-1)^2  -  y^2;
surface  =  Plot3D[f[x,y],{x,0,2},{y,-1,1},
                   AxesLabel->{"x","y","z"},
                   ViewPoint->{1.600,  -2.810,  0.780}];
```

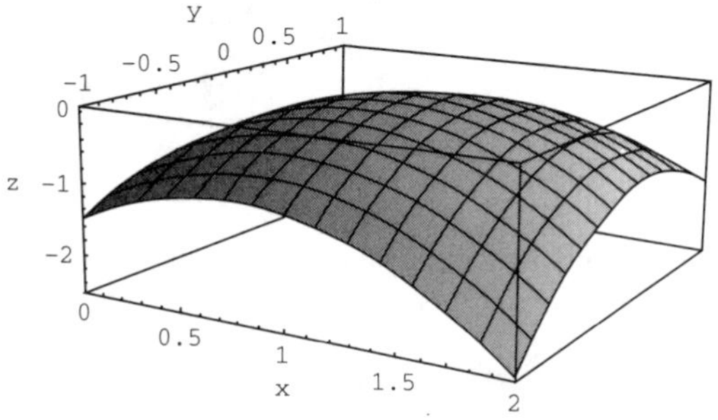


The partial derivative $f_y(x_0,y_0)$ at $(x_0,y_0) = (1.0,-0.5)$ is the rate of change of the function $f(x,y)$ with respect to $y$ at $y_0 = -0.5$ when holding $x$ at $x_0 = 1.0$. Geometrically, these values correspond to the slope of the tangent lines on the surface of the function along a grid line perpendicular to the $x$ axis at $x_0 = 1.0$. To illustrate this concept, we first construct a vertical plane containing the point $(x_0,y_0,z_0)$ where $z_0 = f(x_0,y_0)$ using the function **ParametricPlot3D**.

*In[59]:=*

```
x0  =  1.0;  y0  =  -0.5;
cutter=ParametricPlot3D[{x0,y,z},{y,-1,1},{z,-3,0.5},
                        BoxRatios->{1,1,0.5},
                        AxesLabel->{"x","y","z"},
                         ViewPoint->{1.600,  -2.810,  0.780}];
```

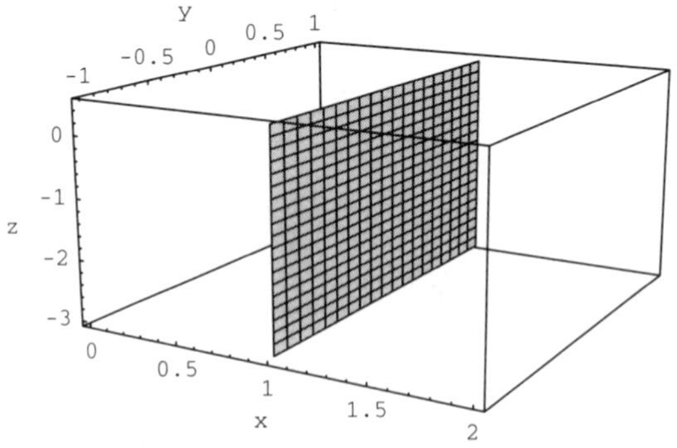


The intersection of this plane and the graph of $f$ is a curve in this vertical plane that has the the equation:

$z = f(x_0,y) = 0.5(x_0-1)y - (x_0-1)^2 - y^2.$

*In[61]:=*
```
Show[surface,cutter];
```

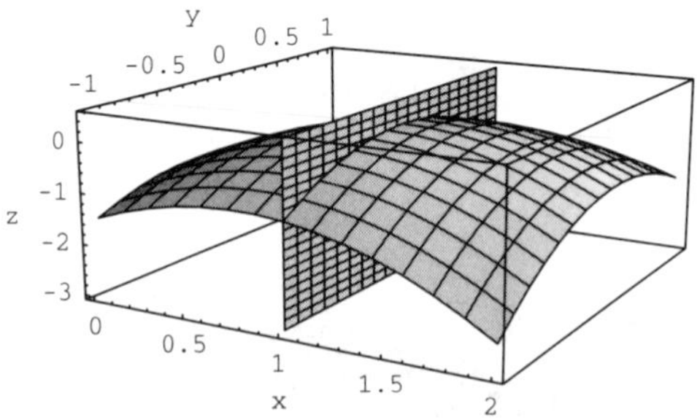


The partial derivative of $f(x,y)$ with respect to $y$ for $x = x_0$ is then the slope of a tangent line on the trace of the surface and is equal to

$f_y(x_0,y) = 0.5\ (x_0-1) - 2y.$

The equation of the tangent line on the surface at the point $(x_0,y_0,z_0)$ in the direction of $y$-axis is

$T(x_0,y) = f(x_0,y_0) + f_y(x_0,y_0)(y - y_0).$

We use **ParametricPlot3D** to graph the tangent line.

*In[62]:=*
```
fy = D[f[x,y],y]/.{x->x0,y->y0};
tyline=ParametricPlot3D[{x0,y,f[x0,y0]+fy*(y-y0),
                          Thickness[0.009]},{y,-1.2,1},
                         BoxRatios->{1,1,0.5},
                          DisplayFunction->Identity];
Show[surface,cutter,tyline];
```

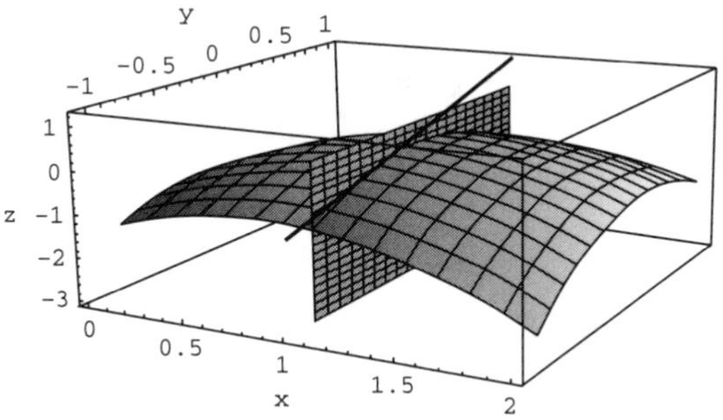


The slope of the tangent line $T(x_0,y)$ at $(1,-0.5)$ is equal to 1 since

$$f_y(x_0,y_0) = 0.5(x_0-1) - 2y_0 = 0.5(1-1) - 2(-0.5) = 1.$$

In a similar fashion, we can illustrate the geometric meaning of the partial derivative $f_x(x,y_0)$. The equation for the tangent line $T(x,y_0)$ on the surface at the point $(x_0,y_0)$ is

$$T(x,y_0) = f(x_0,y_0) + f_x(x_0,y_0)\,(x - x_0)$$

The slope of the tangent line $T(x,y_0)$ at $(1,-0.5)$ is equal to

$$f_x(x_0,y_0) = 0.5y_0 - 2(x_0-1) = -0.25$$

## EXERCISE

1. Using *Mathematica*, draw the tangent lines to the surface

   $$z = 4 - x^2 - y^2$$

   that are parallel to the $x$-axis and to the $y$-axis and pass through the point $(1,-1.2)$.

# □ 8.3 Gradient Vector and Hessian Matrix □

## 8.3.1 Gradient vector and directional derivatives

A sufficiently smooth function of $n$ variables has $n$ first-order partial drivatives and $n^2$ second-order partial derivatives. We shall introduce a vector that is a collection of the $n$ first-order partial derivatives and a matrix that is composed of the $n^2$ second-order partial derivatives.

Suppose $f(x_1,x_2, \ldots ,x_n)$ has $n$ first-order partial derivatives

$$\frac{\partial f}{\partial x_i} = f_{x_i}(x_1,x_2,\ldots,x_n) \equiv f_i,\ i = 1, 2, \ldots, n$$

where $f_i$ is a shorthand notation for the partial derivative with respect to $x_i$. The $n$ partial derivatives can be arranged as an $n$-dimensional vector. This vector is called the *gradient vector* of the function $f$ and is denoted as

$\nabla \mathbf{f} = [f_1 \quad f_2 \quad \ldots \quad f_n]$.

We have written it as a row vector, but it could also be written as a column vector.

**Example 8.15** $f(x,y,z) = x^3y^2 + xz$. The gradient vector is

$\nabla \mathbf{f} = [3x^2y^2{+}z \quad 2x^3y \quad x]$

When the gradient is evaluated at the point (2,1,3), it is the constant vector

$\nabla \mathbf{f} = [15 \quad 16 \quad 2]$

Computation of the gradient vector can be performed using the **MathEcon** function, **gradf**.

*In[66]:=*

```
?gradf
```

**gradf[fct,lst] calculates the gradient of the function fct with respect to the variables specified by lst (a list). For example,**

**gradf[x*y-y^2*z+w,{x,y,z,w}].**

**Example 8.16** Compute the gradient vector of the function in Example 8.15 and evaluate the gradient vector at the point (2,1,3).

*In[67]:=*

```
Clear[f,x,y,z];
f[x_,y_,z_]:= x^3*y^2 + x*z;
gvector = gradf[f[x,y,z],{x,y,z}]
```

*Out[69]=*

$\{3x^2y^2 + z, 2x^3y, x\}$

*In[70]:=*

```
gvector /.{x->2,y->1,z->3}
```

*Out[70]=*

{15, 16, 2}

**Example 8.17** Find the gradient vector of the generic function $f(x,y,z,w)$.

*In[71]:=*

```
Clear[f,x,y,z,w];
gradf[f[x,y,z,w],{x,y,z,w}]
```

*Out[72]=*

$\{f^{(1,0,0,0)}[x,y,z,w], f^{(0,1,0,0)}[x,y,z,w], f^{(0,0,1,0)}[x,y,z,w], f^{(0,0,0,1)}[x,y,z,w]\}$

*Mathematica* uses the notation $\mathbf{f}^{(1,0,0,0)}$**[x,y,z,w]** to represent $f_x(x,y,z,w)$. Similarly, $\mathbf{f}^{(0,1,0,0)}$**[x,y,z,w]** represents $f_y(x,y,z,w)$, and so forth.

Consider the function

$$f(x,y) = y\,(x-1)/2 - (x-1)^2 - y^2.$$

The partial derivative $f_y(x_0,y_0)$ measures the rate of change of the function at $(x_0,y_0)$ parallel to the $y$-axis. Similarly, $f_x(x_0,y_0)$ measures the rate of change of the function parallel to the $x$-axis. These directional changes parallel to the $x$-axis and $y$-axis at the point (1,–0.5) are shown in the following *Mathematica* plot.

*In[73]:=*

```
Clear[f,x,y];
x0  =  1;  y0  =  -0.5;
f[x_,y_]:=  (x-1)*y/2  -(x-1)^2  -  y^2;

surface  =  Plot3D[f[x,y],{x,0,2},{y,-1,1},
                 DisplayFunction->Identity];

fx  =  D[f[x,y],x]/.{x->x0,y->y0};
fy  =  D[f[x,y],y]/.{x->x0,y->y0};
txline=ParametricPlot3D[{x,y0,f[x0,y0]+fx*(x-x0),
           Thickness[0.009]},{x,x0,x0+1},
           BoxRatios->{1,1,0.5},
           DisplayFunction->Identity];

tyline=ParametricPlot3D[{x0,y,f[x0,y0]+fy*(y-y0),
           Thickness[0.009]},{y,y0,y0+1},
           BoxRatios->{1,1,0.5},
           DisplayFunction->Identity];

Show[surface,txline,tyline,
           AxesLabel->{"x","y","z"},
           ViewPoint->{1.600,  -2.810,  0.780},
           DisplayFunction->$DisplayFunction];
```

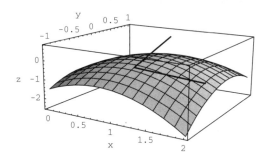

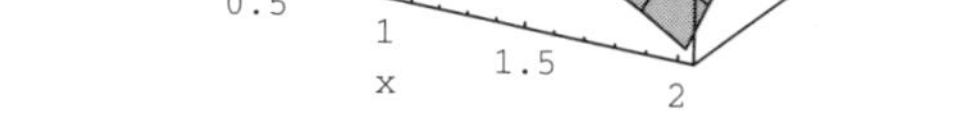


Since $f_x(1,-0.5) = -0.25$ is negative, the thick line parallel to the $x$-axis shown on the surface indicates that the value of the function decreases as $x$ increases from the point (1,–0.5). On the other hand, since $f_y(1,-0.5) = 1$ is positive, the thick line indicates that the value of the function increases as $y$ increases from the point (1,–0.5).

The partial derivatives, shown in the above plot, do not reveal the changes in the value of the function $f(x,y)$ in other directions, for example, as $(x,y)$ moves from $(x_0,y_0)$ to $(x_0+tk_1,y_0+tk_2)$ as shown in figure 8.2.

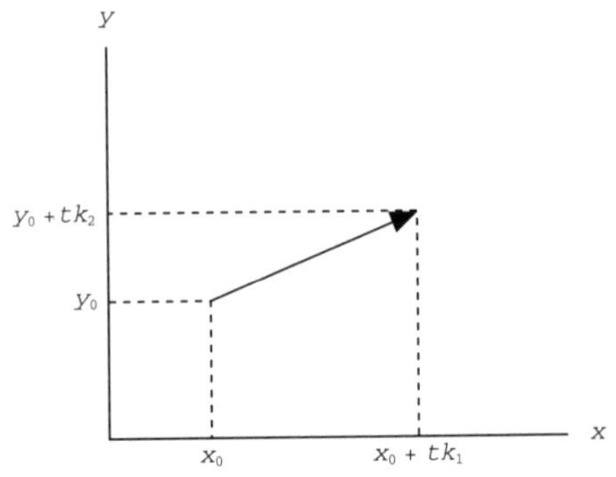


**Figure 8.2** Directional change in $(x, y)$

Let $\mathbf{k} = [k_1\ k_2]^T$ denote a unit vector. The *directional derivative* of $f(x,y)$ at the point $(x_0,y_0)$ in the direction $\mathbf{k}$, denoted as $D_{\mathbf{k}}f(x_0,y_0)$, is defined as

$$D_{\mathbf{k}}f(x_0, y_0) = \lim_{t\to 0}\frac{f(x_0+tk_1,y_0+tk_2) - f(x_0,y_0)}{t}$$

provided the limit exists. It can be shown that the directional derivative at $(x_0,y_0)$ is equal to $\nabla\mathbf{f}(x_0,y_0)\cdot\mathbf{k}$. That is,

$$D_{\mathbf{k}}f(x_0,y_0) = k_1\, f_x(x_0,y_0) + k_2\, f_y(x_0,y_0) = \nabla\mathbf{f}\cdot\mathbf{k}$$

As we can see from this identity, the directional derivative is a linear combination of the partial derivatives. It is a generalization of the partial derivative and measures the rate of change of $f(x,y)$ at $(x_0,y_0)$ in any chosen direction $\mathbf{k}$. In particular, if $\mathbf{k} = [1\ 0]^T$, then $D_{\mathbf{k}}f(x_0,y_0) = f_x(x_0,y_0)$. If $\mathbf{k} = [0\ 1]^T$, then $D_{\mathbf{k}}f(x_0,y_0) = f_y(x_0,y_0)$. The equation for any tangent line on the surface of $f(x,y)$ in the direction $\mathbf{k}$ is

$$T(x_0+k_1t,y_0+k_2t) = f(x_0,y_0) + D_{\mathbf{k}}f(x_0,y_0)t$$

with a slope equal to $D_{\mathbf{k}}f(x_0,y_0)$.

**Example 8.18** Consider the function

$$f(x,y) = y(x-1)/2 - (x-1)^2 - y^2.$$

At the point $(1,-1/2)$ and in the direction of $\mathbf{k} = [1/\sqrt{5}\ 2/\sqrt{5}]^T$, we can compute the directional derivative. Since $f_x(1,-1/2) = -1/4$ and $f_y(1,-1/2) = 1$, the directional derivative is

$$D_{\mathbf{k}}f(1,-0.5) = -1/4\sqrt{5} + 2/\sqrt{5} > 0.$$

The value of $f(x,y)$ is increasing in the neighborhood of $(1,-1/2)$ and in the direction of $\mathbf{k}$. Here is a plot of the surface $z = f(x,y)$ and the tangent line at $(1,-1/2)$.

*In[84]:=*

```
Clear[f,x,y];
k1  =  1/Sqrt[5];  k2  =  2/Sqrt[5];
x0  =  1;  y0  =  -1/2;
f[x_,y_]:=  y*(x-1)/2  -  (x-1)^2  -  y^2;
fx  =  D[f[x,y],x]  /.  {x->x0,y->y0};
fy  =  D[f[x,y],y]  /.  {x->x0,y->y0};
dk  =  k1*fx+k2*fy;

surface  =  Plot3D[f[x,y],{x,0,2},{y,-1,1},
                   DisplayFunction->Identity];

tkline  =  ParametricPlot3D[{x0+t,y0+t,f[x0,y0]+dk*t,
                   Thickness[0.009]},{t,0,0.8},
                   BoxRatios->{1,1,0.5},
                   DisplayFunction->Identity];

Show[surface,tkline,
             AxesLabel->{"x","y","z"},
             ViewPoint->{1.600,  -2.810,  0.780},
             DisplayFunction->$DisplayFunction];
```

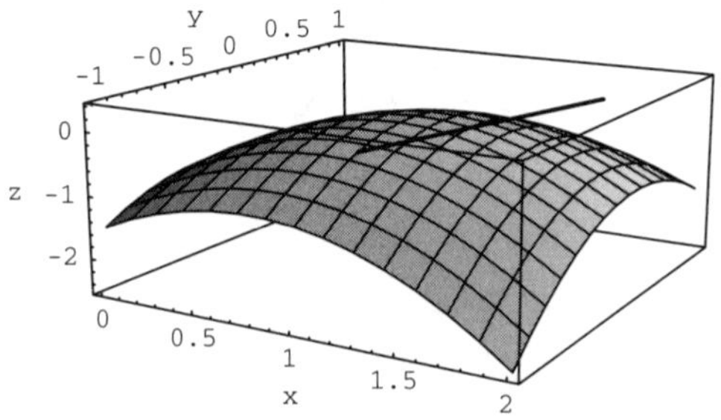


**Example 8.19** Consider $f(x,y) = \log(x^2+y^2)^{1/2}$ where $(x,y) \neq (0,0)$. Find the directional derivative of $f$ at (3,4) in the direction of the vector $\mathbf{k} = [1/\sqrt{10}\ 3/\sqrt{10}]^T$. Using *Mathematica* to do our computations, we can easily find the directional derivative.

*In[95]:=*

```
Clear[f,x,y];
f[x_,y_]:=  Log[Sqrt[x^2+y^2]];
k  =  {1/Sqrt[10],3/Sqrt[10]};
dk  =  gradf[f[x,y],{x,y}].k  /.{x->3,y->4}  //  N
```

*Out[98]=*

```
0.189737
```

Since $D_{\mathbf{k}}f(3,4) \approx 0.189737 > 0$, $f(x,y)$ is increasing in the direction $\mathbf{k} = [1/\sqrt{10}\ 3/\sqrt{10}]^T$.

Recall that for any two vectors $\mathbf{u}$ and $\mathbf{v}$ the dot product can be computed as

$$\mathbf{u} \cdot \mathbf{v} = \|\mathbf{u}\|\,\|\mathbf{v}\|\cos\theta$$

where $\theta$ is the angle between the vectors. Since the directional derivative is a dot product and $\mathbf{k}$ is a unit vector, we have

$D_{\mathbf{k}}f(x_0,y_0) = \nabla\mathbf{f}\cdot\mathbf{k} = \|\nabla\mathbf{f}\|\|\mathbf{k}\|\cos\theta = \|\nabla\mathbf{f}\|\cos\theta$

where $\theta$ is the angle between the gradient vector $\nabla\mathbf{f}$ and the direction vector $\mathbf{k}$. Thus, provided $\nabla\mathbf{f}\neq\mathbf{0}$, the directional derivative takes its largest value when $\theta = 0$, i.e., when $\mathbf{k}$ and $\nabla\mathbf{f}$ are pointing in the same direction. That is, the largest increase of $f(x,y)$ is in the direction of $\nabla\mathbf{f}$. The directional derivative takes its smallest value when $\theta = \pi$. The largest decrease of $f(x,y)$ is in the opposite direction of $\nabla\mathbf{f}$, i.e., $-\nabla\mathbf{f}$. The directional derivative thus provides information about the direction in which the value of $f(x,y)$ increases or decreases most rapidly. Here we summarize this discussion in terms of a theorem.

**THEOREM 8.3** *Suppose $f(x,y)$ is differentiable at $(x_0,y_0)$.*

(1) *If $\nabla\mathbf{f}(x_0,y_0) = 0$, then $D_{\mathbf{k}}f(x_0,y_0) = 0$ for all directions $\mathbf{k}$. The point $(x_0,y_0)$ is called a **stationary** (or **critical**) point of $f(x,y)$.*

(2) *If $\nabla\mathbf{f}(x_0,y_0) \neq 0$, the unit vector*

$$\mathbf{k} = \frac{\nabla\mathbf{f}(x_0,y_0)}{\|\nabla\mathbf{f}(x_0,y_0)\|}$$

*points in the direction of the steepest increases of $f(x,y)$ and $D_{\mathbf{k}}f(x_0,y_0) = \|\nabla\mathbf{f}(x_0,y_0)\|$. On the other hand, $f(x,y)$ has its steepest decrease in the direction $-\mathbf{k}$, and $D_{\mathbf{k}}f(x_0,y_0) = -\|\nabla\mathbf{f}(x_0,y_0)\|$.*

**Example 8.20** Show that the function $f(x,y) = x^2y + xy^2 - 4xy$ has four stationary points at (0,0), (0,4), (5/3,4/3), and (4,0). We use *Mathematica* to obtain these points.

*In[99]:=*

```
Clear[f,x,y];
f[x_,y_]:= x^2*y + x*y^2 - 4*x*y;
gvect = gradf[f[x,y],{x,y}];
Solve[gvect==0,{x,y}]
```

*Out[102]=*

$$\{\{x\to 0,\ y\to 0\},\ \{x\to \frac{4}{3},\ y\to \frac{4}{3}\},\ \{x\to 4,\ y\to 0\},\ \{y\to 4,\ x\to 0\}\}$$

At a different point, say $(x_0,y_0) = (-1,2)$, the gradient vector is $\nabla\mathbf{f}(-1,2) = [-8\ \ 1]$.

*In[103]:=*

```
gvect = gradf[f[x,y],{x,y}] /.{x->-1,y->2}
```

*Out[103]=*

```
{-8, 1}
```

The direction of steepest increase of $f(x,y)$ at $(-1,2)$ is in the direction $\mathbf{k} = [-8/\sqrt{65}\ \ 1/\sqrt{65}]^T$. The maximum value of the directional derivative is equal to $D_{\mathbf{k}}f(-1,2) = \|\nabla\mathbf{f}(-1,2)\| = \sqrt{65}$.

**Example 8.21** The gradient vector of the translog production function given in Example 8.14 in Section 8.2.2 is equal to $\nabla \mathbf{f}(L_0,K_0) = [4.31299 \quad 0.69994]$ at the input levels $(L_0,K_0) = (20,30)$ units. The maximum increment in output is in the direction $\mathbf{k} = [0.987086 \quad 0.160191]^T$ from $(L_0,K_0)$. That is, for every one unit increase in $K$, there is a 6.161931 = (0.987086/0.160191) unit increase in $L$. The maximum increment in output in this direction is $D_{\mathbf{k}}f(L_0,K_0) = 4.36942$ units of output. These calculations are performed below.

*In[104]:=*

```
Clear[f,L,K,fL,fK,a0,a1,a2,a3,a4,a5];
a0=1.5;a1=0.9;a2=0.2;a3=-0.03;a4=-0.01;a5=0.02;
f[L_,K_]:= Exp[a0+a1*Log[L]+a2*Log[K]+a3*(Log[L])^2+
                a4*(Log[K])^2+a5*Log[L]*Log[K]];
gvect = gradf[f[L,K],{L,K}] /.{L->20,K->30} //N
```

*Out[107]=*

{4.31299, 0.69994}

*In[108]:=*

```
k = gvect/Sqrt[gvect.gvect]
```

*Out[108]=*

{0.987086, 0.160191}

*In[109]:=*

```
dk = gvect.k
```

*Out[109]=*

4.36942

## EXERCISES

1. For each of the following functions, find $D_{\mathbf{k}}f(1,1,1)$ in the directions $\mathbf{k} = [1\ 0\ 0]^T$, $[0\ 1\ 0]^T$, and $[1/\sqrt{14}\ 2/\sqrt{14}\ 3/\sqrt{14}]^T$. Also find the directions of the steepest increase and decrease of the functions from (1,1,1). Here $a$, $b$, and $c$ are constants.
   (a) $f(x,y,z) = x^2 + y^2 + z^2 - 2xy + 2yz - 2zx$
   (b) $f(x,y,z) = x^a + xy^bz$
   (c) $f(x,y,z) = x^ay^bz^c$
2. Plot the tangent line of the function $f(x,y) = y(x-1)/2 - (x-1)^2 - y^2$ in the direction $\mathbf{k} = [3/\sqrt{13}\ 2/\sqrt{13}]^T$.
3. Find the directions of the maximum and minimum change of $f(L,K)$ in Example 8.21 at the points $(L_0,K_0) = (10,15)$, (30,20), and (15,15).

### 8.3.2 Hessian matrix

If $f(x_1, x_2, \ldots, x_n)$ is a twice differentiable function, then it has $n^2$ second-order partial derivatives. We denote them as

$$\frac{\partial^2 f}{\partial x_i\, \partial x_j} = f_{ij}, \quad i = 1, \ldots, n;\ j = 1, \ldots, n$$

The second-order partial derivatives can be arranged in a square matrix

$$\mathbf{H} = \begin{bmatrix} f_{11} & f_{12} & \cdots & f_{1n} \\ f_{21} & f_{22} & \cdots & f_{2n} \\ \cdots & \cdots & \cdots & \cdots \\ f_{n1} & f_{n2} & \cdots & f_{nn} \end{bmatrix}$$

The square matrix **H** is called the *Hessian matrix* of $f$. Since $f$ is twice continuously differentiable and using Young's theorem, the Hessian matrix is symmetric.

**Example 8.22** Find the Hessian matrix of the function

$$f(x,y,z) = x^3y^2 + xz,$$

at $(x,y,z) = (2,1,3)$. Computing the second-order partial derivatives, we find

$$\mathbf{H} = \begin{bmatrix} 12 & 24 & 1 \\ 24 & 16 & 0 \\ 1 & 0 & 0 \end{bmatrix}$$

The computation of the Hessian can be accomplished by using the **MathEcon** function **hessian**.

*In[110]:=*

```
?hessian
```

**hessian[fct,lst] generates the hessian matrix of the function fct with respect to the variables specified by lst (a list). For example,**

**hessian[x*y*w-y^2*z+w^3,{x,y,z,w}].**

We use **hessian** to compute the Hessian of $f(x,y,z) = x^3y^2 + xz$.

*In[111]:=*

```
Clear[f,x,y,z];
f[x_,y_,z_]:=  (x^3)*(y^2)  +  x*z;
hmatrix  =  hessian[f[x,y,z],{x,y,z}];
hmatrix  //  MatrixForm
```

*Out[114]//MatrixForm=*

$$\begin{matrix} 6xy^2 & 6x^2y & 1 \\ 6x^2y & 2x^3 & 0 \\ 1 & 0 & 0 \end{matrix}$$

Evaluating the Hessian matrix at the point $(x,y,z) = (2,1,3)$, we have the following.

*In[115]:=*

```
hmatrix  /.{x->2,y->1,z->3}  //  MatrixForm
```

*Out[115]//MatrixForm=*

$$\begin{matrix} 12 & 24 & 1 \\ 24 & 16 & 0 \\ 1 & 0 & 0 \end{matrix}$$

**Example 8.23** Find the Hessian matrix of the generic function $f(x,y,z)$.

*In[116]:=*

```
Clear[f,x,y,z]
hessian[f[x,y,z],{x,y,z}] // MatrixForm
```

*Out[117]//MatrixForm=*

$$\begin{matrix} f^{(2,0,0)}[x,\ y,\ z] & f^{(1,1,0)}[x,\ y,\ z] & f^{(1,0,1)}[x,\ y,\ z] \\ f^{(1,1,0)}[x,\ y,\ z] & f^{(0,2,0)}[x,\ y,\ z] & f^{(0,1,1)}[x,\ y,\ z] \\ f^{(1,0,1)}[x,\ y,\ z] & f^{(0,1,1)}[x,\ y,\ z] & f^{(0,0,2)}[x,\ y,\ z] \end{matrix}$$

The directional derivative $D_{\mathbf{k}}f(x_0,y_0)$ measures the rate of change of $f$ at the point $(x_0,y_0)$ in the direction of the vector $\mathbf{k}$. It can be used to determine if a function is increasing or decreasing in that direction. The second-order partial derivatives and Hessian matrices measure the rate of change of the directional derivatives in a specified direction. For example, the second-order partial derivative

$$f_{xx}(x_0,y_0) = \lim_{\Delta x \to 0} \frac{f_x(x_0+\Delta x, y_0) - f_x(x_0,y_0)}{\Delta x}$$

measures the change of $f_x(x,y)$ at $(x_0,y_0)$ parallel to the $x$-axis. If $f_{xx}(x_0,y_0) > 0$, then the graph of $f(x,y)$ is concave upward in the neighborhood $(x_0,y_0)$ parallel to the $x$-axis, and is concave downward when $f_{xx}(x_0,y_0) < 0$. To generalize the concept, we define the second-order directional derivative to be the directional derivative of the directional derivative. For example, $D_{\mathbf{kk}}f(x_0,y_0)$ is the directional derivative of $D_{\mathbf{k}}f(x,y)$ in the direction $\mathbf{k} = [k_1\ k_2]^T$:

$$D_{\mathbf{kk}}f(x_0,y_0) = \lim_{t \to 0} \frac{\mathbf{D}_{\mathbf{k}}f(x_0+tk_1, y_0+tk_2) - \mathbf{D}_{\mathbf{k}}f(x_0,y_0)}{t}.$$

If $D_{\mathbf{kk}}f(x_0,y_0) > 0$, then in the neighborhood of $(x_0,y_0)$, $f(x,y)$ is concave upward in the direction of $\mathbf{k}$. On the other hand, if $D_{\mathbf{kk}}f(x_0,y_0) < 0$, then $f(x,y)$ is concave downward in that direction. Substituting for the directional derivatives

$$D_{\mathbf{k}}f(x_0,y_0) = k_1 f_x(x_0,y_0) + k_2 f_y(x_0,y_0)$$

$$D_{\mathbf{k}}f(x_0+tk_1,y_0+tk_2) = k_1 f_x(x_0+tk_1,y_0+tk_2) + k_2 f_y(x_0+tk_1,y_0+tk_2)$$

in $D_{\mathbf{kk}}f(x_0,y_0)$, we have

$$\begin{aligned} D_{\mathbf{kk}}f(x_0,y_0) = {} & k_1 \lim_{t\to 0}\left[\frac{f_x(x_0+tk_1,y_0+tk_2) - f_x(x_0,y_0)}{t}\right] \\ & + k_2 \lim_{t\to 0}\left[\frac{f_y(x_0+tk_1,y_0+tk_2) - f_y(x_0,y_0)}{t}\right] \\ = {} & k_1[k_1 f_{xx}(x_0,y_0) + k_2 f_{xy}(x_0,y_0)] + k_2[k_1 f_{yx}(x_0,y_0) + k_2 f_{yy}(x_0,y_0)] \end{aligned}$$

The last equality can be expressed as

$$\begin{aligned} D_{\mathbf{kk}}f(x_0,y_0) &= \begin{bmatrix} k_1 & k_2 \end{bmatrix} \begin{bmatrix} f_{xx}(x_0,y_0) & f_{xy}(x_0,y_0) \\ f_{yx}(x_0,y_0) & f_{yy}(x_0,y_0) \end{bmatrix} \begin{bmatrix} k_1 \\ k_2 \end{bmatrix} \\ &= \mathbf{K}^T\mathbf{H}\mathbf{k} \end{aligned}$$

**Example 8.24** Consider the function $f(x,y) = x^3 + y^2 + 2xy$. The Hessian matrix is

$$\mathbf{H} = \begin{bmatrix} f_{xx} & f_{xy} \\ f_{yx} & f_{yy} \end{bmatrix} = \begin{bmatrix} 6x & 2 \\ 2 & 2 \end{bmatrix}$$

The second-order directional derivative at the point $(x,y) = (0,0)$ in the direction of $\mathbf{k} = [1/\sqrt{2} \;\; 1/\sqrt{2}]^T$ is positive since

$$D_{\mathbf{kk}} f(0,0) = \begin{bmatrix} \frac{1}{\sqrt{2}} & \frac{1}{\sqrt{2}} \end{bmatrix} \begin{bmatrix} 0 & 2 \\ 2 & 2 \end{bmatrix} \begin{bmatrix} \frac{1}{\sqrt{2}} \\ \frac{1}{\sqrt{2}} \end{bmatrix} = 3 > 0$$

Thus, the function is concave upward in that direction as shown in the following *Mathematica* plot where the plane **cutter1** cuts the surface along the direction from (0,0) to (1,1). However, the second-order directional derivative in the direction of $\mathbf{k} = [-1/\sqrt{2} \;\; 1/\sqrt{2}]^T$ is negative since

$$D_{\mathbf{kk}} f(0,0) = \begin{bmatrix} \frac{-1}{\sqrt{2}} & \frac{1}{\sqrt{2}} \end{bmatrix} \begin{bmatrix} 0 & 2 \\ 2 & 2 \end{bmatrix} \begin{bmatrix} \frac{-1}{\sqrt{2}} \\ \frac{1}{\sqrt{2}} \end{bmatrix} = -1 < 0$$

The function is thus concave downward in that direction. The plane **cutter2** cuts the surface along the direction from (0,0) to (–1,1).

*In[118]:=*

```
Clear[f,x,y];
f[x_,y_]:= x^3 + y^2 + 2*x*y;
surface  = Plot3D[f[x,y],{x,-1,1},{y,-1,1},
                DisplayFunction->Identity];
cutter1  = ParametricPlot3D[{t,t,z},{t,0,1},{z,-2,4},
                 DisplayFunction->Identity];
cutter2  = ParametricPlot3D[{-t,t,z},{t,0,1},{z,-2,0.5},
                 DisplayFunction->Identity];
Show[surface,cutter1,cutter2,
          ViewPoint->{-4.000, -1.830, 0.910},
          AxesLabel->{"x","y","z"},
           DisplayFunction->$DisplayFunction];
```

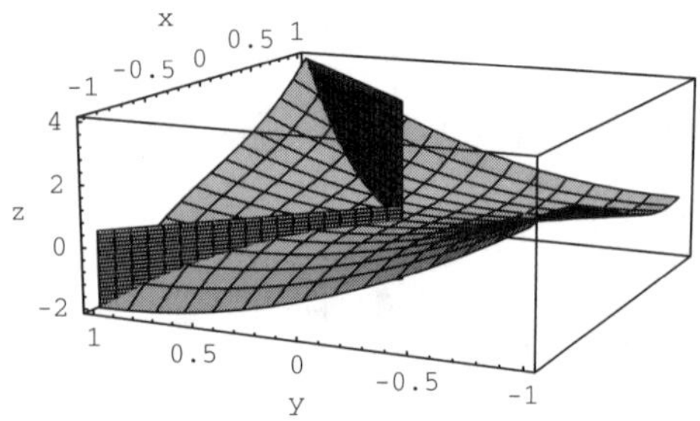

Suppose $f(x,y)$ is twice continuously differentiable in a neighborhood of a point $(x_0,y_0)$. The Hessian matrix $\mathbf{H}(x,y)$ is defined at each point in the neighborhood. Suppose the second-order directional derivative

$$D_{\mathbf{kk}}f(x_0,y_0) = \mathbf{k}^T\mathbf{H}(x_0,y_0)\,\mathbf{k}$$

is nonnegative in any direction. Then $D_{\mathbf{kk}}f(x_0,y_0)$ is a positive semidefinite quadratic form and the Hessian matrix $\mathbf{H}(x_0,y_0)$ is positive semidefinite. If the graph of $f(x,y)$ is concave upward in every direction in the neighborhood of $(x_0,y_0)$, then the function is said to be *convex* in that neighborhood. One can show that $f(x,y)$ is convex if and only if $\mathbf{H}(x,y)$ is positive semidefinite.

**Example 8.25** A twice continuously differentiable function $f(x,y)$ possesses a *relative maximum* at the point $(x_0,y_0)$ if the gradient vector is a zero vector and the Hessian matrix is negative definite. In Chapter 7 we showed that a symmetric matrix is negative definite if the leading principal minors of order $r$ alternate in sign such that $(-1)^r|\mathbf{H}_r| > 0$. To demonstrate that the function

$$f(x,y) = -x^2 + xy - y^2 + 2x - y$$

has a relative maximun value at (1,0), we begin by calculating the gradient vector.

*In[124]:=*
```
Clear[f,x,y];
f[x_,y_]:= -x^2 + x*y - y^2 + 2*x - y;
gvector = gradf[f[x,y],{x,y}]
```

*Out[126]=*
```
{2 - 2x + y, -1 + x - 2y}
```

Next we calculate the critical points.

*In[127]:=*
```
Solve[gvector=={0,0},{x,y}]
```

*Out[127]=*
```
{{x → 1, y → 0}}
```

The **MathEcon** function **signQL** is used to calculate the leading principal minors of the Hessian matrix at (1,0).

*In[128]:=*
```
signQL[hessian[f[x,y],{x,y}]/.{x->1,y->0}]
```

*Out[128]=*
```
{-2, 3}
```

Since $|\mathbf{H}_1| = -2 < 0$, and $|\mathbf{H}_2| = 3 > 0$, the Hessian matrix is negative definite. Thus the function $f(x,y) = -x^2 + xy - y^2 + 2x - y$ has a relative maximum value at $x = 1$ and $y = 0$.

## EXERCISES

1. For each of the following functions, find the Hessian matrices and evaluate them at the point (1,1,1). $a$, $b$, and $c$ are constants.
   (a) $f(x,y,z) = x^2 + y^2 + z^2 - 2xy + 2yz - 2zx$
   (b) $f(x,y,z) = x^a + xy^bz$
   (c) $f(x,y,z) = x^ay^bz^c$

2. Show that the gradient vector of the function

   $$f(x,y,z) = x^3 + y^3 - 3x - 12y - 10$$

   is a zero vector at the point (–1,–2), and that the Hessian matrix is negative definite at this point.

## □ 8.4 Differentials □

### 8.4.1 Total differentials

The derivative $dy/dx$ of a function $y = f(x)$ measures the relative change of $y$ with respect to $x$. However, the symbols, $dy$ and $dx$, have their own special meaning and are called *differentials*.

Consider a differentiable function $y = f(x)$. The increment of $y$ at the point $x_0$, denoted as $\Delta y$, is defined as

$$\Delta y = f(x_0+\Delta x) - f(x_0)$$

which can be rewritten as

$$\Delta y = \frac{f(x_0+\Delta x) - f(x_0)}{\Delta x}\Delta x$$

Here $\Delta x$ is an arbitrary nonzero number. As $\Delta x$ approaches 0, the above equation becomes

$$\Delta y \approx \left[\lim_{\Delta x\to 0}\frac{f(x_0+\Delta x) - f(x_0)}{\Delta x}\right]\Delta x = f'(x_0)\Delta x$$

The quantity $f'(x_0)\Delta x$, which is an approximation to $\Delta y$ and is called *(total) differential* of $y$ at $x_0$ and is denoted as $dy$. The differential of $x$, denoted as $dx$, is defined as $dx = \Delta x \neq 0$. Since $dx \neq 0$, we write

$$dy = f'(x_0)\, dx.$$

Frequently we also write $df$ instead of $dy$ to show the dependence of $y$ on the function $f$ in $y = f(x)$. Figure 8.3 shows the relationship between $\Delta y$ and $dy$. The difference, $\Delta y - dy$, approaches zero as $\Delta x \to 0$.

**Example 8.26** The differential of $y = f(x) = 4x^2$ at any point $x$ is

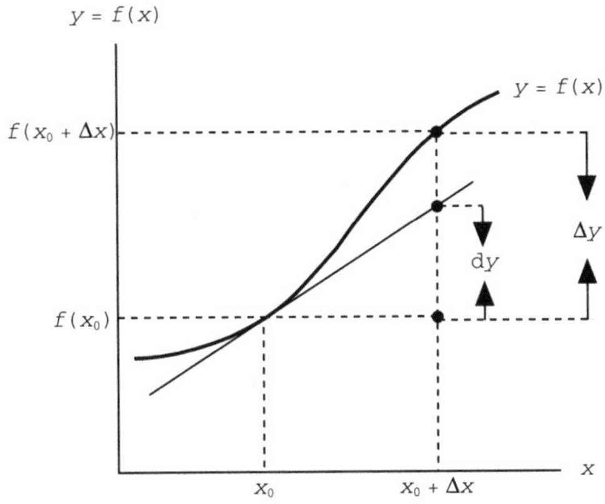


**Figure 8.3** The differential

$df = (8x)\,dx.$

The increment of $y$ at $x_0 = 2$ with $dx = \Delta x = 0.1$ is

$\Delta y = 4(x)^2 - 4(x_0)^2 = 4(2.1)^2 - 4(2)^2 = 1.64.$

The differential at $x_0 = 2$ is

$dy = (8x_0)\,dx = 8(2)(0.1) = 1.6.$

The difference is $|\Delta y - dy| = 0.04$.

*Mathematica* has a built-in function **Dt** to calculate the (total) *differential of a function.*

*In[129]:=*

```
?Dt
```

**Dt[f, x] gives the total derivative of f with respect to x. Dt[f] gives the total differential of f. Dt[f, {x, n}] gives the nth total derivative with respect to x. Dt[f, x1, x2, ...] gives a mixed total derivative.**

For example,

*In[130]:=*

```
Clear[x]
Dt[4*x^2]
```

*Out[131]=*

```
8xDt[x]
```

The notation **Dt[x]** is *Mathematica*'s representation of $dx$.

**Example 8.27** The differential of

$$f(x) = \frac{x-1}{x^2+1}$$

is

$$df = \left[\frac{-2x(x-1)}{(1+x^2)^2} + \frac{1}{(1+x^2)}\right]dx$$

as shown in the following *Mathematica* calculation.

*In[132]:=*
```
Clear[x]
f[x_]:=  (x-1)/(x^2+1);
df  =  Dt[f[x]]
```

*Out[134]=*

$$\frac{-2(-1+x)x\,Dt[x]}{(1+x^2)^2} + \frac{Dt[x]}{1+x^2}$$

The differential of a function of $n$ variables is defined in similar fashion. The *(total) differential* of $f(x_1,x_2,\ldots,x_n)$ at a point $(c_1,c_2,\ldots,c_n)$ is defined as the quantity

$$df = f_1 dx_1 + f_2 dx_2 + \ldots + f_n dx_n$$

where $f_i$ is the partial derivative with respect to $x_i$ at $(c_1,c_2,\ldots,c_n)$. The differential $df$ can be expressed as the dot product of the gradient vector of the function $f$ and the vector of differentials, $\mathbf{dx} = [dx_1\ dx_2\ \ldots\ dx_n]^T$:

$$df = [f_1\quad f_2\quad \ldots\quad f_n]\begin{bmatrix} dx_1 \\ dx_2 \\ \cdot \\ \cdot \\ dx_n \end{bmatrix}$$

$$= \nabla\mathbf{f}\cdot\mathbf{dx}$$

**Example 8.28** Consider a production function with labor, $L$, and capital, $K$, as inputs:

$$Q(L,K) = 4L^{0.5}K^{0.4}.$$

Find the total differential of output, $Q$, at any point $(L,K)$.

*In[135]:=*
```
Clear[Q,K,L];
dQ  =  Dt[4*(L^0.5)*(K^0.4)]
```

*Out[136]=*

$$\frac{1.6L^{0.5}\,Dt[K]}{K^{0.6}} + \frac{2K^{0.4}\,Dt[L]}{L^{0.5}}$$

If the labor input increases from 5 units to 6 units and the capital input decreases from 10 units to 9 units, then the differential in output is equal to 1.34802 units.

*In[137]:=*
```
dQ /. {L->5,Dt[L]->1,K->10,Dt[K]->-1}
```

*Out[137]=*
1.34802

**Example 8.29** Consider a utility function $f(x_1,x_2,x_3)$ with three goods. Find the total differential of the utility function at any point $(x_1,x_2,x_3)$.

*In[138]:=*
```
Clear[f,x1,x2,x3]
Dt[f[x1,x2,x3]]
```

*Out[139]=*
$\mathrm{Dt}[x3]f^{(0,0,1)}[x1, x2, x3] + \mathrm{Dt}[x2]f^{(0,1,0)}[x1, x2, x3] + \mathrm{Dt}[x1]f^{(1,0,0)}[x1, x2, x3]$

Note that *Mathematica* considers all nonnumerics in a function as variables when computing the total differential. For example, in computing the total differential of a general Cobb-Douglas function, $Q(L,K) = L^a K^b$, we find the symbols **Dt[a]** and **Dt[b]**.

*In[140]:=*
```
Clear[K,L,a,b];
Dt[(L^a)*(K^b)]
```

*Out[141]=*
$L^a(bK^{-1+b}\mathrm{Dt}[K] + K^b\mathrm{Dt}[b]\mathrm{Log}[K]) + K^b(aL^{-1+a}\mathrm{Dt}[L] + L^a\mathrm{Dt}[a]\mathrm{Log}[L])$

*Mathematica* treats the coefficients $a$ and $b$ as variables. However, you can specify the coefficients to be constants by using the **SetAttributes** function.

*In[142]:=*
```
SetAttributes[{a,b},Constant];
Dt[(L^a)*(K^b)]
```

*Out[143]=*
$b\,K^{-1+b}L^a\mathrm{Dt}[K] + aK^bL^{-1+a}\mathrm{Dt}[L]$

## EXERCISES

1. Find the total differentials of the following functions where $a$, $b$, and $c$ are constants:
   (a) $f(x,y,z) = xyz$
   (b) $f(x,y,z) = xe^{y+z}$
   (c) $f(x,y,z) = ax^2 + by^2 + cz^2$
   (d) $f(x,y,z) = a\log(x) + b\log(y) + c\log(z)$

2. Suppose $y = f(x_1,x_2, \ldots ,x_n)$ is a utility function, and $z = F(y)$ is an increasing monotonic function of $y$, i.e., $F'(y) > 0$ for all $y$. Find the differential d$z$. What is the relationship between the differentials d$z$ and d$y$?

### 8.4.2 Higher-order differentials

Consider the total differential of a function of two-variables $f(x,y)$:

$$df = f_x dx + f_y dy.$$

The second-order differential is the total differential of $df$. Treating $dx$ and $dy$ as constants, we have

$$\begin{aligned}
d(df) &= d^2f = d(f_x dx + f_y dy) \\
&= d(f_x dx) + d(f_y dy) \\
&= d(f_x)dx + f_x d(dx) + d(f_y)dy + f_y d(dy) \\
&= (f_{xx}dx + f_{xy}dy)dx + f_x(0) + (f_{yy}dy + f_{yx}dx)dy + f_y(0) \\
&= f_{xx}dx^2 + f_{xy}(dy)(dx) + f_{yx}(dx)(dy) + f_{yy}dy^2
\end{aligned}$$

The last expression can be written in terms of the Hessian matrix $\mathbf{H}$ as

$$d^2f = \begin{bmatrix} dx & dy \end{bmatrix} \begin{bmatrix} f_{xx} & f_{xy} \\ f_{yx} & f_{yy} \end{bmatrix} \begin{bmatrix} dx \\ dy \end{bmatrix} = (d\mathbf{x})^T \mathbf{H} (d\mathbf{x})$$

where $d\mathbf{x} = [dx\ dy]^T$. This expression states that $d^2f$ is a quadratic form. Notice that the quadratic form $d^2f(\mathbf{x})$ is similar to the second-order directional derivative $D_{\mathbf{kk}}f(\mathbf{x}) = \mathbf{k}^T\mathbf{H}\mathbf{k}$. Both are associated with the Hessian matrix $\mathbf{H}$. Since $d\mathbf{x}$ represents the change of $\mathbf{x}$ in any direction, $D_{\mathbf{kk}}f(\mathbf{x})$ is a special case of $d^2f$.

**Example 8.30** Consider the function

$$f(x,y) = x^2y - xy^2.$$

The first-order differential of $f$ is

$$df = f_x dx + f_y dy = (2xy - y^2)dx + (x^2 - 2xy)dy,$$

and the second-order differential is

$$\begin{aligned}
d^2f &= f_{xx}dx^2 + (f_{xy} + f_{yx})(dy)(dx) + f_{yy}dy^2 \\
&= 2y dx^2 + 4(x-y)(dy)(dx) - 2x dy^2 \\
&= \begin{bmatrix} dx & dy \end{bmatrix} \begin{bmatrix} 2y & 2(x-y) \\ 2(x-y) & -2x \end{bmatrix} \begin{bmatrix} dx \\ dy \end{bmatrix}
\end{aligned}$$

There are two ways to calculate the second-order differential. You could use the **MathEcon** function, **hessian**, to compute the Hessian matrix and then pre- and post-multiply the Hessian matrix by $d\mathbf{x}$. Alternatively, you could use the *Mathematica* function **Dt** to take the differential of $f(x,y)$ twice. We first calculate the Hessian matrix and then expand the quadratic form.

*In[144]:=*

```
Clear[f,x,y,dx,dy,H];
f[x_,y_]:= x^2*y - x*y^2;
H = hessian[f[x,y],{x,y}];
Expand[{dx,dy}.H.{dx,dy}]
```

*Out[147]=*
```
4dxdyx - 2dy^2x + 2dx^2y - 4dxdyy
```

Next we use the *Mathematica* function **Dt** twice to obtain the second-order differential.

*In[148]:=*
```
Dt[Dt[f[x,y]]]
```

*Out[148]=*
```
2yDt[x]^2 + 4xDt[x]Dt[y] - 4yDt[x]Dt[y] - 2xDt[y]^2 + 2xyDt[Dt[x]]
  - y^2Dt[Dt[x]] + x^2Dt[Dt[y]] - 2xyDt[Dt[y]]
```

Note that since $x$ and $y$ are independent variables, the differentials, **Dt[x]** and **Dt[y]**, are treated as constants and hence **Dt[Dt[x]]** and **Dt[Dt[y]]** are zero. To make the expression easy to read we can replace **Dt[x]** and **Dt[y]** with **dx** and **dy** and replace **Dt[Dt[x]]** and **Dt[Dt[y]]** by zero.

*In[149]:=*
```
Dt[Dt[f[x,y]]]  /.{Dt[x]->dx,Dt[y]->dy,
                   Dt[Dt[x]]->0,Dt[Dt[y]]->0}
```

*Out[149]=*
```
4dxdyx - 2dy^2x + 2dx^2y - 4dxdyy
```

**Example 8.31** Consider a Cobb-Douglas production function $Q = L^aK^b$. The second-order differential is

$$d^2Q = \begin{bmatrix} dL & dK \end{bmatrix} \begin{bmatrix} (a-1)aL^{a-2}K^b & abL^{a-1}K^{b-1} \\ abL^{a-1}K^{b-1} & (b-1)bL^aK^{b-2} \end{bmatrix} \begin{bmatrix} dL \\ dK \end{bmatrix}$$

Here is $d^2Q$ using the **hessian** function.

*In[150]:=*
```
Clear[Q,L,K,a,b,dL,dK];
Q[L_,K_]:=  (L^a)*(K^b);
H  =  hessian[Q[L,K],{L,K}];
Expand[{dL,dK}.H.{dL,dK}]
```

*Out[153]=*
```
-(adL^2K^bL^(-2+a)) + a^2dL^2K^bL^(-2+a) + 2abdKdLK^(-1+b)L^(-1+a)
  - bdK^2K^(-2+b)L^a + b^2dK^2K^(-2+b)L^a
```

The second-order differential of a function $f(x_1,x_2, \ldots ,x_n)$ is computed in a similar fashion. The second-order differential is a quadratic form:

$$d^2f = \begin{bmatrix} dx_1 & dx_2 & \ldots & dx_n \end{bmatrix} \begin{bmatrix} f_{11} & f_{12} & \cdots & f_{1n} \\ f_{21} & f_{22} & \cdots & f_{2n} \\ \cdots & \cdots & \cdots & \cdots \\ \cdots & \cdots & \cdots & \cdots \\ f_{n1} & f_{n2} & \cdots & f_{nn} \end{bmatrix} \begin{bmatrix} dx_1 \\ dx_2 \\ \cdot \\ \cdot \\ \cdot \\ dx_n \end{bmatrix} = (\mathbf{dx})^T\mathbf{H}(\mathbf{dx})$$

## EXERCISES

1. Find the second-order differential for the following functions:
   (a) $f(x,y,z) = x,y,z$
   (b) $f(x,y,z) = xe^{y+z}$
   (c) $f(x,y,z) = ax^2 + by^2 + cz^2$
   (d) $f(x,y,z) = a\log(x) + b\log(y) + c\log(z)$
2. Suppose $y = f(x_1,x_2, \ldots ,x_n)$ is a utility function, and $z = F(y)$ is an increasing monotonic function of $y$, i.e., $F'(y) > 0$ for all $y$. Find the second-order differential of $z$ if all $x$'s are independent variables. What is the relationship between $d^2z$ and $d^2y$?

### 8.4.3 Total differentials with constraints

The total differential of $f(x,y)$ with a side constraint, say $x = g(y)$, is somewhat different from the total differential presented in the previous section. As illustrated schematically in figure 8.4, the variable $x$ is not really an independent variable, but rather is related to $y$ through the constraint.

**Example 8.32** Consider $f(x,y) = xy + y^2$ subject to $x = g(y) = y^2$. Substituting for $x$, we have a function of $y$ only:

$$f(y^2,y) = y^3 + y^2 = F(y)$$

Hence, the differential of f is

$$df = dF = (3y^2 + 2y)\,dy.$$

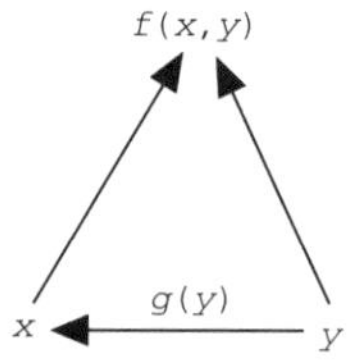


**Figure 8.4** Relation of variable $x$ to $y$

Alternatively using the chain rule, we have

$$df = \left(f_x \frac{dx}{dy} + f_y\right) dy = (f_x g_y + f_y)\,dy = (3y^2 + 2y)\,dy$$

Hence, when some of the variables are related through constraints, the differential changes.

Consider a function $f(x,y)$ subject to a constraint: $x = g(y)$. The first-order differential is

$$df = f_x dx + f_y dy$$

where $dx = g'dy$ and $g'$ is shorthand for the derivative $g'(y)$. Substituting $dx$ in the differential $df$, we have

$$df = f_x g'dy + f_y dy = (f_x g' + f_y)dy.$$

Now we compute the second-order differential of $f$.

$$\begin{aligned} d(df) &= d^2 f = d(f_x dx + f_y dy) \\ &= f_x d(dx) + d(f_x)dx + f_y d(dy) + d(f_y)dy \\ &= f_x d^2x + (f_{xx}dx + f_{xy}dy)dx + f_y(0) + (f_{yy}dy + f_{yx}dx)dy \\ &= f_x d^2x + \begin{bmatrix} dx & dy \end{bmatrix} \begin{bmatrix} f_{xx} & f_{xy} \\ f_{yx} & f_{yy} \end{bmatrix} \begin{bmatrix} dx \\ dy \end{bmatrix} \end{aligned}$$

Notice that $d(dx) = d^2x \neq 0$ and $d(dy) = d^2y = 0$ since $x$ is a function of $y$ and $y$ is an independent varaible. Let us look more closely at $d^2x$, the second-order differential of $x$. From the constraint, $x = g(y)$, we have $dx = g'dy$ and $d(dx) = d^2x = g''(dy)^2$, where $g''$ stands for the second-order derivative $g''(y)$. Expressed in matrix form,

$$d^2x = \begin{bmatrix} dx & dy \end{bmatrix} \begin{bmatrix} 0 & 0 \\ 0 & g'' \end{bmatrix} \begin{bmatrix} dx \\ dy \end{bmatrix}$$

Substituting $d^2x$ into the $d^2f$ equation, we have

$$\begin{aligned} d^2 f &= f_x \begin{bmatrix} dx & dy \end{bmatrix} \begin{bmatrix} 0 & 0 \\ 0 & g'' \end{bmatrix} \begin{bmatrix} dx \\ dy \end{bmatrix} + \begin{bmatrix} dx & dy \end{bmatrix} \begin{bmatrix} f_{xx} & f_{xy} \\ f_{yx} & f_{yy} \end{bmatrix} \begin{bmatrix} dx \\ dy \end{bmatrix} \\ &= \begin{bmatrix} dx & dy \end{bmatrix} \begin{bmatrix} 0 & 0 \\ 0 & f_x g'' \end{bmatrix} \begin{bmatrix} dx \\ dy \end{bmatrix} + \begin{bmatrix} dx & dy \end{bmatrix} \begin{bmatrix} f_{xx} & f_{xy} \\ f_{yx} & f_{yy} \end{bmatrix} \begin{bmatrix} dx \\ dy \end{bmatrix} \\ &= \begin{bmatrix} dx & dy \end{bmatrix} \begin{bmatrix} f_{xx} & f_{xy} \\ f_{yx} & f_{yy} + f_x g'' \end{bmatrix} \begin{bmatrix} dx \\ dy \end{bmatrix} \end{aligned}$$

Notice that the second-order differential $d^2f$ in this case is a quadratic form. However, the matrix that represents the quadratic form is no longer the Hessian matrix of $f$. This new matrix is called a *constrained Hessian matrix.*

**Example 8.33** Given $f(x,y) = x^3y + xy^2$ and $x = g(y) = 4y^2$. Calculate the first and second differentials of $f$. The first and second partial derivatives are

$f_x = 3x^2y + y^2$; $f_y = x^3 + 2xy$;
$f_{xx} = 6xy$; $f_{xy} = f_{yx} = 3x^2 + 2y$; $f_{yy} = 2x$;
$g' = 8y$; $g'' = 8$.

The first-order differential is

$$df = f_x dx + f_y dy = (3x^2y + y^2)dx + (x^3 + 2xy)dy$$

subject to $dx = 8ydy$. The second-order differential is

$$d^2 f = \begin{bmatrix} dx & dy \end{bmatrix} \begin{bmatrix} 6xy & 3x^2 + 2y \\ 3x^2 + 2y & 2x + 8(3x^2y + y^2) \end{bmatrix} \begin{bmatrix} dx \\ dy \end{bmatrix}$$

If the constraint $x = g(y)$ is linear in $y$, then $g''(y) = 0$. In this case, the matrix that represents the second-order differential is identical to the situation without a constraint.

**Example 8.34** Given a utility function $f(x,y) = x^2y^2$ and a budget constraint, $3x + 6y = 30$, find the first- and second-order differentials of the utility function. The linear budget constraint can be written as $x = g(y) = (30–6y)/3$. We express the result in a matrix form.

$$\mathrm{d}f = \begin{bmatrix} f_x & f_y \end{bmatrix}\begin{bmatrix} \mathrm{d}x \\ \mathrm{d}y \end{bmatrix} = \begin{bmatrix} 2xy^2 & 2x^2y \end{bmatrix}\begin{bmatrix} \mathrm{d}x \\ \mathrm{d}y \end{bmatrix}$$

$$\mathrm{d}^2f = \begin{bmatrix} \mathrm{d}x & \mathrm{d}y \end{bmatrix}\begin{bmatrix} f_{xx} & f_{xy} \\ f_{yx} & f_{yy} \end{bmatrix}\begin{bmatrix} \mathrm{d}x \\ \mathrm{d}y \end{bmatrix} = \begin{bmatrix} \mathrm{d}x & \mathrm{d}y \end{bmatrix}\begin{bmatrix} 2y^2 & 4xy \\ 4xy & 2x^2 \end{bmatrix}\begin{bmatrix} \mathrm{d}x \\ \mathrm{d}y \end{bmatrix}$$

Both are subject to $\mathrm{d}x = g'(y)\,\mathrm{d}y = -2\mathrm{d}y$.

Formulas for first-order and second-order differentials can be derived for functions of $n$ variables with one constraint. Consider the function

$$f(x_1,x_2, \ldots ,x_n) \quad \text{subject to} \quad x_1 = g(x_2,x_3, \ldots ,x_n)$$

The first-order differential is

$$\mathrm{d}f = f_1\mathrm{d}x_1 + f_2\mathrm{d}x_2 + \ldots + f_n\mathrm{d}x_n$$

subject to

$$\mathrm{d}x_1 = g_2\mathrm{d}x_2 + g_3\mathrm{d}x_3 + \ldots + g_n\mathrm{d}x_n$$

where $f_i$ and $g_i$ are partial derivatives of $f$ and $g$ with respect to $x_i$. Alternatively, we may write

$$\mathrm{d}f = (f_2+f_1g_2)\,\mathrm{d}x_2 + (f_3+f_1g_3)\,\mathrm{d}x_3 + \ldots + (f_n+f_1g_n)\,\mathrm{d}x_n$$

by substituting for $\mathrm{d}x_1$. The second-order differential is

$$\mathrm{d}^2f = \mathrm{d}(\mathrm{d}f) = \mathrm{d}(f_1\mathrm{d}x_1 + f_2\mathrm{d}x_2 + \ldots + f_n\mathrm{d}x_n).$$

In taking the differentials, one should remember that the differential of $x_1$, i.e., $\mathrm{d}x_1$, is a function of $x_2,x_3, \ldots$, and $x_n$ as given by the constraint $x_1 = g(x_2,x_3, \ldots ,x_n)$. Thus, $\mathrm{d}^2x_1 \neq 0$, but $\mathrm{d}^2x_2 = \mathrm{d}^2x_3 = \ldots = \mathrm{d}^2x_n = 0$. One can show that

$$\mathrm{d}^2f = f_1\mathrm{d}^2x_1 + \begin{bmatrix} \mathrm{d}x_1 & \mathrm{d}x_2 & \ldots & \mathrm{d}x_n \end{bmatrix}\begin{bmatrix} f_{11} & f_{12} & \ldots & f_{1n} \\ f_{21} & f_{22} & \ldots & f_{2n} \\ \ldots & \ldots & \ldots & \ldots \\ f_{n1} & f_{n2} & \ldots & f_{nn} \end{bmatrix}\begin{bmatrix} \mathrm{d}x_1 \\ \mathrm{d}x_2 \\ \cdot \\ \mathrm{d}x_n \end{bmatrix}$$

where

$$d^2x_1 = \begin{bmatrix} dx_1 & dx_2 & \dots & dx_n \end{bmatrix} \begin{bmatrix} 0 & 0 & \dots & 0 \\ 0 & g_{22} & \dots & g_{2n} \\ \dots & \dots & \dots & \dots \\ 0 & g_{n2} & \dots & g_{nn} \end{bmatrix} \begin{bmatrix} dx_1 \\ dx_2 \\ \cdot \\ dx_n \end{bmatrix}$$

Summing these quadratic forms, $d^2f$ and $d^2x_1$, we have

$$d^2f = \begin{bmatrix} dx_1 & dx_2 & \dots & dx_n \end{bmatrix} \begin{bmatrix} f_{11} & f_{12} & \dots & f_{1n} \\ f_{21} & f_{22} + f_1 g_{22} & \dots & f_{2n} + f_1 g_{2n} \\ \dots & \dots & \dots & \dots \\ f_{n1} & f_{n2} + f_1 g_{2n} & \dots & f_{nn} + f_1 g_{nn} \end{bmatrix} \begin{bmatrix} dx_1 \\ dx_2 \\ \cdot \\ dx_n \end{bmatrix}$$

subject to

$$dx_1 = g_2 dx_2 + g_3 dx_3 + \dots + g_n dx_n.$$

The matrix in the formula for $d^2f$ is again a constrained Hessian matrix. It can be computed with the **MathEcon** function **conhess**.

*In[154]:=*

```
?conhess
```

**conhess[fct,lst1,fctlst,lst2] creates the second-order differential (a matrix) of the function fct with respect to the variables specified by lst1 (a list) where the variables in the list lst2 are constrained by functions specified in the list of functions fctlst. For example,**

**conhess[x*y*w-y^2*z+w^3,{x,y,z,w},{x+y*z},{w}].**

This function computes the constrained Hessian matrix of a function (first argument) with respect to a list of variables (second argument), subject to a list of constraint functions (third argument) for a list of the constrained variables (fourth argument).

**Example 8.35** Use the **conhess** function to find the constrained Hessian matrix of the function

$$f(x,y,z) = x^3y + xy^2 + yz$$

such that

$$x = g(y,z) = 4yz^2$$

*In[155]:=*

```
Clear[f,x,y,z,g];
f[x_,y_,z]:=  (x^3)*y  +  x*(y^2)  +  y*z;
g[y_,z_]:=  4*y*z^2;
conhess[f[x,y,z],{x,y,z},{g[y,z]},{x}]  //  MatrixForm
```

*Out[158]//MatrixForm=*

$$\begin{matrix} 6xy & 3x^2 + 2y & 0 \\ 3x^2 + 2y & 2x & 1 + 8(3x^2y + y^2)z \\ 0 & 1 + 8(3x^2y + y^2)z & 8y(3x^2y + y^2) \end{matrix}$$

That is,

$$d^2f = \begin{bmatrix} dx & dy & dz \end{bmatrix} \begin{bmatrix} f_{xx} & f_{xy} & f_{xz} \\ f_{yx} & f_{yy} + f_x g_{yy} & f_{yz} + f_x g_{yz} \\ f_{zx} & f_{zy} + f_x g_{yz} & f_{zz} + f_x g_{zz} \end{bmatrix} \begin{bmatrix} dx \\ dy \\ dz \end{bmatrix}$$

$$= \begin{bmatrix} dx & dy & dz \end{bmatrix} \begin{bmatrix} 6xy & 3x^2+2y & 0 \\ 3x^2+2y & 2x & 1 + 8(3x^2y+y^2)z \\ 0 & 1 + 8(3x^2y+y^2)z & 8y(3x^2y+y^2) \end{bmatrix} \begin{bmatrix} dx \\ dy \\ dz \end{bmatrix}$$

subject to

$$dx = 4z^2dy + 8yz\,dz.$$

If the constraint function $g(x_2, \ldots, x_n)$ is linear in its variables, then the second-order partials $g_{ij}$ are zero. In this case, the constrained Hessian matrix is identical to the Hessian matrix.

**Example 8.36** Given a utility function $f(x,y,z) = x^2y^2z^2$ and a budget constraint, $3x + 5y + 6z = 20$, find the second-order differential, $d^2f$. We note that the budget constraint is linear and we need only the Hessian matrix.

*In[159]:=*

```
Clear[f,g,x,y,z];
f[x_,y_,z_]:=  (x*y*z)^2;
g[x_,y_]:=  (20-3*x-5*y)/6;
hessian[f[x,y,z],{x,y,z}] //  MatrixForm
```

*Out[162]//MatrixForm=*

$$\begin{matrix} 2y^2z^2 & 4xyz^2 & 4xy^2z \\ 4xyz^2 & 2x^2z^2 & 4x^2yz \\ 4xy^2z & 4x^2yz & 2x^2y^2 \end{matrix}$$

This is the same matrix that is produced by constrained Hessian, **conhess**.

*In[163]:=*

```
conhess[f[x,y,z],{x,y,z},{g[x,y]},{z}]  //  MatrixForm
```

*Out[163]//MatrixForm=*

$$\begin{matrix} 2y^2z^2 & 4xyz^2 & 4xy^2z \\ 4xyz^2 & 2x^2z^2 & 4x^2yz \\ 4xy^2z & 4x^2yz & 2x^2y^2 \end{matrix}$$

**Example 8.37** Find the constrained Hessian matrix of the function $f(x,y)$ subject to the constraint $x = g(y)$.

*In[164]:=*

```
Clear[f,g,x,y];
h = conhess[f[x,y],{x,y},{g[y]},{x}]
```

*Out[165]=*

$\{\{f^{(2,0)}[x,y],\ f^{(1,1)}[x,y]\},\ \{f^{(1,1)}[x,y],\ f^{(0,2)}[x,y] + g''[y]f^{(1,0)}[x,y]\}\}$

When there is more than one constraint, the first-order and second-order differentials can be computed in a similar fashion. For example, consider the function

$$f(x_1,x_2, \ldots ,x_n)$$

subject to 2 constraints

$$x_1 = g(x_3, \ldots ,x_n)$$
$$x_2 = h(x_3, \ldots ,x_n).$$

The first-order differential is

$$\begin{aligned} df &= f_1 dx_1 + f_2 dx_2 + \ldots + f_n dx_n \\ &= \nabla \mathbf{f} \cdot \mathbf{dx} \end{aligned}$$

where

$$dx_1 = g_3 dx_3 + g_4 dx_4 + \ldots + g_n dx_n$$
$$dx_2 = h_3 dx_3 + h_4 dx_4 + \ldots + h_n dx_n$$

The second-order differential is

$$d^2f = f_1 d^2x_1 + f_2 d^2x_2 + \begin{bmatrix} dx_1 & dx_2 & \ldots & dx_n \end{bmatrix} \begin{bmatrix} f_{11} & f_{12} & \ldots & f_{1n} \\ f_{21} & f_{22} & \ldots & f_{2n} \\ \ldots & \ldots & \ldots & \ldots \\ f_{n1} & f_{n2} & \ldots & f_{nn} \end{bmatrix} \begin{bmatrix} dx_1 \\ dx_2 \\ \cdot \\ dx_n \end{bmatrix}$$

Replacing $d^2x_1$ and $d^2x_2$, we can write the above expression as

$$d^2f = (\mathbf{dx})^T \begin{bmatrix} f_{11} & f_{12} & f_{13} & \ldots & f_{1n} \\ f_{21} & f_{22} & f_{23} & \ldots & f_{2n} \\ f_{31} & f_{32} & f_{33} + f_1 g_{33} + f_2 h_{33} & \ldots & f_{3n} + f_1 g_{3n} + f_2 h_{3n} \\ \ldots & \ldots & \ldots & \ldots & \ldots \\ \ldots & \ldots & \ldots & \ldots & \ldots \\ f_{n1} & f_{n2} & f_{n3} + f_1 g_{n3} + f_2 h_{n3} & \ldots & f_{nn} + f_1 g_{nn} + f_2 h_{nn} \end{bmatrix} (\mathbf{dx})$$

**Example 8.38** Consider the function

$$f(x,y,z) = x^3yz + xy^3z + xyz^3$$

subject to the constraints: $x = g(z) = 4z^2$ and $y = h(z) = z^3$. Using **conhess**, we compute the constrained Hessian matrix.

*In[166]:=*

```
Clear[f,g,h,x,y,z];
f[x_,y_,z_]:= x^3*y*z + x*y^3*z + x*y*z^3;
g[z_]:= 4*z^2;
h[z_]:= z^3;
conhess[f[x,y,z],{x,y,z},{g[z],h[z]},{x,y}]
```

*Out[170]=*

$$\{\{6xyz,\ 3x^2z + 3y^2z + z^3,\ 3x^2y + y^3 + 3yz^2\},$$
$$\{3x^2z + 3y^2z + z^3,\ 6xyz,\ x^3 + 3xy^2 + 3xz^2\},$$
$$\{3x^2y + y^3 + 3yz^2,\ x^3 + 3xy^2 + 3xz^2,$$
$$6xyz + 6z(x^3z + 3xy^2z + xz^3) + 8(3x^2yz + y^3z + yz^3)\}\}$$

## EXERCISES

1. Find the second-order differential for the following functions and constraints:
   (a) $f(x,y) = x^2 + xy$, subject to $2x + 4y = 3$
   (b) $f(x,y,z) = xyz$, subject to $3xy + 2yz - zx = 5$
   (c) $f(x,y,z) = x - y^2 + zx$, subject to $x^2 + y^2 + z^2 = 1$ and $x + y + z = 0$.
2. Consider the cost function $f(x_1,x_2,x_3) = 5x_1 + 2x_2 + 7x_3$ of using three inputs in production. The production function is of the Cobb-Douglas type:

   $$Q = 5x_1^{0.5}x_2^{0.3}x_3^{0.1}.$$

   Find the second-order differential of the cost function if the output is to set to $Q = 10$ units.

# □ 8.5 Derivatives of a Composite Function □

## 8.5.1 Total derivative of a composite function

Consider a function of two variables $f(x,y)$ such that $x = g(t)$, $y = h(t)$. The relationship among the variables is illustrated schematically in figure 8.5.

If we replace $x$ with $g(t)$ and $y$ with $h(t)$ in $f$, then the function becomes a function of a single variable $t$. We call $f$ a *composite function* of $t$. If $f$, $g$, and $h$ are differentiable, then

$$\frac{df}{dt} = f_x\left(\frac{dx}{dt}\right) + f_y\left(\frac{dy}{dt}\right) = f_x g_t + f_y h_t.$$

This derivative can be computed using the *Mathematica* function **Dt**.

*In[171]:=*

```
Clear[f,x,y];
Dt[f[x,y],t]
```

*Out[172]=*

$$Dt[y,t]f^{(0,1)}[x,y] + Dt[x,t]f^{(1,0)}[x,y]$$

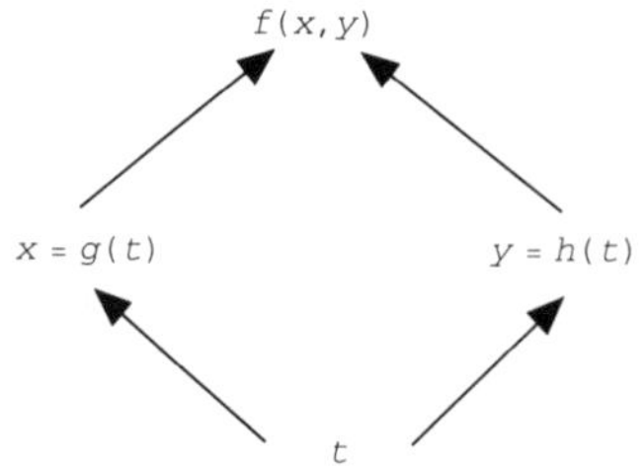


**Figure 8.5** Relationship among the variables

Notice that **Dt[y,t]** represents d$y$/d$t$ and **Dt[x,t]** represents d$x$/d$t$ in the output.

**Example 8.39** Find d$f$/d$t$ for the function $f(x,y) = x^2 + xy + y^2$, subject to $x = t^2 + 2t + 1$ and $y = t^3$.

*In[173]:=*
```
Clear[f,x,y,t];
f[x_,y_]:= x^2 + x*y + y^2;
x[t_]:= t^2 + 2*t + 1;
y[t_]:= t^3;
total = Dt[f[x,y],t]
```

*Out[177]=*
```
2xDt[x, t] + yDt[x, t] + xDt[y, t] + 2yDt[y, t]
```

*In[178]:=*
```
total /. {Dt[x,t]->x'[t],Dt[y,t]->y'[t],
          x->x[t],y->y[t]} // Simplify
```

*Out[178]=*

$4 + 12t + 15t^2 + 12t^3 + 5t^4 + 6t^5$

Alternatively, we could find d$f$/d$t$ directly by substituting for $x$ and $y$ and then differentiating with respect to $t$.

*In[179]:=*
```
Dt[f[x[t],y[t]],t] // Simplify
```

*Out[179]=*

$4 + 12t + 15t^2 + 12t^3 + 5t^4 + 6t^5$

**Example 8.40** Consider a production function $Q = f(L,K)$ where labor, $L$, and capital, $K$, are functions of time, $t$. The growth of output over time is

$$\frac{dQ}{dt} = f_L\left(\frac{dL}{dt}\right) + f_K\left(\frac{dK}{dt}\right).$$

If the production function is of Cobb-Douglas type,

$f(L,K) = AL^aK^b$

then

$$\frac{dQ}{dt} = aAL^{a-1}K^{b}\left(\frac{dL}{dt}\right) + bAL^{a}K^{b-1}\left(\frac{dK}{dt}\right).$$

This is shown in the following *Mathematica* calculation.

*In[180]:=*

```
Clear[f,L,K,a,b,A];
SetAttributes[{A,a,b},Constant];
f[L_,K_]:= A*(L^a)*(K^b);
Dt[f[L,K],t]
```

*Out[183]=*

$$A b K^{-1+b} L^{a} Dt[K, t] + a A K^{b} L^{-1+a} Dt[L, t]$$

Dividing the total derivative by the output, $Q$, we obtain the growth rate of the output as a linear combination of the growth rates in labor and capital,

Consider a function of several variables

$$f(x_1,x_2, \ldots ,x_n)$$

with several constraints

$$x_i = g_i(t), \quad i = 1,2, \ldots ,n.$$

The total derivative is

$$\begin{aligned}\frac{df}{dt} &= f_1\left(\frac{dx_1}{dt}\right) + \ldots + f_n\left(\frac{dx_n}{dt}\right)\\ &= \nabla\mathbf{f} \cdot \frac{d\mathbf{x}}{dt}\end{aligned}$$

where $\nabla\mathbf{f}$ is the gradient vector of $f$ and $d\mathbf{x}/dt$ is defined as

$$\frac{d\mathbf{x}}{dt} = \frac{d}{dt}\begin{bmatrix} x_1 \\ x_2 \\ \cdot \\ \cdot \\ x_n \end{bmatrix} = \begin{bmatrix} \frac{dx_1}{dt} \\ \frac{dx_2}{dt} \\ \cdot \\ \cdot \\ \frac{dx_n}{dt} \end{bmatrix}$$

**Example 8.41** Consider a function $f(x_1,x_2, \ldots ,x_n)$ with the following property.

$$f(tx_1,tx_2, \ldots ,tx_n) = t^r f(x_1,x_2, \ldots ,x_n)$$

A function satisfying this property is called a *homogeneous function of degree r*. Let $z_i = tx_i$. Taking the total derivative with respect to $t$ on both sides of the above equality, we compute

$$x_1 f_{z_1} + x_2 f_{z_2} + , \ldots , + x_n f_{z_n} = r t^{r-1} f(x_1, x_2, \ldots, x_n)$$

If we set $t = 1$, then

$$x_1 f_{x_1} + x_2 f_{x_2} + , \ldots , + x_n f_{x_n} = r f(x_1, x_2, \ldots, x_n).$$

This can be expressed in terms of the gradient of $f$ as

$$\nabla \mathbf{f} \cdot \mathbf{x} = r f(x_1, x_2, \ldots, x_n)$$

where $\mathbf{x}$ is the vector $[x_1\, x_2 \ldots x_n]^T$. This identity is satisfied by every homogeneous function. Homogeneous functions will be discussed in detail in section 8.6.

The second-order total derivative is the total derivative of the first-order total derivative. In the two-variable case, $f = f(x,y)$, $x = g(t)$, and $y = h(t)$, we find that

$$\begin{aligned}
\frac{d^2 f}{dt^2} &= \frac{d}{dt}\left(f_x \frac{dx}{dt} + f_y \frac{dy}{dt}\right) = \frac{d}{dt}\left(f_x \frac{dx}{dt}\right) + \frac{d}{dt}\left(f_y \frac{dy}{dt}\right) \\
&= \left(f_{xx}\frac{dx}{dt} + f_{xy}\frac{dy}{dt}\right)\frac{dx}{dt} + f_x \frac{d^2x}{dt^2} + \left(f_{yx}\frac{dx}{dt} + f_{yy}\frac{dy}{dt}\right)\frac{dy}{dt} + f_y \frac{d^2y}{dt^2} \\
&= \left(f_{xx}\frac{dx}{dt} + f_{xy}\frac{dy}{dt}\right)\frac{dx}{dt} + f_x \frac{d^2x}{dt^2} + \left(f_{yx}\frac{dx}{dt} + f_{yy}\frac{dy}{dt}\right)\frac{dy}{dt} + f_y \frac{d^2y}{dt^2} \\
&= f_x \frac{d^2x}{dt^2} + f_y \frac{d^2y}{dt^2} + \begin{bmatrix} \frac{dx}{dt} & \frac{dy}{dt} \end{bmatrix} \begin{bmatrix} f_{xx} & f_{xy} \\ f_{yx} & f_{yy} \end{bmatrix} \begin{bmatrix} \frac{dx}{dt} \\ \frac{dy}{dt} \end{bmatrix}
\end{aligned}$$

This computation can be perform by **Dt**.

*In[184]:=*

```
Clear[f,x,y,t];
Dt[f[x,y],{t,2}]
```

*Out[185]=*

$$\text{Dt}[y, \{t, 2\}]f^{(0,1)}[x, y] + \text{Dt}[x, \{t, 2\}]f^{(1,0)}[x, y] + \text{Dt}[y, t]\ (\text{Dt}[y, t]f^{(0,2)}[x, y] + \text{Dt}[x, t]f^{(1,1)}[x, y]) + \text{Dt}[x, t](\text{Dt}[y, t]f^{(1,1)}[x, y] + \text{Dt}[x, t]f^{(2,0)}[x, y])$$

For a function of $n$ variables $f(x_1, x_2, \ldots, x_n)$ where

$$\mathbf{x} = \begin{bmatrix} x_1 \\ x_2 \\ \cdot \\ \cdot \\ x_n \end{bmatrix} = \begin{bmatrix} g_1(t) \\ g_2(t) \\ \cdot \\ \cdot \\ g_n(t) \end{bmatrix} \equiv \mathbf{g}(t)$$

the second-order total derivative is

$$\frac{d^2 f}{dt^2} = \nabla \mathbf{f} \cdot \frac{d^2 \mathbf{x}}{dt^2} + \left[\frac{d\mathbf{x}}{dt}\right]^T \mathbf{H} \left[\frac{d\mathbf{x}}{dt}\right]$$

where

$$\frac{\mathrm{d}^2\mathbf{x}}{\mathrm{d}t^2} \equiv \begin{bmatrix} \dfrac{\mathrm{d}^2x_1}{\mathrm{d}t^2} \\ \dfrac{\mathrm{d}^2x_2}{\mathrm{d}t^2} \\ \cdot \\ \cdot \\ \dfrac{\mathrm{d}^2x_n}{\mathrm{d}t^2} \end{bmatrix}$$

**Example 8.42** In sections 8.3.1 and 8.3.2, we introduced the directional derivative. It is equal to the total derivative of $f(\mathbf{x}) = f(x_1,x_2, \ldots ,x_n)$ with respect to $t$, where $x_i = tk_i$, $i = 1,2, \ldots ,n$. Thus,

$$D_{\mathbf{k}}f(\mathbf{x}) = \mathrm{k}_1 f_1 + \mathrm{k}_2 f_2 + \ldots + \mathrm{k}_n f_n = \nabla\mathbf{f} \cdot \mathbf{k}.$$

The second-order directional derivative is

$$D_{\mathbf{kk}}f(\mathbf{x}) = \mathbf{k}^T\mathbf{H}\mathbf{k}.$$

## EXERCISES

1. Find $\mathrm{d}f/\mathrm{d}t$ and $\mathrm{d}^2f/\mathrm{d}t^2$ for the following composite functions:
   (a) $f(x,y) = x\mathrm{e}^y$, $x = t$, and $y = t^2$
   (b) $f(x,y) = \log(x+y)$, $x = \mathrm{e}^t$, and $y = \dfrac{1}{t}$
   (c) $f(x,y,z) = x^2yz + x^2yz + xyz^2$, $x = t$, $y = t^2$, $z = t^3$
2. A Cobb-Douglas function $f(L,K) = L^aK^b$ is a homogeneous function of degree $r = a+b$ since

   $$f(tL,tK) = t^{a+b}f(L,K)$$

   Show that

   $$Lf_L + Kf_K = (a+b)f(L,K)$$

3. Find the second-order total derivative of $f(tL,tK)$ with respect to $t$ in exercise 2 and show that the following equality holds:

   $$\begin{bmatrix} L & K \end{bmatrix} \begin{bmatrix} f_{LL} & f_{LK} \\ f_{KL} & f_{KK} \end{bmatrix} \begin{bmatrix} L \\ K \end{bmatrix} = (a+b)(a+b-1)f(L,K)$$

### 8.5.2 Partial derivatives of composite functions

Sometimes the variables of a function may themselves be functions of more than one variable. For example, consider $f(x,y)$ where $x = g(t_1,t_2)$ and $y = h(t_1,t_2)$. This is illustrated schematically in figure 8.6.

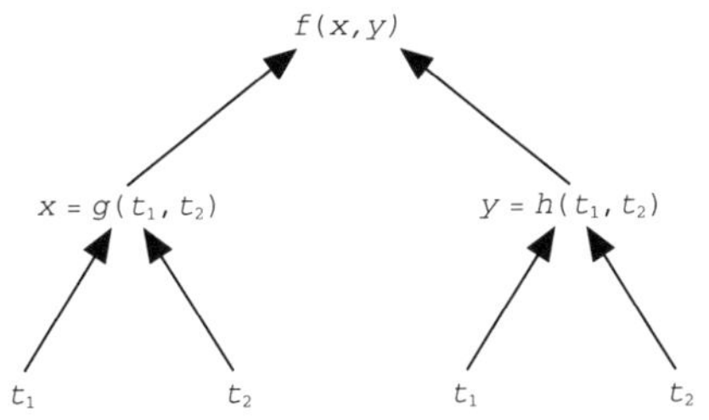


**Figure 8.6** Variables of a function as functions of more than one variable

The composite function $f(g(t_1,t_2),h(t_1,t_2))$ is a function of $t_1$ and $t_2$ and we would like to compute partial derivatives of this function. Using the chain rule, we have

$$\frac{\partial f}{\partial t_1} = f_x \frac{\partial x}{\partial t_1} + f_y \frac{\partial y}{\partial t_1}.$$

The second-order partial derivative with respect to $t_1$ is

$$\begin{aligned}\frac{\partial^2 f}{\partial t_1^2} &= \frac{\partial}{\partial t_1}\left(\frac{\partial f}{\partial t_1}\right) = \frac{\partial}{\partial t_1}\left(f_x \frac{\partial x}{\partial t_1} + f_y \frac{\partial y}{\partial t_1}\right) \\ &= \frac{\partial}{\partial t_1}(f_x)\frac{\partial x}{\partial t_1} + f_x \frac{\partial}{\partial t_1}\left(\frac{\partial x}{\partial t_1}\right) + \frac{\partial}{\partial t_1}(f_y)\frac{\partial y}{\partial t_1} + f_y \frac{\partial}{\partial t_1}\left(\frac{\partial y}{\partial t_1}\right) \\ &= \left(f_{xx}\frac{\partial x}{\partial t_1} + f_{xy}\frac{\partial y}{\partial t_1}\right)\left(\frac{\partial x}{\partial t_1}\right) + f_x \frac{\partial^2 x}{\partial t_1^2} + \left(f_{yx}\frac{\partial x}{\partial t_1} + f_{yy}\frac{\partial y}{\partial t_1}\right)\left(\frac{\partial y}{\partial t_1}\right) + f_y \frac{\partial^2 y}{\partial t_1^2}.\end{aligned}$$

Writing this identity in matrix form, we have

$$\frac{\partial^2 f}{\partial t_1^2} = f_x \frac{\partial^2 x}{\partial t_1^2} + f_y \frac{\partial^2 y}{\partial t_1^2} + \begin{bmatrix} \dfrac{\partial x}{\partial t_1} & \dfrac{\partial y}{\partial t_1} \end{bmatrix} \begin{bmatrix} f_{xx} & f_{xy} \\ f_{yx} & f_{yy} \end{bmatrix} \begin{bmatrix} \dfrac{\partial x}{\partial t_1} \\ \dfrac{\partial y}{\partial t_1} \end{bmatrix}$$

Similarly, the mixed partial derivative can be computed as

$$\frac{\partial^2 f}{\partial t_1 \partial t_2} = f_x \frac{\partial^2 x}{\partial t_1 \partial t_2} + f_y \frac{\partial^2 y}{\partial t_1 \partial t_2} + \begin{bmatrix} \dfrac{\partial x}{\partial t_1} & \dfrac{\partial y}{\partial t_1} \end{bmatrix} \begin{bmatrix} f_{xx} & f_{xy} \\ f_{yx} & f_{yy} \end{bmatrix} \begin{bmatrix} \dfrac{\partial x}{\partial t_2} \\ \dfrac{\partial y}{\partial t_2} \end{bmatrix}$$

Taking the partial derivative is similar to taking the total derivative with *Mathematica*. The above first, second, and mixed partial derivatives can also be obtained using the *Mathematica* function **Dt**. First we compute $\partial f / \partial t_1$.

*In[186]:=*

```
Clear[f,x,y,t1,t2];
Dt[f[x,y],t1]
```

*Out[187]=*

```
Dt[y, t1]f^(0,1)[x, y] + Dt[x, t1]f^(1,0)[x, y]
```

Next, $\partial f^2/\partial t_1{}^2$.

*In[188]:=*

```
Dt[f[x,y],{t1,2}]
```

*Out[188]=*

```
Dt[y, {t1, 2}]f^(0,1)[x, y] + Dt[x, {t1, 2}]f^(1,0)[x, y] + Dt[y, t1](Dt[y, t1]f^(0,2)[x, y]
  + Dt[x, t1]f^(1,1)[x, y]) + Dt[x, t1](Dt[y, t1]f^(1,1)[x, y] + Dt[x, t1]f^(2,0)[x, y])
```

Lastly, $\partial f^2/\partial t_1 \partial t_2$.

*In[189]:=*

```
Dt[f[x,y],t1,t2]
```

*Out[189]=*

```
Dt[y, t1, t2]f^(0,1)[x, y] + Dt[x, t1, t2]f^(1,0)[x, y] + Dt[y, t1](Dt[y, t2]f^(0,2)[x, y]
  + Dt[x, t2]f^(1,1)[x, y]) + Dt[x, t1](Dt[y, t2]f^(1,1)[x, y] + Dt[x, t2]f^(2,0)[x, y])
```

**Example 8.43** (Partial derivatives of an indirect utility function) Consider a utility function that has as its arguments the quantities of goods. The solution to the utility maximization problem yields quantities demanded of these goods as functions of prices and income. The utility function evaluated at the levels of the quantity demanded yields an indirect utility function. The indirect utility is a function of prices and income. Given the indirect utility function, we can see immediately how changes in prices or income affect utility. Suppose we are interested in how utility changes as the price of good $x$ changes (in a two-good world). Consider a utility function,

$$u = f(x,y) = a \log x + b \log y$$

and two demand equations,

$$x = g(p_x, p_y, m) = \frac{a}{a+b}\frac{m}{p_x}$$

$$y = h(p_x, p_y, m) = \frac{b}{a+b}\frac{m}{p_y}$$

where $p_x$ and $p_y$ are prices, and $m$ is income. We compute the change in utility with respect to $p_x$ (price of good $x$) and $m$ (income),

$$\frac{\partial f}{\partial p_x} \quad \text{and} \quad \frac{\partial f}{\partial m}$$

to produce *Roy's Identity*. Roy's Identity states that the demand function, $x = g(p_x,p_y,m)$, should be equal to the negative ratio of the above two partial derivatives,

$$x = -\frac{\frac{\partial f}{\partial p_x}}{\frac{\partial f}{\partial m}} = g(p_x, p_y, m)$$

*In[190]:=*
```
Clear[f,x,y,m,a,b,px,py];
SetAttributes[{a,b},Constant];
f[x_,y_]:= a*Log[x]  + b*Log[y];
x[m_,px_,py_]:=  (a/(a+b))*(m/px);
y[m_,px_,py_]:=  (b/(a+b))*(m/py);
dudpx  =  Dt[f[x[m,px,py],y[m,px,py]],px,
             Constants->{m,py}]
```

*Out[195]=*
```
   a
-(--)
  px
```

*In[196]:=*
```
dudm  =  Dt[f[x[m,px,py],y[m,px,py]],m,
           Constants->{px,py}]
```

*Out[196]=*
```
a   b
- + -
m   m
```

*In[197]:=*
```
x[m,px,py]  ==  -dudpx/dudm  //  Simplify
```

*Out[197]=*
```
True
```

## EXERCISE

1. Find the partial derivatives, $\partial f/\partial t$, $\partial^2 f/\partial t^2$, $\partial^2 f/\partial t\partial s$, for the following composite functions:
   (a) $f(x,y,z) = \log(x+y+z)$, $x = t^2 + s$, $y = ts$, $z = t/s$
   (b) $f(x,y,z) = x^2yz + xy^2z + xyz^2$, $x = t$, $y = s$, $z = t^2 + s^2$

# □ 8.6 Homogeneous Functions □

## 8.6.1 Definition

Suppose $f(x,y)$ is a production function with two inputs, $x$ and $y$. When $x$ and $y$ are increased or decreased by a fixed proportion, we are frequently interested in determining if the corresponding increase or decrease in output $f(x,y)$ is greater than, equal to, or less than the proportion. For example, consider the function

$$f(x,y) = x^2 + y^2 - 2xy.$$

If each variable $x$ and $y$ is multiplied by a positive constant $t$, then

$$f(tx,ty) = (tx)^2 + (ty)^2 - 2(tx)(ty) = t^2(x^2 + y^2 - 2xy) = t^2 f(x,y).$$

The function has the property that $f(tx,ty)$ is proportional to $f(x,y)$ by the factor $t^2$. Hence, $f$ is a homogeneous function of degree 2.

> **DEFINITION 8.4** *If $f(\mathbf{x}) = f(x_1,x_2, \ldots ,x_n)$ is defined on a domain* **S**, *then the function is said to be* ***homogeneous of degree r*** *if*
>
> $$f(tx_1,tx_2, \ldots ,tx_n) = t^r f(x_1,x_2, \ldots ,x_n), \quad or \quad f(t\mathbf{x}) = t^r f(\mathbf{x})$$
>
> *for all points* **x** *and $t\mathbf{x} = (tx_1,tx_2, \ldots ,tx_n)$ in* **S**. *The degree of homogeneity exponent $r$ can take any value, positive, negative, or zero.*

Since most economic variables are taken to be nonnegative, it is normally assumed that $t > 0$. However, this is not required in the definition.

**Example 8.44** The function

$$f(x,y,z) = \frac{x^3 + y^3 + x^2y}{\sqrt{xyz}}$$

is a homogeneous function of degree 3/2 since

$$\begin{aligned} f(tx,ty,tz) &= \frac{(tx)^3 + (ty)^3 + (tx)^2(ty)}{\sqrt{(tx)(ty)(tz)}} \\ &= \frac{t^3(x^3 + y^3 + x^2y)}{\sqrt{t^3(xyz)}} \\ &= t^{3/2} f(x,y,z) \end{aligned}$$

**Example 8.45** The function $f(x,y,z) = \log x^2 + \log y^2 + \log z^2$ is not a homogeneous function since

$$f(tx,ty,tz) = 3\log t^2 + f(x,y,z).$$

An important application of homogeneous functions in economics is the determination of returns to scale in production theory. If a production function is homogeneous of degree $r$, then the production function exhibits a constant returns to scale when $r = 1$. It exhibits a decreasing returns to scale if $r < 1$ and an increasing returns to scale if $r > 1$.

**Example 8.46** The Cobb-Douglas production function

$$f(x_1,x_2, \ldots ,x_n) = \prod_{i=1}^{n} x_i^{a_i}$$

is a homogeneous function since

$$f(tx_1,tx_2,\ldots,tx_n) = \prod_{i=1}^{n}(tx_i)^{a_i} = (t^{\Sigma a_i})\prod_{i=1}^{n}x_i^{a_i}$$
$$= (t^{\Sigma a_i})f(x_1,x_2,\ldots,x_n)$$

The degree of homogeneity, and, hence, returns to scale, is determined by the value of the sum of the exponents. If $r = \Sigma a_i > 1$, then the production function has an increasing returns to scale. If $r = \Sigma a_i < 1$, then it has a decreasing returns to scale. If $r = \Sigma a_i = 1$, and hence is a linear production function, then it exhibits a constant returns to scale.

## EXERCISES

1. Determine whether the following functions are homogeneous. If so, what are their degrees?
   (a) $f(x,y,z) = x^2 + yz$
   (b) $f(x,y,z) = \dfrac{1}{x + y + z}$
   (c) $f(x,y,z) = \dfrac{xyz}{x^4 + y^4 + z^4}$
   (d) $f(x,y,z) = x^2e^{-y/z}$

2. Suppose $f(\mathbf{x})$ and $g(\mathbf{x})$ are homogeneous of degree $m$ and $n$, respectively. Show that $f(\mathbf{x})g(\mathbf{x})$ is homogeneous of degree $mn$. Are $f(\mathbf{x}) + g(\mathbf{x})$, $f(\mathbf{x})/g(\mathbf{x})$, and $f^3(\mathbf{x})$ homogeneous?

### 8.6.2 Geometric view

Homogeneous functions have some interesting geometric properties. Suppose $z = f(x,y)$ is homogeneous of degree $r$. Consider the values of $f$ along a ray **OA** from the origin **O** as shown in figure 8.7. Let $(x_0,y_0)$ be a point distinct from the origin (0,0). Once we know the value of the function, $z_0 = f(x_0,y_0)$, at this point, then we know the values of all other points $(tx_0,ty_0)$ along the ray. That is,

$$f(tx_0,ty_0) = t^r f(x_0,y_0) = t^r z_0$$

as shown in figure 8.7. Geometrically, we are tracing the value of the function $f(tx_0,ty_0)$ by "cutting" the surface $z = f(x,y)$ along the ray **OA**. The tracing on the surface is the curve **OA′**. If we cut the surface along another ray such as **OB**, we find that the trace **OB′** also exhibits the same property, $f(tx_1,ty_1) = t^r f(x_1,y_1) = t^r z_1$.

**Example 8.47** To illustrate this geometric view, consider the function,

$$f(x,y) = \frac{x^3 + y^3}{\sqrt{x} + \sqrt{y}}$$

The function is a homogeneous function of degree 5/2. We draw the graph of the function $f(x,y)$ and intersect it with a vertical plane along the ray $(tx_0,ty_0)$. As $t$

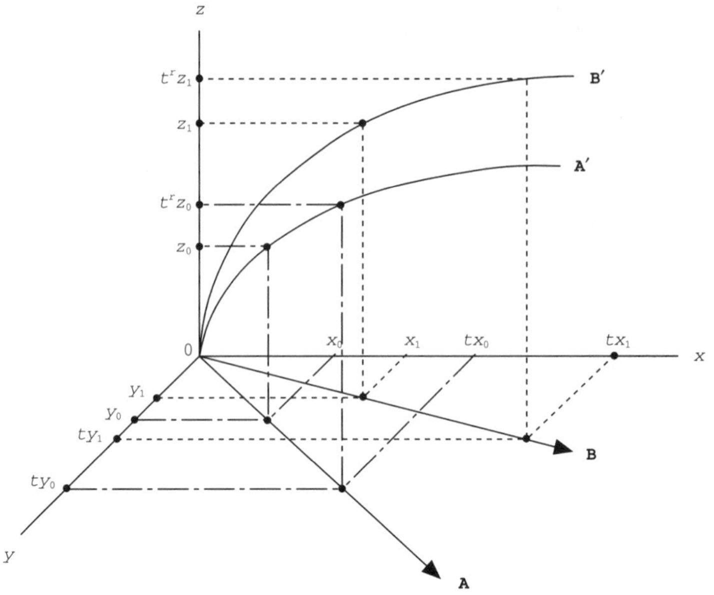


**Figure 8.7** Homogeneous function

increases, the value of the function $f(tx_0,ty_0)$ increases by the factor $t^{5/2}$. That is, $f(tx_0,ty_0) = t^{5/2}f(x_0,y_0)$.

*In[198]:=*

```
Clear[f,x,y];
f[x_,y_]:= (x^3+y^3)/(Sqrt[x]+Sqrt[y]);x0=2;y0=3;
homo  =  Plot3D[f[x,y],{x,0.1,6},{y,0.1,8},
                    DisplayFunction->Identity];
cutter  =  ParametricPlot3D[{t  x0,t  y0,z},
                      {t,0.1,3},{z,0,150},
                       DisplayFunction->Identity];
Show[homo,cutter,DisplayFunction->$DisplayFunction,
         Lighting->True,AxesLabel->{"x","y","z"},
         ViewPoint->{1.059,-3.094,0.867},
         Boxed->False];
```

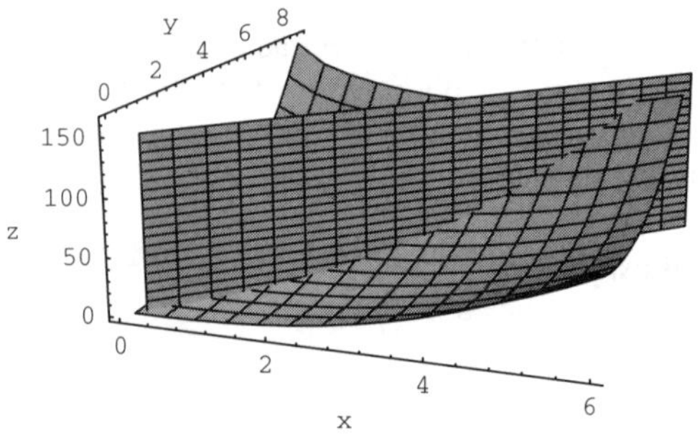


Altenatively, a homogeneous function can be characterized by its level curves. A *level curve* is the set of all points $(x,y)$ such that $f(x,y) = c$, where $c$ is a constant. Level

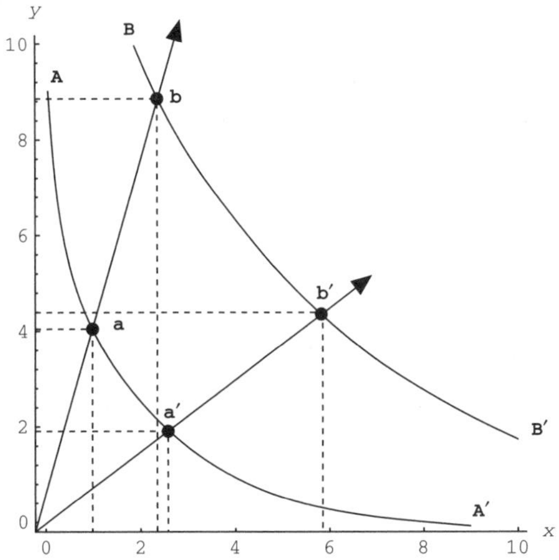


**Figure 8.8** Level curves and homogeneous functions

curves are called *isoquant curves* for production functions and *indifference curves* for utility functions. Suppose there are two such points, $(x_0,y_0)$ and $(x_1,y_1)$, on the level curve $f(x,y) = c$. Hence, $f(x_0,y_0) = f(x_1,y_1) = c$. If the function $f(x,y)$ is homogeneous of degree $r$ and $t$ is a positive number, then $(tx_0,ty_0)$ is a point on the ray from (0,0) to $(x_0,y_0)$ and $(tx_1,ty_1)$ is a point on the ray from (0,0) to $(x_1,y_1)$. Furthermore,

$$f(tx_0,ty_0) = t^r f(x_0,y_0) = t^r c$$
$$f(tx_1,ty_1) = t^r f(x_1,y_1) = t^r c.$$

Thus, $f(tx_0,ty_0) = f(tx_1,ty_1) = t^r c$, namely, the function $f$ has the same value at $(tx_0,ty_0)$ and $(tx_1,ty_1)$ for each value of $t$. Hence, for fixed $t$, $(tx_0,ty_0)$ and $(tx_1,ty_1)$ must be points on the same level curve.

**Example 8.48** The function $f(x,y) = \sqrt{x} + \sqrt{y}$ is homogeneous of degree $r = 1/2$. We consider two level curves of $f$ which we label **AA′** and **BB′** in figure 8.8. The lower level curve (**AA′**) shown in figure 8.8 corresponds to the contour at $c = 3$. Two points on the level curve, $(x_0,y_0) = (1,4)$ and $(x_1,y_1) = (2.56,1.96)$, are shown at points **a** and **a′**. They lie on the intersection with two rays from the origin. The extension of the rays $(tx,ty)$, (supposing $t = 2.25$), must intersect the upper level curve (**BB′**) as shown at points **b** and **b′**. That is,

$$f(2.25(1),2.25(4)) = (2.25)^{0.5}f(1,4) = 4.5$$
$$f(2.25(2.56),2.25(1.96)) = (2.25)^{0.5}f(2.56,1.96) = 4.5$$

## EXERCISES

1. Show that the slope of the tangent line to the level curves of a homogeneous function is constant along rays from the origin. For example, in figure 8.8, the

slopes of the tangent lines to the level curves at points **a** and **b** are equal to those at **a′** and **b′** respectively.

2. A simple consumer demand function has as its arguments the product's price, $P$, and consumers income, $Y$. If both price and income were to increase at a same rate, the demand would remain constant.
   (a) Show that the Cobb-Doglas demand function,

   $$f(P,Y) = 50P^{-0.25}Y^{0.25}$$

   is homogeneous of degree 0.
   (b) Use the function **ContourPlot** to plot the iso-demand (level) curve at $f(P,Y) = 100$ units with the ranges $\{P,1,6\}$ and $\{Y,10,100\}$.
   (c) Suppose the consumer's initial income is $Y_0 = 32$ dollars, and the price paid is $P_0 = 2$ dollars per unit. The demand will remain at $50(2)^{-0.25}(32)^{0.25} = 100$ units. Show that the demand $f(tP_0, tY_0)$ is constant by varying $t$ from 0.1 to 3.

### 8.6.3 Some properties

Several interesting and important properties of a homogeneous function are frequently used in economics. Suppose $f(x_1,x_2, \ldots ,x_n)$ is homogeneous of degree $r$. That is,

$$f(tx_1,tx_2, \ldots ,tx_n) = t^r f(x_1,x_2, \ldots ,x_n).$$

*Property 1 (ratio property)* If $t$ is replaced by $1/x_1$, then

$$\begin{aligned} f(x_1,x_2,\ldots,x_n) &= x_1^r f\left(1,\frac{x_2}{x_1},\frac{x_3}{x_1},\ldots,\frac{x_n}{x_1}\right) \\ &= x_1^r \phi\left(\frac{x_2}{x_1},\frac{x_3}{x_1},\ldots,\frac{x_n}{x_1}\right) \end{aligned}$$

where $\phi$ is a function of ratios of the variables.

**Example 8.49** $f(x,y) = x^2y - 2xy^2 + y^3$ is homogeneous of degree $r = 3$. The function can be rewritten as

$$f(x,y) = x^3\left[\left(\frac{y}{x}\right) - 2\left(\frac{y}{x}\right)^2 + \left(\frac{y}{x}\right)\right] = x^3\phi\left(\frac{y}{x}\right).$$

**Example 8.50** In a linear homogeneous production function, i.e., homogeneous of degree one, the average product of one input is a function of the input ratios. With labor, $L$, and captial, $K$, as inputs, a constant returns to scale production function implies that the average product of labor, $Q/L$, is a function of captial–labor ratio, $K/L$. That is

$$Q = f(L,K) = L\phi(K/L) \quad \text{and} \quad Q/L = \phi(K/L).$$

**Example 8.51** A homogeneous demand function of degree 0 implies that the quantity demand is a function of relative prices and real income. If $D = f(P_1,P_2, \ldots ,P_n,Y)$ is homogeneous of degree zero in $n$ prices, $P_1,P_2, \ldots ,P_n$, and income, $Y$, then

$$f(P_1,P_2,\ldots,P_nY) = \phi\left(\frac{P_2}{P_1},\frac{P_3}{P_1},\ldots,\frac{P_n}{P_1},\frac{Y}{P_1}\right).$$

*Property 2 (derivative property)* The partial derivative of a homogeneous function of degree $r$ is itself a homogeneous function of degree $r$–1. If $f_i(x_1, x_2, \ldots, x_n)$ is the partial derivative with respect to $x_i$, then

$$f_i(tx_1,tx_2,\ldots,tx_n) = t^{r-1}f_i(x_1,x_2,\ldots,x_n).$$

**Example 8.52** The Cobb-Douglas production function $f(L,K) = AL^aK^b$ is homogeneous of degree $a+b$. Since the marginal product of labor $f_L(L,K)$ is equal to

$$f_L(L,K) = aAL^{a-1}K^b$$

and

$$f_L(tL,tK) = aA(tL)^{a-1}(tK)^b = t^{(a+b-1)}f_L(L,K)$$

then $f_L(L,K)$ is homogeneous of degree $a+b-1$. Similarly, the marginal product of capital $f_K(L,K) = bAL^aK^{b-1}$ is homogeneous of degree $a+b-1$.

*Property 3 (Euler's theorem)* If $f(x_1,x_2,\ldots,x_n)$ is a differentiable homogeneous function of degree $r$, then

$$\sum_{i=1}^{n} x_i f_i(x_1,x_2,\ldots,x_n) = rf(x_1,x_2,\ldots,x_n).$$

Expressed in vector form, the relationship is

$$\mathbf{x} \cdot \nabla\mathbf{f} = rf$$

where $\mathbf{x} = [x_1\ x_2\ \ldots\ x_n]^T$ and $\nabla\mathbf{f}$ is the gradient vector of $f$. The converse of Euler's theorem is also true. If

$$\sum_{i=1}^{n} x_i f_i(x_1,x_2,\ldots,x_n) = rf(x_1,x_2,\ldots,x_n)$$

for all $x_1,x_2,\ldots,x_n$, then $f(x_1,x_2,\ldots,x_n)$ is homogeneous of degree $r$.

**Example 8.53** A CES function

$$f(x,y) = [ax^{\mathrm{d}} + by^{\mathrm{d}}]^{r/\mathrm{d}}$$

is homogeneous of degree $r$, since

$$xf_x + yf_y = rf.$$

If $r = 1$, then the CES function is of constant returns to scale, and

$xf_x + yf_y = f(x,y).$

If each input is paid according to its marginal product, e.g., $f_x$ = price of $x$ (wage rate on labor input) and $f_y$ = price of $y$ (interest rate on capital loan), then the total payment to inputs will just exhaust the total output. Hence, we have

$$\frac{xf_x}{f(x,y)} + \frac{yf_y}{f(x,y)} = 1.$$

What happens then in the case of increasing ($r > 1$) or decreasing ($r < 1$) returns to scale?

An extended Euler's theorem can be obtained by applying Euler's theorem to the partial derivative $f_i(x_1,x_2, \ldots ,x_n)$. If the partial derivative is homogeneous of degree $r$–1, then

$$\sum_{j=1}^{n} x_j f_{ij}(x_1,x_2, \ldots ,x_n) = (r-1)\, f_i(x_1,x_2, \ldots ,x_n)$$

where $f_{ij}$ is the second-order cross partial derivative. Substituting the result for the original relation, we have

$$\sum_{i=1}^{n}\sum_{j=1}^{n} x_i x_j f_{ij}(x_1,x_2, \ldots ,x_n) = r(r-1)\, f(x_1,x_2, \ldots ,x_n).$$

In matrix form, this equation can be written as

$$\mathbf{x}^T\mathbf{H}\mathbf{x} = r(r-1)f$$

where $\mathbf{x} = [x_1\ x_2 \ldots x_n]^T$, and $\mathbf{H}$ is the Hessian matrix of $f$ at $(x_1,x_2, \ldots ,x_n)$.

## EXERCISES

1. Consider the following functions

$$f(x,y,z) = (x^2y + y^2z + z^2x)^{1/3}$$

$$f(x,y,z) = \frac{x^3 + y^3 + z^3}{x^2 + y^2 + z^2}$$

   (a) Show that the functions are linear homogeneous functions.
   (b) Express each in the form $x\phi(y/x, z/x)$.
   (c) Show that the partial derivatives $\partial f/\partial x$ and $\partial^2 f/\partial x^2$ are homogeneous functions.
   (d) Verify Euler's theorem in each case.

2. Show that the CES function,

$$f(x,y,z) = [ax^d + by^d + (1-a-b)z^d]^{r/d}$$

is a homogeneous function of degree $r$. Demonstrate the three properties of homogeneous functions.

3. By Euler's theorem, a function $y = f(x_1,x_2, \ldots ,x_n)$ is homogeneous of degree $r$ if

$$\sum_{i=1}^{n} x_i f_i(x_1,x_2, \ldots ,x_n) = rf(x_1,x_2, \ldots ,x_n).$$

We can extend this definition to include the case where the degree of homogeneity $r$ is a function, i.e., $r = g(y)$. What is the degree of homogeneity if

$$ye^{\theta y} = Ax_1^{\alpha(1-\delta)}x_2^{\alpha\delta}.$$

### 8.6.4 Homothetic function

Suppose $y = f(x_1,x_2, \ldots ,x_n)$ is homogeneous of degree $r$, and the level surface, $f(x_1,x_2, \ldots ,x_n) = c$, implicitly defines a function, $x_i = g(x_1, \ldots ,x_{i-1},x_{i+1}, \ldots ,x_n)$. By the Implicit Function Theorem, the partial derivative of $x_i$ with respect to $x_j$ is simply the negative of the ratio of paritial derivatives of $f$ with respect to $x_i$ and $x_j$:

$$\frac{\partial x_i}{\partial x_j} = -\frac{f_j(x_1,x_2, \ldots ,x_n)}{f_i(x_1,x_2, \ldots ,x_n)}.$$

The partial derivatives, $f_j(x_1,x_2, \ldots ,x_n)$ and $f_i(x_1,x_2, \ldots ,x_n)$, are also homogeneous functions of degree $r-1$. Thus, at the point $(tx_1,tx_2, \ldots ,tx_n)$, the above ratio becomes

$$\frac{\partial x_i}{\partial x_j} = -\frac{f_j(tx_1,tx_2, \ldots ,tx_n)}{f_i(tx_1,tx_2, \ldots ,tx_n)} = -\frac{t^{r-1}f_j(x_1,x_2, \ldots ,x_n)}{t^{r-1}f_i(x_1,x_2, \ldots ,x_n)} = -\frac{f_j(x_1,x_2, \ldots ,x_n)}{f_i(x_1,x_2, \ldots ,x_n)}$$

which is identical to $\partial x_i/\partial x_j$ evaluated at the point $(x_1,x_2, \ldots ,x_n)$.

The invariance of the partial derivative $\partial x_i/\partial x_j$ along a ray from the origin is not unique to a homogeneous function. In fact, any monotonic transformation of a homogeneous function has the same property. Let $z = F(y)$ be a monotonic function of a homogeneous function $y = f(x_1,x_2, \ldots ,x_n)$. The composite function $z = F(y)$ is called a *homothetic* function. The partial derivative $\partial x_i/\partial x_j$ is also invariant since

$$\frac{\partial x_i}{\partial x_j} = -\frac{F'(y)f_j(x_1,x_2, \ldots ,x_n)}{F'(y)f_i(x_1,x_2, \ldots ,x_n)} = -\frac{f_j(x_1,x_2, \ldots ,x_n)}{f_i(x_1,x_2, \ldots ,x_n)}$$

**Example 8.54** Consider the function $f(x,y) = \sqrt{x} + \sqrt{y}$. This function is homogeneous of degree $r = 1/2$ since

$$\frac{dy}{dx} = -\frac{f_x(x,y)}{f_y(x,y)} = -\frac{1/2\,x^{-1/2}}{1/2\,y^{-1/2}} = -\sqrt{\frac{y}{x}}$$

The function $z = \log f(x,y)$ is a homothetic function since logarithmic function is monotonic. A direct calculation shows that

$$\frac{dy}{dx} = -\frac{f_x(x,y)/\log[f(x,y)]}{f_y(x,y)/\log[f(x,y)]} = -\frac{1/2\,x^{-1/2}}{1/2\,y^{-1/2}} = -\sqrt{\frac{y}{x}}$$

## EXERCISES

1. Find the ratio of the marginal utility of goods, $x$ and $y$, when the utility function is of Cobb-Douglas form

$$u = f(x,y) = Ax^a y^b$$

Show that the same ratio is obtained when the utility function is written as

(a) $\log u = \log A + a \log x + b \log y$

(b) $g(u) = \dfrac{1}{1 + e^{-u}}$

2. Suppose $u = f(x_1, x_2, \ldots, x_n)$ is a utility function of goods $x_i$. If the index function of utility $U = g(u)$ is an increasing, monotonic function, show that

$$\frac{\partial^2 U}{\partial x_i^2} = F'(u)\frac{\partial^2 u}{\partial x_i^2} + F''(u)\left(\frac{\partial u}{\partial x_i}\right)^2 \quad \text{for} \quad i = 1,2, \ldots, n.$$

Apply the results to the functions given in exercise 1.

# 9

# Taylor Series and Implicit Functions

In Chapter 8, we were concerned primarily with the idea of the differential calculus of functions of several variables. In this chapter, we use this calculus to obtain polynomial approximations for sufficiently smooth functions. These approximations are called Taylor polynomials. Also in this chapter we study equations that define functions implicitly. For example, the equation $F(x,y) = 0$ defines $y$ implicitly in terms of $x$. Under what circumstances can we solve this equation for $y$ in terms of $x$, giving an explicit representation for $y$? This study leads us to the famous Implicit Function Theorem and its consequences.

## □ 9.1 Taylor Series □

### 9.1.1 Taylor polynomials

We begin by recalling (section 8.4.1) that the differential of a function $f(x)$ at $x_0$, $df = f'(x_0)\,dx$, is an approximation to the increment of $f$ at $x_0$, $\Delta f = f(x) - f(x_0)$. Rewriting $\Delta f \approx df$, we have $f(x) \approx f(x_0) + f'(x_0)(x-x_0) = P_1(x)$. The first degree polynomial, $P_1(x)$, can serve as an approximation for $f(x)$. In this section we generalize this type of approximation to higher degree polynomials.

Consider a function $f(x)$ that is differentiable at a point in its domain $x = a$. A first degree polynomial that is equal to $f(x)$ and $f'(x)$ at $x = a$ is

$$P_1(x) = f(a) + f'(a)(x-a).$$

It is easy to verify that $P_1(a) = f(a)$ and $P_1'(a) = f'(a)$. Let

$$\begin{aligned} R_1(x) &= f(x) - P_1(x) \\ &= f(x) - f(a) - f'(a)(x-a). \end{aligned}$$

We call $R_1(x)$ the *remainder* or *error* of the approximation. As $x \to a$, $R_1(x) \to 0$.

**Example 9.1** Consider the exponential function $f(x) = e^x$. Since $f(0) = f'(0) = 1$, a first-degree polynomial approximation is

$P_1(x) = f(0) + f'(0)x = 1 + x.$

Since $P_1(0) = f(0)$ and $P_1'(0) = f'(0)$, $P_1(x)$ has the same tangent line as $f(x)$ at $x = 0$. As shown in the following *Mathematica* plot, the error of the approximation is the gap between $f(x)$ and $P_1(x)$. At $x = 0.5$, the error is defined as

$$\begin{aligned} R_1(0.5) &= f(0.5) - P_1(0.5) \\ &= e^{0.5} - (1 + 0.5) \approx 0.14872 \end{aligned}$$

The error of the approximation gets smaller as $x$ approaches the point $x = 0$.

*In[1]:=*
```
Clear[f,p1,x];
f[x_]:= Exp[x];
p1[x_]:= 1 + x;
Plot[{f[x],p1[x]},{x,-1,1},
       PlotStyle->{{},{Dashing[{0.02}]}}];
```

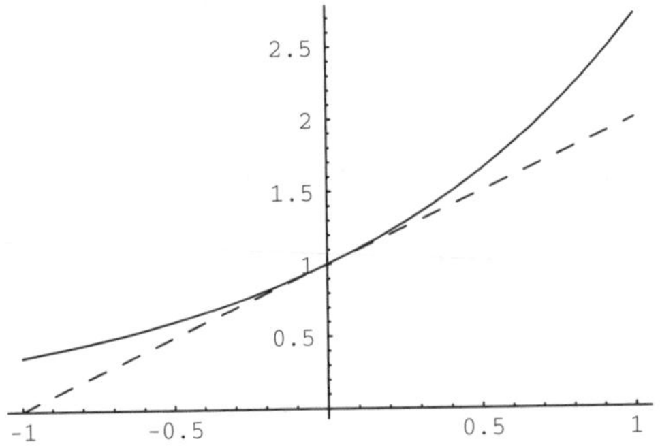


We now look at higher degree polynomial approximation.

> **DEFINITION 9.1** *A **Taylor polynomial** $P_n(x)$ of degree n for an n-times differentiable function $f(x)$ at point $x = a$ is defined as*
>
> $$f(x) = P_n(x) + R_{n+1}(x)$$
>
> *where*
>
> $$P_n(x) = f(a) + f'(a)(x - a) + \frac{f''(a)}{2!}(x - a)^2 + \ldots + \frac{f^{(n)}(a)}{n!}(x - a)^n$$

The point $x = a$ is called the *center of expansion*. The Taylor polynomial and its derivatives satisfy the identities:

(1) $f(a) = P_n(a)$

(2) $f^{(k)}(a) = P_n^{(k)}(a)$, k = 1,2, . . . ,$n$

**Example 9.2** In example 9.1, the approximation can be improved if a second-degree polynomial $P_2(x)$ is used. At $a = 0$, $f''(0) = 1$ for $f(x) = e^x$, and hence

$$P_2(x) = 1 + x + \frac{1}{2}x^2.$$

The error of the approximation at $x = 0.5$ is

$$R_3(0.5) = f(0.5) - P_2(0.5)$$
$$= e^{0.5} - \left(1 + 0.5 + \frac{1}{2}(0.5)^2\right) \approx 0.0237$$

which is much smaller than the error when $P_1(x)$ is used. The following plot shows the graphs $f(x)$, $P_1(x)$, and $P_2(x)$.

*In[5]:=*

```
Clear[f,p1,p2,x];
f[x_]:= Exp[x];
p1[x_]:= 1 + x;
p2[x_]:= 1 + x + x^2/2;
Plot[{f[x],p1[x],p2[x]},{x,-1,1},
PlotStyle->{{},{Dashing[{0.02}]},{Thickness[0.007]}}];
```

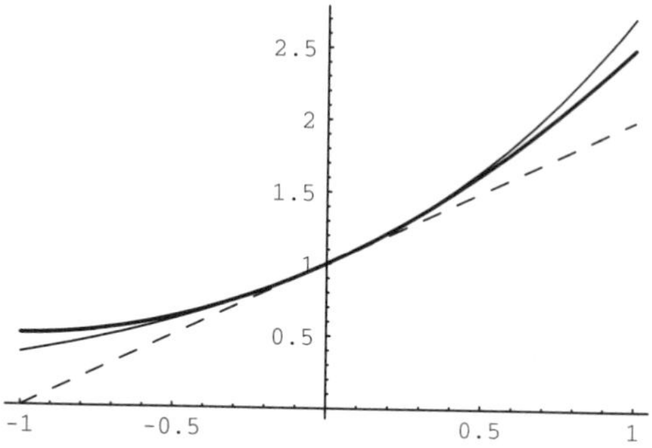


One reason for the improvement of the approximation as $n$ increases is that more information is incorporated into the Taylor polynomial. For example, $P_2(x)$ contains information about $f(x)$, $f'(x)$ and $f''(x)$ at $x = a$, while $P_1(x)$ uses only $f(a)$ and $f'(a)$. Hence, we expect that in a neighborhood of $x = a$

$$\lim_{n\to\infty} R_{n+1}(x) = 0$$

and we infer that $f(x)$ can be approximated arbitrarily closely by its Taylor polynomial in this neighborhood of the center of expansion. This is the case for many infinitely differentiable functions.

Various forms of the remainder exist. For example, the *Lagrange's form* of the remainder is

$$R_{n+1}(x) = \frac{f^{(n+1)}(t)}{(n+1)!}(x - a)^{n+1}$$

where $t$ lies between $x$ and $a$.

From the Lagrange's form of the remainder, an upper bound for the approximation error can sometimes be obtained. If $|f^{(n+1)}(x)| \leq M$, then

$$|R_{n+1}(x)| \le \left|\frac{M(x-a)^{n+1}}{(n+1)!}\right| = \frac{M}{(n+1)!}|x-a|^{n+1}$$

**Example 9.3** Approximate $e^{-0.5}$ around $x = 0$ using a third-degree polynomial. Here $a = 0$. Since $f^{(k)}(x) = e^x$ for $k = 0,1, \ldots ,4$, we have

$$\begin{aligned} f(x) = e^x &= P_3(x) + R_4(x) \\ &= 1 + x + \frac{x^2}{2!} + \frac{x^3}{3!} + R_4(x) \end{aligned}$$

where

$$R_4(x) = \frac{f^{(4)}(t)}{4!}x^4 = \frac{e^t}{4!}x^4$$

for some $t$ between 0 and $x$. Thus, for $x = -0.5$,

$$\begin{aligned} e^{-0.5} &= 1 + (-0.5) + \frac{(-0.5)^2}{2!} + \frac{(-0.5)^3}{3!} + R_4(-0.5) \\ &= 0.60416 + R_4(-0.5) \end{aligned}$$

Since $|R_4(-0.5)| = e^t(-0.5)^4/4!$ for $-0.5 < t < 0$, we have the upper bound

$$0 < |R_4(-0.5)| < \frac{1}{4!}e^0(-0.5)^4 = 0.0026.$$

Hence, we have upper and lower bounds

$$0.60156 < e^{-0.5} < 0.60676$$

## EXERCISES

1. Find the Taylor polynomials of degree $n$ at the point $x = a$ for the following functions:
   (a) $f(x) = \dfrac{1}{x}$, $n = 4$, $a = 1$
   (b) $f(x) = \sin x$, $n = 3$, $a = 0$
   (c) $f(x) = (1 + x)^{3.5}$, $n = 3$, $a = 0$.
2. Plot the function $f(x) = \sin x$ and the Taylor polynomials $P_3(x)$ and $P_4(x)$ at the point $a = 0$. Show that the error of approximation is smaller for $P_4(x)$ than for $P_3(x)$.
3. Prove that if $f(x)$ is an odd function, i.e., $f(-x) = -f(x)$, then the Taylor polynomial of degree $n$ about $x = 0$ contains only terms with odd powers of $x$.
4. Prove that if $f(x)$ is an even function, i.e., $f(-x) = f(x)$, then the Taylor polynomial of degree $n$ about $x = 0$ will contain only terms with even powers of $x$.

5. (The Mean-Value Theorem). Approximate $f(x)$ by $P_0(a)$ and show that there exists at least one point $t$ between $x$ and $a$ such that

$$f'(t) = \frac{f(x) - f(a)}{x - a}$$

## 9.1.2 Computing Taylor polynomials with *Mathematica*

The *Mathematica* function **Series** can be used to compute the Taylor polynomial of a function. Here is the *Mathematica* description of this function.

*In[10]:=*

```
?Series
```

**Series[f, {x, x0, n}] generates a power series expansion for f about the point x = x0 to order (x - x0)^n. Series[f, {x, x0, nx}, {y, y0, ny}] successively finds series expansions with respect to y, then x.**

**Example 9.4** Find the Taylor's series expansion of $f(x) = e^x$ about the point $a = 1/5$ for $n = 4$, using *Mathematica*.

*In[11]:=*

```
Clear[x];
P4 = Series[Exp[x],{x,1/5,4}]
```

*Out[12]=*

$$E^{1/5} + E^{1/5}(-(\frac{1}{5}) + x) + \frac{E^{1/5}(-(\frac{1}{5}) + x)^2}{2} + \frac{E^{1/5}(-(\frac{1}{5}) + x)^3}{6} + \frac{E^{1/5}(-(\frac{1}{5}) + x)^4}{24} + O[-(\frac{1}{5}) + x]^5$$

*In[13]:=*

```
P4 // N
```

*Out[13]=*

$$1.2214 + 1.2214(-0.2 + x) + 0.6107(-0.2 + x)^2 + 0.20357(-0.2 + x)^3 + 0.050892(-0.2 + x)^4 + O[-0.2 + x]^5$$

The remainder term is denoted by *Mathematica* as $\mathbf{O[-0.2+x]^5}$ which stands for terms of order $(-0.2+x)^5$ or higher.

**Example 9.5** *Mathematica* can find the Taylor polynomial of an arbitrary $f(x)$ symbolically in terms of its derivatives.

*In[14]:=*

```
Clear[f,a,x];
Series[f[x],{x,a,3}]
```

*Out[15]=*

$$f[a] + f'[a](-a + x) + \frac{f''[a](-a + x)^2}{2} + \frac{f^{(3)}[a](-a + x)^3}{6} + O[-a + x]^4$$

To obtain only the Taylor polynomial without the remainder in *Mathematica*, we can use the *Mathematica* function **Normal**.

*In[16]:=*

```
?Normal
```

**Normal[expr] converts expr to a normal expression, from a variety of special forms.**

**Example 9.6** Calculate the Taylor polynomial with and without the remainder for $\log x$ about the point $a = 1$ to $n = 6$.

*In[17]:=*

```
Clear[x];
P6 = Series[Log[x],{x,1,6}]
```

*Out[18]=*

$$(-1+x) - \frac{(-1+x)^2}{2} + \frac{(-1+x)^3}{3} - \frac{(-1+x)^4}{4} + \frac{(-1+x)^5}{5} - \frac{(-1+x)^6}{6} + O[-1+x]^7$$

*In[19]:=*

```
Normal[P6]
```

*Out[19]=*

$$-1 - \frac{(-1+x)^2}{2} + \frac{(-1+x)^3}{3} - \frac{(-1+x)^4}{4} + \frac{(-1+x)^5}{5} - \frac{(-1+x)^6}{6} + x$$

We can, of course, combine the **Series** and **Normal** functions to obtain the same result.

*In[20]:=*

```
Normal[Series[Log[x],{x,1,6}]]
```

*Out[20]=*

$$-1 - \frac{(-1+x)^2}{2} + \frac{(-1+x)^3}{3} - \frac{(-1+x)^4}{4} + \frac{(-1+x)^5}{5} - \frac{(-1+x)^6}{6} + x$$

**Example 9.7** A power function, or Box-Cox transformation of a variable $x$ with parameter $r$, is defined as

$$f(x) = \frac{x^r - 1}{r}, \; x > 0$$

The function was first encountered in example 2.5 in section 2.1.1. It includes $\log x$ as a special case when $r$ approaches 0. For a given value of $x$, the power function is a function of $r$:

$$g(r) = \frac{x^r - 1}{r}, \; x > 0$$

We use **Series** to expand the function $g(r)$ about the point $r = 0$ with $n = 2$.

*In[21]:=*

```
Clear[x,r];
Normal[Series[(x^r-1)/r,{r,0,2}]]
```

*Out[22]=*

$$\text{Log}[x] + \frac{r\,\text{Log}[x]^2}{2} + \frac{r^2\,\text{Log}[x]^3}{6}$$

The last two terms of the Taylor polynomial approximate the difference between $f(x)$ and $\log x$,

$$f(x) - \log x \approx \frac{[\log(x)]^2}{2}r + \frac{[\log(x)]^3}{6}r^2$$

**Example 9.8** We previously defined a constant elasticity of substitution, CES, production function (see example 2.6 of section 2.1.1). Let the output $Q$ be related to two inputs, capital, $K$, and labor, $L$, as

$$Q(K,L) = [aK^r + (1-a)L^r]^{1/r}$$

where $r$ is a parameter. We showed that as $r \to 0$, the CES function approaches the Cobb-Douglas(CD) function,

$$Q(K,L) = K^a L^{1-a}.$$

Let us rewrite the CES function in a logarithmic form

$$\begin{aligned}\log Q &= \frac{1}{r}\log[aK^r + (1-a)L^r] \\ &\equiv \frac{1}{r}g(r)\end{aligned}$$

where $g(r)$ is defined as the logarithmic term on the right-hand side of the equation. We use the **Normal** and **Series** functions to obtain the Taylor polynomial $P_2(r)$ of degree 2 for the function $g(r)$ about the point $r = 0$.

*In[23]:=*

```
Clear[f,a,r,K,L,P2];
g[r_]:=  Log[a*K^r  +  (1-a)*L^r];
P2  =  Normal[Series[g[r],{r,0,2}]]  //  Simplify
```

*Out[25]=*

$$\frac{(1-a)\,a r^2\,(-\text{Log}[K] + \text{Log}[L])^2}{2} + r(a\,\text{Log}[K] + \text{Log}[L] - a\,\text{Log}[L])$$

If the polynomial $P_2(r)$ is divided by $r$, the logarithmic approximation of the CES function, $\log Q$, is then obtained as

$$\log Q \approx a\log K + (1-a)\log(L) + \frac{a(1-a)r}{2}[\log L - \log K]^2$$

or

$$\text{log of CES} \approx \text{log of CD} + \frac{a(1-a)r}{2}[\log L - \log K]^2.$$

Thus, the logarithm of a CES function is approximately equal to the logarithm of a Cobb-Douglas function plus a term showing the approximate difference between them. As $r \to 0$, the difference becomes smaller and smaller.

Taylor's series expansions can be generalized to functions of several variables. Consider a function $f(\mathbf{x})$ of $n$ variables, $\mathbf{x} = (x_1, x_2, \ldots, x_n)$ that has continuous partial derivatives at the point $\mathbf{a} = (a_1, a_2, \ldots, a_n)$. Suppose that $f(\mathbf{x})$ is defined in a convex region, i.e., a straight line connecting the two points will lie totally within the region. This is a technical condition of the domain of $f$, but it is essential for providing a formula for the remainder term. Taylor's Theorem for $f(\mathbf{x})$ states that

$$f(\mathbf{x}) = f(\mathbf{a}) + \mathrm{d}f(\mathbf{a};\mathbf{x}-\mathbf{a}) + \frac{1}{2!}\mathrm{d}^2 f(\mathbf{a};\mathbf{x}-\mathbf{a}) + \ldots + \frac{1}{m!}\mathrm{d}^m f(\mathbf{a};\mathbf{x}-\mathbf{a}) + R_{m+1}(\mathbf{x})$$

where the remainder is

$$R_{m+1}(\mathbf{x}) = \frac{1}{(m+1)!}\mathrm{d}^{m+1} f(\mathbf{t};\mathbf{x}-\mathbf{a})$$

and the point $\mathbf{t}$ lies on the line segment between $\mathbf{x}$ and $\mathbf{a}$. The term $\mathrm{d}f^k(\mathbf{a};\mathbf{x}-\mathbf{a})$ is the $k$th order differential of $f(\mathbf{x})$ evaluated at $\mathbf{a}$ with $\mathrm{d}\mathbf{x} = \mathbf{x}-\mathbf{a}$ or, componentwise, $\mathrm{d}x_i = x_i - a_i$, $i = 1, 2, \ldots, n$. For example, the first order differential is

$$\begin{aligned} \mathrm{d}f(\mathbf{a};\mathbf{x}-\mathbf{a}) &= f_1 \mathrm{d}x_1 + f_2 \mathrm{d}x_2 + \ldots + f_n \mathrm{d}x_n \\ &= f_1(x_1-a_1) + f_2(x_2-a_2) + \ldots + f_n(x_n-a_n) \\ &= \nabla f(\mathbf{a}) \cdot (\mathbf{x}-\mathbf{a}) \end{aligned}$$

where all the partial derivatives of f($\mathbf{x}$) are evaluated at $\mathbf{a}$. The second-order differential is the quadratic form

$$\mathrm{d}^2 f(\mathbf{a};\mathbf{x}-\mathbf{a}) = \begin{bmatrix} \mathrm{d}x_1 & \mathrm{d}x_2 & \ldots & \mathrm{d}x_n \end{bmatrix} \begin{bmatrix} f_{11} & f_{12} & \ldots & f_{1n} \\ f_{21} & f_{22} & \ldots & f_{2n} \\ \ldots & \ldots & \ldots & \ldots \\ f_{n1} & f_{n2} & \ldots & f_{nn} \end{bmatrix} \begin{bmatrix} \mathrm{d}x_1 \\ \mathrm{d}x_2 \\ \cdot \\ \cdot \\ \cdot \\ \mathrm{d}x_n \end{bmatrix}$$

$$= \begin{bmatrix} x_1-a_1 & x_2-a_2 & \ldots & x_n-a_n \end{bmatrix} \begin{bmatrix} f_{11} & f_{12} & \ldots & f_{1n} \\ f_{21} & f_{22} & \ldots & f_{2n} \\ \ldots & \ldots & \ldots & \ldots \\ f_{n1} & f_{n2} & \ldots & f_{nn} \end{bmatrix} \begin{bmatrix} x_1-a_1 \\ x_2-a_2 \\ \cdot \\ \cdot \\ \cdot \\ x_n-a_n \end{bmatrix}$$

where all the second-order partial derivatives of $f(\mathbf{x})$ are evaluated at $\mathbf{a}$.

We can write the expansion in a less compact form that indicates its computational complexity. Namely, the Taylor series expansion of $f(\mathbf{x})$ about $\mathbf{x} = \mathbf{a}$ is:

$$f(\mathbf{x}) = f(\mathbf{a}) + \sum_{i=1}^{n} f_i(\mathbf{a})(x_i - a_i) + \frac{1}{2!}\sum_{i,j=1}^{n} f_{ij}(\mathbf{a})(x_i - a_i)(x_j - a_j)$$

$$+ \ldots + \frac{1}{m!}\sum_{i,j,\ldots,k=1}^{n} f_{ij\ldots k}(\mathbf{a})(x_i - a_i)(x_j - a_j)\ldots(x_k - a_k) + R_{m+1}(\mathbf{x})$$

where $f_{ij\ldots k}(\mathbf{a})$ is the $m$-th order mixed partial derivative with respect to the $m$ variables $(x_i, x_j, \ldots, x_k)$, evaluated at $\mathbf{a}$.

The *Mathematica* function **Series** can be used to compute the Taylor's series expansion for these functions. For functions of more than one variable, we must specify the independent variables, the coordinates of **a**, and the degrees in each variable of the polynomial.

**Example 9.9** Expand the function $f(x,y)$ about the point (0,0) with the degrees of $x$ and $y$ equal to 2.

*In[26]:=*

```
Clear[f,x,y];
Series[f[x,y],{x,0,2},{y,0,2}]
```

*Out[27]=*

$$f[0,0] + f^{(0,1)}[0,0]y + \frac{f^{(0,2)}[0,0]y^2}{2} + O[y]^3$$
$$+ (f^{(1,0)}[0,0] + f^{(1,1)}[0,0]y + \frac{f^{(1,2)}[0,0]y^2}{2} + O[y]^3)x$$
$$+ (\frac{f^{(2,0)}[0,0]}{2} + \frac{f^{(2,1)}[0,0]y}{2} + \frac{f^{(2,2)}[0,0]y^2}{4} + O[y]^3)x^2 + O[x]^3$$

**Example 9.10** Find the Taylor polynomial of degree 2 for the function, $f(x,y,z) = 1/(1+x-y+z)$ about the point (0,1,1).

*In[28]:=*

```
Normal[Series[1/(1+x-y+z),{x,0,2},{y,1,2},{z,1,2}]]
```

*Out[28]=*

$$1 - x + x^2 + (1 - 2x + 3x^2)(-1 + y) + (1 - 3x + 6x^2)(-1 + y)^2$$
$$+ (-1 + 2x - 3x^2 + (-2 + 6x - 12x^2)(-1 + y) + (-3 + 12x - 30x^2)(-1 + y)^2)$$
$$(-1 + z) + (1 - 3x + 6x^2 + (3 - 12x + 30x^2)(-1 + y) + (6 - 30x + 90x^2)$$
$$(-1 + y)^2)(-1 + z)^2$$

## EXERCISES

1. Find the Taylor series expansions at $x = a$ of degree $n$ for the following functions:
   (a) $f(x) = \dfrac{1}{1+x}$, $n = 4$, $a = 0$
   (b) $f(x) = e^{-x}$, $n = 3$, $a = 0.5$
   (c) $f(x) = \sqrt{x}$, $n = 4$, $a = 4$
   (d) $f(x) = xe$, $n = 4$, $a = 4$.

2. The CES function

$$f(r) = [aK^r + (1-a)\,L^r]^{1/r}$$

reduces to various special functions. As $r \to 0$, $f(r)$ approaches to Cobb-Douglas function. $f(1)$ is a linear function, and $f(-1)$ is a harmonic mean function.
   (a) Find the Taylor polynomial $P_1(r)$ at $r=1$ and compute the difference $P_1(r) - f(1)$.
   (b) Find the Taylor polynomial $P_1(r)$ at $r=-1$ and compute the difference $P_1(r) - f(-1)$.
3. Find Taylor series expansions for each of the following functions:
   (a) $f(x,y,z) = \log(x+y+z)$, at $(x,y,z) = (1,1,1)$ with $n = 2$.
   (b) $f(x,y) = e^{x+y}$, at $(x,y) = (0,0)$ with $n = 2$.

## □ 9.2 Implicit Functions □

### 9.2.1 Definitions

In economics, we frequently encounter equations of the form $F(x,y) = 0$. For example, $F(x,y) = Ax^a y^b - 10 = 0$, where $x$ and $y$ are inputs required to produce 10 units of output in a Cobb-Douglas production function. In many applications we are interested in solving $F(x,y) = 0$ for $x$ or $y$. In the Cobb-Douglas example, $y = f(x)$ represents an isoquant, that is, the relation between inputs. However, often the function $F$ is so complicated that we cannot explicitly solve for $x$ or $y$. In such cases it is important to know the conditions under which explicit solutions are possible.

As an example, consider the implicit equation

$$F(x,y) = y + x^2 - 4 = 0.$$

This equation expresses a certain condition that a point in the $xy$-plane, $(x,y)$, may or may not satisfy. For example, $(x,y) = (1,3)$ does satisfy the condition, while $(x,y) = (2,1)$ does not. The collection of all points $(x,y)$ which satisfies the condition is called the *locus* of the equation. The locus of points for this equation is obviously all points $(x,y)$ such that

$$y = 4 - x^2$$

which is called a *solution* of $F(x,y) = 0$. Note that this solution is a function that gives $y$ as an explicit function of $x$:

$$y = f(x) = 4 - x^2.$$

To confirm this we replace $y$ in $F(x,y) = 0$ by $f(x)$:

$$F(x,f(x)) = (4 - x^2) + x^2 - 4 = 0.$$

The following is the graph of $f(x)$.

*In[29]:=*

```
Clear[f,x];
f[x_]:= 4 - x^2;
Plot[f[x],{x,-3,3},AxesLabel->{"x","y"}];
```

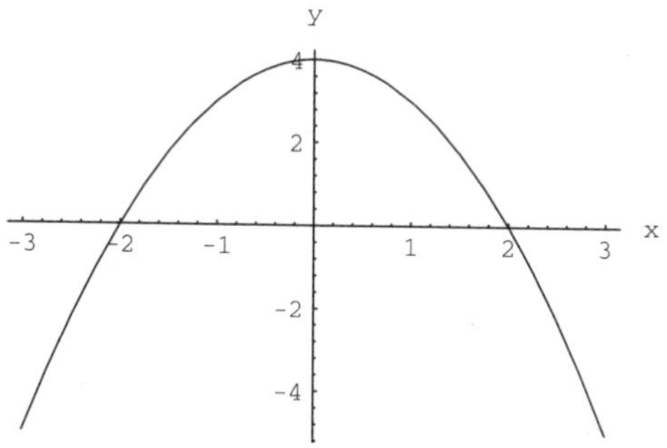


The *Mathematica* package **ImplicitPlot** can be used to graph implicit equations. We first load this package.

*In[32]:=*
```
Needs["Graphics`ImplicitPlot`"];
```

Here is *Mathematica*'s description of the function **ImplicitPlot** that is defined in the package.

*In[33]:=*
```
?ImplicitPlot
```

**ImplicitPlot[eqn, {x, a, b}] draws a graph of the set of points that satisfy the equation eqn. The variable x is associated with the horizontal axis and ranges from a to b. The remaining variable in the equation is associated with the vertical axis. ImplicitPlot[eqn, {x, a, x1, x2, ..., b}] allows the user to specify values of x where special care must be exercised. ImplicitPlot[{eqn1,eqn2,..},{x,a,b}] allows more than one equation to be plotted, with PlotStyles set as in the Plot function. ImplicitPlot[eqn,{x,a,b},{y,a,b}] uses a contour plot method of generating the plot. This form does not allow specification of intermediate points.**

We use the **ImplicitPlot** to graph the locus of the equation

$F(x,y) = y + x^2 - 4 = 0.$

*In[34]:=*
```
Clear[x,y];
ImplicitPlot[y+x^2-4==0,{x,-3,3},{y,-5,5},
                    AxesLabel->{"x","y"},AspectRatio->1];
```

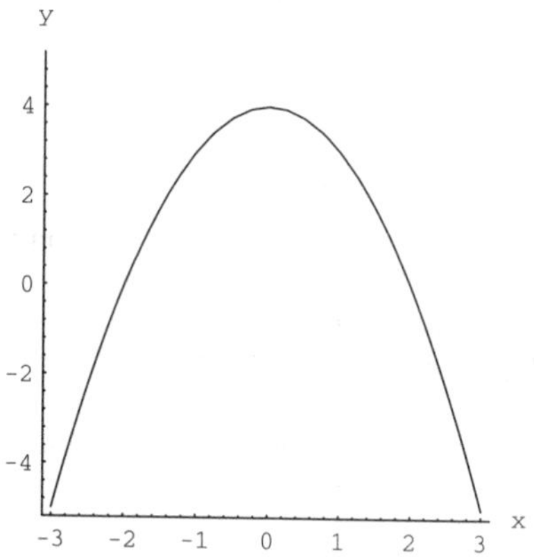

As shown above, the graph of the equation is the same as the graph of the function $f(x) = 4 - x^2$.

**Example 9.11** A Cobb-Douglas production function, $Q = 5L^{0.5}K^{0.4}$, with output $Q = 10$ units, implies an explicit function of isoquant curve, $K = f(L)$. We graph this isoquant with **ImplicitPlot**.

*In[36]:=*

```
Clear[K,L];
isoquant = 10 - 5*(L^0.5)*(K^0.4) == 0;
ImplicitPlot[isoquant,{L,1,5},
                    AxesLabel->{"L","K"},AspectRatio->1];
```

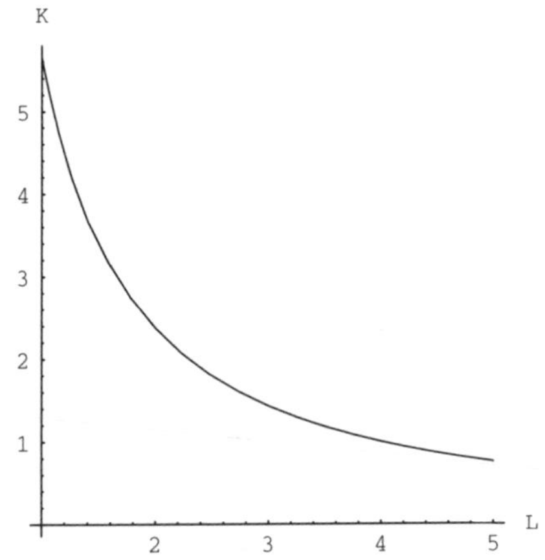


An alternative method of graphing an implicit equation is to use the function **ContourPlot**.

*In[39]:=*

```
?ContourPlot
```

**ContourPlot[f, {x, xmin, xmax}, {y, ymin, ymax}] generates a contour plot of f as a function of x and y.**

This function has several options. The option **Contours** is used to specify the values of $c$ in $F(x,y) = c$ for which the contours will be drawn.

*In[40]:=*

```
?Contours
```

**Contours is an option for ContourGraphics specifying the contours to use. Contours → n chooses n equally spaced contours between the minimum and maximum z values. Contours → {z1, z2, ... } specifies the explicit z values to use for contours.**

**Example 9.12** The following graph displays the isoquant of the Cobb-Douglas function in example 9.11 at $Q = 10$, 12 and 15 units.

*In[41]:=*

```
Clear[f,K,L,isoquant];
f[L_,K_]:= 5*L^0.5*K^0.4;
isoquant  =  ContourPlot[f[L,K],{L,1,5},{K,1,5},
                 Contours->{10,12,15},PlotPoints->30,
                 ContourShading->False,
                 ContourSmoothing->Automatic,
                 AxesLabel->{"L","K"},Axes->True,
                 Frame->False];
```

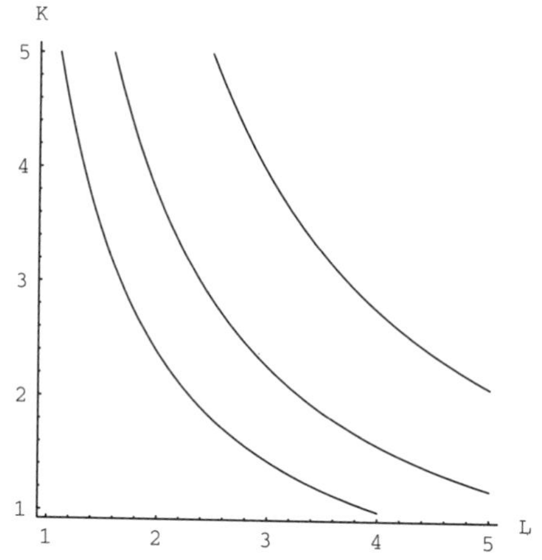


The *Mathematica* function **ContourPlot3D** allows the plotting of a three dimensional contour surface of the form $f(x,y,z) = c$. To use the function, we need to load the package into the *Mathematica* kernel.

*In[44]:=*

```
Needs["Graphics`ContourPlot3D`"];
```

This package defines the function **ContourPlot3D** that can be used to graph the contoursurface $f(x,y,z) = c$.

*In[45]:=*

```
?ContourPlot3D
```

**ContourPlot3D[ fun, {x, xmin, xmax}, {y, ymin, ymax}, {z, zmin, zmax}] plots the surface implicitly defined by fun[ x, y, z] == 0. Setting Contours → {val1, val2,...} will plot the surfaces for values val1, val2, etc.**

**Example 9.13** Expand the Cobb-Douglas production in example 9.12 to include a third input, energy, $R$, so that

$$Q = f(L,K,R) = 5L^{0.4}K^{0.2}R^{0.3}.$$

The following **ContourPlot3D** plots the contour surface at $Q = 10$ units of output.

*In[46]:=*
```
Clear[f,L,K,R];
f[L_,K_,R_]:=  (5*L^0.4)*(K^0.2)*(R^0.3);
ContourPlot3D[f[L,K,R],{L,1,5},{K,1,4},{R,1,3},
                Contours->{10}];
```

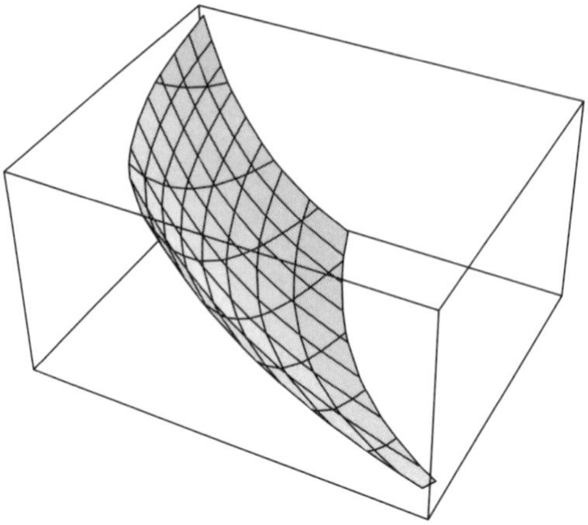

## EXERCISES

1. Consider $F(x,y) = x^3 + y^3 - 3xy = 0$. Show that the points, (2/3,4/3), (2/3, $(-2+\sqrt{6})/3$), and (2/3,$(-2-\sqrt{6})/3$), satisfy the equation. Use **ImplicitPlot** to check your work.
2. Does the implicit equation $F(x,y) = x + y - \sin xy = 0$ have a solution near the point (0,0) that can be expressed in the form $y = f(x)$? Use **ImplicitPlot** to plot the equation.

### 9.2.2 Implicit Function Theorem

Frequently, an implicit equation $F(x,y) = 0$ is so complicated that any attempt to obtain an explicit function $y = f(x)$ may not be possible. Even though an explicit formula for $f(x)$ may not be computable, we would still like to know if $f(x)$ exists in some neighborhood of a point on the graph of $F(x,y) = 0$.

**Example 9.14** It is not possible to solve for $y$ in terms of $x$ for the equation

$$F(x,y) = y + 0.1\log y - 3 + \log x = 0.$$

That is, we cannot find a function $f(x)$ such that $y = f(x)$ and $F(x,y) = 0$. However, the point $(x_0, y_0) = (e^2,1)$ is in the locus of this equation since

$$F(x_0,y_0) = 1 + 0.1\log(1) - 3 + \log(e^2) = 0.$$

This only tells us the value of $f(x)$ at $x_0$. More generally we want to find $f(x)$ at point near $x_0$ or at least know if it exists.

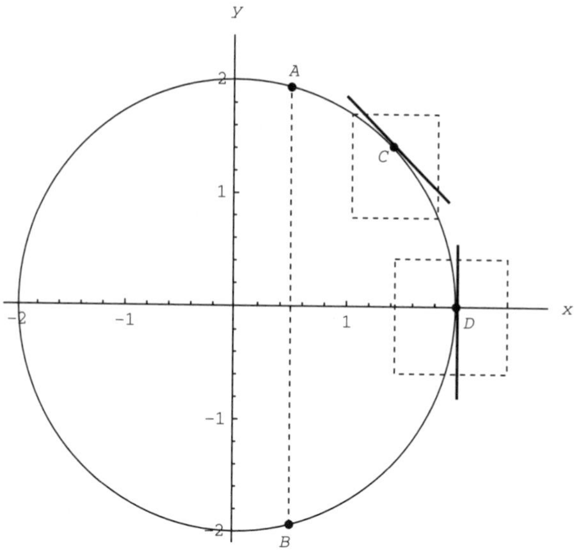


**Figure 9.1** Implicit equation $F(x, y) = 0$

**Example 9.15** The implicit equation

$$F(x,y) = x^2 + y^2 - 4 = 0$$

represents a circle with radius 2 that is centered at (0,0), as demonstrated in figure 9.1. The equation can be solved for $y$ in terms of $x$:

$$y = f(x) = \pm\sqrt{4 - x^2}$$

Technically $y = f(x)$ is not a function, since there are two values of $y$ that correspond to each value of $x$, for $-2 < x < 2$. For example,

$$x = 0.5;\ y = \pm\sqrt{4 - (0.5)^2} = \pm\sqrt{3.75}$$

The two values of $y$, shown at points $A$ and $B$ of figure 9.1, are obtained. If we consider only the relation $y = f(x)$ around a point $(x_0,y_0)$, say,

$$x_0 = 1.5;\ y_0 = +\sqrt{4 - (1.5)^2} = +\sqrt{1.75}$$

as shown in the enclosed box-like region on the upper part of the circle, then for each point $x$ in the neighborhood of $x_0$ (around point $C$), a unique value of $y$ is obtained, i.e., we have the function

$$y = f(x) = +\sqrt{4 - x^2}$$

that is defined in a neighborhood of $(x_0,y_0)$. Since the explicit function $y = f(x)$ exists around the point $(x_0,y_0)$, the derivative of the explicit function at that point can be directly obtained from this function as

$$\frac{\mathrm{d}y}{\mathrm{d}x} = -\frac{x}{\sqrt{4 - x^2}}.$$

The thick line on the upper part of figure 9.1 is the tangent line at the point $(x_0,y_0)$. Alternatively, the derivative can be obtained from the implicit equation $F(x,y) = x^2 + y^2 - 4 = 0$ by the chain rule. Taking the total differential of $F(x,y) = 0$, we have

$$\mathrm{d}F(x,y) = F_x\mathrm{d}x + F_y\mathrm{d}y = 2x\mathrm{d}x + 2y\mathrm{d}y = \mathrm{d}(0) = 0$$

and hence,

$$\frac{\mathrm{d}y}{\mathrm{d}x} = -\frac{F_x}{F_y} = -\frac{2x}{2y} = -\frac{x}{\sqrt{4 - x^2}}.$$

The existence of the explicit function, $y = f(x)$ rests on the assumption that in a neighborhood of the point $(x_0,y_0)$, we have $F_y(x_0,y_0) \neq 0$. This is not the case at the points $(x_0,y_0) = (\pm 2,0)$. As shown at the point $D$ in the above graph, it is impossible to enclose a region of the circle such that for each point in the neighborhood of (2,0), a unique value of $y$ is associated. At $x = 1.9$, say, there are two $y$ values associated. That is, the implicit equation

$$F(x,y) = x^2 + y^2 - 4 = 0$$

does not imply the existence of an explicit function $y = f(x)$ in the neighborhood of $(x_0,y_0) = (2,0)$. Hence the derivative of $f(x)$ does not exist. At the point (2,0), $F_y = -2y = 0$.

The above example raises the following important question: Under what condition does an implicit equation involving $n+1$ variables

$$F(\mathbf{x},y) = F(x_1,x_2, \ldots ,x_n,y) = 0$$

yield an explicit function $y = f(x_1,x_2, \ldots ,x_n) = f(\mathbf{x})$ such that

$$F(\mathbf{x},f(\mathbf{x})) = 0?$$

What is the relationship between the partial derivatives of the explicit function $f(\mathbf{x})$ and the implicit function $F(\mathbf{x},y) = 0$? This question is answered in the following theorem.

**THEOREM 9.1** *(Implicit Function Theorem) Given a function* $F(x_1,x_2, \ldots ,x_n,y) = 0$, *suppose that* $F(x_1,x_2, \ldots x_n,y)$ *has continuous first partial derivatives in the neighborhood of* $(x_1^0,x_2^0, \ldots ,x_n^0,y^0)$. *Furthermore, assume that*

$$F(x_1^0,x_2^0, \ldots ,x_n^0,y^0) = 0 \quad \text{and} \quad F_y(x_1^0,x_2^0, \ldots ,x_n^0,y^0) \neq 0$$

*Under these conditions, there exists a continuous function*

$$y = f(x_1,x_2, \ldots ,x_n)$$

*that is defined in a neighborhood of* $(x_1^0,x_2^0, \ldots ,x_n^0,y^0)$. *The explicit function has continuous first partial derivatives given by*

$$\frac{\partial y}{\partial x_i} = -\frac{F_i(x_1^0,x_2^0,\ldots,x_n^0,y^0)}{F_y(x_1^0,x_2^0,\ldots,x_n^0,y^0)} \quad \text{for} \quad i = 1,2,\ldots,n$$

*where $F_i(x_1^0,x_2^0,\ldots,x_n^0,y^0)$ is the partial derivative of F with respect to $x_i$.*

This method of calculating the partial derivative is called the *Implicit Function Rule.*

**Example 9.16** Consider $F(x,y,z) = z^3 + (x^2 + y^2)z + 2 = 0$. We compute the partial derivatives of the explicit function $z = f(x,y)$ with respect to $x$ and $y$. Solving the function $f(x,y)$ for $z$ explicitly would be somewhat tedious. However, Since $F_z = 3z^2 + x^2 + y^2 \neq 0$ at any point that satisfies $F(x,y,z) = 0$, the explicit function $z = f(x,y)$ exists. Furthermore, the partial derivatives are:

$$\frac{\partial z}{\partial x} = f_x = -\frac{F_x}{F_z} = \frac{-2xz}{3z^2 + x^2 + y^2}$$

$$\frac{\partial z}{\partial y} = f_y = -\frac{F_y}{F_z} = \frac{-2yz}{3z^2 + x^2 + y^2}$$

These are confirmed in the following *Mathematica* calculations.

*In[49]:=*

```
Clear[F,x,y,z,fx,fy];
F[x_,y_,z_]:= z^3 + (x^2 + y^2)*z + 2;
fx = - D[F[x,y,z],x]/D[F[x,y,z],z]
```

*Out[51]=*

$$\frac{-2xz}{x^2 + y^2 + 3z^2}$$

*In[52]:=*

```
fy = - D[F[x,y,z],y]/D[F[x,y,z],z]
```

*Out[52]=*

$$\frac{-2yz}{x^2 + y^2 + 3z^2}$$

It is important to note that the implicit function theorem lists the *sufficient*, but not the *necessary* conditions, for the existence of the function $f$. That is, if the conditions are satisfied we know $f$ exists. However, the explicit function may exist even if the conditions are not satisfied.

**Example 9.17** Consider the equation $F(x,y) = (y-x)^3 = 0$. It is obvious that an explicit function is $y = f(x) = x$, and that it exists at the point (0,0). Yet we cannot confirm this using the implicit function theorem since $F_y = 0$ at this point.

**Example 9.18** Consider a CES production function

$$Q = [aK^d + (1-a)L^d]^{1/d}$$

with output, $Q$, and two inputs, $K$ and $L$. For a given output, say $Q = 100$ units, the implicit equation is

$$F(K,L) = [aK^{d} + (1-a)L^{d}]^{1/d} - 100 = 0$$

which has an isoquant, $K = f(L)$, if $F_K(K^0,L^0) \neq 0$. We calculate the slope of the isoquant, $f_L$, by the Implicit Function Rule. The negative of the slope is of course the marginal rate of substitution (MRTS) between $K$ and $L$,

$$\text{MRTS} = \frac{F_L}{F_K} = -f_L.$$

*In[53]:=*

```
Clear[F,K,L,d];
F[K_,L_]:=  (a*K^d  +  (1-a)*L^d)^(1/d)  -  100;
MRTS  =  D[F[K,L],L]/D[F[K,L],K]
```

*Out[55]=*

$$\frac{(1-a)K^{1-d}L^{-1+d}}{a}$$

## EXERCISES

1. Does each of the following equations $F(x,y,z) = 0$ implicitly define a function $z = f(x,y)$ in the neighborhood of $(x^0,y^0,z^0)$? If so, find the partial derivatives, $\partial z/\partial x$ and $\partial z/\partial y$, for the following functions:
   (a) $F(x,y,z) = x^3 + y^3 + z^3 - xyz - 2 = 0$, at $(1,1,-1)$.
   (b) $F(x,y,z) = x^2 + z^3 - z - xy\sin(z) = 0$, at $(1,1,0)$.
   (c) $F(x,y,z) = (x^2 + y^2 + z^2)^{1/2} - \cos(z) = 0$, at $(0,1,0)$.

2. Are there functions $y = g(x,z)$ defined by the implicit equations in exercise 1? What are the partial derivatives, $\partial y/\partial x$ and $\partial y/\partial z$?

3. Plot the contour of the equation

   $$y - xe^{y} = 1$$

   near the point $(-1,0)$. Compute the derivative $dy/dx$ at that point.

4. A generalized production function $Q = f(K,L)$ is defined implicitly from the equation,

   $$Qe^{rQ} = AK^{a}L^{b}$$

   Find the marginal product of $L$ and $K$, and the marginal rate of marginal substitution.

5. From $\partial z/\partial x = -F_x/F_z$ in example 9.16, show that

   $$\frac{\partial^2 z}{\partial x^2} = \frac{F_z^2F_{xx} - 2F_xF_zF_{xz} + F_x^2F_{zz}}{-F_z^3}$$

   Derive the similar formulas for $\partial^2 z/\partial y^2$ and $\partial^2 z/\partial x\partial y$.

### 9.2.3 Simultaneous equation systems and implicit functions

Consider a system of $n$ linear equations,

$$
\begin{aligned}
a_{11}y_1 + \ldots + a_{1n}y_n &= x_1 \\
a_{21}y_1 + \ldots + a_{2n}y_n &= x_2 \\
\ldots \qquad & \ldots \\
a_{n1}y_1 + \ldots + a_{nn}y_n &= x_n.
\end{aligned}
$$

In matrix notation, the system can be written as

$$\mathbf{Ay} = \mathbf{x}.$$

This system can also be written as a system of implicit equations:

$$
\begin{aligned}
F^1(\mathbf{x},\mathbf{y}) &= a_{11}y_1 + a_{12}y_2 + \ldots + a_{1n}y_n - x_1 = 0 \\
F^2(\mathbf{x},\mathbf{y}) &= a_{21}y_1 + a_{22}y_2 + \ldots + a_{2n}y_n - x_2 = 0 \\
&\ldots\ldots\ldots\ldots\ldots\ldots\ldots\ldots \\
F^n(\mathbf{x},\mathbf{y}) &= a_{n1}y_1 + a_{n2}y_2 + \ldots + a_{nn}y_n - x_n = 0.
\end{aligned}
$$

In matrix notation, the system is

$$\mathbf{F}(\mathbf{x},\mathbf{y}) = \mathbf{Ay} - \mathbf{x} = \mathbf{0}.$$

We note that the elements of the matrix **A** are simply the first partial derivatives of **F**, $a_{ij} = \partial F^i/\partial y_j$. Recall that a unique solution of a linear system exists if

$$
|\mathbf{A}| = \begin{vmatrix} a_{11} & a_{12} & \ldots & a_{1n} \\ a_{21} & a_{22} & \ldots & a_{2n} \\ \ldots & \ldots & \ldots & \ldots \\ a_{n1} & a_{n2} & \ldots & a_{nn} \end{vmatrix} = \begin{vmatrix} \frac{\partial F^1}{\partial y_1} & \frac{\partial F^1}{\partial y_2} & \ldots & \frac{\partial F^1}{\partial y_n} \\ \frac{\partial F^2}{\partial y_1} & \frac{\partial F^2}{\partial y_2} & \ldots & \frac{\partial F^2}{\partial y_n} \\ \ldots & \ldots & \ldots & \ldots \\ \frac{\partial F^n}{\partial y_1} & \frac{\partial F^n}{\partial y_2} & \ldots & \frac{\partial F^n}{\partial y_n} \end{vmatrix} \neq 0
$$

The matrix **A** is the Jacobian matrix of **F**. The existence of the explicit functions, $y_i = f_i(x_1, \ldots, x_n)$, $i=1,2, \ldots, n$, depends upon the Jacobian matrix not being zero. In this case, the explicit functions are given by the equation $\mathbf{y} = \mathbf{f}(\mathbf{x}) = \mathbf{A}^{-1}\mathbf{x}$, i.e., $y_i = (\mathbf{A}^{-1}\mathbf{x})_i$.

Now consider the general system of implicit equations:

$$
\begin{aligned}
F^1(y_1, y_2, \ldots, y_n, x_1, x_2, \ldots, x_m) &= 0 \\
F^2(y_1, y_2, \ldots, y_n, x_1, x_2, \ldots, x_m) &= 0 \\
\vdots \qquad \qquad \vdots \qquad \qquad & \vdots \\
F^n(y_1, y_2, \ldots, y_n, x_1, x_2, \ldots, x_m) &= 0
\end{aligned}
$$

In vector notation,

$$\mathbf{F}(\mathbf{y},\mathbf{x}) = \mathbf{0}$$

where $\mathbf{F} = [F^1\ F^2 \ldots F^n]^T$. Note that in this case we have chosen to write the variables to be solved first. Explicit solutions to this system often take the form of a system of explicit equations,

$$\begin{aligned} y_1 &= f^1(x_1, \ldots, x_m) \\ y_2 &= f^2(x_1, \ldots, x_m) \\ &\cdots\cdots\cdots\cdots \\ &\cdots\cdots\cdots\cdots \\ y_n &= f^n(x_1, \ldots, x_m) \end{aligned}$$

Expressed in vector notation,

$$\mathbf{y} = \mathbf{f}(\mathbf{x})$$

where $\mathbf{f}$ is a vector-valued function. The elements of $\mathbf{y}$ are referred to as *endogenous* variables, while the elements of $\mathbf{x}$ are called *exogenous* variables.

The Implicit Function Theorem generalizes in straightforward manner, allowing us to determine if a solution to this general problem exists. Specifically, if at a point

$$(\mathbf{y}^0,\mathbf{x}^0) = (y_1^0,y_2^0, \ldots ,y_n^0,x_1^0,x_2^0, \ldots ,x_m^0),$$

$\mathbf{F}(\mathbf{y}^0,\mathbf{x}^0) = \mathbf{0}$ and the determinant of the Jacobian matrix is nonzero,

$$|\mathbf{J}| = \begin{vmatrix} \dfrac{\partial F^1(\mathbf{y}^0,\mathbf{x}^0)}{\partial y_1} & \dfrac{\partial F^1(\mathbf{y}^0,\mathbf{x}^0)}{\partial y_2} & \cdots & \dfrac{\partial F^1(\mathbf{y}^0,\mathbf{x}^0)}{\partial y_n} \\ \dfrac{\partial F^2(\mathbf{y}^0,\mathbf{x}^0)}{\partial y_1} & \dfrac{\partial F^2(\mathbf{y}^0,\mathbf{x}^0)}{\partial y_2} & \cdots & \dfrac{\partial F^2(\mathbf{y}^0,\mathbf{x}^0)}{\partial y_n} \\ \cdots & \cdots & \cdots & \cdots \\ \dfrac{\partial F^n(\mathbf{y}^0,\mathbf{x}^0)}{\partial y_1} & \dfrac{\partial F^n(\mathbf{y}^0,\mathbf{x}^0)}{\partial y_2} & \cdots & \dfrac{\partial F^n(\mathbf{y}^0,\mathbf{x}^0)}{\partial y_n} \end{vmatrix} \neq 0$$

then there exists a system of explicit functions in the neighborhood of $(\mathbf{y}^0,\mathbf{x}^0)$:

$$\begin{aligned} y_1 &= f^1(x_1, \ldots, x_m) \\ y_2 &= f^2(x_1, \ldots, x_m) \\ &\cdots\cdots\cdots\cdots \\ y_n &= f^n(x_1, \ldots, x_m). \end{aligned}$$

Once again, the condition of the nonvanishing Jacobian determinant is a sufficient condition, not a necessary condition.

The partial derivaties of $y_i$ with respect to $x_j$ can be obtained directly. Let

$$\mathbf{B} = \begin{bmatrix} \dfrac{\partial F^1}{\partial x_1} & \dfrac{\partial F^1}{\partial x_2} & \cdots & \dfrac{\partial F^1}{\partial x_m} \\ \dfrac{\partial F^2}{\partial x_1} & \dfrac{\partial F^2}{\partial x_2} & \cdots & \dfrac{\partial F^2}{\partial x_m} \\ \cdots & \cdots & \cdots & \cdots \\ \dfrac{\partial F^n}{\partial x_1} & \dfrac{\partial F^n}{\partial x_2} & \cdots & \dfrac{\partial F^n}{\partial x_n} \end{bmatrix}$$

Taking the total differential of $\mathbf{F}(\mathbf{y},\mathbf{x}) = \mathbf{0}$, we have

$$\mathrm{d}\mathbf{F}(\mathbf{y},\mathbf{x}) = \mathbf{J}\,\mathrm{d}\mathbf{y} + \mathbf{B}\,\mathrm{d}\mathbf{x} = \mathbf{0}$$

where

$$\mathrm{d}\mathbf{F}(\mathbf{y},\mathbf{x}) = \begin{bmatrix} \mathrm{d}F^1(\mathbf{y},\mathbf{x}) \\ \mathrm{d}F^2(\mathbf{y},\mathbf{x}) \\ \vdots \\ \mathrm{d}F^n(\mathbf{y},\mathbf{x}) \end{bmatrix}; \ \mathrm{d}\mathbf{y} = \begin{bmatrix} \mathrm{d}y_1 \\ \mathrm{d}y_2 \\ \vdots \\ \mathrm{d}y_{1n} \end{bmatrix}; \ \mathrm{d}\mathbf{x} = \begin{bmatrix} \mathrm{d}x_1 \\ \mathrm{d}x_2 \\ \vdots \\ \mathrm{d}x_m \end{bmatrix}$$

Solving for $\mathrm{d}\mathbf{y}$, we have

$$\mathrm{d}\mathbf{y} = -\mathbf{J}^{-1}\mathbf{B}\,\mathrm{d}\mathbf{x}.$$

This relates to the changes between exogenous and endogenous variables.

**Example 9.19** Consider the following system of implicit equations:

$$F^1(y_1,y_2,x_1,x_2) = y_1^3 + x_1y_2 + x_2y_1 - 2x_2 = 0$$
$$F^2(y_1,y_2,x_1,x_2) = y_2^3 - x_2y_2 + x_1y_1 - 2x_1 = 0.$$

We want to solve for $y_1$ and $y_2$ as functions of $x_1$ and $x_2$ in a neighborhood of $(y_1,y_2,x_1,x_2) = (1,-1,0,1)$. The Jacobian determinant is

$$|\mathbf{J}| = \begin{vmatrix} \dfrac{\partial F^1}{\partial y_1} & \dfrac{\partial F^1}{\partial y_2} \\ \dfrac{\partial F^2}{\partial y_1} & \dfrac{\partial F^2}{\partial y_2} \end{vmatrix} = \begin{vmatrix} 3y_1^2 + x_2 & x_1 \\ x_1 & 3y_2^2 - x_2 \end{vmatrix}$$

At the point $(y_1,y_2,x_1,x_2) = (1,-1,0,1)$, $F^1(1,-1,0,1) = 0$, $F^2(1,-1,0,1) = 0$, and $|\mathbf{J}| = 8$. Thus, there exist functions

$$y_1 = f(x_1,x_2)$$
$$y_2 = g(x_1,x_2)$$

that are defined in a neighborhood of (1,–1,0,1). In the following *Mathematica* calculation, we show that

$$\mathrm{d}y_1 = \frac{1}{4}\mathrm{d}x_1 + \frac{1}{4}\mathrm{d}x_2$$

$$\mathrm{d}y_2 = \frac{1}{2}\mathrm{d}x_1 - \frac{1}{2}\mathrm{d}x_2$$

We use the **MathEcon** function **gradf** to calculate the necessary gradient vectors for **J** and **B**. The differenials $\mathrm{d}y_1$ and $\mathrm{d}y_2$ of the explicit function are then evaluated at the point (1,–1,0,1).

*In[56]:=*

```
Clear[F1,F2,y1,y2,x1,x2,dx1,dx2];
F1[y1_,y2_,x1_,x2_]:= y1^3 + x1*y2 + x2*y1 - 2*x2;
F2[y1_,y2_,x1_,x2_]:= y2^3 - x2*y2 + x1*y1 - 2*x1;
```

```
J  =  {gradf[F1[y1,y2,x1,x2],{y1,y2}],
        gradf[F2[y1,y2,x1,x2],{y1,y2}]};
B  =  {gradf[F1[y1,y2,x1,x2],{x1,x2}],
        gradf[F2[y1,y2,x1,x2],{x1,x2}]};
dx  =  {dx1,dx2};
dy  =  -Inverse[J].B.dx  /.{y1->1,y2->-1,x1->0,x2->1}
```

*Out[62]=*

$$\{\frac{dx1}{4} + \frac{dx2}{4}, \frac{dx1}{2} - \frac{dx2}{2}\}$$

**Example 9.20** Consider a national income model with consumption equation $F^1 = 0$, tax equation $F^2 = 0$, and income identity $F^3 = 0$ where

$$F^1 = C - a - b(Y - T) = 0$$
$$F^2 = T - r - sY = 0$$
$$F^3 = Y - C - I - G = 0$$

Here $Y$ is the income, $C$ is the consumption, $T$ is the tax which are treated as dependent variables. The autonomous investment, $I$, and government expenditure, $G$, are the independent variables. The constants, $a$, $b$, $r$, and $s$, are parameters. These three implicit equations determine three explicit functions,

$$Y = f^1(I, G)$$
$$C = f^2(I, G)$$
$$T = f^3(I, G)$$

if the following Jacobian determinant

$$|\mathbf{J}| = \begin{vmatrix} \frac{\partial F^1}{\partial Y} & \frac{\partial F^1}{\partial C} & \frac{\partial F^1}{\partial T} \\ \frac{\partial F^2}{\partial Y} & \frac{\partial F^2}{\partial C} & \frac{\partial F^2}{\partial T} \\ \frac{\partial F^3}{\partial Y} & \frac{\partial F^3}{\partial C} & \frac{\partial F^3}{\partial T} \end{vmatrix} = \begin{vmatrix} -b & 1 & b \\ -s & 0 & 1 \\ 1 & -1 & 0 \end{vmatrix} = 1 - b(1-s)$$

is nonzero. Suppose $|\mathbf{J}| \neq 0$. We can then find the effect of $I$ and $G$ on $Y$, $C$, and $T$. That is

$$\begin{bmatrix} dY \\ dC \\ dT \end{bmatrix} = -\mathbf{J}^{-1}\mathbf{B}\begin{bmatrix} dI \\ dG \end{bmatrix}$$

where

$$\mathbf{B} = \begin{bmatrix} \frac{\partial F^1}{\partial I} & \frac{\partial F^1}{\partial G} \\ \frac{\partial F^2}{\partial I} & \frac{\partial F^2}{\partial G} \\ \frac{\partial F^3}{\partial I} & \frac{\partial F^3}{\partial G} \end{bmatrix} = \begin{bmatrix} 0 & 0 \\ 0 & 0 \\ -1 & -1 \end{bmatrix}$$

Hence,

$$\begin{bmatrix} dY \\ dC \\ dT \end{bmatrix} = -\begin{bmatrix} -b & 1 & b \\ -s & 0 & 1 \\ 1 & -1 & 0 \end{bmatrix}^{-1} \begin{bmatrix} 0 & 0 \\ 0 & 0 \\ -1 & -1 \end{bmatrix} \begin{bmatrix} dI \\ dG \end{bmatrix}$$

$$= \frac{1}{1-b(1-s)} \begin{bmatrix} (dI + dG) \\ b(1-s)(dI + dG) \\ s(dI + dG) \end{bmatrix}$$

The impact multipliers, i.e., the partial derivatives of the explicit functions, are

$$\frac{\partial Y}{\partial I} = \frac{\partial Y}{\partial G} = \frac{1}{1-b(1-s)}$$

$$\frac{\partial C}{\partial I} = \frac{\partial C}{\partial G} = \frac{b(1-s)}{1-b(1-s)}$$

$$\frac{\partial T}{\partial I} = \frac{\partial T}{\partial G} = \frac{s}{1-b(1-s)}$$

Again, this can be demonstrated in the following *Mathematica* computation.

*In[63]:=*

```
Clear[F1,F2,F3,Y,c,t,i,g,a,b,r,s,di,dg];
SetAttributes[{a,b,r,s},Constant];
F1[y_,c_,t_]:= c - a - b*(y-t);
F2[y_,t_]:= t - r - s*y;
F3[y_,c_,i_,g_]:= y - c - i - g;
J  =  {gradf[F1[y,c,t],{y,c,t}],
       gradf[F2[y,t],{y,c,t}],
        gradf[F3[y,c,i,g],{y,c,t}]};
B  =  {gradf[F1[y,c,t],{i,g}],
       gradf[F2[y,t],{i,g}],
        gradf[F3[y,c,i,g],{i,g}]};
impact  =  -Inverse[J].B.{di,dg};
impact  //  MatrixForm
```

*Out[71]//MatrixForm=*

$$\begin{pmatrix} \frac{dg}{1-b+bs} + \frac{di}{1-b+bs} \\ \frac{dg(b-bs)}{1-b+bs} + \frac{di(b-bs)}{1-b+bs} \\ \frac{dgs}{1-b+bs} + \frac{dis}{1-b+bs} \end{pmatrix}$$

**Example 9.21** In demand theory, we often encounter a system of form:

$$F^1(x,y,\lambda,p_x) = f_x(x,y) - \lambda p_x = 0$$
$$F^2(x,y,\lambda,p_y) = f_y(x,y) - \lambda p_y = 0$$
$$F^3(x,y,\lambda,p_x,p_y,m) = m - xp_x - yp_y = 0$$

where $f_x(x,y)$ and $f_y(x,y)$ are the partial derivatives of a utility function $f(x,y)$, $p_x$ and $p_y$ are prices of $x$ and $y$, and $m$ is income. $\lambda$ is an unknown variable, called the marginal utility of money. These three equations, to be discussed in Chapter 11, are the necessary conditions for maximizing utility function subject to the income constraint, $xp_x + yp_y = m$. A sufficient condition that these equations implicitly define the quantity demands, $x$ and $y$, and the marginal utility of money $\lambda$ as differentiable functions of $p_x$, $p_y$ and $m$ is $|\mathbf{J}| \neq 0$. We first show that

$$\mathbf{J} = \begin{bmatrix} f_{xx} & f_{xy} & -p_x \\ f_{yx} & f_{yy} & -p_y \\ -p_x & -p_y & 0 \end{bmatrix}$$

is the Jacobian matrix of the system.

*In[72]:=*

```
Clear[F1,F2,F3,f,x,y,px,py,lambda];
F1[x_,y_,lambda_,px_]:=  D[f[x,y],x]-lambda*px;
F2[x_,y_,lambda_,py_]:=  D[f[x,y],y]-lambda*py;
F3[x_,y_,px_,py_,m_]:=  m-x*px-y*py;
J   =  {gradf[F1[x,y,lambda,px],{x,y,lambda}],
          gradf[F2[x,y,lambda,py],{x,y,lambda}],
          gradf[F3[x,y,px,py,m],{x,y,lambda}]};  MatrixForm[J]
```

*Out[76]//MatrixForm=*

$$\begin{matrix} f^{(2,0)}[x, y] & f^{(1,1)}[x, y] & -px \\ f^{(1,1)}[x, y] & f^{(0,2)}[x, y] & -py \\ -px & -py & 0 \end{matrix}$$

The effect of the prices, $p_x$, $p_y$, and income, $m$, on the demand for $x$, $y$, and the marginal utility of money $\lambda$ is

$$\begin{bmatrix} \mathrm{d}x \\ \mathrm{d}y \\ \mathrm{d}\lambda \end{bmatrix} = -\mathbf{J}^{-1}\mathbf{B} \begin{bmatrix} \mathrm{d}p_x \\ \mathrm{d}p_y \\ \mathrm{d}m \end{bmatrix}$$

where

$$\mathbf{B} = \begin{bmatrix} \dfrac{\partial F^1}{\partial p_x} & \dfrac{\partial F^1}{\partial p_y} & \dfrac{\partial F^1}{\partial m} \\ \dfrac{\partial F^2}{\partial p_x} & \dfrac{\partial F^2}{\partial p_y} & \dfrac{\partial F^2}{\partial m} \\ \dfrac{\partial F^3}{\partial p_x} & \dfrac{\partial F^3}{\partial p_y} & \dfrac{\partial F^3}{\partial_m} \end{bmatrix} = \begin{bmatrix} -\lambda & 0 & 0 \\ 0 & -\lambda & 0 \\ -x & -y & 1 \end{bmatrix}$$

The matrix **B** is obtained in the following calculation.

*In[77]:=*

```
B  =  {gradf[F1[x,y,lambda,px],{px,py,m}],
       gradf[F2[x,y,lambda,py],{px,py,m}],
       gradf[F3[x,y,px,py,m],{px,py,m}]};  MatrixForm[B]
```

*Out[77]//MatrixForm=*

| | | |
|---|---|---|
| -lambda | 0 | 0 |
| 0 | -lambda | 0 |
| -x | -y | 1 |

The partial price effect of $p_x$, for example, holding $p_y$ and $m$ constant, is the solution obtained by setting $\mathrm{d}p_y = \mathrm{d}m = 0$. That is,

$$\begin{bmatrix}\partial x\\ \partial y\\ \partial\lambda\end{bmatrix} = -\mathbf{J}^{-1}\mathbf{B}\begin{bmatrix}\partial p_x\\ 0\\ 0\end{bmatrix}; \quad \text{or} \quad \begin{bmatrix}\dfrac{\partial x}{\partial p_x}\\ \dfrac{\partial y}{\partial p_x}\\ \dfrac{\partial\lambda}{\partial p_x}\end{bmatrix} = -\mathbf{J}^{-1}\mathbf{B}\begin{bmatrix}1\\ 0\\ 0\end{bmatrix}$$

The following *Mathematica* calculation gives these partial price effects on $x$, $y$ and $\lambda$. We leave the calculation of income effect on $x$, $y$ and $\lambda$ as an exercise. We only demonstrate that

$$\frac{\partial x}{\partial p_x} = \frac{-\lambda p_y^2 + x(p_x f_{yy} - p_y f_{xy})}{-p_x^2 f_{yy} + 2p_x p_y f_{xy} - p_y^2 f_{xx}}$$

by extracting the first element.

*In[78]:=*

```
impact  =  -Inverse[J].B.{1,0,0};
impact[[1]]
```

*Out[79]=*

$$-\left(\frac{\text{lambda py}^2}{-(\text{px}^2\ f^{(0,2)}[x, y]) + 2\ \text{px py}\ f^{(1,1)}[x, y] - \text{py}^2\ f^{(2,0)}[x, y]}\right.$$
$$\left. + \frac{x\ (\text{px}\ f^{(0,2)}[x, y] - \text{py}\ f^{(1,1)}[x, y])}{-(\text{px}^2\ f^{(0,2)}[x, y]) + 2\ \text{px py}\ f^{(1,1)}[x, y] - \text{py}^2\ f^{(2,0)}[x, y]}\right)$$

## EXERCISES

1. Show that the equations

   $$e^x + e^{2y} + e^{3u} + e^{4v} = 4$$
   $$e^x + e^y + e^u + e^v = 4$$

   can be solved for $u$ and $v$ in terms of $x$ and $y$ around the point (0,0,0,0). Compute the partial derivatives, $\partial u/\partial x$, $\partial u/\partial y$, $\partial v/\partial x$ and $\partial v/\partial y$.

2. Under what sufficient conditions can the equations

   $$xy + z^2 = a$$
   $$x^2 - y^2 + z^2 = b$$

be explicitly solved for $x = f(z)$ and $y = g(z)$? Under what sufficient condition do solutions for $x = f(y)$ and $z = g(y)$ exist?

3. Consider the national income model in example 9.20. If $a$, $b$, $r$, $s$ are considered as independent variables, then the three explicit functions are

$$Y = f^1(I,G,a,b,r,s)$$
$$C = f^2(I,G,a,b,r,s)$$
$$T = f^3(I,G,a,b,r,s)$$

Calculate the effects of the marginal propensity to consumer, $b$, and the marginal tax rate, $x$, on the income, $Y$, consumption, $C$, and the tax, $T$.

4. Consider the following macroeconomic model

| | |
|---|---|
| $C = f(Y - T)$ | consumption function |
| $I = g(R)$ | investment function |
| $R = h(M)$ | money market equilibrium |
| $Y = C + I + G$ | income identity |

where $Y$, $C$, $I$, and $R$ are income, consumption, investment, and interest rate, respectively, and $T$, $G$, $M$ are taxes, government expenditure, and money supply, respectively.

(a) State a sufficient condition for the existence of solutions for $Y$, $C$, $I$, and $R$ as functions of $T$, $G$, and $M$.

(b) Find the multiplier, $\partial Y/\partial G$, $\partial C/\partial T$, and $\partial R/\partial M$.

5. Find the effect of $p_y$ and $m$ on the demands for $x$ and $y$ in example 9.21, i.e., the partial derivatives, $\partial x/\partial p_y$, $\partial y/\partial p_x$, $\partial x/\partial m$, and $\partial y/\partial m$.

10

# Concave and Quasiconcave Functions

The concepts of concavity and quasiconcavity play important roles in the study of optimization problems in economics. We briefly encountered these concepts in section 2.2.3 and mentioned that maxima and minima of a function can be distinguished by its curvatures. A differentiable function of a single variable is said to be concave if its second derivative is negative on its domain; it is said to be convex when its second derivative is positive. Thus a function has a maximum (minimum) at a critical point if the function is concave (convex) at that point. Technically, these concepts are not just associated with the derivative of a function. There exist non-differentiable functions that are convex or concave and possess maximum and minimum points. In the next two chapters, we shall discuss the optimization of functions. In this chapter, we shall discuss concavity and quasiconcavity and their connection to calculating the maximum and minimum values of functions.

## □ 10.1 Concave and Convex Functions □

### 10.1.1 Convex sets

Consider the disk in figure 10.1(a). Let $\mathbf{x}_0$ and $\mathbf{x}_1$ be any two points in this disk. Any point, say $\mathbf{x}$, on the line connecting $\mathbf{x}_0$ and $\mathbf{x}_1$ is a linear combination of $\mathbf{x}_0$ and $\mathbf{x}_1$. It can be written in terms of $\mathbf{x}_0$ and $\mathbf{x}_1$ as

$$\mathbf{x} = \theta_0\mathbf{x}_0 + \theta_1\mathbf{x}_1$$

where $\theta_0$ and $\theta_1$ are scalars. A *convex combination* of $\mathbf{x}_0$ and $\mathbf{x}_1$ is a special case of such a linear combination in which the scalars, $\theta_0$ and $\theta_1$, are nonnegative and add up to unity. In particular,

$$\mathbf{x} = \theta\mathbf{x}_0 + (1-\theta)\mathbf{x}_1$$

where $0 \le \theta \le 1$. If $\theta = 1$, the point $\mathbf{x}$ is the same as $\mathbf{x}_0$. If $\theta = 1/2$, $\mathbf{x} = (\mathbf{x}_0+\mathbf{x}_1)/2$, then $\mathbf{x}$ is the midpoint between $\mathbf{x}_0$ and $\mathbf{x}_1$. Thus any point on the line segment between $\mathbf{x}_0$ and $\mathbf{x}_1$ can be represented as a convex combination of $\mathbf{x}_0$ and $\mathbf{x}_1$.

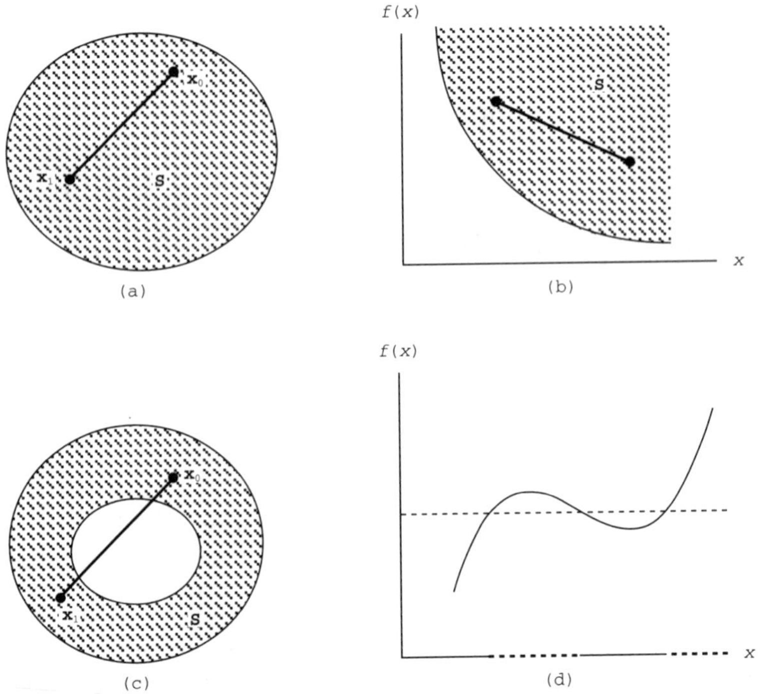


**Figure 10.1** Convex sets: (a) and (b) are convex sets; (c) and (d) are not

> **DEFINITION 10.1** *A set* **S** *in* $\mathbf{R}^n$ *is said to be convex if for any two points* $\mathbf{x}_0$ *and* $\mathbf{x}_1$ *belonging to the set* **S**, *then* $\mathbf{x} = \theta\mathbf{x}_0 + (1-\theta)\mathbf{x}_1$ *also belongs to* **S**.

The set **S** of all points either on or inside the disk in figure 10.1(a) form a convex set. Figure 10.1(b) depicts the graph of the function $f(x) = 4 + 1/x$. The set **S** is the collection of all points $\{x,y\}$ such that $y \geq f(x)$. It is a convex set. In figure 10.1(c), **S** is the shaded area. It is not a convex set since some part of the line segment joining $\mathbf{x}_0$ and $\mathbf{x}_1$ lies outside of the set **S**. Figure 10.1(d) depicts the graph of the function $f(x) = x^3 + x^2 - 2x + 2$. **S** is the set that consists of all points $x$ on the horizontal axis such that $f(x) \geq 2$, i.e.,

$$\mathbf{S} = \{x \mid x^3 + x^2 - 2x + 2 \geq 2\}.$$

**S** consists of two disjointed (dashed) line segments. **S** is not a convex set.

**Example 10.1** The set

$$\mathbf{S} = \{(x,y,z) \mid x + 3y - 2z = 5\}$$

is a convex set. Suppose $(x_0,y_0,z_0)$ and $(x_1,y_1,z_1)$ are points in **S**, i.e.,

$$x_0 + 3y_0 - 2z_0 = 5 \quad \text{and} \quad x_1 + 3y_1 - 2z_1 = 5.$$

Let the third point $(x,y,z)$ be a convex combination of these two points, i.e., if

$$x = \theta x_0 + (1-\theta)x_1;$$
$$y = \theta y_0 + (1-\theta)y_1;$$
$$z = \theta z_0 + (1-\theta)z_1;$$

then

$$\begin{aligned} x + 3y - 2z &= \theta(x_0 + 3y_0 - 2z_0) + (1-\theta)(x_1 + 3y_1 - 2z_1) \\ &= \theta(5) + (1-\theta)(5) = 5. \end{aligned}$$

Thus $(x,y,z)$ is also in **S** and **S** is a convex set.

The equation, $x + 3y - 2z = 5$, represents a plane in $\mathbf{R}^3$. Any set of the form

$$\mathbf{S} = \{\mathbf{x} \mid \mathbf{a}^T\mathbf{x} = b\}$$

is called a *hyperplane* in $\mathbf{R}^n$ where $\mathbf{a}$ is an $n$-dimensional nonzero vector and $b$ is a scalar. Hyperplanes are convex sets.

**Example 10.2** The set

$$\mathbf{S} = \{(x,y,z) \mid x + 3y - 2z \le 5\}$$

is also a convex set. **S** is a collection of points on one side of the plane in Example 10.1. This set forms a *closed half space*. A hyperplane divides $\mathbf{R}^n$ into two closed half spaces defined by

$$\mathbf{S}_1 = \{\mathbf{x} \mid \mathbf{a}^T\mathbf{x} \le b\} \quad \text{and} \quad \mathbf{S}_2 = \{\mathbf{x} \mid \mathbf{a}^T\mathbf{x} \ge b\}$$

Both closed half spaces are convex sets. The sets, $\{\mathbf{x} \mid \mathbf{a}^T\mathbf{x} < b\}$ and $\{\mathbf{x} \mid \mathbf{a}^T\mathbf{x} > b\}$, are called *open half spaces*. They are also convex.

**Example 10.3** Consider the utility function of two commodities,

$$f(x,y) = xy$$

where $x,y > 0$. An indifference curve at the utility level, say $f(x,y) = 5$, is plotted below using the **ContourPlot** function.

*In[1]:=*

```
Clear[f,x,y];
f[x_,y_]:= x*y;
ContourPlot[f[x,y],{x,0,5},{y,0,5},Contours->{5},
            Frame->False,ContourShading->False,
            Axes->True,AxesLabel->{"x","y"}];
```

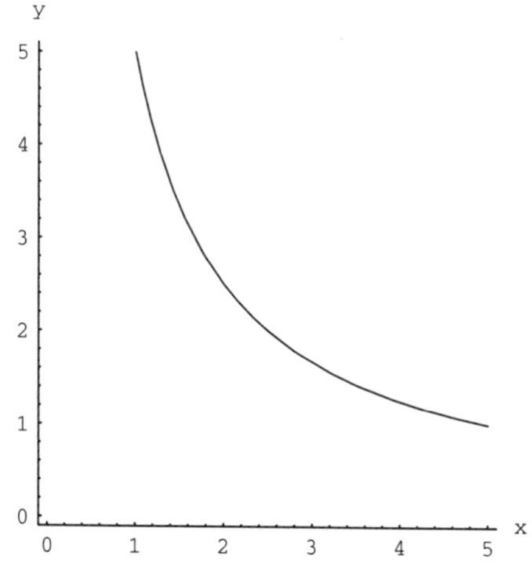

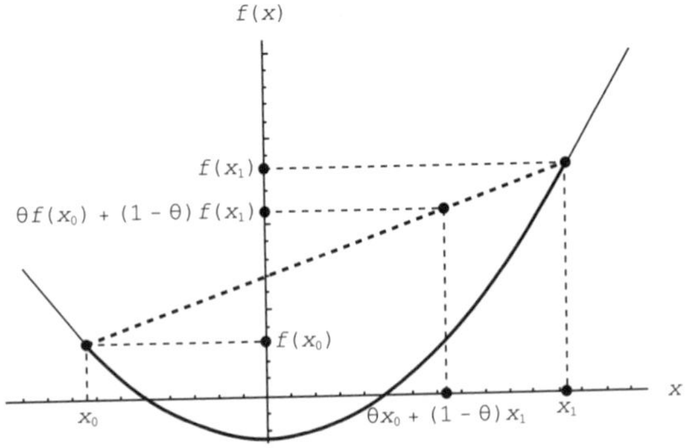


**Figure 10.2** Convex function

The set $\mathbf{S} = \{(x,y) \mid f(x,y) \geq 5\}$ consists of different bundles of commodities which yield the consumer at least 5 units of utility satisfaction. $\mathbf{S}$ is convex.

## EXERCISES

1. Let $\mathbf{S}_1$ and $\mathbf{S}_2$ be convex, nondisjoint sets in $\mathbf{R}^2$. Give examples to show that
   (a) $\mathbf{S} = \mathbf{S}_1 \cap \mathbf{S}_2$ is convex.
   (b) $\mathbf{S} = \mathbf{S}_1 + \mathbf{S}_2 = \{x_1 + x_2 \mid x_1 \in \mathbf{S}_1, x_2 \in \mathbf{S}_2\}$ is convex.
   (c) $\mathbf{S} = \mathbf{S}_1 - \mathbf{S}_2 = \{x_1 - x_2 \mid x_1 \in \mathbf{S}_1, x_2 \in \mathbf{S}_2\}$ is convex.

2. Are the following sets convex?
   (a) $\mathbf{S} = \{(x,y) \mid 1 < x + y < 5\}$.
   (b) $\mathbf{S} = \{(x,y) \mid 1 < x, y < 5\}$.
   (c) $\mathbf{S} = \{x \mid x < 1, x > 2\}$
   (d) $\mathbf{S} = \{(x,y) \mid 1 < x^2 + y^2 < 9\}$.

### 10.1.2 Concave and convex functions

The graph in figure 10.2 depicts a function $f(x)$ and a chord joining the points $(x_0, f(x_0))$ and $(x_1, f(x_1))$ on its graph. The chord (dashed line) lies above the values of the function (thick curve) on the interval $(x_0, x_1)$.

For any two points in the domain of $f(x)$, $x_0$ and $x_1$, the chord joining $(x_0, f(x_0))$ and $(x_1, f(x_1))$ always lies strictly above the graph of $f$. Furthermore, the chord is a linear combination of $f(x_0)$ and $f(x_1)$. Functions that have this property are called *convex*. There is also a related concept called *concave*.

> **DEFINITION 10.2** *A function $f(x)$ defined on a convex set $\mathbf{S}$ of the real line is called **concave (convex)** if for any two points $x_0$ and $x_1$ in $\mathbf{S}$ and $0 < \theta < 1$, we have*
>
> $$f(\theta x_0 + (1-\theta)x_1) \geq (\leq)\ \theta f(x_0) + (1-\theta)f(x_1)$$
>
> *It is **strictly concave (convex)** if for any two distinct points $x_0 \neq x_1$ in $\mathbf{S}$ and $0 < \theta < 1$, we have*
>
> $$f(\theta x_0 + (1-\theta)x_1) > (<)\ \theta f(x_0) + (1-\theta)f(x_1)$$

Most functions are neither concave or convex, but a linear function, $f(x) = a + bx$, is both convex and concave.

To graph a function of a single variable along with the chord defined by the convex combination of two points on the graph of a function, we use the **MathEcon** function **arc2d**. Here is a description of this function.

*In[4]:=*

```
?arc2d
```

**arc2d[fct,dom,seg,opt] generates a 2D Graphics object that illustrates the graph of the function fct over the interval dom (a list) with the graph highlighted on the subinterval seg (a list). The fourth argument is optional. If the fourth argument is chord, then a chord is drawn between points specified by seg. For example,**

**arc2d[x^2-1,{x,-3,4},{x,0,1},chord].**

The first argument contains the function, the second argument is a list that gives the interval over which the function is plotted, and the third argument gives the interval over the portion of the graph that is to be highlighted (this is referred to as the arc). The last argument is optional. If the fourth argument of **arc2d** contains the word **chord**, then a chord is drawn between the points specified by the third argument of **arc2d**. If there is no fourth argument, then no chord is drawn. For example, the function $f(x) = 1 + x^2$ is defined on the interval [–3,2]. We would like to draw the arc and the chord on the interval [–2,1].

*In[5]:=*

```
Clear[f,x];
f[x_]:= 1+x^2;
domain = {x,-3,2}; segment = {x,-2,1};
convex = arc2d[f[x],domain,segment,chord];
Show[convex,Axes->True,AxesLabel->{"x","f(x)"}];
```

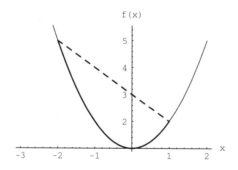

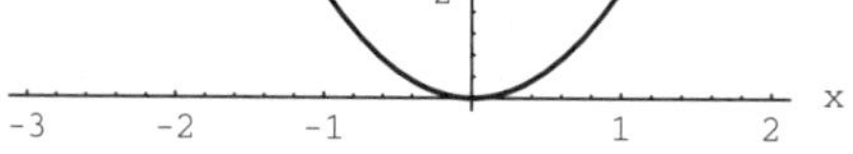


**Example 10.4** Show that $f(x) = \log(3+x)$ is strictly concave on the interval [–2,3]. We pick two points, say $x_0 = -1$ and $x_1 = 2$, and use **arc2d**.

*In[10]:=*

```
Clear[f,x];
f[x_]:= Log[3+x];
domain = {x,-2,3}; segment = {x,-1,2};
concave = arc2d[f[x],domain,segment,chord];
Show[concave,Axes->True,AxesLabel->{"x","f(x)"}];
```

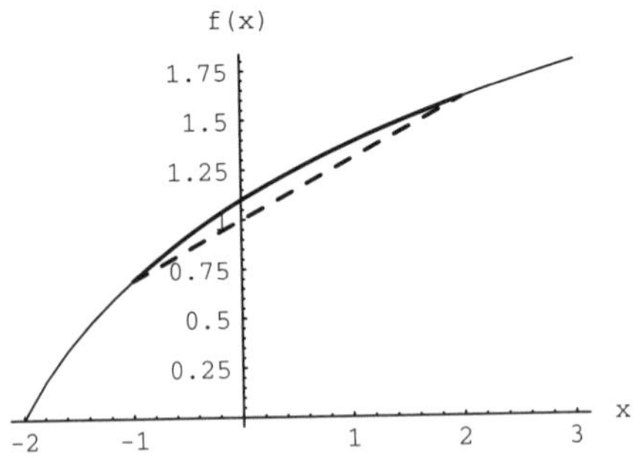


The arc is strictly above the chord. This is true for any two points $x_0$ and $x_1$ in [–2,3]. Hence, $f(x)$ is strictly concave on [–2,3].

**Example 10.5** Show that $f(x) = x^4 - 4x^3 - x^2 - x$ defined on [–1,1] is neither concave nor convex. Picking $x_0 = -0.8$ and $x_1 = 0.9$, we draw the graph using **arc2d**.

*In[15]:=*
```
Clear[f,x];
f[x_]:= x^4 - 4*x^3 - x^2 - x;
domain = {x,-1,1}; segment = {x,-0.8,0.9};
neither = arc2d[f[x],domain,segment,chord];
Show[neither,Axes->True,AxesLabel->{"x","f(x)"}];
```

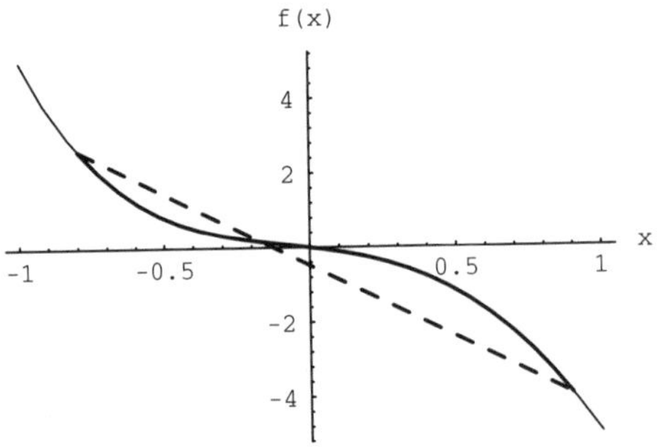


A section of the chord lies above the $f(x)$, and the other lies below, and we conclude that it is neither concave or convex on [–1,1]. However, $f(x)$ is convex on $-1 \leq x \leq 0$, and is concave on $0 \leq x \leq 1$.

Concave or convex functions of several variables is a straightforward generalization. For a function of $n$ variables, $f(\mathbf{x}) = f(x_1, x_2, \ldots, x_n)$, the chord connecting two points on the graph of the function, $(\mathbf{x}_0, f(\mathbf{x}_0))$ and $(\mathbf{x}_1, f(\mathbf{x}_1))$, is the set of points

$$\theta f(\mathbf{x}_0) + (1-\theta) f(\mathbf{x}_1).$$

A function defined on a convex set $\mathbf{S}$ in $\mathbf{R}^n$ is *concave* if for any two points $\mathbf{x}_0$ and $\mathbf{x}_1$ in $\mathbf{S}$ and $0 < \theta < 1$, then

$$f(\theta x_0 + (1-\theta)\mathbf{x}_1) \geq \theta f(\mathbf{x}_0) + (1-\theta) f(\mathbf{x}_1).$$

It is *strictly concave* if for any two distinct points, $\mathbf{x}_0 \neq \mathbf{x}_1$, in $\mathbf{S}$ and $0 < \theta < 1$, then

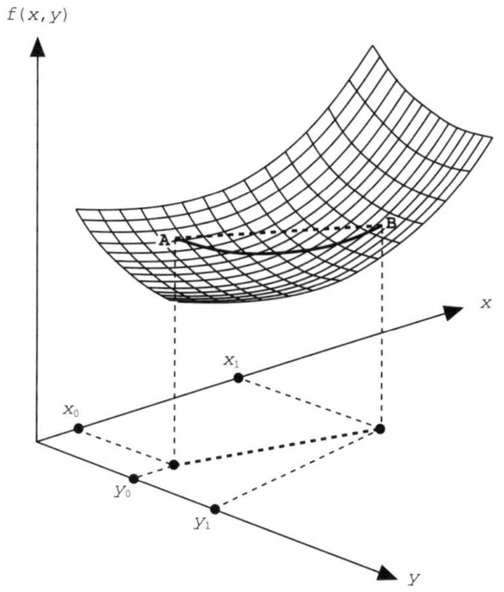


**Figure 10.3** A strictly convex function

$f(\theta x_0 + (1-\theta)\mathbf{x}_1) > \theta f(\mathbf{x}_0) + (1-\theta)f(\mathbf{x}_1).$

For the definitions of convexity and strict convexity, the inequality signs are reversed.

**Example 10.6** Consider the function $f(x,y) = x^3 + y^2$ defined on nonnegative values of $x$ and $y$. As shown in figure 10.3, the chord (dashed line) connecting the points on the surface of $f$, $A$ and $B$, lies strictly above the arc(solid line) on the surface of the function. Hence, the $f(x,y)$ is a strictly convex function.

To show this numerically, both the chord and $f(x,y)$ are evaluated at 9 points of the form, $(\theta x_0 + (1-\theta)x_1, \theta y_0 + (1-\theta)y_1)$, where $\theta$ runs from 0.1 to 0.9 with an increment of 0.1, where $(x_0,y_0) = (0.5,1.5)$ and $(x_1,y_1) = (1.5,0.5)$.

*In[20]:=*
```
Clear[f,x,y];
f[x_,y_]:= x^3 + y^2;
x0=0.5;y0=1.5;x1=1.5;y1=0.5;
dashline = Table[theta*f[x0,y0] + (1-theta)*f[x1,y1],
                 {theta,0.1,0.9,0.1}];
solidline = Table[f[theta*x0 + (1-theta)*x1,
                    theta*y0 + (1-theta)*y1],
                 {theta,0.1,0.9,0.1}];
TableForm[{{dashline,solidline}},
          TableHeadings->{{},{"Chord","f(x)"}}]
```

*Out[25]//TableForm=*

| Chord | f(x) |
|---|---|
| 3.5 | 3.104 |
| 3.375 | 2.687 |

```
3.25     2.368
3.125    2.141
3.       2.
2.875    1.939
2.75     1.952
2.625    2.033
2.5      2.176
```

The first column of the output contains the values of the chord and the second contains those of $f(x,y)$. The chord is always larger than $f(x,y)$. This fact demonstrates, at least for this particular choice of $(x_0,y_0)$ and $(x_1,y_1)$, that $f(x,y)$ is strictly convex over the set $\{ (x,y) \mid x,y \geq 0\}$.

**Example 10.7** Consider the function $f(x,y) = x^3 + y^2$ is defined on $\mathbf{R}^2$. The following plot produces an S-shaped surface.

*In[26]:=*

```
Clear[f,x,y];
f[x_,y_]:=  x^3  +  y^2;
x0=0.5;  y0=1.5;  x1=1.5;  y1=0.5;
Plot3D[f[x,y],{x,-10,10},{y,-10,10},
          ViewPoint->{-1.810,  -3.560,  0.650},
          AxesLabel->{"x","y","f(x)"}];
```

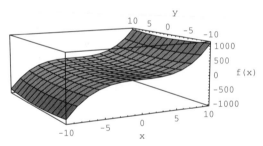

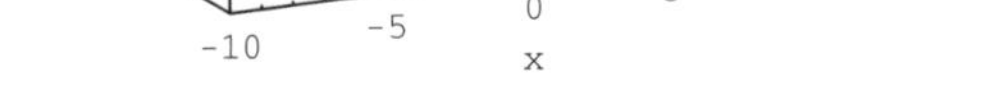


A straight line chord may not always be above or below the corresponding arc on the surface. Thus $f(x,y)$ is neither concave nor convex on $\mathbf{R}^2$.

**Example 10.8** A real quadratic form $Q(\mathbf{x}) = \mathbf{x}^T\mathbf{A}\mathbf{x}$ is (strictly) convex for all $\mathbf{x}$ in $\mathbf{R}^n$ if the symmetric matrix $\mathbf{A}$ is positive semidefinite (definite), and is (strictly) concave if $\mathbf{A}$ is negative semidefinite (definite). To show this, consider any two distinct points, $\mathbf{x}_0$ and $\mathbf{x}_1$, and their convex combination, $\mathbf{x} = \theta\mathbf{x}_0 + (1-\theta)\mathbf{x}_1$ for $0 < \theta < 1$. The difference, denoted as $\Delta$, between the values of $Q$ at $\mathbf{x}$, $Q(\mathbf{x}) = Q(\theta\mathbf{x}_0 + (1-\theta)\mathbf{x}_1)$, and the chord, $\theta Q(\mathbf{x}_0) + (1-\theta)Q(\mathbf{x}_1)$, is equal to

$$\begin{aligned}\Delta &= (\theta\mathbf{x}_0 + (1-\theta)\mathbf{x}_1)^T\mathbf{A}(\theta\mathbf{x}_0 + (1-\theta)\mathbf{x}_1) - \theta\mathbf{x}_0^T\mathbf{A}\mathbf{x}_0 - (1-\theta)\mathbf{x}_1{}^T\mathbf{A}\mathbf{x}_1 \\ &= \theta(\theta-1)\,(\mathbf{x}_1^T\mathbf{A}\mathbf{x}_1 - \mathbf{x}_1^T\mathbf{A}\mathbf{x}_0 - \mathbf{x}_0^T\mathbf{A}\mathbf{x}_1 + \mathbf{x}_0^T\mathbf{A}\mathbf{x}_0) \\ &= \theta(\theta-1)\,(\mathbf{x}_1 - \mathbf{x}_0)^T\mathbf{A}(\mathbf{x}_1 - \mathbf{x}_0)\end{aligned}$$

The difference, $\Delta$, is itself a quadratic form. For any $\mathbf{x}_1 \neq \mathbf{x}_0$, $\Delta \geq 0$ and, hence, $Q(\mathbf{x}) = \mathbf{x}^T\mathbf{A}\mathbf{x}$ is convex if $\mathbf{A}$ is positive semidefinite. Similarly, $\Delta \leq 0$ and $Q(\mathbf{x})$ is concave if $\mathbf{A}$ is negative semidefinite. The quadratic form is strictly convex ($\Delta > 0$) or concave ($\Delta < 0$) if $\mathbf{A}$ is positive or negative definite.

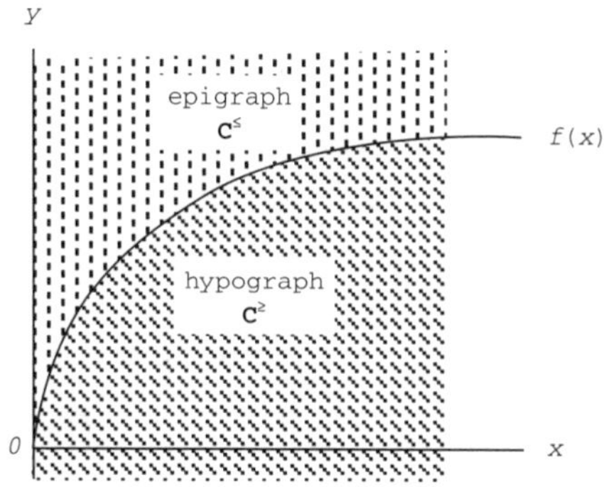


**Figure 10.4** Epigraph and hypograph

## EXERCISES

1. Which of the following functions are concave, convex, or neither?
   (a) $f(x) = 6x - x^2 - 3, \quad -5 \le x \le 30.$
   (b) $f(x) = xe^{-x}, \quad -4 \le x \le 3.$
   (c) $f(x) = \dfrac{1}{\sqrt{2\pi}}e^{-x^2/2}, \quad -2 \le x \le 2.$
   (d) $f(x) = x^{-2}, \quad x > 0.$
2. Are the following quadratic forms concave, convex, or neither?
   (a) $f(\mathbf{x}) = 2x_1^2 - 3x_2^2 - 4x_1x_2$
   (b) $f(\mathbf{x}) = x_1x_2 + x_2x_3 + x_3x_1$
   (c) $f(\mathbf{x}) = -(x_1-2x_2)^2 - (x_2-2x_3)^2 - (x_3-2x_1)^2$

### 10.1.3 Epigraph and hypograph

So far, concave and convex functions have been characterized by comparing the values of the function on its graph, $f(\theta\mathbf{x}_0 + (1-\theta)\mathbf{x}_1)$, to the values of the corresponding chord, $\theta f(\mathbf{x}_0) + (1-\theta)f(\mathbf{x}_1)$. However, concavity and convexity can also be characterized in terms of a set of points in $\mathbf{R}^{n+1}$.

Consider the function $f(x) = \sqrt{x}$ for $x > 0$ shown in figure 10.4. Define the set of all points in $\mathbf{R}^2$ such that

$$\mathbf{C}^{\ge} = \{ (x,y) \mid x > 0 \quad \text{and} \quad f(x) \ge y\}.$$

This set is called the *hypograph* of $f$. In figure 10.4, it is the shaded area on and below the graph of $f$. Similarly, let

$$\mathbf{C}^{\le} = \{ (x,y) \mid x > 0 \quad \text{and} \quad f(x) \le y\}$$

which is the dotted area on and above the graph of $f$. $\mathbf{C}^{\le}$ is called the *epigraph* of $f$.

The hypograph in figure 10.4 is obviously a convex set. A function is concave (convex) if its hypograph (epigraph) is a convex set. The function $f(x) = \sqrt{x}$ is concave and its hypograph is convex. We thus have the following theorem which gives different characterizations of concave and convex functions.

**THEOREM 10.1** *Let $f(\mathbf{x})$ be a real-valued function defined on a convex set* **S** *in* $\mathbf{R}^n$. *$f(\mathbf{x})$ is concave on* **S** *if and only if the hypograph*

$$\mathbf{C}^{\geq} = \{(\mathbf{x},y) \mid \mathbf{x} \in \mathbf{S} \quad \text{and} \quad f(\mathbf{x}) \geq y\}$$

*is a convex set. Similarly, $f(\mathbf{x})$ is convex on* **S** *if and only if the epigraph*

$$\mathbf{C}^{\leq} = \{(\mathbf{x},y) \mid \mathbf{x} \in \mathbf{S} \quad \text{and} \quad f(\mathbf{x}) \leq y\}$$

*is a convex set.*

We leave the proof of this theorem as an exercise, for it follows directly from the definitions of concavity and convexity.

**Example 10.9** The function

$$f(x) = xe^{-x^2}$$

is neither concave nor convex. $f(x)$ is plotted below on the interval [−2,3].

*In[30]:=*

```
Clear[f,x]
f[x_]:= x*Exp[-x^2];
Plot[f[x],{x,-2,3},AxesLabel->{"x","y"}];
```

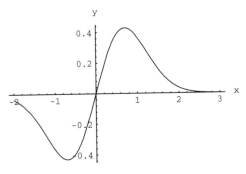

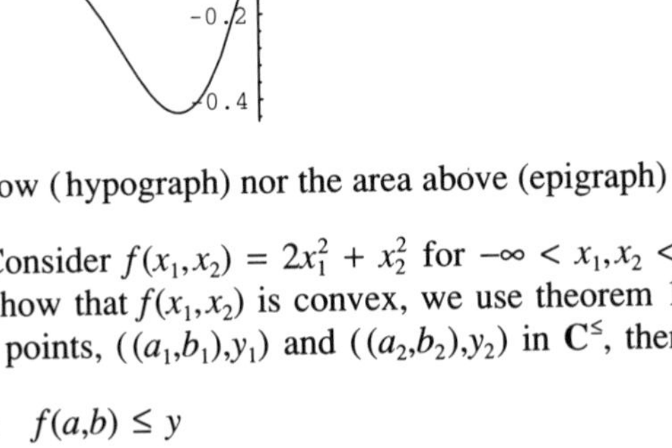


Neither the area below (hypograph) nor the area above (epigraph) the curve is convex.

**Example 10.10** Consider $f(x_1,x_2) = 2x_1^2 + x_2^2$ for $-\infty < x_1,x_2 < \infty$. Show that it is convex on $\mathbf{R}^2$. To show that $f(x_1,x_2)$ is convex, we use theorem 10.1. We must show that if for any two points, $((a_1,b_1),y_1)$ and $((a_2,b_2),y_2)$ in $\mathbf{C}^{\leq}$, then

$$((a,b),y) \in \mathbf{C}^{\leq} \quad \text{or} \quad f(a,b) \leq y$$

where $a = \theta a_1 + (1-\theta)a_2$, $b = \theta b_1 + (1-\theta)b_2$, and $y = \theta y_1 + (1-\theta)y_2$. To illustrate this, consider two points, say $((a_1,b_1),y_1) = ((1,1),4)$, and $((a_2,b_2),y_2) = ((0,-1),2)$. These two points are in $\mathbf{C}^{\leq}$ since $f(1,1) = 3 < y_1 = 4$, and $f(0,-1) = 1 < y_2 = 2$. Moreover, $a = \theta(1) + (1-\theta)(0) = \theta$, $b = \theta(1) + (1-\theta)(-1) = 2\theta - 1$, and $y = \theta(4) + (1-\theta)(2) = 2\theta + 2$. Thus,

$$f(a,b) = 2\theta^2 + (2\theta-1)^2 = 4\theta(\theta-1) + 2\theta^2 + 1$$
$$\leq 2\theta^2 + 1 \leq 2\theta + 1 = y$$

The inequalities follow from $0 \leq \theta \leq 1$. The epigraph $\mathbf{C}^{\leq}$ is a convex set. The following *Mathematica* plot shows that the set $\mathbf{C}^{\leq}$ lies above the surface of $f(x_1,x_2)$ and the epigraph is a convex set.

*In[33]:=*

```
Clear[x,y,f]
f[x_,y_]:= 2*x^2 + y^2;
Plot3D[f[x,y],{x,-2,2},{y,-2,2},
        AxesLabel->{"x","y","f(x,y)"}];
```

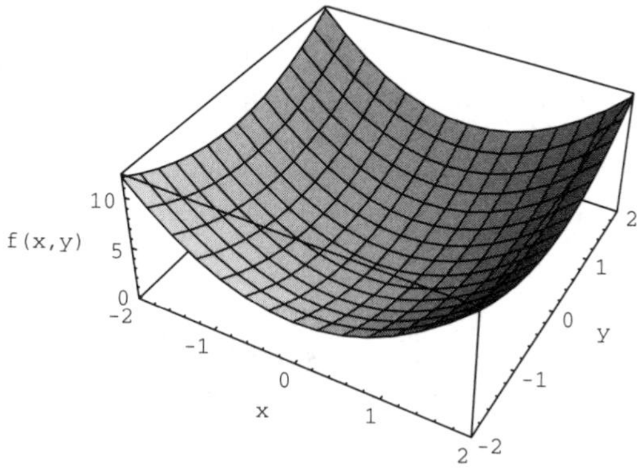


## EXERCISES

1. Find the epigraph and hypograph of the following functions:
   (a) $f(x) = 6x - x^2 - 3$, $-5 \leq x \leq 30$.
   (b) $f(x) = \dfrac{1}{\sqrt{2\pi}}e^{-x^2/2}$, $-2 \leq x \leq 2$.
   (c) $f(x_1,x_2) = 2x_1^2 - 3x_2^2 - 4x_1x_2$, $-\infty < x_1,\ x_2 < \infty$
   Which of them are concave, convex, or neither?
2. Prove theorem 10.1.
3. Show that the hypograph is convex for the CES production function

   $$Q = [0.6L^{-0.8}+0.4K^{-0.8}]^{-1.25}$$

## □ 10.2 Differentiable Concave and Convex Functions □

### 10.2.1 Differentiable functions

In defining concave and convex functions, we did not assume that the functions were differentiable. For a differentiable function, concavity and convexity can be tested by examining the gradient vector or the Hessian matrix of the function.

Recall that a tangent line of a function $f(x)$ at point $x_0$ can be represented by the linear function

$$T(x) = f(x_0) + f'(x_0)(x - x_0)$$

where $f'(x_0)$ is the first derivative of $f$ at $x_0$. The function $T(x)$ can be used to characterize the concavity or convexity of $f$.

**THEOREM 10.2** *A differentiable function $f(x)$ is concave on an open interval I if and only if the graph of $f(x)$ lies everywhere on or below any tangent line to the graph of f, i.e.,*

$$f(x) \leq T(x), \quad \text{or} \quad f(x) - f(x_0) \leq f'(x_0)(x - x_0)$$

*for any x and $x_0$ in I. It is strictly concave if and only if for each $x \neq x_0$ in I, we have*

$$f(x) < T(x), \quad \text{or} \quad f(x) - f(x_0) < f'(x_0)(x - x_0).$$

*For convex and strictly convex, the inequality signs are reversed.*

**Example 10.11** Show that $f(x) = x^2 - 2x$ is strictly convex on the interval (–2,2). The tangent line at $x_0 = -1$ is $T(x) = 3 - 4(1+x)$. This is verified in the calculation below.

*In[36]:=*
```
Clear[f,T,x];
f[x_]:= x^2-2*x; x0=-1;
T[x_] = f[x0]+(D[f[x],x]/.x->x0)*(x-x0)
```

*Out[38]=*
```
3 - 4(1 + x)
```

Both $f(x)$ and $T(x)$ are plotted for $-2 \leq x \leq 2$.

*In[39]:=*
```
Plot[{f[x],T[x]},{x,-2,2},
        PlotStyle->{{},{Thickness[0.008]}}];
```

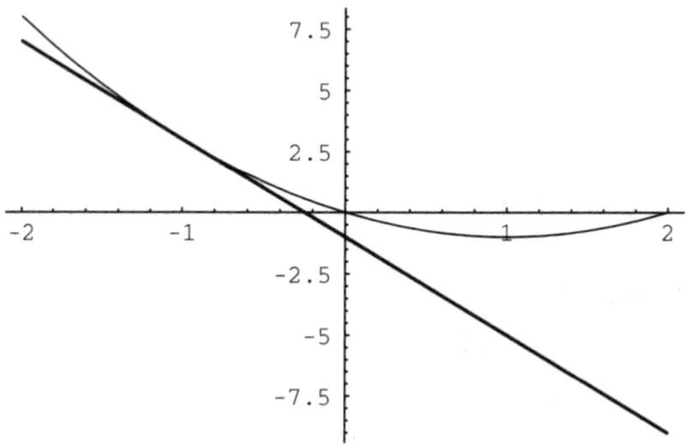

The tangent line clearly lies below (supports) the graph of the $f(x)$. Tangent lines at different points $x_0$ also lie below $f(x)$ on the inteval (–2,2). Hence $f(x) = x^2 - 2x$ is strictly convex on this interval. In fact, the function is convex on the interval $(-\infty,\infty)$.

To graph a tangent line and the function, we can use the **MathEcon** function **tangentline**.

*In[40]:=*

```
?tangentline
```

**tangentline[fct,int,pt] generates a 2D Graphics object that contains the graph of the function fct over the interval int (a list) with the tangent line to the graph of fct at the point pt. The graphics can then be displayed with the Show function. For example,**

**Show[tangentline[Cos[2*Pi*x],{x,-1,1},Pi/4],Axes→True];**

The first argument contains the function, the second argument contains a list that specifies the interval over which the graph of function is to be plotted, and the third argument is the point in the domain of the function where the tangent line is to be drawn.

**Example 10.12** Show that $f(x) = \log(3+x)$ is a strictly concave function on (–2,3). The tangent lines lie above $f(x)$ on $-2 < x < 3$. A tangent line at the point $x_0 = -1$ is shown below.

*In[41]:=*

```
Clear[f,x,x0];
f[x_]:= Log[3+x];
domain = {x,-2,3}; x0 = -1;
concave = tangentline[f[x],domain,x0];
Show[concave,Axes->True,AxesLabel->{"x","f(x)"}];
```

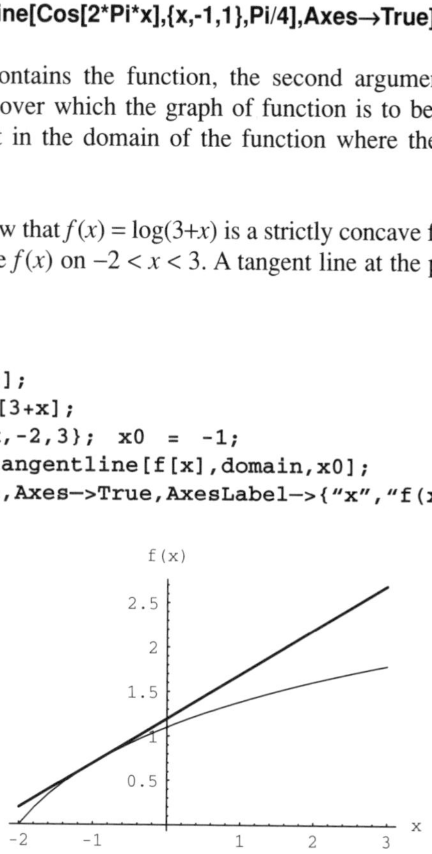


**Example 10.13** The function $f(x) = x^3$ is neither convex nor concave on (–3,2). The tangent line at $x_0 = 1$ neither supports nor lies above $f(x)$ as is shown in the following plot.

*In[46]:=*

```
Clear[x];
Show[tangentline[x^3,{x,-3,2},1],
        Axes->True,AxesLabel->{"x","f(x)"}];
```

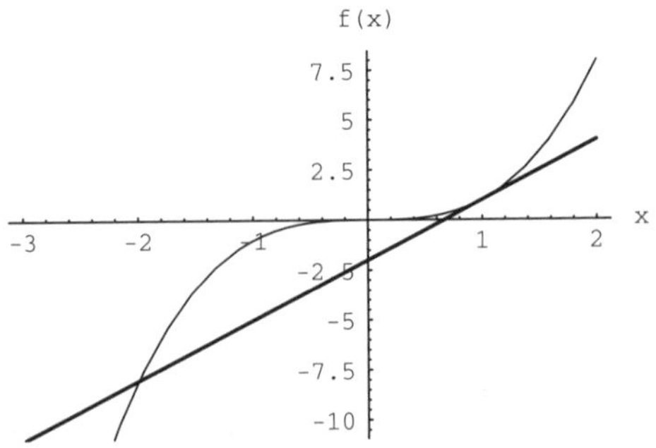


However, $f(x) = x^3$ is convex if $f(x)$ is restricted to $x > 0$, and is concave on $x < 0$.

For a function $f(\mathbf{x}) = f(x_1,x_2, \ldots ,x_n)$ of more than one variable, we can extend the above ideas. If $f(\mathbf{x})$ is differentiable, then it has a tangent hyperplane at each point where it is differentiable. The tangent hyperplane to the graph of $f(\mathbf{x})$ at $\mathbf{x}_0$ is the function

$$T(\mathbf{x}) = f(\mathbf{x}_0) + \nabla f(\mathbf{x}_0) \cdot (\mathbf{x} - \mathbf{x}_0).$$

The gradient $\nabla f(\mathbf{x}_0)$,

$$\nabla f(\mathbf{x}_0) = [f_1(\mathbf{x}_0) \quad f_2(\mathbf{x}_0) \quad \ldots \quad f_n(\mathbf{x}_0)]$$

is a vector of partial derivatives evaluated at $\mathbf{x}_0$. Thus $f(\mathbf{x})$ is concave on an open convex set $\mathbf{S}$ if and only if the surface of $f$ lies everywhere on or below any tangent hyperplane. That is,

$$f(\mathbf{x}) \le T(\mathbf{x}) \quad \text{or} \quad f(\mathbf{x}) - f(\mathbf{x}_0) \le \nabla f(\mathbf{x}_0) \cdot (\mathbf{x} - \mathbf{x}_0)$$

for any two points $\mathbf{x}$ and $\mathbf{x}_0$ in $\mathbf{S}$. $f(\mathbf{x})$ is *strictly concave* if and only if, for each $\mathbf{x} \neq \mathbf{x}_0$ in $\mathbf{S}$,

$$f(\mathbf{x}) < T(\mathbf{x}) \quad \text{or} \quad f(\mathbf{x}) - f(\mathbf{x}_0) < \nabla f(\mathbf{x}_0) \cdot (\mathbf{x} - \mathbf{x}_0)$$

For convex and strictly convex, the inequality signs are reversed.

**Example 10.14** Show that the function $f(x,y) = 5x^4 + 3y^2$ is convex on $\mathbf{R}^2$. The function has the partial derivatives, $f_x = 20x^3$ and $f_y = 6y$. The tangent plane $T(\mathbf{x})$ is given by the function

$$T(x,y) = (5x_0^4 + 3y_0^2) + 20x_0^3(x-x_0) + 6y_0(y-y_0)$$

The following graph shows that at the point $(x_0,y_0) = (1,1)$, $T(x,y)$ supports $f(x,y)$.

*In[48]:=*

```
Clear[f,T,x,y];
f[x_,y_]:= 5*x^4 + 3*y^2;
x0=1; y0=1;
T[x_,y_]  =   f[x0,y0]+(D[f[x,y],x]/.{x->x0,y->y0})(x-x0)+
                  (D[f[x,y],y]/.{x->x0,y->y0})(y-y0);
```

```
surface     =    Plot3D[f[x,y],{x,-2,3},{y,-2,3},
                    DisplayFunction->Identity];
tangentplane    =    Plot3D[T[x,y],{x,-2.5,3.5},{y,-2.5,3.5},
                       DisplayFunction->Identity];
Show[surface,tangentplane,
                      ViewPoint->{-1.164,-3.008,0.788},
                      Axes->False,Boxed->False,AspectRatio->0.5,
                      DisplayFunction->$DisplayFunction];
```

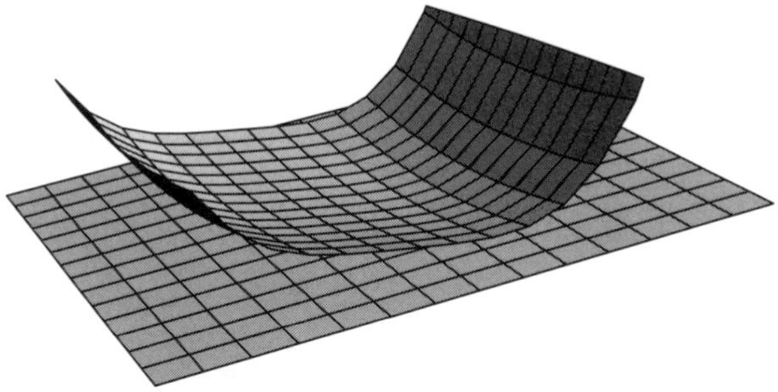

**Example 10.15** Show that the CES function

$f(x,y) = (0.6x^{-0.8} + 0.4y^{-0.8})^{-1.25}$, $x,y > 0$,

is concave on the set $\{(x,y) \mid x,y > 0\}$. We plot the difference between $f(x,y)$ and $T(x,y)$ at $(x_0,y_0) = (5,10)$ over the region $3 \le x \le 7$ and $7 \le y \le 13$.

*In[55]:=*

```
Clear[f,T,x,y];
a=0.6;  d=-0.8;  x0=5;  y0=10;
f[x_,y_]:=  (a*x^d  +  (1-a)*y^d)^(1/d);
T[x_,y_]=   f[x0,y0]+(D[f[x,y],x]/.{x->x0,y->y0})(x-x0)+
                     (D[f[x,y],y]/.{x->x0,y->y0})(y-y0);
Plot3D[f[x,y]-T[x,y],{x,3,7},{y,7,13},
                     AxesLabel->{"x","y","f(x,y)-T(x,y)"},
                     ViewPoint->{-1.240,  -3.560,  0.650}];
```

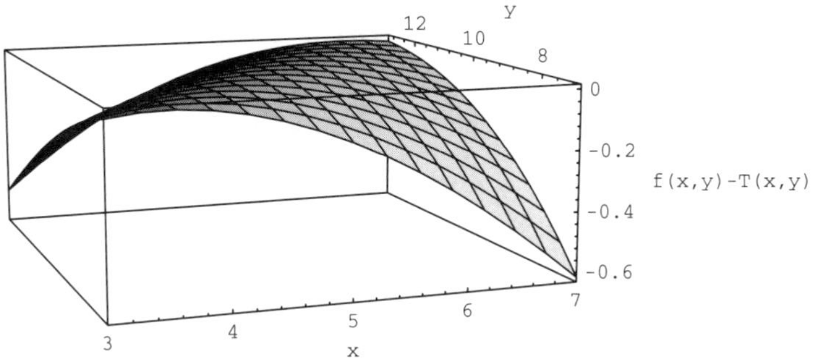


Since the difference is negative, $f(x,y) - T(x,y) < 0$, the CES function is concave.

**Example 10.16** Consider a three variables CES function defined on $x,y,z > 0$,

$f(x,y,z) = (0.3x^{-0.8} + 0.5y^{-0.8} + 0.2z^{-0.8})^{-1.25}$

We define the tangent hyperplane of $f$ at (5,10,6).

*In[60]:=*

```
Clear[T,f,x,y,z];
a=0.3;  b=0.5;  d=-0.8;  x0=5;  y0=10;  z0=6;
f[x_,y_,z_]:=  (a*x^d  +  b*y^d  +  (1-a-b)*z^d)^(1/d);
gvector  =  gradf[f[x,y,z],{x,y,z}]  /.  {x->x0,y->y0,z->z0}
T[x_,y_,z_]  =  f[x0,y0,z0]  +  gvector.{x-x0,y-y0,z-z0};
T[x,y,z]
```

*Out[63]=*

```
{0.556226, 0.266223, 0.267075}
```

*Out[65]=*

```
7.04581 + 0.556226(–5 + x) + 0.266223(–10 + y) + 0.267075(–6 + z)
```

Lastly, the difference, $f(x,y,z) - T(x,y,z)$, is evaluated at various points. For illustration, we pick only two points, (7,3,9) and (4,15,5), to show that the difference is negative.

*In[66]:=*

```
f[7,3,9]  -  T[7,3,9]
```

*Out[66]=*

```
–2.69044
```

*In[67]:=*

```
f[4,15,5]  -  T[4,15,5]
```

*Out[67]=*

```
–0.579271
```

This CES function appears to be concave.

## EXERCISES

1. Prove that a Cobb-Douglas production function, $f(x,y) = Ax^a y^b$, is strictly concave if it is subject to decreasing returns to scale, i.e., $a > 0$, $b > 0$, and $a+b < 1$.

2. Use **tangentline** to determine which of the following functions are convex, concave, or neither:
   (a) $f(x) = -5x + 6x^2 - 3, \quad -1 \le x \le 2$
   (b) $f(x) = x^2 e^{-x}, \quad -2 \le x \le 2$
   (c) $f(x) = x + \log x \quad 0 < x \le 5$

3. Show that $f(x_1,x_2,x_3) = 0.5(x_1^2 + x_2^2 - x_3^2) + x_1 x_2$ is neither concave nor convex.

4. Which of the following functions are convex, concave, or neither?
   (a) $f(x,y) = (x + y)e^{-x}, \quad x, y \ge 0.$
   (b) $f(x,y) = x^2 y^2 \quad x, y \ge 0.$
   (c) $f(x,y) = \sqrt{x} + \sqrt{y}, \quad x, y > 0.$

   If the function is convex or concave is it strictly so?

### 10.2.2 Twice differentiable functions

For twice-differentiable functions of a single variable, the relationship between the second derivative and the convexity is given in the following theorem.

**THEOREM 10.3** *Let $f(x)$ be a function of a single variable that is twice differentiable on an open interval* **S** *in* **R**. *$f(x)$ is concave (convex) on* **S** *if and only if the second derivatives are nonpositive (nonnegative), i.e., $f''(x) \le 0$ ($f''(x) \ge 0$) on* **S**.

**Example 10.17** $f(x) = e^x$ is convex on $-\infty < x < \infty$ since $f''(x) = e^x \ge 0$ for any $x$. $g(x) = \log x$ is concave on $x > 0$ since $g''(x) = -1/x^2 < 0$.

The "if and only if" condition of the above theorem cannot be extended to the cases of strictly concave and convex functions. However, we have the following propositions:

(1) if $f''(x) > 0$, then $f(x)$ is strictly convex;

(2) if $f''(x) < 0$, then $f(x)$ is strictly concave.

The converses of these propositions are not true. For example, $f(x) = x^4 + 1$ is strictly convex, but $f'(x) = f''(x) = 0$ at $x = 0$.

**Example 10.18** The function $f(x) = -x^2/(1+x^2)$ is neither concave nor convex on the interval $-4 < x < 4$. This follows from the second derivative

$$f''(x) = \begin{cases} \text{positive}, & |x| > 1/\sqrt{3} \\ \text{zero}, & |x| = 1/\sqrt{3} \\ \text{negative}, & |x| < 1/\sqrt{3} \end{cases}$$

which changes sign over the interval $(-4,4)$. This is confirmed by plotting the chord joining the points $(-3, f(-3))$ and $(0.5, f(0.5))$.

*In[68]:=*
```
Clear[f,x];
f[x_]:= -x^2/(1+x^2);
domain = {x,-4,4}; segment = {x,-3,0.5};
neither = arc2d[f[x],domain,segment,chord];
Show[neither,Axes->True,AxesLabel->{"x","f(x)"}];
```

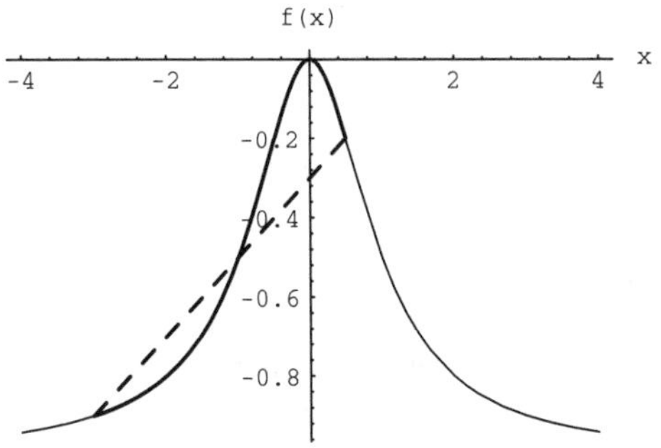

Since the chord is not entirely above or below $f(x)$, $f(x)$ is neither convex nor concave. The indefiniteness of this function is further demonstrated by plotting the tangent line $T(x_0)$ at $x_0 = -1.5$.

*In[73]:=*
```
x0 = -1.5;
Tline = tangentline[f[x],domain,x0];
Show[Tline,Axes->True,AxesLabel->{"x","f(x)"}];
```

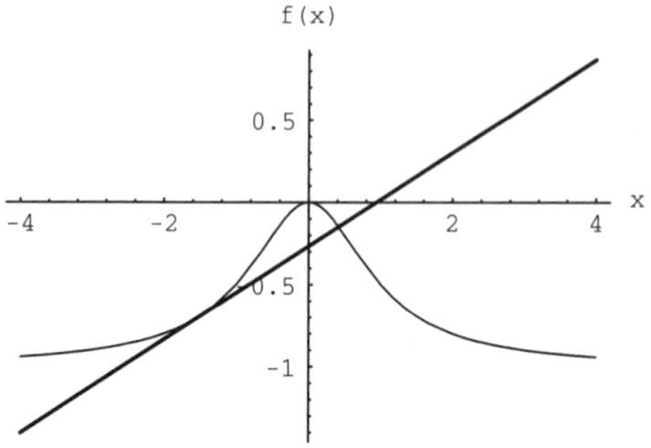


$T(x_0)$ does not support $f(x)$. Hence, $f(x)$ is neither convex nor concave.

**Example 10.19** Show that the function $f(x) = x^3 - 3x^2 + 5$ is neither concave nor convex on **R**. Calculating the second derivative of $f(x)$, we find that it changes sign at $x = 1$. As shown in the following plot, $f(x)$ is concave on the interval $x \le 1$, and convex on the interval $x \ge 1$.

*In[76]:=*
```
Clear[f,x];
f[x_]:= x^3 - 3*x^2 + 5;
Plot[f[x],{x,-1,3},AxesLabel->{"x","f(x)"}];
```

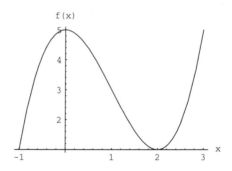

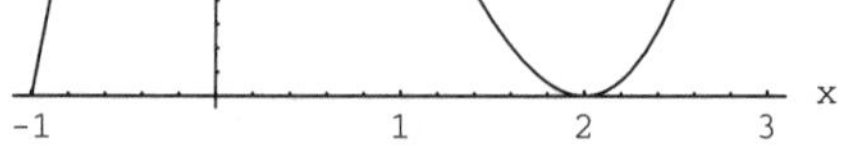


The point $x = 1$ where $f(x)$ changes from being concave to convex is called a *point of inflection.*

**DEFINITION 10.3** *Suppose $f(x)$ is a continuous function of a single variable. A point c is called a* ***point of inflection*** *if in a neighborhood of c, $f(x)$ is concave for $x \le c$ and convex for $x \ge c$ (or vice versa).*

It is easy to prove that if $f(x)$ is twice differentiable in a neighborhood of $x = c$ and $f''(x)$ changes sign at $x = c$, then $c$ is an inflection point.

For a differentiable function $f(\mathbf{x})$ of more than one variable, concavity and convexity can be determined by examining the sign of the second-order differential $d^2f(\mathbf{x})$. As discussed in Chapters 8 and 9, the second-order differential evaluated at $\mathbf{c} = (c_1,c_2, \ldots c_n)$ is the quadratic form

$$d^2f(\mathbf{c};\mathbf{x}-\mathbf{c}) = [x_1-c_1 \quad x_2-c_2 \quad \ldots \quad x_n-c_n]\begin{bmatrix} f_{11} & f_{12} & \cdots & f_{1n} \\ f_{21} & f_{22} & \cdots & f_{2n} \\ \cdots & \cdots & \cdots & \cdots \\ f_{n1} & f_{n2} & \cdots & f_{nn} \end{bmatrix}\begin{bmatrix} x_1-c_1 \\ x_2-c_2 \\ \cdot \\ x_n-c_n \end{bmatrix}$$

$$= (\mathbf{x}-\mathbf{c})^T\mathbf{H}(\mathbf{x}-\mathbf{c})$$

where $\mathbf{H}$ is the Hessian matrix and the differentials $dx_i$ are replaced by $(x_i-c_i)$. The following theorem establishes an equivalence between convexity and the Hessian matrix.

**THEOREM 10.4** Let $f(\mathbf{x}) = f(x_1,x_2, \ldots ,x_n)$ *be twice differentiable on an open convex set* $\mathbf{S}$. *The function is concave (convex) in* $\mathbf{S}$ *if and only if* $d^2f(\mathbf{c};\mathbf{x}-\mathbf{c}) \leq 0$ $(d^2f(\mathbf{c};\mathbf{x}-\mathbf{c}) \geq 0)$ *for all* $\mathbf{x}$ *and* $\mathbf{c}$ *in* $\mathbf{S}$, *or equivalently, if and only if the Hessian matrix* $\mathbf{H}$ *is negative (positive) semidefinite.*

In Chapter 7, we showed that a symmetric matrix, such as the Hessian matrix $\mathbf{H}$, is positive semidefinite if and only if all principal minors of order k are nonnegative, i.e., $|\mathbf{P}_k| \geq 0$ for $k = 1,2, \ldots ,n$. The Hessian matrix is negative semidefinite if and only if $(-1)^k|\mathbf{P}_k| \geq 0$, i.e., the principal minors $|\mathbf{P}_k|$ of odd order are nonpositive and the principal minors of even order are nonnegative.

To calculate the Hessian matrix, we use the **MathEcon** function **hessian**. The signs of the principal minors of the Hessian matrix can be determined by the **MathEcon** function **signQ**.

**Example 10.20** Show that the function $f(x_1,x_2) = x_1 - x_2 - x_1^2$ is concave on $\mathbf{R}^2$. The function has the Hessian matrix

$$\mathbf{H} = \begin{bmatrix} f_{11} & f_{12} \\ f_{21} & f_{22} \end{bmatrix} = \begin{bmatrix} -2 & 0 \\ 0 & 0 \end{bmatrix}$$

The two principal minors $|\mathbf{P}_1|$ of order 1 have values $-2$ and 0, and $|\mathbf{P}_2| = |\mathbf{H}| = 0$. Thus the Hessian matrix is negative semidefinite and $f(x_1,x_2)$ is concave. This is shown in the following calculation.

*In[79]:=*

```
Clear[x1,x2];
H = hessian[x1-x2-x1^2,{x1,x2}];
signQ[H]
```

*Out[81]=*

```
{{-2, 0}, {0}}
```

We confirm its concavity in the following plot.

*In[82]:=*

```
Clear[f,x1,x2];
f[x1_,x2_]:= x1  -  x2  -  x1^2;
Plot3D[f[x1,x2],{x1,-5,5},{x2,-5,5},
                  AxesLabel->{"x1","x2","f(x1,x2)"},
                  ViewPoint->{0.150,  -3.090,  1.010}];
```

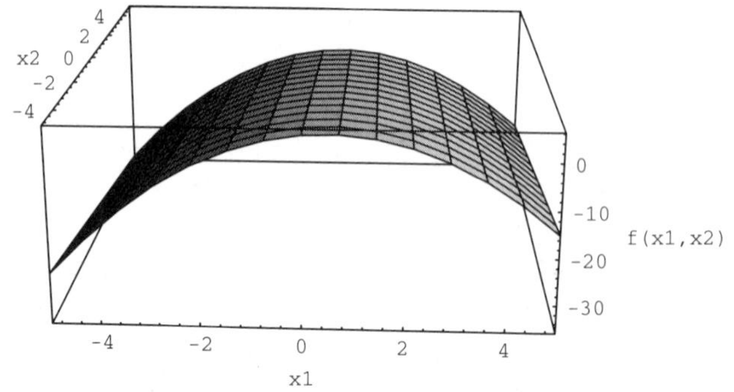


**Example 10.21** A simple Cobb-Douglas production function

$f(x,y) = x^a y^b$

defined for $x,y > 0$ has the Hessian matrix **H**

$$\mathbf{H} = \begin{bmatrix} f_{xx} & f_{xy} \\ f_{yx} & f_{yy} \end{bmatrix} = \begin{bmatrix} a(a-1)x^{a-2}y^b & abx^{a-1}y^{b-1} \\ abx^{a-1}y^{b-1} & b(b-1)x^a y^{b-2} \end{bmatrix}$$

The principal minors $|\mathbf{P}_1|$ of order 1 are

$a(a-1)x^{a-2}y^b$ and $b(b-1)x^a y^{b-2}$

and the principal minor of order 2 is $|\mathbf{H}|$ is

$ab(1-a-b)x^{-2(1-a)}y^{-2(1-b)}$

When $a \geq 0$, $b \geq 0$, and $a+b \leq 1$, the Cobb-Douglas production function is subject to nonincreasing returns to scale. In this case, $|\mathbf{P}_1| \leq 0$ and $|\mathbf{H}| \geq 0$. The Hessian matrix is negative semidefinite and hence the production function is concave. We confirm this with the following calculation.

*In[85]:=*

```
Clear[f,x,y,a,b];
f[x_,y_]:= x^a  y^b;
H  =  hessian[f[x,y],{x,y}];
signQ[H]  //  Simplify
```

*Out[88]=*

$\{\{(-1 + a)a x^{-2+a} y^b, (-1 + b) b x^a y^{-2+b}\}, \{a(1 - a - b) b x^{-2+2a} y^{-2+2b}\}\}$

**Example 10.22** Consider the following CES production function

$f(x,y) = (ax^b + (1-a)y^b)^{1/b},\ x,y > 0$

and $b \neq 0$. For what values of the parameters, $a$ and $b$, is the function convex on $\{ (x,y) \mid x,y > 0\}$? For what values of the parameters is it concave? The principal minors of the Hessian matrix **H** are calculated below.

*In[89]:=*

```
Clear[f,x,y,a,b];
f[x_,y_]:=  (a*x^b+(1-a)*y^b)^(1/b);
H  =  hessian[f[x,y],{x,y}];
signQ[H][[1]]  //  Simplify
signQ[H][[2]]  //  Simplify
```

*Out[91]=*

$$\{\frac{(-1 + a)a(1 - b)x^{-2+b}\, y^b (a\, x^b + y^b - a\, y^b)^{1/b}}{(-(a\, x^b) - y^b + a\, y^b)^2},$$
$$(-1+a)a(1-b)x^b\, y^{-2+b}(a\, x^b + y^b - a\, y^b)^{-2+1/b}\}$$

*Out[92]=*

{0}

The first two entries in the list are the principal minors $|\mathbf{P}_1|$ of order 1. The principal minor of order 2 is zero, $|\mathbf{P}_2| = |\mathbf{H}| = 0$. If $0 < a < 1$ and $b \leq 1$, we have $|\mathbf{P}_1| \leq 0$. The Hessian matrix is negative semidefinite and the CES function is concave. On the other hand, if $0 < a < 1$ and $b \geq 1$, we have $|\mathbf{P}_1| \geq 0$. The Hessian matrix is then positive semidefinite and the CES function is convex.

**Example 10.23** Consider a three-variable CES function

$f(x,y,z) = (0.3x^{-0.8} + 0.5y^{-0.8} + 0.2z^{-0.8})^{-1.25}$

where $x,y,z > 0$. Show that it is concave in a neighborhood of the points (7,3,9) and (4,15,5). At $(x,y,z) = (7,3,9)$, the following calculation shows that the three principal minors of order 1, $|\mathbf{P}_1|$, are negative, and that the three principal minors of order 2, $|\mathbf{P}_2|$, are postive and $|\mathbf{H}| = 0$. Hence the Hessian matrix is negative semidefinite at this point.

*In[93]:=*

```
Clear[H,f,x,y,z];
a=0.3;  b=0.5;  d=-0.8;
f[x_,y_,z_]:=  (a*x^d  +  b*y^d  +  (1-a-b)*z^d)^(1/d);
H[x_,y_,z_]  =  hessian[f[x,y,z],{x,y,z}];
signQ[H[7,3,9]]  //  Chop
```

*Out[97]=*

{{-0.0265774, -0.191747, -0.00980772},
{0.00226795, 0.000251994, 0.00137197}, {0}}

Similar results and conclusions can be reached at another point $(x,y,z) = (4,15,5)$. This again illustrates the concavity of a CES function.

*In[98]:=*

```
signQ[H[4,15,5]]  //  Chop
```

*Out[98]=*

```
{{-0.195352, -0.0110217, -0.0968573},
  {0.00144905, 0.0130415, 0.000927395}, {0}}
```

Similar to the single variable case, the "if and only if" condition of theorem 10.3 cannot be extended to the cases of strictly concave or convex functions.

**Theorem 10.5** *Let $f(\mathbf{x})$ be twice differentiable on an open convex set* **S**. *The function is strictly concave (convex) if the second-order differential is negative (positive) definite, i.e.,* $d^2f(\mathbf{c};\mathbf{x}-\mathbf{c}) < 0$ ($d^2f(\mathbf{c};\mathbf{x}-\mathbf{c}) > 0$), *for all* **x** *and* **c** *in* **S**.

Let $|\mathbf{H}_k|$ be the leading principal minors of order $k$ of the Hessian matrix **H**,

$$|\mathbf{H}_k| = \begin{vmatrix} f_{11} & f_{12} & \cdots & f_{1k} \\ f_{21} & f_{22} & \cdots & f_{2k} \\ \cdots & \cdots & \cdots & \cdots \\ f_{k1} & f_{k2} & \cdots & f_{kk} \end{vmatrix}, \quad k = 1,2, \ldots, n$$

We have the following propositions concerning strict concavity and strict convexity:

(1) If the Hessian matrix is negative definite for all **x** in **S**, $(-1)^k|\mathbf{H}_k| > 0$, for $k = 1,2, \ldots, n$, then $f(\mathbf{x})$ is strictly concave on **S**.

(2) If the Hessian matrix is positive definite for all **x** in **S**, $|\mathbf{H}_k| > 0$, for $k = 1,2, \ldots, n$, then $f(\mathbf{x})$ is strictly convex on **S**.

The leading principal minors of the **H** matrix can be calculated using the **MathEcon** function **signQL**. We use this function in the following example.

**Example 10.24** Consider the function

$$f(x,y) = xe^{x+y}$$

on $\mathbf{S} = \{(x,y) \mid x,y \geq 0\}$. The Hessian matrix is

$$\mathbf{H} = \begin{bmatrix} f_{xx} & f_{xy} \\ f_{yx} & f_{yy} \end{bmatrix} = \begin{bmatrix} (x+2)e^{x+y} & (x+1)e^{x+y} \\ (x+1)e^{x+y} & xe^{x+y} \end{bmatrix}$$

The leading principal minors are

$$|\mathbf{H}_1| = (x+2)e^{x+y} > 0$$
$$|\mathbf{H}| = -e^{2(x+y)} < 0$$

Thus the **H** matrix is neither positive nor negative definite. The function is neither strictly convex nor strictly concave on **S**. In fact, the function is neither convex nor concave on **S**.

*In[99]:=*

```
Clear[f,x,y,H]
f[x_,y_]:= x*Exp[x+y];
H = hessian[f[x,y],{x,y}];
signQL[H]
```

*Out[102]=*

```
{2E^(x+y) + E^(x+y) x, -E^(2x+2y)}
```

**Example 10.25** The function

$$f(x,y,z) = x^2 - 2xy + 4y^2 - 2xz - 6yz + 9z^2$$

is strictly convex since all the leading principal minors are positive, which can be seen in the following calculation.

*In[103]:=*

```
Clear[H,f,x,y,z]
f[x_,y_,z_]:= x^2 - 2*x*y + 4*y^2 - 2*x*z - 6*y*z + 9*z^2;
H = hessian[f[x,y,z],{x,y,z}];
signQL[H]
```

*Out[106]=*

```
{2, 12, 64}
```

## EXERCISE

1. Use the Hessian matrix to test for the concavity and convexity of the functions given in the exercises at the end of section 10.2.1.

## □ 10.3 Some Properties of Concave and Convex Functions □

We list several important properties of concave and convex functions in this section. Assume that all functions are defined on a convex set **S** in $\mathbf{R}^n$.

*Property 1* Linear functions are both concave and convex. For example, $f(x_1,x_2,x_3) = 3x_1 - 2x_2 + 4x_3$ is both concave and convex. The proof follows directly from the definition. In fact, if $f(\mathbf{x})$ is both concave and convex, then the function must be a linear function.

*Property 2* The negative of a (strictly) concave function is (strictly) convex, and vice versa. For example, $f(x) = x^2$ is strictly convex. The chord joining the points $(a,a^2)$ and $(b,b^2)$ lies above the values on the graph of $x^2$. The chord joining the points $(a,-a^2)$ and $(b,-b^2)$, however, lies below the graph of $-x^2$.

*Property 3* The sum of positive scalar multiples of concave (convex) functions is concave (convex). Suppose the functions $f_i(\mathbf{x})$ are concave on a convex set **S**, and $a_i > 0$, for $i = 1,2, \ldots ,n$. Then

$$h(\mathbf{x}) = \sum_{i=1}^{n} a_i f_i(\mathbf{x})$$

is concave. To prove this, let $\mathbf{x}_0$ and $\mathbf{x}_1$ be two points in **S**, then we have

$$\begin{aligned} h(\theta\mathbf{x}_0 + (1-\theta)\mathbf{x}_1) &= \sum_{i=1}^{n} a_i f_i(\theta\mathbf{x}_0 + (1-\theta)\mathbf{x}_1) \\ &\geq \sum_{i=1}^{n} a_i[\theta f_i(\mathbf{x}_0) + (1-\theta) f_i(\mathbf{x}_1)] \\ &= \theta\sum_{i=1}^{n} a_i f(\mathbf{x}_0) + (1-\theta)\sum_{i=1}^{n} a_i f(\mathbf{x}_1) \\ &= \theta h(\mathbf{x}_0) + (1-\theta) h(\mathbf{x}_1) \end{aligned}$$

Hence $h(\mathbf{x})$ is concave. A similar argument applies to the case of linear combinations of convex functions.

**Example 10.26** Suppose $f(\mathbf{x}) = f(x_1, x_2, \ldots, x_n)$ is a concave production function with $n$ inputs. The profit function is defined as

$$\begin{aligned} h(\mathbf{x}) &= pf(\mathbf{x}) - (w_1x_1 + w_2x_2 + \ldots + w_nx_n) \\ &= pf(\mathbf{x}) + (-\sum_{i=1}^{n} w_i x_i) \end{aligned}$$

where $p$ and $w_i$ are positive output and input prices, respectively. Since $(-\Sigma w_i x_i)$ is a linear function, it is concave. By Property 3, the profit function is therefore a concave function.

*Property 4* An increasing, concave (convex) function of a concave (convex) function is concave (convex). Suppose $f(\mathbf{x})$ is concave and $F(y)$ is an increasing, concave function of a single variable defined on the range of $f(\mathbf{x})$. Then the composite function $h(\mathbf{x}) = F(f(\mathbf{x}))$ is concave on $\mathbf{S}$. To prove this, consider two points $\mathbf{x}_0$ and $\mathbf{x}_1$ in $\mathbf{S}$. Then

$$\begin{aligned} h(\theta\mathbf{x}_0 + (1-\theta)\mathbf{x}_1) &= F(f(\theta\mathbf{x}_0 + (1-\theta)\mathbf{x}_1)) \\ &\geq F(\theta f(\mathbf{x}_0) + (1-\theta) f(\mathbf{x}_1)) \\ &\geq \theta F(f(\mathbf{x}_0)) + (1-\theta) F(f(\mathbf{x}_1)) \\ &= \theta h(\mathbf{x}_0) + (1-\theta) h(\mathbf{x}_1) \end{aligned}$$

The first inequality is due to the fact that $f(\mathbf{x})$ is concave, i.e., $f(\theta\mathbf{x}_0 + (1-\theta)\mathbf{x}_1) \geq \theta f(\mathbf{x}_0) + (1-\theta) f(\mathbf{x}_1)$, and $F(y)$ is an increasing function. The second inequality follows from the concavity of $F(y)$.

**Example 10.27** As shown in example 10.22 in section 10.2.2, the CES production function

$$q = (ax_1^b + (1-a)x_2^b)^{1/b},\ 0 < x_i,\ 0 < a < 1$$

is a concave function if $b \leq 1$, and is a convex function if $b \geq 1$. For any $0 < r \leq 1$, $F(q) = q^r$ is an increasing, concave function. Thus the transformed CES function

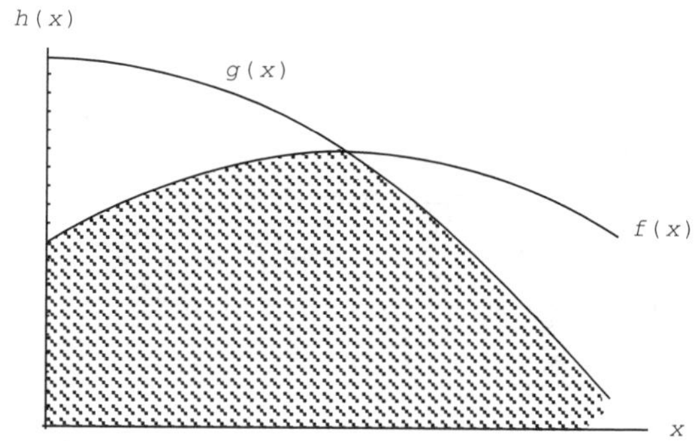


**Figure 10.5** $h(x) = \min\,(f(x), g(x))$

$$Q = F(q) = (ax_1^b + (1-a)x_2^b)^{r/b},\ b \leq 1,\ 0 < r \leq 1,$$

is concave. Similarly, for any $r \geq 1$, $F(q) = q^r$ is an increasing, convex function: then the transformed CES function

$$Q = F(q) = (ax_1^b + (1-a)\,x_2^b)^{r/b},\ b \geq 1,\ r \geq 1,$$

is convex.

*Property 5* If both $f(\mathbf{x})$ and $g(\mathbf{x})$ are concave on a convex set $\mathbf{S}$, then $h(\mathbf{x}) = \min\{f(\mathbf{x}),g(\mathbf{x})\}$ is concave on $\mathbf{S}$. On the other hand, if $f(\mathbf{x})$ and $g(\mathbf{x})$ are convex on $\mathbf{S}$, then $h(\mathbf{x}) = \max\{f(\mathbf{x}),g(\mathbf{x})\}$ is convex on $\mathbf{S}$. Figure 10.5 illustrates this property. The shaded area is an intersection of the hypographs of two concave functions. Hence the hypograph of $h(x)$,

$$\mathbf{C}^{\geq} = \{\,(x,y) \mid x \in \mathbf{S} \ \text{ and } \ h(x) \geq y\}$$

is a convex set. Therefore, $h(x)$ is a concave function.

**Example 10.28** A *Leontief* or *fixed-coefficient* production function is defined as

$$h(x_1,x_2,\ldots,x_n) = \min\left\{\frac{x_1}{a_1}, \frac{x_2}{a_2}, \ldots, \frac{x_n}{a_n}\right\}$$

where $a_i$ is the amount of $i$-th input required to produce a unit of output, and $x_i$ is the total amount of the input available. Since $x_i/a_i$ is concave, the Leontief production function is concave. Suppose there are only two inputs, $x_1$ and $x_2$ with $a_1 = 4$ and $a_2 = 2$. The following *Mathematica* plot shows that the function is concave.

*In[107]:=*
```
Plot3D[Min[x1/4,x2/2],{x1,0,20},{x2,0,10},
        AxesLabel->{"x1","x2","f"},
        ViewPoint->{-1.370, -3.810, 1.020}];
```

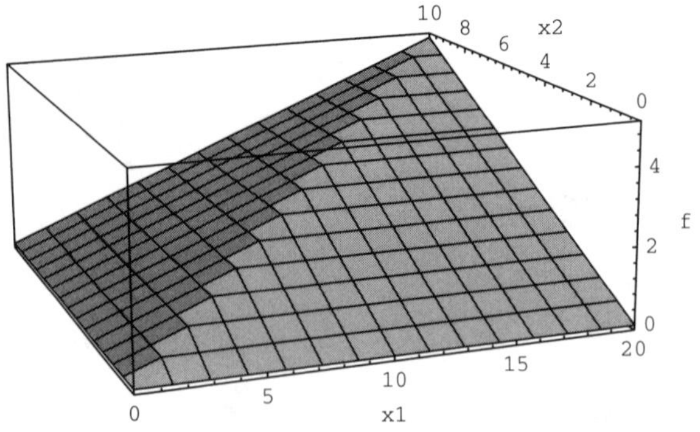


*Property 6* If $f(\mathbf{x})$ is concave, then for any real number $c$, then the set

$$\mathbf{L}^{\geq} = \{\mathbf{x} \mid \mathbf{x} \in \mathbf{S} \quad \text{and} \quad f(\mathbf{x}) \geq c\}$$

in $\mathbf{R}^n$ is a convex set. On the other hand, if $f(\mathbf{x})$ is convex, then the set

$$\mathbf{L}^{\leq} = \{\mathbf{x} \mid \mathbf{x} \in \mathbf{S} \quad \text{and} \quad f(\mathbf{x}) \leq c\}$$

is a convex set. The set $\mathbf{L}^{\geq}$ is called the *upper level set* of $f$ at $c$ and $\mathbf{L}^{\leq}$ is called the *lower level set* of $f$ at $c$.

The function shown in figure 10.6(a) is a concave function. The thick line segment on the $x$-axis is an upper level set $\mathbf{L}^{\geq}$ at $c$, and is a convex set. The function in (b) is a convex function. The lower level set $\mathbf{L}^{\leq}$ at $c$ is a convex set.

**Example 10.29** Consider a concave utility function of two goods, $f(x_1,x_2) = \log x_1 + \log x_2$ for $x_1,x_2 > 0$. The equation

$$f(x_1,x_2) = \log x_1 + \log x_2 = 3$$

implicitly defines an indifference curve (or level curve) at that given level of utility. The indifference curve is plotted below using the **ContourPlot** function. The upper level set $\mathbf{L}^{\geq}$ is the area on and above the indifference curve. $\mathbf{L}^{\geq}$ is a convex set.

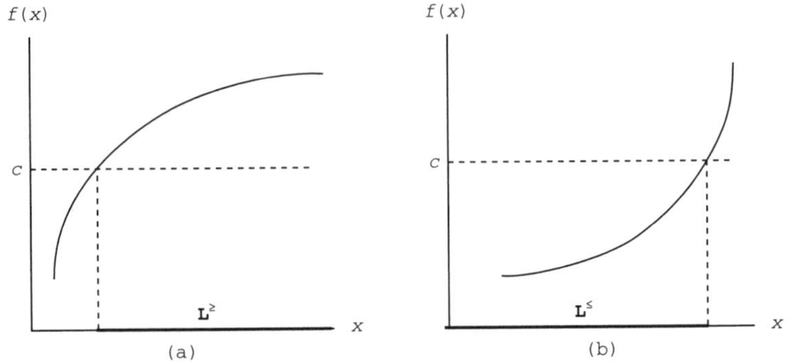


**Figure 10.6** Level sets: (a) upper level set; (b) lower level set

*In[108]:=*

```
Clear[f,x,y];
f[x_,y_]:= Log[x]+Log[y];
ContourPlot[f[x,y],{x,1,10},{y,1,10},Contours->{3},
            Frame->False,ContourShading->False,
            Axes->True,AxesLabel->{"x","y"}];
```

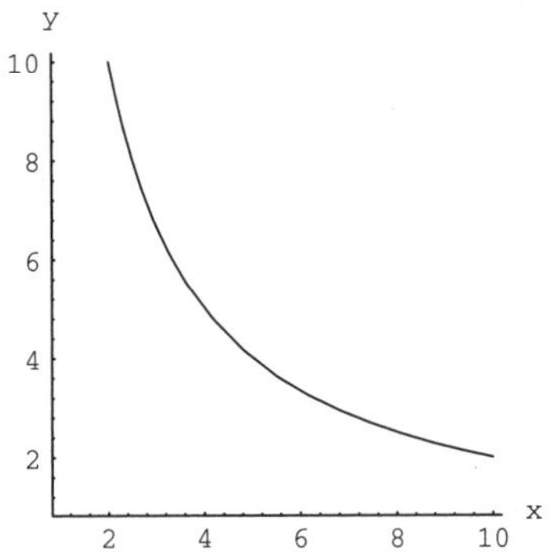


## EXERCISES

1. Suppose the $n \times n$ matrix **A** is positive semidefinite. Is

   $$f(\mathbf{x}) = \mathbf{x}^T \mathbf{A} \mathbf{x} + \mathbf{b} \cdot \mathbf{x} + c$$

   a concave function where **b** is a row vector and $c$ is a scalar?

2. If $f(\mathbf{x})$ and $g(\mathbf{y})$ are convex functions, then is $h(\mathbf{x},\mathbf{y}) = f(\mathbf{x}) + g(\mathbf{y})$ necessarily convex? Give a counterexample.

3. If $f(\mathbf{x}) > 0$ and $f(\mathbf{x})$ is concave on **S**, show that the reciprocal, $g(\mathbf{x}) = 1/f(\mathbf{x})$, is convex on $S$.

# □ 10.4 Quasiconcave and Quasiconvex Functions □

## 10.4.1 Definitions

Consider the illustration in figure 10.7(a). Given any two points, say $x_0$ and $x_1$, consider their corresponding arc (thick line) on the graph of $f$. We observe that

$$f(\theta x_0 + (1-\theta)x_1) \geq \min\{f(x_0), f(x_1)\}$$

for $0 < \theta < 1$. Any point on the graph has the height $f(\theta x_0 + (1-\theta)x_1)$ which is greater than or equal to the smallest of the values at the endpoints of the arc, $f(x_0)$ and $f(x_1)$. Since points on any similar arc cannot be below *both ends* of the arc at the same time, the graph of $f(x)$ cannot have a pit or valley nor can it have two distinct peaks, although it may have one. The function is "unimodal" or "single-humped." A function with this property is called a *quasiconcave function.*

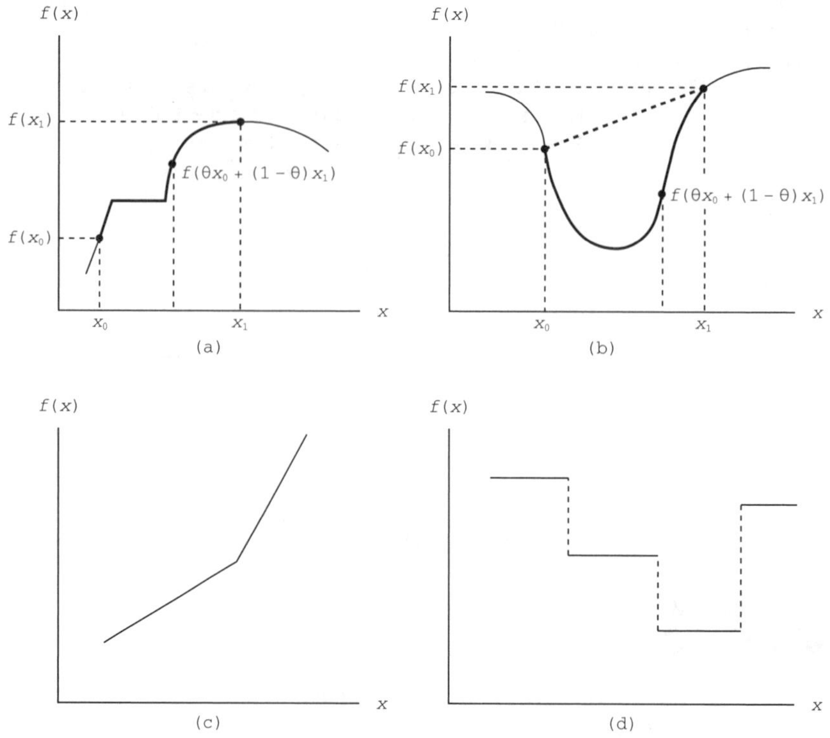


**Figure 10.7** Quasiconcave and quasiconvex functions: (a) quasiconcave; (b) strictly quasiconvex; (c) strictly quasiconcave and strictly quasiconvex; (d) quasiconvex

> **DEFINITION 10.4** *A function of single variable $f(x)$ is called a* ***quasiconcave*** *function on an interval* **S** *if for any two points $x_0$ and $x_1$ in* **S** *and $0 < \theta < 1$,*
>
> $$f(\theta x_0 + (1-\theta)x_1) \geq \min\{f(x_0), f(x_1)\}$$
>
> *Similarly $f(x)$ is called* ***quasiconvex*** *on* **S** *if*
>
> $$f(\theta x_0 + (1-\theta)x_1) \leq \max\{f(x_0), f(x_1)\}$$
>
> *When $x_0 \neq x_1$ and the weak inequalities "≥" and "≤" are changed to strict inequalities ">" and "<", then the function is said to be* ***strictly quasiconcave*** *or* ***strictly quasiconvex*** *on* **S**, *respectively.*

Figure 10.7(a) shows a quasiconcave, but not strictly quasiconcave, function. It is not strict since there exists a part of the graph that contains a flat segment. The function in (b) is both quasiconvex and strictly quasiconvex. Notice that neither the functions in (a) nor in (b) are concave or convex. Convexity and concavity require the comparison of the values of the function on an arc (thick segment) to the values on a chord (thick dashed line) connecting any two points on the graph. On the other hand, quasiconvexity and quasiconcavity compare the values of the function on an arc to only the values on the *ends* of the arc. It is in this sense that quasiconvexity and quasiconcavity are less restrictive requirements on a function than convexity and concavity. The function in (c) is both strictly quasiconcave and strictly quasiconvex. The quasiconvex function in (d) is not even continuous at certain points.

**Example 10.30** $f(x) = 1/x$ for $x > 0$ is both strictly quasiconcave and strictly quasiconvex. If $x_0 < x_1$, then

$$\min\{f(x_0), f(x_1)\} = \min\left\{\frac{1}{x_0}, \frac{1}{x_1}\right\} = \frac{1}{x_1};$$

$$\max\{f(x_0), f(x_1)\} = \max\left\{\frac{1}{x_0}, \frac{1}{x_1}\right\} = \frac{1}{x_0}.$$

Since

$$f(\theta x_0 + (1-\theta)x_1) = \frac{1}{\theta x_0 + (1-\theta)x_1} > \frac{1}{\theta x_1 + (1-\theta)x_1} = \frac{1}{x_1}$$

$f(x)$ is strictly quasiconcave on $x > 0$. Similarly,

$$f(\theta x_0 + (1-\theta)x_1) = \frac{1}{\theta x_0 + (1-\theta)x_1} < \frac{1}{\theta x_0 + (1-\theta)x_0} = \frac{1}{x_0}$$

and therefore, $f(x)$ is strictly quasiconvex on $x > 0$.

**Example 10.31** The function,

$$f(x) = \begin{cases} \log x, \ 0 < x \le 2 \\ \log 2, \ 2 < x \le 3 \\ \log(x-1), \ 3 < x \end{cases}$$

is quasiconcave, but not strictly quasiconcave since its graph contains a flat segement as shown in the following plot. The values of the function on the flat portion of the arc are equal to, but not larger than, the value at the endpoint of the arc.

*In[111]:=*

```
Clear[f,x];
f[x_ /; 0<x<=2]:= Log[x];
f[x_ /; 2<x<=3]:= Log[2];
f[x_ /; x>3]:= Log[x-1];
domain = {x,1,4}; segment = {x,2.5,3.5};
explicit = arc2d[f[x],domain,segment];
Show[explicit,Axes->True,AxesLabel->{"x","f(x)"}];
```

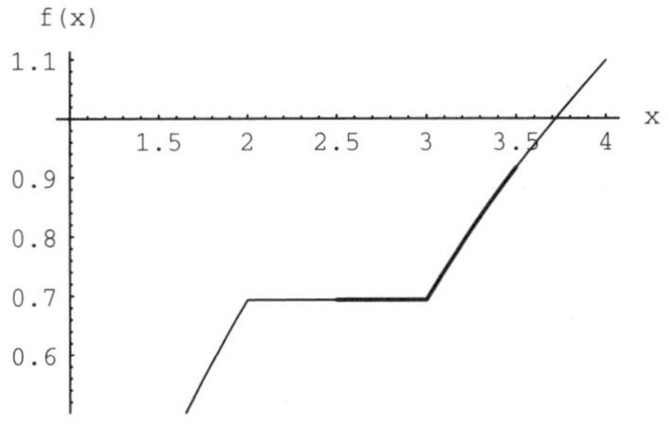

**Example 10.32** The function $f(x) = x^2/(1+x^2)$ is strictly quasiconvex on the interval $\mathbf{S} = [-5,2]$. We illustrate this for specific choices of $x_0$ and $x_1$. Choose $x_0 = -4$ and $x_1 = 0.5$, in **S** and observe that

$$f(\theta x_0 + (1-\theta)x_1) < \max\{f(x_0), f(x_1)\} = f(-4).$$

Here is the picture in this case.

*In[118]:=*
```
Clear[f,x];
f[x_]:= x^2/(1+x^2);
domain = {x,-5,2}; segment = {x,-4,0.5};
Show[arc2d[f[x],domain,segment],
        Axes->True,AxesLabel->{"x","f(x)"}];
```

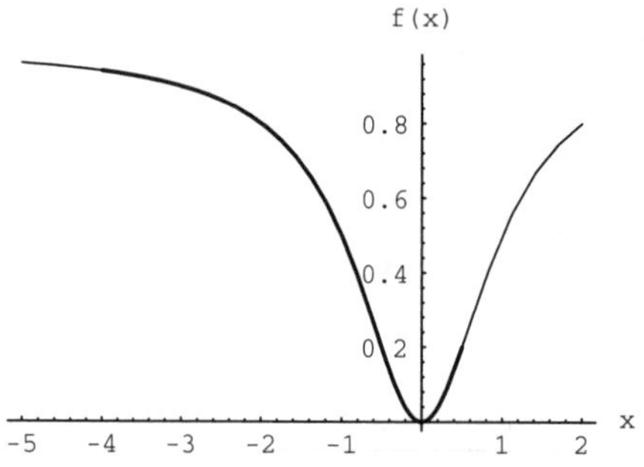


The quasiconcavity and quasiconvexity of functions of more than one variable can be similarly defined.

> **DEFINITION 10.5** *A function* $f(\mathbf{x}) = f(x_1, x_2, \ldots, x_n)$ *defined on a convex set* **S** *is called* ***quasiconcave*** *on* **S** *if for any two points* $\mathbf{x}_0$ *and* $\mathbf{x}_1$ *in* **S**, *we have*
>
> $$f(\theta \mathbf{x}_0 + (1-\theta)\mathbf{x}_1) \geq \min\{f(\mathbf{x}_0), f(\mathbf{x}_1)\}$$
>
> *for* $0 < \theta < 1$. *Similarly* $f(\mathbf{x})$ *is* ***quasiconvex*** *on* **S** *if*
>
> $$f(\theta \mathbf{x}_0 + (1-\theta)\mathbf{x}_1) \leq \max\{f(\mathbf{x}_0), f(\mathbf{x}_1)\}$$
>
> *Furthermore, the function is said to be* ***strictly quasiconcave*** *on* **S** *if for each* $\mathbf{x}_0, \mathbf{x}_1 \in \mathbf{S}$ *with* $\mathbf{x}_0 \neq \mathbf{x}_1$, *we have*
>
> $$f(\theta \mathbf{x}_0 + (1-\theta)\mathbf{x}_1) > \min\{f(\mathbf{x}_0), f(\mathbf{x}_1)\}$$
>
> *and is said to be* ***strictly quasiconvex*** *on* **S** *if*
>
> $$f(\theta \mathbf{x}_0 + (1-\theta)\mathbf{x}_1) < \max\{f(\mathbf{x}_0), f(\mathbf{x}_1)\}$$

**Example 10.33** Consider the function of two variables,

$$f(x) = \begin{cases} -4(x^2 + y^2) + 2,\ 0 \le \sqrt{x^2 + y^2} \le 1 \\ -2,\ 1 < \sqrt{x^2 + y^2} \le 2 \\ -3(x^2 + y^2) + 10,\ 2 < \sqrt{x^2 + y^2} \end{cases}$$

The following *Mathematica* plot shows the surface and an arc (thick line) running from $(x_0,y_0) = (0.3,0.3)$ to $(x_1,y_1) = (1.3,1.3)$ along the straight line $x = y$.

*In[122]:=*

```
Clear[f,x,y];
f[x_,y_ /; x^2+y^2<=1]:= -4(x^2+y^2)+2;
f[x_,y_ /; 1<Sqrt[x^2+y^2]<=2]:= -2;
f[x_,y_ /; 2<Sqrt[x^2+y^2]]:= -3(x^2+y^2)+10;
quasiconcave = Plot3D[f[x,y],{x,0,2.3},{y,0,2.3},
                      PlotRange->{-20,2},
                      DisplayFunction->Identity];
arc = ParametricPlot3D[{x,x,f[x,x],
                      Thickness[0.01]},{x,0.3,1.3},
                      DisplayFunction->Identity];
Show[quasiconcave,arc,
                      ViewPoint->{0.230, 3.470, 1.100},
                      AxesLabel->{"x","y","f(x,y)"},
                      DisplayFunction->$DisplayFunction];
```

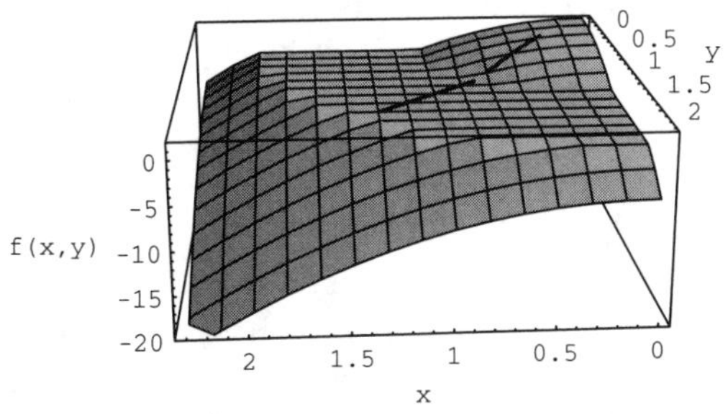


Every point on the arc portion of the graph, even on the flat part of the surface, has a value larger than or equal to the value at the lower end of the arc, $f(1.3,1.3) = -2$. Thus, for any two points, $\mathbf{x}_0$ and $\mathbf{x}_1$,

$$f(\theta\,\mathbf{x}_0 + (1-\theta)\,\mathbf{x}_1) \ge \min\{f(\mathbf{x}_0), f(\mathbf{x}_1)\}$$

for $0 < \theta < 1$. Hence, we conclude that the function is quasiconcave. Furthermore, for two distinct points $\mathbf{x}_0 \ne \mathbf{x}_1$ that are both on the flat part of the surface (where the values of the function are equal), the condition for strict quasiconcavity, $f(\theta\,\mathbf{x}_0 + (1-\theta)\,\mathbf{x}_1) > \min\{f(\mathbf{x}_0), f(\mathbf{x}_1)\}$, is not satisfied. The following plot shows the arc connecting $\mathbf{x}_0 = (x_0,y_0) = (0.5,1.5)$ and $\mathbf{x}_1 = (x_1,y_1) = (1.5,0.5)$ on the straight line $y = 2 - x$. We have $f(\theta\,\mathbf{x}_0 + (1-\theta)\,\mathbf{x}_1) = f(\mathbf{x}_0) = f(\mathbf{x}_1)$.

*In[129]:=*

```
arc = ParametricPlot3D[{x,2-x,f[x,2-x],
                      Thickness[0.01]},{x,0.5,1.5},
                      DisplayFunction->Identity];
```

```
Show[quasiconcave,arc,
                              ViewPoint->{0.230, 3.470, 1.100},
                              AxesLabel->{"x","y","f(x,y)"},
                              DisplayFunction->$DisplayFunction];
```

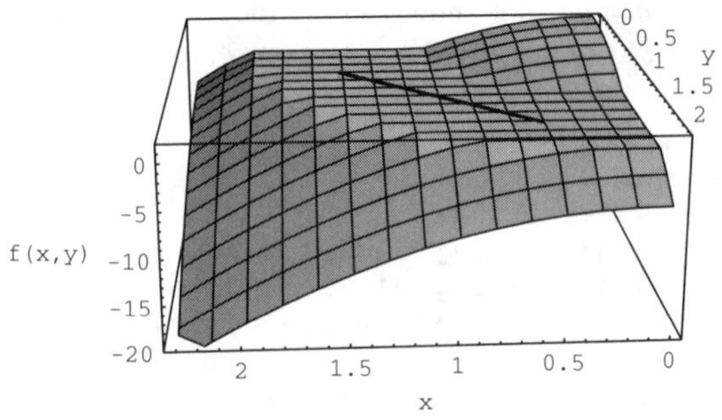


**Example 10.34** A function of the form

$$f(\mathbf{x}) = \frac{1}{\sqrt{2\pi\,|\mathbf{A}|}} e^{(-\frac{1}{2}\mathbf{x}^T\mathbf{A}^{-1}\mathbf{x})}; \quad \text{for} \quad \mathbf{x} \in \mathbf{R}^n$$

is called a *multivariate normal* density function with the symmetric (nonsingular) *correlation matrix* A. It is known that $f(\mathbf{x})$ is strictly quasiconcave. We illustrate its strict quasiconcavity with two variables, $\mathbf{x} = (x,y)$ and the correlation matrix

$$\mathbf{A} = \begin{bmatrix} 1.0 & 0.8 \\ 0.8 & 1.0 \end{bmatrix}$$

Let us pick two distinct points, $(x_0,y_0) = (-1.0,-0.8)$ and $(x_1,y_1) = (1,-1.2)$. The *Mathematica* plot below shows the the surface and the arc (thick curve) running from $(x_0,y_0)$ to $(x_1,y_1)$ along straight line $y = -1 - 0.2x$. (Note: In the **ParametricPlot3D** statement below, a constant 0.01 is added to the function **f**[x,–1–0.2x]. The purpose of adding the constant is to raise the arc line in plotting so that it will be visible above the surface when the two graphs are combined in the **Show** function.)

*In[131]:=*

```
Clear[f,x,y,A];
A  =  {{1,0.8},{0.8,1}};
f[x_,y_]:=  Exp[-0.5{x,y}.Inverse[A].{x,y}]/
               (Sqrt[2*Pi*Det[A]]);
surface  =  Plot3D[f[x,y],{x,-1.5,1.5},{y,-1.5,1.5},
                        AxesLabel->{"x","y","f(x,y)"},
                        DisplayFunction->Identity];
arc  =  ParametricPlot3D[{x,-1-0.2x,f[x,-1-0.2x]+0.01,
                      Thickness[0.01]},{x,-1,1},
                      DisplayFunction->Identity];
Show[surface,arc,ViewPoint->{-2.210,  -3.810,  1.170},
                        DisplayFunction->$DisplayFunction];
```

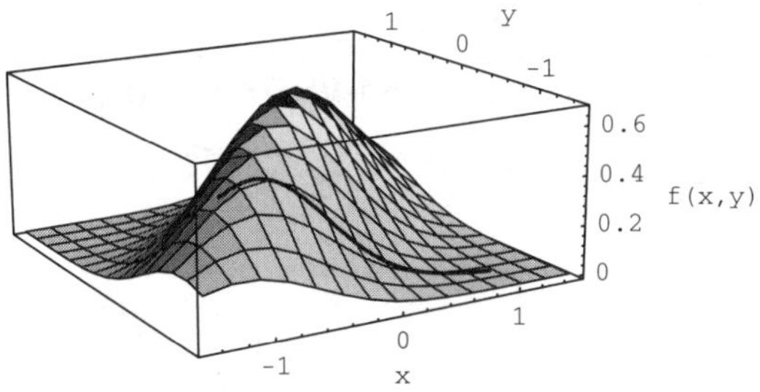


Every point on the arc is higher than the lower end of the arc which is at $(x_1,y_1) = (1,-1.2)$. Thus the bivariate normal density is strictly quasiconcave. Imagining a chord connecting the two endpoints, we can see that the arc is neither entirely above nor below the chord. The bivariate normal density is neither convex nor concave.

From the definition of quasiconcavity and quasiconvexity, the following properties are readily proven.

*Property 1* All concave (convex) functions are quasiconcave (quasiconvex). Similarly, all strictly concave (convex) functions are strictly quasiconcave (quasiconvex). However, the converse of these statements does not hold. For example, suppose $f(\mathbf{x})$ is concave and at the points $\mathbf{x}_0$ and $\mathbf{x}_1$, we have $f(\mathbf{x}_0) \leq f(\mathbf{x}_1)$. Then, for $0 < \theta < 1$, the concavity implies that

$$\begin{aligned} f(\theta\mathbf{x}_0 + (1-\theta)\mathbf{x}_1) &\geq \theta f(\mathbf{x}_0) + (1-\theta)f(\mathbf{x}_1) \\ &\geq \theta f(\mathbf{x}_0) + (1-\theta)f(\mathbf{x}_0) \\ &= f(\mathbf{x}_0) \\ &= \min\{f(\mathbf{x}_0), f(\mathbf{x}_1)\} \end{aligned}$$

Thus the concave function $f(\mathbf{x})$ is also quasiconcave.

*Property 2* If $f(\mathbf{x})$ is (strictly) quasiconcave, then $-f(\mathbf{x})$ is (strictly) quasiconvex.

*Property 3* Any increasing (decreasing) function is both quasiconcave and quasiconvex. Thus a linear function is both quasiconcave and quasiconvex.

*Property 4* Any nondecreasing function of a quasiconcave function is also quasiconcave. For example, the CES production function

$$q = (ax_1^b + (1-a)\,x_2^b)^{1/b}, \; 0 < x_i, \; 0 < a < 1$$

is concave and hence, quasiconcave for $b \leq 1$. The monotonic nondecreasing function

$$F(q) = q^r = (ax_1^b + (1-a)x_2^b)^{r/b}, \; r > 0$$

is quasiconcave. Since $F(q)$ is a homogeneous function of degree $r$, the qausiconcave production function allows increasing returns to scale when $r > 1$.

There is another category of quasiconcave and quasiconvex functions that we want to define.

**DEFINITION 10.6** *A function $f(\mathbf{x})$ defined on a convex set* **S** *is said to be* ***explicitly quasiconcave*** *on* **S** *if for each $\mathbf{x}_0, \mathbf{x}_1 \in$* **S** *with $f(\mathbf{x}_0) \neq f(\mathbf{x}_1)$, we have*

$$f(\theta\,\mathbf{x}_0 + (1-\theta)\,\mathbf{x}_1) > \min\{f(\mathbf{x}_0), f(\mathbf{x}_1)\}$$

*for $0 < \theta < 1$. Similarly, $f(\mathbf{x})$ is* ***explicitly quasiconvex*** *on* **S** *if for each $\mathbf{x}_0, \mathbf{x}_1 \in$* **S** *with $f(\mathbf{x}_0) \neq f(\mathbf{x}_1)$, we have*

$$f(\theta\,\mathbf{x}_0 + (1-\theta)\,\mathbf{x}_1) < \max\{f(\mathbf{x}_0), f(\mathbf{x}_1)\}$$

*for $0 < \theta < 1$.*

The distinction between the "strict" and "explicit" cases of quasiconcavity and quasiconvexity lies in certain provisions given in definition 10.5 and definition 10.6. In both cases, all values of $f(\theta\,\mathbf{x}_0 + (1-\theta)\,\mathbf{x}_1)$ are compared to the endpoints of the arc, $f(\mathbf{x}_0)$ and $f(\mathbf{x}_1)$. However, in the "strict" case, the definition requires that the *endpoints* be distinct points, $\mathbf{x}_0 \neq \mathbf{x}_1$, while in the "explicit" case, the definition requires that the *values* of the function at the endpoints be distinct, $f(\mathbf{x}_0) \neq f(\mathbf{x}_1)$.

**Example 10.35** Consider the piecewise function

$$f(x) = \begin{cases} x^3 - x, & 1 \le x \le 2 \\ 6, & 2 < x < 3 \\ 54/x^2, & 3 \le x \end{cases}$$

We plot the graph $f(x)$ and highlight the segment for $1.5 \le x \le 2.5$.

*In[137]:=*

```
Clear[f,x];
f[x_ /; 1<=x<=2]:= x^3-x;
f[x_ /; 2<x<3]:= 6;
f[x_ /; 3<=x]:= 54/x^2;
domain = {x,1,4}; segment = {x,1.5,2.5};
explicit = arc2d[f[x],domain,segment];
Show[explicit,Axes->True,AxesLabel->{"x","f(x)"}];
```

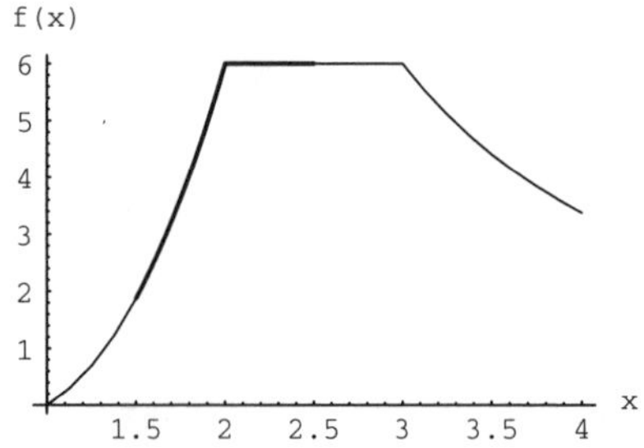


With $x_0 = 1.5$ and $x_1 = 2.5$, every point on the arc is larger than $f(x_0)$. Therefore, $f(x)$ is explicitly quasiconcave. However, consider a point $x$ that lies between two distinct points $x_0$ and $x_1$ on the flat top. We would then have $f(x_0) = f(x) = f(x_1)$. The function is therefore not strictly quasiconcave.

**Example 10.36** The function

$$f(x,y) = \begin{cases} 10x + 2y + 6, & x \le y \\ 2x + 10y + 6, & y < x \end{cases}$$

is explicitly quasiconcave but not strictly quasiconcave for all $-\infty < x,y < \infty$. We can see this by plotting the graph of $f$ and mark the graph along the line $y = x - 1$ in its domain.

*In[144]:=*
```
Clear[f,x,y];
f[x_,y_]:= 10*x+2*y+6 /; x<=y;
f[x_,y_]:= 2*x+10*y+6 /; y<x;
explicit = Plot3D[f[x,y],{x,0,5},{y,0,5},
                  DisplayFunction->Identity];
arc = ParametricPlot3D[{1+y,y,f[1+y,y],
                        Thickness[0.01]},{y,1,3},
                        DisplayFunction->Identity];
Show[explicit,arc,
                ViewPoint->{-1.170, -4.000, 0.960},
                AxesLabel->{"x","y","z"},
                 DisplayFunction->$DisplayFunction];
```

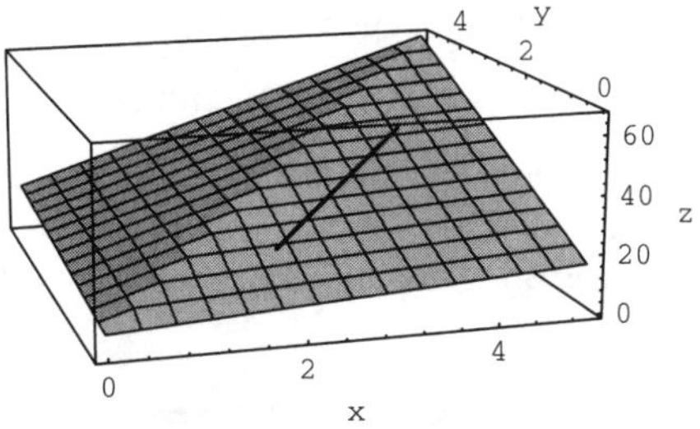


Let us pick any two points, say $(x_0,y_0) = (2,1)$ and $(x_1,y_1) = (4,3)$. Then $f(x_0,y_0) = 20 \neq f(x_1,y_1) = 44$. The arc is a straight line shown on the surface $f(x,y) = 2x + 10y + 6$. Points on this arc have the property that

$$\begin{aligned} &f(\theta x_0 + (1-\theta)x_1, \theta y_0 + (1-\theta)y_1) \\ &\quad = 2(\theta x_0 + (1-\theta)x_1) + 10(\theta y_0 + (1-\theta)y_1) + 6 \\ &\quad = 2(2\theta + 4(1-\theta)) + 10(\theta + 3(1-\theta)) + 6 \\ &\quad = 44 - 24\theta > \min\{f(x_0,y_0), f(x_1,y_1)\} = 20 \end{aligned}$$

for $0 < \theta < 1$. Therefore, $f(x,y)$ is explicitly quasiconcave. However, it is not strictly quasiconcave. For two other distinct points, say $(x_0,y_0) = (2,0.6)$ and $(x_1,y_1) = (3,0.4)$, such that $f(x_0,y_0) = f(x_1,y_1) = 16$, then we have

$$f(\theta x_0 + (1-\theta)x_1, \theta y_0 + (1-\theta)y_1) = \min\{f(x_0,y_0), f(x_1,y_1)\} = 16$$

which violates the strict inequality provision for strict quasiconcavity.

An important remark about these definitions is in order here. In some mathematics textbooks, strictly quasiconcave and strictly quasiconvex functions given in definition

10.5 are sometimes called *strongly quasiconcave* and *strongly quasiconvex* functions; and the explictly quasiconcave functions and explictly quasiconvex functions defined in definition 10.6 are then called *strictly quasiconcave* and *strictly quasiconvex* functions. However, we shall use definitions 10.5 and 10.6 as they are commonly used in economic literature.

## EXERCISES

1. Are the following functions quasiconcave, quasiconvex, both, or neither? Use the function **arc2d** to confirm your answers.
   (a) $f(x) = \dfrac{1}{1+e^{-3x}}, \qquad -\infty < x < \infty.$
   (b) $f(x) = xe^{-x}, \qquad x > 0.$
   (c) $f(x) = x + \log(x), \quad x > 0.$

2. Show that $f(x) = x^3$ and $g(x) = -3x$ are both quasiconcave for all $x$, but $h(x) = f(x) + g(x) = x^3 - 3x$ is not.

3. Prove that any monotonic increasing (or decreasing) function is quasiconcave.

4. Prove that any monotonic nondecreasing function of a quasiconcave function is also quasiconcave.

### 10.4.2 Level sets, quasiconcavity, and quasiconvexity

Analogous to the characterization of concave and convex functions in terms of the hypograph $\mathbf{C}^{\geq}$ and the epigraph $\mathbf{C}^{\leq}$ in section 10.1.3, quasiconcave and quasiconvex functions can be characterized in terms of level sets $\mathbf{L}^{\geq}$ and $\mathbf{L}^{\leq}$.

**THEOREM 10.6** *Let $f(\mathbf{x})$ be defined on a convex set $\mathbf{S}$ in $\mathbf{R}^n$. The function is quasiconcave on $\mathbf{S}$ if and only if the upper level set*

$$\mathbf{L}^{\geq} = \{\mathbf{x} \mid \mathbf{x} \in \mathbf{S}, f(\mathbf{x}) \geq c\}$$

*is convex for any real number c. The function is quasiconvex on $\mathbf{S}$ if and only if the lower level set*

$$\mathbf{L}^{\leq} = \{\mathbf{x} \mid \mathbf{x} \in \mathbf{S}, f(\mathbf{x}) \leq c\}$$

*is convex for any real number c.*

**Example 10.37** Figure 10.8 depicts the graph of the function

$$f(x) = e^{-0.2x^2}$$

and the upper level set at $c = 0.6$,

$$\mathbf{L}^{\geq} = \{x \mid e^{-0.2x^2} \geq 0.6, -\infty < x < \infty\}$$

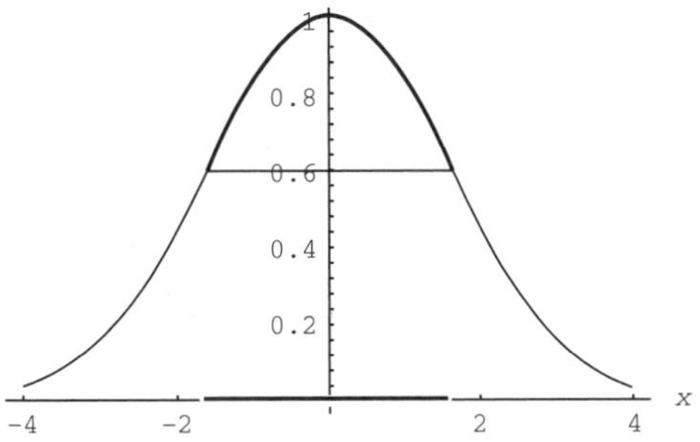


**Figure 10.8** Quasiconcave and upper-level set L

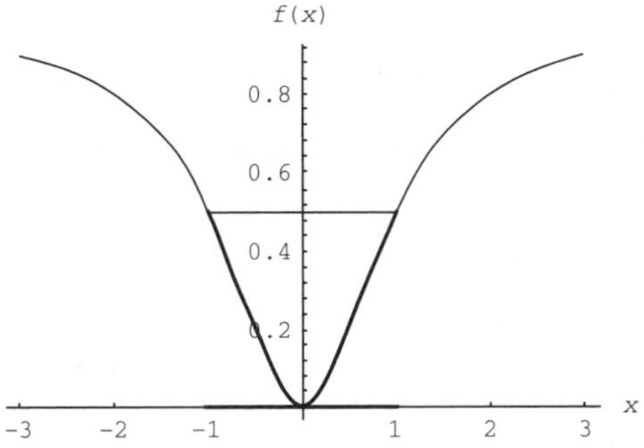


**Figure 10.9** Quasiconvex and lower-level set L

$\mathbf{L}^{\geq}$ consists of points on the thick line segment on the $x$-axis. It is a convex set. In fact, $\mathbf{L}^{\geq}$ is convex for any value $c$. Therefore, $f(x)$ is quasiconcave on **R**.

**Example 10.38** In figure 10.9 the graph of

$$f(x) = \frac{x^2}{x^2 + 1}$$

is shown. This function is quasiconvex on **R** since $\mathbf{L}^{\leq}$ is a convex set. At $c = 0.5$, for example, $\mathbf{L}^{\leq}$ is the line interval $[-1,1]$ which is a convex set.

**Example 10.39** The function $f(x) = x^3 + x^2 - 2x + 2$ for $-\infty < x < \infty$, is neither a quasiconcave nor a quaisconvex function. Let $c = 2$. We plot the function $g(x) = f(x) - c$.

*In[150]:=*

```
Clear[f,g,x];
c = 2;
f[x_]:= x^3+x^2-2*x+2;
g[x_]:= f[x]-c;
Plot[g[x],{x,-2.5,2},AxesLabel->{"x","g(x)"}];
```

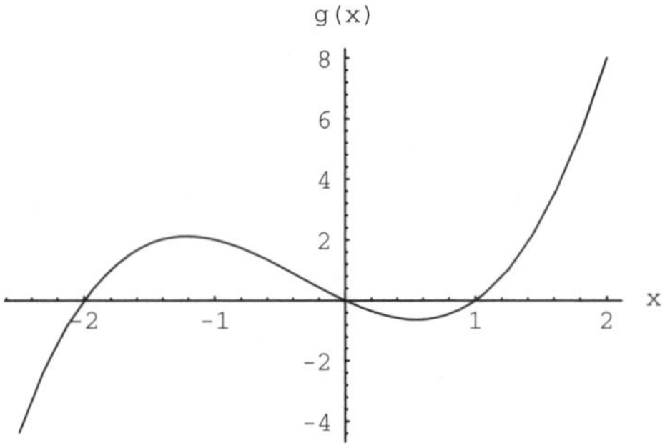


$\mathbf{L}^{\geq}$ consists of two disjointed line segments on the $x$-axis. These segments are union of intervals on the $x$-axis such that $g(x) = f(x) - c \geq 0$:

$$\begin{aligned}\mathbf{L}^{\geq} &= \{x \mid f(x) - 2 \geq 0\} \\ &= \{x \mid -2 \leq x \leq 0\} \cup \{x \mid 1 \leq x < \infty\}\end{aligned}$$

where $\cup$ denotes the union of the two sets. Since $\mathbf{L}^{\geq}$ is not convex, the function is not a quasiconcave function. Similarly, the lower level set

$$\begin{aligned}\mathbf{L}^{\leq} &= \{x \mid f(x) - 2 \leq 0\} \\ &= \{x \mid -\infty \leq x \leq -2\} \cup \{x \mid 0 \leq x \leq 1\}\end{aligned}$$

is not a convex set. This function is not quasiconvex on **R**.

**Example 10.40** Consider the function

$$f(x,y) = \frac{x^2\,y^2}{(1+x^2)(1+y^2)}$$

which is defined on $\mathbf{S} = \{\,(x,y) \mid x,y \geq 0\}$. This function is quasiconcave on **S**. To show this, we plot the function, and the plane $z = 2$ to show an upper level set $\mathbf{L}^{\geq}$.

*In[155]:=*

```
Clear[f,x,y];
c  =  0.2;
f[x_,y_]:=  (x^2  y^2)/((1+x^2)(1+y^2));
surface  =  Plot3D[f[x,y],{x,0,2},{y,0,2},
                DisplayFunction->Identity];
cutter  =  Plot3D[c,{x,0,2},{y,0,2},
                DisplayFunction->Identity];
Show[surface,cutter,AxesLabel->{"x","y","z"},
               ViewPoint->{3.296,  0.000,  0.764},
               DisplayFunction->$DisplayFunction];
```

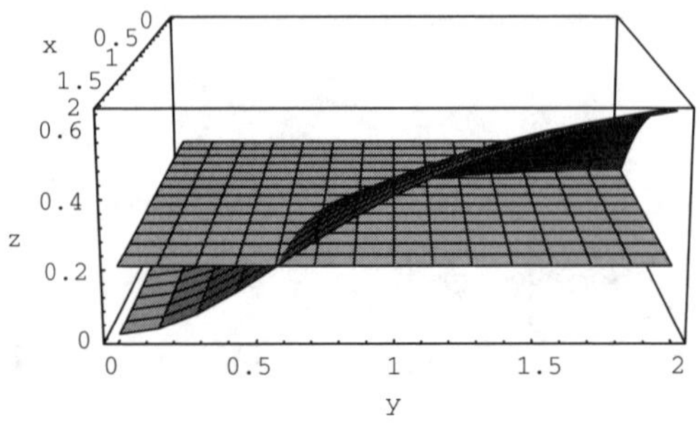

The upper level set $\mathbf{L}^{\geq}$ corresponding to $c = 0.2$ is the collection of $(x,y)$ such that the surface of $f(x,y)$ lies above the flat plane. Analytically, this set is

$$\mathbf{L}^{\geq} = \left\{(x,y) \mid x,y \geq 0, \frac{x^2 y^2}{(1+x^2)(1+y^2)} \geq c\right\}$$

As can be seen from the above plot, the upper level set $\mathbf{L}^{\geq}$ is convex. Thus the function is quasiconcave, although it is not concave.

The level curves of a function $f(x,y)$, $\{ (x,y) \mid f(x,y) = c\}$, can be displayed using the **ContourPlot** function. The following picture shows level curves at five different $c$ values. The areas with higher $f(x,y)$ values are shaded lighter. Each upper level curve defines a level set $\mathbf{L}^{\geq}$ which is the area to the right of each level curve. Since all level sets are convex, the function $f(x,y)$ must be quasiconcave.

*In[161]:=*
```
Clear[f,x,y];
f[x_,y_]:= (x^2 y^2)/((1+x^2)(1+y^2));
c = {0.1,0.2,0.3,0.4,0.5};
ContourPlot[f[x,y],{x,0,2},{y,0,2},Contours->c,
            Frame->False,Axes->True,
            AxesLabel-<{"x","y"}];
```

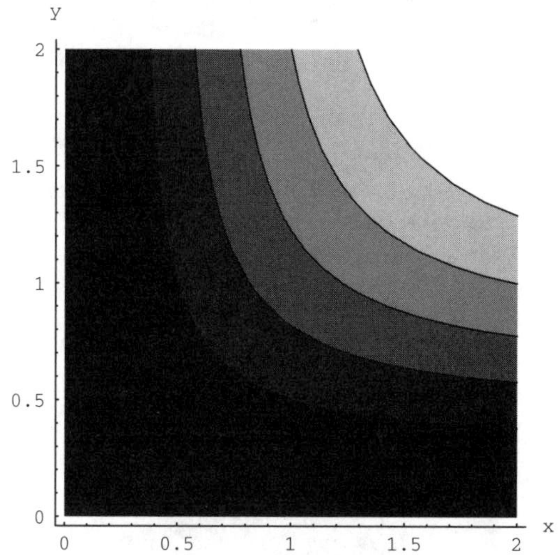


**Example 10.41** The function $f(x,y) = x^2 - \log y$ defined on the set $\mathbf{S} = \{ (x,y) \mid x \in R, y > 0\}$, is quasiconvex, but not quasiconcave on its domain. This can be seen by viewing the graph of $f$ and the cutting plane, $z = 1$.

*In[165]:=*
```
Clear[f,x,y];
c = 1;
f[x_,y_]:= x^2 - Log[y];
surface = Plot3D[f[x,y],{x,-3,3},{y,0.1,3},
                 DisplayFunction->Identity];
cutter = Plot3D[c,{x,-3,3},{y,0.1,3},
                 DisplayFunction->Identity];
```

```
Show[surface,cutter,ViewPoint->{1.046,  2.768,  1.642},
                   AxesLabel->{"x","y","z"},
                    DisplayFunction->$DisplayFunction];
```

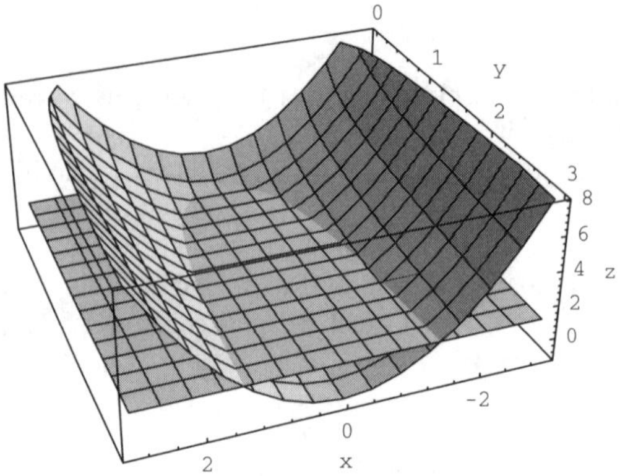


The U-shape lower level set $\mathbf{L}^{\leq}$ at $c = 1$ shown in the plot is convex. Hence the function $f(x,y)$ is quasiconvex. However, the upper level set $\mathbf{L}^{\geq}$, which is outside of the U-shape area, is not convex and hence the function is not quasiconcave. Four level curves are plotted below for $c = 0.5$, 1, 2, and 3. Since the areas with smaller $f(x,y)$ values are darker, the lower level set $\mathbf{L}^{\leq}$ is the shaded area above the associate level curve. Since all lower level sets are convex, the function $f(x,y)$ must be quasiconcave.

*In[171]:=*
```
c  =  {0.5,1,2,3};
ContourPlot[f[x,y],{x,-3,3},{y,0.05,3},Contours->c,
            Frame->False,Axes->True,
            AxesLabel->{"x","y"}];
```

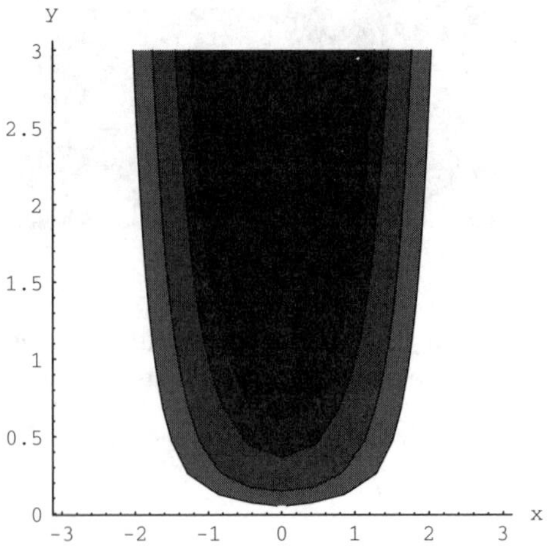


The set

$\mathbf{L}^{=} = \{\mathbf{x} \mid \mathbf{x} \in \mathbf{S}, f(\mathbf{x}) = c\}$

is called a *level surface*. Indifference curves in a utility function and isoquant curves in a production function are examples of level surfaces.

**Example 10.42** Suppose $f(x,y)$ in example 10.40 represents a consumer utility function. Thus a quasiconcave utility function implies the convexity of the upper level sets $\mathbf{L}^{\geq}$ and the convexity of the indifference curves $\mathbf{L}^{=}$. Conversely, if all upper level sets and indifference curves are convex to the origin, then the ultility function must be quasiconcave. We explain below what we mean by convex to the origin.

A strictly quasiconcave or strictly quasiconvex function will have its level surface or curve either "bend-in" or "bend-out" toward the origin. The function

$$f(x,y) = \frac{x^2 y^2}{(1+x^2)(1+y^2)}$$

given in example 10.40 is strictly quasiconcave for $x,y \geq 0$. The level curves strictly "bend-in" toward the orgin (0,0) as shown in the plot of its contours. An explictly, but not strictly, quasiconcave or quasiconvex function has level surfaces or curves that contain linear segments. The function given in example 10.36 in section 10.4.1,

$$f(x,y) = \begin{cases} 10x + 2y + 6, & x \leq y \\ 2x + 10y + 6, & x > y \end{cases}$$

is explicitly, but not strictly, quasiconcave on $\mathbf{R}^2$. A level curve is plotted below for $c =$ 40 and it contains linear segments, which reflect the flatness of the functional surface.

*In[173]:=*
```
Clear[f,x,y];
f[x_,y_]:=  10*x+2*y+6  /;  x<=y
f[x_,y_]:=  2*x+10*y+6  /;  y<x
ContourPlot[f[x,y],{x,2,5},{y,2,5},Contours->{40},
              Frame->False,ContourShading->False,
              Axes->True,AxesLabel->{"x","y"}];
```

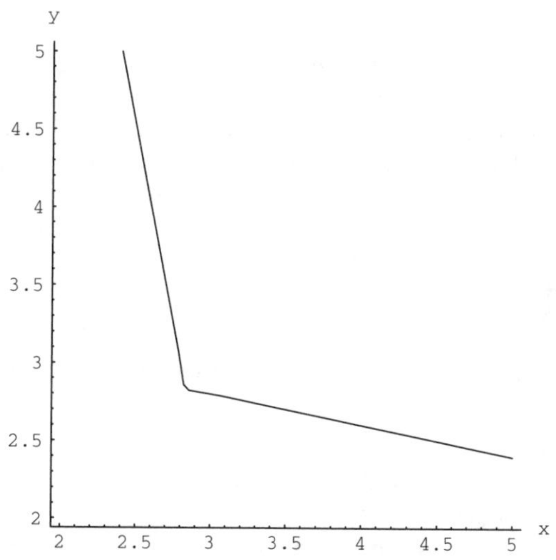

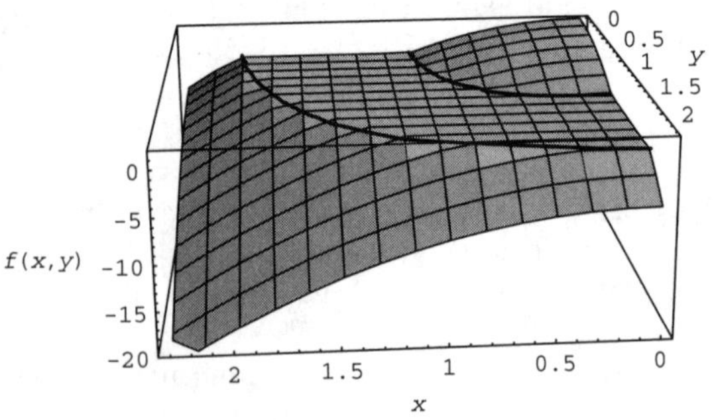


**Figure 10.10** A plane between two curves

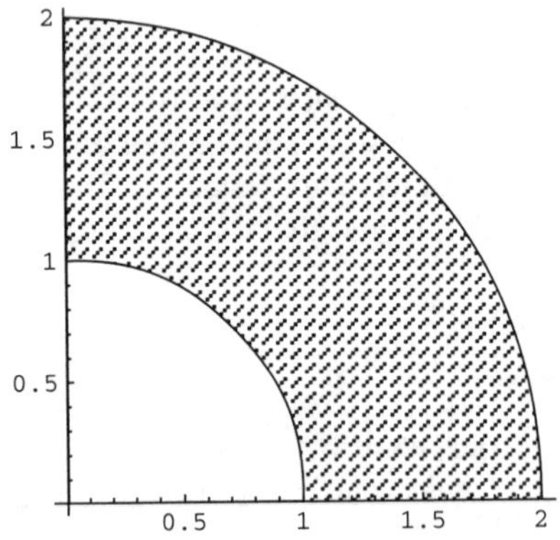


**Figure 10.11** Level set L

The function given in example 10.33 in section 10.4.1,

$$f(x,y) = \begin{cases} -4(x^2 + y^2) + 2, 0 \leq \sqrt{x^2 + y^2} < 1 \\ -2, 1 \leq \sqrt{x^2 + y^2} \leq 2 \\ -3(x^2 + y^2) + 10, 2 < \sqrt{x^2 + y^2} \end{cases}$$

is quasiconcave on $\mathbf{R}^2$, but is neither explicitly nor strictly quasiconcave. The level surface at $f(x,y) = -2$ is a plane within the two curves shown in figure 10.10.

The projection of the level surface on the *xy*-plane, or the level curve at $c = -2$ therefore contains a "band" as shown in shaded area of figure 10.11. Any point $(x,y)$ within the band or region has the property that $f(x,y) = 2$.

## EXERCISES

1. Plot the upper and lower level sets of the following functions:
   (a) $f(x) = \dfrac{1}{1+e^{-3x}}$, $\quad -\infty < x < \infty$.
   (b) $f(x) = xe^{-x}$, $\quad x > 0$.
   (c) $f(x) = x + \log(x)$, $\quad x > 0$.
   Are the functions quasiconcave, quasiconvex, both, or neither?

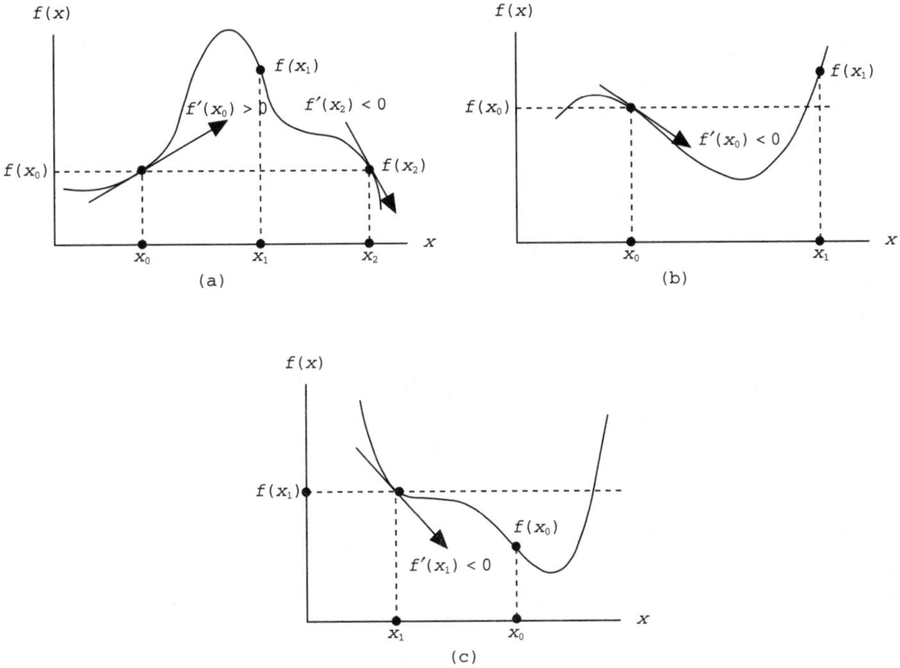


**Figure 10.12** Quasiconcave and quasiconvex:
(a) quasiconcave: $f'(x_0)(x_1 - x_0) > 0$; (b) not quasiconcave: $f'(x_0)(x_1 - x_0) < 0$;
(c) quasiconvex: $f'(x_1)(x_0 - x_1) < 0$

2. Use the **ContourPlot** function to determine if the following functions are quasiconcave, quasiconvex, both, or neither:
   (a) $f(x,y) = \log(x+y), \quad x,y \geq 0.$
   (b) $f(x,y) = x^2y^2, \quad -\infty < x,y < \infty.$
   (c) $f(x,y) = 3$

## □ 10.5 Differentiable Quasiconcave and Quasiconvex Functions □

The function depicted in figure 10.12(a) is quasiconcave. The upper level set

$$\mathbf{L}^{\geq} = \{x \mid -\infty < x < \infty, f(x) \geq c\}$$

is a convex set. Let $x_0$ be a point on the level curve, i.e., $c = f(x_0)$, and consider the tangent line to the graph of $f$ at $x_0$. Suppose $x_1 \in \mathbf{L}^{\geq}$, i.e., $f(x_1) \geq f(x_0) = c$. Since $x_1$ is on the "right" of $x_0$, or $x_1 - x_0 \geq 0$, the slope of the tangent line must point toward the direction of increasing $f(x)$, or $f'(x_0) \geq 0$. Hence, $f'(x_0)(x_1 - x_0) \geq 0$. On the other hand, if $f(x_1) \geq f(x_2)$ and $x_1$ is on the "left" of $x_2$, or $x_1 - x_2 \leq 0$, then the slope of $f(x)$ at $x_2$ is nonpositive, i.e., $f'(x_2) \leq 0$. Hence, $f'(x_2)(x_1 - x_2) \geq 0$. This is not the case in figure 10.12(b). The function is not quasiconcave since the upper level set

$$\mathbf{L}^{\geq} = \{x \mid -\infty < x < \infty, f(x) \geq f(x_0) = c\}$$

is not convex. At point $x_1$, $f(x_1) > f(x_0)$ and $(x_1 - x_0) > 0$, but $f'(x_0)(x_1 - x_0) < 0$. The slope of the tangent line does not point in the direction of increasing $f(x)$. A similar argument applies to the case of the quasiconvex function given in figure 10.12(c). The lower level set

$$\mathbf{L}^{\leq} = \{x \mid -\infty < x < \infty, f(x) \leq f(x_1)\}$$

is convex. Since $f(x_1) \geq f(x_0)$, the slope of the tangent line points toward the decreasing direction of $f(x)$, Thus, $f'(x_1)(x_0 - x_1) \leq 0$. This argument motivates the following theorem.

**THEOREM 10.7** *A differentiable function $f(x)$ defined on an open interval* **S** *is quasiconcave on* **S** *if and only if for all $x_0, x_1 \in$* **S**,

$$f(x_1) \geq f(x_0) \Rightarrow f'(x_0)(x_1 - x_0) \geq 0.$$

*and is quasiconvex on* **S** *if and only if*

$$f(x_1) \geq f(x_0) \Rightarrow f'(x_1)(x_0 - x_1) \leq 0.$$

**Example 10.43** Consider $f(x) = x^3$ on **R**. Suppose $f(x_1) \geq f(x_0)$, that is $x_1^3 \geq x_0^3$. This implies that $x_1 \geq x_0$. We have then $f'(x_1)(x_0 - x_1) = 3x_1^2(x_0 - x_1) \leq 0$ when $x_1 \geq x_0$. Therefore, $f(x_1) \geq f(x_0)$ implies $x_1 \geq x_0$, which, in turn, implies $f'(x_0)(x_0 - x_1) \leq 0$. By the theorem, $f(x) = x^3$ is quasiconvex on **R**. Is it quasiconcave on **R**?

**Example 10.44** $f(x) = \log x - x^2$ is concave for $\mathbf{S} = \{x \mid x > 0\}$. It must then be quasiconcave on **S**. Since $f(1) = -1 > f(2) \approx -3.3$, and $f'(2)(1-2) = 3.5 > 0$, for example, the sufficient condition for quasiconcavity is satisfied at $x_0 = 2$ and $x_1 = 1$.

**Example 10.45** The function

$$f(x) = \frac{1}{1+\mathrm{e}^{-1.5x}}$$

is both quasiconcave and quasiconvex on **R**. We illustrate this by picking $x_0 = -1$ and $x_1 = 2$. It is easy to show that $f(x_1) \approx 0.95 > f(x_0) \approx 0.18$, and $f'(x_0)(x_1 - x_0) \approx 0.67 > 0$, $f'(x_1)(x_0 - x_1) \approx -0.20 < 0$. Thus the conditions for quasiconcave and quasiconvex are satisfied at these two points.

We generalize the above discussion to functions of $n$ variables, $f(\mathbf{x}) = f(x_1, x_2, \ldots, x_n)$.

**THEOREM 10.8** *A differentiable function $f(\mathbf{x})$ defined on an open convex set* **S** *in* $\mathbf{R}^n$ *is quasiconcave on* **S** *if and only if, for any $\mathbf{x}_0, \mathbf{x}_1 \in$* **S**

$$f(\mathbf{x}_1) \geq f(\mathbf{x}_0) \Rightarrow \nabla f(\mathbf{x}_0) \cdot (\mathbf{x}_1 - \mathbf{x}_0) \geq 0.$$

*$f(\mathbf{x})$ is quasiconvex on* **S** *if and only if*

$$f(\mathbf{x}_1) \geq f(\mathbf{x}_0) \Rightarrow \nabla f(\mathbf{x}_1) \cdot (\mathbf{x}_0 - \mathbf{x}_1) \leq 0.$$

**Example 10.46** Consider the CES function $f(x,y) = (0.6x^{-0.8} + 0.4y^{-0.8})^{-1.25}$ on $\mathbf{S} = \{(x,y) \mid x,y > 0\}$. It was shown to be concave in section 10.2.1. Then it must be quasiconcave. As demonstrated in the following *Mathematica* calculation at $(x_0,y_0) = (5,10)$ and $(x_1,y_1) = (6,8)$, we have $f(x_1,y_1) = 6.67937 > f(x_0,y_0) = 6.31383$.

*In[177]:=*
```
Clear[f,x,y,gvector];
x0=5;  y0=10;  x1=6;  y1=8;
f[x_,y_]:=  (0.6  x^(-0.8)  +  0.4  y^(-0.8))^(-1.25);

f[x0,y0]
```

*Out[180]=*
```
6.31383
```

*In[181]:=*
```
f[x1,y1]
```

*Out[181]=*
```
6.67937
```

We calculate $\nabla f(x_0,y_0) \cdot [x_1-x_0 \;\; y_1-y_0]$ to illustrate that the CES function statisfies the condition for quasiconcavity at $(x_0,y_0)$.

*In[182]:=*
```
gvector  =  gradf[f[x,y],{x,y}]/.{x->x0,y->y0};
gvector.{x1-x0,y1-y0}
```

*Out[183]=*
```
0.563492
```

For a twice differentiable function, quasiconcavity and quasiconvexity can be checked by using the first- and second-order partial derivatives of the function.

**THEOREM 10.9** *Let $f(\mathbf{x}) = f(x_1,x_2, \ldots ,x_n)$ be defined in the nonnegative orthant $\mathbf{S} = \{\mathbf{x} \mid \mathbf{x} \geq \mathbf{0}\}$. Let the bordered determinants $|\mathbf{B}_k|$, $k = 1,2, \ldots n$, be defined as*

$$|\mathbf{B}_k| = \begin{vmatrix} 0 & f_1 & f_2 & \cdots & f_k \\ f_1 & f_{11} & f_{12} & \cdots & f_{1k} \\ \cdots & \cdots & \cdots & \cdots & \cdots \\ f_k & f_{k1} & f_{k2} & \cdots & f_{kk} \end{vmatrix}$$

*(1) A necessary condition for $f(\mathbf{x})$ to be quasiconcave on $\mathbf{S}$ is that $(-1)^k|\mathbf{B}_k| \geq 0$, and for $f(\mathbf{x})$ to be quasiconvex, $|\mathbf{B}_k| \leq 0$, for all k.*

*(2) A sufficient condition for $f(\mathbf{x})$ to be quasiconcave on $\mathbf{S}$ is that $(-1)^k|\mathbf{B}_k| > 0$, and for $f(\mathbf{x})$ to be quasiconvex, $|\mathbf{B}_k| < 0$, for all k.*

To calculate all leading principal minors $|\mathbf{B}_k|$ for k = 1,2, . . . ,$n$, we use the **MathEcon** function **borderB**. Once the matrix $\mathbf{B}_n$ is computed, the function **signQL** is then used to evaluate the leading principal minors.

**Example 10.47** We show that the function $f(x,y) = (1+x)(1+y)$ is quasiconcave for all $x,y \geq 0$. The bordered determinant is

$$|\mathbf{B}_2| = \begin{vmatrix} 0 & f_x & f_y \\ f_x & f_{xx} & f_{xy} \\ f_y & f_{yx} & f_{yy} \end{vmatrix} = \begin{vmatrix} 0 & 1+y & 1+x \\ 1+y & 0 & 1 \\ 1+x & 1 & 0 \end{vmatrix}$$

The leading principal minors are

$$|\mathbf{B}_1| = -1 - 2y - y^2 < 0$$
$$|\mathbf{B}_2| = 2 + 2x + 2y + 2xy > 0$$

for all $x,y \geq 0$. The function is thus quasiconcave. We use **borderB** to confirm this result.

*In[184]:=*
```
Clear[f,x,y];
f[x_,y_]:= (1+x)(1+y);
g  =  gradf[f[x,y],{x,y}];
H  =  hessian[f[x,y],{x,y}];
B  =  borderB[H,{g}];
signQL[B]
```

*Out[189]=*
$$\{0, -1 - 2y - y^2, 2 + 2x + 2y + 2xy\}$$

We note that the first element of the output in **signQL[B]** is $|\mathbf{B}_0|$, which is to be ignored.

**Example 10.48** Consider a Cobb-Douglas function

$$f(x,y,z) = x^{0.3}\, y^{0.5}\, z^{0.6}$$

where $x,y,z \geq 0$. As shown in the following calculation, $|\mathbf{B}_1| < 0$, $|\mathbf{B}_2| > 0$, and $|\mathbf{B}_3| < 0$.

*In[190]:=*
```
Clear[f,x,y,z];
f[x_,y_,z_]:= (x^0.3)*(y^0.5)*(z^0.6);
g  =  gradf[f[x,y,z],{x,y,z}];
H  =  hessian[f[x,y,z],{x,y,z}];
B  =  borderB[H,{g}];
signQL[B]
```

*Out[195]=*
$$\{0, \frac{-0.09\,y^{1.}\,z^{1.2}}{x^{1.4}}, \frac{0.12\,z^{1.8}}{x^{1.1}\,y^{1.5}}, \frac{-0.126\,z^{0.4}}{x^{0.8}}\}$$

Therefore, the function is quasiconcave on $x,y,z \geq 0$.

## EXERCISES

1. Show that $f(x,y) = (1-x)(1-y)$ is quasiconvex for $0 < x < 1$ and $1 < y$.

2. Determine which of the following functions are quasiconcave, quasiconvex, or neither.
   (a) $f(x) = x^3 - 3x$.
   (b) $f(x) = \log x + e^{-x}$, $x > 0$
   (c) $f(x) = x^2/(x+x^3)$

3. Show that a polynomial function of degree 3,

   $$f(x) = a + bx + cx^2 + dx^3$$

   is neither quasiconcave nor quasiconvex.

4. It is known that the following CES function

   $$f(x,y,z) = (0.3x^{-0.8} + 0.5y^{-0.8} + 0.2z^{-0.8})^{-1.25}$$

   is quasiconcave. Evaluate the principal minors $|\mathbf{B}_k|$ of the bordered matrix at different values of $(x,y,z)$. Are the sufficient conditions, $(-1)^k|\mathbf{B}_k| \geq 0$, satisfied?

# 11

# Optimization

Optimization deals with the problem of finding the maximum or minimum values of a function $f(\mathbf{x}) = f(x_1,x_2, \ldots ,x_n)$ on a set $\mathbf{S}$ that is contained in its domain. The set

$$\mathbf{S} = \{ (x_1,x_2, \ldots ,x_n) \mid \mathbf{g}(x_1,x_2, \ldots ,x_n) \leq 0,\ \mathbf{h}(x_1,x_2, \ldots ,x_n) = \mathbf{0}\}$$

is often defined in terms of constraints, where $\mathbf{g}$ and $\mathbf{h}$ are given vector-valued functions. For example, consumers might want to maximize a utility function derived from the consumption of $n$ goods subject to their budget constraints. The constraints define the set $\mathbf{S}$. Another example is when a firm attempts to minimize the cost of producing a given quantity of output by choosing a combination of $n$ factor inputs subject to the current state of production technology. The function $f(\mathbf{x})$ is called the *objective function*, and the set $\mathbf{S}$ is called the *opportunity set*. Solutions of an optimization problem depend upon the mathematical properties of the objective function, such as concavity and convexity, and the geometry of the opportunity set. If the solution of an optimization does not vary with time, then the optimization problem is called *static optimization* or *mathematical programming*. On the other hand, if the solution is a function of time, then the optimization problem is called *dynamic optimization* or *dynamic programming*. Dynamic optimization is beyond the scope of this book. In this and the next chapter we shall discuss only static optimization problems.

## □ 11.1 Unconstrained Extreme Values □

### 11.1.1 Some definitions

Generally, we want to compute the maximum or minimum values of a function restricted to some subset of its domain. This can be a difficult problem. Searching for optimal values of a function on an unconstrained set is considerably easier from a computational point of view than looking for optimal values on a set with constraints. Hence, we shall first consider unconstrained optimization. We begin by introducing some terminology.

**DEFINITION 11.1** *Let $f(\mathbf{x}) = f(x_1,x_2, \ldots ,x_n)$ be a real-valued function defined for all* **x** *belonging to some set* **S** *in* $\mathbf{R}^n$, *and let* $\mathbf{c} = (c_1,c_2, \ldots ,c_n)$ *be a point in* **S**.

*(1) If $f(\mathbf{c}) \geq f(\mathbf{x})$ for all $\mathbf{x} \in \mathbf{S}$, then $f(\mathbf{c})$ is called the* ***absolute (global) maximum*** *of f on* **S** *and* **c** *is called an* ***absolute (global) maximum point*** *for $f(\mathbf{x})$ in* **S**. *If $f(\mathbf{c}) > f(\mathbf{x})$, for all $\mathbf{x} \neq \mathbf{c}$, then* **c** *is the* ***unique absolute (global) maximum point***.

*(2) If $f(\mathbf{c}) \leq f(\mathbf{x})$ for all $\mathbf{x} \in \mathbf{S}$, then $f(\mathbf{c})$ is called the* ***absolute (global) minimum*** *of f on* **S**, *and* **c** *is called an* ***absolute (global) minimum point*** *for $f(\mathbf{x})$ in* **S**. *If $f(\mathbf{c}) < f(\mathbf{x})$ for all $\mathbf{x} \neq \mathbf{c}$, then* **c** *is the* ***unique absolute (global) minimum point***.

*(3) An* ***absolute (global) extremum*** *of $f(\mathbf{x})$ on* **S** *is either an absolute maximum or absolute minimum of $f(\mathbf{x})$ on* **S**. *The point* **c** *is an* ***absolute (global) extreme point***.

**Example 11.1** The function $f(x) = x^4 - 2x^2 + 1$ is defined on the closed interval **S** = [−2,2]. The function has two absolute maximum points at $x = 2$ and $x = -2$ (with the absolute maximum $f(2) = f(-2) = 9$), and has two absolute minimum points at x = 1 and x = −1 (with the absolute minimum $f(1) = f(-1) = 0$). We can visualize these observations by plotting $f(x)$ over [−2,2].

*In[1]:=*
```
Clear[f,x];
f[x_]:= x^4-2*x^2+1;
Plot[f[x],{x,-2,2},
                    AxesLabel->{"x","f(x)"},PlotRange->All];
```

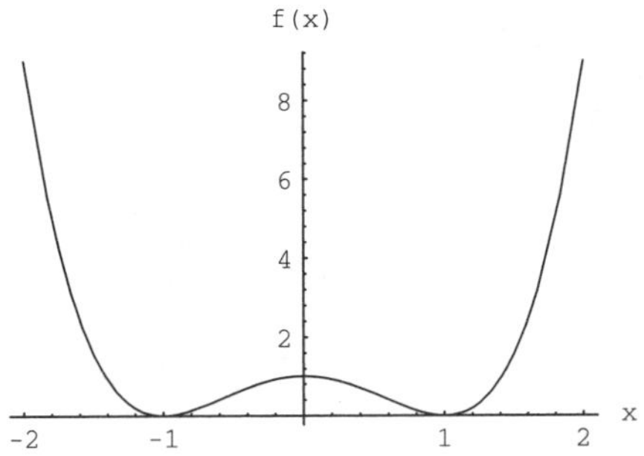


**Example 11.2** The function

$$f(x,y) = e^{-(x^2+y^2)}$$

defined on $\mathbf{S} = \mathbf{R}^2$ has an absolute maximum point at (0,0) with $f(0,0) = 1$. Since $f(x,y) < 1$ for all $(x,y) \neq (0,0)$, the point (0,0) is the unique absolute maximum point. Plotting the graph of $f$ will confirm this observation.

*In[4]:=*
```
Clear[x,y];
Plot3D[Exp[-(x^2+y^2)],{x,-1,1},{y,-1,1},
             ViewPoint->{-2.730, -3.810, 1.170},
              AxesLabel->{"x","y","f(x,y)"}];
```

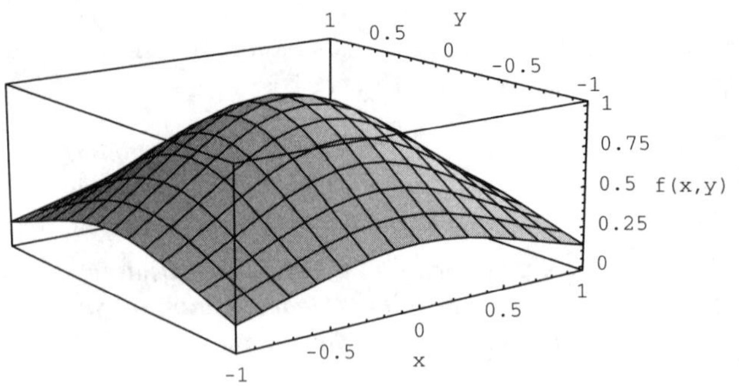


Two remarks about the absolute extrema are in order. First, a function $f(\mathbf{x})$ may fail to have absolute extrema on a given set **S**. For example, $f(x) = x$ on $\mathbf{S} = (-\infty,\infty)$ has neither an absolute maximum nor an absolute minimum. Second, if $f(\mathbf{x})$ is any function defined on **S**, then $-f(\mathbf{x})$ is also defined on **S**. Furthermore, $f(\mathbf{x}) \le f(\mathbf{c})$ for all $\mathbf{x} \in \mathbf{S}$ if and only if $-f(\mathbf{x}) \ge -f(\mathbf{c})$ for all $\mathbf{x} \in \mathbf{S}$. Thus, **c** is a maximum point of $f(\mathbf{x})$ on **S** if and only if **c** is a minimum point of $-f(\mathbf{x})$ on **S**. This implies that a maximization problem can be rephrased as a minimization problem, and vice versa.

**Example 11.3** The function $g(x) = -f(x) = -x^4 + 2x^2 - 1$ reverses the extrema of the function given in Example 11.1. It has two absolute maximum points at $x = 1$ and $x = -1$ (with the absolute maximum $g(1) = g(-1) = 0$) and two absolute minimum points at $x = 2$ and $x = -2$ (with the absolute minimum $g(2) = g(-2) = -9$).

*In[6]:=*
```
Clear[f,g,x];
f[x_]:= x^4-2*x^2+1;
g[x_]:= -f[x]
Plot[g[x],{x,-2,2},
                AxesLabel->{"x","-f(x)"},PlotRange->All];
```

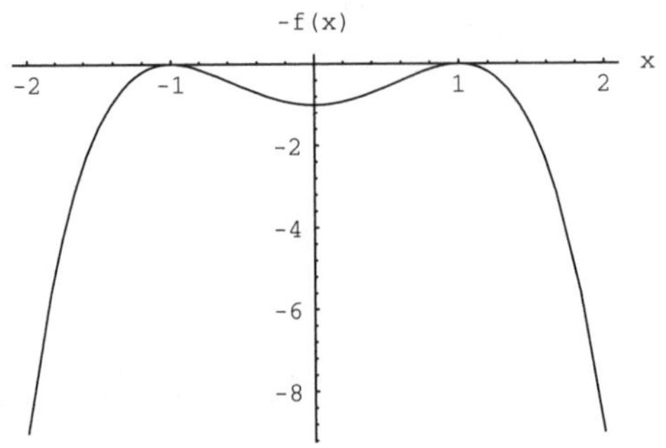


In example 11.1, $f(x) = x^4 - 2x^2 + 1$ defined on $\mathbf{S} = [-2,2]$, has two absolute maximum points at $x = 2$ and $x = -2$. They are absolute maximum points since $f(2) \ge f(x)$ for all $x$ in **S**. However, if we consider only the values of $x$ in the immediate neighborhood of $x = 0$, $f(x)$ has a maximum at $x = 0$ since $f(0) \ge f(x)$ for $x$ in the neighborhood of $x = 0$. This leads us to the following definition.

**DEFINITION 11.2** Let $f(\mathbf{x})$ be a function defined on **S** and **c** be an interior point of **S**.

(1) *If $f(\mathbf{c}) \geq f(\mathbf{x})$ for $\mathbf{x} \in \mathbf{S}$ in the neighborhood of* **c**, *then $f(\mathbf{c})$ is a* ***relative (local) maximum***, *and* **c** *is a* ***relative (local) maximum point***. *$f(\mathbf{c})$ is a* ***strict relative (local) maximum*** *if $f(\mathbf{c}) > f(\mathbf{x})$ in a neighborhood of* **c**.

(2) *If $f(\mathbf{c}) \leq f(\mathbf{x})$ for $\mathbf{x} \in \mathbf{S}$ in the neighborhood of* **c**, *then $f(\mathbf{c})$ is a* ***relative (local) minimum***, *and* **c** *is a* ***relative (local) minimum point***. *$f(\mathbf{c})$ is a* ***strict relative (local) minimum*** *if $f(\mathbf{c}) < f(\mathbf{x})$ in a neighborhood of* **c**.

(3) *A* ***relative (local) extremum*** *of $f(\mathbf{x})$ is either a relative minimum or a relative maximum. The point* **c** *is a* ***relative (local) extreme point***.

**Example 11.4** The function

$$f(x) = \frac{1}{5}x^5 - \frac{5}{2}x^4 + \frac{35}{3}x^3 - 25x^2 + 24x + 1$$

for $1 \leq x < 4$ is plotted below. It has an absolute maximum at the endpoint, $x = 1$, but no absolute minimum. It does, however, have a relative maximum at 3, and a relative minimum at 2. The endpoint $x = 1$ is also a relative maximum.

*In[10]:=*

```
Clear[f,x];
f[x_]:= (1/5)*x^5-(5/2)*x^4+(35/3)*x^3-25*x^2+24*x+1;
Plot[f[x],{x,1,4},PlotRange->{{0,5},{7,10}}];
```

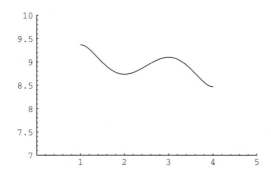

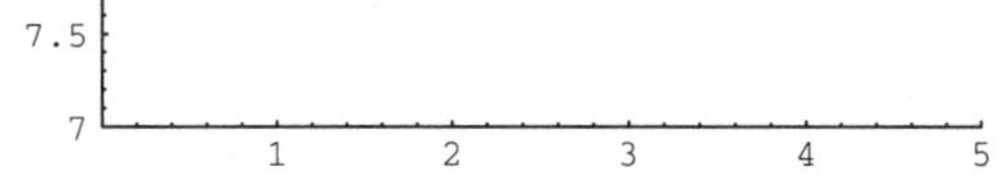


From the above plot, it is clear that a relative maximum (minimum) is not always an absolute maximum (minimum). Absolute extrema are either the largest or the smallest values that $f(\mathbf{x})$ can assume on the entire set **S**. Relative extrema are either the largest or the smallest values that $f(\mathbf{x})$ can assume in some open neighborhood contained in the domain **S**.

**Example 11.5** Consider the function $f(x)$ on $\mathbf{S} = [-1,5]$.

$$f(x) = \begin{cases} -x^2 + 5, & -1 \leq x < 2 \\ x^3 - 11x^2 + 39x - 41, & 2 \leq x \leq 5 \end{cases}$$

It has an absolute maximum at $x = 0$ and an absolute minimum at $x = 2$.

*In[13]:=*

```
Clear[f,x];
f[x_ /; -1<=x<2]:= -x^2 + 5;
f[x_ /; 2<=x<=5]:= x^3 - 11*x^2 + 39*x - 41;
Plot[f[x],{x,-1,5},
        AxesLabel->{"x","f(x)"},PlotRange->All];
```

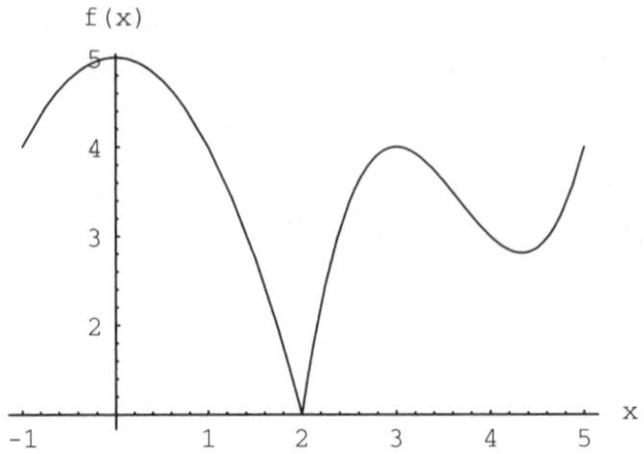


We make an important observation as we examine the above graph. The function has an absolute maximum at $x = 0$ where the derivative $f'(0) = 0$, and has an absolute minimum at $x = 2$ where $f(x)$ is not differentiable. This observation can be generalized. Suppose $f(x)$ is differentiable in **S**, except perhaps at a few points. If $f(x)$ has an absolute extremum at some point $c$, then

(1) $c$ is a point where $f'(c) = 0$, or
(2) $f(x)$ is not differentiable at $c$, or
(3) $c$ is an endpoint.

**Definition 11.3** *Let $f(x)$ be defined on an interval $(a,b)$. A* ***critical point*** *(or a* ***stationary point****) of a function $f(x)$ is an interior point $c \in (a,b)$ such that $f'(c) = 0$ or $f'(c)$ does not exist.*

If a function $f(x)$ is differentiable at any interior point of the set **S**, then an absolute extremum must be located at a point where $f'(x) = 0$ or at an endpoint. Thus the task of finding extrema becomes more manageable. Let $f(x)$ be defined on the interval $[a,b]$ and differentiable $(a,b)$ with $f'(x) = 0$ for $x = x_1, x_2, \ldots, x_n \in (a,b)$. The $n$ critical points and the endpoints, $a$ and $b$, are then the only possible points where $f$ can have an extremum. The function has an absolute maximum at $x_{\max}$ and an absolute minimum at $x_{\min}$ where

$$f(x_{\max}) = \max\{f(x_1), f(x_2), \ldots, f(x_n), f(a), f(b)\}$$
$$f(x_{\min}) = \min\{f(x_1), f(x_2), \ldots, f(x_n), f(a), f(b)\}.$$

**Example 11.6** Consider the function $f(x) = x^3 - 3x^2 - 9x + 3$ on $\mathbf{S} = [-2,5]$. The function is differentiable at all interior points of **S**. Thus the critical points must be the points where $f'(x) = 3x^2 - 6x - 9 = 0$. There are two critical points at $x = -1$ and $x = 3$. We confirm this in the following *Mathematica* calculation.

*In[17]:=*
```
Clear[f,x];
f[x_]:= x^3-3*x^2-9*x+3;
f'[x]
```

*Out[19]=*
```
-9 - 6x + 3x^2
```

*In[20]:=*
```
Solve[f'[x]==0]
```

*Out[20]=*
```
{{x → -1}, {x → 3}}
```

We plot $f(x)$ (thick line) and $f'(x)$ to show that the points $x = -1$ and $x = 3$ are the only two points where $f'(x)$ is zero. The critical point $x = -1$ is a relative maximum point with $f(-1) = 8$ while the critical point $x = 3$ is a relative minimum point with $f(3) = -24$. Since the endpoints have values, $f(-2) = 1$ and $f(5) = 8$, the function has absolute maxima at $x = -1$ and an absolute minimum at $x = 3$.

*In[21]:=*
```
Plot[{f[x],f'[x]},{x,-2,5},
          PlotStyle->{{Thickness[0.008]},{}},
        AxesLabel->{"x","f(x)  and  f'(x)"}];
```

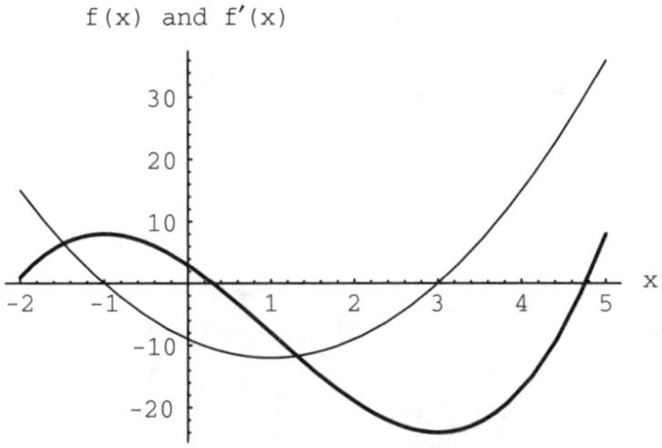


For functions of several variables, $f(\mathbf{x}) = f(x_1,x_2, \ldots ,x_n)$, a point, $\mathbf{c} = (c_1,c_2, \ldots ,c_n)$, is a *critical point (stationary point)* if either

(1) $f_1(\mathbf{c}) = f_2(\mathbf{c}) = \ldots = f_n(\mathbf{c}) = 0$, or

(2) one or more of the first partial derivatives at $\mathbf{c}$ do not exist,

where $f_i(\mathbf{c})$ is the first partial derivative with respect to $x_i$ evaluated at $\mathbf{c}$.

**Example 11.7** Let

$$f(x,y) = (x^2+2y^2)\, e^{-(x^2+y^2)}$$

be defined on $\mathbf{R}^2$. The partial derivatives

$f_x(x,y) = 2x(1-x^2-2y^2)\,e^{-(x^2+y^2)}$
$f_x(x,y) = 2y(2-x^2-2y^2)\,e^{-(x^2+y^2)}$

exist on $\mathbf{R}^2$. Setting the partial derivatives to zero, $f_x(x,y) = 0$ and $f_y(x,y) = 0$, five critical points are obtained at $(x,y) = (-1,0)$, $(0,0)$, $(1,0)$, $(0,-1)$, and $(0,1)$. These points are computed in the following *Mathematica* calculation.

*In[22]:=*

```
Clear[f,x,y];
f[x_,y_]:= (x^2+2*y^2) Exp[-(x^2+y^2)];
Solve[{D[f[x,y],x]==0,D[f[x,y],y]==0},{x,y}]
```

Solve : : ifun : Warning : Inverse functions are being used by Solve, so some solutions may not be found.

*Out[24]=*

```
{{x → -1, y → 0}, {x → 0, y → 0}, {x → 1, y → 0},
  {y → -1, x → 0}, {y → 1, x → 0}}
```

The following 3-dimensional *Mathematica* plot shows that the critical points occur on the rim and the bottom of a volcano (the graph of $f$). Two relative maxima, which are also the absolute maxima, occur at (0,1) and (0,–1) with the maximum value $f(0,1) = f(0,-1) = 2/e$. One relative minimum, which is also the absolute minimum, occurs at (0,0) with the minimum value $f(0,0) = 0$.

*In[25]:=*

```
Plot3D[f[x,y],{x,-2,2},{y,-2,2},
                AxesLabel->{"x","y","f(x,y)"},
               ViewPoint->{-2.270, 0.910, 2.580}];
```

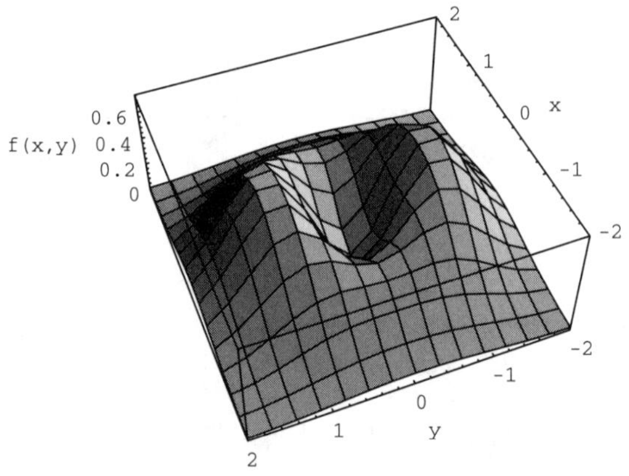


## EXERCISES

1. Find the critical points of the following functions. Plot the function and check if the critical points are absolute extrema relative, extrema, or neither.
   (a) $f(x) = x - x^2, \; -\infty < x < \infty$
   (b) $f(x) = \begin{cases} \dfrac{x+1}{x-1}, & x \neq 1 \\ 0, & x = 1 \end{cases}$

(c) $f(x,y) = 3x^2 - 9xy - 6y^2 + 2x + 16y,\ 0 \le x,y \le 2$
(d) $f(x,y) = x^2 + 2xy + y^2,\ -\infty < x,y < \infty$

2. Show that $f(x,y) = (y-x^2)(y-2x^2)$ has a critical point at the origin (0,0). Is the origin an extremum?

## 11.1.2 Necessary and sufficient conditions for relative extrema

We begin the discussion of the necessary and sufficient conditions for relative extrema in the case of a function of a single variable $f(x)$. Recall that a function $f(x)$ attains a relative minimum (maximum) at a point $c$ when $f(x) - f(c)$ is nonnegative (nonpositive) for all $x$ in a neighborhood of $c$. Assume that the function $f(x)$ has continuous derivatives up to any desired order at the point $x = c$. The Taylor series expansion of the function about the point $c$ is

$$f(x) - f(c) = f'(c)(x-c) + \frac{f''(c)}{2!} + \dots + \frac{f^{(n)}(c)}{n!}(x-c)^n + \frac{f^{(n+1)}(t)}{(n+1)!}(x-c)^{n+1}$$

where $t$ lies between $x$ and $c$. A condition for a relative extremum to exist, i.e., the condition for $f(x) - f(c) \ge 0$ in a relative minimum case and $f(x) - f(c) \le 0$ in the relative maximum case, rests on the sign of the right-hand side of the above equation. We discuss the condition for relative extrema in the following cases with respect to the signs of derivatives.

*Case 1* Suppose $f'(c) \ne 0$. Set $n = 1$ in the above Taylor series.

$$f(x) - f(c) = f'(t)(x-c)$$

Since the derivative is continuous and $x$ is very close to $c$, the derivative $f'(t)$ must have the same sign as $f'(c)$. Suppose $f'(c)$ is nonzero, say positive. If $f'(c) > 0$, then $f'(t) > 0$. The difference, $f(x) - f(c)$, must change sign as $(x - c)$ changes signs, i.e., as $x$ approaches $c$ from different directions, and hence $f$ does not have a relative extremum at $x = c$. Hence, if $x = c$ is a relative extreme point for $f(x)$, then the first derivative must be zero. Thus, a necessary condition for an extremum is then $f'(c) = 0$ when $f$ is differentiable at $x = c$.

*Case 2* Suppose $f'(c) = 0$, and $f''(c) \ne 0$. Set $n = 2$.

$$f(x) - f(c) = \frac{f''(t)}{2!}(x-c)^2$$

The left-hand side is always positive, $f(x) - f(c) > 0$, as long as $f''(t) > 0$, since $(x - c)^2$ is always positive. Again, the sign of $f''(t)$ is the the same as the sign of $f''(c)$. This results in the following sufficient conditions:

(1) If $f'(c) = 0$, and $f''(c) > 0$, then the point $x = c$ gives a relative minimum of $f$.

(2) If $f'(c) = 0$, and $f''(c) < 0$, then the point $x = c$ gives a relative maximum of $f$.

*Case 3* Suppose $f'(c) = f''(c) = 0$, and $f'''(c) \neq 0$. Set $n = 3$.

$$f(x) - f(c) = \frac{f'''(t)}{3!}(x - c)^3$$

Since $(x-c)^3$ changes sign as $x$ approaches $c$ from different directions, the sign of $f'''(c)$ cannot determine the sign of $f(x) - f(c)$. A sufficient condition for a relative extremum cannot be established in this situation. If $f'''(c) > 0$, then $f(x) - f(c)$ is positive when $(x - c) > 0$, and $f(x) - f(c)$ is negative when $(x - c) < 0$. The critical point $c$ does not give a relative extreme value of $f$. In fact, the point $c$ is an inflection point of $f$ since $f''(c) = 0$ and $f'''(c) \neq 0$.

*Case 4* Suppose $f'(c) = f''(c) = \ldots = f^{(n-1)}(c) = 0$, and $f^{(n)}(c) \neq 0$ for $n > 3$. The Taylor series can now be written

$$f(x) - f(c) = \frac{f^{(n)}(t)}{n!}(x - c)^n$$

If $n$ is an odd interger, then the sign of $f(x) - f(c)$ changes with the sign of $(x - c)$ and $c$ is not a relative extreme point. However, since $f''(c) = 0$, the point $x = c$ must be an inflection point. On the other hand, if $n$ is an even interger, then the sign of $f(x) - f(c)$ is determined by the sign of the $n$-th derivative. If $f^{(n)}(c) > 0$, and hence $f^{(n)}(t) > 0$, then we have $f(x) - f(c) > 0$ and the point $c$ is a relative minimum point. If $f^{(n)}(c) < 0$, and hence $f^{(n)}(t) < 0$, then $f(x) - f(c) < 0$ and the point $c$ is a relative maximum point.

We now state the necessary and sufficient conditions for relative extrema.

**THEOREM 11.1** *(Necessary and Sufficient Conditions for Relative Extrema) Suppose a function $f(x)$ has continuous derivative up to order $n$ at $x = c$.*

*(1) (Necessary Condition) If the point $c$ is a relative extremum point, then $f'(c) = 0$.*

*(2) (Sufficient Condition) If $f'(c) = f''(c) = \ldots = f^{(n-1)}(c) = 0$, and $f^{(n)}(c) \neq 0$, then $f(c)$ is:*
*(a) a relative minimum if $n$ is an even integer and $f^{(n)}(c) > 0$;*
*(b) a relative maximum if $n$ is an even integer and $f^{(n)}(c) < 0$;*
*(c) an inflection point if $n \geq 3$ is an odd integer.*

**Example 11.8** Find the relative extrema of the function

$$f(x) = 0.25x^4 - x^3 + x^2, \quad -\infty < x < \infty.$$

We solve $f'(x) = x^3 - 3x^2 + 2x = 0$ for the critical points of $f(x)$.

*In[26]:=*
```
Clear[f,x];
f[x_]:= 0.25*x^4 - x^3 + x^2;
Solve[f'[x]==0]
```

*Out[28]=*
```
{{x → 0.}, {x → 1.}, {x → 2.}}
```

If the function has relative extrema, it must be at these points. We evaluate the second derivative, $f''(x) = 3x^2 - 6x + 2$, at these points.

*In[29]:=*
```
f''[x]  /.  x->0
```

*Out[29]=*
2

*In[30]:=*
```
f''[x]  /.  x->1
```

*Out[30]=*
−1.

*In[31]:=*
```
f''[x]  /.  x->2
```

*Out[31]=*
2.

Since $f''(0) = f''(2) = 2 > 0$, both critical points, $x = 0$, and $x = 2$, are relative minimum points. Since $f''(1) = -1 < 0$, $x = 1$ is a relative maximum point. We plot both $f(x)$ (thick line) and $f'(x)$ to illustrate the correspondence between the relative extrema and the critical points.

*In[32]:=*
```
Plot[{f[x],f'[x]},{x,-1,3},
        PlotStyle->{{Thickness[0.008]},{}},
       AxesLabel->{"x","f(x)  and  f'(x)"}];
```

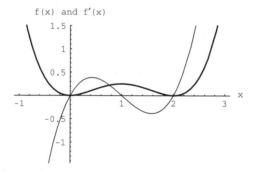

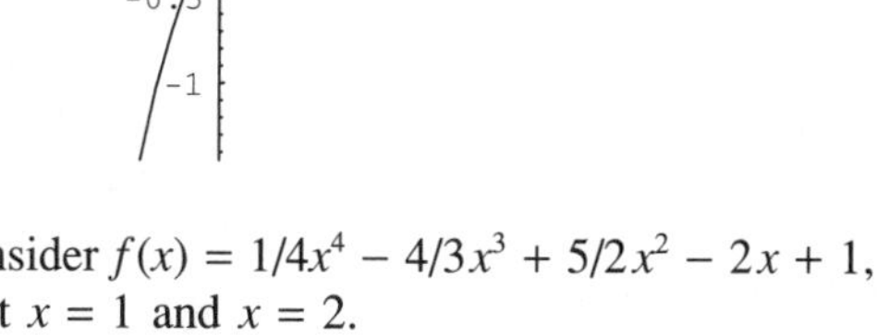


**Example 11.9** Consider $f(x) = 1/4x^4 - 4/3x^3 + 5/2x^2 - 2x + 1$, $-\infty < x < \infty$. It has two critical points at $x = 1$ and $x = 2$.

*In[33]:=*
```
Clear[f,x];
f[x_]:=  (1/4)*x^4  -  (4/3)*x^3  +  (5/2)*x^2  -  2*x  +  1  ;
Solve[f'[x]==0]
```

*Out[35]=*
{{x → 1}, {x → 1}, {x → 2}}

The point $x = 2$ corresponds to a relative minimum since $f''(2) = 1 > 0$.

*In[36]:=*
```
f''[2]
```

*Out[36]=*
```
1
```

The point $x = 1$ is an inflection point since $f''(1) = 0$, and $f'''(1) = -2 \neq 0$.

*In[37]:=*
```
f''[1]
```

*Out[37]=*
```
0
```

*In[38]:=*
```
f'''[1]
```

*Out[38]=*
```
-2
```

Again we plot the function $f(x)$ to show the extreme value and the inflection point.

*In[39]:=*
```
Plot[f[x],{x,0,2.5},
        AspectRatio->1,AxesLabel->{"x","f(x)"}];
```

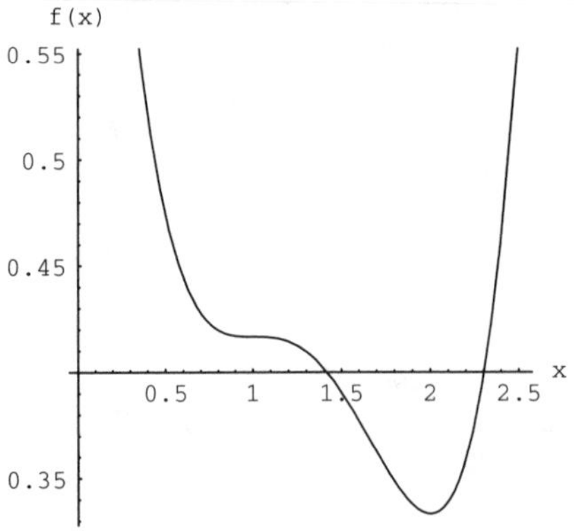


Necessary and sufficient conditions for computing relative extrema can be given for functions of several variables, $f(\mathbf{x}) = f(x_1,x_2, \ldots ,x_n)$. We assume that $\mathbf{S}$ is a convex set in $\mathbf{R}^n$. As shown in Chapter 9, the Taylor series expansion about the point $\mathbf{c} = (c_1,c_2, \ldots ,c_n)$ with its remainder is

$$f(\mathbf{x}) = f(\mathbf{c}) + df(\mathbf{c};\mathbf{x}-\mathbf{c}) + \frac{1}{2!}d^2f(\mathbf{c};\mathbf{x}-\mathbf{c})$$
$$+ \ldots + \frac{1}{n!}d^{(n)}f(\mathbf{x};\mathbf{x}-\mathbf{c}) + \frac{1}{(n+1)!}d^{(n+1)}f(\mathbf{t};\mathbf{x}-\mathbf{c})$$

where $\mathbf{t}$ lies on the line segment between $\mathbf{x}$ and $\mathbf{c}$. The $k$th-order differential $df^k$ $(\mathbf{c};\mathbf{x}-\mathbf{c})$ is evaluated at $\mathbf{c}$ with $d\mathbf{x} = \mathbf{x}-\mathbf{c}$. The function $f(\mathbf{x})$ attains a relative minimum (maximum) at the point **c** if $f(\mathbf{x}) - f(\mathbf{c})$ is nonnegative (nonpositive) in a neighborhood of **c**. To examine for relative extrema, we consider the following cases.

*Case 1* Suppose $df(\mathbf{c};\mathbf{x}-\mathbf{c}) \neq 0$, Set $n = 1$. The Taylor series is

$$f(\mathbf{x}) - f(\mathbf{c}) = df(\mathbf{t};\mathbf{x}-\mathbf{c})$$

where $df(\mathbf{t};\mathbf{x}-\mathbf{c})$ is the first-order differential of $f(\mathbf{x})$ evaluated at the point **t** with $d\mathbf{x} = \mathbf{x}-\mathbf{c}$. For **x** close to **c**, the sign of $f(\mathbf{x}) - f(\mathbf{c})$ is the same as $df(\mathbf{c};\mathbf{x}-\mathbf{c})$. The first-order differential $df(\mathbf{x})$ evaluated at **c** is

$$\begin{aligned} df(\mathbf{c};\mathbf{x}-\mathbf{c}) &= f_1(\mathbf{c})(x_1-c_1) + f_2(\mathbf{c})(x_2-c_2) + \ldots + f_n(\mathbf{c})(x_n-c_n) \\ &= \nabla\mathbf{f}(\mathbf{c}) \cdot (\mathbf{x}-\mathbf{c}) \end{aligned}$$

where $\nabla\mathbf{f}(\mathbf{c})$ is the gradient vector evaluated at **c**. If $df(\mathbf{c};\mathbf{x}-\mathbf{c}) \neq 0$ for $\mathbf{x}-\mathbf{c} \neq \mathbf{0}$, then the gradient vector $\nabla\mathbf{f}(\mathbf{c}) \neq \mathbf{0}$. The sign $f(\mathbf{x}) - f(\mathbf{c})$ could either be positive or negative in the neighborhood of **c** since the elements of **x–c** can be positive or negative. The direction in which **x** approaches **c** varies. Thus, if $df(\mathbf{c};\mathbf{x}-\mathbf{c}) \neq 0$, the point **c** cannot be a relative extreme point. This argument results in the following necessary condition.

**THEOREM 11.2** *(Necessary Condition for Relative Extrema) Suppose* $f(\mathbf{x}) = f(x_1, x_2, \ldots, x_n)$ *is defined on the convex set* **S** *in* $\mathbf{R}^n$ *and* $\mathbf{c} = (c_1, c_2, \ldots, c_n)$ *is an interior point of* **S** *at which* $f(\mathbf{x})$ *is differentiable. Then a necessary condition for* **c** *to be a relative extremum is that*

$$\nabla\mathbf{f}(\mathbf{c}) = \mathbf{0},$$

*i.e.,* $f_i(\mathbf{c}) = 0$ *for* $i = 1, 2, \ldots, n$.

*Case 2* Suppose $df(\mathbf{c};\mathbf{x}-\mathbf{c}) = 0$ and $d^2f(\mathbf{c};\mathbf{x}-\mathbf{c}) \neq 0$. If $n = 2$ in the Taylor series expansion, then

$$f(\mathbf{x}) - f(\mathbf{c}) = \frac{1}{2!} d^2f(\mathbf{t};\mathbf{x}-\mathbf{c}).$$

For **x** close to **c**, the sign of $d^2f(\mathbf{t};\mathbf{x}-\mathbf{c})$ is the same as the sign of $d^2f(\mathbf{c};\mathbf{x}-\mathbf{c})$. The sign of $f(\mathbf{x}) - f(\mathbf{c})$ depends on the second-order differential $d^2f(\mathbf{x};\mathbf{x}-\mathbf{c})$ evaluated at the critical point **c**. As shown in Chapter 8, the second-order differential is the quadratic form

$$\begin{aligned} d^2f(\mathbf{c};\mathbf{x}-\mathbf{c}) &= [dx_1 \quad dx_2 \quad \ldots \quad dx_n] \begin{bmatrix} f_{11} & f_{12} & \cdots & f_{1n} \\ f_{21} & f_{22} & \cdots & f_{2n} \\ \cdots & \cdots & \cdots & \cdots \\ f_{n1} & f_{n2} & \cdots & f_{nn} \end{bmatrix} \begin{bmatrix} dx_1 \\ dx_2 \\ \cdot \\ dx_n \end{bmatrix} \\ &= [x_1-c_1 \quad x_2-c_2 \quad \ldots \quad x_n-c_n] \begin{bmatrix} f_{11} & f_{12} & \cdots & f_{1n} \\ f_{21} & f_{22} & \cdots & f_{2n} \\ \cdots & \cdots & \cdots & \cdots \\ f_{n1} & f_{n2} & \cdots & f_{nn} \end{bmatrix} \begin{bmatrix} x_1-c_1 \\ x_2-c_2 \\ \vdots \\ x_n-c_n \end{bmatrix} \\ &= (\mathbf{x}-\mathbf{c})^T \mathbf{H}(\mathbf{c})(\mathbf{x}-\mathbf{c}) \end{aligned}$$

where **H** denotes the Hessian matrix. If the quadratic form is positive (negative) definite for $\mathbf{x}-\mathbf{c} \neq \mathbf{0}$, then the critical point **c** gives a relative minimum (maximum) value of $f(\mathbf{x})$. If the quadratic form is indefinite, then the critical point is called a *saddle point*.

Recall that the sign of a quadratic form depends upon the Hessian matrix **H**. Let

$$|\mathbf{H}_k| = \begin{vmatrix} f_{11} & f_{12} & \cdots & f_{1k} \\ f_{21} & f_{22} & \cdots & f_{2k} \\ \cdots & \cdots & \cdots & \cdots \\ f_{k1} & f_{k2} & \cdots & f_{kk} \end{vmatrix}$$

denote the leading principal minors of **H**. These minors can be used to determine the sign of **H**. We have the following sufficient conditions for an extremum.

**THEOREM 11.3** *(Sufficient Condition for Relative Extremum) Suppose* $f(\mathbf{x}) = f(x_1, x_2, \ldots, x_n)$ *is twice differentiable and* $\mathbf{c} = (c_1, c_2, \ldots, c_n)$ *is a critical point.*

*(1) If* $|\mathbf{H}_k(\mathbf{c})| > 0$ *for all* $k = 1,2, \ldots, n$*, then* $f(\mathbf{x})$ *has a relative minimum point at* **c**.

*(2) If* $(-1)^k|\mathbf{H}_k(\mathbf{c})| > 0$ *for all* $k = 1,2, \ldots, n$*, then* $f(\mathbf{x})$ *has a relative maximum point at* **c**.

*(3) If* $|\mathbf{H}(\mathbf{c})| \neq 0$*, and* $\mathbf{H}(\mathbf{c})$ *is neither positive nor negative definite, then* **c** *is a saddle point.*

*Case 3* Suppose $df(\mathbf{c};\mathbf{x}-\mathbf{c}) = d^2f(\mathbf{c}) = \ldots = d^{(n-1)}f(\mathbf{c};\mathbf{x}-\mathbf{c}) = 0$, and $d^{(n)}f(\mathbf{c};\mathbf{x}-\mathbf{c}) \neq 0$. The Taylor series in this case is

$$f(\mathbf{x}) - f(\mathbf{c}) = \frac{1}{n!} d^{(n)}f(\mathbf{t};\mathbf{x}-\mathbf{c})$$

It is clear now that necessary and sufficient conditions for the point **c** to be an extreme point depend on the sign of the $n$-th order differential. If $d^{(n)}f(\mathbf{c};\mathbf{x}-\mathbf{c}) > 0$, then the point **c** is a relative minimum point, and if $d^{(n)}f(\mathbf{c};\mathbf{x}-\mathbf{c}) < 0$, then the point **c** is relative maximum point. Differentials of order higher than 2 are more difficult to evaluate. Hence, the precise condition for extrema in terms of the high order differential of $f(\mathbf{x})$ will not be discussed here. (See exercise 4 below.)

**Example 11.10** Show that the following function

$$f(x,y) = (x-1)^2 - (x-1)y/2 + y^2$$

has a relative minimum at $(x,y) = (1,0)$. We first evaluate the partial derivatives, $f_x(x,y)$ and $f_y(x,y)$, and find the critical point by solving $f_x(x,y) = 0$ and $f_y(x,y) = 0$ for $(x,y)$.

*In[40]:=*

```
Clear[f,x,y];
f[x_,y_]:=  (x-1)^2  -  (x-1)y/2  +  y^2;
fx  =  D[f[x,y],x];
fy  =  D[f[x,y],y];
Solve[{fx==0,fy==0},{x,y}]
```

*Out[44]=*

{{x → 1, y → 0}}

The second-order partial derivatives are used to form the Hessian matrix **H**.

*In[45]:=*

```
fxx = D[f[x,y],{x,2}];
fxy = D[f[x,y],x,y];
fyy = D[f[x,y],{y,2}];
H = {{fxx,fxy},{fxy,fyy}} /.{x->1,y->0}; H // MatrixForm
```

*Out[48]//MatrixForm=*

$$\begin{matrix} 2 & -(\frac{1}{2}) \\ -(\frac{1}{2}) & 2 \end{matrix}$$

The leading principal minors are: $|\mathbf{H}_1| = 2 > 0$ and $|\mathbf{H}_2| = 15/4 > 0$. Hence $d^2f(\mathbf{c};\mathbf{x}-\mathbf{c})$ is positive definite. The critical point $\mathbf{c} = (1,0)$ is a relative minimum point. We confirm our calculation by plotting $f(x,y)$.

*In[49]:=*

```
Plot3D[f[x,y],{x,0,2},{y,-1,1},
          BoxRatios->{1,1,0.8},
           AxesLabel->{"x","y","f(x,y)"},
          ViewPoint->{-1.220, -2.790, 0.580}];
```

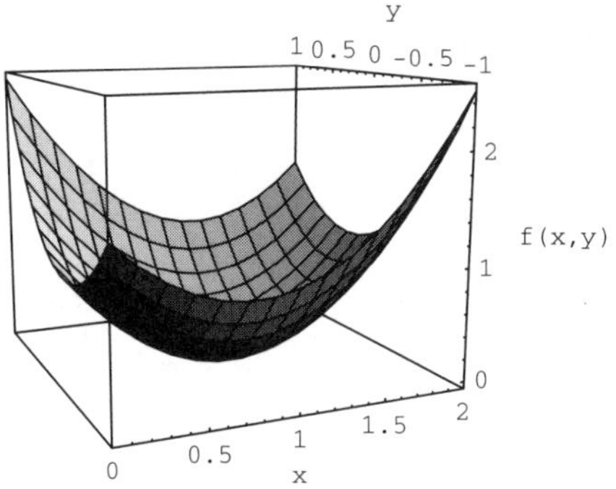


**Example 11.11** Find the relative extrema of the function

$f(x,y,z) = (1 - x - 2y - 3z)^2 + x^2 + y^2 + z^2$.

We first find the critical points.

*In[50]:=*

```
Clear[f,x,y,z,c];
f[x_,y_,z]:= (1-x-2*y-3*z)^2 + x^2 +y^2 + z^2
c = Solve[{D[f[x,y,z],x]==0,D[f[x,y,z],y]==0,
               D[f[x,y,z],z]==0},{x,y,z}]
```

*Out[52]=*

$$\{\{x \to \frac{1}{15}, y \to \frac{2}{15}, z \to \frac{1}{5}\}\}$$

Hence, there is a single critical point, **c** = (1/15,2/15,1/5). We use the **MathEcon** functions, **hessian** and **signQL**, introduced in Chapters 7 and 8, to calculate the Hessian matrix and the sequence of leading principal minors, $|\mathbf{H}_k(\mathbf{c})|$.

*In[53]:=*

```
h = hessian[f[x,y,z],{x,y,z}];
signQL[h /. c[[1]]]
```

*Out[54]=*

{4, 24, 120}

At the critical point, the leading principal minors are positive, $|\mathbf{H}_1| = 4 > 0$, $|\mathbf{H}_2| = 24 > 0$, and $|\mathbf{H}_3| = 120 > 0$. Hence the Hessian matrix is positive definite and the point is a relative minimum point.

**Example 11.12** Find the extrema of

$$f(x,y) = (x^2 + 2y^2)\, e^{-(x^2+y^2)}$$

We first calculate the critical points

*In[55]:=*

```
Clear[f,x,y,h];
f[x_,y_]:= (x^2+2*y^2)*Exp[-(x^2+y^2)];
c = Solve[gradf[f[x,y],{x,y}]=={0,0},{x,y}]
```

Solve : : ifun : Warning : Inverse functions are being used by Solve, so some solutions may not be found.

*Out[57]=*

{{x → −1, y → 0}, {x → 0, y → 0}, {x → 1, y → 0},
{y → −1, x → 0}, {y → 1, x → 0}}

It has five critical points: **c** = (−1,0),(0,0),(1,0),(0,−1), and (0,1). We first check the leading principal minors at **c** = (−1,0).

*In[58]:=*

```
Clear[f,x,y,h];
f[x_,y_]:= (x^2+2*y^2)*Exp[-(x^2+y^2)];
h = hessian[f[x,y],{x,y}];
signQL[h] /. {x->-1,y->0}
```

*Out[61]=*

$$\{\frac{-4}{E}, \frac{-8}{E^2}\}$$

Hence **H**(−1,0) is indefinite, and the critical point is a saddle point. Next we check **c** = (0,0).

*In[62]:=*

```
signQL[h] /. {x->0,y->0}
```

*Out[62]:=*

{2, 8}

Hence **H**(0,0) is positive definite, and the critical point is a relative minimum point. We check the remaining points.

*In[63]:=*
```
signQL[h] /. {x->1,y->0}
```

*Out[63]=*

$$\{\frac{-4}{E}, \frac{-8}{E^2}\}$$

*In[64]:=*
```
signQL[h] /. {x->0,y->-1}
```

*Out[64]=*

$$\{\frac{-2}{E}, \frac{16}{E^2}\}$$

*In[65]:=*
```
signQL[h] /. {x->0,y->1}
```

*Out[65]=*

$$\{\frac{-2}{E}, \frac{16}{E^2}\}$$

**H**(1,0) is indefinite, and the critical point is a saddle point. **H**(0,–1) and **H**(0,1) are negative definite and these two points are relative maximum points. Here is a plot to confirm our calculations.

*In[66]:=*
```
Plot3D[f[x,y],{x,-2,2},{y,-2,2},
       AxesLabel->{"x","y","f(x,y)"}];
```

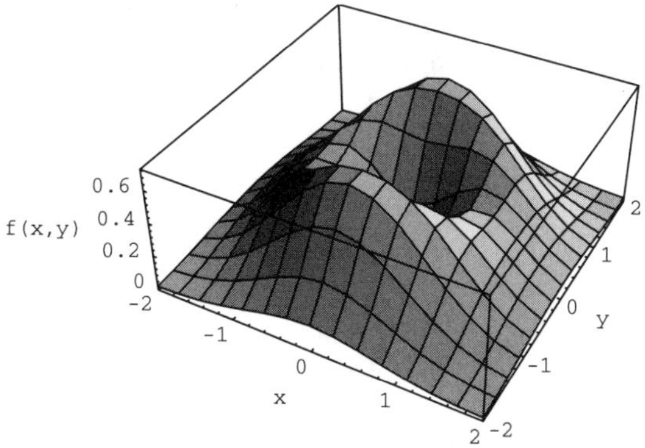


## EXERCISES

1. Find the extreme values and saddle points (if any) for the following functions:
   (a) $f(x) = ax^2 + bx + c, \quad -\infty < x < \infty$
   (b) $f(x) = ax^3 + bx^2 + cx + d, \quad -\infty < x < \infty$
   (c) $f(x) = xe^{-x}, \quad -\infty < x < \infty$
   (d) $f(x) = (x-5)^7 + 2(x-5)^6, \quad -\infty < x < \infty$
   $a$, $b$, $c$, and $d$ are constants with $a > 0$.

2. A monopolist's inverse demand function is $P = f(Q)$, and cost function is $C = g(Q)$, where $P$, $Q$, and $C$ are price, quantity, and total cost, respectively, What are the necessary and sufficient conditions for $Q$ to
   (a) maximize revenue, $QP = Qf(Q)$,
   (b) minimize average cost, $C/Q = g(Q)/Q$,
   (c) maximize profit, $QP - C = Qf(Q) - g(Q)$.

3. Find the extrema of the following functions:
   (a) $f(x,y) = x^3y^2(1-x-y)$ in the first quadrant of the $xy$-plane.
   (b) $f(x,y) = (x-3y)^2 + (y-1)^2$, for all $x$ and $y$.
   (c) $f(x,y,z) = (x-3y-2z)^2 + (y-1)^2 + (z-2)^2$, for all $x$, $y$ and $z$.
   (d) $f(x,y,z) = (x^2+2y^2+3z^2)\, e^{-(xz^2+y^2+z^2)}$

4. Let $f(x,y) = (y-x^2)(y-2x^2)$. The third-order differential is $d^3f(x,y) = f_{xxx}(dx)^3 + 3f_{xxy}(dx)^2(dy) + 3f_{xyy}(dx)(dy)^2 + f_{yyy}(dy)^3$ where $f_{xxx}, f_{xxy}, f_{xyy}$, and $f_{yyy}$ are third-order partial derivatives. Show that the origin (0,0) is a saddle point.

### 11.1.3 Finding relative extrema with *Mathematica*

The *Mathematica* function **FindMinimum** can often be used to locate relative minima. The algorithm used in **FindMinimum** requires an initial guess to the location of the relative minimum. It then searches for the path of steepest descent to find a relative minimum. **FindMinimum** may or may not find an absolute minimum. Here is the *Mathematica* description of this function.

*In[67]:=*

```
?FindMinimum
```

**FindMinimum[f, {x, x0}] searches for a local minimum in f, starting from the point x=x0.**

It can be used to search for extrema of functions of one or more variables. Since the maximization of $f(x)$ is equivalent to the minimization of $-f(x)$, **FindMinimum** can also be used in maximization problems.

**Example 11.13** Use **FindMinimum** to find the relative extrema of

$$f(x) = x^3 + 2x^2 - 30x + 5$$

We choose $x = 0$ as an initial guess of where the minimum is located.

*In[68]:=*

```
Clear[f,x];
f[x_]:= x^3+2*x^2-30*x+5;
FindMinimum[f[x],{x,0}]
```

*Out[70]=*

```
{-41.9158, {x → 2.56512}}
```

*Mathematica* estimated that a relative minimum occurs at $x = 2.56512$ with a value of $f(2.56512) = -41.9158$. To find a relative maximum, the minimum of $-f(x)$ is located.

*In[71]:=*
```
FindMinimum[-f[x],{x,0}]
```

*Out[71]=*
{–93.101, {x → –3.89845}}

A plot of the function confirms these estimates.

*In[72]:=*
```
Plot[f[x],{x,-5,5},AxesLabel->{"x","f(x)"}];
```

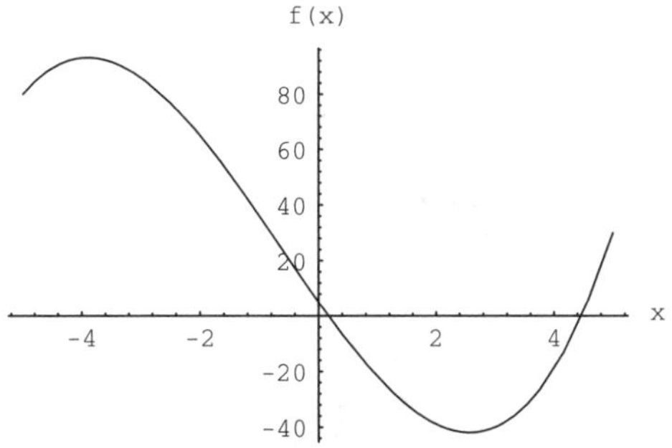


A starting point for **FindMinimum** is often difficult to provide. One approach is to graph the function to find a reasonable guess.

**Example 11.14** Find the extrema of

$f(x) = x\mathrm{e}^{-2x}$

on the internal [0,5]. We plot the graph of the function on $0 \le x \le 5$.

*In[73]:=*
```
Clear[f,x];
f[x_]:= x*Exp[-2x];
Plot[f[x],{x,0,5}];
```

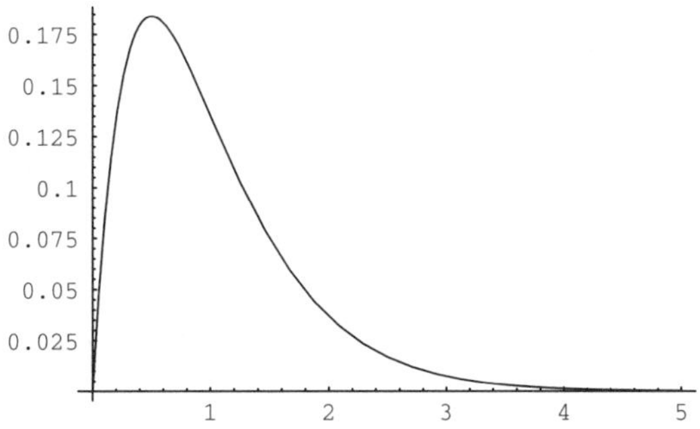


A reasonable initial guess for the maximum is $x_0 = 1$.

*In[76]:=*
```
FindMinimum[-f[x],{x,1}]
```

*Out[76]=*
```
{-0.18394, {x → 0.5}}
```

We thus find a relative maximum at $x = 0.5$ with a value of $f(0.5) = 0.18394$.

**Example 11.15** Find a relative minimum of

$$f(x,y) = 4(x-1)^2 - xy + (y-2)^2$$

on the rectangle $\{ (x,y) \mid 0 \leq x \leq 2, -2 \leq y \leq 4\}$. First we plot this function.

*In[77]:=*
```
Clear[f,x,y];
f[x_,y_]:= 4*(x-1)^2-x*y +(y-2)^2;
Plot3D[f[x,y],{x,-2,2},{y,-2,4},
                AxesLabel->{"x","y","f(x,y)"},
                ViewPoint->{1.058, -3.012, 1.121}];
```

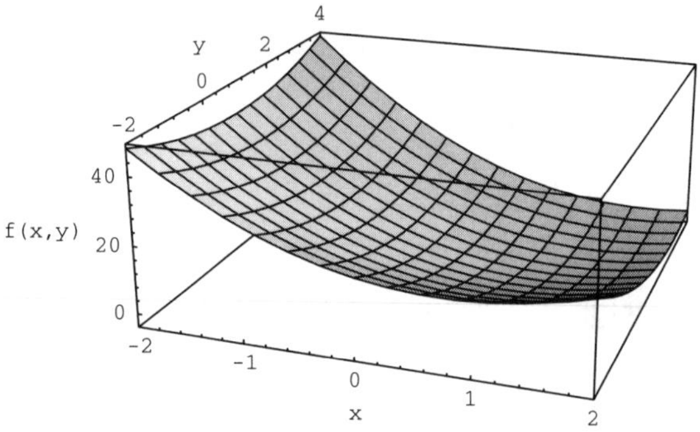


It appears that there may be relative minimum near (1,0). Hence, we will use it as a starting point.

*In[80]:=*
```
FindMinimum[f[x,y],{x,1},{y,0}]
```

*Out[80]=*
```
{-2.66667, {x → 1.33333, y → 2.66667}}
```

*Mathematica* estimates that $f(x,y)$ has a relative minimum near (1.33333,2.66667) and the value of $f(x,y)$ there is –2.6667. In fact, we could venture a guess at the exact minimum point, (4/3,8/3).

*In[81]:=*
```
Solve[gradf[f[x,y],{x,y}]=={0,0},{x,y}]
```

*Out[81]=*

$$\{\{x \to \frac{4}{3}, y \to \frac{8}{3}\}\}$$

Hence, $\mathbf{c} = (4/3,8/3)$ is a critical point and we can verify that $f(x,y)$ has a relative minimum there.

**Example 11.16** A firm employs labor, $L$, and capital, $K$, as inputs in the Cobb-Douglas production function

$$Q(L,K) = 10L^{0.5}K^{0.4}$$

Suppose the unit output price is \$5, and the unit labor cost and unit capital cost are \$12 and \$40, respectively. The firm's profit function is then

$$g(L,K) = 5Q(L,K) - 12L - 40K$$

Find the maximum profit. The profit function is plotted below.

*In[82]:=*
```
Clear[L,K,g];
g[L_,K_]:= 5*(10*L^0.5 K^0.4) - 12*L - 40*K;
Plot3D[g[L,K],{L,3,7},{K,0.5,3},
        AxesLabel->{"L","K","g(L,K)"},
        ViewPoint->{-4.000, -2.220, 1.080}];
```

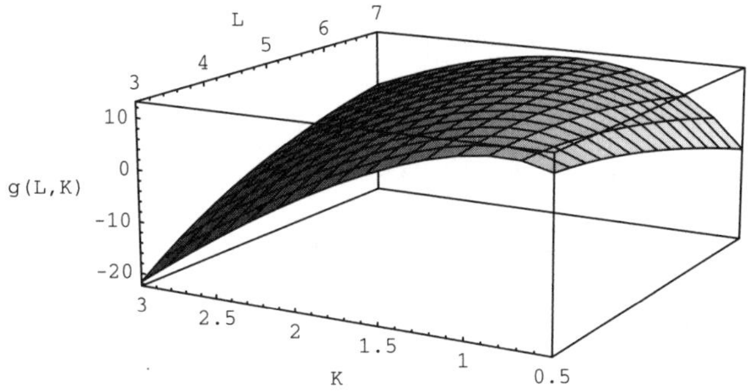


Based on the above graph, we can choose a reasonable initial guess $(L,K) = (6,1)$.

*In[85]:=*
```
FindMinimum[-g[L,K],{L,6},{K,1}]
```

*Out[85]=*
```
{-12.2643, {L → 5.11013, K → 1.22643}}
```

A relative maximum is located at $L = 5.11013$ and $K = 1.22643$ units with value, $-g(L,K) = 12.2643$, i.e., the relative maximum profit is $g(L,K) = \$12.2643$. Of course, the solution can also be obtained by finding critical points using the partial derivatives of the profit function with respect to $L$ and $K$ as illustrated below.

*In[86]:=*
```
c = Solve[{D[g[L,K],L]==0,D[g[L,K],K]==0},{K,L}]
```

*Out[86]=*
```
{{K → 1.22643, L → 5.11014}}
```

At the critical point $(L,K) = (5.11014,1.22643)$, the leading principal minors of the Hessian matrix are $|\mathbf{H}_1| = -1.17414 < 0$, and $|\mathbf{H}_2| = 7.65887 > 0$. Hence $\mathbf{H}$ is negative definite, and the critical point is a relative maximum point.

*In[87]:=*

```
h = hessian[g[L,K],{L,K}];
signQL[h] /. c[[1]]
```

*Out[88]=*

```
{-1.17414, 7.65887}
```

The corresponding maximum profit is, again, \$12.2643

*In[89]:=*

```
g[L,K] /. c[[1]]
```

*Out[89]=*

```
12.2643
```

## EXERCISES

1. Use the **FindMinimum** function to find relative extrema for the following functions:
   (a) $f(x) = x^2 - 6x + 5$.
   (b) $f(x) = (x-1)(x+2)^3$
   (c) $f(x,y) = x^3 + y^3 - 3xy + 20$
2. Find the values of $L$ and $K$ that maximize the profit in example 11.16 if the unit labor input price decreases to \$10 and the unit capital input price decreases to \$35.

### 11.1.4 Concavity, convexity, and absolute extrema

A relative extreme point may or may not be an absolute extreme point. However, a relative extreme point is an absolute extreme point if the function is convex or concave. This fact can be quite useful in determining absolute extrema since relative extrema are easy to locate, especially if the function is continuously differentiable.

Suppose $f(\mathbf{x})$ is a concave function defined on a convex set $\mathbf{S}$ and suppose $\mathbf{c} \in \mathbf{S}$ is a relative maximum point. For any $\mathbf{x} \in \mathbf{S}$ in a neighborhood of $\mathbf{c}$, we have $f(\mathbf{c}) \geq f(\mathbf{x})$. If $\mathbf{c}$ is not an absolute maximum point, then there must exist a point $\mathbf{x}_0 \in \mathbf{S}$ such that $f(\mathbf{x}_0) \geq f(\mathbf{c})$. Since $f(\mathbf{x})$ is a concave function, the values of $f$ are no less than the values of $f$ on a chord between the two points, $(\mathbf{x}_0, f(\mathbf{x}_0))$ and $(\mathbf{c}, f(\mathbf{c}))$. That is, for $0 < \theta < 1$,

$$f(\theta\mathbf{x}_0 + (1-\theta)\mathbf{c}) \geq \theta f(\mathbf{x}_0) + (1-\theta)f(\mathbf{c}) > f(\mathbf{c}) + (1-\theta)f(\mathbf{c}) = f(\mathbf{c}).$$

As $\theta \to 0$, the point $\theta\mathbf{x}_0 + (1-\theta)\mathbf{c}$ is then sufficiently close to $\mathbf{c}$ and hence is in a neighborhood of $\mathbf{c}$. The above inequality therefore contradicts the statement that $\mathbf{c}$ is a relative maximum point. This discussion leads us to the following general theorem.

**THEOREM 11.4** *Suppose* $\mathbf{S}$ *is a convex set and* $\mathbf{c} \in \mathbf{S}$ *is a relative maximum (minimum) point. Then:*

*(1)* $\mathbf{c}$ *is an absolute maximum (minimum) point if* $f(\mathbf{x})$ *is a concave (convex) function on* $\mathbf{S}$.

*(2)* $\mathbf{c}$ *is the unique absolute maximum (minimum) point if* $f(\mathbf{x})$ *is a strictly concave (convex) function on* $\mathbf{S}$.

The proof of (2) is left as an exercise.

**Example 11.17** $f(x) = x^2$ is a strictly convex function on $(-\infty,\infty)$ and $x = 0$ is a relative minimum point. It is therefore the unique absolute minimum point.

**Example 11.18** Consider the function

$$f(x) = \begin{cases} x^2 - 6x + 10, & x \leq 2 \text{ or } x \geq 4 \\ 2, & 2 < x < 4 \end{cases}$$

The function is convex, but not strictly convex, and has a relative minimum point at $x = 3$. While the point $x = 3$ is an absolute minimum point, it is not unique. We plot the function below to illustrate this discussion.

*In[90]:=*

```
Clear[f,x];
f[x_ /; x<=2 || x>=4]:= x^2-6*x+10 ;
f[x_ /; 2<x<4]:= 2 ;
Plot[f[x],{x,0,6},PlotRange->{0,10},
                    AxesLabel->{"x","f(x)"}];
```

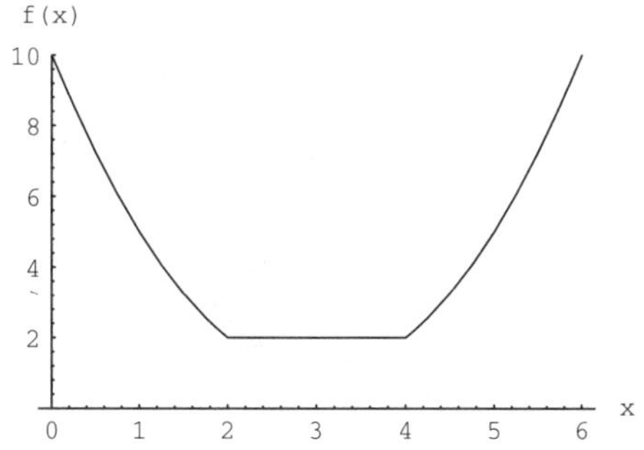


**Example 11.19** The function

$$f(x) = e^{-(x^2+y^2)}$$

given in example 11.2 in section 11.1.1 is a strictly concave function. The origin (0,0) is a relative maximum point and hence is the unique absolute maximum point.

Suppose a differentiable function $f(\mathbf{x})$ is convex on a convex set **S**. As we have shown in Chapter 10, the tangent hyperplane at point **c**, $T(\mathbf{x}) = f(\mathbf{c}) + \nabla \mathbf{f}(\mathbf{c})(\mathbf{x}-\mathbf{c})$, supports the graph of the function, i.e.,

$$f(\mathbf{x}) \geq T(\mathbf{x}) \quad \text{or} \quad f(\mathbf{x}) - f(\mathbf{c}) \geq \nabla f(\mathbf{c}) \cdot (\mathbf{x}-\mathbf{c})$$

for all **x** in **S**. Suppose **c** is a critical point, that is, $f_i(\mathbf{c}) = 0$, $i = 1,2, \ldots ,n$. Hence, $\nabla \mathbf{f}(\mathbf{c}) = \mathbf{0}$. Furthermore, $f(\mathbf{x}) \geq f(\mathbf{c})$ for all **x** and **c** in **S**. The critical point **c** is an absolute minimum point, not just a relative minimum point in **S**. If $f(\mathbf{x})$ is strictly convex, then the weak inequality ($\geq$) changes to strict inequality ($>$). The critical point must then be the unique absolute minimum point. On the other hand, if $f(\mathbf{x})$ is concave and **c** is a critical point, then $f(\mathbf{x}) \leq f(\mathbf{c})$. The critical point is an absolute maximimum point. It is the unique absolute maximum point if $f(\mathbf{x})$ is strictly concave. This discussion leads us to the following theorem.

**THEOREM 11.5** *Suppose $f(\mathbf{x})$ is differentiable on a convex set* **S**, *and* **c** *is an interior point of* **S**.

*(1) If $f(\mathbf{x})$ is a (strictly) concave function, then* **c** *is an (the unique) absolute maximum point if and only if* **c** *is a critical point.*

*(2) If $f(\mathbf{x})$ is a (strictly) convex function, then* **c** *is an (the unique) absolute minimum point if and only if* **c** *is a critical point.*

**Example 11.20** The function $f(x,y) = 4(x-1)^2 - xy + (y-2)^2$ is a strictly convex function on $\mathbf{S} = \mathbf{R}^2$, as shown by the following *Mathematica* plot.

*In[94]:=*

```
Clear[f,x,y];
f[x_,y_]:= 4*(x-1)^2-x*y+(y-2)^2;
Plot3D[f[x,y],{x,0,4},{y,0,4},
        AxesLabel->{"x","y","f(x,y)"}];
```

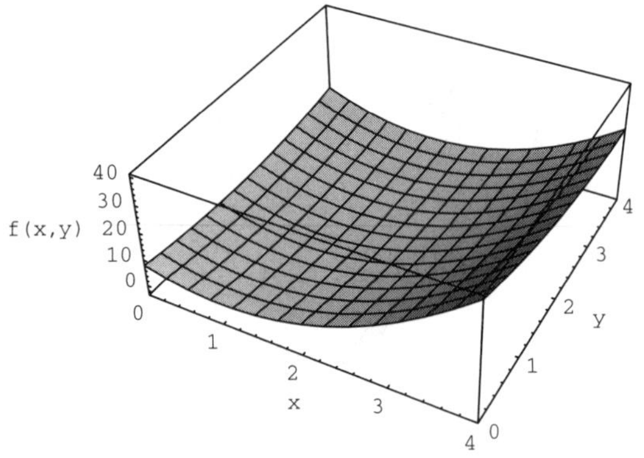


Let us calculate the critical points of $f$.

*In[97]:=*

```
Solve[{D[f[x,y],x]==0,D[f[x,y],y]==0},{x,y}]
```

*Out[97]=*

$$\{\{x \to \frac{4}{3}, y \to \frac{8}{3}\}\}$$

Since $f_x = 0$ and $f_y = 0$ at $(x,y) = (4/3,8/3)$, the critical point is the unique absolute minimum point.

**Example 11.21** Suppose $f(\mathbf{x}) = f(x_1,x_2, \ldots ,x_n)$ is a concave production funtion with $n$ inputs $x_i$. Let $p$ and $w_i$ denote the output and $i$-th input prices, respectively. As shown in example 10.26 in section 10.3, the profit function

$$h(\mathbf{x}) = pf(\mathbf{x}) - \sum_{i=1}^{n} w_i x_i$$

is concave. If $\mathbf{c}$ is a critical point of $f(\mathbf{x})$, then

$$h_i(\mathbf{c}) = pf_i(\mathbf{c}) - w_i = 0,$$

and $\mathbf{c}$ is a point that maximizes the profit. It is also an absolute maximum point. At the critical point $\mathbf{c}$, the marginal-revenue product, $pf_i(\mathbf{c})$, of each input equals its own price, $w_i = pf_i(\mathbf{c})$.

## EXERCISES

1. Find the critical points, if any, of the following functions:

$$f(x) = x^2 e^x, \quad -2 < x < 2$$
$$f(x) = -5x + 6x^2 - 3, \quad -\infty < x < \infty$$
$$f(x,y) = x^2 - 3xy + 10y^2 - 2y + 1, \quad -\infty < x,y < \infty$$
$$f(x,y) = (x+y)e^{-x}, \quad x,y > 0.$$
$$f(x,y) = x^2 + y^2, \quad x,y > 0$$

Are these points relative or absolute extremum points?

2. Write the following functions in the form $f(\mathbf{x}) = \mathbf{x}^T\mathbf{H}\mathbf{x} + \mathbf{b}\mathbf{x} + c$, where $\mathbf{H}$ is a Hessian matrix, $\mathbf{b}$ is a constant vector, and $c$ is a scalar:

$$f(x,y,z) = x^2 + 2xy + 4xz + 3y^2 + 2yz + 5z^2 - 4x + 3z - 8$$
$$f(x,y,z,w) = 5x^2 + 12xy - 16xz + 11y^2 - 26yz + 18z^2 - 2yw - 2zw + 4w^2 - 2x - 4y - 6z + 5w + 10$$

Find the critical points. Are the critical points absolute extreme points?

# □ 11.2 Constrained Extreme Values □

## 11.2.1 Method of direct substitution

Many economics problems involve optimization with certain side constraints. For example, a consumer might want to maximize a utility function subject to a budget constraint. In this section, we discuss this type of optimization.

**Example 11.22** Consider the maximization of the utility function $f(x,y) = xy$, subject to the budget constraint, $g(x,y) = x + 2y - 60 = 0$. Since the constraint implies an explicit restriction, $x = 60 - 2y$, a direct substitution of the restriction in the utility function $f(x,y) = (60 - 2y)y \equiv F(y)$ converts a constrained maximization to an unconstrained one. We obtain a maximum value by setting the first derivative of $F(y)$ to zero i.e., $60 - 4y = 0$. Hence $y = 15$, and from the constraint, $x = 30$. Since $F''(y) = -4 < 0$, the point $(x,y) = (30,15)$ is a relative maximum point with the utility value $f(30,15) = 450$. As shown in the following 3-dimensional plot, the solution of this constrained maximization problem is obtained by searching for extreme points along the constraint $x = 60 - 2y$ on the surface $z = f(x,y)$.

*In[98]:=*

```
Clear[f,x,y];
f[x_,y_]:= x*y;
utility = Plot3D[f[x,y],{x,24,36},{y,12,18},
                    AxesLabel->{"x","y","f(x,y)"},
                    ViewPoint->{-1.220, -2.790, 0.580},
                    DisplayFunction->Identity];
budget = ParametricPlot3D[{60-2*y,y,z},{y,12,18},
                    {z,300,500},DisplayFunction->Identity];
Show[utility,budget,DisplayFunction->$DisplayFunction];
```

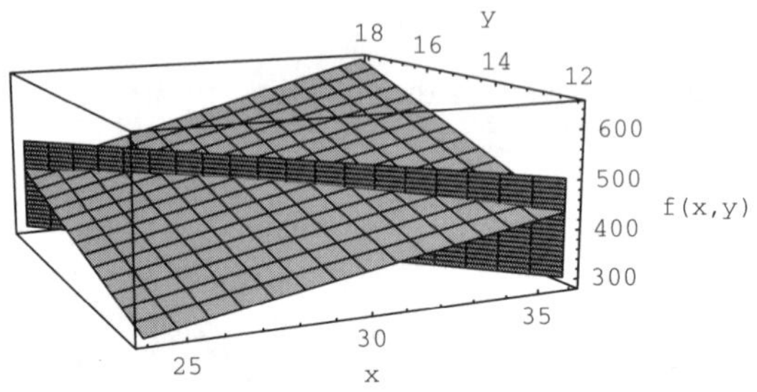


**Example 11.23** Consider the following problem with two constraints:

minimize $f(\mathbf{x}) = f(x_1, x_2, x_3, x_4) = \mathbf{x}^T\mathbf{A}\,\mathbf{x} + \mathbf{a}^T\mathbf{x}$
subject to $\mathbf{g}(\mathbf{x}) = \mathbf{B}\mathbf{x} + \mathbf{b} = \mathbf{0}$

where the matrices are

$$\mathbf{A} = \begin{bmatrix} 2 & 1 & -1 & 1 \\ 1 & 3 & -1 & 1 \\ -1 & -1 & 2 & -1 \\ 1 & 1 & -1 & 1 \end{bmatrix}; \mathbf{a} = \begin{bmatrix} -3 \\ 2 \\ 1 \\ 1 \end{bmatrix}$$

$$\mathbf{B} = \begin{bmatrix} 2 & 1 & 1 & -1 \\ 1 & 1 & 1 & 1 \end{bmatrix}; \mathbf{b} = \begin{bmatrix} 1 \\ 2 \end{bmatrix}$$

The objective function $f(\mathbf{x})$ and the two constraints $\mathbf{g}(\mathbf{x})$ are defined in the *Mathematica* statements below.

*In[103]:=*

```
Clear[f,x,A,a,B,b,f,g,x1,x2,x3,x4];
x = {x1,x2,x3,x4};
A =   {{2,1,-1,1},{1,3,-1,1};{-1,-1,2,-1},{1,1,-1,1}};
a = {-3,2,1,1};
B =  {{2,1,1,-1},{1,1,1,1}};
b = {1,2};
f[x_]:= x.A.x  +  a.x  ;
g[x_]:=  B.x  +  b;
```

The two constraints, $\mathbf{g}(\mathbf{x}) = \mathbf{B}\mathbf{x} + \mathbf{b} = \mathbf{0}$, imply that $x_3$ and $x_4$ could be expressed in terms of $x_1$ and $x_2$, if $\mathbf{B}$ is of rank 2. The solutions,

$$x_3 = -\frac{2}{3}(1+x_1) - x_2;\ x_4 = \frac{1}{2}(-1+x_1)$$

are obtained below.

*In[111]:=*

```
h = Solve[g[x]=={0,0},{x3,x4}]
```

*Out[111]=*

$$\{\{x3 \to -1 + \frac{-1+x1}{2} - 2x1 - x2,\ x4 \to \frac{-1+x1}{2}\}\}$$

Replacing $x_3$ and $x_4$ in $f(\mathbf{x})$, $f(\mathbf{x})$ becomes a function of $x_1$ and $x_2$ only, say

$$F(x_1, x_2) \equiv f\left(x_1, x_2, -\frac{3}{2}(1+x_1)-x_2, \frac{1}{2}(-1+x_1)\right)$$

Here is this substitution using *Mathematica*.

*In[112]:=*

```
F[x1,x2] = f[x] /. h[[1]]
```

*Out[112]=*

$$-2 - 4x1 + (-1 + \frac{-1+x1}{2} - 2x1 - x2)$$
$$(\frac{1-x1}{2} - x1 + 2(-1 + \frac{-1+x1}{2} - 2x1 - x2) - x2) + x2$$
$$+ \frac{(-1+x1)(1 + \frac{1-x1}{2} + \frac{-1+x1}{2} + 3x1 + 2x2)}{2}$$
$$+ x1\ (1 + \frac{1-x1}{2} + \frac{-1+x1}{2} + 4x1 + 2x2)$$
$$+ x2\ (1 + \frac{1-x1}{2} + \frac{-1+x1}{2} + 3x1 + 4x2)$$

This converts the constrained minimization of $f(x_1,x_2,x_3,x_4)$ to an unconstrained minimization of $F(x_1,x_2)$. By setting the partial derivatives to zero, $\partial F/\partial x_1 = \partial F/\partial x_2 = 0$, we obtain the critical point $\mathbf{c} = (x_1,x_2) = (29/118,-197/236)$ of $F(x_1,x_2)$.

*In[113]:=*

```
c = Solve[{D[F[x1,x2],x1]==0,D[F[x1,x2],x2]==0},{x1,x2}]
```

*Out[113]=*

$$\{\{x1 \to \frac{29}{118},\ x2 \to -(\frac{197}{236})\}\}$$

To ensure that the critical point **c** is a relative minimum point, the leading principal minors of the Hessian matrix of $F(\mathbf{x}_1,\mathbf{x}_2)$ are calculated.

*In[114]:=*

```
signQL[hessian[F[x1,x2],{x1,x2}]]
```

*Out[114]=*

$\{\frac{49}{2}, 118\}$

Since $|\mathbf{H}_1| = 49/2 > 0$, and $|\mathbf{H}| = 118 > 0$, the Hessian matrix is positive definite. The point $(\mathbf{x}_1,\mathbf{x}_2) = (29/118,-197/236)$ is indeed a relative minimum point. The rest of the solution is obtained using the constraints, $\mathbf{g}(\mathbf{x}) = \mathbf{B}\mathbf{x} + \mathbf{b} = \mathbf{0}$.

*In[115]:=*

```
Solve[(g[x] /. c[[1]]) == {0,0},{x3,x4}]
```

*Out[115]=*

$\{\{x3 \to -(\frac{61}{59}), x4 \to -(\frac{89}{236})\}\}$

In summation,

$$x_1 = \frac{29}{118}, \; x_2 = \frac{-197}{236}, \; x_3 = \frac{-61}{59}, \; x_4 = \frac{-89}{236}$$

is a relative minimum point of the function

$$f(\mathbf{x}) = f(x_1,x_2,x_3,x_4) = \mathbf{x}^T\mathbf{A}\,\mathbf{x} + \mathbf{a}^T\mathbf{x}$$

subject to the constraints

$$\mathbf{g}(\mathbf{x}) = \mathbf{B}\mathbf{x} + \mathbf{b} = \mathbf{0}$$

with the relative minimum value $-609/472$ as we see in the following calculation.

*In[116]:=*

```
f[x] /. {x1->29/118,x2->-197/236,x3->-61/59,x4->-89/236}
```

*Out[116]=*

$-(\frac{609}{472})$

The constraints $\mathbf{g}(\mathbf{x}) = \mathbf{B}\mathbf{x} + \mathbf{b} = \mathbf{0}$ are satisfied at this point as we confirm in the following calculation.

*In[117]:=*

```
g[x] /. {x1->29/118,x2->-197/236,x3->-61/59,x4->-89/236}
```

*Out[117]=*

{0, 0}

The example above demonstrates a method to solve the constrained optimization problem through a direct substitution. Direct substitution is often used to solve simple problems where the objective function $f(\mathbf{x})$ and the constraints $\mathbf{g}(\mathbf{x}) = \mathbf{0}$ can be manipulated to reduce the problem to optimizing a function with fewer independent variables and no constraints. In many optimization problems, this is not possible. For example, it is not possible to obtain an explicit representation for $x_2$ as a function of $x_1$ with the constraint, $g(x_1,x_2) = \log(x_1+x_2) + x_1 + x_2 + 3 = 0$. In such cases, we often employ an alternative method known as the Lagrange Multiplier Method.

## EXERCISE

1. Use the direct substitution method to find the relative extrema (if any) for the following functions subject to their constraints:
   (a) $f(x,y) = xy$, subject to
   $g(x,y) = x^2 + y^2 - 1 = 0$.
   (b) $f(x,y) = x^2 + 2y^2$, subject to
   $g(x,y) = x + 2y - 5 = 0$.
   (c) $f(x,y,z) = x^2 + 2y^2 + 3z^2$, subject to
   $g(x,y,z) = x + y + z - 5 = 0$.
   (d) $f(x,y,z) = x^2 + 2y^2 + z^2$, subject to
   $g(x,y) = x^2 + 2xy + y^2 - 1 = 0$, and
   $h(y,z) = y + z - 4 = 0$.

### 11.2.2 Lagrangian function

Consider an optimization problem that requires the maximization or minimization of a differentiable function $f(x,y)$ subject to the constraint $g(x,y) = 0$. If the constraint was not present, then a relative extremum occurs at a point $(x_0,y_0)$ where $f_x(x_0,y_0) = f_y(x_0,y_0) = 0$ and hence,

$$df(x_0,y_0) = f_x(x_0,y_0)\,dx + f_y(x_0,y_0)\,dy = 0.$$

With the constraint, we still require $df(x_0,y_0) = 0$, but since $x$ and $y$ are subject to the side restriction $g(x,y) = 0$, the partial derivatives are not necessarily zero. In other words, $dx$ and $dy$ are not independent differentials in $df(x,y)$. To see this, we compute the differential of the constraint

$$dg(x_0,y_0) = g_x(x_0,y_0)\,dx + g_y(x_0,y_0)\,dy = 0.$$

If $g_x(x_0,y_0) \neq 0$, then we have

$$dx = -\frac{g_y(x_0,y_0)}{g_x(x_0,y_0)}\,dy.$$

Thus the differential $dx$ depends on the differential $dy$.

Substituting the above relation $dx$ in $df(x_0,y_0)$, we have

$$df(x_0,y_0) = \left[ f_y(x_0,y_0) - f_x(x_0,y_0)\frac{g_y(x_0,y_0)}{g_x(x_0,y_0)} \right] dy = 0.$$

For constrained optimization, a necessary condition that $df(x_0,y_0) = 0$ subject to $g(x_0,y_0) = 0$ is now

$$f_y(x_0,y_0) - f_x(x_0,y_0)\frac{g_y(x_0,y_0)}{g_x(x_0,y_0)} = 0.$$

Alternatively, if $f_x(x_0,y_0) \neq 0$, then the conditions can be written as

$$\frac{f_y(x_0,y_0)}{f_x(x_0,y_0)} = \frac{g_y(x_0,y_0)}{g_x(x_0,y_0)}.$$

This equation implies that $f_x(x_0,y_0)$ is proportional to $g_x(x_0,y_0)$, and $f_y(x_0,y_0)$ is proportional to $g_y(x_0,y_0)$ with the same proportionality constant, $\lambda$. That is,

$$f_x(x_0,y_0) = -\lambda g_x(x_0,y_0)$$
$$f_y(x_0,y_0) = -\lambda g_y(x_0,y_0).$$

The constant, $\lambda$, is called a *Lagrange multiplier*.

This condition can be derived more directly using the *Lagrangian function*

$$L(x,y,\lambda) = f(x,y) + \lambda g(x,y).$$

We treat the Lagrange multiplier $\lambda$ as a variable along with $x$ and $y$. The Lagrangian function $L(x,y,\lambda)$ is equal to the objective function $f(x,y)$ for all points $(x,y)$ that satisfy the constraint, $g(x,y) = 0$. We next compute the critical points of $L$. Its critical points must satisfy the system of equations:

$$L_x = f_x + \lambda g_x = 0$$
$$L_y = f_y + \lambda g_y = 0$$
$$L_\lambda = g(x,y) = 0.$$

Note that the three equations are identical to the necessary condition

$$df(x,y) = f_x dx + f_y dy = 0$$

subject to $g(x,y) = 0$. If $(x_0,y_0,\lambda_0)$ is a critical point of the Lagrangian function $L(x,y,\lambda)$, then $(x_0,y_0)$ will automatically satisfy the equations

$$df(x_0,y_0) = 0$$
$$g(x_0,y_0) = 0.$$

Furthermore, at $(x_0,y_0,\lambda_0)$, the value of the Lagrangian function is equal to the value of the objective function, $L(x_0,y_0,\lambda_0) = f(x_0,y_0)$ since $g(x_0,y_0) = 0$. This alternative method based on the Lagrangian function is called the *Lagrange Multiplier Method.*

Necessary conditions for the existence of an optimal solution of the constrained optimization of $f(x,y)$ subject to $g(x,y) = 0$ can be summarized in the following three sets of equivalent statements:

(1) $df(x,y) = f_x dx + f_y dy = 0$ and
$g(x,y) = 0$

(2) $\dfrac{f_y}{f_x} = \dfrac{g_y}{g_x}$ and
$g(x,y) = 0$

(3) $L_x = f_x + \lambda g_x = 0$
$L_y = f_y + \lambda g_y = 0$
$L_\lambda = g(x,y) = 0$

**Example 11.24** Find the relative extrema of

$f(x,y) = (x-1)^2 + y^2$

subject to $g(x,y) = y^2 + 2x - 5 = 0$. The Lagrangian function is

$L(x,y,\lambda) = (x-1)^2 + y^2 + \lambda(y^2 + 2x - 5)$.

We first define the Lagrangian function in the following *Mathematica* statements.

*In[118]:=*

```
Clear[f,g,L,x,y,lambda];
f[x_,y_]:=  (x-1)^2  +  y^2;
g[x_,y_]:=  y^2  +  2*x  -  5;
L[x_,y_,lambda_]:=  f[x,y]  +  lambda*g[x,y];
```

Next we compute the critical points of $L(x,y,\lambda)$.

*In[122]:=*

```
Solve[{D[L[x,y,lambda],x]==0,
        D[L[x,y,lambda],y]==0,
         D[L[x,y,lambda],lambda]==0},{x,y,lambda}]
```

*Out[122]=*

$\{\{\text{lambda} \to -(\frac{2}{3}), \text{x} \to \frac{5}{2}, \text{y} \to 0\},$
$\{\text{x} \to 2, \text{lambda} \to -1, \text{y} \to -1\}, \{\text{x} \to 2, \text{lambda} \to -1, \text{y} \to 1\}\}$

Three critical points are:

$(x_0,y_0,\lambda_0) = (5/2,\ 0,\ -3/2)$
$(x_0,y_0,\lambda_0) = (2,\ -1,\ -1)$
$(x_0,y_0,\lambda_0) = (2,\ 1,\ -1)$.

While these three critical points satisfy the necessary conditions for relative extrema, they may or may not be extrema. In the next section we will present sufficient conditions for them to be relative extrema.

To give a geometric interpretation of this method, let us consider the problem of maximizing $f(x,y)$ subject to the constraint $g(x,y) = 0$. A maximum value for $f(x,y)$ can be found by searching for the level curves of $f$, $\{ (x,y) \mid f(x,y) = k\}$. As shown in figure 11.1, when $k$ increases, the level curve moves higher and higher in the direction of increasing $k$: $k_1 < k_2 < \ldots < k_{max}$. The intersections of any level curve with the constraint $g(x,y) = 0$, are possible points where $f$ takes its maximum value and satisfy the constraint. The points $a$, $b$, $c$, $d$ and $e$ are such points. The slope of the tangent line to a level curve is $dx/dy = -f_y/f_x$ since $f_x dx + f_y dy = 0$. Similarly, the slope of the tangent line to the constraint curve is $dx/dy = -g_y/g_x$ since $g_x dx + g_y dy = 0$. A necessary condition for $f$ to have a relative maximum value at $(x_0,y_0)$ is $-f_x(x_0,y_0)/f_y(x_0,y_0) = -g_x(x_0,y_0)/g_y(x_0,y_0)$. The slope $-f_y(x_0,y_0)/f_x(x_0,y_0)$ of the level curve $f(x,y) = k_{max}$ must be equal to the slope of the constraint $-g_y(x_0,y_0)/g_x(x_0,y_0)$. The level curve, $f(x,y) = k_{max}$, is tangent to the constraint curve at this point. In terms of the Lagrange multiplier, the necessary condition can be written as $f_x(x_0,y_0)/g_x(x_0,y_0) = f_y(x_0,y_0)/g_y(x_0,y_0) = -\lambda$.

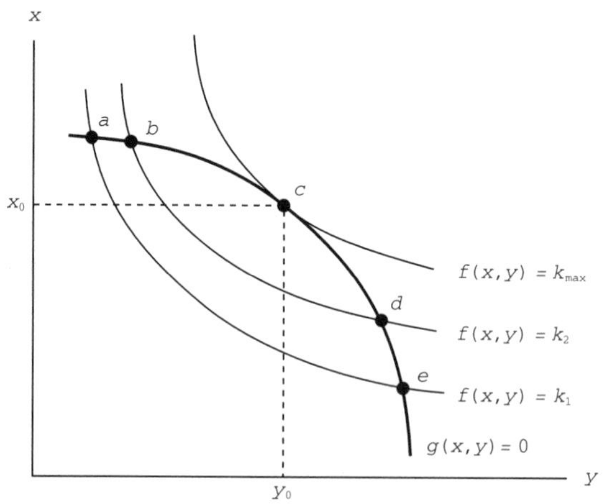


**Figure 11.1** Relative maximum with constraint

**Example 11.25** Find the maximum value of the utility function

$f(x,y) = (1/2)\log x + \log y$

subject to a linear budget constraint, $g(x,y) = 2x + y - 10 = 0$. We use the Lagrangian function.

*In[123]:=*

```
Clear[f,g,L,x,y,lambda];
f[x_,y_]:= (1/2)*Log[x]+Log[y];
g[x_,y_]:= 2*x+y-10;
L[x_,y_,lambda_]:= f[x,y]+lambda*g[x,y];
```

Next we calculate the critical points of $L(x,y,\lambda)$.

*In[127]:=*

```
c = Solve[{D[L[x,y,lambda],x]==0,
           D[L[x,y,lambda],y]==0,
             D[L[x,y,lambda],lambda]==0},{x,y,lambda}]
```

*Out[127]=*

$$\{\{\text{lambda} \to -(\frac{3}{20}),\ \text{x} \to \frac{5}{3},\ \text{y} \to \frac{20}{3}\}\}$$

The only critical point is $(x_0,y_0,\lambda_0) = (5/3,20/3,-3/20)$ and the value of the Lagrangian function is computed below.

*In[128]:=*

```
maxvalue = L[x,y,lambda]/.c[[1]]
```

*Out[128]=*

$$\frac{\text{Log}[\frac{5}{3}]}{2} + \text{Log}[\frac{20}{3}]$$

*In[129]:=*
```
maxvalue // N
```

*Out[129]=*
```
2.15253
```

Hence, $f(x_0,y_0) \approx 2.15253$. We use *Mathematica* to plot four level curves, $\{(x,y) \mid f(x,y) = k\}$ for $k = 2, 2.15253, 2.3$, and $2.5$, and the budget constraint. This plot shows that at the point $(5/3,20/3)$, the level curve $f(x,y) = 2.15253$ is tangent to the constraint curve $g(x,y) = 2x + y - 10 = 0$.

*In[130]:=*
```
utility = ContourPlot[f[x,y],{x,1,3},{y,5,8},
                    Contours->{2,2.15253,2.3,2.5},
                    ContourShading->False,
                    DisplayFunction->Identity];
budget = ContourPlot[g[x,y],{x,1,3},{y,5,8},
                    Contours->{0},ContourShading->False,
                    ContourStyle->Thickness[0.0075],
                    DisplayFunction->Identity];
Show[utility,budget,DisplayFunction->$DisplayFunction];
```

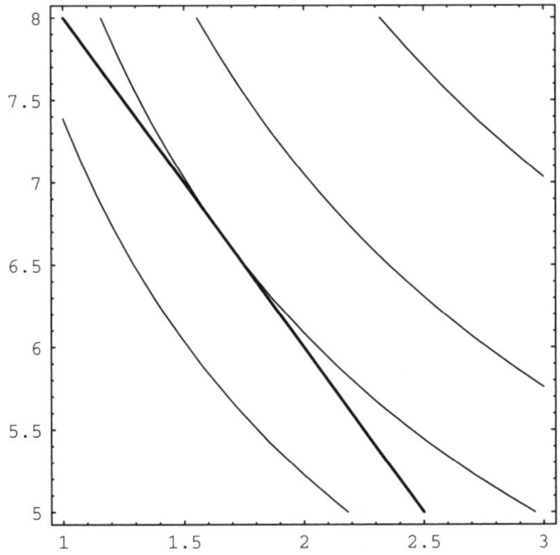


The Lagrange multiplier method can be extended to functions of $n$-variables. Consider the optimization problems:

maximize or minimize $f(\mathbf{x}) = f(x_1,x_2, \ldots ,x_n)$
subject to $g(\mathbf{x}) = g(x_1,x_2, \ldots ,x_n) = 0.$

A necessary condition for $\mathbf{x}_0$ to be a point of relative extremum is

$$df(\mathbf{x}_0) = f_1(\mathbf{x}_0)\,dx_1 + \ldots + f_n(\mathbf{x}_0)\,dx_n = 0$$

such that $g(\mathbf{x}_0) = 0$. This can also be written in terms of a Lagrangian function

$L(\mathbf{x},\lambda) = f(\mathbf{x}) + \lambda g(\mathbf{x})$.

Taking the partial derivatives of $L(\mathbf{x}, \lambda)$ with respect to $\mathbf{x}$ and $\lambda$, we have

$L_i = f_i + \lambda g_i = 0,\ i = 1,2, \ldots ,n$
$L_\lambda = g(\mathbf{x}) = 0.$

These $n$+1 equations can be solved for critical points $\mathbf{c} = (\mathbf{x}_0,\lambda_0)$ of $L$.

**Example 11.26** Consider a utility function of three goods

$$f(x_1,x_2,x_3) = a_1\log(x_1-b_1) + a_2\log(x_2-b_2) + a_3\log(x_3-b_3)$$

where $x_i - b_i > 0$, $b_i > 0$ and $a_i > 0$ with $a_1 + a_2 + a_3 = 1$. The constants $b_i$ can be interpreted as the minimum or "necessary" quantity of the $i$-th good required for consumption. Let $P_i$ and $M$ be the constant prices and income, respectively. Suppose a consumer desires to maximize the utility function subject to the budget constraint

$$g(x_1,x_2,x_3) = p_1x_1 + p_2x_2 + p_3x_3 - M = 0.$$

The Lagrangian function for this problem is

$$L(\mathbf{x},\lambda) = \sum_{i=1}^{3} a_i\log(x_i-b_i) + \lambda(\sum_{i=1}^{3} p_ix_i-Y)$$

*In[133]:=*

```
Clear[f,g,L,x1,x2,x3];
SetAttributes[{a1,a2,a3,b1,b2,b3,p1,p2,p3,Y},Constant];
f[x1_,x2_,x3_]:= a1*Log[x1-b1]  + a2*Log[x2-b2]  +
                    a3*Log[x3-b3];
g[x1_,x2_,x3_]:= p1*x1  + p2*x2  + p3*x3  - Y;
L[x1_,x2_,x3_,lambda_]:= f[x1,x2,x3]+lambda*g[x1,x2,x3];
```

The critical point $\mathbf{c} = (\mathbf{x}_0,\lambda_0)$ is obtained by setting the partials of $L$ to zero.

*In[138]:=*

```
c = Solve[{D[L[x1,x2,x3,lambda],x1]==0,
           D[L[x1,x2,x3,lambda],x2]==0,
           D[L[x1,x2,x3,lambda],x3]==0,
            D[L[x1,x2,x3,lambda],lambda]==0},
          {x1,x2,x3,lambda}];
Simplify[c]
```

*Out[139]=*

$$\{\{x1 \to \frac{a2\ b1\ p1 + a3\ b1\ p1 - a1\ b2\ p2 - a1\ b3\ p3 + a1\ Y}{(a1 + a2 + a3)p1},$$
$$x2 \to \frac{-(a2\ b1\ p1) + a1\ b2\ p2 + a3\ b2\ p2 - a2\ b3\ p3 + a2\ Y}{(a1 + a2 + a3)p2},$$
$$x3 \to \frac{-(a3\ b1\ p1) - a3\ b2\ p2 + a1\ b3\ p3 + a2\ b3\ p3 + a3\ Y}{(a1 + a2 + a3)p3},$$
$$lambda \to \frac{a1 + a2 + a3}{b1\ p1 + b2\ p2 + b3\ p3 - Y}\}\}$$

Setting $a_1 + a_2 + a_3 = 1$, the critical point **c** can be further simplified to yield the well-known demand functions:

$$x_i = b_i + \frac{a_i}{p_i}(Y - \sum_{i=1}^{3} p_i b_i), \quad i=1,2,3$$

$$\lambda = \frac{-1}{Y - \sum_{i=1}^{3} p_i b_i}$$

Multiplying $x_i$ by $p_i$, we obtain the *linear expenditure system*:

$$p_i x_i = p_i b_i + a_i(Y - \sum_{i=1}^{3} p_i b_i), \quad i=1,2,3$$

The first term on the right, $p_i b_i$, is the minimum expenditure to which the consumer is committed. The term, $(Y - \Sigma p_i b_i)$ is the "supernumerary" income beyond the minimum required expenditure. Thus the expenditure $p_i x_i$ on any good is a linear function of the supernumerary income.

An extension to the case of $n$-variables with $m$ multiple constraints is also straightforward. Consider the constrained optimization problem:

maximize or minimize $f(\mathbf{x}) = f(x_1, x_2, \ldots, x_n)$
subject to $g^1(\mathbf{x}) = g^1(x_1, x_2, \ldots, x_n) = 0$
$g^2(\mathbf{x}) = g^2(x_1, x_2, \ldots, x_n) = 0$
. . . . . . . . . . . . . . . . .
$g^m(\mathbf{x}) = g^m(x_1, x_2, \ldots, x_n) = 0.$

A necessary condition for a relative extremum is

$$df(\mathbf{x}) = f_1 dx_1 + f_2 dx_2 + \ldots + f_n dx_n = 0$$

subject to $g^j(\mathbf{x}) = 0$, $j = 1,2, \ldots, m$. To form the Lagrangian function we introduce $m$ Lagrange multipliers, one for each constraint:

$$L(x_1 \ldots x_n, \lambda_1 \ldots \lambda_m) = f(x_1 \ldots x_n) + \sum_{j=1}^{m} \lambda_j g^j(x_1 \ldots x_n).$$

In a compact matrix form, we can write this function as

$$L(\mathbf{x}, \lambda) = f(\mathbf{x}) + \boldsymbol{\lambda}^T \mathbf{g}(\mathbf{x})$$

where $\boldsymbol{\lambda} = [\lambda_1 \ldots \lambda_m]^T$ is a vector of multipliers and $\mathbf{g}(\mathbf{x})$ is a vector-valued function that represents the constraints. A necessary condition for relative extremum is

$$L_i = \frac{\partial L}{\partial x_i} = f_i + \sum_{j=1}^{m} \lambda_j \frac{\partial g^j}{\partial x_i} = f_i + \sum_{j=1}^{m} \lambda_j g_i^j = 0, \quad i = 1,2, \ldots, n$$

$$L_{\lambda_j} = \frac{\partial L}{\partial \lambda_j} = g^j = 0, \quad j = 1,2, \ldots, m$$

These $n{+}m$ equations can be solved for critical points $\mathbf{c} = (\mathbf{x}_0, \lambda_0)$ of $L(\mathbf{x}, \lambda)$.

**Example 11.27** Find the minimum value of

$$f(x,y,z,w) = x^2 + 2y^2 + 2z^2 + w^2 - 2xy - 2yz - 2zw$$

subject to

$$g^1(x,y,z,w) = 2x + y + z + w - 10 = 0$$
$$g^2(x,y,z,w) = 4x - z + w - 12 = 0.$$

We use the Lagrangian function

$$\begin{aligned} L(x,y,z,w,\lambda_1,\lambda_2) = {} & x^2 + 2y^2 + 2z^2 + w^2 - 2xy - 2yz - 2zw \\ & + \lambda_1(2x + y + z + w - 10) \\ & + \lambda_2(4x - z + w - 12) \end{aligned}$$

The Lagrangian function is defined in the following *Mathematica* statements.

*In[140]:=*
```
Clear[f,g1,g2,L,x,y,z,w,lambda1,lambda2,c]
f[x_,y_,z_,w_]= x^2+2*y^2+2*z^2+w^2-2*x*y-2*y*z-2*z*w;
g1[x_,y_,z_,w_]:= 2*x+y+z+w-10;
g2[x_,y_,z_,w_]:= 4*x-z+w-12;
L[x_,y_,z_,w_,lambda1_,lambda2_]:=
     f[x,y,z,w]+lambda1*g1[x,y,z,w]+lambda2*g2[x,y,z,w];
```

Taking the partial derivative of $L(x,y,z,w,\lambda_1,\lambda_2)$, we obtain the critical points as shown below.

*In[145]:=*
```
c = Solve[{D[L[x,y,z,w,lambda1,lambda2],x]==0,
           D[L[x,y,z,w,lambda1,lambda2],y]==0,
           D[L[x,y,z,w,lambda1,lambda2],z]==0,
           D[L[x,y,z,w,lambda1,lambda2],w]==0,
           D[L[x,y,z,w,lambda1,lambda2],lambda1]==0,
           D[L[x,y,z,w,lambda1,lambda2],lambda2]==0},
         {x,y,z,w,lambda1,lambda2}]
```

*Out[145]=*

$$\{\{\text{lambda2} \to -(\frac{200}{209}),\ \text{x} \to \frac{622}{209},\ \text{y} \to \frac{382}{209},\ \text{w} \to \frac{22}{19},\ \text{lambda1} \to \frac{160}{209},\ \text{z} \to \frac{222}{209}\}\}$$

The point (622/209,382/209,222/209,22/19) may or may not be a relative minimum of the constrained problem. Let us compute the value of $f$ there.

*In[146]:=*
```
f[x,y,z,w] /. c[[1]]
```

*Out[146]=*

$$\frac{400}{209}$$

Treating the Lagrange multipliers $\lambda$ as independent variables, we obtain the necessary condition or critical points of the Lagrangian function $L(\mathbf{x},\lambda)$. This procedure is similar to finding critical points in an unconstrained case. However, this similarity cannot be carried over to sufficient conditions. It is incorrect to treat $L(\mathbf{x},\lambda)$ as a strictly unconstrained objective function for two reasons. First, suppose the relative maximum of $f(\mathbf{x})$ subject the constraint $\mathbf{g}(\mathbf{x}) = \mathbf{0}$ occurs at the point $\mathbf{x}_0$. The Lagrangian function at $\mathbf{x}_0$ becomes $L(\mathbf{x}_0,\boldsymbol{\lambda}) = f(\mathbf{x}_0) + \boldsymbol{\lambda}^T\mathbf{g}(\mathbf{x}_0) = f(\mathbf{x}_0)$ since $\mathbf{g}(\mathbf{x}_0) = \mathbf{0}$. The Lagrangian function is invariant with respect to $\boldsymbol{\lambda}$. Second, the values of $\mathbf{x} = (x_1,x_2, \ldots ,x_n)$ are not "free" in maximizing $L(\mathbf{x},\boldsymbol{\lambda})$ since the variation of $\mathbf{x}$ is restricted to be $\mathbf{g}(\mathbf{x}) = \mathbf{0}$, and hence the Lagrangian function cannot be treated as an unconstrained objective function. For these two reasons a new procedure is needed to develop a sufficient condition for relative extrema with constraints.

## EXERCISES

1. Given the utility function $f(x,y) = \log(x-1) + \log(y-2)$ and the budget constraint $2x+y = 10$, do the following:
   (a) Write the Lagrangian function for maximizing the utility function.
   (b) Solve for the relative maximum point $(x_0,y_0)$.
   (c) Use **ContourPlot** to show that the level curve at $(x_0,y_0)$ is tangent to the budget constraint.
2. Write the Lagrangian function for

   $$\min f(\mathbf{x}) = x_1^2 + x_2^2 + \ldots + x_n^2$$

   subject to $\sum x_i = 1$. Find the relative minimum points.
3. Find the relative extreme points (if any) of the functions:
   (a) $f(x,y) = x^2-2xy+y^2$ subject $xy = -1$.
   (b) $f(x,y,z) = (x+y+z-5)$ subject to $x+y^2+z = 4$, and $x+y+z^2 = 1$.
   (c) $f(x,y,z) = x+y+z$ subject to $\log x + \log y + \log z = 3$.

### 11.2.3 Sufficient conditions

Consider the constrained optimization problem of maximizing or minimizing $f(x,y)$ subject to the constraint $g(x,y) = 0$. A necessary condition for $(x_0,y_0)$ to be a relative extremum point is

$$df(x_0,y_0) = f_x(x_0,y_0)\,dx + f_y(x_0,y_0)\,dy = 0$$

subject to $g(x_0,y_0) = 0$. To obtain the sufficient conditions we need to examine the sign of the second-order differential $d^2f(x,y)$ as in the case of unconstrained optimization. Since $x$ and $y$ are subject to the restriction $g(x,y) = 0$, the differential of a variable, say $dx$, is not independent of $dy$. As discussed in Chapter 8, the second-order differential in this case is

$$\begin{aligned}
d^2f(x,y) &= d(f_x dx + f_y dy)\\
&= f_x d(dx) + d(f_x)dx + f_y d(dy) + d(f_y)dy\\
&= f_x d^2x + (f_{xx}dx + f_{xy}dy)dx\\
&\quad + f_y(0) + (f_{yy}dy + f_{yx}dx)dy\\
&= f_x d^2x + [dx \quad dy]\begin{bmatrix} f_{xx} & f_{xy}\\ f_{yx} & f_{yy}\end{bmatrix}\begin{bmatrix} dx\\ dy\end{bmatrix}\\
&= f_x d^2x + [dx \quad dy]\mathbf{H}\begin{bmatrix} dx\\ dy\end{bmatrix}
\end{aligned}$$

where $\mathbf{H}$ is the Hessian matrix of $f(x,y)$. Notice that $d(dx) = d^2x \neq 0$ and $d(dy) = d^2y = 0$ since $x$ is a function of $y$ through the constraint $g(x,y) = 0$. To calculate $d^2x$, we take the second-order differential of $g(x,y) = 0$ and observe the implicit dependency of $x$ on $y$. That is,

$$\begin{aligned}
d^2g(x,y) &= g_x d^2x + [dx \quad dy]\begin{bmatrix} g_{xx} & g_{xy}\\ g_{yx} & g_{yy}\end{bmatrix}\begin{bmatrix} dx\\ dy\end{bmatrix}\\
&= g_x d^2x + [dx \quad dy]\mathbf{G}\begin{bmatrix} dx\\ dy\end{bmatrix} = 0
\end{aligned}$$

where $\mathbf{G}(x,y)$ is the Hessian matrix of $g(x,y)$. Assuming $g_x \neq 0$, we solve for $d^2x$

$$d^2x = -\frac{1}{g_x}[dx \quad dy]\mathbf{G}\begin{bmatrix} dx\\ dy\end{bmatrix}$$

Substituting this result into $d^2f(x,y)$, we have

$$\begin{aligned}
d^2f(x,y) &= -\frac{f_x}{g_x}[dx \quad dy]\mathbf{G}\begin{bmatrix} dx\\ dy\end{bmatrix} + [dx \quad dy]\mathbf{H}\begin{bmatrix} dx\\ dy\end{bmatrix}\\
&= [dx \quad dy](\mathbf{H} - \frac{f_x}{g_x}\mathbf{G})\begin{bmatrix} dx\\ dy\end{bmatrix}
\end{aligned}$$

The second-order differential is a quadratic form with the matrix

$$\mathbf{H} - \frac{f_x}{g_x}\mathbf{G} = \begin{bmatrix} f_{xx} - \frac{f_x}{g_x}g_{xx} & f_{xy} - \frac{f_x}{g_x}g_{xy}\\ f_{yx} - \frac{f_x}{g_x}g_{yx} & f_{yy} - \frac{f_x}{g_x}g_{yy}\end{bmatrix}$$

A sufficient condition for a relative extremum to exist is then related to the sign of the quadratic form $d^2f(x,y)$. However, the "variables" of the quadratic form are the differentials, $dx$ and $dy$, which are subject to the restriction imposed by the constraint equation $g(x,y) = 0$. That is,

$$dg(x,y) = g_x dx + g_y dy = [g_x \quad g_y]\begin{bmatrix} dx\\ dy\end{bmatrix} = 0$$

In Chapter 7 we gave sufficient conditions for a quadratic form to be positive or negative definite subject to constraints. The conditions are stated in terms of the signs of the leading principal minors of the bordered Hessian matrix. We use these conditions to prove the following theorem.

**Theorem 11.6** *(Sufficient Condition) Suppose the objective function $f(x,y)$ and the constraint $g(x,y) = 0$ are twice differentiable, and suppose the point $(x_0,y_0)$ satisfies the necessary conditions for a relative extremum. Define the bordered Hessian determinant evaluated at $(x_0,y_0)$ as*

$$|\mathbf{B}| = \begin{vmatrix} 0 & g_x & g_y \\ g_x & f_{xx} - \dfrac{f_x}{g_x} g_{xx} & f_{xy} - \dfrac{f_x}{g_x} g_{xy} \\ g_y & f_{yx} - \dfrac{f_x}{g_x} g_{yx} & f_{yy} - \dfrac{f_x}{g_x} g_{yy} \end{vmatrix}$$

*We have the following sufficient conditions for relative extrema:*

*(1) If $d^2f(x_0,y_0) > 0$ (positive definite) subject to $dg(x_0,y_0) = 0$, then $(x_0,y_0)$ is a relative minimum point. Equivalently, if $|\mathbf{B}| < 0$, then $(x_0,y_0)$ is a relative minimum point.*

*(2) If $d^2f(x_0,y_0) < 0$ (negative definite) subject to $dg(x_0,y_0) = 0$, then $(x_0,y_0)$ is a relative maximum point. Equivalently, if $|\mathbf{B}| > 0$, then $(x_0,y_0)$ is a relative maximum point.*

From the computational point of view, the bordered Hessian determinant can be calculated directly from the Hessian matrix of the Lagrangian function. That is,

$$|\mathbf{B}| = \begin{vmatrix} L_{\lambda\lambda} & L_{\lambda x} & L_{\lambda y} \\ L_{x\lambda} & L_{xx} & L_{xx} \\ L_{y\lambda} & L_{yx} & L_{yy} \end{vmatrix}$$

where $L_{ij}$ are the second-order partial derivative of

$$L(x,y,\lambda) = f(x,y) + \lambda g(x,y).$$

For example,

$$L_{\lambda\lambda} = 0;\ L_{x\lambda} = L_{\lambda x} = g_x;\ L_{y\lambda} = L_{\lambda y} = g_y$$
$$L_{xx} = f_{xx} + \lambda\, g_{xx};\ L_{xy} = f_{xy} + \lambda g_{xy},\ L_{yy} = f_{yy} + \lambda g_{yy}.$$

It is easy to verify then that after the substitution of these partial derivatives and with the necessary condition, $\lambda = -f_x/g_x$, the Hessian determinant of the Lagrangian function is identical to the bordered Hessian determinant of $f(x,y)$ subject to the constraint $g(x,y) = 0$.

**Example 11.28** As shown in example 11.24 in section 11.2.2, the function $f(x,y) = (x-1)^2 + y^2$ subject to $g(x,y) = y^2 + 2x - 5 = 0$ has three critical points for $L(x,y,\lambda)$ at $(x,y,\lambda) = (5/2,0,-3/2)$, $(2,-1,-1)$, and $(2,1,-1)$. Are these points relative extrema of the constrained optimization problem? We use the sufficient conditions presented in Theorem 11.6. The **MathEcon** functions **hessian** and **signQL** calculate the bodered Hessian matrix **B** of $L(x,y,\lambda)$ and the signs of the leading principal minors evaluated at these critical points. Since $L_{\lambda\lambda}$ is arranged as the first element of the bordered Hessian matrix **B**, the list of the variables in **hessian** should have $\lambda$ as the first element.

*In[147]:=*
```
Clear[f,g,L,x,y,lambda];
f[x_,y_]:= (x-1)^2 + y^2;
g[x_,y_]:= y^2 + 2*x - 5;
L[x_,y_,lambda_]:= f[x,y]+lambda*g[x,y];
B = hessian[L[x,y,lambda],{lambda,x,y}];
```

At the first critical point $(x,y,\lambda) = (5/2,0,-3/2)$,

*In[152]:=*
```
signQL[B] /. {x->5/2,y->0,lambda->-3/2}
```

*Out[152]=*
```
{0, -4, 4}
```

we have $|\mathbf{B}| = 4 > 0$. Thus $(x,y) = (5/2,0)$ is a relative maximum point with $f(5/2,0) = 9/4$. (Note: the smallest dimension of the relevant Hessian matrix **B** is 3×3.) At the other two critical points, $(x,y,\lambda) = (2,-1,-1)$ and $(2,1,-1)$, we have

*In[153]:=*
```
signQL[B] /. {x->2,y->-1,lambda->-1}
```

*Out[153]=*
```
{0, -4, -8}
```

*In[154]:=*
```
signQL[B] /. {x->2,y->1,lambda->-1}
```

*Out[154]=*
```
{0, -4, -8}
```

That is, $|\mathbf{B}| = -8 < 0$. They are relative minimum points with the relative minimum value of $f(2,-1) = f(2,1) = 2$. A plot of $f(x,y)$ with the constraint is given below.

*In[155]:=*
```
surface = Plot3D[f[x,y],{x,0,4},{y,-2,2},
                 AxesLabel->{"x","y","f(x,y)"},
                 ViewPoint->{-4.000, -1.290, 0.590},
                 DisplayFunction->Identity];
constrain = ParametricPlot3D[{5/2-1/2 y^2,y,z},{y,-2,2},
                  {z,0,5},DisplayFunction->Identity];
Show[surface,constrain,
                  DisplayFunction->$DisplayFunction];
```

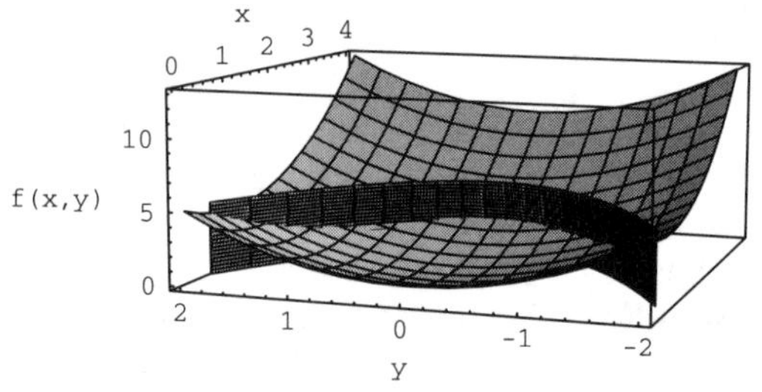

Hence, the problem has a relative maximum at (2/5,0) and two relative minima at (2,–1) and (2,1).

Consider the constrained optimization problem to maximize or minimize the function

$$f(\mathbf{x}) = f(x_1,x_2,\ldots,x_n)$$

subject to

$$g(\mathbf{x}) = g(x_1,x_2,\ldots,x_n) = 0.$$

Sufficient conditions for a solution of this problem to exist depend upon the sign of the second-order differential $d^2f(\mathbf{x})$ subject to the differential of the constraint $dg(\mathbf{x}) = 0$. Without going through details, the second-order differential of $f$ is the quadratic form

$$d^2f(\mathbf{x}) = (d\mathbf{x})^T(\mathbf{H} - \frac{f_x}{g_x}\mathbf{G})(d\mathbf{x})$$

and is subject to $dg(\mathbf{x}) = [g_1\ g_2 \ldots g_n]\cdot d\mathbf{x} = 0$ where $d\mathbf{x} = [dx_1\ dx_2 \ldots dx_n]^T$. The $r$-th order bordered Hessian determinant for this problem is

$$|\mathbf{B}_r| = \begin{vmatrix} 0 & g_1 & g_2 & \cdots & g_r \\ g_1 & f_{11}-\frac{f_1}{g_1}g_{11} & f_{12}-\frac{f_1}{g_1}g_{12} & \cdots & f_{1r}-\frac{f_1}{g_1}g_{1r} \\ g_2 & f_{21}-\frac{f_1}{g_1}g_{21} & f_{22}-\frac{f_1}{g_1}g_{22} & \cdots & f_{2r}-\frac{f_1}{g_1}g_{2r} \\ \cdots & \cdots & \cdots & \cdots & \cdots \\ g_r & f_{r1}-\frac{f_1}{g_1}g_{r1} & f_{r2}-\frac{f_1}{g_1}g_{r2} & \cdots & f_{rr}-\frac{f_1}{g_1}g_{rr} \end{vmatrix}$$

$$= \begin{vmatrix} L_{\lambda\lambda} & L_{\lambda 1} & L_{\lambda 2} & \cdots & L_{\lambda r} \\ L_{1\lambda} & L_{11} & L_{12} & \cdots & L_{1r} \\ L_{2\lambda} & L_{21} & L_{22} & \cdots & L_{2r} \\ \cdots & \cdots & \cdots & \cdots & \cdots \\ L_{r\lambda} & L_{r1} & L_{r2} & \cdots & L_{rr} \end{vmatrix}$$

for $r = 1,2,\ldots,n$. Suppose $\mathbf{x}_0$ satisfies the necessary conditions for a relative extremum. We have the following sufficient conditions (all differentials and determinants are evaluated at $\mathbf{x}_0$):

(1) If $d^2f(\mathbf{x}) > 0$ (positive definite) subject to $dg(\mathbf{x}) = 0$, then $\mathbf{x}_0$ is a relative minimum point. That is, $\mathbf{x}_0$ is a relative minimum point if $|\mathbf{B}_r| < 0$, for $r = 2,\ldots,n$.

(2) If $d^2f(\mathbf{x}) < 0$ (negative definite) subject to $dg(\mathbf{x}) = 0$, then $\mathbf{x}_0$ is a relative maximum point. That is, $\mathbf{x}_0$ is a relative minimum point if $(-1)^r|\mathbf{B}_r| > 0$, for $r = 2,\ldots,n$.

**Example 11.29** We find the relative extrema of the following utility function $f(x,y,z,w)$ subject to a budget constraint $g(x,y,z,w) = 0$.

$$f(x,y,z,w) = 0.3*\log(x-2) + 0.4*\log(y-3) + 0.2*\log(z-4) + 0.1*\log(w-5)$$
$$g(x,y,z,w) = 2x + 3y + 4z + 5w - 100 = 0.$$

We first define the Lagrangian function.

*In[158]:=*

```
Clear[f,g,L,x,y,z,w,lambda];
f[x_,y_,z_,w_]:= 0.3*Log[x-2]  +  0.4*Log[y-3]+
                  0.2*Log[z-4]  +  0.1*Log[w-5];
g[x_,y_,z_,w_]:= 2*x  +  3*y  +  4*z  +  5*w  -  100;
L[x_,y_,z_,w_,lambda_]:= f[x,y,z,w]  +  lambda*g[x,y,z,w];
```

Next we calculate a critical point of the Lagrangian function.

*In[162]:=*

```
c  =  Solve[{D[L[x,y,z,w,lambda],x]==0,
             D[L[x,y,z,w,lambda],y]==0,
             D[L[x,y,z,w,lambda],z]==0,
             D[L[x,y,z,w,lambda],w]==0,
D[L[x,y,z,w,lambda],lambda]==0},{x,y,z,w,lambda}]
```

*Out[162]=*

```
{{x → 8.9, y → 9.13333, z → 6.3, w → 5.92, lambda → -0.0217391}}
```

A possible extremum of $f$ is at the point

$(x,y,z,w) = (8.9,9.13,6.3,5.92)$.

Now we compute the leading principal minors.

*In[163]:=*

```
B  =  hessian[L[x,y,z,w,lambda],{lambda,x,y,z,w}];
signQL[B]  /.  c[[1]]
```

*Out[164]=*

```
{0, -4, 0.0992439, -0.00482417, 0.000633292}
```

At this point, the leading principal minors of the bordered Hessian are $|\mathbf{B}_2| \approx 0.099 > 0$, $|\mathbf{B}_3| \approx -0.0048 < 0$, and $|\mathbf{B}_4| \approx 0.0006 > 0$. Thus $(x,y,z,w) = (8.9,9.13,6.3,5.92)$ is a relative minimum. Let us compute the value of $f$ at this point.

*In[165]:=*

```
f[x,y,z,w]  /.  c[[1]]
```

*Out[165]=*

```
1.4632
```

The bordered Hessian matrix of an $n$-variable objective function $f(\mathbf{x}) = f(x_1,x_2, \ldots ,x_n)$ with $m$ constraints, $g^j(\mathbf{x}) = 0$, $j = 1,2, \ldots ,m$, is

$$|\mathbf{B}_r| = \begin{vmatrix} L_{\lambda_1\lambda_1} & \cdots & L_{\lambda_1\lambda_m} & L_{\lambda_1 1} & \cdots & L_{\lambda_1 r} \\ & & \cdots\cdots\cdots & & & \\ L_{\lambda_m\lambda_1} & \cdots & L_{\lambda_m\lambda_m} & L_{\lambda_m 1} & \cdots & L_{\lambda_m r} \\ L_{1\lambda_1} & \cdots & L_{1\lambda_m} & L_{11} & \cdots & L_{1r} \\ & & \cdots\cdots\cdots & & & \\ L_{r\lambda_1} & \cdots & L_{r\lambda_m} & L_{r1} & \cdots & L_{rr} \end{vmatrix}, \quad r=m+1,m+2, \ldots ,n$$

where the second-order partial derivatives are

$$L_{\lambda_1\lambda_j} = 0, \; L_{\lambda_{ij}} = \frac{\partial^2 L}{\partial \lambda_i \partial x_j} = g_j^i$$

$$L_{ij} = \frac{\partial^2 L}{\partial x_i \partial x_j} = f_{ij} + \sum_{k=1}^{m} \lambda_k g_{ij}^k$$

Suppose $\mathbf{x}_0$ satisfies the necessary condition for a relative extremum. Sufficient conditions are as follows:

(1) The function has a relative minimum if $(-1)^m|\mathbf{B}_r| > 0$, $r = m+1, m+2, \ldots ;n$.

(2) It has a relative maximum if $(-1)^r|\mathbf{B}_r| > 0$, $r = m+1, m+2, \ldots ,n$.

**Example 11.30** Consider the constrained optimization problem:

$$\min f(x,y,z) = x^2 + 2y^2 + 2z^2 + w^2 - 2xy - 2yz - 2zw$$

subject to

$$g^1(x,y,z) = 2x + y + z + w - 10 = 0$$
$$g^2(x,y,z) = 4x - z + w - 12 = 0.$$

The Lagrangian function is

$$L(x,y,z,w,\lambda_1,\lambda_2) = x^2 + 2y^2 + 2z^2 + w^2 - 2xy - 2yz - 2zw + \lambda_1(2x+y+z+w-10) + \lambda_2(4x-z+w-12)$$

*In[166]:=*

```
Clear[f,g1,g2,L,x,y,z,w,lambda1,lambda2,c,h];
f[x_,y_,z_,w_]:= x^2+2*y^2+2*z^2+w^2-2*x*y-2*y z-2*z*w;
g1[x_,y_,z_,w_]:= 2*x+y+z+w-10;
g2[x_,y_,z_,w_]:= 4*x-z+w-12;
L[x_,y_,z_,w_,lambda1_,lambda2_]:= f[x,y,z,w]+
                                   lambda1*g1[x,y,z,w]+
                                   lambda2*g2[x,y,z,w];
```

We next calculate the critical points of $L(x,y,z,w,\lambda_1,\lambda_2)$.

*In[171]:=*

```
c=Solve[{D[L[x,y,z,w,lambda1,lambda2],x]==0,
         D[L[x,y,z,w,lambda1,lambda2],y]==0,
         D[L[x,y,z,w,lambda1,lambda2],z]==0,
         D[L[x,y,z,w,lambda1,lambda2],w]==0,
          D[L[x,y,z,w,lambda1,lambda2],lambda1]==0,
          D[L[x,y,z,w,lambda1,lambda2],lambda2]==0},
       {x,y,z,w,lambda1,lambda2}]
```

*Out[171]=*

$\{\{\text{lambda2} \to -(\frac{200}{209}), \text{x} \to \frac{622}{209}, \text{y} \to \frac{382}{209}, \text{w} \to \frac{22}{19}, \text{lambda1} \to \frac{160}{209},$
$\text{z} \to \frac{222}{209}\}\}$

The leading principal minors of the bordered Hessian matrix at the critical point are computed.

*In[172]:=*

```
B = hessian[L[x,y,z,w,lambda1,lambda2],
            {lambda1,lambda2,x,y,z,w}];
signQL[B] /. c[[1]]
```

*Out[173]=*

```
{0, 0, 0, 16, 330, 836}
```

The associated leading principal minors of the bordered Hessian matrix **B** are $|\mathbf{B}_3| = 330 > 0$, and $|\mathbf{B}_4| = 836 > 0$. Hence the point $(x,y,w,z) = (622/209, 382/209, 22/19, 222/209)$ is a relative minimum point. Lastly, let us compute the value of the objective function there.

*In[174]:=*

```
L[x,y,z,w,lambda1,lambda2]/.c[[1]]
```

*Out[174]=*

$$\frac{400}{209}$$

## EXERCISES

1. Find the relative extrema of the following functions subject to the constraint:
   (a) $f(x,y,z) = 2x^2 + 3y^2 + 4z^2$ subject to $x + y + z = 10$.
   (b) $f(x,y,z) = x + y + z$ subject to $2x^2 + 3y^2 + 4z^2 = 1200/13$.
2. Find the relative extrema of the following functions subject to constraint:
   (a) $f(x,y) = x^2 + y^2 + xy$ subject to
   $g(x,y) = 2x^2 + 6xy + 2y^2 - 9 = 0$.
   (b) $f(x,y) = x^2 + y^2$ subject to
   $g(x,y) = (x-1)^2 - y^2 = 0$.
   Verify your answer by plotting $z = f(x,y)$ and $g(x,y) = 0$.
3. Find the relative extrema of

   $f(x,y,z) = 2x^2 + 3y^2 + 4z^2$ subject to
   $x + y + z = 10$ and $x^2 + y^2 = 4$.

4. Find the relative extrema of

   $f(\mathbf{x}) = \mathbf{x}^T\mathbf{A}\mathbf{x} + \mathbf{b}\mathbf{x} + c$ subject to
   $g(\mathbf{x}) = \mathbf{B}^T\mathbf{x} - d = \mathbf{0}$

   where $\mathbf{x}$ is an $n \times 1$ column vector, $\mathbf{A}$ and $\mathbf{B}$ are $n \times n$ and $m \times n$ matrices ($m < n$), and $\mathbf{b}$ is $1 \times n$ row vector. $c$ and $d$ are scalar constants.

### 11.2.4 Interpretation of the Lagrange multiplier

The Lagrange multiplier $\lambda$ was treated as an additional variable in the Lagrangian function for solving the constrained optimization problem. No significant importance or interpretation was given to $\lambda$. However, one of the reasons for the use of the Lagrange multiplier method in economics is that $\lambda$ often has an interesting interpretation, and its value often yields useful information.

Consider the problem of maximizing $f(x,y)$ subject to a constraint $g(x,y) = k$. Previously we set $k = 0$. For example, in the case of utility maximization, the budget constraint is written as $g(x,y) = ax + by - m = 0$, where $a$ and $b$ are prices, and $m$ is the income. Hence $g(x,y) = ax + by - m = k$ for any arbitrary value $k$ and indicates the change of budget constraint, i.e., the income increase from $m$ to $m+k$. It is intuitively clear that as the constraint varies, the critical point $(x_0,y_0,\lambda_0)$ will change accordingly. The critical points depend upon $k$. We are interested in the effect of $k$ on $(x_0,y_0,\lambda_0)$ and on the maximum value of the objective function, $f(x_0,y_0)$.

Consider the Lagrangian function of the problem

$$L(x,y,\lambda) = f(x,y) + \lambda[g(x,y)-k].$$

A necessary condition for maximization is:

$$\begin{aligned} L_x &= f_x + \lambda g_x = 0 \\ L_y &= f_y + \lambda g_y = 0 \\ L_\lambda &= g(x,y) - k = 0. \end{aligned}$$

Solving these three equations for $x,y$, and $\lambda$, we obtain the critical point, $(x_0,y_0,\lambda_0)$, which is a function of $k$. Namely, we make this functional relationship explicit by writing

$$x_0 = x_0(k),\ y_0 = y_0(k),\ \lambda_0 = \lambda_0(k).$$

Subtituting these values in the Lagrangian function, we have

$$\begin{aligned} L(x_0,y_0,\lambda_0) &= f(x_0,y_0) + \lambda_0[g(x_0,y_0)-k] \\ &= f(x_0,y_0) \end{aligned}$$

The last equality is due to the fact that $g(x_0,y_0) - k = 0$. Since $x_0$ and $y_0$ are both functions of $k$, the maximum value of the objective function must be a function of $k$. That is, let

$$\phi(k) = L(x_0(k),y_0(k),\lambda_0(k)) = f(x_0(k),y_0(k))$$

The function $\phi(k)$ is called the *indirect objective function.* We are interested in the effect of $k$ on $\phi(k)$. To examine it, we take the total derivative of $L(x_0,y_0,\lambda_0)$ with respect to $k$

$$\begin{aligned} \frac{dL(x_0,y_0,\lambda_0)}{dk} &= f_x\frac{dx_0}{dk} + f_y\frac{dy_0}{dk} + \frac{d\lambda_0}{dk}[g(x_0,y_0) - k] + \lambda_0\left(g_x\frac{dx_0}{dk} + g_y\frac{dy_0}{dk} - 1\right) \\ &= (f_x + \lambda_0 g_x)\frac{dx_0}{dk} + (f_y + \lambda_0 g_y)\frac{dy_0}{dk} + \frac{d\lambda_0}{dk}[g(x_0,y_0) - k] - \lambda_0 \\ &= -\lambda_0 \end{aligned}$$

All derivatives are evaluated at $(x_0,y_0,\lambda_0)$. Since $L(x_0,y_0,\lambda_0) = f(x_0,y_0)$, the derivative of $L(x_0,y_0,\lambda_0)$ with respect to $k$ must be identical to the derivative of $f(x_0,y_0)$ with respect to $k$. Thus,

$$\frac{df(x_0,y_0)}{dk} = -\lambda_0$$

If the objective function $f(x,y)$ is the utility function, then $-\lambda_0$ may be interpreted as the change of the maximum value of the utility function with respect to the change in income. That is, $-\lambda_0$ is called the *marginal utility of income*. In other cases, if the objective function $f(x,y)$ is the profit (in dollars) of a firm, and $k$ is regarded as the amount of some resources that are limited according to the constraints, then $-\lambda_0$ may be interpreted as dollars per unit of the resources. The firm would be willing to pay $-\lambda_0$ dollars for an increment in the resources. The Lagrange multiplier is often called the *shadow price* or *opportunity cost* of the resources.

**Example 11.31** Consider a utility maximization problem. The utility function $f(x,y)$ and its budget constraint $g(x,y) - k = 0$ are

$$f(x,y) = (1/2)\log x + \log y$$
$$g(x,y) = 2x + y - k = 0$$

where $k$ is any arbitrary constant. The corresponding Lagrangian function is

$$L(x,y,\lambda) = (1/2)\log x + \log y + \lambda(2x + y - k)$$

The following calculation shows that a critical point is

$$x_0 = x_0(k) = \mathrm{k}/6,$$
$$y_0 = y_0(k) = 2\mathrm{k}/3,$$
$$\lambda_0 = \lambda_0(k) = -3/2\mathrm{k}.$$

*In[175]:=*

```
Clear[f,L,x,y,lambda,k];
SetAttributes[k,Constant];
f[x_,y_]:=  (1/2)*Log[x]+Log[y];
g[x_,y_]:=  2*x+y-k;
L[x_,y_,lambda_]:=  f[x,y]+lambda*g[x,y];
c  =  Solve[{D[L[x,y,lambda],x]==0,
          D[L[x,y,lambda],y]==0,
          D[L[x,y,lambda],lambda]==0},
        {x,y,lambda}]
```

*Out[180]=*

$$\{\{\text{lambda} \rightarrow \frac{-3}{2\text{k}}, \text{x} \rightarrow \frac{\text{k}}{6}, \text{y} \rightarrow \frac{2\text{k}}{3}\}\}$$

The indirect objective function is equal to,

$$f(x_0,y_0) = (1/2)\log(k/6) + \log(2k/3)$$

*In[181]:=*

```
f[x,y]  /.  c[[1]]
```

*Out[181]=*

$$\frac{\text{Log}[\frac{k}{6}]}{2} + \text{Log}[\frac{2k}{3}]$$

If income is equal to $k$ = \$100, then $x_0$ = 100/6 units, $y_0$ = 200/3 units, and the maximum utility is equal to $f(x_0,y_0) \approx 5.606$ units. The marginal utility of income, or the shadow price of income in terms of utility is $-\lambda_0$ = 3/200 = 0.015 units. As the income increases to $k$ = \$150, the point of maximum utility changes to $x_1$ = 25 units and $y_1$ = 100 units. The corresponding shadow price of income is now $-\lambda_1$ = 3/300 = 0.010 units.

*In[182]:=*

```
c /. k->150
```

*Out[182]=*

$$\{\{\text{lambda} \to -(\frac{1}{100}), x \to 25, y \to 100\}\}$$

The maximum utility is approximately equal to $f(x_0,y_0) \approx 6.21461$ units.

*In[183]:=*

```
maxvalue = f[x,y] /. c[[1]] /. k->150
```

*Out[183]=*

$$\frac{\text{Log}[25]}{2} + \text{Log}[100]$$

*In[184]:=*

```
maxvalue // N
```

*Out[184]=*

6.21461

The following plot shows the change of utility maximization. As the income $k$ increases from 100 to 150, the budget constraint (the vertical cutting surface) moves further out and results in the increment in consumption from $(x_0,y_0)$ = (100/6,200/3) to (25,100).

*In[185]:=*

```
utility = Plot3D[f[x,y],{x,1,40},{y,60,110},
                  AxesLabel->{"x","y","f(x,y)"},
                  ViewPoint->{-4.000, -1.290, 2.360},
                  DisplayFunction->Identity];
k100 = ParametricPlot3D[{50-1/2 y,y,z},{y,60,100},
                  {z,1,7},
                    DisplayFunction->Identity];
k150 = ParametricPlot3D[{75-1/2 y,y,z},{y,60,110},
                  {z,1,7},
                    DisplayFunction->Identity];
Show[utility,k100,k150,
                  DisplayFunction->$DisplayFunction];
```

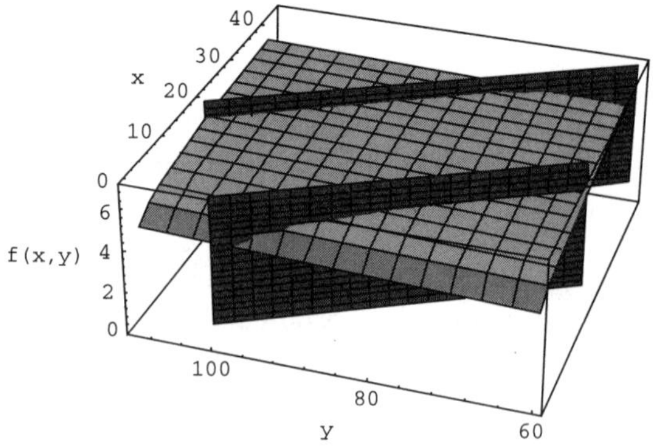


## EXERCISES

1. Consider the maximization of the quadratic utility function

   $f(x,y) = 100x + 120y - 2x^2 + 2xy - y^2$

   subject to $2x + y = k$ where $k$ is income.
   (a) Find the quantity demanded for $x$ and $y$.
   (b) Is the sufficient condition for maximization satisfied?
   (c) If $k$ = \$50, what are the demands for $x$ and $y$? What is the corresponding marginal utility of income?

2. Given the same quadratic utility function as in exercise 1, suppose the budget constraint is changed to

   $ax + by = k$

   where $a$ and $b$ are prices for $x$ and $y$, respectively.
   (a) Find the demand function for $x$ and $y$ as a function of prices and income.
   (b) If $a$=\$2, $b$=\$4, and $k$=\$50, what are the demands for $x$ and $y$?
   (c) What is the corresponding marginal utility of income now?

### 11.2.5 Quasiconcavity, quasiconvexity, and absolute extrema

In theorem 11.4 in section 11.1.4, we stated that a relative extreme point is an absolute extreme point if a function is convex or concave. Although this result is quite useful, it is not practical in most economic applications. The requirement that functions be concave or convex is too restrictive. As mentioned in Chapter 10, neither the utility functions nor an increasing returns to scale production functions are concave. The assumption of concavity and convexity in theorem 11.4, however, can be relaxed and replaced by the weaker alternative theorem below.

**THEOREM 11.7** *Suppose* **S** *is a convex set and* **c** $\in$ **S** *is a relative maximum (minimum) point. Then:*

*(1)* **c** *is an absolute maximum (minimum) point iff f*(**x**) *is an explicitly quasiconcave (quasiconvex) function on* **S**;

*(2)* **c** *is the unique absolute maximum (minimum) point if f*(**x**) *is a strictly quasiconcave (quasiconvex) function on* **S**.

We prove part (1) of the theorem and leave part (2) for readers to prove. The proof is similar to the one given in theorem 11.4.

Suppose $f(\mathbf{x})$ is an explicit quasiconcave function defined on a convex set $\mathbf{S}$ and suppose $\mathbf{c} \in \mathbf{S}$ is a relative maximum point. We have $f(\mathbf{c}) \geq f(\mathbf{x})$ for any $\mathbf{x} \in \mathbf{S}$ and in a neighborhood of $\mathbf{c}$. If $\mathbf{c}$ is not an absolute maximum point, then there must exist a point $\mathbf{x}_0 \in \mathbf{S}$ such that $f(\mathbf{x}_0) \geq f(\mathbf{c})$. Since $f(\mathbf{x})$ is an explicitly quasiconcave function, we have

$$f(\theta \mathbf{x}_0 + (1-\theta)\mathbf{c}) > \min\{ f(\mathbf{x}_0), f(\mathbf{c}) \} = f(\mathbf{c})$$

for $0 < \theta < 1$. Letting $\theta \to 0$, the point $\mathbf{x} = \theta \mathbf{x}_0 + (1-\theta)\mathbf{c}$ is then in the neighborhood of $\mathbf{c}$. The above inequality therefore contradicts the statement that $\mathbf{c}$ is a relative maximum point, or $f(\mathbf{c}) \geq f(\mathbf{x})$ for any $\mathbf{x} \in \mathbf{S}$ and in the neigborhood of $\mathbf{c}$. This completes the proof.

**Example 11.32** The explicit quasiconcave function given in example 10.35 of section 10.4.1 has a relative maximum point c in the interval [2,3]. Since $f(x)$ is explicitly quasiconcave, $c$ is an absolute maximum point.

**Example 11.33** The bivariate normal density function

$$f(\mathbf{x}) = \frac{1}{\sqrt{2\pi\, |\mathbf{R}|}} e^{(-1/2\mathbf{x}^T \mathbf{R}^{-1} \mathbf{x})}$$

given in example 10.34 of section 10.4.1 is a strictly quasiconcave function on the convex set $\mathbf{S}$ in $\mathbf{R}^2$. Here $\mathbf{x} = (x,y)$ and the correlation matrix is

$$\mathbf{R} = \begin{bmatrix} 1.0 & 0.8 \\ 0.8 & 1.0 \end{bmatrix}$$

We plot the function below.

*In[189]:=*
```
Clear[f,x,y];
R = {{1,0.8},{0.8,1}};
f[x_,y_]:= Exp[-0.5{x,y}.Inverse[R].{x,y}]/
             (Sqrt[2*Pi*Det[R]]);
surface = Plot3D[f[x,y],{x,-1.4,1},{y,-1.4,1.4},
                 AxesLabel->{"x","y","z"},
                  ViewPoint->{-2.210, -3.810, 1.170}];
```

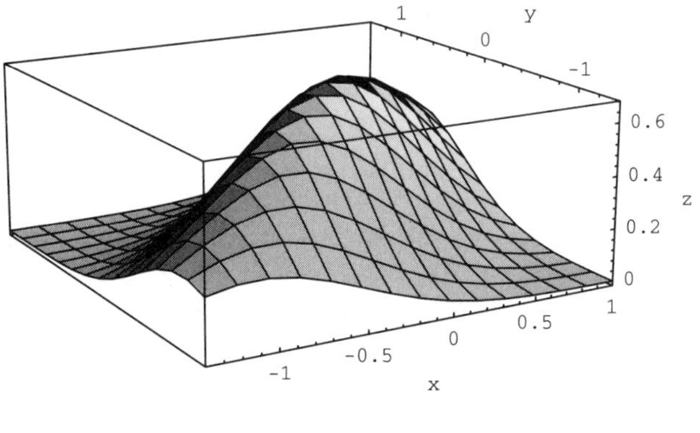

It is quite clear that the point $\mathbf{x} = (0,0)$ is a relative maximum point and hence, it is the unique absolute maximum point.

**Example 11.34** Suppose the above bivariate normal density function is to be maximized subject to a linear constraint $g(x,y) = 0.2x + y + 1 = 0$. That is $f(x,y)$ is restricted to the set

$$\mathbf{S} = \{(x,y) \mid g(x,y) = 0.2x + y + 1 = 0\}.$$

The set $\mathbf{S}$ is a convex set. If $(x_0,y_0)$ is a relative maximum point, it must be the unique maximum point of $f(x,y)$ subject to the linear constraint $g(x,y) = 0$. In the following graph, the constraint $g(x,y) = 0.2x + y + 1 = 0$ "cuts" the graph of $f(x,y)$. The objective function reaches an unique peak at (–0.735,–0.853) with the unique absolute maximum value being 0.460.

*In[193]:=*
```
constrain = ParametricPlot3D[{x,-1-0.2x,z},
              {x,-1.4,0.5},{z,0,0.5},
                DisplayFunction->Identity];
Show[surface,constrain,ViewPoint->{-2.210,-3.810,1.170},
              DisplayFunction->$DisplayFunction];
```

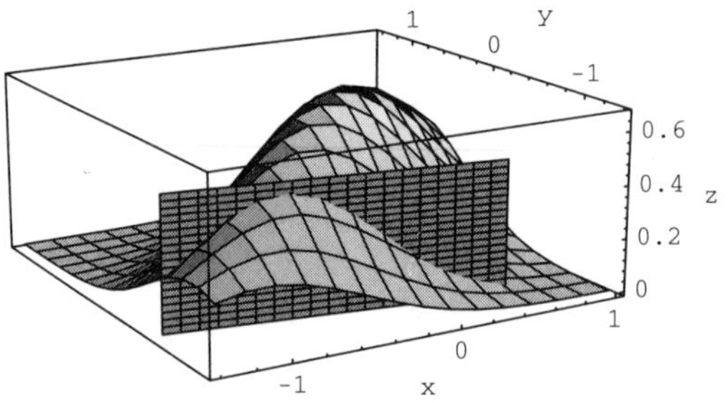


**Example 11.35** Suppose the constraint in example 11.34 is changed to the nonlinear function

$$g(x,y) = (x+0.6)^2 - y - 1.3 = 0.$$

That is, $f(x,y)$ is to be maximized on the set

$$\mathbf{S} = \{(x,y) \mid g(x,y) = (x+0.6)^2 - y - 1.3 = 0\}.$$

Since the restriction is nonlinear, the set $\mathbf{S}$ is not a convex set. The following graph shows a relative maximum point at (–1.071,–1.078). From the graph, it is obvious that the point is not an absolute maximum point. The relative maximum value at (–1.071,–1.078) is $f(-1.071,-1.078) = 0.35$, while the absolute maximum value is 0.500 at (0.716,0.432). A relative minimum value is 0.171 at (–0.245,–1.17), which is also the absolute minimum point.

*In[195]:=*

```
constrain  =  ParametricPlot3D[{x,(x+0.6)^2-1.3,z},
                   {x,-1.4,1},{z,0,0.5},
                   DisplayFunction->Identity];
Show[surface,constrain,ViewPoint->{-2.210,-3.810,1.170},
                        DisplayFunction->$DisplayFunction];
```

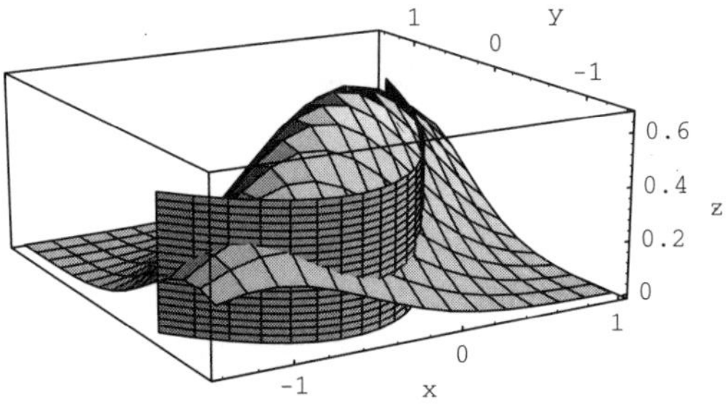


## EXERCISES

1. Give an example to illustrate that a relative maximum is not necessarily an absolute maximum if $f(x)$ is quasiconcave.
2. Give an example to illustrate that a relative maximum is an absolute maximum if $f(x)$ is explicitly quasiconcave.
3. Show that the point (−0.245,−1.17) in example 11.35 is the unique absolute minimum point, and that (0.716,0.432) is the unique absolute maximum point.
4. Prove the second part of theorem 11.7.

# 12

# Mathematical Programming

In previous chapters, we discussed in some detail the classical methods of optimization of an objective function $f(\mathbf{x})$ when $\mathbf{x}$ is unconstrained or when $\mathbf{x}$ satisfies some equality constraints. However, most optimization problems that arise in economics involve inequality constraints for $\mathbf{x}$. The most common type of inequality constraint is the nonnegative restriction on the independent variables of the objective function. For example, negative prices of goods are not meaningful in economics. In this chapter we shall study the problem of finding the maximum and/or minimum values of an objective function $f(\mathbf{x})$ on a set $\mathbf{S}$ in $\mathbf{R}^n$. The set $\mathbf{S}$ will be specified by a system of inequalities which we abbreviate as $\mathbf{g}(\mathbf{x}) \leq \mathbf{0}$. The problem of finding the optimal values of $f$ on $\mathbf{S}$ is called a *mathematical programming problem* and, generally, is harder to solve than unconstrained problems or problems involving equality contraints.

## □ 12.1 Extrema with Inequality Constraints □

### 12.1.1 Feasible region and inequality constraints

Let $f(\mathbf{x}) = f(x_1,x_2, \ldots x_n)$ be a scalar-valued function and

$$\mathbf{g}(\mathbf{x}) = \mathbf{g}(x_1,x_2, \ldots x_n) = [g_1(\mathbf{x})\ g_2(\mathbf{x}) \ldots g_m(\mathbf{x})]^T$$

a vector-valued function. The optimization problem that we will discuss in this chapter involves either maximizing or minimizing the *objective function* $f(\mathbf{x})$ on the set $\mathbf{S} = \{\mathbf{x} \in \mathbf{R}^n \mid \mathbf{g}(\mathbf{x}) \leq \mathbf{0}\}$. The set $\mathbf{S}$ is called the *feasible region* of the optimization problem. We begin with several examples to illustrate the concept of feasible region and inequality constraints, and their relation to the optimization problem.

**Example 12.1** Consider the maximization of the function

$$f(x) = 5 - (x-1)^2$$

subject to the constraint: $x \geq 0$. The inequality constraint can be written as $g(x) = -x \leq 0$, and the feasible region is then

$$\mathbf{S} = \{x \in \mathbf{R} \mid g(x) \leq 0\}.$$

As shown in the following plot, the optimal value occurs at $x = 0$, as opposed to $x = -1$ which is not in the feasible region.

*In[1]:=*

```
Plot[5-(x+1)^2,{x,-2,2},AxesLabel->{"x","f(x)"}];
```

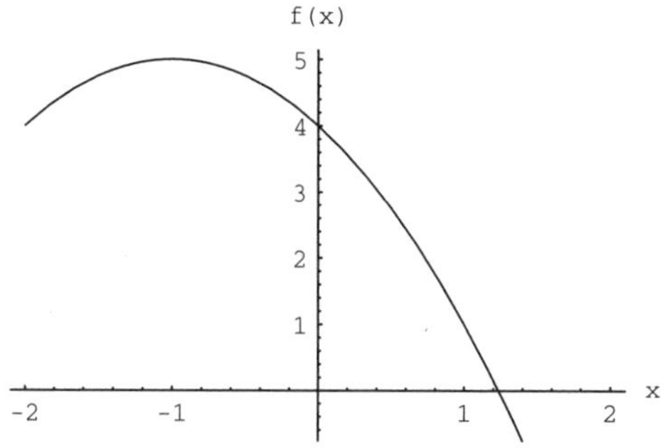


**Example 12.2** Consider the minimization of

$f(\mathbf{x}) = f(x,y) = 2 - x^2 - y^2$

subject to the inequality constraints:

$g_1(x,y) = x + y - 1 \leq 0,$
$g_2(x,y) = 3x - y - 1 \leq 0,$
$g_3(x,y) = 2x + y \leq 0.$

The feasible region is

$\mathbf{S} = \{ (x,y) \in \mathbf{R}^2 \mid g_1(x,y) \leq 0,\ g_2(x,y) \leq 0,\ g_3(x,y) \leq 0 \}.$

**S** is bounded by the three straight lines: $y = 1 - x$, $y = 3x - 1$, and $y = -2x$ which form the boundary of **S** as shown in the following *Mathematica* plot.

*In[2]:=*

```
Plot[{1-x,3*x-1,-2*x},{x,-3,3},
     AxesLabel->{"x","y"},AspectRatio->Automatic,
     PlotRange->{{-2,2},{-4,4}},
     Ticks->{{-2,2},{-4,-2,2,4}},
     PlotStyle->Thickness[0.02]];
```

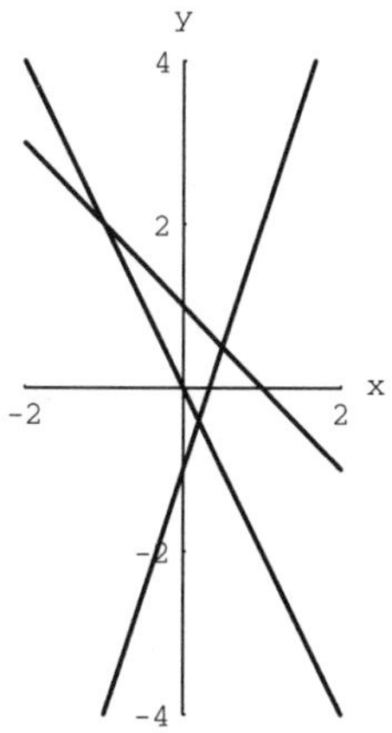

The feasible region **S** consists of the set of points on and in the interior of the triangle formed by these three lines. The optimization problem is to minimize $f(x,y)$ over the set **S**. In the picture below, the graph of $f$ is shown with the region **S** projected upward onto this surface. The optimization problem is to find the smallest value of $f$ on the part of the surface enclosed by the surface curves.

*In[3]:=*

```
Clear[f,x,y];
f[x_,y_]:= 2 - x^2 - y^2;
objectf  = Plot3D[f[x,y],{x,-2,2},{y,-2,2},
                DisplayFunction->Identity];
constg1  = ParametricPlot3D[{x,-x+1,f[x,x-1],
                Thickness[0.01]},{x,-1,1},
                DisplayFunction->Identity];
constg2  = ParametricPlot3D[{x,3*x-1,f[x,3*x-1],
                Thickness[0.01]},{x,-1,1},
                DisplayFunction->Identity];
constg3  = ParametricPlot3D[{x,-2*x,f[x,-2*x],
                Thickness[0.01]},{x,-1,1},
                DisplayFunction->Identity];
Show[constg1,constg2,constg3,objectf,
                DisplayFunction->$DisplayFunction,
               ViewPoint->{-0.965, 1.632, 3.385},
                AxesLabel->{"x","y","z"}];
```

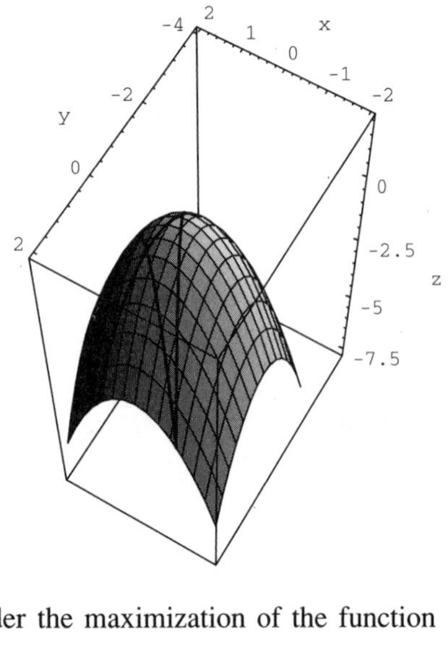


**Example 12.3** Consider the maximization of the function

$$f(\mathbf{x}) = f(x,y) = -x^2 + 4xy - 3y^2$$

subject to the nonnegative constraints, $x \geq 0$, $y \geq 0$, and

$$g_1(x,y) = 0.5x^2 + y - 2 \leq 0$$
$$g_2(x,y) = y - 0.5x^2 \leq 0.$$

The nonnegative constraints can be expressed as

$g_3(x,y) = -x \leq 0$
$g_4(x,y) = -y \leq 0.$

The feasible region is

$$\mathbf{S} = \{ (x,y) \in \mathbf{R}^2 \mid g_1(x,y) \leq 0,\ g_2(x,y) \leq 0,\ g_3(x,y) \leq 0,\ g_4(x,y) \leq 0\}.$$

The objective function is plotted below with the feasible region projected onto the graph of the objective function. The optimization problem is to maximize $f(x,y)$ on the part of the surface that is enclosed by the projected constraints.

*In[10]:=*

```
Clear[f,x,y];
f[x_,y_]:= -x^2 + 4*x*y - 3*y^2;
objectf = Plot3D[f[x,y],{x,-1,2},{y,-1,2},
            AxesLabel->{"x","y","z"},
            DisplayFunction->Identity];
constg1 = ParametricPlot3D[{x,2-0.5*x^2,f[x,2-0.5*x^2],
            Thickness[0.0075]},{x,0,1.6},
            DisplayFunction->Identity];
constg2 = ParametricPlot3D[{x,0.5*x^2,f[x,0.5*x^2],
            Thickness[0.0075]},{x,0,1.6},
            DisplayFunction->Identity];
constg3 = ParametricPlot3D[{x,0,f[x,0],
            Thickness[0.0075]},{x,0,2},
            DisplayFunction->Identity];
constg4 = ParametricPlot3D[{0,y,f[0,y],
            Thickness[0.0075]},{y,0,2},
            DisplayFunction->Identity];
Show[objectf,constg1,constg2,constg3,constg4,
            DisplayFunction->$DisplayFunction,
           ViewPoint->{-4.000, -3.000, 2.860},
            AxesLabel->{"x","y","z"}];
```

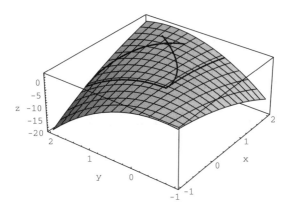

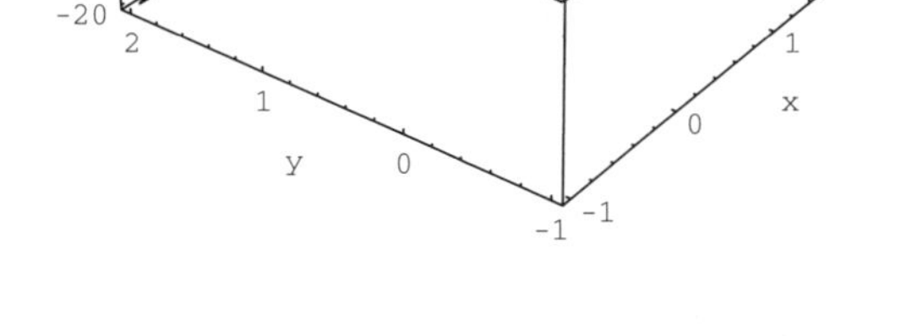


**Example 12.4** Consider a Cobb-Douglas production function $Q = L^a K^b$ with two inputs. The input prices are $P_L$ and $P_K$, respectively. The optimization problem is to minimize the cost function, $C(L,K)$, subject to some minimum production $Q_0$. That is,

minimize $C(L,K) = P_L L + P_K K$
subject to $Q = L^a K^b \geq Q_0$
$L,K \geq 0.$

In this chapter, we will discuss methods that can be used to calculate the minimum value of $C(L,K)$ for specific values of $a, b, Q_0, P_L$, and $P_K$.

## EXERCISES

1. Using *Mathematica*, sketch the feasible region for the following optimization problem:

   minimize $f(\mathbf{x})$
   subject to $\mathbf{S} = \{\mathbf{x} \in \mathbf{R}^2 \mid g(\mathbf{x}) \leq \mathbf{0}\}$

   where

   $$\mathbf{g}(\mathbf{x}) = \mathbf{g}(x,y) = \begin{bmatrix} x^2 + y^2 - 8 \\ y^2 - 2x \\ xy - 4 \end{bmatrix}$$

2. Using *Mathematica*, sketch the feasible region and the surface $z = f(x,y)$ for the following optimization problem:

   minimize $f(\mathbf{x}) = x^2 - y + 1$, subject to
   $\mathbf{S} = \{(x,y) \in \mathbf{R}^2 \mid x + 2y - 6 \leq 0, x-2 \leq 0, x \geq 0, y \geq 0\}$

## 12.1.2 The geometry of optimization problems

**DEFINITION 12.1** *An optimization problem of the type*

*minimize* $f(\mathbf{x})$
*subject to* $\mathbf{S} = \{x \in \mathbf{R}^n \mid \mathbf{g}(\mathbf{x}) \leq \mathbf{0}\}$

*where* $g(\mathbf{x}) = [g_1(\mathbf{x})\ g_2(\mathbf{x})\ \ldots\ g_m(\mathbf{x})]^T$ *is a vector-valued function and is called a* ***mathematical programming problem.***

The above definition is quite general. In fact, any mathematical programming problem for maximizing an objective function can be rephrased as a minimization problem. That is, the maximization problem

maximize $f(\mathbf{x})$
subject to $\mathbf{S} = \{\mathbf{x} \in \mathbf{R}^n \mid \mathbf{g}(\mathbf{x}) \leq \mathbf{0}\}$

can always be rephrased as the minimization problem

minimize $-f(\mathbf{x})$
subject to $\mathbf{S} = \{\mathbf{x} \in \mathbf{R}^n \mid \mathbf{g}(\mathbf{x}) \leq \mathbf{0}\}$.

Furthermore, any nonnegative constraint $g_i(\mathbf{x}) \geq 0$ can be converted to a nonpositive constraint $-g_i(\mathbf{x}) \leq 0$, and any equality constraint $g_i(\mathbf{x}) = 0$ is equivalent to a pair of inequality constraints, $g_i(\mathbf{x}) \leq 0$ and $-g_i(\mathbf{x}) \leq 0$.

**Example 12.5** Consider the mathematical programming problem:

minimize $f(x,y) = 2x + y$
subject to $g_1(x,y) = x^2 + y^2 - 5 \leq 0,$
$g_2(x,y) = x - y - 1 \leq 0.$

The following *Mathematica* plot traces the equations $g_1(x,y) = 0$, and $g_2(x,y) = 0$ on the surface $z = f(x,y)$.

*In[18]:=*

```
Clear[f,x,y];
f[x_,y_]:=  2*x  +  y;
objectf  =  Plot3D[f[x,y],{x,-3,3},{y,-3,3},
                  DisplayFunction->Identity];
constg1  =  ParametricPlot3D[{Sqrt[5]*Cos[t],
               Sqrt[5]*Sin[t],
               f[Sqrt[5]*Cos[t],Sqrt[5]*Sin[t]],
               Thickness[0.0075]},{t,0,2*Pi},
               DisplayFunction->Identity];
constg2  =  ParametricPlot3D[{x,x-1,f[x,x-1],
               Thickness[0.0075]},{x,-2,3},
               DisplayFunction->Identity];
Show[objectf,constg1,constg2,
               DisplayFunction->$DisplayFunction,
               AxesLabel->{"x","y","z"}];
```

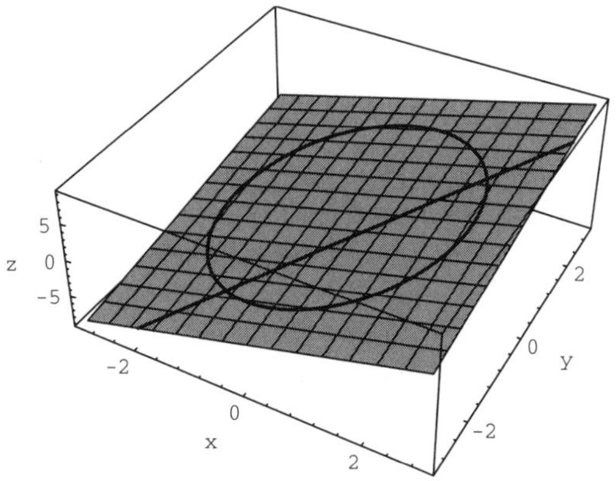


In the above *Mathematica* code, we have used a parametric form of the equation $x^2 + y^2 - 5 = 0$ by introducing the parametrization:

$x = \sqrt{5}\cos t$, and $y = \sqrt{5}\sin t$.

When the surface is projected onto the $xy$-plane as shown in figure 12.1, the shaded area is the feasible region

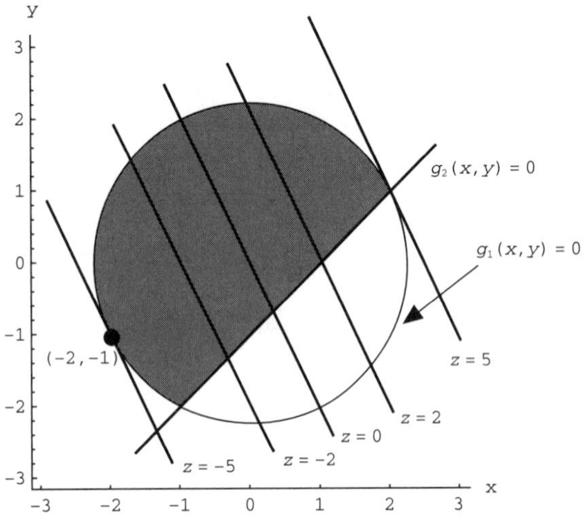


**Figure 12.1** Minimization

$\mathbf{S} = \{ (x,y) \in \mathbf{R}^2 \mid g_1(x,y) \leq 0,\ g_2(x,y) \leq 0 \}.$

The family of straight lines are contours of the objective function, $z = f(x,y)$, and are plotted for $z = -5,-2,0,2,5$. The smallest value of $f(x,y)$ lies on the contour $f(x,y) = -5$ and occurs at the point $(-2,-1)$. We note that the optimal point is located at the point of tangency of this contour and the boundary of the first constraint $g_1(x,y) = 0$. We say that the constraint $g_1(x,y)$ is *binding* or *active* at the optimal point $(-2,-1)$. As shown in the figure, the second constraint, $g_2(x,y) \leq 0$, is not binding, and is inactive at this point. We can calculate the optimal point by using the fact that at this optimal point, the slope of the tangent line to the contour of the objective function, $f(x,y) = -5$, and the slope of the binding constraint, $g_1(x,y) = 0$, are the same. On $f(x,y) = 2x + y = 5$, we have

$$df = 2dx + dy = 0,$$

which implies that the slope of the contour at $z = -5$ is $dy/dx = -2$. On the binding constraint, $g_1(x,y) = x^2 + y^2 - 5 = 0$, we have

$$dg_1(x,y) = (2x)dx + (2y)dy = 0$$

and the slope is $dy/dx = -x/y$. Equality of the slopes of the contour at $z = -5$ and the binding constraint requires that

$$-2 = -x/y, \quad \text{or} \quad x = 2y.$$

This equality together with the binding constraint

$$g_1(x,y) = x^2 + y^2 - 5 = 0$$

can be used to solve for the optimal point

$$x = -2, \quad \text{and} \quad y = -1.$$

**Example 12.6** Consider the optimization problem:

maximize $f(x,y) = xy - x^2$
subject to $g_1(x,y) = x^2 - y \leq 0,$
$g_2(x,y) = y^2 - x \leq 0,$
$x,y \geq 0.$

The graph of the objective function and the projection of the feasible region onto this surface are plotted below.

*In[24]:=*

```
Clear[f,x,y];
f[x_,y_]:= x*y  -  x^2;
objectf  =  Plot3D[f[x,y],{x,0,1},{y,0,1},
                DisplayFunction->Identity];
constg1  =  ParametricPlot3D[{x,x^2,f[x,x^2],
                Thickness[0.0075]},{x,0,1},
                DisplayFunction->Identity];
constg2  =  ParametricPlot3D[{x,Sqrt[x],f[x,Sqrt[x]],
                Thickness[0.0075]},{x,0,1},
                DisplayFunction->Identity];
Show[objectf,constg1,constg2,
                DisplayFunction->$DisplayFunction,
                AxesLabel->{"x","y","z"}];
```

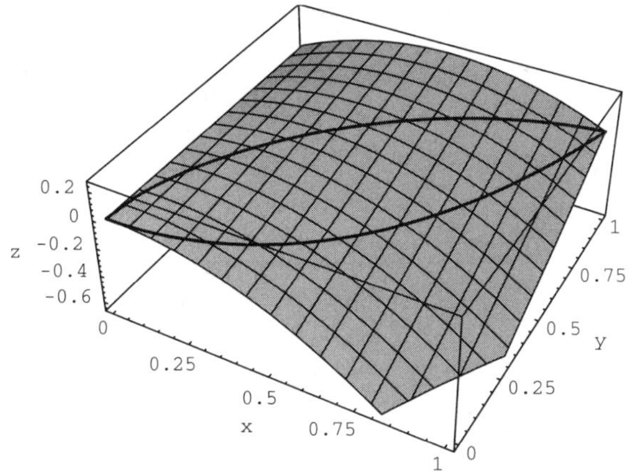


As shown in the following contour plot, the feasible region **S** is enclosed by equations, $g_1(x,y) = 0$, and $g_2(x,y) = 0$. The contours of $f(x,y)$ are plotted in heavier lines at $z = 1/20, 27/256, 1/5$.

*In[30]:=*

```
Clear[g1,g2,x,y];
g1[x_,y_]:= x^2  -  y;
g2[x_,y_]:= y^2  -  x;
objectf=ContourPlot[f[x,y],{x,0,1},{y,0,1},
                    Contours->{0.2,27/256,0.05},
                    ContourStyle->{{Thickness[0.0075]},
                    {Thickness[0.01]},
```

```
                        {Thickness[0.0125]}},
                        ContourShading->False,
                        ContourSmoothing->30,
                        DisplayFunction->Identity];
constg1=ContourPlot[g1[x,y],{x,0,1},{y,0,1},
                        Contours->{0},ContourShading->False,
                        ContourStyle->{Thickness[0.02]}
                        ContourSmoothing->30,
                        DisplayFunction->Identity];
constg2=ContourPlot[g2[x,y],{x,0,1},{y,0,1},
                        Contours->{0},ContourShading->False,
                        ContourSmoothing->30,
                        DisplayFunction->Identity];
Show[objectf,constg1,constg2,
                        DisplayFunction->$DisplayFunction];
```

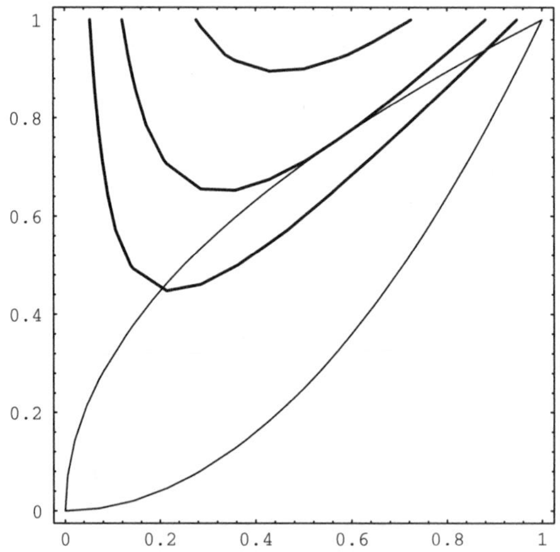


The maximum value of $f(x,y)$ occurs on the binding constraint $g_2(x,y) = 0$ and at the point of tangency between $f(x,y) = xy - x^2 = 27/256$ and $g_2(x,y) = y^2 - x = 0$. By the Implicit Function Theorem, the slopes of the tangent lines to $f(x,y) = 27/256$ and $g_2(x,y) = 0$ can be calculated as

$$\frac{\mathrm{d}y}{\mathrm{d}x} = -\frac{\partial f/\partial x}{\partial f/\partial y}, \quad \text{and} \quad \frac{\mathrm{d}y}{\mathrm{d}x} = -\frac{\partial g_2/\partial x}{\partial g_2/\partial y}$$

The optimal point is then the solution of

$$-\frac{\partial f/\partial x}{\partial f/\partial y} = -\frac{\partial g_2/\partial x}{\partial g_2/\partial y}, \quad \text{and} \quad g_2(x,y) = 0$$

Solving this system of equations, we find that the optimal point is at $(x,y) = (9/16, 3/4)$.

*In[35]:=*

```
Solve[{-D[f[x,y],x]/D[f[x,y],y]==
                -D[g2[x,y],x]/D[g2[x,y],y],g2[x,y]==0},{x,y}]
```

*Out[35]=*

$$\{\{x \to \frac{9}{16}, y \to \frac{3}{4}\}\}$$

Note that, in examples 12.5 and 12.6, the optimal solutions are located on the boundary of the feasible regions. However, as shown in the next example, the optimal solution may occur at an interior point of the feasible region, and consequently, none of the constraints may be binding.

**Example 12.7** Minimize

$$f(x,y) = (x - 0.6)^2 + (y - 0.4)^2$$

subject to

$$g_1(x,y) = xy \leq 1,$$
$$g_2(x,y) = -x \leq 0,$$
$$g_3(x,y) = -y \leq 0.$$

The optimal solution of the mathemtical programming problem occurs at $(x,y) = (0.6,0.4)$. Since

$$g_1(0.6, 0.4) = 0.24 < 1$$
$$g_2(0.6, 0.4) = -0.6 < 0$$
$$g_3(0.6, 0.4) = -0.4 < 0$$

none of the constraints are binding.

## EXERCISES

1. Use *Mathematica* to solve the following optimization problems:
   (a) Minimize $f(x,y) = x^2 + y^2 - 25x - 10y + 5$
   subject to $x + 2y \leq 0$
   $0 \leq x \leq 3$
   $0 \leq y \leq 2$
   (b) Maximize $f(x,y) = 5(x-2)^2 + 3(y-2)^2$
   subject to $x + y \leq 6$
   $x - y \geq -2$
   $x + y \geq 2$
   $x,y \geq 0$

2. Suppose $f(x,y)$ in example 12.6 is to be minimized subject to the same constraints.
   (a) Find the point of minimization.
   (b) Is the optimal point a boundary point or an interior point?
   (c) Use *Mathematica* to confirm your solution.

# □ 12.2 Fritz John Necessary Conditions □

## 12.2.1 Feasible and descent directions sets

In this section we establish necessary conditions for a feasible point **a** in **S** to be an optimal solution of the optimization problem:

minimize $f(\mathbf{x})$
subject to $\mathbf{S} = \{\mathbf{x} \in \mathbf{R}^n \mid \mathbf{g}(\mathbf{x}) \leq \mathbf{0}\}$

Our approach to developing necessary conditions for a point to be an optimal solution will first be geometric. Using the geometric insight, we shall then develop an analytical characterization of the necessary conditions in terms of constraints $\mathbf{g}(\mathbf{x}) \leq \mathbf{0}$ in **S** and an objective function $f(\mathbf{x})$.

Consider the minimization problem given in example 12.6 in section 12.1.2.

minimize $z = f(x,y) = xy - x^2$
subject to $g_1(x,y) = x^2 - y \leq 0,$
$g_2(x,y) = y^2 - x \leq 0,$
$x \geq 0,\ y \geq 0.$

The graph of the objective function and the projection of the feasible region onto this surface is presented below.

*In[36]:=*

```
Clear[f,x,y];
f[x_,y_]:= x*y-x^2;
objectf  =  Plot3D[f[x,y],{x,1,0.0},{y,0,1.0},
               DisplayFunction->Identity];
constg1  =  ParametricPlot3D[{x,x^2,f[x,x^2],
               Thickness[0.0075]},{x,0,1},
               DisplayFunction->Identity];
constg2  =  ParametricPlot3D[{y^2,y,f[y^2,y],
               Thickness[0.0075]},{y,0,1},
               DisplayFunction->Identity];
Show[objectf,constg1,constg2,
               DisplayFunction->$DisplayFunction,
               AxesLabel->{"x","y","z"},
              ViewPoint->{-2.994,  -2.724,  2.143}];
```

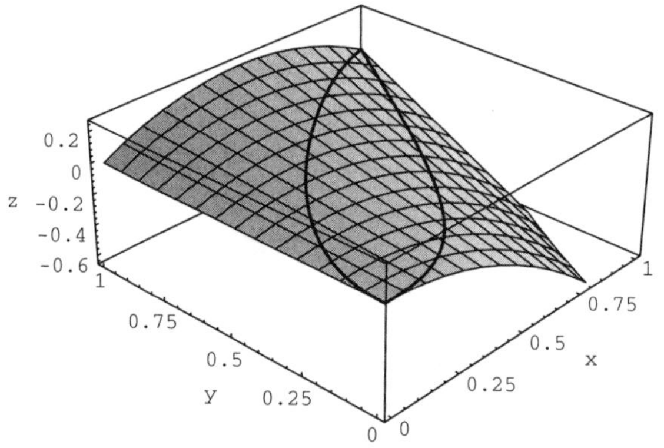

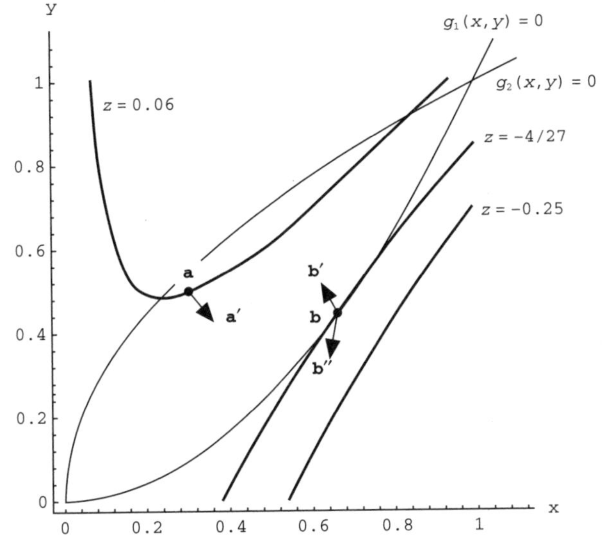


**Figure 12.2** Feasible and descent directions

We can view our optimization problem by imagining ourselves standing on a mountainous region (i.e., the surface $z = f(x,y)$) that is enclosed by a fence (i.e., the projection of **S** on this surface). We walk around the region, staying within the fence, and search for the region's lowest point. It is clear that we always want to walk in directions that lead us downhill. Of course, such a direction might result in walking into the fence. Hence, we must develop a strategy of heading downhill, but not bumping into the fence. Let us try to put this situation into mathematical terms.

Figure 12.2 shows the feasible region and some of the contour curves of the objective function. The feasible region **S** is on and enclosed by the two thin lines bounded by the equations, $g_1(x,y) = 0$, and $g_2(x,y) = 0$, and three contours are displayed for $f(x,y) = 0.06$, $-4/27$, and $-0.25$.

Suppose that we are standing at a fixed point **a**, say (0.3, 0.5), in the feasible set **S** and we want to head in a direction that will make $f(x,y)$ smaller. It is useful to view the point **a** as a vector, i.e., $\mathbf{a} = [0.3\ 0.5]^T$, since we are moving from **a** in a certain direction. In moving, the first thing that we want is to stay in the feasible set **S**. Let $\mathbf{d} = [d_1\ d_2]^T$ be a nonzero vector. The vector **d** is called a *feasible direction* at **a** if $(\mathbf{a} + \varepsilon\mathbf{d}) \in \mathbf{S}$ for a sufficiently small positive scalar $\varepsilon$. For example, if $\mathbf{d} = [0.5\ -0.5]^T$ and $\varepsilon = 0.1$, then $\mathbf{a}' = \mathbf{a} + \varepsilon\mathbf{d} = [0.35\ 0.45]^T$. As shown in figure 12.2, the vector $\mathbf{a}'$ lies within the feasible region **S**. The vector **d** is thus a *feasible direction*. Similarly, at the point $\mathbf{b} = [2/3\ 4/9]^T$, the vector $\mathbf{d} = [-6\ 4]^T$ is also a feasible direction. If we let $\varepsilon = 0.01$, then

$$\mathbf{b}' = \mathbf{b} + \varepsilon\mathbf{d} = [182/300 \quad 436/900]^T \approx [0.607 \quad 0.484]^T$$

which is within the feasible region **S**. However, the vector **d** that moves from point **b** to **b**″ in figure 12.2 is not a feasible direction at **b**. For a given point **a**, the set of vectors

$$\Omega(\mathbf{a}) = \{\mathbf{d} \mid \mathbf{d} \text{ is a feasible direction at } \mathbf{a}\}$$

is called the *set of feasible directions* at **a**. It is clear from its definition that we stay within the set **S** when we move along a direction in $\Omega(\mathbf{a})$.

In figure 12.2, the value of $f$ decreases as we move from point **a** to $\mathbf{a}' = \mathbf{a} + \varepsilon\mathbf{d}$ in the direction $\mathbf{d} = [0.5\ -0.5]^T$ since

$$f(\mathbf{a} + \varepsilon\mathbf{d}) = f(0.35, 0.45) = 0.035 < f(\mathbf{a}) = f(0.3, 0.5) = 0.06.$$

A vector **d** is called a *descent direction* at point **a** if

$$f(\mathbf{a} + \varepsilon\mathbf{d}) < f(\mathbf{a})$$

for a sufficiently small scalar $\varepsilon$. The vector $\mathbf{d} = [-6\ 4]^T$ that moves from point **b** to $\mathbf{b}' = \mathbf{b} + \varepsilon\mathbf{d}$ is not a descent direction at b since $f(\mathbf{b} + \varepsilon\mathbf{d}) > f(\mathbf{b})$. For a given point **a**, the set of directions

$$\Lambda(\mathbf{a}) = \{\mathbf{d} \mid f(\mathbf{a} + \varepsilon\mathbf{d}) < f(\mathbf{a})\}$$

is called the *set of descent directions* at **a** where $\varepsilon$ is a sufficiently small number.

At a given point **a**, we have defined two sets, one that gives us downhill directions, $\Lambda(\mathbf{a})$, and another, $\Omega(\mathbf{a})$, which keeps us from moving outside of the feasible set. From the above discussion, it is clear that in search for the optimal point, we want a direction that is both feasible and descending. Suppose $f$ has a local minimum at **a**. If **a** is an interior point of **S**, then it is clear that any feasible direction at **a** cannot be a descent direction at **a**; otherwise, we would violate the fact that we are at a local minimum. In this case, $\Lambda(\mathbf{a})$ must be the empty set and $\Omega(\mathbf{a})$ contains all directions. Therefore, the intersection of the two sets, $\Omega(\mathbf{a})$ and $\Lambda(\mathbf{a})$, is an empty set, which is denoted by the symbol $\varnothing$. In mathematical terms, we have $\Omega(\mathbf{a}) \cap \Lambda(\mathbf{a}) = \varnothing$. On the other hand, if a local minimum point **b** is a boundary point, i.e., a point such that $g_i(\mathbf{b}) = 0$ for at least one of the constraint $g_i(\mathbf{x}) \le 0$, then any feasible direction cannot be a descent direction. An example of such a point is point **b** in figure 12.2. At point **b**, $\Lambda(\mathbf{b})$ is not empty (since $f(\mathbf{b}) > f(\mathbf{b}''))$, but any descent direction (from **b** to $\mathbf{b}''$) will not be feasible because it will lead us out of the region **S**. Hence $\Omega(\mathbf{a}) = \varnothing$ and again, $\Omega(\mathbf{b}) \cap \Lambda(\mathbf{b}) = \varnothing$. We have illustrated the following theorem concerning an optimal solution to our problem.

**THEOREM 12.1** *Suppose $x = a$ is a local minimum point of the optimization problem:*

*minimize* $f(\mathbf{x})$
*subject to* $\mathbf{S} = \{\mathbf{x} \mid \mathbf{g}(\mathbf{x}) \le \mathbf{0}\}$.

*Then*

$$\Omega(\mathbf{a}) \cap \Lambda(\mathbf{a}) = \varnothing.$$

Theorem 12.1 gives us the necessary conditions for the point **a** to be a solution of our problem. We will discuss sufficient conditions in another section.

Although the above theorem gives a simple criterion for deciding when a point **a** will be a local solution of the minimization problem, it is often difficult to apply. The criterion requires that sets $\Omega(\mathbf{a})$ and $\Lambda(\mathbf{a})$ be constructed and their intersection computed. To construct such sets, we must have the point **a** which is not generally known. Although the sets $\Omega(\mathbf{a})$ and $\Lambda(\mathbf{a})$ are easy to interpret as geometric entities, they lack an analytical framework. It would be helpful, then, if $\Omega(\mathbf{a})$ and $\Lambda(\mathbf{a})$ could be characterized in terms of the objective function $f(\mathbf{x})$ and the constraints $\mathbf{g}(\mathbf{x})$.

If $f(\mathbf{x})$ is differentiable at a point **a**, then the directional derivative at **a** in the direction **d** is $D_{\mathbf{d}}f(\mathbf{a}) = \nabla f(\mathbf{a}) \cdot \mathbf{d}$. The directional derivative measures the rate at which $f(\mathbf{x})$ increases or decreases as we move away from a point **a** in the direction of **d**. Suppose there is a vector **d** such that $\nabla f(\mathbf{a}) \cdot \mathbf{d} < 0$. The function $f(\mathbf{x})$ then decreases in the direction of **d**. In this case, there exists a positive number $\varepsilon > 0$ such that $f(\mathbf{a} + \varepsilon\mathbf{d}) < f(\mathbf{a})$. The set of descent direction, $\Lambda(\mathbf{a}) = \{\mathbf{d} \mid f(\mathbf{a} + \varepsilon\mathbf{d}) < f(\mathbf{a})\}$, can then be characterized as the set

$$\Lambda(\mathbf{a}) = \{\mathbf{d} \mid \nabla f(\mathbf{a}) \cdot \mathbf{d} < 0\}.$$

Similarly, if the $i$-th constraint, $g_i(\mathbf{x})$, is differentiable at **a**, then the directional derivative, $D_{\mathbf{d}}g(\mathbf{a}) = \nabla g_i(\mathbf{a}) \cdot \mathbf{d}$, measures the change of $g_i(\mathbf{x})$ at **a** in the direction **d**. If **a** is on the boundary of the constraint $g_i(\mathbf{a}) = 0$ and $\nabla g_i(\mathbf{a}) \cdot \mathbf{d} > 0$, then the directional vector **d** is not feasible since $g_i(\mathbf{a} + \varepsilon\mathbf{d}) > 0$. Suppose **a** lies on the boundaries of k constraints, $g_1(\mathbf{a}) = g_2(\mathbf{a}) = \ldots = g_k(\mathbf{a}) = 0$. The directional vector is feasible if $\nabla g_i(\mathbf{a}) \cdot \mathbf{d} < 0$, for $i=1,2,\ldots,k$. Define the set

$$\Omega(\mathbf{a}) = \{\mathbf{d} \mid \nabla g_i(\mathbf{a}) \cdot \mathbf{d} < 0,\ i=1,2,\ldots,k\}.$$

What characterization can we give to a local minimum point in terms of the sets $\Omega(\mathbf{a})$ and $\Lambda(\mathbf{a})$? Suppose **a** is a local minimum point. We consider two cases:

(1) If **a** is an interior point, then

$$\Lambda(\mathbf{a}) = \{\mathbf{d} \mid \nabla f(\mathbf{a}) \cdot \mathbf{d} < 0\} = \varnothing$$

since **a** is a local minimum point, i.e., $f(\mathbf{a}) < f(\mathbf{a} + \varepsilon\mathbf{d})$ in any direction **d**. The intersections of $\Omega(\mathbf{a})$ and $\Lambda(\mathbf{a})$ must be empty,

$$\Omega(\mathbf{a}) \cap \Lambda(\mathbf{a}) = \varnothing.$$

(2) If **a** is on the boundaries of k constraints, $g_1(\mathbf{a}) = g_2(\mathbf{a}) = \ldots = g_k(\mathbf{a}) = 0$, then it is also true that

$$\Omega(\mathbf{a}) \cap \Lambda(\mathbf{a}) = \varnothing.$$

Otherwise, if $\Omega(\mathbf{a}) \cap \Lambda(\mathbf{a}) \neq \varnothing$, then neither $\Lambda(\mathbf{a})$ nor $\Omega(\mathbf{a})$ are empty sets. In this case, we could then find a directional vector **d** that decreases $f$, i.e., $f(\mathbf{a}) < f(\mathbf{a} + \varepsilon\mathbf{d})$ since $\nabla f(\mathbf{a}) \cdot \mathbf{d} < 0$, and at the same time keep $g_i(\mathbf{a})$ within bounds, i.e., $g_i(\mathbf{a} + \varepsilon\mathbf{d}) < g_i(\mathbf{a}) = 0$ since $\nabla g_i(\mathbf{a}) \cdot \mathbf{d} < 0$. This contradicts the fact that **a** is a local minimum point.

**Example 12.8** Show that the point $\mathbf{a} = (1-\sqrt{2}/2, -\sqrt{2}/2)$ satisfies $\Omega(\mathbf{a}) \cap \Lambda(\mathbf{a}) = \varnothing$ for the problem:

$$\begin{aligned} &\text{minimize } f(x,y) = x + y \\ &\text{subject to } g_1(x,y) = x^2 + y^2 - 1 \le 0 \\ &\qquad\qquad\ g_2(x,y) = x^2 + y^2 - 2x \le 0 \end{aligned}$$

One can show that $\nabla f(\mathbf{a}) = [1\ 1]^T$, $\nabla g_1(\mathbf{a}) = [2x\ 2y]^T$, and $\nabla g_2(\mathbf{a}) = [2(x-1)\ 2y]^T$. At the point **a**, we have,

$$g_1(1-\sqrt{2}/2, -\sqrt{2}/2) = 1 - \sqrt{2} < 0,$$
$$g_2(1-\sqrt{2}/2, -\sqrt{2}/2) = 0.$$

Thus **a** is a boundary point of $g_2(x,y) = 0$. Since $f(\mathbf{a}) = [1\ 1]^T$, and $\nabla g_2(\mathbf{a}) = [-\sqrt{2}\ -\sqrt{2}]^T$, we have with $\mathbf{d} = [d_1\ d_2]$

$$\Lambda(\mathbf{a}) = \{\mathbf{d} \mid d_1 + d_2 < 0\}$$
$$\Omega(\mathbf{a}) = \{\mathbf{d} \mid -\sqrt{2}(d_1 + d_2) < 0\}$$

It is impossible to find a directional vector **d** such that $d_1 + d_2 < 0$ and $(d_1 + d_2) > 0$, and hence,

$$\Omega(\mathbf{a}) \cap \Lambda(\mathbf{a}) = \varnothing.$$

Therefore, **a** satisfies the requirement to be a local minimum point.

Now consider another point $\mathbf{a} = (1/2, \sqrt{3}/2)$. Both constraints are now binding since $g_1(\mathbf{a}) = g_2(\mathbf{a}) = 0$. There exists a directional vector, say $\mathbf{d} = [-1\ -1]^T$, such that

$$\nabla f(\mathbf{a}) \cdot \mathbf{d} = d_1 + d_2 < 0$$
$$\nabla g_1(\mathbf{a}) \cdot \mathbf{d} = d_1 + \sqrt{3}d_2 < 0$$
$$\nabla g_2(\mathbf{a}) \cdot \mathbf{d} = -d_1 + \sqrt{3}d_2 < 0$$

Hence, the intersection of $\Omega(\mathbf{a}) = \{\mathbf{d} \mid \nabla g_1(\mathbf{a}) \cdot \mathbf{d} < 0, \nabla g_2(\mathbf{a}) \cdot \mathbf{d} < 0\}$ and $\Lambda(\mathbf{a}) = \{\mathbf{d} \mid \nabla f(\mathbf{a}) \cdot \mathbf{d} < 0\}$ is not empty. Therefore, the point $\mathbf{a} = (1/2, -\sqrt{3}/2)$ is not a local minimum point.

**Example 12.9** Show that $\mathbf{a} = (0, 3, 3)$ is a possible minimum point of the optimization problem:

$$\begin{aligned} &\text{minimize } f(x,y,z) = x^2 + y^2 + z^2 + xy - yz + zx \\ &\text{subject to } x^2 + y - z \le 0 \\ &\qquad x + y^2 + z \le 15 \\ &\qquad x + y \ge 3 \\ &\qquad x,y,z \ge 0. \end{aligned}$$

The above inequality constraints can be stated as

$$g_1(\mathbf{x}) = x^2 + y - z \le 0,$$
$$g_2(\mathbf{x}) = x + y^2 + z - 15 \le 0$$
$$g_3(\mathbf{x}) = -x - y + 3 \le 0$$
$$g_4(\mathbf{x}) = -x \le 0$$
$$g_5(\mathbf{x}) = -y \le 0$$
$$g_6(\mathbf{x}) = -z \le 0.$$

It is easy to show that **a** is a feasible point, and

$$g_1(\mathbf{a}) = g_3(\mathbf{a}) = g_4(\mathbf{a}) = 0.$$

We use the **MathEcon** function **gradf** to calculate the directional derivatives: $\nabla f(\mathbf{a}) \cdot \mathbf{d}$, $\nabla g_1(\mathbf{a}) \cdot \mathbf{d}$, $\nabla g_3(\mathbf{a}) \cdot \mathbf{d}$, and $\nabla g_4(\mathbf{a}) \cdot \mathbf{d}$.

*In[42]:=*
```
Clear[f,g1,g2,g3,g4,x,y,z,d1,d2,d3];
f[x_,y_,z_]:=x^2+y^2+z^2+x*y-y*z+x*z;
g1[x_,y_,z_]:=x^2+y-z;
g3[x_,y_,z_]:=-x-y+3;
g4[x_,y_,z_]:=-x;
d={d1,d2,d3};
gradf[f[x,y,z],{x,y,z}].d  /.{x->0,y->3,z->3}
```

*Out[48]=*
```
6d1 + 3d2 + 3d3
```

*In[49]:=*
```
gradf[g1[x,y,z],{x,y,z}].d/.{x->0,y->3,z->3}
```

*Out[49]=*
```
d2 - d3
```

*In[50]:=*
```
gradf[g3[x,y,z],{x,y,z}].d  /.{x->0,y->3,z->3}
```

*Out[50]=*
```
-d1 - d2
```

*In[51]:=*
```
gradf[g4[x,y,z],{x,y,z}].d  /.{x->0,y->3,z->3}
```

*Out[51]=*
```
-d1
```

For $\mathbf{a}$ to be a local minimum point we need

$$\begin{aligned}
\nabla f(\mathbf{a}) \cdot \mathbf{d} &= 6d_1 + 3d_2 + 3d_3 < 0 \\
\nabla g_1(\mathbf{a}) \cdot \mathbf{d} &= d_2 - d_3 < 0 \\
\nabla g_3(\mathbf{a}) \cdot \mathbf{d} &= -d_1 - d_2 < 0 \\
\nabla g_4(\mathbf{a}) \cdot \mathbf{d} &= -d_1 < 0
\end{aligned}$$

From $\nabla g_4(\mathbf{a}) \cdot \mathbf{d} < 0$ we have $d_1 > 0$. From $\nabla g_3(\mathbf{a}) \cdot \mathbf{d} < 0$ and $\nabla g_1(\mathbf{a}) \cdot \mathbf{d} < 0$ we have $d_2 > -d_1$, and $d_3 > d_2$. Using these inequalities in $\nabla f(\mathbf{a}) \cdot \mathbf{d}$, we have

$$\nabla f(\mathbf{a}) \cdot \mathbf{d} = 6d_1 + 3d_2 + 3d_3 > 6d_1 - 3d_1 + 3d_2 > 6d_1 - 3d_1 - 3d_1 = 0$$

which is inconsistent with the condition that $\nabla f(\mathbf{a}) \cdot \mathbf{d} < 0$. Thus the point $\mathbf{a} = (0,3,3)$ is not a local minimum point.

**Example 12.10** Consider the problem of minimizing the cost, $C$, of producing at least $Q_0$ quantity of output ($Q$), with labor ($L$), and capital ($K$), inputs. That is,

$$\begin{aligned}\text{minimize } & C(L,K) = P_L L + P_K K \\ \text{subject to } & g_1(L,K) = Q_0 - Q(L,K) \le 0 \\ & g_2(L,K) = -L \le 0 \\ & g_3(L,K) = -K \le 0\end{aligned}$$

where $P_L$ and $P_K$ are constant input prices, and $Q(L,K)$ is the production function. Let $\mathbf{d} = [dL\ dK]^T$ be the directional vector indicating the change of $L$ and $K$, and let $Q_L$ and $Q_K$ be the partial derivative (i.e., the marginal products) of $Q(L,K)$. If $(L,K)$ is a local minimum point, then

$$\begin{aligned}&\nabla C(L,K)\cdot\mathbf{d} = P_L dL + P_K dK \le 0, \\ &\nabla g_1(L,K)\cdot\mathbf{d} = -Q_L dL - Q_K dK \le 0 \\ &\nabla g_2(L,K)\cdot\mathbf{d} = -dL \le 0 \\ &\nabla g_3(L,K)\cdot\mathbf{d} = -dK \le 0.\end{aligned}$$

This system of inequalities implies that it is impossible to find a directional vector **d** of changing inputs such that there are simultaneously,

(1) nonnegative increments in inputs, $dL > 0$ and $dK > 0$;

(2) nonnegative increments in output, $Q_L dL + Q_K dK \ge 0$; and

(3) nonpositive increments in the cost of production, $P_L dL + P_K dK \le 0$.

## EXERCISES

1. Find $\Omega(\mathbf{a}) \cap \Lambda(\mathbf{a})$ where $\mathbf{a} = (1/2, 1/2)$ and

$$\begin{aligned}\text{minimize } & f(x,y) = (x-1)^2 + (y-1)^2, \\ \text{subject to } & g(x,y) = (x+y-1)^3 \le 0.\end{aligned}$$

2. Find $\Omega(\text{a}) \cap \Lambda(\text{a})$ where $\text{a} = (1,1)$ and

$$\begin{aligned}\text{minimize } & f(x,y) = (x-2)^2 + (y-1)^2, \\ \text{subject to } & g_1(x,y) = x^2 - y \le 0, \\ & g_2(x,y) = 2 + x + y \le 0,\end{aligned}$$

### 12.2.2 Fritz John necessary condition

There are alternative ways to characterize a necessary condition for optimality. One such characterization is the *Fritz John necessary condition.* Before we develop the characterization, we make the following observations about the necessary condition presented in the previous section.

Suppose $\mathbf{x} = \mathbf{a}$ is a local minimum point of $f(\mathbf{x})$ on $\mathbf{S} = \{\mathbf{x}\in\mathbf{R}^n \mid g(\mathbf{x}) \le \mathbf{0}\}$. Then $\Omega(\mathbf{a}) \cap \Lambda(\mathbf{a}) = \varnothing$, or in particular,

$$\{\mathbf{d} \mid \nabla f(\mathbf{a})\cdot\mathbf{d} < 0\} \cap \{\mathbf{d} \mid \nabla g_j(\mathbf{x})\cdot\mathbf{d} < 0,\ j\in J(\mathbf{a})\} = \varnothing$$

where $J(\mathbf{a}) = \{j \mid g_j(\mathbf{a}) = 0\}$ denotes an index set of the binding constraints. It may be a difficult problem to find candidates for **a**. If **a** is a point where $f(\mathbf{x})$ has a local minimum and is an interior point of **S**, then $\nabla f(\mathbf{a}) = \mathbf{0}$, and $\Lambda(\mathbf{a}) = \{\mathbf{d} \mid \nabla f(\mathbf{a})\cdot\mathbf{d} < 0\} = \varnothing$ which implies that $\Omega(\mathbf{a}) \cap \Lambda(\mathbf{a}) = \varnothing$, and a necessary condition for minimization is satisfied. In this case, no constraints are binding, i.e., $g_i(\mathbf{a}) < 0$ for $i = 1,2, \ldots m$, and the constraints do not play any role in the minimization. In fact, the point

**a** can be obtained by solving $\nabla f(\mathbf{a}) = \mathbf{0}$. This is essentially an "unconstrained" optimization problem. However, if **a** is on the boundary of **S**, $g_j(\mathbf{a}) = 0$ for some $j \in J(\mathbf{a})$, we must show that there are no directions **d** such that $\nabla f(\mathbf{a}) \cdot \mathbf{d} < 0$ and $\nabla g_j(\mathbf{a}) \cdot \mathbf{d} < 0$. In this case, only the gradients of the binding contraints and $f$ will play a role.

Suppose there is only a single binding constraint at **a**, say the first constraint, and hence, $g_1(\mathbf{a}) = 0$. The gradient vectors, $\nabla f(\mathbf{a})$ and $\nabla g_1(\mathbf{a})$, show the direction of increase in $f(\mathbf{x})$ and $g_1(\mathbf{x})$, respectively. Since $g_1(\mathbf{a}) = 0$, $\nabla g_1(\mathbf{a})$ points out of the feasible region. If **a** is a local minimum point of $f(\mathbf{x})$ on **S**, then the gradient vector $\nabla f(\mathbf{a})$ must point into **S**. Otherwise, if the direction of increasing values of $f(\mathbf{x})$ points outward of **S**, we can always decrease the value of $f(\mathbf{x})$ by moving in the direction $-\nabla f(\mathbf{a})$ which points into **S** and still be within **S**, thus contradicting the fact that **a** is a local minimum point. These arguments imply that the gradient vectors, $\nabla f(\mathbf{a})$ and $\nabla g_1(\mathbf{a})$, must point in opposite directions from each other and thus, there must exist nonnegative constants $\lambda_0$ and $\lambda_1$, not both zero, such that

$$\lambda_0 \nabla f(\mathbf{a}) + \lambda_1 \nabla g_1(\mathbf{a}) = \mathbf{0}.$$

This condition ensures that the gradients of $f(\mathbf{x})$ and $g_1(\mathbf{x})$ are opposite in sign. This is an alternative way of characterizing a necessary condition for **a** to be a local minimum point.

**Example 12.11** Consider the problem to

$$\begin{aligned} &\text{minimize } f(x,y) = x^2 + 2y^2 \\ &\text{subject to } g(x,y) = 4 - x - y \leq 0. \end{aligned}$$

We show that $\mathbf{a} = (8/3, 4/3)$ is a possible local minimum point. It is obvious that the constraint $g(x,y)$ is binding at this point since $g(\mathbf{a}) = 0$. Also, $\nabla f(\mathbf{x}) = [2x\ 4y]^T$ and $\nabla g(\mathbf{x}) = [-1\ -1]^T$ and there exists nonnegative constants, $\lambda_0 = 3/16$ and $\lambda_1 = 1$, such that

$$\lambda_0 \nabla f(\mathbf{a}) + \lambda_1 \nabla g(\mathbf{a}) = \frac{3}{16}\begin{bmatrix} \frac{16}{3} \\ \frac{16}{3} \end{bmatrix} + 1\begin{bmatrix} -1 \\ -1 \end{bmatrix} = \begin{bmatrix} 0 \\ 0 \end{bmatrix}$$

Thus the point $\mathbf{a} = (8/3, 4/3)$ satisfies the condition to be a local minimum point. Figure 12.3 shows that the gradient vector $\nabla f(\mathbf{a}) = [16/3\ 16/3]^T$ points into the feasible region $\mathbf{S} = \{(x,y) \mid g(x,y) \leq 0\}$ while $\nabla g(\mathbf{a}) = [-1\ -1]^T$ points out of **S**.

The **MathEcon** function **fjohn** creates a graphic of the gradient vector $\nabla f(\mathbf{a})$ and the gradient vectors $\nabla g_i(\mathbf{a})$ of the constraints that are binding at point **a**. Here is a description of this function.

*In[52]:=*

```
?fjohn
```

**fjohn[pt,const,objfct,var,options] generates a 2D Graphic to illustrate the gradients of an objective function objfct and binding constraint const (a list) at the point pt in a nonlinear programming problem. The fourth argument of fjohn contains a list of the variables for the objective and constraint functions. The last argument is optional. If it is the string "label", then the gradient vectors are labeled; if it is the**

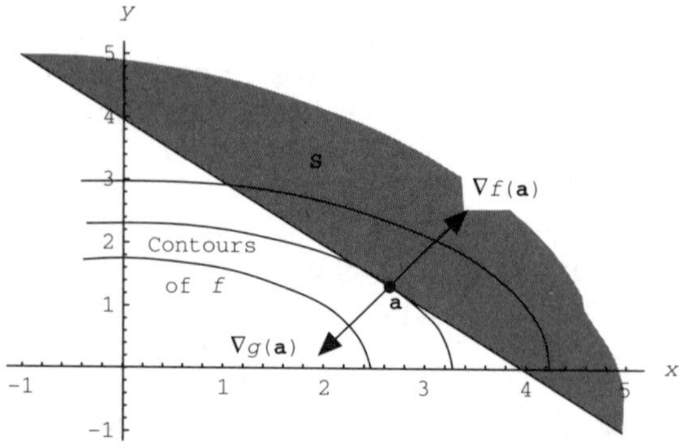


**Figure 12.3** Gradient vectors $\nabla f(\mathbf{a})$ and $\nabla g(\mathbf{a})$

**string "cone", then the gradients of the binding constraints and the negative of the gradient of the objective function is drawn and labeled. For example,**

**fjohn[{1,1},{x-y,x^2-y},x^2+x^3,{x,y},"label"].**

We shall discuss the purpose of having the "cone" option in the function **fjohn** later. The function creates a graphic with the origin of the axes at **a**. For uniformity, the gradient vectors are all normalized to have unit length. The gradients $\nabla f(\mathbf{a}) = [16/3\ 16/3]^T$ and $\nabla g(\mathbf{a}) = [-1\ -1]^T$ in example 12.11 are normalized and plotted below using **fjohn**.

*In[53]:=*

```
Clear[f,g,x,y];
f[x_,y_]:=x^2+2*y^2;
g[x_,y_]:=4-x-y;
graph=fjohn[{8/3,4/3},{g[x,y]},f[x,y],{x,y},"label"];
Show[graph,AspectRatio->Automatic,
         PlotRange->{{-1,1},{-1,1}},Axes->True,
         AxesLabel->{"x","y"},Ticks->None];
```

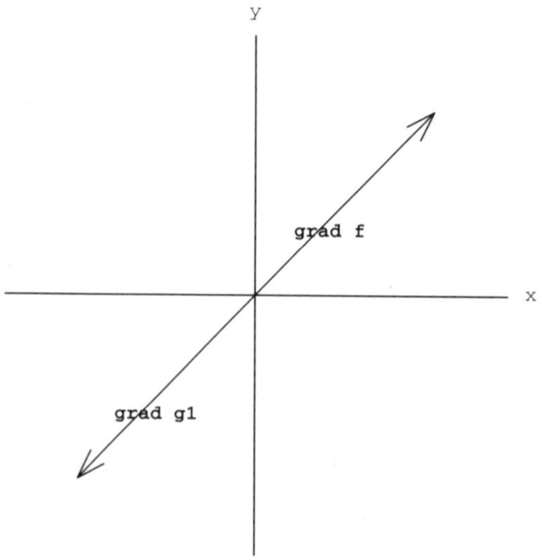

Since $\nabla f(\mathbf{a})$ and $\nabla g(\mathbf{a})$ are pointing in opposite directions, the point $\mathbf{a} = (8/3, 4/3)$ satisfies the condition to be a local minimum point. On the other hand, $\mathbf{a} = (2,2)$ does not meet the condition since $\nabla f(\mathbf{a})$ and $\nabla g(\mathbf{a})$ are not pointing in opposite directions of each other, as shown in the following plot.

*In[58]:=*

```
graph=fjohn[{2,2},{g[x,y]},f[x,y],{x,y},label];
Show[graph,AspectRatio->Automatic,
          PlotRange->{{-1,1},{-1,1}},Axes->True,
          AxesLabel->{"x","y"},Ticks->None];
```

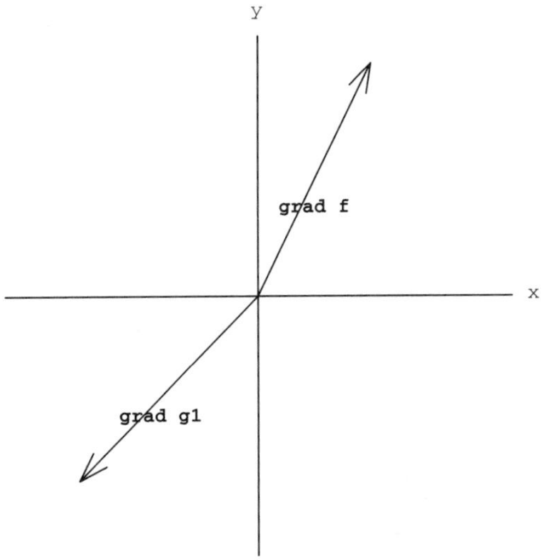


The generalization of the above condition to a case with more than one binding constraint at point $\mathbf{a}$ is straightforward. The condition is stated in the following theorem.

**THEOREM 12.2** *(Fritz John necessary condition) Suppose $f(\mathbf{x})$ and $\mathbf{g}(\mathbf{x})$ are differentiable on $\mathbf{R}^n$ and consider the problem of minimizing $f(\mathbf{x})$ subject to $\mathbf{S} = \{\mathbf{x} \in \mathbf{R}^n \mid g(\mathbf{x}) \leq 0\}$. Suppose $\mathbf{a}$ is a local minimum point. Let $J(\mathbf{a}) = \{ j \mid g_j(\mathbf{a}) = 0\}$ be an index of binding constraints. Then there is a set of nonnegative scalars, $\lambda_0$ and $\lambda_j$ for $j \in J(\mathbf{a})$, not all zero, such that*

$$\lambda_0 \nabla f(\mathbf{a}) + \sum_{j \in J(\mathbf{a})} \lambda_j \nabla g_j(\mathbf{a}) = 0$$

In theorem 12.2 the equation for the gradients can be writtten as

$$\sum_{j \in J(\mathbf{a})} \lambda_j \nabla g_j(\mathbf{a}) = -\lambda_0 \nabla f(\mathbf{a})$$

Geometrically, $\Sigma_{j\in J(\mathbf{a})} \lambda_j \nabla g_j(\mathbf{a})$ with $\lambda_j \geq 0$ forms a cone generated by the gradients of the binding constraints. The Fritz John necessary condition implies that $-\lambda_0 \nabla f(\mathbf{a})$ lies inside the cone as shown in the following example.

**Example 12.12** Consider the following problem:

$$\begin{aligned} &\text{minimize } f(x,y) = (x-8)^2 + (y-6)^2 \\ &\text{subject to } g_1(x,y) = x + y - 7 \leq 0 \\ &\qquad g_2(x,y) = 4x + y - 16 \leq 0 \\ &\qquad g_3(x,y) = -x + y - 5 \leq 0 \\ &\qquad x \geq 0,\ y \geq 0. \end{aligned}$$

We show that the point $\mathbf{a} = (3,4)$ satisfies the Fritz John necessary condition. Both $g_1(x,y)$ and $g_2(x,y)$ are binding constraints since $g_1(\mathbf{a}) = g_2(\mathbf{a}) = 0$. The gradient vectors are:

$$\nabla f(\mathbf{a}) = \begin{bmatrix} -10 \\ -4 \end{bmatrix};\ \nabla g_1(\mathbf{a}) = \begin{bmatrix} 1 \\ 1 \end{bmatrix};\ \nabla g_2(\mathbf{a}) = \begin{bmatrix} 4 \\ 1 \end{bmatrix}.$$

In the following *Mathematica* calculation, we solve the equation, $\lambda_0 \nabla f(\mathbf{a}) + \lambda_1 \nabla g_1(\mathbf{a}) + \lambda_2 \nabla g_2(\mathbf{a}) = \mathbf{0}$, for $\lambda_1$ and $\lambda_2$ in terms of $\lambda_0$.

*In[60]:=*

```
Clear[f,x,y,g1,g2,g3,g4,g5,lambda0,lambda1,lambda2,fjnc]
f[x_,y_]:=(x-8)^2+(y-6)^2;
g1[x_,y_]:=x+y-7;
g2[x_,y_]:=4*x+y-16;
g3[x_,y_]:=-x+y-5;
g4[x_,y_]:=-x;
g5[x_,y_]:=-y;
fjnc  =  lambda0*gradf[f[x,y],{x,y}]+
         lambda1*gradf[g1[x,y],{x,y}]+
        lambda2*gradf[g2[x,y],{x,y}]  /.  {x->3,y->4};
Solve[fjnc  ==  0,{lambda1,lambda2}]
```

*Out[68]=*

```
{{lambda1 → 2 lambda0, lambda2 → 2 lambda0}}
```

This calculation shows that if $\lambda_0 > 0$, then $\lambda_1 = 2\lambda_0 > 0$ and $\lambda_2 = 2\lambda_0 > 0$. Thus, the point $\mathbf{a} = (3,4)$ satisfies the Fritz John necessary condition. Below we plot the gradient vectors $\nabla f(\mathbf{a})$, $\nabla g_1(\mathbf{a})$ and $\nabla g_2(\mathbf{a})$ using the **fjohn** function.

*In[[69]:=*

```
graph=fjohn[{3,4},{g1[x,y],g2[x,y],g3[x,y],
              g4[x,y],g5[x,y]},f[x,y],{x,y},"label"];
Show[graph,AspectRatio->Automatic,
             PlotRange->{{-1,1},{-1,1}},Axes->True,
             AxesLabel->{"x","y"},Ticks->None];
```

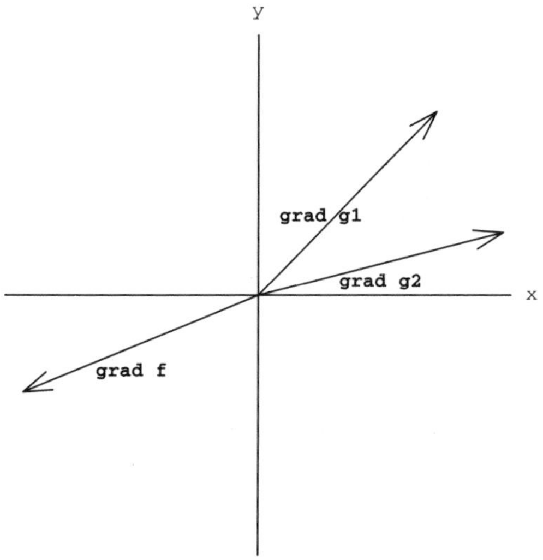


The graph shows that the gradient $-\nabla f(\mathbf{a})$ lies in a cone formed by the vectors $\nabla g_1(\mathbf{a})$ and $\nabla g_2(\mathbf{a})$. The **fjohn** function illustrates this fact by using the optional argument.

*In[71]:=*

```
graph=fjohn[{3,4},{g1[x,y],g2[x,y],g3[x,y],
          g4[x,y],g5[x,y]},f[x,y],{x,y},"cone"];
Show[graph,AspectRatio->Automatic,
         PlotRange->{{-1,1},{-1,1}},Axes->True,
         AxesLabel->{"x","y"},Ticks->None];
```

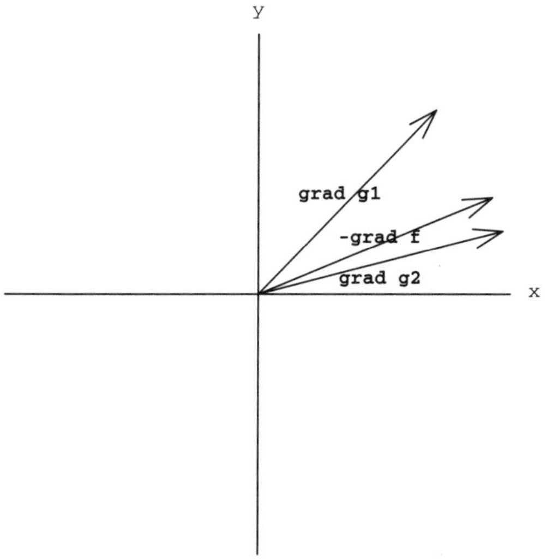


Now consider the boundary point $\mathbf{b} = (1,6)$. At point $\mathbf{b}$, we have $g_1(\mathbf{b}) = g_3(\mathbf{b}) = 0$. The constraints $g_1(x,y) \leq 0$ and $g_3(x,y) \leq 0$ are now binding. As shown below, the equation

$$\lambda_0 \nabla f(\mathbf{b}) + \lambda_1 \nabla g_1(\mathbf{b}) + \lambda_3 \nabla g_3(\mathbf{b}) = \mathbf{0}$$

is satisfied by $\lambda_1 = 7\lambda_0$, and $\lambda_3 = -7\lambda_0$.

*In[73]:=*

```
Clear[fjnc,lambda0,lambda1,lambda3];
fjnc  =  lambda0*gradf[f[x,y],{x,y}]+
         lambda1*gradf[g1[x,y],{x,y}]+
         lambda3*gradf[g3[x,y],{x,y}]  /.{x->1,y->6};
Solve[fjnc  ==  0,{lambda1,lambda3}]
```

*Out[75]=*

{{lambda1 → 7 lambda0, lambda3 → –7 lambda0}}

If $\lambda_0 > 0$, then $\lambda_3 < 0$ which implies that the Fritz John necessary condition is not satisfied and the point $\mathbf{b} = (1,6)$ cannot be a local minimum point. We plot the gradient vectors $\nabla f(\mathbf{b})$, $\nabla g_1(\mathbf{b})$ and $\nabla g_3(\mathbf{b})$ using the **fjohn**.

*In[76]:=*

```
graph=fjohn[{1,6},{g1[x,y],g2[x,y],g3[x,y],
            g4[x,y],g5[x,y]},f[x,y],{x,y},"cone"];
Show[graph,AspectRatio->Automatic,
           PlotRange->{{-1,1},{-1,1}},Axes->True,
           AxesLabel->{"x","y"},Ticks->None];
```

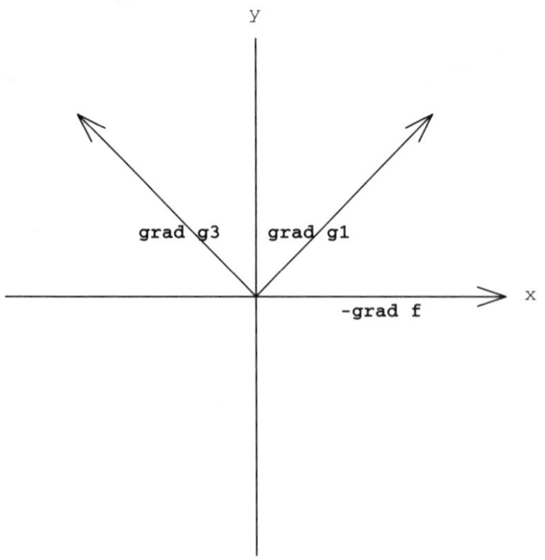


The gradient vector $-\nabla f(\mathbf{a})$ lies outside the cone formed by the gradient vectors $\nabla g_1(\mathbf{a})$ and $\nabla g_3(\mathbf{a})$.

We now make some remarks about the Fritz John necessary condition

$$\lambda_0 \nabla f(\mathbf{a}) + \sum_{j \in J(\mathbf{a})} \lambda_j \nabla g_j(\mathbf{a}) = 0$$

(1) The problem of maximizing $f(\mathbf{x})$ subject to $\mathbf{S} = \{\mathbf{x} \in \mathbf{R}^n \mid \mathbf{g}(\mathbf{x}) \leq \mathbf{0}\}$ is equivalent to minimizing $-f(\mathbf{x})$. The Fritz John necessary condition for $\mathbf{a}$ to be a solution of the maximization problem is

$$-\lambda_0 \nabla f(\mathbf{a}) + \sum_{j \in J(\mathbf{a})} \lambda_j \nabla g_j(\mathbf{a}) = 0$$

(2) In the Fritz John necessary condition, only the binding constraints, $g_j(\mathbf{a}) = \mathbf{0}$, $j \in J(\mathbf{a})$, are involved. However, the necessary condition can be stated in an equivalent form that includes all constraints, $g_i(\mathbf{x}) \leq 0$, $i=1,2, \ldots, m$, whether they are binding or not. If $\mathbf{a}$ is a point of local minimum of $f(\mathbf{x})$ in $\mathbf{S}$, then

$$\lambda_0 \nabla f(\mathbf{a}) + \sum_{i=1}^{m} \lambda_i \nabla g_i(\mathbf{a}) = 0$$

$$\begin{array}{ll} \lambda_i \, g_i(\mathbf{a}) = 0 & \text{for } \ i = 1,2, \ldots, m \\ g_i(\mathbf{a}) \leq 0 & \text{for } \ i = 1,2, \ldots, m \\ \lambda_0, \lambda_i \geq 0 & \text{for } \ i = 1,2, \ldots, m \\ (\lambda_0, \boldsymbol{\lambda}) \neq (0, \mathbf{0}) & \end{array}$$

where $\boldsymbol{\lambda} = [\lambda_1 \, \lambda_2 \ldots \lambda_m]^T$. It is evident that $\lambda_i = 0$ for the nonbinding constraint, $g_i(\mathbf{a}) < 0$, since $\lambda_i g_i(\mathbf{a}) = 0$. The scalars $\lambda_0$ and $\lambda_i$ for $i = 1,2, \ldots, m$, are called *Lagrangian multipliers*. The conditions that $\lambda_i g_i(\mathbf{a}) = 0$, for $i = 1,2, \ldots, m$ are called the *complementary slackness conditions*. If a constraint is not binding, that is, if $g_i(\mathbf{a}) < 0$, then it requires that $\lambda_i = 0$. Whenever $\lambda_i > 0$, the constraint must be binding, $g_i(\mathbf{a}) = 0$.

(3) The necessary condition does not allow all of the parameters $\lambda_0$ and $\lambda_i$ to be zero.

(4) If a local minimum occurs at an interior of $\mathbf{S}$, then $J(\mathbf{a})$ is empty. The necessary condition becomes

$$\lambda_0 \nabla f(\mathbf{a}) = \mathbf{0}.$$

By choosing any $\lambda_0 > 0$, the condition is $\nabla f(\mathbf{a}) = 0$, which is essentially the necessary condition for the unconstrained minimization problem.

(5) If the $\lambda_0 = 0$, then

$$\sum_{j \in J(\mathbf{a})} \lambda_j \nabla g_j(\mathbf{a}) = 0$$

In this case, the gradient vector $\nabla f(\mathbf{a})$ drops out completely. The Fritz John necessary condition does not make use of any information about the objective function $f(\mathbf{x})$. The necessary condition only requires that gradient vectors $\nabla g_j(\mathbf{a})$ of the binding constraints be linearly dependent. The Fritz John necessary condition provides no practical value in finding a local minimum of $f(\mathbf{x})$. For this reason, we are more interested in alternative necessary conditions that impose restrictions on constraints that will guarantee a positive Lagrangian multiplier $\lambda_0 > 0$. This additional restriction on the constraint set $\mathbf{S}$ is called *constraint qualification*. For an illustration, we consider the following example.

**Example 12.13** Consider the mathematical problem

$$\begin{array}{ll} \text{minimize} & f(x,y) = -x \\ \text{subject to} & g_1(x,y) = y - x^3 \leq 0, \\ & g_2(x,y) = -y \leq 0. \end{array}$$

At the point $\mathbf{a}$ = (0,0), both $g_1(\mathbf{x}) \le 0$ and $g_2(\mathbf{x}) \le 0$ are binding constraints. The gradient vectors are: $\nabla f(\mathbf{a}) = [-1\ 0]^T$, $\nabla g_1(\mathbf{a}) = [0\ 1]^T$, and $\nabla g_2(\mathbf{a}) = [0\ -1]^T$. At $\mathbf{a}$, the equation

$$\lambda_0\begin{bmatrix}-1\\0\end{bmatrix}+\lambda_1\begin{bmatrix}0\\1\end{bmatrix}+\lambda_2\begin{bmatrix}0\\-1\end{bmatrix}=\begin{bmatrix}0\\0\end{bmatrix}$$

is satisfied if and only if $\lambda_0 = 0$. In the following plot, the gradient vectors are plotted. The feasible region **S** is the area between the horizontal axis and the heavy curve in the second quadrant.

*In[78]:=*

```
Clear[f,g1,g2,constrain,graph];
f[x_,y_]:=-x;
g1[x_,y_]:=y-x^3;  g2[x_,y_]:=-y;
graph=fjohn[{0,0},{g1[x,y],g2[x,y]},f[x,y],
          {x,y},"label"];
constrain=Plot[(-x)^3,{x,-1,0.5},
          PlotStyle->{Thickness[0.008]},Ticks->None,
          PlotRange->All,AxesLabel->{"x","y"},
          DisplayFunction->Identity];
Show[constrain,graph,DisplayFunction->$DisplayFunction];
```

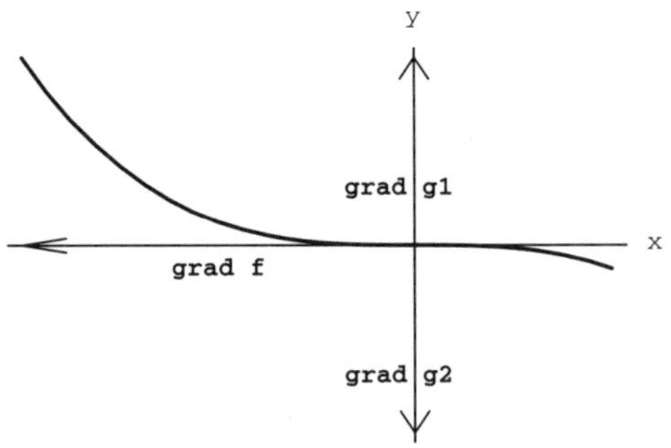


In this example, the vectors $\nabla g_1(\mathbf{a})$ and $\nabla g_2(\mathbf{a})$ are linearly dependent.

## EXERCISES

1. Consider the following problem

$$\begin{aligned}\text{minimize } & f(x,y) = (x-3)^2 + (y-2)^2,\\ \text{subject to } & g_1(x,y) = x^2 + y^2 - 5 \le 0\\ & g_2(x,y) = x + 2y - 4 \le 0\\ & x,y \ge 0.\end{aligned}$$

   (a) Verify the Fritz John necessary condition at the point $\mathbf{a}_1 = (2,1)$.
   (b) Use the **fjohn** function to graph the gradient vectors $\nabla f(\mathbf{a}_1)$, $\nabla g_i(\mathbf{a}_1)$ and confirm the results given in (a).
   (c) Show that $\mathbf{a}_2 = (0,0)$ does not satisfy the necessary condition.

2. Consider the following optimization problem:

maximize $3x + y$,
subject to $x^2 + y^2 \leq 5$
$x - y \leq 1$.

(a) Show that $\mathbf{a}_1 = (2,1)$ satisfies the Fritz John necessary condition, but $\mathbf{a}_2 = (3/\sqrt{2}, 1/\sqrt{2})$ does not.
(b) Use the function **fjohn** to graph to confirm these results.

## □ 12.3 Kuhn-Tucker Necessary and Sufficient Conditions □

### 12.3.1 Kuhn-Tucker necessary conditions

In this section we discuss well-known necessary optimality conditions that are similar to the Fritz John necessary condition with an additional qualification imposed on the constraints in order to ensure the Lagrangian multiplier $\lambda_0$ is positive.

**THEOREM 12.3** *(Kuhn-Tucker necessary conditions) Suppose $f(\mathbf{x})$ and $\mathbf{g}(\mathbf{x})$ are differentiable on $\mathbf{R}^n$ and consider the problem of minimizing $f(\mathbf{x})$ subject to $\mathbf{S} = \{\mathbf{x} \in \mathbf{R}^n \mid g(\mathbf{x}) \leq \mathbf{0}\}$. Suppose $\mathbf{a}$ is a point where $f(\mathbf{x})$ has a local minimum. Furthermore, suppose that the gradient vectors of the binding constraints*

$$\{\nabla g_j(\mathbf{a}) = \mathbf{0} \mid j \in J(\mathbf{a})\}$$

*are linearly independent. Then there is a set of nonnegative scalars, $\{\lambda_j \mid j \in J(\mathbf{a})\}$ such that*

$$\nabla f(\mathbf{a}) + \sum_{j \in J(\mathbf{a})} \lambda_j \nabla g_j(\mathbf{a}) = 0$$

The Kuhn-Tucker necessary conditions are similar to the Fritz John necessary condition. The Kuhn-Tucker necessary conditions require $\lambda_0 > 0$ and the gradient vectors of the binding constraints $\{\nabla g_j(\mathbf{a}) \mid j \in J(\mathbf{a})\}$ are linearly independent. If $\lambda_0 > 0$, then the Lagrangian multipliers in the Fritz John necessary condition can be rescaled to make $\lambda_0 = 1$. To guarantee that $\lambda_0 > 0$, we have to place a restriction on the binding constraint $g_j(\mathbf{a}) = 0$. This type of restriction is called a *constraint qualification.*

**Example 12.14** Consider the optimization problem

minimize $f(x,y) = x + y$
subject to $g_1(x,y) = x + y^2 - 1 \leq 0$
$g_2(x,y) = x^2 + y^2 - 2x \leq 0$.

Show that the point $\mathbf{a} = (1-\sqrt{2}/2, -\sqrt{2}/2)$ satisfies the Kuhn-Tucker necessary conditions

$$\nabla f(\mathbf{a}) + \lambda_2 \nabla g_2(\mathbf{a}) = \mathbf{0}$$

where $\lambda_2 > 0$. The following calculation shows that $\lambda_2 = 1/\sqrt{2} > 0$.

*In[84]:=*

```
Clear[f,x,y,g1,g2,lambda2,ktnc];
a1  =  1-Sqrt[2]/2;  a2  =  -Sqrt[2]/2;
f[x_,y_]:=  x  +  y;
g1[x_,y_]:=  x+y^2-1;  g2[x_,y_]:=  x^2+y^2-2*x;
ktnc  =  gradf[f[x,y],{x,y}]+
            lambda2*gradf[g2[x,y],{x,y}]  /.  {x->a1,y->a2};
Solve[ktnc  ==  0,{lambda2}]
```

*Out[89]=*

$$\{\{\text{lambda2} \to \frac{1}{\text{Sqrt[2]}}\}\}$$

Using the **fjohn** function, we plot the gradient vectors $\nabla f(\mathbf{a})$ and $\nabla g_2(\mathbf{a})$.

*In[90]:=*

```
graph=fjohn[{a1,a2},{g1[x,y],g2[x,y]},f[x,y],
            {x,y},"label"];
Show[graph,AspectRatio->Automatic,
           PlotRange->{{-1,1},{-1,1}},Axes->True,
           AxesLabel->{"x","y"},Ticks->None];
```

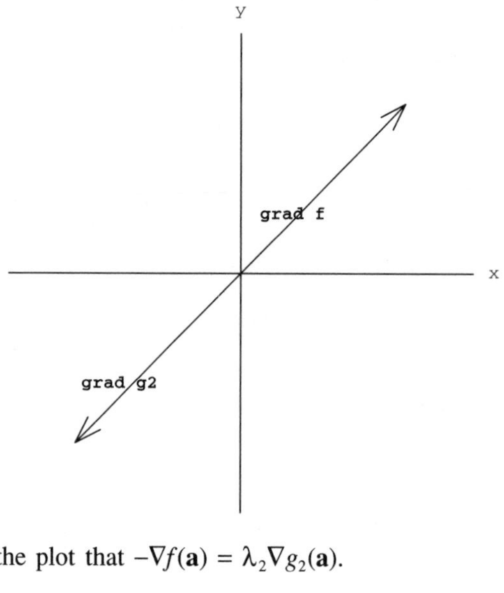


We observe from the plot that $-\nabla f(\mathbf{a}) = \lambda_2 \nabla g_2(\mathbf{a})$.

**Example 12.15** Show that $\mathbf{a} = (2,1)$ satisfies the Kuhn-Tucker necessary conditions for the following minimization problem:

minimize $f(x,y) = x^2 + y^2 - 4x$
subject to $g_1(x,y) = 2 - xy \leq 0$
$g_2(x,y) = x^2 + y - 5 \leq 0$
$g_3(x,y) = -x \leq 0$
$g_4(x,y) = -y \leq 0.$

First, we observe that $g_1(\mathbf{a}) = 0$ and $g_2(\mathbf{a}) = 0$. The following calculations show that there exists nonnegative $\lambda_1$ and $\lambda_2$ such that $\nabla f(\mathbf{a}) + \lambda_1 \nabla g_1(\mathbf{a}) + \lambda_2 \nabla g_2(\mathbf{a}) = \mathbf{0}$.

*In[92]:*

```
Clear[f,x,y,g1,g2,lambda1,lambda2];
f[x_,y_]:= x^2+y^2-4*x;
g1[x_,y_]:= 2-x*y;  g2[x_,y_]:= x^2+y-5;
ktnc  =  gradf[f[x,y],{x,y}]+
                    lambda1*gradf[g1[x,y],{x,y}]+
                     lambda2*gradf[g2[x,y],{x,y}] /.{x->2,y->1};
Solve[ktnc  ==  0,{lambda1,lambda2}]
```

*Out[96]=*

$\{\{\text{lambda1} \to \frac{8}{7}, \text{lambda2} \to \frac{2}{7}\}\}$

Furthermore, since the rank of $[\nabla g_1(\mathbf{a})\ \nabla g_2(\mathbf{a})]$ is two, $\nabla g_1(\mathbf{a})$ and $\nabla g_2(\mathbf{a})$ are linearly independent.

*In[97]:=*

```
rank[{gradf[g1[x,y],{x,y}]  /.  {x->2,y->1},
      gradf[g2[x,y],{x,y}]  /.  {x->2,y->1}}]
```

*Out[97]=*

2

Hence, the Kuhn-Tucker necessary conditions are satisfied. The following plot shows that $-\nabla f(\mathbf{a})$ lies in the cone generated by $\nabla g_1(\mathbf{a})$ and $\nabla g_2(\mathbf{a})$.

*In[98]:=*

```
graph=fjohn[{2,1},{g1[x,y],g2[x,y],g3[x,y],g4[x,y]},
            f[x,y],{x,y},"cone"];
Show[graph,AspectRatio->Automatic,
           PlotRange->{{-1,1},{-1,1}},Axes->True,
           AxesLabel->{"x","y"},Ticks->None];
```

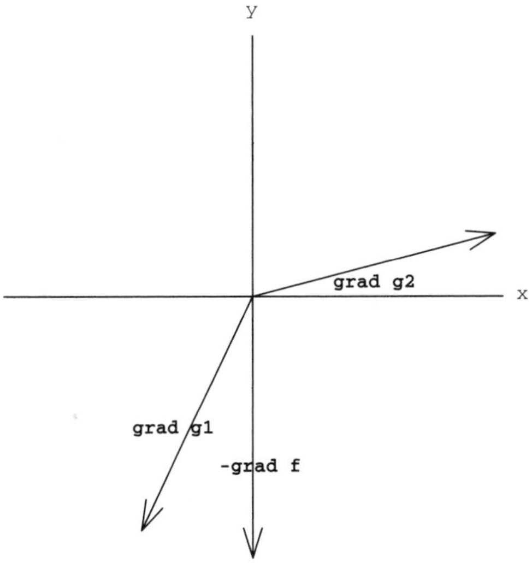

We make some remarks about the Kuhn-Tucker necessary conditions:

$$\nabla f(\mathbf{a}) + \sum_{j\in J(\mathbf{a})} \lambda_j \nabla g_j(\mathbf{a}) = 0$$

where $\lambda_j \geq 0$ and the set of vectors $\{\nabla g_j(\mathbf{a}) \mid j\in J(\mathbf{a})\}$ are linearly independent vectors.

(1) The Kuhn-Tucker necessary conditions for maximizing $f(\mathbf{x})$ subject to $\mathbf{S} = \{\mathbf{x}\in\mathbf{R}^n \mid g(\mathbf{x}) \leq \mathbf{0}\}$ are

$$-\nabla f(\mathbf{a}) + \sum_{j\in J(\mathbf{a})} \lambda_j \nabla g_j(\mathbf{a}) = 0$$

where $\lambda_j \geq 0$ and the set of vectors $\{\nabla g_j(\mathbf{a}) \mid j\in J(\mathbf{a})\}$ are linearly independent vectors.

(2) The necessary conditions can be stated in the following equivalent form that includes all constraints $g_i(x) \leq 0$, $i = 1,2, \ldots ,m$, whether they are binding or not. That is, necessary conditions for **a** to be a local minimum point are

$$\nabla f(\mathbf{a}) + \sum_{i=1}^{m} \lambda_i \nabla g_i(\mathbf{a}) = 0$$
$$\lambda_i g_i(\mathbf{a}) = 0 \quad \text{for} \quad i = 1,2, \ldots ,m$$
$$g_i(\mathbf{a}) \leq 0 \quad \text{for} \quad i = 1,2, \ldots ,m$$
$$\lambda_i \geq 0 \quad \text{for} \quad i = 1,2, \ldots ,m$$
$$\{\nabla g_j(\mathbf{a}) \mid j\in J(\mathbf{a})\} \text{ are linearly independent vectors.}$$

The conditions $\lambda_i g_i(\mathbf{a}) = 0$, $g_i(\mathbf{a}) \leq 0$, and $\lambda_i \geq 0$ imply that if a constraint is not binding, then $\lambda_i = 0$. Whenever $\lambda_i > 0$, the constraint must be binding.

(3) The Kuhn-Tucker necessary conditions are closely related to the necessary conditions with equality constraints introduced in the last chapter. Consider the problem of minimization subject to $m$ constraints:

minimize $f(x_1,x_2, \ldots ,x_n)$
subject to $g_i(x_1,x_2, \ldots ,x_n) \leq 0$, $i = 1,2, \ldots ,m$.

Let us define a Lagrangian function

$$L(\mathbf{x},\mathbf{u}) = f(\mathbf{x}) + \lambda_1 g_1(\mathbf{x}) + \lambda_2 g_2(\mathbf{x}) + \ldots + \lambda_m g_m(\mathbf{x})$$

where $\lambda_i$ are Lagrangian multipliers, or *Kuhn-Tucker multipliers*. The Kuhn-Tucker necessary conditions can be written in terms of the partial derivatives of $L$ as

$$\frac{\partial L}{\partial x_i} = \frac{\partial f}{\partial x_i} + \sum_{j=1}^{m} \lambda_j \frac{\partial g_j}{\partial x_i} = 0, i = 1,2, \ldots ,n$$

$$\lambda_j \frac{\partial L}{\partial \lambda_j} = \lambda_j g_j = 0, j = 1,2, \ldots ,m$$

$$\frac{\partial L}{\partial \lambda_j} = g_j \leq 0, j = 1,2, \ldots ,m$$

$$\lambda_j \geq 0, j = 1,2, \ldots ,m$$

where all functions and derivatives are evaluated at local minimum point. If the number of variables $n$ and the number of constraints $m$ are small, it is possible to use *Mathematica* to solve for points where the above identities are satisfied.

**Example 12.16** Find the points that satisfy the Kuhn-Tucker necessary conditions for the optimization problem:

minimize $f(x,y,z) = x - y^2$
subject to $g_1(x,y,z) = x^2 + y^2 + z^2 - 9 \le 0$
$g_2(x,y,z) = -x + 3y + z - 6 \le 0.$

We define the Lagrangian function as

$$L(x,y,z,\lambda_1,\lambda_2) = f(x,y,z) + \lambda_1 g_1(x,y,z) + \lambda_2 g_2(x,y,z).$$

The Kuhn-Tucker necessary conditions require

$$\frac{\partial L}{\partial x} = 1 + 2\lambda_1 x - \lambda_2 = 0$$

$$\frac{\partial L}{\partial y} = -2y + 2\lambda_1 y + 3\lambda_2 = 0$$

$$\frac{\partial L}{\partial z} = 2\lambda_1 z + \lambda_2 = 0$$

$$\lambda_1 \frac{\partial L}{\partial \lambda_1} = \lambda_1(x^2 + y^2 + z^2 - 9) = 0$$

$$\lambda_2 \frac{\partial L}{\partial \lambda_2} = \lambda_2(-x + 3y + z - 6) = 0$$

$$\frac{\partial L}{\partial \lambda_1} = x^2 + y^2 + z^2 - 9 \le 0$$

$$\frac{\partial L}{\partial \lambda_2} = -x + 3y + z - 6 \le 0$$

$$\lambda_1, \lambda_2 \ge 0$$

We first solve for points $(x,y,z,\lambda_1,\lambda_2)$ that satisfy only the equality conditions, i.e.,

$$\frac{\partial L}{\partial x} = 0,\ \frac{\partial L}{\partial y} = 0,\ \frac{\partial L}{\partial z} = 0,\ \lambda_1 \frac{\partial L}{\partial \lambda_1} = 0,\ \lambda_2 \frac{\partial L}{\partial \lambda_2} = 0$$

*In[100]:=*

```
Clear[f,x,y,z,L,lambda1,lambda2,g1,g2,sol];
f[x_,y_,z_]:= x-y^2;
g1[x_,y_,z_]:= x^2+y^2+z^2-9;
g2[x_,y_,z_]:= -x+3*y+z-6;
L[x_,y_,z_,lambda1_,lambda2_]:=
              f[x,y,z]+lambda1*g1[x,y,z]+lambda2*g2[x,y,z];
```

```
sol=NSolve[{D[L[x,y,z,lambda1,lambda2],x]==0,
            D[L[x,y,z,lambda1,lambda2],y]==0,
            D[L[x,y,z,lambda1,lambda2],z]==0,
        lambda1*D[L[x,y,z,lambda1,lambda2],lambda1]==0,
         lambda2*D[L[x,y,z,lambda1,lambda2],lambda2]==0},
             {x,y,z,lambda1,lambda2}];
sol={x,y,z,lambda1,lambda2} /. sol
```

Infinity : : indet :
  Indeterminate expression 0. ComplexInfinity encountered.

*Out[106]=*

{{-0.5, -2.95804, 0., 1., 0.}, {-0.5, 2.95804, 0., 1., 0.}, {-4.00054 + 0.186305 I, 0.517711 - 0.80628 I, 0.446325 + 2.60514 I, 0.087008 + 0.0683353 I, 0.278379 - 0.514336 I},
{-4.00054 - 0.186305 I, 0.517711 + 0.80628 I, 0.446325 - 2.60514 I, 0.087008 - 0.0683353 I, 0.278379+0.514336 I}, {0.266751, 1.1728, 2.74834, -0.165832, 0.911528}, {0.143426, 2.5645, -1.55008, 0.355453, 1.10196}}

There are six possible solutions. However, not all solutions are real and some have nonnegative scalars $\lambda_1, \lambda_2 \geq 0$. By inspection, only the first, second, and sixth solutions satisfy the nonnegativity conditions. These solutions are

*In[107]:=*

```
sol[[1]]
```

*Out[107]=*

{-0.5, -2.95804, 0., 1., 0.}

*In[108]:=*

```
sol[[2]]
```

*Out[108]=*

{-0.5, 2.95804, 0., 1., 0.}

*In[109]:=*

```
sol[[6]]
```

*Out[109]=*

{0.143426, 2.5645, -1.55008, 0.355453, 1.10196}

These solutions must also satisfy the inequalities: $\partial L/\partial\lambda_1 = g_1 \leq 0$ and $\partial L/\partial\lambda_2 = g_2 \leq 0$.

*In[110]:=*

```
a1  =  Take[sol[[1]],3]
```

*Out[110]=*

{-0.5, -2.95804, 0.}

*In[111]:=*

```
Apply[g1,a1]  //  Chop
```

*Out[111]=*
```
0
```

*In[112]:=*
```
Apply[g2,a1]
```

*Out[112]=*
```
-14.3741
```

These results show that at the point $\mathbf{a}_1 = (x,y,z) = (-0.5,-2.95804,0)$, $g_1(\mathbf{a}_1) = 0$ and $g_2(\mathbf{a}_1) < 0$. At $\mathbf{a}_1$, the first constraint is binding, but not the second. Therefore, $\mathbf{a}_1$ satisfies the Kuhn-Tucker necessary conditions for a local minimum. Next we examine the point $\mathbf{a}_2 = (-0.5, 2.95804, 0)$.

*In[113]:=*
```
a2 = Take[sol[[2]],3];
Apply[g1,a2] // Chop
```

*Out[114]=*
```
0
```

*In[115]:=*
```
Apply[g2,a2]
```

*Out[115]=*
```
3.37412
```

Since $g_2(\mathbf{a}_2) = 3.37412 > 0$, the point $\mathbf{a}_2 = (-0.5, 2.95804, 0)$ is not a feasible point. Lastly, we check the point $\mathbf{a}_3 = (0.143426, 2.5645, -1.55008)$.

*In[116]:=*
```
a3 = Take[sol[[6]],3];
Apply[g1,a3] // Chop
```

*Out[117]=*
```
0
```

*In[118]:=*
```
Apply[g2,a3] // Chop
```

*Out[118]=*
```
0
```

Since $g_1(\mathbf{a}_3) = g_2(\mathbf{a}_3) = 0$, both constraints are binding. Furthermore, the gradient vectors $\nabla g_1(\mathbf{a}_3)$ and $\nabla g_2(\mathbf{a}_3)$ are linearly independent from the following calculation.

*In[119]:=*
```
dg1 = gradf[g1[x,y,z],{x,y,z}] /.
     {x->a3[[1]],y->a3[[2]],z->a3[[3]]};
dg2 = gradf[g2[x,y,z],{x,y,z}] /.
     {x->a3[[1]],y->a3[[2]],z->a3[[3]]};
rank[{dg1,dg2}]
```

*Out[121]=*
```
2
```

The point $\mathbf{a}_3$ satisfies the Kuhn-Tucker necessary conditions. Are $\mathbf{a}_1$ and $\mathbf{a}_3$ global or local minimum points? We shall examine this question in the next section.

**Example 12.17** Consider the following problem

maximize $f(x,y) = 18x - x^2 + xy - y^2$
subject to $g_1(x,y) = x + y - 12 \leq 0$
$g_2(x,y) = -x + y - 6 \leq 0$
$g_3(x,y) = -x \leq 0$
$g_4(x,y) = -y \leq 0.$

We find possible local maximum points. Since this is a maximization problem, we set the problem and the Lagrangian function to minimize $-f(x,y)$ subject to the same constraints.

$$L(x,y,\lambda_1,\lambda_2,\lambda_3,\lambda_4) = -f(x,y) + \lambda_1 g_1(x,y) + \lambda_2 g_2(x,y) + \lambda_3 g_3(x,y) + \lambda_4 g_4(x,y).$$

The Kuhn-Tucker necessary conditions require

$$\frac{\partial L}{\partial x} = 0; \frac{\partial L}{\partial y} = 0; \lambda_i \frac{\partial L}{\partial \lambda_i} = 0,\ i = 1,2,3,4;$$

$$\frac{\partial L}{\partial \lambda_i} = g_i \leq 0,\ \lambda_i \geq 0,\ i = 1,2,3,4.$$

We first solve for $(x,y,\lambda_1,\lambda_2,\lambda_3,\lambda_4)$ from the set of equations.

*In[122]:=*
```
Clear[f,x,y,g1,g2,g3,g4];
Clear[L,lambda1,lambda2,lambda3,lambda4,sol];
f[x_,y_]:= 18*x-x^2+x*y-y^2;
g1[x_,y_]:= x+y-12;
g2[x_,y_]:= -x+y-6;
g3[x_,y_]:= -x;
g4[x_,y_]:= -y;
L[x_,y_,lambda1_,lambda2_,lambda3_,lambda4_]:=
        -f[x,y]+lambda1*g1[x,y]+lambda2*g2[x,y]+
              lambda3*g3[x,y]+lambda4*g4[x,y];
sol  =  NSolve[{
              D[L[x,y,lambda1,lambda2,lambda3,lambda4],x]==0,
          D[L[x,y,lambda1,lambda2,lambda3,lambda4],y]==0,
        lambda1*D[L[x,y,lambda1,lambda2,lambda3,lambda4],
                lambda1]==0,
        lambda2*D[L[x,y,lambda1,lambda2,lambda3,lambda4],
                lambda2]==0,
        lambda3*D[L[x,y,lambda1,lambda2,lambda3,lambda4],
                lambda3]==0,
        lambda4*D[L[x,y,lambda1,lambda2,lambda3,lambda4],
                lambda4]==0},
        {x,y,lambda1,lambda2,lambda3,lambda4}];
sol  =  {x,y,lambda1,lambda2,lambda3,lambda4}  /.  sol
```

*Out[131]=*

```
{{-6., 0., 0., -30., 0., -24.}, {0., 0., 0., 0., -18., 0.}, {0., 0., 0., 0., -18., 0.},
 {0., 6., 0., -12., -12., 0.}, {0., 12., -24., 0., -54., 0.}, {3., 9., 3., -18., 0., 0.},
 {6., 12., 0., -18., 0., 0.}, {9., 0., 0., 0., 0., -9.}, {9., 3., 3., 0., 0., 0.},
 {12., 0., -6., 0., 0., -18.}, {12., 6., 0., 0., 0., 0.},
 {-11. + 0. lambda1 + 0. lambda2 + 0. lambda3 + 0. lambda4 + 0. y,
  -6. + 0. lambda1 + 0. lambda2 + 0. lambda3 + 0. lambda4,
  0. + 0. lambda2 + 0. lambda3 + 0. lambda4,
  1.08086 10^17 + 0. lambda3 + 0. lambda4, -1.08086 10^17 + 0. lambda4,
  1.08086 10^17}}
```

By inspection, only the 9th solution satisfies the requirements: $x,y \geq 0$, and $\lambda_i \geq 0$, $i=1,2,3,4$.

*In[132]:=*

```
sol[[9]]
```

*Out[132]=*

```
{9., 3., 3., 0., 0., 0.}
```

Thus the point $(x,y) = (9,3)$ with the binding constraint $g_1(x,y) = 0$ and $\lambda_1 = 3$ satisfy the Kuhn-Tucker necessary conditions.

**Example 12.18** Demand for long-distance telephone calls varies by the hour of day so that during peak periods the capacity is fully utilized, while at the off-peak periods the capacity is underutilized. Suppose that AT&T wants to charge a higher rate during peak periods and a lower rate during off-peak periods. What should be the pricing policy so that the profit is maximized? This example is adapted from William Baumol, *Economic Theory and Operations Analysis*, Prentice Hall, 1977, pp. 173–5.

Let the demand for telephone calls and the corresponding prices per minute at each hour of the day be denoted by the vectors

$$\mathbf{Q} = [q_1 \quad q_2 \quad \ldots \quad q_{24}]^T$$
$$\mathbf{P} = [p_1 \quad p_2 \quad \ldots \quad p_{24}]^T$$

respectively. Furthermore, let the daily total operating cost be a function of the quantity of telephone calls at each hour, which we denote by the function

$$C(\mathbf{Q}) = C(q_1, q_2, \ldots, q_{24}).$$

Lastly, let $F(x)$ denote the daily cost of capital or capacity as a function of hourly output capacity, $x$. The optimization problem is to maximize the daily profit $\Pi$, subject to the hourly capacity constraints. That is,

$$\text{maximize } \Pi = \sum_{i=1}^{24} p_i q_i - C(q_1, q_2, \ldots, q_{24}) - F(x)$$
$$\text{subject to } q_i - x \leq 0,\ i = 1,2, \ldots, 24$$

We assume that the prices $p_i$ are independent of the outputs $q_i$, i.e., $\partial p_i / \partial q_i = 0$. Since this is a maximization problem, we reformulate the problem to minimize the Lagrangian function:

$$L(\mathbf{Q},\lambda) = -\left[\sum_{i=1}^{24} p_i q_i - C(q_1,q_2,\ldots,q_{24}) - F(x)\right] + \sum_{i=1}^{24} \lambda_i (q_i - x)$$

The Kuhn-Tucker necessary conditions require that

$$\frac{\partial L}{\partial q_i} = -p_i + \frac{\partial C}{\partial q_i} + \lambda_i = 0,\ i = 1,2,\ldots,24$$

$$\frac{\partial L}{\partial x} = \frac{\partial F}{\partial x} - \sum_{i=1}^{24} \lambda_i = 0,$$

$$\lambda_i \frac{\partial L}{\partial \lambda_i} = \lambda_i (q_i - x) \leq 0,\ i = 1,2,\ldots,24$$

$$\lambda_i \geq 0,\ i = 1,2,\ \ldots\ ,24$$

Suppose the $i$-th hour capacity constraints are not binding, i.e., $\partial L/\partial \lambda_i = (q_i - x) < 0$. Hence, we take $\lambda_i = 0$ so that the necessary condition $\lambda_i\ \partial L/\partial \lambda_i = 0$ are satisfied. This implies

$$\frac{\partial L}{\partial q_i} = -p_i + \frac{\partial C}{\partial q_i} = 0, \quad \text{or} \quad p_i = \frac{\partial C}{\partial q_i}$$

Thus, during the off-peak periods, the optimal price should be equal to the marginal operating cost, $\partial C/\partial q_i$. On the other hand, if the constraint is binding, i.e., $\partial L/\partial \lambda_i = (q_i - x) = 0$, we have $\lambda_i > 0$. This implies

$$\frac{\partial L}{\partial q_i} = -p_i + \frac{\partial C}{\partial q_i} + \lambda_i = 0, \quad \text{or} \quad p_i = \frac{\partial C}{\partial q_i} + \lambda_i$$

That is, during the peak period, the optimal price should exceed the marginal cost plus a nonnegative supplementary cost, $\lambda_i$. Since $\partial L/\partial x = 0$ implies

$$\frac{\partial F}{\partial x} = \sum_{i=1}^{24} \lambda_i$$

the sum of all supplementary costs for all peak periods is equal to the marginal capacity cost. From the profit maximization point of view, AT&T shall charge higher rates during the peak hours and lower rates during the off-peak hours.

## EXERCISES

1. Consider the optimization problem:

   mimimize $f(x,y) = 2x^2 - 2xy + 2y^2 - 6x$
   subject to $g_1(x,y) = 3x + 4y - 6 \leq 0$
   $g_2(x,y) = -x + 4y^2 - 2 \leq 0$
   $x, y \geq 0.$

(a) State the Kuhn-Tucker necessary conditions for this problem.
(b) Find the points that satisfy it.

2. Consider the following problem:

maximize $x^2 - x - y$
subject to $x + 5y \leq 6$
$x + y \geq 5$
$x, y \geq 0.$

(a) State the Kuhn-Tucker necessary conditions for this problem.
(b) Find points that satisfy it.

### 12.3.2 Kuhn-Tucker sufficient conditions

In the previous section we discussed the necessary conditions for an optimization problem to have a local extremum in terms of the first-order conditions of a Lagrangian function

$$L(\mathbf{x},\lambda) = f(\mathbf{x}) + \lambda_1 g_1(\mathbf{x}) + \lambda_2 g_2(\mathbf{x}) + \ldots + \lambda_m g_m(\mathbf{x}).$$

Suppose the point **a** satisfies the Kuhn-Tucker necessary conditions. Furthermore, suppose **a** is an interior point of the feasible region **S**. In this case, the Lagrangian multipliers $\lambda_i$ are all zero. Since there are no binding constraints at point **a**, the sufficient conditions for **a** to be a local extremum point are the same as in the case of unconstrained optimization discussed in Chapter 11. In particular, we investigate the successive leading principal minors at **a**

$$|\mathbf{H}_r| = \begin{vmatrix} f_{11} & f_{12} & \cdots & f_{1r} \\ f_{21} & f_{22} & \cdots & f_{2r} \\ \cdots & \cdots & \cdots & \cdots \\ f_{r1} & f_{r2} & \cdots & f_{rr} \end{vmatrix}, \quad r = 1,2, \ldots ,n.$$

We can characterize **a** according to the following:

(1) **a** is a local minimum point if **a** satisfies the Kuhn-Tucker necessary conditions and $|\mathbf{H}_r| > 0$ for all $r = 1,2, \ldots ,n$;

(2) **a** is local maximum point if **a** satisfies the Kuhn-Tucker necessary conditions and $(-1)^r|\mathbf{H}_r| > 0$ for all $r = 1,2, \ldots ,n$.

Suppose that the point **a** is not an interior point and that there are $k$ binding constraints. To simplify the discussion we assume that the first $k$ constraints are binding, $g_i(\mathbf{a})=0$, $i=1,2, \ldots k$, and the remaining constraints are not binding. For the nonbinding constraints we can choose $\lambda_j=0$, $j=k+1,k+2, \ldots ,m$. The Lagrangian function in this situation is

$$L^*(\mathbf{x},\lambda_1,\lambda_2, \ldots ,\lambda_k) = f(\mathbf{x}) + \lambda_1 g_1(\mathbf{x}) + \lambda_2 g_2(\mathbf{x}) + \ldots + \lambda_k g_k(\mathbf{x}).$$

Sufficient conditions for **a** to be a local extremum subject to $m$ inequality constraints are now equivalent to the conditions that $f(\mathbf{x})$ has a local extremum at **a** subject to the $k$ binding constraints. Sufficient conditions in this situation are related to the bordered Hessian determinants discussed in Chapter 11. Hence, we consider the determinants:

$$|\mathbf{B}_r| = \begin{vmatrix} L^*_{\lambda_1\lambda_1} & \dots & L^*_{\lambda_1\lambda_k} & L^*_{\lambda_1 1} & \dots & L^*_{\lambda_1 r} \\ \dots & \dots & \dots & \dots & \dots & \dots \\ L^*_{\lambda_k\lambda_1} & \dots & L^*_{\lambda_k\lambda_k} & L^*_{\lambda_k 1} & \dots & L^*_{\lambda_k r} \\ L^*_{1\lambda_1} & \dots & L^*_{1\lambda_k} & L^*_{11} & \dots & L^*_{1r} \\ \dots & \dots & \dots & \dots & \dots & \dots \\ L^*_{r\lambda_1} & \dots & L^*_{r\lambda_k} & L^*_{r1} & \dots & L^*_{rr} \end{vmatrix}, \; r=k+1,k+2,\ldots,n$$

where the second-order partial derivatives are evaluated at the point **a** and

$$L^*_{\lambda_i\lambda_j} = 0,\; L^*_{\lambda_i j} = L^*_{j\lambda_i} = \frac{\partial^2 L^*}{\partial\lambda_i \partial x_j},\; L^*_{ij} = \frac{\partial^2 L^*}{\partial x_i \partial x_j}$$

If **a** satisfies the Kuhn-Tucker necessary conditions, then the sufficient conditions for **a** to be a local minimum point are

$(-1)^k|\mathbf{B}_r| > 0$, for $r = k+1, k+2, \ldots, n$.

Note that if $k = n$, there is no bordered determinant $|\mathbf{B}_r|$ to be checked. For the problem of maximizing $f(\mathbf{x})$ on **S**, we replace $f(\mathbf{x})$ by $-f(\mathbf{x})$ in $L^*(\mathbf{x},\lambda_1, \lambda_2, \ldots, \lambda_k)$ and check the same conditions for minimization. In Exercise 1 below, the sufficient conditions for maximimization without replacing $f(\mathbf{x})$ by $-f(\mathbf{x})$ are given.

**Example 12.19** Consider the optimization problem

minimize $f(x,y,z) = x - y^2$
subject to $g_1(x,y,z) = x^2 + y^2 + z^2 - 9 \leq 0$,
$g_2(x,y,z) = -x + 3y + z - 6 \leq 0$.

that was given in example 12.16 in section 12.3.1. We showed that there are two points that satisfy the Kuhn-Tucker necessary conditions for a local minimum. These points are $\mathbf{a}_1 = (x,y,z) = (-0.5,-2.95804,0)$ and $\mathbf{a}_3 = (x,y,z) = (0.143426,2.5645, -1.55008)$. We check to see if these points satisfy the sufficient conditions. For $\mathbf{a}_1$, the Lagrangian function is

$L^*(x,y,z,\lambda_1) = f(x,y,z) + \lambda_1 g_1(x,y,z)$.

We use the **MathEcon** functions **hessian** and **signQL** to calculate the Hessian matrix **B** of $L^*(x,y,z,\lambda_1)$ and the signs of the leading principal minors evaluated at $\mathbf{a}_1$.

*In[133]:=*

```
Clear[f,x,y,z,g1,g2];
f[x_,y_,z_]:= x-y^2;
g1[x_,y_,z_]:= x^2+y^2+z^2-9;
g2[x_,y_,z_]:= -x+3*y+z-6;
```

*In[137]:=*

```
Clear[a1,lambda1,Lstar,B]
a1 = {-0.5,-2.95804,0};
Lstar[x_,y_,z_,lambda1_]:= f[x,y,z]+lambda1*g1[x,y,z];
B = hessian[Lstar[x,y,z,lambda1],{lambda1,x,y,z}];
signQL[B]/.{x->a1[[1]],y->a1[[2]],z->a1[[3]],lambda1->1}
```

*Out[141]=*
```
{0, -1., -70., -140.}
```

In this case there is only one binding constraint and $\lambda_1 = 1$. The relevant leading principal minors are $|\mathbf{B}_2| = -70$ and $|\mathbf{B}_3| = -140$. Since $(-1)^k|\mathbf{B}_2| > 0$, and $(-1)^k|\mathbf{B}_3| > 0$, the point $\mathbf{a}_1 = (-0.5,-2.95804,0)$ is a local minimum point. At the point $\mathbf{a}_3 = (0.143426,2.5645,-1.55008)$, both constraints are binding with $\lambda_1 = 0.355453$ and $\lambda_2 = 1.10196$. The Lagrangian function is:

$$L^*(x,y,z,\lambda_1,\lambda_2) = f(x,y,z) + \lambda_1 g_1(x,y,z) + \lambda_2 g_2(x,y,z).$$

The determinants of the leading principal minors of $\mathbf{B}$ evaluated at $\mathbf{a}_3$ are

*In[142]:=*
```
Clear[a3,lambda1,lambda2,Lstar,B];
a3 = {0.143426, 2.5645, -1.55008};
Lstar[x_,y_,z_,lambda1_,lambda2_]:=
        f[x,y,z]+lambda1*g1[x,y,z]+lambda2*g2[x,y,z];
B=hessian[Lstar[x,y,z,lambda1,lambda2],
          {lambda1,lambda2,x,y,z}];
signQL[B] /.{x->a3[[1]],y->a3[[2]],z->a3[[3]],
          lambda1->0.355453,lambda2->1.10196}
```

*Out[146]=*
```
{0, 0, 0, 35.8748, 163.318}
```

With $k = 2$, we only need to check the sign of $|\mathbf{B}_3| = 163.318$. Since $(-1)^2|\mathbf{B}_3| = 163.318 > 0$, point $\mathbf{a}_3$ is also a local minimum point.

**Example 12.20** Consider the problem

$$\begin{aligned}
\text{maximize } & f(x,y) = 18x - x^2 + xy - y^2 \\
\text{subject to } & g_1(x,y) = x + y - 12 \le 0 \\
& g_2(x,y) = -x + y - 6 \le 0 \\
& g_3(x,y) = -x \le 0 \\
& g_4(x,y) = -y \le 0
\end{aligned}$$

presented in example 12.17 in section 12.3.1. The point $\mathbf{a} = (9,3)$ statisfies the Kuhn-Tucker necessary conditions for a local maximum and $g_1(x,y) = 0$ is the only binding constraint with $\lambda_1 = 3$. Since this is a maximization problem, we form the Lagrangian function

$$L^*(x,y,\lambda_1) = -f(x,y) + \lambda_1 g_1(x,y).$$

*In[147]:=*
```
Clear[f,x,y,g1,lambda1,Lstar,B];
f[x_,y_]:= 18*x-x^2+x*y-y^2;
g1[x_,y_]:= x+y-12;
Lstar[x_,y_,lambda1_]:=-f[x,y]+lambda1*g1[x,y];
B=hessian[Lstar[x,y,lambda1],{lambda1,x,y}];
signQL[B] /. {x->9,y->3,lambda1->3}
```

*Out[152]=*
```
{0, -1, -6}
```

Since $|\mathbf{B}_2| = -6$ and $(-1)^1|\mathbf{B}_2| > 0$, the sufficient conditions are satisfied. Subject to the constraints, $(9,3)$ is a local minimum point for $-f(x,y)$ and a local maximum point for $f(x,y)$ with $f(9,3) = 99$.

**Example 12.21** Consider the following problem

$$\begin{aligned} &\text{maximize } f(x,y) = x - x^2 + y - 2y^2 \\ &\text{subject to } g_1(x,y) = 2x - 2y + 1 \leq 0 \\ &\qquad\qquad g_2(x,y) = x - 1 \leq 0 \\ &\qquad\qquad g_3(x,y) = -x + 2y \leq 0. \end{aligned}$$

Since this is a maximization problem, the Lagrangian function is

$$L(x,y,\lambda_1,\lambda_2,\lambda_3) = -f(x,y) + \lambda_1 g_1(x,y) + \lambda_2 g_2(x,y) + \lambda_3 g_3(x,y).$$

The Kuhn-Tucker necessary conditions require

$$\frac{\partial L}{\partial x} = 0; \ \frac{\partial L}{\partial y} = 0; \ \lambda_i \frac{\partial L}{\partial \lambda_i} = 0, \ i = 1,2,3;$$

$$\frac{\partial L}{\partial \lambda_i} = g_i \leq 0, \ \lambda_i \geq 0, \ i = 1,2,3$$

We first solve for $(x,y,\lambda_1,\lambda_2,\lambda_3)$.

*In[153]:=*

```
Clear[f,x,y,g1,g2,g3,L,lambda1,lambda2,lambda3,sol];
f[x_,y_]:= x-x^2+y-2*y^2;
g1[x_,y_]:= 2*x-2*y+1;
g2[x_,y_]:= x-1;
g3[x_,y_]:= -x+2*y;
L[x_,y_,lambda1_,lambda2_,lambda3_]:= -f[x,y]+
          lambda1*g1[x,y]+lambda2*g2[x,y]+lambda3*g3[x,y];
sol=NSolve[{D[L[x,y,lambda1,lambda2,lambda3],x]==0,
           D[L[x,y,lambda1,lambda2,lambda3],y]==0,
              lambda1*D[L[x,y,lambda1,lambda2,lambda3],
                    lambda1]==0,
              lambda2*D[L[x,y,lambda1,lambda2,lambda3],
                    lambda2]==0,
              lambda3*D[L[x,y,lambda1,lambda2,lambda3],
                    lambda3]==0},
              {x,y,lambda1,lambda2,lambda3}];
sol={x,y,lambda1,lambda2,lambda3} /.sol
```

*Out[160]=*

```
{{-1., -0.5, 4.5, 0., 6.}, {0., 0.5, 0.5, 0., 0.}, {0.5, 0.25, 0., 0., 0.},
 {0.5, 0.25, 0., 0., 0.}, {1., 0.25, 0., -1., 0.}, {1., 0.5, 0., -1.5, -0.5},
 {1., 1.5, 2.5, -6., 0.},
 {0. + 0. lambda1 + 0. lambda2 + 0. lambda3 + 0. y, 0. + 0. lambda1
  + 0. lambda2 + 0. lambda3, 1.20096 10^16 + 0. lambda2 + 0. lambda3,
  -1.20096 10^16 + 0. lambda3, 1.20096 10^16}}
```

By inspection, only the following sets meet the conditions: $\lambda_1,\lambda_2,\lambda_3 \geq 0$. Hence, possible extremum points are:

$(x,y,\lambda_1,\lambda_2,\lambda_3) = (-1, -0.5, 4.5, 0, 6)$
$(x,y,\lambda_1,\lambda_2,\lambda_3) = (0, 0.5, 0.5, 0, 0)$
$(x,y,\lambda_1,\lambda_2,\lambda_3) = (0.5, 0.25, 0, 0, 0).$

Only the first possibility, $\mathbf{a} = (x,y) = (-1, -0.5)$, is feasible since $g_1(\mathbf{a}) = g_3(\mathbf{a}) = 0$ and $g_2(\mathbf{a}) = -2 \leq 0$. In this case the number of constraints is equal to the number of varibles, $k = n$, and hence, there is no bordered Hessian determinant to be checked. Therefore, **a** is a local maximum point.

Our discussion so far has dealt with the necessary and sufficient conditions for a local extremum. Of course, local extrema are not necessarily global extrema. As we have shown in Chapter 11, the sufficient conditions for a local extremum to be a global extremum requires that the objective function be explicitly quasiconcave or quasiconvex over a convex feasible set. Since the feasible set **S** in the optimization with inequality constraints need not be a convex set, the sufficient conditions for a local extremum to be a global extremum are more stringent. Different sets of sufficient conditions for global optimality exist, but we state one of the more famous sufficient conditions below.

**THEOREM 12.4** *(Kuhn-Tucker sufficient conditions) Suppose $f(\mathbf{x})$ and all the constraint functions $g_i(\mathbf{x})$ are convex functions. Consider the problem to minimize $f(\mathbf{x})$ on $\mathbf{S} = \{\mathbf{x} \in \mathbf{R}^n \mid \mathbf{g}(\mathbf{x}) \leq 0\}$. If **a** satisfies the Kuhn-Tucker necessary conditions, then **a** is a global miniumum. More generally, if $f(\mathbf{x})$ is a convex function and **S** is a convex set, then a point that satisfies the Kuhn-Tucker necessary conditions is a global minumum. If $f(\mathbf{x})$ is a concave function and **S** is convex, then a point that satisfies the Kuhn-Tucker necessary conditions is a global maximum.*

A differential function is convex (concave) if and only if the Hessian matrix **H** is positive (negative) semidefinite, or if and only if all principal minors are nonnegative (alternative in sign).

**Example 12.22** Consider the optimization problem:

minimize $f(x,y) = x + y,$
subject to $g_1(x,y) = x^2 + y^2 - 1 \leq 0$
$g_2(x,y) = x^2 + y^2 - 2x \leq 0.$

We showed in example 12.14 in section 12.3.1 that the point $\mathbf{a} = (1-\sqrt{2}/2,-\sqrt{2}/2)$ satisfied the Kuhn-Tucker necessary conditions. It is obvious that $f(x,y)$ is convex since it is linear. In the calculations below, both constraint functions $g_1(x,y)$ and $g_2(x,y)$ are shown to be convex.

*In[161]:=*
```
Clear[g1,g2,x,y];
g1[x_,y_]:= x^2 + y^2 - 1;
signQ[hessian[g1[x,y],{x,y}]]
```

*Out[163]=*
```
{{2, 2}, {4}}
```

*In[164]:=*

```
g2[x_,y_]:= x^2 + y^2 - 2*x;
signQ[hessian[g2[x,y],{x,y}]]
```

*Out[165]=*

```
{{2, 2}, {4}}
```

Both $g_1(x,y)$ and $g_2(x,y)$ have principal minors of order 1, $|\mathbf{P}_1| = 2$, and of order 2, $|\mathbf{P}_1| = 4$. Thus the constraint functions are convex, and we conclude that $\mathbf{a} = (1-\sqrt{2}/2, -\sqrt{2}/2)$ is a global minimum point.

## EXERCISES

1. Suppose the point **a** satisfies the Kuhn-Tucker necessary conditions for maximization of $f(\mathbf{x})$ subject to $\mathbf{g}(\mathbf{x}) \leq \mathbf{0}$. Suppose $g_i(\mathbf{a}) = 0$ for $i = 1,2, \ldots ,k$. Consider the Lagrangian function

$$L^*(\mathbf{x},\lambda_1, \lambda_2, \ldots ,\lambda_k) = f(\mathbf{x}) + \lambda_1 g_1(\mathbf{x}) + \lambda_2 g_2(\mathbf{x}) + \ldots + \lambda_k g_k(\mathbf{x}).$$

Show that the sufficient conditions for **a** to be a local maximum are $(-1)^r|\mathbf{B}_r| > 0$, for $r = k+1, k+2, \ldots , n$.

2. Show that $\mathbf{a} = (5,1)$ is a global minimum point for the problem

$$\begin{aligned} &\text{mimimize } f(x,y) = (x-10)^2 + 2(y-2)^2 \\ &\text{subject to } x + y \geq 2 \\ &\qquad -x + y \leq 3 \\ &\qquad x + y \leq 6 \\ &\qquad x - 3y \leq 2 \\ &\qquad x,\ y \geq 0. \end{aligned}$$

3. Find local extrema of $f(x,y) = xy$ subject to $2x + y \leq 12$, and $x, y \geq 0$. Are they global extrema?

### 12.3.3 Optimization with equality and inequality constraints

Consider the optimization problem

$$\begin{aligned} &\text{minimize } f(x) \\ &\text{subject to } \mathbf{S} = \{\mathbf{x} \in \mathbf{R}^n \mid \mathbf{g}(\mathbf{x}) \leq 0,\ \mathbf{h}(\mathbf{x}) = \mathbf{0}\} \end{aligned}$$

where

$$\begin{aligned} \mathbf{g}(\mathbf{x}) &= [g_1(\mathbf{x}) \quad g_2(\mathbf{x}) \quad \ldots \quad g_m(\mathbf{x})]^T \\ \mathbf{h}(\mathbf{x}) &= [h_1(\mathbf{x}) \quad h_2(\mathbf{x}) \quad \ldots \quad h_s(\mathbf{x})]^T \end{aligned}$$

are vector-valued functions. We will give necessary and sufficient conditions for a point to be an extremum point. The next theorem gives the requirements for a point to be a local minimum point of this optimization problem.

**THEOREM 12.5** *(Kuhn-Tucker necessary conditions) Suppose* $f(\mathbf{x})$, $\mathbf{g}(\mathbf{x}) = [g_1(\mathbf{x})\ g_2(\mathbf{x})\ \ldots\ g_m(\mathbf{x})]^T$, *and* $h(\mathbf{x}) = [h_1(\mathbf{x})\ h_2(\mathbf{x})\ \ldots\ h_s(\mathbf{x})]^T$ *are differentiable on* $\mathbf{R}^n$. *Consider the optimization problem:*

*minimize* $f(\mathbf{x})$
*subject to* $\mathbf{S} = \{\mathbf{x} \in \mathbf{R}^n \mid g(\mathbf{x}) \le \mathbf{0},\ h(\mathbf{x}) = \mathbf{0}\}$.

*If* **a** *is a local minimum point and the set of vectors*

$$\{\nabla g_j(\mathbf{a}) = 0,\ \nabla h_t(\mathbf{a}) = 0 \mid j \in J(\mathbf{a}),\ t = 1,2, \ldots, s\}$$

*is linearly independent, then there are two sets of scalars,* $\{\lambda_j \ge 0 \mid j \in J(\mathbf{a})\}$ and $\{\mu_1, \ldots, \mu_s\}$, *such that*

$$\nabla f(\mathbf{a}) + \sum_{j \in J(\mathbf{a})} \lambda_j \nabla g_j(\mathbf{a}) + \sum_{t=1}^{s} \mu_t \nabla h_t(\mathbf{a}) = 0$$

**Example 12.23** Consider the optimization problem:

minimize $f(x,y,z) = -x + 3y + z^2$
subject to $g(x,y,z) = -x - y - z \le 0$
$h(x,y,z) = 2x - y + z^2 = 0.$

Show the point $\mathbf{a} = (-95/588, -115/588, 5/14)$ satisfies the Kuhn-Tucker necessary conditions in theorem 12.5. First, we solve the equation

$$\nabla f(\mathbf{a}) + \lambda_1 \nabla g(\mathbf{a}) + \mu_1 \nabla h(\mathbf{a}) = \mathbf{0}$$

for $\lambda_1$ and $\mu_1$.

*In[166]:=*

```
Clear[f,g,h,x,y,z,lambda1,mu1,ktnc];
f[x_,y_,z_]:=  -x+3*y+z^2;
g[x_,y_,z_]:=  -x-y-z;
h[x_,y_,z_]:=  2*x-y+z^2;
a  =  {-95/588,  -115/588,  5/14};
ktnc  =     gradf[f[x,y,z],{x,y,z}]+
          lambda1*gradf[g[x,y,z],{x,y,z}]+
         mu1*gradf[h[x,y,z],{x,y,z}]  /.
             {x->a[[1]],y->a[[2]],z->a[[3]]};
Solve[ktnc  ==  0,  {lambda1,mu1}]
```

*Out[172]=*

$$\{\{\text{lambda1} \to \frac{5}{3},\ \text{mu1} \to \frac{4}{3}\}\}$$

The solution shows that $\lambda_1 = 5/3 > 0$ and $\mu_1 = 4/3$. Furthermore, $g(\mathbf{a}) = 0$ and the gradient vectors

$\nabla g(\mathbf{a}) = [-1 \quad -1 \quad -1]^T$
$\nabla h(\mathbf{a}) = [2 \quad -1 \quad 10/14]^T$

are linearly independent, satisfying the constraint qualification. Thus, the point **a** satisfies the Kuhn-Tucker necessary conditions.

The Kuhn-Tucker necessary conditions can be stated in terms of the Lagrangian function

$$L(\mathbf{x},\lambda,\mu) = f(\mathbf{x}) + \lambda_1 g_1(\mathbf{x}) + \ldots + \lambda_m g_m(\mathbf{x}) + \mu_1 h_1(\mathbf{x}) + \ldots + \mu_s h_s(\mathbf{x}).$$

In particular, the following equations and inequalities must be satisfied:

$$\frac{\partial L}{\partial x_i} = \frac{\partial f}{\partial x_i} + \sum_{j=1}^{m} \lambda_j \frac{\partial g_j}{\partial x_i} + \sum_{t=1}^{s} \mu_t \frac{\partial h_t}{\partial x_i} = 0, \quad i = 1,2,\ldots,n$$

$$\lambda_j \frac{\partial L}{\partial \lambda_j} = \lambda_j g_j = 0, \quad j = 1,2,\ldots,m$$

$$\frac{\partial L}{\partial \lambda_j} = g_j \le 0, \quad j = 1,2,\ldots,m$$

$$\lambda_j \ge 0, \qquad j = 1,2,\ldots,m$$

$$\frac{\partial L}{\partial \mu_t} = h_t = 0, \quad t = 1,2,\ldots,s$$

along with the constraint qualification.

**Example 12.24** Consider the optimization problem,

minimize $f(x,y) = x$
subject to $g(x,y) = (x-4)^2 + y^2 - 16 \le 0$
$h(x,y) = (x-3)^2 + (y-2)^2 - 13 = 0.$

First we find candidates for local minimum points. We first set up the Lagrangian function

$$L(x,y,\lambda_1,\mu_1) = f(x,y) + \lambda_1 g(x,y) + \mu_1 h(x,y)$$

and solve

$\partial L/\partial x = 0$
$\partial L/\partial y = 0$
$\lambda \partial L/\partial \lambda_1 = 0$
$\partial L/\partial \mu_1 = 0$

for $(x,y,\lambda_1,\mu_1)$.

*In[173]:=*

```
Clear[L,f,g,h,lambda1,mu1,sol];
f[x_,y_]:= x;
g[x_,y_]:= (x-4)^2+y^2-16;
h[x_,y_]:= (x-3)^2+(y-2)^2-13;
```

```
L[x_,y_,u1_,v1_]:=  f[x,y]+lambda1*g[x,y]+mu1*h[x,y];
sol  =  NSolve[{D[L[x,y,lambda1,mu1],x]==0,
                D[L[x,y,lambda1,mu1],y]==0,
                  lambda1*D[L[x,y,lambda1,mu1],lambda1]==0,
                D[L[x,y,lambda1,mu1],mu1]==0},
              {x,y,lambda1,mu1}];
sol  =  {x,y,lambda1,mu1}  /.  sol
```

*Out[179]=*

```
{{6.60555, 2., 0., -0.138675}, {-0.605551, 2., 0., 0.138675},
  {6.4, 3.2, 0.075, -0.2}, {0., 0., 0.125, 0.}}
```

There are four possible solutions

$\mathbf{a}_1 = (6.60555, 2)$ with $\lambda_1 = 0,$ $\mu_1 = -0.138675$
$\mathbf{a}_2 = (-0.605551, 2)$ with $\lambda_1 = 0,$ $\mu_1 = 0.138675$
$\mathbf{a}_3 = (6.4, 3.2)$ with $\lambda_1 = 0.075,$ $\mu_1 = -0.2$
$\mathbf{a}_4 = (0, 0)$ with $\lambda_1 = 0.125,$ $\mu_1 = 0.$

It is easy to show that $\mathbf{a}_2$ is not feasible since $g(\mathbf{a}_2) > 0$. The other three points $\mathbf{a}_1$, $\mathbf{a}_3$, and $\mathbf{a}_4$ all satisfy the Kuhn-Tucker necessary conditions. We plot the feasible region **S** below. The graph of the constraint $g(x,y) = 0$ is a circle of radius 4 centered at (4,0). The graph of the constraint $h(x,y) = 0$ is another circle of radius $\sqrt{13}$ that is centered at (3,2). The feasible region **S** is the thick curve that lies inside the circle $g(x,y) = 0$.

*In[180]:=*

```
circleg  =  Graphics[Circle[{4,0},4]];
circleh  =  Graphics[Circle[{3,2},Sqrt[13]]];
S  =  ParametricPlot[{Sqrt[13]*Cos[t]+3,
        Sqrt[13]*Sin[t]+2},{t,-ArcCos[-3/Sqrt[13]],
        ArcCos[3.4/Sqrt[13]]},
        PlotStyle->Thickness[0.01],
        DisplayFunction->Identity];
Show[circleg,circleh,S,
        PlotRange->All,
        AspectRatio->Automatic,Axes->True,
        AxesLabel->{"x","y"},
        DisplayFunction->$DisplayFunction];
```

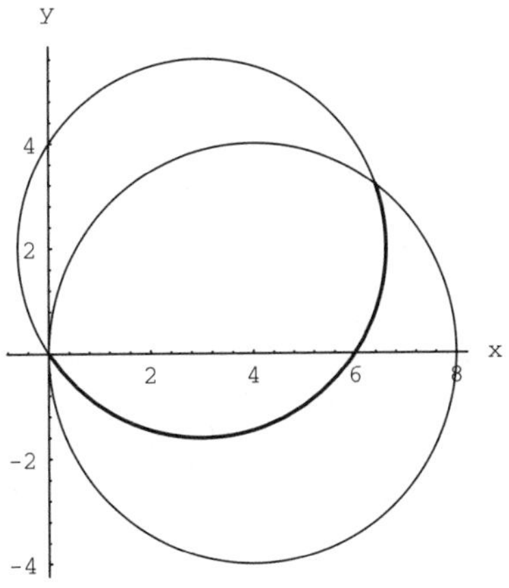

Points $\mathbf{a}_3$ and $\mathbf{a}_4$ are the intersection points of the two circles. Where are the points $\mathbf{a}_1$ and $\mathbf{a}_2$ on the graph? Are points $\mathbf{a}_1$, $\mathbf{a}_3$, and $\mathbf{a}_4$ local minimum points?

Suppose $g_j(\mathbf{a}) = 0$, $j=1,2,\ldots,k$ are the binding constraints along with $h_t(\mathbf{a}) = 0$, $t=1,2,\ldots,s$. There are a total of $k+s$ equality constraints at $\mathbf{a}$. The sufficient conditions for $\mathbf{a}$ to be a local extremum can be stated in terms of the principal minors of the Hessian matrix associated with the constrained Lagrangian function

$$L^*(\mathbf{x},\lambda,\mu) = f(\mathbf{x}) + \sum_{j=1}^{k} \lambda_j g_j(\mathbf{x}) + \sum_{t=1}^{s} \mu_t g_t(\mathbf{x})$$

We arrange the second-order partial derivatives of the Lagrangian function to form the bordered Hessian determinants

$$|\mathbf{B}_r| = \begin{vmatrix} L^*_{\lambda\lambda} & L^*_{\lambda\mu} & L^*_{\lambda r} \\ L^*_{\mu\lambda} & L^*_{\mu\mu} & L^*_{\mu r} \\ L^*_{r\lambda} & L^*_{r\mu} & L^*_{rr} \end{vmatrix}, \; r = k+s+1,\; k+s+2, \ldots, n$$

where

$$\boldsymbol{L}^*_{\lambda\lambda} + \left[\frac{\partial^2 L^*}{\partial\lambda_i\lambda_j}\right] = \mathbf{0},\; \boldsymbol{L}^*_{\mu\mu} = \left[\frac{\partial^2 L^*}{\partial\mu_i\mu_j}\right] = \mathbf{0},\; \boldsymbol{L}^*_{\lambda\mu} = \left[\frac{\partial^2 L^*}{\partial\lambda_i\mu_j}\right] = (\boldsymbol{L}^*_{\mu\lambda})^T = \mathbf{0}$$

are matrices with elements composed of the second-order partial and cross partial derivatives of $L^*$ with respect to $\lambda = [\lambda_1\ \lambda_2 \ldots \lambda_k]^T$ and $\mu = [\mu_1\ \mu_2 \ldots \mu_s]^T$. The zero matrices are of dimension $k \times k$, $s \times s$, and $k \times s$, respectively. Other matrices are

$$\boldsymbol{L}^*_{\lambda r} = \left[\frac{\partial^2 L^*}{\partial\lambda_i x_j}\right] = (\boldsymbol{L}^*_{r\lambda})^T,\; i = 1,2,\ldots,k;\; j=1,2,\ldots,r$$

$$\boldsymbol{L}^*_{\mu r} = \left[\frac{\partial^2 L^*}{\partial\mu_i x_j}\right] = (\boldsymbol{L}^*_{r\mu})^T,\; i = 1,2,\ldots,s;\; j=1,2,\ldots,r$$

$$\boldsymbol{L}^*_{rr} = \left[\frac{\partial^2 L^*}{\partial x_i x_j}\right],\; i = 1,2,\ldots,r;\; j=1,2,\ldots,r$$

of dimensions $k \times r$, $s \times r$, and $r \times r$, respectively. A sufficient condition for $\mathbf{a}$ to be a local minimum is

$$(-1)^{k+s}|\mathbf{B}_r| > 0, \quad \text{for} \quad r = k+s+1,\; k+s+2, \ldots, n.$$

If $k+s = n$, then there are no borded determinants to be checked.

**Example 12.25** In example 12.24, the point $\mathbf{a}_1$ satisfies the necessary conditions for it to be a local minimum point. Show that it does not satisfy the sufficient conditions. Since $g(\mathbf{a}_1) = -0.5211 < 0$, we have $k = 0$. The corresponding Lagrangian function is $L^*(x,y,\mu_1) = f(x,y) + \mu_1 h(x,y)$. The following calculation shows that $|\mathbf{B}_2| = 14.4219$, and $(-1)^1|\mathbf{B}_2| < 0$.

*In[184]:=*
```
Clear[f,h,Lstar,mu1,B];
f[x_,y_]:= x;
h[x_,y_]:= (x-3)^2+(y-2)^2-13;
a1 = {6.60551,2};
Lstar[x_,y_,mu1_]:= f[x,y]+mu1*h[x,y];
B = hessian[Lstar[x,y,mu1],{mu1,x,y}];
signQL[B] /. {x->a1[[1]],y->a1[[2]],mu1->-0.138675}
```

*Out[190]=*
```
{0, -51.9991, 14.4219}
```

Hence, the point $\mathbf{a}_1$ does not satisfy the sufficient conditions for a local minimum.

To develop the sufficient conditions for a global extremum, the necessary conditions given in theorem 12.5

$$\nabla f(\mathbf{a}) + \sum_{j \in J(\mathbf{a})} \lambda_j \nabla g_j(\mathbf{a}) + \sum_{t=1}^{s} \mu_t \nabla h_t(\mathbf{a}) = 0$$

place no restriction on the Lagrangian multipliers $\mu_t$. They can take any value, positive, negative, or zero. In light of this, the sufficient conditions for global extremum given in theorem 12.4 can now be modified.

**THEOREM 12.6** *(Kuhn-Tucker sufficient conditions) Suppose $f(\mathbf{x})$ and all the constraint functions $g_i(\mathbf{x})$ are convex functions. Consider the optimization problem:*

*minimize $f(x)$*
*subject to $\mathbf{S} = \{\mathbf{x} \in \mathbf{R}^n \mid g(\mathbf{x}) \leq \mathbf{0},\ h(\mathbf{x}) = \mathbf{0}\}$.*

*If $\mathbf{a}$ satisfies the Kuhn-Tucker necessary conditions*

$$\nabla f(\mathbf{a}) + \sum_{j \in J(\mathbf{a})} \lambda_j \nabla g_j(\mathbf{a}) + \sum_{t=1}^{s} \mu_t \nabla h_t(\mathbf{a}) = 0$$

*and $h_t(\mathbf{x})$ is convex for $\mu_t > 0$, and is concave for $\mu_t < 0$, then $\mathbf{a}$ is a global minimum point.*

Note that if $\mu_t = 0$, $t = 1,2,\ldots,5$, then the necessary conditions reduce to

$$\nabla f(\mathbf{a}) + \sum_{j \in J(\mathbf{a})} \lambda_j \nabla g_j(\mathbf{a}) = 0$$

which is equivalent to the case without equality constraints. In this case, the constraint functions, $h_t(\mathbf{x}) = 0$, play no role in determining the sufficient conditions. Thus the Kuhn-Tucker sufficient conditions stated in theorem 12.4 apply directly to the case where $\mu_t = 0$.

**Example 12.26** Let us consider example 12.25 again. The objective function $f(x,y) = x$ is convex and both $g(x,y)$ and $h(x,y)$ are convex since all the principal minors are nonnegative as shown below.

*In[191]:*
```
g[x_,y_]:= (x-4)^2+y^2-16;
h[x_,y_]:= (x-3)^2+(y-2)^2-13;
signQ[hessian[g[x,y],{x,y}]]
```

*Out[193]*
```
{{2, 2}, {4}}
```

*In[194]:=*
```
signQ[hessian[h[x,y],{x,y}]]
```

*Out[194]=*
```
{{2, 2}, {4}}
```

At point $\mathbf{a}_3 = (6.4, 3.2)$, we have $\mu_1 = -0.2 < 0$. The sufficient conditions require that $h(x,y)$ be concave. Hence the point $\mathbf{a}_3$ is not a global minimum. However, at $\mathbf{a}_4 =$ (0,0), we have $\mu_1 = 0$, and $g(x,y)$ is convex. Hence $\mathbf{a}_4$ is a global minimum point.

## EXERCISES

1. What are the Kuhn-Tucker necessary and sufficient conditions for

$$\begin{aligned} &\text{maximize } f(x,y) = x \\ &\text{subject to } g(x,y) = (x-4)^2 + y^2 - 16 \leq 0 \\ &\qquad\qquad h(x,y) = (x-3)^2 + (y-2)^2 - 13 = 0. \end{aligned}$$

2. Write the Kuhn-Tucker necessary and sufficient conditions for

$$\begin{aligned} &\text{minimize } f(x,y) = x^2 + y^2 \\ &\text{subject to } 1 - 2x - y \leq 0 \\ &\qquad\qquad y - 1/2 = 0. \end{aligned}$$

Using these conditions, find the local minimum points.

## □ 12.4 Linear Programming □

We have established necessary and sufficient conditions for a particular point to be the optimal solution of the problem:

$$\begin{aligned} &\text{minimize } f(\mathbf{x}) \\ &\text{subject to } \mathbf{g}(\mathbf{x}) \leq \mathbf{0}, \\ &\qquad\qquad \mathbf{h}(\mathbf{x}) = \mathbf{0}. \end{aligned}$$

As we have illustrated, it is often very difficult to find a candidate for optimality. For this reason, computational methods have been developed to help find points of optimality. If the objective functions $f(\mathbf{x})$, and the constraints $\mathbf{g}(\mathbf{x})$ and $\mathbf{h}(\mathbf{x})$ are linear in $\mathbf{x}$, the optimization problem is called a *linear programming problem*. Computational algorithms for a linear programming problem are abundant. *Mathematica* has two built-in functions to find the optimal solution for these types of optimization problems. The functions are called **ConstrainedMin** and **ConstrainedMax**. Here is *Mathematica*'s description of the function **ConstrainedMin**.

*In[195]:=*
```
?ConstrainedMin
```

**ConstrainedMin[f, {inequalities}, {x, y, ...}] finds the global minimum of f in the domain specified by the inequalities. The variables x, y, ... are all assumed to be nonnegative.**

The **ConstrainedMin** function has the objective function $f(\mathbf{x})$ as its first argument, followed by a list of inequality constraints, and a list of variables. The variables are restricted to be nonnegative. The inequalities can be in any form, $g_i(\mathbf{x}) \leq 0$, $g_i(\mathbf{x}) \geq 0$, $g_i(\mathbf{x}) < 0$, $g_i(\mathbf{x}) > 0$, or an equality, $g_i(\mathbf{x}) = 0$.

**Example 12.27** Find the optimal solution of the following problem.

minimize $f(x,y,z) = x - 4y + 3z$
subject to $x + y + z - 12 \leq 0$
$2x + y + z \leq 24$
$x, y, z \geq 0.$

We use the **ConstrainedMin** function.

*In[196]:=*
```
Clear[f,g1,g2,x,y,z];
f[x_,y_,z_]:= x - 4*y + 3*z;
g1[x_,y_,z_]:= x + y - z - 12;
g2[x_,y_,z_]:= 2*x + y + z;
ConstrainedMin[f[x,y,z],
              {g1[x,y,z]<=0,g2[x,y,z]<=24},{x,y,z}]
```

*Out[200]=*
```
{-54, {x → 0, y → 18, z → 6}}
```

The output states that the global minimum occurs at $\mathbf{a} = (0,18,6)$ and $f(\mathbf{a}) = -54$.

**Example 12.28** Find the optimal solution of the following problem.

maximize $f(x,y,z) = x + 2y + 3z$
subject to $x + y + 5z \leq 10,$
$3x + 2y + 4z \leq 25$
$x + 3y + z \leq 15$
$x, y, z \geq 0.$

We use the **ConstrainedMax** function.

*In[201]:=*
```
Clear[f,g1,g2,g3,x,y,z];
f[x_,y_,z_]:= x + 2*y + 3*z;
g1[x_,y_,z_]:= x + y + 5*z ;
g2[x_,y_,z_]:= 3*x + 2*y + 4*z;
```

```
g3[x_,y_,z_]:=  x  +  3*y  +  z;
ConstrainedMax[f[x,y,z],
                {g1[x,y,z]<=10,g2[x,y,z]<=25,
                g3[x,y,z]<=15},{x,y,z}]
```

*Out[206]=*

$$\{\frac{25}{2}, \{x \to \frac{80}{13}, y \to \frac{75}{26}, z \to \frac{5}{26}\}\}$$

Thus, $\mathbf{a} = (80/13, 75/26, 5/26)$ and $f(\mathbf{a}) = 25/2$.

In a linear programming problem, $f(\mathbf{x})$ and $g(\mathbf{x})$ are linear functions. It is convenient to write the optimization problem in terms of vectors and matrices. In particular, suppose that $f(\mathbf{x}) = \mathbf{c}^T\mathbf{x}$ and $\mathbf{g}(\mathbf{x}) = \mathbf{b} - \mathbf{A}\mathbf{x}$ where $\mathbf{c}$ and $\mathbf{b}$ are fixed vectors, and $\mathbf{A}$ is a matrix. Then our optimization problem takes the form

minimize $f(\mathbf{x}) = \mathbf{c}^T\mathbf{x} = c_1x_1 + c_2x_2 + \ldots + c_nx_n$
subject to $x_i \geq 0,\ i = 1,2, \ldots ,n$
$\mathbf{g}(\mathbf{x}) = \mathbf{b} - \mathbf{A}\mathbf{x} \leq \mathbf{0}$

*Mathematica* has a built-in function to solve the linear programming problem. It is called **LinearProgramming**. Here is *Mathematica*'s explanation of this function.

*In[207]:=*

```
?LinearProgramming
```

**LinearProgramming[c, m, b] finds the vector x which minimizes the quantity c.x subject to the constraints m.x >= b and x >= 0.**

**Example 12.29** Find the optimal solution of the following problem.

minimize $f(x) = c^T\mathbf{x} = 2x_1 + x_2 + 3x_3 + 2x_4$
subject to $x_i \geq 0,\ i = 1,2,3,4$
$\mathbf{g}(\mathbf{x}) = \mathbf{b} - \mathbf{A}\mathbf{x} \leq \mathbf{0}$, or

$$\begin{bmatrix} 4 \\ 7 \end{bmatrix} - \begin{bmatrix} 1 & 1 & 1 & 1 \\ 2 & 1 & 2 & 3 \end{bmatrix} \begin{bmatrix} x_1 \\ x_2 \\ x_3 \\ x_4 \end{bmatrix} \leq \begin{bmatrix} 0 \\ 0 \end{bmatrix}$$

*In[208]:=*

```
c  =  {2,1,3,2};
b  =  {4,7};
A  =  {{1,1,1,1},{2,1,2,3}};
sol  =  LinearProgramming[c,A,b]
c.sol
```

*Out[211]=*

$$\{0, \frac{5}{2}, 0, \frac{3}{2}\}$$

*Out[212]=*

$$\frac{11}{2}$$

The optimal solution is at the point (0,5/2,0,3/2) and the optimal value of $f(\mathbf{x}) = 11/2$.

## EXERCISES

1. Using *Mathematica*, find the optimal solution of

$$\begin{aligned} &\text{minimize } 4x + 3y \\ &\text{subject to } y \le 5 \\ &\qquad x + 4 \le 8 \\ &\qquad x - y \le 2 \\ &\qquad x,y \ge 0. \end{aligned}$$

2. Using *Mathematica*, find the optimal solution of

$$\begin{aligned} &\text{maximize } 2x + 3y - z \\ &\text{subject to } x + 2y + 2z \le 6 \\ &\qquad 3x - y + z \le 9 \\ &\qquad 2x + 3y + 5z \le 20 \\ &\qquad x,y,z \ge 0. \end{aligned}$$

3. Using *Mathematica*, find the optimal solution to

$$\begin{aligned} &\text{minimize } f(\mathbf{x}) = 2x_1 + x_2 + 3x_3 + 2x_4 \\ &\text{subject to } x_i \ge 0,\ i = 1,2,3,4 \\ &\qquad \mathbf{g}(\mathbf{x}) = \mathrm{b} - \mathbf{A}\mathbf{x} \le \mathbf{0}, \text{ or} \end{aligned}$$

$$\begin{bmatrix} 6 \\ 5 \end{bmatrix} - \begin{bmatrix} 3 & 4 & 1 & -2 \\ 2 & 3 & -1 & 3 \end{bmatrix} \begin{bmatrix} x_1 \\ x_2 \\ x_3 \\ x_4 \end{bmatrix} \le \begin{bmatrix} 0 \\ 0 \end{bmatrix}$$

# 13

# Ordinary Differential Equations

In the formulation of economic problems, the mathematical model is often an equation that involves an unknown function and its derivatives. For example, the differential equation $\mathrm{d}y/\mathrm{d}t = ky(t)$ models a population that grows at a rate, $k$, proportional to the number of individuals at time $t$, $y(t)$. In this chapter we discuss methods that can be used to solve these types of equations.

## □ 13.1 Introduction □

### 13.1.1 Basic terminology

**DEFINITION 13.1** *An **ordinary differential equation** is an equation involving an unknown function y(x) and one or more of its derivatives. Mathematically, we write this as*

$$F(x,y,y',y'', \ldots ,y^{(n)}) = 0,\ x \in I.$$

*The interval I is the **domain**, x is the **independent variable**, and y is the **dependent variable** of the differential equation. The highest order derivative n that appears in the equation is called the **order** of the differential equation.*

If the unknown function depends upon two or more independent variables, then the equation is called a *partial differential equation.* In this book we restrict our discussion to ordinary differential equations (or simply differential equations).

**Example 13.1** The following equation is a second-order differential equation:

$$xy' + y'' - e^x y^2 = 0,\ -1 < x < 2.$$

The domain of the differential equation is the interval $(-1,2)$.

Instead of using the notation $F(x,y,y',y'', \ldots y^{(n)}) = 0$, we can often solve for the highest order derivative $y^{(n)}$ and write the differential equation as $y^{(n)} = f(x,y,y',$

$\ldots, y^{(n-1)}$). This convention is sometimes called the *standard form* of the differential equation.

**Example 13.2** In example 13.1, we could rewrite the differential equation as

$$y'' = -xy' + e^x y^2.$$

This equation is now in standard form.

**Example 13.3** Let $D = f(p)$ and $S = g(p)$ be the demand and supply of quantity, and assume that they are functions of price $p$, which changes over time. We assume that the price adjustment over time, $dp(t)/dt$, is proportional to the excess demand, i.e.,

$$\frac{dp(t)}{dt} = k(D - S) = k(f(p) - g(p)) \equiv kh(p)$$

where $k$ is a positive constant. The equation $dp/dt = kh(p)$ is a first-order differential equation in standard form.

Ordinary differential equations are classified into two broad categories: *linear* and *nonlinear*.

**DEFINITION 13.2** *An nth-order differential equation is said to be* ***linear*** *in y if it can be written in the form*

$$a_n(x)y^{(n)} + a_{n-1}(x)y^{(n-1)} + \ldots + a_1(x)y' + a_0(x)y = g(x)$$

*where $a_0(x), a_1(x), \ldots, a_n(x)$, and $g(x)$ are known functions of x. A differential equation that is not linear is said to be* ***nonlinear****. The functions $a_i(x)$ are called the* ***coefficient functions****. A linear differential equation is* ***homogeneous*** *if $g(x) \equiv 0$; otherwise it is* ***nonhomogeneous*** *or* ***inhomogeneous****.*

**Example 13.4** The third-order linear differential equation

$$5y''' + \sin(x)y'' - e^x y = 0$$

is homogeneous.

**Example 13.5** The second-order differential equation

$$y'' + (x^2+1)y' - 2y^2 = x$$

is nonlinear because of the $y^2$ term.

**Example 13.6** Suppose the demand and supply equations in example 13.3 are linear functions of price, $D = a_0 + a_1 p$ and $S = b_0 + b_1 p$, where $a_i$ and $b_i$ are constant. The price adjustment equation is a first-order, inhomogeneous, linear differential equation

$$dp/dt - k(a_1 - b_1)p = k(a_0 - b_0).$$

Consider a first-order differential equation in the standard form

$$dy/dx = f(x,y).$$

Assuming that $f(x,y)$ can be written as the ratio of two functions,

$$f(x,y) = -\frac{P(x,y)}{Q(x,y)}$$

the differential equation can now be written as an equation involving differentials,

$$P(x,y)dx + Q(x,y)dy = 0.$$

This form is called the *differential form* of a first-order differential equation.

**Example 13.7** The first-order differential equation

$$y' = x(1 + \sin xy)$$

can be written in the differential form,

$$x dx - \frac{1}{1 + \sin(xy)} dy = 0$$

When we solve first-order differential equations, it is convenient to have the equation in standard form or differential form.

## EXERCISES

1. For each of the following ordinary differential equations, identify the order, dependent and independent variables, and determine if the differential equation is linear or nonlinear:
   (a) $(y''')^2 - y' + 9y = \sin x$
   (b) $w' + e^z w = 5$
   (c) $(x + y^2)dx + \frac{y}{\sin xy} dy = 0$
2. Rewrite the differential equation
   $$\frac{dy}{dx} = \frac{e^{x+y^2}}{x^2 + y^2}$$
   in differential form.

### 13.1.2 Solutions of differential equations

Solving a differential equation is very much like solving an equation in algebra. For example, a solution of the equation $x^2 + 3x + 2 = 0$ is a number (in this case, $x = -1$ or $-2$) that satisfies the equation. In the case of a differential equation, the solution is a function that satisfies the differential equation.

**DEFINITION 13.3** *A **solution** of a differential equation* $F(x,y(x),y'(x), \ldots y^{(n)}(x)) = 0$ *for* $x \in I$ *is a function* $\phi(x)$ *that satisfies the differential equation, i.e.*

$$F(x,\phi(x),\phi'(x), \ldots \phi^{(n)}(x)) = 0, \; x \in I.$$

**Example 13.8** The function $\phi(x) = \sin 2x$ is a solution of the second-order differential equation $y'' + 4y = 0$. We calculate $\phi''(x) + 4\phi(x)$ and show that it is equal to 0. In the following *Mathematica* expressions, the symbol **phi[x]** is used to represent $\phi(x)$.

*In[1]:=*

```
Clear[phi,x];
phi[x_]:= Sin[2x];
phi''[x] + 4*phi[x] == 0
```

*Out[3]=*

```
True
```

If the dependent variable of a differential equation is $y$ and the independent variable is $x$, then a solution is often written as $y(x)$, instead of $\phi(x)$.

**Example 13.9** The function

$$y(x) = \log \frac{1}{1 + e^{-x}}$$

is a solution of the first-order differential equation

$$(1 + e^{-x})y' = e^{-x}.$$

We can check it with *Mathematica*.

*In[4]:=*

```
Clear[y,x];
y[x_]:= Log[1/(1+Exp[-x])];
(1+Exp[-x])*y'[x] == Exp[-x] // Simplify
```

*Out[6]=*

```
True
```

**Example 13.10** A model for the demand, $D(p)$, supply $S(p)$, excess inventory, $Q(t)$, and the price adjustment, $p(t)$, at time $t$ is given by the first-order differential equation:

$$dp/dt = k(D - S) + rQ$$

where $k$ and $r$ are constants and

$$Q(t) = \int_0^t [S(\tau) - D(\tau)]\,d\tau$$

Assuming the demand and supply as functions of price are given by the functions

$D(p) = 12 - 2p$
$S(p) = 2 + 3p,$

with $k = 0.2$, $r = -0.25$, the differential equation becomes

$$\frac{dp}{dt} = 0.2(D\text{–S}) - 0.25\text{Q}.$$

Upon differentiating this equation with respect to $t$, we obtain the second-order, linear, inhomogeneous differential equation

$$d^2p/dt^2 + dp/dt + 1.25p = 2.5.$$

This equation has the solution

$$p(t) = e^{-0.5t}(c_1\cos t + c_2\sin t) + 2$$

where $c_1$ and $c_2$ are any arbitrary constants. We confirm the solution by the following *Mathematica* calculation.

*In[7]:=*
```
Clear[p,t,c1,c2];
p[t_]:= Exp[-0.5*t]*(c1*Cos[t]+c2*Sin[t])  +  2;
p"[t]  +  p'[t]  +  1.25*p[t]  ==  2.5  //  Simplify
```

*Out[9]=*
```
True
```

We will discuss the constants $c_1$ and $c_2$ at a later point in this chapter. For the moment, suppose $c_1 = -0.5$ and $c_2 = 1.55$. The graph of the solution of the price equation

$$p(t) = e^{-0.5t}\,(-0.5\cos t + 1.55\sin t) + 2$$

is shown below.

*In[10]:=*
```
Plot[p[t]  /.  {c1->-0.5,c2->1.55},{t,0,10},
               AxesLabel->{"t","p"}];
```

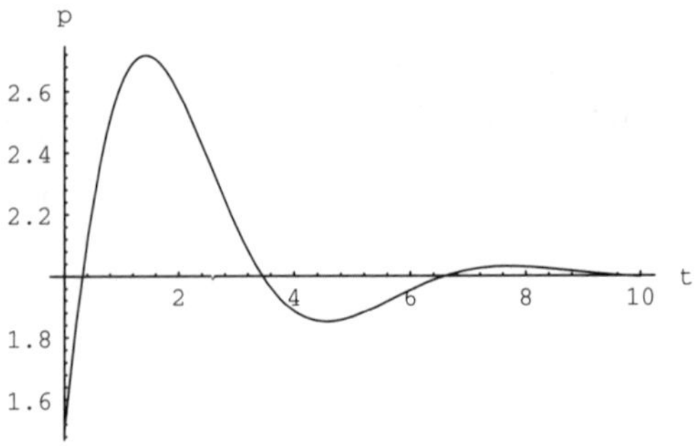

If the dependent variable is expressed explicitly in terms of the independent variable, say $y = \phi(x)$, then we call the function $\phi(x)$ an *explicit solution* of the differential equation. If the dependent and independent variables are expressed together as an equation, say $G(x,y) = 0$, then we call this equation an *implicit solution*. In what sense is this a solution of the differential equation? To understand this type of solution, consider the first-order differential equation

$$3y^2y' + 2x = 0.$$

The equation $g(x,y) = y^3 + x^2 - 9 = 0$ is an implicit solution of this differential equation. If we differentiate the equation $G(x,y) = 0$ implicitly with respect to $x$, then we find precisely the differential equation.

*In[11]:=*

```
Clear[G,x,y];
g[x_,y_]:= y[x]^3 + x^2 - 9 == 0;
D[g[x,y],x]
```

*Out[13]=*

```
2x + 3y[x]^2y'[x] == 0
```

It is possible to graph the implicit solution of a first-order differential equation using the function **ImplicitPlot** which is defined in the package called **ImplicitPlot**.

*In[14]:=*

```
Needs["Graphics`ImplicitPlot`"];
```

Here is *Mathematica*'s description of this function.

*In[15]:=*

```
?ImplicitPlot
```

**ImplicitPlot[eqn, {x, a, b}] draws a graph of the set of points that satisfy the equation eqn. The variable x is associated with the horizontal axis and ranges from a to b. The remaining variable in the equation is associated with the vertical axis. ImplicitPlot[eqn, {x, a, x1, x2, ..., b}] allows the user to specify values of x where special care must be exercised. ImplicitPlot[{eqn1,eqn2,..},{x,a,b}] allows more than one equation to be plotted, with PlotStyles set as in the Plot function. ImplicitPlot[eqn,{x,a,b},{y,a,b}] uses a contour plot method of generating the plot. This form does not allow specification of intermediate points.**

*In[16]:=*

```
Clear[x,y];
ImplicitPlot[y^3+x^2-9==0,{x,-10,10},{y,-10,10},
     AxesLabel->{"x","y"},PlotPoints->100,
     AxesOrigin->{0,0}];
```

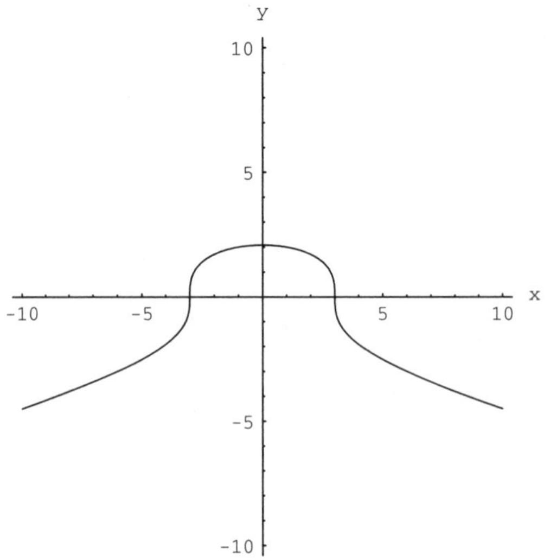


We see that an implicit solution of a differential equation is an equation that when differentiated implicitly with respect to the independent variable yields the differential equation itself. In this example, we can obtain an explicit solution $y = \phi(x)$ from the implicit solution $G(x,y) = 0$ by solving for $y$ in terms of $x$. That is,

$$\phi(x) = \sqrt[3]{9 - x^2}$$

However, it is not always possible to obtain an explicit solution from an implicit solution. For example, the differential equation

$$(3x^4y^2 - \frac{1}{y})y' + 4x^3y^3 + \frac{1}{x} = 0$$

has the implicit solution

$$G(x,y) = x^4y^3 + \log x - \log y - 2 = 0$$

which is confirmed by implicitly differentiating $G(x,y) = 0$ with respect to $x$.

*In[18]:=*

```
Clear[G,x,y];
G[x,y]  =  x^4*y[x]^3  +  Log[x]  -  Log[y[x]]  -  2  ==  0;
D[G[x,y],x] // Simplify
```

*Out[20]=*

$$\frac{1}{x} + 4x^3y[x]^3 - \frac{y'[x]}{y[x]} + 3x^4y[x]^2y'[x] == 0$$

However, it is impossible to solve for an explicit solution $y = \phi(x)$ from the implicit solution $G(x,y) = 0$. Hence, an implicit solution is often the only type of solution that can be found.

## EXERCISES

1. Use *Mathematica* to show that the following functions are solutions to the accompanying differential equations:
   (a) $x^3y''' + 3x^3y'' + 3xy' - 3y = 0,$
   $y(x) = \cos(\sqrt{3}\log x)$
   (b) $x^2y' = y^2 - xy + x^2,$
   $y(x) = x(1 - \dfrac{1}{\log(x) - 10})$
   (c) $x^2y'' + 2xy' - 6y = 50\dfrac{\log x}{x^3},\ x > 0$
   $y(x) = c_1x^2 + c_2x^{-3} - x^{-3}[5(\log x)^2 + 2\log x]$
   where $c_1$ and $c_2$ are arbitrary constants.

2. Show that

$$\frac{y^3}{3} = \frac{x^2}{2} - 5x + c$$

is an implicit solution of $y' = (x-5)/y^2$ for any constant $c$. Assign a value for $c$ and use **ImplicitPlot** to plot the implicit solution.

3. Show that an alternative expression for the solution in example 13.10 is

$$p(t) = a_1e^{-0.5t}\cos(t + a_2) + 2.$$

Corresponding to $c_1 = -0.5$ and $c_2 = 1.55$, the arbitrary constants are $a_1 = 1.5$ and $a_2 = -2$. Plot this solution.

### 13.1.3 General and particular solutions

In the previous section, we discovered that it is possible for a solution (both implicit and explicit) to contain arbitrary constants. We give a name to these types of solutions.

**DEFINITION 13.4** *A solution of an nth-order differential equation that contains n arbitrary constants is called a* ***general solution*** *of the differential equation. Any solution that can be obtained from the general solution by choosing specific values for the arbitrary constants is called a* ***particular solution****. Any solution of a differential equation that cannot be obtained from a general solution is called a* ***singular solution****.*

**Example 13.11** The second-order differential equation $y'' + y = 0$ has a general solution

$$y(x) = c_1\cos x + c_2\sin x.$$

Here $c_1$ and $c_2$ are arbitrary constants. This is confirmed in the following *Mathematica* calculation.

*In[21]:=*

```
Clear[y,x,c1,c2];
y[x_]:= c1*Cos[x] + c2*Sin[x];
y''[x] + y[x] == 0
```

*Out[23]=*

```
True
```

If we assign different values to $c_1$ and $c_2$, it is easy to check that the following are four particular solutions:

$y(x) = \cos x$; $\quad y(x) = \cos x - 3\sin x$;
$y(x) = -\pi \sin x$; $y(x) = 0$.

This differential equation does not have any singular solution.

Many differential equations do not have a singular solution. However, the following differential equation is an example of one that does have a singular solution.

**Example 13.12** The differential equation

$$(y')^3 - y = 0$$

has the general solution

$$y(x) = \left(\frac{2}{3}x + c_1\right)^{3/2}.$$

Letting $c_1 = 0$, a particular solution is

$$y(x) = \left(\frac{2}{3}x\right)^{3/2}.$$

We can see by inspection that $y(x) \equiv 0$ is also a solution. However, this solution cannot be obtained from the general solution by choosing a specific value of $c_1$. Hence it is a singular solution.

It is possible to have implicit general solutions as in the following example.

**Example 13.13** The equation

$$G(x,y) = x^2 + \log\left(\frac{y}{y-2}\right) - c_1 = 0$$

is a general implicit solution of the first-order differential equation

$$y' = y(y-2).$$

We note that $y(x) \equiv 0$ and $y(x) \equiv 2$ are singular solutions since they cannot be obtained from the implicit general solution.

Particular solutions are often determined from a general solution by imposing certain conditions on the solution functions. For example, if the compound growth rate of the US population, $y(t)$, is 1 percent over time, $t$, then this situation can be expressed as the first-order differential equation: $dy/dt = 0.01y$. The differential equation has the general solution

$$y(t) = c_1 e^{0.1t}$$

where $c_1$ is an arbitrary constant. The general solution gives a family of curves over time depending upon the values of $c_1$. Suppose in the year $t = 1995$, the population size is 250 million. This fact can be expressed as $y(1995) = 225{,}000{,}000$. Using this value for the population, we can determine the value of $c_1$ and hence a particular member of the family of curves. That is,

$$y(1995) = 250{,}000{,}000 = c_1 e^{0.01(1995)}.$$

Solving for $c_1 = 0.541708$, we have then the particular solution

$$y(t) = 0.541708 e^{0.01t}.$$

For different specifications of the population size at time $t = 1995$, different particular solutions are obtained. For example, if $y(1995) = 260{,}000{,}000$, then $y(t) = 0.563376 e^{0.01t}$. If $y(1995) = 270{,}000{,}000$, then $y(t) = 0.585044 e^{0.01t}$. The following plot shows some of these population curves.

*In[24]:=*

```
Clear[t];
Plot[{0.5417*Exp[0.01*t],0.563376*Exp[0.01*t],
      0.585044*Exp[0.01*t]},{t,1995,2000},
      PlotStyle->{{},Dashing[{0.02}],Thickness[0.008]},
      AxesLabel->{"t","y"}];
```

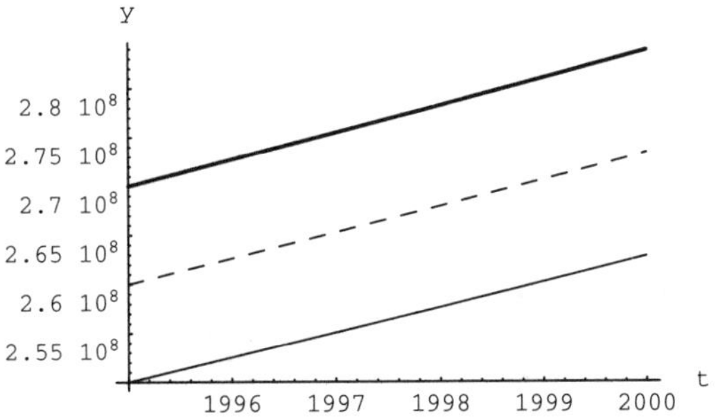


**Example 13.14** Consider the demand and supply model given in example 13.1 of section 13.1.2. The second-order differential equation

$$d^2p/dt^2 + dp/dt + 1.25p = 2.5$$

has the general solution

$$p(t) = e^{-0.5t}(c_1 \cos t + c_2 \sin t) + 2$$

It contains two arbitrary constants, $c_1$ and $c_2$. Suppose two initial pieces of information are known, say $t = 0$, $p(0) = 1.5$ and $p'(0) = 1.8$. Hence,

$1.5 = p(0) = c_1 + 2$
$1.8 = p'(0) = -0.5c_1 + c_2$

Solving for $c_1$ and $c_2$, we find that $c_1 = -0.5$, and $c_2 = 1.55$. These values are confirmed in the following *Mathematica* calculation.

*In[26]:=*
```
Clear[p,c1,c2,t];
p[t_]:= Exp[-0.5*t]*(c1*Cos[t]  +  c2*Sin[t])  +  2;
Solve[{p[0]==1.5,p'[0]==1.8},{c1,c2}]
```

*Out[28]=*
{{c1 → −0.5, c2 → 1.55}}

The corresponding particular solution is

$p(t) = e^{-0.5t}(-0.5\cos t + 1.55\sin t) + 2$

Now suppose $p(0) = 2.3$ and $p'(0) = 3.0$.

*In[29]:=*
```
Solve[{p[0]==2.3,p'[0]==3.0},{c1,c2}]
```

*Out[29]=*
{{c1 → 0.3, c2 → 3.15}}

Lastly suppose $p(0) = 2.8$ and $p'(0) = -0.5$.

*In[30]:=*
```
Solve[{p[0]==2.8,p'[0]==-0.5},{c1,c2}]
```

*Out[30]=*
{{c1 → 0.8, c2 → −0.1}}

The information about $p(0)$ and $p'(0)$ identifies a particular member of the family of solutions that is represented by the general solution. Here are the graphs of some of these curves for three different sets of values for $p(0)$ and $p'(0)$.

*In[31]:=*
```
Plot[{p[t]  /.  {c1->-0.5,  c2->1.55},
        p[t]  /.  {c1-> 0.3,  c2->3.15},
        p[t]  /.  {c1-> 0.8,  c2->-0.1}},{t,0,10},
         PlotStyle->{{},Dashing[{0.02}],Thickness[0.008]},
         AxesLabel->{"t","p"},PlotRange->{0,4}];
```

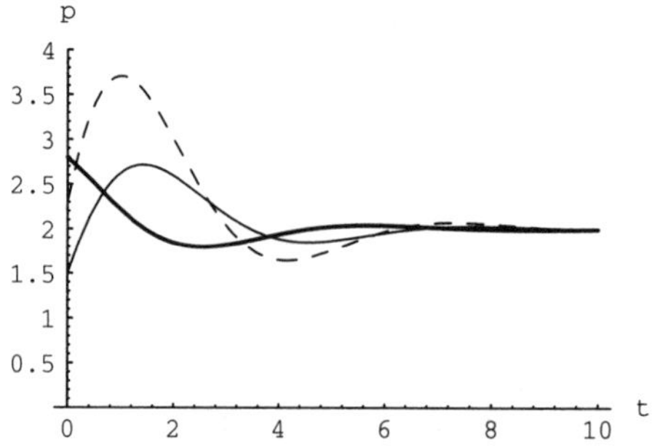

The general solution defines a family of solutions and its members are the particular solutions. If the general solution of an $n$th order differential equation is composed of $n$ arbitrary constants, then we need to impose $n$ conditions on the solution or its derivatives to determine a specific particular solution. Hence, the number of conditions will correspond to the order of the differential equation. If these conditions are imposed at some specific point, then the conditions are called *initial conditions* of the differential equation. A differential equation with initial conditions is called an *initial-value problem.* If the conditions are imposed at more than one point, then the conditions are called *boundary conditions.* A differential equation with boundary conditions is called a *boundary-value problem.*

**Example 13.15** Consider the initial-value problem for the price adjustment, $\mathrm{d}p/\mathrm{d}t$, over time, $t$,

$$\frac{\mathrm{d}p}{\mathrm{d}t} + 2p = 6$$

with the initial condition

$$p(0) = 4.$$

It is easy to verify that

$$p(t) = 3 + \mathrm{e}^{-2t}$$

is the solution of this initial-value problem.

**Example 13.16** The following is an initial-value problem.

$$y'' - 3y' - 4y = x^3$$
$$y(1) = 1,\ y'(1) = 2.$$

We can confirm that

$$y(x) = \frac{153}{128} - \frac{39}{32}x + \frac{9}{16}x^2 - \frac{1}{4}x^3 + \frac{91}{128}\mathrm{e}^{-4(1-x)}$$

is the solution of the initial-value problem by using *Mathematica.*

*In[32]:=*
```
Clear[x,y];
y[x_]:= 153/128 - (39/32)*x + (9/16)*x^2 - (1/4)*x^3 +
            (91/128)*Exp[-4*(1-x)];
y''[x] - 3*y'[x] - 4*y[x] == x^3 // Simplify
```

*Out[34]=*
```
True
```

*In[35]:=*
```
y[1] == 1
```

*Out[35]=*
True

*In[36]:=*
```
y'[1] == 2
```

*Out[36]=*
True

**Example 13.17** The differential equation

$$y'' + y' - 2y = 2,$$

and boundary conditions, $y(0) = -1$, $y(1) = 0$, form a boundary-value problem. This boundary-value problem has the solution

$$y(x) = \frac{e^2}{1 - e^3}(e^{-2x} - e^x) - 1 \approx -0.387155(e^{-2x} - e^x) - 1.$$

If the boundary conditions are changed to

$$y(0) = -1, \ y'(1) = 1,$$

then the solution of the boundary-value problem becomes

$$y(x) = \frac{-e^2}{2 + e^3}(e^{-2x} - e^x) - 1 \approx -0.334565(e^{-2x} - e^x) - 1.$$

These two particular solutions of the boundary-value problem are plotted below.

*In[37]:=*
```
Clear[x];
Plot[{-0.387155*(Exp[-2x]-Exp[x])-1,
      -0.334565*(Exp[-2x]-Exp[x])-1},{x,-1,2},
            PlotStyle->{{},Thickness[0.008]},
            AxesLabel->{"x","y"}];
```

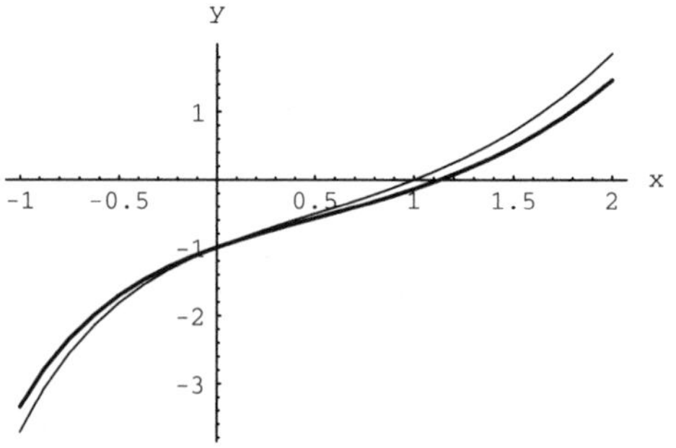


One might wonder if solutions of initial-value problems and boundary-value problems are unique. In other words, is it possible for a given initial-value problem or boundary-value problem to have more than one solution? It turns out that it is quite common to have more than one solution to a given problem. The following boundary-value problem is an example.

**Example 13.18** Consider the following boundary-value problem.

$$y'' + y = 0, \ -\pi < x < \pi$$
$$y(-\pi) = 0, \ y(\pi) = 0.$$

The general solution for this differential equation is

$$y(x) = c_1 \cos x + c_2 \sin x.$$

Using the boundary conditions, we have

$$0 = y(-\pi) = c_1 \cos(-\pi) + c_2 \sin(-\pi) = c_1$$
$$0 = y(\pi) = c_1 \cos(\pi) + c_2 \sin(\pi) = c_1$$

which implies that $c_1 = 0$ and $c_2$ is arbitrary. Hence, there are an infinite number of solutions to this boundary-value problem.

The situation for initial-value problems not having unique solutions is not quite as bad. One can give relatively mild conditions on the differential equation and the initial conditions that will guarantee that an initial-value problem has a unique solution.

## EXERCISES

1. Show that $\sin y + e^y = x^6 - x^2 + x + c$ is the general (implicit) solution of

$$y' = \frac{6x^5 - 2x + 1}{\cos y + e^y}$$

2. Show that $y(x) = c_1 + c_2 e^{-x} + 5(x-1)$ is the general (explicit) solution of

$$y'' + y' = 5.$$

3. The fourth-order differential equation

$$y^{(4)} + 4y''' + 6y'' + 4y' + y = 2, \ x > 0$$

has the general solution

$$y(x) = 2 + (c_1 + c_2 x + c_3 x^2 + c_4 x^3)e^{-x}.$$

With the following initial conditions

$$y(0) = 1, \ y'(0) = 0, \ y''(0) = 0, \ y'''(0) = -2$$

find a particular solution.

4. Given that $y(x) = c_1 e^{-2x} + c_2 x e^{-2x}$ is the general solution of $y'' + 4y' + 4y = 0$, find the solution of the initial-value problem with the initial conditions: $y(0) = 2$, $y'(0) = -3$.

5. Given that $\log|y-1| - \log|x+3| = c$ is the general solution of $dy/dx = (y-1)/(x+3)$, find the solution of the initial-value problem:

$$y' = \frac{y-1}{x+3},\ y(1) = 10.$$

6. The initial-value problem

$$[(\cos x)(\sin x) - xy^2]dx + y(1 - x^2)dy = 0,\ y(0) = 1$$

has an implicit general solution

$$\cos^2 x - y^2(1-x^2) = c.$$

Find an implicit solution of the initial-value problem.

## □ 13.2 First-Order Differential Equations □

### 13.2.1 Separable differential equation

In this section we present some methods for finding the general solutions of a first-order differential equation. There are no general methods for finding solutions of all first-order differential equations. However, there are certain classes of first-order differential equations for which we can present an algorithm to find solutions of differential equations that arise often in applications.

**DEFINITION 13.5** *A first-order differential equation is said to be* ***separable*** *if it can be written in the differential form*

$$P(x)dx + Q(y)dy = 0.$$

The name of this type of differential equation is quite descriptive. Namely, a separable differential equation is one where the dependent and independent variables can be separated in the differential equation.

**Example 13.19** The differential equation

$$\frac{xy}{y^2+1}\frac{dy}{dx} + \cos x = 0$$

is separable since we can rewrite it as

$$\frac{\cos x}{x}dx + \frac{y}{y^2+1}dy = 0$$

provided $x \neq 0$.

To find the general solution of a separable differential equation, we simply integrate the differential form of the equation. That is,

$$\int P(x)\mathrm{d}x + \int Q(y)\mathrm{d}y = c_1.$$

The arbitrary constant $c_1$ arises from the constant of integration for each indefinite integral. This equation is an implicit general solution of the separable differential equation.

**Example 13.20** Find the general solution of

$$\frac{\mathrm{d}y}{\mathrm{d}x} = \frac{1 + x^2}{x\sin y}$$

Let us assume that $x > 0$. We first separate the variables,

$$\left[\frac{1 + x^2}{x}\right]\mathrm{d}x + [-\sin y]\mathrm{d}y = 0$$

Hence,

$$\int \frac{1 + x^2}{x}\mathrm{d}x + \int(-\sin y)\mathrm{d}y = c_1$$

We use *Mathematica* to do the integrations.

*In[39]:=*

```
Clear[x,y,c1];
gensol = Integrate[(1+x^2)/x,x]+Integrate[-Sin[y],y]==c1
```

*Out[40]=*

$$\frac{x^2}{2} + \mathrm{Cos}[y] + \mathrm{Log}[x] == c1$$

Notice that in this case it is possible to find an explicit general solution by solving for $y$.

*In[41]:=*

```
Solve[gensol,y]
```

Solve : : ifun : Warning : Inverse functions are being used by Solve, so some solutions may not be found.

*Out[41]=*

$$\{\{y \to \mathrm{ArcCos}[\frac{2c1 - x^2 - 2\mathrm{Log}[x]}{2}]\}\}$$

Hence, an explicit general solution is

$$y(x) = \cos^{-1}\left(c_1 - \log x - \frac{1}{2}x^2\right)$$

The **MathEcon** function **separableode** can be used to solve a separable differential equation. Solutions are expressed in both the implicit form and the corresponding explicit form (if possible). Here is a description of this function.

*In[42]:=*
```
?separableode
```

**separableode[var1,var2,fct1,fct2] attempts to find the general implicit and explicit solutions of the separable, first order differential equation: fct1 d(var1) + fct2 d(var2) = 0. The solutions are presented as a list of rules. The arbitrary constant is denoted by C[1]. For example,**

**separableode[x,y,Cos[x],-y*Sin[y^2]].**

The first two arguments are the variables in the differential equation, and the last two arguments are functions that are the coefficients of the differentials in the differential equation.

**Example 13.21** Solve the differential equation $y\,dx + 2x\,dy = 0$. We first rewrite the equation as

$$\frac{1}{2x}dx + \frac{1}{y}dy = 0$$

Thus $P(x) = 1/2x$ and $Q(y) = 1/y$.

*In[43]:=*
```
Clear[x,y,P,Q];
P[x_]  =  1/(2*x);
Q[y_]  =  1/y;
separableode[x,y,P[x],Q[y]]
```

*Out[46]=*

$$\{\frac{\text{Log}[x]}{2} + \text{Log}[y] == C[1],\ \{\{x \to E^{2(C[1] - \text{Log}[y])}\}\},\ \{\{y \to E^{(2C[1] - \text{Log}[x])/2}\}\}\}$$

The output from **separableode** is a list of solutions. The first element in the list is the implicit general solution. The remaining solution in the lists contain possible explicit solutions, either in the form $y = \phi(x)$ or in the form $x = \psi(y)$. The arbitrary constant is denoted by $C[1]$. In this example, the implicit general solution is

$$\frac{\log(x)}{2} + \log(y) = c_1$$

An explicit solution in the form $y = \phi(x)$ is

$$y(x) = e^{(2c_1 - \log(x))/2} = \frac{A}{\sqrt{x}}$$

An explicit solution in the form $x = \psi(y)$ is also given.

**Example 13.22** Find the solution of the initial-value problem

$$\frac{dy}{dx} + \frac{1 + y^2}{1 + x^2} = 0, \; y(1) = \sqrt{3}$$

The variables can be separated as

$$\frac{1}{1 + x^2} dx + \frac{1}{1 + y^2} dy = 0.$$

We now find the general solution using **separableode**.

*In[47]:=*

```
Clear[x,y,P,Q];
P[x_]  =  1/(1+x^2);
Q[y_]  =  1/(1+y^2);
gensol  =  separableode[x,y,P[x],Q[y]]
```

*Out[50]=*

```
{ArcTan[x] + ArcTan[y] == C[1], {{x → -Tan[ArcTan[y] - C[1]]}},
  {{y → -Tan[ArcTan[x] - C[1]]}}}
```

The explicit general solution for $y$ as a function of $x$ is therefore

$$y(x) = -\tan(\tan^{-1}x - c_1)$$

The third element in the list of solution is $y(x)$.

*In[51]:=*

```
y[x_]  =  y  /.  gensol[[3,1]]
```

*Out[51]=*

```
-Tan[ArcTan[x] - C[1]]
```

If $y(1) = \sqrt{3}$, then we find that $c_1 = 7\pi/12$.

*In[52]:=*

```
Solve[y[1]==Sqrt[3],C[1]]
```

```
Solve : : ifun : Warning : Inverse functions are being used by Solve, so some
  solutions may not be found.
```

*Out[52]=*

$$\{\{C[1] \rightarrow \frac{7Pi}{12}\}\}$$

Hence, the solution of the initial-value problem is

$$y(x) = \tan(\frac{7\pi}{12} - \tan^{-1}(x))$$

## EXERCISES

1. Find a general solution for each of the following first-order differential equations:
   (a) $y' = \dfrac{x^4 - 1}{y^3}$
   (b) $y' = \dfrac{\sec^2 y}{x^2 + 1}$
   (c) $y' = x^2(y + 1)$
   (d) $\sqrt{y}\,\mathrm{d}x - (1 + x^2)\mathrm{d}y = 0$
2. Find the general solution of

   $$y' = \sin(x + y)$$

3. Find the solution of the initial-value problem:

   $$x\frac{\mathrm{d}y}{\mathrm{d}x} = \frac{x^2 + 1}{\sin y},\ y(1) = -2.$$

4. The number of auto parts stores $S(t)$ in the United States that sell PSC spark plugs is modeled by the initial-value problem

   $$\frac{\mathrm{d}S}{\mathrm{d}t} = \frac{S(1 + 0.00002\,S)}{10},\ t > 0$$
   $$S(0) = 1,$$

   where $t$ is measured in months. How many stores will be selling this brand of spark plugs one year after its introduction into stores?

### 13.2.2 Linear differential equation

We introduced the notion of a linear differential equation in the first section of this chapter. A first-order linear differential equation has the form

$$a_1(x)y' + a_0(x)y = g(x)$$

where $a_1(x)$, $a_0(x)$, and $g(x)$ are given functions. We shall assume that $a_1(x) \neq 0$ on the domain of the differential equation. Dividing the equation by $a_1(x)$, we have the form for a first-order, linear differential equation:

$$y' + P(x)y = Q(x).$$

**Example 13.23** The first-order differential equation

$$y' + \frac{1}{1 + x^2}y = \cos x$$

is linear. Namely, $P(x) = 1/(1+x^2)$ and $Q(x) = \cos x$.

**Example 13.24** The differential equation

$$(\sin x)y' + 5y = e^{-x}$$

is linear since it can be written as

$$y' + (5\csc x)y = e^{-x}\csc x.$$

The domain of this differential equation is restricted to those values of $x$ for which $\sin x \neq 0$.

First-order linear differential equations can be solved by constructing an *integrating factor*. Let us define the function

$$\mu(x) = e^{\int P(x)\,dx}.$$

Multiply the differential equation, $y' + P(x)y = Q(x)$, by $\mu(x)$, we have

$$\mu(x)y'(x) + \mu(x)P(x)y(x) = \mu(x)Q(x).$$

The last equation implies that

$$\frac{d}{dx}[\mu(x)y(x)] = \mu(x)Q(x).$$

Integrating both sides of the above equation, we have

$$\mu(x)y(x) = \int \mu(x)Q(x)\,dx + c_1$$

where $c_1$ is a constant of integration. Dividing both sides by $\mu(x)$, we obtain a formula for the general solution of the first-order linear differential equation,

$$y(x) = \frac{1}{\mu(x)}\left[\int \mu(x)Q(x)\,dx + c_1\right].$$

**Example 13.25** Find the general solution of the first-order linear differential equation,

$$y' + y = 2x + 5.$$

Here $P(x) \equiv 1$ and $Q(x) = 2x + 5$. We will use *Mathematica* to find the integrating factor and evaluate the formula for $y(x)$.

*In[53]:=*
```
Clear[x,y,mu,P,Q,c1];
P[x_]:=  1;
Q[x_]:=  2*x+5;
mu[x_]  =  Exp[Integrate[P[x],x]]
```

*Out[56]=*
$E^x$

*In[57]:=*
```
y[x_]  =  (1/mu[x])*(Integrate[mu[x]*Q[x],x]+c1)
```

*Out[57]=*

$$\frac{c1 + E^{x}(3 + 2x)}{E^{x}}$$

Since finding the general solution of a first-order linear differential equation simply involves evaluating a formula, the **MathEcon** function **linearode** automates this process. We assume that the differential equation is written in its standard form:

$$y' + P(x)y = Q(x).$$

Here is a description of this function.

*In[58]:=*

```
?linearode
```

**linearode[var1,fct1,fct2] attempts to find the general, explicit solution of the first order, linear ODE: d(var2)/d(var1) + fct1(var1) var2 = fct2(var1). The output is an expression involving the symbol var1 and the arbitrary constant C[1]. For example,**

**linearode[x,1/x,x^2].**

The first argument is the independent variable, the second argument is the coefficient of the $y$ term, $P(x)$, and the third argument is the inhomogeneous term $Q(x)$.

**Example 13.26** Find the general solution

$$\frac{dy}{dx} + \frac{1}{x}y = e^{x},\ x > 0.$$

Here $P(x) = 1/x$ and $Q(x) = e^{x}$.

*In[59]:=*

```
Clear[x];
linearode[x,1/x,Exp[x]]
```

*Out[60]=*

$$\frac{E^{x}(-1 + x) + C[1]}{x}$$

The symbol **C[1]** is an arbitrary constant.

An interesting aspect of linear differential equations is that the general solution can be split into two pieces. Let $y_c(x)$ be the general solution of the corresponding *homogeneous differential equation*

$$y' + P(x)y = 0.$$

The general solution of this differential equation, $y_c(x)$, is called the *complementary solution* of the inhomogeneous equation. Let $y_p(x)$ be any *particular solution* of the inhomogenous differential equation

$$y' + P(x)y = Q(x).$$

By direct substitution, it is easy to show that $y(x) = y_c(x) + y_p(x)$ is the general solution of the inhomogeneous equation

$$y' + P(x)y = Q(x).$$

As we shall see later, dividing the solution of an inhomogeneous linear differential equation into a complementary solution and a particular solution is an important method of solving higher-order linear differential equations.

**Example 13.27** Suppose the demand, $D$, and supply, $S$, for a particular commodity take the form

$$D = a_0 + a_1 p$$
$$S = b_0 + b_1 p$$

where $a_i$ and $b_i$ are constant, and $p(t)$ is the market price at time $t$. Assuming that the rate of change of price over time is directly proportional to excess demand, we have the differential equation

$$\frac{dp}{dt} = k(D - S) = k(a_0 + a_1 p - b_0 - b_1 p)$$

which can be written as a first-order linear differential equation,

$$\frac{dp}{dt} - k(a_1 - b_1)p = k(a_0 - b_0).$$

It is easy to show that the corresponding homogeneous differential equation

$$\frac{dp}{dt} - k(a_1 - b_1)p = 0$$

has the complementary solution

$$p_c(t) = c_1 e^{(a_1 - b_1)kt}.$$

The inhomogeneous differential equation has a particular solution

$$p_p(t) = \frac{b_0 - a_0}{a_1 - b_1}.$$

The general solution of the inhomogeneous equation is then

$$p(t) = p_p(x) + p_c(x) = \frac{b_0 - a_0}{a_1 - b_1} + c_1 e^{(a_1 - b_1)kt}$$

We use the **MathEcon** function **linearode** to find the general solution.

*In[61]:=*

```
Clear[p,t,a0,a1,b0,b1,k];
p[t_] = linearode[t,-k*(a1-b1),k*(a0-b0)] // Simplify
```

*Out[62]=*

$$\frac{b0}{a1-b1}+\frac{a0}{-a1+b1}+E^{(a1-b1)kt}C[1]$$

Suppose the initial price at time $t = 0$ is equal to $p_0$. The arbitrary constant $c_1$ is found to be

$$c_1 = \left[p_0 - \frac{b_0 - a_0}{a_1 - b_1}\right].$$

Substituting the constant $c_1$ into the price equation, we obtain the solution of the initial-value problem,

$$p(t) = \frac{b_0 - a_0}{a_1 - b_1} + \left[p_0 - \frac{b_0 - a_0}{a_1 - b_1}\right] e^{(a_1 - b_1)kt}$$

It is interesting to observe that if $k > 0$, $a_1 < 0$ (i.e., demand is downward sloping), and $b_1 > 0$ (i.e., supply is upward sloping), then the exponent in the above particular solution is negative, $(a_1 - b_1)kt < 0$. As $t \to \infty$, the price approaches

$$\lim_{t\to\infty} p(t) = \frac{b_0 - a_0}{a_1 - b_1}$$

which is called the equilibrium price.

## EXERCISES

1. Find the general solutions for the following linear differential equations:
   (a) $y' = 2\pi y + 3$
   (b) $y' + y/x = \log(x)$
   (c) $y' + \dfrac{e^x}{1 + x^2} = y$
   (d) $(2xy)y' + y^2 = (\sin y)y'$
2. Find the solution of the initial-value problem:

$$\sqrt{x+1}\,y' + (\sin x)y = \sec x,\; y(\pi) = \frac{\pi}{2}$$

### 13.2.3 Tangent fields and graphical solutions

Most first-order differential equations are neither separable nor linear. In fact, the majority of first-order differential equations cannot be solved. For example,

$$\frac{dy}{dx} = \sin\left[\frac{y + e^{x^2}}{\sqrt{1 + x^2}}\right] + \sqrt[3]{y}$$

cannot be solved using techniques that are known to mathematicians today. If one is willing to accept an approximation to the solution, then there are several methods for approximating the solution of initial-value problems. However, there is much information about the solution that is contained in the differential equation itself. Suppose we write the first-order differential equation in the standard form

$$y' = f(x,y),\ x \in I$$

If $y = \phi(x)$ is a solution, then the differential equation gives us the slope of the tangent line to the graph of $\phi$ at every point that the solution passes through in the $xy$-plane. That is, if $y = \phi(x)$ passes through the point $(x_0,y_0)$, then the slope of the tangent line to the solution at $(x_0,y_0)$ is $f(x_0,y_0)$. The problem is that if we do not know the solution, then we cannot find points through which it passes in the $xy$-plane. However, we could draw the tangent lines at any array of points in the $xy$-plane that would be tangent to the solution if the solution passed through these points. This would give us a picture of the qualitative behavior of the solution. We call this picture the *tangent field* or *direction field* of the differential equation. The **MathEcon** function **tangentfield** generates the tangent field for a given first-order differential equation in standard form. Here is a description of this function

*In[63]:=*

```
?tangentfield
```

**tangentfield[fct,var1range,var2range,int,opt] generates a 2D Graphics object that illustrates the tangent field of the differential equation: d(var2)/d(var1) = fct where fct is a function of var1 and var2, var1range is a list that is the range of the variable var1, and var2range is a list for the range of the variable var2 over which the tangent field will be displayed. The fourth argument int is a positive integer that is related to the number of tangent lines to be drawn. The last argument is optional and can include 2D Graphics options. For example,**

**tangentfield[x*y^3,{x,-1,2},{y,0,2},10,AxesLabel→{"x","y"}].**

For a differential equation $dy/dx = f(x,y)$, the first argument of **tangentfield** is the function $f(x,y)$, the second argument is a range for the independent variable $x$, a third argument is the range for the dependent variable $y$, the fourth argument is a positive integer that tells the program how many tangent lines are to be computed in the $x$ and $y$ directions, and the last argument contains **Graphics** options that the user would like to apply to the graph. This last argument is optional. The function generates a two-dimensional graphics object which can be displayed with the **Show** function. Let us look at two examples.

**Example 13.28** If $y = \phi(x)$ is a solution of the differential equation

$$y' = f(x,y) = 2x + y,$$

then the slope of the tangent line to $\phi(x)$ as it passes through the point $(-2,2)$ is $-2$. At point $(1,-2)$, the slope of the tangent line is zero and hence the segment of $\phi(x)$ is flat. The tangent line of $\phi(x)$ is positively sloped at point $(1,1)$. The following plot shows the tangent field of the differential equation.

*In[64]:=*
```
Clear[f,x,y,tangent];
f[x_,y_]:= 2*x + y;
tangent = tangentfield[f[x,y],{x,-2,2},{y,-2,2},8];
Show[tangent,Axes->True,AxesLabel->{"x","y"}];
```

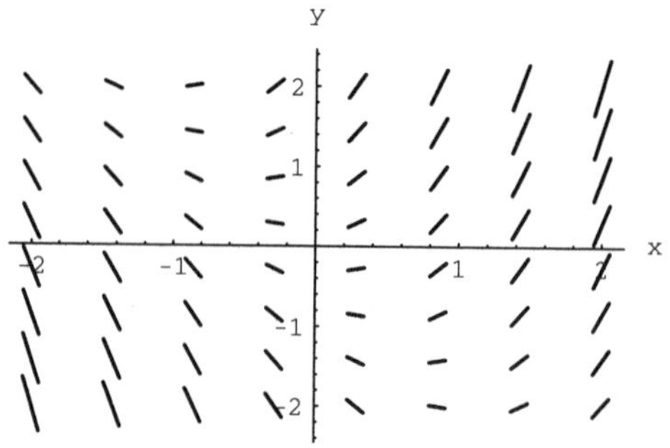


It is easy to show that the general solution of $y' = 2x + y$ is

$$y = \phi(x) = c_1 e^x - 2(1 + x)$$

where $c_1$ is an arbitrary constant. Suppose the initial condition, $y(0) = 3$, is given. Then $c_1 = 1$. We superimpose this particular solution, $y = e^x - 2(1 + x)$, on the graph of the tangent field to illustrate the use of the tangent field in sketching a particular solution of a differential equation.

*In[68]:=*
```
Clear[phi,x,c1,graph];
phi[x_]:= c1*Exp[x]-2(1+x);
graph = Plot[phi[x]/.{c1->1},{x,-2,2},
             DisplayFunction->Identity];
Show[tangent,graph,Axes->True,AxesLabel->{"x","y"},
             DisplayFunction->$DisplayFunction];
```

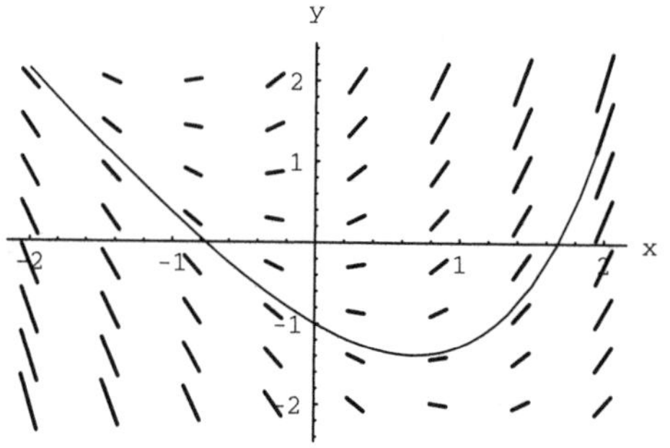


**Example 13.29** Graph the tangent field of the differential equation

$$y' = f(x,y) = -\sqrt{1 - y^2}, 0 \leq y \leq 1$$

along with the particular solution

$y = \phi(x) = \cos x.$

*In[72]:=*

```
Clear[f,x,y,tangent,graph,phi];
f[x_,y_]:=  -Sqrt[1-y^2];
tangent  =  tangentfield[f[x,y],{x,0,Pi},{y,-1,1},8];
phi[x_]:=  Cos[x];
graph=Plot[phi[x],{x,0,Pi},DisplayFunction->Identity];
Show[tangent,graph,DisplayFunction->$DisplayFunction,
                Axes->True,AxesLabel->{"x","y"}];
```

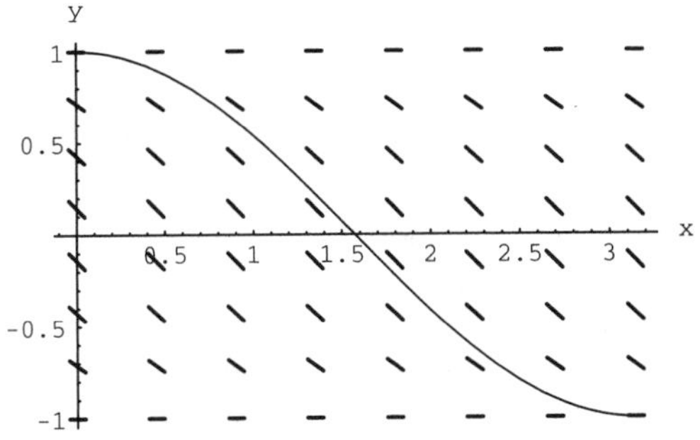


Suppose the differential equation $y' = f(x,y)$ depends only upon the dependent variable $y$; that is,

$y' = f(y),\ x \in I$

A differential equation of this type is said to be *autonomous*. Since $y' = f(y)$ is independent of $x$, the slopes of the tangent segments for a given value of $y$ do not change with $x$. This has an interesting effect on the tangent field.

**Example 13.30** The following autonomous differential equation

$y' = f(y) = -y + 1$

has the general solution

$y = \phi(x) = 1 + c_1 e^{-x}$

We graph the tangent field and two particular solutions corresponding to $c_1 = 0.05$ and $-0.1$.

*In[78]:=*

```
Clear[f,x,y,tangent,graph];
f[x_,y_]:=  -(y-1);
tangent  =  tangentfield[f[x,y],{x,-5,5},{y,-3,3},8];
graph  =  Plot[{1+0.05*Exp[-x],1-0.1*Exp[-x]},{x,-4,5},
                DisplayFunction->Identity];
Show[tangent,graph,DisplayFunction->$DisplayFunction,
                Axes->True,AxesLabel->{"x","y"}];
```

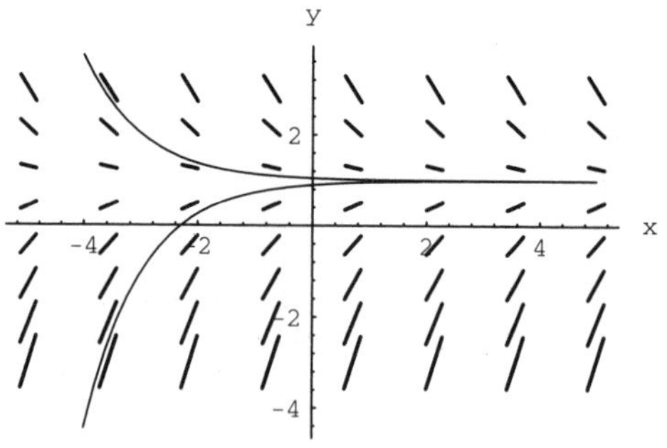


From this example, we can make the following observations:

(1) The slopes of the tangent segments across any horizontal line $y = y_0$ are identical.

(2) If $y' = f(y) > 0$ at a point $y_0$, then the tangent segment at the point $(x,y_0)$ in the $xy$-plane must have a positive slope. The solution $y = \phi(x)$ at point $(x,y_0)$ must then be an increasing function of $y$. The lower curve in the tangent field illustrates this case. On the other hand, for all values of $y$ such that $y' = f(y) < 0$, $y = \phi(x)$ is a decreasing function of $y$. The upper curve illustrates this case.

(3) If $y' = f(y) = 0$ at a point $y = y_e$, then the tangent segment at the point $(x,y_e)$ is horizontal. The solution $y = \phi(x)$ at point $(x,y_e)$ is constant regardless of $x$. That is $y(x) \equiv y_e$. This constant solution is called an *equilibrium solution* of the differential equation. In the example, $f(y) = -y + 1 = 0$ has the equilibrium solution $y_e = 1$.

The relationship between the autonomous differential equation $y' = f(y)$ and the solution $y = \phi(x)$ is more evident if we plot the *phase diagram*, i.e., the graph obtained by plotting $y$ and $y' = f(y)$.

*In[83]:=*

```
Clear[f,y];
f[y_]:= -y + 1;
Plot[f[y],{y,-3,3},AxesLabel->{"y","y'"}];
```

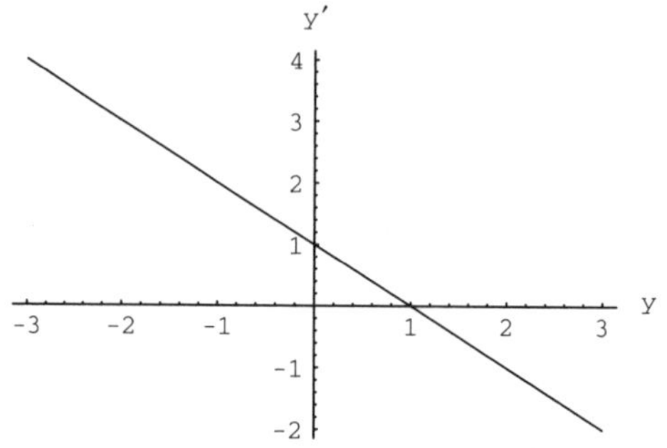


An equilibrium solution $y_e$ occurs at $y = 1$ since $y' = f(1) = 0$. Suppose that we assign the initial condition $y(0) = -1$. The initial condition implies that $y' = f(-1) = 2 > 0$. The function $y(x)$ must be increasing and moving toward the right of the initial value $-1$ along the $y$-axis. As long as $f(y)$ is positive, $y$ will keep increasing until it reaches

$y_e = 1$. On the other hand, if $y(0) = 3$, then the derivative at that point is $y' = f(3) = -2 < 0$ as shown in the phase diagram. In this case, $y(x)$ must be decreasing and moving toward the left of the initial value 3 along the $y$-axis until the equilibrium point $y_e = 1$ is reached. We have inferred the behavior of the solution of the differential equation without actually finding it.

**Example 13.31** Consider the autonomous differential equation

$$y' = f(y) = (y+1)(y-1)$$

The following phase diagram shows that two equilibrium solutions are $y(x) \equiv -1$ and $y(x) \equiv 1$ since $f(-1) = f(1) = 0$. If the initial value of $y(x)$ is $y_0$ such that $y_0 < -1$, then we have $y'(x) > 0$, and $y(x)$ will be increasing and moving toward $y_e = -1$. On the other hand, if the initial value is between $-1$ and 1, then we have $y'(x) < 0$. $y(x)$ will be decreasing and moving toward $y_e = -1$ again. In fact, any small departure from $y_e = -1$ will force $y(x)$ to move back to the equilibrium solution $y_e = -1$. We call the equilibrium solution $y_e = -1$ a *stable equilibrium solution*. On the other hand, if the initial value $y_0$ is larger than the other equilibrium point $y_e = 1$, $y$ will continue to increase since $y'(x) > 0$ at $y_0$. It will move away from $y_e = 1$. The equilibrium solution at $y_e = 1$ is an *unstable equilibrium solution*. Here is a picture of the phase plane for this example.

*In[86]:=*

```
Clear[f,y];
f[y_]:= (y+1)*(y-1);
Plot[f[y],{y,-2,2},AxesLabel->{"y","y'"}];
```

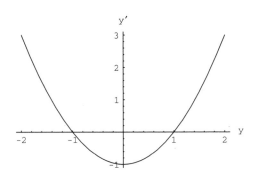

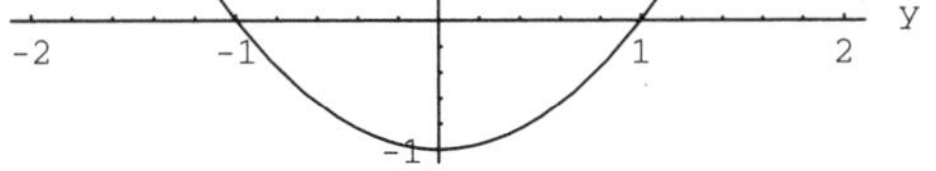


The above example suggests that, in general, the slope of the phase diagram at the points where $y' = f(y) = 0$ determines the stability of an equilibrium solution. Suppose $y(x) \equiv y_e$ is an equilibrium point, i.e., $f(y_e) = 0$. If $f(y)$ is a decreasing function in the neighborhood of $y_e$, then $y_e$ is a stable equilibrium solution. On the other hand, if $f(y)$ is a nondecreasing function in the neighborhood of $y_e$, then $y_e$ is an unstable equilbrium solution. Thus, the sign of the derivative of $f(y)$ with respect to $y$ offers a simple test for the stability of an equilibrium solution:

(1) $y_e$ is a stable equilibrium solution if $f(y_e) = 0$ and $f'(y_e) < 0$.

(2) $y_e$ is an unstable equilibrium solution if $f(y_e) = 0$ and $f'(y_e) \geq 0$.

**Example 13.32** The autonomous differential equation

$$y' = f(y) = 2y - y^2$$

has two equilibrium solutions, $y_e = 0$ and $y_e = 2$. Since $f'(0) = 2 > 0$, $y_e = 0$ is an unstable equilibrium solution. However, $y_e = 2$ is a stable solution since $f'(2) = -2 < 0$. We plot the phase diagram below.

*In[89]:=*

```
Clear[f,y];
f[y_]:=  2*y  -  y^2;
Plot[f[y],{y,-2,3},AxesLabel->{"y","y'"}];
```

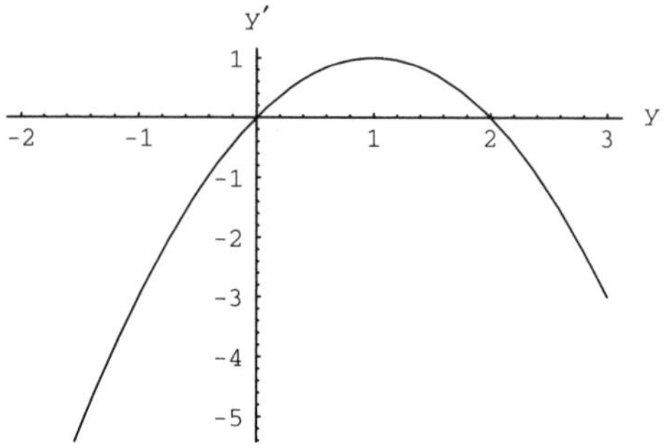


**Example 13.33** The autonomous differential equation

$$y' = f(y) = (y - 2)^2$$

has the equilibrium solution $y_e = 2$. However, since

$$f'(y_e) = 2(y_e - 2) = 0,$$

$y_e = 2$ is unstable. By plotting the phase diagram we observe that $f(y)$ is decreasing on one side and increasing on the other side of the point $y_e = 2$. The equilibrium solution is sometimes called *neutrally stable*.

*In[92]:=*

```
Clear[f,x,y];
f[y_]:=  (y-2)^2;
Plot[f[y],{y,1,3},AxesLabel->{"y","y'=f(y)"}];
```

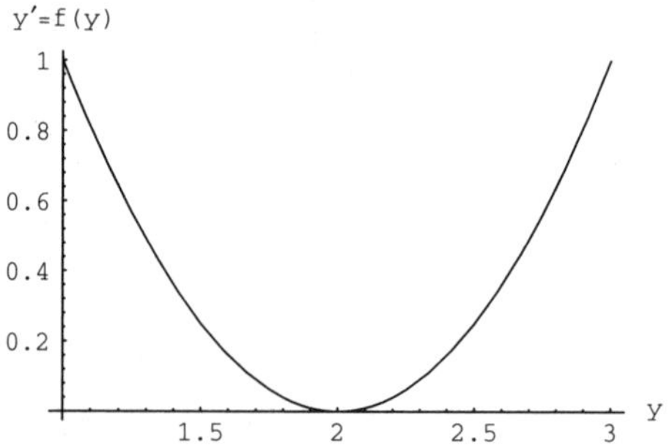

The following tangent field shows that $y$ moves toward $y_e = 2$ if $y$ initially starts below $y_e$. However, it moves away from $y_e$ if $y$ initially begins above $y_e$. The thick line is the graph of the equilibrium solution.

*In[95]:=*

```
Clear[x,y];
el  =  Graphics[{Thickness[0.015],
                 Line[{{0,2},{4,2}}]}];
tangent  =  tangentfield[(y-2)^2,{x,0,4},{y,1,3},8];
Show[tangent,el,Axes->True,AxesLabel->{"x","y"}];
```

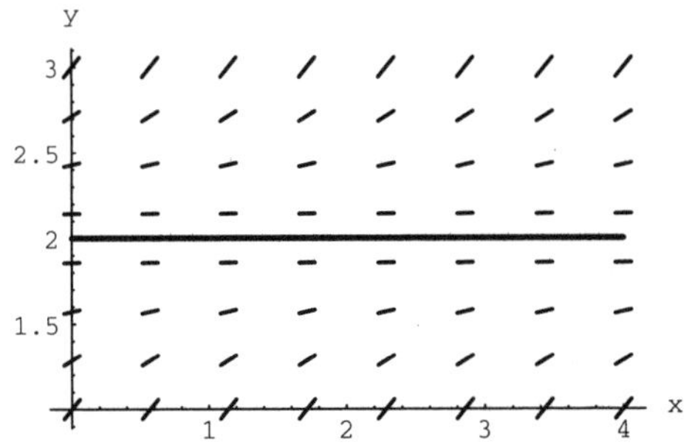


It can be shown that this autonomous differential equation has the general solution

$$y = \phi(x) = 2 - \frac{1}{x + c}$$

The following plot shows that $y$ approaches $y_e = 2$ if the initial value of $y$ is less than 2. However, $y$ breaks away from $y_e$ if the initial value of $y$ is greater than $y_e = 2$. Note that $y_e = 2$ is the singular solution of differential equation since it cannot be obtained from the general solution $y = \phi(x)$. Here is the graph of a particular solution.

*In[99]:=*

```
Clear[x];
graph=Plot[2-1/(x-1),{x,0.5,1.5},AxesLabel->{"x","y"}];
```

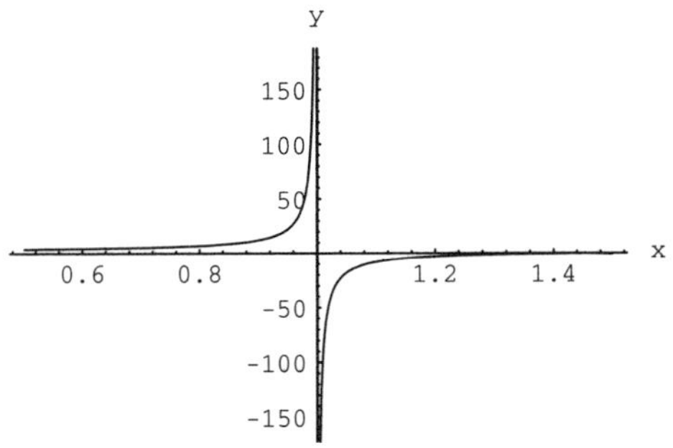


**Example 13.34** Consider the price adjustment model first discussed in example 13.10 in section 13.1.2. Let $D = f(p)$ and $S = g(p)$ be the demand and supply, which are functions of price $p$. The price adjustment $dp(t)/dt$ at time $t$ is proportional to the excess demand,

$$\frac{\mathrm{d}p}{\mathrm{d}t} = k(D - S) = k(f(p) - g(p)) \equiv kh(p).$$

The differential equation is autonomous. Suppose $p_e$ is an equilibrium price such that

$$\frac{\mathrm{d}p}{\mathrm{d}t} = kh(p_e) = 0$$

$p_e$ is a stable equilibrium price if

$$\frac{\mathrm{d}}{\mathrm{d}p}(kh(p)) = k(f'(p) - g'(p)) < 0$$

where all derivatives, $f'(p)$, $g'(p)$, and $h'(p)$, are evaluated at $p_e$. If $k > 0$, the demand is downward sloping ($f'(p) < 0$), and the supply is upward sloping ($g'(p) > 0$), then $p_e$ must be a stable equilibrium.

**Example 13.35** The *Solow growth model* describes the growth path of output and capital–labor ratio of an economy. Consider the following aggregrate Cobb-Douglas production function of a country,

$$Q(t) = K(t)^a L(t)^{1-a} \equiv L(t)k(t)^a$$

where $Q(t)$, $K(t)$, and $L(t)$ are, respectively, output, capital, and labor inputs at time $t$. The lower-case $k(t)$ represents the capital–labor ratio ($K/L$). Assume that $L$ grows exponentially over time at a constant rate $r$,

$$\mathrm{d}L(t)/\mathrm{d}t = L' = rL,$$

and the growth rate of $K$ is proportional to output $Q$,

$$K' = sQ = sLk.$$

Differentiating $K \equiv kL$, we have

$$K' = kL' + Lk'.$$

Substituting for the growth rates of labor and capital, we obtain the following differential equation

$$sLk^a = rLk + Lk'$$

or

$$k' = sk^a - rk \equiv f(k).$$

This is an autonomous differential equation. The capital–labor ratio $k$ is at equilibrium solution $k_e$ when $f(k_e) = 0$, or

$$k_e = \left(\frac{s}{r}\right)^{1/(1-a)}$$

$k_e$ is a stable equilibrium solution if

$$f'(k_e) = as(k_e)^{a-1} - b < 0,$$

and is an unstable equilibrium solution if $f'(k_e) \geq 0$. For a numerical illustration, suppose $a = 0.4$, $r = 0.02$, and $s = 0.1$, we have $k_e = 14.6201$ and $f'(k_e) = -0.012 < 0$. Thus $k_e$ is a stable equilibrium.

*In[101]:=*
```
Clear[f,k];
a=0.4;r=0.02;s=0.1;
f[k_]:=  s*k^a  -  r*k;
ke=Solve[f[k]==0,k]
```

*Out[104]=*
```
{{k → 0.}, {k → 14.6201}}
```

*In[105]:=*
```
D[f[k],k]  /.ke[[2]]
```

*Out[105]=*
```
-0.012
```

The plot of $k$ versus $k'$ shows a negative slope at $(k_e,0)$.

*In[106]:=*
```
Plot[f[k],{k,0,20},AxesLabel->{"k","k'"}];
```

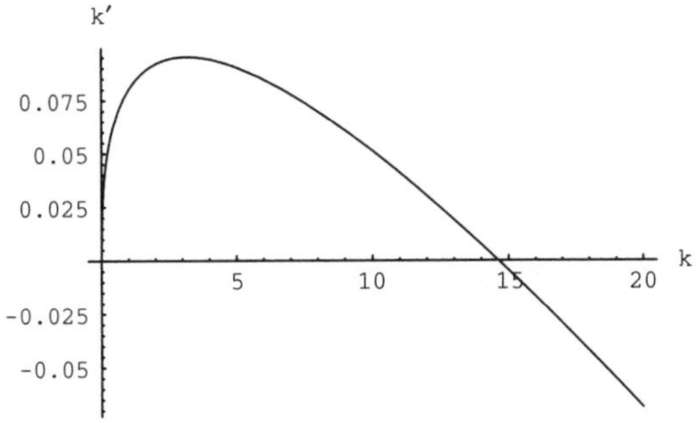


## EXERCISES

1. Consider the differential equation

   $$y' = f(x,y) = x + y$$

   (a) Compute the tangent field for $-1 \leq x \leq 1$, $-10 \leq y \leq 5$.
   (b) Does the differential equation appear to have any equilibrium solutions?
   (c) Confirm that

$$y = \phi(x) = c_1 e^{-x} - (1+x)$$

is the general solution. Superimpose the graphs of two particular solutions with $c_1 = -3$ and $c_1 = 3$ on the tangent field to confirm your answer to (b).

2. Graph the tangent field of the differential equation

$$y' = x - \sqrt{8 - y^2}\,,\ x \in [0,1]$$

3. Consider the differential equation

$$\frac{dy}{dx} = \frac{1}{10} e^{y} \sin(y^2).$$

Plot the tangent field in the region $-2 \le x \le 2$, $-2 \le y \le 2$. Does the differential equation appear to have any equilibrium solutions in this rectangle?

4. Graph the phase diagram of the following autonomous differential equations $y' = f(y)$ and check the stability of each equilibrium solution:
(a) $f(y) = y(y-1)(y+3)$
(b) $f(y) = \sin(y^2)$
(c) $f(y) = y^3 + y^2 - y - 1$

## □ 13.3 Higher-Order Linear Differential Equations □

### 13.3.1 Theory of $L[y] = 0$

An $n$th-order linear differential equation can be written as

$$L[y] = a_n(x)\frac{d^n y}{dx} + a_{n-1}(x)\frac{d^{n-1} y}{dx^{n-1}} + \ldots + a_1(x)\frac{dy}{dx} + a_0(x)y = g(x).$$

In this section we shall discuss methods of finding the general solution when $g(x) \equiv 0$. We have introduced the operation notation $L[y]$ to simplify the writing of the differential equation.

Consider a second-order linear differential equation,

$$L[y] = y'' - 4y = 0.$$

It is easy to show that the functions,

$$y_1(x) = e^{-2x}, \quad \text{and} \quad y_2(x) = e^{2x},$$

are solutions of $L[y] = 0$. Furthermore, it is also easy to confirm that a linear combination

$$y(x) = c_1 y_1(x) + c_2 y_1(x) = c_1 e^{-2x} + c_2 e^{2x}$$

is also a solution for any constants $c_1$ and $c_2$. The following theorem generalizes the idea of forming a linear combination of solutions to find a solution of $L[y] = 0$. The theorem is also known as the *superposition principle*.

**THEOREM 13.1** *Suppose $y_1(x), \ldots, y_n(x)$ are solutions of the nth-order homogeneous linear differential equation*

$$L[y] = a_n(x)y^{(n)} + a_{n-1}(x)y^{(n-1)} + \ldots + a_1(x)y' + a_0(x)y = 0$$

*If $c_1, \ldots, c_n$ are constants, then the linear combination*

$$y[x] = c_1y_1(x) + c_2y_2(x) + \ldots + c_ny_n(x) = \sum_{k=1}^{n} c_ky_k(x)$$

*is also a solution of $L[y] = 0$.*

The theorem is easily proven by noting that $L$ is a linear operator, i.e., it satisfies the properties:

(1) $L[u+v] = L[u] + L[v]$

(2) $L[au] = aL[u]$

for any $n$-times differentiable functions $u(x)$ and $v(x)$, and constant $a$.

**Example 13.36** The third-order differential equation

$$L[y] = x^3y''' - 5x^2y'' + 12xy' - 12y = 0$$

has three solutions:

$$y_1(x) = x, \; y_2(x) = x^3, \quad \text{and} \quad y_3(x) = x^4.$$

If $c_1$, $c_2$, and $c_3$ are arbitrary constants, then the linear combination

$$y(x) = c_1y_1(x) + c_2y_2(x) + c_3y_3(x)$$

is also a solution. We confirm this by the following *Mathematica* calculation.

```
In[107]:=
    Clear[x,c1,c2,c3];
    y1[x_]:= x; y2[x_]:= x^3; y3[x_]:= x^4;
    y[x_]:= c1*y1[x] + c2*y2[x] + c3*y3[x];
    x^3*y'''[x]-5*x^2*y''[x]+12*x*y'[x]-12*y[x] == 0 //Simplify

Out[110]=
    True
```

Theorem 13.1 provides a convenient method of constructing the general solution of an $n$th-order linear differential equation by forming a linear combination of $n$ solutions. However, this method works only if none of the $n$ solutions, $y_1(x), y_2(x), \ldots, y_n(x)$, are linearly dependent on any of the others. We illustrate this problem in the following example.

**Example 13.37** The functions $y_1(x) = \cos 2x$ and $y_2(x) = -3\cos 2x$ are solutions of $L[y] = y'' + 4y = 0$. By the superposition principle, the function

$$y(x) = c_1\cos 2x - 3c_2\cos 2x$$

is also a solution. However, it is not the general solution since it can be reduced to

$$y(x) = (c_1 - 3c_2)\cos 2x = \alpha\cos 2x$$

which has only a single arbitrary constant $\alpha$. A general solution of second-order differential equations must have two arbitrary constants. Hence, the above linear combination $y(x)$ cannot be a general solution.

The explanation for why we could construct a general solution from two solutions in example 13.36 but not in example 13.37 lies in the following observations. In example 13.37, the two solutions, $y_1(x) = \cos 2x$ and $y_2(x) = -3\cos 2x$, are linearly dependent functions, namely, $y_2(x) = -3y_1(x)$. In example 13.36, the three solutions, $y_1(x) = x$, $y_2(x) = x^3$, and $y_3(x) = x$, are linearly independent functions.

**Definition 13.6** *A set of functions $\{y_1(x), y_2(x), \ldots, y_n(x)\}$ is said to be* ***linearly independent*** *on the interval I if the only way that the equation*

$$c_1y_1(x) + c_2y_2(x) + \ldots + c_ny_n(x) = \sum_{k=1}^{n} c_ky_k(x) = 0$$

*can be satisfied on the interval I is to set $c_1 = c_2 = \ldots c_n = 0$. If $\{y_1(x), y_2(x), \ldots, y_n(x)\}$ are not linearly independent on I, then we say that they are* ***linearly dependent*** *on the interval I.*

**Example 13.38** The set of functions $\{1, x, x^2\}$ is linearly independent on the interval $[0,1]$. The only way to satisfy the equation

$$c_1 + c_2x + c_1x^2 = 0$$

on $x \in [0,1]$ is to set $c_1 = c_2 = c_3 = 0$.

**Example 13.39** The set of functions $\{1, x, 0\}$ is linearly dependent on the interval $[-1,1]$. It is possible to find values for the constants $c_1 = 0$, $c_2 = 0$, $c_3 = 9$ such that

$$c_1 + c_2x + c_10 = 0$$

we now develop an easy way to determine if a set of solutions to $L[y] = 0$ is linearly independent.

**Definition 13.7** *Suppose $y_1(x)$, $y_2(x)$, ..., $y_n(x)$ are $(n-1)$ times differentiable functions on I. The* ***Wronskian*** *of these functions is defined as the determinant*

$$W(y_1, y_2, \ldots y_n) = \begin{vmatrix} y_1 & y_2 & \cdots & y_n \\ y_1' & y_2' & \cdots & y_n' \\ \cdots & \cdots & \cdots & \cdots \\ y_1^{(n-1)} & y_2^{(n-1)} & \cdots & y_n^{(n-1)} \end{vmatrix}$$

**Example 13.40** The Wronskian of the functions, $y_1(x) = 1$, $y_2(x) = e^x$, $y_3(x) = e^{-x}$ is

$$W(y_1,y_2,y_3) = \begin{vmatrix} 1 & e^x & e^{-x} \\ 0 & e^x & -e^{-x} \\ 0 & e^x & e^{-x} \end{vmatrix} = 2$$

We can use *Mathematica* to evaluate the determinant.

*In[111]:=*

```
Clear[y1,y2,y3,x,w];
y1[x_]:= 1; y2[x_]:= Exp[x]; y3[x_]:= Exp[-x];
w = Det[{{y1[x],y2[x],y3[x]},
         {y1'[x],y2'[x],y3'[x]},
          {y1''[x],y2''[x],y3''[x]}}] //Simplify
```

*Out[113]=*

2

The **MathEcon** function **wronskian** evaluates the Wronskian of a set of functions. Here is a description of this function.

*In[114]:=*

```
?wronskian
```

**wronskian[fctlst,var] computes the Wronskian determinant of a list of functions in the first argument whose independent variable is the second argument var. For example,**

**wronskian[{1,x,x^2},x].**

The first argument is the list of functions and the second argument is the independent variable of the functions.

**Example 13.41** Evaluate the Wronskian of the functions

$$y_1(x) = e^{2x}\sin(3x),$$
$$y_2(x) = e^{2x}\cos(3x),$$
$$y_3(x) = e^{-x}.$$

*In[115]:=*

```
Clear[y1,y2,y3,x];
y1[x_]:= Exp[2*x]*Sin[3*x];
y2[x_]:= Exp[2*x]*Cos[3*x];
y3[x_]:= Exp[-x];
wronskian[{y1[x],y2[x],y3[x]},x] //Simplify
```

*Out[119]=*

$-54 E^{3x}$

We now state without proof two important theorems that relate the Wronskian to the determination of linear independence of the solutions of $L[y] = 0$ and to the construction of the general solution of $L[y] = 0$.

**THEOREM 13.2** *Suppose $y_1(x), y_2(x), \ldots, y_n(x)$ are solutions of $L[y] = 0$, $x \in I$. A necessary and sufficient condition that these functions are linearly independent on $I$ is that $W(y_1(x_0), \ldots, y_n(x_0)) \neq 0$ for some $x_0$ in $I$.*

**Example 13.42** The differential equation

$$y^{(4)} - 9y^{(3)} + 22y'' + 28y' - 120y = 0$$

has the solutions

$$y_1(x) = e^{4x}\sin(2x),$$
$$y_2(x) = e^{4x}\cos(2x),$$
$$y_3(x) = e^{-2x}$$
$$y_4(x) = e^{3x}$$

We calculate the Wronskian with the function **wronskian**.

*In[120]:=*

```
Clear[y1,y2,y3,y4,x];
y1[x_]:= Exp[4*x]*Sin[2*x]; y2[x_]:= Exp[4*x]*Cos[2*x];
y3[x_]:= Exp[-2*x]; y4[x_]:= Exp[3*x];
wronskian[{y1[x],y2[x],y3[x],y4[x]},x] //Simplify
```

*Out[123]=*

$$-2000E^{9x}$$

Since the Wronskian is never zero, these four solutions are linearly independent.

**THEOREM 13.3** *Suppose $y_1(x), y_2(x), \ldots, y_n(x)$ are linearly independent solutions of $L[y] = 0$, $x \in I$.* If $c_1, c_2, \ldots, c_n$ *are arbitrary constants, then*

$$y(x) = c_1y_1(x) + \ldots + c_ny_n(x)$$

*is the general solution of $L[y] = 0$.*

**Example 13.43** The functions

$$y_1(x) = 1,\ y_2(x) = x,\ y_3(x) = e^{2x}$$

are solutions of the differential equation

$$L[y] = y'''(x) - 2y''(x) = 0.$$

Since the Wronskian, $W[1, x, e^{2x}] = 4e^{2x} \neq 0$, the linear combination

$$y(x) = c_1 + c_2x + c_3e^{2x}$$

is the general solution of $L[y]$.

*In[124]:=*

```
Clear[y1,y2,y3,x];
y1[x_]:= 1;
y2[x_]:= x;
y3[x_]:= Exp[2*x];
wronskian[{y1[x],y2[x],y3[x]},x]
```

*Out[128]=*

$4E^{2x}$

## EXERCISES

1. The functions, $\{e^x, e^{-x}, 10e^{-3x}\}$, are solutions of the differential equation, $y''' + 3y'' - y' - 3y = 0$. Are they linearly independent? If so, find the general solution.
2. $\{x^{1/3}, x^{-3}\}$ are solutions of $3x^2y'' + 11xy' - 3y = 0$, $x > 0$. Are they linearly independent on $(0,\infty)$? If so, then find the general solution.
3. $\{\sin(x+\pi/4), \sin x, \cos x\}$ are solutions of $y^{(4)} - y = 0$. Are they linearly independent?

### 13.3.2 Theory of $L[y] = g(x)$

Recall that we observed that the general solution of a first-order linear inhomogeneous differential equation is the sum of two solutions – the complementary solution and a particular solution. This same construction applies to higher-order inhomogeneous differential equations.

**THEOREM 13.4** *If $y_c(x)$ is the general solution of the homogeneous differential equation $L[y] = 0$ and $y_p(x)$ is any particular solution of the inhomogeneous differential equation $L[y] = g(x)$, then $y(x) = y_c(x) + y_p(x)$ is the general solution of $L[y] = g(x)$.*

The proof of the theorem is elementary and is left as an exercise. The function $y_c(x)$ is called the *complementary solution* of the inhomogeneous differential equation $L[y] = g(x)$.

**Example 13.44** The differential equation $L[y] = y'' + 9y = e^x$ has the complementary solution

$$y_c(x) = c_1\cos 3x + c_2\sin 3x$$

and a particular solution

$$y_p(x) = e^x/4.$$

Hence,

$$y(x) = y_c(x) + y_p(x) = c_1\cos 3x + c_2\sin 3x + e^x/4$$

is the general solution of $L[y] = e^x$.

**Example 13.45** The third-order inhomogeneous differential equation

$$L[y] = y'''(x) - 3y'(x) - 2y(x) = \sin x$$

has the three solutions of $L[y] = 0$:

$$y_1(x) = e^{-x}, \; y_2(x) = xe^{-x}, \quad \text{and} \quad y_3(x) = e^{2x}.$$

The Wronskian is nonzero,

*In[129]:=*
```
Clear[x,y1,y2,y3];
y1[x_]:= Exp[-x];
y2[x_]:= x*Exp[-x];
y3[x_]:= Exp[2*x];
wronskian[{y1[x],y2[x],y3[x]},x]
```

*Out[133]=*
```
9
```

Hence, the functions are linearly independent and the complementary solution is

$$y_c(x) = c_1 e^{-x} + c_2 x e^{-x} + c_3 e^{2x}.$$

We check this by showing $L[y_c(x)] = 0$ in the following calculation,

*In[134]:=*
```
Clear[yc,x];
yc[x_]:= c1*y1[x]  +  c2*y2[x]  +  c3*y3[x];
yc'''[x]  -  3*yc'[x]  -  2*yc[x]  ==  0 //Simplify
```

*Out[136]=*
```
True
```

It can also be shown that

$$y_p(x) = \frac{1}{5}\cos x - \frac{1}{10}\sin x$$

is a particular solution of $L[y] = \sin x$. We check this with *Mathematica.*

*In[137]:=*
```
Clear[yp,x];
yp[x_]:= 1/5*Cos[x]  -  1/10*Sin[x];
yp'''[x]  -  3*yp'[x]  -  2*yp[x]  ==  Sin[x]  //Simplify
```

*Out[139]=*
```
True
```

Hence the general solution of $L[y] = \sin x$ is

$$y(x) = y_c(x) + y_p(x)$$
$$= c_1 e^{-x} + c_2 x e^{-x} + c_3 e^{2x} + \frac{1}{5}\cos x - \frac{1}{10}\sin x$$

Again, we check this by showing that $y(x)$ satisfies the differential equation.

*In[140]:=*
```
Clear[y,x];
y[x_]:= yc[x] + yp[x];
y'''[x] - 3*y'[x] - 2*y[x] == Sin[x] //Simplify
```

*Out[142]=*
```
True
```

## EXERCISES

1. Verify that

$$y(x) = c_1 \frac{1}{x} + c_2 x + c_3 x^2 + \cos x - \frac{\sin x}{x}$$

is the general solution of

$$y''' + \frac{1}{x} y'' - \frac{2}{x^2} y' + \frac{2}{x^3} y = \sin x,\ x > 0$$

Identify $y_c(x)$ and $y_p(x)$.

2. Verify that

$$y(x) = c_1 x + c_2 x^3 + c_3 x^{-2} - (5/6)x - 5x\log x$$

is the general solution of

$$x^3 y''' + x^2 y'' - 6xy' + 6y = 30x.$$

Identify $y_c(x)$ and $y_p(x)$.

3. Verify that

$$y(x) = c_1 \cos 2x + c_2 \sin 2x + (3/4)x^3 - (9/8)x$$

is the general solution of

$$y'' + 4y = 3x.$$

Identify $y_c(x)$ and $y_p(x)$.

### 13.3.3 Finding the general solution of $L[y] = 0$

Consider a first-order linear homogeneous differential equation

$$L[y] = a_1 \frac{dy}{dx} + a_0 y = 0$$

where $a_1$ and $a_0$ are constants. The differential equation has a solution

$$y(x) = e^{rx}$$

where $r = -a_0/a_1$. In particular, the solution is an exponential function. Can we expect similar exponential functions to be a solution for higher-order linear differential equations?

Consider the case of an $n$th-order differential equation

$$L[y] = a_n y^{(n)} + a_{n-1} y^{(n-1)} + \ldots + a_1 y' + a_0 y = 0$$

where $a_0, a_1, \ldots, a_n$ are constants. Suppose $e^{rx}$ is a solution where $r$ is some constant. Substituting $y(x) = e^{rx}$ in $L[y] = 0$, we have

$$L[e^{rx}] = a r^n e^{rx} + a_{n-1} r^{n-1} e^{rx} + \ldots + a_1 r e^{rx} + a_0 e^{rx} = 0.$$

This implies that

$$[a_n r^n + a_{n-1} r^{n-1} + \ldots + a_1 r + a_0] e^{rx} = 0.$$

Since $e^{rx} \neq 0$, $r$ must satisfy the polynomial equation

$$P(r) = a_n r^n + a_{n-1} r^{n-1} + \ldots + a_1 r + a_0 = 0.$$

Hence, if $y(x) = e^{rx}$ is a solution of $L[y] = 0$, then the constant $r$ must be a root of the polynomial, $P(r)$. The polynomial is called the *characteristic* or *auxiliary polynomial* of $L[y] = 0$.

Let $r_1, \ldots, r_n$ denote the roots of the characteristic equation. These roots can be real or complex, and distinct or repeated. In the case that all of the roots are real and distinct, i.e., $r_1 \neq r_2 \neq \ldots \neq r_n$, each root generates a solution of $L[y] = 0$. That is,

$$y_1(x) = e^{r_1 x},\ y_2(x) = e^{r_2 x},\ \ldots,\ y_n(x) = e^{r_n x}$$

are solutions. Futhermore, it can be shown, using the Wronskian, that they are linearly independent. Here are Wronskian calculations for $n = 3$.

*In[143]:=*

```
Clear[r1,r2,r3,x,y1,y2,y3];
y1[x_]:=  Exp[r1*x];
y2[x_]:=  Exp[r2*x];
y3[x_]:=  Exp[r3*x];
wronskian[{y1[x],y2[x],y3[x]},x]  //Simplify
```

*Out[147]=*

$E^{(r1+r2+r3)x}(-r1 + r2)(r1 - r3)(r2 - r3)$

Note that $W(x) \neq 0$ if $r_1 \neq r_2 \neq r_3$. Having the $n$ linearly independent solutions, we can form the general solution of $L[y] = 0$ as the linear combination

$$y(x) = c_1 e^{r_1 x} + c_2 e^{r_2 x} + \ldots + c_n e^{r_n x}$$

where $c_1, \ldots, c_n$ are arbitrary constants.

**Example 13.46** Find the general solution of the differential equation

$$L[y] = y''' - 2y'' - y' + 2y = 0.$$

The characteristic equation is

$$P(r) = r^3 - 2r^2 - r + 2 = 0.$$

We find the roots of the characteristic polynomial.

*In[148]:=*

```
Clear[p,r];
p[r_]:= r^3  -  2*r^2  -  r  +  2;
Solve[p[r]==0,r]
```

*Out[150]=*

{{r → −1}, {r → 1}, {r → 2}}

The three roots are real and distinct. Each one will generate a linearly independent solution of $L[y] = 0$. These solutions are $y_1(x) = e^{-x}$, $y_2(x) = e^x$, and $y_3(x) = e^{2x}$. The general solution is therefore

$$y(x) = c_1 e^{-x} + c_2 e^x + c_3 e^{2x}.$$

The arbitrary constants $c_1$, $c_2$, and $c_3$ are determined by three initial conditions, say $y(0) = 6$, $y'(0) = 5$, and $y''(0) = 15$.

*In[151]:=*

```
Clear[c1,c2,c3,y,x];
y[x_]:= c1*Exp[-x]+c2*Exp[x]+c3*Exp[2*x];
Solve[{y[0]==6,  y'[0]==5,  y''[0]==15},{c1,c2,c3}]
```

*Out[153]=*

{{c1 → 2, c2 → 1, c3 → 3}}

The particular solution is then

$$y(x) = 2e^{-x} + e^x + 3e^{2x}.$$

We plot the particular solution of the differential equation.

*In[154]:=*

```
Plot[y[x] /.{c1->2,c2->1,c3->3},{x,-2,3},
          AxesLabel->{"x","y(x)"}];
```

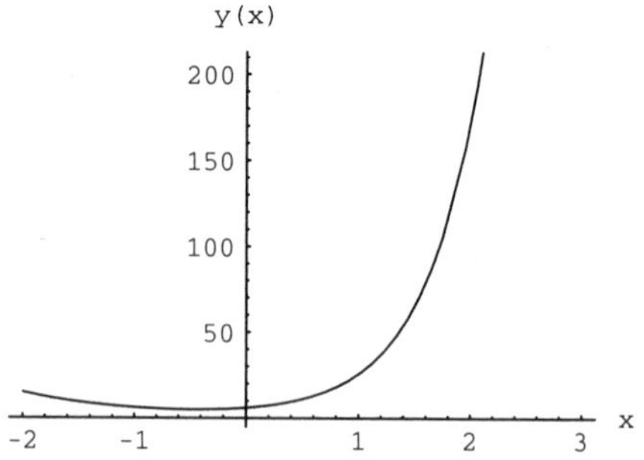


Now suppose that the roots of the characteristic equation $P(x) = 0$ are real, but not all distinct. For example, the third-order differential equation

$$L[y] = y''' - 4y'' + 5y' - 2y = 0$$

has the characteristic equation

$$P(r) = r^3 - 4r^2 + 5r - 2 = (r-1)^2(r-2) = 0.$$

It has two repeated roots, $r_1 = r_2 = 1$, and a distinct root $r_3 = 2$. These roots generate three solutions, $y_1(x) = e^x$, $y_2(x) = e^x$, and $y_3(x) = e^{2x}$. It is obvious that $y_1(x)$ and $y_2(x)$ are not linearly independent functions. Any linear combination of the three functions results in only two arbitrary constants, not three as required for a third-order differential equation. That is,

$$\begin{aligned} y(x) &= c_1 e^x + c_2 e^x + c_3 e^{2x} \\ &= (c_1 + c_2)e^x + c_3 e^{2x} \\ &= c_0 e^x + c_3 e^{2x} \end{aligned}$$

How do we then generate an additional linearly independent solution function in the case of repeated roots? The following theorem provides the answer to this question.

**THEOREM 13.5** *Suppose r is a root of multiplicity k of the characteristic equation $P(r) = 0$ for $L[y] = 0$. Then $e^{rx}, xe^{rx}, x^2e^{rx}, x^3e^{rx}, \ldots, x^{k-1}e^{rx}$ are linearly independent solutions of $L[y] = 0$.*

This theorem is not difficult to prove and we will leave the proof as an exercise.

Theorem 13.5 allows us to "fill in" the necessary number of linearly independent solutions when we have a repeated root of the auxiliary polynomial.

**Example 13.47** Find the general solution of

$$L[y] = y^{(7)} + y^{(6)} - 6y^{(5)} - 6y^{(4)} + 9y''' + 9y'' - 4y' - 4y = 0$$

The characteristic polynomial is

$P(r) = r^7 + r^6 - 6r^5 - 6r^4 + 9r^3 + 9r^2 - 4r - 4.$

The roots are,

*In[155]:=*
```
Clear[p,r];
p[r_]:= r^7+r^6-6*r^5-6*r^4+9*r^3+9*r^2-4*r-4;
Solve[p[r]==0,r]
```

*Out[157]=*
```
{{r → -2}, {r → -1}, {r → -1}, {r → -1}, {r → 1}, {r → 1}, {r → 2}}
```

The seven roots are −2,2,−1,−1,−1,1,1. $r_1 = -2$, and $r_2 = 2$ are distinct. $r_3 = r_4 = r_5 = -1$ and $r_6 = r_7 = 1$ are repeated roots. Corresponding to the the distinct roots, we have the solutions

$y_1(x) = e^{-2x},\ y_2(x) = e^{2x}.$

To obtain the three linearly independent solutions from the repeated root $r_3 = r_4 = r_5 = -1$ of multiplicity 3, we form the solutions:

$y_3(x) = e^{-x},\ y_4(x) = xe^{-x},\ y_5(x) = x^2e^{-x}.$

Finally, with respect to the double root $r_6 = r_7 = 1$, we have the solutions:

$y_6(x) = e^{x},\ y_7(x) = xe^{x}.$

The general solution is therefore the linear combination of these solutions with seven arbitrary constants:

$y(x) = c_1e^{-2x} + c_2e^{2x} + c_3e^{-x} + c_4xe^{-x} + c_5x^2e^{-x} + c_6e^{x} + c_7xe^{x}.$

It is certainly a possibility for the roots of the characteristic polynomial to be complex numbers. For example, the differential equation

$L[y] = y'' - 2y' + 5y = 0$

has the characteristic polynomial $P(r) = r^2 - 2r + 5$ which has the complex roots

$r_1 = 1 + 2i, \quad \text{and} \quad r_2 = 1 - 2i.$

Since these two complex roots are distinct, each root generates a solution,

$y_1(x) = e^{(1+2i)x},\ y_2(x) = e^{(1-2i)x}$

Since $y_1(x)$ and $y_2(x)$ are linearly independent, the general solution must be

$y(x) = c_1e^{(1+2i)x} + c_2e^{(1-2i)x}$

However, this solution appears to be complex-valued and is not a satisfactory answer.

In general, suppose the characteristic polynomial, $P(r)$, of a second-order linear differential equation, $L[y] = 0$, has a pair of roots of the form:

$r_1 = h + iv,\ r_2 = h - iv$

The general solution can be written as

$$\begin{aligned} y(x) &= k_1 e^{(h+iv)x} + k_2 e^{(h-iv)x} \\ &= e^{hx}[k_1 e^{ivx} + k_2 e^{-ivx}]. \end{aligned}$$

Notice that we change the notations for the arbitrary constants to $k_1$ and $k_2$. The exponential functions in the brackets can be expressed in terms of trigonometric functions using the *Euler formula*:

$$e^{i\theta} = \cos\theta + i\sin\theta.$$

Rewriting the general solution, using the Euler formula, we have

$$\begin{aligned} y(x) &= e^{hx}[k_1(\cos vx + i\sin vx) + k_2(\cos vx - i\sin vx)] \\ &= e^{hx}[(k_1 + k_2)\cos vx + (k_1 - k_2)i\sin vx] \end{aligned}$$

Letting $c_1 = (k_1 + k_2)$ and $c_2 = (k_1 - k_2)i$, general solution becomes

$$y(x) = e^{hx}[c_1\cos vx + c_2\sin vx]$$

The general solution can be interpreted as a linear combination of two linearly independent solution, $y(x) = c_1y_1(x) + c_2y_2(x)$, where

$$y_1(x) = e^{hx}\cos vx, \quad \text{and} \quad y_2(x) = e^{hx}\sin vx$$

An alternate form for the general solution

$$y(x) = Ce^{hx}\cos(vx - \delta)$$

where $C$ and $\delta$ are the real arbitrary constants and are related to the constants $c_1$ and $c_2$ by the equations:

$$C = \sqrt{c_1^2 + c_2^2} \quad \text{and} \quad \tan\delta = \frac{c_2}{c_1}$$

**Example 13.48** Find the solution of the initial-value problem

$$L[y] = y''' - 3y'' + 9y' + 13y = 0$$

such that $y(0) = 2$, $y'(0) = 1$, and $y''(0) = 50$. The characteristic polynomial in this case is

$$P(r) = r^3 - 3r^2 + 9r + 13$$

and it has the roots, $r_1 = -1$, $r_2 = 2 + 3i$, $r_3 = 2 - 3i$ as can be seen from the following *Mathematica* calculation.

*In[158]:=*

```
Clear[p,r];
p[r_]:= r^3 - 3*r^2 + 9*r + 13;
Solve[p[r]==0,r]
```

*Out[160]=*

```
{{r → -1}, {r → 2 - 3I}, {r → 2 + 3I}}
```

For the distinct real root $r_1 = -1$, we have the solution $y_1(x) = e^{-x}$. For the pair of conjugate complex roots $r_2$ and $r_3$, we have the two linearly independent solutions

$$y_2(x) = e^{2x}\cos 3x,\ y_3(x) = e^{2x}\sin 3x.$$

The general solution is therefore

$$y(x) = c_1 e^{-x} + c_2 e^{2x}\cos 3x + c_3 e^{2x}\sin 3x$$

or

$$y(x) = c_1 e^{-x} + C e^{2x}\cos(3x - \delta).$$

To find the particular solution, we set

$$y(0) = 2,\ y'(0) = 1, \quad \text{and} \quad y''(0) = 50$$

and solve for the arbitrary constants, $c_1$, $c_2$, and $c_3$.

*In[161]:=*

```
Clear[c1,c2,c3,y,x];
y[x_]:=c1*Exp[-x]+c2*Exp[2*x]*Cos[3*x]+c3*Exp[2*x]*Sin[3*x];
Solve[{y[0]==2, y'[0]==1, y''[0]==50},{c1,c2,c3}]
```

*Out[163]=*

```
{{c3 → 3, c1 → 4, c2 → -2}}
```

From the above calculation, we have the solution of the initial-value problem:

$$y(x) = 4e^{-x} - 2e^{2x}\cos 3x + 3e^{2x}\sin 3x.$$

This solution is plotted below.

*In[164]:=*

```
Plot[y[x] /. {c1->4,c2->-2,c3->3},{x,-2,3},
        AxesLabel->{"x","y(x)"}];
```

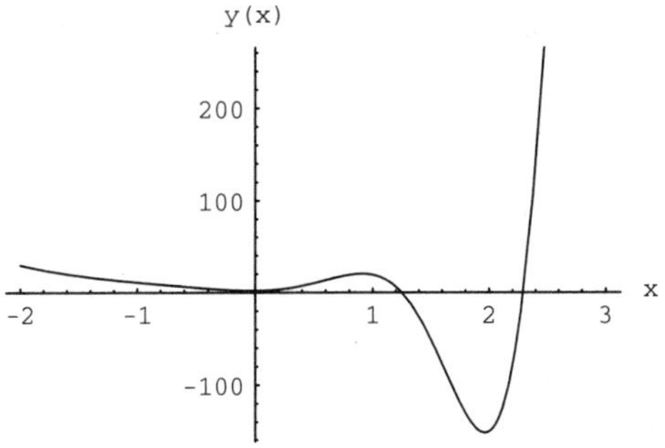

We have seen how to construct the general solution of $L[y] = 0$ when the roots of the characteristic equation are real distinct, real repeated, and complex distinct. If we have repeated complex roots, the we proceed in a manner that is similar to the real repeated case.

Suppose $r = h \pm iv$ are complex roots of multiplicity $k$. Corresponding to these $2k$ roots, the following are then $2k$ linearly independent solutions of $L[y] = 0$:

$$\begin{array}{ll} y_1(x) = e^{hx}\cos vx, & y_2(x) = e^{hx}\sin vx \\ y_3(x) = xe^{hx}\cos vx, & y_4(x) = xe^{hx}\sin vx \\ y_5(x) = x^2e^{hx}\cos vx, & y_6(x) = x^2e^{hx}\sin vx \\ \dots\dots\dots & \dots\dots\dots \\ y_{2k-1}(x) = x^{k-1}e^{hx}\cos vx, & y_{2k}(x) = x^{k-1}e^{hx}\sin vx. \end{array}$$

**Example 13.49** Find the general solution of

$$L[y] = y^{(6)} - 5y^{(5)} + 32y''' - 84y'' + 92y' - 48y = 0$$

Using *Mathematica*, we calculate the roots of the characteristic polynomial

$$P(r) = r^6 - 5r^5 + 32r^3 - 84r^2 + 92r - 48.$$

*In[165]:=*

```
Clear[r,p];
p[r_]:=r^6  -  5*r^5  +  32*r^3  -  84*r^2  +  92*r  -  48;
Solve[p[r]==0,r]
```

*Out[167]=*

```
{{r → -3}, {r → 1 - I}, {r → 1 - I}, {r → 1 + I}, {r → 1 + I}, {r → 4}}
```

Hence, we have two real distinct roots, −3 and 4, and two complex roots, $1 \pm i$, of multiplicity 2. Linearly independent solutions are therefore

$$\begin{array}{ll} y_1(x) = e^{-3x}, & y_2(x) = e^{4x}, \\ y_3(x) = e^{x}\cos x, & y_4(x) = e^{x}\sin x, \\ y_5(x) = xe^{x}\cos x, & y_6(x) = xe^{x}\sin x. \end{array}$$

The general solution is

$$y(x) = c_1e^{-3x} + c_2e^{4x} + e^x(c_3\cos x + c_4\sin x) + xe^x(c_5\cos x + c_6\sin x).$$

A remark is in order about the general solutions $y(x)$ derived from the conjugate complex roots, $r = h \pm iv$:

$$\begin{aligned} y(x) &= k_1e^{(h+iv)x} + k_2e^{(h-iv)x} \\ &= c_1e^{hx}\cos vx + c_2e^{hx}\sin vx. \end{aligned}$$

By Euler's formula,

$$\begin{aligned} e^{(h+iv)x} &= e^{hx}\cos(vx) + ie^{hx}\sin(vx) \\ &= \mathrm{Re}\{e^{(h+iv)x}\} + i\,\mathrm{Im}\{e^{(h+iv)x}\} \end{aligned}$$

where *Re* and *Im* are the real part and imaginary part of their argument, respectively. This calculation can be done by *Mathematica* using the built-in functions **Re**, **Im**, and **ComplexExpand**.

*In[168]:=*

```
Clear[r,h,v,x,f];
f[x] = Exp[(h+v*I)*x];
ComplexExpand[Re[f[x]]]
```

*Out[170]=*

$E^{hx}Cos[v\,x]$

*In[171]:=*

```
ComplexExpand[Im[f[x]]]
```

*Out[171]=*

$E^{hx}Sin[v\,x]$

## EXERCISES

1. Find the general solution for each of the following differential equations:
   (a) $y'' + 7y = 0$
   (b) $2y'' + 2y' + 9y = 0$
   (c) $y''' + y'' - 4y' - 4y = 0$
2. Solve the initial-value problem:

   $$y''' - 3y'' + 3y' - y = 0,$$
   $$y(0) = 1,\ y'(0) = -2,\ y''(0) = 0$$

3. For the second order differential equation

   $$ay'' + by' + cy = 0$$

   where $a$, $b$, and $c$ are constants, show that every solution must approach zero as $x \to +\infty$, when $b > 0$.

### 13.3.4 Finding the general solution of $L[y] = g(x)$

From the theory section, we know that in order to find the general solution of the inhomogeneous differential equation $L[y] = g(x)$, we must find the general solution of $L[y] = 0$, $y_c(x)$, the complementary solution, and any particular solution of the inhomogeneous differential equation $L[y] = g(x)$, $y_p(x)$. The general solution of the inhomogeneous differential equation is then $y(x) = y_c(x) + y_p(x)$. In this section, we present the method of *Variation of Parameters* for finding a particular solution of $L[y] = g(x)$.

Consider a second-order linear differential equation,

$$L[y] = y''(x) + a_1 y'(x) + a_0 y(x) = g(x)$$

Note that we have normalized the coefficient of $y''(x)$ to 1. Assume that $y_1(x)$ and $y_2(x)$ are the two linearly independent solutions of $L[y] = 0$. We seek a particular solution of $L[y] = g(x)$ in the form:

$$y_p(x) = u_1(x)y_1(x) + u_2(x)y_2(x)$$

where $u_1(x)$ and $u_2(x)$ are two unknown functions to be determined. These functions will be determined by substituting $y_p(x)$ into the differential equation.

Differentiating the particular solution with respect to $x$, we calculate

$$\begin{aligned} y_p' &= u_1'y_1 + u_1y_1' + u_2'y_2 + u_2y_2' \\ &= (u_1'y_1 + u_2'y_2) + u_1y_1' + u_2y_2'. \end{aligned}$$

The above derivative is very complicated since it involves so many terms. To reduce the complexity, we choose the functions $u_1(x)$ and $u_2(x)$ so that

$$u_1'y_1 + u_2'y_2 = 0.$$

This greatly simplifies the derivative of $y_p(x)$:

$$y_p' = u_1y_1' + u_2y_2'.$$

Taking the derivative of $y_p'(x)$ with respect to $x$, we have

$$y_p'' = u_1'y_1' + u_1y_1'' + u_2'y_2' + u_2y_2''.$$

Substituting $y_p$, $y_p'$, and $y_p''$ into the inhomogeneous equation, $L[y_p] = g(x)$, we find

$$(u_1'y_1' + u_1y_1'' + u_2'y_2' + u_2y_2'') + a_1(u_1y_1' + u_2y_2') + a_0(u_1y_1 + u_2y_2) = g(x).$$

Rearranging terms,

$$u_1(y_1'' + a_1y_1' + a_0y_1) + u_2(y_2'' + a_1y_2' + a_0y_2) + (u_1'y_1' + u_2'y_2') = g(x),$$

the first two terms are zero since $y_1$ and $y_2$ are solutions of the homogeneous equation $L[y] = 0$. Hence, the equation can be simplified to

$$u_1'y_1' + u_2'y_2' = g(x).$$

This equation and the assumptions we made in choosing $u_1(x)$ and $u_2(x)$ constitute a system of linear equations in $u_1'(x)$ and $u_2'(x)$:

$$\begin{aligned} &u_1'(x)y_1(x) + u_2'(x)y_2(x) = 0 \\ &u_1'(x)y_1'(x) + u_2'(x)y_2'(x) = g(x) \end{aligned}$$

Using Cramer's rule to solve for $u_1'$ and $u_2'$, we have

$$u_1' = \frac{\begin{vmatrix} 0 & y_2 \\ g(x) & y_2' \end{vmatrix}}{\begin{vmatrix} y_1 & y_2 \\ y_1' & y_2' \end{vmatrix}}; \quad u_2' = \frac{\begin{vmatrix} y_1 & 0 \\ y_1' & g(x) \end{vmatrix}}{\begin{vmatrix} y_1 & y_2 \\ y_1' & y_2' \end{vmatrix}}$$

The denominator in these fractions is the Wronskian $W(x)$ of $y_1(x)$ and $y_2(x)$. Since $y_1(x)$ and $y_2(x)$ are linearly independent solutions of $L[y]=0$, $W(x)$ is never zero. Once $u_1'(x)$ and $u_2'(x)$ are obtained, we can find $u_1(x)$ and $u_2(x)$ by integration. Defining

$$W_1(x) = \begin{vmatrix} 0 & y_2 \\ g(x) & y_2' \end{vmatrix}; \; W_2(x) = \begin{vmatrix} y_1 & 0 \\ y_1' & g(x) \end{vmatrix}; \; W(x) = \begin{vmatrix} y_1 & y_2 \\ y_1' & y_2' \end{vmatrix}$$

the expressions for $u_1(x)$ and $u_2(x)$ are

$$u_1(x) = \int \frac{W_1(x)}{W(x)} \mathrm{d}x; \; u_2(x) = \int \frac{W_2(x)}{W(x)} \mathrm{d}x.$$

The particular solution of the inhomogeneous linear differential equation $L[y] = g(x)$ is

$$\begin{aligned} y_p(x) &= u_1(x) y_1(x) + u_2(x) y_2(x) \\ &= y_1(x) \int \frac{W_1(x)}{W(x)} \mathrm{d}x + y_2(x) \int \frac{W_2(x)}{W(x)} \mathrm{d}x. \end{aligned}$$

This method of finding the particular solution is called *Variation of Parameters* and gives a formula for a particular solution of the inhomogeneous differential equation.

**Example 13.50** Find the the general solution of

$$L[y] = y'' + 9y = \sin x$$

We first find the complementary solution to $L[y] = 0$ by finding the roots of the characteristic polynomial, $P(r) = r^2 + 9$.

*In[172]:=*

```
Clear[r,p];
p[r_]:= r^2 + 9;
Solve[p[r]==0,r]
```

*Out[174]=*

```
{{r → -3 I}, {r → 3 I}}
```

Since the roots are complex, we have two linearly independent solutions: $y_1(x) = \cos 3x$ and $y_2(x) = \sin 3x$ which imply that the complementary solution is

$$y_c(x) = c_1 \cos 3x + c_2 \sin 3x.$$

*In[175]:=*

```
Clear[c1,c2,y1,y2,x];
y1[x_]:= Cos[3*x]; y2[x_]:= Sin[3*x];
yc[x_] = c1*y1[x] + c2*y2[x]
```

*Out[177]=*

```
c1 Cos[3x] + c2 Sin[3x]
```

Now we find a particular solution of the inhomogeneous problem $L[y] = g(x)$ using the method of Variation of Parameters. We must evaluate the formula

$$y_p(x) = y_1(x)\int\frac{W_1(x)}{W(x)}\mathrm{d}x + y_2(x)\int\frac{W_2(x)}{W(x)}\mathrm{d}x.$$

We use the **MathEcon** function, **wronskian**, to calculate the Wronskian $W(x)$. The other determinants, $W_1(x)$ and $W_2(x)$, are evaluated by the *Mathematica* function **Det**.

*In[178]:=*

```
Clear[g,x,W,W1,W2,yp];
g[x_]:=  Sin[x];
W[x_]:=  wronskian[{y1[x],y2[x]},x];
W1[x_]:=  Det[{{0,y2[x]},{g[x],y2'[x]}}];
W2[x_]:=  Det[{{y1[x],0},{y1'[x],g[x]}}];
yp[x_]  =  y1[x]*Integrate[W1[x]/W[x],x]  +
           y2[x]*Integrate[W2[x]/W[x],x]
```

*Out[183]=*

$$\frac{(2\mathrm{Cos}[2x] - \mathrm{Cos}[4x])\,\mathrm{Sin}[3x]}{24} + \frac{\mathrm{Cos}[3x]\,(-2\mathrm{Sin}[2x] + \mathrm{Sin}[4x])}{24}$$

The general solution is then the sum of the complementary solution and this particular solution. That is,

*In[184]:=*

```
Clear[y];
y[x_]  =  yc[x]  +  yp[x]
```

*Out[185]=*

$$\mathrm{c1Cos}[3x] + C_2\mathrm{Sin}[3x] + \frac{(2\mathrm{Cos}[2x] - \mathrm{Cos}[4x])\mathrm{Sin}[3x]}{24} + \frac{\mathrm{Cos}[3x]\,(-2\mathrm{Sin}[2x] + \mathrm{Sin}[4x])}{24}$$

The variation of parameters formula can be generalized to higher order linear differential equations

$$L[y] = y^{(n)}(x) + a_{n-1}y^{(n-1)}(x) + \ldots + a_1y'(x) + a_0y(x) = g(x)$$

If $y_1(x), y_2(x), \ldots, y_n(x)$ are linearly independent solutions of the homogeneous equation, $L[y] = 0$, then one can use the arguments above to show that a particular solution of the inhomogeneous equation, $L[y] = g(x)$ is given by

$$y_p(x) = y_1(x)\int\frac{W_1(x)}{W(x)}dx + y_2(x)\int\frac{W_2(x)}{W(x)}dx + \ldots + y_n(x)\int\frac{W_n(x)}{W(x)}dx$$

where $W(x)$ is the Wronskian of the functions $y_1(x), y_2(x), \ldots, y_n(x)$ and the numerators in the integrals are the determinants

$$W_i(x) = \begin{vmatrix} y_1 & \ldots & y_{i-1} & 0 & y_{i+1} & \ldots & y_n \\ y_1' & \ldots & y_{i-1}' & 0 & y_{i+1}' & \ldots & y_n' \\ y_1'' & \ldots & y_{i-1}'' & 0 & y_{i+1}'' & \ldots & y_n'' \\ \ldots & \ldots & \ldots & \ldots & \ldots & \ldots & \ldots \\ y_1^{(n-1)} & \ldots & y_{i-1}^{(n-1)} & g(x) & y_{i+1}^{(n-1)} & \ldots & y_n^{(n-1)} \end{vmatrix};\ i = 1,2, \ldots, n$$

The **MathEcon** function, **wis**, computes these $W_i(x)$'s determinants.

*In[186]:=*

```
?wis
```

**wis[fct,fctlst,var] computes the determinants that are used in the Variation of Parameters Method. For example,**

**wis[Exp[x],{1,x,x^2},x].**

The first argument of **wis** is the right-side of the differential equation, the second argument is a list of the linearly independent solutions of L[y] = 0, and the third argument is the independent variable. The output of **wis** is a list that contains the functions $W_1(x), \ldots, W_n(x)$.

**Example 13.51** Find the general solution of

$$L[y] = y''' - y'' - y' + y = e^x$$

We first find the general solution of $L[y] = 0$. The roots of the characteristic equation are −1, 1, and 1.

*In[187]:=*

```
Clear[r,p];
p[r_]:= r^3  - r^2  - r + 1;
Solve[p[r]==0,r]
```

*Out[189]=*

$\{\{r \to -1\}, \{r \to 1\}, \{r \to 1\}\}$

Since the roots are real with one of the roots repeated, the three linearly independent solutions are: $y_1(x) = e^{-x}$, $y_2(x) = e^x$, and $y_3(x) = xe^x$. The complementary solution is therefore

$$y_c(x) = c_1e^{-x} + c_2e^x + c_3xe^x.$$

*In[190]:=*

```
Clear[x,y1,y2,y3,yc];
y1[x_]:= Exp[-x]; y2[x_]:= Exp[x]; y3[x_]:= x*Exp[x];
yc[x_]  = c1*y1[x]  + c2*y2[x]  + c3*y3[x]
```

*Out[192]=*

$\frac{c1}{E^x} + c2E^x + c3E^x x$

Using the function, **wis**, we calculate the determinants: $W_1(x) = e^{3x}$, $W_2(x) = -e^x - 2xe^x$, and $W_3(x) = 2e^x$.

*In[193]:=*

```
{W1[x],W2[x],W3[x]}  =  wis[Exp[x],{y1[x],y2[x],y3[x]},x]
```

*Out[193]=*

$\{E^{3x}, -E^x - 2E^x x, 2E^x\}$

Having these parts of the Variation of Parameters formula, we can calculate the particular solution by integrating.

*In[194]:=*

```
Clear[W,yp];
W[x_]  =  wronskian[{y1[x],y2[x],y3[x]},x];
yp[x_]  =  y1[x]*Integrate[W1[x]/W[x],x]  +
           y2[x]*Integrate[W2[x]/W[x],x]  +
           y3[x]*Integrate[W3[x]/W[x],x]  //  Simplify
```

*Out[196]=*

$$\frac{E^x(1 - 2x + 2x^2)}{8}$$

The general solution is therefore $y(x) = y_c(x) + y_p(x)$.

*In[197]:=*

```
Clear[y];
y[x_]  =  yc[x]  +  yp[x]
```

*Out[198]=*

$$\frac{c1}{E^x} + c2E^x + c3E^x x + \frac{E^x(1 - 2x + 2x^2)}{8}$$

## EXERCISES

1. Find the general solution of the following differential equations:
   (a) $y'' - 9y = 9xe^{-3x}$
   (b) $2y''' - 6y'' = x^2$
   (c) $y^{(4)} - y = \sin x$
2. Find the solution of the initial-value problem

   $$y^{(4)} - y''' = x + e^x$$

   with $y(0) = 0$, $y'(0) = 2$, $y''(0) = 0$, $y'''(0) = 1$.

## □ 13.4 Solving Differential Equations with *Mathematica* □

The built-in *Mathematica* function **DSolve** is capable of solving many differential equations. There is also a *Mathematica* package, called **DSolve**, that vastly expands the capabilities of the **DSolve** function to solve differential equations (both linear and nonlinear). We first discuss the funtion **DSolve** in its basic form.

### 13.4.1 The **DSolve** function

The **DSolve** function can be used to find the general solution of a differential equation. Here is *Mathematica*'s description of this function.

*In[199]:=*

```
?DSolve
```

**DSolve[eqn, y[x], x] solves a differential equation for the functions y[x], with independent variable x. DSolve[{eqn1, eqn2, ...}, {y1[x1, ...], ...}, {x1, ...}] solves a list of differential equations.**

The first argument contains the differential equation as an equation i.e., specified with ==. The second argument contains the dependent variable (including its argument), and the last argument is the independent variable.

**Example 13.52** Find the general solution of

$$y' - 2y = 4x.$$

*In[200]:=*

```
Clear[x,y];
gensol = DSolve[y'[x]-2*y[x]==4*x,y[x],x]
```

*Out[201]=*

$$\{\{y[x] \to -1 - 2x + E^{2x}C[1]\}\}$$

The **DSolve** function uses the reserved symbol **C** for arbitrary constants. The general solution of this differential equation is therefore

$$y = -1 - 2x + c_1 e^{2x}$$

where $c_1$ is an arbitrary constant. Let us define the symbol **y[x]** to be the solution obtained by **DSolve**.

*In[202]:=*

```
y[x_] = y[x] /. gensol[[1]]
```

*Out[202]=*

$$-1 - 2x + E^{2x}C[1]$$

**Example 13.53** Find the general solution of

$$y^{(4)} - 8y^{(3)} + 26y'' - 32y' + 13y = 2x.$$

*In[203]:=*

```
Clear[x,y,L];
L = D[y[x],{x,4}] - 8*D[y[x],{x,3}] + 26*y''[x] -
      32*y'[x] + 13*y[x];
DSolve[L == 2x, y[x], x]
```

*Out[205]=*

$$\{\{y[x] \to \frac{64}{169} + \frac{2x}{13} + E^{x}C[1] + E^{x}xC[2] + E^{3x}C[4]Cos[2x] - E^{3x}C[3]Sin[2x]\}\}$$

**DSolve** can also solve initial-value problems. The only difference is that the first argument is a list that contains the differential equation and the initial conditions.

**Example 13.54** Find the solution of the initial-value problem

$$y''' - y' = 0$$

such that $y(0) = 1$, $y'(0) = 0$, and $y''(0) = -3$.

*In[206]:=*
```
Clear[x,y];
gensol = DSolve[{y'''[x]-y'[x]==0,
           y[0]==1,y'[0]==0,y''[0]==-3},y[x],x]
```

*Out[207]=*

$$\{\{y[x] \to 4 - \frac{3}{2E^x} - \frac{3E^x}{2}\}\}$$

We can then plot the solution of the initial-value problem.

*In[208]:=*
```
y[x_] = y[x] /. gensol[[1]];
Plot[y[x],{x,-2,2},AxesLabel->{"x","y(x)"}];
```

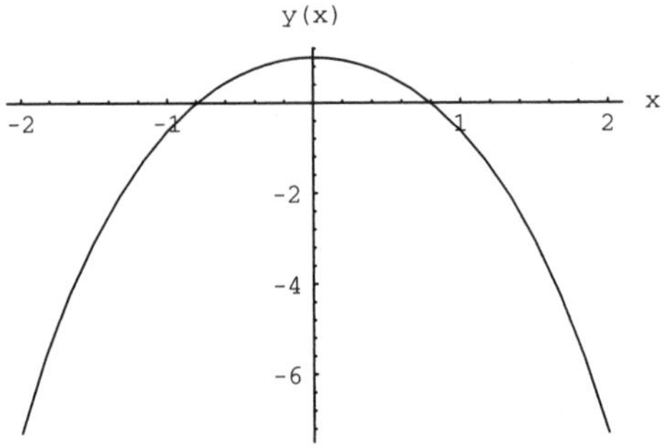


**Example 13.55** The capital–labor ratio $k(t)$ of the Solow growth model given in example 13.35 in section 13.2.3 satisfies the autonomous differential equation

$$k'(t) = sk(t)^a - rk(t).$$

We use the **DSolve** function to find its general solution

*In[210]:=*
```
Clear[k,t,a,r,s];
DSolve[k'[t]==s*k[t]^a-r*k[t],k[t],t]
```

*Out[211]=*

$$\{\{k[t] \to (\frac{s}{r} + E^{(-1+a)rt}\, C[1])^{1/(1-a)}\}\}$$

That is

$$k(t) = \left[\frac{s}{r} + c_1 e^{(a-1)rt}\right]^{1/(1-a)}$$

where $c_1$ is an arbitrary constant. Suppose $a = 0.4$, $r = 0.02$, and $s = 0.1$. The solution of the initial-value problem with $k(0) = 3$ can be computed.

*In[212]:=*

```
a=0.4;r=0.02;s=0.1;
gensol=DSolve[{k'[t]==s*k[t]^a-r*k[t],k[0]==3},k[t],t]
```

*Out[213]=*

$$\{\{k[t] \to 1.\ (5. - \frac{3.06682}{E^{0.012t}})^{1.66667}\}\}$$

We plot the growth path of $k(t)$.

*In[214]:=*

```
k[t_]= k[t] /. gensol[[1]];
Plot[k[t],{t,0,500},AxesLabel->{"t","k(t)"}];
```

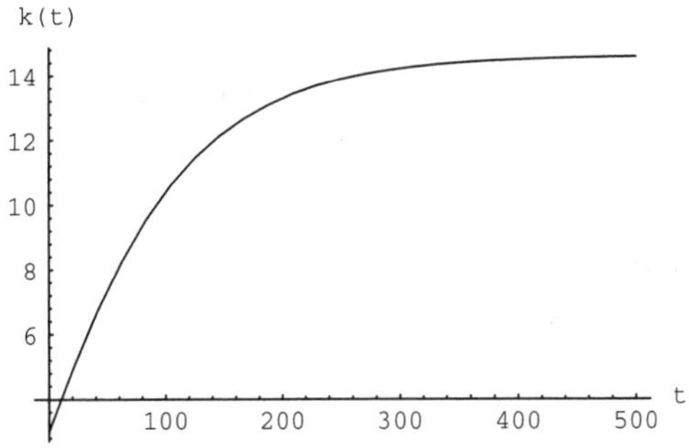


As t $\to \infty$, the capital–labor ratio approaches the stable equilibrium value $k_e = 14.6201$, which is the value of the solution given previously in example 13.35 in section 13.2.3,

$$k_e = \left(\frac{s}{r}\right)^{1/(1-a)}$$

## EXERCISES

1. Use the **DSolve** function to find the general solution of the following differential equations:
   (a) $y'' + 4y' + 4y = \sin x$
   (b) $y''' - y'' + y' - y = 2e^x$
   (c) $y^{(4)} + 5y'' + 4y = 40\cos 3x$

2. Use the **DSolve** function to find the solution of the initial-value problem:

$$y''' - 3y'' + 2y' = 4x - 8 + \frac{2e^{2x}}{e^x + 1}$$

$$y(0) = 1,\ y'(0) = 0,\ y''(0) = -1.$$

### 13.4.2 The DSolve package

*Mathematica* has a package that greatly enhances the capabilities of the **DSolve** function. Let us try to solve a differential equation for which the basic form of the **DSolve** function is unable to find a general solution.

**Example 13.56** Find the general solution of $y' = e^{x+2y}$.

*In[216]:=*

```
Clear[x,y];
DSolve[y'[x]==Exp[x+2*y[x]],y[x],x]
```

*Out[217]=*

$$\text{DSolve}[y'[x] == E^{x+2y[x]},\ y[x],\ x]$$

Since the **DSolve** function is unable to solve the differential equation, it returns the input statement. However, the equation is in fact a separable differential equation and hence,

$$e^x dx - e^{-2y} dy = 0$$

could be solved by the method of separable variable. The **MathEcon** function, **separableode**, is used here to find solutions.

*In[218]:=*

```
separableode[x,y,Exp[x],-Exp[-2y]]
```

Solve : : ifun : Warning : Inverse functions are being used by Solve, so some solutions may not be found.

*Out[218]=*

$$\{E^X + \frac{1}{2E^{2y}} == C[1],\ \{\{x \to -2y + \text{Log}[\frac{-1 + 2E^{2y}C[1]}{2}]\}\},$$
$$\{\{y \to \text{Log}[\frac{-I}{\text{Sqrt}[2E^x - 2C[1]]}]\},\ \{y \to \text{Log}[\frac{I}{\text{Sqrt}[2E^x - 2C[1]]}]\}\}\}$$

The output from **separableode** yields an implicit solution, and three explicit solutions, one in the form $x = \psi(y)$ and two in the form $y = \phi(x)$ are found. If we multiply the argument of the **Log** function in the explicit solution for $y$ by **I/I**, the solutions become

$$y(x) = \log\left(\frac{\pm 1}{\sqrt{(2c_1 - 2e^x)}}\right)$$

We now load the package **DSolve** and use it to solve this differential equation.

*In[219]:=*

```
Needs["Calculus`DSolve`"];
```

The format of using the enhanced **DSolve** function in the package is the same as the regular **DSolve** function.

*In[220]:=*

```
Clear[x,y];
DSolve[y'[x]==Exp[x+2*y[x]],y[x],x]
```

Solve : : ifun : Warning : Inverse functions are being used by Solve, so some solutions may not be found.

*Out[221]=*

$$\{\{y[x] \to \mathrm{Log}[\frac{-I}{\mathrm{Sqrt}[2E^x + 2C[1]]}]\}, \{y[x] \to \mathrm{Log}[\frac{I}{\mathrm{Sqrt}[2E^x + 2C[1]]}]\}\}$$

Note that these solutions can be "rationalized" to yield real-value solutions of the differential equation.

**Example 13.57** Find the solution of the initial-value problem

$$3x^2y'' + 11xy' - 3y = 0$$

such that $y(1) = 0$ and $y'(1) = -2$.

*In[222]:=*

```
Clear[x,y];
DSolve[{3*x^2*y"[x]+11*x*y'[x]-3*y[x]==0,
        y[1]==0,y'[1]==-2},y[x],x]
```

*Out[223]=*

$$\{\{y[x] \to \frac{3}{5x^3} - \frac{3x^{1/3}}{5}\}\}$$

## EXERCISES

1. Use the **DSolve** package to find solutions to the following differential equations:
   (a) $x^3y''' - 6x^2y'' + 18xy' - 24y = 0$
   (b) $x^2y'' + xy' + (x^2 - 4)y = 0$
   (c) $(1 - x^2)y'' - 2xy' + 2y = 0$
2. Use the **DSolve** package to find the solutions of the following initial value problem:

   $$y' = 1 - x - y + xy^2,\ y(0) = 0.$$

   Graph the solution.
3. Use the **DSolve** package to find the general solution of

   $$y'' = 2x(y')^2.$$

### 13.4.3 The **NDSolve** function

Many differential equations that arise in applications cannot be solved analytically. In these cases, the best that we can do is to generate a function that approximates the solution to the differential equation. In these situations, we approximate the *values* of the solution to an initial-value problem at specific points in the domain of the differential equation. Several approximation methods are available, such as Euler's method, the Runge-Kutta method, and the Adams-Bashforth methods, to name a few. Another way to approximate the solution is to find a *function* that approximates the solution over its domain. Of course, if one has an approximating function, then we can make approximations to the solution at specific points. *Mathematica* has a function called

**NDSolve** that will generate an approximating function to the solution of an initial-value problem. Here is the description of this function.

*In[224]:=*

```
?NDSolve
```

**NDSolve[eqns, y, {x, xmin, xmax}] finds a numerical solution to the differential equations eqns for the function y with the independent variable x in the range xmin to xmax. NDSolve[eqns, {y1, y2, ...}, {x, xmin, xmax}] finds numerical solutions for the functions yi. NDSolve[eqns, y, {x, x1, x2, ...}] forces a function evaluation at each of x1, x2, ... The range of numerical integration is from Min[x1, x2, ...] to Max[x1, x2, ...].**

The first argument is a list that contains the differential equation and the initial conditions, the second argument contains the dependent variable of the differential equation, and the third argument is a list that gives the independent variable, and the interval over which the approximating function is defined. The output from **NDSolve** is a rule that can be used to define the approximating function.

**Example 13.58** Plot an approximating function for the solution of the first-order, initial-value problem

$$y' = \sin(\pi x + e^{x+y}),\ y(0) = 1.$$

over the interval $0 \leq x \leq 2$. Let us first try to solve it with **DSolve**.

*In[225]:=*

```
Clear[x,y];
DSolve[{y'[x]==Sin[Pi*x+Exp[x+y]],y[0]==1},y[x],x]
```

General : : intinit : Loading integration packages – please wait.

*Out[226]=*

{{y[x] → 1 + Integrate[Sin[E^(DSolve`t + y) + Pi DSolve`t], {DSolve`t, 0, x}]}}

Now we use the **NDSolve** function to find an approximating function to the solution.

*In[227]:=*

```
Clear[x,y];
sol = NDSolve[{y'[x] == Sin[Pi*x+Exp[x+y[x]]],y[0]==1},
              y[x],{x,0,2}]
```

*Out[228]=*

{{y[x] → InterpolatingFunction[{0., 2.}, <>] [x]}}

The *Mathematica* output is expressed as a rule. We use the **ReplaceAll** function (/.) to define a function.

*In[229]:=*

```
y[x_] = y[x] /. sol[[1]];
```

Let us compute the value of the approximating function at some points in its domain.

*In[230]:=*
```
{y[0],y[0.5],y[0.75],y[1.5],y[2]}
```

*Out[230]=*
{1., 0.693951, 0.4951, 0.362051, 0.279493}

We can even plot the approximating function.

*In[231]:=*
```
Plot[y[x],{x,0,2},
     AxesLabel->{"x","y"},PlotRange->{0,1.2}];
```

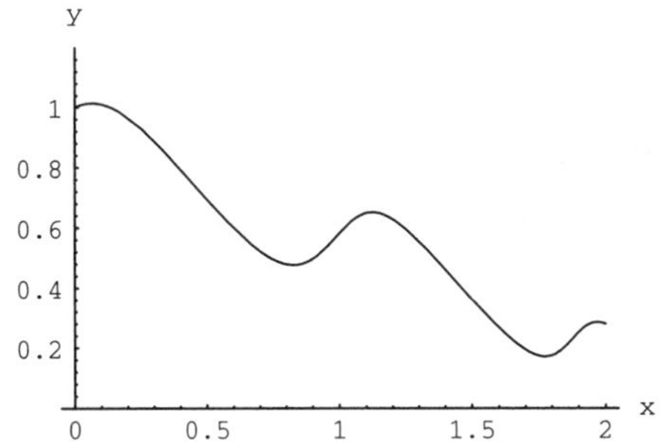


**Example 13.59** Plot an approximating function for the solution of the third order, initial-value problem

$$y''' + 5xy'' + 9y' - y^2 = 1 + x^3$$

with the initial values, y(0) = −1, y′(0) = 1, and y″(0) = 0, over the interval $-1 \le x \le 1$.

*In[232]:=*
```
Clear[x,y];
eqn  =  y'''[x]+5*x*y''[x]+9*y'[x]-y[x]^2==1+x^3;
sol  =  NDSolve[{eqn,y[0]==-1,y'[0]==1,y''[0]==0},
                 y[x],{x,-1,1}];
y[x_]  =  y[x]  /.  sol[[1]];
Plot[y[x],{x,-1,1},AxesLabel->{"x","y"},PlotRange->All];
```

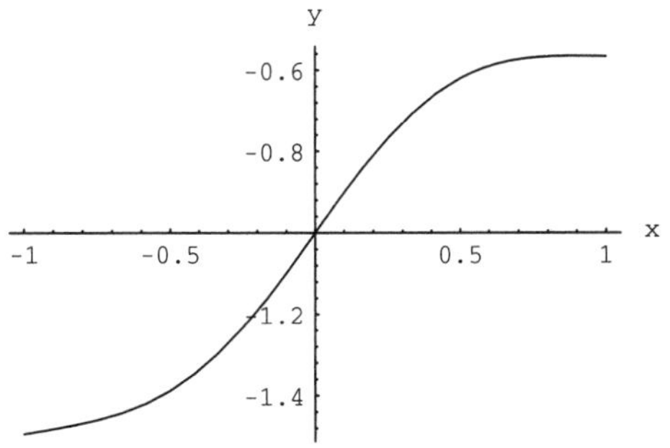

## EXERCISES

1. Use the **NDSolve** function to plot an approximation to the solutions to the initial-value problem:

   $$e^x y'' + xy' - 5y = \sin x$$

   with $y(0) = 0$, and $y'(0) = -1$.

2. Use the **NDSolve** function to plot an approximation to the solutions to the initial-value problem:

   $$\sin y' = \cos(x+y)$$

   with $y(0) = 0$.

3. Use the **NDSolve** function to plot an approximation to the solutions to the initial-value problem:

   $$y'' + xy' + y^2 = 1$$

   with $y(0) = 0$ and $y'(0) = 0$.

# 14

# Systems of Differential Equations

Many mathematical models in economics involve solving a system of differential equations. Economic variables and their variations over time are often interrelated. For example, the price adjustment of one good often depends upon the prices of its complements as well as the prices of its substitutes. We are then faced with the problem of simultaneously solving a system of differential equations. As in the last chapter we shall confine our discussion to ordinary differential equations.

## □ 14.1 Systems of First-Order Differential Equations □

### 14.1.1 First-order systems and fundamental solutions

The terminology used for systems of differential equations is similar to that used for scalar differential equations. A *first-order system* of differential equations is a set of first-order differential equations

$$
\begin{aligned}
y_1' &= F_1(x, y_1, y_2, \ldots, y_n)\\
y_2' &= F_2(x, y_1, y_2, \ldots, y_n)\\
&\cdots\cdots\cdots\cdots\\
y_n' &= F_n(x, y_1, y_2, \ldots, y_n)
\end{aligned}
$$

where $y_1(x), y_2(x), \ldots, y_n(x)$ are functions of a single variable $x$ that are restricted to some interval $I$, called the *domain* of the system.

**Example 14.1** The following is a first-order system:

$$
\begin{aligned}
y_1' &= xy_1y_2 + y_3\\
y_2' &= y_1y_2^2 + \cos(xy_1) + e^x\\
y_3' &= 45
\end{aligned}
$$

for $-1 < x < 3$. Its domain is the interval (1,3).

It is convenient to write a first-order system of differential equations in vector notation. Defining the vector-valued functions $\mathbf{y}(x)$ and $\mathbf{F}(x, \mathbf{y})$ such that

$$\mathbf{y} = \begin{bmatrix} y_1(x) \\ y_2(x) \\ \cdots \\ y_n(x) \end{bmatrix}; \quad \mathbf{F}(x,\mathbf{y}) = \begin{bmatrix} F_1(x,y_1,y_2,\ldots,y_n) \\ F_2(x,y_1,y_2,\ldots,y_n) \\ \cdots\cdots\cdots \\ F_n(x,y_1,y_2,\ldots,y_n) \end{bmatrix}$$

the system can be written as $d\mathbf{y}/dx = \mathbf{F}(x,\mathbf{y})$ or $\mathbf{y}' = \mathbf{F}(x,\mathbf{y})$. If the functions $F_i(x,y_1,y_2,\ldots,y_n)$, $i = 1,2,\ldots,n$, are linear functions of the variables $y_1,y_2,\ldots,y_n$, then the first-order system is said to be *linear*.

**Example 14.2** The price-adjustment of coffee, $dp_1/dt$ over time, $t$, varies with the price of coffee, $p_1$, and the price of the substitute, $p_2$, say tea, and vice versa. Thus,

$$\frac{dp_1}{dt} = a_{10} + a_{11}p_1 + a_{12}p_2$$

$$\frac{dp_2}{dt} = a_{20} + a_{21}p_1 + a_{22}p_2$$

is a system of first-order linear differential equations where $a_{ij}$ are constants.

For systems of linear differential equations, it is convenient to introduce matrix notation. Suppose

$$\begin{aligned} F_1(x,y_1,y_2,\ldots,y_n) &= a_{11}(x)y_1 + a_{12}(x)y_2 + \ldots + a_{1n}(x)y_n + g_1(x), \\ F_2(x,y_1,y_2,\ldots,y_n) &= a_{21}(x)y_1 + a_{22}(x)y_2 + \ldots + a_{2n}(x)y_n + g_2(x), \\ &\cdots\cdots\cdots \\ F_n(x,y_1,y_2,\ldots,y_n) &= a_{n1}(x)y_1 + a_{n2}(x)y_2 + \ldots + a_{nn}(x)y_n + g_n(x), \end{aligned}$$

where $a_{11}(x), \ldots, a_{nn}(x)$, and $g_1(x), \ldots, g_n(x)$ are functions that are defined on the domain of the system. Let $\mathbf{A}(x)$ be a matrix-valued function that is composed of the coefficients in the linear system. The system can then be written as

$$\mathbf{y}' = \mathbf{A}(x)\mathbf{y} + \mathbf{g}(x)$$

where

$$\mathbf{A}(x) = \begin{bmatrix} a_{11}(x) & a_{12}(x) & \ldots & a_{1n}(x) \\ a_{21}(x) & a_{22}(x) & \ldots & a_{2n}(x) \\ \cdots & \cdots & \cdots & \cdots \\ a_{n1}(x) & a_{n2}(x) & \ldots & a_{nn}(x) \end{bmatrix}; \quad \mathbf{g}(x) = \begin{bmatrix} g_1(x) \\ g_2(x) \\ \ldots \\ g_n(x) \end{bmatrix}$$

**Example 14.3** The following is a system of first-order linear differential equations:

$$\begin{bmatrix} y_1' \\ y_2' \\ y_3' \end{bmatrix} = \begin{bmatrix} \sin(x) & -3x & 1 \\ -5 & -3x^3 & 1/x \\ x^2 & 5x^2 & 56 \end{bmatrix} \begin{bmatrix} y_1 \\ y_2 \\ y_3 \end{bmatrix} + \begin{bmatrix} 5x \\ -\tan(x) \\ 56 \end{bmatrix}$$

for $-\pi < x < 9$.

As in the case of scalar differential equations, we can classify a system of linear differential equations into one of two types. The system $\mathbf{y}' = \mathbf{A}(x)\mathbf{y} + \mathbf{g}(x)$, $x \in I$, is said to be *homogeneous* if $\mathbf{g}(x) \equiv \mathbf{0}$. Otherwise, the system is said to be *inhomogeneous* or *nonhomogeneous*.

Every $n$th-order, scalar differential equation in the form

$$y^{(n)} = f(x, y, y', \ldots, y^{(n-1)})$$

can be converted into a first-order system. We demonstrate this transformation in the following example.

**Example 14.4** Consider a fourth-order linear differential equation

$$y^{(4)} + a_3 y^{(3)} + a_2 y'' + a_1 y' + a_0 y = g(x)$$

Define a set of four new variables, $z_1$, $z_2$, $z_3$, $z_4$, such that

$$\begin{aligned} z_1 &= y \\ z_2 &= z_1' = y' \\ z_3 &= z_2' = y'' \\ z_4 &= z_3' = y^{(3)}. \end{aligned}$$

Since $y^{(4)} = z_4'$, the differential equation can be written as

$$z_4' = -a_3 z_4 - a_2 z_3 - a_1 z_2 - a_0 z_1 + g(x)$$

The derivatives of the four new variables can now be expressed as a system of four equations

$$\begin{bmatrix} z_1' \\ z_2' \\ z_3' \\ z_4' \end{bmatrix} = \begin{bmatrix} 0 & 1 & 0 & 0 \\ 0 & 0 & 1 & 0 \\ 0 & 0 & 0 & 1 \\ -a_0 & -a_1 & -a_2 & -a_3 \end{bmatrix} \begin{bmatrix} z_1 \\ z_2 \\ z_3 \\ z_4 \end{bmatrix} + \begin{bmatrix} 0 \\ 0 \\ 0 \\ g(x) \end{bmatrix}$$

In matrix form, this system can be written as

$$\mathbf{z}' = \mathbf{A}\,\mathbf{z} + \mathbf{g}(x).$$

This reduction to a system of first-order equations can be extended to a system of high-order differential equations.

**Example 14.5** Consider the system

$$\begin{aligned} y_1^{(3)} &= 2y_1'' - 5y_1' + 3y_1 + 4y_2 \\ y_2' &= y_1'' - 6y_1 + 2y_2 \end{aligned}$$

Define the new variables, $z_1$, $z_2$, $z_3$, $z_4$, such that

$$\begin{aligned} z_1 &= y_1 \\ z_2 &= z_1' = y_1' \\ z_3 &= z_2' = y_1'' \\ z_4 &= y_2 \end{aligned}$$

Therefore,

$z_1' = y_1' = z_2$
$z_2' = y_1'' = z_3$
$z_3' = y_1^{(3)} = 2z_3 - 5z_2 + 3z_1 + 4z_4$
$z_4' = y_2' = z_3 - 6z_1 + 2z_4$

If we express this system in matrix form $\mathbf{z}' = \mathbf{A}\mathbf{z}$, we have

$$\begin{bmatrix} z_1' \\ z_2' \\ z_3' \\ z_4' \end{bmatrix} = \begin{bmatrix} 0 & 1 & 0 & 0 \\ 0 & 0 & 1 & 0 \\ 3 & -5 & 2 & 4 \\ -6 & 0 & 1 & 2 \end{bmatrix} \begin{bmatrix} z_1 \\ z_2 \\ z_3 \\ z_4 \end{bmatrix}$$

A **solution** $\mathbf{y} = \phi(x)$ of a first-order system $\mathbf{y}' = \mathbf{F}(x,\mathbf{y})$, $x \in I$, is a differentiable vector-valued function that satisfies the system of differential equations on its domain $I$. That is, $\phi'(x) = \mathbf{F}(x,\phi(x))$.

**Example 14.6** The following system

$$\begin{bmatrix} y_1' \\ y_2' \end{bmatrix} = \begin{bmatrix} 0 & 2 \\ 1 & 1 \end{bmatrix} \begin{bmatrix} y_1 \\ y_2 \end{bmatrix} + \begin{bmatrix} x \\ 0 \end{bmatrix}$$

has the solution

$$y_1 = c_1 e^{-x} + c_2 e^{2x} + \frac{x}{2} - \frac{3}{4}$$

$$y_2 = \frac{-c_1}{2} e^{-x} + c_2 e^{2x} - \frac{x}{2} + \frac{1}{4}$$

We confirm that this is a solution by taking the derivatives of the functions and showing that $y_1'(x) = 2y_2 + x$, and $y_2'(x) = y_1 + y_2$.

*In[1]:=*
```
Clear[y1,y2,x,c1,c2];
y1[x_]:= c1*Exp[-x]  +  c2*Exp[2*x]  +  x/2  -  3/4;
y2[x_]:= -c1/2*Exp[-x]  +  c2*Exp[2*x]  -  x/2  +  1/4;
y1'[x]  ==  2*y2[x]  +  x  //Simplify
```

*Out[4]=*
```
True
```

*In[5]:=*
```
y2'[x]  ==  y1[x]  +  y2[x]  //Simplify
```

*Out[5]=*
```
True
```

Alternatively, we could define a vector-valued function and substitute it into the first-order system.

*In[6]:=*

```
Clear[y,G];
A = {{0,2},{1,1}};
G[x_]:= {x,0};
y[x_]:= {y1[x],y2[x]};
y'[x] == A.y[x] + G[x] // Simplify
```

*Out[10]=*

```
True
```

An initial-value problem for a first-order system of differential equations, $\mathbf{y}' = \mathbf{F}(x,\mathbf{y})$, $x \in I$, is the system and an initial condition, $\mathbf{y}(x_0) \equiv \mathbf{y}_0$, $x_0 \in I$. Here $\mathbf{y}_0$ is a fixed vector that specifies the values of $y_1(x), \ldots ,y_n(x)$ at $x_0$.

A linear homogeneous system of first-order differential equations with *constant coefficients* has the form

$$y_1'(x) = a_{11}y_1(x) + a_{12}y_2(x) + \ldots + a_{1n}y_n(x)$$
$$y_2'(x) = a_{21}y_1(x) + a_{22}y_2(x) + \ldots + a_{2n}y_n(x)$$
$$\vdots$$
$$y_n'(x) = a_{n1}y_1(x) + a_{n2}y_2(x) + \ldots + a_{nn}y_n(x).$$

If we express this system in matrix form, we have

$$\mathbf{y}' = \mathbf{A}\mathbf{y}$$

where $\mathbf{A}$ is an $n \times n$ matrix with entries that are constants.

The theory behind homogeneous systems, $\mathbf{y}' = \mathbf{A}(x)\mathbf{y}$, leads us to a method for solving these systems. We state below three important properties about the solutions of homogeneous, first-order systems.

*Property 1* Solutions of $\mathbf{y}' = \mathbf{A}(x)\mathbf{y}$ satisfy the superposition principle. Suppose $\mathbf{y}_1(x)$, $\mathbf{y}_2(x), \ldots ,\mathbf{y}_m(x)$ are solutions of $\mathbf{y}' = \mathbf{A}(x)\mathbf{y}$, then any linear combination of them, i.e.,

$$\phi(x) = c_1\mathbf{y}_1(x) + c_2\mathbf{y}_2(x) + \ldots + c_m\mathbf{y}_m(x)$$

for arbitrary constants $c_1, c_2, \ldots , c_m$ is also a solution. If one has $n$ solutions, $\mathbf{y}_1(x)$, $\ldots ,\mathbf{y}_n(x)$, then one can form an $n \times n$ matrix by placing the solutions in columns of the matrix. That is,

$$\Psi(x) = [\mathbf{y}_1(x) \quad \mathbf{y}_2(x) \quad \ldots \quad \mathbf{y}_n(x)].$$

This matrix is called a *solution matrix* of the system. It can be shown that this matrix satisfies the system i.e., $\Psi'(x) = \mathbf{A}(x)\Psi(x)$.

*Property 2* A homogeneous system of $n$ differential equations has $n$ linearly independent solutions. Any set of $n$ linearly independent solutions, $\{\mathbf{y}_1(x),\mathbf{y}_2(x), \ldots ,\mathbf{y}_n(x)\}$, is called a *fundamental solution set*. The solution matrix formed by this set

$$\Phi(\mathrm{x}) = [\mathbf{y}_1(x) \quad \mathbf{y}_2(x) \quad \ldots \quad \mathbf{y}_n(x)]$$

is called a *fundamental matrix* of $\mathbf{y}' = \mathbf{A}(x)\mathbf{y}$. A fundamental solution set is a basis for the vector space formed by the solutions of the homogeneous system of differential equations. One can prove that a set of solutions is a fundamental solution set if and only if the **Wronskian** $W(x)$ of the solution matrix is never zero on the domain of the system. That is,

$$W(x) = |\Phi(x)| = \det|\mathbf{y}_1(x) \quad \mathbf{y}_2(x) \quad \dots \quad \mathbf{y}_n(x)| \neq 0, \ x \in I.$$

*Property 3* Let $\mathbf{c} = [c_1 \ c_2 \dots c_n]^T$ be an arbitrary vector. If $\{\mathbf{y}_1(x), \mathbf{y}_2(x), \dots, \mathbf{y}_n(x)\}$ is a fundamental set, then the general solution of the system $\mathbf{y}' = \mathbf{A}(x)\mathbf{y}$ is given by the function

$$\mathbf{y}(x) = \Phi(x)\mathbf{c} = c_1\mathbf{y}_1(x) + c_2\mathbf{y}_2(x) + \dots + c_n\mathbf{y}_n(x).$$

By general solution, we mean that every solution of the first-order system can be obtained from the general solution by appropriate choices of the constants $c_1, c_2, \dots, c_n$.

**Example 14.7** Consider the first-order system of differential equations:

$$y_1' = y_1$$
$$y_2' = y_1 + 3y_2$$
$$y_3' = y_2 + y_3.$$

Here we take $I = \mathbf{R}$. It is easy to show that

$$\mathbf{y}_1 = \begin{bmatrix} y_1 \\ y_2 \\ y_3 \end{bmatrix} = \begin{bmatrix} 0 \\ 0 \\ e^x \end{bmatrix}; \ \mathbf{y}_2 = \begin{bmatrix} y_1 \\ y_2 \\ y_3 \end{bmatrix} = \begin{bmatrix} -2e^{3x} \\ e^x \\ xe^x \end{bmatrix}; \ \mathbf{y}_3 = \begin{bmatrix} y_1 \\ y_2 \\ y_3 \end{bmatrix} = \begin{bmatrix} 0 \\ 2e^{3x} \\ e^{3x} \end{bmatrix};$$

are three solutions of the system, and that they form a fundamental matrix

$$\Phi(x) = [\mathbf{y}_1(x) \quad \mathbf{y}_2(x) \quad \mathbf{y}_3(x)] = \begin{bmatrix} 0 & -2e^{3x} & 0 \\ 0 & e^x & 2e^{3x} \\ e^x & xe^x & e^{3x} \end{bmatrix}$$

This follows from the the Wronskian.

*In[11]:=*

```
Clear[phi,x];
y1[x_]:= {0, 0, Exp[x]};
y2[x_]:= {-2*Exp[3*x], Exp[x], x*Exp[x]};
y3[x_]:= {0, 2*Exp[3*x], Exp[3*x]};
phi[x_]:= {y1[x],y2[x],y3[x]} // Transpose;
Det[phi[x]]
```

*Out[16]=*

$-4E^{7x}$

The general solution is therefore

$$\begin{bmatrix} y_1 \\ y_2 \\ y_3 \end{bmatrix} = c_1 \begin{bmatrix} 0 \\ 0 \\ e^x \end{bmatrix} + c_2 \begin{bmatrix} -2e^{3x} \\ e^x \\ xe^x \end{bmatrix} + c_3 \begin{bmatrix} 0 \\ 2e^{3x} \\ e^{3x} \end{bmatrix}$$

We construct this solution by using *Mathematica*.

*In[17]:=*

```
Clear[y,x,c1,c2,c3];
c = {c1,c2,c3};
y[x_] = phi[x].c; y[x] // MatrixForm
```

*Out[19]//MatrixForm=*

```
-2c2E^{3x}
c2E^x + 2c3E^{3x}
c1E^x +c3E^{3x} + c2E^x x
```

## EXERCISES

1. Write the system of differential equations

$$\begin{aligned} y_1' &= 9y_1 - y_2/x + y_3 + 5 \\ y_2' &= 2y_1 - 3xy_2 + e^x y_3 \\ y_3' &= 4y_1 - 58y_2 + 56y_3 \end{aligned}$$

in matrix notation. Is it linear? Is it homogeneous?

2. Show that

$$\begin{bmatrix} y_1 \\ y_2 \\ y_3 \end{bmatrix} = e^{-x}\begin{bmatrix} c_1 \\ c_2 - c_1 \\ 2c_3 - 2c_2 + c_1 \end{bmatrix} + xe^{-x}\begin{bmatrix} c_2 \\ 2c_3 - c_2 \\ -4c_3 + c_2 \end{bmatrix} + x^2e^{-x}\begin{bmatrix} c_3 \\ -c_3 \\ c_3 \end{bmatrix}$$

is a solution of the following system of differential equations

$$\begin{bmatrix} y_1' \\ y_2' \\ y_3' \end{bmatrix} = \begin{bmatrix} 0 & 1 & 0 \\ 0 & 0 & 1 \\ -1 & -3 & -3 \end{bmatrix}\begin{bmatrix} y_1 \\ y_2 \\ y_3 \end{bmatrix}$$

3. Show that the following initial value problem:

$$\begin{bmatrix} y_1' \\ y_2' \end{bmatrix} = \begin{bmatrix} 4 & -1 \\ 2 & 1 \end{bmatrix}\begin{bmatrix} y_1 \\ y_2 \end{bmatrix}; \begin{bmatrix} y_1(0) \\ y_2(0) \end{bmatrix} = \begin{bmatrix} 5 \\ 8 \end{bmatrix}$$

has the solution,

$$\begin{bmatrix} y_1 \\ y_2 \end{bmatrix} = \begin{bmatrix} 3e^{2x} + 2e^{3x} \\ 6e^{2x} + 2e^{3x} \end{bmatrix}$$

4. Show that

$$\Phi(x) = \begin{bmatrix} 2e^{3x} & 2e^{-x} \\ e^{3x} & -e^{-x} \end{bmatrix}$$

is a fundamental matrix of $\mathbf{y}' = \mathbf{A}\mathbf{y}$ where

$$\mathbf{A} = \begin{bmatrix} 1 & 4 \\ 1 & 1 \end{bmatrix}$$

5. Reduce the following system to a first-order system:

$$y_1'' = 2y_1' - y_2' + y_1 - 3y_2$$
$$y_2'' = y_1' - 2y_2' + 3y_1 - y_2$$

### 14.1.2 Linear constant coefficient homogeneous systems

The scalar differential equation $y' = ay$, where $a$ is a constant, has the general solution $y = ce^{ax}$. This suggests that the system, $\mathbf{y}' = \mathbf{A}\mathbf{y}$, may have a solution of the form

$$\mathbf{y} = e^{\lambda x}\mathbf{v}$$

where $\lambda$ is an unknown constant and $\mathbf{v}$ is an unknown constant vector. Substituting $\mathbf{y} = e^{\lambda x}\mathbf{v}$ into the system of differential equations $\mathbf{y}' = \mathbf{A}\mathbf{y}$, we find that

$$\lambda e^{\lambda x}\mathbf{v} = \mathbf{A}e^{\lambda x}\mathbf{v}.$$

For $\mathbf{y} = e^{\lambda x}\mathbf{v}$ to be a nontrivial solution, we must have $\mathbf{v} \neq \mathbf{0}$. Hence, $\mathbf{y} = e^{\lambda x}\mathbf{v}$ is a solution if $\lambda$ and $\mathbf{v}$ satisfy the vector equation:

$$\lambda\mathbf{v} = \mathbf{A}\mathbf{v}, \quad \text{or} \quad (\mathbf{A} - \lambda\mathbf{I})\mathbf{v} = \mathbf{0}.$$

The above equation implies that the unknown constant $\lambda$ is an eigenvalue of the matrix $\mathbf{A}$ and the unknown vector $\mathbf{v}$ is its eigenvector. Since $\mathbf{A}$ is an $n \times n$, there are $n$ eigenvalues, $\lambda_1, \lambda_2, \ldots, \lambda_n$, and corresponding eigenvectors $\mathbf{v}_1, \mathbf{v}_2, \ldots, \mathbf{v}_k$, $k \leq n$. Of course, the eigenvalues are not necessarily distinct, nor are the eigenvectors necessarily linearly independent. Suppose $k = n$. They produce $n$ solutions:

$$e^{\lambda_1 x}\mathbf{v}_1, e^{\lambda_2 x}\mathbf{v}_2, \ldots, e^{\lambda_n x}\mathbf{v}_n.$$

If these $n$ solutions are linearly independent, then these solutions can be used to form a fundamental matrix

$$\Phi(x) = [\, e^{\lambda_1 x}\mathbf{v}_1 \quad e^{\lambda_2 x}\mathbf{v}_2 \quad \ldots \quad e^{\lambda_n x}\mathbf{v}_n]$$

The general solution of the system of differential equations is then

$$\begin{aligned}\mathbf{y}(x) &= \Phi(x)\mathbf{c} \\ &= c_1 e^{\lambda_1 x}\mathbf{v}_1 + c_2 e^{\lambda_2 x}\mathbf{v}_2 + \ldots + c_n e^{\lambda_n x}\mathbf{v}_n\end{aligned}$$

where $\mathbf{c}$ is a column vector of arbitrary constants.

Before we provide some examples, we recall from Chapter 6 that the *Mathematica* functions for calculating eigenvalues and eigenvectors of a square matrix are **Eigenvalues, Eigenvectors**, and **Eigensystem**. Here is a description of **Eigensystem**.

*In[20]:=*

```
?Eigensystem
```

**Eigensystem[m] gives a list {values, vectors} of the eigenvalues and eigenvectors of the square matrix m.**

**Example 14.8** Find a fundamental matrix and the general solution of the homogenous system

$$y_1' = -y_1 + 6y_2$$
$$y_2' = y_1 - 2y_2$$

Writing the differential equations in matrix form, $\mathbf{y}' = \mathbf{A}\mathbf{y}$, we have

$$\begin{bmatrix} y_1' \\ y_2' \end{bmatrix} = \begin{bmatrix} -1 & 6 \\ 1 & -2 \end{bmatrix} \begin{bmatrix} y_1 \\ y_2 \end{bmatrix}.$$

The eigenvalues and eigenvectors of **A** are

$$\lambda_1 = -4,\ \mathbf{v}_1 = \begin{bmatrix} -2 \\ 1 \end{bmatrix};\ \lambda_2 = 1,\ \mathbf{v}_2 = \begin{bmatrix} 3 \\ 1 \end{bmatrix}.$$

These results are confirmed in the following calculation.

*In[21]:=*

```
A = {{-1,6},{1,-2}};
Eigensystem[A]
```

*Out[22]=*

```
{{-4, 1}, {{-2, 1}, {3, 1}}}
```

Two solutions of the system are then

$$\mathbf{y}_1(x) = e^{\lambda_1 x}\mathbf{v}_1 = \begin{bmatrix} -2e^{-4x} \\ e^{-4x} \end{bmatrix};\ \mathbf{y}_2(x) = e^{\lambda_2 x}\mathbf{v}_2 = \begin{bmatrix} 3e^{x} \\ e^{x} \end{bmatrix}.$$

The two solutions are linearly independent since the Wronskian is nonzero

$$W(x) = |\Phi(x)| = \begin{vmatrix} -2e^{-4x} & 3e^{x} \\ e^{-4x} & e^{x} \end{vmatrix} = \frac{-5}{e^{3x}} \neq 0.$$

The general solution is therefore

$$\begin{bmatrix} y_1(x) \\ y_2(x) \end{bmatrix} = c_1\mathbf{y}_1(\mathbf{x}) + c_2\mathbf{y}_2(\mathbf{x}) = \begin{bmatrix} -2c_1e^{-4x} + 3c_2e^{x} \\ c_1e^{-4x} + c_2e^{x} \end{bmatrix}.$$

**Example 14.9** Find the solution of the initial-value problem:

$$y_1'(x) = 3y_1(x) - 2y_2(x) - 4y_3(x)$$
$$y_2'(x) = 3y_1(x) - 2y_2\ (x) - 6y_3(x)$$
$$y_3'(x) = -3y_1(x) + 3y_2(x) + 5y_3(x)$$
$$y_1(0) = -5,\ y_2(0) = -9,\ y_3(0) = 5.$$

The eigenvalues and eigenvectors of the coefficient matrix **A** are calculated first.

*In[23]:=*

```
Clear[r,v];
A = {{3,-2,-4},{3,-2,-6},{-3,3,5}};
{r,v} = Eigensystem[A]
```

*Out[25]=*
```
{{1, 2, 3}, {{1, 1, 0}, {-2, -3, 1}, {-4, -6, 3}}}
```

Using the eigenvalues and eigenvectors, three solution of this system are expressed below.

*In[26]:=*
```
Clear[y1,y2,y3,x];
y1[x_] = Exp[r[[1]]x]*v[[1]]
y2[x_] = Exp[r[[2]]x]*v[[2]]
y3[x_] = Exp[r[[3]]x]*v[[3]]
```

*Out[27]=*
$\{E^x, E^x, 0\}$

*Out[28]=*
$\{-2E^{2x}, -3E^{2x}, E^{2x}\}$

*Out[29]=*
$\{-4E^{3x}, -6E^{3x}, 3E^{3x}\}$

The three solutions are linearly independent since the Wronskian $|\Phi(x)| = -e^{6x} \neq 0$,

*In[30]:=*
```
phi[x_] = {y1[x],y2[x],y3[x]};
Det[phi[x]]
```

*Out[31]=*
$-E^{6x}$

The system has the general solution $\mathbf{y}(x) = c_1\mathbf{y}_1(x)+c_2\mathbf{y}_2(x)+c_3\mathbf{y}_3(x)$, or

$$\begin{bmatrix} y_1(x) \\ y_2(x) \\ y_3(x) \end{bmatrix} = \begin{bmatrix} c_1e^x - 2c_2e^{2x} - 4c_3e^{3x} \\ c_1e^x - 3c_2e^{2x} - 6c_3e^{3x} \\ c_2e^{2x} + 3c_3e^{3x} \end{bmatrix}$$

*In[32]:=*
```
Clear[c,c1,c2,c3,y];
c = {c1,c2,c3};
y[x_] = c.phi[x];
y[x] // MatrixForm
```

*Out[35]//MatrixForm=*
$$\begin{matrix} c1E^x - 2c2E^{2x} - 4c3E^{3x} \\ c1E^x - 3c2E^{2x} - 6c3E^{3x} \\ c2E^{2x} + 3c3E^{3x} \end{matrix}$$

The initial conditions determine the values for the arbitrary constants, $c_1$, $c_2$, and $c_3$. At $x = 0$, we have

$$\begin{bmatrix} y_1(0) \\ y_2(0) \\ y_3(0) \end{bmatrix} = \begin{bmatrix} c_1 - 2c_2 - 4c_3 \\ c_1 - 3c_2 - 6c_3 \\ c_2 + 3c_3 \end{bmatrix} = \begin{bmatrix} -5 \\ -9 \\ 5 \end{bmatrix}$$

The solution of these equations is computed next.

*In[36]:=*
```
sol = Solve[y[0]=={-5,-9,5},{c1,c2,c3}]
```

*Out[36]=*
```
{{c1 → 3, c2 → 2, c3 → 1}}
```

Substituting these values into the general solution, we obtain the the solution of the initial-value problem.

*In[37]:=*
```
y[x_] = y[x] /. sol[[1]];
y[x] // MatrixForm
```

*Out[38]//MatrixForm=*
```
3E^x - 4E^2x - 4E^3x
3E^x - 6E^2x - 6E^3x
2E^2x + 3E^3x
```

Thus the initial-value problem has the solution

$$\begin{bmatrix} y_1(x) \\ y_2(x) \\ y_3(x) \end{bmatrix} = \begin{bmatrix} 3e^x - 4e^{2x} - 4e^{3x} \\ 3e^x - 6e^{2x} - 6e^{3x} \\ 2e^{2x} + 3e^{3x} \end{bmatrix}$$

We can verify that this is the solution of the initial-value problem.

*In[39]:=*
```
y'[x] == A.y[x] // Simplify
```

*Out[39]=*
```
True
```

*In[40]:=*
```
y[0]
```

*Out[40]=*
```
{-5, -9, 5}
```

In the above examples, we were able to find $n$ linearly independent eigenvectors $\mathbf{v}_i$ for $\mathbf{A}$ to form a fundamental solution set $\{\mathbf{y}_1(x), \mathbf{y}_2(x), \ldots, \mathbf{y}_n(x)\}$ where

$$\mathbf{y}_1(x) = e^{\lambda_1 x}\mathbf{v}_1,\ \mathbf{y}_2(x) = e^{\lambda_2 x}\mathbf{v}_2,\ \ldots,\ \mathbf{y}_n(x) = e^{\lambda_n x}\mathbf{v}_n.$$

However, if there are repeated eigenvalues, then the solutions may not be linearly independent. For example, consider the system $\mathbf{y}' = \mathbf{Ay}$ where

$$\mathbf{A} = \begin{bmatrix} 1 & 1 \\ 0 & 1 \end{bmatrix}$$

Let us calculate its eigenvalues and eigenvectors.

*In[41]:=*

```
A = {{1,1},{0,1}};
Eigensystem[A]
```

*Out[42]=*

```
{{1, 1}, {{1, 0}, {0, 0}}}
```

The matrix **A** has repeated eigenvalues, $\lambda_1 = \lambda_2 = 1$, and there is a single eigenvector $\mathbf{v} = [1\ \ 0]^T$. Hence we cannot construct two linearly independent solutions of the system.

Before we look at a method to find additional linearly independent solutions when the matrix **A** has repeated eigenvalues, we introduce some terminology. The eigenvalues of **A** are the roots of the characteristic equation: $\det(\mathbf{A} - \lambda\mathbf{I}) = 0$. The multiplicity of these roots (how many times the roots are repeated) is called the *algebraic multiplicity* of the eigenvalue. There is a second type of multiplicity for eigenvalue problems. An eigenvalue of **A** has one or more linearly independent eigenvectors associated with it. The number of linearly independent eigenvectors associated with a particular eigenvalue is called the *geometric multiplicity* of the eigenvalue. This geometric multiplicity is simply the dimension of the subspace of $\mathbf{V}^n$ spanned by the eigenvectors associated with a particular eigenvalue. The geometric multiplicity of an eigenvalue is always less than or equal to its algebraic multiplicity. In the case of repeated eigenvalues, difficulty in finding additional linearly independent solutions will arise only when the geometric multiplicity is strictly less than the algebraic multiplicity. If the algebraic multiplicity is equal to the geometric multiplicity, then a sufficient number of linearly independent solutions exists to form a fundamental set of solutions or to construct a fundamental matrix. Below, we present a method for finding the additional linearly independent solutions when the geometric multiplicity is less than the algebraic multiplicity.

We first introduce the concept of the *matrix exponential* to find additional linearly independent solutions of $\mathbf{y}' = \mathbf{A}\mathbf{y}$ when the matrix **A** has repeated eigenvalues. As motivation, we consider the scalar equation $y' = a\,y$, which has a solution $y = e^{ax}$. The solution can be expanded as an infinite power series

$$e^{ax} = 1 + ax + a^2\frac{x^2}{2!} + a^3\frac{x^3}{3!} + \ldots$$

This power series for the solution of a scalar equation suggests that the solution of a system of differential equation $\mathbf{y}' = \mathbf{A}\mathbf{y}$ is $\mathbf{y}(x) = e^{x\mathbf{A}}\mathbf{v}$ where **v** is some vector. For this solution to make sense, $e^{x\mathbf{A}}$ must be a matrix which we define below as a power series.

Let **A** be a square matrix. The $n \times n$ matrix $e^{x\mathbf{A}}$ is called an *exponential matrix* and is defined as the power series

$$e^{x\mathbf{A}} = \mathbf{I} + x\mathbf{A} + \frac{x^2}{2!}\mathbf{A}^2 + \frac{x^3}{3!}\mathbf{A}^3 + \ldots$$

where **I** is the $n \times n$ identity matrix. One can show that this infinite series converges for every constant square matrix **A**, and that the matrix $e^{x\mathbf{A}}$ satisfies the usual properties of the exponential function. For example, if $x$ is a scalar, then $e^{x(\mathbf{A}+\mathbf{B})} = e^{x\mathbf{A}}e^{x\mathbf{B}}$ for any $n \times n$ matrices **A** and **B** that commute, i.e., $\mathbf{A}\mathbf{B} = \mathbf{B}\mathbf{A}$. If $\mathbf{B} = -\mathbf{A}$, then $e^{x\mathbf{A}}$ is nonsingular and its inverse is $e^{-x\mathbf{A}}$.

Let $\mathbf{y}(x) = e^{x\mathbf{A}}\mathbf{v}$. Taking the derivative of this vector-valued function with respect to $x$, we have

$$\begin{aligned}\frac{d}{dx}(e^{x\mathbf{A}}\mathbf{v}) &= (\mathbf{A} + x\mathbf{A}^2 + \frac{x^2}{2!}\mathbf{A}^3 + \frac{x^3}{3!}\mathbf{A}^4 + \ldots)\mathbf{v} \\ &= \mathbf{A}(\mathbf{I} + x\mathbf{A} + \frac{x^2}{2!}\mathbf{A}^2 + \frac{x^3}{3!}\mathbf{A}^3 + \ldots)\mathbf{v} \\ &= \mathbf{A}e^{x\mathbf{A}}\mathbf{v}.\end{aligned}$$

This result shows that if $\mathbf{y}(x) = e^{x\mathbf{A}}\mathbf{v}$, then it satisfies the first-order system $\mathbf{y}' = \mathbf{A}\mathbf{y}$, and hence $e^{x\mathbf{A}}\mathbf{v}$ is a solution for any vector $\mathbf{v}$. We rewrite this solution as

$$\begin{aligned}\mathbf{y} &= e^{x\mathbf{A}}\mathbf{v} = e^{\lambda x}e^{(\mathbf{A}-\lambda\mathbf{I})x}\mathbf{v} \\ &= e^{\lambda x}\left[\mathbf{v} + x(\mathbf{A} - \lambda\mathbf{I})\mathbf{v} + \frac{x^2}{2!}(\mathbf{A} - \lambda\mathbf{I})^2\mathbf{v} + \frac{x^3}{3!}(\mathbf{A} - \lambda\mathbf{I})^3\mathbf{v} + \ldots\right]\end{aligned}$$

Suppose $\lambda_1, \lambda_2, \ldots, \lambda_n$ and $\mathbf{v}_1, \mathbf{v}_2, \ldots, \mathbf{v}_n$ are the eigenvalues and corresponding eigenvectors of the $\mathbf{A}$. If we choose $\lambda = \lambda_1$ and $\mathbf{v} = \mathbf{v}_1$ in the above expansion, then we have a solution

$$\begin{aligned}\mathbf{y}_1 &= e^{\lambda_1 x}\left[\mathbf{v}_1 + x(\mathbf{A} - \lambda_1\mathbf{I})\mathbf{v}_1 + \frac{x^2}{2!}(\mathbf{A} - \lambda_1\mathbf{I})^2\mathbf{v}_1 + \ldots\right] \\ &= e^{\lambda_1 x}\mathbf{v}_1\end{aligned}$$

The last equality is due to the fact that

$$\begin{aligned}&(\mathbf{A} - \lambda_1\mathbf{I})\mathbf{v}_1 = \mathbf{0}, \\ &(\mathbf{A} - \lambda_1\mathbf{I})^2\mathbf{v}_1 = (\mathbf{A} - \lambda_1\mathbf{I})(\mathbf{A} - \lambda_1\mathbf{I})\mathbf{v}_1 = \mathbf{0}, \ldots.\end{aligned}$$

i.e., $\lambda_1$ is an eigenvalue and $\mathbf{v}_1$ is the corresponding eigenvector of $\mathbf{A}$. If all other eigenvectors are linearly independent, then we can obtain $n$ linearly independent solutions by substituting $\lambda = \lambda_i$ and $\mathbf{v} = \mathbf{v}_i$ such that

$$\mathbf{y}_i = e^{\lambda_i x}\mathbf{v}_i, \; i = 1,2, \ldots, n.$$

Note that we have found $n$ linearly independent solutions even if the eigenvalues are repeated. As long as there are $n$ linearly independent eigenvectors $\mathbf{v}_i$, we have a sufficient number of linearly independent solutions $\mathbf{y}_i$ to form a fundamental set or a fundamental matrix $\mathbf{\Phi}(x)$. The general solution of $\mathbf{y}' = \mathbf{A}\mathbf{y}$ is then a linear combination of these functions:

$$\mathbf{y}(x) = c_1e^{\lambda_1 x}\mathbf{v}_1 + c_2e^{\lambda_2 x}\mathbf{v}_2 + \ldots + c_ne^{\lambda_n x}\mathbf{v}_n.$$

However, this method will not work if we do not have $n$ linearly independent eigenvectors. This situation occurs when the geometric multiplicity of any of the eigenvalues is less than its algebraic multiplicity. Suppose $\lambda_1 = \lambda_2$ and only one linearly independent eigenvector $\mathbf{v}_1$ exists. Let us define a new vector $\mathbf{w}_2$ such that

$$(\mathbf{A} - \lambda_1\mathbf{I})\mathbf{w}_2 = \mathbf{v}_1.$$

This definition implies that

$$(\mathbf{A} - \lambda_1\mathbf{I})^2\mathbf{w}_2 = (\mathbf{A} - \lambda_1\mathbf{I})(\mathbf{A} - \lambda_1\mathbf{I})\mathbf{w}_2 = (\mathbf{A} - \lambda_1\mathbf{I})\mathbf{v}_1 = \mathbf{0},$$
$$(\mathbf{A} - \lambda_1\mathbf{I})^3\mathbf{w}_2 = \mathbf{0}, \ldots.$$

Substituting $\lambda = \lambda_1$ and $\mathbf{v} = \mathbf{w}_2$ in the expansion of the matrix exponential, we obtain a second solution of the system:

$$\begin{aligned}\mathbf{y}_2 &= e^{\lambda_1 x}\left[\mathbf{w}_2 + x(\mathbf{A} - \lambda_1\mathbf{I})\mathbf{w}_2 + \frac{x^2}{2!}(\mathbf{A} - \lambda_1\mathbf{I})^2\mathbf{w}_2 + \ldots\right] \\ &= e^{\lambda_1 x}\left[\mathbf{w}_2 + x(\mathbf{A} - \lambda_1\mathbf{I})\mathbf{w}_2\right] \\ &= e^{\lambda_1 x}\left[\mathbf{w}_2 + x\mathbf{v}_1\right]\end{aligned}$$

The vector $\mathbf{w}_2$ is called a *generalized eigenvector* of the eigenvalue $\lambda_1$. It is not an eigenvector, but satisfies equations that are similar to those satisfied by an eigenvector:

$$(\mathbf{A} - \lambda_1\mathbf{I})\mathbf{w}_2 = \mathbf{v}_1 \neq \mathbf{0},$$
$$(\mathbf{A} - \lambda_1\mathbf{I})^2\mathbf{w}_2 = \mathbf{0}.$$

A vector $\mathbf{w}$ is called a generalized eigenvector of rank $k$ of the eigenvalue $\lambda^*$ if $(\mathbf{A} - \lambda^*\mathbf{I})^{k-1}\mathbf{w} \neq \mathbf{0}$, but $(\mathbf{A} - \lambda^*\mathbf{I})^k\mathbf{w} = \mathbf{0}$. We can use these generalized eigenvectors to define new linearly independent solutions for $\mathbf{y}' = \mathbf{A}\mathbf{y}$.

We introduce the notion of a chain of generalized eigenvectors that is important in the construction of linearly independent solutions when the geometric multiplicity is less than the algebraic multiplicity.

**Definition 14.1** *Let $\mathbf{w}_k$ be a generalized eigenvector of rank k corresponding to the eigenvalue $\lambda^*$ of the matrix* **A**. *Suppose $\lambda^*$ has algebraic multiplicity k. A* ***chain of generalized eigenvectors*** *is a set of vectors $\{\mathbf{w}_1, \mathbf{w}_2, \ldots, \mathbf{w}_k\}$ such that*

$$\begin{aligned}(\mathbf{A} - \lambda^*\mathbf{I})\mathbf{w}_1 &= 0, \\ (\mathbf{A} - \lambda^*\mathbf{I})\mathbf{w}_2 &= \mathbf{w}_1, \\ (\mathbf{A} - \lambda^*\mathbf{I})\mathbf{w}_3 &= \mathbf{w}_2, \\ &\cdots\cdots \\ (\mathbf{A} - \lambda^*\mathbf{I})\mathbf{w}_k &= \mathbf{w}_{k-1}.\end{aligned}$$

Notice that $\mathbf{w}_1$ is, in fact, an eigenvector of **A** corresponding to the eigenvalue $\lambda^*$ since $(\mathbf{A} - \lambda^*\mathbf{I})\mathbf{w}_1 = \mathbf{0}$. The other vectors $\mathbf{w}_i$ in the chain are generalized eigenvectors of different ranks. For example, $(\mathbf{A} - \lambda^*\mathbf{I})\mathbf{w}_2 = \mathbf{w}_1 \neq \mathbf{0}$, but $(\mathbf{A} - \lambda^*\mathbf{I})^2\mathbf{w}_2 = (\mathbf{A} - \lambda^*\mathbf{I})\mathbf{w}_1 = \mathbf{0}$.

Constructing a chain of the generalized eigenvectors is not an easy task. We start with an eigenvector $\mathbf{w}_1$ and build from it iteratively. First, $\mathbf{w}_2$ is found such that $(\mathbf{A} - \lambda^*\mathbf{I})\mathbf{w}_2 = \mathbf{w}_1$ and then $\mathbf{w}_3$ is found such that $(\mathbf{A} - \lambda^*\mathbf{I})\mathbf{w}_3 = \mathbf{w}_2$, and so on.

A chain of generalized eigenvectors can be used to construct $k$ linearly independent solutions of $\mathbf{y}' = \mathbf{A}\mathbf{y}$ when we have a repeated eigenvalue and an insufficient number of linearly independent eigenvectors. Recall that $\mathbf{y}(x) = e^{x\mathbf{A}}\mathbf{v}$ is a solution which can be expanded as

$$\mathbf{y}(x) = e^{\lambda x}\left[\mathbf{v} + x(\mathbf{A} - \lambda\mathbf{I})\mathbf{v} + \frac{x^2}{2!}(\mathbf{A} - \lambda\mathbf{I})^2\mathbf{v} + \frac{x^3}{3!}(\mathbf{A} - \lambda\mathbf{I})^3\mathbf{v} + \ldots\right].$$

Replace $\lambda$ by $\lambda^*$ and $\mathbf{v}$ by $\mathbf{w}_1$. Since

$$(\mathbf{A} - \lambda^*\mathbf{I})\mathbf{w}_1 = (\mathbf{A} - \lambda^*\mathbf{I})^2\mathbf{w}_1 = \ldots = \mathbf{0},$$

we have the first solution

$$\mathbf{y}_1(x) = e^{\lambda^* x}\mathbf{w}_1.$$

Replace $\lambda$ by $\lambda^*$ and $\mathbf{v}$ by $\mathbf{w}_2$. Since

$$(\mathbf{A} - \lambda^*\mathbf{I})\mathbf{w}_2 = \mathbf{w}_1,$$
$$(\mathbf{A} - \lambda^*\mathbf{I})^2\mathbf{w}_2 = (\mathbf{A} - \lambda^*\mathbf{I})^3\mathbf{w}_2 = \ldots = \mathbf{0},$$

we have a second solution $\mathbf{y}_2(x)$ which is linearly independent of $\mathbf{y}_1(x)$ and has the form:

$$\mathbf{y}_2(x) = e^{\lambda^* x}[\mathbf{w}_2 + x\mathbf{w}_1]$$

Next replace $\lambda$ by $\lambda^*$ and $\mathbf{v}$ by $\mathbf{w}_3$. This implies that

$$(\mathbf{A} - \lambda^*\mathbf{I})\mathbf{w}_3 = \mathbf{w}_2,$$
$$(\mathbf{A} - \lambda^*\mathbf{I})^3\mathbf{w}_3 = (\mathbf{A} - \lambda^*\mathbf{I})^4\mathbf{w}_3 = \ldots = \mathbf{0},$$

and we have a third solution $\mathbf{y}_3(x)$ which is linearly independent of both $\mathbf{y}_1(x)$ and $\mathbf{y}_2(x)$ and has the form:

$$\mathbf{y}_3(x) = e^{\lambda^* x}\left[\mathbf{w}_3 + x\mathbf{w}_2 + \frac{x^2}{2!}\mathbf{w}_1\right]$$

This process can continue until a sufficient number of linearly independent solutions has been calculated.

The above procedure is summarized in the following theorem.

**THEOREM 14.1** *Suppose $\lambda^*$ is an eigenvalue of the matrix $\mathbf{A}$ and $\{\mathbf{w}_1, \mathbf{w}_2, \ldots, \mathbf{w}_k\}$ is a chain of generalized eigenvectors with $\mathbf{w}_1$ being an eigenvector of $\mathbf{A}$ corresponding to $\lambda^*$. The following are k linearly independent solutions of $\mathbf{y}' = \mathbf{A}\mathbf{y}$:*

$$\mathbf{y}_1(x) = e^{\lambda^* x}\mathbf{w}_1$$

$$\mathbf{y}_2(x) = e^{\lambda^* x}[\mathbf{w}_2 + x\mathbf{w}_1]$$

$$\mathbf{y}_3(x) = e^{\lambda^* x}\left[\mathbf{w}_3 + x\mathbf{w}_2 + \frac{x^2}{2!}\mathbf{w}_1\right].$$

$$\vdots$$

$$\mathbf{y}_k(x) = e^{\lambda^* x}\left[\mathbf{w}_k + x\mathbf{w}_{k-1} + \ldots + \frac{x^{k-1}}{(k-1)!}\mathbf{w}_1\right]$$

**Example 14.10** The matrix **A** for the homogeneous system

$$\mathbf{y}' = \begin{bmatrix} y_1' \\ y_2' \\ y_3' \end{bmatrix} = \begin{bmatrix} 2 & 2 & 2 \\ 2 & 1 & 2 \\ 1 & 0 & -1 \end{bmatrix} \begin{bmatrix} y_1 \\ y_2 \\ y_3 \end{bmatrix} = \mathbf{A}\,\mathbf{y}$$

has the eigenvalues, $\lambda_1 = \lambda_2 = -1$, and $\lambda_3 = 4$ and eigenvectors:

$$\mathbf{v}_1 = \begin{bmatrix} 0 \\ -1 \\ 1 \end{bmatrix};\ \mathbf{v}_3 = \begin{bmatrix} 5 \\ 4 \\ 1 \end{bmatrix}$$

*In[43]:=*

```
Clear[r,v]
A  =  {{2,2,2},{2,1,2},{1,0,-1}};
{r,v}  =  Eigensystem[A]
```

*Out[45]=*

```
{{-1, -1, 4}, {{0, -1, 1}, {0, 0, 0}, {5, 4, 1}}}
```

Two linearly independent eigenvectors $\mathbf{v}_1$, and $\mathbf{v}_3$ exist, which generate two linearly independent solutions

$$\mathbf{y}_1(x) = e^{-x}\begin{bmatrix} 0 \\ -1 \\ 1 \end{bmatrix};\ \mathbf{y}_3(x) = e^{4x}\begin{bmatrix} 5 \\ 4 \\ 1 \end{bmatrix}$$

To obtain the third linearly independent solution, we generate a chain of generalized eigenvectors $\{\mathbf{w}_1,\mathbf{w}_2\}$ corresponding to $\lambda_1 = -1$. Set $\mathbf{w}_1 = \mathbf{v}_1$. To obtain $\mathbf{w}_2$, we solve the equations

$$(\mathbf{A} - \lambda_1\mathbf{I})\,\mathbf{w}_2 = \mathbf{w}_1 \quad \text{or} \quad \begin{bmatrix} 3 & 2 & 2 \\ 2 & 2 & 2 \\ 1 & 0 & 0 \end{bmatrix} \begin{bmatrix} a \\ b \\ c \end{bmatrix} = \begin{bmatrix} 0 \\ -1 \\ 1 \end{bmatrix}$$

for $a$, $b$, and $c$, the components of $\mathbf{w}_2$. The following calculation shows that $\mathbf{w}_2 = [1\ -(3/2)-c\ c]^T$.

*In[46]:=*

```
Clear[w2,a,b,c];
w2  =  {a,b,c};
Solve[(A-r[[1]]*IdentityMatrix[3]).w2  ==  v[[1]],w2]
```

*Out[48]=*

$$\{\{b \to -\left(\frac{2}{3}\right) - c,\ a \to 1\}\}$$

If we choose a value for $c$, say, $c = 1$, a second solution is

$$\mathbf{y}_2(x) = e^{-x}(\mathbf{w}_2 + \mathbf{w}_1\mathbf{x}) \quad \text{or} \quad \mathbf{y}_2(x) = e^{-x}\begin{bmatrix} 1 \\ -\frac{5}{2} - x \\ 1 + x \end{bmatrix}$$

The general solution of the system is

$$\mathbf{y}(x) = c_1\mathbf{y}_1(x) + c_2\mathbf{y}_2(x) + c_3\mathbf{y}_3(x)$$

$$= c_1 e^{-x}\begin{bmatrix} 0 \\ -1 \\ 1 \end{bmatrix} + c_2 e^{-x}\begin{bmatrix} 1 \\ -\dfrac{5}{2} - x \\ 1 + x \end{bmatrix} + c_3 e^{4x}\begin{bmatrix} 5 \\ 4 \\ 1 \end{bmatrix}$$

For some systems of differential equations, the eigenvalues and eigenvectors of **A** are complex. For example, the coefficient matrix for the system of differential equations

$$\begin{bmatrix} y_1' \\ y_2' \end{bmatrix} = \begin{bmatrix} 1 & 5 \\ -1 & 3 \end{bmatrix}\begin{bmatrix} y_1 \\ y_2 \end{bmatrix}$$

has the eigenvalues $\lambda_1 = 2 + 2i$, $\lambda_2 = 2 - 2i$ and eigenvectors,

$$\mathbf{v}_1 = \begin{bmatrix} 1 + 2i \\ 1 \end{bmatrix}; \; \mathbf{v}_2 = \begin{bmatrix} 1 - 2i \\ 1 \end{bmatrix}$$

The corresponding two solutions are

$$\mathbf{y}_1(x) = e^{\lambda_1 x}\mathbf{v}_1 = e^{(2+2i)x}\begin{bmatrix} 1 + 2i \\ 1 \end{bmatrix},$$

$$\mathbf{y}_2(x) = e^{\lambda_2 x}\mathbf{v}_2 = e^{(2-2i)x}\begin{bmatrix} 1 - 2i \\ 1 \end{bmatrix}$$

The general solution, $\mathbf{y}(x) = c_1\mathbf{y}_1(x) + c_2\mathbf{y}_2(x)$, is then

$$\mathbf{y}(x) = c_1 e^{(2+2i)x}\begin{bmatrix} 1 + 2i \\ 1 \end{bmatrix} + c_2 e^{(2-2i)x}\begin{bmatrix} 1 - 2i \\ 1 \end{bmatrix}$$

However, this solution is not a satisfactory expression since $\mathbf{y}(x)$ is complex-valued. Below we demonstrate a method to derive real-valued solutions when the eigenvalues and eigenvectors of **A** are complex.

Suppose that the coefficient matrix of a system of two differential equations has complex eigenvalues and eigenvectors,

$$\lambda_1 = a + ib, \quad \lambda_2 = a - ib,$$
$$\mathbf{v}_1 = \mathbf{v} + i\mathbf{u}, \quad \mathbf{v}_2 = \mathbf{v} - i\mathbf{u}.$$

where $a$ and $b$ are the real part and imaginary part of the eigenvalue $\lambda_1$, respectively, and $\mathbf{v}$ and $\mathbf{u}$ are respectively the real and imaginary parts of the eigenvector $\mathbf{v}_1$, respectively. The general solution is then

$$\mathbf{y} = c_1 e^{\lambda_1 x}\mathbf{v}_1 + c_2 e^{\lambda_2 x}\mathbf{v}_2$$
$$= c_1 e^{(a+ib)x}(\mathbf{v}+i\mathbf{u}) + c_2 e^{(a-ib)x}(\mathbf{v}-i\mathbf{u}).$$

As shown in Chapter 13, the complex exponential function $e^{(a\pm ib)x}$ can be expressed in terms of trigonometric functions using the Euler formula,

$$e^{(a\pm ib)x} = e^{ax}(\cos bx \pm i\sin bx).$$

Rewriting and simplify the general solution, we have

$$\begin{aligned}\mathbf{y} &= c_1e^{ax}(\cos bx + i\sin bx)\,(\mathbf{v} + i\mathbf{u}) + c_2e^{ax}(\cos bx - i\sin bx)\,(\mathbf{v} - i\mathbf{u})\\ &= c_1e^{ax}(\cos bx + i\sin bx)\mathbf{v} + c_2e^{ax}(\cos bx - i\sin bx)\mathbf{v} + c_1e^{ax}(\cos bx + i\sin bx)i\mathbf{u}\\ &\quad - c_2e^{ax}(\cos bx - i\sin bx)i\mathbf{u}\end{aligned}$$

Setting $C_1 = (c_1+c_2)$ and $C_2 = i(c_1-c_2)$, the solution becomes

$$\mathbf{y}(x) = C_1e^{ax}(\mathbf{v}\cos bx - \mathbf{u}\sin bx) + C_2e^{ax}(\mathbf{u}\cos bx + \mathbf{v}\sin bx)$$

Applying a remark made in section 13.3.3, the general solution can be interpreted as a linear combination of the real and imaginary parts of $\mathbf{y}_1(x)$ or $\mathbf{y}_2(x)$ where

$$\mathbf{y}_1(x) = e^{\lambda_1 x}\mathbf{v}_1 = e^{(a+ib)x}(\mathbf{v}+i\mathbf{u})$$
$$\mathbf{y}_2(x) = e^{\lambda_2 x}\mathbf{v}_2 = e^{(a-ib)x}(\mathbf{v}-i\mathbf{u})$$

That is,

$$\mathbf{y}(\mathbf{x}) = C_1\mathrm{Re}[\mathbf{y}_1(x)] + C_2\mathrm{Im}[\mathbf{y}_1(x)],$$
$$\mathbf{y}(\mathbf{x}) = C_1\mathrm{Re}[\mathbf{y}_2(x)] + C_2\mathrm{Im}[\mathbf{y}_2(x)]$$

**Example 14.11** Consider the system

$$\begin{bmatrix} y_1' \\ y_2' \\ y_3' \end{bmatrix} = \begin{bmatrix} 0 & 1 & 2 \\ 1 & 0 & 3 \\ -1 & -1 & -3 \end{bmatrix}\begin{bmatrix} y_1 \\ y_2 \\ y_3 \end{bmatrix} = \mathbf{Ay}$$

The eigenvalues and eigenvectors of **A** are $\lambda_1 = -1$, $\lambda_2 = -1 - i$, and $\lambda_3 = -1 + i$ and its corresponding eigenvectors are:

$$\mathbf{v}_1 = \begin{bmatrix} -1 \\ 1 \\ 0 \end{bmatrix};$$

$$\mathbf{v}_2 = \begin{bmatrix} -1 \\ -1+i \\ 1 \end{bmatrix} = \begin{bmatrix} -1 \\ -1 \\ 1 \end{bmatrix} + i\begin{bmatrix} 0 \\ 1 \\ 0 \end{bmatrix} = \mathbf{v} + i\mathbf{u};$$

$$\mathbf{v}_3 = \begin{bmatrix} -1 \\ -1-i \\ 1 \end{bmatrix} = \begin{bmatrix} -1 \\ -1 \\ 1 \end{bmatrix} - i\begin{bmatrix} 0 \\ 1 \\ 0 \end{bmatrix} = \mathbf{v} - i\mathbf{u}$$

*In[49]:=*

```
Clear[roots,vectors];
A = {{0,1,2},{1,0,3},{-1,-1,-3}};
{roots,vectors} = Eigensystem[A]
```

*Out[51]=*

```
{{-1, -1 - I, -1 + I}, {{-1, 1, 0}, {-1, -1 + I, 1}, {-1, -1 - I, 1}}}
```

The general solution is then

$$\mathbf{y}(x) = C_1 e^{-x}\mathbf{v}_1 + C_2 e^{-x}[\mathbf{v}\cos x + \mathbf{u}\sin x] + C_3 e^{-x}[\mathbf{u}\cos x - \mathbf{v}\sin x]$$

Combining the coefficients, we have

$$\begin{bmatrix} y_1(x) \\ y_2(x) \\ y_3(x) \end{bmatrix} = e^{-x}\begin{bmatrix} -c_1 - c_2\cos x + c_3\sin x \\ c_1 + c_2(-\cos x + \sin x) + c_3(\cos x + \sin x) \\ c_2\cos x - c_3\sin x \end{bmatrix}$$

We use the **ComplexExpand** function to extract the real and imaginary parts of the solution associated with the complex roots to obtain the solution

$$\mathbf{y}(x) = C_1\mathbf{y}_1(x) + C_2\text{Re}[\mathbf{y}_2(x)] + C_3\text{Im}[\mathbf{y}_2(x)]$$

where $\mathbf{y}_1(x)$ and $\mathbf{y}_2(x)$ are the solutions associated with the real root, $\lambda_1 = -1$, and the complex roots, $\lambda_2 = -1 \pm i$, respectively.

*In[52]:=*

```
Clear[x,y1,y2];
y1[x_] = Exp[roots[[1]]*x]*vectors[[1]];
y2[x_] = Exp[roots[[2]]*x]*vectors[[2]];
real =Re[y2[x]] // ComplexExpand
```

*Out[55]=*

$$\{-(\frac{\text{Cos[x]}}{\text{E}^{\text{x}}}), -(\frac{\text{Cos[x]}}{\text{E}^{\text{x}}}) + \frac{\text{Sin[x]}}{\text{E}^{\text{x}}}, \frac{\text{Cos[x]}}{\text{E}^{\text{x}}}\}$$

*In[56]:=*

```
imaginary = Im[y2[x]] // ComplexExpand
```

*Out[56]=*

$$\{\frac{\text{Sin[x]}}{\text{E}^{\text{x}}}, \frac{\text{Cos[x]}}{\text{E}^{\text{x}}} + \frac{\text{Sin[x]}}{\text{E}^{\text{x}}}, -(\frac{\text{Sin[x]}}{\text{E}^{\text{x}}})\}$$

*In[57]:=*

```
Clear[y];
y[x_]=c1*y1[x]+c2*real+c3*imaginary
```

*Out[58]=*

$$\{-(\frac{\text{c1}}{\text{E}^{\text{x}}}) - \frac{\text{c2Cos[x]}}{\text{E}^{\text{x}}} + \frac{\text{c3Sin[x]}}{\text{E}^{\text{x}}},$$
$$\frac{\text{c1}}{\text{E}^{\text{x}}} + \text{c2}(-(\frac{\text{Cos[x]}}{\text{E}^{\text{x}}}) + \frac{\text{Sin[x]}}{\text{E}^{\text{x}}}) + \text{c3}(\frac{\text{Cos[x]}}{\text{E}^{\text{x}}} + \frac{\text{Sin[x]}}{\text{E}^{\text{x}}}), \frac{\text{c2Cos[x]}}{\text{E}^{\text{x}}} - \frac{\text{c3Sin[x]}}{\text{E}^{\text{x}}}\}$$

## EXERCISES

1. Find the general solutions of the following homogeneous system of differential equations $\mathbf{y}' = \mathbf{A}\mathbf{y}$ where

   (a) $\mathbf{A} = \begin{bmatrix} 1 & -2 & 2 \\ -2 & 1 & -2 \\ 2 & -2 & 1 \end{bmatrix}$

(b) $\mathbf{A} = \begin{bmatrix} 1 & 2 & -1 & -1 \\ -4 & 0 & 1 & 4 \\ -1 & 5 & -2 & -1 \\ -4 & -4 & 3 & 6 \end{bmatrix}$

(c) $\mathbf{A} = \begin{bmatrix} 1 & -1 & -1 \\ 1 & -1 & 0 \\ 1 & 0 & -1 \end{bmatrix}$

2. Find the solution of the initial-value problem $\mathbf{y}' = \mathbf{A}\mathbf{y}$ such that $\mathbf{y}(0) = [1\ -2]^{\mathrm{T}}$, where

$$\mathbf{A} = \begin{bmatrix} 1.0 & 2 \\ -0.5 & 1 \end{bmatrix}$$

### 14.1.3 Inhomogeneous linear systems

As in the case of homogeneous systems, the method for finding solutions of inhomogeneous systems parallels that for the scalar differential equation case. Consider the inhomogeneous system of $n$ linear differential equations

$$\begin{aligned} y_1'(x) &= a_{11}y_1(x) + a_{12}y_2(x) + \ldots + a_{1n}y_n(x) + g_1(x) \\ y_2'(x) &= a_{21}y_1(x) + a_{22}y_2(x) + \ldots + a_{2n}y_n(x) + g_2(x) \\ &\cdots\cdots\cdots\cdots\cdots\cdots\cdots\cdots\cdots\cdots \\ y_n'(x) &= a_{n1}y_1(x) + a_{n2}y_2(x) + \ldots + a_{nn}y_n(x) + g_n(x) \end{aligned}$$

or, as a matrix equation

$$\mathbf{y}'(x) = \mathbf{A}(x)\mathbf{y}(x) + \mathbf{g}(x).$$

If $\mathbf{y}_c(x)$ denotes the complementary solution, i.e., the general solution of the corresponding homogeneous system $\mathbf{y}' = \mathbf{A}(x)\mathbf{y}$, and $\mathbf{y}_p(x)$ is any particular solution of the inhomogeneous system $\mathbf{y}'(x) = \mathbf{A}(x)\mathbf{y}(x) + \mathbf{g}(x)$, then

$$\mathbf{y}(x) = \mathbf{y}_c(x) + \mathbf{y}_p(x)$$

is the general solution of the inhomogeneous system. We have already discussed how to find $\mathbf{y}_c(x)$ when $\mathbf{A}$ is a constant matrix and we shall concentrate on a technique to find $\mathbf{y}_p(x)$. Although the discussion below is valid when $\mathbf{A}(x)$ is a matrix-valued function, we will restrict our attention to the case when $\mathbf{A}$ is a constant matrix.

Suppose $\mathbf{g}(x) = \mathbf{b}$ is a constant vector and consider the inhomogeneous system

$$\mathbf{y}'(x) = \mathbf{A}\mathbf{y}(x) + \mathbf{b}.$$

It is easy to show that

$$\mathbf{y}_p(x) = -\mathbf{A}^{-1}\mathbf{b}$$

is a solution, provided $\mathbf{A}$ is nonsingular. In this case, the general solution of the inhomogeneous system is

$\mathbf{y}(x) = \mathbf{y}_c(x) - \mathbf{A}^{-1}\mathbf{b}.$

**Example 14.12** Find the general solution of the system

$$
\begin{aligned}
y_1' &= -y_1 + 6y_2 + 5 \\
y_2' &= \ \ y_1 - 2y_2 + 15
\end{aligned}
$$

Since $\mathbf{b} = [5 \ 15]^T$, we have

$$\mathbf{y}_p = -\mathbf{A}^{-1}\mathbf{b} = \begin{bmatrix} -19 \\ -4 \end{bmatrix}$$

*In[59]:=*

```
A  =  {{-1,6},{1,-1}};
b  =  {5,15};
yp  =  -Inverse[A].b
```

*Out[61]=*

```
{-19, -4}
```

As shown in example 14.8 in section 14.1.2, the complementary solution is

$$\mathbf{y}_c = c_1 e^{-4x}\begin{bmatrix} -2 \\ 1 \end{bmatrix} + c_2 e^{x}\begin{bmatrix} 3 \\ 1 \end{bmatrix}$$

The general solution of $\mathbf{y}' = \mathbf{A}\mathbf{y}$ is then

$$\mathbf{y} = c_1 e^{-4x}\begin{bmatrix} -2 \\ 1 \end{bmatrix} + c_2 e^{x}\begin{bmatrix} 3 \\ 1 \end{bmatrix} + \begin{bmatrix} -19 \\ -4 \end{bmatrix}$$

When $\mathbf{g}(x)$ is not a constant function, the particular problem can be solved by using a method similar to the Variation of Parameters method introduced in last chapter. The complementary solution has the form:

$$\mathbf{y}_c = \mathbf{\Phi}(x)\mathbf{c}$$

where $\mathbf{\Phi}(x)$ is a fundamental matrix and $\mathbf{c}$ is an $n \times 1$ column vector of arbitrary constants. Since $\mathbf{\Phi}(x)$ is the general solution of $\mathbf{y}' = \mathbf{A}\mathbf{y}$, we have $\mathbf{\Phi}'(x) = \mathbf{A}\mathbf{\Phi}(x)$. Suppose we seek a particular solution of $\mathbf{y}' = \mathbf{A}\mathbf{y} + \mathbf{g}(x)$ of the form:

$$\mathbf{y}_p(x) = \mathbf{\Phi}(x)\mathbf{u}(x).$$

where $\mathbf{u}(x)$ is an unknown vector-valued function. Substituting $\mathbf{y}_p(x)$ into $\mathbf{y}' = \mathbf{A}\mathbf{y} + \mathbf{g}(x)$, we have

$$\mathbf{y}_p'(x) = \mathbf{\Phi}'(x)\mathbf{u}(x) + \mathbf{\Phi}(x)\mathbf{u}'(x) = \mathbf{A}\mathbf{\Phi}(x)\mathbf{u}(x) + \mathbf{g}(x)$$

Since $\mathbf{\Phi}(x)$ is a fundamental matrix, the above equation reduces to

$$\mathbf{\Phi}(x)\mathbf{u}'(x) = \mathbf{g}(x).$$

Furthermore, since $\Phi(x)$ is nonsingular, we have

$$\mathbf{u}'(x) = \Phi^{-1}(x)\mathbf{g}(x)$$

Now, integrating this equation, we obtain the formula:

$$\mathbf{u}(x) = \int \Phi^{-1}(x)\mathbf{g}(x)\mathrm{d}x.$$

Hence, a particular solution of the inhomogeneous is given by

$$\mathbf{y}_p(x) = \Phi(x)\mathbf{u}(x) = \Phi(x)\int \Phi^{-1}(x)\mathbf{g}(x)\mathrm{d}x.$$

The general solution of the inhomogeneous system is therefore

$$\mathbf{y}(x) = \mathbf{y}_c(x) + \mathbf{y}_p(x) = \Phi(x)\mathbf{c} + \Phi(x)\int \Phi^{-1}(x)\mathbf{g}(x)\mathrm{d}x.$$

**Example 14.13** Consider the inhomogeneous system, $\mathbf{y}' = \mathbf{A}\mathbf{y} + \mathbf{g}(x)$, where

$$\mathbf{y}(x) = \begin{bmatrix} y_1(x) \\ y_2(x) \end{bmatrix}; \ \mathbf{A} = \begin{bmatrix} 1 & 2 \\ 2 & 1 \end{bmatrix}; \ \mathbf{g}(x) = \begin{bmatrix} 2x \\ x^2 \end{bmatrix}$$

We compute the eigenvalues and eigenvectors of **A**.

*In[62]:=*

```
A = {{1,2},{2,1}};
Eigensystem[A]
```

*Out[63]=*

```
{{-1, 3}, {{-1, 1}, {1, 1}}}
```

Hence a fundamental matrix of the homogeneous system is

$$\Phi(x) = \begin{bmatrix} e^{-x}\mathbf{v}_1 & e^{3x}\mathbf{v}_2 \end{bmatrix} = \begin{bmatrix} -e^{-x} & e^{3x} \\ e^{-x} & e^{3x} \end{bmatrix}$$

We use *Mathematica* to construct the general solution

$$\mathbf{y}(x) = \mathbf{y}_c(x) + \mathbf{y}_p(x).$$

*In[64]:=*

```
Clear[phi,g,c1,c2,x,yc,yp,y];
phi[x_]:= {{-Exp[-x],Exp[3*x]},{Exp[-x],Exp[3x]}};
g[x_]:= {2*x,x^2};
c = {c1,c2};
yc[x_] = phi[x].c;
yp[x_] = phi[x].Integrate[Inverse[phi[x]].g[x],x];
y[x_] = yc[x] + yp[x];
y[x] // Simplify // MatrixForm
```

*Out[71]//MatrixForm=*

$$-(\frac{58}{27}) - \frac{c1}{E^x} + c2\, E^{3x} + \frac{14x}{9} - \frac{2x^2}{3}$$
$$\frac{50}{27} + \frac{c1}{E^x} + c2E^{3x} - \frac{22x}{9} + \frac{x^2}{3}$$

That is, the general solution is

$$\mathbf{y}(x) = c_1\begin{bmatrix} -e^{-x} \\ e^{-x} \end{bmatrix} + c_2\begin{bmatrix} e^{3x} \\ e^{3x} \end{bmatrix} + \begin{bmatrix} -\frac{58}{27} + \frac{14}{9}x - \frac{2}{3}x^2 \\ \frac{50}{27} - \frac{22}{9}x + \frac{1}{3}x^2 \end{bmatrix}$$

## EXERCISES

1. Find the general solutions of $\mathbf{y}' = \mathbf{A}\mathbf{y} + \mathbf{g}(x)$ for the following matrices $\mathbf{A}$ and inhomogeneous terms $\mathbf{g}(x)$:

   (a) $\mathbf{A} = \begin{bmatrix} 1 & -1 \\ 2 & -1 \end{bmatrix}$; $\mathbf{g}(x) = \begin{bmatrix} \sin(x) \\ 0 \end{bmatrix}$

   (b) $\mathbf{A} = \begin{bmatrix} -5 & -2 \\ 4 & 1 \end{bmatrix}$; $\mathbf{g}(x) = \begin{bmatrix} 2e^{x} \\ 12e^{3x} \end{bmatrix}$

2. Solve the initial-value problem $\mathbf{y}' = \mathbf{A}\mathbf{y} + \mathbf{g}(x)$ when

   $$\mathbf{A} = \begin{bmatrix} 2 & 1 & 1 \\ 2 & 3 & 2 \\ 1 & 1 & 2 \end{bmatrix}; \mathbf{g}(x) = \begin{bmatrix} 16e^{3x} \\ 16e^{x} \\ 0 \end{bmatrix}; \mathbf{y}(0) = \begin{bmatrix} 2 \\ -4 \\ -2 \end{bmatrix}$$

## □ 14.2 The DSolve and NDSolve Functions for Systems □

The *Mathematica* functions **DSolve** and **NDSolve** can be used for either scalar differential equations or systems of differential equations.

### 14.2.1 The **DSolve** function

Linear systems of differential equations can be solved with the **DSolve** function. Recall *Mathematica*'s description of this function.

*In[72]:=*

```
?DSolve
```

**DSolve[eqn, y[x], x] solves a differential equation for the functions y[x], with independent variable x. DSolve[{eqn1, eqn2, ...}, {y1[x1, ...], ...}, {x1, ...}] solves a list of differential equations.**

The system of differential equations is a list in the first argument. The second argument is a list of the dependent variables, and the third argument is the independent variable.

**Example 14.14** Solve the system

$$y_1' = y_1 + y_2 + 2x$$
$$y_2' = 4y_1 + y_2 - x^2$$

using the **DSolve** function.

*In[73]:=*

```
Clear[x,y1,y2];
DSolve[{y1'[x]==y1[x]+y2[x]+2*x,
        y2'[x]==4*y1[x]+y2[x]-x^2},
       {y1[x],y2[x]},x] // Simplify
```

*Out[74]=*

$$\{\{y1[x] \to -(\frac{16}{27}) + \frac{2x}{9} + \frac{x^2}{3} - \frac{C[1]}{E^x} + E^{3x}\,C[2],$$
$$y2[x] \to \frac{22}{27} - \frac{14x}{9} - \frac{x^2}{3} + \frac{2C[1]}{E^x} + 2\,E^{3x}\,C[2]\}\}$$

**Example 14.15** Solve the system:

$$y_1' = 2y_1 + 2y_2 + 2y_3$$
$$y_2' = 2y_1 + y_2 + 2y_3$$
$$y_3' = y_1 - y_3$$

using the **DSolve** function.

*In[75]:=*

```
Clear[x,y1,y2,y3,y];
sol = DSolve[{y1'[x]==2*y1[x]+2*y2[x]+2*y3[x],
        y2'[x]==2*y1[x]+y2[x]+2*y3[x],
        y3'[x]==y1[x]-y3[x]},
       {y1[x],y2[x],y3[x]},x] // Simplify;
y1[x_] = y1[x] /. sol;
y2[x_] = y2[x] /. sol;
y3[x_] = y3[x] /. sol;
y[x_] = {y1[x],y2[x],y3[x]};
y[x] // MatrixForm
```

*Out[81]//MatrixForm=*

$$(2C[1] + 3E^{5x}C[1] - 2C[2] + 2E^{5x}C[2] - 2C[3] + 2E^{5x}C[3]) \,/\, (5E^x)$$
$$(-12C[1] + 12E^{5x}C[1] - 10xC[1] + 17C[2] + 8E^{5x}C[2] + 10xC[2] - 8C[3] + 8E^{5x}C[3] + 10xC[3]) \,/\, (25E^x)$$
$$(-3C[1] + 3E^{5x}C[1] + 10xC[1] - 2C[2] + 2E^{5x}C[2] - 10xC[2] + 23C[3] + 2E^{5x}C[3] - 10xC[3]) \,/\, (25E^x)$$

If we have an initial-value problem for a system, then we include the initial conditions in the first argument of **DSolve**.

**Example 14.16** Find the solution of the initial-value problem:

$y_1' = y_1 - y_2,\ y_1(-2) = 0$
$y_2' = 2y_1 + 4y_2,\ y_2(-2) = 1$

using **DSolve**.

*In[82]:=*
```
Clear[x,y1,y2];
sol=DSolve[{y1'[x]==y1[x]-y2[x],
            y2'[x]==2*y1[x]+4*y2[x],
            y1[-2]==0,y2[-2]==1},
           {y1[x],y2[x]},x]  //  Simplify
```

*Out[83]=*
$\{\{y1[x] \to E^{4+2x} - E^{6+3x},\ y2[x] \to E^{4+2x}\,(-1 + 2E^{2+x})\}\}$

Below we plot the solutions $y_1(x)$ (solid line) and $y_2(x)$ **(dashed line) for** $0 \le x \le 2$.

*In[84]:=*
```
y1[x_]  =  y1[x]  /.  sol[[1,1]];
y2[x_]  =  y2[x]  /.  sol[[1,2]];
Plot[{y1[x],y2[x]},{x,0,2},
          PlotStyle->{{},Dashing[{0.01}]},
          Axes->True,AxesLabel->{"y","x"}];
```

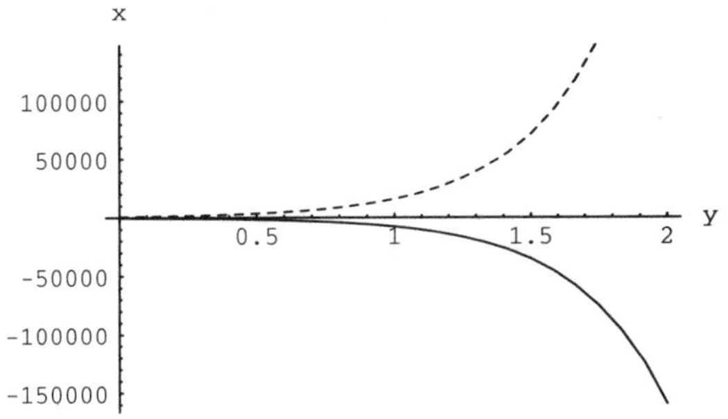


## EXERCISES

1. Use the **DSolve** function to find the general solution of the following differential equations:
   (a) $y_1' = -y_1 - y_2$
   $y_2' = y_1 - y_2 + y_3$
   $y_3' = y_2 - y_3$
   (b) $y_1' = 2y_1 + y_2 - 2y_3 + e^x$
   $y_2' = -3y_1 + 4y_3 + e^x$
   $y_3' = -2y_1 - y_2 + 4y_3 + e^x$

2. Use the **DSolve** function to solve the initial-value problem:
   $y_1' = -2y_1 + 2y_2 + e^x,\ y_1(0) = 2/3$
   $y_2' = -4y_1 + 4y_2, \qquad y_2(0) = 2/3.$

### 14.2.2 The **NDSolve** function

In the previous chapter we used the **NDSolve** function to find an approximation to the solution of an initial-value problem. It can also be used on a system of differential equations. Here is a description of this function.

*In[87]:=*

```
?NDSolve
```

**NDSolve[eqns, y, {x, xmin, xmax}] finds a numerical solution to the differential equations eqns for the function y with the independent variable x in the range xmin to xmax. NDSolve[eqns, {y1, y2, ...}, {x, xmin, xmax}] finds numerical solutions for the functions yi. NDSolve[eqns, y, {x, x1, x2, ...}] forces a function evaluation at each of x1, x2, ... The range of numerical integration is from Min[x1, x2, ...] to Max[x1, x2, ...].**

**Example 14.17** Find an approximating function for the solution of the initial-value problem:

$$y_1' = y_1 - y_2^2, \quad y_1(0) = 0$$
$$y_2' = y_1^2 - y_2, \quad y_2(0) = 1$$

over the interval $0 \leq x \leq 1$.

*In[88]:=*

```
Clear[y1,y2,x];
sol = NDSolve[{y1'[x] == y1[x] - y2[x]^2,
               y2'[x] == y1[x]^2 - y2[x],
                y1[0]==0,y2[0]==1},
               {y1[x],y2[x]},{x,0,1}];
y1[x_] = y1[x] /. sol[[1,1]];
y2[x_] = y2[x] /. sol[[1,2]];
```

Next, we plot these approximations. The solid curve is the graph of the approximation for $y_1(x)$ and the dashed curve is the approximation for $y_2(x)$.

*In[92]:=*

```
Plot[{y1[x],y2[x]},{x,0,1},
     PlotStyle->{{},Dashing[{0.02}]}];
```

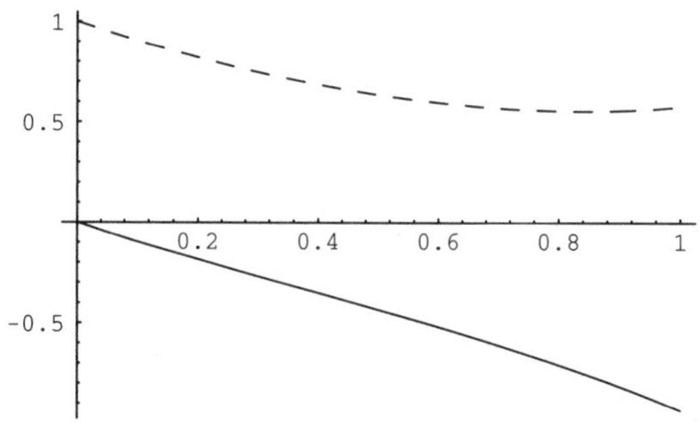

**Example 14.18** Find an approximation for the solution of the nonlinear initial-value problem,

$$y_1' = -y_1 + y_1 y_2,\ y_1(0) = 2$$
$$y_2' = \frac{1}{5} y_1 + 2y_2 - y_1 y_2,\ y_2(0) = 1$$

over the interval $0 \le x \le 10$.

*In[93]:=*

```
Clear[y1,y2,x];
sol = NDSolve[{y1'[x] == -y1[x]+y1[x]*y2[x],
              y2'[x] == y1[x]/5+2*y2[x]-y1[x]*y2[x],
               y1[0]==2,y2[0]==1},
              {y1[x],y2[x]},{x,0,10}];
y1[x_] = y1[x] /. sol[[1,1]];
y2[x_] = y2[x] /. sol[[1,2]];
```

The approximation for each component is plotted below.

*In[97]:=*

```
Plot[{y1[x],y2[x]},{x,0,10},AxesLabel->{"x","y1,y2"},
     PlotStyle->{{},Dashing[{0.02}]}];
```

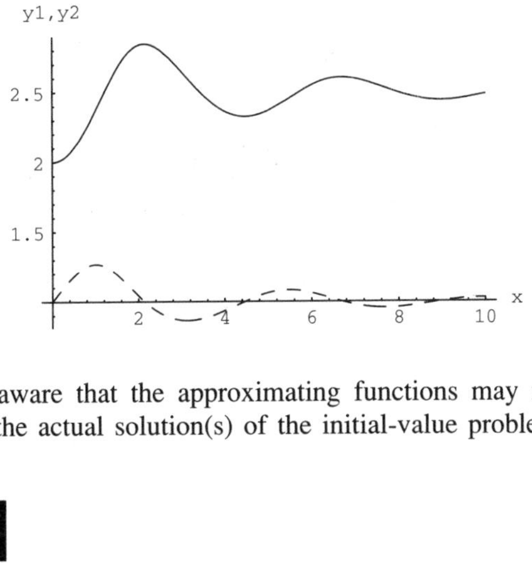


One should be aware that the approximating functions may not be an accurate representation for the actual solution(s) of the initial-value problem.

## EXERCISES

1. Plot the approximation for the solution of the initial-value problem over $0 \le x \le 1$.

$$y_1' = y_1 - y_2^2,\quad y_1(0) = 0$$
$$y_2' = y_1^2 - y_2,\quad y_2(0) = 1$$

2. Plot the approximation for the solution of the initial-value problem over $0 \le x \le 2$.

$$y_1' = y_1(y_2 - y_1 + 2),\ y_1(0) = 2$$
$$y_2' = y_2(y_1 - y_2 - 3),\ y_2(0) = 1$$

## □ 14.3 Autonomous Systems and the Phase Plane □

In previous sections, we restricted our attention to linear systems of differential equations. In most instances, nonlinear first-order systems are not solvable. However, we can often investigate the qualitative behavior of their solutions without explicitly finding their solutions.

In this section we shall discuss a first-order system that has the following form:

$$y_1' = F_1(y_1,y_2, \ldots ,y_n)$$
$$y_2' = F_2(y_1,y_2, \ldots ,y_n)$$
$$\ldots\ldots\ldots\ldots\ldots\ldots$$
$$y_n' = F_n(y_1,y_2, \ldots ,y_n)$$

This first-order system is called an **autonomous** system. Note that the independent variable $x$ does not occur explicitly on the right-side of the differential equations. In short, we write a first-order autonomous system as

$$\mathbf{y}' = \mathbf{F}(\mathbf{y})$$

where $\mathbf{y}(x) = [y_1(x)\ y_2(x) \ldots y_n(x)]^T$ is a vector-valued function of $x$, and $\mathbf{F}$ is a vector-valued function of $(y_1,y_2, \ldots ,y_n)$.

### 14.3.1 Phase space for linear systems

The phase space is one way of visualizing solutions to autonomous systems.

> **DEFINITION 14.2** *Consider* $\mathbf{y}' = \mathbf{F}(\mathbf{y})$. *If* $\phi(x)$ *is a solution of the autonomous system, then its graph is called an* ***orbit***, ***trajectory***, *or* ***path*** *of* $\mathbf{y}' = \mathbf{F}(\mathbf{y})$ *when plotted in* $y_1y_2 \ldots y_n$*-space. This space is called the* ***Poincare phase space***.

Any linear homogeneous system with constant coefficients is an example of an autonomous system. Consider the homogeneous system:

$$\begin{bmatrix} y_1' \\ y_2' \end{bmatrix} = \begin{bmatrix} -1 & 2 \\ 2 & -1 \end{bmatrix} \begin{bmatrix} y_1 \\ y_2 \end{bmatrix} = \mathbf{A}\mathbf{y}$$

The system has eigenvalues $\lambda_1 = -3$, $\lambda_2 = 1$, and eigenvectors

$$\mathbf{v}_1 = \begin{bmatrix} -1 \\ 1 \end{bmatrix}; \ \mathbf{v}_2 = \begin{bmatrix} 1 \\ 1 \end{bmatrix}$$

*In[98]:=*

```
A = {{-1,2},{2,-1}};
Eigensystem[A]
```

*Out[99]=*

```
{{-3, 1}, {{-1, 1}, {1, 1}}}
```

The general solution is then

$$\begin{bmatrix} y_1(x) \\ y_2(x) \end{bmatrix} = c_1 e^{-3x} \begin{bmatrix} -1 \\ 1 \end{bmatrix} + c_2 e^{x} \begin{bmatrix} 1 \\ 1 \end{bmatrix}$$

If

$$\mathbf{y}(0) = \begin{bmatrix} y_1(0) \\ y_2(0) \end{bmatrix} = \begin{bmatrix} -1 \\ 3 \end{bmatrix}$$

then $c_1 = 2$ and $c_2 = 1$, and the solution of the initial-value problem is:

$$\mathbf{y}(x) = \begin{bmatrix} y_1(x) \\ y_2(x) \end{bmatrix} = 2e^{-3x} \begin{bmatrix} -1 \\ 1 \end{bmatrix} + e^{x} \begin{bmatrix} 1 \\ 1 \end{bmatrix}$$

Suppose we treat $x$ as a parameter so that points $(y_1(x), y_2(x))$ in $y_1y_2$-plane trace out a curve. The following parametric plot shows this trajectory.

*In[100]:=*

```
Clear[y1,y2,x]
v1  =  {-1,1};  v2  =  {1,1};
c1  =  2;  c2  =  1;
y1[x_]:=  c1*Exp[-3*x]*(-1)+c2*Exp[x]*1;
y2[x_]:=  c1*Exp[-3*x]*1+c2*Exp[x]*1;
ParametricPlot[{y1[x],y2[x]},{x,0,2},
                    AxesLabel->{"y1","y2"}];
```

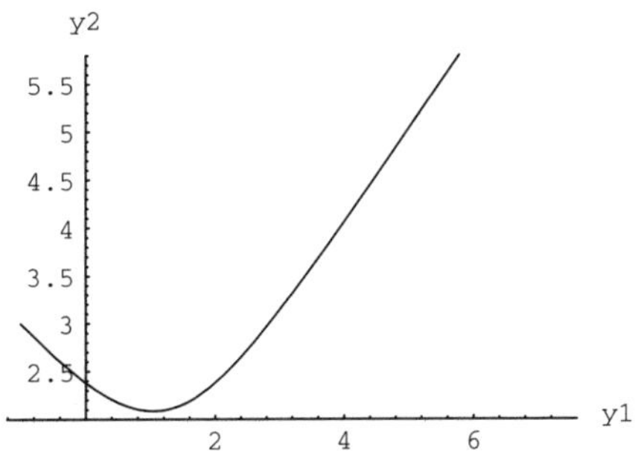


To show more clearly the direction of the trajectory or the solution curve as $x$ increases, we use the **MathEcon** function **trajectory** to plot the trajectory. Here is a description of this function.

*In[106]:=*

```
?trajectory
```

**trajectory[fcts,dom,opt] displays the trajectory of the list of functions fcts given on the domain dom (a list). The last argument is optional and can contain any option for ParametricPlot. Arrows are placed on the graph of the parametric functions to indicate the direction of increasing values of the independent variable. For example,**

**trajectory[{x^2+1,Cos[x]},{x,-1,3}, AxesLabel->{"y1","y2"}].**

The first argument is a list that contains the components of the solution and the second argument is a list that specifies the domain of the solution. The third argument is optional and can contain graphics directives such as labeling the axes or specifying the style of the trajectory. An arrowhead is placed on the trajectory to indicate the direction of increasing values of $x$.

*In[107]:=*

```
trajectory[{y1[x],y2[x]},{x,0,2},
           PlotRange->All,AxesLabel->{"y1","y2"}];
```

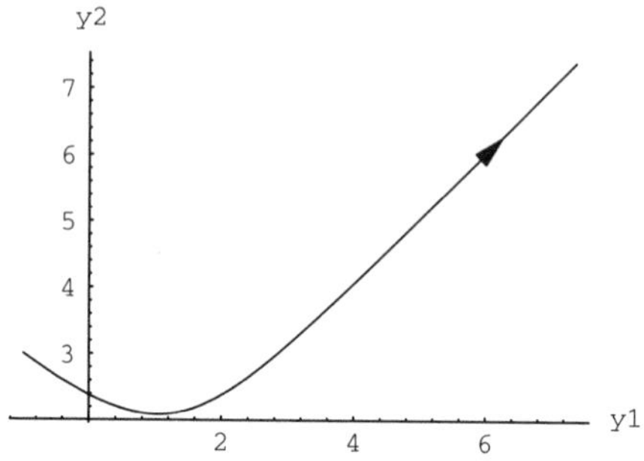


A constant vector $\mathbf{y}_e$ such that $\mathbf{F}(\mathbf{y}_e) = \mathbf{0}$ is called an *equilibrium point* of the system. Note that an equilibrium point is a constant solution of the autonomous system. For this reason, $\mathbf{y}_e$ is also called an *equilibrium solution.* A linear autonomous system $\mathbf{y}' = \mathbf{A}\,\mathbf{y}$ has an equilibrium solution $\mathbf{y}_e \equiv \mathbf{0}$, which corresponds to the origin of the phase space. If the matrix $\mathbf{A}$ is nonsingular, then this solution is the only equilibrium point of the system.

In order to discuss the behavior of trajectories, we introduce the following terminology.

**DEFINITION 14.3** *Suppose* $\mathbf{y}(x)$ *is any solution of an initial-value problem* $\mathbf{y}' = \mathbf{F}(\mathbf{y})$. *An equilibrium point* $\mathbf{y}_e$ *is said to be* ***stable*** *if for every* $\varepsilon > 0$, *there exists a number* $\delta > 0$ *such that, for all* $x \geq x_0$,

$$|\mathbf{y}(x) - \mathbf{y}_e| < \varepsilon \quad \text{if} \quad |\mathbf{y}(x_0) - \mathbf{y}_e| < \delta.$$

*An equilibrium point* $\mathbf{y}_e$ *is said to be* ***asymptotically stable*** *if it is stable and there exists a number* $\nu > 0$ *such that*

$$\lim_{x \to +\infty} \mathbf{y}(x) = \mathbf{y}_e \text{ when } |\mathbf{y}(x_0) - \mathbf{y}_e| < \nu.$$

*An equilibrium point that is not stable is said to be* ***unstable***. *An equilibrium point that is stable, but not asymptotically stable, is said to be* ***neutrally stable***.

Figure 14.1 depicts three cases of the trajectory $\mathbf{y}(x)$ of a two-dimensional system. Panel (a) shows that for every circle with a center at $\mathbf{y}_e$ and with radius $\varepsilon$, there exists a smaller circle with center at $\mathbf{y}_e$ and with radius $\delta$, that once a point $\mathbf{y}(x_0)$ on the trajectory is inside the smaller circle ($|\mathbf{y}(x_0) - \mathbf{y}_e| < \delta$), then the trajectory stays within the larger circle ($|\mathbf{y}(x) - \mathbf{y}_e| < \varepsilon$) for all $x \geq x_0$. The equilibrium point $\mathbf{y}_e$ in (a) is stable. However, $\mathbf{y}_e$ in panel (c) is unstable. Panel (b) illustrates the case when the trajectory is asymptotically stable. In particular, the equilibrium point $\mathbf{y}_e$ is stable and any trajectory that is sufficiently close to $\mathbf{y}_e$ must approach it as $x \to \infty$.

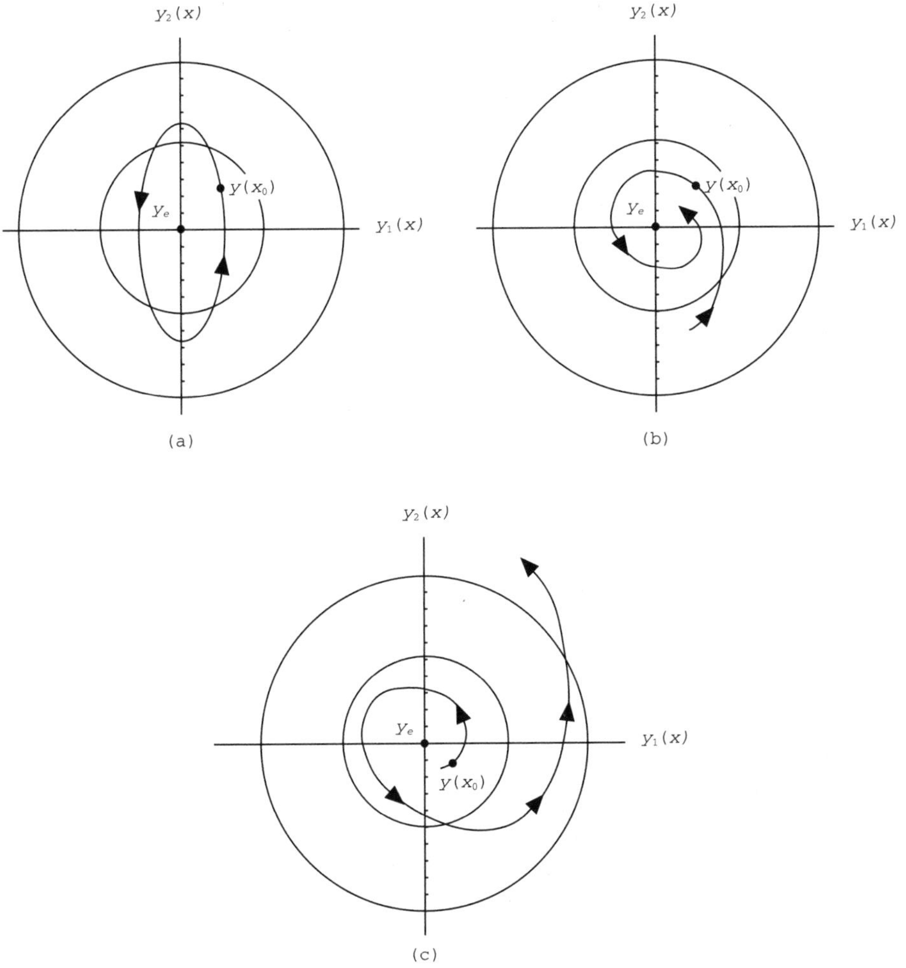


**Figure 14.1** Trajectory and stability: (a) $y_e$ is neutrally stable; (b) $y_e$ is asymptotically stable; (c) $y_e$ is unstable

For the homogeneous system $\mathbf{y}' = \mathbf{A}\mathbf{y}$, the stability of an equilibrium point can be checked by examining the eigenvalues of the matrix $\mathbf{A}$, as stated in the following theorem.

**THEOREM 14.2** *Consider a system of n equations,* $\mathbf{y}' = \mathbf{A}\mathbf{y}$. *Suppose* $\lambda_1, \lambda_2, \ldots, \lambda_k$ *are the eigenvalues of* $\mathbf{A}$. *Denote the multiplicities of the eigenvalues by* $n_1, n_2, \ldots, n_k$.

*(1) If* $\mathrm{Re}[\lambda_i] \le 0$ *when* $n_i = 1$, *and* $\mathrm{Re}[\lambda_i] < 0$ *when* $n_i > 1$, *then the equilibrium point* $\mathbf{y}_e \equiv \mathbf{0}$ *is stable.*

*(2) If* $\mathrm{Re}[\lambda_i] < 0$, *then* $\mathbf{y}_e \equiv \mathbf{0}$ *is asymptotically stable.*

*(3) If* $\mathrm{Re}[\lambda_i] > 0$ *for some eigenvalue* $\lambda_i$, *then* $\mathbf{y}_e \equiv \mathbf{0}$ *is unstable.*

In the above theorem, the multiplicity of an eigenvalue refers to its algebraic multiplicity, that is, it is the multiplicity as a root of the characteristic polynomial $P(\lambda) = |\mathbf{A} - \lambda\mathbf{I}|$.

**Example 14.19** Consider the system of differential equations:

$$\begin{bmatrix} y_1' \\ y_2' \end{bmatrix} = \begin{bmatrix} -2 & 1 \\ 1 & -2 \end{bmatrix} \begin{bmatrix} y_1 \\ y_2 \end{bmatrix} = \mathbf{A}\mathbf{y}$$

Determine the stability of any equilibrium solutions. We first compute the eigenvalues and eigenvectors of **A**.

*In[108]:=*

```
A = {{-2,1},{1,-2}};
Eigensystem[A]
```

*Out[109]=*

```
{{-3, -1}, {{-1, 1}, {1, 1}}}
```

Since **A** is nonsingular (why?), there is only one equilibrium, $\mathbf{y}_e = \mathbf{0}$. This equilibrium solution is asymptotically stable since all of the eigenvalues are negative.

Suppose the initial values, $y_1(0) = 1$ and $y_2(0) = 0$, are given for the system. We solve this initial-value problem with **DSolve**.

*In[110]:=*

```
Clear[y,y1,y2,x];
y[x_] = DSolve[{y1'[x]  ==  -2*y1[x]  +  y2[x],
              y2'[x]  ==  y1[x]  -  2*y2[x],
              y1[0]  ==  1,y2[0]  ==  0},{y1[x],y2[x]},x]
```

*Out[111]=*

$$\{\{y1[x] \rightarrow \frac{1}{2E^{3x}} + \frac{1}{2E^{x}},\ y2[x] \rightarrow \frac{-1}{2E^{3x}} + \frac{1}{2E^{x}}\}\}$$

Thus the components of $\mathbf{y}(x)$ are:

$$y_1(x) = \frac{1}{2}e^{-3x} + \frac{1}{2}e^{-x}$$

$$y_2(x) = -\frac{1}{2}e^{-3x} + \frac{1}{2}e^{-x}$$

Plotting the solution in the phase plane for $0 \le x \le 3$, we observe that $\mathbf{y}(x)$ approaches the origin.

*In[112]:=*

```
{y1[x_],y2[x_]} = {y1[x],y2[x]} /. y[x][[1]];
trajectory[{y1[x],y2[x]},{x,0,3},
            PlotRange->All,AxesLabel->{"y1","y2"}];
```

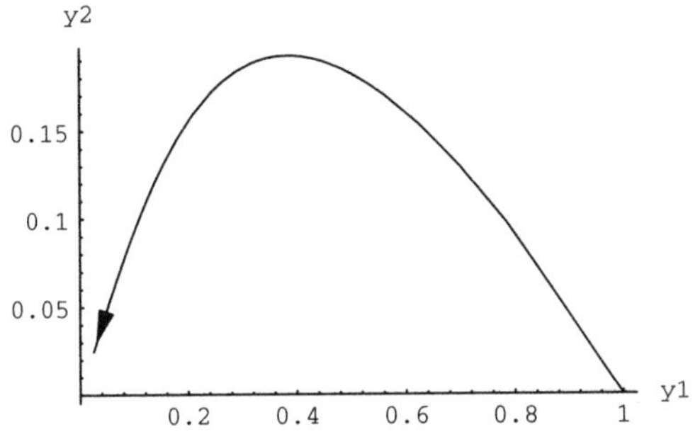


**Example 14.20** Check the stability of the equilibrium solutions of the system

$$\begin{bmatrix} y_1' \\ y_2' \\ y_3' \end{bmatrix} = \begin{bmatrix} 1 & 2 & 1 \\ 1 & -1 & 0 \\ 0 & 0 & -3 \end{bmatrix} \begin{bmatrix} y_1 \\ y_2 \\ y_3 \end{bmatrix} = \mathbf{Ay}$$

The matrix $\mathbf{A}$ of the system has eigenvalues, $\lambda_1 = -3$, $\lambda_2 = -\sqrt{3}$, and $\lambda_3 = \sqrt{3}$. Hence, $\mathbf{y}_e = \mathbf{0}$ is the only equilibrium solution.

*In[114]:=*
```
A = {{1,2,1},{1,-1,0},{0,0,-3}};
Eigensystem[A]
```

*Out[115]=*
```
{{-3, -Sqrt[3], Sqrt[3]}, {{-2, 1, 6}, {1 - Sqrt[3], 1, 0}, {1 + Sqrt[3], 1, 0}}}
```

Two of the eigenvalues are negative and one is positive. Hence, the equilibrium solution $\mathbf{y}_e = \mathbf{0}$ is unstable. The general solution

$$\begin{bmatrix} y_1(x) \\ y_2(x) \\ y_3(x) \end{bmatrix} = c_1 e^{-3x}\mathbf{v}_1 + c_2 e^{-\sqrt{3}x}\mathbf{v}_2 + c_3 e^{\sqrt{3}x}\mathbf{v}_3$$

contains $e^{-3x}$, $e^{-\sqrt{3}x}$ and $e^{\sqrt{3}x}$ terms, but the third term $e^{\sqrt{3}x}$ dominates the first two terms as $x$ increases. The graph of the solution will eventually move away from (0,0,0) in phase space.

**Example 14.21** Consider the linear autonomous system:

$$\begin{bmatrix} y_1' \\ y_2' \end{bmatrix} = \begin{bmatrix} \frac{1}{10} & -1 \\ 1 & \frac{1}{10} \end{bmatrix} \begin{bmatrix} y_1 \\ y_2 \end{bmatrix}$$

The system has complex eigenvalues, $\lambda_1 = 1/10 + i$ and $\lambda_2 = 1/10 - i$. Since the real parts of the eigenvalues, $\mathrm{Re}[\lambda_1] = \mathrm{Re}[\lambda_2] = 1/10$, are positive, the equilibrium solution $\mathbf{y}_e = \mathbf{0}$ is unstable.

Suppose the initial conditions, $y_1(0) = 1$ and $y_2(0) = -1/2$, are imposed. We solve the initial-value problem and then plot the trajectory of this solution for $0 \le x \le 14$.

*In[116]:=*

```
Clear[y,y1,y2,x];
y[x_]  =  DSolve[{y1'[x]==y1[x]/10-y2[x],
                  y2'[x]==y1[x]+y2[x]/10,
                  y1[0]==1,y2[0]==-1/2},{y1[x],y2[x]},x];
{y1[x_],y2[x_]}  =  {y1[x],y2[x]}  /.  y[x][[1]];
trajectory[{y1[x],y2[x]},{x,0,14},
              PlotRange->All,AxesLabel->{"y1","y2"}];
```

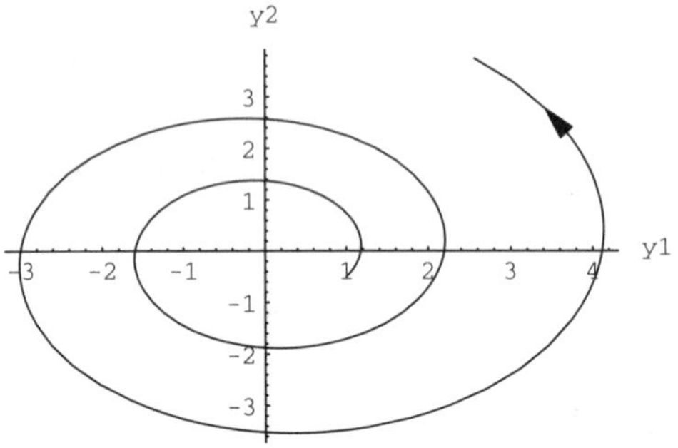


This picture confirms that the equilibrium solution is unstable.

## EXERCISES

1. Determine the stability or instability of the equilibrium solutions for each of the systems $\mathbf{y}' = \mathbf{A}\mathbf{y}$:

   (a) $\mathbf{A} = \begin{bmatrix} 1 & 1 \\ -2 & -2 \end{bmatrix}$

   (b) $\mathbf{A} = \begin{bmatrix} -7 & 1 & -6 \\ 10 & -4 & 12 \\ 2 & -1 & 1 \end{bmatrix}$

   (c) $\mathbf{A} = \begin{bmatrix} 0 & 2 & 1 & 0 \\ -2 & 0 & 0 & 1 \\ 0 & 0 & 0 & 2 \\ 0 & 0 & -2 & 0 \end{bmatrix}$

2. Show that equilibrium solutions of $\mathbf{y}' = \mathbf{A}\mathbf{y}$ where

   $$\mathbf{A} = \begin{bmatrix} 0 & -3 \\ 2 & 0 \end{bmatrix}$$

   are stable, but not asymptotically stable.

### 14.3.2 Linearization of nonlinear systems

For linear systems of differential equations with constant coefficients, it is generally possible to find the general solutions. For nonlinear autonomous systems $\mathbf{y}' = \mathbf{F}(\mathbf{y})$, it is usually impossible to find the general solutions. Without being able to find the general solution, we cannot sketch trajectories for the autonomous system, unless we use some numerical technique to find an approximation to the solution. However, we

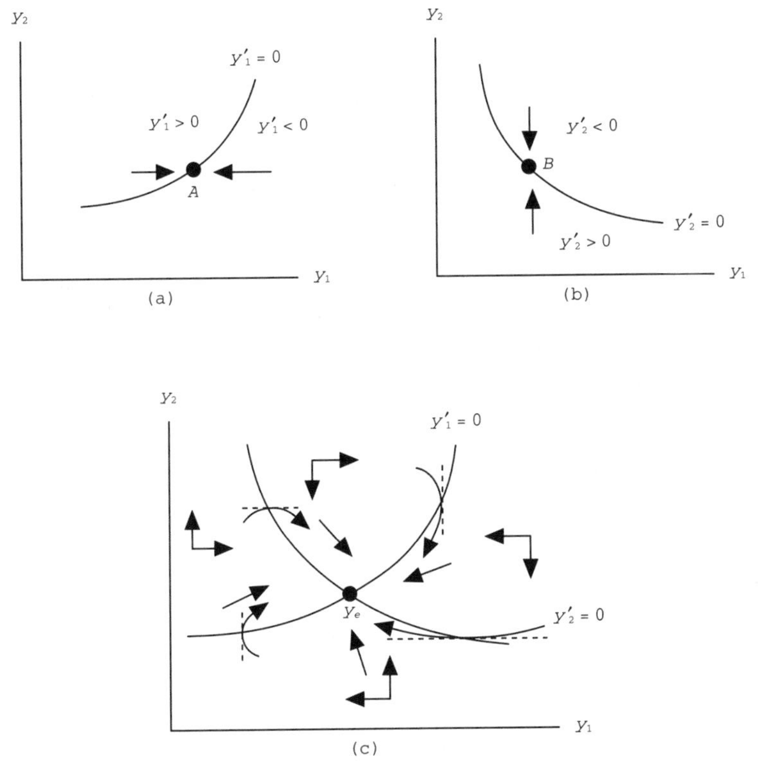


**Figure 14.2** Phase portrait

could try to sketch the phase plane portrait by plotting the direction of change of each variable at various points in the phase plane. For example, consider a nonlinear autonomous system

$$\frac{dy_1}{dx} = y_1' = F_1(y_1,y_2)$$

$$\frac{dy_2}{dx} = y_2' = F_2(y_1,y_2)$$

Panel (a) of figure 14.2 depicts the graph of the equation $F_1(y_1,y_2) = 0$. Any point $(y_1,y_2)$ on the curve satisfies the differential equation $dy_1/dx = 0$. The curve divides the phase space into two regions: an "upper" region with $dy_1/dx > 0$, and a "lower" region with $dy_1/dx < 0$. Given a value for $y_2$, the direction of change of $y_1$ is toward the point $A$ on the line, $dy_1/dx = 0$. Similarly, Panel (b) shows the division of the phase space by the equation $F_2(y_1,y_2) = 0$ and the direction of change of $y_2$ toward the point $B$ when $y_1$ is held constant. When these two curves are combined, the system of two autonomous equations divides the phase space into four regions as shown in panel (c). The direction of simultaneous movements of $(y_1,y_2)$ are indicated by the arrow on the diagram. At any point on the phase space, the directional movement seems to point toward the intersection of the two curves,

$$y_1' = F_1(y_1,y_2) = 0$$
$$y_2' = F_2(y_1,y_2) = 0$$

The point of intersection, $\mathbf{y}_e = (y_{1e},y_{2e})$, is an equilibrium solution of the system. In this case, this solution is asymptotically stable.

Even though this method of sketching the phase plane portrait is useful, the sketches give only local portraits of the solutions in the neighborhood of a point of phase space and do not produce a global picture of the solution. In addition, the sketches do not provide an analytical approximation to the trajectory. In many practical problems, we may only be interested in the solution and its characteristics in the neighborhood around an equilibrium point. If this is the case, the local behavior of the solution can be obtained by using a linear approximation to the solution of the system in the neighborhood of the equilibrium point.

A linear approximation of the system, $y_1' = F_1(y_1,y_2)$ and $y_2' = F_2(y_1,y_2)$, is obtained by computing the Taylor series expansion of the functions $F_1(y_1,y_2)$ and $F_2(y_1,y_2)$ around an equilibrium point $\mathbf{y}_e = (y_{1e},y_{2e})$, and ignoring the second and higher-order terms. That is,

$$y_1' = \frac{\partial F_1}{\partial y_1}(y_1 - y_{1e}) + \frac{\partial F_1}{\partial y_2}(y_2 - y_{2e})$$

$$y_2' = \frac{\partial F_2}{\partial y_1}(y_1 - y_{1e}) + \frac{\partial F_2}{\partial y_2}(y_2 - y_{2e})$$

where the partial derivatives are evaluated at $\mathbf{y}_e$. $F_1(y_{1e},y_{2e}) = 0$ and $F_2(y_{1e},y_{2e}) = 0$ are used in the expansion. This is a linear system of differential equations for $y_1(x)$ and $y_2(x)$ and, in many cases, a good approximation to the nonlinear system. We define the variations of $y_1$ and $y_2$ from the equilibrium point as

$$z_1 = y_1 - y_{1e}, \quad z_2 = y_2 - y_{2e}$$

and observe that $z_1' = y_1'$ and $z_2' = y_2'$. The linear approximation can then be written in a matrix form

$$\begin{bmatrix} z_1' \\ z_2' \end{bmatrix} = \begin{bmatrix} \dfrac{\partial F_1}{\partial y_1} & \dfrac{\partial F_1}{\partial y_2} \\ \dfrac{\partial F_2}{\partial y_1} & \dfrac{\partial F_2}{\partial y_2} \end{bmatrix} \begin{bmatrix} z_1 \\ z_2 \end{bmatrix}$$

or

$$\mathbf{z}' = \mathbf{A}\,\mathbf{z}.$$

We note that $\mathbf{A}$ is the Jacobian matrix of $\mathbf{F}$ at $\mathbf{y}_e$.

It can be shown that the behavior of $\mathbf{y}(x)$ around $\mathbf{y}_e$ in phase space is similar to the behavior of $\mathbf{z}(x)$ around $\mathbf{z} = \mathbf{0}$ for the linear system $\mathbf{z}' = \mathbf{A}\mathbf{z}$. For example, if all eigenvalues or the real parts of the complex eigenvalues are negative, then the equilibrium solution is asymptotically stable.

**Example 14.22** Check the stability of these equilibrium points.

$$\frac{dy_1}{dx} = F_1(y_1, y_2) = 2y_1 - 2y_1^2 - 5y_1y_2$$
$$\frac{dy_1}{dx} = F_2(y_1, y_2) = y_2 - y_2^2 - 2y_1y_2.$$

Setting $F_1 = 0$ and $F_2 = 0$, four equilibrium points are found at (0,0), (3/8,1/4), (1,0), and (0,1).

*In[120]:=*
```
Clear[F1,F2,y1,y2,ye];
F1[y1_,y2_]:= 2*y1-2*y1^2-5*y1*y2;
F2[y1_,y2_]:= y2-y2^2-2*y1*y2;
ye = Solve[{F1[y1,y2]==0,F2[y1,y2]==0},{y1,y2}]
```

*Out[123]=*

$$\{\{y1 \to 0,\ y2 \to 0\},\ \{y1 \to \frac{3}{8},\ y2 \to \frac{1}{4}\},\ \{y1 \to 1,\ y2 \to 0\},\ \{y2 \to 1,\ y1 \to 0\}\}$$

Using the **MathEcon** function **gradf**, we calculate the Jacobian matrix **A**.

*In[124]:=*
```
A = {gradf[F1[y1,y2],{y1,y2}],gradf[F2[y1,y2],{y1,y2}]};
A // MatrixForm
```

*Out[125]//MatrixForm=*

$$\begin{matrix} 2 - 4y1 - 5y2 & -5y1 \\ -2y2 & 1 - 2y1 - 2y2 \end{matrix}$$

Thus

$$\mathbf{A} = \begin{bmatrix} 2-4y_1-5y_2 & -5y_1 \\ -2y_2 & 1-2y_1-2y_2 \end{bmatrix}$$

At the first equilibrium point $y_e = (1,0)$, the eigenvalues of **A** are $\lambda_1 = 1$ and $\lambda_2 = 2$.

*In[126]:=*
```
Eigenvalues[A /. ye[[1]]]
```

*Out[126]=*
```
{1, 2}
```

Since both eigenvalues are positive, the point (1,0) is an unstable equilibrium point. At the second equilibrium point $y_e = (3/8,1/4)$, we have $\lambda_1 = -3/2$ and $\lambda_2 = 1/2$. This point is unstable.

*In[127]:=*
```
Eigenvalues[A /. ye[[2]]]
```

*Out[127]=*

$$\{-(\frac{3}{2}),\ \frac{1}{2}\}$$

The other two equilibrium points, (1,0), and (0,1), are stable.

**Example 14.23** The system

$$y_1' = F_1(y_1, y_2) = y_1 - y_2$$
$$y_2' = F_2(y_1, y_2) = 2y_1^2 + y_2^2 - 3$$

has two equilibrium points at (–1,–1) and (1,1).

*In[128]:=*

```
Clear[F1,F2,y1,y2,ye];
F1[y1_,y2_]:= y1-y2;
F2[y1_,y2_]:= 2*y1^2+y2^2-3;
ye = Solve[{F1[y1,y2]==0,F2[y1,y2]==0},{y1,y2}]
```

*Out[131]=*

{{y1 → –1, y2 → –1}, {y1 → 1, y2 → 1}}

The equilibrium point $\mathbf{y}_e = (-1,-1)$ is unstable since one of the eigenvalues is positive.

*In[132]:=*

```
A = {gradf[F1[y1,y2],{y1,y2}],gradf[F2[y1,y2],{y1,y2}]};
Eigenvalues[A /. ye[[1]]]
```

*Out[133]=*

{–3, 2}

At the second equilibrium point $\mathbf{y}_e = (1,1)$, the eigenvalues are complex.

*In[134]:=*

```
Eigenvalues[A /. ye[[2]]]
```

*Out[134]=*

$$\{\frac{3 - I\,Sqrt[15]}{2}, \frac{3 + I\,Sqrt[15]}{2}\}$$

Since the real part of each eigenvalue is positive, the equilibrium point is unstable.

## EXERCISES

1. Find linearizations for the following autonomous systems about the indicated equilibrium points:
   (a) $y_1' = y_1 + \dfrac{y_1 y_1^3}{(1+y_1^2)^2}$; $y_2' = 2y_1 - 3y_2$; $\mathbf{y}_e = (0, 0)$
   (b) $y_1' = y_1^2 - e^{y_2}$; $y_2' = y_2(1 + y_2)$; $\mathbf{y}_e = (e^{-1/2}, 1)$
2. Find the local phase plane portraits for the following nonlinear autonomous systems:
   (a) $y_1' = 2y_1 - y_1^2$; $y_2' = -y_2 + y_1 y_2$
   (b) $y_1' = y_1(1 - y_1^2)$; $y_2' = y_2$

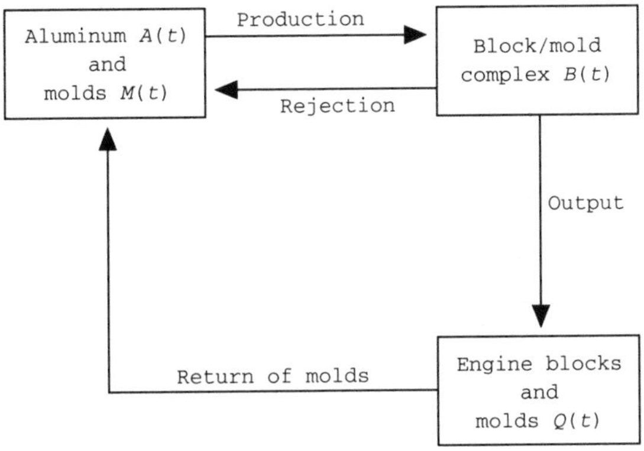


**Figure 14.3** Three-stage casting process

3. Check the stability of the equilibrium points for the following systems:
   (a) $y_1' = 1 - y_1 y_2;\ y_2' = y_1 - y_2^3$
   (b) $y_1' = -y_1 + 3y_2 + y_1 y_2;\ y_2' = y_1 + y_2 + y_1^4$
   (c) $y_1' = -2y_1 - 2y_2;\ y_2' = 4y_1 + 2y_2 + y_1 y_2^2$
   (d) $y_1' = y_1 y_2 + 2y_2 + y_3^2;\ y_2' = y_1 - y_2;\ y_3' = (y_1 - y_2)^2 - 3y_3$

### 14.3.3 Two economic examples

**Example 14.24** Suppose the C-H Motor Company casts engine blocks for an automobile company. The casting process involves three stages as shown in the flow diagram in figure 14.3. The first stage (production stage) involves pouring the raw material (melted aluminum) into molds to form block/mold complexes. After the complexes have cooled, the engine blocks are inspected. If a block passes inspection, then it is stamped OK and sent out for distribution and the mold is immediately returned to the casting shop for reuse. If it does not pass inspection, the mold returns to the casting shop and the aluminum is used as raw material. Let $A(t)$ denote the amount of alumnium that is available for casting at time $t$, $M(t)$ the number of molds that are in the casting shop, $B(t)$ the number of block/mold complex in the casting shop, and $Q(t)$ the number of engine blocks that pass inspection. We assume that $A(t)$, $M(t)$, $B(t)$, and $Q(t)$ are differentiable functions of $t$.

In this model, the production rate in the first stage, denoted as $P'(t) = \mathrm{d}P(t)/\mathrm{d}t$, of making block/mold complexes by pouring melted aluminum into molds is assumed to be proportional to the *product* of the amount of raw material and the number of molds available at time $t$ with the proportionality constant $k_1$, i.e.,

$$P'(t) = \mathrm{d}P(t)/\mathrm{d}t = k_1 A(t) M(t).$$

The rate of change of block/mold complexes that are rejected and returned to the casting shop, denoted as $R'(t)$, is assumed to be proportional to the number of block/mold complexes in the casting shop $B(t)$ with a proportionality constant $k_2$, i.e.,

$$R'(t) = \mathrm{d}R(t)/\mathrm{d}t = k_2 B(t).$$

Furthermore, we assume that the rate of change of output $Q(t)$ is proportional to $B(t)$ with a proportionality constant $k_3$, i.e.,

$$Q'(t) = dQ(t)/dt = k_3 B(t).$$

With these assumptions, the manufacturing process can then be modeled by a system of differential equations.

Consider the availability of raw material (aluminum) for casting at time $t$. We assume that the only source of raw material beyond some initial inventory is the defective blocks that are returned for reuse. Hence, the rate of change of availability of raw material consumptions is equal to the difference between the rate of return and the rate of production,

$$dA(t)/dt = R'(t) - P'(t) = k_2 B(t) - k_1 A(t) M(t).$$

The rate of change of the block/mold complex $B(t)$ is the difference between the shipping in (production) and shipping out (rejection and output) from the second stage of casting process,

$$\begin{aligned} dB(t)/dt &= P'(t) - R'(t) - Q'(t) \\ &= k_1 A(t) M(t) - (k_2 + k_3) B(t). \end{aligned}$$

On the other hand, the rate of change of the availability of molds for casting is the difference between the shipping in (rejection and output) and shipping out (production),

$$\begin{aligned} dM(t)/dt &= R'(t) + Q'(t) - P'(t) \\ &= (k_2 + k_3) B(t) - k_1 A(t) M(t). \end{aligned}$$

We now collect the various equations with respect to the raw material $A(t)$, mold $M(t)$, block/mold complex $B(t)$, and the engine block output $Q(t)$ to form a system of differential equations:

$$\begin{aligned} dA(t)/dt &= k_2 B(t) - k_1 A(t) M(t) \\ dM(t)/dt &= (k_2 + k_3) B(t) - k_1 A(t) M(t) \\ dB(t)/dt &= k_1 A(t) M(t) - (k_2 + k_3) B(t) \\ dQ(t)/dt &= k_3 B(t). \end{aligned}$$

Suppose the following initial conditions for the manufacturing process are stipulated: $A(0) = A_0$, $M(0) = M_0$, $B(0) = 0$, and $Q(0) = 0$. We shall now solve the initial-value problem.

We first note that the system has a *conservation law*, i.e., $dM(t)/dt + dB(t)/dt = 0$. Upon integrating this equation and using the initial conditions for $M(t)$ and $B(t)$, we have $M(t) + B(t) = M_0$. Substituting $M(t) = M_0 - B(t)$ into the first and third equations of the system, we have a system of nonlinear autonomous differential equations,

$$\begin{aligned} dA(t)/dt &= -k_1 M_0 A(t) + (k_1 A(t) + k_2) B(t) \\ dB(t)/dt &= k_1 M_0 A(t) - (k_1 A(t) + k_2 + k_3) B(t). \end{aligned}$$

If we can solve for $A(t)$ and $B(t)$ from the above system of two differential equations, then the other two quantities $M(t)$ and $Q(t)$ can be solved from the relations:

$M(t) = M_0 - B(t)$
$Q(t) = k_3 \int_0^t B(x)\mathrm{d}x$

As shown in the following calculation, the above system of differential equations for $A(t)$ and $B(t)$ has an equilibrium point $\mathbf{y}_e = (A_e, B_e) = (0,0)$ when

$F_1(A,B) \equiv \mathrm{d}A(t)/\mathrm{d}t = -k_1 M_0 A(t) + (k_1 A(t) + k_2) B(t) = 0$
$F_2(A,B) \equiv \mathrm{d}B(t)/\mathrm{d}t = k_1 M_0 A(t) - (k_1 A(t) + k_2 + k_3) B(t) = 0$

*In[135]:=*

```
Clear[M0,A,B,k1,k2,k3,F1,F2];
F1[A_,B_]:=  -k1*M0*A+(k1*A+k2)*B;
F2[A_,B_]:=  k1*M0*A-(k1*A+k2+k3)*B;
ye  =  Solve[{F1[A,B]==0,F2[A,B]==0},{A,B}]
```

*Out[138]=*

{{A → 0, B → 0}}

To study the stability of the equilibrium point, let us linearize the system about this point $\mathbf{y}_e = (A_e, B_e) = (0,0)$ in the *AB*-phase plane. That is,

$$\begin{bmatrix} \dfrac{\mathrm{d}A(t)}{\mathrm{d}t} \\ \dfrac{\mathrm{d}B(t)}{\mathrm{d}t} \end{bmatrix} = \begin{bmatrix} \dfrac{\partial F_1}{\partial A} & \dfrac{\partial F_1}{\partial B} \\ \dfrac{\partial F_2}{\partial A} & \dfrac{\partial F_2}{\partial B} \end{bmatrix} \begin{bmatrix} A(t) - A_e \\ B(t) - B_e \end{bmatrix}$$
$$= \mathbf{J} \begin{bmatrix} A(t) - A_e \\ B(t) - B_e \end{bmatrix}$$

where $\mathbf{J}$ is the Jacobian matrix. Using the **MathEcon** function, **gradf**, the Jacobian matrix evaluated at $\mathbf{y}_e$ can be computed.

*In[139]:=*

```
J  =  {gradf[F1[A,B],{A,B}],gradf[F2[A,B],{A,B}]};
J  =  J  /.  {A->0,B->0}
```

*Out[140]=*

{-{k1, M0), k2}, {k1 M0, -k1 - k3}}

That is,

$$\mathbf{J} = \begin{bmatrix} -k_1 M_0 & k_2 \\ k_1 M_0 & -k_2 - k_3 \end{bmatrix}$$

The two eigenvalues $\lambda_1$ and $\lambda_2$ of $\mathbf{J}$ are

$$\lambda_1 = -\frac{a + \sqrt{a^2 - b}}{2}$$

$$\lambda_2 = -\frac{a - \sqrt{a^2 - b}}{2}$$

where

$a = (k_2+k_3+k_1M_0) > 0$
$b = 4k_1k_3M_0 > 0.$

*In[141]:=*

```
Eigenvalues[J /.{A->0,B->0}]
```

*Out[141]=*

$$\{\frac{-k2 - k3 - k1\,M0 - Sqrt[-4\,k1\,k3\,M0 + (k2 + k3 + k1\,M0)^2]}{2},$$
$$\frac{-k2 - k3 - k1\,M0 + Sqrt[-4\,k1\,k3\,M0 + (k2 + k3 + k1\,M0)^2]}{2}\}$$

If $a^2 - b \geq 0$, then both eigenvalues are real and negative. On the other hand, if $a^2 - b < 0$, $\lambda_1$ and $\lambda_2$ are conjugate complex eigenvalues and the real part $-a/2 < 0$ is negative. Thus, the equilibrium points $\mathbf{y}_e = (A_e, B_e) = (0,0)$ is stable.

For a numerical illustration, let us choose some specific values for $k_1, k_2, k_3$, and an initial value for $M(t)$. Namely, suppose

$k_1 = 0.4$, $k_2 = 0.1$, $k_3 = 0.9$, $M_0 = 5$.

We then solve numerically the system of two differential equations with the initial values, $A(0) = 5$, and $B(0) = 0$, i.e., with 5 tons of aluminum and zero unit of block/mold complex initially,

$dA(t)/dt = -k_1M_0A(t) + (k_1A(t)+k_2)B(t)$, $A(0) = 5$,
$dB(t)/dt = k_1M_0A(t) - (k_1A(t)+k_2+k_3)B(t)$, $B(0) = 0$.

A plot of the trajectories in the *AB*-phase plane is then given.

*In[142]:=*

```
Clear[M0,A,B,k1,k2,k3];
k1=0.4;  k2=0.1;  k3=0.9;  M0=5;
sol  =  NDSolve[{A'[t]  ==  -k1*M0*A[t]+(k1*A[t]+k2)*B[t],
                    B'[t]  ==  k1*M0*A[t]-(k1*A[t]+k2+k3)*B[t],
                  A[0]  ==  5,  B[0]  ==  0},
                  {A[t],B[t]},{t,0,10}];
A[t_]  =  A[t]  /.  sol[[1,1]];
B[t_]  =  B[t]  /.  sol[[1,2]];
```

*In[147]:=*

```
trajectory[{A[t],B[t]},{t,0,3},
                AxesLabel->{"A(t)","B(t)"}];
```

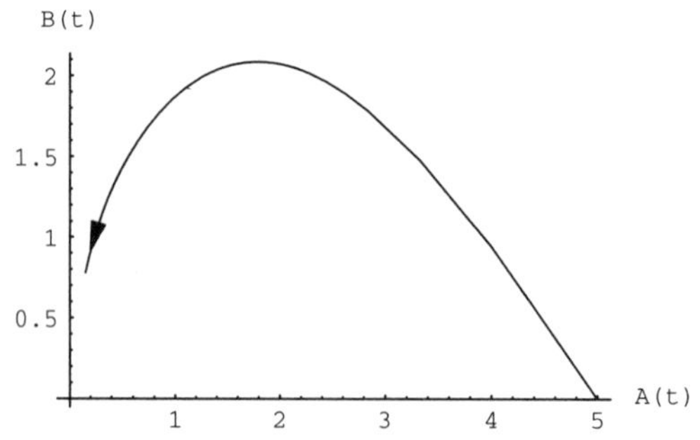

It is clear that $A(t)$ and $B(t)$ are approaching the equilibrium points $\mathbf{y}_e = (A_e, B_e) = (0,0)$ as $t \to \infty$. The solutions for mold $M(t)$ and engine block output $Q(t)$ are obtained as follows:

$$Q(t) = k_3 \int_0^t B(x)\mathrm{d}x$$
$$M(t) = M_0 - B(t)$$

We use the numerical integration function, **NIntegrate**, to find $Q(t)$. Both $Q(t)$ and $M(t)$ are then plotted as functions of time.

*In[148]:=*

```
Clear[Q,M,t];
M[t_]:= M0  -  B[t];
Q[t_]:= k3*NIntegrate[B[x],{x,0,t}]
Plot[{M[t],Q[t]},{t,0,10},
        AxesLabel->{"t","M(t)  &  Q(t)"},
          PlotStyle->{{},Dashing[{0.015}]}];
```

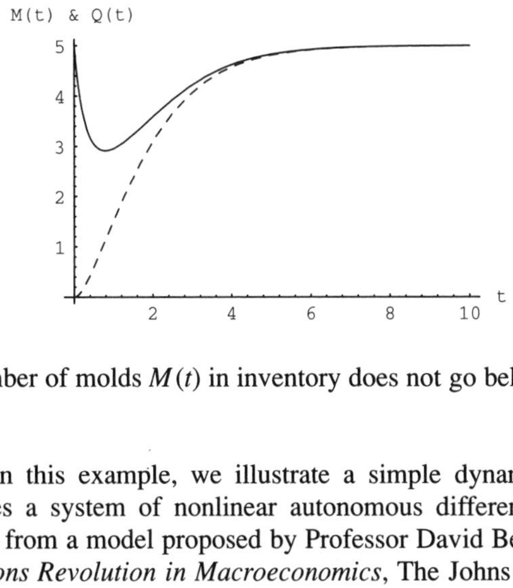


Notice that the number of molds $M(t)$ in inventory does not go below 3 for this choice of the parameters.

**Example 14.25** In this example, we illustrate a simple dynamic macroeconomic model that involves a system of nonlinear autonomous differential equations. The example is adapted from a model proposed by Professor David Begg in his book, *The Rational Expectations Revolution in Macroeconomics*, The Johns Hopkins University Press, 1982.

Consider the national income identity,

$$Y(t) = C(t) + I(t) + D(t).$$

where $Y(t)$ denotes the real income, $C(t)$ real consumption, $I(t)$ the investment, and $D(t)$ the depreciation of capital, as functions of time $t$. Suppose that real comsumption is proportional to the real income so that $C(t) = a_1 Y(t)$, and invesment $I(t) = \mathrm{d}K(t)/\mathrm{d}t = K'(t)$. Furthermore, assume that depreciation $D(t)$ of capital is proportional to $K(t)$ so that $D(t) = a_2 Y(t)$. We assume that the proportionality constants satisfy $0 < a_1 < 1$, $0 < a_2$. Then

$$Y(t) = a_1 Y + K' + a_2 Y.$$

The production function for the economy is assumed to be proportional to $K$,

$$Y = b_0 + b_1 K \quad 0 < b_0,\ 0 < b_1$$

where $b_1$ is the marginal product of capital. Substituting the production function into the income identity, we have the differential equation in $K$,

$$K' = b_0(1-a_1) + [b_1(1-a_1)-a_2]K.$$

Let us now consider the monetary side of the economy. The nominal interest rate $R^*(t)$ consists of two components,

$$\begin{aligned} R^*(t) &= R(t) + \Pi(t) = b_1 + \frac{dP(t)/dt}{P(t)} \\ &\equiv b_1 + P'/P \end{aligned}$$

where the real interest rate $R(t) = b_1$ is assumed to be equal to the real return on capital, or the marginal product of capital in production. The inflation rate $\Pi(t) = P'(t)/P(t)$ is the percentage change in price level $P(t)$.

Suppose the nominal money supply $M^*(t)$ grows at a constant rate $c_0$ so that

$$\frac{dM^*(t)/dt}{M^*(t)} = c_0, \quad 0 < c_0$$

and the real money demand $M(t) = M^*(t)/P(t)$ is a linear function of income and nominal interest rate

$$M(t) = \frac{M^*(t)}{P(t)} = c_1 Y(t) - c_2 R^*(t) \quad 0 < c_1,\ 0 < c_2.$$

It is easy to show that, by differentiating $M^*(t) = M(t)P(t)$, we have

$$\frac{dM(t)/dt}{M(t)} \equiv \frac{M'}{M} = \frac{dM^*(t)/dt}{M^*(t)} - \frac{dP(t)/dt}{P(t)}$$

i.e., the growth rate of real money demand is equal to the growth rate of nominal money supply minus the inflation rate. Substituting $[dM^*(t)/dt]/M^*(t) = c_0$ and $[dP(t)/dt]/P(t) = (R^* - b_1)$, we have

$$\begin{aligned} \frac{M'}{M} &= c_0 - (R^* - b_1) = c_0 - \left[\frac{c_1 Y - M}{c_2} - b_1\right] \\ &= (c_0 + b_1 - \frac{b_0 c_1}{c_2}) - \frac{b_1 c_1}{c_2} K + \frac{1}{c_2} M \end{aligned}$$

where $R^* = (c_1 Y - M)/c_2$ comes from the real money demand equation, and $Y = b_0 + b_1 K$ from the production function. Summarizing, we have a dynamic macroeconomic model consisting of a system of two autonomous differential equations,

$$\frac{dK}{dt} = K' = F_1(K, M) = b_0(1 - a_1) + [b_1(1 - a_1) - a_2]K$$

$$\frac{dM}{dt} = M' = F_2(K, M) = \left[c_0 + b_1 - \frac{b_0 c_1}{c_2}\right]M - \frac{b_1 c_1}{c_2}KM + \frac{1}{c_2}M^2.$$

The system has two equilibrium points $(K_e, M_e)$ as shown in the following calculation. We consider only the second equilibrium point,

$$K_e = \frac{b_0(1-a_1)}{a_2-b_1(1-a_1)}$$

$$M_e = b_0c_1 + \frac{b_0b_1c_1(1-a_1)}{a_2-b_1(1-a_1)} - b_1c_2 - c_0c_2$$

*In[152]:=*

```
Clear[F1,F2,K,M,a1,a2,b0,b1,c0,c1,c2];
F1[K_,M_]:=  b0*(1-a1)+(b1*(1-a1)-a2)*K;
F2[K_,M_]:=  (c0+b1-b0*c1/c2)*M-(b1*c1/c2)*K*M+M^2/c2;
ye=  Solve[{F1[K,M]==0,F2[K,M]==0},{K,M}]
```

*Out[155]=*

$$\{\{M \to 0,\ K \to -(\frac{(1 - a1)b0}{-a2 + b1 - a1b1})\},$$
$$\{M \to b0c1 - \frac{(1 - a1)b0b1c1}{-a2 + b1 - a1b1} - b1c2 - c0c2,$$
$$K \to -(\frac{(1 - a1)b0}{-a2 + b1 - a1b1})\}\}$$

For a numerical illustration, we choose values for the parameters of our model:

$a_1 = 4/5$, $a_2 = 1/10$; $b_0 = 20$, $b_1 = 1/5$;
$c_0 = 1/10$, $c_1 = 2/5$, $c_2 = 3/2$.

The numeric solution of the equilibrium $K$ and $M$ are $K_e = 200/3 \approx 66.6667$ and $M_e = 773/60 \approx 12.8833$.

*In[156]:=*

```
a1=4/5;a2=1/10;b0=20;b1=1/5;c0=1/10;c1=2/5;c2=3/2;
ye[[2]]
```

*Out[157]=*

$$\{M \to \frac{773}{60},\ K \to \frac{200}{3}\}$$

The equilibrium point is unstable since one of the eigenvalues is positive.

*In[158]:=*

```
A={gradf[F1[K,M],{K,M}],gradf[F2[K,M],{K,M}]};
Eigenvalues[A /. ye[[2]]]
```

*Out[159]=*

$$\{-(\frac{3}{50}),\ \frac{773}{90}\}$$

To further illustrate the unstable equilibrium point, we graph $M(t)$ and $K(t)$. Since $F_1(K,M)$ is not a function of $M$, the phase line, $F_1(K,M) = 0$, is a vertical line. The two phase lines intersect at $(K_e, M_e) = (66.6667, 12.8833)$.

*In[160]:=*
```
Needs["Graphics`ImplicitPlot`"];
```

*In[161]:=*
```
ImplicitPlot[{F1[K,M]==0,F2[K,M]==0},
                    {K,55,75},{M,10,15},
                      AxesLabel->{"K","M"},AspectRatio->0.5];
```

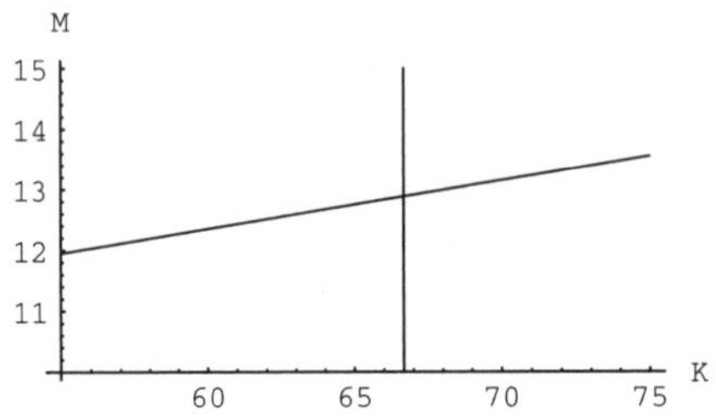


The phase lines, $F_1(K,M) = 0$ and $F_2(K,M) = 0$, divide the phase space into four regions. It can be shown that $F_1(K,M) < 0$ for $K > K_e$, and $F_1(K,M) > 0$ for $K < K_e$. For example, $F_1(67,M) = -1/50 < 0$, and $F_1(65,M) = 1/10 > 0$.

*In[162]:=*
```
F1[67,M]
```

*Out[162]=*

$$-(\frac{1}{50})$$

*In[163]:=*
```
F1[65,M]
```

*Out[163]=*

$$\frac{1}{10}$$

Any point above the second phase line $F_2(K,M) = 0$ will have positive slope $F_2(K,M) > 0$ and vice versa. For example, the point $(K,M) = (545/8,13)$ is on the phase line since $F_2(545/8,13) = 0$. The point $(545/8,14)$ is above the line and hence $F_2(545/8,14) = 28/3 > 0$. On the other hand, the point $(545/8,12)$ is below the line and $F_2(545/8,12) = -8 < 0$.

*In[164]:=*
```
F2[545/8,13]
```

*Out[164]=*

0

*In[165]:=*
```
F2[545/8,14]
```

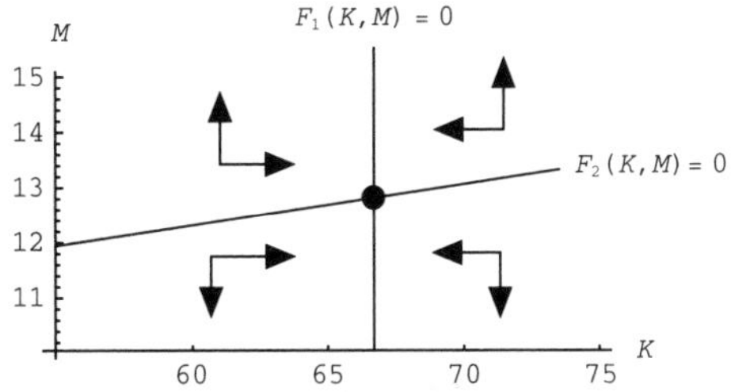


**Figure 14.4** Phase portrait of $F_1(K, M)$ and $F_2(K, M)$

*Out[165]=*

$$\frac{28}{3}$$

*In[166]:=*

```
F2[545/8,12]
```

*Out[166]=*

-8

In figure 14.4 the phase plane portrait of this system is illustrated. The directions of the arrows clearly show that $K$ and $M$ move away from the intersection point. Hence the equilibrium point is unstable.

15

# Difference Equations

Difference equations are similar to differential equations. A difference equation can be viewed as the discrete approximation of a differential equation in which the derivatives have been replaced by differences. Since difference equations are used in many areas of economics and mathematics, we shall treat it as a separate mathematical topic. However, many of the concepts introduced in this chapter for difference equations are analogous to those for differential equations.

## □ 15.1 The Difference Calculus □

### 15.1.1 Forward difference operators

In differential calculus, we studied the properties of differentiation operators, such as the ordinary derivative, partial derivatives, and the total derivative. Difference calculus deals with different types of operators, called difference operators. Difference operators are operators that act on sequences of numbers which we shall denote as $\{y_t\}$. The subscript $t$ denotes the position of a particular element in the sequence.

**DEFINITION 15.1** *Let $\{y_t\}$ be a sequence of numbers. The **(first) forward difference** operator $\Delta$ on the sequence is defined as*

$$\Delta y_t = y_{t+1} - y_t.$$

*By repeated applications of $\Delta$, we can define higher-order forward difference operators such as $\Delta^n y_t = \Delta^{n-1}(\Delta y_t)$, $n = 1,2,\ldots$. The symbol $\Delta^0$ is defined as the identity operator, i.e., $\Delta^0 y_t = y_t$.*

**Example 15.1** Compute the first, second, and third order forward difference operators for the sequence $\{y_1,y_2,y_3,y_4\} = \{2,-3,9,2\}$.

$\Delta y_1 = -3 - 2 = -5$; $\Delta y_2 = 9 - (-3) = 12$; $\Delta y_3 = 2 - 9 = -7$;
$\Delta^2 y_1 = 12 - (-5) = 17$; $\Delta^2 y_2 = -7 - 12 = -19$;
$\Delta^3 y_1 = -19 - 17 = -36$.

We can use the *Mathematica* function **Table** to construct sets of $\Delta y_t$, $\Delta^2 y_t$, and $\Delta^3 y_t$.

*In[1]:=*
```
Clear[y,dy,d2y,d3y];
y  =  {2,-3,9,2};
dy  =  Table[y[[t+1]]-y[[t]],{t,1,3,1}]
```

*Out[3]=*
```
{-5, 12, -7}
```

*In[4]:=*
```
d2y  =  Table[dy[[t+1]]-dy[[t]],{t,1,2,1}]
```

*Out[4]=*
```
{17, -19}
```

*In[5]:=*
```
d3y  =  Table[d2y[[t+1]]-d2y[[t]],{t,1,1}]
```

*Out[5]=*
```
{-36}
```

As seen in this example, the set of first differences of a sequence containing $n$ elements contains $n-1$ elements, the set of second differences contains $n-2$ elements, and so forth.

**Example 15.2** Let the sequence $\{p_1,p_2,p_3, \ldots\}$ denote the prices of a commodity in successive periods. The price changes over these periods are the first-order forward differences, $\Delta p_t = p_{t+1} - p_t$. In economics, the study of discrete changes over periods is often called *period analysis.*

It is possible to express higher-order forward difference operators of sequences in terms of elements in the sequence. For example,

$$\begin{aligned}\Delta^2 y_t &= \Delta(\Delta y_t) = \Delta(y_{t+1} - y_t) = \Delta y_{t+1} - \Delta y_t \\ &= (y_{t+2} - y_{t+1}) - (y_{t+1} - y_t) \\ &= y_{t+2} - 2y_{t+1} + y_t\end{aligned}$$

Similarly,

$$\begin{aligned}\Delta^3 y_t &= \Delta(\Delta^2 y_t) = \Delta(y_{t+2} - 2y_{t+1} + y_t) \\ &= y_{t+3} - 3y_{t+2} + 3y_{t+1} - y_t\end{aligned}$$

and so on. We have just shown some of the special cases of the following theorem.

**THEOREM 15.1** *If $\{y_t\}$ is a sequence of numbers, then*

$$\Delta^n y_t = \sum_{i=0}^{n} (-1)^i \frac{n!}{i!(n-i)!} y_{t+n-i}$$

*Note that the term $n!/(i!(n-1)!)$ is a binomial coefficient.*

We illustrate the use of *Mathematica* to compute the above formula in the following example.

**Example 15.3** We use the *Mathematica* function **Array** to generate a sequence $\{y_1, y_2, \ldots, y_5\}$. The *Mathematica* function **Binomial** to compute the binomial coefficients. We have defined a function **delta[n,t]** to calculate the third- and fourth-order forward differences, $\Delta^3 y_t$ and $\Delta^4 y_t$.

*In[6]:=*
```
Clear[y,n,t,delta];
Array[y,5]
```

*Out[7]=*
```
{y[1], y[2], y[3], y[4], y[5]}
```

*In[8]:=*
```
delta[n_,t_]:= Sum[(-1)^i*Binomial[n,i]*y[t+n-i],
                   {i,0,n}];
delta[3,1]
```

*Out[9]=*
```
-y[1] + 3y[2] - 3y[3] + y[4]
```

*In[10]:=*
```
delta[4,1]
```

*Out[10]=*
```
y[1] - 4y[2] + 6y[3] - 4y[4] + y[5]
```

Properties of the forward difference operators are very much like the properties of ordinary differentiation. Suppose $\{x_t\}$ and $\{y_t\}$ are sequences of numbers and $c$ is a constant. Then

(1) $\Delta(x_t \pm y_t) = \Delta x_t \pm \Delta y_t$

(2) $\Delta(cx_t) = c\Delta x_t$

(3) $\Delta(x_t y_t) = x_{t+1}\Delta y_t + y_t \Delta x_t$

(4) $\Delta\left[\dfrac{x_t}{y_t}\right] = \dfrac{y_t \Delta x_t - x_t \Delta y_t}{y_y y_{t+1}}$

(5) If $\{y_t\}$ is a polynomial sequence of degree $n$, i.e.,

$$y_t = a_0 + a_1 t + a_2 t^2 + \ldots + a_n t^n,$$

then the $k$th-order forward difference is a polynomial of degreee $(n-k)$, i.e.,

$$\Delta^k y_t = b_0 + b_1 t + b_2 t^2 + \ldots + b_{n-k} t^{n-k}$$

In particular,

$$\Delta^n y_t = a_n n! \quad \text{and} \quad \Delta^m y_t = 0,\ m > n.$$

## EXERCISES

1. Find $\Delta y_t$, $\Delta^2 y_t$, and $\Delta^3 y_t$ for the following sequences:
   (a) $\{-10,-5,6,23,46,75\}$
   (b) $\{-10,-7,-4,-1,2,5\}$
   (c) $\{-1,-3,1,17,51,109\}$
2. If each element of the sequence $\{y_t\}$ is a polynomial in $t$ of degree $n$, then $\Delta^m y_t = 0$ for $m > n$. Which of the sequences in exercise 1 are polynomial sequences and what are the degrees of the polynomials?
3. The *backwards difference operator* on a sequence $y_t$ is defined as $\nabla y_t = y_t - y_{t-1}$. Simplify the following expressions.
   (a) $\Delta(\nabla y_k)$
   (b) $\nabla(\Delta y_k)$
   (c) $\nabla(\nabla y_k) = \nabla^2 y_k$

### 15.1.2 Difference equations

A differential equation is an equation involving a function and its derivatives. A forward difference equation is an equation involving a sequence and its forward differences

$$F(t, y_t, \Delta y_t, \Delta^2 y_t, \ldots, \Delta^n y_t) = 0.$$

For example,

$$\Delta^4 y_t + 5\Delta^2 y_t - (y_t)^2 \Delta y_t - 4y_t = e^t$$

is a forward difference equation. Using theorem 15.1, the forward differences $\Delta^n y_t$, $n = 1,2,3,4$, can be expressed in terms of the element of $\{y_t\}$. Hence, a forward difference equation is often written without the forward difference operators. With this in mind, we make the following definition.

**Definition 15.2** *An* ***nth-order difference*** *equation is an equation of the form*

$$F(t, y_t, y_{t+1}, y_{t+2}, \ldots, y_{t+n}) = 0$$

*where $\{y_t\}$ is a sequence and n is a natural number.*

The *order* of a difference equation is defined to be the difference between the smallest and largest subscript in the equation. For the diffence equation, $F(t, y_t, y_{t+1}, y_{t+2}, \ldots, y_{t+n}) = 0$, the order is $n = (t+n)-t$. If we replace $t$ by $t-k$ in the above definition, then the equation becomes

$$F(t-k, y_{t-k}, y_{t-k+1}, y_{t-k+2}, \ldots, y_{t-k+n}) = 0$$

which is still a difference equation of order $n$.

**Example 15.4** Consider the difference equation

$$\Delta^2 y_t + y_t = t^2$$

If we expand the second-order forward difference,

$$\Delta^2 y_t = y_{t+2} - 2y_{t+1} + y_t,$$

then the difference equation can be written as

$$y_{t+2} - 2y_{t+1} + 2y_t = t^2$$

which is a second-order difference equation.

**Example 15.5** The difference equation

$$\Delta^3 y_t + \Delta^2 y_t + \Delta y_t + y_t = c$$

is the same as the difference equation

$$y_{t+3} - 2y_{t+2} + 2y_{t+1} = c.$$

It is also the same as $y_{t+2} - 2y_{t+1} + 2y_t = c$ or $y_{t+1} - 2y_t + 2y_{t-1} = c$. The difference equation is second-order, even though it contains a third-order forward difference operator $\Delta^3 y$. The maximum difference in subscripted indices in the elements of the sequence is 2.

**DEFINITION 15.3** *A difference equation for a sequence* $\{y_t\}$ *is said to be linear if it can be written in the form*

$$a_n(t)y_{t+n} + a_{n-1}(t)y_{t+n-1} + \ldots + a_1(t)y_{t+1} + a_0(t)y_t = g(t)$$

*where* $a_0(t), a_1(t), \ldots, a_n(t)$, *and* $g(t)$ *are functions that depend only upon the index* $t$ *and not on any elements in* $\{y_t\}$.

If a difference equation is not linear, then it is said to be *nonlinear*. If $g(t) = 0$, then the linear difference equation is *homogeneous*; otherwise, it is *inhomogeneous* or *nonhomogeneous*. If the coefficients $a_0(t), a_1(t), \ldots, a_n(t)$ are constant, then the difference equation is said to have *constant coefficients*.

**Example 15.6** The second-order difference equation

$$y_t - t^2 y_t = \cos \pi t$$

is linear.

**Example 15.7** The third-order difference equation

$$y_{t+3} + 5y_{t+1} - y_t^2 = e^t$$

is nonlinear.

In this chapter we are primarily concerned with linear difference equations with constant coefficients.

## EXERCISES

1. Express the following difference equations in the form

$$F(t, y_t, y_{t+1}, y_{t+2}, \ldots, y_{t+n}) = 0,$$

and determine their orders:
(a) $\Delta^2 y_t + \Delta y_t - \Delta y_t = 4t$
(b) $\Delta^3 y_t + \Delta y_t + y_t = -t + 3$
(c) $\Delta^3 y_t + \Delta^2 y_t = \sin t$

2. Express the following difference equations in the form

$$F(t, y_t, \Delta y_t, \Delta^2 y_t, \ldots, \Delta^n y_t) = 0,$$

and determine their orders:
(a) $y_{t+3} - 2y_t + y_{t-1} = t^2$
(b) $y_{t+1} - 2y_t + y_t^3 = t + 2$
(c) $3y_t - 2y_{t-1} + y_{t-2} = t$
(d) $\dfrac{y_{t+1} - 2y_t}{y_{t+3}} = \sin(\dfrac{t\pi}{2})$

### 15.1.3 Solutions of difference equations

The solution of a differential equation is a differentiable function that satisfies the equation. An analogous concept exists for difference equations.

> **DEFINITION 15.4** *A* ***solution*** *of an nth-order difference equation,*
>
> $$F(t, y_t, y_{t+1}, y_{t+2}, \ldots, y_{t+n}) = 0,$$
>
> *is a sequence* $\{y_t\}$ *whose members satisfy the difference equation.*

**Example 15.8** Consider the first-order linear difference equation

$$(t+1)y_{t+1} + ty_t = 2t - 3$$

The sequence,

$$y_t = 1 - \frac{2}{t}, \; t = 1,2, \ldots$$

is a solution of the difference equation. We can easily check this result with *Mathematica*.

*In[11]:=*
```
Clear[y,t]
y[t_]:= 1 - 2/t
(t+1)*y[t+1]+t*y[t] == 2*t-3 // Simplify
```

*Out[13]=*
```
True
```

**Example 15.9** Consider the first-order nonlinear difference equation

$$y_{t+1} = \frac{y_t}{1 + y_t}$$

The sequence

$$y_t = \frac{c}{1 + ct},\ t = 1,2, \ldots$$

is a solution for any constant $c$ as we check with *Mathematica*.

*In[14]:=*
```
Clear[y,t,c]
y[t_]:= c/(1+c*t);
y[t+1] == y[t]/(1+y[t]) // Simplify
```

*Out[16]=*
```
True
```

It is not unusual for solutions of difference equations to contain arbitrary constants. If a solution of a linear $n$th-order difference equation contains $n$ arbitrary constants, then this solution is called a *general solution.* If we choose specific values for the arbitrary constants in the general solution, then the solution is a *particular solution.*

**Example 15.10** The sequence $\{y_t\}$ such that

$$y_t = c_1 + c_2 2^t - t,\ t = 0,1,2, \ldots$$

is the general solution of the second-order linear difference equation

$$y_{t+2} - 3y_{t+1} + 2y_t = 1$$

*In[17]:=*
```
Clear[y,t,c1,c2]
y[t_]:= c1 + c2*2^t - t;
y[t+2]-3*y[t+1]+2*y[t] == 1 // Simplify
```

*Out[19]=*
```
True
```

If the first $n$ elements of a solution to an $n$th-order difference equation are prescribed, then these elements are called *initial conditions* for the difference equation.

**Example 15.11** The second-order difference equation

$$y_{t+2} - y_t = 0$$

has the general solution

$$y_t = c_1 + c_2(-1)^t.$$

The requirements, $y_0 = 2$ and $y_1 = -3$, are initial conditions for this difference equation. These initial conditions specify particular values for the two arbitrary constants, $c_1$ and $c_2$. That is,

$$y_0 = c_1 + c_2(-1)^0 = c_1 + c_2 = 2$$
$$y_1 = c_1 + c_2(-1)^1 = c_1 - c_2 = -3$$

We solve these equations for $c_1$ and $c_2$ and find that $c_1 = -1/2$ and $c_2 = 5/2$. Substituting these values into our general solution, we obtain a particular solution of the difference equation,

$$y_t = -\frac{1}{2} + \frac{5}{2}(-1)^t.$$

**Example 15.12** Consider a simple national income model. In period $t$, the national income $Y_t$, consumption $C_t$, investment $I_t$, and government expenditure $G_t$ are related in the accounting identity

$$Y_t = C_t + I_t + G_t.$$

We assume that the consumption is proportional to income,

$$C_t = aY_{t-1},$$

and that the investment is proportional to change in the consumption

$$I_t = b(C_t - C_{t-1})$$

where both $a$ and $b$ are positive constants. Finally, we assume that the government expenditure is constant

$$G_t \equiv G.$$

If we substitute $C_t$, $I_t$, and $G_t$ into the national income accounting identity, then we can show that the national income satisfies the following second-order linear difference equation

$$Y_{t+2} - a(1+b)Y_{t+1} + abY_t = G$$

Suppose we specify $G = 1$, $a = 0.8$, $b = 0.5$, and the initial conditions $Y_0 = 2$ and $Y_1 = 3$. In a later section of this chapter, we shall demonstrate how to find a general solution to this type of problem. However, to compute the first few terms of $\{Y_t\}$, we can use *Mathematica* directly. Let us shift the index of the sequence in the difference equation by replacing $t$ by $t$–2 and express the difference equation equivalently as

$$Y_t = a(1+b)Y_{t-1} - abY_{t-2} + G$$

The following *Mathematica* statements specify the initial conditions and iteratively compute the sequence $\{t, Y_t\}$ for $t = 2,3, \ldots 10$.

*In[20]:=*

```
Clear[Y,t,a,b,G,income];
G = 1; a = 0.8; b = 0.5;
Y[0] = 2; Y[1] = 3;
Y[t_]:= G+a*(1+b)*Y[t-1]-a*b*Y[t-2];
income = Table[{t,Y[t]},{t,0,10}]; income // TableForm
```

*Out[24]//TableForm=*

| | |
|---|---|
| 0 | 2 |
| 1 | 3 |
| 2 | 3.8 |
| 3 | 4.36 |
| 4 | 4.712 |
| 5 | 4.9104 |
| 6 | 5.00768 |
| 7 | 5.04506 |
| 8 | 5.051 |
| 9 | 5.04317 |
| 10 | 5.03141 |

Using the *Mathematica* function **ListPlot**, we can plot the income list over 10 periods.

*In[25]:=*

```
ListPlot[income,AxesLabel->{"period","Income"}];
```

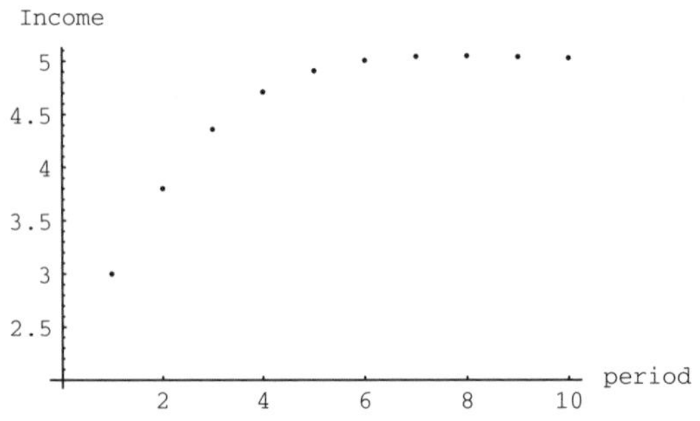


## EXERCISES

1. Show that

$$y_t = c_1 + c_2 t + c_3 t^2 + 2t^3 + t^4$$

is the general solution of the third-order difference equation

$$y_{t+3} - 3y_{t+2} + 3y_{t+1} - y_t = 24(t+2).$$

2. Show that the sequence

$$y_t = \frac{2}{t^2 - t + 1}$$

is a solution of the initial value problem:

$$y_{t+1} - y_t + t y_{t+1} y_t = 0,$$
$$y_1 = 2.$$

## □ 15.2 Solving Linear Difference Equations □

In this section we develop methods for finding the general solutions of linear difference equations with constant coefficients.

Recall that an $n$th-order, linear difference equation with constant coefficients has the form

$$a_n y_{t+n} + a_{n-1} y_{t+n-1} + \ldots + a_1 y_{t+1} + a_0 y_t = g(t)$$

where the coefficients $a_i$, $i = 0,1, \ldots ,n$, are constant and $g(t)$ is a function of the index $t$. The general solution is a sequence whose members depend on $n$ arbitrary constants. That is,

$$y_t = F(t; c_1, c_2, \ldots ,c_n).$$

It is not important what the smallest index of the sequence is, but we shall choose $t = 0$ as the starting index for convenience. Once $n$ initial conditions or the initial sequence $\{y_0, y_1, \ldots, y_{n-1}\}$ are specified, a particular solution can be derived from the general solution by determining values for the arbitrary constants. We shall begin with methods for finding the general solution of a first-order linear difference equation.

### 15.2.1 First-order linear difference equations

Consider the first-order difference equation

$$a_1 y_{t+1} + a_0 y_t = b.$$

Assuming $a_1 \neq 0$, the equation can be rewritten as

$$y_{t+1} = A y_t + B$$

where

$$A = -\frac{a_0}{a_1} \quad \text{and} \quad B = \frac{b}{a_1}$$

By iteration, we have

$$y_1 = Ay_0 + B$$
$$y_2 = Ay_1 + B = A(Ay_0 + B) + B = A^2y_0 + AB + B$$
$$y_3 = Ay_2 + B = A(A^2y_0 + AB + B) + B = A^3y_0 + A^2B + AB + B$$
$$\cdots\cdots\cdots\cdots\cdots\cdots$$
$$y_t = A^ty_0 + A^{t-1}B + \ldots + A^2B + AB + B$$

Using a standard formula for a geometric sum, we have

$$A^{t-1}B + \ldots + AB + B = \begin{cases} B\dfrac{1-A^t}{1-A}, & A \neq 1 \\ tB, & A = 1 \end{cases}.$$

Hence, the general solution is:

$$y_t = \begin{cases} A^ty_0 + B\left(\dfrac{1-A^t}{1-A}\right), & A \neq 1 \\ y_0 + tB, & A = 1 \end{cases}$$

where $y_0$ is an initial value.

**Example 15.13** Find the general solution of the first-order difference equation

$$3y_{t+1} - 2y_t = 3$$

Here $A = 2/3$ and $B = 1$. Since $A \neq 1$, we have

$$y_t = \left(\frac{2}{3}\right)^t y_0 + \frac{1-(2/3)^t}{1-2/3} = \left(\frac{2}{3}\right)^t y_0 + 3\left[1 - \left(\frac{2}{3}\right)^t\right]$$

If we give an initial value, $y_0 = 5$, then we obtain a particular solution that is plotted below.

*In[26]:=*
```
Clear[y,t];
y[0]  =  5;
y[t_]  =  y[0]*(2/3)^t  +  3(1-(2/3)^t);
ListPlot[Table[{t,y[t]},{t,0,10}],AxesLabel->{"t","y(t)"}];
```

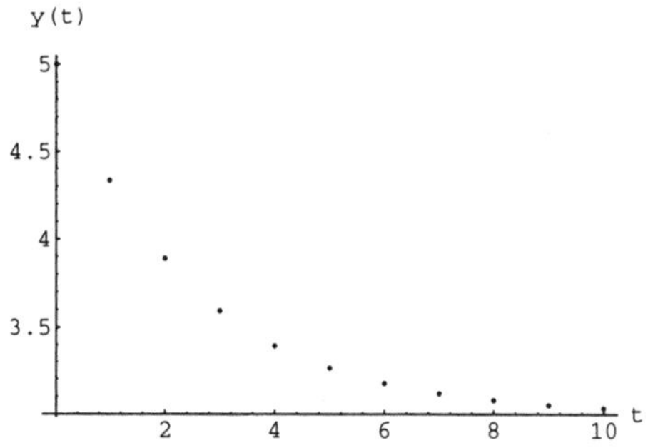


Evidently, as $t \to \infty$, $y_t \to 3$. This value, $y_e = 3$, is called an *equilibrium point* of the sequence. In general, an equilibrium point is a number $y_e$ such that $\lim_{t\to\infty} y_t = y_e$.

The behavior of the general solution depends upon the coefficients in the difference equation. Consider the case when $A \neq 1$. The general solution is:

$$y_t = A^t y_0 + B\left(\frac{1 - A^t}{1 - A}\right)$$

If $|A| < 1$, i.e., $-1 < A < 1$, then $A^t \to 0$ as $t \to \infty$. Hence $y_t$ converges to $B/(1-A)$ $= b/(a_1+a_0)$, an equilibrium point. Depending upon the sign of $A$, the convergence may either be monotonic or oscillatory. If $0 < A < 1$, $y_t$ converges monotonically to $B/(1-A)$, and if $-1 < A < 0$, then $y_t$ converges to $B/(1-A)$ as a damped oscillation around this equilibirum point. If $|A| > 1$, then $|A^t| \to \infty$ as $t \to \infty$ and $y_t$ is divergent and $y_t$ is called an *explosive solution.* If $A > 1$, the divergence is monotonic, or if $A < -1$, the divergence is an *explosive oscillation.*

**Example 15.14** Plot the solution of the initial-value problem:

$y_{t+1} + 0.8\,y_t = 10, \quad y_0 = 5.$

Since $A = -0.8$ and $B = 10$, the particular solution is

$$y_t = 5(-0.8)^t + 10\left(\frac{1 - (-0.8)^t}{1.8}\right)$$

We plot the solution points joined by a line to illustrate the damped oscillation around the equilibrium point, $B/(1-A) \approx 5.55$.

*In[30]:=*
```
Clear[y,t];
A = -0.8; B = 10; y[0] = 5;
y[t_]:= y[0]*A^t + B*(1-A^t)/(1-A);
solution=Table[{t,y[t]},{t,0,20}];
ListPlot[solution,AxesLabel->{"t","y(t)"},
                    PlotJoined->True];
```

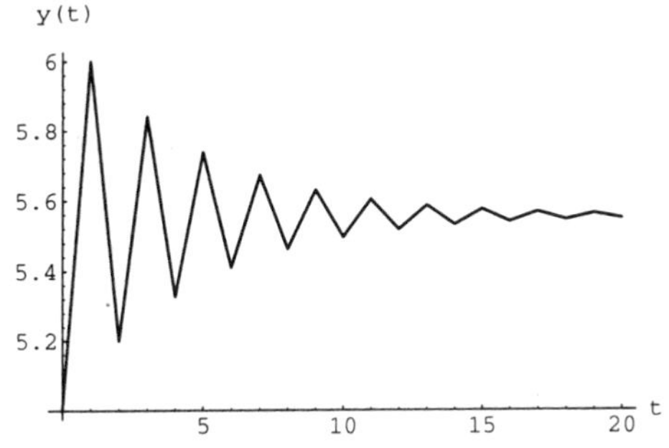


The solution is oscillatory and approaches the value 5.5555.

**Example 15.15** The solution of the initial value problem

$y_{t+1} + 1.2y_t = 4$, $y_0 = 5$

is an explosive oscillation. In this example, $A = -1.2$ and $B = 4$.

*In[35]:=*

```
Clear[y,t];
A = -1.2; B = 4; y[0] = 5;
y[t_]:= y[0]*A^t + B*(1-A^t)/(1-A);
solution = Table[{t,y[t]},{t,0,20}];
ListPlot[solution,AxesLabel->{"t","y(t)"},
                    PlotJoined->True];
```

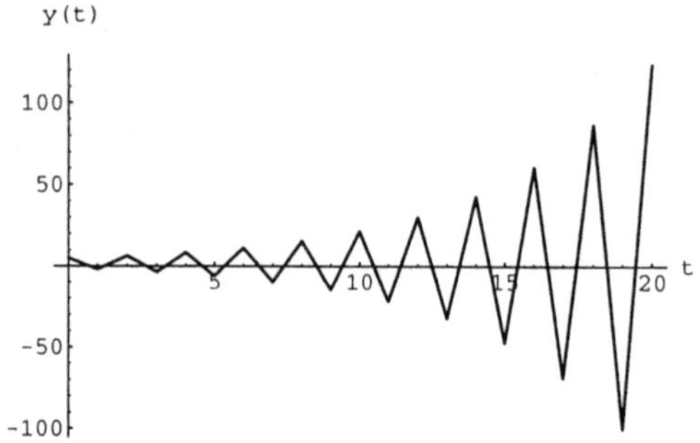


## EXERCISES

1. Find the general solution of the following first-order difference equations:
   (a) $y_{t+1} - y_t = -1$
   (b) $y_{t+1} = 2y_t + 3$
   (c) $y_{t+1} + 0.6y_t = 4.8$
   (d) $y_{t+1} + y_t = 2$

2. Plot the solutions of the following initial-value problems, and determine whether the solutions are divergent and convergent:
   (a) $y_{t+1} - 1.3y_t = 5,\ y_0 = 2.$
   (b) $y_{t+1} + 2y_t = 0,\ y_0 = 1.$
   (c) $y_{t+1} + 0.2y_t = 4,\ y_0 = -5.$
   (d) $y_{t+1} - 0.5y_t = 1,\ y_0 = 1.$

### 15.2.2 Higher-order homogeneous difference equations

Consider the $n$th-order linear, homogeneous difference equation with constant coefficients

$$a_n y_{t+n} + a_{n-1} y_{t+n-1} + \ldots + a_1 y_{t+1} + a_0 y_t = 0.$$

If $n = 1$, then the general solution is $y_t = A^t y_0$. We seek a solution for the higher-order difference equation of the form: $y_t = r^t$ where $r$ is a number that is to be determined. Substituting $y_t = r^t$ into the difference equation, we have

$$a_n r^{t+n} + a_{n-1} r^{t+n-1} + \ldots + a_1 r^{t+1} + a_0 r^t = 0$$

or,

$$r^t(a_n r^n + a_{n-1} r^{n-1} + \ldots + a_1 r + a_0) = 0.$$

For a nontrivial solution ($r \neq 0$) to exist, $r$ must satisfy the polynomial equation:

$$P(r) = a_n r^n + a_{n-1} r^{n-1} + \ldots + a_1 r + a_0 = 0.$$

The polynomial is called the *auxiliary* or *characteristic polynomial* of the difference equation. $P(r) = 0$ is called the *characteristic equation.*

Suppose $r_1, \ldots, r_n$ are the roots of the characteristic equation. These roots can be real or complex, and distinct or repeated. If all roots are real and distinct, i.e., $r_1 \neq r_2 \neq \ldots \neq r_n$, then each root generates a solution of the difference equation. That is,

$$y_t^{(1)} = r_1^t,\ y_t^{(2)} = r_2^t, \ldots,\ y_t^{(n)} = r_n^t$$

Furthermore, these $n$ solutions are linearly independent. Applying the superposition principle, the general solution of the $n$th-order homogeneous difference equation is then a linear combination of these $n$ linearly independent solutions:

$$\begin{aligned} y_t &= c_1 y_t^{(1)} + c_2 y_t^{(2)} + \ldots + c_n y_t^{(n)} \\ &= c_1 r_1^t + c_2 r_2^t + \ldots + c_n r_n^t \end{aligned}$$

**Example 15.16** Find the general solution of

$$y_{t+3} - 2y_{t+2} - 5y_{t+1} + 6y_t = 0.$$

We compute the roots of the characteristic polynomial

$$P(r) = r^3 - 2r^2 - 5r + 6.$$

*In[40]:=*

```
Clear[P,r];
P[r_]:= r^3 - 2*r^2 - 5*r + 6;
Solve[P[r]==0,r]
```

*Out[42]=*

```
{{r → -2}, {r → 1}, {r → 3}}
```

Since all roots are real, distinct roots, the general solution is

$$\begin{aligned} y_t &= c_1(-2)^t + c_2 1^t + c_3 3^t \\ &= c_2 + c_1(-2)^t + c_3 3^t \end{aligned}$$

If $y_0 = 2$, $y_1 = 10$, $y_2 = 4$, then we can solve for the arbitrary constants from the equations:

$$\begin{aligned} 2 &= c_2 + c_1(-2)^0 + c_3(3)^0 = c_2 + c_1 + c_3 \\ 10 &= c_2 + c_1(-2)^1 + c_3(3)^1 = c_2 - 2c_1 + 3c_3 \\ 4 &= c_2 + c_1(-2)^2 + c_3(3)^2 = c_2 + 4c_1 + 9c_3 \end{aligned}$$

*In[43]:=*

```
Clear[y,t,c1,c2,c3];
y[t_]:= c1*(-2)^t + c2 + c3*(3)^t;
Solve[{y[0]==2,y[1]==10,y[2]==4},{c1,c2,c3}]
```

*Out[45]=*

```
{{c1 → -2, c2 → 3, c3 → 1}}
```

The particular solution corresponding to these initial conditions is then

$$y_t = 3 - 2(-2)^t + 3^t$$

which is plotted below for $t = 0,1,2, \ldots ,5$.

*In[46]:=*

```
solution = Table[{t,y[t]} /.{c1->-2,c2->3,c3->1} ,{t,0,5}];
ListPlot[solution,AxesLabel->{"t","y(t)"},
         PlotJoined->True];
```

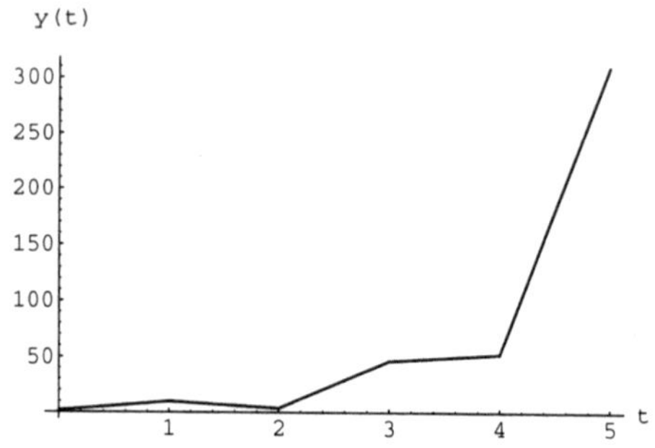


We can use the same line of reasoning to find the general solutions of higher-order difference equations as we did for higher-order differential equations discussed in Chapter 13 in the cases of repeated roots or complex roots.

Suppose $r_1$ is a real root of multiplicity $k$ of the characteristic equation $P(r) = 0$, and the remaining roots, $r_{k+1}, \ldots ,r_n$ are distinct real roots. As illustrated in exercise 15.17, the following are solutions of the difference equation and are linearly independent:

$$y_t^{(1)} = r_1^t,\ y_t^{(2)} = tr_1^t,\ \ldots,\ y_t^{(k)} = t^{k-1}r_1^t$$

The general solution of the $n$th-order homogeneous difference equation with a repeated real root is thus

$$\begin{aligned} y_t &= c_1r_1^t + c_2tr_1^t + \ldots + c_kt^{k-1}r_1^t + c_{k+1}r_{k+1}^t + \ldots + c_nr_n^t \\ &= (c_1 + \ldots c_kt^{k-1})r_1^t + c_{k+1}r_{k+1}^t + \ldots + c_nr_n^t. \end{aligned}$$

In Chapter 13, we tested the linear independence of $n$ solutions of a differential equation by evaluating a determinant (Wronskian). There is a discrete version of the Wronskian determinant for difference equations. Suppose

$$y_t^{(1)},\ y_t^{(2)},\ \ldots,\ y_t^{(n)}$$

are $n$ solutions of a difference equation. These $n$ solutions are linearly independent if and only if the determinant

$$W = \begin{vmatrix} y_0^{(1)} & y_0^{(2)} & \ldots & y_0^{(n)} \\ y_1^{(1)} & y_1^{(2)} & \ldots & y_1^{(n)} \\ \ldots & \ldots & \ldots & \ldots \\ y_{n-1}^{(1)} & y_{n-1}^{(2)} & \ldots & y_{n-1}^{(n)} \end{vmatrix}$$

is nonzero.

**Example 15.17** Find the general solution of

$$y_{t+4} - 9y_{t+3} + 30y_{t+2} - 44y_{t+1} + 24y_t = 0$$

First, we compute the roots of the characteristic polynomial

$$P(r) = r^4 - 9r^3 + 30r^2 - 44r + 24.$$

*In[48]:=*
```
Clear[P,r];
P[r_]:= r^4 - 9*r^3 + 30*r^2 - 44*r + 24;
Solve[P[r]==0,r]
```

*Out[50]=*
```
{{r → 2}, {r → 2}, {r → 2}, {r → 3}}
```

The roots are real and the root $r = 2$ has multiplicity 3, i.e., $r_1 = r_2 = r_3 = 2$. The four linearly independent solutions are therefore

$$y_t^{(1)} = 2^t,\ y_t^{(2)} = t2^t,\ y_t^{(3)} = t^2 2^t,\ y_t^{(4)} = 3^t.$$

The Wronskian determinant is nonzero.

*In[51]:=*
```
Clear[y1,y2,y3];
y1[t_]:= (2)^t; y2[t_]:=t*(2)^t;
y3[t_]:= t^2*(2)^t; y4[t_]:=(3)^t;
w = Det[{{y1[0],y2[0],y3[0],y4[0]},
         {y1[1],y2[1],y3[1],y4[1]},
         {y1[2],y2[2],y3[2],y4[2]},
         {y1[3],y2[3],y3[3],y4[3]}}]
```

*Out[54]=*
```
16
```

Hence, the four solutions are linearly independent. The general solution is then

$$y_t = c_1 2^t + c_2 t 2^t + c_3 t^2 2^t + c_4 3^t$$

We now look at the case of complex roots of the characteristic polynomial. Let us assume that the difference equation is second order and the roots of the characteristic polynomial are $r_1 = h + iv$ and $r_2 = h - iv$. The general solution is a complex-valued sequence whose elements are

$$y_t = k_1(h + iv)^t + k_2(h - iv)^t$$

Note that we have changed the notation for the arbitrary constants to $k_1$ and $k_2$. Recall that in Chapter 13, we used the Euler formula

$$e^{h \pm iv} = e^h(\cos\surd \pm i \sin\surd)$$

to convert a complex number exponential function into a combination of trigonometric functions. Equivalently, a complex number power function can also be converted into terms involving trigonometric functions by *De Moivre's formula*,

$(h \pm iv)^t = R^t(\cos\theta t \pm i\sin\theta t)$

where $R = |h \pm iv|$ and

$$\theta = \tan^{-1}(\frac{v}{h}).$$

The general solution then becomes

$$y_t = k_1R^t(\cos\theta t + i\sin\theta t) + k_2R^t(\cos\theta t - i\sin\theta t)$$
$$= R^t(c_1\cos\theta t + c_1\sin\theta t)$$

where $c_1 = (k_1 + k_2)$ and $c_2 = i(k_1 - k_2)$. Sometimes this solution is also expressed in the form

$$y_t = CR^t\cos(\theta t - \delta).$$

where $C$ and $\delta$ are constants. The general solution can also be interpreted as a linear combination of the real part and the imaginary part of the function $(h + iv)^t$, i.e.,

$$y_t = c_1\text{Re}[(h + iv)^t] + c_2\text{Im}[(h + iv)^t],$$

where $\text{Re}[(h + iv)^t] = R^t\cos\theta t$ and $\text{Im}[(h + iv)^t] = R^t\sin\theta t$.

**Example 15.18** Consider the difference equation

$$y_{t+3} - 0.5y_{t+2} - 0.23y_{t+1} + 0.427y_t = 0.$$

The roots of the characteristic polynomial are: $r_1 = -0.7$, $r_2 = 0.6 - 0.5i$, and $r_3 = 0.6 + 0.5i$.

*In[55]:=*
```
Clear[P,r];
P[r_]:= r^3 - 0.5*r^2 - 0.23*r + 0.427;
Solve[P[r]==0,r]
```

*Out[57]=*
```
{{r → -0.7}, {r → 0.6 - 0.5I}, {r → 0.6 + 0.5I}}
```

The general solution is

$$y_t = c_1(-0.7)^t + R^t(c_2\cos\theta t + c_3\sin\theta t)$$

where $R = [(0.6)^2 + (0.5)^2]^{1/2} \approx 0.781025$ and $\theta = \tan^{-1}(0.5/0.6) \approx 0.694738$.

*In[58]:=*
```
R = Abs[0.6-0.5*I]
```

*Out[58]=*
```
0.781025
```

*In[59]:=*
```
theta = ArcTan[0.5/0.6]
```

*Out[59]=*
```
0.694738
```

Given initial conditions

$y_0 = -1,\ y_1 = -0.7,\ y_2 = 3.65.$

we can solve for the arbitrary constants $c_1$, $c_2$, and $c_3$.

*In[60]:=*
```
Clear[y,t,c1,c2,c3];
y[t_] = c1*(-0.7)^t +
        R^t*(c2*Cos[theta*t]+c3*Sin[theta*t]);
Solve[{y[0]==-1,y[1]==-0.7,y[2]==3.65},{c1,c2,c3}]
```

*Out[60]=*
```
{{c1 → 2., c2 → -3., c3 → 5.}}
```

The particular solution is then

$y_t = 2(-0.7)^t + R^t(-3\cos\theta t + 5\sin\theta t).$

Here is a plot of this solution.

*In[63]:=*
```
solution=Table[{t,y[t]} /.{c1->2,c2->-3,c3->5} ,{t,0,20}];
ListPlot[solution,AxesLabel->{"t","y(t)"},
                  PlotJoined->True,PlotRange->All];
```

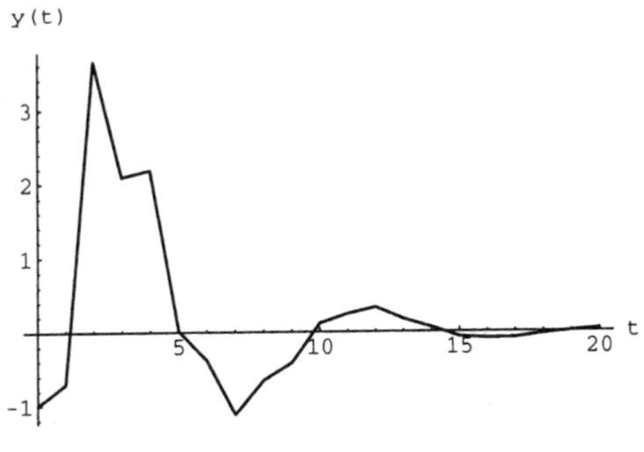


## EXERCISES

1. Find the general solutions of the following homogeneous difference equations:
   (a) $y_{t+2} - 6y_{t+1} + 8y_t = 0$
   (b) $y_{t+3} - 4y_{t+2} + y_{t+1} + 6y_t = 0$
   (c) $y_{t+3} - 3y_{t+2} + 4y_t = 0$
   (d) $y_{t+3} - 3y_{t+2} + 4y_{t+1} + 8y_t = 0$

2. (a) Show that the second-order difference equation, $y_{t+2} + a_1 y_{t+1} + a_0 y_t = 0$, has repeated real roots if and only if $a_1^2 = 4a_0$, and the roots are $r_1 = r_2 = -a_1/2$.
   (b) Show that

$$y_t^{(1)} = \left[-\frac{a_1}{2}\right]^t, \quad y_t^{(2)} = t\left[-\frac{a_1}{2}\right]^t$$

are linearly independent solutions of the difference equation.

3. Find solutions of the problems in Exercise 1 with the following initial conditions and use **ListPlot** to plot the solutions:
   (a) $y_0 = 5$ and $y_1 = 8$.
   (b) $y_0 = 0$, $y_1 = 4$, and $y_2 = 5$.
   (c) $y_0 = -3$, $y_1 = 0$, and $y_2 = 8$.
   (d) $y_0 = 1$, $y_1 = 5$, and $y_2 = 8$.

## 15.2.3 Inhomogeneous difference equations

Consider the inhomogeneous difference equation with constant coefficients

$$y_{t+n} + a_{n-1}y_{t+n-1} + \ldots + a_1 y_{t+1} + a_0 y_t = g(t).$$

Note that we normalized the coefficients in the equation so that $a_n = 1$. Analogous to the general solution of a differential equation, the general solution of an inhomogeneous difference equation consists of two parts: the complementary solution, i.e., the general solution of the corresponding homogeneous difference equation, and a particular solution of the inhomogenous equation. We have already discussed how to find the complementary solution in the last section. Now we are concerned with finding a particular solution of the inhomogeneous difference equation.

Two methods are available for finding the particular solution: the *Method of Undetermined Coefficients* and the *Method of Variation of Parameters*. The former method is easy to implement, but is restricted to certain types of $g(t)$. The latter method, which was first introduced for differential equations in Chapter 13, is applicable to general types of $g(t)$, but is sometimes more difficult to use.

Suppose $g(t)$ is one of the following functional forms:

$$g(t) = b,\ b^t,\ t^b,\ \cos bt, \text{ or } \sin bt,$$

where $b$ is a constant. We also allow $g(t)$ to be linear combinations or products of these functions. The method of undetermined coefficients assumes that the particular solution is similar in form to $g(t)$. For example, if $g(t) \equiv 3$, we try a constant solution, say, $y_t = B$. If $g(t) = 5 + t + e^{2t}$, then we try a solution of the form

$$y_t = B_0 + B_1 t + B_2 e^{2t}.$$

We must determine the coefficients, $B_0$, $B_1$, and $B_2$, so that $y_t$ is a solution of the inhomogeneous difference equation. Suppose the difference equation is

$$y_{t+n} + a_{n-1}y_{t+n-1} + \ldots + a_1 y_{t+1} + a_0 y_t = b.$$

We seek a constant particular solution of the form: $y_p = B$. Subtituting $y_p$ in the difference equation, we have

$$B + a_{n-1}B + \ldots + a_1 B + a_0 B = b.$$

Solving for $B$, we find that

$$y_p = B = \frac{b}{1 + \sum_{i=0}^{n-1} a_i}, \quad \text{if} \quad 1 + \sum_{i=0}^{n-1} a_i \neq 0.$$

If

$$\sum_{i=0}^{n-1} a_i = -1$$

then the denominator of $y_p$ is zero and this solution is invalid. It can be shown that if

$$\sum_{i=0}^{n-1} a_i = -1$$

then the particular solution is of the form $y_p = Bt$.

**Example 15.19** Consider the inhomogeneous difference equation

$$y_{t+3} + y_{t+2} - 32y_{t+1} - 60y_t = 180.$$

Notice that $g(t) \equiv 180$. It is easy to show that

$$y_c = c_1(-5)^t + c_2(-2)^t + c_3 6^t$$

is the complementary solution. The particular solution is

$$y_p = 180/(1+1-32-60) = -180/90 = -2.$$

Thus the general solution of the inhomogeneous equation is

$$y_t = y_c + y_p = c_1(-5)^t + c_2(-2)^t + c_3 6^t - 2.$$

Let us check this solution with *Mathematica.*

*In[65]:=*

```
Clear[t,y,c1,c2,c3];
y[t_]:= c1*(-5)^t + c2*(-2)^t + c3*6^t - 2;
y[t+3]+y[t+2]-32*y[t+1]-60*y[t]==180 // Simplify
```

*Out[67]=*

```
True
```

**Example 15.20** Consider the difference equation

$$y_{t+3} - 4y_{t+2} + y_{t+1} + 2y_t = 16.$$

The complementary solution of the homogeneous equation can be shown to be

$$y_c = c_1 + c_2\left(\frac{3-\sqrt{17}}{2}\right)^t + c_3\left(\frac{3+\sqrt{17}}{2}\right)^t.$$

Notice that in this case the sum of the coefficients on the left-side of the difference equation is zero. Hence, the particular solution will be of the form $y_p = Bt$. Upon substitution we have

$$B(t+3) - 4B(t+2) + B(t+1) + 2B(t) = 16.$$

Solving for $B$, we have $B = -4$. Hence $y_p = -4t$. The general solution of the inhomogeneous equation is therefore

$$y_t = c_1 + c_2\left(\frac{3-\sqrt{17}}{2}\right)^t + c_3\left(\frac{3+\sqrt{17}}{2}\right)^t - 4t.$$

Let us check this with *Mathematica*.

*In[68]:=*
```
Clear[t,y,c1,c2,c3];
r1  =  (3-Sqrt[17])/2;
r2  =  (3+Sqrt[17])/2;
y[t_]:= c1+ c2*r1^t  +  c3*r2^t  -  4*t;
y[t+3]-4*y[t+2]+y[t+1]+2*y[t]==16  //  Simplify
```

*Out[72]=*
```
True
```

**Example 15.21** Find a particular solution of

$$y_{t+2} - 4y_{t+1} + 5y_t = 3^t.$$

Here $g(t) = 3^t$, and we seek a particular solution of the form: $y_p = B\,3^t$. Substituting $y_p$ in the equation, the following calculation shows that $B = 1/2$. Hence $y_p = (1/2)\,3^t$.

*In[73]:=*
```
Clear[g,yp,t,B];
g[t_]:= 3^t;
yp[t_]:= B*3^t;
Solve[yp[t+2]-4*yp[t+1]+5*yp[t]==g[t],{B}]
```

*Out[76]=*

$$\{\{B \to \frac{1}{2}\}\}$$

If $g(t) = \cos bt$ or $g(t) = \sin bt$, we try a solution of the form

$$y_p = B_1 \sin bt + B_2 \cos bt$$

where $B_1$ and $B_2$ are undetermined coefficients.

**Example 15.22** Find a particular solution of

$$y_{t+2} - y_t = \sin \frac{\pi t}{2}.$$

We seek a solution of the form

$$y_p = B_1 \sin \frac{\pi t}{2} + B_2 \cos \frac{\pi t}{2}$$

where $B_1$ and $B_2$ are undetermined coefficients. Upon substitution, the left-hand side of the difference equation becomes

$$B_1 \left[ \sin \frac{\pi(t+2)}{2} - \sin \frac{\pi t}{2} \right] + B_2 \left[ \cos \frac{\pi(t+2)}{2} - \cos \frac{\pi t}{2} \right].$$

We can simplify this expression by using the trigonometric identities:

$$\sin \frac{\pi(2+t)}{2} = -\sin \frac{\pi t}{2}$$

$$\cos \frac{\pi(2+t)}{2} = -\cos \frac{\pi t}{2}.$$

Using these identities, we have

$$-2B_2 \cos \frac{\pi t}{2} - 2B_1 \sin \frac{\pi t}{2} = \sin \frac{\pi t}{2}$$

This identity implies that $B_2 = 0$ and $B_1 = -1/2$. The particular solution is then

$$y_p = -\frac{1}{2} \sin \frac{\pi t}{2}.$$

Suppose $g(t)$ is a polynomial, say

$$g(t) = b_0 + b_1 t + b_2 t^2 + \ldots + b_m t^m.$$

We seek a particular solution in the form of a polynomial

$$y_p = B_0 + B_1 t + B_2 t^2 + \ldots + B_m t^m$$

where $B_0, B_1, \ldots, B_m$ are constants. The method of mimicking may not work in certain situations, and some modifications may be needed. For example, we may want to try

$y_p = t(B_0 + B_1t + B_2t^2 + \ldots + B_mt^m).$

If it fails again, then try

$y_p = t^2(B_0 + B_1t + B_2t^2 + \ldots + B_mt^m)$

and so on.

**Example 15.23** Find a particular solution of

$y_{t+2} - 4y_{t+1} + 5y_t = t - t^2.$

Let the particular solution be of the form

$y_p = B_0 + B_1t + B_2t^2.$

We use *Mathematica* to substitute $y_p$ into the difference equation and determine the unknown coefficients.

*In[77]:=*

```
Clear[y,yp,ypnew,t,B0,B1,B2];
diffeq  =  yp[t+2]-4*yp[t+1]+5*yp[t]==t-t^2;
yp[t_]:=  B0  +  B1*t  +  B2*t^2;
diffeq  //  Simplify
```

*Out[80]=*

$2(B0 - B1 + B1t - 2B2t + B2t^2) == t - t^2$

Equating the coefficients of the $t^0$, $t$ and $t^2$ terms in the above equation, we have

$2(B_0 - B_1) = 0$
$2(B1 - 2B_2) = 1$
$2(B_2) = -1.$

Solving for the coefficients, we have $B_0 = B_1 = B_2 = -1/2$.

*In[81]:=*

```
eqn1  =  2*(B0  -  B1)  ==  0;
eqn2  =  2*(B1  -  2*B2)  ==  1;
eqn3  =  2*B2  ==  -1;
sol  =  Solve[{eqn1,eqn2,eqn3},{B0,B1,B2}]
```

*Out[84]=*

$\{\{B0 \to -(\frac{1}{2}), B1 \to -(\frac{1}{2}), B2 \to -(\frac{1}{2})\}\}$

Hence, a particular solution is

$$y_p = -\frac{1}{2} - \frac{1}{2}t - \frac{1}{2}t^2.$$

Let us check this solution.

*In[85]:=*
```
Clear[yp,t];
yp[t_]:=  (-1/2)*(1  +  t  +t^2);
yp[t+2]  -  4*yp[t+1]  +  5*yp[t]  ==  t  -  t^2  //  Simplify
```

*Out[87]=*
True

The method of undetermined coefficients is restricted to certain types of inhomogeneous terms. We shall briefly cover a more general method of finding particular solutions. The method of Variation of Parameters was first introduced in chapter 13 for finding particular solutions of differential equations. The extension of this method to difference equations is straightfoward.

Consider a second-order difference equation

$$y_{t+2} + a_1 y_{t+1} + a_0 y_t = g(t)$$

The method of variation of parameters seeks a particular solution of the form

$$y_t = u_1(t)\, y_t^{(1)} + u_2(t)\, y_t^{(2)}$$

where $u_1(t)$ and $u_2(t)$ are two unknown functions of $t$, and $y_t^{(1)}$ and $y_t^{(2)}$ are two linearly independent solutions of the homogeneous difference equation

$$y_{t+2} + a_1 y_{t+1} + a_0 y_t = 0.$$

Define the first-order forward differences as

$$\Delta u_1(t) = u_1(t+1) - u_1(t)$$
$$\Delta u_2(t) = u_2(t+1) - u_2(t).$$

We determine the unknown function $u_1(t)$ and $u_2(t)$ by solving for $\Delta u_1(t)$ and $\Delta u_2(t)$ in the following equations:

$$\Delta u_1(t) y_{t+1}^{(1)} + \Delta u_2(t) y_{t+1}^{(2)} = 0$$
$$\Delta u_1(t) y_{t+2}^{(1)} + \Delta u_2(t) y_{t+2}^{(2)} = g(t).$$

Solving these equations for $\Delta u_1(t)$ and $\Delta u_2(t)$, we have

$$\Delta u_1(t) = \frac{\begin{vmatrix} 0 & y_{t+1}^{(2)} \\ g(t) & y_{t+2}^{(2)} \end{vmatrix}}{\begin{vmatrix} y_{t+1}^{(1)} & y_{t+1}^{(2)} \\ y_{t+2}^{(1)} & y_{t+2}^{(2)} \end{vmatrix}} \equiv \frac{W_1(t)}{W(t)}; \quad \Delta u_2(t) = \frac{\begin{vmatrix} y_{t+1}^{(1)} & 0 \\ y_{t+2}^{(1)} & g(t) \end{vmatrix}}{\begin{vmatrix} y_{t+1}^{(1)} & y_{t+1}^{(2)} \\ y_{t+2}^{(1)} & y_{t+2}^{(2)} \end{vmatrix}} \equiv \frac{W_2(t)}{W(t)}.$$

The denominator of these ratios is the Wronskian determinant. To obtain the functions $u_1(t)$ and $u_2(t)$, we note that

$$u_1(t) = u_1(0) + \sum_{k=0}^{t-1} \Delta u_1(k)$$

$$u_2(t) = u_2(0) + \sum_{k=0}^{t-1} \Delta u_2(k).$$

If $c_1 = u_1(0)$ and $c_2 = u_2(0)$ are arbitrary constants, then the **general** solution is

$$y_t = c_1 y_t^{(1)} + c_2 y_t^{(2)} + \left[\sum_{k=0}^{t-1} \Delta u_1(k)\right] y_t^{(1)} + \left[\sum_{k=0}^{t-1} \Delta u_2(k)\right] y_t^{(2)}.$$

The first part of the above expression is the complementary solution

$$y_c = c_1 y_t^{(1)} + c_2 y_t^{(2)}$$

and the second part is a particular solution

$$y_p = \left[\sum_{k=0}^{t-1} \Delta u_1(k)\right] y_t^{(1)} + \left[\sum_{k=0}^{t-1} \Delta u_2(k)\right] y_t^{(2)}.$$

**Example 15.24** Find the general solution for the difference equation

$$y_{t+2} - 5y_{t+1} + 6y_t = t.$$

The roots of the characteristic polynomial are 2, and 3, and hence, the sequences

$$y_t^{(1)} = 2^t, \quad \text{and} \quad y_t^{(2)} = 3^t$$

are two linearly independent solutions of the homogeneous equation. To obtain particular solutions by the method of variation of parameters, we have

$$\Delta u_1(t) = \frac{\begin{vmatrix} 0 & 3^{t+1} \\ t & 3^{t+2} \end{vmatrix}}{\begin{vmatrix} 2^{t+1} & 3^{t+1} \\ 2^{t+2} & 3^{t+2} \end{vmatrix}} = -t\left(\frac{1}{2}\right)^{t+1}, \quad \Delta u_2(t) = \frac{\begin{vmatrix} 3^{t+1} & 0 \\ 3^{t+2} & t \end{vmatrix}}{\begin{vmatrix} 2^{t+1} & 3^{t+1} \\ 2^{t+2} & 3^{t+2} \end{vmatrix}} = t\left(\frac{1}{3}\right)^{t+1}.$$

With some algebraic simplifications, we have

$$\left[\sum_{k=0}^{t-1} \Delta u_1(k)\right] = -1 + \left(\frac{1}{2}\right)^t (1+t), \quad \left[\sum_{k=0}^{t-1} \Delta u_2(k)\right] = \frac{1}{4} - \left(\frac{1}{3}\right)^t \left(\frac{1}{4} + \frac{t}{2}\right)$$

Therefore the general solution of the difference equation is

$$y_t = c_1 2^t + c_2 3^t + \left[-1 + \left(\frac{1}{2}\right)^t (1+t)\right] 2^t + \left[\frac{1}{4} - \left(\frac{1}{3}\right)^t \left(\frac{1}{4} + \frac{t}{2}\right)\right] 3^t$$

$$= (c_1 - 1)2^t + \left(c_1 + \frac{1}{4}\right) 3^t + \left(\frac{3}{4} + \frac{t}{2}\right)$$

The second part is the particular solution

$$y_p = \frac{3}{4} + \frac{t}{2}$$

We check our general solution with *Mathematica*.

*In[88]:=*
```
Clear[y,t,c1,c2];
y[t_]:= c1*2^t + c2*3^t + (3/4) + t/2;
y[t+2] - 5*y[t+1] + 6*y[t] == t // Simplify
```

*Out[90]=*
```
True
```

Since the original inhomogeneous difference equation has $g(t) = t$, the particular solution could have been found by the method of undetermined coefficients.

## EXERCISES

1. Find the general solution of the following difference equations:
   (a) $y_{t+2} - 4y_{t+1} + 4y_t = 5(4^t)$
   (b) $y_{t+2} - 6y_{t+1} + 8y_t = 3t^2 + 2$
   (c) $y_{t+2} + 4y_t = \cos \pi t$
   (d) $y_{t+3} + y_t = 2^t \cos 3t$
   (e) $y_{t+4} - 16y_t = 3t$
   (f) $y_{t+3} - 3y_{t+2} + 3y_{t+1} - y_t = 48 + 24t$
2. Show that

$$y_p = \frac{bt}{n + \sum_{i=1}^{n-1} ia_i}$$

is a particular solution of the difference equation

$$y_{t+n} + a_{n-1}y_{t+n-1} + \ldots + a_1 y_{t+1} + a_0 y_t = b$$

when

$$\sum_{i=1}^{n} a_i = -1 \quad \text{and} \quad \sum_{i=1}^{n-1} ia_i \neq -n.$$

### 15.2.4 Solving difference equations with **RSolve**

The *Mathematica* package, **RSolve**, can be used to solve some elementary difference equations. It computes general solutions of difference equations as well as initial-value problems. The package **RSolve** is part of the **DiscreteMath** collection of packages.

*In[91]:=*
```
Needs["DiscreteMath`RSolve`"];
```

*In[92]:=*
```
?RSolve
```

**RSolve[{eqn1, eqn2, ...}, {a1[n], a2[n], ...}, n, opts] solves the recurrence equations eqn1, eqn2, ... for the sequences a1[n], a2[n], ... If there is a single sequence or equation, it need not be given in a list. Equations can either be recurrences or initial/boundary conditions. An equation may have the form eqn /; cond where cond is an inequality specifying the range of values of n for which eqn is valid; when no condition is given it is assumed to be n >= 0.**

The first argument contains the difference equation, the second argument the sequence in the difference equation, and the third argument is the index for the difference equation. We shall demonstrate the package by using it in some examples.

**Example 15.25** Use **RSolve** to show that the difference equation

$$y_{t+2} - y_t = 0$$

has the general solution

$$y_t = c_1 1^t + c_2(-1)^t = c_1 + c_2(-1)^t.$$

We apply **RSolve** to this difference equation.

*In[93]:=*

```
Clear[y,t];
eqn  =  y[t+2]  -  y[t]  ==  0;
sol  =  RSolve[eqn,y[t],t]
```

*Out[95]=*

$$\{\{y[t] \to (\frac{1}{2} + \frac{(-1)^t}{2})y[0] + (\frac{1}{2} + \frac{(-1)^{-1+t}}{2})y[1]\}\}$$

**RSolve** uses the initial values, $y_0$ and $y_1$, as arbitrary constants in the general solution. The constants are related through the equations:

$$c_1 = (y_0 + y_1)/2$$
$$c_2 = (y_0 - y_1)/2.$$

We verify below that these solutions are the same.

*In[96]:=*

```
Clear[y1,y2,t];
y1[t_]  =  y[t]  /.  sol[[1]];
y2[t_]=  c1  +  c2*(-1)^t  /.  {c1->(y[0]+y[1])/2,
             c2->(y[0]-y[1])/2};
y1[t]==y2[t]  //  Simplify
```

*Out[99]=*

True

**Example 15.26** Solve the initial-value problem:

$$y_{t+2} + y_{t+1} + 2y_t = 6$$
$$y_0 = 1$$
$$y_1 = 3.$$

We use **RSolve** directly on the initial-value problem.

*In[100]:=*
```
Clear[y,t];
eqn  =  y[t+2]  +  y[t+1]  +  2y[t]  ==  6;
sol  =  RSolve[{eqn,y[0]==1,y[1]==3},y[t],t]  ;
y[t_]  =  y[t]  /.  sol[[1]]
```

*Out[103]=*

$$\frac{3}{2} - 2\text{Sqrt}[\frac{2}{7}]\ 2^{t/2}\text{Cos}[\text{Pi } t - t\ \text{ArcTan}[\text{Sqrt}[7]] - \text{ArcTan}[4(\frac{-3}{8\text{Sqrt}[7]} - \frac{\text{Sqrt}[7]}{8})]]$$

The following plot illustrates that the absolute value $|y_t| \to \infty$ as $t \to \infty$. Hence, the solution is unstable.

*In[104]:=*
```
graph  =  Table[{t,y[t]},{t,0,10}];
ListPlot[graph,AxesLabel->{"t","y(t)"},
                    PlotJoined->True];
```

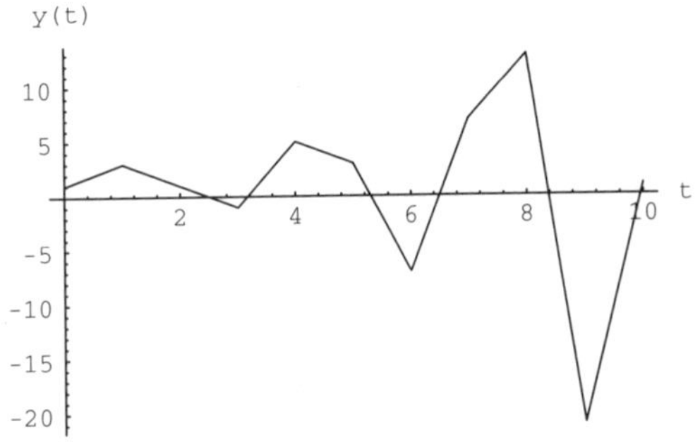


**Example 15.27** Solve the initial-value problem:

$y_{t+2} + 6y_{t+1} + 25y_t = 0$
$y_0 = 0$
$y_1 = -1/10.$

*In[106]:=*
```
Clear[y,t,eqn];
eqn  =  y[t+2]  +  6*y[t+1]  +  25*y[t]  ==  0;
sol  =  RSolve[{eqn,y[0]==0,y[1]==-1/10},y[t],t]
```

*Out[108]=*
```
{{y[t] → -(5^(-1 + t)*Cos[ArcTan[3/4] - (-1 + t)*(-Pi + ArcTan[4/3])]
   *If[t >= 1, 1, 0])/8}}
```

Note that the answer contains a factor **If[t>=1,1,0]** which means that the factor is 1 if the sequence index $t$ is greater than or equal to 1, and zero otherwise.

## EXERCISES

1. Using **RSolve**, find and plot the solution of the initial-value problem:

$$y_{t+3} - 2y_{t+1} + y_t = 0,$$
$$y_0 = 0, y_1 = -1, \quad \text{and} \quad y_2 = 0.$$

2. Using **RSolve**, find and plot the solution of the initial-value problem:

$$y_{t+2} + y_t = k$$
$$y_0 = 0, \quad \text{and} \quad y_1 = -1.$$

### 15.2.5 Stability of linear difference equations

Consider an *n*th order linear difference equation

$$y_{t+n} + a_{n-1}y_{t+n-1} + \ldots + a_1 y_{t+1} + a_0 y_t = g(t).$$

The general solution consists of two parts, the complementary solution, $y_c$, and the particular solution, $y_p$, so that

$$y_t = y_c + y_p$$

We are interested in the limiting behavior of the complementary function $y_c$. We say that the particular solution is *stable* if and only if

$$\lim_{t \to \infty} y_c = 0$$

Hence, as t $\to \infty$, the behavior of the general solution of the difference equation is essentially that of the particular solution.

**Example 15.28** The first-order difference equation

$$y_{t+1} + a y_t = b$$

where $a$ and $b$ are constants has the general solution

$$y_t = \begin{cases} c_1(-a)^t + \dfrac{b}{1+a}, a \neq -1 \\ c_1 + bt, a = -1 \end{cases}.$$

If $|a| < 1$, then the particular solution $y_p = b/(1+a)$ is stable since

$$\lim_{t \to \infty} y_c = c_1(-a)^t = 0.$$

Furthermore for large $t$, $y_t \approx b/(1+a)$.

For an *n*th order, linear difference equation with constant coefficient, the complementary solution has the form

$$y_c = c_1 r_1^t + c_2 r_2^t + \ldots + c_n r_n^t$$

when $r_i$, $i = 1,2, \ldots, n$, are distinct real roots of the characteristic polynomial. In the case of a repeated root $r_1$ and distinct remaining $n-k$ roots, the complementary solution is

$$y_c = [c_1 + c_2 t + \ldots + c_2 t^{k-1}]r_1^t + c_{k+1}r_{k+1}^t + \ldots + c_n r_n^t.$$

In the case where $r_1$ and $r_2$ are complex and the remaining $n-2$ roots are real and distinct, the complementary solution can be written as

$$y_c = c_1 R^t \cos(\theta t) + c_2 R^t \sin(\theta t) + c_3 r_3^t + \ldots + c_n r_n^t$$

In all three cases, a necessary and sufficient condition for the particular solution to be stable is that $|r_i| < 1$, $i=1,2, \ldots ,n$.

**Example 15.29** Consider the difference equation

$$y_{t+3} + \frac{7}{2}y_{t+2} + 2y_{t+1} - 2y_t = 18$$

The roots of the characteristic polynomial are $r_1 = r_2 = -2$, and $r_3 = 1/2$. A particular solution is $y_p \equiv 4$ and the complementary solution is

$$y_c = (c_1 + c_2 t)(-2)^t + c_3\left(\frac{1}{2}\right)^t.$$

Since $|r_1| = |r_2| = |-2| > 1$, the general solution is unstable. If $y_0 = 1$, $y_1 = 2$, and $y_2 = 3$ are initial values, then the arbitrary constants are $c_1 = -1/5$, $c_2 = 9/25$, and $c_3 = -84/25$.

*In[109]:=*
```
Clear[y,t,c1,c2,c3,c];
y[t_] = (c1+c2*t)(-2)^t + c3*(1/2)^t + 4;
{c} = Solve[{y[0]==1,y[1]==2,y[2]==3},{c1,c2,c3}]
```

*Out[111]=*

$$\{\{c2 \to -(\frac{1}{5}),\ c1 \to \frac{9}{25},\ c3 \to -(\frac{84}{25})\}\}$$

The following plot indicates that $y_t \to -\infty$ as $t \to \infty$.

*In[112]:=*
```
tab = Table[{t,y[t]} /. c, {t,0,20}];
ListPlot[tab,AxesLabel->{"t","y(t)"},
                    PlotJoined->True];
```

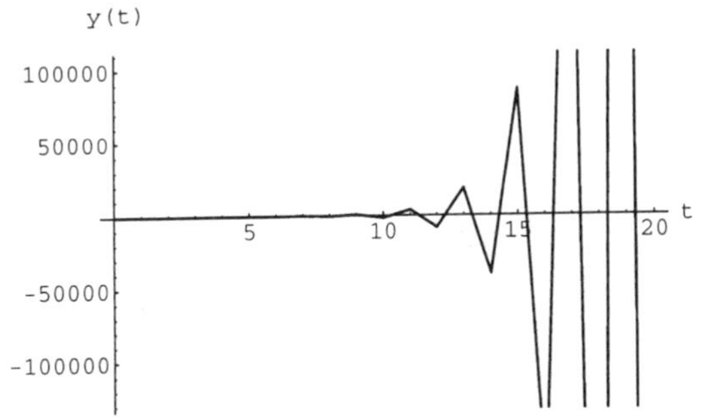

**Example 15.30** Consider the 4th order difference equation

$$y_{t+4} - 0.18y_{t+3} - 0.32y_{t+2} + 0.22y_{t+1} - 0.08y_t = 3.2.$$

The roots of the charactertistic polynomial are $r_1 = -0.8$, $r_2 = 0.5$, $r_3 = 0.2 + 0.4i$, and $r_4 = 0.2 - 0.4i$. The complementary solution is

$$y_c = c_1(-0.8)^t + c_2(0.5)^t + c_3R^t\cos(\theta t) + c_4R^t\sin(\theta t)$$

where $R = [(0.2)^2+(0.4)^2]^{1/2} \approx 0.4472$, and $\theta = \tan^{-1}(0.4/0.2) \approx 1.1071$. A particular solution is

$$y_p = \frac{3.2}{1 - 0.18 - 0.32 + 0.22 - 0.08} = 5$$

Since the roots of the characteristic polynomial are less than 1 in absolute value, the particular solution is stable. Suppose the initial conditions, $y_0 = 9$, $y_1 = 2.7$, $y_2 = 5.35$, and $y_3 = 3.619$, are specified. Then it can be shown that $c_1 = 2$, $c_2 = -1$, $c_3 = 3$, and $c_4 = -2$. We plot the solution of the initial-value problem below.

*In[114]:=*

```
Clear[R,theta,y,yc,yp,t,c1,c2,c3,c4];
R=Sqrt[0.2^2+0.4^2];  theta=ArcTan[0.4/0.2];
r1  =  -0.8;  r2  =  1/2;
c1  =  2;  c2  =  -1;  c3  =  3;  c4  =  -2;
yc[t_]  =  c1*r1^t+c2*r2^t+c3*R^t*Cos[theta*t]+
          c4*R^t*Sin[theta*t];
yp[t_]:=  5;
y[t_]  =  yc[t]  +  yp[t];
tab  =  Table[{t,y[t]},{t,0,20}];
ListPlot[tab,AxesLabel->{"t","y(t)"},
                 PlotJoined->True,
                  PlotRange->{{0,20},{0,10}}];
```

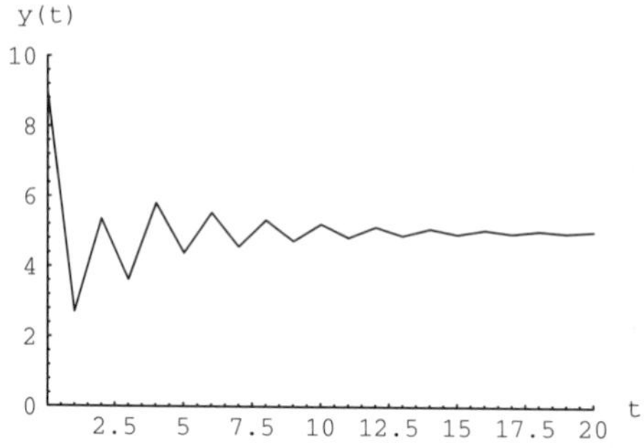


## EXERCISES

1. Check the stability of particular solutions of the following difference equations:
   (a) $9y_{t+2} - 6y_{t+1} + y_t = 0$
   (b) $y_{t+2} - y_{t+1} + 2y_t = 3$
   (c) $y_{t+2} - 4y_{t+1} + y_t = 3 + 2t$

2. For what values of $a$ will the trivial solution of

$$y_{t+2} - a y_{t+1} + a y_t = 0$$

be stable?

## □ 15.3 Systems of Difference Equations □

Systems of difference equations are similar to the systems of differential equations that were discussed in Chapter 14. In this section, we shall briefly discuss both systems of linear and nonlinear first-order difference equations. As with differential equations, higher-order systems can always be reduced to first-order systems as shown in the next section.

### 15.3.1 Systems of linear difference equations

A system of linear difference equations with constant coefficients is a set of difference equations of the form:

$$\begin{aligned}
y_{1,t+1} &= a_{11}y_{1,t} + a_{12}y_{2,t} + \ldots + a_{1n}y_{n,t} + g_1(t)\\
y_{2,t+1} &= a_{21}y_{1,t} + a_{22}y_{2,t} + \ldots + a_{2n}y_{n,t} + g_2(t)\\
&\cdots\cdots\cdots\cdots\cdots\cdots\cdots\cdots\cdots\\
y_{n,t+1} &= a_{n1}y_{1,t} + a_{n2}y_{2,t} + \ldots + a_{nn}y_{n,t} + g_n(t).
\end{aligned}$$

In matrix notation, we write the system as

$$\mathbf{y}_{t+1} = \mathbf{A}\mathbf{y}_t + \mathbf{g}(t)$$

where $\mathbf{A} = [a_{ij}]$ is an $n \times n$ matrix. Here

$$\begin{aligned}
y_t &= [y_{1,t} \quad y_{2,t} \quad \ldots \quad y_{n,t}]^{\mathrm{T}}\\
g(t) &= [g_1(t) \quad g_2(t) \quad \ldots \quad g_n(t)]^{\mathrm{T}}.
\end{aligned}$$

We can find elements of the vector sequence $\{\mathbf{y}_t\}$ by iteration:

$$\begin{aligned}
\mathbf{y}_1 &= \mathbf{A}\mathbf{y}_0 + \mathbf{g}(0)\\
\mathbf{y}_2 &= \mathbf{A}\mathbf{y}_1 + \mathbf{g}(1) = \mathbf{A}[\mathbf{A}\mathbf{y}_0 + \mathbf{g}(0)] + \mathbf{g}(1)\\
&= \mathbf{A}^2\mathbf{y}_0 + \mathbf{A}\mathbf{g}(0) + \mathbf{g}(1)\\
\mathbf{y}_3 &= \mathbf{A}\mathbf{y}_2 + \mathbf{g}(2) = \mathbf{A}[\mathbf{A}^2\mathbf{y}_0 + \mathbf{A}\mathbf{g}(0) + \mathbf{g}(1)] + \mathbf{g}(2)\\
&= \mathbf{A}^3\mathbf{y}_0 + \mathbf{A}^2\mathbf{g}(0) + \mathbf{A}\mathbf{g}(1) + \mathbf{g}(2)\\
&\cdots\cdots\cdots\cdots\cdots\cdots\cdots\cdots\cdots\\
\mathbf{y}_t &= \mathbf{A}^t\mathbf{y}_0 + \mathbf{A}^{t-1}\mathbf{g}(0) + \mathbf{A}^{t-2}\mathbf{g}(1) + \ldots + \mathbf{A}\mathbf{g}(t-2) + \mathbf{g}(t-1)
\end{aligned}$$

Thus the general solution of the system is given by

$$\mathbf{y}_t = \mathbf{A}^t\mathbf{y}_0 + \sum_{i=0}^{t-1}\mathbf{A}^i\mathbf{g}(t-i)$$

The first term in this expression is the complementary solution of the system and the second term is a particular solution. This iterative method of solving systems of difference equations is very inefficient since it requires the computation of $\mathbf{A}, \mathbf{A}^2, \ldots, \mathbf{A}^t$. If $t$ is large, this is cumbersome. We shall present an alternative way of solving a system of difference equations.

The general solution of an inhomogeneous system consists of a complementary solution $\mathbf{y}_c$ and a particular solution $\mathbf{y}_p$, i.e.,

$$\mathbf{y}_t = \mathbf{y}_c + \mathbf{y}_p.$$

The complementary solution is computed from the homogeneous system

$$\mathbf{y}_{t+1} = \mathbf{A}\mathbf{y}_t$$

and the particular solution is any particular solution of the inhomogeneous system.

The particular solution $\mathbf{y}_p$ is easy to find if $\mathbf{g}(t)$ is a constant vector, $\mathbf{g}(t) \equiv \mathbf{b}$. In this case, we seek a solution of the form: $\mathbf{y}_p = \mathbf{k}$ which is independent of $t$. Substituting this form into the difference equations, we have

$$\mathbf{k} = \mathbf{A}\mathbf{k} + \mathbf{b} \quad \text{or} \quad (\mathbf{I} - \mathbf{A})\mathbf{k} = \mathbf{b}.$$

If $\mathbf{I} - \mathbf{A}$ is nonsingular, then we have

$$\mathbf{y}_p \equiv (\mathbf{I} - \mathbf{A})^{-1}\mathbf{b}.$$

**Example 15.31** Find a particular solution of the system of difference equations:

$$\begin{aligned} y_{1,t+1} &= 11y_{1,t} - 3y_{2,t} - 2y_{3,t} + 2 \\ y_{2,t+1} &= \ \ 8y_{1,t} - 2y_{3,t} + 1 \\ y_{3,t+1} &= 19y_{1,t} - 7y_{2,t} - 2y_{3,t} + 4. \end{aligned}$$

The particular solution is computed using the formula:

$$\mathbf{y}_p = (\mathbf{I} - \mathbf{A})^{-1}\mathbf{b} = [1/6 \quad 2/3 \quad 5/6]^{\mathrm{T}}.$$

We can verify this solution using *Mathematica*.

*In[123]:=*

```
A  =  {{11,-3,-2},{8,0,-2},{19,-7,-2}};
b  =  {2,1,4};
yp  =  Inverse[IdentityMatrix[3]-A].b
```

*Out[125]=*

$$\left\{\frac{1}{6}, \frac{2}{3}, \frac{5}{6}\right\}$$

Consider the problem of finding the complementary solution. Successive iterations of the homogeneous system show that $\mathbf{y}_c = \mathbf{A}^t\mathbf{y}_0$. Suppose the matrix $\mathbf{A}$ has $n$ eigenvalues, $r_1, r_2, \ldots, r_n$, and $n$ linearly independent eigenvectors, $\mathbf{v}_1, \mathbf{v}_2, \ldots, \mathbf{v}_n$. That is, they satisfy the set of equations

$$\mathbf{A}\mathbf{v}_i = r_i\mathbf{v}_i, \quad i = 1,2, \ldots, n.$$

Recall that this case occurs when the algebraic and geometric multiplicities are equal. We arrange these equations in matrix form so that

$$\mathbf{A}[\mathbf{v}_1 \;\; \mathbf{v}_2 \;\; \ldots \;\; \mathbf{v}_n] = [\mathbf{v}_1 \;\; \mathbf{v}_2 \;\; \ldots \;\; \mathbf{v}_n]\begin{bmatrix} r_1 & 0 & \ldots & 0 \\ 0 & r_2 & \ldots & 0 \\ \ldots & \ldots & \ldots & \ldots \\ 0 & 0 & \ldots & r_n \end{bmatrix}$$

or more compactly,

$$\mathbf{AP} = \mathbf{PD}$$

where $\mathbf{P}$ is the modal matrix of $\mathbf{A}$ and $\mathbf{D}$ is the diagonal matrix with the eigenvalues as the diagonal elements. Since the vectors $\mathbf{v}_i$ are linearly independent, the matrix $\mathbf{P}$ is nonsingular. Thus

$$\mathbf{A} = \mathbf{PDP}^{-1}.$$

Computing matrix products with A, this equation becomes:

$$\mathbf{A}^2 = \mathbf{AA} = (\mathbf{PDP}^{-1})(\mathbf{PDP}^{-1}) = \mathbf{PD}^2\mathbf{P}^{-1}$$
$$\mathbf{A}^3 = \mathbf{A}^2\mathbf{A} = (\mathbf{PD}^2\mathbf{P}^{-1})(\mathbf{PDP}^{-1}) = \mathbf{PD}^3\mathbf{P}^{-1}$$
$$\ldots\ldots\ldots\ldots\ldots\ldots\ldots\ldots\ldots\ldots$$
$$\mathbf{A}^t = \mathbf{PD}^t\mathbf{P}^{-1}.$$

We note that

$$\mathbf{D}^t = \begin{bmatrix} r_1^t & 0 & \ldots & 0 \\ 0 & r_2^t & \ldots & 0 \\ \ldots & \ldots & \ldots & \ldots \\ 0 & 0 & \ldots & r_n^t \end{bmatrix}$$

is a diagonal matrix. Substituting the result $\mathbf{A}^t = \mathbf{PD}^t\mathbf{P}^{-1}$ in the complementary solution, we have

$$\mathbf{y}_c = \mathbf{A}^t\mathbf{y}_0 = \mathbf{PD}^t\mathbf{P}^{-1}\mathbf{y}_0.$$

If we define $\mathbf{c} = \mathbf{P}^{-1}\mathbf{y}_0$ to be a column vector of arbitrary constants that can be determined from the initial condition $\mathbf{y}_0$, then the complementary solution can be written as

$$\mathbf{y}_c = [\mathbf{v}_1 \;\; \mathbf{v}_2 \;\; \ldots \;\; \mathbf{v}_n]\begin{bmatrix} r_1 & 0 & \ldots & 0 \\ 0 & r_2 & \ldots & 0 \\ \ldots & \ldots & \ldots & \ldots \\ 0 & 0 & \ldots & r_n \end{bmatrix}\begin{bmatrix} c_1 \\ c_2 \\ \ldots \\ c_n \end{bmatrix}$$
$$= c_1 r_1^t \mathbf{v}_1 + c_2 r_2^t \mathbf{v}_2 + \ldots + c_n r_n^t \mathbf{v}_n.$$

**Example 15.32** Find the complementary solution of the system of difference equations in Example 15.31. In this case, the eigenvalues and eigenvectors of $\mathbf{A}$ are computed below.

*In[126]:=*
```
Clear[r,v];
A = {{11,-3,-2},{8,0,-2},{19,-7,-2}};
{r,v} = Eigensystem[A]
```

*Out[128]=*
```
{{2, 3, 4}, {{1, 1, 3}, {1, 2, 1}, {1, 1, 2}}}
```

Thus, the system has the complementary solution

$$\mathbf{y}_c = c_1(2)^t\begin{bmatrix}1\\1\\3\end{bmatrix} + c_2(3)^t\begin{bmatrix}1\\2\\1\end{bmatrix} + c_3(4)^t\begin{bmatrix}1\\1\\2\end{bmatrix}$$

With the particular solution from Example 15.31, the general solution is

$$\mathbf{y}_t = \mathbf{y}_c + \mathbf{y}_p = c_1(2)^t\begin{bmatrix}1\\1\\3\end{bmatrix} + c_2(3)^t\begin{bmatrix}1\\2\\1\end{bmatrix} + c_3(4)^t\begin{bmatrix}1\\1\\2\end{bmatrix} + \begin{bmatrix}1/6\\2/3\\5/6\end{bmatrix}$$

Suppose the initial conditions

$$\mathbf{y}_0 = \begin{bmatrix}y_{1,0}\\y_{2,0}\\y_{3,0}\end{bmatrix} = \begin{bmatrix}5\\8\\12\end{bmatrix}$$

are specified. Substituting these initial conditions into the general solution, we solve for the arbitrary constants.

*In[129]:=*
```
Clear[c1,c2,c3,y,t];
yp = {1/6,2/3,5/6};
y[t_]:= c1*r[[1]]^t*v[[1]]+c2*r[[2]]^t*v[[2]]+
        c3*r[[3]]^t*v[[3]]+yp;
Solve[y[0]=={5,8,12},{c1,c2,c3}]
```

*Out[132]=*

$$\{\{c1 \to 4,\ c2 \to \frac{5}{2},\ c3 \to -(\frac{5}{3})\}\}$$

The solution of the initial-value problem is therefore

$$\mathbf{y}_t = 4(2)^t\begin{bmatrix}1\\1\\3\end{bmatrix} + \frac{5}{2}(3)^t\begin{bmatrix}1\\2\\1\end{bmatrix} - \frac{5}{3}(4)^t\begin{bmatrix}1\\1\\2\end{bmatrix} + \begin{bmatrix}1/6\\2/3\\5/6\end{bmatrix}$$

We note that the solution gets arbitrarily larger as $t$ increases. Note that the **RSolve** function can be used to find the solution of the above initial-value problem.

*In[133]:=*

```
Clear[y1,y2,y3,t];
solution = RSolve[{y1[t+1]==11*y1[t]-3*y2[t]-2*y3[t]+2,
                y2[t+1]==8*y1[t]-2*y3[t]+1,
                y3[t+1]==19*y1[t]-7*y2[t]-2*y3[t]+4,
                y1[0]==5,y2[0]==8,y3[0]==12},
               {y1[t],y2[t],y3[t]},t]
```

*Out[134]=*

$$\{\{y1[t] \to \frac{1}{6} + 4\ 2^t + \frac{5\ 3^t}{2} - \frac{5\ 4^t}{3},\ y2[t] \to \frac{2}{3} + 4\ 2^t + 5\ 3^t - \frac{5\ 4^t}{3},$$
$$y3[t] \to \frac{5}{6} + 12\ 2^t + \frac{5\ 3^t}{2} - \frac{10\ 4^t}{3}\}\}$$

We now examine the case when the algebraic multiplicity of the eigenvalues of $\mathbf{A}$ exceeds the geometric multiplicity. Consider a system of two difference equations: $\mathbf{y}_{t+1} = \mathbf{A}\mathbf{y}_t$. Suppose that the two eigenvalues of $\mathbf{A}$ are repeated eigenvalues, say $r_1 = r_2$, and the corresponding eigenvectors $\mathbf{v}_1$ and $\mathbf{v}_2$ are not linearly independent. In this case, the solutions,

$$r_1^t\mathbf{v}_1 \quad \text{and} \quad r_2^t\mathbf{v}_2$$

are not linearly independent. We encountered a similar problem in Chapter 14 for a system of differential equations. In this case we define a vector $\mathbf{w}_2$ such that

$$(\mathbf{A} - r_1\mathbf{I})\mathbf{w}_2 = \mathbf{v}_1.$$

By substitution, it is easy to show that

$$[t\mathbf{v}_1 + r_1\mathbf{w}_2]r_1^{t-1}$$

is a solution of the system $\mathbf{y}_{t+1} = \mathbf{A}\mathbf{y}_t$, and the two vectors, $r_1^t\mathbf{v}_1$ and $(t\mathbf{v}_1 + r_1\mathbf{w}_2)r_1^{t-1}$, are linearly independent. Hence the general solution of the system is

$$\mathbf{y}_t = c_1 r_1^t\mathbf{v}_1 + c_2(t\mathbf{v}_1 + r_1\mathbf{w}_2)r_1^{t-1}.$$

**Example 15.33** Consider the system of homogeneous difference equations

$$\mathbf{y}_{t+1} = \begin{bmatrix} y_{1,t+1} \\ y_{2,t+1} \\ y_{3,t+1} \end{bmatrix} = \begin{bmatrix} 2 & 2 & 2 \\ 2 & 1 & 2 \\ 1 & 0 & -1 \end{bmatrix}\begin{bmatrix} y_{1,t} \\ y_{2,t} \\ y_{3,t} \end{bmatrix} = \mathbf{A}\mathbf{y}_t$$

The matrix $\mathbf{A}$ has eigenvalues, $r_1 = r_2 = -1$, and $r_3 = 4$. The repeated eigenvalue has a single eigenvector, $\mathbf{v}_1 = [0\ -1\ 1]^T$. Here is confirmation of this from *Mathematica*.

*In[135]:=*

```
A = {{2,2,2},{2,1,2},{1,0,-1}};
Eigensystem[A]
```

*Out[136]=*

```
{{-1, -1, 4}, {{0, -1, 1}, {0, 0, 0}, {5, 4, 1}}}
```

We find the vector $\mathbf{w}_2$ such that

$$(\mathbf{A} - r_1\mathbf{I})\,\mathbf{w}_2 = \mathrm{v}_1 \quad \text{or} \quad \begin{bmatrix} 3 & 2 & 2 \\ 2 & 2 & 2 \\ 1 & 0 & 0 \end{bmatrix}\begin{bmatrix} a \\ b \\ c \end{bmatrix} = \begin{bmatrix} 0 \\ -1 \\ 1 \end{bmatrix}$$

where $a$, $b$, and $c$ are elements of $\mathbf{w}_2$. One solution of this set of equations is

$\mathbf{w}_2 = [1 \;\; -(5/2) \;\; 1]^{\mathrm{T}}$.

Thus the general solution is

$$\mathbf{y}_t = c_1 r_1^t \mathbf{v}_1 + c_2 r_1^{t-1}(t\mathbf{v}_1 + r_1\mathbf{w}_2) + c_3 r_3^t \mathbf{v}_3$$

$$= c_1(-1)^t\begin{bmatrix} 0 \\ -1 \\ 1 \end{bmatrix} + c_2(-1)^{t-1}\begin{bmatrix} -1 \\ -t+5/2 \\ t-1 \end{bmatrix} + c_3(4)^t\begin{bmatrix} 5 \\ 4 \\ 1 \end{bmatrix}$$

When $\mathbf{A}$ has complex eigenvalues, we can still obtain real-valued solutions of the homogeneous system. Consider the case ($n = 2$) when the eigenvalues are complex

$r_1 = a + ib$, and $r_2 = a - ib$,

with complex eigenvectors,

$\mathrm{v}_1 = \mathbf{v} + i\mathbf{u}$ and $\mathrm{v}_2 = \mathbf{v} - i\mathbf{u}$.

The general solution of the homogeneous system

$$\mathbf{y}_t = c_1(a + ib)^t(\mathbf{v} + i\mathbf{u}) + c_2(a - ib)^t(\mathbf{v} - i\mathbf{u})$$

can be expressed in terms of trigonometric functions by using the De Moivre's formula. Thus

$$\mathbf{y}_t = c_1 R^t[\mathbf{v}\cos(\theta t) - \mathbf{u}\sin(\theta t)] + c_2 R^t[\mathbf{u}\cos(\theta t) + \mathbf{v}\sin(\theta t)]$$

where

$$R = \sqrt{a^2 + b^2}\,,\; \theta = \tan^{-1}\left(\frac{b}{a}\right)$$

**Example 15.34** Consider the homogeneous system $\mathbf{y}_{t+1} = \mathbf{A}\mathbf{y}_t$ where

$$\mathbf{A} = \begin{bmatrix} 1 & -1 & -1 \\ 1 & -1 & 0 \\ 1 & 0 & -1 \end{bmatrix}$$

First, we calculate the eigenvalues and eigenvectors of the matrix $\mathbf{A}$.

*In[137]:=*

```
A = {{1,-1,-1},{1,-1,0},{1,0,-1}};
{r,vect} = Eigensystem[A]
```

*Out[138]=*
```
{{-1, -I, I}, {{0, -1, 1}, {1 - I, 1, 1}, {1 + I, 1, 1}}}
```

The roots are $r_1 = -1$, $r_2 = -i$, and $r_3 = i$. For the complex roots $r_2$ and $r_3$, we see immediately that $R = 1$ and $\theta = \pi/2$. Using *Mathematica*, we construct the general solution for $y_{1,t}$, $y_{2,t}$, and $y_{3,t}$.

*In[139]:=*
```
Clear[c1,c2,c3,y,t];
R = 1; theta = -Pi/2;
v = Re[vect[[2]]]; u = Im[vect[[2]]];
y[t_] = c1*r[[1]]^t*vect[[1]] +
            c2*R^t*(Cos[theta*t]*v-Sin[theta*t]*u) +
            c3*R^t*(Cos[theta*t]*u+Sin[theta*t]*v);
y[t] // MatrixForm
```

*Out[143]//MatrixForm=*

$$\begin{array}{l} c3(-\text{Cos}[\frac{\text{Pi t}}{2}] - \text{Sin}[\frac{\text{Pi t}}{2}]) + c2(\text{Cos}[\frac{\text{Pi t}}{2}] - \text{Sin}[\frac{\text{Pi t}}{2}]) \\ -((-1)^t c1) + c2\,\text{Cos}[\frac{\text{Pi t}}{2}] - c3\,\text{Sin}[\frac{\text{Pi t}}{2}] \\ (-1)^t c1 + c2\,\text{Cos}[\frac{\text{Pi t}}{2}] - c3\,\text{Sin}[\frac{\text{Pi t}}{2}] \end{array}$$

Suppose the initial values are $y_{1,0} = -1$, $y_{2,0} = 4$, and $y_{3,0} = -1$. The arbitrary constants satisfy the following system of equations.

*In[144]:=*
```
eqn1 = y[0][[1]] == -1
eqn2 = y[0][[2]] == 4
eqn3 = y[0][[3]] == -2
```

*Out[144]=*
```
c2 - c3 == -1
```

*Out[145]=*
```
-c1 + c2 == 4
```

*Out[146]=*
```
c1 + c2 == -2
```

Solving for the arbitrary constants, we have $c_1 = -3$, $c_2 = 1$, and $c_3 = 2$.

*In[147]:=*
```
sol = Solve[{eqn1,eqn2,eqn3},{c1,c2,c3}]
```

*Out[147]=*
```
{{c3 → 2, c1 → -3, c2 → 1}}
```

The solution of the initial-value problem is therefore

$$y_{1,t} = -\cos\frac{\pi t}{2} - 3\sin\frac{\pi t}{2}$$

$$y_{2,t} = 3(-1)^t + \cos\frac{\pi t}{2} - 2\sin\frac{\pi t}{2}$$

$$y_{3,t} = -3(-1)^t + \cos\frac{\pi t}{2} - 2\sin\frac{\pi t}{2}$$

which is obtained from the following *Mathematica* calculations.

*In[148]:=*

```
Clear[yip];
yip[t]  =  y[t]  /.  sol[[1]]  //  Simplify;
yip[t]  //  MatrixForm
```

*Out[150]//MatrixForm=*

$$\begin{pmatrix} -\text{Cos}[\frac{\text{Pi t}}{2}] - 3\text{Sin}[\frac{\text{Pi t}}{2}] \\ 3(-1)^t + \text{Cos}[\frac{\text{Pi t}}{2}] - 2\text{Sin}[\frac{\text{Pi t}}{2}] \\ -3(-1)^t + \text{Cos}[\frac{\text{Pi t}}{2}] - 2\text{Sin}[\frac{\text{Pi t}}{2}] \end{pmatrix}$$

We can use the **RSolve** function directly to solve the initial-value problem. Recall that the *Mathematica* **RSolve** package must be loaded before the function is used.

*In[151]:=*

```
Needs["DiscreteMath`RSolve`"];
```

*In[152]:=*

```
Clear[y1,y2,y3,t];
solution  =  RSolve[{y1[t+1]==y1[t]-y2[t]-y3[t],
                     y2[t+1]==y1[t]-y2[t],
                     y3[t+1]==y1[t]-y3[t],
                     y1[0]==-1,y2[0]==4,y3[0]==-2},
                    {y1[t],y2[t],y3[t]},t];
solution[[1]]  //  MatrixForm
```

*Out[154]//MatrixForm=*

$$\begin{pmatrix} \text{y1[t]} \to -\text{Cos}[\frac{\text{Pi t}}{2}] - 3\text{Sin}[\frac{\text{Pi t}}{2}] \\ \text{y2[t]} \to 3(-1)^t + \text{Cos}[\frac{\text{Pi t}}{2}] - 2\text{Sin}[\frac{\text{Pi t}}{2}] \\ \text{y3[t]} \to -3(-1)^t + \text{Cos}[\frac{\text{Pi t}}{2}] - 2\text{Sin}[\frac{\text{Pi t}}{2}] \end{pmatrix}$$

The three solutions, $y_1(t)$, $y_2(t)$, and $y_3(t)$, can be plotted on a single graph by the *Mathematica* **MultipleListPlot** function.

*In[155]:=*

```
Needs["Graphics`MultipleListPlot`"];
```

Here is the description of the function **MultipleListPlot**.

*In[156]:=*

```
?MultipleListPlot
```

**MultipleListPlot[ l1, l2, ... ] allows many lists of data to be plotted on the same graph. Each list can be either a list of pairs of numbers, in which case the pairs are taken as x,y-coordinates, or else a list of numbers, in which case the numbers are taken as y-coordinates and successive integers starting with 1 are supplied as x-coordinates. The DotShapes option specifies plotting symbols to be used for the lists of data, and (if the option PlotJoined→True is specified) the option LineStyles specifies styles for the lines connecting the points.**

The solid line corresponds to the component $y_{1,t}$, the narrowly dashed line to $y_{2,t}$, and the remaining line to $y_{3,t}$.

*In[157]:=*

```
{y1[t_],y2[t_],y3[t_]} =
                        {y1[t],y2[t],y3[t]} /.solution[[1]];
tab1 = Table[{t,y1[t]},{t,0,10}];
tab2 = Table[{t,y2[t]},{t,0,10}];
tab3 = Table[{t,y3[t]},{t,0,10}];
MultipleListPlot[tab1,tab2,tab3,
                         AxesLabel->{"t","y(t)"},
                        PlotJoined->True,
                         LineStyles->{{},{Dashing[{0.01}]},
                        {Dashing[{0.02}]}}];
```

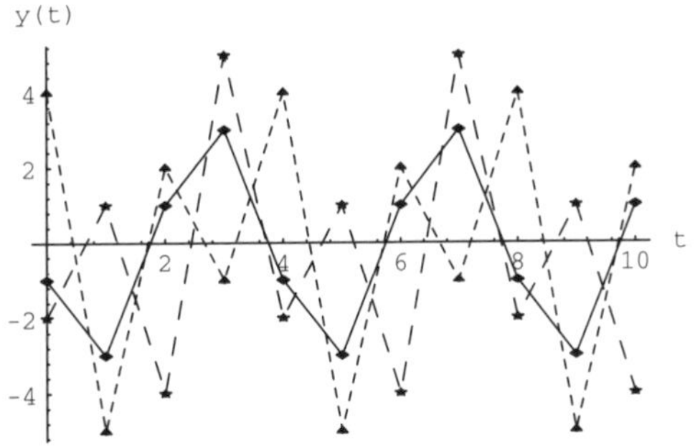


## EXERCISES

1. Solve the following systems of difference equations:
   (a) $y_{1,t+1} = 0.9y_{1,t} - 1.5y_{2,t} + 3.1y_{3,t}$
   $y_{2,t+1} = 3.5y_{1,t} - 10.1y_{2,t} + 25.3y_{3,t}$
   $y_{3,t+1} = 1.3y_{1,t} - 3.9y_{2,t} + 9.9y_{3,t}$
   (b) $y_{1,t+1} = -7/4y_{1,t} - 15/4y_{2,t} + 15/2y_{3,t} - 2$
   $y_{2,t+1} = -9/4y_{1,t} + 15/4y_{2,t} + 1/2y_{3,t} + 3$
   $y_{3,t+1} = -1/2y_{1,t} + 3/2y_{2,t} + y_{3,t} + 1$
   (c) $y_{1,t+1} = 2y_{2,t} + 8$
   $y_{2,t+1} = -4y_{1,t} + 6y_{2,t} + 1$
   $y_{3,t+1} = -2y_{1,t} + 2y_{2,t} + 2y_{3,t} + 7$

(d) $y_{1,t+1} = -3y_{1,t} + 2y_{3,t}$
$y_{2,t+1} = y_{1,t} - y_{2,t}$
$y_{3,t+1} = -2y_{1,t} - y_{2,t}$

2. Consider the fourth-order difference equation

$$y_{t+4} + a_3 y_{t+3} + a_2 y_{t+2} + a_1 y_{t+1} + a_0 y_t = g(t).$$

Define the following transformations

$$\begin{aligned} z_{1,t} &= y_t \\ z_{2,t} &= z_{1,t+1} = y_{t+1} \\ z_{3,t} &= z_{2,t+1} = y_{t+2} \\ z_{4,t} &= z_{3,t+1} = y_{t+3} \\ z_{4,t+1} &= y_{t+4} \\ &= -a_3 z_{4,t} - a_2 z_{3,t} - a_1 z_{2,t} + a_0 z_{1,t} + g(t) \end{aligned}$$

Show that the difference equation can be reduced to a system of first-order equations in terms of $z_{1,t}$, $z_{2,t}$, $z_{3,t}$, and $z_{4,t}$.

3. Solve the following difference equations:
(a) $y_{t+4} + 2y_{t+3} - 3y_{t+2} + 4y_{t+1} - 5y_t = 10$
(b) $y_{1,t+2} = y_{1,t+1} + y_{1,t} + y_{2,t}$
$y_{2,t+1} = 4y_{1,t} + 2y_{2,t}$

### 15.3.2 Systems of nonlinear difference equations

In the previous section we discussed techniques to solve systems of linear difference equations. In this section we discuss a technique to approximate the behavior of the solutions of systems of nonlinear difference equations.

Consider a system of two nonlinear difference equations:

$$\begin{aligned} y_{1,t+1} &= F_1(y_{1,t}, y_{2,t}) \\ y_{2,t+1} &= F_2(y_{1,t}, y_{2,t}). \end{aligned}$$

An *equilibrium point*, $\mathbf{y}_e = (y_{1e}, y_{2e})$, of this system is a point in the domains of $F_1$ and $F_2$ such that

$$\begin{aligned} y_{1e} &= F_1(y_{1e}, y_{2e}) \\ y_{2e} &= F_2(y_{1e}, y_{2e}). \end{aligned}$$

As in the case of nonlinear systems of differential equations, we attempt to approximate the solutions of the nonlinear system in a neighborhood of $\mathbf{y}_e$ by solutions of some linear system. The linear system is obtained by expanding in a Taylor series around $\mathbf{y}_e$ the functions $F_1(y_{1,t}, y_{2,t})$ and $F_2(y_{1,t}, y_{2,t})$, and ignoring the second and higher-degree terms:

$$\begin{aligned} y_{1,t+1} &= y_{1e} + \frac{\partial F_1}{\partial y_1}\left[y_{1,t} - y_{1e}\right] + \frac{\partial F_1}{\partial y_2}\left[y_{2,t} - y_{2e}\right] \\ y_{2,t+1} &= y_{2e} + \frac{\partial F_2}{\partial y_1}\left[y_{1,t} - y_{1e}\right] + \frac{\partial F_2}{\partial y_2}\left[y_{2,t} - y_{2e}\right] \end{aligned}$$

The partial derivatives are evaluated at $\mathbf{y}_e$. Defining the intermediate variables

$z_{1,t} = y_{1,t} - y_{1e}$, $z_{2,t} = y_{2,t} - y_{2e}$,

the linear system can be written in a matrix form

$$\begin{bmatrix} z_{1,t+1} \\ z_{2,t+1} \end{bmatrix} = \begin{bmatrix} \dfrac{\partial F_1}{\partial y_1} & \dfrac{\partial F_1}{\partial y_2} \\ \dfrac{\partial F_2}{\partial y_1} & \dfrac{\partial F_2}{\partial y_2} \end{bmatrix} \begin{bmatrix} z_{1,t} \\ z_{2,t} \end{bmatrix}, \quad \text{or} \quad \mathbf{z}_{t+1} = \mathbf{A}\,\mathbf{z}_t.$$

We can then solve this linear constant coefficient system for the $z_{1,t}$ and $z_{2,t}$. These functions yield the approximation

$$y_{1,t} \approx z_{1,t} + y_{1e}$$
$$y_{2,t} \approx z_{2,t} + y_{2e}.$$

## EXERCISES

1. Linearize the system

$$y_{1,t+1} = y_{1,t} + y_{1,t}y_{2,t}$$
$$y_{2,t+1} = -y_{1,t}y_{2,t} + 2y_{1,t} - 3y_{2,t}$$

and then solve the resulting linear system in the neighborhood of the equilibrium point.

### 15.3.3 An economic example

Suppose that two countries are engaged in trade. We model the national incomes of each country at a discrete time (e.g., quarters or years). The following notations for the $i$-th country at time $t$ are used: $NI_t^{(i)}$(national income), $CS_t^{(i)}$(consumption), $IV_t^{(i)}$(investment), $GS_t^{(i)}$(government spending), $EX_t^{(i)}$(exports), and $IM_t^{(i)}$(imports from the other country). For each country, we have the following national income identity:

$$NI_t^{(i)} = CS_t^{(i)} + IV_t^{(i)} + GS_t^{(i)} + EX_t^{(i)} - IM_t^{(i)},$$

for $i = 1,2$ and $t = 1,2,3, \ldots$. For simplicity, we make the following two assumptions:

(1) Both investment and government spending are constant over time, i.e.,

$$IV_t^{(i)} = IV_0^{(i)},\ GS_t^{(i)} = GS_0^{(i)}.$$

(2) Both consumption and imports at time $t$ are linear functions of national income at time $t$–1. That is,

$$CS_t^{(i)} = CS_0^{(i)} + a_i NI_{t-1}^{(i)},$$
$$IM_t^{(i)} = IM_0^{(i)} + b_i NI_{t-1}^{(i)},$$

where $CS_0^{(i)}$ and $IM_0^{(i)}$ are initial levels of consumption and imports. The constant coefficients, $a_i$ and $b_i$, are the marginal propensity to consume and to import. Futhermore, since there are only two countries, one country's export is the other country's import.

$$EX_t^{(1)} = IM_t^{(2)},\ EX_t^{(2)} = IM_t^{(1)}.$$

With these assumptions, the national incomes for the two countries can then be written as a system of difference equations

$$NI_t^{(1)} = k_{10} + k_{11}NI_{t-1}^{(1)} + k_{12}NI_{t-1}^{(2)}$$
$$NI_t^{(2)} = k_{20} + k_{21}NI_{t-1}^{(1)} + k_{22}NI_{t-1}^{(2)}$$

where the constant coefficients are

$$k_{10} = CS_0^{(1)} + IV_0^{(1)} + GS_0^{(1)} - IM_0^{(1)} + IM_0^{(2)},$$
$$k_{11} = a_1 - b_1,$$
$$k_{12} = b_2,$$
$$k_{20} = CS_0^{(2)} + IV_0^{(2)} + GS_0^{(2)} - IM_0^{(2)} + IM_0^{(1)},$$
$$k_{21} = b_1,$$
$$k_{22} = a_2 - b_2.$$

For an illustration, we choose values for the parameters and the initial conditions for the national incomes. Suppose $NI_0^{(1)} = 15$, $NI_0^{(2)} = 10$, $CS_0^{(1)} = 5$, $CS_0^{(2)} = 4$, $IV_0^{(1)} = 1$, $IV_0^{(2)} = 3$, $GS_0^{(1)} = 2$, $GS_0^{(2)} = 1.5$, $IM_0^{(1)} = 1$, $IM_0^{(2)} = 0.8$, and $a_1 = 0.4$, $a_2 = 0.3$, $b_1 = 0.1$, and $b_2 = 0.05$.

*In[162]:=*

```
Clear[CS1,CS2,GS1,GS2,IM1,IM2,IV1,IV2,NI1,NI2];
CS1[0]=5;  CS2[0]=4;
IV1[0]=1;  IV2[0]=3;
GS1[0]=2;  GS2[0]=1.5;
IM1[0]=1;  IM2[0]=0.8;
NI1[0]=15;  NI2[0]=10;
a1=0.4;  a2=0.3;  b1=0.1;  b2=0.05;
k10=CS1[0]  +  IV1[0]  +  GS1[0]  -  IM1[0]  +  IM2[0];
k11  =  a1  -  b1;
k12  =  b2;
k20  =  CS2[0]  +  IV2[0]  +  GS2[0]  -  IM2[0]  +  IM1[0];
k21  =  b1;
k22  =  a2-b2;
{k10,k11,k12,k20,k21,k22}
```

*Out[175]=*

```
{7.8, 0.3, 0.05, 8.7, 0.1, 0.25}
```

Next we calculate some the values of the national income for each country over 10 periods and plot the results.

*In[176]:=*

```
Clear[t];
NI1[t_ /;  t>=1]:=  NI1[t]  =
                    k10+k11*NI1[t-1]+k12*NI2[t-1];
```

```
NI2[t_ /; t>=1]:= NI2[t] =
                  k20+k21*NI1[t-1]+k22*NI2[t-1];
country1 = Table[{t,NI1[t]},{t,0,10}];
country2 = Table[{t,NI2[t]},{t,0,10}];
Needs["Graphics`MultipleListPlot`"];
MultipleListPlot[country1,country2,PlotRange->{0,20},
            PlotJoined->True,
            AxesLabel->{"Period","National Income"}];
```

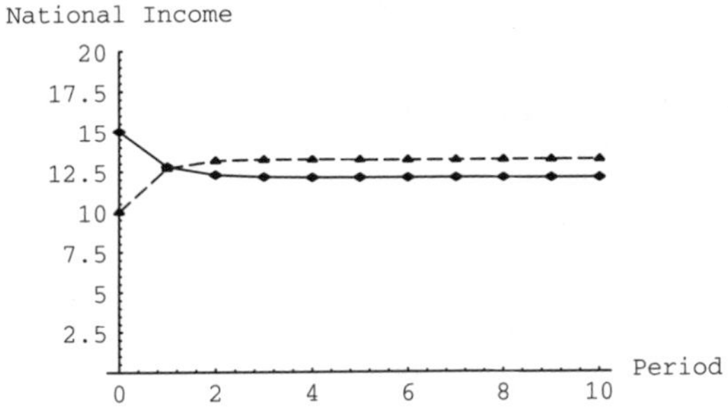


Notice that how Country 1's national income immediately falls below the national income of Country 2 and both countries appear to approach constant values.

We can also obtain a solution of the initial-value problem using the theory developed in this chapter. If $\mathbf{y}_t = [NI_t^{(1)}\ NI_t^{(2)}]^{\mathrm{T}}$, then the system is of the form $\mathbf{y}_{t+1} = \mathbf{A}\mathbf{y}_t + \mathbf{b}$ where

$$\mathbf{A} = \begin{bmatrix} k_{11} & k_{12} \\ k_{21} & k_{22} \end{bmatrix};\ \mathbf{b} = \begin{bmatrix} k_{10} \\ k_{20} \end{bmatrix}$$

*In[183]:=*

```
Clear[A,g];
A = {{k11, k12},{k21,k22}};
b = {k10,k20};
```

Since **b** is a constant vector, a particular solution is

$$\mathbf{y}_p = (\mathbf{I} - \mathbf{A})^{-1}\mathbf{b} = \begin{bmatrix} 12.0865 \\ 13.2115 \end{bmatrix}$$

*In[186]:=*

```
Clear[yp,t];
yp[t_] = Inverse[IdentityMatrix[2]-A].b;
yp[t] // MatrixForm
```

*Out[188]//MatrixForm=*

```
12.0865
13.2115
```

To construct the complementary solutions we find the eigenvalues and eigenvectors of the matrix **A**.

*In[189]:=*

```
{r,v} = Eigensystem[A]
```

*Out[189]=*

```
{{0.35, 0.2}, {{0.707107, 0.707107}, {-0.447214, 0.894427}}}
```

Hence, the complementary solution is given by the following Mathematica calculation.

*In[190]:=*

```
Clear[c1,c2,yc];
yc[t_] = c1*r[[1]]^t*v[[1]] + c2*r[[2]]^t*v[[2]];
yc[t] // MatrixForm
```

*Out[192]//MatrixForm=*

$$\begin{matrix} 0.707107\ 0.35^t c1 - 0.447214\ 0.2^t c2 \\ 0.707107\ 0.35^t c1 + 0.894427\ 0.2^t c2 \end{matrix}$$

The general solution is then $\mathbf{y}_t = \mathbf{y}_c + \mathbf{y}_p$.

*In[193]:=*

```
Clear[y,t];
y[t_] = yc[t] + yp[t];
y[t] // MatrixForm
```

*Out[195]//MatrixForm=*

$$\begin{matrix} 12.0865 + 0.707107\ 0.35^t\ c1 - 0.447214\ 0.2^t\ c2 \\ 13.2115 + 0.707107\ 0.35^t\ c1 + 0.894427\ 0.2^t\ c2 \end{matrix}$$

Now we use the initial conditions, $NI_0^{(1)} = 15$, $NI_0^{(2)} = 10$, to determine values for the arbitrary constants, and hence, the solution of the initial-value problem.

*In[196]:=*

```
c=Solve[y[0]=={15,10},{c1,c2}]
y[t_] = y[t] /. c[[1]];
y[t] // MatrixForm
```

*Out[196]=*

```
{{c1 → 1.2329, c2 → -4.56531}}
```

*Out[198]//MatrixForm=*

$$\begin{matrix} 12.0865 + 2.04167\ 0.2^t + 0.871795\ 0.35^t \\ 13.2115 - 4.08333\ 0.2^t + 0.871795\ 0.35^t \end{matrix}$$

The national incomes for these countries during period $t$ are

$$\mathbf{y} = \begin{bmatrix} NI_t^1 \\ NI_t^2 \end{bmatrix} = \begin{bmatrix} 12.0865 + 2.04167(0.2)^t + 0.871795(0.35)^t \\ 13.2115 - 4.08333(0.2)^t + 0.871795(0.35)^t \end{bmatrix}$$

Notice that $\mathbf{y}_t$ approaches a constant vector as $t \rightarrow \infty$.

*In[199]:=*

```
Limit[y[t],t->Infinity]
```

*Out[199]=*

```
{12.0865, 13.2115}
```

These values are the same as we observed in the graph of the national incomes.

# Appendix: MathEcon Package

## □ Introduction □

A collection of *Mathematica* functions have been written to accompany *Mathematics and Mathematica for Economists*. These functions have been assembled into a package that we entitled **MathEcon**. The functions are defined in a *Mathematica* notebook (file) called **MathEcon.m.** In order to use the functions in the package, the definitions of the function must be loaded into the Kernel by using the **Needs** or the **Get** (<<) functions. Before the **MathEcon** package can be loaded, a path must be established to inform *Mathematica* the location of the package. Suppose the notebook **MathEcon.m** (Macintosh) or **MathEcon.ma** (PC) is stored in a folder named **MathFunctions** on the hard-disk drive called **mydisk**. The following statement establishes a path to the package:

```
AppendTo[$Path,"mydisk:MathFunctions"];
```

Once the path is established, we can load the **MathEcon.m** or **MathEcon.ma** package into the *Mathematica* Kernel using the **Needs** function.

```
Needs["MathEcon`"]
```

The functions that are defined in **MathEcon.m**, are now available to use. An alternative method to define these functions is to open the **MathEcon** notebook and execute all of the input cells. Using *Mathematica*'s help facilities, descriptions of the functions can be queried. Here is a description of the package itself:

*In[1]:=*

```
?MathEcon
```

**MathEcon is a package of functions that is used with the book:**

**Mathematics and Mathematica for Economists**
**by Cliff Huang and Philip Crooke.**

**It contains the following functions:**

**fibprime directed directed3d**
**vector2d vector3d addition2d**
**subtraction2d projection2d projection3d**
**rotation2d rank rowop**
**colop submatrix minor**
**cofactor aug colrep**
**signQ signQL borderB**
**gradf hessian conhess**
**arc2d tangentline fjohn**
**separableode linearode tangentfield**
**wronskian wis trajectory**

Descriptions of the individual function can also be obtained using the help facility.

*In[2]:=*

```
?rank
```

**rank[lst] calculates the dimension of the space spanned by the vectors contained in its argument (list). For example,**

**rank[{{1,-1,9},{1,-2,-3}}].**

*In[3]:=*

```
?hessian
```

**hessian[fct,lst] generates the hessian matrix of the function fct with respect to the variables specified by lst (a list). For example,**

**hessian[x*y*w-y^2*z+w^3,{x,y,z,w}].**

## □ Loading the MathEcon Package □

It is good idea to load the **MathEcon** package at the beginning of your session with *Mathematica*. Here is a listing of the package.

```
(*MathEcon Package*)
(*Philip Crooke & Cliff Huang*)
(*Vanderbilt University*)
(*May 22, 1996*)


BeginPackage["MathEcon`"];
Needs["Graphics`Arrow`"];

Unprotect[fibprime,directed,vector2d,directed3d,
vector3d,addition2d,subtraction2d,projection2d,
projection3d,rotation2d,rank,rowop,colop,submatrix,
minor,cofactor,aug,colrep,signQ,signQL,borderB,gradf,hes
sian,conhess,arc2d,tangentline,fjohn,separableode,linear
ode,tangentfield,wronskian,wis,trajectory];
```

```
Clear[fibprime,directed,vector2d,directed3d,
vector3d,addition2d,subtraction2d,projection2d,
projection3d,rotation2d,rank,rowop,colop,submatrix,
minor,cofactor,aug,colrep,signQ,signQL,borderB,gradf,hes
sian,conhess,arc2d,tangentline,fjohn,separableode,linear
ode,tangentfield,wronskian,wis,trajectory];

MathEcon::usage = "MathEcon is a package of functions
that is used with the book:\r\r
Mathematics and Mathematica for Economists \r
   by Cliff Huang and Philip Crooke.\r\r
It contains the following functions: \r\r
fibprime   directed   directed3d \r
vector2d vector3d   addition2d \r
subtraction2d   projection2d   projection3d \r
rotation2d   rank   rowop \r
colop   submatrix   minor \r
cofactor   aug   colrep \r
signQ   signQL   borderB \r
gradf   hessian   conhess \r
arc2d   tangentline   fjohn \r
separableode   linearode tangentfield \r
wronskian   wis   trajectory \r";

fibprime::usage = "fibprime[n] calculates the prime
Fibonaci numbers that are less than or equal to an
integer n. For example,
\r\rfibprime[37].";

directed::usage = "directed[pt1,pt2,\"label\",opt]
generates a 2D Graphics object for a directed line
segment that begins at the point pt1 and ends at the
point pt2. It allows the line segment to have a
\"label\" (a string), and a dashed line style is used
when the fourth argument is present. For example,
\r\rdirected[{-1,2},{3,2},\"a\",dash].";

vector2d::usage = "vector2d[pt,\"label\",opt] generates a
2D Grapbics object for a vector from the origin to the
point specified in the first argument. It allows the
vector to have a label (a string) and a dashed line
style is used when the third argument is present. For
example, \r\rvector[{3,4},\"a\",dash].";

directed3d::usage = "directed3d[pt1,pt2,\"label\",opt]
generates a 3D Graphics object for a directed line
segment that begins at the point pt1 and ends at the
point pt2. It allows the line segment to have a label
(a string) and a dashed line style can be used when
the fourth argument is present.  For example,
\r\rdirected3d[{0,1,-1},{3,4,-2},\"a\",dash].";

vector3d::usage = "vector3d[pt,\"label\",opt] generates a
3D Grapbics object for a vector from the origin to the
```

```
point specified in the first argument. It allows the
vector to have a label (string) and a dashed line style
is used when the third argument is present.  For
example, \r\rvector3d[{1,-9,0},\"a\",dash].";

addition2d::usage =
"addition2d[pt1,\"label1\",pt2,\"label2\"] generates a
2D Graphics object that illustrates the addition of two
vectors from the origin that terminate at the points
pt1 and pt2, respectively. Each vector has a label
(string) and the vector that is the sum is labeled.
For example, \r\raddition2d[{-1,2},\"a\",{0,-1},\"b\"].";

subtraction2d::usage =
"subtraction2d[pt1,\"label1\",pt2,\"label2\"] generates a
2D Graphics object that illustrates the difference of
two vectors from the origin that terminate at the
points pt1 and pt2, respectively.  Each vector has a
label (a string) and the vector that is the difference
is labeled.  For example,
\r\rsubtraction2d[{-1,2},\"a\",{0,-1},\"b\"].";

projection2d::usage =  "projection2d[pt1,\"label1\",pt2]
generates a 2D Graphics object that illustrates the
projection of a vector that starts at the origin and
ends at pt1 onto another vector that starts at the
origin and ends at pt2.  The first vector can have a
label (a string).  For example,
\r\rprojection2d[{-2,1},\"a\",{1,4}].";

projection3d::usage =  "projection3d[pt1,\"label1\",pt2]
generates a 3D Graphics object that illustrates the
projection of a vector that starts at the origin and
ends at pt1 onto another vector that starts at the
origin and ends at pt2. The first vector can have a
label (a string).  For example,
\r\rprojection3d[{1,0,2},\"a\",{3,1,2}].";

rotation2d::usage = "rotation2d[pt,\"label\",ang]
generates a 2D Graphics object that illustrates the
rotation of the vector that starts at the origin and
ends at the point pt through the angle ang.  The
vector can have a label (a string).  For example,
\r\rrotation2d[{-1,2},\"a\",Pi/4].";

rank::usage = "rank[lst] calculates the dimension of the
space spanned by the vectors contained in its argument
(list).  For example, \r\rrank[{{1,-1,9},{1,-2,-3}}].";

rowop::usage = "rowop[rowlist] generates the elementary
row operation matrix that are dictated by its argument
which is a list of elementary row operations that are
to be performed. For example,
\r\rrowop[{row[3],row[2],row[1]}].";
```

```
colop::usage = "colop[collist] generates the elementary
column operation matrix that are dictated by its
argument which is a list of elemntary column operations
that are to be performed.  For example,
\r\r colop[{col[2],col[3],col[1]}].";

row::usage = "row[i] is a function used in the rowop
function to represent the ith row of the identity
matrix.  For example, \r\rrow[3].";

col::usage = "col[i] is a function used in the colop
function to represent the ith column of the identity
matrix.  For example,  \r\rcol[2].";

submatrix::usage = "submatrix[mat,irow,jcol] calculates
the submatrix of a given matrix mat by removing row
irow and column jcol.  For example,
\r\rsubmatrix[{{1,9},{6,-5}},1,2].";

minor::usage = "minor[mat,irow,jcol] calculates the
(irow,jcol) minor of a given matrix mat.  For example,
\r\rminor[{{1,9},{6,-5}},1,2].";

cofactor::usage = "cofactor[mat,irow,jcol] calculates the
(irow,jcol) cofactor of a given matrix mat.  For
example, \r\rcofactor[{{1,9},{6,-5}},1,2].";

aug::usage = "aug[mat,vect] forms the augmented matrix
of the matrix mat and the vector vect.  For example,
\r\raug[{{1,2},{0,1}},{-3,2}].";

colrep::usage = "colrep[mat,vect,icol] replaces the icol
column of a given matrix mat by the vector vect.  For
example, \r\rcolrep[{{1,2},{0,1}},{-3,2},2].";

changebasis::usage =
"changebasis[vect1,bas,\"label1\",\"basislabel\"] creates a
graphic that illustrates how the vector vect1 given in
the usual basis {{1,0},{0,1}} appears in the basis bas.
The given vector and the basis vectors can have labels
(strings).  For example,
\r\rchangebasis[{-1,3},{{-1,1},{0,1}},\"a\",\"b\"].";

signQ::usage = "signQ[mat] creates a list of the
principal minors of the matrix mat.  For example,
\r\rsignQ[{{2,3,1},{4,3,1},{0,9,-3}}].";

signQL::usage = "signQL[mat] creates a list of the
leading principal minors of the matrix mat.  For
example, \r\rsignQL[{{2,3,1},{4,3,1},{0,9,-3}}].";

borderB::usage = "borderB[mat,vect] generates the border
matrix of the matrix mat and the vector vect.  For
example,
\r\rborderB[{{2,3,1},{4,3,1},{0,9,-3}},{-1,0,4}].";
```

```
gradf::usage = "gradf[fct,lst] calculates the gradient of
the function fct with respect to the variables specified
by lst (a list).  For example,
\r\rgradf[x*y-y^2*z+w,{x,y,z,w}].";

hessian::usage = "hessian[fct,lst] generates the hessian
matrix of the function fct with respect to the
variables specified by lst (a list).  For example,
\r\rhessian[x*y*w-y^2*z+w^3,{x,y,z,w}].";

conhess::usage = "conhess[fct,lst1,fctlst,lst2] creates
the second-order differential (a matrix) of the function
fct with respect to the variables specified by lst1 (a
list) where the variables in the list lst2 are
constrained by functions specified in the list of
functions fctlst.  For example,
\r\rconhess[x*y*w-y^2*z+w^3,{x,y,z,w},{x+y*z},{w}].";

arc2d::usage = "arc2d[fct,dom,seg,opt] generates a 2D
Graphics object that illustrates the graph of the
function fct over the interval dom (a list) with the
graph highlighted on the subinterval seg (a list).  The
fourth argument is optional.  If the fourth argument is
chord, then a chord is drawned between points specified
by seg. For example,
\r\rarc2d[x^2-1,{x,-3,4},{x,0,1},chord].";

tangentline::usage = "tangentline[fct,int,pt] generates a
2D Graphics object that contains the graph of the
function fct over the interval int (a list) with the
tangent line to the graph of fct at the point pt. The
graphics can then be display with the Show function.
For example, \r\r
Show[tangentline[Cos[2*Pi*x],{x,-1,1},Pi/4],Axes->True];";

fjohn::usage = "fjohn[pt,const,objfct,var,options]
generates a 2D Graphics to illustrate the gradients of
an objective function objfct and binding constraint
const (a list) at the point pt in a nonlinear
programming problem.  The fourth argument of fjohn
contains a list of the variables for the objective and
constraint functions.  The last argument is optional.
If it is the string \"label\", then the gradient
vectors are labeled; if it is the string \"cone\", then
the gradients of the binding contraints and the negative
of the gradinet of the objective function is drawn and
labeled. For example,
\r\rfjohn[{1,1},{x-y,x^2-y},x^2+x^3,{x,y},\"label\"].";

separableode::usage = "separableode[var1,var2,fct1,fct2]
attempts to find the general implicit and explicit
solutions of the separable, first order differential
equation: fct1 d(var1) + fct2 d(var2) = 0. The
solutions are presented as a list of rules.  The
arbitrary constant is denoted by C[1].  For example,
\r\rseparableode[x,y,Cos[x],-y*Sin[y^2]].";
```

```
linearode::usage = "linearode[var1,fct1,fct2] attempts to
find the general, explicit solution of the first order,
linear ODE: d(var2)/d(var1) + fct1(var1) var2 =
fct2(var1).  The output is an expression involving the
symbol var1 and the arbitrary constant C[1].  For
example, \r\rlinearode[x,1/x,x^2].";

tangentfield::usage =
"tangentfield[fct,var1range,var2range,int,opt] generates a
2D Graphics object that illustrate the tangent field of
the differential equation: d(var2)/d(var1) = fct where
fct is a function of var1 and var2, var1range is a
list that is the range of the variable var1, and
var2range is a list for the range of the variable var2
over which the tangent field will be displayed.  The
fourth argument int is a positive integer that is
related to the number of tangent lines to be drawn. The
last argument is optional and can include 2D Graphics
options.  For example,
\r\rtangentfield[x*y^3,{x,-1,2},{y,0,2},10,AxesLabel->{\
"x\",\"y\"}].";

wronskian::usage = "wronskian[fctlst,var] computes the
Wronskian determinant of a list of functions in the
first argument whose independent variable is the second
argument var.  For example, \r\rwronskian[{1,x,x^2},x].";

wis::usage = "wis[fct,fctlst,var] computes the
determinants that are used in the Variation of
Parameters Method. For example,
\r\rwis[Exp[x],{1,x,x^2},x].";

trajectory::usage = "trajectory[fcts,dom,opt] displays the
trajectory of the list of functions fcts given on the
domain dom (a list).  The last argument is optional and
can contain any option for ParametricPlot. Arrows are
placed on the graph of the parametric functions to
indicate the direction of increasing values of the
independent variable.  For example,
\r\rtrajectory[{x^2+1,Cos[x]},{x,-1,3},
AxesLabel->{\"y1\",\"y2\"}].";

Begin["`Private`"];
fibprime[n_Integer]:= Module[{k,t,lessprime,x},
Clear[f,m];
f[0]=1;
f[1]=1;
f[m_ /; m>=2]:= f[m] = f[m-1]+f[m-2];
t = Table[f[k],{k,0,n}];
lessprime[x_]:= PrimeQ[x] && (x <= n);

Select[t,lessprime]];

directed[start_List,end_List,label_String,dash___]:=
Module[{p,f,aa,bb,cc,dd,len,setdash,
```

```
A,B,temp,end1,end2},
{p=Pi/10;f=0.12;setdash={N[1/72]};
If[dash==Null,setdash={}];
aa=start[[1]];bb=start[[2]];
cc=end[[1]];dd=end[[2]];
len=Sqrt[(aa-cc)^2+(bb-dd)^2];
A={{Cos[p],Sin[p]},{-Sin[p],Cos[p]}};
B={{Cos[-p],Sin[-p]},{-Sin[-p],Cos[-p]}};
temp=end-start;
end1=end-(f/len)*A.temp;
end2=end-(f/len)*B.temp;
Graphics[{AbsoluteThickness[N[1/72]],
AbsoluteDashing[{}],
Line[{end,end1}],
Line[{end,end2}],Dashing[setdash],
Line[{start,end}],Text[FontForm[label,
{"Courier-Bold",12}],
{(aa+cc)/2,(bb+dd)/2},{0,2}]}]}];

vector2d[v_List,lab_String,styl___]:=
directed[{0,0},v,lab,styl];


directed3d[start_List,end_List,label_String,dash___]:=
Module[{p,hd,len,AA,BB,aa,bb,cc,
dd,ee,ff,setdash,end1,end2},
{p=Pi/10;hd=0.25;setdash={N[1/72]};
If[dash==Null,setdash={}];
aa=start[[1]];bb=start[[2]];cc=start[[3]];
dd=end[[1]];ee=end[[2]];ff=end[[3]];
len=Sqrt[(aa-dd)^2+(bb-ee)^2+(cc-ff)^2];
AA={{Cos[p],Sin[p],0},{-Sin[p],Cos[p],0},{0,0,1}};
BB={{Cos[-p],Sin[-p],0},{-Sin[-p],Cos[-p],0},{0,0,1}};
end1=end-(hd/len)*AA.(end-start);
end2=end-(hd/len)*BB.(end-start);
Graphics3D[{AbsoluteThickness[N[9/72]],
Dashing[{}],
Line[{end,end1}],
Line[{end,end2}],
Dashing[setdash],
Line[{start,end}],
Text[
FontForm[label,{"Geneva-Bold",12}],
{(aa+dd)/2,(bb+ee)/2,(cc+ff)/2},{0,2}]}]}]


vector3d[v_List,label_String,dash___]:=
directed3d[{0,0,0},v,label,dash];


addition2d[a_List,labela_String,b_List,labelb_String]:=
Module[{sumab},
{directed[{0,0},a,labela],
directed[{0,0},b,labelb],
directed[a,b+a," ",dash],
directed[{0,0},a+b,StringJoin[{labela,"+",labelb}]]}];
```

```
subtraction2d[a_List,labela_String,b_List,labelb_String]
:=Module[{subab},
{directed[{0,0},a,labela],
directed[{0,0},b,labelb],
directed[a,a-b," ",dash],
directed[{0,0},a-b,StringJoin[{labela,"-",labelb}]]}];


projection2d[a_List,labela_String,b_List]:=
Module[{temp},
{directed[{0,0},a,labela],directed[{0,0},b,""],
directed[{0,0},((a.b)/(b.b))*b,"proj"],
Graphics[{Dashing[{0.01}],Line[{a,((a.b)/(b.b))*b}]}]}];


projection3d[a_List,labela_String,b_List]:=
Module[{temp},
{directed3d[{0,0,0},a,labela],directed3d[{0,0,0},b,""],
directed3d[{0,0,0},((a.b)/(b.b))*b,"proj"],
Graphics3D[{Dashing[{0.02}],Line[{a,((a.b)/(b.b))*b}]}]}];


rotation2d[a_List,labela_String,angle_]:=
Module[{A,temp,p},
{A={{Cos[angle],-Sin[angle]},{Sin[angle],Cos[angle]}};
temp=A.a;
p=ArcTan[a[[1]],a[[2]]];
{directed[{0,0},a,labela],
directed[{0,0},temp,"rot"],
Graphics[{Dashing[{0.02}],
Circle[{0,0},Sqrt[a.a],{p,p+angle}]}]}}];


rank[v_List]:=Length[Transpose[v]]-Length[NullSpace[v]];
Clear[rowop];
rowop[x_List]:= Module[{n},
n=Length[x];
row[y_]:=IdentityMatrix[n][[y]];
x];


colop[x_List]:= Module[{n},
n=Length[x];
col[y_]:=IdentityMatrix[n][[y]];
Transpose[x]];


submatrix[A_List,irow_Integer,jcol_Integer]:=
Module[{index},
index=Table[k,{k,Length[A]}];
A[[Drop[index,{irow,irow}],Drop[index,{jcol,jcol}]]]];


minor[A_List,irow_Integer,jcol_Integer]:=
Module[{index},
index=Table[k,{k,Length[A]}];
Det[A[[Drop[index,{irow,irow}],Drop[index,{jcol,jcol}]]]]];
```

```
cofactor[A_List,irow_Integer,jcol_Integer]:=
Module[{index},
index=Table[k,{k,Length[A]}];
(-1)^(irow+jcol)*
Det[A[[Drop[index,{irow,irow}],Drop[index,{jcol,jcol}]]]]];


aug[a_List,v_List]:= Transpose[Append[Transpose[a],v]];


colrep[a_List,v_List,i_Integer]:=
Transpose[ReplacePart[Transpose[a],v,i]];
Clear[changebasis];
changebasis[x_List,p_List,xlabel_String:"x",
plabel_String:"p"]:= Module[{origin,y,points,lines,
vectx,vectp1,vectp2,vectI1,vecI2},
origin = {0,0};
y = Inverse[p].x;
points = Graphics[{
PointSize[0.02],Point[x],
Point[{1,0}],
Point[{0,1}],
Point[{x[[1]],0}],
Text[StringJoin[xlabel,"1"],{x[[1]],0},{1,-1}],
Point[{0,x[[2]]}],
Text[StringJoin[xlabel,"2"],{0,x[[2]]},{-1,1}],
Point[p[[1]]],
Point[p[[2]]],
Point[y[[1]]*p[[1]]],
Text[" y1",y[[1]]*p[[1]],{-1,0}],
Point[y[[2]]*p[[2]]],
Text["y2 ",y[[2]]*p[[2]],{1,0}]}];
lines = Graphics[{
Line[{origin,y[[1]]*p[[1]]}],
Line[{origin,y[[2]]*p[[2]]}],
Dashing[{0.01}],
Line[{x,{x[[1]],0}}],
Line[{x,{0,x[[2]]}}],
Line[{x,y[[1]]*p[[1]]}],
Line[{x,y[[2]]*p[[2]]}]}];
vectx = vector2d[x,xlabel];
vectp1 = vector2d[p[[1]],StringJoin[plabel,"1"]];
vectp2 = vector2d[p[[2]],StringJoin[plabel,"2"]];
vectI1 = vector2d[{1,0},""];
vectI2 = vector2d[{0,1},""];
{points,lines,vectx,vectp1,vectp2,vectI1,vectI2}];


signQ[A_List]:= Module[{k},
k=Length[A];
Table[Minors[A,i][[j,j]],{i,k},{j,Binomial[k,i]}]];


signQL[A_List]:= Module[{k},
k=Length[A];
Table[Minors[A,i][[1,1]],{i,k}]];
```

```
borderB[A_List,b_List]:= Module[{cons,consrow,conscol},
cons=If[VectorQ[b],{b},b];
consrow=0*IdentityMatrix[Length[cons]];
Do[consrow[[i]]=Join[consrow[[i]],cons[[i]]],
{i,Length[cons]}];
conscol=Transpose[cons];
Do[conscol[[i]]=Join[conscol[[i]],A[[i]]],
{i,Length[A]}];
bord=Join[consrow,conscol];
bord];
Clear[gradf];
gradf[f_,v_List]:= Module[{n,i},
n=Length[v];
Table[D[f,v[[i]]],{i,1,n}]];

hessian[f_,v_List]:= Module[{n,i,j},
n=Length[v];
Table[D[f,v[[i]],v[[j]]],{i,1,n},{j,1,n}]];

conhess[f_,v_List,g_,u_List]:= Module[{m,ch,k},
m=Length[u];
ch=hessian[f,v];
Do[ch=ch  +  D[f,u[[k]]]*hessian[g[[k]],v],{k,1,m}];
ch];

signQL[A_List]:= Module[{k},
k=Length[A];
Table[Minors[A,i][[1,1]],{i,k}]];

gradf[f_,v_List]:= Module[{n,i},
n=Length[v];
Table[D[f,v[[i]]],{i,1,n}]];

arc2d[f_,s_List,r_List,dh___]:=
Module[{chrds,funcx,arcx},
chrdx=Graphics[{Dashing[{0.02}],
Thickness[0.008],
Line[{{r[[2]],f/.r[[1]]->r[[2]]},
{r[[3]],f/.r[[1]]->r[[3]]}}]}];
If[dh==Null,chrdx=Graphics[{}]];
funcx=Plot[f,s,DisplayFunction->Identity];
arcx=Plot[f,r,PlotStyle->{Thickness[0.009]},
DisplayFunction->Identity];
{chrdx,funcx,arcx}];

tangentline[f_,s_List,r_]:= Block[
{tx,$DisplayFunction=Identity},
tx=(f/.s[[1]]->r)+
(D[f,s[[1]]]/.s[[1]]->r)*(s[[1]]-r);
{Graphics[{}],
Plot[{f,tx},s,PlotStyle->{{},{Thickness[0.008]}}]}];

fjohn[a_List,constraints_List,object_,v_List,label___]:=
Module[
{temp,n,i,j,rul1,m,vlist,glist,vectf,tempf,index,nl,nw},
Clear[i,n,rul1,x,y];
```

```
nl=True;
nw=False;
If[label=="cone",nw=True];
If[label==Null,{nl=False,nw=False}];
rul1 = {v[[1]]->a[[1]],v[[2]]->a[[2]]};
n=Length[constraints];
binding={};
glist={};
vlist={};
index={};
Do[If[Chop[N[constraints[[i]] /. rul1]]==0,
{binding=Append[binding,constraints[[i]]],index=Append
[index,i]}],{i,1,n}];
tempf = gradf[object,v] /. rul1;
tempf = tempf/Sqrt[tempf.tempf];
If[nw,tempf=-tempf];
vectf=vector2d[tempf,If[nl,If[nw,"-grad f","grad
f"],""]];
m=Length[binding];
Do[vlist=Append[vlist,gradf[binding[[k]],v] /.
rul1],{k,1,m}];
Do[glist=Append[glist,vector2d[vlist[[j]]/Sqrt[vlist[[j]].
vlist[[j]]],
If[nl,ToString[StringForm["grad
g``",index[[j]]]],""]]],{j,1,m}];
glist=Append[glist,vectf];
glist];

Clear[separableode];
separableode[x_,y_,P_,Q_]:= Module[{z,w,Pz,Qw,solz,solw,
testz,testw,lst},
testz=True;
testw=True;
Pz = P /. x->z;
Qw = Q /. y->w;
gensol = Integrate[Pz,z]+Integrate[Qw,w]==C[1];
solz = Solve[gensol,z];
If[solz=={} || Head[solz]==Solve,testz=False];
solw = Solve[gensol,w];
lst={gensol};
If[solw=={} || Head[solw]==Solve,testw=False];
If[testz,lst=Append[lst,solz]];
If[testw,lst=Append[lst,solw]];
lst=lst /. {z->x,w->y}];

linearode[x_,P_,Q_]:= Module[{z,mu,temp,Pz,Qz},
Pz = P /. x->z;
Qz = Q /. x->z;
mu=Exp[Integrate[Pz,z]];
temp=(1/mu)*(Integrate[mu*Qz,z]+C[1]);
temp /. z->x];

tangentfield[f_,{x_,a_,b_},{y_,c_,d_},n_Integer,opt___]
:= Module[{incx,incy,slope,pt,del,i,j,m,lineset,ptset},
{incrx=(b-a)/(n-1);
```

```
incry=(d-c)/(n-1);
del=incrx/10;
slope={};
pt={};
Do[Do[pt=Append[pt,{a+i*incrx,c+j*incry}],
{i,0,n-1}],{j,0,n-1}];
Do[Do[slope=Append[slope,f
/.{x->a+i*incrx,y->c+j*incry}],
{i,0,n-1}],{j,0,n-1}];
lineset={};
ptset={};
Do[
{end1={pt[[m,1]]-del,pt[[m,2]]-slope[[m]]*del},
end2={pt[[m,1]]+del,pt[[m,2]]+slope[[m]]*del},
lineset=Append[lineset,Line[{end1,end2}]],
ptset=Append[ptset,Point[pt[[m]]]]},{m,1,n^2}];
Graphics[{Thickness[0.0075],lineset,PointSize[0.01],ptset},
opt]}];

wronskian[lst_List,x_]:=   Module[{k,i},
Det[Table[D[lst,{x,k}],{k,0,Length[lst]-1}]]];

wis[F_,lst_List,x_]:= Module[{n,k,i,col,w,an,wdet},
an=1;
n=Length[lst];
wdet={};
w=Table[D[lst,{x,kk}],{kk,0,Length[lst]-1}];
col=Table[If[i!=n,0,F/an],{i,1,n}];
Do[wdet=Append[wdet,Det[Transpose[ReplacePart[Transpose[
w],col,k]]]],
{k,1,n}];
wdet];

Clear[trajectory,yy,ran];
trajectory[yy_List,ran_List,opts___]:=
Module[{u,len,t,ptlst,maxdis,maxpos,n1,plt},
plt  =  ParametricPlot[{yy[[1]],yy[[2]]},ran,
DisplayFunction->Identity,opts];
u=Position[plt,Line][[1]];
len  =  Length[u];
u[[len]]=u[[len]]+1;
t=Prepend[u,plt];
ptlst  =  Apply[Part,t];
len=Length[ptlst];
maxdis=0;
maxpos=1;
For[i=1,i<len,i++,
If[(ptlst[[i]]-ptlst[[i+1]]).(ptlst[[i]]-
ptlst[[i+1]])>m  axdis^2,
maxpos=i]];
If[maxpos==len-1,maxpos=maxpos-1];
If[maxpos==1,maxpos=maxpos+2];
n1  =  maxpos-1;
Show[plt,Graphics[Arrow[ptlst[[n1]],ptlst[[n1+1]]]],
DisplayFunction->$DisplayFunction];];
```

```
End[];

Protect[fibprime,directed,vector2d,directed3d,vector3d,
addition2d,subtraction2d,projection2d,projection3d,
rotation2d,rank,rowop,colop,submatrix,minor,cofactor,
aug,colrep,signQ,signQL,borderB,gradf,hessian,conhess,
arc2d,tangentline,fjohn,separableode,linearode,
tangentfield,wronskian,wis,trajectory];

EndPackage[];
```

# Index